SPANISH COMPUTING DICTIONARY

Spanish-English
English-Spanish

DICCIONARIO BILINGÜE DE INFORMÁTICA

Español-Inglés
Spanish-English

S.M.H. Collin
Jordi Piqué
Universitat de Valéncia, Spain
Santiago Posteguillo
Universitat Jaume I at Castelló, Spain
Lourdes Melcion
University of Surrey, United Kingdom

BLOOMSBURY

A BLOOMSBURY REFERENCE BOOK

www.bloomsbury.com/reference

First published 2004

Bloomsbury Publishing Plc
38 Soho Square, London W1D 3HB

Copyright © Bloomsbury Publishing Plc 2004

British Library Cataloguing-in-Publication Data
A catalogue record for this book is available from the British Library

ISBN 0 7475 6986 X

Text Production and Proofreading
Katy McAdam, Edmund Wright, Heather Bateman, Cécile Guinard,
Emma Harris, Sarah Lusznat

All papers used by Bloomsbury Publishing are natural, recyclable products made
from wood grown in well-managed forests. The manufacturing processes conform
to the environmental regulations of the country of origin.

Text processed and computer typeset by Bloomsbury
Printed and bound in Finland by WS Bookwell

Preface

The aim of this bilingual English-Spanish / Spanish-English dictionary is to fill a lexicographical gap in the area of computing and Internet terminology. For the first time we are able to offer a comprehensive volume that includes over 35,000 entries, examples and translated terms from this ever-expanding subject area.

The initial word list is based on a monolingual dictionary also published by Bloomsbury, namely the *Dictionary of Computing*. New terms relating to the computer industry and its products have been added to both the English and the Spanish sections. Only terms directly related to computer technology have been included, and every effort has been made to clarify the meaning of each word by the use of examples, collocates, encyclopedic comments and quotations from trade publications.

In the Spanish word list we have incorporated English words accepted in the Spanish dictionary of the Real Academia Española (2001), such as *hardware* and *software*, which can be considered as fully assimilated into the Spanish language. We have also included English borrowings such as *buffer* or *bus* which, although not totally assimilated into Spanish, are nevertheless in common use among Spanish-speaking users and experts. When compiling quotations in both sections of the dictionary, we have relied mainly on recent periodicals, and sources are acknowledged under individual entries.

Prefacio

El objetivo de este diccionario bilingüe, inglés-español / español-inglés, es el de cubrir un espacio lexicográfico que hasta la fecha no había sido objeto de un esfuerzo de esta magnitud en el campo de la terminología informática e Internet.

En el proceso de selección de términos hemos tomado como base el diccionario monolingüe de Bloomsbury Publishing *Dictionary of Computing*. Se han añadido asimismo términos, tanto en la parte inglesa como española, relacionados con los nuevos productos informáticos que sistemáticamente la industria va creando. Se han incluido sólo términos directamente relacionados con la tecnología informática y se ha hecho todo el esfuerzo necesario para clarificar al máximo el significado de cada palabra, ilustrándolo mediante ejemplo, colocaciones, comentarios o citas.

Por otro lado, se incluyen palabras que ya han sido incorporadas en la nueva edición del diccionario de la Real Academia Española (2001), por ejemplo *hardware* y *software*, como calcos integrados en el español. También se han incluido calcos no integrados, como *buffer* y *bus*, de uso frecuente entre los usuarios y expertos de la informática en los países de habla hispana. En el trabajo de recopilación de citas, en ambas secciones del diccionario, nos hemos servido principalmente de revistas recientes, así como de otras fuentes que han sido debidamente indicadas.

CÓMO USAR EL DICCIONARIO

El dicionario presenta una estructura clara y fácil de manejar. Está dividido en dos partes: español–inglés, inglés–español.

Las palabras principales de cada entrada aparecen en **negrita** y, en la parte de inglés-español, van acompañadas de su transcripción fonética.

En cada una de las entradas se indican las distintas funciones gramaticales mediante ■

Los números 1, 2, etc. introducen divisiones semánticas con sus correspondientes traducciones. En casos en los que hay más de una traducción posible, dentro de la misma división, se incluyen ejemplos contextualizados.

Las glosas entre paréntesis indican la traducción de una palabra cuyo significado es de uso poco frecuente. También se utilizan paréntesis en los casos de ambigüedad.

Para ilustrar ejemplos de uso se incluyen, al final de la entrada en casillas, citas extraídas de revistas y periódicos especializados.

El uso de las abreviaturas se ha mantenido al mínimo y éstas son las que aparecen:

f	femenino
fpl	nombre femenino plural
m	masculino
mpl	nombre masculino plural
UK	Reino Unido
US	Estados Unidos
vi	verbo intransitivo
vr	verbo reflexivo
vt	verbo transitivo

USING THE DICTIONARY

The dictionary aims to provide a clear layout which will help the user find the required translation as easily as possible.

Each entry contains a headword in **bold** type, followed by a pronunciation in the case of English headwords.

Within the entry different parts of speech are introduced by ■.

Different meanings are introduced by numbers (1, 2, etc). Within each meaning division main translations are grouped together first, if there is more than one, followed by examples showing how the headword is used in context.

Glosses in brackets clarify the exact meaning of a word that is being translated, in cases where the meaning is less familiar or the word has more than one possible interpretation.

Boxes after an entry contain extracts from magazines or journals giving more in-depth information on how the word is used.

As far as is possible, abbreviations are not used in the dictionary, with the exception of the following:

f	feminine
fpl	feminine plural
m	masculine
mpl	masculine plural
UK	British English
US	American English
vi	intransitive verb
vr	reflexive verb
vt	transitive verb

ESPAÑOL-INGLÉS
SPANISH-ENGLISH

A

A *símbolo* A ∎ *abrev* A

A: (*controlador de discos*) A:

ábaco *m sustantivo* nomogram *o* nomograph

abandonar *verbo vt* to abort ◊ **el programa se interrumpió pulsando el botón rojo** the program was aborted by pressing the red button

abarcar *verbo vt* to span

abastecedor *m sustantivo* provider

aberración *f sustantivo* **1.** aberration **2.** distortion

aberración *f* **por defecto** *sustantivo* drop out

aberración *f* **por exceso** *sustantivo* drop in

abertura ◊ **abertura** *f* (**de un objetivo**) aperture

abierto *adj* open ◊ **bucle abierto** open loop ◊ **interconexión de sistemas abiertos (de acuerdo con las normas ISO)** Open Systems Interconnection (OSI) ◊ **no se puede acceder a los datos a no ser que el archivo esté abierto** you cannot access the data unless the file is open

abonado *sustantivo* subscriber ◊ **abonado** *m* **que llama (por teléfono)** caller ◊ **identificación de abonado que llama (por teléfono)** caller ID ◊ **selección directa del abonado llamado** subscriber trunk dialling (STD)

abortar *verbo vt* to abort

abreviatura *f sustantivo* abbreviation ◊ **en el texto, se utiliza la abreviatura 'proc' en vez de procesador** within the text, the abbreviation 'proc' is used instead of processor

abrir *verbo vt* to open ◊ **no puede acceder a los datos sin abrir el fichero antes** you cannot access the data unless the file has been opened

abscisa *f sustantivo* x-coordinate

absorber *verbo vt* to absorb

absorción *f sustantivo* absorption

acabar *verbo vi* to close

acarreo *m* **negativo** *sustantivo* borrow

acceder *verbo vi* to access ◊ **ella accedió al fichero del empleado archivado en el ordenador** she accessed the employee's file stored in the computer

acceso *sustantivo* access ◊ **acceso** *m* **básico RDSI** basic rate access; BRA ◊ **acceso** *m* **directo a la memoria mediante utilización en robo de ciclo** DMA cycle stealing ◊ **acceso** *m* **múltiple con detección de portadora evitando colisiones** carrier sense multiple access-collision avoidance; CSMA-CA ◊ **acceso** *m* **múltiple de detección de portadora con detección de colisión** carrier sense multiple access-collision detection; CSMA-CD ◊ **acceso** *m* **por demanda de la memoria paginada** demand fetching ◊ **acceso** *m* **por nivel de operaciones compartidas** share-level access ◊ **después de que se descubriera que estaba accediendo ilegalmente al sistema, se le prohibió el acceso** after he was discovered hacking, he was barred access to the system ◊ **dispositivo de almacenamiento de acceso directo** direct access storage device (DASD) ◊ **el acceso instantáneo al disco RAM fue bien acogido** the instantaneous access of the RAM disk was welcome ◊ **él tiene acceso a numerosos ficheros confidenciales** he has access to numerous sensitive files ◊ **prohibir al acceso a un sistema** to bar access to a system ◊ **tarjeta de acceso** access card ◊ **tener acceso a algo** to have access to something ◊ **tener acceso** *o* **acceder a un fichero de datos** to have access to a file of data ◊ **tiempo de acceso (a un fichero, etc.)** the access time of this dynamic RAM chip is around 200ns – we have faster versions if your system clock is running faster

'En la actualidad, la ciencia de lo diminuto sirve para construir láseres semiconductores y memorias de acceso aleatorias basadas en la magnetoresistencia gigante.' [*Ciberp@ís*]

acceso *m* **a distancia** *sustantivo* remote access ◊ **software de acceso remoto** remote access software

acceso *m* **al azar** *sustantivo* random access

acceso *m* **al disco** *sustantivo* disk access

acceso *m* **aleatorio** *sustantivo* random access ◊ **los lectores de disquetes son de acceso aleatorio, mientras que las cintas magnéticas son de memoria de acceso secuencial** disk drives are random access, magnetic tape is sequential access memory

acceso *m* **al ordenador principal** *sustantivo* mainframe access

acceso *m* **asíncrono** *sustantivo* asynchronous access

acceso *m* **automático a una sesión** *sustantivo* automatic log on

acceso *m* **cíclico** *sustantivo* cyclic access

acceso *m* **compartido** *sustantivo* shared access

acceso *m* **concurrente** *sustantivo* concurrency

acceso *m* **de mercado** *sustantivo* dial-up access

acceso *m* **directo** *sustantivo* **1.** direct access **2.** key combination **3.** key shortcut **4.** random access ◇ **los lectores de disquetes son de acceso aleatorio, mientras que las cintas magnéticas son de memoria de acceso secuencial** disk drives are random access, magnetic tape is sequential access memory

acceso *m* **directo a la memoria** *sustantivo* **1.** direct memory access **2.** DMA

acceso *m* **directo al menú** *sustantivo* menu shortcut

acceso *m* **en serie** *sustantivo* serial access

acceso *m* **instantáneo** *sustantivo* instantaneous access ◇ **el acceso instantáneo al disco RAM fue bien acogido** the instantaneous access of the RAM disk was welcome

acceso *m* **múltiple según demanda** *abrev* DAMA ■ *sustantivo* demand assigned multiple access

acceso *m* **(en) paralelo** *sustantivo* parallel access

acceso *m* **rápido** *sustantivo* rapid access

accesorio *m sustantivo* accessory ◇ **este popular ordenador personal dispone de una amplia gama de accesorios** this popular home computer has a large range of accessories ◇ **la impresora viene con diversos accesorios, como por ejemplo una cubierta insonorizada** the printer comes with several accessories, such as a soundproof hood

accesorio *m* **de escritorio** *abrev* DA ■ *sustantivo* desk accessory

accesorio *m* **de tecnología avanzada** *sustantivo* advanced technology attachment packet interface ■ *abrev* ATAPI

accesorio *m* **rápido de tecnología avanzada** *sustantivo* ATA Fast

accesorios *mpl sustantivo* ancillary equipment

accesorio *m* **ultra-rápido de tecnología avanzada** *sustantivo* ATA Ultra

acceso *m* **secuencial** *sustantivo* **1.** sequential access **2.** serial access

acceso *m* **serial** *sustantivo* serial access

acceso *m* **sin limitaciones** *sustantivo* open access

accidental *adj* accidental

acción *f sustantivo* action ◇ **acción** *f* **inmediata** *(en caso de un sector defectuoso)* hot fix ◇ **campo de acción** *o* **de movimiento** action field

accionado, ◇ **accionado, -a por la tecla Ctrl** control-driven ◇ **accionado, -a por la tecla de control** control-driven ◇ **accionado, -a por un suceso** event-driven

accionador *m sustantivo* actuator

accionar una tecla *verbo* to key ◇ **introducir (un texto** *o* **datos) con** *o* **mediante el teclado** *o* **teclar** *o* **mecanografiar** to key in

acelerador *m* **binario** *sustantivo* blitter

acentuación *f sustantivo* emphasis

aceptado, -a por anticipado *adj* pre-agreed

aceptar *verbo vt* to accept

Acerca de ... About...

acercar *verbo vt* to zoom ◇ **acercar** *o* **ampliar la imagen** *o* **enfocar en primer plano** zoom in

acierto *m sustantivo* hit

acimut *m sustantivo* azimuth ◇ **la alineación acimutal puede no ser la correcta para cintas grabadas en una máquina distinta** azimuth alignment might not be correct for tape recorded on a different machine

ACL *sustantivo* **1.** access control list **2.** ACL

acomodaticio *adj* compliant

acontecimiento *m sustantivo* event

acoplador *m sustantivo* **1.** coupler **2.** MIDI Mapper ◇ **se podría utilizar el acoplador MIDI para desviar al piano electrónico todas las notas destinadas a la batería** you could use the MIDI Mapper to re-direct all the notes meant for the drum machine to the electronic piano

acoplador *m* **acústico** *sustantivo* acoustic coupler ◇ **utilizo un acoplador acústico en mi ordenador portátil** I use an acoustic coupler with my lap-top computer

acoplador *m* **de impedancia** *sustantivo* cable matcher

acoplados mecánicamente *adj* ganged

acoplamiento *m sustantivo* linkage

acoplamiento *m* **de entrada/salida** *sustantivo* I/O mapping

acoplamiento *m* **mutuo** *sustantivo* interface

acoplar *verbo vt* to dock

'Como complemento al 'Yahoo! Messenger' se puede también instalar 'Companion', una barra de herramientas suplementaria que se acopla al navegador 'Explorer'.' [*Ciberp@ís*]

ACPI *sustantivo* ACPI

ActionMedia (*marca comercial*) ActionMedia

activado, ◇ **activado, -a por reconocimiento de datos** data-driven

activado por un suceso *adj* event-driven

activador *m sustantivo* actuator

activador *m* **de la instrucción ANSI** *sustantivo* ANSI driver

activar *verbo* **1.** *vt* to activate **2.** *vt* to arm **3.** *vt* to enable ◇ **al pulsar la tecla CR se activa la impresora** pressing CR activates the printer

ActiveVRML *sustantivo* ActiveVRML

ActiveX (*marca comercial*) ActiveX

activo *adj* **1.** active **2.** enabled ◇ **circuito activo** active circuit

actualización *f sustantivo* **1.** update **2.** upkeep ◇ **agentes de actualización** update agents

actualización *f* **de ficheros** *sustantivo* file maintenance

actualización *f* **de la división silábica** *sustantivo* rehyphenation

actualización *f* **después de cálculos** *sustantivo* post-editing

actualización *f* **después de una compilación** *sustantivo* post-editing

actualización *f* **dinámica** *sustantivo* dynamic update

actualizar *verbo* **1.** *vt* to post **2.** *vt* to refresh **3.** *vt* to regenerate **4.** *vt* to update ◇ **señal de actualización de la memoria** memory refresh signal ◇ **tenemos los documentos originales y los actualizados en discos** we have the original and updated documents on disks

acuerdo *m* **de conjunto** *sustantivo* package deal ◇ **llegaron a un acuerdo de conjunto que incluye el desarrollo de software, la personalización del hardware y la formación del personal** they agreed a package deal, which involves the development of software, customizing hardware and training of staff

acuerdo *m* **de licencia** *sustantivo* licence agreement

acuerdo *m* **global** *sustantivo* package deal ◇ **hemos propuesto una oferta global que comprende un sistema informático completo para la oficina, la formación del personal y el mantenimiento del equipo** we are offering a package deal which includes the whole office computer system, staff training and hardware maintenance

acumulador *m* *sustantivo* **1.** ACC **2.** accumulator *o* accumulator register

acumular *verbo* *vt* to accumulate ◇ **hemos acumulado de forma gradual un gran banco de datos de nombres y direcciones** we have gradually accumulated a large databank of names and addresses

acusar ◇ **acusar recibo (de un mensaje)** acknowledge

acuse ◇ **acuse** *m* **de recibo (electrónico)** receipt notification

acuse *m* **de recibo negativo** *abrev* NAK ■ *sustantivo* negative acknowledgement

acuse *m* **de recibo positivo** *sustantivo* affirmative acknowledgement

acústica *f* **ambiental** *sustantivo* ambience

acústico *adj* acoustic

adaptación *f* *sustantivo* adaptation ◇ **la adaptación del ojo para responder a los distintos niveles de luminosidad** the adaptation of the eye to respond to different levels of brightness

adaptado al ordenador *adj* machine-intimate

adaptador *sustantivo* **1.** adapter *o* adaptor **2.** adapter plug **3.** adaptor ◇ **adaptador** *m* **de canal de transmisión de datos** data adapter unit ◇ **adaptador** *m* **de interfaces de interconexión general** general purpose interface adapter ◇ **adaptador** *m* **de vídeo de animación completa** full-motion video adapter ◇ **adaptador** *m* **para interfaz de comunicaciones asíncronas** ACIA; asynchronous communications interface adapter ◇ **el adaptador de cable permite conectar el escáner a la interfaz SCSI** the cable adapter allows attachment of the scanner to the SCSI interface ◇ **el paquete informático incluye el cable para conectar el escáner al adaptador** the cable to connect the scanner to the adapter is included in the package

adaptador *m* **controlador de vídeo** *sustantivo* video board

adaptador *m* **controlador** *m* **de vídeo** *sustantivo* **1.** video adapter **2.** video controller

adaptador *m* **de canal de transmisión** *sustantivo* channel adapter

adaptador *m* **de FAX** *sustantivo* fax card *o* fax adapter *o* fax board

adaptador *m* **de interconexiones de periféricos** *sustantivo* peripheral interface adapter

adaptador *m* **de línea** *sustantivo* line adapter

adaptador *m* **del ordenador principal** *sustantivo* host adapter ◇ **se incluye el cable para conectar el escáner con el adaptador huésped** the cable to connect the scanner to the host adapter is included

adaptador *m* **de pantalla** *sustantivo* display adapter

adaptador *m* **de pantalla monocromo** *sustantivo* **1.** MDA **2.** monochrome display adapter

adaptador *m* **de red** *sustantivo* network adapter

adaptador *m* **de terminal** *sustantivo* terminal adapter

adaptador *m* **gráfico** *sustantivo* graphics adapter ◇ **el nuevo adaptador gráfico es capaz de producir gráficos de mayor definición** the new graphics adapter is capable of displaying higher resolution graphics

adaptador *m* **hembra** *sustantivo* sex changer

adaptador *m* **macho** *sustantivo* sex changer

adaptador *m* **maestro de enlaces** *sustantivo* bus master adapter ◇ **el adaptador maestro de enlaces de red proporciona una trasferencia mucho más rápida que el adaptador antiguo** the bus master network adapter provides much faster data throughput than the old adapter

adaptar *verbo* **1.** *vt* to adapt **2.** *vt* to condition **3.** *vt* to modify ◇ **adapte los datos en bruto a un formato estándar** condition the raw data to a standard format ◇ **¿se puede adaptar este ordenador para que acepte disquetes de 5,25 pulgadas?** can this computer be adapted to take 5.25 inch disks?

adaptator *m* **de interfaz de comunicaciones** *sustantivo* communications interface adapter

adición *f* *sustantivo* **1.** addition **2.** sum ◇ **adición** *f* **a tecnología avanzada** advanced technology attachment; ATA; AT attachment

adicional *adj* **1.** add-in **2.** additional **3.** add-on ◇ **¿podemos añadir tres estaciones de trabajo adicionales a la red?** can we add three additional workstations to the network? ◇ **un disco duro adicional aumentará la capacidad de memoria del ordenador** the add-on hard disk will boost the computer's storage capabilities

adición *f* **destructiva** *sustantivo* destructive addition

a distancia *adj* remote ◇ **llamada de procedimiento a distancia** remote procedure call

(RPC) ◇ **los usuarios pueden imprimir informes en impresoras a distancia** users can print reports on remote printers

administración ◇ **administración** *f* **avanzada de corriente** advanced power management; APM

administración *f* **de tareas** *sustantivo* task management

administración *f* **de texto** *sustantivo* text management

administrador *m* *sustantivo* administrator ◇ **administrador** *m* **de (base de) datos** data administrator

administrador *m* **de base de datos** *sustantivo* 1. database administrator 2. DBA

administrador *m* **de información personal** *sustantivo* 1. personal information manager 2. PIM

administrador *m* **de memoria extendida** *sustantivo* extended memory manager

administrador *m* **de red** *sustantivo* 1. network administrator 2. system administrator

administrator *mf* **ACPI** *sustantivo* ACPI

admitir *verbo vt* to recognise *o* to recognize

Adobe™ Adobe Systems

Adobe Acrobat (*marca comercial*) Adobe Acrobat

adquisición *f* *sustantivo* 1. acquisition 2. logging

adquisición *f* **de datos** *sustantivo* data acquisition

adulterado *adj* doped

adulterante *m* *sustantivo* dopant

advertir *verbo vt* to warn

aerógrafo *m* *sustantivo* airbrush

aficionado, *mf* ◇ **aficionado, -a a la informática** hacker

afirmativo *adj* 1. affirmative 2. positive

agencia *f* *sustantivo* bureau ◇ **agencia** *f* **de servicios editoriales (informáticos)** service bureau ◇ **nuestros datos son gestionados por una agencia de servicios** our data manipulation is handled by a bureau

agencia *f* **de información** *sustantivo* information provider

agencia *f* **de tratamiento de textos** *sustantivo* word-processing bureau

agenda *f* *sustantivo* planner

agenda *f* **electrónica** *sustantivo* electronic agenda

agente *sustantivo* agent

'...los agentes de actualización son trozos de código que se insertan en los programas que se inventaron, en principio, para que los usuarios pudieran olvidarse de las tareas de adecentamiento del software.' [*Ciberp@ís*]

agente *m* **impurificador** *sustantivo* dopant

agente *m* **intermediario** *sustantivo* proxy agent

agente *m* **usuario** *sustantivo* 1. UA 2. user agent

aglomeración *f* *sustantivo* congestion

a gran escala *adj* large-scale

agregado *m* *sustantivo* aggregate

agregado *m* **de datos** *sustantivo* data aggregate

agregar *verbo vt* to append

agrupación *sustantivo* character assembly ◇ **agrupación** *f* **adaptable de datos para corrección de errores MNP** adaptive packet assembly

agrupamiento *m* *sustantivo* cluster

agrupar *verbo* 1. *vt* to batch 2. *vt* to gather 3. *vt* to group

aguja *f* *sustantivo* 1. needle 2. stylus

aislamiento *m* **de canales** *sustantivo* channel isolation

aislante *m* *sustantivo* isolator

aislar *verbo vt* to isolate ◇ **direccionamiento adaptable aislado** *o* **ruta adaptable aislada** isolated adaptive routing

ajustar *verbo* 1. *vt* to calibrate 2. *vt* to fit 3. *vt* to normalise *o* to normalize 4. *vt* to regulate 5. *vt* to tune ◇ **ajustar el espacio entre dos caracteres** to kern ◇ **hemos reducido el espacio entre la 'T' y la 'o' para que estén más juntas** we have kerned 'T' and 'o' so they are closer together ◇ **todos los datos nuevos han sido ajustados a diez puntos decimales** all the new data has been normalized to 10 decimal places

ajustar (las cabezas) *verbo* to centre

ajustar con precisión *verbo* to fine-tune

ajuste *m* *sustantivo* adjustment ◇ **ajuste** *m* **de la tasa en bps** bps rate adjust ◇ **creo que el mando de juegos necesita un ajuste ya que a veces se atasca** I think the joystick needs adjustment as it sometimes gets stuck ◇ **el brillo necesita ajuste** the brightness needs adjustment

ajuste *m* **automático de decimales** *sustantivo* automatic decimal adjustment

alambre *m* *sustantivo* wire

alambre *m* **de conducción** *sustantivo* lead

álbum *m* **de recortes** *sustantivo* scrapbook ◇ **guardamos nuestro logotipo en el álbum de recortes** we store our logo in the scrapbook

alcanzar ◇ **alcanzar su nivel más alto** peak ◇ **alcanzar su punto máximo** peak ◇ **la energía alcanzó su máximo nivel de 1.200 voltios** the power peaked at 1,200 volts

al día *phrase* per day ■ *adj* state-of-the-art

aleatoria *sustantivo* hash total

alejar *verbo vt* to zoom ◇ **alejar** *o* **reducir la imagen** zoom out

alerta *f* *sustantivo* alert

alfabetizar *verbo vt* to alphabetise *o* to alphabetize ◇ **introduzca la información bibliográfica y póngala en orden alfabético** enter the bibliographical information and alphabetize it

alfafotográfico *adj* alphaphotographic

alfageométrico *adj* alphageometric

alfamosaico *adj* alphamosaic

alfanumérico *adj* **1.** alphameric **2.** alphanumeric

alfombrilla *f* **antiestática** *sustantivo* anti-static mat

álgebra *f sustantivo* algebra

álgebra *f* **booleana** *sustantivo* **1.** Boolean algebra **2.** Boolean logic

álgebra *f* **de Boole** *sustantivo* Boolean logic

ALGOL *sustantivo* **1.** ALGOL **2.** algorithmic language

algorítmico *adj* algorithmic

algoritmo *sustantivo* algorithm ◇ **algoritmo** *m* **de la página menos utilizada recientemente** least recently used algorithm

'De los débiles algoritmos de cifrado empleados a finales de los años 80 se ha pasado a complejas técnicas de polimorfismo y metamorfismo, que alteran la secuencia de instrucciones del código vírico y, mediante sistemas de mutación, son capaces de generar millones de variantes de un mismo espécimen, haciendo imposible su detección por medio de productos antivirus convencionales.' [*Ciberp@ís*]

algoritmo *m* **criptográfico** *sustantivo* cryptographic algorithm

algoritmo *m* **de compactación** *sustantivo* compacting algorithm

algoritmo *m* **de encriptación estándar** *sustantivo* DES

algoritmo *m* **de líneas ocultas** *sustantivo* hidden line algorithm

algoritmo *m* **del primer emplazamiento posible** *sustantivo* first fit

algoritmo *m* **de paginación** *sustantivo* paging algorithm

algoritmo *m* **de Shell** *sustantivo* shell sort

algoritmo *m* **usado menos recientemente** *sustantivo* least recently used algorithm

alias *sustantivo* **1.** alias **2.** alias name ◇ **el sistema operativo utiliza el alias COM1 para designar la terminal de dirección 3FCh del puerto en serie** the operating system uses the alias COM1 to represent the serial port address 3FCh

'En variedades de comunicación sincrónica como el chat, los apodos o alias son muy comunes.' [*Ciberpragmática*]

alimentación *sustantivo* feed ◇ **(instrucción de) alimentación de página** feed form

'Conviene asegurarse de que la fuente de alimentación es fiable, de que el bastidor es robusto y que el ventilador sea de dimensiones generosas.' [*Ciberp@ís*]

alimentación *f* **automática del papel** *sustantivo* auto advance

alimentación *f* **continua** *sustantivo* continuous feed

alimentación *f* **de papel** *sustantivo* paper feed

alimentación *f* **hoja a hoja** *sustantivo* **1.** sheet feed **2.** single sheet feed ◇ **dispositivo de alimentación automática de hojas** sheet feed attachment

alimentación *f* **ininterrumpida** *sustantivo* continuous feed

alimentación *f* **por guías** *sustantivo* tractor feed

alimentador *m* **de arrastre** *sustantivo* sprocket feed

alimentador *m* **de folios** *sustantivo* cut sheet feeder

alimentador *m* **de papel cortado** *sustantivo* cut sheet feeder

alimentador *m* **de sobres** *sustantivo* envelope feeder

alimentador *m* **hoja a hoja** *sustantivo* cut sheet feeder

alimentar *verbo vt* to power ◇ **el monitor se alimenta del suministro eléctrico de la unidad central** the monitor is powered from a supply in the main PC

alineación ◇ **alineación** *f* **de los ángulos de acimut** azimuth alignment ◇ **con este pequeño tornillo se ajusta la alineación acimutal** azimuth alignment is adjusted with this small screw ◇ **la alineación acimutal puede no ser la correcta para cintas grabadas en una máquina distinta** azimuth alignment might not be correct for tape recorded on a different machine

alineación *f* **acimutal** *sustantivo* azimuth alignment ◇ **con este pequeño tornillo se ajusta la alineación acimutal** azimuth alignment is adjusted with this small screw ◇ **la alineación acimutal puede no ser la correcta para cintas grabadas en una máquina distinta** azimuth alignment might not be correct for tape recorded on a different machine

alineación *f* **automática de decimales** *sustantivo* automatic decimal adjustment

alineación *f* **de cabezas** *sustantivo* azimuth alignment ◇ **con este pequeño tornillo se ajusta la alineación acimutal** azimuth alignment is adjusted with this small screw ◇ **la alineación acimutal puede no ser la correcta para cintas grabadas en una máquina distinta** azimuth alignment might not be correct for tape recorded on a different machine

alineamiento *m sustantivo* alignment

alinear *verbo* **1.** *vt* to align **2.** *vt* to justify **3.** *vt* to range

alinear (las cabezas) *verbo* to centre

alinear mal *verbo* to skew ◇ **esta página está mal alineada** this page is badly skewed

alma *f sustantivo* core

almacenamiento *sustantivo* storage ◇ **almacenamiento** *m* **(de datos) en línea** online storage ◇ **almacenamiento** *m* **en memoria intermedia de entrada** *or* **salida** I/O buffer ◇ **almacenamiento** *m* **secundario rápido de discos múltiples** RAID; redundant array of inexpensive disks ◇ **almacenamiento** *m* **temporal que funciona bajo el principio de 'primero en entrar primero en salir'** FIFO queue

almacenamiento *m* **activo** *sustantivo* active storage

almacenamiento *m* **asociativo** *sustantivo* associative storage

almacenamiento *m* **auxiliar** *sustantivo* **1.** auxiliary memory **2.** auxiliary storage *o* auxiliary store

almacenamiento *m* **borrable** *sustantivo* **1.** erasable memory **2.** erasable storage

almacenamiento *m* **con discos fijos e intercambiables** *sustantivo* **1.** FEDS **2.** fixed and exchangeable disk storage

almacenamiento *m* **de datos** *sustantivo* **1.** data storage **2.** information storage **3.** information storage and retrieval ■ *abrev* ISR

almacenamiento *m* **de discos intercambiables** *sustantivo* **1.** EDS **2.** exchangeable disk storage

almacenamiento *m* **de ficheros** *sustantivo* file storage

almacenamiento *m* **de gran capacidad** *sustantivo* mass storage

almacenamiento *m* **de holograma** *sustantivo* holographic storage

almacenamiento *m* **de la información** *sustantivo* **1.** information storage **2.** information storage and retrieval ■ *abrev* ISR

almacenamiento *m* **FIFO** *sustantivo* first in first out

almacenamiento *m* **fuera de red** *sustantivo* off-line storage

almacenamiento *m* **intermedio** *sustantivo* intermediate storage

almacenamiento *m* **masivo** *sustantivo* mass storage

almacenamiento *m* **no volátil** *sustantivo* **1.** non volatile memory **2.** non volatile storage *o* non-volatile store

almacenamiento *m* **óptico** *sustantivo* optical storage

almacenamiento *m* **reutilizable** *sustantivo* erasable storage

almacenamiento *m* **temporal** *sustantivo* temporary storage

almacenamiento *m* **temporal de entrada/salida** *sustantivo* I/O buffer

almacenar *verbo vt* to plant

almacenar en memoria temporal *verbo* to cache ◊ **este programa puede almacenar en memoria temporal fuentes de caracteres de cualquier tamaño** this program can cache any size font ◊ **las instrucciones de la memoria temporal de este procesador mejoran su rendimiento en un 15 por ciento** this CPU cache instructions improve performance by 15 percent

almacén *m* **de datos** *sustantivo* data warehouse

almacén *m* **temporal** *sustantivo* clipboard ◊ **copie el texto en el bloc de ntoas, luego péguelo en un nuevo documento** copy the text to the clipboard, then paste it back into a new document

al mismo nivel *adj* flush

ALPHA™ *sustantivo* ALPHA

alquilar *verbo vt* to lease ◊ **la empresa alquila todos sus ordenadores** the company leases all its computers ◊ **la política de la empresa es utilizar sólo material alquilado** the company has a policy of only using leased equipment

alta definición *f sustantivo* hi-res

alta definición *f sustantivo* high-resolution *o* high-res ◊ **la pantalla de alta definición puede obtener una resolución de 640 por 450 pixels** the high resolution screen can display 640 by 450 pixels

alta fidelidad *f sustantivo* high fidelity

alta precisión *f sustantivo* high specification

alta resolución *f sustantivo* hi-res

alta resolución *f sustantivo* high-resolution *o* high-res

alta tecnología *f sustantivo* high specification ■ *adj* high-tech ■ *sustantivo* high technology

altavoz *m sustantivo* loudspeaker

altavoz *m* **secundario de frecuencias bajas** *sustantivo* sub-woofer

alteración *f sustantivo* distortion

alternancia *f sustantivo* alternation

alternar *verbo* **1.** *vi* to alternate **2.** *vi* to toggle

alto *m* **rendimiento** *adj* high-end

ALU *sustantivo* ALU

aludir *verbo vi* to reference

alumbrado *m* **UV** *sustantivo* UV light

al vuelo *adv* on the fly

ambiental *adj* ambient

ambiente *adj* ambient

ambiente *m* **universitario** *sustantivo* campus environment

ambigüedad *f sustantivo* ambiguity ◊ **ambigüedad** *f* **(causada) por un error** error ambiguity

ambiguo *adj* ambiguous

ámbito *m sustantivo* **1.** range **2.** scope

ámbito *m* **normal** *sustantivo* normal range

AMD (*empresa productora de procesadores*) AMD

America Online (*gran proveedor de servicios de internet*) America Online

amigable *adj* user-friendly ◊ **comparada con la versión anterior, ésta es muy fácil de usar** compared with the previous version this one is very user-friendly ◊ **es una máquina tan fácil de usar** it's such a user-friendly machine

amortiguar *verbo vt* to deaden ◊ **se utilizan unas cubiertas insonorizadas para amortiguar el ruido de las impresoras** acoustic hoods are used to deaden the noise of printers

amovible *adj* exchangeable

amperio *m sustantivo* ampere

amperio *m* **(A)** *sustantivo* amp

ampliable *adj* scalable

ampliación *f sustantivo* **1.** addition **2.** amplification **3.** enhancement **4.** zooming

ampliar la pantalla *verbo* to maximise *o* to maximize

amplificación *f sustantivo* **1.** amplification **2.** gain ◇ **aumente la amplificación de la señal de entrada** increase the amplification of the input signal ◇ **la amplificación es tan alta que distorsiona la señal** the amplification is so high, the signal is distorting

amplificación *f* **de imágenes** *sustantivo* image enhancement

amplificador *m sustantivo* amplifier ◇ **amplificador de audio** audio amplifier ◇ **amplificador de bajo ruido** low noise amplifier ◇ **tipo de amplificador** amplifier class

amplificador *m* **de señal** *sustantivo* **1.** line driver **2.** regenerator

amplificar *verbo vt* to amplify ◇ **la señal recibida necesita ser amplificada antes de que se pueda procesar** the received signal needs to be amplified before it can be processed ◇ **teléfono amplificado** amplified telephone

amplitud *f sustantivo* **1.** amplitude **2.** magnitude ◇ **amplitud de una señal** signal magnitude ◇ **codificación por desplazamiento de amplitud** amplitude shift keying (ASK) ◇ **distorsión de amplitud** amplitude distortion

añadido *adj* add-on

añadir *verbo* **1.** *vt* to add **2.** *vt* to append **3.** *vt* to insert ◇ **con las teclas de función es muy fácil añadir o suprimir material de un texto** adding or deleting material from the text is easy using function keys ◇ **la empresa de software ha añadido un nuevo paquete de gestión a su gama de productos** the software house has added a new management package to its range of products ◇ **si se utiliza la instrucción de DOS COPY A+B, el fichero B se añade al final del fichero A** if you enter the DOS command COPY A+B, the file B will be appended to the end of file A

analfabeto, -a en informática *adj* computer illiterate

análisis ◇ **análisis** *m* **del contenido de la memoria** memory dump

análisis *m* **criptográfico** *sustantivo* cryptanalysis

análisis *m* **de datos** *sustantivo* data analysis

análisis *m* **de los costes** *sustantivo* cost analysis

análisis *m* **del tráfico** *sustantivo* traffic analysis

análisis *m* **de red** *sustantivo* network analysis

análisis *m* **de ruta crítica** *sustantivo* critical path analysis

análisis *m* **de sistemas** *sustantivo* systems analysis

análisis *m* **funcional** *sustantivo* functional specification

análisis *m* **léxico** *sustantivo* lexical analysis

análisis *m* **numérico** *sustantivo* numerical analysis

análisis *m* **sintáctico** *sustantivo* syntax analysis

analista *m&f sustantivo* analyst

analista *m&f* **de sistemas** *sustantivo* systems analyst

analizador *m sustantivo* analyser ◇ **analizador de frecuencias** frequency analyzer

analizador *m* **de circuitos** *sustantivo* circuit analyser

analizador *m* **de comunicaciones** *sustantivo* communications scanner

analizador *m* **de control de llamadas** *sustantivo* communications scanner

analizador *m* **de estado lógico** *sustantivo* logic state analyser

analizador *m* **de la imagen** *sustantivo* image processor

analizador *m* **de línea** *sustantivo* line analyser

analizador *m* **sintáctico** *sustantivo* parser

analizar gramaticalmente *verbo* to parse

analizar sintácticamente *verbo* to parse

analógico a digital *abrev* A/D ■ *adj* analog to digital

analógico a numérico *abrev* A/D ■ *adj* analog to digital

analógico-digital *adj* A to D

anamórfico *adj* anamorphic

ancho *m* **de banda** *sustantivo* bandwidth

ancho *m* **de banda a petición** *sustantivo* bandwidth on demand

ancho *m* **de banda de sonido** *sustantivo* sound bandwidth

ancho *m* **de banda de vídeo** *sustantivo* video bandwidth

anchura ◇ **anchura** *f* **de banda (de frecuencias)** bandwidth ◇ **este cable de fibra óptica tiene una mayor capacidad de transferencia que el viejo cable de cobre, por lo que puede transportar datos a mayor velocidad** this fibre-optic cable has a greater bandwidth than the old copper cable and so it can carry data at higher speeds ◇ **la capacidad de transferencia de un teléfono es de 3100Hz** telephone bandwidth is 3100Hz

anchura *f* **de banda agregada** *sustantivo* aggregate bandwidth

anchura *f* **de banda de vídeo** *sustantivo* video bandwidth

anchura *f* **de página** *sustantivo* page width

anchura *f* **de una línea** *sustantivo* measure

Andorra *abrev* ad

anexar *verbo vt* to append

angstrom *m abrev* Å

ángstrom *m sustantivo* angstrom

angstromio *m sustantivo* angstrom

ángulo *m sustantivo* angle

ángulo *m* **de pantalla** *sustantivo* screen angle

anidar *verbo vi* to nest

anillo *m sustantivo* ring ◇ **red en anillo** ring network ◇ **red en anillo** o red 'Token Ring' Token Ring network

anillo *m* **de contrarrotación** *sustantivo* counter-rotating ring

anillo *m* **de protección de escritura** *sustantivo* write-permit ring

anillo *m* **de red principal** *sustantivo* backbone ring

anillo *m* **lógico** *sustantivo* logical ring

animación *f sustantivo* animation ◇ **animación** *f* **(de imágenes) por ordenador** computer animation

animación *f* **en tiempo real** *sustantivo* realtime animation

animación *f* **por ordenador** *sustantivo* computer animation

animatronics *sustantivo* animatronics

ánodo *m sustantivo* anode

anomalía *f sustantivo* 1. aberration 2. error

anomalía *f* **permanente** *sustantivo* hard error

anotación *f sustantivo* annotation

anotación *f* **a pie de página** *sustantivo* footnote

anotar *verbo vt* to log

anotar registros *verbo* to record ◇ **este dispositvo registra las señales sobre cinta magnética** this device records signals onto magnetic tape ◇ **los datos registrados digitalmente se utilizan para generar imágenes** digitally recorded data are used to generate images ◇ **registre los resultados en este columna** record the results in this column

anteceder *verbo vt* to precede ◇ **instrucción que anula la instrucción anterior** instruction which cancels the instruction which precedes it

antememoria *f sustantivo* 1. cache 2. cache memory 3. RAM cache ◇ **el tiempo de acceso a los ficheros es mucho menor si los datos usados con mayor frecuencia se almacenan en la memoria temporal** file access time is much quicker if the most frequently used data is stored in cache memory

anticipado ◇ **anticipado** *m* **(de una imagen)** pre-imaging

anticuado *adj* out of date ◇ **su sistema informático está muy anticuado** their computer system is years out of date ◇ **todavía están utilizando un equipo anticuado** they are still using out-of-date equipment

antimelladura *f sustantivo* dejagging

antirrebote *m sustantivo* de-bounce

antirreflejo *m sustantivo* glare filter

anulación *f sustantivo* cancellation

anular *verbo* 1. *vt* to cancel 2. *vt* to undo ◇ **acaba de borrar el párrafo, pero puede anular esta acción desde el menú Editar** you've just deleted the paragraph, but you can undo it from the option in the Edit menu

anunciador *m sustantivo* annunciator

anunciar *verbo vt* to announce o to

anycast *m sustantivo* anycast

Apache™ HTTP *sustantivo* Apache™ HTTPD

apagado *m* **automático** *sustantivo* automatic power off

apagar *verbo vt* to power down ∎ *sustantivo vt* suspend

Apagar el equipo *sustantivo* ShutDown

apagón *m sustantivo* power failure

apagón *m* **parcial** *sustantivo* brown-out

apaisado *sustantivo* landscape

aparato *m sustantivo* 1. device 2. output device

aparato *m* **de entrada/salida** *sustantivo* I/O device

aparato *m* **de televisión** *sustantivo* television ◇ **cámara de televisión** television camera ◇ **proyector de televisión** television projector ◇ **receptor de televisión** television receiver ◇ **televisor** television receiver

aparato *m* **en buen estado** *sustantivo* functional unit

aparcar *verbo vt* to park ◇ **cuando está aparcada, la cabeza del disco no daña los datos si toca la superficie del disco** when parked, the disk head will not damage any data if it touches the disk surface

apertura *f* **automática de una sesión** *sustantivo* auto-login o auto-logon

aplicación *sustantivo* 1. application 2. applications software ◇ **aplicación** *f* **en la memoria del servidor** server-based application ◇ **aplicación principal** application parent ◇ **aplicación** *f* **que tolera y resuelve posibles fallos** hazard-free implementation

'Las aplicaciones que más se están desarrollando en estos momentos fuera del ámbito de los ordenadores personales son las operaciones 'sin manos', por ejemplo las que se desarrollan en un coche: establecer una llamada telefónica (sin que el vehículo empiece a hacer peligrosas eses), pedir una información al ordenador de a bordo, enviar un correo o dictar una breve nota-recordatorio.' [*Internet y el español*]

aplicación *f* **activa** *sustantivo* active application

aplicación *f* **compartida** *sustantivo* server-based application

aplicación *f* **de red** *sustantivo* network-intrinsic application

aplicaciones *fpl* **informáticas** *plural noun* computer applications

aplicación *f* **para Netware™** (*marca comercial*) NetWare Loadable Module

aplicación *f* **que usa una red** *sustantivo* network-intrinsic application

aplicación *f* **vertical** *sustantivo* vertical application ◇ **su nuevo programa para la gestión de una floristería es una buena aplicación vertical** your new software to manage a florist's is a good vertical application

aplicación *f* **web** *sustantivo* web application

aplique *m sustantivo* applet

APM *sustantivo* **1.** advanced power management **2.** APM

apoyar *verbo vt* to back up ◇ **trajo consigo un fichero con documentos para apoyar su reclamación** he brought along a file of documents to back up his claim

apoyo *sustantivo* support ◇ **de apoyo** backup

apoyo *m* **técnico** *sustantivo* **1.** backup **2.** technical support

Apple Computer Corporation (*empresa de technología de la información*) Apple Computer Corporation

Appleshare™ (*marca comercial*) Appleshare

AppleTalk™ (*marca comercial de un protocolo de comunicaciones*) AppleTalk™

appoyo *m sustantivo* backup

aprendizaje *m* **asistido por ordenador** *sustantivo* **1.** CAL **2.** CBL **3.** computer-aided learning **4.** computer-assisted learning **5.** computer-based learning **6.** programmed learning

araña *f sustantivo* crawler

arbitraje *m* **del bus** *sustantivo* bus arbitration

árbol *m sustantivo* tree ◇ **estructura en árbol** *o* **arborescencia** tree structure

árbol *m* **binario** *sustantivo* **1.** binary tree **2.** btree

árbol *m* **de carpetas** *sustantivo* tree of folders

árbol *m* **de decisiones** *sustantivo* decision tree

árbol *m* **de ejecución mínima** *sustantivo* minimal tree

árbol *m* **de extensión** *sustantivo* spanning tree

árbol *m* **sumidero** *sustantivo* sink tree

arborescencia *f sustantivo* forest

arborescencia *f* **encadenada** *sustantivo* threaded tree

Archie *sustantivo* Archie

archivar *verbo* **1.** *vt* to archive **2.** *vt* to file

archivo *m sustantivo* file

archivo *m* **autoextraíble** *sustantivo* self extracting archive

archivo *m* **comprimido** *sustantivo* zip file

archivo *m* **de disco** *sustantivo* disk file

archivo *m* **de entrada/salida** *sustantivo* I/O file

archivo *m* **de firma** *sustantivo* signature file

archivo *m* **de registro** *sustantivo* log file

archivo *m* **incrustado** *sustantivo* embedded object

archivo *m* **invertido** *sustantivo* inverted file

archivo *m* **padre** *sustantivo* father file

archivos *mpl sustantivo* archive

arder *verbo vi* to burn

área ◇ **área** *f* **de instrucción en la memoria** instruction area ◇ **área** *f* **de salida (de la memoria)** output area

área *f* **activa de píxeles** *sustantivo* active pixel region

área *f* **de almacenamiento de variables** *sustantivo* string area

área *f* **de búsqueda** *sustantivo* seek area

área *f* **de datos** *sustantivo* data area

área *f* **de entrada** *sustantivo* input area

área *f* **de imagen** *sustantivo* image area

área *f* **de memoria alta** *sustantivo* high memory area ■ *abrev* HMA

área *f* **de segmento de recubrimiento** *sustantivo* overlay region

área *f* **de trabajo** *f sustantivo* **1.** work area **2.** workspace

área *f* **de visualización** *sustantivo* image area

área *f* **transitoria** *sustantivo* transient area

argumento ◇ **argumento** *m* **(de una función)** arg; argument

argumento *m* **decisivo** *sustantivo* deciding factor ◇ **el factor decisivo fue la excelente calidad de los gráficos** the deciding factor was the superb graphics

argumento *m* **de línea de instrucciones** *sustantivo* command line argument ◇ **utilice la instrucción DIR para ver los ficheros en el disco; añada el argumento de línea de instrucciones A: para ver los ficheros en la disquetera A:** use the command 'DIR' to view the files on disk, add the command line argument 'A:' to view the files on drive A:

aritmética *f* **de coma fija** *sustantivo* fixed-point arithmetic

aritmética *f* **de coma flotante** *sustantivo* floating point arithmetic

aritmética *f* **de doble precisión** *sustantivo* double-length arithmetic

aritmética *f* **externa** *sustantivo* external arithmetic

aritmética *f* **interna** *sustantivo* internal arithmetic

armar *verbo* **1.** *vt* to arm **2.** *vt* to mount

armazón *f* **fija** *sustantivo* rack

armónicos *mpl sustantivo* harmonics

ARPA *sustantivo* Advanced Research Projects Agency Network

arquitectura *sustantivo* architecture ◇ **arquitectura** *f* **a SNA arquitectura** *f* **de red(es) de sistemas** Systems Network Architecture ◇ **arquitectura** *f* **común de agente de solicitud de objetos** common object request broker architecture ◇ **(arquitectura de gestión de redes) NetView™** NetView

'La nueva arquitectura de las redes -basada en la conexión entre el usuario y los servidores- facilita que millones de personas puedan consultar casi a la vez el mismo servicio electrónico de información y obtener respuesta con relativa rapidez.' [*La Red*]

arquitectura *f* **abierta** *sustantivo* open architecture

arquitectura *f* **ampliada de CD-ROM** *sustantivo* CD-ROM Extended Architecture ■ XA

arquitectura *f* **cliente-servidor** *sustantivo* client-server architecture

arquitectura *f* **de aplicaciones de sistemas** *sustantivo* Systems Application Architecture

arquitectura *f* **de bus múltiple** *sustantivo* multiple bus architecture

arquitectura *f* **de contenido de documentos** *sustantivo* **1.** DIA/DCA **2.** document interchange architecture/document content architecture

arquitectura *f* **de microordenador** *sustantivo* microcomputer architecture

arquitectura *f* **de objetos** *sustantivo* **1.** object architecture **2.** object-orientated architecture

arquitectura *f* **de ordenador** *sustantivo* **1.** computer architecture **2.** computer organisation *o* computer organization

arquitectura *f* **de piel de cebolla** *sustantivo* onion skin architecture ◇ **la arquitectura de piel de cebolla de este ordenador consiste en un núcleo central, un sistema operativo, un lenguaje de bajo nivel y a continuación el programa del usuario** the onion skin architecture of this computer is made up of a kernel at the centre, an operating system, a low-level language and then the user's program ◇ **la arquitectura de piel de cebolla de este ordenador consiste en un núcleo central, un sistema operativo, un lenguaje de bajo nivel y a continuación los programas de usuario** the onion skin architecture of this computer is made up of a kernel at the centre, an operating system, a low-level language and then the user's programs

arquitectura *f* **de procesador escalar** (*de Sun Microsystems*) Scalar Processor Architecture

arquitectura *f* **de protocolo de demanda** *sustantivo* demand protocol architecture

arquitectura *f* **de red** *sustantivo* network architecture

arquitectura *f* **de redes** *sustantivo* SNA

arquitectura *f* **de transmisión de documentos** *sustantivo* **1.** DIA/DCA **2.** document interchange architecture/document content architecture

arquitectura *f* **de un chip** *sustantivo* chip architecture

arquitectura *f* **de un circuito integrado** *sustantivo* chip architecture

arquitectura *f* **de un microprocesador** *sustantivo* microprocessor architecture

arquitectura *f* **DPA** *sustantivo* demand protocol architecture

arquitectura *f* **en elementos de bits** *sustantivo* bit-slice architecture *o* bit-slice design

arquitectura *f* **estándar industrial, Arquitectura** *f* **ISA** *sustantivo* ISA

arquitectura *f* **ISA** *sustantivo* **1.** Industry Standard Architecture **2.** ISA

arquitectura *f* **ISO/OSI** *sustantivo* International Standards Organization Open System Interconnection

arquitectura *f* **MCA 1.** (*marca comercial*) MCA **2.** Micro Channel Architecture

arquitectura *f* **micro channel** *abrev* MCA ■ *sustantivo* media control architecture

arquitectura *f* **monoflujo de instrucciones monoflujo de datos** *sustantivo* **1.** single instruction stream single data stream **2.** SISD

arquitectura *f* **monoflujo de instrucciones multiflujo de datos** *sustantivo* **1.** SIMD **2.** single instruction stream multiple data stream

arquitectura *f* **orientada a objetos** *sustantivo* **1.** object architecture **2.** object-orientated architecture

arquitectura *f* **SIMD** *sustantivo* **1.** SIMD **2.** single instruction stream multiple data stream

arquitectura *f* **SISD** *sustantivo* **1.** single instruction stream single data stream **2.** SISD

arquitectura SPARC™ (*de Sun Microsystems*) Scalar Processor Architecture

arrancar *verbo* *vt* to boot ◇ **arrancar en caliente** to warmboot ◇ **arrancar en frío** to coldboot

arranque *sustantivo* start ◇ **arranque** *m* (**de un sistema**) bootstrap ◇ **arranque** *m* **automático** (**de un sistema**) auto-boot

arranque *m* *sustantivo* **1.** booting **2.** boot up

arranque *m* **automático** *sustantivo* auto start

arranque *m* **en caliente** *sustantivo* **1.** warm boot **2.** warm start

arranque *m* **en frío** *sustantivo* **1.** cold boot **2.** cold start

arranquer en frío *verbo* to hardboot

arrastrar ◇ **arrastrar y hacer clic** drag and click

arrastrar y soltar *verbo* to drag and drop ◇ **arrastre y suelte el icono del documento sobre el icono del tratamiento de textos y el sistema arrancará el programa y cargará el documento** drag and drop the document icon onto the word-processor icon and the system will start the program and load the document

arrastre *m* *sustantivo* **1.** carry **2.** feed **3.** pinfeed ◇ (**dispositivo de**) **arrastre** *m* **de cinta de papel** paper tape feed ◇ **arrastre** *m* **en esquema circular** *or* **en bucle** end around carry

arrastre *m* **de la tonalidad** *sustantivo* hangover

arrastre *m* **del papel** *sustantivo* paper feed

arrastre *m* **en bucle** *sustantivo* end about carry

arrastre *m* **en cascada** *sustantivo* cascade carry

arrastre *m* **en esquema circular** *sustantivo* end about carry

arrastre *m* **hacia adelante** *sustantivo* carry look ahead

arrastre *m* **parcial** *sustantivo* partial carry

arrastre *m* **rápido** *sustantivo* ripple-through carry

arrastre *m* **simultáneo de transmisión** *sustantivo* ripple-through carry

arreglo *m* **provisional** *sustantivo* bug patch

arrendar *verbo vt* to lease ◇ **circuito arrendado** leased circuit

arseniuro *m* **de galio** *sustantivo* gallium arsenide

artefacto *m* *sustantivo* **1.** artefact *o* artifact **2.** artifact

artículo *m* *sustantivo* article ◇ **escribió un artículo para el periódico local sobre el grupo de usuarios** he wrote an article about the user group for the local newspaper

artículo *m* **lógico** *sustantivo* logical record

ascender *verbo vi* to ascend

ascensor *m* *sustantivo* elevator

asentir *verbo vt* to acknowledge

aserción *f sustantivo* assertion

aserto *m sustantivo* assertion

asignación *f* *sustantivo* allocation ◇ **asignación de bandas (de frecuencias o de longitud de ondas)** band allocation ◇ **la nueva asignación de bandas de frecuencias significa que tendremos más canales (de transmisión)** the new band allocation means we will have more channels

asignación *f sustantivo* assignment

asignación *f* **de canal adaptable** *sustantivo* adaptive channel allocation

asignación *f* **de ida y vuelta** *sustantivo* round robin

asignación *f* **de memoria** *sustantivo* **1.** memory allocation **2.** storage allocation

asignación *f* **de recursos** *sustantivo* resource allocation

asignación *f* **dinámica** *sustantivo* dynamic allocation

asignación *f* **dinámica de la memoria** *sustantivo* dynamic storage allocation

asignación *f* **previa** *sustantivo* pre-allocation

asignar *verbo* **1.** *vt* to allocate **2.** *vt* to assign **3.** *vt* to map ◇ **asignar una zona de la memoria a una tarea determinada** to assign ◇ **el sistema operativo asignó la mayor parte de la memoria principal a la hoja de cálculo** the operating system allocated most of main memory to the spreadsheet program ◇ **frecuencia asignada** assigned frequency ◇ **se han asignado dos ordenadores PC para producir las etiquetas** two PCs have been assigned to outputting the labels

asincrónico *m adj* **1.** async **2.** asynchronous **3.** unclocked

asíncrono *m adj* **1.** async **2.** asynchronous **3.** unclocked ◇ **cuando se utilizan puertos asíncronos de acceso no se requiere ningún hardware especial** when asynchronous ports are used no special hardware is required ◇ **modo asíncrono de respuesta** asynchronous response

mode (ARM) ◇ **modo asíncrono equilibrado** asynchronous balanced mode (ABM) ◇ **modo asíncrono equilibrado extendido** asynchronous balanced mode extended (ABME)

asistencia *f* **en línea** *sustantivo* online help

asistencia *f* **técnica de un sistema** *sustantivo* system support

asistencia *f* **técnica para un sistema** *sustantivo* system support

asistido, -a por ordenador *adj* **1.** computer-aided **2.** computer-assisted

asociación ◇ **asociación** *f* británica de normativa sobre diseño y seguridad** British Standards Institute; BSI ◇ **asociación** *f* **de estándares de vídeo y electrónica** VESA; Video Electronics Standards Association ◇ **asociación** *f* **de industrias electrónicas** EIA ◇ **asociación** *f* **europea de fabricantes de ordenadores** ECMA

Asociación ◇ **Asociación** *f* **de transferencia de datos por infrarrojo** Infrared Data Association

asociación *f* **de sistemas multimedia interactivos** *sustantivo* **1.** IMA **2.** Interactive Multimedia Association

asociar *verbo vt* to connect

ASP *abrev* ASP

asterisco *m sustantivo* asterisk

AT *sustantivo* AT

ATA *sustantivo* **1.** advanced technology attachment **2.** ATA

ataque *m sustantivo* attack

ATD *sustantivo* ATD

atenuación *f sustantivo* attenuation

atenuar *verbo vt* to deaden

atenuarse *verbo vr* to fade

Athlon XP (*marca comercial de un procesador*) Athlon XP

atómico *adj* atomic

átomo *m sustantivo* atom

atractivo *adj* sticky

atribución *f sustantivo* allocation

atribuir *verbo vt* to allocate

atributo *m sustantivo* attribute ◇ **al pulsar al mismo tiempo las teclas Ctrl y B se activa el atributo negrita para este párrafo de texto** pressing Ctrl and B keys at the same time will set the bold attribute for this paragraph of text ◇ **este atributo controla el color de la pantalla** this attribute controls the colour of the screen

atributo *m* **de archivos** *sustantivo* archive attribute *o* archive bit

atributo *m* **del sistema** *sustantivo* system attribute

atributo *m* **de pantalla** *sustantivo* **1.** display attribute **2.** screen attribute

atributo *m* **de sólo lectura** *sustantivo* read only attribute

atributo *m* **de un fichero** *plural noun* file attribute

atributos *mpl* **seleccionables** *plural noun* selectable attributes

audible *adj* audible ◇ **la impresora emite una señal audible cuando se le acaba el papel** the printer makes an audible signal when it runs out of paper

audio *adj* audio ◇ **audioconferencia** audio conferencing ◇ **audio** *or* **vídeo intercalados** audio/video interleaved (AVI) ◇ **diapositiva (de) audio** audio slide ◇ **frecuencia audio** *o* **audiofrecuencia** audio frequency ◇ **puerto (de) audio** audio port ◇ **reductor (de la señal) de audio** audio compressor ◇ **sistema de audio interactivo** active audio system

audiotex *m sustantivo* audiotex

audio/vídeo intercalados *sustantivo* **1.** audio/video interleaved **2.** AVI

auditoría *f sustantivo* audit

aumentar *verbo* **1.** *vt* to ascend **2.** *vt* to increment ◇ **el contador se incrementa cada vez que se ejecuta una instrucción** the counter is incremented each time an instruction is executed

aumentar la escala *verbo* to scale up

aumento *m sustantivo* increment

autenticador *m sustantivo* authenticator

autentificación *f* **de mensajes** *sustantivo* authentication of messages

auto- *prefijo* self- ◇ **bucle con retorno automático a cero** *o* **con retorno automático a los parámetros de salida** self-resetting *o* self-restoring loop ◇ **lista autoreferencial** self-referent list

autocorrector *adj* self-correcting

autodiagnóstico *m sustantivo* self-diagnostic

autoedición *f sustantivo* DTP

autoescaneado *m* **de baudios** *sustantivo* auto-baud scanning *o* auto-baud sensing

autoexec.bat *sustantivo* AUTOEXEC.BAT

autoflujo *m sustantivo* autoflow

automatización *f* **de la oficina** *sustantivo* office automation

automatización *f* **de oficinas** *abrev* OA

autónomo *adj* stand-alone *o* standalone

autor *m sustantivo* author

auto-respuesta *f sustantivo* auto-answer

autoridad *f* **certificadora** *abrev* CA ■ *sustantivo* certificate authority

autorización *f sustantivo* **1.** authorisation *o* authorization **2.** permission ◇ **autorización** authorization to copy (ATC) ◇ **este usuario no puede acceder al fichero del servidor porque no tiene autorización** this user cannot access the file on the server because he does not have permission

autorización *f sustantivo* clearance ◇ **usted no tiene la autorización necesaria para este procesador** you do not have the required clearance for this processor

autorización *f* **de acceso** *sustantivo* access authority

autorización *f* **en tiempo real** *sustantivo* real-time authorisation *o* real-time authentication

autorización *f* **para copiar** *sustantivo* **1.** ATC **2.** authorisation to copy

autorizado *adj* legal

auto-test *m* **de encendido** *sustantivo* power on self test

A/UX (*marca comercial*) A/UX

auxiliar back-end ■ *sustantivo* **1.** backing **2.** satellite ■ *adj* standby ◇ **al añadir otra disquetera aumentaré la capacidad de la memoria auxiliar** by adding another disk drive, I will increase the backing store capabilities ◇ **auxiliar** *m* **de bajo consumo de energía** low-power standby

auxiliares de una red *sustantivo* network redundancy

avalancha *f sustantivo* avalanche ◇ **fotodiodo de avalanchas** avalanche photodiode (APD) ◇ **hubo una avalancha de errores después de apretar la tecla equivocada** there was an avalanche of errors after I pressed the wrong key

avance ◇ **avance** *m* **(del papel) por tracción** tractor feed

avance *m* **de línea** *abrev* LF ■ *sustantivo* line feed

avance *m* **rápido del papel** *sustantivo* slew

avance *m* **tecnológico** *sustantivo* sophistication ◇ **el avance tecnológico del nuevo programa es sobresaliente** the sophistication of the new package is remarkable

avanzado *adj* **1.** sophisticated **2.** state-of-the-art ◇ **un programa avanzado de publicación asistida por ordenador** a sophisticated desktop publishing program

avanzar *verbo vi* to increment

avanzar fotograma a fotograma *verbo* to step frame

avanzar un paso *verbo* to step ◇ **avanzamos por el archivo registro a registro** we stepped forward through the file one record at a time

avatar *m sustantivo* avatar

avería *f* **provocada por el equipo** *sustantivo* hardware failure

averiarse *verbo vr* to fail

avería *f* **total de un disco** *sustantivo* disk crash

avisar *verbo vt* to warn

aviso ◇ **aviso** *m* **de recepción de copia discreta** blind copy receipt

ayuda *f sustantivo* help

ayuda *f* **en función del contexto** *sustantivo* context-sensitive help

ayuda *f* **para el diagnóstico** *sustantivo* diagnostic aid

ayudar *verbo vt* to back up

azimut *m sustantivo* azimuth

B

b *abrev* b ◇ **bit(s) por segundo** bps (bits per second)
B *abrev* B ■ *símbolo* B ◇ **KB** *o* **kilo-byte** KB (kilobyte)
B: B:
BACKUP *sustantivo* BACKUP
bafle *m sustantivo* loudspeaker
bajada *f* **de energía** *sustantivo* sag
bajada *f* **de la corriente** *sustantivo* brown-out
bajar *verbo* **1.** *vt* to download **2.** *vi* to fade
balún *m sustantivo* balun
banco *sustantivo* bank

'Cuando hace dos meses el Banco… anunció el lanzamiento en la Red de su nuevo banco virtual, consistente en un portal-supermercado financiero con comercio electrónico, me confirmé en algo que venía barruntando desde tiempo atrás: lo de la nueva economía electrónica va en serio y sin retorno.' [*Nueva economía*]

banco *m* **de canales** *sustantivo* channel bank
banco *m* **de conocimientos** *sustantivo* knowledge base
banco *m* **de datos** *sustantivo* databank
banco *m* **de ensayo** *sustantivo* test bed
banco *m* **de memoria** *sustantivo* memory bank ◇ **una tarjeta de extensión tiene un banco de memoria de 128KB formado por 16 chips** an add-on card has a 128KB memory bank made up of 16 chips
banco *m* **de pruebas** *sustantivo* test bed
banda *f sustantivo* band ◇ **la banda de base de frecuencias vocales oscila entre 20Hz y 15Hz** voice base band ranges from 20Hz to 15KHz
banda *f* **ancha** *sustantivo* **1.** broadband **2.** wideband
banda *f* **ancha ISDN** *sustantivo* broadband ISDN
banda *f* **base** *sustantivo* baseband *o* base band
banda *f* **B-ISDN** *sustantivo* broadband ISDN
banda *f* **de frecuencia no utilizada** *sustantivo* guard band
banda *f* **de guarda** *sustantivo* guard band
banda *f* **de papel** *sustantivo* paper tape
banda *f* **de protección** *sustantivo* guard band
banda *f* **intermedia** *sustantivo* guard band
banda *f* **multipista** *sustantivo* band
banda *f* **original** *sustantivo* magnetic master
banda *f* **perforada** *sustantivo* perforated tape
bandeja ◇ **bandeja** *f* **de entrada del correo electrónico** InBox ◇ **bandeja** *f* **de papel (para alimentación hoja a hoja)** paper tray
bandeja *f* **de papel** *sustantivo* bin ◇ **bandeja inferior** (*icono*) lower bin ◇ **bandeja superior** upper bin
baratija *f sustantivo* junk
barra *f sustantivo* **1.** bar **2.** block ◇ **barra** *f* **de conexiones (del terminal)** terminal strip ◇ **barra** *f* **de selección** (*de opciones del menú desplegable*) highlight bar
barra *f* **de desplazamiento** *sustantivo* scroll bar ◇ **el indicador se encuentra en la mitad de la barra de desplazamiento de modo que sé que estoy en la mitad del documento** the marker is in the middle of the scroll bar so I know I am in the middle of the document
barra *f* **de desplazamiento horizontal** *sustantivo* horizontal scrollbar
barra *f* **de espaciado** *sustantivo* space bar
barra *f* **de espacio** *sustantivo* space bar
barra *f* **de estado** *sustantivo* status bar
barra *f* **de herramientas** *sustantivo* toolbar
barra *f* **del menú** *sustantivo* **1.** action bar **2.** menu-bar
barra *f* **desplegable del menú** *sustantivo* action bar pull-down
barra *f* **de tareas** *sustantivo* taskbar
barra *f* **de título** *sustantivo* title bar
barra *f* **graduada** *sustantivo* ruler
barra *f* **oblicua** *sustantivo* slash
barra *f* **oblicua inversa (\)** *sustantivo* backslash
barra *f* **ómnibus** *sustantivo* bus bar
barrer *verbo* *vi* to scan
barrido *m sustantivo* **1.** scan **2.** scanning ◇ **dispositivo de lectura por barrido** scanning device ◇ **haz de barrido** *o* **de exploración** scanning spot beam
barrido *m* **de pantalla** *sustantivo* television scan
barrido *m* **por trama** *sustantivo* raster scan
barrido *m* **progresivo** *sustantivo* progressive scanning
barrido *m* **vectorial** *sustantivo* vector scan
barril *m sustantivo* barrel
basada en caracteres *adj* character-based
basado en disquetes *adj* disk-based

basar *verbo vt* to base

basar(se) en *verbo* to base

base *f sustantivo* **1.** base **2.** foot **3.** radix ◇ **base** *f* **de datos con estructura libre** free form database ◇ **el número hexadecimal tiene una base de 16** the hexadecimal number has a radix of 16

base *f* **2** *sustantivo* base 2

base *f* **8** *sustantivo* base 8

base *f* **10** *sustantivo* base 10

base *f* **16** *sustantivo* base 16

base *f* **binaria** *sustantivo* base 2

base *f* **decimal** *sustantivo* base 10

base *f* **de datos** *sustantivo* database

base *f* **de datos activa** *sustantivo* active database

base *f* **de datos en línea** *sustantivo* online database

base *f* **de datos en red** *sustantivo* network database

base *f* **de datos entrelazada** *sustantivo* plex database

base *f* **de datos física** *sustantivo* physical database

base *f* **de datos integrada** *sustantivo* integrated database

base *f* **de datos jerárquica** *sustantivo* hierarchical database

base *f* **de datos lineal** *sustantivo* flat file database

base *f* **de datos relacional** *abrev* RDBMS ■ *sustantivo* relational database *o* relational database management system

base *f* **de dirección** *sustantivo* address base

base *f* **de tiempo** *sustantivo* time base

base *f* **de tiempo rápida** *sustantivo* fast timescale

base *f* **de tiempo reducida** *sustantivo* fast time-scale

base *f* **doble** *sustantivo* dual homing

base *f* **hexadecimal** *sustantivo* base 16

base *f* **octal** *sustantivo* **1.** base 8 **2.** octal scale

basura *f sustantivo* **1.** garbage **2.** junk ◇ **basura** *f* **en la entrada, basura** *f* **en la salida** garbage in garbage out ◇ **basura** *f* **en la entrada, basura en la salida** GIGO ◇ **correo basura** *o* **propaganda sin interés** junk mail

BAT *sustantivo* BAT

batería ◇ **equipado, -a con una batería (auxiliar)** battery-backed ◇ **la memoria CMOS, equipada con una batería auxiliar, sustituye la disquetera en este (modelo de ordenador) portátil** battery-backed CMOS memory replaces a disk drive in this portable ◇ **la tarjeta RAM puede ir opcionalmente equipada con una pila auxiliar** the RAM disk card has the option to be battery-backed

batería *f* **auxiliar** *sustantivo* battery backup

batería *f* **de ion-litio** *sustantivo* lithium-Ion battery

batería *f* **de níquel y cadmio** *sustantivo* NiCad

batería *f* **de reserva** *sustantivo* battery backup

batería *f* **recargable** *sustantivo* re-chargeable battery ◇ **se utiliza una batería recargable como alimentación auxiliar para la memoria RAM cuando se apaga el sistema** a re-chargeable battery is used for RAM back-up when the system is switched off

baudio *m sustantivo* baud

BCD *sustantivo* BCD

biblioteca *sustantivo* library ◇ **biblioteca** *f* **de enlaces (Netware)** Bindery ◇ **biblioteca** *f* **(de programas) de entrada** *or* **salida** input/output library ◇ **busque las referencias bibliográficas en el catálogo de la biblioteca** look up the bibliographical details in the library catalogue ◇ **la función de la raíz cuadrada ya está en el programa de biblioteca** the square root function is already in the library program ◇ **los editores han verificado todas las referencias en la biblioteca local** the editors have checked all the references in the local library ◇ **tiene una enorme biblioteca de juegos de ordenador** he has a large library of computer games

biblioteca *f* **de cintas** *sustantivo* tape library

biblioteca *f* **de funciones** *sustantivo* function library

biblioteca *f* **de gráficos** *sustantivo* graphics library

biblioteca *f* **de macros** *sustantivo* macro library

biblioteca *f* **de programas** *sustantivo* **1.** program library **2.** software library

biblioteca *f* **de rutinas de aplicaciones** *sustantivo* run-time library ◇ **el software ha sido diseñado con todas las rutinas gráficas accesibles en la biblioteca de rutinas de aplicaciones** the software is designed with all the graphics routines in this run-time library file

biblioteca *f* **de un sistema** *sustantivo* system library

biblioteca *f* **dinámica de enlaces** *sustantivo* **1.** DLL **2.** dynamic link library

biblioteca *f* **gráfica** *sustantivo* graphics library

bidireccional *adj* two-dimensional

bienes *mpl* **disponibles** *plural noun* assets

biestable *adj* bistable

bifurcación *f sustantivo* **1.** branch **2.** jump **3.** resource fork **4.** switch ◇ **la estación defectuosa está en esta bifurcación** the faulty station is on this branch

bifurcación *f* **condicional** *sustantivo* **1.** case branch **2.** conditional branch **3.** conditional jump

bifurcación *f* **de un programa** *sustantivo* program branch

bifurcación *f* **incondicional** *sustantivo* unconditional branch *o* unconditional jump *o* unconditional transfer

billón *m sustantivo* billion

binario *adj* binary ◇ **su carta es un fichero de texto, no un fichero binario** your letter is a text file, not a binary file

BIND *sustantivo* BIND

BinHex *sustantivo* BinHex

biopastilla *f sustantivo* biochip

bipolar *adj* bipolar ◇ **transistor de conexión bipolar** bipolar junction transistor (BJT)

bit *m abrev* b ■ *sustantivo* **1.** binary digit **2.** bit **3.** bit ◇ **bit** *m* **de desbordamiento (de la capacidad)** overflow bit; overflow flag ◇ **(el) bit más significativo** most significant bit (MSB) ◇ **bit menos significativo** least significant bit (LSB) ◇ **bit(s) por segundo** bps (bits per second) ◇ **(el) bit significativo** significant bit ◇ **(número de) bits por píxel** bits per pixel (BPP) ◇ **(número de) bits por segundo** *o* **bps** bits per second (bps) ◇ **bit** *m* **suplementario para detección de errores** overhead bit ◇ **el diseño en elementos de bits utiliza cuatro procesadores de texto de 4 bits para crear un procesador de 16 bits** the bit slice design uses four 4-bit word processors to construct a 16-bit processor ◇ **la prueba del sexto bit de un byte que contiene un carácter ASCII determina si el carácter es bit significativo y si debe ir en mayúscula o en minúscula** testing bit six of a byte containing an ASCII character is bit significant and determines if the ASCII character is upper or lower case

bit *m* **binario** *sustantivo* binary bit

bit *m* **de archivos** *sustantivo* archive attribute *o* archive bit

bit *m* **de arrastre** *sustantivo* carry bit

bit *m* **de código** *sustantivo* code bit

bit *m* **de comprobación** *sustantivo* check bit

bit *m* **de control** *sustantivo* check bit

bit *m* **de estado** *sustantivo* status bit

bit *m* **de guarda** *sustantivo* guard bit

bit *m* **de inicio** *sustantivo* **1.** start bit **2.** start element

bit *m* **de máscara** *sustantivo* mask bit

bit *m* **de parada** *sustantivo* **1.** stop bit **2.** stop element

bit *m* **de paridad** *sustantivo* parity bit

bit *m* **de protección** *sustantivo* bozo bit

bit *m* **de señal** *sustantivo* **1.** sign bit **2.** sign indicator

bit *m* **de servicio** *sustantivo* service bit

bit *m* **de sincronización** *sustantivo* sync bit

bit *m* **de transferencia** *sustantivo* carry bit

bitio *m abrev* b ■ *sustantivo* bit

bitio *m* **marcado** *sustantivo* dirty bit

bitio *m* **sucio** *sustantivo* dirty bit

bit *m* **marcado** *sustantivo* dirty bit

bit *m* **más significativo** *sustantivo* **1.** most significant bit **2.** msb *o* MSB

bit *m* **menos significativo** *sustantivo* **1.** least significant bit **2.** LSB

BitNet *sustantivo* BitNet

bit *m* **ponderado** *sustantivo* weighted bit

bits *mpl* **de descripción de color** *plural noun* colour bits

bits *mpl* **por píxel** *sustantivo* BPP

bits por píxel *sustantivo* bits per pixel

bits por pulgada *sustantivo* bits per inch

bits por segundo *sustantivo* bits per second

BIX *sustantivo* BIX

biz *sustantivo* biz

blanco y negro *sustantivo* black and white ◇ **(en) blanco y negro** monochrome

'bleeding edge' *adj* bleeding edge

blindar *verbo vt* to shield

bloatware *m sustantivo* bloatware

bloc *m sustantivo* block

bloc *m* **(de datos)** *sustantivo* tablet

bloc *m* **de notas** *sustantivo* **1.** clipboard **2.** notepad **3.** writing pad

Bloc *m* **de Notas™** *sustantivo* clipboard

bloc *m* **de notas de pantalla** *sustantivo* screen notepad

blocque ◇ **borrar bloques** block-delete ◇ **copiar bloques (de datos)** block-copy ◇ **mover bloques (de texto)** block move

blog *m sustantivo* blog

blogger *m sustantivo* blogger

blogging *m sustantivo* blogging

blogosfera *f sustantivo* blogosphere

blogware *m sustantivo* blogware

Bloq Mayús *sustantivo* caps lock

bloque *m sustantivo* bank ◇ **bloque** *m* **(de datos) de control** control block ◇ **bloque** *m* **de identificación de un programa de carga** initial program header ◇ **bloque** *m* **de párrafo (de memoria)** paragraph

bloquear *verbo* **1.** *vt* to block **2.** *vt* to inhibit **3.** *vt* to lock ◇ **bloquear (el acceso a) un fichero** locking a file ◇ **el director del sistema bloqueó su petición de más tiempo en la unidad central** the system manager blocked his request for more CPU time

bloquear(se) *sustantivo vr* lock up

bloquearse *verbo* **1.** *vr* to crash **2.** *vr* to go down

bloque *m* **de alimentación** *sustantivo* power pack

bloque *m* **de arranque** *sustantivo* **1.** boot block **2.** boot record

bloque *m* **de bits** *sustantivo* bit block

bloque *m* **de caracteres** *sustantivo* character block

bloque *m* **de datos** *sustantivo* data block

bloque *m* **de enchufe** *sustantivo* (de cable de red local) punch-down block

bloque *m* **de energía** *sustantivo* power pack

bloque *m* **de entrada** *sustantivo* input block

bloque *m* **de identificación** *sustantivo* **1.** header **2.** header block

bloque *m* **de página** *sustantivo* page frame

bloqueo *m sustantivo* 1. crash 2. file locking 3. lockdown 4. (*radiocommunications*) lockout ◇ **sistema de bloqueo de receptores** receiver lockout system

bloqueo *m* **de protección** *sustantivo* advisory lock

bloqueo *m* **de registros** *sustantivo* record locking

bloqueo *m* **de un programa** *sustantivo* program crash

Bluetooth (*marca comercial*) Bluetooth

BMS *sustantivo* 1. most significant bit 2. msb *o* MSB

bobina *f sustantivo* spool

bobina *f* **de inducción** *sustantivo* inductor

bobina *f* **de recepción** *sustantivo* take-up reel ◇ **coloque la bobina llena en este eje y la bobina de recepción en el otro** put the full reel on this spindle, and feed the tape into the take-up reel on the other spindle

bobina *f* **receptora** *sustantivo* 1. pickup reel 2. take-up reel ◇ **coloque la bobina llena en este eje y la bobina de recepción en el otro** put the full reel on this spindle, and feed the tape into the take-up reel on the other spindle

boca *f* **de conexiones** *sustantivo* hub

boca *f* **de conexiones apilable** *sustantivo* stackable hub

boca *f* **de conexiones múltiple** *sustantivo* stackable hub

boca *f* **de conexión inteligente** *sustantivo* intelligent wiring hub

bof *abrev* bof *o* BOF

BOF *abrev* bof

bola *f* **de guía** *sustantivo* trackball

bola *f* **de seguimiento** *sustantivo* trackball

bolsa *f sustantivo* bag

bomba *sustantivo* bomb

'Mandar una bomba es enviar a una dirección del correo electrónico una cantidad tal de datos que se colapsa el sistema del receptor.' [*Computer Hoy*]

bomba *f* **de tiempo** *sustantivo* time bomb

bomba *f* **lógica** *sustantivo* 1. logic bomb 2. time bomb ◇ **el programador de sistemas instaló una bomba lógica cuando le despidieron** the system programmer installed a logic bomb when they made him redundant

bombardear *verbo vt* to bomb

borde *m sustantivo* 1. border 2. edge 3. mat

borde *m* **anterior** *sustantivo* leading edge

borde *m* **de alineación** *sustantivo* aligning edge

borde *m* **de entrada** *sustantivo* leading edge

borde *m* **de guía** *sustantivo* leading edge

borde *m* **de (la) pantalla** *sustantivo* screen border

borde *m* **de referencia** *sustantivo* aligning edge

borne *m sustantivo* terminal

borne *m* **positivo** *sustantivo* positive terminal

borrada ◇ **que no puede ser borrada** non-erasable storage

borrado *sustantivo* deletion ◇ **borrado** *m* **parcial (de la memoria)** checkerboarding

borrado *m* **de líneas ocultas** *sustantivo* hidden line removal

borrador *m sustantivo* 1. eraser 2. rough copy

borrar *verbo* 1. *vt* to clear 2. *vt* to delete 3. *vt* to erase 4. *vt* to rub out 5. *vt* to scratch 6. *vt* to scrub 7. *vt* to wipe ◇ **al reformatear un disco se borrarán todos sus datos** by reformatting you will wipe the disk clean ◇ **borre todos los ficheros con la extensión BAK** scrub all files with the .BAK extension

borrar *m* **completamente** *verbo* to bulk erase

borrar datos por superposición *verbo* to overwrite ◇ **los nuevos datos introducidos han reemplazado la información anterior** the latest data input has overwritten the old information

borrar un fichero *verbo* to zero

bosque *m sustantivo* forest

bot *m sustantivo* bot

botón *m sustantivo* 1. (*de un ratón o de un mando de juego*) button 2. button 3. knob ◇ **botón** *m* **derecho (del ratón)** right-hand button ◇ **seleccione el botón de la izquierda para cancelar la operación o el de la derecha para continuar** there are two buttons at the bottom of the status line, select the left button to cancel the operation or the right to continue ◇ **utilice el ratón para situar el cursor sobre el icono e inicie la aplicación pulsando el botón del ratón** use the mouse to move the cursor to the icon and start the application by pressing the mouse button

botón *m* **de contraste** *sustantivo* contrast

botón *m* **de registro** *sustantivo* record button

botón *m* **de reinicio** *sustantivo* reset button *o* reset key

botón *m* **Inicio** *sustantivo* Start button

bozo *m* **(Apple Macintosh)** *sustantivo* bozo bit

bpp (bitios por pulgada) *sustantivo* BPI *o* bpi

bps *sustantivo* bits per second ◇ **su velocidad de transmisión es de 60.000 bits por segundo (bps) a través de una conexión en paralelo** their transmission rate is 60,000 bits per second (bps) through a parallel connection

bps (bitios por segundo) *sustantivo* bps

brazo *m* **de acceso** *sustantivo* access arm

brazo *m* **de lectura** *sustantivo* actuator

brazo *m* **de lectura/escritura** *sustantivo* access arm ◇ **el brazo de acceso se sitúa en la posición de 'parking' durante el transporte** the access arm moves to the parking region during transport

brillante *adj* brilliant ◇ **el color de fondo es rojo brillante** the background colour is a brilliant red ◇ **empleó blanco brillante para lo más**

destacado he used brilliant white for the highlights

brillo *m sustantivo* brightness ◇ **el brillo del monitor puede dañar la vista** the brightness of the monitor can hurt the eyes ◇ **un mando de control le permite ajustar el brillo y el contraste** a control knob allows you to adjust brightness and contrast

brillo *m* **fotométrico** *sustantivo* luminance

brocha *f sustantivo* brush

bucle *m sustantivo* loop ◇ **bucle** *m* **con retorno automático a cero** self-resetting loop ◇ **bucle** *m* **con retorno automático a los parámetros de salida** self-resetting loop; self-restoring loop ◇ **película en bucle** loop film ◇ **red en anillo** *o* **en bucle** loop network

bucle *m* **analógico** *sustantivo* analog loopback

bucle *m* **anidado** *sustantivo* nested loop

bucle *m* **cerrado** *sustantivo* closed loop

bucle *m* **continuo** *sustantivo* **1.** continuous loop **2.** endless loop

bucle *m* **de cadena margarita** *sustantivo* daisy chain recursion

bucle *m* **de corrección** *sustantivo* loopback

bucle *m* **de espera** *sustantivo* wait loop

bucle *m* **de mantenimiento** *sustantivo* holding loop

bucle *m* **de modificación** *sustantivo* modification loop

bucle *m* **de recurrencia** *sustantivo* daisy chain recursion

bucle *m* **de sincronización** *sustantivo* timing loop

bucle *m* **de soporte** *sustantivo* holding loop

bucle *m* **de temporización** *sustantivo* timing loop

bucle *m* **FOR-NEXT** *sustantivo* for-next loop

bucle *m* **infinito** *sustantivo* **1.** endless loop **2.** infinite loop

bucle *m* **interior** *sustantivo* inner loop

bucle *m* **jerarquizado** *sustantivo* nested loop

bucle *m* **mientras** *sustantivo* while-loop

bucle *m* **principal (de un programa)** *sustantivo* main loop

bucle *m* **sin fin** *sustantivo* **1.** endless loop **2.** infinite loop

bucle *m* **(condicional) 'WHILE'** *sustantivo* while-loop

búfer *m sustantivo* buffer

bufér *m* **secundario** *sustantivo* back buffer

'buffer' *m sustantivo* buffer

'buffer' *m* **de E/S** *sustantivo* I/O buffer

bus *m sustantivo* **1.** bus **2.** microcomputer bus ◇ **bus** *m* **dual independiente** DIB ◇ **bus** *m* **(de tipo) S-100** S100 bus

bus *m* **A** *sustantivo* A-bus

bus *m* **AT** *sustantivo* AT-bus

buscador *sustantivo* **1.** search engine **2.** web browser

'Ningún buscador indiza más allá del 50% de la Red, afirmaba Search Engine Watch en noviembre del 2000, y en estos momentos es difícil saber qué proporción de la Web abarca la suma de todos los buscadores (o, en otras palabras, qué porción de la Web es opaca a cualquier búsqueda).' [*Internet y el español*]

buscador *m* **web** *sustantivo* web crawler

buscar *verbo vt* to search ◇ **(función de) buscar y reemplazar en todo el texto** global search and replace ◇ **(dispositivo de) buscar y sustituir** find and replace; search and replace ◇ **que se puede buscarse** to searchable

buscar hacia atrás *verbo* to backtrack

bus *m* **de Apple Desktop** (*marca comercial*) Apple Desktop Bus

bus *m* **de arbitraje** *sustantivo* contention bus

bus *m* **de control** *sustantivo* control bus

bus *m* **de datos** *sustantivo* data bus

bus *m* **de direcciones** *sustantivo* **1.** address bus **2.** address highway

bus *m* **de entrada de datos** *sustantivo* **1.** data input bus **2.** DIB

bus *m* **de entrada/salida** *sustantivo* I/O bus

bus *m* **de extensión** *sustantivo* expansion bus

bus *m* **de interfaz HP** Hewlett Packard Interface Bus ■ *abrev* HPIB

bus *m* **de regulación** *sustantivo* contention bus

bus *m* **de transferencia de datos** *sustantivo* data highway

bus *m* **IEEE** *sustantivo* IEEE bus

bus *m* **local** *sustantivo* **1.** local bus **2.** PCI **3.** peripheral component interconnect ◇ **las tarjetas de extensión más rápidas encajan en este conector de enlace local** the fastest expansion cards fit into this local bus connector

bus *m* **local VESA** *sustantivo* **1.** VESA local bus **2.** VL-bus *o* VL local bus

bus *m* **MCA** (*de IBM*) Micro Channel Bus

bus *m* **Micro-Channel** Micro Channel Bus

bus *m* **multiplexado** *sustantivo* multiplexed bus

bus *m* **principal** *sustantivo* A-bus

búsqueda *sustantivo* **1.** look-up **2.** search ◇ **búsqueda** *f* **(de una instrucción)** fetch phase ◇ **búsqueda** *f* **que distingue las mayúsculas de las minúsculas** case sensitive search

búsqueda *f* **asociativa** *sustantivo* chaining search

búsqueda *f* **binaria** *sustantivo* **1.** binary chop **2.** binary look-up **3.** binary search

búsqueda *f* **de Boole** *sustantivo* Boolean search

búsqueda *f* **de una instrucción** *sustantivo* fetch instruction

búsqueda *f* **de zona** *sustantivo* area search

búsqueda *f* **dicotómica** *sustantivo* dichotomising search *o* dichotomizing search

búsqueda *f* **disyuntiva** *sustantivo* disjunctive search

búsqueda *f* **documental** *sustantivo* data retrieval

búsqueda *f* **en cadena** *sustantivo* chaining search

búsqueda *f* **en retroceso** *sustantivo* backwards search

búsqueda *f* **en tablas** *sustantivo* table lookup

búsqueda *f* **en todo el texto** *sustantivo* full-text search

búsqueda *f* **exhaustiva** *sustantivo* exhaustive search

búsqueda *f* **global** *sustantivo* full-text search

búsqueda *f* **hacia atrás** *sustantivo* backwards search

búsqueda *f* **lineal** *sustantivo* linear search

búsqueda *f* **lógica** *adj* logic-seeking

búsqueda *f* **mediante palabras clave** *sustantivo* disjunctive search

búsqueda *f* **por dicotomía** *sustantivo* dichotomising search *o* dichotomizing search

búsqueda *f* **retrospectiva** *sustantivo* retrospective search

búsqueda *f* **secuencial** *sustantivo* **1.** linear search **2.** sequential search ◇ **algoritmo de búsqueda secuencial** sequential search algorithm

búsqueda *f* **selectiva** *sustantivo* area search

búsqueda y carga de instrucciones *sustantivo* fetch

bus *m* **serial universal** *sustantivo* universal serial bus

bus *m* **serie universal** *sustantivo* USB

bus *m* **VLB** *sustantivo* **1.** VESA local bus **2.** VL-bus *o* VL local bus

bus *m* **VME** *sustantivo* VME bus

buzón ◇ **buzón** *m* **(de mensajes electrónicos)** mailbox

'Los buzones electrónicos se llenan de correspondencia no deseada, mientras los anunciantes avispados ensayan métodos que tratan de comprometer al consumidor, que muchas veces desvela contra su voluntad, y sin saberlo siquiera, su dirección electrónica.' [*La Red*]

buzón *m* **electrónico** *sustantivo* electronic mailbox ◇ **cuando contacto con la red, siempre examino mi buzón electrónico por si hay algún mensaje nuevo** when I log onto the network, I always check my electronic mailbox for new messages

byte *m* *abrev* B ■ *sustantivo* byte ◇ **byte** *m* **de datos con bits de error y control** envelope ◇ **KB** *o* **kilo-byte** KB (kilobyte)

byte *m* **de caracteres** *sustantivo* character byte

byte *m* **de control de acceso** *sustantivo* access control byte

bytes *mpl* **por pulgada** *sustantivo* bytes-per-inch

bytes *mpl* **por segundo** *sustantivo* **1.** Bps **2.** bytes per second

C

C *símbolo* C

C++ *sustantivo* C++

caballo *m* **de Troya** *sustantivo* Trojan Horse

cabecera *sustantivo* **1.** head **2.** header **3.** heading **4.** running head **5.** tape header ◇ **cabecera** *f* **de una página (de una lista)** head of form ◇ **cabecera** *f* **preestablecida (guardada en memoria)** form flash

cabecera *f* **de cinta** *sustantivo* tape header

cabecera *f* **de cinta magnética** *sustantivo* leader

cabecera *f* **de fichero** *sustantivo* **1.** file header **2.** header ◇ **la cabecera del fichero de la base de datos muestra el número total de registros y hace un listado de los campos indexados** the file header in the database file shows the total number of records and lists the index fields

cabecera *f* **de mensaje** *sustantivo* message header

cabeza *f* *sustantivo* head ◇ **cabeza** *f* **de disco (magnético) móvil** movable head disk ◇ **cabeza** *f* **de escritura de cinta magnética** tape head ◇ **cabeza** *f* **de lectura (de cintas magnéticas)** tape head

cabeza *f* **de bobina** *sustantivo* head

cabeza *f* **de borrado** *sustantivo* erase head

cabeza *f* **de escáner** *sustantivo* scan head ◇ **este modelo usa una cabeza de escáner que puede reconocer 256 colores diferentes** this model uses a scan head that can distinguish 256 different colours

cabeza *f* **de escritura** *sustantivo* **1.** record head **2.** write head

cabeza *f* **de impresora** *sustantivo* printhead

cabeza *f* **de lectura** *sustantivo* **1.** disk head **2.** playback head **3.** read head **4.** tape head ◇ **cabeza de lectura de cintas** tape playback head ◇ **cabeza de lectura de discos** disk playback head

cabeza *f* **de lectura desalineada** *sustantivo* nonaligned read head

cabeza *f* **de lectura/escritura** *sustantivo* **1.** combined head **2.** read/write head **3.** R/W head

cabeza *f* **de lectura/escritura de disquetes** *sustantivo* disk head

cabeza *f* **de red** *sustantivo* head end

cabeza *f* **de registro** *sustantivo* **1.** record head **2.** write head

cabeza *f* **flotante** *sustantivo* flying head

cabeza *f* **magnética** *sustantivo* magnetic head

cabeza *f* **múltiple rotativa** *sustantivo* head wheel

cable *sustantivo* **1.** cable **2.** lead **3.** line **4.** wire ◇ **cable** *m* **de par retorcido no recubierto** unshielded twisted-pair cable; UTP cable ◇ **cable** *m* **(modelo) 'Type' (de IBM)** Type cable ◇ **carga de una línea** line load ◇ **dispositivo de final de línea** line terminator ◇ **impedancia de línea** line impedance ◇ **repetidor de televisión por cable** cable TV relay station ◇ **sobretensiones transitorias de línea** line transient ◇ **televisión por cable** *o* **TV por cable** cable television *o* cable TV ◇ **tráfico** line load ◇ **unidad de extensión de una línea** line extender

'El consumo de televisión por cable también crece gracias a la red de fibra óptica. El Gobierno y AOL Time Warner han acordado que los estadounidenses retransmitirán en algunas zonas del sur, a cambio de que las agencias de noticias chinas hagan lo mismo, a través de AOL, en Nueva York y California, con gran presencia de emigrantes.' [*Ciberp@ís*]

cableado *m* *sustantivo* **1.** cable plant **2.** cabling **3.** wiring ◇ **cableado** *m* **según categoría (de cable)** category wiring ◇ **cada pie (30,5 cms) de cableado cuesta hasta dos libras** cabling costs up to £2 a foot ◇ **se tuvo que cambiar el cableado del sistema** the wiring in the system had to be replaced

cableado *m* **estructurado** *sustantivo* **1.** structured cabling **2.** structured wiring

cablear *verbo* *vt* to wire

cable *m* **coaxial** *sustantivo* co-axial cable *o* coax

cable *m* **de bajada** *sustantivo* drop cable

cable *m* **de bifurcación** *sustantivo* branch cable

cable *m* **de cinta** *sustantivo* **1.** ribbon cable **2.** tape cable

cable *m* **de conexión** *sustantivo* patch cord

cable *m* **de derivación** *sustantivo* drop cable

cable *m* **de entrada** *sustantivo* input lead

cable *m* **de fibra óptica** *sustantivo* fibre optic cable *o* fibre optic connection

cable *m* **de par retorcido** *sustantivo* twisted-pair cable

cable *m* **de par retorcido recubierto** *sustantivo* shielded twisted pair cable ■ *abrev* STP

cable *m* **de tierra** *sustantivo* earth wire

cable *m* **de toma de tierra** *sustantivo* earth wire

cable *m* **óptico** *sustantivo* fibre optic cable *o* fibre optic connection

cable *m* **plano** *sustantivo* tape cable

cable *m* **recubierto** *sustantivo* shielded cable

cables *mpl sustantivo* cabling ◇ **el uso de cables de alta calidad permite al usuario alcanzar una velocidad de transferencia de datos muy alta** using high-quality cabling will allow the user to achieve very high data transfer rates

cable *m* **terrestre** *sustantivo* landline

cabrestante *m* **de arrastre** *sustantivo* capstan

caché *m* **de nivel 1** *sustantivo* L1 cache

caché *m* **de nivel 2** *sustantivo* L2 cache

CAD *sustantivo* CAD ◇ **todos nuestros ingenieros diseñan en terminales equipados con CAD** all our engineers design on CAD workstations

CAD/CAM *sustantivo* CAD/CAM

cadena *f sustantivo* **1.** chain **2.** network **3.** string ◇ **barrido de cadenas** string scanning ◇ **cadena de caracteres** character string ◇ **cadena** *f* **de caracteres terminada en un carácter nulo** null terminated string ◇ **cadena** *f* **(de caracteres) prohibida** forbidden character ◇ **correspondencia de cadenas** string matching ◇ **cuando se imprime, se pueden encadenar más de 1.000 artículos o capítulos** more than 1,000 articles or chapters can be chained together when printing ◇ **mecanismo alimentador (de hojas) en cadena** chain delivery mechanism ◇ **red** *o* **cadena** *o* **canal de televisión** television network ◇ **red radiofónica** *o* **cadena de radio** radio network

cadena *f* **de caracteres** *sustantivo* **1.** catena **2.** character string

cadena *f* **de caracteres alfabéticos** *sustantivo* alphabetic string

cadena *f* **de caracteres alfanuméricos** *sustantivo* alphanumeric string

cadena *f* **de caracteres ASCIIZ** *sustantivo* ASCIIZ string

cadena *f* **de caracteres de identificación** *abrev* ID ■ *sustantivo* identifier

cadena *f* **de comando** *sustantivo* command string

cadena *f* **de elementos de datos** *sustantivo* data element chain

cadena *f* **de inicialización** *sustantivo* initialisation string *o* initialization string

cadena *f* **de instrucciones** *sustantivo* command chain

cadena *f* **en blanco** *sustantivo* blank string

cadena *f* **margarita** *sustantivo* daisy chain

cadena *f* **mariposa** *sustantivo* daisy chain

cadena *f* **nula** *sustantivo* null string

cadena *f* **numérica** *sustantivo* numeric string

cadena *f* **vacía** *sustantivo* **1.** blank string **2.** null string

cadmio-níquel *m sustantivo* nickel cadmium

caer *verbo vi* to drop

caída *f* **de potencia** *sustantivo* power loss

caja *f sustantivo* housing ◇ **cuando el ordenador se cayó al suelo, su caja se estropeó** the computer housing was damaged when it fell on the floor

caja *f* **de cableado** *sustantivo* wiring closet

caja *f* **de conexiones** *sustantivo* junction box

caja *f* **de control** *sustantivo* check box ◇ **seleccione la opción desplazando el cursor a la caja de selección y pulsando el botón del ratón** select the option by moving the cursor to the check box and pressing the mouse button

caja *f* **de decisión** *sustantivo* decision box

caja *f* **de derivación** *sustantivo* junction box

caja *f* **de diálogo** *sustantivo* dialog box

caja *f* **de empalme(s)** *sustantivo* junction box

caja *f* **de expansión** *sustantivo* expansion box

caja *f* **de Faraday** *sustantivo* Faraday cage

caja *f* **de herramientas** *sustantivo* toolkit

caja *f* **delimitadora** *sustantivo* bounding box

caja *f* **de objetos de E/S** *sustantivo* combo box

caja *f* **de placa de circuito** *sustantivo* card cage

caja *f* **de selección** *sustantivo* check box ◇ **seleccione la opción desplazando el cursor a la caja de selección y pulsando el botón del ratón** select the option by moving the cursor to the check box and pressing the mouse button

caja *f* **de útiles** *sustantivo* combo box

caja *f* **negra** *sustantivo* black box

caja *f* **secundaria** *sustantivo* B box

cajero *m* **automático** *sustantivo* **1.** ATM **2.** automated teller machine

cajista *m sustantivo* typesetter

calco *m sustantivo* carbon copy

Calculadora *f* **(de Microsoft Windows)** Calculator

calculadora *f* **digital electrónica** *sustantivo* electronic digital computer

calculadora *f* **programable** *sustantivo* programmable calculator

calcular *verbo vt* to crunch

calcular el tiempo *verbo* to time ◇ **reloj de temporización** timing clock ◇ **señales de temporización** timing signals

cálculo *m adj, sustantivo* computing

cálculo *m* **automático nuevo** *sustantivo* automatic recalculation

cálculo *m* **binario** *sustantivo* binary arithmetic

cálculo *m* **de coma fija** *sustantivo* fixed-point arithmetic

cálculo *m* **de coma flotante** *sustantivo* floating point arithmetic

cálculo *m* **de dimensiones** *sustantivo* dimensioning ◇ **el cálculo de las dimensiones de la red tiene lugar en esta línea** array dimensioning occurs at this line

cálculo *m* **de imágenes intermedias** *sustantivo* tweening ◇ **con el procedimiento de transformación en serie, se puede mostrar como una rana se convierte en una princesa en cinco pasos** using tweening, we can show how a frog turns into a princess in five steps

cálculo *m* **de una dirección** *sustantivo* address computation

cálculo *m* **subordinado** *sustantivo* background recalculation

cálculo *m* **ultra rápido** *sustantivo* number crunching ◇ **se necesita un procesador muy potente para las aplicaciones gráficas ya que éstas requieren una capacidad de cálculo ultra rápido** a very powerful processor is needed for graphics applications which require extensive number crunching capabilities

calibrado *m* *sustantivo* calibration

calibrar *verbo vt* to calibrate

calidad ◇ **calidad** *f* **del servicio (de transmisión de información)** quality of service

calidad *f* **borrador** *sustantivo* draft quality

calidad *m* **casi de impresión alta** *abrev* NLQ

calidad *f* **de datos** *sustantivo* data reliability

calidad *f* **de impresión** *sustantivo* 1. printer quality 2. print quality ◇ **una impresora gráfica con una resolución de 600 puntos por pulgada proporciona una buena calidad de impresión** a desktop printer with a resolution of 600dpi provides good print quality

calidad *f* **de impresora** *sustantivo* printer quality

calidad *f* **de la palabra** *sustantivo* speech quality

calidad *f* **del servicio (de transmisión de información)** *abrev* QOS

calidad *f* **de transmisión** *sustantivo* broadcast quality ◇ **podemos utilizar su presentación multimedia como anuncio en televisión si tiene calidad para ser emitido** we can use your multimedia presentation as the advert on TV if it's of broadcast quality

caliente *adj* hot ◇ **carácter fundido** *o* **composición caliente** *o* **al plomo** hot type ◇ **composición al plomo** *o* **composición caliente** hot metal composition

cámara *f* **anecoica** *sustantivo* anechoic chamber

cámara *f* **de compensación electrónica** *sustantivo* ACH

cámara *f* **de vídeo web** *sustantivo* web cam

cámara *f* **digital** *sustantivo* digital camera

cámara *f* **estéril** *sustantivo* clean room

cambiador *m* **de género** *sustantivo* gender changer

cambiar *sustantivo vt* change over ■ *verbo* 1. *vt* to negate 2. *vt* to swap

cambiar de dirección *verbo* to relocate ◇ **se cambia la dirección de los datos durante la ejecución** the data is relocated during execution

cambiar de lugar *verbo* to move

cambiar el nombre de *verbo* to rename ◇ **guarde el fichero y cambie el nombre a 'CLIENT'** save the file and rename it CLIENT

cambiar la ruta *verbo* to re-route

cambio *m* *sustantivo* 1. change 2. modification 3. shift 4. swap 5. swapping ◇ **cambio** *m* **de una tarea a otra** task swapping

cambio *m* **de aplicación** *sustantivo* context-switching

cambio *m* **de control** *sustantivo* control change

cambio *m* **de fuente de caracteres** *sustantivo* font change

cambio *m* **de página** *verbo* to form feed ■ *sustantivo* page break

cambio *m* **de tramos** *sustantivo* frame relay

cambio *m* **gradual** *sustantivo* 1. phased change-over 2. staged change-over

cambio *m* **progresivo** *sustantivo* phased change-over

camino *m* *sustantivo* 1. path 2. route 3. thread

camino *m* **completo** *sustantivo* full path

camino *m* **de acceso** *sustantivo* access path

camino *m* **de acceso (DOS)** *sustantivo* path

camino *m* **de datos** *sustantivo* data path

campana *f* **de insonorización** *sustantivo* 1. acoustic hood 2. sound hood

campo *sustantivo* 1. field 2. range ◇ **campo** *m* **(de gran capacidad) para datos binarios** binary large object; blob ◇ **el registro 'empleado' tiene un campo para la (variable) 'edad'** the employee record has a field for age ◇ **intensidad de campo** field strength

campo *m* **binario** *sustantivo* binary field

campo *m* **calculado** *sustantivo* calculated field

campo *m* **clave** *sustantivo* key field

campo *m* **de aplicación** *sustantivo* scope

campo *m* **de audiofrecuencias** *sustantivo* audio range

campo *m* **de clasificación** *sustantivo* sortkey *o* sort field ◇ **las instrucciones se clasificaron por fechas al tomar el campo de fechas como la clave de clasificación** the orders were sorted according to dates by assigning the date field as the sortkey

campo *m* **de control** *sustantivo* control field

campo *m* **de datos** *sustantivo* data field

campo *m* **de datos del operador** *sustantivo* operand field

campo *m* **de dirección** *sustantivo* address field

campo *m* **de etiqueta** *sustantivo* label field

campo *m* **de identificación** *sustantivo* label field

campo *m* **de longitud fija** *sustantivo* fixed-length field

campo *m* **de memorándum** *sustantivo* memo field

campo *m* **de notas** *sustantivo* comment field

campo *m* **de operación** *sustantivo* operation field

campo *m* **de operando** *sustantivo* operand field

campo *m* **de signo** *sustantivo* signed field

campo *m* **de tamaño fijo** *sustantivo* constant length field

campo *m* **estimado** *sustantivo* calculated field

campo *m* **fijo** *sustantivo* fixed field

campo *m* **magnético** *sustantivo* magnetic field

campo *m* **no protegido** *sustantivo* unprotected field

campo *m* **protegido** *sustantivo* protected field

canal *sustantivo* channel ◊ **campo de control de canales** channel control field ◊ **canal** *m* **(de transmisión) de datos** data channel ◊ **canal** *m* **de retorno de una red local** backward LAN channel ◊ **canal** *m* **de transmisión de la información** information transfer channel ◊ **canal** *m* **Q que identifica un corte del CD y su duración** Q Channel ◊ **canal** *m* **T (portador de 1.544 megabits para manejar canales de voz y de datos a 64kbits** *or* **seg.)** T1 ◊ **canal** *m* **universal de transmisión por bloques** universal block channel ◊ **condición de estado del canal** channel status condition ◊ **conector de canales** channel connector ◊ **conmutación de canal** channel switching ◊ **controlador de canal** channel controler ◊ **error de canal** channel error ◊ **extensión de área de memoria para la gestión de canales** channel work area expansion ◊ **grupo de canales** *o* **de vías** channel group ◊ **palabra de dirección de canal** channel address word ◊ **respuesta de tiempo de canal** channel time response

canal *m* **alfa** *sustantivo* alpha channel

canal *m* **analógico** *sustantivo* analog channel

canal *m* **central** *sustantivo* centre channel

canal *m* **común** *sustantivo* common carrier

canal *m* **de comunicaciones** *sustantivo* communications channel

canal *m* **de datos** *sustantivo* data channel

canal *m* **dedicado** *sustantivo* dedicated channel

canal *m* **de entrada/salida** *sustantivo* **1.** input/output channel **2.** I/O channel

canal *m* **de fibra** *sustantivo* fibre channel

canal *m* **de retorno** *sustantivo* reverse channel

canal *m* **de transmisión** *sustantivo* **1.** communications channel **2.** transmission channel

canal *m* **digital** *sustantivo* digital channel

canal *m* **doble** *sustantivo* dual channel

canal *m* **E/S** *sustantivo* I/O channel

canal *m* **especializado** *sustantivo* dedicated channel

canal *m* **hacia atrás** *sustantivo* backward channel

canalización *sustantivo* **1.** channelling **2.** conduit **3.** tunnelling

> 'Las páginas web, además de ser portadoras de la información empresarial, contienen los elementos de canalización del tráfico de los usuarios y de obtención de datos de interés para los responsables del márketing.' [*PC Plus*]

canalizar *verbo vt* to channel

canal *m* **lógico** *sustantivo* logical channel

canal *m* **MIDI** *sustantivo* MIDI channel

canal *m* **principal** *sustantivo* primary channel

canal *m* **secundario** *sustantivo* secondary channel

canal *m* **universal de transmisión por bloques** *abrev* UBC

cancelación *f sustantivo* cancellation

cancelar *verbo vt* to cancel

cancelar anormalmente *verbo* to abort

canjeable *adj* exchangeable

cañón *m sustantivo* **1.** data projector **2.** gun

cañón *m* **de electrones** *sustantivo* electron gun

C ANSI *sustantivo* ANSI C

cantidad *f sustantivo* quantity ◊ **(gran) cantidad** quantity ◊ **compró una gran cantidad de piezas de repuesto** he bought a large quantity of spare parts ◊ **se ha importado una pequeña cantidad de copias ilegales del programa** a small quantity of illegal copies of the program have been imported

capa *sustantivo* **1.** layer **2.** presentation layer ◊ **capa** *f* **de adaptación en modo de transferencia asíncrona** AAL; ATM adaptation layer ◊ **capa** *f* **de sesiones de función de protocolo de red** session layer

capa *f* **binaria** *sustantivo* bit plane

capacidad *f sustantivo* **1.** capacity **2.** microprocessor addressing capabilities **3.** storage capacity ◊ **capacidad** *f* **de proceso (electrónico) de datos** EDP capability ◊ **capacidad** *f* **de proceso electrónico de datos** electronic data processing capability

capacidad *f* **de cálculo** *sustantivo* computing power

capacidad *f* **de cálculo aritmético** *sustantivo* arithmetic capability

capacidad *f* **de canal** *sustantivo* channel capacity

capacidad *f* **de direccionamiento** *sustantivo* **1.** addressability **2.** addressing capacity

capacidad *f* **de emulación** *sustantivo* emulation facility

capacidad *f* **de memoria** *sustantivo* **1.** memory capacity **2.** storage capacity ◊ **la capacidad total de la memoria es ahora de 3 MB** total storage capacity is now 3MB

capacidad *f* **de producción** *sustantivo* producing capacity

capacidad *f* **de salto** *sustantivo* skip capability

capacidad *f* **de transferencia** *sustantivo* bandwidth ◊ **este cable de fibra óptica tiene una mayor capacidad de transferencia que el viejo cable de cobre, por lo que puede transportar datos a mayor velocidad** this fibre-optic cable has a greater bandwidth than the old copper cable and so it can carry data at higher speeds ◊ **la capacidad de transferencia de un teléfono es de 3100Hz** telephone bandwidth is 3100Hz

capacidad *f* **de transmisión de información** *sustantivo* information rate

capacidad *f* **de un circuito** *sustantivo* circuit capacity

capacidad *f* **máxima** *sustantivo* maximum capacity

capacidad *f* **máxima absoluta** *sustantivo* absolute maximum rating

capacidad *f* **no formateada** *sustantivo* unformatted capacity

capacitancia *f* *sustantivo* capacitance

capacitivo *adj* capacitative *o* capacititive

capa *f* **de adaptación ATM** *sustantivo* ATM adaptation layer

capa *f* **de aplicación** *sustantivo* application layer

capa *f* **de enlace de datos** *sustantivo* data link layer

capa *f* **de fósforo** *sustantivo* phosphor coating

capa *f* **de presentación** *sustantivo* presentation layer

capa *f* **de protocolo** *sustantivo* layer

capa *f* **de red** *sustantivo* network layer

capa *f* **de sesión** *sustantivo* session layer

capa *f* **fina** *sustantivo* thin film

capa *f* **física** *sustantivo* physical layer

capa *f* **fosforescente** *sustantivo* phosphor coating

capa *f* **gruesa** *sustantivo* thick film

capas ◊ **capas** *fpl* **en modo de transferencia asíncrona** ATM layers

capas *fpl* **ATM** *sustantivo* ATM layers

capa *f* **(de) transporte** *sustantivo* transport layer

cápsula *f* *sustantivo* shell

captación *f* **de datos** *sustantivo* data capture

captador *sustantivo* 1. grabber 2. sensor ◊ **captador** *m* **de imágenes (de vídeo)** frame grabber

captador *m* **de imágenes** *sustantivo* frame grabber

captura *f* *sustantivo* 1. capture 2. fetch cycle ◊ **captura** *f* **por demanda de la memoria paginada** demand fetching

captura *f* **de datos** *sustantivo* data capture ◊ **la recogida de datos se inicia cuando se recibe una señal de interrupción** data capture starts when an interrupt is received

captura *f* **de pantalla** *verbo* to screen capture ■ *sustantivo* 1. screen grab 2. screen shot

capturar *verbo* 1. *vt* to capture 2. *vt* to fetch

carácter *m* *sustantivo* 1. character 2. function digit 3. special sort ◊ **carácter** *m* **de control de la impresión** print control character ◊ **carácter** *m* **de redirección (del DOS)** redirect operator ◊ **inclinación de un carácter** character skew ◊ **protocolos orientados al carácter** character oriented protocols (COP) ◊ **tecla (de) carácter** character key

carácter *m* **ASCII** *sustantivo* ASCII character

carácter *m* **BS** *abrev* BS

carácter *m* **comodín** *sustantivo* 1. question mark 2. wild card *o* wild card character

carácter *m* **completo** *plural noun* fully formed character ◊ **una impresora de margarita produce caracteres completos** a daisy wheel printer produces fully formed characters

carácter *m* **de acuse de recibo** *sustantivo* acknowledge character

carácter *m* **de alarma** *sustantivo* bell character *o* BEL

carácter *m* **de anulación** *sustantivo* cancel character ◊ **después de cualquier error, el programa envía automáticamente un carácter de cancelación** the software automatically sends a cancel character after any error

carácter *m* **de borrado** *sustantivo* erase character

carácter *m* **de consulta** *sustantivo* inquiry character

carácter *m* **de control** *sustantivo* 1. check character 2. control character 3. device control character

carácter *m* **de control de dispositivo** *sustantivo* device control character

carácter *m* **de control de precisión** *sustantivo* accuracy control character

carácter *m* **de desplazamiento** *sustantivo* shift character

carácter *m* **de eliminación** *sustantivo* delete character

carácter *m* **de escape** *sustantivo* escape character

carácter *m* **de espaciado** *sustantivo* space character

carácter *m* **de espacio** *sustantivo* 1. blank character 2. space character

carácter *m* **de final de línea** *sustantivo* line ending

carácter *m* **de identificación** *abrev* ID ■ *sustantivo* 1. identification character 2. identifier

carácter *m* **de instrucción** *sustantivo* instruction character

carácter *m* **de instrucción de periféricos** *sustantivo* device control character

carácter *m* **de línea nueva** *sustantivo* new line character

carácter *m* **de pantalla** *sustantivo* display character

carácter *m* **de periféricos** *sustantivo* device control character

carácter *m* **de petición** *sustantivo* enquiry character

carácter *m* **de rechazo de bloque** *sustantivo* block ignore character

carácter *m* **de redundancia** *sustantivo* redundant character

carácter *m* **de relleno** *sustantivo* **1.** fill character **2.** gap character **3.** ignore character **4.** NUL character **5.** null character **6.** pad character

carácter *m* **de retorno de línea** *sustantivo* new line character

carácter *m* **de retroceso** *sustantivo* backspace character

carácter *m* **de sincronización** *sustantivo* sync character

carácter *m* **de supresión** *sustantivo* delete character

carácter *m* **de sustitución** *sustantivo* substitute character

carácter *m* **de tabulación** *sustantivo* tab character

carácter *m* **de tabulado** *sustantivo* tab character

carácter *m* **disponible sincrónico** *sustantivo* synchronous idle character

carácter *m* **en blanco** *sustantivo* **1.** blank character **2.** space character

carácter *m* **en negrita** *sustantivo* bold face

caracteres *sustantivo* type ◇ **(fuente de) caracteres (de la impresora)** type ◇ **caracteres** *mpl* **que se destacan visualmente** display highlights ◇ **fuente de caracteres** type font ◇ **para la cabecera, cambiaron la fuente de caracteres a cursiva** they switched to italic type for the heading

caracteres *mpl* **alfanuméricos** *plural noun* **1.** alphanumeric characters **2.** alphanumerics

caracteres *mpl* **alfanuméricos mostrados** *plural noun* (*sobre una pantalla de videotexto*) blast-through alphanumerics

caracteres *mpl* **codificados en binario** *plural noun* binary coded characters

caracteres *mpl* **de control de impresión** *sustantivo* printer control characters

caracteres *mpl* **de llamada selectiva** *plural noun* polling characters

caracteres *mpl* **dóricos** *plural noun* **1.** block capitals **2.** block letters

carácter *m* **especial** *sustantivo* special character

caracteres *mpl* **por pulgada** *plural noun* characters per inch ■ *sustantivo* cpi

caracteres *mpl* **por segundo (cps)** *sustantivo* **1.** characters per second **2.** cps

caracteres *mpl* **programados por el usuario** *plural noun* user-defined character

caracteres *mpl* **TrueType™** (*marca comercial*) TrueType

carácter *m* **gráfico** *sustantivo* graphics character

carácter *m* **intermitente** *sustantivo* flashing character

característica *f sustantivo* attribute

característica *f* **esencial** *sustantivo* prime attribute

característica *f* **más importante** *sustantivo* key feature ◇ **las principales características de este sistema son: 20 Mb de memoria formateada con un tiempo de acceso de 60 ms** the key features of this system are: 20Mb of formatted storage with an access time of 60ms

característica *f* **principal** *sustantivo* key feature ◇ **las principales características de este sistema son: 20 Mb de memoria formateada con un tiempo de acceso de 60 ms** the key features of this system are: 20Mb of formatted storage with an access time of 60ms

característico *m sustantivo* characteristic ◇ **este defecto es característico de esta marca y modelo de ordenador personal** this fault is characteristic of this make and model of personal computer

carácter *m* **más significativo** *sustantivo* **1.** most significant digit *o* most significant character **2.** MSD

carácter *m* **no válido** *sustantivo* illegal character

carácter *m* **nulo** *sustantivo* **1.** idle character **2.** NUL character **3.** null character

carácter *m* **numérico** *sustantivo* numeric character

carácter *m* **prohibido** *sustantivo* **1.** forbidden character *o* forbidden combination **2.** illegal character

carácter *m* **redundante** *sustantivo* redundant character

carácter *m* **reservado** *sustantivo* reserved character ◇ **en el DOS, el carácter reservado \ se utiliza para representar el camino de un directorio** in DOS, the reserved character \ is used to represent a directory path

carácter *m* **tab** *sustantivo* tab character

carga *sustantivo* **1.** charge **2.** loading ◇ **carga** *f* **automática de fuentes de caracteres** automatic font downloading ◇ **carga** *f* **en modo de transferencia asíncrona** ATM payload ◇ **cargar (un programa) puede ser un proceso largo** loading can be a long process

carga *f* **de trabajo** *f sustantivo* workload

carga *f* **de una batería** *sustantivo* battery charging

cargador *sustantivo* **1.** cartridge **2.** loader ◇ **este ordenador portátil no tiene disqueteras, pero dispone de una ranura para cargadores ROM** the portable computer has no disk drives, but has a slot for ROM cartridges

'Gracias a los cargadores de arranque podrás tener varios sistemas en tu ordenador y decidir cada vez cuál de ellos cargar al encenderlo.' [*Computer Hoy*]

cargador *m* **absoluto** *sustantivo* absolute loader

cargador *m* **automático** *sustantivo* automatic loader

cargador *m* **binario** *sustantivo* binary loader

cargador *m* **de cinta** *sustantivo* tape cartridge

cargador *m* **de cinta magnética** *sustantivo* **1.** magnetic tape cartridge **2.** magnetic tape cassette

cargador *m* **de datos** *sustantivo* data cartridge

cargador *m* **de disco(s)** *sustantivo* disk cartridge

cargador *m* **de discos** *sustantivo* disk pack

cargador *m* **de enlaces** *sustantivo* linking loader

cargador *m* **de información** *sustantivo* data cartridge

cargador *m* **de tarjetas perforadas** *sustantivo* hopper

cargador *m* **ROM** *sustantivo* ROM cartridge ◊ **este ordenador portátil no tiene disqueteras, pero dispone de una ranura para cargadores ROM** the portable computer has no disk drives, but has a slot for ROM cartridges

carga *f* **eléctrica** *sustantivo* electric charge

carga *f* **estática** *sustantivo* corona

cargar *verbo* **1.** *vt* to charge **2.** to load **3.** *vt* to upload ◊ **carga equilibrada** matched load ◊ **impedancia de carga** load impedance ◊ **que se puede cargar** bootable ◊ **tiempo de descarga** load life

carga *f* **útil ATM** *sustantivo* ATM payload

carpeta *f* *sustantivo* folder ◊ **carpeta** *f* **de fuentes (de caracteres)** Fonts Folder

carpeta *f* **compartida** *sustantivo* shared folder

carpeta *f* **de inicio** *sustantivo* Startup folder

carpeta *f* **del sistema** *sustantivo* system folder

carpeta *f* **padre** *sustantivo* parent folder

carpeta *f* **preferencial (Macintosh)** *sustantivo* blessed folder

carrera *f* *sustantivo* race ◊ **condición de carrera** race condition

carrete *m* *sustantivo* spool

carro *m* *sustantivo* carriage ◊ **retorno de carro** *or* **avance de línea** carriage return/line feed (CR/LF)

carta *f* **estándar** *sustantivo* **1.** form letter **2.** repetitive letter

carta *f* **modelo** *sustantivo* form letter

carta *f* **tipo** *sustantivo* **1.** form letter **2.** repetitive letter **3.** template

cartucho *m* *sustantivo* **1.** cartridge **2.** tape cartridge ◊ **cartucho** *m* **(de banda magnética)** magnetic cartridge ◊ **cartucho** *m* **de (una unidad de) cinta con flujo continuo** stringy floppy; tape streamer

cartucho *m* **de cinta** *sustantivo* tape cartridge

cartucho *m* **de cinta magnética** *sustantivo* **1.** magnetic tape cartridge **2.** magnetic tape cassette

cartucho *m* **de datos** *sustantivo* data cartridge

cartucho *m* **de juego** *sustantivo* game cartridge

cartucho *m* **de tinta** *sustantivo* ink cartridge

cartucho *m* **de tóner** *sustantivo* toner cartridge ◊ **cambie el cartucho de tóner según se indique en el manual** change toner cartridge according to the manual

cartucho *m* **RAM** *sustantivo* RAM cartridge

cartucho *m* **ROM** *sustantivo* ROM cartridge

CASE *sustantivo* case

casete *mf* *sustantivo* **1.** cassette **2.** cassette recorder **3.** cassette tape ◊ **casete** *f* **(de banda magnética)** magnetic cassette ◊ **debe hacer una copia de seguridad de la información del ordenador en una casete** you must back up the information from the computer onto a cassette ◊ **videocasete** *o* **casete de vídeo** video cassette

casete *f* **(de cinta)** *sustantivo* tape cassette

casete *f* **audionumérica** *sustantivo* digital cassette

casete *f* **de datos** *sustantivo* data cassette

casete *f* **de memoria de burbujas** *sustantivo* bubble memory cassette

casete *f* **digital** *sustantivo* digital cassette

casete *f* **digital compacto** *sustantivo* **1.** DCC **2.** digital compact cassette

casi- *prefijo* quasi-

casi instrucción *f* *sustantivo* quasi-instruction

casillero *m* *sustantivo* rack

CAST *sustantivo* cast

catalogación *f* **electrónica** *sustantivo* electronic filing

catalogación *f* **por ordenador** *sustantivo* electronic filing

catalogar *verbo* *vt* to catalogue ◊ **todos los terminales son catalogados con su ubicación, signo de llamada y tabla de atributos** all the terminals are catalogued, with their location, call sign and attribute table

catálogo *m* *sustantivo* catalogue ◊ **catálogo disk** disk catalogue ◊ **la entrada en el catálogo de ficheros de disco queda eliminada cuando se borra el fichero** the entry in the disk catalogue is removed when the file is deleted

catástrofe *f* *sustantivo* catastrophe

categoría 1 *sustantivo* Category 1

categoría 2 *sustantivo* Category 2

categoría 3 *sustantivo* Category 3

categoría 4 *sustantivo* Category 4

categoría 5 *sustantivo* Category 5

categoría *f* **de acceso** *sustantivo* access category

categoría *f* **de presentación** *sustantivo* presentation layer

categoría *f* **de sesiones** *sustantivo* session layer

CCD *abrev* CCD

CD *abrev* CD ■ *sustantivo* compact disc ◇ **de calidad CD** CD quality

'Las nuevas tecnologías de la información han ocasionado transformaciones notables en la definición de los negocios y de los sectores. Las innovaciones tecnológicas … desmantelan a una velocidad vertiginosa cualquier fortaleza de la empresa mejor enfocada … Eso le pasó a la Encyclopaedia Britannica, empresa excelente durante más de doscientos años, casi arrumbada por los CD-ROM.' [*Nueva economía*]

CD *m* **grabable** *sustantivo* recordable CD

CD-I *sustantivo* CD-I

CD *m* **interactivo** *sustantivo* compact disc-interactive

CD *m* **para vídeo digital** *sustantivo* video-CD

CD-R *sustantivo* CD-R

CD *m* **regrabable** *sustantivo* CD-ROM Re-Writable

CD-RW *m sustantivo* CD-RW

celda *f sustantivo* cell

celda *f* **activa** *sustantivo* active cell

celda *f* **de anclaje** *sustantivo* anchor cell

celda *f* **de control de colores** *sustantivo* colour cell

celda *f* **de memoria** *sustantivo* memory cell

celda *f* **de (la) memoria** *sustantivo* store cell

celda *f* **de respuesta** *sustantivo* response position

celda *f* **de trabajo** *sustantivo* active cell

celda *f* **magnética** *sustantivo* magnetic cell

celda *f* **vacía** *sustantivo* blank cell

célula *f sustantivo* element

célula *f* **binaria** *sustantivo* binary cell

centellear *verbo vi* to flicker

centelleo *m sustantivo* flicker

central *f* **telefónica** *sustantivo* exchange

centrar *verbo vt* to centre

centrar las cabezas *verbo* to centre

centro *sustantivo* hub ◇ **centro** *m* **de recuperación de (la) información** information retrieval centre ◇ **centro** *m* **nacional de aplicaciones de supercomputación** NCSA

'El centro comercial virtual de bancos y cajas de ahorro sirve para promocionar y popularizar el uso de sus herramientas para el comercio electrónico, como son sus TPV virtual (el sistema para pagar con tarjeta por Internet) y su pasarela de pagos (el sistema de seguridad para las transacciones electrónicas).' [*Ciberp@ís*]

centro *m* **de conmutación** *sustantivo* switching centre

centro *m* **de servidores** *sustantivo* server farm

centro Xerox (*centro de desarrollo*) Xerox PARC

cerebro *m* **humano** *sustantivo* wetware

cero *m sustantivo* zero ◇ **el código de llamadas internacionales es cero cero (00)** the code for international calls is zero zero (00)

cero *m* **barrado** *sustantivo* slashed zero

cero *m* **de cabeza** *sustantivo* leading zero

cerrado *adj* hard

cerrar *verbo* 1. *vt* to close 2. *vt* to lock 3. *vt* to quit 4. *vt* to shut down ◇ **televisión en circuito cerrado** closed circuit television (CCTV)

certificado *m sustantivo* certificate

certificado *m* **de homologación** *sustantivo* certificate of approval

cesto *m* **de la compra** *sustantivo* shopping basket *o* shopping cart

CF32 *sustantivo* CD32

charlar *verbo vi* to chat

chasis *m sustantivo* chassis

chasis *m* **bajo tensión** *sustantivo* hot chassis

chasis *m* **de cableado** *sustantivo* wiring frame

chasis *m* **fijo** *sustantivo* rack

chasis *m* **magnetofónico** *sustantivo* tape deck

chasis *m* **preparado** *adj* rack mounted

CHCP *sustantivo* CHCP

chip *m sustantivo* 1. chip 2. silicon chip ◇ **chip** *m* **de (síntesis de) voz** speech chip ◇ **la línea de validación de datos está conectada a la línea de selección del chip de pestillo** the data strobe line is connected to the latch chip select line

chip *m* **de diagnóstico** *sustantivo* diagnostic chip ◇ **están haciendo una investigación sobre chips de diagnóstico para probar ordenadores equipados con procesadores** they are carrying out research on diagnostic chips to test computers that contain processors

chip *m* **de memoria** *sustantivo* memory chip

chip *m* **de microprocesador** *sustantivo* microprocessor chip

chip *m* **de sonido** *sustantivo* sound chip

chip *m* **matemático** *sustantivo* maths chip

chip *m* **RAM** *sustantivo* RAM chip

choque *m sustantivo* collision

cianotipo *m sustantivo* blueprint

ciber- *prefijo* cyber-

cibercafé *sustantivo* 1. cybercafé 2. Internet café

'Proliferan los cibercafés, las charlas, los clubes de todo género en los que adolescentes soñadores, amas de casa hastiadas e individuos en paro despeñan sus horas polemizando sobre los temas más inimaginables.' [*La Red*]

ciberespacio *sustantivo* cyberspace

'En el caso de Internet, los navegantes del ciberespacio (como los de los océanos) necesitan tiempo para adentrarse en las aguas excesivas, a veces procelosas, y no siempre limpias de la WWW.' [*La Red*]

ciberley *f sustantivo* cyberlaw

cibernética *f sustantivo* cybernetics
ciberocupación *f sustantivo* cybersquatting
cíclico *adj* cyclic
ciclo *m sustantivo* **1.** cycle **2.** loop ◊ **ciclo** *m* **de captura (de una instrucción)** fetch-execute cycle ◊ **ciclo** *m* **de ejecución (de una instrucción)** fetch-execute cycle ◊ **ciclo** *m* **de rotación de los ficheros de seguridad** grandfather cycle ◊ **ciclo** *m* **de vida de un programa** software life cycle ◊ **ciclo** *m* **de vida de un sistema** system life cycle
ciclo *m* **abuelo** *sustantivo* grandfather cycle
ciclo *m* **de acción** *sustantivo* action cycle
ciclo *m* **de actualización** *sustantivo* refresh cycle
ciclo *m* **de control** *sustantivo* control cycle
ciclo *m* **de ejecución** *sustantivo* **1.** execute cycle **2.** execution cycle
ciclo *m* **de instrucciones** *sustantivo* instruction cycle
ciclo *m* **de la CPU** *sustantivo* CPU cycle
ciclo *m* **de la unidad central** *sustantivo* CPU cycle
ciclo *m* **de lectura** *sustantivo* **1.** fetch cycle **2.** read cycle
ciclo *m* **de lectura/escritura** *sustantivo* **1.** read/write cycle **2.** R/W cycle
ciclo *m* **del reloj** *sustantivo* clock cycle
ciclo *m* **de máquina** *sustantivo* machine cycle
ciclo *m* **de memoria** *sustantivo* memory cycle
ciclo *m* **de operación** *sustantivo* operation cycle
ciclo *m* **funcional** *sustantivo* action cycle
ciclo *m* **principal** *sustantivo* major cycle
ciclo *m* **sin fin** *sustantivo* continuous loop
ciego *adj* blind
cierre *m* **de ficheros** *sustantivo* file locking
cierre *m* **de línea** *sustantivo* (*radiocommunications*) lockout
cierre *m* **de protección** *sustantivo* advisory lock
cierre *m* **de sesión** *sustantivo* **1.** logging off **2.** logging out
cifra *sustantivo* **1.** check number **2.** cypher **3.** digit **4.** number **5.** numeral **6.** unallowable digit ◊ **cifra** *f* **(numérica) de control** check digit ◊ **un número de teléfono de ocho cifras** a phone number with eight digits *o* an eight-digit phone number
cifra *f* **de alto nivel** *sustantivo* high order
cifra *f* **de orden inferior** *sustantivo* low-order digit ◊ **el 6 es la cifra menos significativa del número 234156** the number 234156 has a low-order digit of 6
cifra *f* **menos significativa** *sustantivo* low-order digit ◊ **el 6 es la cifra menos significativa del número 234156** the number 234156 has a low-order digit of 6
cifrar *verbo* **1.** *vt* to code **2.** *vt* to encipher **3.** *vt* to encode **4.** *vt* to encrypt ◊ **están en lenguaje**

cifrado our competitors cannot understand our files – they have all been enciphered
cilindro *m sustantivo* **1.** cylinder **2.** drum
cinta *f* **audiodigital** *sustantivo* **1.** DAT **2.** digital audio tape
cinta *f* **casete** *sustantivo* cassette tape
cinta *f* **continua** *sustantivo* streamer
cinta *f* **de carbón** *sustantivo* carbon ribbon
cinta *f* **de cartucho** *sustantivo* cartridge ribbon
cinta *f* **de empalmar** *sustantivo* splicing tape
cinta *f* **de empalme** *sustantivo* splicing tape
cinta *f* **de impresora** *sustantivo* printer ribbon
cinta *f* **de modificaciones** *sustantivo* change tape
cinta *f* **de papel** *sustantivo* paper tape
cinta *f* **de trabajo** *sustantivo* scratch tape
cinta *f* **de una sola pasada** *sustantivo* single-strike ribbon
cinta *f* **de vídeo** *sustantivo* video tape
cinta *f* **maestra** *sustantivo* master tape
cinta *f* **magnética** *sustantivo* **1.** cassette tape **2.** magnetic tape **3.** mag tape
cinta *f* **no reutilizable** *sustantivo* single-strike ribbon
cinta *f* **original** *sustantivo* master tape
cinta *f* **perforada** *sustantivo* **1.** perforated tape **2.** punched tape *o* punched paper tape **3.** punched tape
cinta *f* **sin formato** *sustantivo* unjustified tape
cinta *f* **sin justificar** *sustantivo* unjustified tape
cinta *f* **virgen** *sustantivo* blank tape
circuito *m sustantivo* **1.** circuit **2.** loop ◊ **características de un circuito** circuit grade ◊ **circuito** *m* **de respuesta en nanosegundos** (*electrónico or lógico*) nanocircuit ◊ **circuito** *m* **(integrado generador) de sonido** music chip ◊ **circuito** *m* **encriptado de protección de software** dongle ◊ **circuito** *m* **(dispuesto) en serie** series circuit ◊ **(tarjeta de) circuito impreso** printed circuit board (PCB) ◊ **circuito** *m* **integrado de entrada** *or* **salida en paralelo** parallel input/output chip ◊ **circuito** *m* **integrado de tarjeta de vídeo** video interface chip ◊ **conjunto digital conmutado de circuitos** circuit switched digital circuitry (CSDC) ◊ **nivel de ruido de un circuito** circuit noise level ◊ **red conmutada de circuitos** circuit switched network
circuito *m sustantivo* nonequivalence gate
circuito *m* **alquilado** *sustantivo* leased line
circuito *m* **analógico** *sustantivo* analog gate
circuito *m* **antirrebote** *sustantivo* de-bounce circuit
circuito *m* **basculante** *sustantivo* flip-flop
circuito *m* **biestable** *sustantivo* flip-flop
circuito *m* **biestable de tipo JK** *sustantivo* JK-flip-flop
circuito *m* **cíclico** *sustantivo* round robin

circuito *m* **combinatorio** *sustantivo* combinational circuit

circuito *m* **compensado** *sustantivo* balanced circuit

circuito *m* **compuesto** *sustantivo* 1. composite circuit 2. hybrid circuit

circuito *m* **de anti-coincidencia** *sustantivo* anticoincidence circuit *o* anticoincidence function

circuito *m* **de coincidencia** *sustantivo* 1. AND circuit *o* AND element 2. coincidence circuit *o* coincidence element 3. coincidence gate *o* coincidence circuit *o* coincidence element

circuito *m* **de conmutación** *sustantivo* switching circuit

circuito *m* **de datos** *sustantivo* data circuit

circuito *m* **de decisión** *sustantivo* decision circuit

circuito *m* **de equivalencia** *sustantivo* equivalence gate

circuito *m* **de extensión** *sustantivo* plug-in unit

circuito *m* **de muestreo** *sustantivo* sampler

circuito *m* **de muestreo y retención** *sustantivo* sample and hold circuit

circuito *m* **de respuesta en nanosegundos** *sustantivo* nanosecond circuit

circuito *m* **de unión** *sustantivo* trunk

circuito *m* **digital** *sustantivo* digital circuit

circuito *m* **dúplex** *sustantivo* duplex circuit

circuito *m* **en red** *sustantivo* gate array

circuito *m* **equilibrado** *sustantivo* balanced circuit

circuito *m* **híbrido** *sustantivo* hybrid circuit

circuito *m* **integrado** *sustantivo* chip ■ *abrev* IC ■ *sustantivo* 1. integrated circuit 2. on chip

circuito *m* **integrado de silicio** *sustantivo* silicon chip

circuito *m* **integrado para aplicaciones específicas** *sustantivo* application specific integrated circuits ■ *plural noun* ASIC

circuito *m* **intermedio** *sustantivo* buffer

circuito *m* **lógico** *sustantivo* 1. gate circuit 2. logic circuit 3. logic gate

circuito *m* **lógico complejo** *sustantivo* gate array

circuito *m* **lógico de tres estados** *sustantivo* three state logic

circuito *m* **lógico no conectado** *sustantivo* 1. ULA 2. uncommitted logic array

circuito *m* **mixto** *sustantivo* hybrid circuit

circuito *m* **multipunto** *sustantivo* multidrop circuit

circuito *m* **NO** *sustantivo* 1. negation gate 2. NOT gate

circuito *m* **NO-O** *sustantivo* NOR gate

circuito *m* **NO-Y** *sustantivo* NAND gate

circuito *m* **O** *sustantivo* OR gate

circuito *m* **O exclusivo** *sustantivo* NEQ gate

circuitos *mpl* **programados** *sustantivo* scheduled circuits

circuito *m* **virtual** *sustantivo* virtual circuit

circuito *m* **Y** *sustantivo* AND circuit *o* AND element

circular *adj* cyclic ◇ **(hacer) circular** circulate

cita *f sustantivo* quotation

citar *verbo* 1. *vt* to quote 2. to quote

citas *fpl* **por ordenador** *sustantivo* computer dating

clase *f sustantivo* 1. class 2. sort

clasificación *f* **con soporte externo** *sustantivo* external sort

clasificación *f* **de ficheros** *verbo* to file sort

clasificación *f* **de Shell** *sustantivo* shell sort

clasificación *f* **electrónica** *sustantivo* electronic filing

clasificación *f* **en orden creciente** *sustantivo* forward mode

clasificación *f* **externa** *sustantivo* external sort

clasificación *f* **interna** *sustantivo* internal sort

clasificación *f* **por burbujas** *sustantivo* bubble sort

clasificación *f* **por selección arbórea** *sustantivo* tree selection sort

clasificación *f* **rápida** *sustantivo* quicksort

clasificación *f* **selectiva** *sustantivo* selective sort

clasificador *m sustantivo* 1. collator 2. folder

clasificar *verbo* 1. *vt* to match 2. *vt* to order 3. *vt* to sort ◇ **clasificar (datos) en orden alfabético** alphasort ◇ **(función de) clasificar y fusionar** to merge sort

clasificar por rango *verbo* to rank

clave *f sustantivo* 1. key 2. sortkey *o* sort field ◇ **las instrucciones se clasificaron por fechas al tomar el campo de fechas como la clave de clasificación** the orders were sorted according to dates by assigning the date field as the sortkey

clave *f* **cifrada** *sustantivo* 1. cipher key 2. cryptographic key

clave *f* **criptográfica** *sustantivo* cryptographic key

clave *f* **de acceso** *sustantivo* password ◇ **el usuario debe escribir su contraseña para poder acceder a la base de datos** the user has to key in the password before he can access the database ◇ **protegido, -a por una contraseña** password-protected

clave *f* **de control** *sustantivo* check key

clave *f* **(numérica) de control** *sustantivo* 1. check digit 2. check number

clave *f* **de identificación** *sustantivo* key

clave *f* **de índice** *sustantivo* index key

clave *f* **de protección** *sustantivo* protection key

clave *f* **de un código** *sustantivo* key ◇ **eso descodificará el último mensaje** type this key into the machine, that will decode the last message ◇ **gestión de la clave** key management ◇ **tecla**

de carácter character key ◇ **teclee esta clave en la máquina** type this key into the machine, that will decode the last message

clave *f* **electrónica** *sustantivo* dongle

clave *f* **personal** *sustantivo* signature

clave *f* **primaria** *sustantivo* primary key

clave *f* **principal** *sustantivo* primary key

clave *f* **única** *sustantivo* one-time pad

clavija *f* *sustantivo* **1.** jack *o* jack plug **2.** pin **3.** plug ◇ **tablero de clavijas** *o* **de terminales de conexión** pin board ◇ **utilice un enchufe de tres clavijas para conectar la impresora a la red** use a three-pin plug to connect the printer to the mains

clavija *f* **de alineamiento** *sustantivo* alignment pin

clavija *f* **para módem** *sustantivo* data jack

clavija *f* **para teléfono** *sustantivo* data jack

clavija *f* **tomacorriente polarizada** *sustantivo* polarised plug

clic *m* *sustantivo* click ◇ **al pinchar el ratón uno se puede desplazar por el texto y los gráficos** you move through text and graphics with a click of the button

clic *m* **de tecla** *sustantivo* key click

cliché *m* *sustantivo* stencil

cliente *m* *sustantivo* client ◇ **protocolo cliente a cliente** client-to-client protocol (CTCP)

cliente *m* **remoto** *sustantivo* (*no conectado a la red local*) remote client

clon *m* *sustantivo* clone

CMOT *sustantivo* CMOT

coacción *f* *sustantivo* restriction

COBOL *sustantivo* **1.** common business orientated language **2.** common ordinary business-oriented language

cociente *m* *sustantivo* quotient

codificación *sustantivo* **1.** coding **2.** encoding **3.** encryption **4.** folding ◇ **línea de codificación** coding line

'Las compañías de software han desarrollado diversos métodos de codificación que, aseguran, garantizan una confidencialidad total sobre los datos transmitidos, pero la desconfianza de los usuarios es todavía grande.' [*La Red*]

codificación *f* **anticopia** *sustantivo* copy protection ◇ **el nuevo programa no tendrá protección contra la copia** the new program will come without copy protection ◇ **un disco duro puede fallar debido a una protección contra la copia defectuosa** a hard disk may crash because of faulty copy protection

codificación *f* **ARLL** *sustantivo* advanced run-length limited ■ *abrev* ARLL

codificación *f* **binaria** *sustantivo* binary encoding

codificación *f* **bipolar** *sustantivo* bipolar coding

codificación *f* **de Hamming** *sustantivo* H & J

codificación *f* **de usuario a usuario** *sustantivo* Uuencoding

codificación *f* **directa** *sustantivo* **1.** cloud **2.** direct coding

codificación *f* **en binario** *sustantivo* binary encoding

codificación *f* **en cuadrícula** *sustantivo* trellis coding

codificación *f* **en línea directa** *sustantivo* straight-line coding

codificación *f* **específica** *sustantivo* specific coding

codificación *f* **magnética** *sustantivo* magnetic encoding

codificación *f* **Manchester** *sustantivo* Manchester coding

codificación *f* **relativa** *sustantivo* relative coding

codificado *m* **en cuadratura** *sustantivo* quadrature encoding

codificador *m* *sustantivo* **1.** coder **2.** encoder **3.** scrambler ◇ **codificador de colores** colour encoder

codificador *m* **de bandas magnéticas** *sustantivo* magnetic tape encoder

codificador/descodificador *m* *sustantivo* coder/decoder

codificador *m* **/ descodificador** *sustantivo* CODEC

codificador *m* **de teclado** *sustantivo* keyboard encoder

codificador *m* **de teclas** *sustantivo* keyboard encoder

codificador *m* **para bandas magnéticas** *sustantivo* magnetic tape encoder

codificar *verbo* **1.** *vt* to code **2.** *vt* to encipher **3.** *vt* to encode **4.** *vt* to encrypt **5.** *vt* to scramble ◇ **se puede transmitir un texto codificado por una línea de teléfono normal de forma que nadie pueda entenderlo** the encrypted text can be sent along ordinary telephone lines, and no one will be able to understand it

código *sustantivo* code ◇ **código** *m* **con tiempo de acceso mínimo** optimum code ◇ **código** *m* **(de instrucción) de dirección única** single address code ◇ **código de escape** escape code ◇ **código de existencias** *o* **de 'stock'** stock code ◇ **código** *m* **de identificación de una tecla** scan code ◇ **código** *m* **de intercambio decimal de codificación binaria extendida** EBCDIC; extended binary coded decimal interchange code ◇ **código** *m* **de marca de cinta de papel** tape code ◇ **código** *m* **de un (solo) nivel** one-level code ◇ **código** *m* **de verificación y corrección de errores** error checking code ◇ **código** *m* **estándar americano para el intercambio de información** American Standard Code for Information Interchange; ASCII ◇ **código postal** post code =; *US* zip code ◇ **dispositivo de conversión de códigos** code translator feature

'Compilar software sigue siendo muy importante, ya que muchos de los programas que puedes des-

cargar se encuentran en código fuente.'
[*Computer Hoy*]

código *m* **abierto** *sustantivo* open code

código *m* **absoluto** *sustantivo* **1.** absolute code **2.** actual code **3.** specific code

código *m* **AT** *sustantivo* attention code

código *m* **autocomprobador** *sustantivo* self-checking code

código *m* **autoverificador** *sustantivo* self-checking code

código *m* **básico** *sustantivo* basic code

código *m* **BCH** *sustantivo* **1.** BCH code **2.** Bose-Chandhuri-Hocquenghem code

código *m* **binario** *sustantivo* binary code

código *m* **biquinario** *sustantivo* biquinary code

código *m* **byte** *sustantivo* bytecode

código *m* **cíclico** *sustantivo* cyclic code

código *m* **cifrado** *sustantivo* cipher

código *m* **compacto** *sustantivo* compact code

código *m* **corrector de error(es)** *sustantivo* error correcting code

código *m* **de acceso** *sustantivo* **1.** access code **2.** authorisation code

código *m* **de acción** *sustantivo* action code

código *m* **de alerta** *sustantivo* wake-up code

código *m* **de autenticación de mensajes** *sustantivo* message code authentication

código *m* **de barras** *sustantivo* **1.** bar code **2.** bar graph **3.** bar graphics **4.** universal product code ■ *abrev* UPC

código *m* **de base** *sustantivo* skeletal code

código *m* **de bloques** *sustantivo* block code

código *m* **de caracteres** *sustantivo* character code

código *m* **de caracteres interno** *sustantivo* internal character code

código *m* **decimal cíclico** *sustantivo* cyclic decimal code

código *m* **de comprobación al azar** *sustantivo* hash code

código *m* **de condición** *sustantivo* condition code

código *m* **de desplazamiento** *sustantivo* shift code

código *m* **de direcciones** *sustantivo* address code

código *m* **de dirección múltiple** *sustantivo* multiple address code

código *m* **de dispositivo** *sustantivo* device code

código *m* **de ensamblaje** *sustantivo* assembly code

código *m* **de errores** *sustantivo* error code

código *m* **de escape** *sustantivo* escape code

código *m* **de espera** *sustantivo* stop code

código *m* **de exceso de 3** *sustantivo* excess-3 code ◊ **la representación del código de exceso de 3 del número 6 es 1001** the excess-3 code representation of 6 is 1001

código *m* **de final de bloque** *sustantivo* end of block

código *m* **de final de datos** *sustantivo* end of data

código *m* **de final de dirección** *sustantivo* end of address

código *m* **de final de documento** *sustantivo* end of document

código *m* **de final de línea** *sustantivo* end of line

código *m* **de final de medio** *sustantivo* end of medium

código *m* **de final de mensaje** *sustantivo* **1.** end of message **2.** tail

código *m* **de final de párrafo** *sustantivo* hard return

código *m* **de final de registro** *sustantivo* end of record

código *m* **de final de tarea** *sustantivo* end of job

código *m* **de final de texto** *sustantivo* end of text

código *m* **de función** *sustantivo* **1.** function code **2.** function digit

código *m* **de Gray** *sustantivo* Gray code

código *m* **de Hamming** *sustantivo* **1.** Hamming code **2.** H & J

código *m* **de Huffman** *sustantivo* Huffman code

código *m* **de identificación** *sustantivo* ID code ◊ **después de activar el sistema, tiene que introducir su código de identificación y a continuación su contraseña** after you wake up the system, you have to input your ID code then your password

código *m* **de identificación de periféricos** *sustantivo* device code

código *m* **de identificación de usuario** *sustantivo* user ID ◊ **si se olvida de su código personal, no podrá conectarse** if you forget your user ID, you will not be able to logon

código *m* **de inicio de cabecera** *sustantivo* start of header

código *m* **de inicio de texto** *abrev* SOT ■ *sustantivo* start of text ■ *abrev* STX

código *m* **de instrucción** *sustantivo* computer code

código *m* **de instrucciones** *sustantivo* command code

código *m* **de interrupción anormal** *sustantivo* abend code

código *m* **de intervención** *sustantivo* attention code

código *m* **de macros** *sustantivo* macro code

código *m* **de maquina** *sustantivo* machine language

código *m* **de máquina** *sustantivo* machine code

código *m* **de Murray** *sustantivo* Murray code

código *m* **de operación** *sustantivo* **1.** command code **2.** op code **3.** operation code **4.** order code

código *m* **de página activo** *sustantivo* active code page

código *m* **de página en vigor** *sustantivo* active code page

código *m* **de perforación** *sustantivo* **1.** punched code **2.** tape code

código *m* **de posición independiente** *sustantivo* relocatable program ◇ **el sistema operativo puede cargar y ejecutar un programa reubicable desde cualquier área de la memoria** the operating system can load and run a relocatable program from any area of memory

código *m* **de proporción constante** *sustantivo* constant ratio code

código *m* **de redundancia** *sustantivo* redundant code

código *m* **de redundancia cíclica** *abrev* CRC

código *m* **de resultado** *sustantivo* result code

código *m* **de soporte de datos** *sustantivo* end of medium

código *m* **detector de error** *sustantivo* **1.** error detecting code **2.** self-checking code

código *m* **de terminación** *sustantivo* abend code

código *m* **de una sola dirección** *sustantivo* single address code

código *m* **directo** *sustantivo* direct code

código *m* **EBCDIC** *sustantivo* **1.** EBCDIC **2.** extended binary coded decimal interchange code

código *m* **elemental** *sustantivo* basic code

código *m* **en cadena** *sustantivo* chain code

código *m* **encadenado** *sustantivo* chain code

código *m* **erróneo** *sustantivo* false code

código *m* **ESC** *sustantivo* ESC

código *m* **específico** *sustantivo* specific code

código *m* **fuente** *sustantivo* source code

código *m* **horario** *sustantivo* time code

código *m* **identificador** *sustantivo* form type

código *m* **incompleto** *sustantivo* skeletal code

código *m* **incorporado** *sustantivo* embedded code

código *m* **indicador** *sustantivo* flag code

código *m* **indicador de error** *sustantivo* error code

código *m* **intermedio** *sustantivo* intermediate code

código *m* **interpretativo** *sustantivo* interpretative code

código *m* **legible por máquina** *sustantivo* machine-readable code

código *m* **macro** *sustantivo* macro code

código *m* **máquina** *sustantivo* **1.** actual code **2.** computer code

código *m* **M de N** *sustantivo* M out of N code

código *m* **no impresor** *plural noun* nonprinting code

código *m* **numérico de una tecla** *sustantivo* key number

código *m* **objeto** *sustantivo* object code

código *m* **operativo** *sustantivo* operating code

código *m* **optimizado** *sustantivo* optimised code *o* optimized code

código *m* **óptimo** *sustantivo* optimum code

código *m* **parametrizable** *sustantivo* skeletal code

código *m* **personal** *sustantivo* **1.** ID code **2.** signature **3.** user ID ◇ **después de activar el sistema, tiene que introducir su código de identificación y a continuación su contraseña** after you wake up the system, you have to input your ID code then your password ◇ **si se olvida de su código personal, no podrá conectarse** if you forget your user ID, you will not be able to logon

código *m* **polinómico** *sustantivo* (*de detección de errores por algoritmo de cálculo*) polynomial code

código *m* **por facetas** *sustantivo* faceted code

código *m* **precompilado** *sustantivo* precompiled code

código *m* **puro** *sustantivo* pure code

código *m* **que no imprime** *plural noun* nonprinting code

código *m* **redundante** *sustantivo* redundant code

código *m* **reflejado** *sustantivo* reflected code

códigos *mpl* **correctores** *plural noun* self-correcting codes

códigos *mpl* **de instrucción** *plural noun* instruction codes

código *m* **separador de información** *sustantivo* separator

código *m* **simbólico** *sustantivo* **1.** symbolic code **2.** symbolic instruction

códigos *mpl* **significativos** *plural noun* significant digit codes

código *m* **suplementario** *sustantivo* overhead

código *m* **temporal MIDI** *sustantivo* **1.** MIDI time code **2.** MTC

coeficiente *m* *sustantivo* **1.** factor **2.** ratio

coeficiente *m* **de amortiguación** *sustantivo* decrement

coeficiente *m* **de clics en anuncios** *sustantivo* click rate

coemplazamiento *m* *sustantivo* co-location

cola *sustantivo* **1.** FIFO queue **2.** hangover **3.** tail ◇ **cola** *f* (**descendente de una letra**) descender ◇ **cola** *f* **de espera** (**de periféricos**) device queue ◇ **cola** *f* **de espera de entrada de datos** input work queue ◇ **cola** *f* **de tareas** (**en espera**) job queue

cola *f* **de espera** *sustantivo* **1.** (*de petición de servicio de datos para transmitir*) channel queue **2.** first in first out **3.** queue ◊ **gestor de lista** *o* **de cola de espera** queue manager

cola *f* **de ficheros** *sustantivo* file queue ◊ **los periféricos como las impresoras láser entán conectados en línea con una cola automática de ficheros en espera** output devices such as laser printers are connected on-line with an automatic file queue

cola *f* **de impresión** *sustantivo* print queue

cola *f* **de tareas para ejecutar** *sustantivo* task queue

cola *f* **de transmisión de datos** *sustantivo* channel queue

colgado *adv* on-hook

colisión *f sustantivo* collision

colocación *f* **de un indicador** *sustantivo* flagging

colocar *verbo* **1.** *vt* to plant **2.** *vt* to set

colocar texto alrededor *verbo* to run around

color *sustantivo* hue ◊ **colores** *m* **personalizados** custom colours

color *m* **acromático** *sustantivo* achromatic colour

color *m* **aditivo** *sustantivo* additive colour

color *m* **de fondo** *sustantivo* background colour

color *m* **de pantalla** *sustantivo* display colour

color *m* **de primer plano** *sustantivo* foreground colour

color *m* **de visualización** *sustantivo* display colour

colorear *verbo* *vt* to paint

colores *mpl* **del sistema** *plural noun* system colours

color *m* **estándar** *sustantivo* colour standard

color *m* **saturado** *sustantivo* saturated colour

color *m* **suavizado** *sustantivo* dithered colour

columna *f sustantivo* column ◊ **el precio incluye una impresora de 80 columnas** an 80-column printer is included in the price ◊ **escriba el total al final de la columna** put the total at the bottom of the column ◊ **sumar una columna de cifras** to add up a column of figures

columna *f* **doble** *sustantivo* dual column

com *suffix* com

COM1 *sustantivo* COM1

coma *f sustantivo* comma ◊ **coma** *f* **separadora de fracción de decimal** radix point

coma *f* **binaria** *sustantivo* binary point

COMAL *sustantivo* common algorithmic language

comando *sustantivo* command

'La interfaz basada en iconos permite también - como la textual- una disposición de elementos jerarquizada, introduciendo así un cierto 'orden' en los comandos a disposición del usuario.' [*Internet y el español*]

combinación *f sustantivo* permutation

combinación *f* **de teclas** *sustantivo* **1.** key combination **2.** key shortcut

combinador *m sustantivo* multiplexor ◊ **un multiplexor de 4 a 1 combina 4 entradas con una sola salida** a 4 to 1 multiplexor combines four inputs into a single output

combinar *verbo* **1.** *vt* to coalesce **2.** *vt* to merge ◊ **el sistema fusiona** *o* **combina automáticamente texto e ilustraciones dentro del documento** the system automatically merges text and illustrations into the document

comentario *m sustantivo* **1.** annotation **2.** comment **3.** narrative **4.** REM **5.** remark ◊ **comentario** *m* **que inhabilita una instrucción** comment out ◊ **en BASIC se pueden introducir comentarios después de la instrucción REM** BASIC allows comments to be written after a REM instruction

comercialización *f sustantivo* release

comercializar *verbo* *vt* (*un nuevo producto*) to release

comercio commerce ◊ **comercio** *m* **a través de la TV interactiva** T-commerce

'El comercio electrónico tiene un impacto directo en las políticas de aprovisionamiento, permite que empresas y distribuidores compartan previsiones de demanda y mejoren el suministro en una planificación colaborativa.' [*Nueva economía*]

comercio *m* **electrónico** *sustantivo* **1.** e-commerce **2.** electronic commerce

comillas *fpl plural noun* inverted commas ■ *sustantivo* quotation marks ■ *plural noun* quotes

comillas *fpl* **sencillas** *plural noun* single quotes

comité ◊ **comité** *m* **consultivo internacional en teléfonos y telégrafos** CCITT ◊ **comité** *m* **Consultivo Internacional en Teléfonos y Telégrafos** Comité Consultatif Internationale de Télégraphie et Téléphonie ◊ **comité** *m* **de normalización de internet** Internet engineering task force ◊ **comité** *m* **de sistemas avanzados** Advanced Television Systems Committee; ATSC

comité *m* **de actividades de internet** *sustantivo* **1.** IAB **2.** Internet Activities Board **3.** Internet architecture board

comité *m* **de ingeniería de internet** *sustantivo* Internet engineering task force

comité *m* **de investigación de internet** *sustantivo* **1.** Internet research task force **2.** IRTF

comité *m* **(ANSI) T1** *sustantivo* T1 committee

compactación *f* **de datos** *sustantivo* data compacting

compactar *verbo* *vt* to concentrate ◊ **los datos comprimidos fueron transmitidos con poco gasto** the concentrated data was transmitted cheaply

compact Flash *abrev* CF ■ *sustantivo* compact Flash

Compaq™ COMPAQ

comparación *f* **lógica** *sustantivo* logical comparison

comparador *m sustantivo* comparator

compartición *f* **del tiempo** *sustantivo* time-sharing

compartición *f* **de recursos** *sustantivo* resource sharing

compatibilidad *f sustantivo* compatibility ◇ **compatibilidad** *f* **con un sistema de nivel inferior** downward compatibility

compatibilidad *f* **del equipo** *sustantivo* hardware compatibility

compatibilidad *f* **de un programa** *sustantivo* program compatibility

compatible *adj* **1.** compatible **2.** compliant ◇ **compatible con el correo electrónico** mail-enabled ◇ **compatible con un sistema de nivel inferior** downward compatible ◇ **compatible con un sistema de nivel superior** upward compatible ◇ **este tratamiento de textos es compatible con el correo electrónico y puede enviar mensajes a otros usuarios sin salir del programa** this word-processor is mail-enabled – you can send messages to other users from within it ◇ **si desea leer discos compactos de tipo PhotoCD en su ordenador, asegúrese de que su disquetera de CD-ROM es compatible con PhotoCD o con CD-ROM XA** if you want to read PhotoCD compact discs in your computer you must be sure that the CD-ROM drive is PhotoCD or CD-ROM XA compliant

compatible con ficheros de versiones anteriores *adj* backwards compatible

compatible con la asignación *adj* assignment compatible

compatible con un programa *adj* software compatible

compatible con versiones anteriores *adj* backwards compatible

compatible hacia atrás *adj* backwards compatible

compatible Hayes *adj* Hayes-compatible

compatible TTL *adj* TTL-compatible

compilación *f sustantivo* compilation

compilación *f* **de programa** *sustantivo* program compilation

compilado parcialmente *adj* semicompiled

compilador *m sustantivo* **1.** compiler *o* compiler program **2.** language compiler ◇ **compilador** *m* **(de un lenguaje)** language compiler

compilador *m* **cruzado** *sustantivo* cross-compiler ◇ **podemos utilizar el compilador cruzado para desarrollar el software antes de que llegue el nuevo sistema** we can use the cross-compiler to develop the software before the new system arrives

compilador *m* **del programa fuente** *sustantivo* source machine

compilador *m* **de optimización** *sustantivo* optimising compiler

compilador *m* **en cruce** *sustantivo* cross-compiler

compilador *m* **en lenguaje máquina** *sustantivo* machine language compile

compilador *m* **nativo** *sustantivo* native compiler

compilador *m* **original** *sustantivo* native compiler

compilar *verbo vt* to compile ◇ **con esta versión antigua del programa se tarda mucho en compilar** compiling takes a long time with this old version ◇ **corrija los errores de su programa antes de compilarlo** debug your program, then compile it ◇ **los programas de BASIC compilados son mucho más rápidos que la versión intérprete** compiled BASIC programs run much faster than the interpretor version

'Hemos intentado compilar una misma aplicación en cada distribución tras realizar una instalación típica, para comprobar si ésta copia todo lo necesario.' [*Computer Hoy*]

complementado *adj* complemented

complementario *adj* **1.** add-in **2.** additional **3.** add-on ◇ **equipo complementario** add-on equipment ◇ **la nueva tarjeta de ampliación permite mostrar gráficos en color** the new add-on board allows colour graphics to be displayed ◇ **productos complementarios** add-on products ◇ **tarjeta** add-on board ◇ **un disco duro adicional aumentará la capacidad de memoria del ordenador** the add-on hard disk will boost the computer's storage capabilities

complemento *m sustantivo* complement ◇ **determinar el complemento (de una cantidad)** complement ◇ **se encuentra el complemento cambiando los unos a ceros y los ceros a unos** the complement is found by changing the 1s to 0s and 0s to 1s

complemento *m* **de 1** *sustantivo* one's complement ◇ **el complemento de 1 de 10011 es 01100** the one's complement of 10011 is 01100

complemento *m* **de 2** *sustantivo* two's complement

complemento *m* **de 9** *sustantivo* nine's complement

complemento *m* **de 10** *sustantivo* ten's complement

complemento *m* **de base** *sustantivo* radix complement

complemento *m* **de diez** *sustantivo* ten's complement

complemento *m* **de raíz reducida** *sustantivo* diminished radix complement

completar *verbo vt* to fill

componente *m sustantivo* **1.** chip **2.** element ◇ **componente** *m* **sustitutivo (de un programa)** stub

componente *m* **de dimensiones muy pequeñas** *sustantivo* microdevice

componente *m* **semiconductor** *sustantivo* semiconductor device

componer ◇ **componer un texto (con ordenador)** word-process ◇ **es muy fácil leer ficheros de textos procesados por ordenador** it is quite easy to read word-processed files

componer texto sin interrupción *verbo* to run on ◇ **el texto puede continuar en la línea siguiente sin dejar espacios** the line can run on to the next without any space

composición ◇ **composición** *f* **automática de tipos de cartas** automatic letter writing

composición *f* **de página** *sustantivo* page layout

compositor *m* **tipógrafo** *sustantivo* typesetter ◇ **el texto está preparado para ser enviado al tipógrafo** the text is ready to be sent to the typesetter

compra *f* **por ordenador** *sustantivo* electronic shopping

compresión *f* *sustantivo* **1.** companding **2.** compression **3.** packing ◇ **compresión** *f* **de imágenes con pérdida de información** lossy compression ◇ **compresión** *f* **de imágenes sin pérdida de información** lossless compression ◇ **compresión** *f* **de los datos del disco** DoubleSpace

compresión *f* **asimétrica** *sustantivo* asymmetric compression

compresión *f* **asimétrica de vídeo** *sustantivo* asymmetric video compression

compresión *f* **de datos** *sustantivo* **1.** data compacting **2.** data compression ◇ **se grabaron todos los ficheros en un solo disco mediante esta nueva rutina de compresión de datos** all the files were stored on one disk with this new data compacting routine

compresión *f* **de (la) imagen** *sustantivo* image compression

compresión *f* **de información** *sustantivo* data compacting ◇ **se grabaron todos los ficheros en un solo disco mediante esta nueva rutina de compresión de datos** all the files were stored on one disk with this new data compacting routine

compresión *f* **de la imagen** *sustantivo* picture image compression

compresión *f* **de texto** *sustantivo* text compression

compresión *f* **de vídeo** *sustantivo* video compression ◇ **compresor, -a de vídeo (para emisión por un canal digital)** video compressor

compresión *f* **fractal** *sustantivo* fractal compression

compresión *f* **simétrica** *sustantivo* symmetrical compression

comprimir *verbo* **1.** *vt* to concentrate **2.** *vt* to reduce ◇ **los datos comprimidos fueron transmitidos con poco gasto** the concentrated data was transmitted cheaply

comprobación ◇ **comprobación** *f* **del buen funcionamiento del sistema** system check ◇ **comprobación** *f* **de validez (de datos)** validity check

comprobación *f* **asistida por ordenador** *sustantivo* **1.** CAT **2.** computer-assisted testing

comprobación *f* **beta** *sustantivo* beta test

comprobación *f* **de datos** *sustantivo* **1.** data check **2.** data validation

comprobación *f* **de un programa** *sustantivo* program testing

comprobación *f* **interna total de lectura/escritura** *sustantivo* leap-frog test

comprobación *f* **numérica** *sustantivo* test numeric

comprobación *f* **por suma** *sustantivo* summation check

compuesto *adj* compound

CompuServe™ CompuServe

computarizar *verbo* *vt* to computerise *o* to computerize

comunicación *sustantivo* data communications ◇ **comunicación** *f* **agrupada (por lotes)** batched communication

comunicación *f* **asíncrona** *sustantivo* asynchronous communication

comunicación *f* **de datos en serie** *sustantivo* **1.** serial data communications **2.** serial data transmission

comunicación *f* **entre ordenadores** *sustantivo* computer conferencing

comunicaciones ◇ **comunicaciones** *fpl* **avanzadas programa a programa** APPC ◇ **comunicaciones** *fpl* **avanzadas programa a programa (APPC)** advanced program to program communications ◇ **comunicaciones** *fpl* **en condiciones de igualdad** advanced program to program communications ◇ **comunicaciones** *fpl* **en condiciones de igualdad** APPC

comunicaciones *fpl* **de baja velocidad** *plural noun* low-speed communications

comunicaciones *fpl* **de datos** *sustantivo* data communications

comunicaciones *fpl* **de información** *sustantivo* data communications

comunicaciones *fpl* **por cable** *plural noun* line communications

comunicaciones *fpl* **por línea** *plural noun* line communications

comunicaciones *fpl* **sincrónicas en binario** *sustantivo* **1.** binary synchronous communications **2.** BSC

comunicación *f* **no prioritaria** *sustantivo* background communication

comunicación *f* **radiofónica** *sustantivo* broadcast

comunicación *f* **subordinada** *sustantivo* background communication

comunicante *m&f* *sustantivo* called party

comunidad *f* **virtual** *sustantivo* **1.** community **2.** virtual community

con ◇ **con alimentación automática de papel** paper-fed

con anticipación *prefijo* pre-

concatenación ◇ **concatenación** *f* **de (muchas) cadenas** string concatenation

concatenación *f* **de datos** *sustantivo* concatenated data set

concatenar *verbo* 1. *vt* to catenate 2. *vt* to concatenate

concentración *f* **de datos** *sustantivo* 1. data compacting 2. data compression ◇ **los escáners utilizan una técnica denominada compresión de datos que consigue reducir, hasta un tercio, la memoria necesaria** scanners use a technique called data compression which manages to reduce, even by a third, the storage required ◇ **se grabaron todos los ficheros en un solo disco mediante esta nueva rutina de compresión de datos** all the files were stored on one disk with this new data compacting routine

concentrador *m sustantivo* concentrator

concentrador *m* **10base-T** *sustantivo* concentrator

concentrador *m* **activo** *sustantivo* active hub

concentradora *f* **de datos** *sustantivo* milking machine

concentrador *m* **de datos** *sustantivo* data concentrator

concentrador *m* **de información** *sustantivo* data concentrator

concentrador *m* **de red** *sustantivo* concentrator

concentrador *m* **inteligente** *sustantivo* smart wiring hub ◇ **con este software de gestión puedo desconectar el puerto de Tom del concentrador inteligente remoto** using this management software, I can shut down Tom's port on the remote smart wiring hub

concentrador *m* **multirepetidor** *sustantivo* hub

concentrar *verbo vt* to concentrate ◇ **concentrar un rayo de luz con una lente** to concentrate a beam of light on a lens

con conector compatible *adj* plug-compatible ◇ **esta nueva placa de conexión es mucho más rápida que cualquier otra; se instala simplemente enchufándola en el puerto de extensión** this new plug-compatible board works much faster than any of its rivals, we can install it by simply plugging it into the expansion port ◇ **fabricante de enchufes conectores** plug-compatible manufacturer (PCM)

con conmutación de paquetes *adj* packet-switched

condensación *f sustantivo* packing

condensación *f* **de datos** *sustantivo* 1. data compacting 2. data compression ◇ **los escáners utilizan una técnica denominada compresión de datos que consigue reducir, hasta un tercio, la memoria necesaria** scanners use a technique called data compression which manages to reduce, even by a third, the storage required ◇ **se grabaron todos los ficheros en un solo disco mediante esta nueva rutina de compresión de datos** all the files were stored on one disk with this new data compacting routine

condensación *f* **de información** *sustantivo* data compression ◇ **los escáners utilizan una técnica denominada compresión de datos que consigue reducir, hasta un tercio, la memoria necesaria** scanners use a technique called data compression which manages to reduce, even by a third, the storage required

condensador *sustantivo* capacitor ◇ **condensador** *m* **(en memoria RAM)** bucket ◇ **condensador cerámico** ceramic capacitor ◇ **condensador** *m* **de seguridad de la memoria** memory backup capacitor ◇ **condensador electrolítico** electrolytic capacitor ◇ **condensador no electrolítico** non-electrolytic capacitor ◇ **condensador variable** variable capacitor ◇ **micrófono electrostático (de condensador)** capacitor microphone

condensador *m* **para la memoria RAM** *sustantivo* memory backup capacitor

condensar *verbo vt* to concentrate

condición *f sustantivo* condition

condicional *adj* conditional ◇ **la bifurcación condicional seleccionará la rutina 1 ó la 2 según sea la respuesta sí o no** the conditional branch will select routine one if the response is yes and routine two if no

condicionamiento *f* **de señal** *sustantivo* signal conditioning

condicionar *verbo vt* to condition

condicionar previamente *verbo* to precondition

condición *f* **de alerta** *sustantivo* alert condition

condición *f* **de entrada** *sustantivo* entry condition

condición *f* **de error** *sustantivo* error condition

condición *f* **de espera** *sustantivo* 1. wait condition 2. waiting state 3. wait state

condición *f* **de parada** *sustantivo* halt condition

condición *f* **de un evento** *sustantivo* flag event

condición *f* **inicial** *sustantivo* initial condition

condición *f* **que provoca un indicador** *sustantivo* flag event

con diseño *adj* patterned

conducción *f sustantivo* conduction ◇ **la conducción de electricidad mediante contactos de oro** the conduction of electricity by gold contacts

conducir *verbo vt* to conduct ◇ **conducir la electricidad** to conduct electricity

conductibilidad *f sustantivo* conduction

conducto *m sustantivo* 1. channelling 2. conduit 3. duct 4. pipeline ◇ **los cables de cada terminal se canalizan al servicio de informática mediante un conducto metálico** the cables from each terminal are channelled to the computer centre by metal conduit

conductor *adj* conductive ■ *sustantivo* 1. conductor 2. lead ◇ **el cobre es un buen conductor de la electricidad** copper is a good conductor of electricity

conductor *m* **común** *sustantivo* 1. bus 2. highway 3. I/O bus

conectable directamente *adj* plug-compatible ◇ **esta nueva placa de conexión es mucho más rápida que cualquier otra; se instala simplemente enchufándola en el puerto de extensión** this new plug-compatible board works much faster than any of its rivals, we can install it by simply plugging it into the expansion port

conectado *adv, adj* online ■ *adv* online ◇ **el terminal está conectado al ordenador principal** the terminal is on-line to the mainframe

conectador *m sustantivo* connector

conectar *verbo* **1.** *vt* to connect **2.** *vt* to link ◇ **apagar** to switch off ◇ **cambiar (a)** to switch over to ◇ **conectar (con la ayuda de un conmutador)** to switch ◇ **(dispositivo) conectar y listo** to plug and play; to PNP ◇ **desconectar** to switch off ◇ **encender** *o* **poner en funcionamiento** *o* **en marcha** to switch on ◇ **llamada virtual conmutada** switched virtual call ◇ **los dos ordenadores están conectados** the two computers are linked ◇ **red conmutada de datos** switched data network ◇ **red conmutada en estrella** switched star

conectar a tierra *verbo* to earth ◇ **todos los aparatos eléctricos deben tener toma de tierra** all appliances must be earthed

conectarse *verbo vt* (*a un nodo a un servidor de red*) to attach ◇ **he dado la instrucción para conectarme al servidor local** I issued the command to attach to the local server

conectividad *f sustantivo* connectivity ◇ **conectividad** *f* **de una base de datos Java** (*marca comercial*) Java Database Connectivity

conector *sustantivo* **1.** connective **2.** connector **3.** expansion slot **4.** joystick port **5.** pin ◇ **conector** *m* **(de un transistor)** gate ◇ **conector** *m* **BNC en forma de T** BNC T-piece connector ◇ **conector** *m* **de un solo borde de enchufe** polarised edge connector ◇ **conector** *m* **(de tarjeta adicional)** vacío empty slot ◇ **el conector al final del cable se adapta a cualquier puerta estándar en serie** the connector at the end of the cable will fit any standard serial port

conector *m* **(de cable)** *sustantivo* cable connector

conector *m* **AUI** *sustantivo* AUI connector

conector *m* **(coaxial) BNC** *sustantivo* BNC connector

conector *m* **booleano** *sustantivo* Boolean connective

conector *m* **DB** *sustantivo* **1.** data bus connector **2.** DB connector

conector *m* **de borde** *sustantivo* edge connector

conector *m* **de borde de tarjetas** *sustantivo* card edge connector

conector *m* **de borde polarizado** *sustantivo* polarised edge connector

conector *m* **de fibra óptica** *sustantivo* fibre connector

conector *m* **de tipo D** *sustantivo* D-type connector ◇ **el puerto en serie de un PC usa un**

conector de tipo D con nueve contactos the serial port on a PC uses a 9-pin D-type connector

conector *m* **D-SUB** *sustantivo* D-SUB connector

conector *m* **en D** *sustantivo* D-type connector ◇ **el puerto en serie de un PC usa un conector de tipo D con nueve contactos** the serial port on a PC uses a 9-pin D-type connector

conector *m* **en T** *sustantivo* T connector

conector *m* **hembra** *sustantivo* female connector

conector *m* **IEC** *sustantivo* IEC connector

conector *m* **macho** *sustantivo* male connector

conector *m* **MIDI** *sustantivo* MIDI connector

conector *m* **PCMCIA** *sustantivo* PCMCIA connector

conector *m* **SCART** *sustantivo* SCART connector

conector *m* **ST** *sustantivo* ST connector

conector *m* **VGA** *sustantivo* VGA feature connector

conexión *sustantivo* **1.** contact **2.** interfacing **3.** junction **4.** linking **5.** nexus **6.** port **7.** switching ◇ **conexión** *f* **(por transmisión) de datos** data connection ◇ **conexión** *f* **de ordenadores en modo conversacional** computer conferencing ◇ **conexión** *f* **de un periférico de entrada** input lead ◇ **conexión** *f* **(de ordenadores) en red** networking ◇ **conexión segura** reliable connection ◇ **de conexión directa** direct connect ◇ **el circuito no funciona porque la conexión está sucia** the circuit is not working because the contact is dirty ◇ **el multiusuario del sistema de tablón de anuncios tiene un servicio de comunicación entre ordenadores** *or* **de teleconferencia** the multi-user BBS has a computer conferencing facility ◇ **enlace** *o* **conexión entre segmentos** intersegment linking

conexíon ◇ **servicio** *m* **de red orientado a la conexión** CONS

conexión *f* **abortada** *sustantivo* aborted connection

conexión *f* **activa** *sustantivo* active link

conexión *f* **cableada** *sustantivo* hardwired connection

conexión *f* **de fibra óptica** *sustantivo* fibre optic cable *o* fibre optic connection

conexión *f* **de mercado** *sustantivo* dial-up connection

conexión *f* **directa** *sustantivo* **1.** direct connection **2.** null modem ◇ **este cable está configurado como una conexión directa, lo que me permite interconectar fácilmente estos dos ordenadores** this cable is configured as a null modem, which will allow me to connect these 2 computers together easily

conexión *f* **directa entre canales** *sustantivo* channel-to-channel connection

conexión *f* **directa por cable** *sustantivo* direct cable connection

conexión *f* **en cadena** *sustantivo* daisy-chaining ◇ **la conexión en cadena ahorra mucho cable** daisy-chaining saves a lot of cable

conexión *f* **en cascada** *sustantivo* **1.** cascade connection **2.** daisy-chaining ◇ **la conexión en cadena ahorra mucho cable** daisy-chaining saves a lot of cable

conexión *f* **en paralelo** *sustantivo* parallel connection ◇ **la velocidad de transmisión es de 60.000 bps mediante una conexión en paralelo** their transmission rate is 60,000 bps through parallel connection

conexión *f* **fija** *sustantivo* hardwired connection

conexión *f* **Megastream™** (*marca comercial de un enlace de datos*) Megastream

conexión *f* **por enrollamiento de hilos** *sustantivo* wire wrap

confidencialidad *sustantivo* privacy ◇ **codificación (de la información) para asegurar la confidencialidad** privacy transformation

'La confidencialidad es una exigencia de compradores y comerciantes para que los datos de una transacción no sean conocidos nada más que por las partes que intervienen en la transacción.' [*PC Plus*]

confidencialidad *f* **de datos** *sustantivo* privacy of data

confidencialidad *f* **de información** *sustantivo* privacy of information

confidencialidad *f* **segura** *sustantivo* **1.** PGP **2.** pretty good privacy

CONFIG.SYS *sustantivo* (*fichero de configuración de MS-DOS*) CONFIG.SYS ◇ **si añade una nueva tarjeta adaptadora a su ordenador personal, tendrá que añadir una instrucción nueva al fichero CONFIG.SYS** if you add a new adapter card to your PC you will have to add a new command to the CONFIG.SYS file

configuración *sustantivo* **1.** configuration **2.** database mapping **3.** map **4.** network topology **5.** page setup ◇ **configuración** *f* **avanzada e interfaz de potencia** advanced configuration and power interface ◇ **configuración** *f* **de una base de datos** database mapping ◇ **(con) configuración válida** configured-in

'Muchas distribuciones han desarrollado utilidades que, cual 'Panel de Control' de Windows, permite modificar la configuración del sistema.' [*Computer Hoy*]

configuración *f* **de entrada/salida** *sustantivo* I/O mapping

configuración *f* **de la memoria** *sustantivo* memory map

configuración *f* **del equipo** *sustantivo* hardware configuration

configuración *f* **de red** *sustantivo* networking

configuración *f* **de un conector** *sustantivo* pinout

configuración *f* **lógica** *sustantivo* logic map

configuración *f* **MIDI** *sustantivo* MIDI mapping

configuración *f* **normal** *sustantivo* normal form

configurado *adj* configured-in

configurado, ◇ configurado, -a en (la) memoria memory-mapped ◇ **una pantalla configurada en la memoria dispone de una dirección asignada para cada píxel, lo que permite el acceso directo de la unidad central de proceso a la pantalla** a memory-mapped screen has an address allocated to each pixel, allowing direct access to the screen by the CPU

configurar *verbo* **1.** *vt* to configure **2.** *vt* to set up ◇ **este terminal ha sido configurado para visualizar gráficos** this terminal has been configured to display graphics ◇ **sólo tiene que configurar su ordenador personal una vez, cuando lo compra** you only have to configure the PC once – when you first buy it

configurar en red *verbo* to network

confirmación *f* **positiva** *sustantivo* affirmative acknowledgement

confirmar *verbo* *vt* to acknowledge

conformidad *f* *sustantivo* maintenance release ◇ **la puesta a punto correctiva de la base de datos, versión 2.01, corrige el problema de los márgenes** the maintenance release of the database program, version 2.01, corrects the problem with the margins

congelar *verbo* *vt* to freeze ◇ **congelar** *o* **fijar** *o* **parar (una imagen)** to freeze (frame) ◇ **el procesador de imágenes puede congelar una imagen de televisión aislada** the image processor will freeze a single TV frame

con guías *adj* rack mounted

con impurezas *adj* doped

conjunción *f* *sustantivo* **1.** conjunction **2.** meet

conjuntamente *sustantivo* tandem

conjunto *m* *sustantivo* **1.** character set **2.** set ◇ **conjunto** *m* **de caracteres redefinibles dinámicamente** dynamically redefinable character set

conjunto *m* **de aplicaciones multimedia** *sustantivo* **1.** MDK **2.** multimedia developer's kit

conjunto *m* **de caracteres** *sustantivo* character set

conjunto *m* **de caracteres alternos** *sustantivo* alternate character set ◇ **podemos imprimir caracteres griegos al seleccionar el conjunto de caracteres alternos** we can print Greek characters by selecting the alternate character set

conjunto *m* **de caracteres de terminal** *sustantivo* terminal character set

conjunto *m* **de chips** *sustantivo* chip set

conjunto *m* **de circuitos integrados** *sustantivo* chip set

conjunto *m* **de conmutadores** *sustantivo* ganged switch ◇ **un reagrupamiento de conmutadores se emplea para seleccionar el bus de datos al que responde una impresora**

a ganged switch is used to select which data bus a printer will respond to

conjunto m **de datos encadenados** *sustantivo* concatenated data set

conjunto m **de estructuras** *sustantivo* platform ◇ **este software sólo funcionará sobre una plataforma IBM** this software will only work on the IBM PC platform

conjunto m **de instrucciones** *sustantivo* instruction repertoire o instruction set

conjunto m **de instrucciones Hayes AT** *sustantivo* Hayes AT command set

conjunto m **de tareas en curso** *sustantivo* job mix

conjunto m **de trabajos** *sustantivo* job mix

conjunto m **nulo** *sustantivo* null set

conjuntor m *sustantivo* jack o jack plug

conjunto m **universal** *sustantivo* universal set ◇ **el conjunto universal de números primos inferiores a diez y superiores a dos es 3,5,7** the universal set of prime numbers less than ten and greater than two is 3,5,7

conjunto m **vacío** *sustantivo* null set

conmutación f *sustantivo* switching

conmutación f **automática de frecuencias** *sustantivo* 1. automatic frequency switching 2. automatic mode

conmutación f **automática de modo** *sustantivo* 1. automatic frequency switching 2. automatic mode

conmutación f **de bancos** *sustantivo* bank switching

conmutación f **de circuitos** *sustantivo* circuit switching

conmutación f **de paquetes** *sustantivo* packet switching

conmutación f **de seguridad** *sustantivo* switched network backup

conmutación f **de tareas** *sustantivo* (*de un programa a otro*) task switching

conmutación f **digital** *sustantivo* digital switching

conmutación f **temporal asíncrona** *sustantivo* 1. asynchronous transfer mode 2. ATM

conmutador *sustantivo* 1. sense switch 2. switch ◇ **conmutador** m **privado (conectado con la red pública)** private branch exchange ◇ **serie de conmutadores** o **conmutadores en serie** switch train

conmutador m **basculante** *sustantivo* toggle switch

conmutador m **de acción momentánea** *sustantivo* momentary switch

conmutador m **de género** *sustantivo* gender changer

conmutador m **DIP** *sustantivo* DIP switch

conmutador m **electrónico** *sustantivo* sampler

conmutadores mpl **montados en serie** *sustantivo* ganged switch ◇ **un reagrupamiento de conmutadores se emplea para seleccion-**

ar el bus de datos al que responde una impresora a ganged switch is used to select which data bus a printer will respond to

conmutador m **privado (conectado con la red pública)** *abrev* PBX

conocimiento m **global** *sustantivo* global knowledge

conocimientos ◇ **que tiene conocimientos de informática** computer-literate

conocimientos mpl **informáticos** *sustantivo* computer literacy

Consejo ◇ **Consejo** m **Europeo para la Investigación Nuclear** CERN

conservabilidad f *sustantivo* maintainability

conservación f *sustantivo* maintenance

conservación f *sustantivo* 1. maintenance 2. upkeep

conservar *verbo vt* to maintain

con sistema automático *adj* hands off

consistencia f *sustantivo* texture

consola *sustantivo* console ◇ **consola** f **(IBM o compatible)** CON ◇ **la consola consiste en un dispositivo de entrada de datos, como el teclado, y un dispositivo de salida de datos, como una impresora o una pantalla** the console consists of input device such as a keyboard, and an output device such as a printer or CRT

consola f **(de instrucciones)** *sustantivo* console

consola f **de instrucciones a distancia** *sustantivo* 1. remote console 2. remote device

consola f **de juego** *sustantivo* 1. game console 2. games console

consola f **del sistema** *sustantivo* system console

constante f *sustantivo* constant ■ *adj* constant ◇ **el motor de la disquetera gira a una velocidad constante** the disk drive motor spins at a constant velocity ◇ **velocidad angular constante** constant angular velocity (CAV)

constante f **de reasignación** *sustantivo* relocation constant

constante f **de reubicación** *sustantivo* relocation constant

constituir *vt sustantivo* form ◇ **el sistema está constituido por cinco módulos independientes** the system is formed of five separate modules

constreñir *verbo vt* to constrain

consulta f *abrev* ENQ ■ *sustantivo* inquiry

consulta f **de una tabla de referencia** *sustantivo* table lookup

consulta f **en tablas** *sustantivo* table lookup

consulta f **relacional** *sustantivo* relational query ◇ **la consulta relacional 'encontrar todos los hombres de menos de 35 años' no funciona en este sistema** the relational query 'find all men under 35 years old' will not work on this system

consulta/respuesta f *sustantivo* inquiry/response

consultar la red *verbo* to browse

consumir *verbo vt* to use ◇ **consume demasiada electricidad** it's using too much electricity

contabilizar *verbo vt* to account

contactar *verbo vt* to contact

contacto *m sustantivo* **1.** contact **2.** pin ◇ **(film) negativo de contacto** contact negative ◇ **prueba (impresa) de contacto** contact print

contacto *m* **en circuito sin corriente** *sustantivo* dry contact

contacto *m* **seco** *sustantivo* dry contact

contador *m sustantivo* counter

contador *m* **binario** *sustantivo* binary counter

contador *m* **de bucles** *sustantivo* loop counter

contador *m* **de incremento/decremento** *sustantivo* up/down counter

contador *m* **de instrucciones** *sustantivo* instruction counter

contador *m* **de microprograma** *sustantivo* microprogram counter

contador *m* **de programas** *abrev* PC ■ *sustantivo* **1.** program address counter **2.** program counter

contador *m* **de repeticiones** *sustantivo* repeat counter

contaminación *f sustantivo* smog

contaminación *f* **electrónica** *sustantivo* electronic smog

contención *f sustantivo* contention

contenido *m sustantivo* content ■ *plural noun* contents

contenido *m* **de la información** *sustantivo* information content

contestador *m* **automático** *sustantivo* voicemail ◇ **he escuchado mi contestador para ver si alguien me había dejado algún mensaje** I checked my voice mail to see if anyone had left me a message

contestador *m* **(telefónico) automático** *sustantivo* answering machine

contestador *m* **con mensaje vocal** *sustantivo* voice answer back

contestar *verbo vi* to reply

contexto *m sustantivo* context

continuación *f sustantivo* continuation page

continuar *verbo vi* to resume

continuidad *f sustantivo* continuity

con todos sus componentes *adj* fully-populated

contra ◇ **protección** *f* **contra la subida de tensión** over-voltage protection

contrario *adj* reverse

contraseña *f sustantivo* password ◇ **el usuario debe escribir su contraseña para poder acceder a la base de datos** the user has to key in the password before he can access the database ◇ **protegido, -a por una contraseña** password-protected

contraste *m sustantivo* contrast ◇ **la tecla le permite ajustar el brillo y el contraste** the control allows you to adjust brightness and contrast

contraste *m* **del rendimiento** *sustantivo* benchmarking

contratación *f* **contenido electrónica** *sustantivo* program trading

contrato *m* **de arrendamiento** *sustantivo* lease

contrato *m* **de mantenimiento** *sustantivo* **1.** maintenance contract **2.** service contract

contrato *m* **global** *sustantivo* package deal ◇ **llegaron a un acuerdo de conjunto que incluye el desarrollo de software, la personalización del hardware y la formación del personal** they agreed a package deal, which involves the development of software, customizing hardware and training of staff

control *sustantivo* **1.** control **2.** desk check **3.** verification ◇ **control** *m* **a distancia por rayos infrarrojos** infrared controller ◇ **control** *m* **de acceso (al sistema)** access control; access controller ◇ **control** *m* **de acceso al medio** MAC ◇ **control** *m* **de acceso a medios (de transmisión)** MAC; media access control ◇ **control** *m* **de desbordamiento de la capacidad** overflow check ◇ **(dispositivo de) control** *m* **de (alimentación de) electricidad** power monitor ◇ **control** *m* **de enlace de datos de alto nivel** high-level data link control ◇ **control** *m* **de intercambio de comunicaciones entrada** *or* **salida** handshake I/O control ◇ **control** *m* **del flujo (de datos)** flow control ◇ **control** *m* **del flujo de la información** information flow control ◇ **unidad de control** control unit (CU)

control *m* **a distancia** *sustantivo* remote control

controlado por un ratón *adj* mouse-driven

controlador *sustantivo* plotter driver ◇ **controlador** *m* **de acceso directo a la memoria** DMA controller ◇ **controlador** *m* **de emisor** *or* **receptor asíncrono universal** UART controller ◇ **controlador** *m* **de instalación del acoplador MIDI** MIDI setup map

controlador *m sustantivo* **1.** driver **2.** handler

controlador *m* **básico** *sustantivo* basic controller

controlador *m* **de comunicaciones** *sustantivo* communications control unit

controlador *m* **de disco** *sustantivo* disk controller

controlador *m* **de disco duro** *sustantivo* **1.** hard disk drive **2.** hard drive

controlador *m* **de discos** *sustantivo* disk drive

controlador *m* **de discos flexibles** *sustantivo* **1.** FDC **2.** floppy disk controller

controlador *m* **de disquete** *sustantivo* disk controller

controlador *m* **de disquetes** *sustantivo* **1.** FDC **2.** floppy disk controller

controlador *m* **de enlaces** *sustantivo* bus driver

controlador *m* **de entrada/salida** *sustantivo* input/output controller

controlador *m* **de errores** *sustantivo* error handler

controlador *m* **de impresora** *sustantivo* printer's controller

controlador *m* **de interrupciones** *abrev* IH ■ *sustantivo* interrupt handler

controlador *m* **de interrupciones programable** *sustantivo* PIC

controlador *m* **de interrupción programable** *sustantivo* programmable interrupt controller

controlador *m* **de la instrucción ANSI** *sustantivo* ANSI driver

controlador *m* **de la representación visual** *sustantivo* display controller

controlador *m* **de memoria temporal** *sustantivo* cache controller

controlador *m* **de pantalla** *sustantivo* display controller

controlador *m* **de periférico(s)** *sustantivo* controller

controlador *m* **de periféricos** *sustantivo* 1. PCU 2. peripheral control unit 3. peripheral driver

controlador *m* **de red** *sustantivo* network controller

controlador *m* **de seguridad por dominio(s)** *sustantivo* backup domain controller

controlador *m* **de selección** *sustantivo* selection handle

controlador *m* **de terminal** *sustantivo* terminal controller

controlador *m* **de transmisiones** *sustantivo* communications control unit

controlador *m* **DMA** *sustantivo* DMA controller

controlador *m* **monolítico** *sustantivo* monolithic driver

controlar *verbo* 1. *vt* to monitor 2. *vt* to regulate 3. *vt* to test 4. *vt* to verify ◇ **la máquina controla cada señal al mismo tiempo que la envía** the machine monitors each signal as it is sent out

control *m* **automático de amplificación** *sustantivo* 1. AGC 2. automatic gain control

control *m* **cíclico** *sustantivo* cyclic check

control *m* **de bifurcación** *sustantivo* transfer control

control *m* **de bloques de caracteres** *sustantivo* 1. BCC 2. block character check

control *m* **de bucle** *sustantivo* loop check

control *m* **de calidad** *sustantivo* quality control

control *m* **de canal** *sustantivo* line control

control *m* **de caracteres** *sustantivo* character check

control *m* **de carro** *sustantivo* carriage control ◇ **los códigos de control de carro pueden** emplearse para hacer avanzar el papel dos líneas entre cada línea de texto carriage control codes can be used to move the paper forward two lines between each line of text

control *m* **de coherencia** *sustantivo* consistency check

control *m* **de datos** *sustantivo* data control

control *m* **de ejecución de tareas** *sustantivo* job statement control

control *m* **de enlace de comunicaciones** *sustantivo* communications link control

control *m* **de enlace de datos** *sustantivo* data link control

control *m* **de enlace de datos de alto nivel** *abrev* 1. HDLC 2. HLDLC

control *m* **de errores** *sustantivo* error control

control *m* **de inferencia** *sustantivo* inference control

control *m* **de intercambio E/S** *sustantivo* handshake I/O control

control *m* **del canal de acceso** *sustantivo* access channel control

control *m* **del sistema** *sustantivo* system check

control *m* **de pantalla ANSI** *sustantivo* ANSI screen control

control *m* **de paridad** *sustantivo* parity check

control *m* **de paridad par** *sustantivo* even parity *o* even parity check

control *m* **de paridad par-impar** *sustantivo* odd-even check

control *m* **de paridad vertical** *sustantivo* vertical parity check

control *m* **de proceso** *sustantivo* process control

control *m* **de producción** *sustantivo* production control

control *m* **de pulsaciones** *sustantivo* keystroke verification

control *m* **de regularidad** *sustantivo* consistency check

control *m* **de retorno** *sustantivo* feedback control

control *m* **de secuencia** *sustantivo* sequence check

control *m* **de seguridad** *sustantivo* security check

control *m* **de teclas** *sustantivo* keystroke verification

control *m* **de trabajos por lotes** *sustantivo* stacked job control

control *m* **de transferencia** *sustantivo* 1. transfer check 2. transfer control

control *m* **de transmisiones** *sustantivo* communications link control

control *m* **de un programa** *sustantivo* desk check

control *m* **digital directo** *sustantivo* 1. DDC 2. direct digital control

control *m* **en cascada** *sustantivo* cascade control

control *m* **estándar de enlaces** *sustantivo* basic mode link control

control *m* **hacia atrás** *sustantivo* backwards supervision

control *m* **horizontal** *sustantivo* horizontal check

control *m* **integrado** *sustantivo* built-in check

control *m* **lógico de enlaces** *sustantivo* **1.** LLC **2.** logical link control

control *m* **numérico** *sustantivo* computer numerical control ■ *abrev* NC ■ *sustantivo* numerical control

control *m* **por eco** *sustantivo* echo check

control *m* **por lectura** *sustantivo* read back check

control *m* **por redundancia longitudinal** *sustantivo* longitudinal redundancy check

control *m* **por redundancia vertical** *sustantivo* **1.** vertical redundancy check **2.** VRC

control *m* **remoto** *sustantivo* remote control ◇ **el vídeo tiene un dispositivo de control remoto** the video recorder has a remote control facility

control *m* **ROM** *sustantivo* control ROM

control *m* **y validación** *sustantivo* V & V

control y validación *sustantivo* verification and validation

convención *f sustantivo* **1.** Backus-Naur-Form **2.** convention

convergencia *f sustantivo* convergence

conversación *f sustantivo* conversation

conversacional *adj* interactive

conversar *verbo vt* to converse

conversión *f sustantivo* conversion ◇ **conversión f de soporte (de datos)** media conversion ◇ **conversión f de una onda en numérica** waveform digitisation ◇ **factor de conversión** conversion factor ◇ **para transferir de una cinta magnética a un disquete, se necesita un dispositivo de conversión de soporte (de datos)** to transfer from magnetic tape to floppy disk, you need a media conversion device

conversión *f* **binario a decimal** *sustantivo* binary-to-decimal conversion

conversión *f* **de asignación** *sustantivo* assignment conversion

conversión *f* **de barrido** *sustantivo* **1.** line doubling **2.** scan conversion **3.** up conversion

conversión *f* **decimal-binaria** *sustantivo* decimal-to-binary conversion

conversión *f* **de código(s)** *sustantivo* code conversion

conversión *f* **de datos** *sustantivo* data translation

conversión *f* **de ficheros** *sustantivo* file conversion

conversión *f* **de señal** *sustantivo* signal conversion ◇ **convertidor de señal** signal converter

conversor *m sustantivo* changer ◇ **cambiadiscos** record changer ◇ **se pueden interconectar todos estos periféricos con sólo dos cables y un conversor de género** you can interconnect all these peripherals with just two cables and a gender changer

conversor *m* **de género** *sustantivo* gender changer ◇ **se pueden interconectar todos estos periféricos con sólo dos cables y un conversor de género** you can interconnect all these peripherals with just two cables and a gender changer

convertibilidad *f sustantivo* convertibility

convertible *adj* convertible

convertidor *m sustantivo* **1.** conversion equipment **2.** converter **3.** convertor ◇ **convertidor de analógico a digital** analog to digital converter (ADC) ◇ **convertidor** *m* **de cinta a tarjeta perforada** tape to card converter ◇ **convertidor de digital a analógico** digital to analog converter (DAC) ◇ **convertidor** *m* **de digital a analógico de acceso aleatorio** random access digital to analog converter ◇ **convertidor** *m* **en paralelo de señales analógicas-digitales** flash A/D ◇ **el convertidor permitió que se usaran los datos antiguos en el nuevo sistema** the convertor allowed the old data to be used on the new system

convertidor *m* **A/D** *sustantivo* flash A/D

convertidor *m* **analógico-digital** *sustantivo* A to D converter ◇ **la señal de voz se pasó primero a través de un convertidor analógico-digital antes de ser analizada** the speech signal was first passed through an A to D converter before being analysed

convertidor *m* **de digital a analógico** *sustantivo* **1.** ADC **2.** analog to digital converter

convertidor *m* **de estándares** *sustantivo* standards converter

convertidor *m* **de normas** *sustantivo* standards converter

convertidor *m* **de señal** *sustantivo* dataset

convertidor *m* **de serial a paralelo** *sustantivo* serial to parallel converter

convertidor *m* **de texto a voz** *sustantivo* text-to-speech converter

convertidor *m* **digital-analógico** *sustantivo* DAC

convertidor *m* **digital/analógico** *sustantivo* **1.** d/a converter **2.** digital to analog converter **3.** D to A converter

convertir *verbo vt* to translate

cookie *m sustantivo* cookie

cookie sin el nombre del usuario *sustantivo* blind certificate

coordenada *f sustantivo* vector

coordenada *f* **horizontal** *sustantivo* x-coordinate

coordenadas *fpl plural noun* coordinates

coordenadas *fpl* **absolutas** *plural noun* absolute coordinates

coordenadas *fpl* **cartesianas** *plural noun* cartesian coordinates

coordenadas *fpl* **polares** *sustantivo* polar coordinates

coordenadas *fpl* **relativas** *plural noun* relative coordinates

coordenadas *fpl* **X-Y** *sustantivo* x-y

coordenada *f* **vertical** *sustantivo* y-coordinate

coordinación *f sustantivo* coordination

coordinación *f* **inductiva** *sustantivo* inductive coordination

copia *sustantivo* **1.** mastering **2.** print **3.** replication ◊ **copia** *f* **de cortesía** bcc; cc ◊ **copia** *f* **espejo de datos (sobre un disco espejo)** disk duplexing; disk mirroring ◊ **relación de contraste de una copia** print contrast ratio

copia *f sustantivo* replication

copia *f* **archivada** *sustantivo* archived copy

copia *f* **automática de seguridad** *sustantivo* automatic backup

copia *f* **de archivos** *sustantivo* archived copy

copia *f* **del original** *sustantivo* protection master

copia *f* **de papel carbón** *sustantivo* carbon copy

copia *f* **de protección** *sustantivo* backup

copia *f* **de reserva** *sustantivo* backup

copia *f* **de seguridad** *sustantivo* **1.** backup **2.** backup copy **3.** backup version **4.** security backup

copia *f* **de seguridad de cinta** *sustantivo* tape backup

copia *f* **de seguridad del sistema** *sustantivo* system backup

copia *f* **de seguridad incremental** *sustantivo* incremental backup

copia *f* **de seguridad programada** *sustantivo* timed backup

copia *f* **facsímil** *sustantivo* facsimile copy

copia *f* **final** *sustantivo* clean copy

copia *f* **ilegal** *sustantivo* **1.** bootleg **2.** pirate copy ◊ **una copia pirateada de un programa de ordenador** a pirate copy of a computer program

copia *f* **impresa** *sustantivo* **1.** computer printout **2.** hard copy **3.** printout

copia *f* **oculta** *sustantivo* blind carbon copy

copia *f* **original de seguridad** *sustantivo* protection master

copia *f* **para archivar** *sustantivo* file copy

copia *f* **pirata** *sustantivo* **1.** bootleg **2.** pirate copy ◊ **una copia pirateada de un programa de ordenador** a pirate copy of a computer program

copia *f* **pirateada** *sustantivo* pirate copy ◊ **una copia pirateada de un programa de ordenador** a pirate copy of a computer program

copiar *verbo* **1.** *vt* to copy **2.** *vt* to download **3.** *vti* to dump ◊ **me llevé el ejemplar de 'The Times' de ayer** I kept yesterday's copy of 'The Times' ◊ **no es necesario pagar para copiar software de dominio público procedente de**

un tablón de anuncios (de la red) there is no charge for downloading public domain software from the BBS

copia *f* **temporal** *sustantivo* soft copy

coprocesador *m sustantivo* coprocessor

coprocesador *m* **gráfico** *sustantivo* graphics coprocessor

coprocesador *m* **matemático** *sustantivo* maths coprocessor

CORAL *sustantivo* CORAL

corazón *m sustantivo* kernel

corchete *m sustantivo* bracket

corchetes *mpl plural noun* square brackets

corrección *f sustantivo* perspective correction ◊ **agentes de actualización** update agents ◊ **corrección** *f* **(de un fichero, etc.)** update

corrección *f* **automática de errores** *sustantivo* automatic error correction

corrección *f* **de errores** *sustantivo* **1.** data cleaning **2.** error correction

corrección *f* **de errores hacia adelante** *sustantivo* forward error correction

corrección *f* **de errores hacia atrás** *sustantivo* backward error correction

corrección *f* **en retroceso** *sustantivo* backward error correction

corrección *f* **inmediata** *sustantivo* hot fix

corrección *f* **provisional** *sustantivo* patch

corrector, -a de estilo *sustantivo* editor

corrector *m* **de disco** *sustantivo* disk doctor

corrector *m* **gramatical** *sustantivo* grammar checker

corrector *m* **ortográfico** *sustantivo* spellchecker *o* spelling checker ◊ **actualizaremos el programa mediante un procesador de textos y un corrector ortográfico** the program will be upgraded with a word-processor and a spelling checker

corregir *verbo* **1.** *vt* to edit **2.** *vt* to revise **3.** *vt* to update ◊ **la versión corregida no contiene errores** the revised version has no mistakes

corregir errores *verbo* to troubleshoot

corregir previamente *verbo* to pre-edit

correo ◊ **correo que va lentamente** snail mail

'Un asunto polémico tratado por el Parlamento Europeo ha sido el del correo comercial no solicitado. El debate está entre exigir que el cliente acepte expresamente (opt-in) que se le remita este tipo de correo o bien autorizarlo genéricamente salvo que el cliente exprese su deseo (opt-out), inscribiéndose en una lista, de no recibirlo.' [*Ciberp@ís*]

'El correo electrónico puede ser visto como una continuación de forma electrónica de las tradicionales prácticas de correo o mailing.' [*PC Plus*]

correo *m* **de caracoles** *sustantivo* snail mail

correo *m* **electrónico** *sustantivo* **1.** electronic mail **2.** email *o* e-mail

corresidente *adj* coresident

corriente *f sustantivo* **1.** electricity **2.** power ◊ **hubo un corte de la corriente eléctrica y el**

ordenador falló the electricity was cut off, and the computer crashed

corriente *f* **alterna** *abrev* AC ∎ *sustantivo* alternating current

corriente *f* **continua** *sustantivo* direct current

corriente *m* **continua** *abrev* DC

corriente *f* **de bits** *sustantivo* bit stream

corriente *f* **eléctrica** *sustantivo* electric current

corriente *f* **transitoria** *sustantivo* power transient

corromper *verbo vt* to corrupt

corrompido *adj* corrupt

corrupción *f* *sustantivo* corruption

corrupción *f* **de datos** *sustantivo* data corruption ◇ **el deterioro de datos en el disco ha resultado en un fichero ilegible** data corruption on the disk has made one file unreadable ◇ **los acopladores acústicos son más susceptibles al deterioro de los datos que el módem de conexión directa a la línea** acoustic couplers suffer from data corruption more than the direct connect form of modem

corrupto *adj* corrupt

corrutina *f* *sustantivo* coroutine

cortacircuitos *m* *sustantivo* circuit breaker

cortar *verbo* 1. *vt* to cut 2. *vt* to scissor

cortar y insertar *sustantivo* cut and paste

corte *m* *sustantivo* cut ◇ **los editores han pedido que se hagan algunos recortes en el primer capítulo** the editors have asked for cuts in the first chapter

corte *m* **(de palabra)** *sustantivo* break

corte *m* **accidental** *sustantivo* holdup

corte *m* **de la corriente** *sustantivo* power failure

corte *m* **del fluido eléctrico** *sustantivo* power failure

corte *m* **de líneas** *sustantivo* line break

corte *m* **de una señal** *sustantivo* breakup

coste *m* **de conexión** *sustantivo* connect charge

creación *f* *sustantivo* 1. generation 2. origination

creación *f* **de datos** *sustantivo* data origination

creación *f* **de enlaces** *sustantivo* linkage

creación *f* **de ficheros** *sustantivo* file creation

creación *f* **de modelos de programas** *sustantivo* modelling

creación *f* **de un programa** *sustantivo* program generation

creado por ordenador *adj* computer-generated

creador *m* **de programas** *sustantivo* software developer

crear *verbo* 1. *vt* to generate 2. *vt* to originate 3. *vt* to produce ◇ **crear una imagen a partir de datos grabados digitalmente** to generate an image from digitally recorded data

criptografía *f* *sustantivo* cryptography

criptográfico *adj* cryptographic

cristal *m* *sustantivo* crystal ◇ **micrófono de cristal** *o* **piezoeléctrico** crystal microphone ◇ **oscilador de cristal** crystal oscillator

crítico *adj* mission-critical

croma *f* *sustantivo* 1. chroma 2. chrominance ◇ **control de croma** chroma control ◇ **detector de croma** chroma detector

crominancia *f* *sustantivo* 1. chroma 2. chrominance

cronometraje *m* **doble** *sustantivo* dual clocking

cronometrar *verbo vt* to time

cronómetro *m* *sustantivo* 1. clock 2. timer

cruce *m* *sustantivo* crossover

Ctrl *sustantivo* CTR *o* CTRL *o* Ctrl

CTRL *sustantivo* CTR *also* Ctrl

CTS *sustantivo* 1. clear to send 2. CTS

cuadr- *prefijo* quadr-

cuadrángulo *m* *adj* quad

cuadrante *m* *sustantivo* dial

cuadrar *verbo vi* to crop

cuadro *sustantivo* 1. panel 2. table ◇ **cuadro** *m* **pequeño de manipulación de una figura** handle ◇ **para agrandar un recuadro en el programa DTP, selecciónelo primero (con el ratón) y a continuación arrastre uno de los cuadros pequeños de manipulación hasta lograr la figura deseada** to stretch the box in the DTP program, select it once to display the handles then drag one handle to change its shape

cuadro *m* **de cableado** *sustantivo* wiring frame

cuadro *m* **de control** *sustantivo* control panel

cuadro *m* **de mensaje** *sustantivo* message box

cuadro *m* **de respuesta** *sustantivo* response frame

cuadro *m* **numérico** *sustantivo* numeric array

cuádruple *m* *adj* quad ∎ *sustantivo* quadruplex

cuantificable *adj* quantifiable

cuantificación *f* **de la amplitud** *sustantivo* amplitude quantisation

cuantificación *f* **de nivel cuaternario** *sustantivo* quaternary level quantization

cuantificación *f* **de nivel cuatro** *sustantivo* quaternary level quantization

cuantificador *m* *sustantivo* quantifier

cuantificar *verbo vt* to quantify ◇ **cuantificar** *o* **calcular el efecto de algo** to quantify the effect of something ◇ **es imposible cuantificar el efecto del nuevo sistema informático en la producción** it is impossible to quantify the effect of the new computer system on our production

cuanto *m* *sustantivo* quantum

cuarto ◇ **cuarto** *m* **de charlas en el Internet** chat room

cuaternario *adj* quaternary

cubierta *f sustantivo* **1.** banner page **2.** bezel **3.** cladding **4.** deck **5.** hood

cubierta *f* **insonorizada** *sustantivo* **1.** acoustic hood **2.** sound hood

cubrir *verbo* to mask ◊ **la primera instrucción, UMASK, asigna un valor a una máscara de bits interna al sistema, utilizada para enmascarar automáticamente los bits de protección cuando se crea un fichero** the first instruction, UMASK, sets an internal bit mask within the system, which is used to mask off mode bits when a file is created

cuenta *f sustantivo* account ◊ **el nombre de la cuenta de John Smith es JSMITH** John Smith's account name is JSMITH ◊ **si es usted un nuevo usuario, deberá solicitar del operador la creación de una nueva cuenta (de acceso)** if you are a new user, you will have to ask the supervisor to create an account for you

cuenta *f* **de acceso privilegiada/prioritaria** *sustantivo* privileged account ◊ **el director del sistema puede acceder a cualquier otra cuenta desde su cuenta privilegiada** the system manager can access anyone else's account from his privileged account

cuenta *f* **de usuario** *sustantivo* user account ◊ **tengo una nueva cuenta de usuario en esta red local, pero no me acuerdo de la contraseña** I have a new user account on this LAN but I cannot remember my password

cuerpo *m sustantivo* **1.** body **2.** type size ◊ **cuerpo (de un carácter)** body size

cuerpo *m* **del bucle** *sustantivo* loop body

cuerpo *m* **de un texto** *sustantivo* matter ◊ **impresos** printed matter ◊ **material publicitario** publicity matter

cuota *f* **fija** *sustantivo* flat rate

curiosear *verbo vi* to browse

cursiva *f sustantivo* italic ◊ **apriete CTRL I para imprimir el texto en cursiva** hit CTRL I to print the text in italics ◊ **el título viene impreso en cursiva y subrayado** the headline is printed in italic and underlined ◊ **todas las notas a pie de página están impresas en cursiva** all the footnotes are printed in italics

cursor *sustantivo* cursor ◊ **cursor** *m* **de la barra lateral** *(de desplazamiento)* elevator ◊ **cursor** *m* **(de forma) rectangular** block cursor ◊ **un usuario se puede mover por la imagen o por el texto arrastrando el cursor de la barra lateral de desplazamiento hacia arriba o hacia abajo** the user can scroll through the image or text by dragging the elevator up or down the scroll bar

cursor *m* **destructivo** *sustantivo* destructive cursor ◊ **resulta difícil leer la pantalla sin un cursor destructivo** reading the screen becomes difficult without a destructive cursor

cursor *m* **direccionable** *sustantivo* addressable cursor

cursor *m* **en I** *sustantivo* I-beam

cursor *m* **no destructivo** *sustantivo* non destructive cursor

cursor *m* **secundario** *sustantivo* ghost cursor

cursor *m* **supresor** *sustantivo* destructive cursor

curva *f sustantivo* plot

curva *f* **de aprendizaje** *sustantivo* learning curve

curva de aprendizaje difícil *sustantivo* steep learning curve

curva *f* **de Bézier** *sustantivo* Bézier curve

curva *f* **envolvente** *sustantivo* envelope

D

D *símbolo* D

dar algo como válido *verbo* to validate

dar el último toque *verbo* to tweak

dar formato *verbo* **1.** to edit **2.** to format ◇ **ésta da un nuevo formato al texto** there are several special edit keys – this one will re-format the text ◇ **se utilizan hojas de estilo para dar formato a los documentos** style sheets are used to format documents

dar la vuelta *verbo* to round

dar realce *verbo* to highlight

dar una instrucción *verbo* to order

dar un paso *verbo* to step

datagrama *m sustantivo* datagram

datagrama *m* **IP** *sustantivo* IP Datagram

dato *m* **absoluto** *sustantivo* atom

datos *mpl sustantivo* **1.** data **2.** information ◇ **área de datos** data area ◇ **bus de entrada de datos** data input bus (DIB) ◇ **cada vez que se enciende el motor hay un deterioro de los datos** data corruption occurs each time the motor is switched on ◇ **(transmisión de) datos infravocales** data below voice (DBV) ◇ **(transmisión de) datos supravocales** data above voice (DAV) ◇ **diagrama de flujo datos** data flow diagram (DFD) ◇ **diccionario** *or* **directorio de datos** data dictionary/directory (DD/D) ◇ **el diagrama de flujo de datos nos permitió mejorar los resultados al utilizar una estructura mejor** the data flowchart allowed us to improve throughput, by using a better structure ◇ **equipo de comunicación de datos** *o* **de información** data communications equipment (DCE) ◇ **estándar de puesta en clave de datos** data encryption standard (DES) ◇ **formato de intercambio de datos** *o* **formato DIF** data interchange format (DIF) ◇ **lenguaje de descripción de datos** *o* **de información** data description language (DDL) ◇ **los datos se introducen en una de las diversas estaciones de trabajo** data is input at one of several workstations ◇ **los escáners utilizan una técnica denominada compresión de datos que consigue reducir, hasta un tercio, la memoria necesaria** scanners use a technique called data compression which manages to reduce, even by a third, the storage required ◇ **se grabaron todos los ficheros en un solo disco mediante esta nueva rutina de compresión de datos** all the files were stored on one disk with this new data compacting routine ◇ **se tiene que analizar el fichero de datos** the data file has to be analysed ◇ **un**

usuario necesita una contraseña para acceder a los datos a user needs a password to access data

datos *mpl* **adicionales** *sustantivo* incremental data

datos *mpl* **alfanuméricos** *sustantivo* alphanumeric data

datos *mpl* **analógicos** *sustantivo* analog data

datos *mpl* **de base** *sustantivo* master data

datos *mpl* **de control** *sustantivo* **1.** control **2.** control data **3.** test data ◇ **para reiniciar su ordenador personal, pulse Ctrl-Alt-Del** to reset your PC, press Ctrl-Alt-Del ◇ **programa de control para microordenadores** control program for microcomputers (CP/M) ◇ **señal de control** *o* **de instrucciones** control signal ◇ **tarjeta de control** control card

datos *mpl* **de entrada** *sustantivo* input ◇ **la unidad de entrada acepta información codificada que proviene de operadores humanos, de dispositivos electromagnéticos o de otras computadoras** the input unit accepts coded information from human operators, from electromechanical devices, or from other computers ◇ **velocidad de entrada (de datos)** input speed

datos *mpl* **de entrada/salida (E/S)** *sustantivo* input/output

datos *mpl* **de instrucción** *sustantivo* control data

datos *mpl* **de llegada** *sustantivo* incoming traffic

datos *mpl* **de magnitud escalar** *sustantivo* scalar data

datos *mpl* **de prueba** *sustantivo* test data

datos *mpl* **de referencia** *sustantivo* master data

datos *mpl* **de salida** *sustantivo* computer output

datos *mpl* **de tipo general** *sustantivo* abstract data type ◇ **la pila es una estructura de datos de tipo abstracto que puede almacenar cualquier tipo de datos, desde un número entero hasta una dirección** the stack is a structure of abstract data types, it can store any type of data from an integer to an address

datos *mpl* **digitales** *sustantivo* digital data

datos *mpl* **en bruto** *sustantivo* raw data

datos *mpl* **erróneos, resultados erróneos** *sustantivo* **1.** garbage in garbage out **2.** GIGO

datos *mpl* **fijos** *sustantivo* fixed data

datos *mpl* **gráficos** *sustantivo* graphic data

datos *mpl* **incrementales** *sustantivo* incremental data

datos *mpl* **maestros** *sustantivo* master data

datos *mpl* **modificables** *sustantivo* variable data

datos *mpl* **numerados** *sustantivo* enumerated type

datos *mpl* **permanentes** *sustantivo* fixed data

datos *mpl* **procesados parcialmente** *sustantivo* semi-processed data

datos *mpl* **recibidos** *sustantivo* incoming traffic

datos *mpl* **relativos** *sustantivo* relative data

dato(s) *m(pl)* **variable(s)** *sustantivo* variable data

de acceso prohibido *adj* access-barred

de alta precisión *plural noun* high-spec

de alta velocidad *adj* high-speed

de base *adj* primitive

de biblioteca *adj* primitive

debido *m* **a una causa externa** *sustantivo* induced failure

debilitamiento *sustantivo* 1. attenuation 2. decay ◇ **debilitamiento** *m* **(de la señal)** attenuation ◇ **si el cable es demasiado largo, el debilitamiento de la señal comenzará a ocasionar errores en los datos** if the cable is too long, the signal attenuation will start to cause data errors

debilitamiento *m* **por inserción** *sustantivo* insertion loss

debilitarse *verbo vr* to fade

débito *m* **debe** *sustantivo* debit

de bobina a bobina *sustantivo* reel to reel

de borde activado *adj* edge-triggered

de botones *adj* pushbutton ◇ **teléfono de teclado** *o* **de botones** pushbutton telephone

DEBUG *sustantivo* DEBUG

década *f* *sustantivo* decade

decaimiento ◇ **con una pequeña debilitación, suena de forma muy aguda** with a short decay, it sounds very sharp ◇ **decaimiento** *m* **(de un sonido)** decay ◇ **intervalo de amortiguamiento** *o* **descenso** *o* **decaimiento de una señal** decay time ◇ **tiempo** decay time

de calidad fotográfica *adj* photorealistic

de capas múltiples *adj* multilayer ◇ **dispositivo de capas múltiples** multilayer device

decena *f* *sustantivo* decade ◇ **contador de decenas** decade counter

decibelio (dB) *m* *abrev* dB

decibelio *m* **(dB)** *sustantivo* decibel

decimal *m* **codificado binario natural** *sustantivo* natural binary coded decimal ■ *abrev* NBCD

decimal *m* **codificado en binario** *sustantivo* 1. BCD 2. binary coded decimal ◇ **la representación decimal codificada en binario del**

decimal 8 es 1000 the BCD representation of decimal 8 is 1000

decimal *m* **condensado** *sustantivo* packed decimal

decisión *f* **lógica** *sustantivo* logical decision

declaración *f* *sustantivo* 1. declaration 2. declarative statement 3. statement

declaración *f* *sustantivo* statement

declaración *f* **de procedimiento** *sustantivo* 1. narrative statement 2. procedure declaration

declaración *f* **de una variable local** *sustantivo* local declaration

decodificador *m* *sustantivo* decode unit

de contacto *adj* touch

de contactos/conectores compatibles *adj* pin-compatible

de control *adj* supervisory

decrecer *verbo vi* to decrement

dedicado, -a *adj* dedicated

'En principio, los ordenadores son máquinas universales que adoptan funciones según los programas. Pero determinadas necesidades de interfaz o de procesamiento motivan que existan ordenadores que sólo hacen una cosa: e-books (o libros electrónicos) que sólo sirven para leer, consolas de juegos que sólo son para la diversión, máquinas GPS que sólo sirven para situarnos en el espacio… Todos son dispositivos dedicados, en el sentido de que sólo hacen una cosa.' [*Ciberp@ís*]

dedo *m* *sustantivo* finger

de dos dimensiones *adj* two-dimensional

deducción *f* *sustantivo* inference

de emergencia *adj* 1. redundant 2. standby

de expansión *adj* add-in

de fácil uso *adj* user-friendly

defecto *m* *sustantivo* bug ■ *adj* default ■ *sustantivo* fault ◇ **la anchura de la pantalla tiene un valor por defecto de 80** screen width has a default value of 80 ◇ **por defecto** *o* **implícito** by default

definible por el usuario *adj* user-selectable

definición *f* *sustantivo* 1. definition 2. display resolution 3. resolution

definición *f* **de barrido** *sustantivo* scanning resolution

definición *f* **de celda** *sustantivo* cell definition

definición *f* **de lectura** *sustantivo* scanning resolution

definición *f* **de macro** *sustantivo* macro definition

definición *f* **de un problema** *sustantivo* problem definition

definición *f* **de visualización gráfica** *sustantivo* graphic display resolution

definición *f* **límite** *sustantivo* limiting resolution

definido, -a previamente *adj* predefined

definir *verbo* 1. *vt* to assign 2. *vt* to define 3. *vt* to set up ◇ **definir una tabla (de direccionamiento binario)** to bit-map ◇ **todas las variables**

fueron definidas en la inicialización all the variables were defined at initialization

definir de nuevo *verbo* to redefine ◇ **redefinimos los parámetros iniciales** we redefined the initial parameters ◇ **redefinir (la función) de una tecla** *o* **reprogramar una tecla** to redefine a key

definir una dirección *verbo* to address

deflector *m sustantivo* baffle

deformación *f sustantivo* corruption

de forma manual *adv* manually ◇ **hay que introducir el papel en la impresora de forma manual** the paper has to be fed into the printer manually

deformar *verbo vt* to distort

de forma secuencial *adv* sequentially

DEFRAG *sustantivo* DEFRAG

defragmentación *f sustantivo* defragmentation

defragmentación *f* **de ficheros** *sustantivo* file defragmentation

degradación *f sustantivo* degradation

degradación *f* **de la imagen** *sustantivo* image degradation

degradación *f* **del funcionamiento** *sustantivo* degradation

degradación *f* **gradual** *sustantivo* shading

degradación *f* **leve** *sustantivo* graceful degradation

degradación *f* **limitada** *sustantivo* graceful degradation

degradación *f* **progresiva** *sustantivo* graceful degradation

de intensidad media *adj* half-intensity

dejar a cero *verbo* to erase

dejar de funcionar *verbo vi* to go down

delimitador *m sustantivo* delimiter

delimitador *m* **(de información)** *sustantivo* delimiter

delimitador *m* **de datos** *sustantivo* data delimiter

delimitar *verbo vt* to delimit

delito *m* **informático** *sustantivo* computer crime

Delphi *(servicio proveedor de información en línea)* Delphi

demanda *f* **de lectura/escritura** *sustantivo* demand reading/writing

demanda *f* **de página** *sustantivo* demand paging

demanda *f* **de transferencia de datos** *sustantivo* demand reading/writing

demarcación *f sustantivo* 1. demarcation 2. flagging

demi- *prefijo* semi-

demo *f sustantivo* demonstration software ◇ **la compañía proporcionó un programa de demostración que permite hacerlo todo menos guardar los datos** the company gave away demonstration software that lets you do everything except save your data

demodulación *f sustantivo* demodulation

demonio *m sustantivo* daemon ◇ **demonio** *m* **de protocolo de transferencia de hipertexto** HTTPd; hypertext transfer protocol daemon

demora *f* **de propagación** *sustantivo* propagation delay

demorar *verbo vt* to phase ◇ **ángulo de fase** *o* **de desfasamiento** phase angle ◇ **compensador de fase** phase equalizer ◇ **modulación de fase** phase modulation ◇ **recorte de fase** phase clipping

denegación *sustantivo* denial

'DoS son las siglas correspondientes a Denial of Service (denegación de servicio), referidas al tipo de ataque que pretende bloquear un servidor a partir de la solicitud masiva de información por medio de varias máquinas 'hackeadas'.' [*Ciberp@ís*]

denegación *f* **alternativa** *sustantivo* alternative denial

de niveles múltiples *adj* multilevel

densidad *f sustantivo* density

densidad *f* **binaria** *sustantivo* bit density

densidad *f* **cuádruple** *sustantivo* quad density

densidad *f* **de almacenamiento** *sustantivo* packing density

densidad *f* **de bits** *sustantivo* bit density

densidad *f* **de caracteres** *sustantivo* 1. character density 2. pitch

densidad *f* **de los componentes** *sustantivo* component density

densidad *f* **del tráfico** *sustantivo* traffic density

densidad *f* **de memoria** *sustantivo* storage density

densidad *f* **de registro** *sustantivo* 1. packing density 2. recording density

dentado *m plural noun* jaggies

de ocho bits *adj* eight-bit *o* 8-bit

departamento *m* **de servicio al cliente** *sustantivo* customer service department

departamento *m* **informático** *sustantivo* computer department

departamento *m* **posventa** *sustantivo* customer service department

dependiente *adj* dependent

dependiente del dispositivo *adj* device-dependent

dependiente del equipo *adj* hardware dependent ◇ **los componentes lógicos de comunicaciones dependen del equipo y sólo funcionan con un módem compatible de tipo Hayes** the communications software is hardware dependent and will only work with Hayes-compatible modems

dependiente del procesador *adj* processor-limited

de plataforma *adj* flatbed

deposición *f sustantivo* deposition

depósito *m sustantivo* deposition

depósito *m* **de datos** *sustantivo* **1.** data sink **2.** sink ◇ **corriente de drenaje** sink current ◇ **disipador térmico** heat sink

depósito *m* **de la clave** *sustantivo* key escrow

depósito *m* **de memoria** *sustantivo* file storage

de procedimiento *adj* procedural

depuración *f* **de datos** *sustantivo* data cleaning

depuración *f* **de errores** *sustantivo* error recovery

depuración *f* **de ficheros** *sustantivo* file purge

depurador *m sustantivo* debugger ◇ **el depurador de errores no puede gestionar instrucciones compuestas** the debugger cannot handle compound statements

depurar *verbo* **1.** *vt* to debug **2.** *vt* to strip **3.** *vt* to troubleshoot

derechos *mpl* **de acceso** *plural noun* access rights

de reserva *adj* standby

derivación *f sustantivo* bridging

derivar (de) *verbo vi* to derive ◇ **indexación derivada** derived indexing ◇ **sonido derivado** derived sound

des- *prefijo* non- ◇ **instrucciones no desplegables** non-scrollable instructions ◇ **lectura no destructiva** non-destructive readout (NDR) ◇ **realizaré una serie de pruebas no destructivas en su ordenador y, si las pasa, podrá empezar a utilizarlo de nuevo** I will carry out a number of non-destructive tests on your computer: if it passes, you can start using it again

desactivado *adj* quiescent

desactivar *verbo vt* to disarm

desagrupar *verbo vt* to ungroup

desajustado *adj* out of alignment

desajuste *m* **(de pantalla)** *sustantivo* bleed

desaparecer progresivamente (la imagen) *sustantivo* dissolve

desarmar *verbo vt* to disassemble

desarrollo *m* **de un programa** *sustantivo* program development

desbloquear *verbo vt* to unlock

desbordamiento *sustantivo* spillage ◇ **desbordamiento** *m* **(de capacidad)** OV ◇ **desbordamiento** *m* **de capacidad (de una línea)** overflow

desbordamiento *m* **de la característica** *sustantivo* characteristic overflow

desbordamiento *m* **de pila** *sustantivo* stack overflow

desbordamiento *m* **negativo** *sustantivo* underflow

descargar *verbo vt* to offload

'A la hora de descargar software de Internet, estamos ya muy acostumbrados a términos como shareware (que significa 'probar antes de comprar') o freeware (programas que se utilizan de manera gratuita). A caballo entre estas dos maneras de distribuir aplicaciones podemos encontrar el careware. En este tipo de programas el autor no pide compensación económica alguna por su trabajo. Se conforma con una muestra de agradecimiento si el programa resulta de utilidad para el usuario que lo copia.' [*Ciberp@ís*]

descargar a la memoria externa *verbo* to roll out

descargar al disco *verbo* to roll out

descifrado *m sustantivo* decryption ◇ **el descifrado se realiza utilizando el hardware para aumentar la velocidad** decryption is done using hardware to increase speed

descifrar *verbo* **1.** *vt* to decipher **2.** *vt* to decode **3.** *vt* to decrypt **4.** *vt* to de-scramble

descodificador *m sustantivo* **1.** decoder **2.** descrambler

descodificador *m* **de direcciones** *sustantivo* address decoder

descodificador *m* **de instrucciones** *sustantivo* instruction decoder

descodificador *m* **de operación** *sustantivo* operation decoder

descodificar *verbo* **1.** *vt* to decode **2.** *vt* to descramble

descolgado *adv* off-hook

descompilación *f sustantivo* decompilation

descompresión *f sustantivo* decompression

descomprimir *verbo* **1.** *vt* to decompress **2.** *vi* to decompress **3.** *vi* to unpack **4.** *vt* to unzip ◇ **esta rutina descomprime los ficheros archivados** this routine unpacks the archived file

descondensar *verbo vi* to unpack ◇ **esta rutina descomprime los ficheros archivados** this routine unpacks the archived file

desconectado *adv, adj* off-line

desconectador *m* **disyuntor** *sustantivo* isolator

desconectar *verbo* **1.** *vt* to disarm **2.** *vt* to disconnect **3.** *vt* to power down **4.** *vt* to unplug ◇ **no olvide desconectar el cable antes de trasladar la impresora** do not forget to disconnect the cable before moving the printer ◇ **no traslade el sistema sin haberlo desconectado antes** do not move the system without unplugging it ◇ **simplemente desconecte la unidad de disco y conecte una nueva en su lugar** simply unplug the old drive and plug-in a new one

describir un círculo *verbo* to circulate

descriptografía *f sustantivo* decryption

descriptor *m sustantivo* descriptor

descriptor *m* **de ficheros** *sustantivo* **1.** file descriptor **2.** file label

desdibujar(se) *verbo* to blur

desdoblamiento *m sustantivo* folding

desechos *mpl sustantivo* garbage

de seguridad *adj* redundant

deseleccionar *verbo vt* to deselect

desempaquetar *verbo vt* to unpack

desenchufar *verbo vt* to unplug

desensamblador *m sustantivo* disassembler

desensamblar *verbo vt* to disassemble

desfase *m sustantivo* **1.** lag **2.** skew ◇ **se percibe un desfase horario en las llamadas telefónicas internacionales** time lag is noticeable on international phone calls

desfilar *verbo vi* to pass

desglosar *verbo vt* to partition

desimantador *m* **de cabezas** *sustantivo* head demagnetiser

desinstalar *verbo* **1.** *vt* to takedown **2.** *vt* to uninstall

deslizamiento *m sustantivo* SLIP

deslizamiento *m* **a la derecha** *sustantivo* right shift

deslizar *verbo vt* to drag

desmagnetizador *m sustantivo* **1.** degausser **2.** demagnetiser *o* demagnetizer ◇ **utilizó un desmagnetizador para desmagnetizar los cabezales de lectura** he used the demagnetizer to degauss the tape heads

desmagnetizador *m* **de cabezas** *sustantivo* head demagnetiser

desmagnetizar *verbo* **1.** *vt* to bloop **2.** *vt* to degauss **3.** *vt* to demagnetise *o* to demagnetize ◇ **hay que desmagnetizar los cabezales de lectura** *or* **escritura para asegurar un funcionamiento óptimo** the R/W heads have to be degaussed each week to ensure optimum performance

desmontable *adj* removable

desmontar *verbo vt* to disassemble ◇ **desmontar (entre dos tareas)** to takedown

desocupado *adv* on-hook

desordenado *adj* unsorted

desplazamiento *sustantivo* **1.** displacement **2.** float **3.** relocation **4.** scroll **5.** shift ◇ **contador de desplazamiento** shift counter ◇ **desplazamiento ascendente** *o* **hacia arriba** scrolling up ◇ **desplazamiento** *m* **de bits (en memoria)** bit blit ◇ **desplazamiento** *m* **de la paleta de colores** palette shift ◇ **desplazamiento** *m* **del texto sobre la pantalla** display scrolling ◇ **desplazamiento descendente** *o* **hacia abajo** scrolling down

desplazamiento *m* **a la derecha** *sustantivo* right shift

desplazamiento *m* **aritmético** *sustantivo* arithmetic shift

desplazamiento *m* **cíclico** *sustantivo* cyclic shift

desplazamiento *m* **circular** *sustantivo* **1.** circular shift **2.** end about shift **3.** ring shift

desplazamiento *m* **de ciclo** *verbo* to cycle shift

desplazamiento *m* **dinámico** *sustantivo* dynamic relocation program

desplazamiento *m* **horizontal** *sustantivo* horizontal scrolling

desplazamiento *m* **lógico** *sustantivo* **1.** logical shift **2.** non arithmetic shift

desplazamiento *m* **no aritmético** *sustantivo* **1.** logical shift **2.** non arithmetic shift

desplazamiento *m* **vertical** *sustantivo* vertical scrolling

desplazar *verbo* **1.** *vt* to drag **2.** *vt* to move **3.** *vt* to scroll **4.** *vt* to shift **5.** *vt* to smooth scroll ◇ **desplazar la imagen en la pantalla línea a línea** to roll scroll

desplazar(se) a la derecha *sustantivo* shift right

desplazar(se) a la izquierda *sustantivo* shift left

desplazarse ◇ **desplazarse (con un transmisor inalámbrico)** *vr* roam

destacar *verbo* **1.** *vt* to highlight **2.** *vt* to underline

destino *m* **de datos** *sustantivo* data sink

destrucción ◇ **destrucción** *f* **(accidental) del disco** disk crash

destruir *verbo* **1.** *vt* to delete **2.** *vt* to erase **3.** *vt* to kill **4.** *vt* to wipe ◇ **al reformatear un disco se borrarán todos sus datos** by reformatting you will wipe the disk clean

'Periódicamente adquieren notoriedad los virus, programas informáticos cuya presencia en el ordenador propio nadie desea, que son capaces de crear, modificar o destruir información haciéndola inservible y que pueden propagarse a otros programas y sistemas de forma espontánea.' [*PC Plus*]

desubscribirse *verbo vi* to unsubscribe

de superficie plana *adj* flatbed ◇ **los escáners son o bien de superficie plana o de rodillo con autoalimentación de papel** scanners are either flatbed models or platen type, paper-fed models ◇ **transmisor de superficie plana** *o* **de tipo 'flatbed'** flatbed transmitter

de supervisión *adj* supervisory

desviación *f sustantivo* **1.** alternate route **2.** bypass **3.** deflection

desviación *f* **de un rayo** *sustantivo* beam deflection ◇ **se utiliza un campo magnético para la desviación de un haz en un tubo de rayos catódicos (CRT)** a magnetic field is used for beam deflection in a CRT

desviar *verbo vt* to redirect ◇ **puede clasificar los resultados de la instrucción DIR desviándola a la instrucción SORT** you can sort the results from a DIR command by redirecting to the SORT command

desviar (por ruta distinta) *verbo* to redirect

desvío *m sustantivo* **1.** bypass **2.** trap

detección *sustantivo* sense ◇ **detección** *f* **(automática) de fallos** fault detection

detección *f* **automática de errores** *sustantivo* automatic error detection

detección *f* **de bordes** *sustantivo* edge detection

detección *f* **de colisión** *sustantivo* collision detection

detección f **de errores** *sustantivo* **1.** error detection **2.** error trapping

detección f **de límites** *sustantivo* edge detection

detección f **de portadora de datos** *sustantivo* DCD

detección y corrección de errores *sustantivo* **1.** EDAC **2.** error detection and correction

de teclas *adj* pushbutton

de tecnología avanzada *plural noun* highspec

detectar *verbo* **1.** *vt* to find **2.** *vt* to sense ◊ **el detector (de fallos) localizó el error rápidamente** the debugger found the error very quickly

detector m **de imágenes por contacto** *sustantivo* **1.** CIS **2.** contact image sensor

detector m **de virus** *sustantivo* virus detector

deteriorar *verbo* *vt* to corrupt ◊ **la pérdida de energía durante el acceso al disco puede deteriorar los datos** power loss during disk access can corrupt the data

deteriorar(se) *verbo* *vr* to crash

deterioro m *sustantivo* corruption ◊ **los acopladores acústicos son más susceptibles al deterioro de los datos que el módem de conexión directa a la línea** acoustic couplers suffer from data corruption more than the direct connect form of modem

deterioro m **de datos** *sustantivo* data corruption ◊ **cada vez que se enciende el motor hay un deterioro de los datos** data corruption occurs each time the motor is switched on

deterioro m **de los datos** *sustantivo* data corruption ◊ **el deterioro de datos en el disco ha resultado en un fichero ilegible** data corruption on the disk has made one file unreadable ◊ **los acopladores acústicos son más susceptibles al deterioro de los datos que el módem de conexión directa a la línea** acoustic couplers suffer from data corruption more than the direct connect form of modem

determinador m **de pilas** *sustantivo* battery meter

determinista *adj* deterministic

de tipo 'flatbed' *adj* flatbed ◊ **transmisor de superficie plana** o **de tipo 'flatbed'** flatbed transmitter

de tres dimensiones *adj* three-dimensional

de valor absoluto *adj* unsigned

de vez en cuando *adv* periodically

de vigilancia *adj* supervisory

diafonía f *sustantivo* **1.** babble **2.** crosstalk

diafragma m *sustantivo* diaphragm

diagnosis f *sustantivo* diagnosis

diagnosticar *verbo* *vt* to diagnose

diagnóstico m *sustantivo* diagnostic ■ *plural noun* diagnostics

diagnóstico m **de errores** *sustantivo* **1.** error diagnosis **2.** error diagnostics

diagnóstico m **de fallos** *sustantivo* fault diagnosis

diagnóstico m **de la memoria** *sustantivo* memory diagnostic

diagnóstico m **de problemas** *sustantivo* problem diagnosis

diagnóstico m **de prueba** *sustantivo* loopback test

diagnóstico m **mediante el compilador** *plural noun* compiler diagnostics ◊ **un detallado diagnóstico mediante el compilador facilita el proceso de corrección de errores** thorough compiler diagnostics make debugging easy

diagrama m *sustantivo* **1.** chart **2.** map **3.** pattern **4.** schema ◊ **diagrama** m **de red** (*con configuración de topología*) network diagram ◊ **este diagrama de sectores muestra la asignación de memoria** the memory allocation is shown on this pie chart

diagrama m **cableado** *sustantivo* cabling diagram

diagrama m **circular** *sustantivo* pie chart ◊ **este diagrama de sectores muestra la asignación de memoria** the memory allocation is shown on this pie chart

diagrama m **de bloques** *sustantivo* block diagram ◊ **el primer paso para diseñar un nuevo ordenador es dibujar un diagrama (de bloques) de sus componentes principales** the first step to designing a new computer is to draw out a block diagram of its main components

diagrama m **de circuito cableado** *sustantivo* cabling diagram

diagrama m **de datos** *sustantivo* datagram

diagrama m **de flujo** *sustantivo* **1.** flowchart **2.** flow diagram ◊ **el ordinograma representa el primer paso de un programa bien diseñado** a flowchart is the first step to a well designed program ◊ **plantilla** flowchart template

diagrama m **de flujo de datos** *sustantivo* **1.** data flow diagram **2.** DFD

diagrama m **del flujo de datos** *sustantivo* data flowchart ◊ **el diagrama de flujo de datos nos permitió mejorar los resultados al utilizar una estructura mejor** the data flowchart allowed us to improve throughput, by using a better structure

diagrama m **de procedimiento** *sustantivo* process chart

diagrama m **de proceso** *sustantivo* process chart

diagrama m **de sectores** *sustantivo* pie chart ◊ **este diagrama de sectores muestra la asignación de memoria** the memory allocation is shown on this pie chart

diagrama m **de un circuito** *sustantivo* circuit diagram ◊ **el programa CAD traza el diagrama del circuito con rapidez** the CAD program will plot the circuit diagram rapidly

diagrama m **de Veitch** *sustantivo* Veitch diagram

diagrama m **de Venn** *sustantivo* Venn diagram

diagrama *m* **en columnas** *sustantivo* columnar graph

diagrama *m* **funcional** *sustantivo* functional diagram

diagrama *m* **lógico** *sustantivo* **1.** logical chart **2.** logic flowchart

diagrama *m* **principal** *sustantivo* outline flowchart

diagramas *mpl plural noun* presentation graphics ◇ **las ventas del último mes parecieron aún mejores gracias a la presentación gráfica** the sales for last month looked even better thanks to the use of presentation graphics

dial *m* *sustantivo* dial ◇ **para sintonizar emisora de radio, gire el dial** to tune into the radio station, turn the dial

dialecto *m* *sustantivo* dialect ◇ **el dialecto de BASIC de este fabricante es un poco diferente al que yo estoy acostumbrado** this manufacturer's dialect of BASIC is a little different to the one I'm used to

dialogado *adj* interactive

diálogo *m* *sustantivo* **1.** dialog **2.** dialogue *o* dialog

diapositiva *f sustantivo* **1.** slide **2.** transparency ◇ **magnetófono con interfaz sincronizado para (la proyección de) diapositivas** slide/sync recorder ◇ **proyector de diapositivas** slide projector

diario *m* *sustantivo* journal ◇ **los registros modificados fueron añadidos al fichero maestro y anotados en el diario de modificaciones** the modified records were added to the master file and noted in the journal

diario *m* **de un sistema** *sustantivo* system log

dibit *m* *sustantivo* dibit

dibujo *m* *sustantivo* picture

dibujo *m* **lineal** *sustantivo* line drawing

diccionario *m* *sustantivo* dictionary

diccionario *m* **de ideas afines** *sustantivo* thesaurus

diccionario/directorio *m* **de datos** *sustantivo* **1.** data dictionary/directory **2.** DD/D

diccionario *m* **ideológico** *sustantivo* thesaurus

dicroico *adj* dichroic

dieciséis bits 16-bit ■ *adj* sixteen-bit

dieléctrico *m adj* dielectric

diferencia *f sustantivo* float

diferencia *f* **de potencial** *sustantivo* potential difference

diferencia *f* **simétrica** *sustantivo* symmetric difference

difundir *verbo vi* to propagate

difusión *f sustantivo* diffusion

difusión *f* **por la red** *sustantivo* networking

digital *adj* digital

digitalización *f* **de una onda** *sustantivo* waveform digitisation

digitalizador *m sustantivo* digitiser *o* digitizer

digitalizador *m* **de vídeo** *sustantivo* video digitiser

digitalizar *verbo vt* to digitise *o* to digitize

dígito *m* *sustantivo* **1.** bit **2.** digit **3.** function digit **4.** number ◇ **cuando se suman 5 más 7, hay una respuesta de dos y un dígito, que se suma a la columna siguiente, lo cual da 12** when 5 and 7 are added, there is an answer of 2 and a carry which is put in the next column, giving 12 ◇ **dígito** *m* **que se lleva en una suma** carry ◇ **el sistema de números de base decimal utiliza los dígitos 0123456789** the decimal number system uses the digits 0123456789

dígito *m* **binario** *abrev* b ■ *sustantivo* **1.** binary **2.** binary digit

dígito *m* **de alto nivel** *sustantivo* high order

dígito *m* **de relleno** *sustantivo* gap digit

dígito *m* **de signo** *sustantivo* sign digit

dígito *m* **más significativo (MSD)** *sustantivo* **1.** most significant digit *o* most significant character **2.** MSD

dígito *m* **menos significativo** *sustantivo* **1.** least significant digit **2.** LSD

dígito *m* **no permitido** *sustantivo* unallowable digit

dígito *m* **octal** *sustantivo* octal digit

dígito *m* **ruidoso** *sustantivo* noisy digit

dimensión *f sustantivo* **1.** dimension **2.** size ◇ **dimensión** *f* **de una unidad de información** item size

dimensionar *verbo vt* to size

dimensión *f* **de una matriz** *sustantivo* array dimension

dimensión *f* **de una serie** *sustantivo* array dimension

dimensiones *fpl plural noun* measurements ◇ **anotar las medidas de un paquete** to write down the measurements of a package

dimensión *f* **multiusuario** *sustantivo* MUD

DIN *sustantivo* **1.** Deutsche Industrienorm **2.** DIN

dinámico *adj* dynamic ◇ **lenguaje de escritura hipertextual dinámico** dynamic hypertext markup language (DHTML) ◇ **micrófono dinámico** dynamic microphone ◇ **RAM dinámico** *o* **memoria de acceso aleatorio dinámica** dynamic RAM *o* dynamic random access memory (DRAM)

dinero *m* **electrónico** *sustantivo* digital cash

Dingbat™ *sustantivo* Dingbat™

diodo *m* *sustantivo* diode

diodo *m* **electroluminescente** *sustantivo* **1.** LED **2.** light-emitting diode

diodo *m* **emisor de luz** *sustantivo* **1.** LED **2.** light-emitting diode

dipolo *m* *sustantivo* doublet

dirección *sustantivo* address ◇ **dirección** *f* **de los puertos de entrada** *or* **salida** I/O address ◇ **dirección** *f* **de un (solo) nivel** one-level address ◇ **dirección** *f* **origen de la primera instrucción**

de un programa program origin ◇ **dirección** *f* **(de la memoria) virtual** virtual address

'La dirección electrónica es de poca utilidad a la hora de procesar el mensaje electrónico, con la excepción del importante filtrado inicial del destinatario acerca de si el mensaje va dirigido personalmente, o genéricamente desde una lista de distribución.' [*Ciberpragmática*]

direccionable *adj* addressable ◇ **con el nuevo sistema operativo, la totalidad de los 5 MB de RAM resulta direccionable** with the new operating system, all of the 5MB of RAM is addressable

direccionable de píxeles *adj* dot addressable

dirección *f* **abreviada** *sustantivo* abbreviated address ◇ **mi dirección electrónica completa tiene más de 60 caracteres, por lo que le será más fácil utilizar mi dirección abreviada** my full network address is over 60 characters long, so you will find it easier to use my abbreviated address

dirección *f* **absoluta** *sustantivo* real address

dirección *f* **absoluta de máquina** *sustantivo* absolute address

dirección *f* **actual** *sustantivo* current address

direccionador *m sustantivo* router

direccionamiento *m sustantivo* 1. addressing 2. brouter 3. routing ◇ **el puente de direccionamiento proporciona una ruta dinámica y puede unir dos redes locales** the brouter provides dynamic routing and can bridge two local area networks

direccionamiento *m* **abreviado** *abrev* abb. add. ■ *sustantivo* abbreviated addressing

direccionamiento *m* **absoluto** *sustantivo* absolute addressing

direccionamiento *m* **adaptable** *sustantivo* adaptive routing

direccionamiento *m* **adaptable distribuido** *sustantivo* distributed adaptive routing

direccionamiento *m* **ampliado** *sustantivo* augmented addressing

direccionamiento *m* **asociativo** *sustantivo* 1. associative addressing 2. content-addressable addressing

direccionamiento *m* **binario** *sustantivo* bit addressing

direccionamiento *m* **de contenido direccionable** *sustantivo* 1. associative addressing 2. content-addressable addressing

direccionamiento *m* **de página** *sustantivo* page addressing

direccionamiento *m* **de registro(s)** *sustantivo* register addressing

direccionamiento *m* **de segundo nivel** *sustantivo* second-level addressing

direccionamiento *m* **diferido** *sustantivo* deferred addressing

direccionamiento *m* **directo** *sustantivo* 1. deferred addressing 2. direct addressing

direccionamiento *m* **implicado** *sustantivo* implied addressing ◇ **el direccionamiento inherente del acumulador se utiliza en la instrucción LDA, 16** implied addressing for the accumulator is used in the instruction LDA,16

direccionamiento *m* **implícito** *sustantivo* inherent addressing

direccionamiento *m* **indexado** *sustantivo* indexed addressing

direccionamiento *m* **indirecto** *sustantivo* indirect addressing

direccionamiento *m* **indizado** *sustantivo* indexed addressing

direccionamiento *m* **inherente** *sustantivo* 1. implied addressing 2. inherent addressing ◇ **el direccionamiento inherente del acumulador se utiliza en la instrucción LDA, 16** implied addressing for the accumulator is used in the instruction LDA,16

direccionamiento *m* **inmediato** *sustantivo* immediate addressing

direccionamiento *m* **simplificado** *abrev* abb. add. ■ *sustantivo* abbreviated addressing

direccionar *verbo vt* to address

dirección *f* **base** *sustantivo* base address

dirección *f* **de base** *sustantivo* 1. base address 2. presumptive address

dirección *f* **de celda** *sustantivo* cell address

dirección *f* **de control de periféricos** *sustantivo* device address

dirección *f* **de destino** *sustantivo* destination address

dirección *f* **de ejecución** *sustantivo* execution address

dirección *f* **de entrada** *sustantivo* entry point

dirección *f* **de instrucción** *sustantivo* instruction address

dirección *f* **de internet** *sustantivo* Internet protocol address

dirección *f* **del acumulador** *sustantivo* accumulator address

dirección *f* **de la subred** *sustantivo* subnet address *o* subnet number

dirección *f* **del flujo** *sustantivo* flow direction

dirección *f* **de origen** *sustantivo* initial address

dirección *f* **de (una) pila** *sustantivo* stack address

dirección *f* **de pista** *sustantivo* track address

dirección *f* **de primer nivel** *sustantivo* first-level address

dirección *f* **de red** *sustantivo* network address

dirección *f* **de referencia** *sustantivo* reference address

dirección *f* **de referencia directa** *sustantivo* direct reference address

dirección *f* **de retorno** *sustantivo* return address

dirección *f* **directa** *sustantivo* 1. immediate address 2. zero-level address

dirección *f* **efectiva** *sustantivo* effective address

dirección *f* **en internet** *sustantivo* **1.** Internet protocol address **2.** IP address

direcciones *fpl* **de bytes** *plural noun* byte address

direcciones *fpl* **de octetos** *plural noun* byte address

dirección *f* **específica** *sustantivo* specific address

dirección *f* **explícita** *sustantivo* explicit address

dirección *f* **física** *sustantivo* physical address

dirección *f* **flotante** *sustantivo* floating address

dirección *f* **generada** *sustantivo* generated address

dirección *f* **indexada** *sustantivo* indexed address

dirección *f* **inicial** *sustantivo* initial address

dirección *f* **inmediata** *sustantivo* **1.** immediate address **2.** zero-level address

dirección *f* **Internet** *sustantivo* **1.** host address **2.** host number **3.** Internet address **4.** Internet number

dirección *f* **(de) máquina** *sustantivo* machine address

dirección *f* **múltiple** *sustantivo* multi-address *o* multi-address instruction

dirección *f* **origen** *sustantivo* origin

dirección *f* **paginada** *sustantivo* paged address

dirección *f* **real** *sustantivo* **1.** actual address **2.** effective address **3.** first-level address

dirección *f* **relativa** *sustantivo* **1.** floating address **2.** indirect address **3.** offset value *o* offset word **4.** relative address

dirección *f* **secundaria** *sustantivo* subaddress

dirección *f* **simbólica** *sustantivo* **1.** symbolic address **2.** tag

dirección *f* **simbólica flotante** *sustantivo* floating symbolic address

dirección *f* **simbólica relativa** *sustantivo* floating symbolic address

dirección *f* **simplificada** *sustantivo* abbreviated address ◇ **mi dirección electrónica completa tiene más de 60 caracteres, por lo que le será más fácil utilizar mi dirección abreviada** my full network address is over 60 characters long, so you will find it easier to use my abbreviated address

dirección *f* **sintética** *sustantivo* synthetic address

dirección *f* **supuesta** *sustantivo* presumptive address

dirección *f* **uno más uno** *sustantivo* one-plus-one address

dirección *f* **válida de memoria** *sustantivo* valid memory address

directamente *adj, adv* direct ◇ **marcar (el número) directamente** to dial direct ◇ **si quiere puede llamar a Nueva York desde Londres marcando el número directamente** you can dial New York direct from London if you want

directiva *f* *sustantivo* directive

directo *adj, adv* direct

director *m* **de ruta** *sustantivo* router

director *m* **informático** *sustantivo* computer manager

directorio *sustantivo* directory ◇ **MKDIR (de creación de un directorio)** make directory

> 'Los directorios mantienen una información estructurada, que permite la búsqueda sistemática de la información deseada.' [*PC Plus*]

directorio *m* **(de ficheros)** *sustantivo* disk directory ◇ **el drectorio del disco muestra el nombre, la fecha y la hora de creación de un fichero** the disk directory shows file name, date and time of creation

directorio *m* **actual** *sustantivo* current directory

directorio *m* **compartido** *sustantivo* shared directory

directorio *m* **de ficheros** *sustantivo* file directory

directorio *m* **de red** *sustantivo* network directory

directorio *m* **de red compartido** *sustantivo* shared network directory

directorio *m* **jerárquico** *sustantivo* hierarchical directory

directorio *m* **padre** *sustantivo* parent directory

directorio *m* **raíz** *sustantivo* root directory ◇ **en el sistema DOS, el directorio raíz de la unidad de disco C: se llama C:** in DOS, the root directory on drive C: is called C:\

dirigido por un ratón *adj* mouse-driven

dirigir *verbo* *vt* to address ◇ **dirigir una carta** *o* **un paquete** to address a letter *o* a parcel

disco *sustantivo* **1.** disk **2.** milk disk ◇ **disco** *m* **compacto de una sola grabación** compact disc write once ◇ **disco óptico** optical disk ◇ **disco** *m* **que permite una sola escritura, pero lecturas múltiples** write once, read many times memory

disco *m* **compacto** *sustantivo* **1.** compact disc **2.** disc

disco *m* **compacto borrable** *sustantivo* compact disc erasable

disco *m* **compacto CD-ROM** *sustantivo* compact disc ROM

disco *m* **compacto de audio** *sustantivo* compact disc-digital audio

disco *m* **compacto de sólo lectura** *sustantivo* CD-ROM

disco *m* **compacto grabable** *sustantivo* recordable CD

disco *m* **compacto interactivo** *sustantivo* compact disc-interactive

disco *m* **comprimido** *sustantivo* Zip disk

disco *m* **de arranque** *sustantivo* **1.** boot disk **2.** startup disk ◇ **después de encender el orde-**

nador, inserte el disquete de arranque after you switch on the computer, insert the boot disk

disco *m* **de destino** *sustantivo* target disk

disco *m* **de inicio** *sustantivo* startup disk

disco *m* **del sistema** *sustantivo* system disk

disco *m* **de memoria** *sustantivo* 1. RAM disk 2. storage disk

disco *m* **de ochenta pistas** *sustantivo* eighty-track disk *o* 80-track disk

disco *m* **de registro** *sustantivo* work disk

disco *m* **de seguridad** *sustantivo* backup disk

disco *m* **de trabajo** *sustantivo* work disk

disco *m* **de vídeo digital** *sustantivo* digital videodisc ◇ **disco** *m* **de vídeo digital recordable** DVD-Recordable

disco *m* **duro** *sustantivo* 1. hard disk 2. rigid disk

disco *m* **duro C:** *sustantivo* C: drive

disco *m* **duro fijo** *sustantivo* fixed disk

disco *m* **duro interno** *sustantivo* internal hard disk

disco DVD *m* *sustantivo* DVD

disco *m* **fijo** *sustantivo* fixed disk

disco *m* **flexible** *abrev* fd *o* FD ■ *sustantivo* floppy disk *o* floppy

disco *m* **intercambiable Winchester** *sustantivo* removable Winchester disk

disco *m* **láser** *sustantivo* laser disc

disco *m* **maestro** *sustantivo* 1. master disc 2. master disk

disco *m* **magnético** *sustantivo* magnetic disk

disco *m* **magnetoóptico** *sustantivo* magneto-optical disc

disco *m* **no formateado** *sustantivo* unformatted disk ◇ **es imposible copiar algo en un disco no formateado** it is impossible to copy to an unformatted disk

disco *m* **no intercambiable** *sustantivo* fixed disk

disco *m* **óptico** *sustantivo* optical disk

disco *m* **óptico de transmisión** *sustantivo* transmissive disk

disco *m* **óptico WORM** *sustantivo* write once, read many times memory

disco *m* **original** *sustantivo* 1. magnetic master 2. master disc 3. master disk

disco *m* **RAM** *sustantivo* RAM disk

disco *m* **RAM silicio** *sustantivo* silicon disk

disco *m* **sectorizado suave** *sustantivo* soft-sectored disk

disco *m* **simple** *sustantivo* platter

disco *m* **vacío** *sustantivo* blank disk

disco *m* **vídeo digital** *sustantivo* digital versatile disc

disco *m* **virtual** *sustantivo* virtual disk

disco *m* **(duro) Winchester** *sustantivo* Winchester disk *o* Winchester drive

discreto *adj* discrete ◇ **una palabra de datos se compone de (una serie de) bits discretos** a data word is made up of discrete bits

diseñado, -a por ordenador *adj* computer-generated ◇ **analizaron la imagen diseñada por ordenador** they analyzed the computer-generated image ◇ **gráficos** *mpl* **diseñados por ordenador** *or* **infografía** *f* computer-generated graphics

diseñador *m* *sustantivo* developer

diseñador *m* **de aplicaciones** *sustantivo* application developer

diseñador *m* **de 'software'** *sustantivo* software developer

diseñados ◇ **gráficos** *mpl* **diseñados con (un dispositivo) tortuga** turtle graphics ◇ **la presentación gráfica se preparó con gráficos de tortuga** the charts were prepared using turtle graphics

diseño *m* *sustantivo* 1. layout 2. outline 3. page layout 4. pattern ◇ **el equipo de diseño está realizando la maquetación de la nueva revista** = the design team is working on the layouts for the new magazine

diseño *m* **asistido por ordenador** *sustantivo* CAD ◇ **todos nuestros ingenieros diseñan en terminales equipados con CAD** all our engineers design on CAD workstations

diseño *m* **asistido por ordenador (CAD)** *sustantivo* 1. computer-aided design 2. computer-assisted design

diseño *m* **de menor coste** *sustantivo* least cost design ◇ **el presupuesto es de sólo 1.000 libras esterlinas; necesitamos el diseño más económico para el nuevo circuito** the budget is only £1,000, we need the least cost design for the new circuit

diseño *m* **de productos** *sustantivo* product design

diseño *m* **de programas** *sustantivo* software development

diseño *m* **de un circuito** *sustantivo* circuit design

diseño *m* **de un fichero** *sustantivo* 1. file layout 2. file organisation

diseño *m* **de un registro** *sustantivo* 1. record format 2. record layout

diseño *m* **de un sistema** *sustantivo* system design

diseño *m* **en elementos de bits** *sustantivo* bit-slice architecture *o* bit-slice design

diseño *m* **estructurado** *sustantivo* structured design

diseño *m* **gráfico** *sustantivo* blueprint

diseño *m* **más económico** *sustantivo* least cost design ◇ **el presupuesto es de sólo 1.000 libras esterlinas; necesitamos el diseño más económico para el nuevo circuito** the budget is only £1,000, we need the least cost design for the new circuit

diseño *m* **previo** *sustantivo* pre-imaging

disimular *verbo vt* to conceal

disipador *m* **térmico** *sustantivo* heat-sink

disolver(se) *sustantivo vr* dissolve

dispersión *f sustantivo* dispersion

disponer *verbo* **1.** *vt* to arm **2.** *vt* to network **3.**
vt to tab ◇ **disponer en tabla** to tabulate

disponer en mosaico *verbo* to tile

disponibilidad *f* **de ciclo** *sustantivo* cycle
availability

disponibilidad *f* **de memoria** *sustantivo* addressing capacity

disponible *adj* **1.** configured-in **2.** idle

disposición *f* *sustantivo* balance ◇ **disposición** *f* **de las teclas de un teclado** keyboard
layout ◇ **el paquete de software DTP permite
al usuario ver si la disposición general de la
página es correcta** the DTP package allows the
user to see if the overall page balance is correct

disposición *f* **de los contactos** *sustantivo*
pinout

dispositivo *sustantivo* **1.** device **2.** eraser **3.**
microdevice ◇ **dispositivo** *m* **con memoria de
estado sólido** solid-state memory device ◇ **dispositivo** *m* **de almacenamiento de acceso directo** DASD; direct access storage device ◇ **dispositivo** *m* **de protección de la escritura de
un fichero** file protect tab ◇ **dispositivo** *m* **de
rejilla (en pantalla)** grid snap ◇ **dispositivo** *m*
de selección de señal máxima auctioneering
device ◇ **dispositivo** *m* **de selección de señal
mínima** auctioneering device ◇ **si quiere dibujar con líneas precisas, le resultará más fácil
con el dispositivo de rejilla activado** if you
want to draw accurate lines, you'll find it easier
with grid snap turned on

dispositivo *m* **absoluto** *sustantivo* absolute
device

dispositivo *m* **acoplado de carga** *sustantivo* charge-coupled device

dispositivo *m* **activo** *sustantivo* active device

dispositivo *m* **adicional** *sustantivo*, *adj* add-
in ■ *sustantivo* add-on

dispositivo *m* **ALU** *sustantivo* ALU

dispositivo *m* **añadido** *sustantivo* add-on

dispositivo *m* **anticopia** *sustantivo* copy
protect ◇ **el programa no está protegido (contra la copia)** the program is not copy protected ◇
**todos los disquetes tienen un dispositivo an-
ticopia** all the disks are copy protected

dispositivo *m* **antiparásito** *sustantivo* suppressor

dispositivo *m* **autónomo** *sustantivo* stand-
alone *o* standalone

dispositivo *m* **auxiliar** *sustantivo* **1.** safety
net **2.** standby ◇ **en caso de fallo eléctrico, tenemos un dispositivo UPS de emergencia** if
there is a power failure, we have a safety net in the
form of a UPS

dispositivo *m* **CCD** *sustantivo* charge-coupled device

dispositivo *m* **complementario** *sustantivo*,
adj add-in ■ *sustantivo* add-on

dispositivo *m* **compuesto** *sustantivo* compound device

dispositivo *m* **de acceso** *sustantivo* facility
◇ **almacén** storage facilities ◇ **medios de almacenamiento** storage facilities

dispositivo *m* **de acceso aleatorio** *sustantivo* random access device

dispositivo *m* **de alineación** *sustantivo*
aligner

dispositivo *m* **de almacenamiento** *sustantivo* storage device

dispositivo *m* **de almacenamiento
masivo** *sustantivo* mass storage device

dispositivo *m* **de arrastre de cinta** *sustantivo* tape transport

dispositivo *m* **de bloqueo** *sustantivo* latch

dispositivo *m* **de bloques** *sustantivo* block
device ◇ **la disquetera es un dispositivo de
bloques que puede transferir 256 bytes de
datos a la vez** the disk drive is a block device that
can transfer 256 bytes of data at a time

dispositivo *m* **de cargamentos adyacentes** *abrev* CCD

dispositivo *m* **de contacto** *sustantivo* touch
pad

dispositivo *m* **de control multimedia** *sustantivo* MCI device

dispositivo *m* **de emergencia** *sustantivo* **1.**
safety net **2.** standby ◇ **en caso de fallo eléctrico, tenemos un dispositivo UPS de emergencia** if there is a power failure, we have a safety net
in the form of a UPS

dispositivo *m* **de entrada/salida** *sustantivo*
1. input/output device **2.** input/output unit **3.** I/O
device

dispositivo *m* **de estado sólido** *sustantivo*
solid-state device

dispositivo *m* **de grabación de imágenes** *sustantivo* frame grabber

dispositivo *m* **de identificación personal**
sustantivo **1.** personal identification device **2.** PID

dispositivo *m* **de instrucciones a distancia** *sustantivo* **1.** remote console **2.** remote device

dispositivo *m* **de intercambio de datos**
sustantivo data switching exchange

dispositivo *m* **de justificación** *sustantivo*
aligner

dispositivo *m* **de marcas detectables**
sustantivo mark sense device

dispositivo *m* **de posicionamiento** *sustantivo* aligner

dispositivo *m* **de protección de escritura**
sustantivo write-protect tab

dispositivo *m* **de reserva** *sustantivo* standby

dispositivo *m* **de ruta** *sustantivo* router

dispositivo *m* **de salida** *sustantivo* output
device

dispositivo *m* **de seguridad** *sustantivo*
safety net ◇ **en caso de fallo eléctrico, tenemos un dispositivo UPS de emergencia** if

there is a power failure, we have a safety net in the form of a UPS

dispositivo *m* **de señalización relativa** *sustantivo* relative pointing device

dispositivo *m* **de visualización** *sustantivo* readout device

dispositivo *m* **emisor** *sustantivo* send-only device

dispositivo *m* **emisor-receptor** *sustantivo* transceiver

dispositivo *m* **externo** *sustantivo* external device

dispositivo *m* **independiente** *sustantivo* stand-alone *o* standalone

dispositivo *m* **indicador** *sustantivo* pointing device

dispositivo *m* **inteligente** *sustantivo* intelligent device

dispositivo *m* **lógico programable** *sustantivo* PLA ■ *abrev* PLD ■ *sustantivo* **1.** programmable logic array **2.** programmable logic device

dispositivo *m* **MIDI** *sustantivo* MIDI device

dispositivo *m* **programable de campo** *sustantivo* field programmable device

dispositivo *m* **PROM** *abrev* FROM ■ *sustantivo* fusible read only memory

dispositivo *m* **táctil** *sustantivo* touch pad

dispositivo *m* **universal** *sustantivo* universal device

dispuesto *adj* ready

dispuesto, -a en capas *adj* layered

dispuesto en serie *adv* serially

disquete *sustantivo* **1.** disk **2.** diskette **3.** disk memory **4.** floppy disk *o* floppy ◇ **disquete** *m* **de 3,5 pulgadas** microfloppy

'Los contagios vía disquete han desaparecido y la única vía de propagación de un virus es el correo electrónico.' [*Ciberp@ís*]

disquete *m* **de almacenamiento** *sustantivo* storage disk

disquete *m* **de arranque** *sustantivo* boot disk ◇ **después de encender el ordenador, inserte el disquete de arranque** after you switch on the computer, insert the boot disk

disquete *m* **de densidad simple** *sustantivo* single density disk

disquete *m* **de doble cara** *sustantivo* double-sided disk

disquete *m* **de doble densidad** *sustantivo* double density disk

disquete *m* **de enlace** *sustantivo* milk disk

disquete *m* **de fuentes** *sustantivo* font disk

disquete *m* **de limpieza de cabezales** *sustantivo* head cleaning disk ◇ **utilice un disquete de limpieza de cabezas una vez por semana** use a head cleaning disk every week

disquete *m* **de limpieza de cabezas** *sustantivo* head cleaning disk

disquete *m* **de ocho pulgadas** *sustantivo* eight-inch disk *o* 8-inch disk

disquete *m* **de seguridad** *sustantivo* backup disk

disquete *m* **de una sola cara** *sustantivo* single-sided disk

disquete *m* **de un solo lado** *sustantivo* single-sided disk ■ *abrev* SSD

disquete *m* **en blanco** *sustantivo* blank disk

disquete *m* **flexible** *abrev* fd *o* FD

disquete *m* **no compatible** *sustantivo* alien disk

disquetera *f sustantivo* floppy disk drive

disquetera *f sustantivo* fixed head disk *o* fixed head disk drive

disquetera *f* **actual** *sustantivo* current drive

disquetera *f* **de altura media** *sustantivo* half-height drive

disquetera *f* **externa** *sustantivo* external disk drive

disquete *m* **reversible** *sustantivo* flippy

distancia *f* **de Hamming** *sustantivo* Hamming distance

distancia *f* **de señal** *sustantivo* signal distance

distancia *f* **sobre el eje X** *sustantivo* x distance

distancia *f* **sobre el eje Y** *sustantivo* y-distance

distintivo *m sustantivo* logo

distorsión *f sustantivo* **1.** aberration **2.** distortion ◇ **deformación** *o* **distorsión de una imagen** image distortion ◇ **óptica de distorsión** distortion optics

distorsionar *verbo vt* to distort

distorsión *f* **de una señal** *sustantivo* breakup

distorsión *f* **en cojín** *sustantivo* pincushion distortion

distorsión *f* **trapezoidal** *sustantivo* **1.** keystone distortion **2.** trapezoidal distortion

distribución *f sustantivo* **1.** allocation **2.** assignment **3.** distribution ◇ **centro de distribución** distribution point

distribución *f* **automática de llamadas** *sustantivo* **1.** ACD **2.** automatic call distribution

distribución *f* **de memoria** *sustantivo* memory allocation

distribución *f* **de página** *sustantivo* page setup

distribuidor *m* **automático de llamadas** *sustantivo* **1.** ACD **2.** automatic call distribution

distribuir *verbo vt* to distribute ◇ **proceso de datos distribuido** distributed data processing (DDP)

disyunción *f sustantivo* **1.** disjunction **2.** exjunction

dividendo *m sustantivo* dividend

dividir *verbo* **1.** *vt* to cut **2.** *vt* to partition **3.** *vt* to segment

dividir en sectores *verbo* to sector

división *sustantivo* partition ◇ **división** *f* **con parámetros de identificación** (*de un programa en COBOL*) identification division ◇ **división** *f* **silábica (por guiones)** hyphenation

división *f* **automática** *sustantivo* automatic hyphenation

divisor *m sustantivo* divisor

DLL *sustantivo* **1.** DLL **2.** dynamic link library

DMA *sustantivo* DMA

doblador *m* **de reloj** *sustantivo* clock doubler ◇ **el nuevo procesador de Intel tiene un doblador opcional de reloj que dobla el rendimiento** the new CPU from Intel has an optional clock doubler that will double performance

doblar *verbo vt* to dub ◇ **sonido doblado** dubbed sound

doble-clic *m sustantivo* double-click

doble densidad *f abrev* DD

doble subrayado *m sustantivo* double strike

doblete *m sustantivo* doublet

documentar *verbo vt* to document

documento *sustantivo* **1.** document **2.** record

'El modelo 7650 es un teléfono móvil que incorpora una cámara digital y que permite enviar las fotografías como un documento adjunto en un correo electrónico.' [*Ciberp@ís*]

documento *m* **activo** *sustantivo* Active Document

documento *m* **adjunto** *sustantivo* attachment

documento *m* **asociado** *sustantivo* associated document *o* associated file

documento *m* **compuesto** *sustantivo* compound document

documento *m* **definitivo** *sustantivo* (*creado a partir de otros textos*) boilerplate

documento *m* **de origen** *sustantivo* source document

documento *m* **estándar** *sustantivo* standard document *o* standard form

documento *m* **impreso** *sustantivo* hard copy

documento *m* **original** *sustantivo* source document

documento *m* **retornable** *sustantivo* turnaround document

documentos *mpl sustantivo* documentation

Dolby Digital™ (*marca comercial*) Dolby Digital™

Dolby system™ (*marca comercial*) Dolby system™

domicilio *m sustantivo* address

dominar *verbo vt* to master

dominio *sustantivo* domain

'La galería comercial (mall) está constituida por un conjunto de tiendas que aparecen en un domin-

io común y bajo la cobertura de un nombre comercialmente conocido.' [*PC Plus*]

dominio *m* **de nivel superior** *sustantivo* top-level domain

dominio *m* **público** *abrev* PD ■ *sustantivo* public domain

dominios *mpl* **adyacentes** *plural noun* adjacent domains

dos bits *mpl sustantivo* dibit

dual *adj* dual ◇ **multifrecuencia de tono dual** dual tone multi-frequency (DTMF)

dualidad *f* **funcional** *sustantivo* folding

duende *m sustantivo* **1.** gremlin **2.** sprite

dúplex *m sustantivo* duplex

duplexado *m sustantivo* duplexing

dúplex *m* **bidireccional** *sustantivo* full duplex

dúplex *m* **completo** *abrev* fdx *o* FDX

dúplex *m* **en alternativa** *sustantivo* **1.** half duplex **2.** HD ■ *abrev* HDX

dúplex *m* **integral** *abrev* fdx *o* FDX

duplicación *f sustantivo* backup ◇ **duplicación** *f* **de datos sobre un disco espejo** disk duplexing; disk mirroring

duplicado *m sustantivo* replication

duración *f sustantivo* fault time ◇ **duración** *f* **media de funcionamiento correcto entre fallos** mean time between failures; MTBF ◇ **duración** *f* **media necesaria para una reparación** mean time to repair; MTTR

duración *f* **de ejecución** *sustantivo* **1.** execute time **2.** run-time *o* run duration

duración *f* **de ensamblaje** *sustantivo* assembly time

duración *f* **de la compilación** *sustantivo* compilation time

duración *f* **de una llamada** *sustantivo* call duration ◇ **la duración de una llamada depende de la complejidad de la transmisión** call duration depends on the complexity of the transaction ◇ **los precios están relacionados con la duración de la llamada** charges are related to call duration

duración *f* **de un sistema** *sustantivo* system life cycle

duración *f* **de vida** *sustantivo* lifetime ◇ **este nuevo ordenador tiene una duración de vida de cuatro años** this new computer has a four-year lifetime

duro *adj* hard

DVD-R *abrev* DVD-R

DVD-RAM *sustantivo* DVD-RAM

DVD-ROM *sustantivo* DVD-ROM

DVD+RW *sustantivo* DVD+RW

DVD-vídeo *m sustantivo* DVD-video

E

E *símbolo* E

eco *m sustantivo* echo ◇ **cámara de ecos** echo chamber ◇ **supresor de eco** echo suppressor

ecuación *f* **de Mandlebrot** *sustantivo* Mandlebrot set

ecuación *f* **máquina** *sustantivo* machine equation

edición ◇ **edición** *f* **de vídeo asistida por ordenador** desktop video; DTV

'La posibilidad de patentar no sólo los programas sino también el formato electrónico en que se publica la información puede provocar graves restricciones a la libertad de expresión cuando la edición electrónica se extienda.' [*Ciberp@ís*]

edición *f* **de enlaces** *sustantivo* linkage editing

edición *f* **de imágenes** *sustantivo* image editing

edición *f* **de vídeo** *sustantivo* video editing

edición *f* **electrónica** *sustantivo* desktop publishing

edición *f* **en línea** *sustantivo* online editing

edición *f* **fuera de línea** *sustantivo* off-line editing

editar *verbo* **1.** *vt* to edit **2.** *vt* to word-process ◇ **editar en forma de lista** to list ◇ **hacer una lista de (las líneas de instrucción de) un programa** to list a program

editor *m sustantivo* **1.** editor **2.** linkage editing ◇ **editor** *o* **montador de enlaces** linkage editor

editor *m* **de enlaces** *sustantivo* binder

editor *m* **de imagen** *sustantivo* image editor

editor *m* **de línea** *sustantivo* **1.** EDLIN **2.** line editor

editor *m* **del programa fuente** *sustantivo* source editor

editor *m* **de pantalla** *sustantivo* screen editor

editor *m* **de programa** *sustantivo* **1.** editor program **2.** program editor

editor *m* **de texto(s)** *sustantivo* text editor

editor *m* **de una onda** *sustantivo* waveform editor

editor *m* **de vídeo** *sustantivo* video editor

editor *m* **línea a línea** *sustantivo* line editor

-edu *suffix* edu

efecto *m sustantivo* transient

efecto *m* **corona** *sustantivo* corona

efecto *m* **en cascada** *sustantivo* ripple-through effect

efecto *m* **escalera** *sustantivo* aliasing ■ *plural noun* jaggies

efecto *m* **Hall** *sustantivo* Hall effect

efecto *m* **memoria** *sustantivo* memory effect

efecto *m* **muaré** *sustantivo* moiré effect

efecto *m* **niebla** *sustantivo* **1.** fogging **2.** haze

efectuar una bifurcación *verbo* to jump on zero

efectuar una nueva compilación *verbo* to recompile

efectuar una partición *verbo* to partition

EISA *sustantivo* **1.** EISA **2.** Electronics Industry Standards Association

eje *m sustantivo* **1.** axis **2.** spindle ◇ **el paquete de diseño asistido por ordenador (CAD) permite colocar el eje en cualquier sitio (de la pantalla)** the CAD package allows an axis to be placed anywhere

ejecución *sustantivo* **1.** execution **2.** run ◇ **codificación de ejecución longitud** run-length encoding (RLE) ◇ **ejecución** *f* **de un programa de edición** (*por control*) editing run

ejecución *f* **de prueba** *sustantivo* test run

ejecución *f* **de un programa** *sustantivo* **1.** computer run **2.** machine run **3.** program execution **4.** program run

ejecución *f* **en paralelo** *sustantivo* parallel running

ejecución *f* **en seco** *sustantivo* dry run

ejecución *f* **seca** *sustantivo* dry run

ejecutar *verbo* **1.** *vt* to execute **2.** *vt* to launch **3.** *vt* to run ◇ **ejecutar de nuevo (un programa)** to rerun ◇ **ejecutar (las instrucciones) por encauzamiento** to pipeline

ejecutivo *adj* executive ■ *sustantivo* supervisor

eje *m* **de abscisas** *sustantivo* **1.** horizontal axis **2.** x-axis

eje *m* **de coordenadas** *sustantivo* axis

eje *m* **de la ordenada** *sustantivo* y-axis

eje *m* **de ordenadas** *sustantivo* vertical axis

eje *m* **horizontal** *sustantivo* horizontal axis

eje *m* **principal (de red)** *sustantivo* backbone ◇ **hemos interconectado las redes en cada oficina mediante una red principal de alta velocidad** we have linked the networks in each office using a high-speed backbone

eje *m* **vertical** *sustantivo* vertical axis

eje *m* **X** *sustantivo* x-axis

eje *m* **Y** *sustantivo* y-axis

eje *m* **Z** *sustantivo* z-axis

electricidad *f sustantivo* electricity ◇ **los precios de la electricidad son un factor importante en los costos de producción** electricity prices are an important factor in the production costs

electricidad *f* **disponible** *sustantivo* available power

electricidad *f* **estática** *sustantivo* static electricity

electrofotográfico *adj* electrophotographic

electroluminiscencia *f sustantivo* electroluminescence

electroluminiscente *adj* **1.** electroluminescent **2.** electroluminescing ◇ **la pantalla está recubierta de una capa electroluminiscente** the screen coating is electroluminescent

electromagnético *adj* electromagnetic ◇ **espectro electromagnético** electromagnetic spectrum

electrónica *f sustantivo* electronics ◇ **electrónica** *f* **de unidad (de lectura) integrada ampliada** extended integrated drive electronics ◇ **especialista en electrónica** electronics specialist ◇ **experto, -a en electrónica** electronics specialist ◇ **la industria electrónica** the electronics industry

electrónica *f* **de dispositivo integrado** *sustantivo* integrated device electronics *o* integrated drive electronics ◇ **las disqueteras electrónicas de dispositivo integrado son el estándar incorporado en la mayoría de los ordenadores personales** IDE drives are the standard fitted to most PCs

electrónico *símbolo* E ◇ **consultor, -a** *o* **asesor, -a de comercio electrónico** e-commerce consultant

electrosensible *adj* electrosensitive

electrostático *adj* electrostatic ◇ **altavoz electrostático** electrostatic speaker

elegible *adj* selectable

elegir *verbo vt* to select

elegir/fusionar *sustantivo vt* sort/merge

elemental *adj* **1.** elementary **2.** low-end **3.** primary ◇ **sección elemental de cable** elementary cable section

elemento *m sustantivo* **1.** building block **2.** element **3.** menu item **4.** unit ◇ **elemento** *m* **(de un campo)** member

elemento *m* **aritmético extendido** *sustantivo* extended arithmetic element

elemento *m* **de coincidencia** *sustantivo* **1.** AND circuit *o* AND element **2.** coincidence circuit *o* coincidence element **3.** coincidence gate *o* coincidence circuit *o* coincidence element

elemento *m* **de datos** *sustantivo* **1.** data element **2.** data item

elemento *m* **de identidad** *sustantivo* identity gate *o* identity element

elemento *m* **de imagen** *sustantivo* **1.** available point **2.** picture element

elemento *m* **de inicio** *sustantivo* **1.** start bit **2.** start element

elemento *m* **de macro** *sustantivo* macroelement

elemento *m* **de parada** *sustantivo* **1.** stop bit **2.** stop element

elemento *m* **de una imagen** *sustantivo* pixel

elemento *m* **de una matriz** *sustantivo* array element

elemento *m* **de una señal** *sustantivo* signal element ◇ **el elemento de señal de este sistema es un breve impulso de voltaje, que indica uno binario** the signal element in this system is a short voltage pulse, indicating a binary one ◇ **los elementos de señal del sistema de transmisión por radio son 10 ms de 40 KHz para el binario 0 y 10 ms de 60 KHz para el binario 1** the signal elements for the radio transmission system are 10ms of 40KHz and 10ms of 60KHz for binary 0 and 1 respectively

elemento *m* **de un código** *sustantivo* code element

elemento *m* **final de una arborescencia** *sustantivo* leaf

elemento *m* **fusible** *sustantivo* fusible link

elemento *m* **lógico** *sustantivo* logic element

elemento *m* **lógico compuesto** *sustantivo* compound logical element

elemento *m* **lógico múltiple** *sustantivo* compound logical element

elementos *mpl* **de la CPU** *plural noun* CPU elements

elementos *mpl* **de la unidad central** *plural noun* CPU elements

elementos *mpl* **disponibles** *plural noun* assets

elemento *m* **único** *sustantivo* one element

elemento *m* **visualizado** *sustantivo* display element

elemento *m* **Y** *sustantivo* AND circuit *o* AND element

eliminación *f sustantivo* deletion ◇ **eliminación** *f* **de ceros (no significativos)** zero compression

eliminación *f* **de ceros (no significativos)** *sustantivo* zero suppression

eliminación *f* **de errores** *sustantivo* data cleaning

eliminación *f* **de ficheros** *sustantivo* file deletion

eliminación *f* **de una señal** *sustantivo* blanking

eliminador *m* **de corriente transitoria** *sustantivo* transient suppressor

eliminar *verbo* **1.** *vt* to clean **2.** *vt* to delete **3.** *vt* to erase **4.** *vt* to kill **5.** *vt* to scratch **6.** *vt* to scrub

'Los archivos más comunes de eliminar son los llamados 'temporales'. Estos los crea y emplea el sistema para realizar alguna operación concreta en un determinado momento y luego no los elimina aunque ya no sean necesarios.' [*Ciberp@ís*]

eliminar errores *verbo* to debug
eliminar mediante un filtrado *verbo* to filter
e-mail ◇ **e-mail** *m* **enriquecido** rich e-mail
'El e-mail es un medio eficaz y barato para acercarse a los que están lejos y alejarse de los más cercanos.' [*Ciberp@ís*]
embalaje *m sustantivo* packaging
embalar *verbo vt* to pack
emigración *f sustantivo* migration
emisión *f sustantivo* broadcast ◇ **emisión** *f* **constante de mensajes de alerta por error** stuck beacon ◇ **emisión** *f* **de señales por canales independientes** separate channel signalling ◇ **técnica de difusión por satélite** *o* **de emisión vía satélite** broadcast satellite technique
emisión *f* **por la Web** *sustantivo* webcast
emisor *m* **de cinta** *sustantivo* tape transmitter
emisor *m* **de respuestas automáticas** *sustantivo* autoresponder
emisor *m* **emisora** *sustantivo* sender
emisor/receptor *m* **asíncrono universal** *sustantivo* **1.** UART **2.** universal asynchronous receiver/transmitter **3.** universal device
emisor-receptor *m* **automático** *sustantivo* ASR
emisor/receptor *m* **automático** *sustantivo* automatic send/receive
emisor /transmisor *m* **síncrono asíncrono universal** *sustantivo* universal synchronous asynchronous receiver/transmitter
emisor/transmisor *m* **síncrono asíncrono universal** *sustantivo* USART
emisor/transmisor *m* **síncrono universal** *sustantivo* **1.** universal synchronous receiver/transmitter **2.** USRT
emitir *verbo* **1.** *vt* to broadcast **2.** *vt* to poll
emitir impulsos *verbo* to pulse ◇ **emitimos la señal de entrada pero tampoco funcionó** we pulsed the input but it still would not work
emitir una señal *verbo* to signal
emoticón, emoticono *sustantivo* emoticon
'La sonrisa, que en los chats suele comunicarse con el emoticono simple [:-)], es una de estas acciones no verbales que suele favorecer una interpretación óptima, puesto que es una expresión típicamente humana que puede observarse plenamente ya en los niños de corta edad.' [*Ciberpragmática*]
emoticono *m sustantivo* smiley
empalmar *verbo* **1.** *vt* to join **2.** *vt* to splice ◇ **prensa de empalmar** splicing block
empalme *m sustantivo* junction
empaquetamiento *m* **doble en línea** *sustantivo* **1.** DIP **2.** dual-in-line package
empaquetar *verbo vt* to pack ◇ **los disquetes están empaquetados en un envoltorio de plástico** the diskettes are packed in plastic wrappers
emparejar *verbo vt* to match

emplazamiento *sustantivo* location ◇ **emplazamiento** *m* **para la tarjeta de extensión** expansion slot
emplazamiento *m* **de la disquetera** *sustantivo* **1.** bay **2.** drive bay
emplazamiento *m* **de la memoria** *sustantivo* store location
emplazamiento *m* **del lector de discos** *sustantivo* **1.** bay **2.** drive bay
empresa *f* **de montaje** *sustantivo* **1.** OEM **2.** original equipment manufacturer ◇ **empezó su carrera como montador de ordenadores personales para el mercado de fabricantes de equipos informáticos originales** he started in business as a manufacturer of PCs for the OEM market
empresa *f* **de pruebas beta** *sustantivo* beta site
empresa *f* **de servicios** *sustantivo* bureau ◇ **confiamos nuestros escritos de oficina a una empresa informática local** we farm out the office typing to a local bureau ◇ **la empresa ofrece diversos servicios ofimáticos, como los de impresión y recogida de datos** the company offers a number of bureau services, such as printing and data collection ◇ **nuestros datos son gestionados por una agencia de servicios** our data manipulation is handled by a bureau
empresa *f* **de servicios informáticos** *sustantivo* computer bureau
empresa *f* **de software** *sustantivo* software house
empresa *f* **de tratamiento de textos** *sustantivo* word-processing bureau
empresa *f* **electrónica** *sustantivo* e-business
empresa *f* **pública de servicios informativos** *sustantivo* common carrier
emulación *f sustantivo* emulation
emulación *f* **de impresora** *sustantivo* printer emulation ◇ **esta emulación de impresora permite que mi impresora NEC emule una Epsom** this printer emulation allows my NEC printer to emulate an Epsom
emulación *f* **de terminal** *sustantivo* terminal emulation
emulación *f* **de terminal VT** *sustantivo* VT-terminal emulation
emulador *m sustantivo* emulator
emulador *m* **integrado** *sustantivo* integrated emulator
emulador *m* **integrado en el circuito** *sustantivo* in-circuit emulator ◇ **este emulador incorporado al circuito actúa como emulador de una disquetera para comprobar el funcionamiento del controlador de disquetes** this in-circuit emulator is used to test the floppy disk controller by emulating a disk drive
emular *verbo vt* to emulate ◇ **una impresora láser que puede emular una amplia gama de impresoras de oficina** a laser printer which emulates a wide range of office printers
en *sustantivo* en

en anillo *sustantivo* ring ◇ **red en anillo** ring network ◇ **red en anillo** *o* **red 'Token Ring'** Token Ring network

en buen estado *adv* up

encabezado *m sustantivo* heading

encabezamiento *m sustantivo* **1.** caption **2.** heading **3.** message header ◇ **encabezamiento** *m* **preestablecido (guardado en memoria)** form flash ◇ **las leyendas se imprimen en cursiva** the captions are printed in italics

encabezamiento *m* **actual** *sustantivo* running head

encabezamiento *m* **de bloque** *sustantivo* block header

encabezar *verbo vt* to head ◇ **mi fichero encabezaba la cola** the queue was headed by my file

encadenado *m sustantivo* chaining

encadenado *m* **de imágenes** *sustantivo* AB roll

encadenamiento *m sustantivo* **1.** chaining **2.** linking

encadenamiento *m* **de datos** *sustantivo* data chaining

encadenamiento *m* **de información** *sustantivo* data chaining

encadenamiento *m* **en retroceso** *sustantivo* backward chaining

encadenamiento *m* **hacia atrás** *sustantivo* backward chaining

encadenamiento *m* **margarita** *sustantivo* daisy chain bus

encadenamiento *m* **mariposa** *sustantivo* daisy chain bus

encadenar *verbo* **1.** *vt* to catenate **2.** *vt* to concatenate

encadenar(se) *verbo vr* to chain

encaminador *m sustantivo* router

encaminamiento *m sustantivo* **1.** data routing **2.** routing

encaminamiento *m* **de fuente transparente** *sustantivo* source transparent routing ■ *abrev* SRT

encaminamiento *m* **de mensajes** *sustantivo* message routing

encaminamiento *m* **fuente** *sustantivo* source routing

encapsulación *f sustantivo* encapsulation

encapsulado *adj* encapsulated

encapsulado *m* **dual en línea** *sustantivo* **1.** DIP **2.** dual-in-line package

encauzar *verbo vt* to pipeline

encender *verbo vt* to power up

enchufable *m sustantivo* plug-in

enchufar *verbo vt* to plug ◇ **enchufar** to plug in ◇ **enchufar y usar** to plug and play

'Los ordenadores de última generación, con sistemas operativos recientes, reconocen automáticamente cuando se conecta un nuevo aparato, como en el caso de una impresora. Es lo que se conoce como plug and play (enchufar y usar).' [*Ciberp@ís*]

enchufe *m sustantivo* **1.** plug **2.** socket ◇ **la impresora va provista de un enchufe** the printer is supplied with a plug

enchufe *m* **hembra** *sustantivo* female socket

enchufe *m* **polarizado** *sustantivo* polarised plug

encontrar *verbo* **1.** *vt* to diagnose **2.** *vt* to find

encontrar(se) *verbo vr* to locate ◇ **el ordenador se encuentra en el edificio de la oficina principal** the computer is located in the main office building

encriptado *m* **de clave pública** *sustantivo* public key encryption

encriptado *m* **de datos** *sustantivo* data encryption

encriptado *m* **de información** *sustantivo* data encryption

encriptar *verbo vt* to encrypt

en equipo *sustantivo* tandem

energía *f sustantivo* power ◇ **'apagado'** *o* **'energía desconectada'** 'power off' ◇ **'encendido'** *o* **'energía conectada'** 'power on'

energía *f* **disponible** *sustantivo* available power

en estado sólido *adj* solid-state

enfocar *verbo vt* to focus ◇ **han ajustado la posición de la lente de modo que el rayo de luz esté correctamente enfocado** they adjusted the lens position so that the beam focused correctly ◇ **la cámara está enfocando un primer plano** the camera is focused on the foreground

enfoque *m sustantivo* focus

en forma de diagrama *adj* schematic

en forma de tabla *adj* tabular ◇ **en forma de tabla** *o* **dispuesto, -a en tabla** in tabular form

en funcionamiento *adv* up ■ *adj* working

en función del contexto *adj* context-sensitive

engancharse en un bucle *verbo* to hang

enlace *sustantivo* **1.** channel **2.** data bus **3.** I/O bus **4.** link **5.** linking ◇ **enlace** *m* **común de Apple Desktop** ABD ◇ **enlace** *m* **común IEEE** (*conforme a las normas del instituto de ingeniería eléctrica y electrónica*) IEEE bus ◇ **enlace** *o* **conexión entre segmentos** intersegment linking ◇ **enlace** *o* **transmisión por satélite** satellite link ◇ **para una transmisión más rápida, se puede utilizar un enlace directo con el ordenador principal** to transmit faster, you can use the direct link with the mainframe ◇ **pérdida de enlace** *o* **de transmisión** link loss

enlace *m* **activo** *sustantivo* active link

enlace *m* **compartido** *sustantivo* shared bus

enlace *m* **común** *sustantivo* **1.** A-bus **2.** address highway **3.** bus **4.** data highway **5.** highway **6.** trunk ◇ **enlace común de entrada** *or* **salida** *o* **enlace común E** *or* **S** input/output data bus (I/O bus)

enlace *m* **común bidireccional** *sustantivo* bi-directional bus

enlace *m* **común central** *sustantivo* bus

enlace *m* **común de Apple Desktop** (*marca comercial*) Apple Desktop Bus

enlace *m* **común de cadena mariposa** *sustantivo* daisy chain bus

enlace *m* **común de control** *sustantivo* control bus

enlace *m* **común de datos** *sustantivo* data bus

enlace *m* **común de direcciones** *sustantivo* address bus

enlace *m* **común de entrada/salida** *sustantivo* input/output bus

enlace *m* **común de expansión** *sustantivo* expansion bus

enlace *m* **común de interconexión general** *sustantivo* **1.** general purpose interface bus **2.** GPIB

enlace *m* **común de memoria** *sustantivo* memory bus

enlace *m* **común de un microordenador** *sustantivo* microcomputer bus

enlace *m* **común PCI** *sustantivo* peripheral component interconnect

enlace *m* **de cadena (margarita)** *sustantivo* daisy chain bus

enlace *m* **de comunicaciones** *sustantivo* communications link

enlace *m* **de datos** *sustantivo* **1.** data link **2.** optical data link

enlace *m* **de datos en cadena** *sustantivo* data chaining

enlace *m* **de interfaz HP** Hewlett Packard Interface Bus ■ *abrev* HPIB

enlace *m* **de transferencia de datos** *sustantivo* data highway

enlace *m* **de transmisiones** *sustantivo* communications link

enlace *m* **fusible** *sustantivo* fusible link

enlace *m* **local** *sustantivo* local bus ◇ **las tarjetas de extensión más rápidas encajan en este conector de enlace local** the fastest expansion cards fit into this local bus connector

enlace *m* **local VESA** *sustantivo* VESA local bus

enlace *m* **óptico de datos** *sustantivo* optical data link

enlace *m* **por infrarrojo** *sustantivo* infra-red link

enlaces *mpl* **redundantes** *sustantivo* network redundancy

enlace *m* **T1** *sustantivo* T1 link

enlace *m* **T2** *sustantivo* T2 link

enlace *m* **T3** *sustantivo* T3 link

enlazar *verbo* **1.** *vt* to bind **2.** *vt* to link

enlazar (con un servidor) *verbo* to attach ◇ **he dado la instrucción para conectarme al servidor local** I issued the command to attach to the local server

en lenguaje máquina *adj* machine readable ◇ **el disco almacena los datos en lenguaje máquina** the disk stores data in machine-readable form

en línea *adj* in-line ■ *sustantivo* in-line ■ *adv*, *adj* online ■ *adv* online

en línea con *verbo* to flush ■ *adj* flush ◇ **la cubierta se recorta en línea con las páginas** the cover is trimmed flush with the pages

enmascarable *adj* maskable

enmascaramiento *m* *sustantivo* masking

enmascarar *verbo* *vt* to conceal

en paralelo *adj* parallel ◇ **entrada en paralelo** *or* **salida en paralelo** parallel input/parallel output (PIPO) ◇ **entrada** *or* **salida en paralelo** parallel input/output (PIO) ◇ **su velocidad normal de transmisión es de 60.000 bps mediante una conexión en paralelo** their average transmission rate is 60,000 bps through parallel connection

en red *adv*, *adj* online

en reposo *adj* **1.** idle **2.** quiescent

enrollamiento *m* **automático** *sustantivo* **1.** word wrap **2.** wraparound

enrutador *m* *sustantivo* router

ensamblador *m* *sustantivo* **1.** assembler **2.** base language

ensambladora *f* *sustantivo* collator

ensamblador *m* **absoluto** *sustantivo* absolute assembler

ensamblador *m* **cruzado** *sustantivo* cross-assembler

ensamblador *m* **de doble paso** *sustantivo* two-pass assembler

ensamblador *m* **de dos pasos** *sustantivo* two-pass assembler

ensamblador *m* **de macros** *sustantivo* macro assembler *o* macro assembly program

ensamblador *m* **de paso único** *sustantivo* single-pass assembler

ensamblador/desensamblador *m* **de paquetes** *sustantivo* packet assembler/disassembler ■ *abrev* PAD

ensamblador *m* **de una sola pasada** *sustantivo* one-pass assembler ◇ **este nuevo ensamblador de una sola pasada es muy rápido** this new one-pass assembler is very quick in operation

ensamblador *m* **de un solo paso** *sustantivo* single-pass assembler

ensamblaje *m* *sustantivo* **1.** assembly **2.** linking

ensamblaje *m* **adaptable de paquetes** *sustantivo* adaptive packet assembly

ensamblaje *m* **de documentos** *sustantivo* **1.** document assembly **2.** document merge

ensamblar *verbo* *vt* to assemble ◇ **hay una espera breve durante la que el programa se ensambla en código objeto** there is a short wait during which time the program is assembled into object code ◇ **las piezas de la disquetera se manufacturan en Japón y se ensamblan en España** the parts for the disk drive are made in Japan and assembled in Spain ◇ **los errores de sintaxis detectados mientras se ensambla el programa fuente** syntax errors spotted whilst the source program is being assembled

ensayar *verbo vt* to pilot ◇ **están poniendo a prueba el nuevo sistema** they are piloting the new system

ensayo *m sustantivo* operation trial

ensayo *m* **comparativo del rendimiento** *sustantivo* benchmark ◇ **la revista dio los resultados de la prueba de evaluación del nuevo programa** the magazine gave the new program's benchmark test results ◇ **prueba comparativa** *o* **de contraste** benchmark test

ensayo *m* **del programa** *sustantivo* test run ◇ **la prueba de funcionamiento pronto descubrirá posibles errores** a test run will soon show up any errors

ensayo *m* **verificación** *sustantivo* test

ensemblador *m sustantivo* assembler program

en serie *adv* sequentially

en tándem *sustantivo* tandem

Enter *sustantivo* return

entidad *f sustantivo* entity

entintar *verbo vt* to ink

entorno *m sustantivo* environment ◇ **entorno** *m* **de soporte de un lenguaje** language support environment ◇ **entorno** *m* **gráfico WIMP (con ventana, icono, ratón, puntero)** window, icon, mouse, pointer

entorno *m* **de desarrollos integrados** *sustantivo* IDE

Entorno *m* **de Red** *sustantivo* Network Neighborhood

entornos *mpl* **integrados de proyectos** *abrev* IPSE

entorno *m* **universitario** *sustantivo* campus environment

entrada *sustantivo* **1.** entering **2.** entry **3.** fan-in **4.** input ■ *abrev* i/p *o* I/P ◇ **entrada** *f* **(en un registro de funcionamiento)** log ◇ **entrada** *f* **con una clave de acceso pirateada** piggyback entry ◇ **entrada** *f* **de datos mediante el teclado** manual input ◇ **entrada** *f* **directa de datos (mediante el teclado)** DDE; direct data entry ◇ **entrada** *f* **en paralelo** *or* **salida en paralelo** parallel input/parallel output ◇ **entrada** *f* **en paralelo** *or* **salida en serie** parallel input/serial output ◇ **entrada** *f* **en serie** *or* **salida** *f* **en serie** serial input/serial output ◇ **entrada** *or* **salida** *f* **configurada en la memoria** memory-mapped input/output ◇ **entrada** *f* **serial** *or* **salida en paralelo** serial input/parallel output; SIPO ◇ **entrada** *f* **(de datos) vocal** voice data entry ◇ **la unidad de entrada acepta información codificada que proviene de operadores humanos, de dispositivos electromagnéticos o de otras computadoras** the input unit accepts

coded information from human operators, from electromechanical devices, or from other computers ◇ **velocidad de entrada (de datos)** input speed

entrada *f* **de datos** *sustantivo* **1.** data entry **2.** data input

entrada *f* **de datos manual** *sustantivo* manual entry

entrada *f* **de información** *sustantivo* information input

entrada *f* **de tareas remotas** *sustantivo* **1.** remote job entry **2.** RJE

entrada *f* **de trabajos a distancia** *sustantivo* **1.** remote job entry **2.** RJE

entrada *f* **en paralelo/salida en paralelo** *sustantivo* PIPO

entrada *f* **en paralelo/salida en serie** *sustantivo* PISO

entrada *f* **en tiempo real** *sustantivo* real-time input

entrada *f* **principal** *sustantivo* main entry

entrada/salida *f sustantivo* I/O ◇ **entrada** *or* **salida** *f* **configurada en la memoria** memory-mapped I/O ◇ **petición de entrada** *or* **salida** I/O request ◇ **procesador de entrada** *or* **salida** I/O processor

entrada/salida *f* **(E/S)** *sustantivo* input/output

entrada/salida *f* **de la memoria intermedia** *sustantivo* buffered input/output

entrada/salida *f* **en paralelo** *sustantivo* **1.** parallel input/output **2.** PIO

entrada/salida *f* **en serie** *sustantivo* serial input/output ■ *abrev* **1.** SIO **2.** SISO

entrada *f* **serial/salida serial** *sustantivo* serial input/serial output

entrar *verbo* **1.** *vt* to enter **2.** *vt* to read in

entre bloques *adj* interblock

entrelazado *m* **de bits** *sustantivo* bit interleaving

entrelazado *m* **de caracteres** *sustantivo* character interleaving

entrelazar *verbo vt* to interlace

en tres dimensiones *adj* 3D

enumeración *f sustantivo* enumeration

enumerar *verbo vt* to list

envasar *verbo vt* to pack

envejecimiento *m sustantivo* burn-in

enviar *verbo* **1.** *vt* to address **2.** *vt* to forward ◇ **enviar un acuse de recibo** acknowledge

enviar (por ruta distinta) *verbo* to redirect

enviar por fax *verbo* to fax *o* to FAX

enviar una señal *verbo* to signal

envío *m sustantivo* **1.** despatch **2.** dispatch *o* despatch **3.** routing

envío *m* **por correo** *sustantivo* mailing ◇ **comprar una lista de direcciones** to buy a mailing list ◇ **elaborar una lista de direcciones** to build up a mailing list ◇ **el envío por correo (electrónico) de material publicitario** the mailing of publicity material ◇ **envío de fol-**

letos publicitarios mailing shot ◊ **envío por correo directo** o **publicidad directa** o **'mailing' directo** direct mailing ◊ **folleto enviado por correo** mailing piece ◊ **prospecto** mailing piece

envío m **por correo electrónico** sustantivo mailing

envolvente m sustantivo envelope ◊ **detección de (curva) envolvente** envelope detection ◊ **(forma de la) parte inicial de un envolvente** attack envelope ◊ **retardo de envolvente** envelope delay

EPS sustantivo encapsulated PostScript

EPSF sustantivo encapsulated PostScript file

equilibrar verbo vt to match ◊ **carga equilibrada** matched load

equilibrio m sustantivo balance

equilibrio m **de colores** sustantivo colour balance

equilibrio m **de las columnas** sustantivo column balance

equipamiento m **informático** sustantivo installation

equipo sustantivo hardware ◊ **equipo** m **de desarrollo de un microordenador** microcomputer development kit ◊ **equipo** m **de limpieza de la pantalla** screen cleaning kit ◊ **equipo** m **de red (informática)** network hardware ◊ **equipo** m **para la gestión de formularios** form handling equipment

equipo m **accesorio** sustantivo ancillary equipment

equipo m **automático de verificación** sustantivo **1.** ATE **2.** automatic test equipment

equipo m **auxiliar** sustantivo **1.** auxiliary equipment **2.** standby equipment

equipo m **base** sustantivo base hardware

equipo m **convertidor** sustantivo conversion equipment

equipo m **de adaptación** sustantivo bridgeware

equipo m **de comunicación de datos** sustantivo data communications equipment ■ abrev DCE

equipo m **de emergencia** sustantivo standby equipment

equipo m **de impresos** sustantivo form handling equipment

equipo m **de información** sustantivo data communications equipment

equipo m **de pruebas** sustantivo test equipment ◊ **el ingeniero tiene equipo especial de pruebas para este modelo** the engineer has special test equipment for this model

equipo m **de repuesto** sustantivo auxiliary equipment

equipo m **en red** sustantivo networking hardware

equipo m **informático no terminado** sustantivo vapourware

equipo m **periférico** sustantivo peripheral equipment

equipo m **sólo para demostraciones** sustantivo kludge o kluge

equivalencia f sustantivo equivalence

equívoco adj ambiguous

errata f sustantivo literal

erróneo adj false

error m sustantivo error

error sustantivo **1.** bug **2.** error **3.** fault ◊ **códigos de corrección de errores** error correcting codes ◊ **códigos de detección de errores** error detecting codes ◊ **cometió un error al calcular el total** he made an error in calculating the total ◊ **detección y corrección de errores** error detection and correction (EDAC) ◊ **entre las características del programa se incluye el registro (automático) de errores** features of the program include error logging ◊ **error de imprenta** printer's error ◊ **error** m **de un componente (defectuoso)** component error ◊ **error** m **generado (por redondeo)** generated error ◊ **(señal de) interrupción por un error** o **por un incidente** error interrupt ◊ **la secretaria** o **el secretario debe haber cometido un error mecanográfico** the secretary must have made a typing error ◊ **mensaje de diagnóstico de error** diagnostic (error) message ◊ **pensamos que existe un error de base en el diseño del producto** we think there is a basic fault in the product design ◊ **por error** in error o by error ◊ **una página arrugada o rota puede ser la causa de un error de exploración** a wrinkled or torn page may be the cause of scanning errors

'Así son las cosas cuando se trata de hablar con un ordenador. Todo son bits, la unidad mínima. La publicidad, sobre todo en Navidad, se llena de bits. Pero hay que ir con cuidado: no confundir un bit con un byte. Un error de imprenta puede hacer perder mucho tiempo.' [*Ciberp@ís*]

error m **absoluto** sustantivo absolute error

error m **catastrófico** sustantivo catastrophic error

error m **causado por el soporte** sustantivo media error

error m **causado por la máquina** sustantivo machine error

error m **compensado** sustantivo balanced error

error m **consciente** sustantivo conscious error

error m **crítico** sustantivo critical error

error m **de ambigüedad** sustantivo **1.** ambiguity error **2.** error ambiguity

error m **de arranque** sustantivo cold fault

error m **de barrido** sustantivo scanning error

error m **de código** sustantivo false code

error m **de compilación** sustantivo compilation error ◊ **los errores de compilación hacen que se aborte la tarea** compilation errors result in the job being aborted

error *m* **de cuantificación** *sustantivo* quantisation error

error *m* **de datos** *sustantivo* data error

error *m* **de ejecución** *sustantivo* **1.** execution error **2.** run-time error

error *m* **de escaneado** *sustantivo* scanning error

error *m* **de escritura** *sustantivo* write error

error *m* **de estimación** *sustantivo* approximation error

error *m* **de exploración** *sustantivo* scanning error ◊ **una página arrugada o rota puede ser la causa de un error de exploración** a wrinkled or torn page may be the cause of scanning errors

error *m* **de lectura** *sustantivo* read error

error *m* **de lectura transitorio** *sustantivo* transient read error

error *m* **del ordenador** *sustantivo* computer error

error *m* **de rechazo** *sustantivo* rejection error

error *m* **de redondeo** *sustantivo* **1.** approximation error **2.** truncation error

error *m* **de sección** *sustantivo* frame error

error *m* **de semántica** *sustantivo* semantic error

error *m* **de sintaxis** *sustantivo* **1.** grammatical error **2.** syntactic error **3.** syntax error

error *m* **de sustitución** *sustantivo* substitution error

error *m* **detectado** *sustantivo* detected error

error *m* **de tramo** *sustantivo* frame error

error *m* **de transmisión** *sustantivo* transmission error

error *m* **de truncamiento** *sustantivo* truncation error

error *m* **en la línea** *sustantivo* line gremlin

error *m* **en ráfagas** *sustantivo* error burst

error *m* **equilibrado** *sustantivo* balanced error

error *m* **esporádico** *sustantivo* sporadic fault

error *m* **falso** *sustantivo* false error

error *m* **fatal** *sustantivo* **1.** catastrophic error **2.** fatal error

error *m* **heredado** *sustantivo* inherited error

error *m* **imposible de corregir** *sustantivo* unrecoverable error

error *m* **inexplicable** *sustantivo* gremlin

error *m* **inicial** *sustantivo* initial error

error *m* **intermitente** *sustantivo* intermittent error

error *m* **irrecuperable** *sustantivo* unrecoverable error

error *m* **lógico** *sustantivo* logical error

error *m* **momentáneo** *sustantivo* **1.** soft error **2.** transient error

error *m* **no detectado** *sustantivo* undetected error

error *m* **notificado** *sustantivo* detected error

error *m* **pasajero** *sustantivo* transient error

error *m* **permanente** *sustantivo* **1.** hard error **2.** permanent error **3.** solid error

error *m* **por redondeo** *sustantivo* rounding error *o* round-off error

error *m* **propagado** *sustantivo* propagated error

error *m* **que se propaga** *sustantivo* propagating error

error *m* **recuperable** *sustantivo* recoverable error

error *m* **relativo** *sustantivo* relative error

error *m* **reparable** *sustantivo* recoverable error

error *m* **semántico** *sustantivo* semantic error

error *m* **sintáctico** *sustantivo* **1.** syntactic error **2.** syntax error

error *m* **temporal** *sustantivo* transient error

error *m* **transitorio** *sustantivo* **1.** soft error **2.** transient error

error *m* **transmitido** *sustantivo* inherited error

E/S ◊ **E** *or* **S configurada en la memoria** memory-mapped I/O

esbozo *m* *sustantivo* **1.** layout **2.** rough copy

escala *f* *sustantivo* **1.** octal scale **2.** scale ◊ **integración a escala muy grande** very large scale integration (VLSI) ◊ **integración a escala super grande** super large scale integration (SLSI) ◊ **integración a media escala** medium scale integration (MSI) ◊ **integración a pequeña escala** small scale integration (SSI)

escala *f* **binaria** *sustantivo* binary scale ◊ **en una palabra de cuatro bits, la escala binaria es 1,2,4,8** in a four bit word, the binary scale is 1,2,4,8

escalable *adj* scalable

escalada *f* **ascendente** *sustantivo* hill climbing

escala *f* **de grises** *sustantivo* **1.** gray scale **2.** grey scale

escala *f* **de tiempo rápida** *sustantivo* fast time-scale

escalar *m* *sustantivo* scalar ◊ **una magnitud escalar tiene un valor de magnitud único, un vector tiene dos o más valores posicionales** a scalar has a single magnitude value, a vector has two or more positional values

escaneado *m* *sustantivo* **1.** scan **2.** scanning ◊ **el escaneado detectó rápidamente cual de los componentes se estaba recalentando** the heat scan of the computer quickly showed which component was overheating ◊ **el escaneado reveló qué registros se encontraban anticuados** the scan revealed which records were now out of date

escaneado *m* **dirigido** *sustantivo* directed scan

escanear *verbo* *vt* to scan ◊ **la máquina escanea con una resolución de hasta 300 puntos por pulgada** the machine scans at up to 300 dpi resolution ◊ **un fax escanea la imagen y la convierte en formato digital antes de trans-**

mitirla a facsimile machine scans the picture and converts this to digital form before transmission

escáner *sustantivo* **1.** page reader **2.** scanner ◇ **escáner** *m* **(de reconocimiento) óptico** optical scanner

escáner *m* **de bolsillo** *sustantivo* hand-held scanner

escáner *m* **de comunicaciones** *sustantivo* communications scanner

escáner *m* **de imágenes** *sustantivo* **1.** image scanner **2.** video scanner

escáner *m* **de mano** *sustantivo* hand-held scanner

escáner *m* **de reconocimiento óptico** *sustantivo* optical scanner

escáner *m* **de superficie plana** *sustantivo* flatbed scanner ◇ **no se puede hacer rodar el papel a través de escáners de superficie plana** paper cannot be rolled through flatbed scanners

escáner *m* **de vídeo** *sustantivo* video scanner

escape *m sustantivo* **1.** ESC **2.** ESC **3.** ESC **4.** Esc key

esclavo *m sustantivo* slave

esclavo *m* **de un enlace común** *sustantivo* bus slave

escribir *verbo vt* to blast ◇ **escribir una vez – leer muchas** to WORM

escribir a máquina *verbo* to type ◇ **escribe con bastante rapidez** he can type quite fast ◇ **todos los informes están escritos en su máquina de escribir portátil** all his reports are typed on his portable typewriter

escribir en mayúsculas *verbo* to shout

escribir un programa *verbo* to program

escritor *m sustantivo* writer

escritorio *m adj* desktop ■ *sustantivo* desktop

escritorio multimedia *plural noun* desktop media

escritorio *m* **virtual** *sustantivo* virtual desktop

escritura *f* **agrupada** *verbo* to gather write

escritura *f* **cifrada** *sustantivo* cipher

esencial *adj* prime

esfera *f sustantivo* dial

espaciado *sustantivo* **1.** pitch **2.** spacing ◇ **el espaciado entre caracteres de algunas líneas no es siempre el mismo** the spacing on some lines is very uneven ◇ **espaciado** *m* **(proporcional) de caracteres** intercharacter spacing

espaciado *m* **interlineal** *sustantivo* space

espaciado *m* **proporcional** *adj* proportionally spaced

espaciador *m sustantivo* spacer

espaciador *m* **inteligente** *sustantivo* intelligent spacer

espaciar *verbo vt* to space ◇ **cada línea de caracteres estaba espaciada de forma regular a lo largo de toda la página** the line of characters was evenly spaced out across the page

espacio *sustantivo* space ◇ **espacio** *m* **(que ocupa un ordenador)** footprint ◇ **espacio** *m* **de memoria reservada para utilización de un usuario** private address space

espacio *m* **(de tiempo)** *sustantivo* period ◇ **durante algunos meses** for a period of months ◇ **durante seis años** *o* **en un periodo de seis años** for a six-year period ◇ **durante un espacio** *o* **periodo de tiempo** for a period of time

espacio *m* **de dirección en segmentos** *sustantivo* segmented address space

espacio *m* **de direcciones** *sustantivo* address space

espacio *m* **de dirección plana** *sustantivo* flat address space

espacio *m* **de marca** *sustantivo* mark space

espacio *m* **de memoria de imágenes** *sustantivo* image storage space

espacio *m* **de retroceso** *sustantivo* backspace ■ *abrev* BS ◇ **si comete un error al introducir datos, utilice la tecla de retroceso para corregirlo** if you make a mistake entering data, use the backspace key to correct it

espacio *m* **de trabajo** *sustantivo* workspace

espacio *m* **de visualización** *sustantivo* display space

espacio *m* **direccionable** *sustantivo* address space

espacio *m* **entre bloques** *abrev* IBG ■ *sustantivo* **1.** interblock gap **2.** interrecord gap

espacio *m* **entre dos registros** *sustantivo* record gap

espacio *m* **entre palabra y palabra** *sustantivo* interword spacing

espacio *m* **entre puntos** *sustantivo* dot pitch

espacio *m* **hacia atrás** *sustantivo* backspace ■ *abrev* BS

espacio *m* **intermedio** *sustantivo* gap

espacio *m* **neutro** *sustantivo* file gap

espacio *m* **nominal** *sustantivo* namespace

espacio *m* **para dar la vuelta** *sustantivo* turnaround time

espacios *mpl sustantivo* spacing

espacio *m* **sin interrupción** *sustantivo* non breaking space

espacio *m* **sin ruptura** *sustantivo* non breaking space

especial back-end

especialista *f sustantivo* specialist

especialista *m&f* **en redes informáticas** *sustantivo* networking specialist ◇ **esta empresa informática es una sociedad británica especializada en redes** this computer firm is a UK networking specialist

especializado *adj* dedicated

especializarse *verbo* to specialise ◇ **está especializado en el diseño de sistemas CAD** he specializes in the design of CAD systems

especificación *f sustantivo* **1.** spec **2.** specification

especificaciones *fpl* sustantivo blueprint ■ *plural noun* design parameters ◇ **especificaciones** *fpl* **de la presentación de datos** layout

especificaciones *fpl* **de un programa** sustantivo software specification

especificaciones *fpl* **de un sistema** plural noun system specifications

especificación *f* **funcional** sustantivo functional specification

especificidad *f* sustantivo specificity

espera sustantivo waiting state ◇ **sistema** *m* **en espera (de recibir una señal)** sleep

esquema *m* sustantivo 1. framework 2. layout 3. outline 4. schema

esquema *m* **de base de datos** sustantivo database schema

esquema *m* **de bloques** sustantivo block diagram ◇ **el primer paso para diseñar un nuevo ordenador es dibujar un diagrama (de bloques) de sus componentes principales** the first step to designing a new computer is to draw out a block diagram of its main components

esquema *m* **del usuario** sustantivo (desde el punto de vista) external schema

esquema *m* **estándar** sustantivo canonical schema

esquema *m* **externo** sustantivo external schema

esquema *m* **funcional** sustantivo functional diagram

esquema *m* **principal** sustantivo outline flowchart

esquemático *adj* schematic

esquematizador *m* **de texto** sustantivo outliner

esquina *f* **izquierda superior** sustantivo cursor home

estabilidad *f* **de (la) imagen** sustantivo image stability

estabilizador *m* **de impedancia** sustantivo balun ◇ **hemos utilizado un estabilizador de impedancia para conectar el cable coaxial al circuito de par retorcido** we have used a balun to connect the coaxial cable to the twisted-pair circuit

estabilizador *m* **de la señal** sustantivo clamper

establecer verbo 1. vt to preset 2. vt to set

establecer una comunicación verbo to connect

establecer un enlace verbo to bind

estación sustantivo 1. inquiry station 2. station ◇ **estación** *f* **de datos** data station

estación *f* **a distancia** sustantivo remote station

estacionamiento *m* **de la cabeza** sustantivo head park

estación *f* **base** sustantivo base station

estación *f* **combinada** sustantivo combined station

estación *f* **de atrancamiento** sustantivo docking station

estación *f* **de conexión única** abrev SAS ■ sustantivo single attachment station

estación *f* **de doble conexión** abrev DAS ■ sustantivo dual attachment o dual attached station

estación *f* **de enlace único** sustantivo single attachment station

estación *f* **de trabajo** sustantivo 1. operating console 2. workstation ◇ **el sistema incluye cinco terminales conectados en anillo** the system includes five workstations linked together in a ring network ◇ **la memoria de archivo tiene una capacidad total de 1200 Mb entre siete estaciones de trabajo** the archive storage has a total capacity of 1200 Mb between seven workstations

estación *f* **de trabajo multifunción** sustantivo multifunction workstation

estación *f* **primaria** sustantivo primary station

estación *f* **remota** sustantivo remote station

estación *f* **secundaria** sustantivo secondary station

estadística *f* sustantivo statistics

estadísticas *fpl* plural noun statistics

estadístico *adj* statistical

estado sustantivo stage ◇ **estado** *m* **de conexión** connect state ◇ **estado** *m* **de configuración** configuration state

estado *m* **de espera** sustantivo 1. wait condition 2. wait state

estado *m* **desactivado** sustantivo disarmed state

estado *m* **estable** sustantivo stable state

estado *m* **estacionario** sustantivo steady state

estado *m* **listo** sustantivo ready state

estado *m* **lógico** sustantivo logic state

estado *m* **lógico bajo** adj logical low

estado *m* **para recepción de instrucciones** sustantivo command state

estado *m* **preparado** sustantivo ready state

estándar *adj* machine-independent ■ sustantivo standard ■ adj universal ◇ **estándar** *m* **de puesta en clave de datos** data encryption standard ◇ **estándar** *m* **francés de TV y vídeo** SECAM SECAM ◇ **estándar** *m* **IEEE 802.2 que define los enlaces entre los datos** IEEE-802.2 ◇ **estándar** *m* **IEEE 802.3 que define el sistema de red Ethernet** IEEE-802.3 ◇ **estándar** *m* **IEEE 802.4 que define el bus en anillo** IEEE-802.4 ◇ **estándar** *m* **IEEE-802.5 que define la red en anillo de IBM** IEEE-802.5 ◇ **estándar** *m* **X.25** (conexión entre un terminal y una red de transferencia por paquetes) X.25 ◇ **estándar** *m* **X.400** (transferencia de mensajes electrónicos) X.400 ◇ **estándar** *m* **X.500** (gestión de nombres y de transferencia de mensajes) X.500 ◇ **estándar** *m* **XMS (de memoria extendida)** XMS; extended memory specification

estándar 10Base2 10Base2

estándar 10Base5 10Base5

estándar 10BaseT 10BaseT

estándar *m* **común** *sustantivo* de facto standard

estándares *mpl* **de producción** *plural noun* production standards

estándares *mpl* **de programación** *plural noun* programming standards

estándar *m* **FDDI II** *sustantivo* FDDI II

estandarizar *verbo vt* to standardise ◇ **el control estandarizado de los enlaces de transmisión** the standardized control of transmission links

estándar *m* **LAP** *sustantivo* **1.** LAP **2.** link control protocol

estándar *m* **MNP 5** *sustantivo* MNP 5

estándar *m* **MSX** *sustantivo* MSX

estándar *m* **SAA** *sustantivo* Systems Application Architecture

estándar *m* **ST506** *sustantivo* ST506 standard ◇ **el estándar ST506 ha sido sustituido ya por los estandares IDE y SCSI** the ST506 standard has now been replaced by IDE and SCSI

estandarte *m sustantivo* banner *o* banner advertisement *o* banner ad

estándar *m* **VT-52** *sustantivo* VT-52

estándar *m* **XGA** *sustantivo* **1.** extended graphics array **2.** XGA

estanographia *f sustantivo* steganography

estar al frente de *verbo* to head

estar en marcha *verbo* to run ◇ **el ordenador ha estado funcionando diez horas al día** the computer has been running ten hours a day ◇ **no interrumpa el verificador ortográfico mientras está en marcha** do not interrupt the spelling checker while it is running

estar especializado en *verbo* to specialise ◇ **está especializado en el diseño de sistemas CAD** he specializes in the design of CAD systems

estático *adj* static

estéreo *adj* stereo *o* stereophonic

estereofónico *adj* stereo *o* stereophonic

estilo *m sustantivo* style

estilo *m* **de carácter** *sustantivo* type style

estilo *m* **de impresión** *sustantivo* print style

estilo *m* **de letra** *sustantivo* **1.** face **2.** typeface

estilo *m* **de pincel** *sustantivo* brush style ◇ **para rellenar un área grande, selecciono un estilo de pincel ancho y cuadrado** to fill in a big area, I select a wide, square brush style

estratificador *adj* layered

estrella *f* **activa** *sustantivo* active star

estropear(se) *verbo vr* to crash ◇ **la cabeza del disco se ha estropeado y puede que los datos se hayan perdido** the disk head has crashed and the data may have been lost

estropearse *verbo vr* to fail ◇ **si al encender el ordenador no pasa nada, es que está estropeado** a computer has failed if you turn on the power supply and nothing happens

estructura *sustantivo* **1.** framework **2.** structure ◇ **primero se diseñó la estructura del programa** the program framework was designed first

'La estructura de la web permite una aproximación atractiva y didáctica a las obras de numerosos artistas.' [*Ciberp@ís*]

estructura *f* **anidada** *sustantivo* nested structure

estructura *f* **cartesiana** *sustantivo* cartesian structure

estructura *f* **de control** *sustantivo* control structure

estructura *f* **de datos** *sustantivo* data structure

estructura *f* **de datos dinámica** *sustantivo* dynamic data structure

estructura *f* **de la información** *sustantivo* information structure

estructura *f* **de red** *sustantivo* network structure

estructura *f* **de un enlace común** *sustantivo* bus structure

estructura *f* **de un fichero** *sustantivo* file structure

estructura *f* **de un programa** *sustantivo* program structure

estructura *f* **de un registro** *sustantivo* record structure

estructura *f* **en red** *sustantivo* network structure

estructura *f* **entrelazada** *sustantivo* plex structure

estructura *f* **jerárquica de datos** *sustantivo* data hierarchy

estructura *f* **jerarquizada** *sustantivo* nested structure

estructurar *verbo vt* to structure ◇ **primero usted estructura un documento para que se ajuste a sus necesidades de forma que luego sólo tiene que rellenar los espacios en blanco** you first structure a document to meet your requirements and then fill in the blanks

estuche *m sustantivo* housing

estuche *m* **de circuito** *sustantivo* card cage

estudio *m* **de viabilidad** *sustantivo* feasibility study

etapa *f sustantivo* **1.** stage **2.** step

etapa *f* **de programación** *sustantivo* program step

etapa *f* **de un trabajo** *sustantivo* job step

Ethernet *f sustantivo* Ethernet

Ethernet *f* **Blue Book** *sustantivo* Blue Book Ethernet

Ethernet *f* **de cable fino** *sustantivo* thin-Ethernet

Ethernet *f* **de cable pesado** *sustantivo* thick-Ethernet

Ethernet *f* **de par retorcido** *sustantivo* twisted-pair Ethernet

EtherTalk EtherTalk

etiqueta *sustantivo* **1.** file label **2.** label **3.** tag **4.** trailer ◇ **cada fichero tiene una etiqueta de tres letras para una identificación rápida** each file has a three letter tag for rapid identification ◇ **etiqueta** *f* **de ayuda (que identifica la función del icono)** bubble-help ◇ **etiqueta** *f* **(de cabecera) de cinta** tape label ◇ **etiqueta** *f* **interior (de identificación)** interior label ◇ **etiqueta interna (de identificación en soporte magnético)** internal label ◇ **los programas en lenguaje BASIC utilizan numerosas etiquetas de programa tales como la numeración de las líneas** BASIC uses many program labels such as line numbers

etiqueta *f* **(de instrucciones)** *sustantivo* quasi-instruction

etiqueta *f* **de calidad** *sustantivo* label

etiqueta *f* **de campo** *sustantivo* **1.** field label **2.** field name

etiqueta *f* **de final de cinta** *sustantivo* tape trailer

etiqueta *f* **de identificación** *sustantivo* header label

etiqueta *f* **del volumen** *sustantivo* volume label *o* volume name

etiqueta *f* **de reconocimiento de banda** *sustantivo* header label

etiquetado *m* *sustantivo* labelling

etiqueta *f* **externa** *sustantivo* external label

etiqueta *f* **fijada en el exterior** *sustantivo* external label

etiqueta *f* **perforada** *sustantivo* punched tag

etiquetas *fpl* **continuas** *plural noun* continuous labels

Eudora Eudora

evaluación *f* *sustantivo* measurement

evaluación *f* **asistida por ordenador** *sustantivo* computer-aided testing

evaluación *f* **comparativa del rendimiento** *sustantivo* benchmarking

evento *m* *sustantivo* event

exactitud *f* *sustantivo* **1.** accuracy **2.** precision

exacto *adj* precise

examinar *verbo* *vt* to browse

examinar (algo) atentamente *verbo* to scan ◇ **examinó el mapa para encontrar Teddington** he scanned the map for Teddington

excepción *f* *sustantivo* exception

exceso *m* *sustantivo* spillage

exceso *m* **de velocidad** *sustantivo* overrun

excitación *f* *sustantivo* impulse

excitador *m* *sustantivo* driver

exclusión *f* *sustantivo* exclusion

exclusión *f* **recíproca** *sustantivo* inequivalence

exhibición *f* **de diapositivas** *sustantivo* slide show

exigencias *fpl* *plural noun* requirements

EXIT *sustantivo* EXIT

éxito *m* *sustantivo* hit
'La Fábrica Nacional de Moneda y Timbre ha tenido que parar las descargas desde su servidor por falta de ancho de banda, ante el éxito de la demanda.' [*Ciberp@ís*]

EXOR *sustantivo* exclusive OR

expansión *f* *sustantivo* **1.** companding **2.** expansion

expansión *f* **de la memoria** *sustantivo* memory expansion

expediente *m* *sustantivo* file ◇ **colocar (un documento) en un expediente** *o* **introducir (información) en un fichero** to place (something) on file

experto *m* *sustantivo* **1.** networking specialist **2.** specialist ◇ **esta empresa informática es una sociedad británica especializada en redes** this computer firm is a UK networking specialist ◇ **necesita un programador experto que le ayude a diseñar una nueva aplicación de tratamiento de textos** you need a specialist programmer to help devise a new word-processing program

explicación *f* *sustantivo* comment

exploración *f* *sustantivo* **1.** scan **2.** scanning ◇ **haz de barrido** *o* **de exploración** scanning spot beam ◇ **receptor panorámico de radio** *o* **receptor de exploración de señal (radiofónica)** scanning radio receiver

exploración *f* **de trama** *sustantivo* raster scan

exploración *f* **dirigida** *sustantivo* directed scan

exploración *f* **entrelazada** *sustantivo* interlaced scanning

exploración *f* **helicoidal** *sustantivo* helical scan

explorador *m* *sustantivo* **1.** browser **2.** web browser ◇ **explorador** *m* **de internet (de Microsoft)** IE

explorador *m* **de comunicaciones** *sustantivo* communications scanner

explorar *verbo* *vt* to scan

Explorer™ (*programa de gestión de ficheros*) Explorer™

explotación *f* *sustantivo* parallel running

exponente *m* *sustantivo* **1.** characteristic **2.** superior number **3.** superscript

exponente *m* **binario** *sustantivo* binary exponent

exponente *m* **sesgado** *sustantivo* biased exponent

exportar *verbo* *vt* to export ◇ **para utilizar estos datos con dBase, se tienen que exportar como fichero DBF** to use this data with dBASE, you will have to export it as a DBF file

exposición *f* **de un problema** *sustantivo* problem definition

expreicono *m* *sustantivo* emoticon

expresión *f* *sustantivo* expression

expresión *f* **absoluta** *sustantivo* absolute expression

expresión *f* **lógica** *sustantivo* logical expression

extenderse *verbo vr* to span

extensión *sustantivo* expansion ◇ **este paquete de software de dibujo permite importar ficheros BMP** this paint package lets you import BMP files ◇ **extensión** *f* **(de un fichero) BAT** BAT file extension ◇ **extensión** *f* **BMP** (*de un fichero gráfico*) BMP ◇ **inserte la tarjeta en la ranura de extensión disponible** insert the board in the free expansion slot

extensión *f* **BAK** *sustantivo* BAK file extension

extensión *f* **del fichero** *sustantivo* file extent

extensión *f* **del nombre** *sustantivo* (*de un fichero*) filename extension ◇ **en MS-DOS, el nombre del fichero puede tener hasta ocho caracteres además de una extensión de tres caracteres** in MS-DOS, a filename can be up to eight characters long together with a three character filename extension ◇ **la extensión SYS que se añade al nombre de un fichero indica que es un fichero del sistema** the filename extension SYS indicates that this is a system file

extensión *f* **del nombre del fichero** *sustantivo* filename extension

extensión *f* **EPS** *abrev* EPS

extensiones ◇ **extensiones** *fpl* **multimedia** (*marca comercial*) MMX

extensiones *fpl* **de CD-ROM** *plural noun* CD-ROM Extensions

extensiones *fpl* **multimedia** *plural noun* multimedia extensions

extinción *f* *sustantivo* decay

extracción ◇ **extracción** *f* **(de una instrucción)** fetch cycle

extracción *f* **de datos** *sustantivo* data mining

extracódigo *m* *sustantivo* extracode

extractor *m* *sustantivo* extractor

extraer *verbo* **1.** *vt* to extract **2.** *vt* to pull **3.** *vt* to read **4.** *vt* to retrieve ◇ **podemos extraer los ficheros necesarios para la composición (de tipos)** we can extract the files required for typesetting

extraíble *adj* movable

extranet *m* *sustantivo* extranet

extraño *adj* alien

F

f *símbolo* f

fabricación *f sustantivo* production

fabricación *f* **asistida por ordenador** *sustantivo* **1.** CAM **2.** CIM **3.** computer-aided manufacture **4.** computer-assisted manufacture

fabricación *f* **de prototipos** *sustantivo* prototyping

fabricación *f* **integrada por ordenador** *sustantivo* **1.** CIM **2.** computer-integrated manufacturing

fábrica *f* **de montaje** *sustantivo* assembly plant

fabricante ◇ **fabricante** *mf* **de equipos (informáticos) originales** OEM; original equipment manufacturer

fabricante *mf* **de enchufes conectores** *sustantivo* **1.** PCM **2.** plug-compatible manufacturer

fabricar por encargo *verbo* to customise *o* to customize

fácil de usar *adj* **1.** simple to use **2.** user-friendly

facilidad *f sustantivo* facility ◇ **facilidad** *f* **de direccionamiento de un microprocesador** microprocessor addressing capabilities ◇ **facilidad** *f* **de uso** usability

facilidad *f* **de conservación técnica** *sustantivo* maintainability

facilidad *f* **de utilización** *sustantivo* usability ◇ **hemos estudiado diversas pruebas sobre facilidad de uso de programas y hemos descubierto que la interfaz gráfica (GUI) es más fácil para los nuevos usuarios que una línea de instrucción** we have studied usability tests and found that a GUI is easier for new users than a command line

facsímil *m sustantivo* facsimile copy

factor *m sustantivo* factor ◇ **factor** *m* **flotante** float factor ◇ **por un factor de diez** *o* **diez veces** *o* **multiplicado por diez** by a factor of ten

factor *m* **de bloques** *sustantivo* blocking factor

factor *m* **de decisión** *sustantivo* deciding factor ◇ **el factor decisivo fue la excelente calidad de los gráficos** the deciding factor was the superb graphics

factor *m* **de eliminación** *sustantivo* elimination factor

factor *m* **de forma** *sustantivo* form factor

factor *m* **de intercalación** *sustantivo* interleave factor

factor *m* **de omisión** *sustantivo* omission factor

factor *m* **de silencio** *sustantivo* omission factor

factorial *m sustantivo* factorial

factor *m* **piramidal** *sustantivo* fan-out

fallar *verbo* **1.** *vi* to bomb **2.** *vi* to crash **3.** *vi* to fail ◇ **el programa falló y perdimos totos los datos** the program bombed, and we lost all the data ◇ **el prototipo de la unidad de disco falló en su primera prueba** the prototype disk drive failed its first test ◇ **el sistema puede fallar si se instalan al mismo tiempo varios accesorios de escritorio o programas de memoria residente** the system can bomb if you set up several desk accessories or memory-resident programs at the same time

fallo *m sustantivo* **1.** crash **2.** fault **3.** glitch **4.** malfunction **5.** problem ◇ **el personal técnico intenta corregir un fallo de programación** the technical staff are trying to correct a programming fault ◇ **fallo** *m* **(por defecto del reloj)** hazard ◇ **fallo** *m* **de la cabeza de lectura** head crash ◇ **fallo** *m* **provocado (por una causa externa)** induced failure ◇ **localizador de fallos** fault tracer ◇ **los datos se perdieron a causa de un fallo de funcionamiento en el programa** the data was lost due to a software malfunction

fallo *m* **catastrófico** *sustantivo* catastrophic failure

fallo *m* **del equipo** *sustantivo* hardware failure

fallo *m* **del material** *sustantivo* equipment failure

fallo *m* **del ordenador** *sustantivo* equipment failure

fallo *m* **del sistema** *sustantivo* system crash

fallo *m* **de sintaxis** *sustantivo* grammatical error

fallo *m* **de un disquete** *sustantivo* disk crash

fallo *m* **de un programa** *sustantivo* program crash

fallo *m* **inducido** *sustantivo* induced failure

fallo *m* **leve** *adj* soft-fail

fallo *m* **por avería** *sustantivo* burn out

fallo *m* **por calentamiento** *sustantivo* burn out

fallo *m* **serio** *sustantivo* hard failure ◇ **el fallo del equipo se debió a un chip quemado** the hard failure was due to a burnt-out chip

falso *adj* false

falta *f sustantivo* error
falta *f sustantivo* error
falta *f* **de lógica** *sustantivo* circularity
familia *f sustantivo* family
fanático, -a *mf* ◊ **fanático, -a de la información** nerd
fanático, -a informático, -a *sustantivo* hacker
fase *f sustantivo* **1.** fetch phase **2.** phase **3.** stage **4.** step ◊ **el texto está preparado para la fase de impresión** the text is ready for the printing stage ◊ **estamos en la primera fase de pruebas del nuevo sistema informático** we are in the first stage of running in the new computer system
fase *f* **de compilación** *sustantivo* compile phase
fase *f* **de ejecución** *sustantivo* **1.** execute phase **2.** execution phase **3.** target phase
fase *f* **objetivo** *sustantivo* **1.** run phase **2.** target phase
fatal *adj* terminal
FatBits FatBits
fax *sustantivo* **1.** facsimile copy **2.** fax o FAX ◊ **el fax está junto a la centralita (de teléfonos)** the fax machine is next to the telephone switchboard ◊ **enviaremos los planos por fax** we will send a fax of the design plan ◊ **fax** fax machine ◊ **papel para fax** fax paper
'El constante aumento de popularidad del correo electrónico ha provocado la disminución o la reconversión en el uso de otros medios de comunicación como, por ejemplo, el telegrama o el correo tradicional, e incluso ha reducido el uso del teléfono y el fax.' [*Ciberpragmática*]
fax *m* **de telecopia** *sustantivo* fax gateway ◊ **para enviar mensajes por fax en vez de por red, hay que instalar una puerta de fax** to send messages by fax instead of across the network, you'll need to install a fax gateway
FDISK *sustantivo* FDISK
fecha *f sustantivo* date
fecha/hora *f sustantivo* date-time
fecha *f* **juliana** *sustantivo* Julian date
federación ◊ **federación** *f* **americana de sociedades de tratamiento de información** AFIPS
FEDS *sustantivo* **1.** FEDS **2.** fixed and exchangeable disk storage
femto- *símbolo* (*prefijo que representa el factor 10 elevado a −15*) f ■ *prefijo* femto-
femtosegundo *m sustantivo* femtosecond
fenómeno *m* **transitorio** *sustantivo* transient
ferrita *f sustantivo* ferrite
fiabilidad *f sustantivo* reliability ◊ **el producto ha superado las pruebas de fiabilidad** the product has passed its reliability tests ◊ **tiene una excelente fiabilidad** it has an excellent reliability record
fiabilidad *f* **de datos** *sustantivo* data reliability

fiabilidad *f* **del equipo** *sustantivo* hardware reliability
fiabilidad *f* **de un programa** *sustantivo* software reliability
fiable *adj* reliable ◊ **las primeras versiones del software no resultaron completamente fiables** the early versions of the software were not completely reliable
fibra *f sustantivo* fibre
fibra *f* **monomoda** *sustantivo* single mode fibre
fibra *f* **(óptica) monomodo** *sustantivo* monomode fibre
fibra *f* **multimoda** *sustantivo* multimode fibre
fibra *f* **(óptica) multimodal** *sustantivo* multimode fibre
fibra *f* **óptica** *sustantivo* **1.** optical fibre **2.** optic fibre
fibra *f* **sin señal** *sustantivo* dark fibre
fibra *f* **vacía** *sustantivo* dark fibre
fibroóptica *f plural noun* fibre optics
ficha *f sustantivo* **1.** card **2.** token ◊ **ficha** index card
ficha *f* **de control** *sustantivo* control token
ficha *f* **perforada** *sustantivo* **1.** punch card **2.** punched card
fichero *sustantivo* file ◊ **bloque de control de ficheros** file control block (FCB) ◊ **es imposible encontrar un fichero perdido sin un programa de recuperación de ficheros** a lost file cannot be found without a file-recovery utility ◊ **fichero** *m* **de comunicaciones diarias entre el usuario y el ordenador central** journal file ◊ **fichero** *m* **de escritorio (Apple Macintosh)** desktop file ◊ **fichero** *m* **de espera de dos entradas** deque; double ended queue ◊ **fichero escondido** hidden file ◊ **fichero** *m* **PIF (de información de un programa en el entorno MS-Windows)** PIF; program information file ◊ **fichero** *m* **(con formato) RIFF** RIFF file ◊ **fichero** *m* **(de acceso) secuencial** sequential file ◊ **gestión, acceso y transferencia de ficheros** *o* **método FTAM** file transfer access and management (FTAM) ◊ **la cabecera del fichero de la base de datos muestra el número total de registros y hace un listado de los campos indexados** the file header in the database file shows the total number of records and lists the index fields ◊ **los ficheros con la extensión EXE son tipos de ficheros que contienen un código de programa** files with the extension EXE are file types that contain program code ◊ **los nuevos datos son introducidos en el fichero identificado con el número 1** the new data is written to the file identified by file handle 1 ◊ **transferencia, acceso y gestión de ficheros** FTAM
fichero *m* **abierto** *sustantivo* open file
fichero *m* **abuelo** *sustantivo* grandfather file
fichero *m* **activo** *sustantivo* active file
fichero *m* **actualizado** *sustantivo* update
fichero *m* **ancestral** *sustantivo* ancestral file

fichero *m* **ASCII** *sustantivo* ASCII file

fichero *m* **asociado** *sustantivo* associated document *o* associated file

fichero *m* **bidimensional** *sustantivo* flat file

fichero *m* **binario** *sustantivo* binary file ◊ **las instrucciones del programa se guardan en un fichero binario** the program instructions are stored in the binary file ◊ **su carta es un fichero de texto, no un fichero binario** your letter is a text file, not a binary file

fichero *m* **binario ejecutable** *sustantivo* COM file ◊ **para iniciar un programa, escriba el nombre del fichero COM en el (indicador del) MS-DOS** to start the program, type the name of the COM file at the MS-DOS prompt

fichero *m* **circular** *sustantivo* circular file

fichero *m* **COM** *sustantivo* COM file ◊ **para iniciar un programa, escriba el nombre del fichero COM en el (indicador del) MS-DOS** to start the program, type the name of the COM file at the MS-DOS prompt

fichero *m* **COMMAND.COM** *sustantivo* COMMAND.COM

fichero *m* **compartido** *sustantivo* shared file

fichero *m* **compuesto** *sustantivo* compound file

fichero *m* **contiguo** *sustantivo* contiguous file

fichero *m* **de acceso secuencial** *sustantivo* serial file

fichero *m* **de aplicaciones** *sustantivo* application file

fichero *m* **de archivos** *sustantivo* archive file

fichero *m* **de audio** *sustantivo* audio file

fichero *m* **de campos delimitados** *sustantivo* delimited-field file

fichero *m* **de configuración** *sustantivo* configuration file

fichero *m* **de control de tareas** *sustantivo* job control file

fichero *m* **de correcciones** *sustantivo* deletion record

fichero *m* **de datos** *sustantivo* data file ◊ **se tiene que analizar el fichero de datos** the data file has to be analysed

fichero *m* **de datos externo** *sustantivo* external data file

fichero *m* **de direcciones** *sustantivo* mailing list

fichero *m* **de disco** *sustantivo* disk file

fichero *m* **de disquete** *sustantivo* disk file

fichero *m* **de enlaces** *sustantivo* Bindery

fichero *m* **de entrada/salida** *sustantivo* I/O file

fichero *m* **de gráficos CGM** *sustantivo* 1. CGM 2. computer graphics metafile

fichero *m* **de instrucciones** *sustantivo* 1. batch file 2. command file ◊ **este fichero de instrucciones se utiliza para ahorrar tiempo y esfuerzo al realizar una rutina** this batch file is used to save time and effort when carrying out a routine task

fichero *m* **de intercambio** *sustantivo* swap file

fichero *m* **de intercambio permanente** *sustantivo* permanent swap file

fichero *m* **de intercambio temporal** *sustantivo* temporary swap file

fichero *m* **delimitado por una coma** *sustantivo* comma-delimited file ◊ **todas las bases de datos pueden importar y exportar datos a un formato de archivo delimitado por una coma** all databases can import and export to a comma-delimited file format

fichero *m* **de localización** *sustantivo* country file

fichero *m* **de modificaciones** *sustantivo* change file

fichero *m* **de movimientos** *sustantivo* 1. detail file 2. movement file 3. transaction file 4. update file

fichero *m* **de ordenador** *sustantivo* computer file

fichero *m* **de país** *sustantivo* country file

fichero *m* **de programa** *sustantivo* program file

fichero *m* **de programa maestro** *sustantivo* master program file

fichero *m* **de punteros** *sustantivo* pointer file

fichero *m* **de referencia** *sustantivo* 1. authority file *o* authority list 2. reference file

fichero *m* **de registros** *sustantivo* register file

fichero *m* **de salida** *sustantivo* output file

fichero *m* **de seguridad** *sustantivo* backup file

fichero *m* **de serie extensible** *sustantivo* extending serial file

fichero *m* **de sonido** *sustantivo* sound file

fichero *m* **de suma** *sustantivo* addition record

fichero *m* **de supresiones** *sustantivo* deletion record

fichero *m* **de tareas** *sustantivo* job file

fichero *m* **de tercera generación** *sustantivo* son file

fichero *m* **de texto** *sustantivo* text file

fichero *m* **de trabajo** *sustantivo* 1. scratch file 2. work file

fichero *m* **de trabajos** *sustantivo* job file

fichero *m* **de transacciones** *sustantivo* 1. transaction file 2. update file

fichero *m* **DIF** *sustantivo* DIF file

fichero *m* **direccionable por el contenido** *sustantivo* content-addressable file

fichero *m* **dividido en varias partes** *sustantivo* partitioned file

fichero *m* **DLL** *sustantivo* DLL file

fichero *m* **ejecutable** *sustantivo* executable file

fichero *m* **en bucle** *sustantivo* circular file

fichero *m* **encadenado** *sustantivo* 1. chained file 2. threaded file

fichero *m* **ensartado** *sustantivo* threaded file

fichero *m* **favorito** *sustantivo* cookie file

fichero *m* **fuente** *sustantivo* source file

fichero *m* **gráfico** *sustantivo* **1.** GIF file **2.** graphics file ◇ **hay muchos estándares para ficheros gráficos como TIFF, IMG y EPS** there are many standards for graphics files including TIFF, IMG and EPS

fichero *m* **hijo** *sustantivo* son file

fichero *m* **indexado** *sustantivo* indexed file

fichero *m* **informático** *sustantivo* computer file

fichero *m* **intermedio** *sustantivo* intermediate file

fichero *m* **invertido** *sustantivo* inverted file

fichero *m* **'léame'** *sustantivo* readme file

fichero *m* **maestro** *sustantivo* master file

fichero *m* **MIDI** *sustantivo* MIDI file

fichero *m* **objeto** *sustantivo* object file

fichero *m* **padre** *sustantivo* father file

fichero *m* **PCX** *sustantivo* PCX file

fichero *m* **permanente** *sustantivo* permanent file

fichero *m* **plano** *sustantivo* flat file

fichero *m* **por lotes** *sustantivo* batch file ◇ **este fichero de instrucciones se utiliza para ahorrar tiempo y esfuerzo al realizar una rutina** this batch file is used to save time and effort when carrying out a routine task

fichero *m* **PostScript encapsulado** *sustantivo* encapsulated PostScript file

fichero *m* **precursor** *sustantivo* ancestral file

fichero *m* **principal** *sustantivo* master file

ficheros *mpl* **de acceso aleatorio/directo** *sustantivo* random access files

ficheros *mpl* **en cola de espera** *sustantivo* file queue ◇ **los periféricos como las impresoras láser entán conectados en línea con una cola automática de ficheros en espera** output devices such as laser printers are connected on-line with an automatic file queue

ficheros *mpl* **en memoria** *sustantivo* file store

ficheros *mpl* **mezclados** *plural noun* cross-linked files

ficheros *mpl* **ocultos** *plural noun* hidden files

fichero *m* **subdividido** *sustantivo* partitioned file

fichero *m* **temporal** *sustantivo* work file

FIFO *sustantivo* FIFO

fijación *f* **positiva** *sustantivo* positive display

fijar *verbo vt* to preset

fijo *m sustantivo* **1.** constant **2.** still

fila *f sustantivo* row ◇ **las cifras se presentan en filas, no en columnas** the figures are presented in rows, not in columns

filigrana *f sustantivo* watermark

filtrado *m* **bilineal** *sustantivo* bilinear filtering

filtrado *m* **de direcciones fuente** *sustantivo* source address filtering

filtrar *verbo vt* to filter

filtro *m sustantivo* filter ◇ **filtro de paso alto** high pass filter ◇ **filtro de paso bajo** low pass filter

filtro *m* **decroico** *sustantivo* dichroic filter

filtro *m* **de mejora del contraste** *sustantivo* contrast enhancement filter

filtro *m* **de pantalla** *sustantivo* glare filter

filtro *m* **de paso de banda** *sustantivo* band-pass filter

filtro *m* **de peine** *sustantivo* comb filter

fin *m sustantivo* objective

final *m sustantivo* end

final *m* **de lista** *sustantivo* tail

final *m* **de transmisión** *sustantivo* end of transmission

finalidad *f sustantivo* objective

finalización *f sustantivo* **1.** abend **2.** completion

finalización *f* **anormal** *sustantivo* abnormal end

finalizador *m sustantivo* **1.** trailer **2.** trailer record

fin *m* **de archivo** *sustantivo* end of file ■ *abrev* EOF

fin *m* **de bloque** *abrev* EOB

fin *m* **de datos** *abrev* EOD

fin *m* **de dirección** *abrev* EOA

fin *m* **de línea** *abrev* EOL

fin *m* **de mensaje** *abrev* EOM

Finder™ *m* Finder

fin *m* **de registro** *abrev* EOR

fin *m* **de tarea** *abrev* EOJ

fin *m* **de texto** *abrev* **1.** EOT **2.** ETX

fin *m* **de transmisión** *abrev* EOT

Firewire (*marca comercial*) Firewire

firma *sustantivo* signature ◇ **¿reconoce usted la firma del cheque?** do you recognize the signature on the cheque?

'La firma es un breve texto que el remitente adjunta a sus mensajes y que muestra su afiliación, dirección, número de teléfono, dirección de la página personal, etc.' [*Ciberpragmática*]

'De la misma forma que la firma manuscrita garantiza la autenticidad de un escrito, la firma digital es el procedimiento según el cual se consigue la autenticación de un escrito, pero con un grado de protección mayor, porque al mismo tiempo se garantiza la confidencialidad y la integridad de los mensajes y documentos.' [*PC Plus*]

'La firma tiene previsto este mes un lanzamiento espectacular: lo anuncia como el mayor conjunto de aplicaciones integradas de negocio.' [*Ciberp@ís*]

firma *f* **digital** *sustantivo* digital signature

firma *f* **electrónica** *sustantivo* electronic signature

firmar *verbo vt* to sign

'firmware' *m sustantivo* firmware

fisgonear *verbo vi* to browse

flecha *f sustantivo* arrow pointer

flecha *f* **direccional** *sustantivo* vector

flechas *fpl* **de desplazamiento** *plural noun* scroll arrows

flotante *adj* floating ◊ **acento flotante** floating accent ◊ **coma flotante** floating point ◊ **el procesador de coma flotante acelera el tratamiento del programa de gráficos** the floating point processor speeds up the processing of the graphics software ◊ **en un cálculo de coma flotante, el número 56,47 sería 0,5647 elevado a la potencia de 2** the fixed number 56.47 in floating-point arithmetic would be 0.5647 and a power of 2 ◊ **este modelo tiene incorporado un procesador de coma flotante** this model includes a built-in floating point processor ◊ **notación de coma flotante** floating point notation ◊ **voltaje flotante** floating voltage

fluctuación *f sustantivo* jitter

flujo *sustantivo* stream ◊ **flujo** *m* **(de datos) de salida** output stream

flujo *m* **continuo** *sustantivo* continuous data stream

flujo *m* **de bits** *sustantivo* bit stream

flujo *m* **de datos** *sustantivo* **1.** data flow **2.** data stream

flujo *m* **de información** *sustantivo* data stream

flujo *m* **de tareas** *sustantivo* job stream

flujo *m* **de trabajos** *sustantivo* job stream

flujo *m* **ininterrumpido de datos** *sustantivo* continuous data stream

flujo *m* **magnético** *sustantivo* magnetic flux

foco *m sustantivo* focus

foco *m* **de evento** *sustantivo* event focus

folletín *m* **electrónico** *sustantivo* **1.** e-zine **2.** webzine

folleto *m* **electrónico** *sustantivo* brochure site

fondo *m sustantivo* background ◊ **el texto en negro sobre un fondo blanco fatiga menos la vista** black text on a white background is less stressful for the eyes ◊ **fondo** *m* **del escritorio (de la pantalla de Windows)** desktop background

fondo *m* **animado** *adj* busy

fonema *m sustantivo* phoneme ◊ **las palabras 'too' y 'zoo' contienen el fonema 'oo'** the phoneme 'oo' is present in the words too and zoo

forma *f* **BNF** *sustantivo* **1.** Backus-Naur-Form **2.** BNF

formación *sustantivo* array

'Al retraso en la formación de los desempleados se une la renuncia del Gobierno a alfabetizar este año en Internet a un millón de españoles, con un presupuesto de 400 millones, plan anunciado por Aznar en enero de 2001.' [*Ciberp@ís*]

formación *f* **asistida por ordenador** *sustantivo* programmed learning

formación *f* **por ordenador** *abrev* CBI ■ *sustantivo* **1.** CBT **2.** computer-assisted training

formación *f* **práctica** *adj* hands on

forma *f* **de base** *sustantivo* graphics primitive

forma *f* **de onda** *sustantivo* waveform

forma *f* **normal** *sustantivo* normal form

forma *f* **normalizada** *sustantivo* normalised form

forma *f* **primitiva** *sustantivo* **1.** graphics primitive **2.** primitive **3.** (*en un programa de gráficos*) primitive

formar *vt sustantivo* form

format ◊ **formato** *m* **gráfico de intercambio** (*marca comercial*) GIF

formateado, -a previamente *adj* preformatted ◊ **un disco preformateado** a preformatted disk

formateado *m* **de disco** *sustantivo* disk formatting

formateado *m* **de disquete** *sustantivo* disk formatting

formateado *m* **de seguridad** *sustantivo* safe format

formateador *m* **de salida** *sustantivo* output formatter

formatear *verbo* to format

formateo *m* **de un disco** *sustantivo* disk formatting ◊ **antes de utilizar un disco flexible hay que formatearlo** disk formatting has to be done before you can use a new floppy disk

formateo *m* **de un disquete** *sustantivo* disk formatting

formato *sustantivo* format ◊ **formato** *m* **de fichero de imágenes exploradas** tag image file format; TIFF ◊ **formato** *m* **de ficheros gráficos desarrollado por Adobe Acrobat** Acrobat ◊ **formato** *m* **de pantalla (para introducir datos)** form ◊ **formato** *m* **en modo de transferencia asíncrona** ATM cell format ◊ **formato** *m* **intermedio común (para vídeo)** CIF; common intermediate format ◊ **ha sido fácil preparar a los operadores en la utilización del nuevo programa ya que su presentación en pantalla se parece a los impresos existentes** it's been easy to train the operators to use the new software since its display looks like the existing printed forms ◊ **la impresora puede gestionar todo tipo de formatos hasta tamaño en cuarto** the printer can deal with all formats up to quarto

formato *m* **activo de flujo continuo** *sustantivo* **1.** active streaming format **2.** ASF

formato *m* **BCNF** *sustantivo* Boyce-Codd normal form

formato *m* **condensado** *sustantivo* packed format

formato *m* **de bajo nivel** *sustantivo* low-level format

formato *m* **de celda** *sustantivo* cell format ◊ **las celdas tienen un formato de justificación a la derecha y negrita** the cell format is right-aligned and emboldened

formato *m* **de célula ATM** *sustantivo* ATM cell format

formato *m* **de cinta** *sustantivo* tape format

formato *m* **de codificación** *sustantivo* encoding format

formato *m* **de datos** *sustantivo* data format

formato *m* **de direccion(es)** *sustantivo* address format

formato *m* **de documento transferible** *sustantivo* 1. PDF 2. portable document format

formato *m* **de fichero** *sustantivo* file format

formato *m* **de fichero de propietario** *sustantivo* proprietary file format ◇ **no se puede leer este fichero de hoja de cálculo porque mi programa lo guarda en un formato de marca registrada** you cannot read this spreadsheet file because my software saves it in a proprietary file format

formato *m* **de fichero gráfico** *sustantivo* graphics file format

formato *m* **de fichero intercambiable** *sustantivo* 1. IFF 2. interchange file format

formato *m* **de fichero internacional** *sustantivo* 1. IFF 2. international file format

formato *m* **de fichero original** *sustantivo* native file format

formato *m* **de hora TMSF** *sustantivo* 1. TMSF time format 2. tracks, minutes, seconds, frames time format

formato *m* **de imagen fractal** *sustantivo* 1. FIF 2. fractal image format

formato *m* **de impresión** *sustantivo* print format

formato *m* **de instrucción** *sustantivo* instruction format

formato *m* **de instrucciones** *sustantivo* instruction format

formato *m* **de intercambio de datos** *sustantivo* data interchange format

formato *m* **de intercambio de ficheros** *sustantivo* 1. resource interchange file format 2. RIFF

formato *m* **de intercambio gráfico** *sustantivo* graphics interface format

formato *m* **de lenguaje simbólico** *sustantivo* symbolic-coding format

formato *m* **de marca registrada** *sustantivo* proprietary file format ◇ **no se puede leer este fichero de hoja de cálculo porque mi programa lo guarda en un formato de marca registrada** you cannot read this spreadsheet file because my software saves it in a proprietary file format

formato *m* **de mensaje** *sustantivo* message format

formato *m* **de pantalla** *sustantivo* 1. display format 2. format mode 3. screen format

formato *m* **de texto enriquecido** *sustantivo* rich text format ∎ *abrev* RTF

formato *m* **de un registro** *sustantivo* 1. record format 2. record layout

formato *m* **DIF** *sustantivo* data interchange format

formato *m* **estándar** *sustantivo* normal format

formato *m* **estándar de intercambio** *sustantivo* basic exchange format

formato *m* **FIF** *sustantivo* FIF

formato *m* **interno** *sustantivo* internal format

formato *m* **normal** *sustantivo* normal format

formato *m* **normal Boyce-Codd** *sustantivo* Boyce-Codd normal form

formato *m* **original** *sustantivo* native format

formato *m* **para ejecutar** *sustantivo* executable form

formato *m* **TIFF** *sustantivo* 1. tag image file format 2. TIFF

formato *m* **V** *sustantivo* V format

formato *m* **variable** *sustantivo* 1. variable format 2. V format

formato *m* **Vxtreme** *sustantivo* Vxtreme

fórmula *f sustantivo* 1. expression 2. formula

formulario *m sustantivo* form

formulario *m* **de codificación** *sustantivo* coding form

formulario *m* **de programación** *sustantivo* 1. coding form 2. program coding sheet

formulario *m* **de solicitud** *sustantivo* application form

formulario *m* **estándar** *sustantivo* standard document *o* standard form

formularios *mpl* **impresos** *sustantivo* preprinted stationery

foro *m sustantivo* 1. forum 2. newsgroup ◇ **foro** *m* **de discusión (en Internet)** newsgroup ◇ **lector de grupos de noticias** newsgroup reader

fósforo *m sustantivo* phosphor

fósforo *m* **de gran persistencia** *sustantivo* long persistence phosphor

fósforo *m* **de larga persistencia** *sustantivo* long persistence phosphor

foto *f sustantivo* picture ◇ **esta foto muestra el nuevo diseño** this picture shows the new design

foto- *prefijo* photo-

fotocompositora *f sustantivo* phototypesetter

fotografía *sustantivo* picture

'El modelo 7650 es un teléfono móvil que incorpora una cámara digital y que permite enviar las fotografías como mensajes cortos si se dirigen a otro terminal que soporte este sistema o como un documento adjunto en un correo electrónico.' [*Ciberp@ís*]

fotografía *f* **digitalizada** *sustantivo* digitised photograph *o* digitized photograph

fotografía *f* **instantánea** *sustantivo* snapshot

fotografía instantánea *f sustantivo* snapshot

fotograma *m sustantivo* frame ◇ **con el procesador de imágenes se puede congelar un fotograma del vídeo** with the image processor you can freeze a video frame ◇ **imagen de vídeo** *o* **fotograma** video frame

fotograma *m* **de animación digital** *sustantivo* cel

fotos *fpl plural noun* pix

fracción *f sustantivo* fraction

fraccional *m sustantivo* mantissa

fraccionamiento *m sustantivo* fragmentation

fracción *f* **binaria** *sustantivo* binary fraction ◇ **la fracción binaria 0,011 es igual a un cuarto más un octavo (es decir, tres octavos)** the binary fraction 0.011 is equal to one quarter plus one eighth (i.e. three eighths)

fracción *f* **de tiempo** *sustantivo* time slice

fractal *m sustantivo* fractal

fragmentación *f sustantivo* fragmentation

fragmentación *sustantivo* fragmentation
> 'El teléfono móvil, el ordenador personal, la fragmentación temática de los canales de televisión, el vídeo a la carta, los auriculares de alta fidelidad, los walkman, son todos ellos inventos dedicados al individuo.' [*La Red*]

fragmentación *f* **de ficheros** *sustantivo* file fragmentation

fragmento *m sustantivo* fragment

fragmento *m* **adaptador** *sustantivo* stub

fragmento *m* **de película** *verbo* to clip

franja *f* **horaria** *sustantivo* time slice

fraude *m* **informático** *sustantivo* 1. computer crime 2. computer fraud

frecuencia *f sustantivo* frequency ◇ **ámbito de frecuencias** frequency range ◇ **convertidor de frecuencia** frequency changer ◇ **desviación de frecuencia** frequency deviation ◇ **distribución de frecuencia** frequency distribution ◇ **divisor de frecuencia** frequency divider ◇ **dominio de frecuencias** frequency domain ◇ **excursión de frecuencia** frequency swing ◇ **frecuencia** *f* **de actualización de la memoria RAM** RAM refresh rate ◇ **frecuencia** *f* **(de barrido) de líneas** line frequency ◇ **frecuencia de ondas extremadamente altas** *o* **de ondas milimétricas** extremely high frequency (EHF) ◇ **frecuencia de ondas extremadamente bajas** *o* **de ondas miriamétricas** extremely low frequency (ELF) ◇ **la multiplexión de división de frecuencias permite transferir 100 llamadas telefónicas con un único cable principal** using FDM we can transmit 100 telephone calls along one main cable ◇ **la principal frecuencia de reloj es de 10 MHz** the main clock frequency is 10MHz ◇ **(sistema de) modulación** *o* **manipulación por desplazamiento de frecuencias** frequency shift keying (FSK) ◇ **respuesta de frecuencias** frequency response ◇ **variación de frecuencias** frequency variation

frecuencia *f* **crítica de fusión** *sustantivo* critical fusion frequency

frecuencia *f* **de barrido** *sustantivo* scan rate

frecuencia *f* **de líneas** *sustantivo* line frequency

frecuencia *f* **de portadora** *sustantivo* carrier frequency

frecuencia *f* **de radio** *sustantivo* 1. radio frequency 2. RF *o* R/F ◇ **modulador de frecuencia**

de radio RF modulator *o* radio frequency modulator

frecuencia *f* **de reloj** *sustantivo* clock frequency ◇ **la principal frecuencia de reloj es de 10 MHz** the main clock frequency is 10MHz

FTP *sustantivo* FTP

FTP *m* **anónimo** *sustantivo* anonymous FTP

fuente *sustantivo* source ◇ **fuente** *f* **(de caracteres tipográficos)** font ◇ **fuente** *f* **(de caracteres) base** base font ◇ **fuente** *f* **de caracteres para lectura óptica** optical font ◇ **fuente** *f* **de caracteres que se puede copiar** downloadable font ◇ **fuente** *f* **de caracteres reconocible por un lector óptico** OCR font ◇ **fuente** *f* **(de caracteres) del programa** soft font ◇ **fuente** *f* **(de caracteres) incorporada** built-in font ◇ **fuente** *f* **(de caracteres) modelo** outline font ◇ **fuente** *f* **(de caracteres) residente** resident fonts ◇ **fuente** *f* **(de caracteres) transformada por bits** bit-mapped font ◇ **fuente** *f* **(de caracteres) uniforme** monospaced font ◇ **fuente** *f* **vectorial (de caracteres)** vector font
> 'Los remedios más usuales para la protección de la funcionalidad de los equipos son las fuentes interrumpidas (UPS), las copias de seguridad en dispositivos de reserva (backup) y los sistemas de recuperación de la información.' [*PC Plus*]

fuente *f* **de alimentación** *sustantivo* PSU

fuente *f* **de alimentación/de energía** *sustantivo* power supply

fuente *f* **de caracteres** *sustantivo* 1. character set 2. face 3. typeface

fuente *f* **de caracteres de pantalla** *sustantivo* screen font ◇ **la fuente de caracteres de pantalla se muestra a 72 puntos por pulgada en un monitor, en lugar de aparecer impresa a 300 puntos por pulgada mediante esta impresora láser** the screen font is displayed at 72dpi on a monitor, rather than printed at 300dpi on this laser printer

fuente *f* **de caracteres especiales** *sustantivo* Dingbat™ ◇ **para insertar el símbolo de 'copyright', emplee la fuente Dingbat** to insert a copyright symbol, use the Dingbat font

fuente *f* **de caracteres pica** *sustantivo* pica

fuente *f* **de caracteres 'Symbol'** *sustantivo* Symbol font

fuente *f* **de datos** *sustantivo* data source

fuente *f* **de energía** *sustantivo* PSU

fuente *f* **de información** *sustantivo* information provider

fuente *f* **monoespaciada** *sustantivo* monospaced font

fuente *f* **OCR** *sustantivo* OCR font

fuente *f* **óptica de caracteres** *sustantivo* optical font

fuente *f* **por defecto** *sustantivo* base font

fuentes *fpl* **de caracteres** *sustantivo* character repertoire

fuentes *fpl* **de caracteres de cargador** *plural noun* cartridge fonts

fuente *f* **suave** *sustantivo* soft font

fuera de alcance *adj* out of range

fuera de control *adj* out of control

fuera de red *adv, adj* off-line ◇ **antes de cambiar el papel de la impresora, sitúe el interruptor en fuera de red** before changing the paper in the printer, switch it off-line

fuera de servicio *adj* dead

fuerte *adj* robust

fugaz *adj* transient

función *f sustantivo* 1. bead 2. function ◇ **el procesador de textos disponía de una función de corrección ortográfica, pero no de una función de edición de textos** the word-processor had a spelling-checker function but no built-in text-editing function ◇ **función f que genera una señalización** flag event ◇ **la función de insertar se activa pulsando la tecla F5** hitting F5 will put you into insert mode

funciona ◇ **que funciona bien** well-behaved ◇ **que funciona en la mayoría de los ordenadores** machine-independent ◇ **que sólo funciona con un solo tipo de ordenador** machine-dependent

función f absoluta *sustantivo* ABS

función f agregada *sustantivo* aggregate function

funcionamiento *m sustantivo* 1. parallel running 2. performance ◇ **para su evaluación, se pone a prueba el funcionamiento de varios sistemas o dispositivos mediante una prueba estándar** in benchmarking, the performances of several systems or devices are tested against a standard benchmark

funcionamiento m defectuoso *sustantivo* malfunction

funcionamiento m en tándem *sustantivo* working in tandem

funcionar *verbo* 1. *vi* to operate 2. *vi* to perform 3. *vi* to run ◇ **el nuevo software funciona en nuestro ordenador personal** the new package runs on our PC ◇ **el ordenador ha estado funcionando diez horas al día** the computer has been running ten hours a day ◇ **precio de una tirada adicional** run-on price ◇ **¿sabe cómo hacer funcionar la centralita telefónica?** do you know how to operate the telephone switchboard?

funcionar a menor capacidad *verbo* to run in

funcionar mal *verbo* to malfunction ◇ **algunas de las teclas del teclado han empezado a funcionar mal** some of the keys on the keyboard have started to malfunction

función f avanzada de comunicaciones *abrev* ACF

función f (de) biblioteca *sustantivo* library function

función f (de) cadena *sustantivo* string function

función f complementaria *sustantivo* NOT function

función f de Ackerman *sustantivo* Ackerman's function

función f de anti-coincidencia *sustantivo* anticoincidence circuit *o* anticoincidence function

función f de coincidencia *sustantivo* 1. AND 2. AND function 3. coincidence function

función f de comprobación al azar *sustantivo* hashing function

función f de comprobación aleatoria *sustantivo* hashing function

función f de dibujo *sustantivo* drawing tool

función f de disyunción *abrev* NEQ ■ *sustantivo* 1. NEQ function 2. nonequivalence function

función f de equivalencia *sustantivo* 1. equivalence function 2. equivalence operation

función f de globalización *sustantivo* aggregate function

función f de tratamiento de texto *sustantivo* text-editing function ◇ **el programa lleva una función de tratamiento de textos incorporada** the program includes a built-in text-editing function

función f de un evento *sustantivo* flag event

función f de valor absoluto *sustantivo* ABS

funciones fpl aritméticas *plural noun* arithmetic functions

función f estándar *sustantivo* standard function

función f incorporada *sustantivo* built-in function

función f mayúsculas *sustantivo* capitalisation *o* capitalization

función f NAND *sustantivo* 1. NAND function 2. NOT-AND

función f NI *sustantivo* 1. neither-nor function 2. NOR function

función f NO *sustantivo* NOT function

función f NO-O *sustantivo* neither-nor function

función f NOY *sustantivo* 1. NAND function 2. NOT-AND

función f O *sustantivo* OR function

función f OR *sustantivo* 1. disjunction 2. OR function

función f Y *sustantivo* 1. AND 2. AND function 3. coincidence function

funda f (de disquete) *sustantivo* sleeve

fundamental *adj* primary ◇ **colores primarios** *o* **fundamentales** primary colours

fundición f de silicio *sustantivo* silicon foundry

fundido m en negro *sustantivo* fade out

fundir *verbo vt* to coalesce

fusible m *sustantivo* limiter

fusión *sustantivo* file collating

'En esta época de fusiones de empresas, de venta de datos, de banners que nos tapan la página que queremos ver y de spam, es bueno recordar al anunciante quién manda: nosotros, los del otro lado del monitor.' [*Ciberp@ís*]

fusionar *verbo* **1.** *vt* to coalesce **2.** *vt* to merge ◇ **el sistema fusiona** *o* **combina automáticamente texto e ilustraciones dentro del documento** the system automatically merges text and illustrations into the document

fusión *f* **de documentos** *sustantivo* **1.** document assembly **2.** document merge

fusión *f* **de ficheros** *sustantivo* file merger

FYI *sustantivo* for your information

G

G *prefijo* giga-

galería *f* **de imágenes** *sustantivo* clip-art

gama *f sustantivo* **1.** family **2.** range ◇ **gama de frecuencias** frequency range ◇ **la transmisión por teléfono acepta señales dentro de una gama de frecuencias que va de los 300 a los 3400 Hz** the telephone channel can accept signals in the frequency range 300 – 3400Hz

gama *f* **de audiofrecuencias** *sustantivo* audio range

gama *f* **de productos** *sustantivo* **1.** product line *o* product range **2.** product range

gama *f* **de valores** *sustantivo* number range

gama *f* **normal** *sustantivo* normal range

ganancia *f sustantivo* gain ◇ **control de amplificación** *o* **de ganancia** gain control

garantía ◇ **garantía** *f* **de calidad de un programa** software quality assurance

'El Parlamento Europeo aprobó la semana pasada, en primera lectura, una serie de medidas sobre las garantías de privacidad que debe disfrutar el ciudadano europeo en Internet.' [*Ciberp@ís*]

garantía *f* **de calidad de un programa** *abrev* SQA

gasto *m* **horario** *sustantivo* **1.** production rate **2.** rate of production

gastos *mpl* **de acceso al sistema** *sustantivo* access charge

generación *sustantivo* generation ◇ **el fichero padre es una copia de seguridad de primera generación** the father file is a first generation backup

'Los ordenadores de última generación, con sistemas operativos recientes, reconocen automáticamente cuando se conecta un nuevo aparato, como en el caso de una impresora. Es lo que se conoce como plug and play (enchufar y usar).' [*Ciberp@ís*]

generación *f* **aleatoria de números** *sustantivo* random number generation

generación *f* **de datos** *sustantivo* data origination

generación *f* **de ordenadores** *sustantivo* computer generation

generación *f* **de un sistema** *sustantivo* **1.** sysgen **2.** system generation

generado por ordenador *adj* computer-generated

generador *sustantivo* generator ◇ **generador** *m* **de la tasa en baudios** baud rate generator

'El microchip, que se implanta en la base de la espina dorsal de los pacientes, actúa como un generador de impulsos controlado por un ordenador.' [*Ciberp@ís*]

generador *m* **de aplicaciones** *sustantivo* application generator

generador *m* **de caracteres** *sustantivo* character generator ◇ **la ROM utilizada como generadora de caracteres se puede cambiar para proporcionar fuentes distintas** the ROM used as a character generator can be changed to provide different fonts

generador *m* **de caracteres de pantalla** *sustantivo* display character generator

generador *m* **de caracteres facsímiles** *sustantivo* facsimile character generator

generador *m* **de enlaces** *sustantivo* linkage software ◇ **los gráficos y el texto se unen sin el programa generador de enlaces** graphics and text are joined without linkage software

generador *m* **de informes** *sustantivo* report generator

generador *m* **de informes de programas** *sustantivo* program report generator

generador *m* **de números aleatorios** *sustantivo* random number generator

generador *m* **de números pseudo-aleatorios** *sustantivo* pseudo-random number generator

generador *m* **de programa** *sustantivo* program generator

generador *m* **de referencias cruzadas** *sustantivo* cross-reference generator

generador *m* **de sincronismos** *sustantivo* **1.** generator lock **2.** genlock

generar *verbo vt* to generate ◇ **cada vez que se mueve el lápiz óptico la pizarra gráfica genera un par de coordenadas** the graphics tablet generates a pair of co-ordinates each time the pen is moved ◇ **generar un código de comprobación al azar** to hash

genérico *adj* generic

geometría *f sustantivo* geometry

gestión ◇ **gestión, acceso y transferencia de ficheros** file transfer access and management ◇ **gestión** *f* **avanzada de la memoria extendida** enhanced expanded memory specification ◇ **gestión** *f* **de acceso a los datos** data access management ◇ **gestión** *f* **de acceso a los discos** disk access management ◇ **gestión** *f* **de im-**

presión (por periféricos) print spooling ◇ **gestión** *f* **de lista de espera** queue management

gestionar colas *verbo* to spool

gestionar periféricos *verbo* to spool

gestión *f* **de colas** *sustantivo* spool

gestión *f* **de datos** *sustantivo* data management

gestión *f* **de documentos de imágenes** *sustantivo* 1. DIM 2. document image management

gestión *f* **de enlace común** *sustantivo* bus arbitration

gestión *f* **de fallos** *sustantivo* fault management

gestión *f* **de ficheros** *sustantivo* file management *o* file management system

gestión *f* **de la memoria** *sustantivo* memory management

gestión *f* **de periféricos** *sustantivo* spooling

gestión *f* **de red** *sustantivo* network management

gestión *f* **de tareas** *sustantivo* task management

gestión *f* **de terminal** *sustantivo* station management

gestión *f* **de texto** *sustantivo* text management

gestión *f* **de trabajos** *sustantivo* job scheduling

gestor *sustantivo* manager ◇ **gestor** *m* **de fuentes y accesorios del escritorio** Font/DA Mover

gestor *m* **de colas** *sustantivo* spooler

gestor *m* **de datos** *sustantivo* data administrator

gestor *m* **de espacios** *sustantivo* spacer

gestor *m* **de espacios inteligente** *sustantivo* intelligent spacer

gestor *m* **de eventos** *sustantivo* event handler

gestor *m* **de ficheros** *sustantivo* file manager

gestor *m* **de fuentes Adobe** (*marca comercial*) Adobe Type Manager ■ *abrev* ATM

gestor *m* **de impresión** *sustantivo* printer driver ■ (*de Microsoft Windows*) Print Manager

gestor *m* **de la energía** *sustantivo* power management

gestor *m* **de memoria extendida** *sustantivo* 1. EMM 2. expanded memory manager

gestor *m* **de notificaciones** *sustantivo* notify handler

gestor *m* **de periféricos** *sustantivo* 1. device driver 2. device handler 3. handler 4. spooler

gestor *m* **de periféricos en red** *sustantivo* network device driver

gestor *m* **de periféricos instalable** *sustantivo* installable device driver

gestor *m* **de prioridades** *sustantivo* priority scheduler

gestor *m* **de programas** *sustantivo* Program Manager

gestor *m* **de registros** *sustantivo* records manager ◇ (**programa de**) **gestión de registros** *o* **de ficheros** records management

gestor *m* **de segmento superpuesto** *sustantivo* overlay manager

gestor *m* **de sucesos** *sustantivo* event handler

gestor *m* **de tareas** *sustantivo* scheduler

gestor *m* **de telecomunicaciones** *sustantivo* communications executive

gestor *m* **de texto** *sustantivo* text manager

GHz *abrev* GHz ■ *sustantivo* gigahertz

giga- *prefijo* giga-

gigabit *m* *sustantivo* gigabit

gigabyte (Gb) *m* *abrev* Gb

gigabyte *m* **(Gb)** *sustantivo* gigabyte

gigaflop *m* *sustantivo* gigaflop

gigahercio (GHz) *m* *abrev* GHz

gigahercio (GHz) *m* *sustantivo* gigahertz

gigaocteto *m* *abrev* Gb ■ *sustantivo* gigabyte

girar *verbo vt* to rotate

glifo *m* *sustantivo* glyph

global *adj* global

'El comerciante que se lanza a la arena del comercio electrónico disfrutará de una presencia global en el mercado. Su campo de actuación no vendrá limitado por distancias ni por área de actividad.' [*PC Plus*]

goma *f* *sustantivo* eraser tool

Google (*marca comercial*) Google

Gopher *sustantivo* Gopher

GOSUB *sustantivo* GOSUB

GOTO *sustantivo* GOTO

grabación *f* *sustantivo* 1. DAT 2. recording ◇ **grabación** *f* **por medio de un haz electrónico** electron beam recording

grabación *f* *sustantivo* digital audio tape

grabación *f* **agrupada** *verbo* to gather write

grabación *f* **analógica** *sustantivo* analog recording

grabación *f* **con soporte magnético** *sustantivo* magnetic recording

grabación *f* **digital** *sustantivo* sound capture

grabación *f* **en discos magnetoópticos** *sustantivo* magneto-optical recording

grabación *f* **por capa polimerizada** *sustantivo* dye-polymer recording

grabado *m* *sustantivo* print

grabadora *f* *sustantivo* 1. cassette recorder 2. recorder

grabadora *f* **de banda** *sustantivo* magnetic tape recorder

grabadora *f* **de bobina a bobina** *sustantivo* reel to reel recorder

grabadora *f* **de cintas magnéticas** *sustantivo* magnetic tape recorder

grabadora *f* **de sonidos** (*utilidad de Microsoft Windows*) Sound Recorder

grabador *m* **de vídeo** *sustantivo* **1.** VCR **2.** video cassette recorder **3.** video tape recorder **4.** VTR

grabador *m* **en dos fases** *sustantivo* two-phase commit

grabar *verbo vt* to burn in

grabar en la memoria *verbo* to store ◇ **guardar en memoria gráficos de alta definición puede requerir hasta 3 Mb** storing a page of high resolution graphics can require 3Mb

gradiente *sustantivo* gradient

grado ◇ **grado** *m* **de segmentación de la memoria** granularity

gradual *adj* staged

gráfico *m sustantivo* chart ■ *adj* graphic ■ *sustantivo* schema ◇ **gráfico** *m* **(expresado) en co-ordenadas** coordinate graph ◇ **gráfico** *m* **preestablecido (guardado en memoria)** form overlay ◇ **registrador gráfico** *o* **de gráficos** chart recorder

gráfico *m* **circular** *sustantivo* pie chart

gráfico *m* **de barras** *sustantivo* bar chart

gráfico *m* **de derivación** *sustantivo* derivation graph

gráfico *m* **en columnas** *sustantivo* columnar graph

gráfico *m* **plano** *sustantivo* planar

gráficos *mpl sustantivo* graphics ■ *plural noun* presentation graphics ◇ **hay muchos estándares para ficheros gráficos como TIFF, IMG y EPS** there are many standards for graphics files including TIFF, IMG and EPS ◇ **las representaciones gráficas como los histogramas, los gráficos sectoriales, etc.** graphics output such as bar charts, pie charts, etc. ◇ **las ventas del último mes parecieron aún mejores gracias a la presentación gráfica** the sales for last month looked even better thanks to the use of presentation graphics

gráficos *mpl* **contiguos** *plural noun* contiguous graphics ◇ **la mayoría de pantallas no disponen de visualización de gráficos contiguos; cada carácter (gráfico) tiene un pequeño espacio a cada lado para mejorar la legibilidad** most display units do not provide contiguous graphics: their characters have a small space on each side to improve legibility

gráficos *mpl* **de alta definición** *sustantivo* **1.** high resolution graphics **2.** HRG

gráficos *mpl* **de baja definición** *plural noun* low-resolution graphics *o* low-res graphics

gráficos *mpl* **de baja resolución** *plural noun* low-resolution graphics *o* low-res graphics

gráficos *mpl* **de ordenador** *plural noun* computer graphics

gráficos *mpl* **de tortuga** *plural noun* turtle graphics ◇ **la presentación gráfica se preparó con gráficos de tortuga** the charts were prepared using turtle graphics

gráficos *mpl* **interactivos** *plural noun* interactive graphics

gráficos *mpl* **orientados a objetos** *plural noun* object-oriented graphics

gráficos *mpl* **por ordenador** *plural noun* computer graphics

gráficos *mpl* **separados** *plural noun* separated graphics

gráficos *mpl* **transformados por bits** *plural noun* bit-mapped graphics

gráficos *mpl* **vectoriales** *sustantivo* **1.** VDRV **2.** vector graphics *o* vector image **3.** vector scan

grafo *m sustantivo* plot

grafo *m* **de área** *sustantivo* area graph

gramática *f sustantivo* grammar

gramola *f sustantivo* jukebox

granulosidad *f sustantivo* granularity

Green Book *sustantivo* (*estándar de Philips*) Green Book

gritar *verbo vi* to shout

grupo *m sustantivo* **1.** bank **2.** group ◇ **este tratamiento de textos facilita el trabajo en grupo al incluir una conexión con el correo electrónico desde los menús estándares** this word-processor is workgroup enabled which adds an email gateway from the standard menus ◇ **grupo** *m* **(de caracteres** *or* **de palabras)** group ◇ **grupo** *m* **de ficheros (conectados)** file set ◇ **grupo** *m* **de instrucciones de un microprograma** microprogram instruction set ◇ **grupo** *m* **(de datos) de repetición** repeating group ◇ **grupo** *m* **de tareas de ingeniería de Internet** IETF ◇ **grupo** *m* **de un proyecto interconectado por red** workgroup ◇ **grupo** *m* **(de datos) perdido** lost cluster ◇ **un grupo de miniordenadores procesa todos los datos en bruto** a bank of minicomputers process all the raw data

grupo *m* **de bytes** *sustantivo* gulp

grupo *m* **de caracteres** *sustantivo* character assembly

grupo *m* **de caracteres alternativos** *sustantivo* alternate character set ◇ **podemos imprimir caracteres griegos al seleccionar el conjunto de caracteres alternos** we can print Greek characters by selecting the alternate character set

grupo *m* **de código** *sustantivo* (*de distribución por fibra óptica*) code group

grupo *m* **de control** *sustantivo* control group

grupo *m* **de discusión** *sustantivo* **1.** chat group **2.** discussion group

grupo *m* **de dos bytes** *sustantivo* gulp

grupo *m* **de dos cifras binarias** *sustantivo* dibit

grupo *m* **de expertos en imagen en movimiento** *sustantivo* **1.** Moving Pictures Expert Group **2.** MPEG

grupo *m* **de interés especial** *sustantivo* **1.** SIG **2.** special interest group

grupo de noticias ◇ **(grupo de noticias) comp (sobre ordenadores y programación)** comp

grupo *m* **de noticias** *sustantivo* newsgroup ◊
lector de grupos de noticias newsgroup reader

grupo *m* **de periféricos** *sustantivo* cluster

grupo *m* **de píxeles** *sustantivo* texel

grupo *m* **de programas** *sustantivo* **1.** group
2. program group ◊ **todos los iconos de este
grupo están relacionados con la pintura** all
the icons in this group are to do with painting

grupo *m* **de terminales** *sustantivo* cluster

grupo *m* **de trabajo** *sustantivo* workgroup

grupo *m* **de usuario cerrado** *sustantivo* **1.**
closed user group **2.** CUG

grupo *m* **de usuarios** *sustantivo* **1.** group **2.**
user group ◊ **encontré la solución al problema
preguntando a otros en la reunión del grupo
de usuarios** I found how to solve the problem by
asking people at the user group meeting

grupo *m* **racimo** *sustantivo* cluster

grupo *m* **testigo** *sustantivo* control group

grupo *m* **X/OPEN** *sustantivo* X/OPEN

guante *m* **de datos** *sustantivo* data glove

guante *m* **electrónico** *sustantivo* data glove

guardar *verbo* **1.** *vt* to hold **2.** *vt* to save ◊ **este
procesador guarda el texto cada 15 minutos
por si tiene lugar algún fallo** this WP saves the
text every 15 minutes in case of a fault ◊ **no olvide guardar el archivo antes de apagar (el
ordenador)** don't forget to save the file before
switching off

'Todo lo que se guarda en el ordenador, si no se
protege debidamente está siempre a la vista de
cualquier intruso, ya sea accediendo directamente
al ordenador o a través de cualquier red a la que se
esté conectado, como es el caso de Internet.' [*Ci-
berp@ís*]

guardar de nuevo *verbo* to resave ◊ **automáticamente guarda de nuevo el texto** it
automatically resaves the text

guardar en la memoria *verbo* to store ◊
**guardar en memoria gráficos de alta
definición puede requerir hasta 3 Mb** storing
a page of high resolution graphics can require
3Mb

GUI *sustantivo* **1.** graphical user interface **2.** GUI

guía *m sustantivo* column guide ◊ **guía** *f* **de arrastre (del papel)** feed hole

guía *f* **de búsqueda** *sustantivo* search directory

guía *f* **de cinta** *sustantivo* tape guide ◊ **la cinta
no está alineada porque una de las guías se
ha roto** the tape is out of alignment because one
of the tape guides has broken

guión *m* **de shell** *sustantivo* shell script

guión *m* **discrecional** *sustantivo* discretionary hyphen

guión *m* **gráfico** *sustantivo* story board

guión *m* **suave** *sustantivo* soft hyphen

H

hacer ◊ **el programa permite a los usuarios hacer copias de seguridad de ficheros del disco duro con una sola instrucción** the program enables users to back up hard disk files with a single command ◊ **hacer clic dos veces (con el ratón)** double-click ◊ **hacer según los requisitos del cliente** customise ◊ **hacer una copia de seguridad** back up ◊ **hacer un quemado de pantalla** burn in ◊ **se hizo una copia de seguridad de la contabilidad de la empresa en un disco para protegerla en caso de incendio** the company accounts were backed up on disk as a protection against fire damage ◊ **sitúe el puntero sobre el icono y pulse dos veces el ratón para iniciar el programa** move the pointer to the icon then start the program with a double-click

hacer aparecer *verbo* to reveal

hacer(se) borroso *verbo* to blur ◊ **la imagen se hace borrosa al girar el mando de enfocar** the image becomes blurred when you turn the focus knob

hacer circular *verbo* to distribute

hacer desviar *verbo* to deflect

hacer eco *verbo* to echo

hacer funcionar *verbo* to operate ◊ **¿sabe cómo hacer funcionar la centralita telefónica?** do you know how to operate the telephone switchboard?

hacer llegar *verbo* to forward

hacer marcas detectables *verbo* to mark sense

hacer marcha atrás *verbo* to reverse

hacer parpadear *verbo* to flash

hacer pasar *verbo* to pass

hacer referencia a *verbo* to quote ◊ **al responder haga referencia a este número, por favor** in reply please quote this number ◊ **cuando presente una reclamación por favor haga referencia al número del lote situado en la caja del ordenador** when making a complaint please quote the batch number printed on the computer case ◊ **mencionó unas cifras procedentes del artículo del periódico** he quoted figures from the newspaper report

hacer saltar *verbo* to bomb

hacer saltar *verbo* to pop

hacer una auditoría *verbo* to audit

hacer una búsqueda *verbo* to search

hacer una copia *verbo* to copy ◊ **haga una copia de sus datos con la instrucción COPY antes de modificarlos** make a copy of your data using the COPY command before you edit it ◊ **hay una utilidad residente que copia los últimos ficheros en memoria auxiliar cada 40 minutos** there is a memory resident utility which copies the latest files onto backing store every 40 minutes

hacer una copia idéntica *verbo* to mirror

hacer una lista *verbo* to list ◊ **hacer una lista de (las líneas de instrucción de) un programa** to list a program

hacer una oferta global *verbo* to bundle

hacer una prueba *verbo* to test

hacer un barrido *verbo* to scan

hacer un intercambio *verbo* to exchange

hacer un listado *verbo* to catalogue

hacer un sangrado *verbo* to indent ◊ **la primera línea de cada párrafo tiene un sangrado de dos espacios** the first line of the paragraph is indented two spaces

hacer un 'spooling' *verbo* to spool

hacer un 'zoom' *verbo* to zoom

hacia *f* **adelante** *sustantivo* forward mode

hardware *sustantivo* hardware

'Los expertos en hardware y los creadores de software trabajan denodadamente en la fabricación de máquinas y programas que humanicen y faciliten el uso de los ordenadores.' [*La Red*]

hardware *m* **base** *sustantivo* base hardware

hardware *m* **común** *sustantivo* common hardware

hardware *m* **corriente** *sustantivo* common hardware

hartley *m sustantivo* hartley

Hayes Corporation™ Hayes Corporation

haz *m sustantivo* beam ◊ **anchura de un haz** beam width ◊ **haz** *m* **(de fibras ópticas)** bundle

haz *m* **de electrones** *sustantivo* electron beam ◊ **el haz de electrones dibuja la imagen en el interior de una pantalla de rayos catódicos** the electron beam draws the image on the inside of a CRT screen

haz *m* **de imagen** *sustantivo* picture beam

haz *m* **electrónico** *sustantivo* electron beam ◊ **el haz de electrones dibuja la imagen en el interior de una pantalla de rayos catódicos** the electron beam draws the image on the inside of a CRT screen

hecho a medida *adj* 1. custom-built 2. machine-intimate

hembra *adj* female

hercio *m sustantivo* hertz

heredar ◇ **heredar (características de otro objeto)** inherit

herencia *f sustantivo* inheritance

herramienta *sustantivo* tool

'Tanto Netscape como el Explorer de Microsoft, las dos herramientas de navegación más populares y extendidas en el mundo, estimulan constantes novedades en sus productos a fin de facilitar y orientar la tarea de los usuarios.' [*La Red*]

herramienta *f* **de borrar** *sustantivo* eraser tool

herramienta *f* **de dibujo** *sustantivo* drawing tool

herramienta *f* **de programación** *sustantivo* software tool

herramienta *f* **de selección** *sustantivo* selection tool

herramientas ◇ **herramientas** *fpl* **de diagnóstico de un sistema** system diagnostics ◇ **herramientas** *fpl* **de programación automática** APT; automatically programmed tools

herramientas *fpl* **de diagnóstico de errores** *sustantivo* error diagnostics

herramientas *fpl* **de diagnóstico del compilador** *plural noun* compiler diagnostics ◇ **un detallado diagnóstico mediante el compilador facilita el proceso de corrección de errores** thorough compiler diagnostics make debugging easy

herramientas *fpl* **de programación** *sustantivo* tools

hertz *m sustantivo* hertz

heurístico *adj* heuristic ◇ **un programa heurístico aprende de sus acciones y decisiones previas** a heuristic program learns from its previous actions and decisions

Hewlett Packard™ Hewlett Packard ◇ **bus** Hewlett Packard Interface Bus (HPIB) ◇ **enlace de interfaz HP** Hewlett Packard Interface Bus (HPIB) ◇ **lenguaje de control de la impresora HP** *o* **lenguaje HP-PCL** Hewlett Packard Printer Control Language (HP-PCL)

hidruro *m* **metálico de níquel** *sustantivo* **1.** nickel metal hydride **2.** NiMH

hi-fi *sustantivo* high fidelity

hilo *m sustantivo* **1.** thread **2.** wire

hilo *m* **conductor** *sustantivo* lead

hilo *m* **de carga estática** *sustantivo* corona wire ◇ **si la impresión sale borrosa, quizá deba limpiar el hilo de carga estática** if your printouts are smudged, you may have to clean the corona wire

hiperdocumento ◇ **hiperdocumento** *m* **(con imágenes y sonido)** hypermedia

hiperenlace *m sustantivo* hyperlink

hiperterminal *m sustantivo* HyperTerminal

hipertexto *m sustantivo* hypertext ◇ **en esta página de hipertexto, pulse una vez sobre la palabra 'ordenador' y le explicará qué es un ordenador** in this hypertext page, click once on the word 'computer' and it will tell you what a computer is ◇ **protocolo de transferencia de hipertexto** hypertext transfer protocol (HTTP)

hipervínculo *m sustantivo* hyperlink

histograma *m sustantivo* **1.** bar chart **2.** columnar graph **3.** histogram

historial *m sustantivo* (*de páginas consultadas en Internet*) history

hoja *f sustantivo* form ◇ **hoja** *f* **de codificación de un programa** program coding sheet

hoja *f sustantivo* **1.** leaf **2.** sheet

hoja *f* **de cálculo** *sustantivo* spreadsheet

hoja *f* **de codificación** *sustantivo* coding sheet

hoja *f* **de estilo** *sustantivo* style sheet

hoja *f* **de estilo en cascada** *sustantivo* cascading style sheet

hoja *f* **de programación** *sustantivo* coding sheet

hoja *f* **de trabajo** *sustantivo* worksheet

holograma *m sustantivo* **1.** hologram **2.** holographic image

hora *f* **de entrada** *sustantivo* entry time

hora(s) *f(pl)* **de máximo consumo** *sustantivo* peak period

horario *m sustantivo* schedule

horario *m* **de verano** *sustantivo* daylight saving time

horizontal *f sustantivo* x direction

hormado *m sustantivo* contouring

HP *abrev* HP

HTML *sustantivo* **1.** HTML **2.** hypertext markup language

HTTP *sustantivo* **1.** HTTP **2.** hypertext transfer protocol

huella ◇ **huella** *f* **(de un haz luminoso, etc.)** footprint

huésped *m&f sustantivo, adj* host

HyperCard™ HyperCard

HyperTalk™ HyperTalk

I

IBM (*gran empresa productora de procesadores*) IBM

IBM compatible *adj* IBM-compatible

IBM PS/2 (*marca comercial*) IBM PS/2 *o* IBM Personal System/2

IBM-XT (*marca comercial*) IBM XT

icono *sustantivo* **1.** icon *o* ikon **2.** ikon ◇ **el icono del programa de gráficos tiene la forma de paleta de pintor** the icon for the graphics program is a small picture of a palette ◇ **haga clic dos veces sobre el icono del tratamiento de textos-el dibujo de una máquina de escribir** click twice over the wordprocessor icon – the picture of the typewriter

> 'En la película Tienes un e-mail, cada vez que los protagonistas se conectan aparece un icono que reproduce un buzón del que sobresale una carta y, además, el programa genera el mensaje audible 'tienes un e-mail'.' [*Ciberpragmática*]

icono *m* **de aplicaciones** *sustantivo* application icon

icono *m* **de fuentes de caracteres** *sustantivo* suitcase

icono *m* **de grupo** *sustantivo* group icon

icono *m* **de programa** *sustantivo* **1.** program icon **2.** program item

icono *m* **de radio** *sustantivo* radio button

iconos *sustantivo* group ◇ **iconos** *mpl* **del escritorio (de Windows)** desktop icons ◇ **todos los iconos de este grupo están relacionados con la pintura** all the icons in this group are to do with painting

idear *verbo vt* to devise

identificación *abrev* ID ■ *sustantivo* **1.** identification **2.** signature ◇ **análisis seguro de firmas mediante un análisis funcional** *o* **técnica de identificación SAFE** safe signature analysis using functional analysis (SAFE) ◇ **identificación** *f* **automática de los números (de teléfono)** ANI; automatic number identification

identificación *f* **de ficheros** *sustantivo* file identification

identificación *f* **de llamadas** *sustantivo* call discrimination

identificación *f* **de usuario** *sustantivo* user ID ◇ **si se olvida de su código personal, no podrá conectarse** if you forget your user ID, you will not be able to logon

identificador *m abrev* ID ■ *sustantivo* **1.** identifier **2.** identifier word **3.** label **4.** tag

identificador *m* **único** *sustantivo* unique identifier

identificar *verbo vt* to locate ◇ **el ordenador se encuentra en el edificio de la oficina principal** the computer is located in the main office building

idioma *m sustantivo* language ◇ **habla varios idiomas europeos** he speaks several European languages ◇ **lengua extranjera** *o* **idioma extranjero** foreign language

igual *m sustantivo* peer

igualar *verbo vt* to match

igualdad *f sustantivo* **1.** equality **2.** parity

ilegal *adj* illegal

ilustración *f sustantivo* picture

ilustraciones *fpl sustantivo* artwork ■ *plural noun* pix

imagen *sustantivo* image ◇ **distorsión de la imagen** image distortion ◇ **intensificador de (la) imagen** image enhancer ◇ **plano focal** *o* **de imagen** image plane ◇ **portadora de imagen** *o* **de señal de vídeo** image carrier

> 'La multinacional finlandesa Nokia presentó la pasada semana durante la Nokia Mobile Internet Conference celebrada en Barcelona, varios de sus nuevos modelos que permiten incluir imagen y sonido en los mensajes cortos.' [*Ciberp@ís*]

imagen *f* **binaria** *sustantivo* bit image

imagen *f* **borrosa** *sustantivo* blur

imagen *f* **completa** *sustantivo* frame

imagen *f* **copia** *sustantivo* after-image

imagen *f* **de arrastre** *sustantivo* **1.** drag image **2.** no-drop image

imagen *f* **de fondo** *sustantivo* background image

imagen *f* **de primera generación** *sustantivo* first generation image

imagen *f* **de salida** *sustantivo* after-image

imagen *f* **de segundo plano** *sustantivo* background image

imagen *f* **de sistema único** *sustantivo* single-system image

imágenes *fpl plural noun* pix ■ *sustantivo* scrapbook

imágenes *fpl* **de biblioteca** *sustantivo* clipart

imagen *f* **fantasma** *sustantivo* ghost

imagen *f* **fuera de campo** *sustantivo* off-screen image

imagen *f* **fuera de pantalla** *sustantivo* off-screen image

imagen *f* **original** *sustantivo* first generation image

imagen *f* **virtual** *sustantivo* virtual image

imaginar *verbo vt* to picture

imán *m sustantivo* magnet

imantado *adj* magnetic

impedancia *f sustantivo* impedance ◇ **adaptación de impedancia** impedance matching ◇ **desacoplo de impedancia** impedance mismatch ◇ **igualación de impedancia** impedance matching ◇ **la adaptación de impedancia entre un transmisor y un receptor minimiza las pérdidas de potencia de las señales transmitidas** impedance matching between a transmitter and a receiver minimizes power losses to transmitted signals

impedir *verbo vt* to inhibit

implicación *f sustantivo* implication

importante *adj* significant

importar *verbo vt* to import ◇ **puede importar imágenes procedentes de un paquete de CAD en el programa de edición DTP** you can import images from the CAD package into the DTP program ◇ **señal importada** imported signal

impregnar con tinta *verbo* to ink

impresión *sustantivo* 1. printing 2. run ◇ **impresión** *f* **de un programa de montaje** assembly listing ◇ **la próxima impresión de facturas será el viernes** the next invoice run will be on Friday

impresión *f* **de baja calidad** *sustantivo* draft printing

impresión *f* **de calidad de borrador** *sustantivo* draft printing

impresión *f* **de etiquetas** *sustantivo* labelling ◇ **el tratamiento de textos tiene una utilidad especial que permite una simple y rápida impresión de etiquetas** the word-processor has a special utility allowing simple and rapid labelling

impresión *f* **de fondo** *sustantivo* background printing ◇ **se puede ejecutar una impresión de segundo plano mientras corriges otro documento** background printing can be carried out whilst you are editing another document

impresión *f* **del contenido de una memoria)** *sustantivo* deposit

impresión *f* **de ordenador** *sustantivo* computer printout

impresión *f* **de pantalla** *sustantivo* hard copy

impresión *f* **diferida** *sustantivo* deferred printing

impresión *f* **electrosensible** *sustantivo* electrosensitive printing

impresión *f* **en cola** *sustantivo* background printing ◇ **se puede ejecutar una impresión de segundo plano mientras corriges otro documento** background printing can be carried out whilst you are editing another document

impresiones *fpl* **de páginas** *sustantivo* page impression

impresión *f* **fuera de red** *sustantivo* off-line printing

impresión *f* **subordinada** *sustantivo* background printing ◇ **se puede ejecutar una impresión de segundo plano mientras corriges otro documento** background printing can be carried out whilst you are editing another document

impresión *f* **térmica** *sustantivo* electrosensitive printing

impreso *m sustantivo* form ◇ **ha sido fácil preparar a los operadores en la utilización del nuevo programa ya que su presentación en pantalla se parece a los impresos existentes** it's been easy to train the operators to use the new software since its display looks like the existing printed forms

impresor, -a *sustantivo* printer

'Uno de los elementos más importantes de todo entorno informático es, sin duda, la impresora. Desde las matriciales, reservadas a grandes trabajos, hasta las más sofisticadas en color de impresión láser o inyección de tinta, todos necesitamos una. Instalarla y saber solucionar problemas es importante.' [*Ciberp@ís*]

impresora *sustantivo* printer ◇ **impresora** *f* **(en el MS-DOS)** PRN ◇ **impresora** *f* **con definición de tonos negros** black writer ◇ **impresora** *f* **de chorro de tinta térmica** thermal inkjet printer

impresora *f* **(para ordenador)** *sustantivo* computer printer

impresora *f* **activa** *sustantivo* active printer

impresora *f* **bidireccional** *sustantivo* bi-directional printer

impresora *f* **carácter por carácter** *sustantivo* character printer ◇ **la impresora de margarita imprime carácter por carácter** a daisy-wheel printer is a character printer

impresora *f* **compartida** *sustantivo* network printer

impresora *f* **con sublimación térmica** *sustantivo* dye-sublimation printer ◇ **la nueva impresora con sublimación térmica puede producir imágenes con una resolución de 300 puntos por pulgada** the new dye-sublimation printer can produce colour images at a resolution of 300dpi

impresora *f* **de agujas** *sustantivo* stylus printer

impresora *f* **de cadena** *sustantivo* chain printer

impresora *f* **de caracteres plenos** *sustantivo* solid font printer

impresora *f* **de chorro de tinta** *sustantivo* 1. bubble jet printer 2. ink-jet printer

impresora *f* **de color** *sustantivo* colour printer

impresora *f* **de dedal** *sustantivo* thimble printer

impresora *f* **de escritura en blanco** *sustantivo* white writer

impresora *f* **de escritura en negro** *sustantivo* write black printer

impresora *f* **de etiquetas** *sustantivo* label printer

impresora *f* **de matriz por puntos** *sustantivo* dot-matrix printer

impresora *f* **de ordenador** *sustantivo* computer printer

impresora *f* **de red** *sustantivo* network printer

impresora *f* **de sobres** *sustantivo* envelope printer

impresora *f* **de transferencia LCD** *sustantivo* crystal shutter printer

impresora *f* **electrostática** *sustantivo* **1.** electrographic printer **2.** electrostatic printer

impresora *f* **electrotérmica** *sustantivo* electrothermal printer

impresora *f* **en cadena** *sustantivo* chain printer

impresora *f* **en paralelo** *sustantivo* parallel printer

impresora *f* **en serie** *sustantivo* serial printer

impresora *f* **gráfica** *sustantivo* **1.** graphics printer **2.** printer-plotter

impresora *f* **gráfica HP Laserjet** (*marca comercial*) Hewlett Packard LaserJet

impresora *f* **láser** *sustantivo* laser printer

impresora *f* **LaserJet de Hewlett Packard™** LaserJet

impresora *f* **LaserWriter de Apple™** LaserWriter

impresora *f* **LED** *sustantivo* LED printer

impresora *f* **local** *sustantivo* local printer

impresora *f* **matricial** *sustantivo* **1.** dot-matrix printer **2.** matrix printer **3.** stylus printer **4.** wire printer

impresora *f* **no compartida** *sustantivo* local printer

impresora *f* **por defecto** *sustantivo* default printer

impresora *f* **por diodos** *sustantivo* LED printer

impresora *f* **por líneas** *sustantivo* line printer

impresora *f* **por páginas** *sustantivo* page printer ◊ **esta impresora matricial no es una impresora de página por página** this dot-matrix printer is not a page printer, it only prints one line at a time

impresora *f* **por puntos** *sustantivo* dot-matrix printer

impresora *f* **por transmisión LCD** *sustantivo* **1.** LCD shutter printer **2.** liquid crystal display shutter printer

impresora *f* **sin impacto** *sustantivo* non impact printer

impresora *f* **térmica** *sustantivo* **1.** spark printer **2.** thermal printer

impresora *f* **xerográfica** *sustantivo* xerographic printer

imprimir *verbo vt* to print ◊ **documento impreso** *o* **escrito** printed document ◊ **el texto puede continuar en la línea siguiente sin dejar espacios** the line can run on to the next without any space ◊ **esta impresora imprime 60 caracteres por segundo** the printer prints at 60 characters per second ◊ **imprimir la cola de impresión** despool ◊ **imprimir más copias** to run on

impulso *sustantivo* **1.** impulse **2.** pulse ◊ **generador de impulsos** pulse generator ◊ **impulso** *m* **de validez de la dirección** address strobe ◊ **modulación de amplitud de impulsos** *o* **de impulsos en amplitud** pulse amplitude modulation (PAM) ◊ **modulación de duración de impulsos** pulse width modulation (PWM) ◊ **modulación de impulsos** pulse modulation ◊ **modulación por** *o* **de duración de impulsos** pulse duration modulation (PDM) ◊ **modulación por posición de impulsos** *o* **por impulsos de posición variable** pulse position modulation (PPM)

'El microchip, que se implanta en la base de la espina dorsal de los pacientes, actúa como un generador de impulsos controlado por un ordenador.' [*Ciberp@ís*]

impulso *m* **de reloj** *sustantivo* clock pulse

impulso *m* **eléctrico** *sustantivo* strobe

impulso *m* **electrónico** *sustantivo* electronic pulse

impulsos *mpl* **de sincronización** *plural noun* **1.** synchronisation pulses **2.** sync pulses

incidente *m sustantivo* fault

inclinación *f sustantivo* skew

inclusión *f sustantivo* inclusion

incompatibilidad *f sustantivo* noncompatibility

incompatible *adj* incompatible ◊ **intentaron conectar los dos sistemas, pero se encontraron con que eran incompatibles** they tried to link the two systems, but found they were incompatible

incondicional *adj* unconditional ◊ **transferencia automática** *o* **incondicional** unconditional transfer

incorporado *adj* **1.** built-in **2.** inbuilt ◊ **este software tiene incorporado un sistema de corrección de errores** this software has inbuilt error correction

incorporado *m* **al circuito** *sustantivo* in-circuit emulator ◊ **este emulador incorporado al circuito actúa como emulador de una disquetera para comprobar el funcionamiento del controlador de disquetes** this in-circuit emulator is used to test the floppy disk controller by emulating a disk drive

incorporar *verbo vt* to piggyback

incorrecto *adj* false

incorrupto *adj* uncorrupted

incrementar *verbo vt* to increment ◊ **el contador se incrementa cada vez que se ejecuta**

una instrucción the counter is incremented each time an instruction is executed

incremento *m sustantivo* increment ◇ **aumente el incremento a tres** increase the increment to three ◇ **cada vez que se detecta un impulso se añade un incremento al contador** an increment is added to the counter each time a pulse is detected

incumplimiento *m sustantivo* breach

Indeo 1. Indeo **2.** (*marca comercial*) Intel Indeo

independencia ◇ **independencia** *f* **del entorno (de trabajo)** platform independence

independencia *f* **de datos** *sustantivo* data independence

independencia *f* **de plataforma** *sustantivo* platform independence

independiente *adj* device-independent ■ *adv*, *adj* off-line ■ *adj* stand-alone *o* standalone ◇ **los terminales de trabajo han sido interconectados en lugar de dejarlos como sistemas independientes** the workstations have been networked together rather than used as stand-alone systems

independiente del constructor *adj* vendor-independent

indexación *f sustantivo* **1.** index build **2.** indexing

indexación *f* **asistida por ordenador** *sustantivo* computer indexing

indexación *f* **informática** *sustantivo* computer indexing

indexar *verbo vt* to index

index.html *sustantivo* index.html

indicación *f sustantivo* **1.** prompt **2.** tracing

indicación *f* **de instrucción** *sustantivo* command prompt

indicación *f* **del sistema** *sustantivo* system prompt

indicador *sustantivo* **1.** flag **2.** indicator **3.** indicator flag **4.** marker **5.** pointer **6.** sentinel ◇ **aumente los contenidos del indicador hasta la dirección de la siguiente instrucción** increment the contents of the pointer to the address of the next instruction ◇ **indicador** *m* **(binario) de cero** zero flag ◇ **indicador** *m* **de desbordamiento (de la capacidad)** overflow bit; overflow flag ◇ **indicador** *m* **del principio de la cinta** beginning of tape marker ◇ **indicador** *m* **del principio de la información** beginning of information mark; BIM ◇ **indicador** *m* **(luminoso) de marcha** run indicator ◇ **indicador** *m* **(de control) de paridad** parity flag ◇ **indicador** *m* **(en forma de) flecha** arrow pointer ◇ **la instrucción de bifurcación condicional de cero verifica el indicador de cero** the jump on zero instruction tests the zero flag ◇ **si el resultado es cero se activa el indicador cero** if the result is zero, the zero flag is set ◇ **testigo** *o* **indicador de retención** *o* **de arrastre** carry flag

indicador *m* **binario** *sustantivo* flag bit

indicador *m* **de archivos** *sustantivo* archive flag

indicador *m* **de arrastre** *sustantivo* carry flag

indicador *m* **de bit** *sustantivo* flag bit

indicador *m* **de cero** *sustantivo* zero flag

indicador *m* **de columna** *sustantivo* (*de un tratamiento de textos*) column indicator

indicador *m* **de control** *sustantivo* **1.** check indicator **2.** rogue indicator

indicador *m* **de datos** *sustantivo* data pointer

indicador *m* **de estado** *sustantivo* sense switch

indicador *m* **de final de papel** *sustantivo* form stop

indicador *m* **de función** *sustantivo* role indicator

indicador *m* **de funcionamiento** *sustantivo* **1.** device flag **2.** run indicator

indicador *m* **del DOS** *sustantivo* DOS prompt

indicador *m* **del sistema** *sustantivo* system prompt

indicador *m* **del trazador** *sustantivo* plotter driver

indicador *m* **de punto** *sustantivo* dot prompt

indicador *m* **de registro** *sustantivo* recording indicator

indicador *m* **de retención** *sustantivo* carry flag

indicador *m* **de retorno** *sustantivo* back pointer

indicador *m* **hacia adelante** *sustantivo* forward pointer

indicador *m* **luminoso** *sustantivo* activity light

indicador *m* **relativo** *sustantivo* relative pointing device

indicador *m* **sonoro** *sustantivo* howler

indicador *m* **visual** *sustantivo* display

indicar *verbo* **1.** *vt* to flag **2.** *vt* to mark

indicativo *m* **de búsqueda** *sustantivo* search key

índice *sustantivo* **1.** index **2.** rate ◇ **índice** *m* **de movimiento de un fichero** file activity ratio

índice *m* **completo** *sustantivo* dense index

índice *m* **de actividad** *sustantivo* file activity ratio

índice *m* **de ciclo** *sustantivo* cycle index

índice *m* **de comprobación al azar** *sustantivo* hash index

índice *m* **de error residual** *sustantivo* residual error rate

índice *m* **de fallos** *sustantivo* failure rate

índice *m* **de ficheros** *sustantivo* file index

índice *m* **de materias** *sustantivo* table of contents

índice *m* **de renovación** *sustantivo* refresh rate

índice *m* **de repetición** *sustantivo* repeat rate

índice *m* **general** *sustantivo* main index

índice *m* **inverso** *sustantivo* reverse index

índice *m* **principal** *sustantivo* main index

indicio *m* **de un fallo** *sustantivo* fault trace

inducción *f sustantivo* induction ◇ **bobina de inducción** induction coil

inducir *verbo vt* to induce

inductancia *f sustantivo* inductance

inductor *m sustantivo* inductor

inestabilidad *f sustantivo* jitter

infectar *verbo vt* to infect

inferencia *f sustantivo* inference

infinito *m sustantivo* infinity

infografía *f plural noun* computer graphics

infografía *f* **interactiva** *plural noun* interactive graphics

información *f sustantivo* **1.** data **2.** information ◇ **arquitecto, -a de la información** information architect ◇ **equipo de comunicación de datos o de información** data communications equipment (DCE) ◇ **la empresa almacena la información sobre los clientes en su ordenador central** the company stores data on customers in its main computer file

información *f* **de uso** *sustantivo* operational information

información *f* **no válida** *sustantivo* garbage

información *f* **operacional** *sustantivo* operational information

información *f* **para el usuario** *sustantivo* user documentation ◇ **la excelente información proporcionada al usuario facilitó la utilización del programa** using the package was easy with the excellent user documentation

información *f* **parásita** *sustantivo* drop in

informática *f sustantivo* computer science ■ *adj, sustantivo* computing ■ *sustantivo* informatics ■ *abrev* IT

informática *f sustantivo* **1.** computing **2.** information technology

informática *f* **defensiva** *sustantivo* defensive computing

informático *adj, sustantivo* computing

informatización *f sustantivo* computerisation *o* computerization ◇ **la informatización del sector financiero se está produciendo muy rápidamente** computerization of the financial sector is proceeding very fast

informatizar *verbo vt* to computerise *o* to computerize ◇ **funcionan con un sistema informatizado de facturación** they operate a computerized invoicing system ◇ **nuestra gestión de existencias ha sido totalmente informatizada** our stock control has been completely computerized

informe *m* **en columnas** *sustantivo* column report

infraestructura *f sustantivo* infrastructure

infrarrojo *sustantivo* infrared

ingeniería *f* **asistida por ordenador** *sustantivo* **1.** CAE **2.** computer-aided engineering **3.** computer-assisted engineering

ingeniería *f* **del conocimiento** *sustantivo* knowledge engineering

ingeniería *f* **de software** *sustantivo* software engineering

ingeniería *f* **inversa** *sustantivo* reverse engineering

ingeniero ◇ **ingeniero** *m* **de mantenimiento (en el lugar)** field engineer ◇ **instituto** *m* **de ingenieros eléctricos y electrónicos** IEEE

ingeniero *m* **de campo post venta** *sustantivo* field engineer

ingeniero *m* **de empresa** *sustantivo* resident engineer

ingeniero *m* **de productos** *sustantivo* product engineer

ingeniero *m* **de software** *sustantivo* software engineer

ingeniero *m* **informático** *sustantivo* computer engineer

inhibición *f* **de la transmisión** *sustantivo* inhibiting input

inhibición *f* **de una señal** *sustantivo* blanking

inhibir *verbo vt* to inhibit

iniciación *sustantivo* **1.** booting **2.** boot up ◇ **iniciación** *f* **automática (de un sistema)** autoboot

inicial *adj* low-end

inicialización *f sustantivo* initialisation *o* initialization

inicializar *verbo* **1.** *vt* to boot **2.** *vt* to initialise *o* to initialize **3.** *vt* to set up

iniciar *verbo vt* to launch ◇ **que puede iniciarse** bootable ◇ **se inicia el tratamiento de textos al pulsar dos veces sobre este icono** you launch the word-processor by double-clicking on this icon

inicio *m sustantivo* start

inicio *m* **automático** *sustantivo* auto start

inicio *m* **de banda** *sustantivo* tape header

inicio *m* **de la pantalla** *sustantivo* cursor home

inicio *m* **de sesión** *sustantivo* **1.** logging in **2.** logging on ■ *verbo* to logon

injustificado *adj* unjustified

inmovilizado *adj* quiescent

inmunidad *f sustantivo* noise immunity

inscribir *verbo vt* to record

inscripción *f* **de datos** *sustantivo* data logging

inscripción *f* **de información** *sustantivo* data logging

insensibilidad *f* **del ratón** *sustantivo* mouse tracking

inserción ◇ **inserción** *f* **de caracteres (en memoria)** character fill

inserción *f* **de bits** *sustantivo* bit stuffing

inserción *f* **de caracteres de relleno** *sustantivo* character stuffing

inserción f **de caracteres en blanco** *sustantivo* character stuffing

inserción f **de espacios** *sustantivo* quadding

inserción f **de un bloque** *sustantivo* block transfer

insertar *verbo* 1. *vt* to mount 2. *vt* to paste

insertar en una ranura *verbo* to slot ◇ **el disquete se inserta en la ranura de una de las disqueteras** the disk slots into one of the floppy drive apertures

instalación f *sustantivo* installation ◇ **la instalación del equipo sólo llevó unas pocas horas** the installation of the equipment took only a few hours

instalación f **de un nuevo hardware** *sustantivo* rightsizing

instalación f **eléctrica** *sustantivo* wiring

instalación f **informática** *sustantivo* installation

instalación f **simplificada** *sustantivo* abbreviated installation

instalar *verbo* 1. *vt* to install 2. *vt* to mount 3. *vt* to set up ◇ **el sistema es fácil de instalar y sencillo de utilizar** the system is easy to install and simple to use ◇ **instalar una toma de tierra** earth ◇ **los chips se instalan en enchufes sobre la placa del circuito impreso** the chips are mounted in sockets on the PCB ◇ **todos los aparatos eléctricos deben tener toma de tierra** all appliances must be earthed

instituto ◇ **instituto** *m* **nacional americano de estándares** American National Standards Institute

instituto *m* **de ingenieros eléctricos** *abrev* IEE

instrucción f *sustantivo* 1. assignment statement 2. command 3. instruction 4. keyword 5. operation decoder 6. order 7. statement ◇ **escriba la instrucción DIR para obtener la lista de ficheros** type the command 'DIR' to get the list of files ◇ **instrucción** f **(de un programa)** program instruction ◇ **instrucción** f **de ejecución (de un programa)** Run command ◇ **instrucción** f **de entrada en la pila** non-synchronous sound ◇ **instrucción** f **de estabilización de la señal** hold ◇ **instrucción** f **de formato (de párrafo, etc.)** template command ◇ **instrucción de interrupción (de un programa)** interrupt command ◇ **instrucción** f **de n (direcciones) más una** n-plus-one address instruction; n-plus-one instruction ◇ **instrucción de salto** jump instruction ◇ **instrucción** f **de supresión de una interrupción** disable interrupt ◇ **instrucción** f **de vuelta a la situación inicial** revert command ◇ **instrucción e no hacer nada** o **instrucción en efecto** do-nothing instruction ◇ **instrucción** f **IF-THEN-ELSE (si, en otro caso si, si no)** IF-THEN-ELSE ◇ **instrucción nula** o **ficticia** o **simulada** dummy instruction ◇ **instrucción** f **para dar formato a los datos de salida** output formatter ◇ **instrucción** f **para ejecutar una función de formateado** formatter ◇ **instrucción** f **PEEK (de lectura directa de la memoria)** peek ◇ **instrucción** f **(precedida de un) punto** dot command ◇ **la instrucción PRINT se utiliza en este dialecto de BASIC como un operando para mostrar los siguientes datos** the instruction PRINT is used in this BASIC dialect as an operand to display the following data ◇ **los fabricantes de esta unidad central de proceso decidieron que JMP será la palabra de instrucción para llamar la función de salto** the manufacturers of this CPU have decided that JMP will be the instruction word to call the jump function ◇ **macro-instrucción** macro instruction ◇ **RUN es la instrucción de ejecución de un programa** the command to execute the program is RUN ◇ **se necesita la instrucción PEEK 1452 para examinar los contenidos en el lugar 1452 de la memoria** you need the instruction PEEK 1452 here to examine the contents of memory location 1452 ◇ **utilice la instrucción DIR para ver los ficheros en el disco** use the command 'DIR' to view the files on disk, add the command line argument 'A:' to view the files on drive A:

instrucción f *sustantivo* statement

instrucción f **absoluta** *sustantivo* 1. absolute instruction 2. actual instruction

instrucción f **aritmética** *sustantivo* arithmetic instruction

instrucción f **asistida por ordenador** *sustantivo* 1. CAI 2. computer-aided instruction 3. computer-aided training 4. computer-assisted instruction 5. computer-based training

instrucción f **básica** *sustantivo* basic instruction

instrucción f **'buscar'** *sustantivo* get

instrucción f **compuesta** *sustantivo* compound statement ◇ **el depurador de errores no puede gestionar instrucciones compuestas** the debugger cannot handle compound statements

instrucción f **condicional** *sustantivo* 1. conditional statement 2. decision instruction

instrucción f **condicional de bifurcación** *sustantivo* conditional transfer

instrucción f **de aceleración** *sustantivo* accelerator key ◇ **en vez de seleccionar el menú Archivo y a continuación la opción Guardar, utilice la instrucción de aceleración Alt-G para guardar el fichero** instead of selecting the File menu then the Save option, use the accelerator keys Alt and S to do the same thing and save the file

instrucción f **de asignación** *sustantivo* allocation routine

instrucción f **de base** *sustantivo* 1. presumptive instruction 2. reference instruction

instrucción f **de bifurcación** *sustantivo* 1. branch instruction 2. control 3. control statement 4. transfer command

instrucción f **de bifurcación condicional** *sustantivo* case

instrucción f **de borrar** *sustantivo* DEL ◇ **para borrar todos los ficheros con la extensión BAK, utilice la instrucción DEL** o **.BAK**

to delete all files with the extension BAK, use the command DEL *o* .BAK ◇ **para eliminar una palabra de la pantalla, apriete la tecla DEL de forma repetida** to remove a word from the screen, press the DEL key repeatedly

instrucción *f* **de canal** *sustantivo* channel command

instrucción *f* **de captura** *sustantivo* fetch instruction

instrucción *f* **declarativa** *sustantivo* narrative statement

instrucción *f* **de control** *sustantivo* **1.** control instruction **2.** control statement **3.** supervisory instruction ◇ **la próxima intrucción de control cambiará a letra cursiva** the next control instruction will switch to italics

instrucción *f* **de conversión** *sustantivo* conversion program

instrucción *f* **de cuatro direcciones** *sustantivo* four-address instruction

instrucción *f* **de decisión** *sustantivo* decision instruction

instrucción *f* **de desplazamiento** *sustantivo* shift instruction

instrucción *f* **de desplazamiento del acumulador** *sustantivo* accumulator shift instruction

instrucción *f* **de dirección única** *sustantivo* **1.** one-address instruction **2.** single address instruction

instrucción *f* **de dos direcciones** *sustantivo* two-address instruction

instrucción *f* **de edición** *plural noun* edit command ■ *sustantivo* editing term

instrucción *f* **de ejecución** *sustantivo* execute statement

instrucción *f* **de ensamblaje** *sustantivo* pseudo-operation

instrucción *f* **de entrada** *sustantivo* **1.** entry instruction **2.** input statement

instrucción *f* **de entrada/salida** *sustantivo* **1.** input/output instruction **2.** I/O instruction

instrucción *f* **de espacios en blanco** *sustantivo* blank instruction

instrucción *f* **de extracción** *sustantivo* extract instruction

instrucción *f* **de interrupción** *sustantivo* **1.** breakpoint halt **2.** breakpoint instruction

instrucción *f* **de línea** *sustantivo* line control

instrucción *f* **de llamada** *sustantivo* call instruction ◇ **la subrutina de instrucción de llamada debería encontrarse en este punto** the subroutine call instruction should be at this point

instrucción *f* **de macro** *sustantivo* macro command

instrucción *f* **de multidirección** *sustantivo* multi-address *o* multi-address instruction

instrucción *f* **de no hacer nada** *sustantivo* do-nothing instruction

instrucción *f* **de parada** *sustantivo* **1.** breakpoint halt **2.** breakpoint instruction **3.** halt instruction **4.** stop instruction

instrucción *f* **de programa** *sustantivo* program statement

instrucción *f* **de referencia** *sustantivo* reference instruction

instrucción *f* **de relleno** *sustantivo* **1.** blank instruction **2.** non operable instruction **3.** no-op instruction *o* no op **4.** null instruction **5.** pseudo-instruction **6.** waste instruction

instrucción *f* **de salto** *sustantivo* **1.** branch instruction **2.** jump instruction **3.** skip instruction

instrucción *f* **de salto condicional** *sustantivo* discrimination instruction

instrucción *f* **de supervisión** *sustantivo* **1.** executive instruction **2.** supervisory instruction

instrucción *f* **de transferencia** *sustantivo* transfer command

instrucción *f* **de tres direcciones** *sustantivo* three-address instruction

instrucción *f* **de una sola dirección** *sustantivo* single address instruction

instrucción *f* **de un solo operando** *sustantivo* single operand instruction

instrucción *f* **directa** *sustantivo* direct instruction

instrucción *f* **directiva** *sustantivo* directive statement

instrucción *f* **efectiva** *sustantivo* effective instruction

instrucción *f* **ejecutiva** *sustantivo* executive instruction

instrucción *f* **eliminar** *sustantivo* DEL

instrucción *f* **en código** *sustantivo* machine code format

instrucción *f* **en código máquina** *sustantivo* machine code instruction

instrucción *f* **en lenguaje máquina** *sustantivo* **1.** machine code format **2.** machine instruction

instrucción *f* **en su forma inicial** *sustantivo* unmodified instruction

instrucción *f* **Enviar A** *sustantivo* Send To command

instrucciones ◇ **(procesador de) corriente** *f* **de instrucciones múltiples – corriente de un solo dato** MISD ◇ **instrucciones** *fpl* **de control de la impresora** PCL; printer control language

instrucciones *fpl* **de acceso** *plural noun* access method routines

instrucciones *fpl* **de base** *sustantivo* primitive

instrucciones *fpl* **de línea** *sustantivo* line control

instrucciones *fpl* **de trabajo** *plural noun* operating instructions

instrucciones *fpl* **iniciales** *plural noun* initial instructions

instrucciones *fpl* **prioritarias** *plural noun* privileged instructions

instrucción *f* **falsa** *sustantivo* dummy instruction

instrucción *f* **ficticia** *sustantivo* dummy instruction

instrucción *f* **'GET'** *sustantivo* get

instrucción *f* **IF (si)** *sustantivo* IF statement

instrucción *f* **indexada** *sustantivo* indexed instruction

instrucción *f* **inmediata** *sustantivo* immediate instruction

instrucción *f* **intercalada** *sustantivo* embedded command

instrucción *f* **interna** *sustantivo* internal command ◊ **en MS-DOS, la instrucción interna DIR se emplea con frecuencia** in MS-DOS, the internal command DIR is used frequently

instrucción LOAD HIGH *verbo* to load high

instrucción *f* **MD** *sustantivo* **1.** make directory **2.** MD ■ *abrev* MKDIR

instrucción *f* **narrativa** *sustantivo* narrative statement

instrucción *f* **no modificada** *sustantivo* unmodified instruction

instrucción *f* **no válida** *sustantivo* illegal instruction

instrucción *f* **nula** *sustantivo* **1.** dummy instruction **2.** non operable instruction **3.** no-op instruction *o* no op **4.** null instruction

instrucción *f* **para formatear** *sustantivo* formatter

instrucción *f* **para formato de impresión** *sustantivo* print formatter

instrucción *f* **para formato de texto** *sustantivo* text formatter

instrucción *f* **prohibida** *sustantivo* illegal instruction

instrucción *f* **simulada** *sustantivo* **1.** dummy instruction **2.** non operable instruction **3.** no-op instruction *o* no op

instrucción *f* **sin efecto** *sustantivo* do-nothing instruction

instrucción *f* **supuesta** *sustantivo* presumptive instruction

instrumento *m* *sustantivo* instrument

insultar (por la red) *verbo* to flame

integración *f* *sustantivo* integration ◊ **integración a gran escala** large scale integration (LSI) ◊ **integración a media escala** medium scale integration (MSI) ◊ **integración a muy gran escala** very large scale integration (VLSI) ◊ **integración a super gran escala** super large scale integration (SLSI)

integración *f* **a escala de oblea** *sustantivo* wafer scale integration

integración *f* **a gran escala** *sustantivo* large-scale integration

integración *f* **a pequeña escala** *sustantivo* small scale integration ■ *abrev* SSI

integración *f* **de sistemas** *sustantivo* systems integration

integración *f* **de telefonía e informática** *sustantivo* **1.** computer-telephony integration **2.** CTI

integración *f* **en lámina de silicio** *sustantivo* wafer scale integration

integración *f* **en láminas** *sustantivo* wafer scale integration

integración *f* **en muy gran escala** *sustantivo* **1.** very large scale integration **2.** VLSI

integración *f* **en super gran escala** *sustantivo* super large scale integration

integración *f* **media** *sustantivo* medium scale integration ■ *abrev* MSI

integración *f* **perfecta** *sustantivo* seamless integration ◊ **fue necesaria una muy detallada planificación, pero conseguimos una integración perfecta de la nueva aplicación** it took a lot of careful planning, but we succeeded in a seamless integration of the new application

integración *f* **sin costura** *sustantivo* seamless integration ◊ **fue necesaria una muy detallada planificación, pero conseguimos una integración perfecta de la nueva aplicación** it took a lot of careful planning, but we succeeded in a seamless integration of the new application

integrado *adj* **1.** built-in **2.** inbuilt **3.** integrated **4.** on-chip ◊ **acceso digital integrado** integrated digital access (IDA) ◊ **circuito óptico integrado** integrated optical circuit ◊ **dispositivo integrado** integrated device ◊ **el ordenador de nuestro competidor no dispone de una disquetera integrada como este modelo** our competitor's computer doesn't have an integrated disk drive like this model ◊ **entorno de apoyo a proyectos integrados** integrated project support environment (IPSE) ◊ **programa integrado** integrated program ◊ **red digital integrada** integrated digital network

integrado, ◊ **integrado, -a en el circuito** onboard

integral *adj* integral

integrar *verbo vt* to merge

integridad *f* *sustantivo* integrity ◊ **integridad de un fichero** integrity of a file ◊ **los datos de este fichero tienen integridad** the data in this file has integrity

integridad *f* **de datos** *sustantivo* data integrity

integridad *f* **de información** *sustantivo* data integrity

Intel™ Intel

Intel 8086 (*marca comercial*) Intel 8086

Intel 8088 (*marca comercial*) Intel 8088

Intel 80286 (*marca comercial*) Intel 80286

Intel 80386 (*marca comercial*) Intel 80386

Intel 80486 (*marca comercial*) Intel 80486

inteligencia *f* *sustantivo* intelligence

inteligencia *f* **artificial** *sustantivo* **1.** AI **2.** artificial intelligence **3.** machine intelligence

inteligencia f **distribuida** *sustantivo* distributed intelligence

inteligente *adj* intelligent

intensidad f *sustantivo* intensity

intensidad f **de color** *sustantivo* colour depth

intensidad f **del tráfico** *sustantivo* traffic intensity

intensificación f **de imágenes** *sustantivo* image enhancement

interactividad *sustantivo* interactivity

'El atractivo de la interactividad visual y del chat priman sobre la línea editorial y los contenidos elaborados.' [*Nueva economía*]

interactivo *adj* interactive ◊ **el juego de los invasores del espacio tiene unos gráficos interactivos excelentes** the space invaders machine has great interactive graphics, the player controls the position of his spaceship with the joystick ◊ **este programa multimedia interactivo permite que el usuario componga música con un programa de sintetizador** this interactive multimedia title allows a user to make music with a synthesizer program

interactuar *verbo vi* to interface

interbloquear *verbo vt* to interlock

interbloqueo m *sustantivo* **1.** deadlock o deadly embrace **2.** interlock

intercalación f **de correo** *sustantivo* mailmerge

intercalación f **de ficheros** *sustantivo* file collating

intercalación f **de sectores** *sustantivo* sector interleave

intercalar hojas *sustantivo* interleave

intercambiable *adj* **1.** exchangeable **2.** removable ◊ **un disco duro intercambiable** a removable hard disk

intercambiar *verbo vt* to exchange

intercambio *sustantivo* swap

'Dentro del comercio entre empresas deben señalarse las ventas que utilizan los protocolos EDI (intercambio electrónico de datos) y la distribución de servicios turísticos y de transporte (SMD: sistemas mundiales de distribución) entre compañías aéreas y agencias de viajes.' [*PC Plus*]

intercambio m **(de programa)** *sustantivo* swapping

intercambio m **comercial internet** *abrev* CIX ■ *sustantivo* commercial Internet exchange

intercambio m **de ficheros Apple™** (*marca comercial*) Apple file exchange

intercambio m **de información** *sustantivo* feedback

intercambio m **de tareas** *sustantivo* task swapping

intercambio m **de una pieza** *sustantivo* part exchange

intercambio m **dinámico de datos** *sustantivo* **1.** DDE **2.** dynamic data exchange

intercambio m **electrónico de datos** *sustantivo* **1.** EDI **2.** electronic data interchange

intercambio m **secuencial de paquetes** *sustantivo* sequential packet exchange

intercomunicación f *sustantivo* interfacing

interconectar *verbo vt* to network ◊ **gestionan un sistema de microordenadores interconectados** they run a system of networked micros ◊ **se han interconectado los terminales en lugar de usarlos como sistemas independientes** the workstations have been networked together rather than used as standalone systems

interconexión *adj* front end ■ *sustantivo* **1.** interconnection **2.** interface ◊ **interconexión** f **de datos distribuidos por fibra óptica** FDDI; fibre distributed data interface ◊ **interconexión** f **de datos distribuidos por fibra óptica II** fibre distributed data interface II ◊ **interconexión** f **de sistemas abiertos (de acuerdo con las normas ISO)** open system interconnection

interconexión f **de redes** *sustantivo* Internetwork

interconexión f **estándar** *sustantivo* standard interface

interconexión f **normalizada** *sustantivo* standard interface

interfase ◊ **interfase de los programas de Microsoft que sirve para conectar los programas con los datos** DAO

interfaz *sustantivo* interface ◊ **interfaz** f **de control de medios (multimedia)** MCI; media control interface ◊ **interfaz** f **de datos distribuidos por fibra óptica** FDDI; fibre distributed data interface ◊ **interfaz** f **de datos distribuidos por fibra óptica II** fibre distributed data interface II ◊ **interfaz** f **de programación de aplicaciones** API; application programming interface ◊ **interfaz** f **de programación de aplicaciones para el correo electrónico** mail application programming interface; MAPI ◊ **interfaz** f **de programación de aplicaciones telefónicas** TAPI; telephony application programming interface ◊ **interfaz** f **de programación de aplicaciones y servicios telefónicos** telephony services application programming interface ◊ **interfaz** f **de rendimiento primario (de la transmisión)** PRI; primary rate interface ◊ **interfaz** f **eléctrica RS-232C entre ordenador y dispositivo periférico** RS-232C ◊ **interfaz en serie** serial interface ◊ **interfaz** f **en serie de alta velocidad** high-speed serial interface ◊ **interfaz** f **gráfica (del usuario)** graphical user interface ◊ **interfaz** f **para microordenadores SCSI (se pronuncia 'escasi')** small computer systems interface ◊ **si sigo la interfaz de programas de la aplicación (API), publicada para este sistema, el programa funcionará adecuadamente** if I follow the published API for this system, my program will work properly

'Los estudios sobre las interfaces del usuario están, por su parte, orientados a devolver la inteligencia a la red -proceso contrario al ideado por Bill Gates cuando decidió depositarla en la terminal del ordenador personal-.' [*La Red*]

interfaz f **(de usuario)** *adj* front end ◊ **el programa es de fácil utilización gracias a la in-**

terfaz poco complicada the program is very easy to use thanks to the uncomplicated front-end

interfaz *f* **Centronics** *sustantivo* Centronics interface

interfaz *f* **común de pasarela** *sustantivo* common gateway interface

interfaz *f* **de acceso común** *sustantivo* CGI

interfaz *f* **de canal de transmisión** *sustantivo* channel adapter

interfaz *f* **de control** *sustantivo* command interface

interfaz *f* **de copia impresa** *sustantivo* hard copy interface

interfaz *f* **de entrada/salida** *sustantivo* input/output interface

interfaz *f* **de fácil utilización** *sustantivo* friendly front end

interfaz *f* **de instrucciones** *sustantivo* command interface

interfaz *f* **de línea de instrucciones** *sustantivo* command line interface

interfaz *f* **de normas EIA** *sustantivo* 1. EIA interface 2. electronics industry association interface

interfaz *f* **de pequeño dispositivo avanzado** *sustantivo* enhanced small device interface

interfaz *f* **de programación de aplicaciones y servicios telefónicos** *abrev* TSAPI

interfaz *f* **de tecnología avanzada** *sustantivo* ATA packet interface

interfaz *f* **de teleimpresora** *sustantivo* teleprinter interface

interfaz *f* **de terminal** *sustantivo* terminal interface ◇ **el controlador de red tiene 16 interfaces para terminales** the network controller has 16 terminal interfaces

interfaz *f* **de transición** *sustantivo* bridging product

interfaz *f* **de usuario** *sustantivo* user interface

interfaz *f* **de velocidad primaria** *sustantivo* 1. basic rate interface 2. BRI

interfaz *f* **EIA** *sustantivo* EIA interface

interfaz *f* **en paralelo** *sustantivo* 1. parallel interface 2. parallel port

interfaz *f* **ESDI** *sustantivo* enhanced small device interface

interfaz *f* **estándar** *sustantivo* standard interface

interfaz *f* **gráfico (del usuario)** *sustantivo* GUI

interfaz *f* **híbrida** *sustantivo* hybrid interface

interfaz *f* **hombre/máquina** *abrev* HMI ■ *sustantivo* 1. human-computer interface 2. human-machine interface 3. man machine interface

interfaz *f* **normalizada RS-232C** *sustantivo* RS-232C

interfaz *f* **para microordenadores** *sustantivo* SCSI

interfaz *f* **SCSI** *sustantivo* 1. SCSI 2. small computer systems interface

interfaz *f* **SCSI-2** *sustantivo* SCSI-2

interfaz *f* **SCSI-ancho** *sustantivo* Wide-SCSI

interfaz *f* **SCSI-rápido** *sustantivo* Fast-SCSI

interfaz *f* **Ultra-2 SCSI** *sustantivo* Ultra-2 SCSI

interfaz *f* **Ultra SCSI** *sustantivo* Ultra SCSI

interfaz *f* **usuario/máquina** *abrev* HMI ■ *sustantivo* 1. human-computer interface 2. human-machine interface 3. man machine interface

interferencia *sustantivo* 1. interference 2. noise 3. static ◇ **interferencia** *f* **(entre canales de comunicación)** crosstalk ◇ **la interferencia era tan fuerte que la señal era ilegible** the crosstalk was so bad, the signal was unreadable

interferencia *f* **causada por las máquinas** *sustantivo* induced interference

interferencia *f* **causada por otra máquina** *sustantivo* induced interference

interferencia *f* **de ficheros** *plural noun* cross-linked files

interferencia *f* **electromagnética** *sustantivo* 1. electromagnetic interference 2. EMI

interferencia *f* **impulsiva** *sustantivo* impulsive noise

interferencia *f* **inducida** *sustantivo* induced interference

interferencias *fpl* *sustantivo* 1. garbage 2. static

interlínea *f* *sustantivo* 1. leading 2. line spacing

interlineado *m* *sustantivo* 1. leading 2. line spacing

interlocutor *sustantivo* called party

intermediario *m* *sustantivo* 1. interface 2. mid-user

intermedio *m* *sustantivo* interlude

intermitencia *f* *sustantivo* blinking

internet *f* *sustantivo* Internet ◇ **corporación de asignación de números y nombres Internet** Internet coorporation for assigned names and numbers (ICANN) ◇ **extensiones** *fpl* **multipropósito de correo Internet** MIME

Internet ◇ **etiqueta** *f* **de Internet** netiquette

'Internet, como un gigantesco Rastro cibernético repleto de tenderetes (webs) en los que se compra, se vende y sobre todo se charla ininterrumpidamente en una conversación icónica, movida por la curiosidad, es la autopista que nos conduce, o mejor, que nos arrastra a la mítica aldea global.' [*Nueva economía*]

interoperabilidad *f* *sustantivo* interoperability

interpaginar *sustantivo* interleave

interpolación *f* *sustantivo* interpolation

interpretador *m* *sustantivo* interpreter

interpretar *verbo* *vt* to interpret

interpretativo *adj* interpretative

intérprete *m* **de instrucciones** *sustantivo* command interpreter

interrogación *f* **de fichero** *sustantivo* file interrogation

interrogar *verbo* 1. *vt* to interrogate 2. *vt* to poll

interrupción *f sustantivo* **1.** abend **2.** break **3.** interrupt **4.** termination **5.** trap ◇ **interrupción** *f* **(de transmisión) de datos** data break ◇ **interrupción** *f* **del servicio (de un aparato)** outage ◇ **interrupción** *f* **(de control) de paridad** parity interrupt ◇ **(señal de) interrupción** *f* **por un error** error interrupt ◇ **(señal de) interrupción** *f* **por un incidente** error interrupt ◇ **interrupción** *f* **que no puede ser invalidada** non maskable interrupt; NMI ◇ **interrupción** *f* **que puede ser invalidada** maskable interrupt ◇ **interrupción** *f* **total de la alimentación eléctrica** power dump ◇ **una señal de interrupción debida a una impresora defectuosa provocó una terminación anormal** an interrupt from a faulty printer caused an abend

interrupción *f* **activada** *sustantivo* armed interrupt

interrupción *f* **causada por el software** *sustantivo* software interrupt

interrupción *f* **controlada** *sustantivo* transparent interrupt

interrupción *f* **de información** *sustantivo* data break

interrupción *f* **de la corriente** *sustantivo* power failure

interrupción *f* **de la intervención** *sustantivo* attention interruption

interrupción *f* **de llamada** *sustantivo* polled interrupt

interrupción *f* **en cadena** *sustantivo* daisy chain interrupt

interrupción *f* **enmascarable** *sustantivo* maskable interrupt

interrupción *f* **en serie** *sustantivo* daisy chain interrupt

interrupción *f* **externa** *sustantivo* external interrupt

interrupción *f* **impropia** *sustantivo* bad break

interrupción *f* **inadecuada** *sustantivo* bad break

interrupción *f* **invalidable** *sustantivo* maskable interrupt

interrupción *f* **inversa** *sustantivo* reverse interrupt

interrupción *f* **obligatoria** *abrev* NMI ■ *sustantivo* non maskable interrupt

interrupción *f* **prioritaria** *sustantivo* priority interrupt

interrupción *f* **programada** *sustantivo* software interrupt

interrupción *f* **transparente** *sustantivo* transparent interrupt

interrupción *f* **validada** *sustantivo* armed interrupt

interrupción *f* **vectorial** *sustantivo* vectored interrupt

interrupción *f* **vectorizada** *sustantivo* vectored interrupt

interruptor *m sustantivo* circuit breaker

interruptor *m* **con dos posiciones** *sustantivo* toggle switch

interruptor *m* **de corriente** *sustantivo* circuit breaker

interruptor *m* **para reiniciar el equipo** *sustantivo* hardware reset

interruptor *m* **temporal** *sustantivo* momentary switch

intersección *f sustantivo* intersection

intervalo *m sustantivo* **1.** gap **2.** interlude **3.** interval ◇ **había un intervalo entre el instante en el que se apretaba la tecla y el comienzo de la impresión** there was an interval between pressing the key and the starting of the printout

intervalo *m* **de borrado vertical** *sustantivo* vertical blanking interval

intervalo *m* **de captura** *sustantivo* fetch phase

intervalo *m* **de clase** *sustantivo* class interval

intervalo *m* **de llamadas** *sustantivo* polling interval

intervalo *m* **de muestreo** *sustantivo* **1.** sample interval **2.** sampling interval

intervalo *m* **de supresión** *sustantivo* blanking interval

intervalo *m* **en blanco** *sustantivo* record gap

intervalo *m* **entre bloques** *abrev* IBG ■ *sustantivo* **1.** interblock gap **2.** interrecord gap

intervalo *m* **vacío** *sustantivo* gap

Intro *sustantivo* return ◇ **escriba su nombre y número de código, y luego pulse la tecla Intro** you type in your name and code number then press return

introducción *f sustantivo* entering ◇ **el coste de la introducción de datos se calcula por el número de pulsaciones por hora** the cost of keyboarding is calculated in keystrokes per hour ◇ **introducción** *f* **de datos (mediante un teclado)** keyboarding

introducción *f* **(de datos)** *sustantivo* input ◇ **la unidad de entrada acepta información codificada que proviene de operadores humanos, de dispositivos electromagnéticos o de otras computadoras** the input unit accepts coded information from human operators, from electromechanical devices, or from other computers ◇ **velocidad de entrada (de datos)** input speed

introducción *f* **de datos** *sustantivo* **1.** data entry **2.** data input **3.** information input

introducción *f* **de información** *sustantivo* data entry

introducción *f* **doble en memoria intermedia** *sustantivo* double buffering

introducción *f* **en memoria** *sustantivo* instruction storage

introducción *f* **en memoria intermedia** *sustantivo* buffering

introdución ◇ **introducción** *f* **directa en un disco mediante el teclado** keyboard to disk entry

introducir *verbo* **1.** *vt* to enter **2.** *vt* to input **3.** *vt* to mount **4.** *vt* to put **5.** *vt* to read in ◇ **introducir datos en un ordenador** to keyboard ◇ **introducir en la memoria auxiliar** deposit ◇ **introducir un nombre en una lista** to enter a name on a list ◇ **los datos se introducen mediante un módem** the data is input via a modem ◇ **resultaba más barato dejar que otra compañía pasara el manuscrito al ordenador** it was cheaper to have the manuscript keyboarded by another company ◇ **se han introducido los datos** the data has been entered

introducir (un texto) *verbo* (*documento*) to flow text

introducir datos en memoria *verbo* to write ◇ **el tiempo de acceso es el tiempo que se requiere para consultar o escribir un dato en la memoria** access time is the time taken to read from or write to a location in memory ◇ **la memoria caché diferida mejora el rendimiento, pero puede ser peligrosa** write-back cacheing improves performance, but can be dangerous

introducir en un registro *verbo* to deposit

intruso *m sustantivo* intruder

intruso *m* **informático** *sustantivo* hacker

inutilizado *adj* dead

invalidar *verbo vt* to negate

inventar *verbo vt* to devise

inversión *f sustantivo* **1.** inversion **2.** negation ◇ **la inversión de un dígito binario tiene lugar en el complemento de uno** the inversion of a binary digit takes place in one's complement

inversión *f* **binaria** *sustantivo* bit flipping

inversión *f* **de polaridad** *sustantivo* reverse polarity

inverso *sustantivo* inverse ■ *adj* reverse

inversor *m sustantivo* inverter ◇ **inversor de corriente** inverter (AC/DC)

invertir *verbo* **1.** *vt* to invert **2.** *vt* to negate **3.** *vt* to reverse

investigación *sustantivo* **1.** enquiry **2.** research ◇ **investigación y desarrollo** research and development (R & D) ◇ **la empresa ha gastado millones de dólares en investigación y desarrollo** the company has spent millions of dollars on R & D

'Se sabe que la experiencia, las habilidades y las capacidades residen en las inteligencias de los ingenieros de I + D, los trabajadores de producción, las gentes de márketing, los directivos, los proveedores, o los clientes.' [*Nueva economía*]

investigación y desarrollo *sustantivo* **1.** R & D **2.** research and development

invisible *adj* invisible

invitación *f sustantivo* invitation

invitación *f* **a transmitir** *sustantivo* invitation to send ■ *abrev* ITS

irreparable *adj* terminal ◇ **el ordenador tiene un fallo irreparable** the computer has a terminal fault

ISDN *m* **de banda estrecha** *sustantivo* narrow band ISDN

ítem *m* **del menú** *sustantivo* menu item

iteración *f sustantivo* iteration

JK

jaula *f* de **Faraday** *sustantivo* Faraday cage
Java *m* (*marca comercial*) Java
Java Beans (*marca comercial*) Java Beans
JavaScript (*marca comercial*) JavaScript
jerarquía *f sustantivo* hierarchy
jerarquía *f* de **datos** *sustantivo* data hierarchy
jerarquía *f* de la **memoria** *sustantivo* memory hierarchy
jerárquico *adj* hierarchical
jerarquizar *verbo vt* to nest
'joystick' *m sustantivo* joystick
JPEG *sustantivo* **1.** Joint Photographic Experts Group **2.** JPEG
JPEG++ *sustantivo* JPEG++
Jscript (*marca comercial*) JScript
juego *sustantivo* microprogram instruction set ◇
juego *m* de **herramientas** (*de Macintosh*) Toolbox

'Los cibercafés no podrán dar acceso a los juegos en Internet. Ésta es la pretensión de la Comisión Sectorial del Juego, que agrupa a todas las autonomías, con el apoyo del Ministerio del Interior.' [*Ciberp@ís*]

juego *m* de **caracteres** *sustantivo* character set
juego *m* de **caracteres ampliado** *sustantivo* extended character set
juego *m* de **componentes MCA** *sustantivo* MCA chipset ■ Micro Channel Architecture chipset
juego *m* de **herramientas** *sustantivo* toolbox
juego *m* de **instrucciones AT** *sustantivo* AT command set
juego *m* de **limpieza de pantalla** *sustantivo* screen cleaning kit
juego *m* de **ordenador** *sustantivo* computer game
juego *m* de **vídeo** *sustantivo* video game

juego *m* **electrónico** *sustantivo* computer game
juego *m* **fuente** *sustantivo* source deck
juego *m* (de **tarjetas**) **objeto** *sustantivo* object deck
juego *m* **original** *sustantivo* **1.** source deck **2.** source pack
junta *f sustantivo* board
juntar *verbo* **1.** *vt* to add **2.** *vt* to join
justificación *f sustantivo* justification
justificación *f* a la **derecha** *sustantivo* right justification
justificación *f* a la **izquierda** *sustantivo* left justification
justificación *f* **vertical** *sustantivo* vertical justification
justificar *verbo* **1.** *vt* to align **2.** *vt* to justify **3.** *vt* to range
k *símbolo* K
K *símbolo* K
K6™ K6
Kermit *sustantivo* Kermit
kilo *símbolo* K ■ *prefijo* kilo ◇ **kilo-palabra** kiloword (KW)
kilobaudio *m sustantivo* kilobaud
kilobit *m sustantivo* kilobit
kilobits *mpl* **por segundo** *sustantivo* Kbps
kilobits por segundo *sustantivo* kilo bits per second
kilo-byte *m* (**KB**) *sustantivo* kilobyte
kilohercio *m* (**kHz**) *abrev* KHz ■ *sustantivo* kilohertz
kilo-octeto *m* (**Ko**) *sustantivo* kilobyte
kilopalabra *f sustantivo* kiloword
Kilostream (*marca comercial*) Kilostream
Klamath™ Klamath
K palabras *sustantivo* kiloword

L

la empresa f IBM *sustantivo* Big Blue

la (elección) más adecuada *sustantivo* best fit

la mejor elección *sustantivo* best fit

lámina f *sustantivo* wafer

LAN Manager™ (*marca comercial*) LAN Manager

LAN Server™ (*marca comercial*) LAN Server

lanzamiento m *sustantivo* launch ◇ **el lanzamiento del nuevo ordenador personal ha sido retrasado seis meses** the launch of the new PC has been put back six months ◇ **la fecha de lanzamiento de la red es el mes de septiembre** the launch date for the network will be September

lanzar *verbo* 1. *vt* to cast 2. *vt* to launch 3. *vt* to release

lápiz m *sustantivo* pen

lápiz m electrónico *sustantivo* stylus ◇ **para dibujar emplee el lápiz electrónico sobre la tabla gráfica** use the stylus on the graphics tablet to draw

lápiz m fotosensible *sustantivo* 1. light pen 2. pen

lápiz m óptico *sustantivo* 1. bar code reader 2. electronic pen 3. electronic stylus 4. electronic wand 5. light pen 6. pen 7. wand

lápiz m óptico gráfico *sustantivo* graphics light pen

laptop m *sustantivo* laptop *o* laptop computer

la Red *sustantivo* 1. web 2. World Wide Web ■ *abrev* www

láser m *sustantivo* laser ◇ **comunicaciones por rayos láser** laser beam communications ◇ **grabación por rayos láser** laser beam recording (LBR)

lector *sustantivo* 1. drive 2. reader 3. stylus ◇ **lector m (de discos)** fixed head disk ◇ **lector m de cintas de papel perforadas** paper tape reader ◇ **lector m (óptico) de código de barras** bar code reader ◇ **lector m (CD-ROM) de cuatro velocidades** quad-speed drive ◇ **lector m de disquetes de doble cara** double-sided disk drive ◇ **lector m de disquetes de ocho pulgadas** eight-inch drive ◇ **lector m (de disquetes) local** local drive ◇ **lector m óptico de códigos de barras** optical bar reader

lector m audio digital *sustantivo* DAT drive

lector m DAT *sustantivo* DAT drive ◇ **utilizamos un lector DAT como dispositivo de seg-**

uridad de la red we use a DAT drive as the backup device for our network

lector m de bandas *sustantivo* 1. magnetic tape reader 2. tape drive ◇ **nuestro nuevo producto tiene una unidad de flujo de cinta de 96 Mb** our new product has a 96Mb streaming tape drive

lector m de CD *sustantivo* compact disc player

lector m de CD-ROM *sustantivo* CD-ROM player

lector m de cinta audio digital *sustantivo* 1. DAT drive 2. device flag ◇ **utilizamos un lector DAT como dispositivo de seguridad de la red** we use a DAT drive as the backup device for our network

lector m de cinta audionumérica *sustantivo* DAT drive

lector m de cintas de papel perforadas *abrev* PTR

lector m de cintas magnéticas *sustantivo* 1. magnetic tape reader 2. tape reader

lector m de cintas perforadas *sustantivo* tape reader

lector m de disco(s) *sustantivo* disk unit

lector m de discos compactos *sustantivo* compact disc player

lector m de disquetes no compatibles *sustantivo* alien disk reader ◇ **cuando tenga un disquete no compatible seleccione la opción multidisco para que la disquetera se convierta en un lector de discos no compatibles** when you have an alien disk select the multi-disk option to allow you to turn the disk drive into an alien disk reader

lector m de documentos *sustantivo* document reader

lector m de marcas detectables *sustantivo* mark sense reader

lector m de noticias *sustantivo* news reader

lector m de páginas *sustantivo* page reader

lector m de placas de identificación *sustantivo* badge reader ◇ **un lector de tarjetas de identificación garantiza que sólo el personal autorizado pueda acceder a la sala de ordenadores** a badge reader makes sure that only authorized personnel can gain access to a computer room

lector m de red *sustantivo* network drive

lector m de tarjetas *sustantivo* 1. badge reader 2. card reader ◇ **un lector de tarjetas de identificación garantiza que sólo el personal** autorizado pueda acceder a la sala de ordenadores a badge reader makes sure that only authorized personnel can gain access to a computer room

lector *m* **de tarjetas magnéticas** *sustantivo* **1.** magnetic card reader **2.** magnetic strip reader

lector *m* **de tarjetas perforadas** *sustantivo* punched card reader

lector *m* **externo** *sustantivo* external disk drive

lector *m* **multidisco** *sustantivo* **1.** alien disk reader **2.** multi-disk reader ◇ **cuando tenga un disquete no compatible seleccione la opción multidisco para que la disquetera se convierta en un lector de discos no compatibles** when you have an alien disk select the multi-disk option to allow you to turn the disk drive into an alien disk reader

lector *m* **óptico** *sustantivo* optical scanner

lector *m* **óptico de caracteres** *sustantivo* **1.** OCR **2.** optical character reader

lector *m* **óptico de marcas** *sustantivo* **1.** OMR **2.** optical mark reader

lectura *f sustantivo* **1.** browsing **2.** reading **3.** readout **4.** sense ◇ **el reloj tenía una lectura digital** the clock had a digital readout ◇ **la lectura mostraba la hora** the readout displayed the time ◇ **lectura óptica** optical reading ◇ **lectura** *f* **óptica digital (de datos)** digital optical recording; DOR

lectura *f* **(por escáner)** *sustantivo* scanning ◇ **dispositivo de lectura por barrido** scanning device ◇ **escáner** scanning device ◇ **exploración de trama** raster scanning ◇ **haz de barrido** *o* **de exploración** scanning spot beam ◇ **la velocidad de lectura es de 9,9 segundos para un documento de 8,5 por 11 pulgadas** its scanning speed is 9.9 seconds for an 8.5 inch by 11 inch document ◇ **receptor panorámico de radio** *o* **receptor de exploración de señal (radiofónica)** scanning radio receiver

lectura *f* **anticipada** *sustantivo* look-ahead

lectura *f* **destructiva** *sustantivo* **1.** destructive read **2.** destructive readout **3.** DRO

lectura/escritura *f abrev* R/W

lectura *f* **helicoidal** *sustantivo* helical scan

lectura *f* **no destructiva** *sustantivo* **1.** NDR **2.** non destructive readout

lectura *f* **regenerativa** *sustantivo* regenerative reading

leer *verbo* **1.** *vt* to read **2.** *vt* to scan ◇ **el tiempo de acceso es el que se requiere para leer un registro** access time can be the time taken to read from a record

legal *adj* legal

legible *adj* readable

LEGS *sustantivo* SGML

lengua *sustantivo* language ◇ **lengua extranjera** *o* **idioma extranjero** foreign language

'Más del 7% de los usuarios que se conectan a Internet usan una segunda lengua además del inglés. El 51% recurren al español, y el 25% al francés.' [*Ciberp@ís*]

lengua *f* **de destino** *sustantivo* target language ◇ **el lenguaje meta para este programa en PASCAL es el código máquina** the target language for this PASCAL program is machine code

lengua *f* **de partida** *sustantivo* source language

lenguage *m* **COBOL** *sustantivo* COBOL

lenguage *m* **estándar generalizado de señalamiento** *sustantivo* SGML

lenguage *m* **XHTML** *sustantivo* extensible hypertext markup language

lenguage *m* **XML** *sustantivo* extensible markup language

lenguaje *sustantivo* language ◇ **lenguaje** *m* **(de programación) ADA** ADA ◇ **lenguaje** *m* **(de programación) APL** APL ◇ **lenguaje** *m* **(de alto nivel) BASIC** BASIC ◇ **lenguaje** *m* **(de alto nivel) BCPL** BCPL ◇ **lenguaje** *m* **(de alto nivel) C** C ◇ **lenguaje** *m* **de acceso a los datos** data access language ◇ **lenguaje** *m* **de consulta** SQL; structured query language ◇ **lenguaje** *m* **de control de la impresora HP** Hewlett Packard Printer Control Language; HP-PCL ◇ **lenguaje** *m* **de descripción de datos** data description language; DDL ◇ **lenguaje** *m* **de programación (de alto nivel)** formula translator ◇ **lenguaje** *m* **de programación de alto nivel** high-level language; HLL ◇ **lenguaje de programación de alto nivel** *m* **FORTRAN** FORTRAN ◇ **lenguaje** *m* **(de programación) FORTH** FORTH ◇ **lenguaje** *m* **(de alto nivel) Modula-2** Modula-2 ◇ **lenguaje** *m* **(de programación) OCCAM** OCCAM ◇ **lenguaje** *m* **orientado a problemas** problem-orientated language ◇ **lenguaje** *m* **(de programación) para crear imágenes virtuales** virtual reality modelling language; VRML ◇ **lenguaje** *m* **práctico de extracción y formateado** Perl; practical extraction and report language ◇ **lenguaje** *m* **simbólico orientado a cadenas (de caracteres)** SNOBOL; string orientated symbolic language

'El sniffer es una aplicación, generalmente programada en lenguaje C, que se introduce en un sistema hackeado para interceptar información en tránsito, habitualmente con el fin de averiguar contraseñas de usuarios.' [*Ciberp@ís*]

lenguaje *m* **adaptable** *sustantivo* extensible language

lenguaje *m* **algebraico** *sustantivo* algebraic language

lenguaje *m* **algorítmico** *sustantivo* **1.** ALGOL **2.** algorithmic language

lenguaje *m* **a procedimientos** *sustantivo* procedure-orientated language

lenguaje *m* **base** *sustantivo* **1.** base **2.** base language

lenguaje *m* **compartido** *sustantivo* common language

lenguaje *m* **compilador** *sustantivo* language compiler

lenguaje *m* **común** *sustantivo* common language

lenguaje *m* **de acceso a los datos** *abrev* DAL

lenguaje *m* **de alto nivel BASIC** *sustantivo* beginner's all-purpose symbolic instruction code

lenguaje *m* **de aplicación** *sustantivo* application orientated language

lenguaje *m* **de autor** *sustantivo* authoring language

lenguaje *m* **de bajo nivel** *sustantivo* low-level language

lenguaje *m* **de base de datos** *sustantivo* database language

lenguaje *m* **declarativo** *sustantivo* declarative language

lenguaje *m* **de compilación** *sustantivo* compiler language

lenguaje *m* **de consulta** *sustantivo* QBE ■ *abrev* QL ■ *sustantivo* 1. query by example 2. query language

lenguaje *m* **de control** *sustantivo* control language

lenguaje *m* **de control de instrucciones** *sustantivo* command control language

lenguaje *m* **de control de tareas** *sustantivo* 1. JCL 2. job control language 3. job orientated language

lenguaje *m* **de control de trabajos** *sustantivo* job orientated language

lenguaje *m* **de cuarta generación** *abrev* 4GL ■ *sustantivo* fourth generation language

lenguaje *m* **de descripción de página** *sustantivo* 1. page description language 2. page description programming language ■ *abrev* PDL

lenguaje *m* **de diseño de programas** *abrev* PDL ■ *sustantivo* program design language

lenguaje *m* **de ensamblaje** *sustantivo* 1. assembler language 2. assembly language

lenguaje *m* **de información** *sustantivo* 1. data description language 2. DDL ◇ **muchas de las ventajas de un lenguaje de descripción de datos provienen del hecho de que se trata de un lenguaje de segunda generación** many of DDL's advantages come from the fact that it is a second generation language

lenguaje *m* **de instrucción** *sustantivo* command language

lenguaje *m* **de instrucciones** *sustantivo* command language

lenguaje *m* **de macros** *sustantivo* macro language

lenguaje *m* **de manipulación de datos** *sustantivo* data manipulation language ■ *abrev* DML

lenguaje *m* **de máquina** *sustantivo* native language

lenguaje *m* **de marcado de hipertexto** *sustantivo* 1. HTML 2. hypertext markup language

lenguaje *m* **de marcas** *sustantivo* markup language

lenguaje *m* **de modelado de comercio electrónico** *abrev* ECML

lenguaje *m* **de piel de cebolla** *sustantivo* onion skin language

lenguaje *m* **de procedimiento** *sustantivo* procedural language

lenguaje *m* **de programación** *sustantivo* 1. programming language 2. scripting language

lenguaje *m* **de programación APL** *sustantivo* A programming language

lenguaje *m* **de síntesis** *sustantivo* synthetic language

lenguaje *m* **destino** *sustantivo* target language

lenguaje *m* **de usuario** *sustantivo* user-operated language

lenguaje *m* **encadenado** *sustantivo* threaded language

lenguaje *m* **ensamblador** *sustantivo* language assembler

lenguaje *m* **ensamblador de un microprograma** *sustantivo* microprogram assembly language

lenguaje *m* **estándar** *sustantivo* machine-independent language

lenguaje *m* **estándar de marcado general** *sustantivo* Standard Generalized Markup Language

lenguaje *m* **extensible** *sustantivo* extensible language

lenguaje *m* **fuente** *sustantivo* source language

lenguaje *m* **gráfico** *sustantivo* graphic language ◇ **este lenguaje gráfico puede trazar líneas, círculos y gráficos con una sola instrucción** this graphic language can plot lines, circles and graphs with a single command

lenguaje *m* **gráfico HP** Hewlett Packard Graphics Language ■ *abrev* HPGL

lenguaje *m* **HPGL** Hewlett Packard Graphics Language

lenguaje HP-PCL *m* *abrev* HP-PCL

lenguaje *m* **HP-PCL** Hewlett Packard Printer Control Language

lenguaje *m* **independiente de la máquina** *sustantivo* machine-independent language

lenguaje *m* **informático** *sustantivo* computer language

lenguaje *m* **informático estándar** *sustantivo* computer-independent language

lenguaje *m* **informático independiente** *sustantivo* computer-independent language

lenguaje *m* **interno** *sustantivo* internal language

lenguaje *m* **interpretado** *sustantivo* interpreted language

lenguaje *m* **interpretador** *sustantivo* language interpreter

lenguaje *m* **LISP** *sustantivo* 1. LISP 2. list processing

lenguaje *m* **LLL** *sustantivo* low-level language

lenguaje *m* **LOGO** *sustantivo* LOGO

lenguaje *m* **máquina** *sustantivo* **1.** internal language **2.** machine language

lenguaje *m* **multidimensional** *sustantivo* multidimensional language

lenguaje *m* **multinivel** *sustantivo* multidimensional language

lenguaje *m* **nativo** *sustantivo* native language

lenguaje *m* **natural** *sustantivo* natural language ◇ **el sistema experto puede programarse en lenguaje natural** the expert system can be programmed in a natural language

lenguaje *m* **no procedimental** *sustantivo* non-procedural language

lenguaje *m* **objeto** *sustantivo* **1.** object language **2.** target language

lenguaje *m* **orientado al procedimiento** *sustantivo* procedure-orientated language

lenguaje *m* **orientado a objetos** *sustantivo* object-oriented language

lenguaje *m* **orientado a problemas** *abrev* POL

lenguaje *m* **PASCAL** *sustantivo* PASCAL

lenguaje *m* **PCL** *sustantivo* **1.** PCL **2.** printer control language

lenguaje *m* **Perl** *sustantivo* **1.** Perl **2.** practical extraction and report language

lenguaje *m* **PLAN** *sustantivo* PLAN

lenguaje *m* **POP 2** *sustantivo* POP 2

lenguaje *m* **procedimental** *sustantivo* procedural language

lenguaje *m* **SGML** *sustantivo* Standard Generalized Markup Language

lenguaje *m* **simbólico** *sustantivo* symbolic language

lenguaje *m* **sintético** *sustantivo* synthetic language

lenguaje sistema *m* **HPGL** *abrev* HPGL

lenguaje *m* **SNOBOL** *sustantivo* **1.** SNOBOL **2.** string orientated symbolic language

lenguaje *m* **SQL** *sustantivo* **1.** SQL **2.** structured query language

lenguaje *m* **universal** *sustantivo* machine-independent language

lengua *f* **meta** *sustantivo* target language ◇ **el lenguaje meta para este programa en PASCAL es el código máquina** the target language for this PASCAL program is machine code

lengua *f* **origen** *sustantivo* source language

lento ◇ **lento en la introducción de datos** input-bound

lesión *f* **por esfuerzo repetitivo** *sustantivo* repetitive strain injury *o* repetitive stress injury

lesión *f* **por fatiga crónica** *sustantivo* **1.** carpal tunnel syndrome **2.** cumulative trauma disorder ■ *abrev* RSI

lesión *f* **por tensión repetitiva** *sustantivo* repetitive strain injury *o* repetitive stress injury

letra ◇ **letra** *f* **de identificación de la unidad de disco** drive designator; drive letter ◇ **letra** *f* **de identificación de un lector** drive designator; drive letter

letra *f* **estándar** *sustantivo* standard letter

letra *f* **indicativa** *sustantivo* index letter

letras *fpl* **del alfabeto** *sustantivo* alphabetic character set

levantador *m* **de banda** *sustantivo* lifter

levantador *m* **de cinta** *sustantivo* lifter

Ley *f* **de Protección de Datos** *sustantivo* Data Protection Act

ley *f* **de seguridad informática** *sustantivo* Data Protection Act

ley *f* **de Shannon** *sustantivo* Shannon's Law

leyenda *f* *sustantivo* caption ◇ **las leyendas se imprimen en cursiva** the captions are printed in italics

LH *verbo vt* to load high

liberación *f* **anticipada de ficha** *sustantivo* early token release

liberar *verbo* **1.** *vt* to deallocate **2.** *vt* to release ◇ **cuando se presiona la tecla de reinicio se liberan todos los recursos** when a reset button is pressed all resources are deallocated ◇ **liberar (espacio en la memoria)** to free

liberar la línea *verbo* to clear

liberar memoria *verbo* to blast

libertad *f* **de información** *sustantivo* freedom of information

libre *adj* free ■ *sustantivo* free ■ *adj* idle ◇ **indexado libre** free indexing ◇ **línea libre** free line ◇ **pérdida de espacios libres** free space loss ◇ **soportes de espacios libres** free space media

libre acceso *m* *sustantivo* open access

libro *sustantivo* book ◇ **el libro está disponible en rústica y en tapas duras** the book is available in paperback and hard cover ◇ **pueden imprimir libros de hasta 96 páginas** they can print books of up to 96 pages

'Con el libro electrónico no se pretende sustituir al tradicional, sino dar la oportunidad de leer más, con más obras y artículos accesibles en todo momento.' [*Ciberp@ís*]

libro *m* **amarillo** *sustantivo* Yellow Book

libro *m* **de direcciones** *sustantivo* address book

libro *m* **electrónico** *sustantivo* **1.** ebook **2.** electronic book

licencia *f* *sustantivo* licence ◇ **este software está fabricado bajo licencia** this software is manufactured under licence

licencia *f* **de sitio** *sustantivo* site licence ◇ **hemos negociado un buen acuerdo para la licencia de sitios (en la red) para los 1.200 empleados de nuestras oficinas centrales** we have negotiated a good deal for the site licence for our 1200 employees in our HQ

licencia *f* **de software** *sustantivo* software licence

licencia *f* **de utilización** *sustantivo* run-time licence

LIFO *adj* LIFO

liga *f sustantivo* link

ligero *adj* lightweight ◊ **un ordenador ligero que pueda fácilmente caber en una maleta** a lightweight computer which can easily fit into a suitcase

LILO *adj* LILO

limitado ◊ **limitado a la unidad central** CPU bound ◊ **limitado por la (velocidad de) salida (de datos)** output-bound; output-limited

limitado a entrada/salida *adj* I/O bound

limitado en la entrada de datos *adj* input-limited

limitado por el procesador *adj* processor-limited

limitado por el proceso *sustantivo* process bound

limitador *m sustantivo* limiter

limitador *m* **de corriente transitoria** *sustantivo* transient suppressor

limitador *m* **de tensión** *sustantivo* surge protector

limitar *verbo vt* to restrict ◊ **el documento es de acceso restringido y, por lo tanto, no debe disponer de acceso público** the document is restricted, and cannot be placed on open access

límite *m sustantivo* **1.** boundary **2.** edge **3.** restriction

límite *m* **de página** *sustantivo* page boundary

límites *mpl sustantivo* limits

límites *mpl* **de audiofrecuencias** *sustantivo* audio range

límites *mpl* **de matriz** *plural noun* array bounds

limpiar *verbo* **1.** *vt* to clean **2.** *vt* to zap ◊ **ocurren errores de escritura si no utiliza con regularidad un juego de limpieza de cabezas** write errors occur if you do not use a head cleaning kit regularly

limpieza *f* **de datos** *sustantivo* data cleaning

limpieza *f* **de ficheros** *sustantivo* file cleanup

limpieza *f* **de información** *sustantivo* data cleaning

limpieza *f* **de memoria** *sustantivo* garbage collection

limpio *adj* clean

línea *sustantivo* **1.** bar **2.** line **3.** row ◊ **la línea de validación de datos está conectada a la línea de selección del chip de pestillo** the data strobe line is connected to the latch chip select line ◊ **línea** *f* **de instrucción de un programa** program line ◊ **línea** *f* **de validación de un chip** chip select line ◊ **línea** *f* **E-1 (de telecomunicaciones)** E-1

'Un conjunto más bien grande de líneas de control (alambres) transmiten las señales que se utilizan para medir el tiempo y sincroniza hechos en todas las unidades.' [*Organización de computadoras*]

línea *f* **activa** *sustantivo* active line

línea *f* **ADSL** *sustantivo* ADSL

línea *f* **analógica** *sustantivo* analog line

línea *f* **arrendada** *sustantivo* leased line

línea *f* **base** *sustantivo* base line

línea *f* **común** *sustantivo* common carrier

línea *f* **de abonado digital** *sustantivo* **1.** digital subscriber line **2.** DSL

línea *f* **de acceso** *sustantivo* access line

línea *f* **de asunto** *sustantivo* subject line

línea *f* **de barrido** *sustantivo* **1.** scan line **2.** scanning line

línea *f* **de código** *sustantivo* (*de un programa*) code line

línea *f* **dedicada** *sustantivo* dedicated line

línea *f* **de estado** *sustantivo* status line

línea *f* **de flujo** *sustantivo* flowline

línea *f* **de información** *sustantivo* information line

línea *f* **de instrucciones** *sustantivo* command line

línea *f* **de interrupción** *sustantivo* interrupt line

línea *f* **de pantalla** *sustantivo* display line

línea *f* **de productos** *sustantivo* **1.** product line *o* product range **2.** product range

línea *f* **de programa** *sustantivo* line

línea *f* **de referencia** *sustantivo* guide bar

línea *f* **de retardo** *sustantivo* delay line

línea *f* **de retraso** *sustantivo* mercury delay line

línea *f* **de retraso acústico** *sustantivo* acoustic delay line

línea *f* **de selección** *sustantivo* chip select line ◊ **la línea de validación de datos está conectada a la línea de selección del chip de pestillo** the data strobe line is connected to the latch chip select line

línea *f* **de título** *sustantivo* title bar

línea *f* **de transmisión rápida** *sustantivo* fast line

línea *f* **de unión** *sustantivo* (*en un ordinograma*) flowline

línea *f* **digital asimétrica de abonado** *sustantivo* Asymmetric Digital Subscriber Line

línea *f* **equilibrada** *sustantivo* balanced line

línea *f* **especializada** *sustantivo* leased line

línea *f* **guía** *sustantivo* guide bar

lineal *adj* linear ◊ **circuito integrado lineal** linear integrated circuit ◊ **función lineal** linear function ◊ **la expresión Y = 10 + 5X – 3W es una función lineal** the expression $Y = 10 + 5X - 3W$ is a linear function ◊ **la expresión Y = (10 + 5X2) no es una función lineal** the expression $Y = (10 + 5X2)$ is not a linear function ◊ **ordenamiento lineal** linear array

linealidad *f sustantivo* linearity

línea *f* **rápida** *sustantivo* fast line

líneas ◊ **líneas de transmisión de datos de un enlace común** bus data lines

líneas *fpl* **de control de enlaces** *plural noun* bus control lines

líneas ocultas *plural noun* hidden lines

líneas por minuto *sustantivo* lines per minute ■ *abrev* LPM

línea *f* **telefónica** *sustantivo* telephone line

línea *f* **telefónica especializada** *sustantivo* dedicated line

línea *f* **terrestre** *sustantivo* landline

Linux (*marca comercial*) Linux

lista *sustantivo* **1.** exception dictionary **2.** list **3.** listing **4.** polling list ◇ **lista** *f* **de direcciones** automatic mailing list ◇ **lista** *f* **de dirreciones suscripción activa** opt-in mailing list ◇ **lista** *f* **de emplazamientos disponibles no asignados** (*en memoria*) uncommitted storage list

lista *f* **circular** *sustantivo* ring

lista *f* **completa** *sustantivo* dense list

lista *f* **de acciones** *sustantivo* action list

lista *f* **de bloques** *sustantivo* block list

lista *f* **de capacidades** *sustantivo* capability list

lista *f* **de control de acceso** *sustantivo* **1.** access control list **2.** ACL

lista *f* **de desplazamiento ascendente** *sustantivo* push-up list *o* push-up stack

lista *f* **de desplazamiento descendente** *sustantivo* push-down list *o* push-down stack

lista *f* **de direcciones** *sustantivo* mailing list ◇ **su nombre está en nuestra lista de direcciones** his name is on our mailing list

lista *f* **de ensamblaje** *sustantivo* (*de un programa*) assembly listing

lista *f* **de espera** *sustantivo* waiting list

lista *f* **de modificaciones** *sustantivo* journal ◇ **los registros modificados fueron añadidos al fichero maestro y anotados en el diario de modificaciones** the modified records were added to the master file and noted in the journal

lista *f* **de palabras prohibidas** *sustantivo* stop list

lista *f* **de prohibiciones** *sustantivo* stop list

lista *f* **de recursos disponibles** *sustantivo* available list

lista *f* **de referencia** *sustantivo* **1.** authority file *o* authority list **2.** reference list

lista *f* **descriptiva** *sustantivo* description list

lista *f* **desplegable** *sustantivo* drop-down list box

listado *sustantivo* listing ◇ **listado** *m* **de ensamblaje** (*de un programa*) assembly listing

listado *m* *sustantivo* printout

listado *m* **de archivos** *sustantivo* FAT

listado *m* **de excepciones** *sustantivo* exception dictionary

listado *m* **de un programa** *sustantivo* program listing

listado *m* **de un programa fuente** *sustantivo* source listing

listado *m* **informático** *sustantivo* computer listing

lista *f* **en anillo** *sustantivo* ring

lista *f* **en bucle** *sustantivo* circular list

lista *f* **en cadena** *sustantivo* **1.** chained list **2.** chain list

lista *f* **encadenada** *sustantivo* **1.** chained list **2.** chain list **3.** linked list

lista *f* **enlazada** *sustantivo* **1.** chained list **2.** linked list

lista *f* **lineal** *sustantivo* linear list

lista *f* **moderada** *sustantivo* moderated list *o* moderated mailing list

lista *f* **no controlada** *sustantivo* unmoderated list

lista *f* **no verificada** *sustantivo* unmoderated list

lista *f* **ordenada** *sustantivo* ordered list

lista *f* **secuencial** *sustantivo* linear list

lista *f* **vacía** *sustantivo* null list

lista *f* **verificada** *sustantivo* moderated list *o* moderated mailing list

listo *m* *sustantivo* OK

literal *m* *sustantivo* literal

llamada ◇ **llamada** *f* **(selectiva) de grupo** group poll

llamada *f* **de función** *sustantivo* function call

llamada *f* **de macro anidada** *sustantivo* nested macro call

llamada *f* **de procedimiento a distancia** *sustantivo* **1.** remote procedure call **2.** RPC

llamada *f* **de procedimiento asíncrono** *abrev* APC ■ *sustantivo* asynchronous procedure call

llamada *f* **de un subprograma** *sustantivo* subroutine call

llamada *f* **por pulsaciones** *sustantivo* pulse-dialling

llamada *f* **recursiva** *sustantivo* recursive call

llamada *f* **selectiva** *sustantivo* polling

llamar *verbo* **1.** *vt* to call **2.** *vt* to call up **3.** *vt* to fetch **4.** *vt* to invoke **5.** *vt* to poll ◇ **le llamaré mañana a su oficina** I'll call you at your office tomorrow ◇ **llamar anticipadamente (una instrucción)** to pre-fetch

llamar un programa *verbo* to call

llave *f* **de protección** *sustantivo* protection key

llaves *fpl plural noun* **1.** braces **2.** curly brackets *o* curly braces

llenar *verbo* **1.** *vt* to bridge **2.** *vt* to fill ◇ **el disquete se llenó en seguida** the disk was quickly filled up

llevar un diario *verbo* to log

lo ◇ **lo que ve es lo que consigue** What-You-See-Is-What-You-Get ◇ **lo que ve es todo lo que consigue** What-You-See-Is-All-You-Get

local *adj* local ◇ **central urbana** *o* **estación local** local exchange ◇ **las tarjetas de extensión más rápidas encajan en este conector de en-**

lace local the fastest expansion cards fit into this local bus connector ◇ **red inalámbrica de área local** local area wireless network (LAWN)

localización *f sustantivo* fault detection

localización *f* **de la memoria** *sustantivo* store location

localizado *adj* local

localizador *m* **uniforme de recursos** *sustantivo* **1.** uniform resource locator **2.** URL

localizar *verbo* **1.** *vt* to find **2.** *vt* to locate **3.** *vt* to track ◇ **el detector (de fallos) localizó el error rápidamente** the debugger found the error very quickly ◇ **¿ha conseguido localizar el error de programación?** have you managed to locate the programming fault? ◇ **la cabeza lectora no localiza correctamente la pista grabada** the read head is not tracking the recorded track correctly ◇ **llevó mucho tiempo localizar el chip defectuoso** it took a lot of time to find the faulty chip ◇ **localizar (y reparar) un fallo** to troubleshoot

localizar y leer *verbo* to fetch

lógica *sustantivo* logic ◇ **circuito lógico no conectado** uncommitted logic array (ULA) ◇ **lógica** *f* **(de un sistema)** logic ◇ **lógica** *f* **de emisor acoplado (ECL)** emitter-coupled logic ◇ **orden lógica** *o* **circuito lógico** logic array

lógica *f* **booleana** *sustantivo* Boolean logic

lógica *f* **cableada** *sustantivo* hardwired logic

lógica *f* **combinatoria** *sustantivo* combinational logic

lógica *f* **confusa** *sustantivo* fuzzy logic *o* fuzzy theory

lógica *f* **de inyección integrada** *sustantivo* integrated injection logic

lógica *f* **de máquina** *sustantivo* machine equation

lógica *f* **de nivel n** *sustantivo* n-level logic

lógica *f* **de ordenador** *sustantivo* computer logic

lógica *f* **de reconocimiento** *sustantivo* recognition logic

lógica *f* **de transistor-transistor** *sustantivo* **1.** transistor-transistor logic **2.** TTL

lógica *f* **digital** *sustantivo* digital logic

lógica *f* **especializada** *sustantivo* dedicated logic ◇ **la persona seleccionada debería tener conocimientos de hardware para microordenadores y de lógica especializada** the person appointed should have a knowledge of micro-based hardware and dedicated logic

lógica *f* **informática** *sustantivo* computer logic

lógica *f* **negativa** *sustantivo* negative-true logic

lógica *f* **positiva** *sustantivo* positive logic

lógica *f* **secuencial** *sustantivo* sequential logic ◇ **si la secuencia de entrada al circuito de lógica secuencial es 1101 la salida siempre es (0)** if the input sequence to the sequential logic circuit is 1101 the output will always be zero (0)

lógica *f* **simbólica** *sustantivo* symbolic logic

lógica *f* **transistor-transistor** *sustantivo* TTL logic

lógica *f* **TTL** *sustantivo* TTL logic

lógico *adj* logical ◇ **el razonamiento lógico puede simularse mediante una máquina de inteligencia artificial** logical reasoning can be simulated by an artificial intelligence machine

logotipo *m sustantivo* logo

lo más destacado *sustantivo* highlight

longitud *sustantivo* **1.** field length **2.** file length **3.** length ◇ **longitud** *f* **de la zona de barrido** scan length ◇ **longitud** *f* **del nombre de un fichero** length of filename ◇ **longitud** *f* **de una palabra de información** data word length

longitud *f* **de bloque** *sustantivo* block length

longitud *f* **de campo** *sustantivo* field length

longitud *f* **de la memoria intermedia** *sustantivo* buffer length

longitud *f* **de línea** *sustantivo* **1.** line length **2.** line width

longitud *f* **de onda** *sustantivo* wavelength

longitud *f* **de página** *sustantivo* page length

longitud *f* **de palabra** *sustantivo* word length

longitud *f* **de palabra de entrada** *sustantivo* block length

longitud *f* **de una cadena** *sustantivo* string length

longitud *f* **de una línea** *sustantivo* line length

longitud *f* **de un registro** *sustantivo* record length

lote *m sustantivo* batch ◇ **procesador por lotes** batch processor

lote *m* **cargador** *sustantivo* disk pack

lote *m* **de interrupciones** *sustantivo* interrupt stacking

Lotus™ Lotus

lugar *sustantivo* place ◇ **en el lugar (de trabajo)** on-site

lugar *m* **de la disquetera** *sustantivo* bay

lugar *m* **del lector de discos** *sustantivo* bay

lugar *m* **de una cifra** *sustantivo* digit place *o* digit position

luminancia *f sustantivo* luminance ◇ **señal de luminancia** luminance signal

luminosidad *f sustantivo* brightness

luz *f sustantivo* light ◇ **conductor de luz** light conduit ◇ **guía de luz** *o* **guía óptico, -a** light guide ◇ **la pantalla no debería colocarse bajo una luz demasiado intensa** the VDU should not be placed under a bright light ◇ **luz coherente** coherent light ◇ **luz ultravioleta** *o* **radiación ultravioleta** ultra-violet light (UV light) ◇ **luz visible** visible light

luz *f* **de alarma** *sustantivo* warning light ◇ **cuando la luz de alarma en la parte frontal se enciende, hay que apagar el sistema** when the warning light on the front panel comes on, switch off the system

luz *f* **de fondo** *sustantivo* (*de una pantalla de cristal líquido*) backlight

luz *f* **indicadora** *sustantivo* indicator light

luz *f* **testigo** *sustantivo* activity light

luz *f* **ultravioleta** *sustantivo* ultraviolet light

M

Mac *sustantivo* Mac

MacBinario™ *m* **1.** MacBinary **2.** (*marca comercial*) MacBinary

Macintosh™ (*marca comercial*) Macintosh ◇ **los ordenadores Macintosh no son compatibles con un ordenador IBM a no ser que utilice un programa de emulación** Macintosh computers are not compatible with an IBM PC unless you use special emulation software

macro *f sustantivo* **1.** macro **2.** macroinstruction

macro- *prefijo* macro-

macrobloque *m sustantivo* macro block

macrocódigo *m sustantivo* macro code

macrodefinición *f sustantivo* macro definition

macroelemento *m sustantivo* macroelement

macro ensamblador *m sustantivo* macro assembler *o* macro assembly program

macroexpansión *f sustantivo* macro expansion

macroinstrucción *f sustantivo* **1.** macro call **2.** macro command **3.** macroinstruction

macroinstrucción *f sustantivo* macro

macroinstrucciones *fpl sustantivo* macro assembler *o* macro assembly program

macrolenguaje *m sustantivo* macro language

macroordinograma *m sustantivo* macro flowchart

macroprogramación *f sustantivo* macro programming

macrovirus *m sustantivo* macro virus

maestro *adj* master ◇ **programa de control maestro** master control program (MCP)

magacín *m sustantivo* magazine

magnético *adj* magnetic ◇ **enfoque magnético** *o* **concentración magnética** magnetic focusing

magnetizar *verbo vt* to magnetise *o* to magnetize

magnetófono *m* **de cinta magnética** *sustantivo* magnetic tape recorder

magnitud *f sustantivo* magnitude

magnitud *f* **con signo** *sustantivo* **1.** sign and magnitude **2.** signed magnitude

magnitud *f* **escalar** *sustantivo* scalar

'mailing' *m sustantivo* mailing ◇ **envío por correo directo** *o* **publicidad directa** *o* **'mailing' directo** direct mailing

mal *m* **funcionamiento** *sustantivo* malfunction ■ *adj* malfunctioning ■ *sustantivo* problem

malla *f sustantivo* mesh

mando *m sustantivo* **1.** dial **2.** joystick **3.** paddle ◇ **mando de densidad** density dial ◇ **mando de juego** games paddle ◇ **si el texto sale muy claro, gire el mando de densidad de la impresora a negro** if the text fades, turn the density dial on the printer to full black

mando *m* **(de regulación)** *sustantivo* knob ◇ **el brillo puede regularse al girar un mando que está en la parte posterior del monitor** the brightness can be regulated by turning a knob at the back of the monitor ◇ **girar el mando de encedido** *or* **apagado** *o* **conectado** *or* **desconectado** turn the on/off knob

mando *m* **a distancia** *sustantivo* remote control

manejable *adj* manageable ◇ **los datos se deberían dividir en ficheros manejables** data should be split into manageable files

manguera *f sustantivo* conduit

manipulación *f sustantivo* manipulation

manipulación *f* **de bits** *sustantivo* **1.** bit handling **2.** bit manipulation

manipulación *f* **de bloques** *sustantivo* block operation

manipulación *f* **de bytes** *sustantivo* byte manipulation

manipulación *f* **de octetos** *sustantivo* byte manipulation

manipulación *f* **de texto** *sustantivo* text manipulation

manipulador *m* **de interrupción** *sustantivo* trap handler

manipular *verbo vt* to manipulate ◇ **un procesador de imágenes que recoge, muestra y manipula imágenes de vídeo** an image processor that captures, displays and manipulates video images

mano *f sustantivo* hand ◇ **(equipo) de segunda mano** second hand; second user ◇ **visor de mano** hand viewer

mantener *verbo* **1.** *vt* to hold **2.** *vt* to maintain ◇ **corriente de mantenimiento** hold current

mantenimiento *m sustantivo* **1.** file maintenance **2.** maintenance

mantenimiento *m sustantivo* upkeep

mantenimiento *m* **correctivo** *sustantivo* **1.** corrective maintenance **2.** remedial maintenance

mantenimiento *m* **de la línea** *sustantivo* line conditioning

mantenimiento *m* **del equipo de clientes** *sustantivo* customer engineering

mantenimiento *m* **del software** *sustantivo* software maintenance

mantenimiento *m* **de reparación** *sustantivo* remedial maintenance

mantenimiento *m* **de un fichero** *sustantivo* file maintenance

mantenimiento *m* **de un programa** *sustantivo* program maintenance

mantenimiento *m* **preventivo** *sustantivo* preventive maintenance

mantisa *f sustantivo* mantissa ◊ **la mantisa del número 45,897 es 0,897** the mantissa of the number 45.897 is 0.897

mantisa *f* **binaria** *sustantivo* binary mantissa

manual *m sustantivo* manual ◊ **manual** *m* **de uso de un programa** software documentation

manual *m* **de instalación** *sustantivo* installation manual

manual *m* **de instrucciones** *sustantivo* instruction manual

manual *m* **de uso** *sustantivo* **1.** instruction manual **2.** operations manual **3.** user guide **4.** user's manual

manual *m* **de utilización** *sustantivo* **1.** user guide **2.** user's manual

manual *m* **elemental** *sustantivo* primer

manualmente *adv* manually

mapa *m sustantivo* map

mapa *m* **de bits** *sustantivo* bitmap ■ *abrev* bitmp

mapa *m* **de caracteres** *sustantivo* Character Map

mapa *m* **de Karnaugh** *sustantivo* Karnaugh map ◊ **se comprobó si el prototipo tenía riesgos mediante un mapa de Karnaugh** the prototype was checked for hazards with a Karnaugh map

mapa *m* **de la memoria** *sustantivo* memory map

mapa *m* **de sector** *sustantivo* sector map

mapa *m* **lógico** *sustantivo* logic map

maqueta *f sustantivo* **1.** dummy **2.** mock-up **3.** model ◊ **nos mostró una maqueta del nuevo edificio del centro informático** he showed us a model of the new computer centre building

maquetación *f sustantivo* markup

máquina *f sustantivo* **1.** engine **2.** machine ◊ **(instrucción** *o* **datos) en lenguaje máquina** machine-readable ◊ **(programa) propio de la máquina** *o* **hecho a medida** *o* **adaptado al ordenador** machine-intimate

máquina *f* **analítica** *sustantivo* analytical engine

máquina *f* **de base de datos** *sustantivo* database machine

máquina *f* **de bytes** *sustantivo* byte machine

máquina *f* **de componer** *sustantivo* typesetter

máquina *f* **de fotocomposición** *sustantivo* phototypesetter

máquina *f* **de inferencia** *sustantivo* inference engine *o* inference machine

máquina *f* **de octetos** *sustantivo* byte machine

máquina *f* **desnuda** *sustantivo* (*con lo mínimo para funcionar*) clean machine

máquina *f* **de Turing** *sustantivo* Turing machine

máquina *f* **en modalidad carácter** *sustantivo* character machine

máquina *f* **fuente** *sustantivo* source machine

máquina *f* **inteligente** *sustantivo* intelligent device

máquina *f* **virtual** *sustantivo* virtual machine ■ *abrev* VM

marca *sustantivo* **1.** mark **2.** rogue value **3.** scratch ◊ **marca** *f* **del principio de la cinta** beginning of tape marker ◊ **marca** *f* **del principio de la información** beginning of information mark; BIM ◊ **marca** *f* **para localizar una sección del documento** bookmark ◊ **marcas de corrección de las galeradas** proof correction marks

marca *f* **de bloque** *sustantivo* block mark

marca *f* **de direcciones** *sustantivo* address mark

marca *f* **de final de fichero** *sustantivo* trailer

marca *f* **de grupo** *sustantivo* group mark *o* group marker

marca *f* **de inicio de cinta** *sustantivo* BOT marker

marca *f* **de intercalación** *sustantivo* caret

marca *f* **de referencia** *sustantivo* reference mark

marca *f* **de verificación** *sustantivo* check mark

marcado ◊ **marcado** *m* **de límites (de un fichero)** boundary punctuation

marcado *m* **en un teclado tonal** *sustantivo* tone dialling

marcador *m sustantivo* **1.** flag **2.** indicator flag **3.** marker ◊ **marcador** marker pen ◊ **marcador** *m* **de final (de una lista)** terminator

marcador *m* **de campo** *sustantivo* **1.** field marker **2.** field separator

marcador *m* **de enumeración** *sustantivo* bullet

marcador *m* **de final de fichero** *sustantivo* rogue value

marcador *m* **de final de lista** *sustantivo* nil pointer

marcador *m* **de grupo** *sustantivo* group mark *o* group marker

marcador *m* **de inicio de palabra** *sustantivo* word marker

marcador *m* **de lista** *sustantivo* rogue value

marcador *m* **de palabra** *sustantivo* word marker

marcador *m* **de párrafo** *sustantivo* paragraph marker

marcador *m* **en rojo** *sustantivo* redliner

marcadores *mpl* **de tabulación** *plural noun* tabulation markers

marcador *m* **nulo** *sustantivo* nil pointer

marcador *m* **telefónico** (*utilidad de Microsoft Windows*) Dialer ■ *sustantivo* Phone Dialer

marca *f* **lógica** *sustantivo* mark

marcar *verbo* 1. *vt* to flag 2. *vt* to mark ◊ **intervalo de marca** marking interval

marcar un bloque *verbo* to mark block

marcas *fpl* **de tabulación** *plural noun* tab settings *o* tab stops

marcha *f* **atrás** *sustantivo* backward mode

marco *sustantivo* border ◊ **marco** *m* **de tarjetas (de circuitos impresos)** card chassis; card frame ◊ **marco** *m* **de ventana (en pantalla)** frame window ◊ **marco** *m* **frontal (de un ordenador)** bezel

marco *m* **de encuadre** *sustantivo* crop mark

margen *m* *sustantivo* margin ◊ **el margen izquierdo y el margen derecho son las dos secciones de papel en blanco a cada lado de la página** the left margin and right margin are the two sections of blank paper on either side of the page ◊ **fijar un margen** to set a margin ◊ **margen inferior** foot margin ◊ **margen superior** top margin

margen *m* **de encuadernación** *sustantivo* binding offset

margen *m* **de error** *sustantivo* margin of error

margen *m* **de seguridad** *sustantivo* safety margin

margen *m* **interior** *sustantivo* gutter

MARISA *f* *sustantivo* OSI

marketing *m* **de empresas afiliadas** *sustantivo* affiliate marketing

martillo *m* **impresor** *sustantivo* print hammer

más *m* *sustantivo* plus *o* plus sign

mascador *m* *sustantivo* number cruncher

máscara *f* *sustantivo* 1. filter 2. mask ◊ **máscara** *f* **(para introducción) de datos** form mode ◊ **máscara** *f* **(para introducir) de datos** form mode ◊ **se emplea una máscara o clisé para transferir el diseño del transistor al silicio** a mask or stencil is used to transfer the transistor design onto silicon

máscara *f* **de abertura** *sustantivo* aperture mask

máscara *f* **de dirección** *sustantivo* address mask

máscara *f* **de interrupción** *sustantivo* interrupt mask

máscara *f* **de sombra** *sustantivo* shadow-mask

matemáticas *fpl* *sustantivo* 1. math 2. mathematics 3. maths

matemático *adj* mathematical

materia *f* **gris** *sustantivo* wetware

material *m* *sustantivo* 1. installation 2. material 3. network hardware ◊ **el oro es el material ideal para las conexiones eléctricas** gold is the ideal material for electrical connections

material *m* **auxiliar** *sustantivo* auxiliary equipment

material *m* **de red** *sustantivo* networking hardware

material *m* **de tipo N** *sustantivo* n-type material *o* n-type semiconductor

materiales *mpl* **auxiliares** *sustantivo* ancillary equipment

material *m* **ferromagnético** *sustantivo* ferromagnetic material

material *m* **fungible** *plural noun* consumables

material *m* **gráfico** *sustantivo* artwork

matriz *f* *sustantivo* 1. array 2. matrix ◊ **el procesador de matrices permite que la matriz que contiene la imagen de la pantalla pueda girar con una sola instrucción** the array processor allows the array that contains the screen image to be rotated with one simple command ◊ **matriz** *f* **de impresión de alta definición** enhanced dot matrix ◊ **matriz** *f* **gráfica de vídeo (VGA)** video graphics array ◊ **orden lógica** *o* **matriz lógica** logic array

matriz *f* **bidimensional** *sustantivo* two-dimensional array

matriz *f* **de caracteres** *sustantivo* character matrix

matriz *f* **de dos dimensiones** *sustantivo* two-dimensional array

matriz *f* **de gráficos ampliada** *sustantivo* 1. extended graphics array 2. XGA

matriz *f* **del teclado** *sustantivo* key matrix

matriz *f* **de puntos** *sustantivo* dot matrix

matriz *f* **de relación** *sustantivo* matrix

matriz *f* **de tres dimensiones** *sustantivo* three-dimensional array

matriz *f* **exigua** *sustantivo* sparse array

matriz *f* **flexible** *sustantivo* flexible array

matriz *f* **gráfica** *sustantivo* matrix

matriz *f* **multidimensional** *sustantivo* multidimensional array

matriz *f* **negra** *sustantivo* black matrix

matriz *f* **numérica** *sustantivo* numeric array

matriz *f* **pobre** *sustantivo* sparse array

matriz *f* **tridimensional** *sustantivo* three-dimensional array

maximizar *verbo* *vt* to maximise *o* to maximize

máximo *m* *sustantivo* maximum ■ *adj* maximum

mayúscula *f* *sustantivo* uppercase

mayúsculas *fpl* *plural noun* capitals *o* caps ◊ **la contraseña tiene en cuenta las mayúsculas y las minúsculas** the password is case sensitive ◊ **que distingue las mayúsculas de las minúsculas** case sensitive

Mb *sustantivo* megabyte

Mbps *abrev* Mbps

mecánico *adj* mechanical

mecanismo *sustantivo* mechanism ◇ **el mecanismo de la disquetera parece que no funciona bien** the drive mechanism appears to be faulty ◇ **el mecanismo de la impresora es muy simple** the printer mechanism is very simple ◇ **mecanismo** *m* **de protección en caso de fallos** fail safe system ◇ **mecanismo** *m* **de seguridad en caso de fallos** fail safe system

mecanismo *m* **de acceso** *sustantivo* access mechanism

mecanismo *m* **de parada** *sustantivo* shut-off mechanism

media *f* **palabra** *sustantivo* half word

Media Player™ (*marca comercial*) Media Player

media *f* **ponderada** *sustantivo* weighted average

MediaServer™ (*marca comercial*) MediaServer

media tinta *f sustantivo* halftone

medición *f sustantivo* measurement

medición *f* **espacial** *sustantivo* spatial measurement

medida *sustantivo* 1. measure 2. measurement ◇ **anotar las medidas de un paquete** to write down the measurements of a package ◇ **metro** tape measure

'El Parlamento Europeo aprobó la semana pasada, en primera lectura, una serie de medidas sobre las garantías de privacidad que debe disfrutar el ciudadano europeo en Internet. El punto más polémico es el que prohíbe el uso de cookies en los sitios salvo con el consentimiento del navegante, al que el sitio deberá preguntar expresamente si admite el uso de cookies.' [*Ciberp@ís*]

medida *f* **de complejidad** *sustantivo* complexity measure

medida *f* **de precaución** *sustantivo* safety net ◇ **en caso de fallo eléctrico, tenemos un dispositivo UPS de emergencia** if there is a power failure, we have a safety net in the form of a UPS

medida *f* **de superficie** *sustantivo* square measure

medidas *fpl plural noun* measurements ◇ **anotar las medidas de un paquete** to write down the measurements of a package

medidas *fpl* **de seguridad** *plural noun* safety measures

medido por el coeficiente de trabajo *adj* duty-rated

medidor *m* **de batería** *sustantivo* power management

medio *sustantivo, adj* mean ■ *adj* medium ■ *sustantivo* medium ◇ **la cinta magnética es un medio muy fiable de almacenamiento de gran capacidad** magnetic tape is a reliable bulk storage medium ◇ **medio** *m* **de almacenamiento (de datos)** file storage ◇ **medio** *m* **de almacenamiento de gran capacidad** bulk storage

medium ◇ **un sistema informático de tamaño medio** a medium-sized computer system

medio *m* **de almacenamiento** *sustantivo* storage medium

medio *m* **de transmisión** *sustantivo* transmission medium

medio *m* **em** *sustantivo* en

medios ◇ **medios** *mpl* **de comunicación (de masas)** media

medios *mpl* **de comunicación interactivos** *plural noun* interactive media

mediotono *m sustantivo* halftone

medio *m* **vacío** *sustantivo* empty medium

medir *verbo vt* to measure ◇ **tomar medidas para evitar que algo ocurra** to take measures to prevent something happening

mega- *prefijo* mega- ◇ **megabyte** megabyte (MB *o* Mb) ◇ **megaocteto** megabyte (MB *o* Mb)

megabit *m sustantivo* megabit

megabits *mpl* **por segundo** *sustantivo* megabits per second

megabyte *f sustantivo* 1. meg 2. megabyte

megaflops *mpl sustantivo* MFLOPS

megaflops *mpl* **(Mflops)** *sustantivo* megaflop

megahercio (MHz) *m abrev* MHz

megahercio *m* **(MHz)** *sustantivo* megahertz

megaocteto *m sustantivo* 1. meg 2. megabyte

mejora *f sustantivo* enhancement

mejorar *verbo vt* to upgrade

membrete *m sustantivo* heading

memoria *sustantivo* 1. memory 2. storage 3. store ◇ **celda de (la) memoria** store cell ◇ **especificación** *f* **de memoria expandida** EMS ◇ **los dos ordenadores funcionan a velocidades distintas, pero pueden transmitir datos mediante el sistema FIFO** the two computers operate at different rates, but can transmit data using a FIFO memory ◇ **memoria** *f* **(que contiene los ficheros)** file storage ◇ **memoria** *f* **ampliada de salida de datos** extended data output memory ◇ **memoria** *f* **caché de ráfagas de canal** pipeline burst cache ◇ **memoria** *f* **de acceso aleatorio de vídeo** video memory; video RAM; video random access memory; VRAM ◇ **memoria** *f* **de acceso aleatorio dinámica multiuso** MDRAM; multibank dynamic random access memory ◇ **memoria** *f* **de acceso aleatorio no volátil** nonvolatile random access memory; NVRAM ◇ **memoria** *f* **de burbujas (magnéticas)** bubble memory ◇ **memoria** *f* **de dispositivo acoplado de carga** charge-coupled device memory ◇ **memoria** *f* **de lectura programable y borrable eléctricamente** electrically erasable programmable read-only memory ◇ **memoria** *f* **de solo lectura programable y borrable** erasable programmable read-only memory ◇ **memoria** *f* **de sólo lectura que puede borrarse** erasable read-only memory; EROM ◇ **memoria** *f* **de un (solo) nivel** one-level store ◇ **memoria** *f* **dinámica sincrónica de acceso aleatorio** synchronised dynamic RAM; synchronous DRAM ◇ **memoria** *f* **inter-**

media de teclado de n pulsaciones n-key roll-over ◇ **memoria** f **intermedia de transmisión de datos** data communications buffer ◇ **memoria** f **PROM borrable por radiación ultravioleta** ultraviolet erasable PROM ◇ **memoria** f **que funciona bajo el principio de primero en entrar primero en salir** FIFO memory ◇ **memoria** f **ROM programable y borrable** erasable programmable read-only memory ◇ **memoria** f **(de almacenamiento) temporal** cache ◇ **memoria volátil** volatile storage ◇ **registro de datos en memoria** store data register (SDR) ◇ **tamaño de la memoria** storage size ◇ **utilizar una memoria intermedia** buffer

memoria f **a corto plazo** *sustantivo* **1.** scratchpad **2.** scratchpad memory

memoria f **acústica** *sustantivo* **1.** acoustic memory **2.** acoustic store

memoria f **almacenada temporalmente** *sustantivo* buffered memory

memoria f **alta** *sustantivo* **1.** high memory **2.** upper memory

memoria f **amortiguadora** *sustantivo* buffer

memoria f **ampliada** *sustantivo* extended memory

memoria f **asociativa** *sustantivo* associative memory ■ *abrev* CAM ■ *sustantivo* **1.** content-addressable memory *o* content-addressable storage **2.** parallel search storage **3.** searching storage **4.** search memory

memoria f **auxiliar** *sustantivo* **1.** backing memory **2.** backing storage **3.** backing store *o* backing storage *o* backing memory **4.** external memory **5.** slave cache ◇ **al añadir otra disquetera aumentaré la capacidad de la memoria auxiliar** by adding another disk drive, I will increase the backing store capabilities ◇ **la cinta de papel (perforada) es una de las memorias auxiliares de acceso más lento** paper tape is one of the slowest access backing stores

memoria f **baja** *sustantivo* low memory

memoria f **base** *sustantivo* **1.** base memory *o* base RAM **2.** conventional memory

memoria f **borrable** *sustantivo* **1.** erasable memory **2.** erasable storage

memoria f **caché** *sustantivo* **1.** cache **2.** RAM cache

memoria f **caché asíncrona** *sustantivo* asynchronous cache

memoria f **caché integrada** *sustantivo* on-chip cache

memoria f **caché sincrónica** *sustantivo* synchronous cache

memoria f **CCD** *sustantivo* **1.** CCD memory **2.** charge-coupled device memory

memoria f **central** *sustantivo* **1.** central memory **2.** CM **3.** core memory **4.** main memory **5.** main storage **6.** primary memory

memoria f **central rápida** *sustantivo* fast core ◇ **en este sistema, se emplea la memoria central rápida como bloc de notas para todas las operaciones de cálculo** the fast core is used as a scratchpad for all calculations in this system

memoria f **circulante** *sustantivo* circulating storage

memoria f **compartida** *sustantivo* shared memory

memoria f **común** *sustantivo* working store

memoria f **con condensador** *sustantivo* capacitor storage

memoria f **con doble acceso** *sustantivo* dual port memory

memoria f **convencional** *sustantivo* conventional memory

memoria f **criogénica** *sustantivo* cryogenic memory

memoria f **de acceso al azar** *sustantivo* RAM ◇ **disco RAM** *o* **disco de memoria** RAM disk ◇ **(memoria) RAM dinámica** dynamic RAM ◇ **se puede aumentar la memoria de la impresora conectándole otro cartucho RAM** you can increase the printer's memory by plugging in another RAM cartridge

memoria f **de acceso aleatorio** *sustantivo* **1.** RAM **2.** random access memory **3.** random access storage ◇ **al pulsar Ctrl-F5 se activa el programa residente RAM y muestra la agenda del día** when you hit Ctrl-F5, you will activate the RAM resident program and it will display your day's diary ◇ **(memoria) RAM dinámica** dynamic RAM ◇ **se puede aumentar la memoria de la impresora conectándole otro cartucho RAM** you can increase the printer's memory by plugging in another RAM cartridge

memoria f **de acceso aleatorio dinámica** *abrev* DRAM ■ *sustantivo* dynamic random access memory

memoria f **de acceso inmediato** *sustantivo* **1.** IAS **2.** immediate access store

memoria f **de acceso intermedio** *sustantivo* **1.** IAM **2.** intermediate access memory

memoria f **de acceso rápido** *abrev* FAM ■ *sustantivo* **1.** fast access memory **2.** rapid access memory

memoria f **de acceso secuencial** *sustantivo* **1.** SAM **2.** sequential access storage **3.** serial-access memory **4.** serial storage

memoria f **de almacenamiento temporal** *sustantivo* cache memory

memoria f **de alta densidad** *sustantivo* high density storage ◇ **un disco duro, comparado con una cinta perforada, es un medio de almacenamiento de alta densidad** a hard disk is a high density storage medium compared to paper tape

memoria f **de anidamiento** *sustantivo* nesting store

memoria f **de archivo** *sustantivo* archive storage

memoria f **de arranque** *sustantivo* bootstrap memory

memoria f **de bloc de notas** *sustantivo* **1.** scratchpad **2.** scratchpad memory

memoria *f* **de burbujas magnéticas** *sustantivo* magnetic bubble memory

memoria *f* **de búsqueda** *sustantivo* search memory

memoria *f* **de búsquedas paralelas** *sustantivo* parallel search storage

memoria *f* **de control** *sustantivo* control memory

memoria *f* **de datos** *sustantivo* data storage

memoria *f* **de disco** *sustantivo* **1.** disk memory **2.** disk storage

memoria *f* **de entrada** *sustantivo* input storage

memoria *f* **de escáner** *sustantivo* scanner memory

memoria *f* **de escritura láser** *sustantivo* laser emulsion storage

memoria *f* **de extensión** *sustantivo* extension memory

memoria *f* **de formato local** *sustantivo* local format storage

memoria *f* **de imagen de página** *sustantivo* page image buffer

memoria *f* **de imágenes ópticas** *sustantivo* scanner memory

memoria *f* **de instrucción** *sustantivo* instruction storage

memoria *f* **del disco duro** *sustantivo* fixed disk storage

memoria *f* **de lectura borrable eléctricamente** *sustantivo* electrically erasable read-only memory

memoria *f* **de lectura/escritura** *sustantivo* read/write memory

memoria *f* **de línea de retardo** *sustantivo* delay line store

memoria *f* **de núcleos** *sustantivo* core store

memoria *f* **de pantalla** *sustantivo* screen memory

memoria *f* **de película delgada** *sustantivo* thin-film memory

memoria *f* **de proceso preferente** *sustantivo* foreground processing memory

memoria *f* **de sólo lectura** *sustantivo* read only memory ■ *abrev* ROM

memoria *f* **de sólo lectura programable electrónicamente** *abrev* EPROM

memoria *f* **de tabulación** *sustantivo* tab memory

memoria *f* **de transmisión de datos** *sustantivo* communications buffer

memoria *f* **dinámica** *sustantivo* **1.** circulating storage **2.** dynamic memory **3.** dynamic storage

memoria *f* **dinámica permanente** *sustantivo* permanent dynamic memory

memoria *f* **direccionable por contenido** *sustantivo* searching storage

memoria *f* **direccionable por el contenido** *abrev* CAM ■ *sustantivo* content-addressable memory *o* content-addressable storage

memoria *f* **duplicada** *sustantivo* shadow memory *o* shadow page

memoria *f* **EAPROM** *sustantivo* **1.** EAPROM **2.** electrically alterable programmable read-only memory

memoria *f* **EAPROM, modificable eléctricamente** *sustantivo* electrically alterable read-only memory

memoria *f* **EAROM** *sustantivo* EAROM

memoria *f* **EDO** *sustantivo* EDO memory

memoria *f* **EEMS** *sustantivo* enhanced expanded memory specification

memoria *f* **EEPROM** *abrev* EEPROM ■ *sustantivo* electrically erasable programmable read-only memory

memoria *f* **EEROM** *abrev* EEROM ■ *sustantivo* electrically erasable read-only memory

memoria *f* **electrostática** *sustantivo* electrostatic storage

memoria *f* **en curso** *sustantivo* local format storage

memoria *f* **en serie** *sustantivo* serial memory ◇ **la cinta magnética constituye una memoria secuencial de gran capacidad** magnetic tape is a high capacity serial memory

memoria *f* **EPROM** *sustantivo* erasable programmable read-only memory

memoria *f* **estándar** *sustantivo* standard memory

memoria *f* **estática** *sustantivo* **1.** static memory **2.** static storage

memoria *f* **estática de acceso aleatorio** *sustantivo* **1.** SRAM **2.** static RAM

memoria *f* **extendida** *sustantivo* **1.** expanded memory **2.** extended memory

memoria *f* **extendida LIM EMS** *sustantivo* Lotus-Intel-Microsoft Expanded Memory System

memoria *f* **externa** *sustantivo* **1.** external memory **2.** external storage *o* external store

memoria *f* **FIFO** *sustantivo* FIFO memory ◇ **los dos ordenadores funcionan a velocidades distintas, pero pueden transmitir datos mediante el sistema FIFO** the two computers operate at different rates, but can transmit data using a FIFO memory

memoria *f* **física** *sustantivo* physical memory

memoria *f* **'flash'** *sustantivo* flash memory

memoria *f* **fotodigital** *sustantivo* photodigital memory

memoria *f* **global** *sustantivo* global memory

memoria *f* **holográfica** *sustantivo* holographic storage

memoria *f* **intercalada** *sustantivo* interleaved memory

memoria *f* **intermedia** *sustantivo* **1.** buffer **2.** intermediate storage **3.** secondary memory **4.** secondary storage

memoria *f* **intermedia circular** *sustantivo* circular buffer

memoria *f* **intermedia de capacidad variable** *sustantivo* elastic buffer

memoria *f* **intermedia de comunicaciones** *sustantivo* communications buffer

memoria *f* **intermedia de datos** *sustantivo* data buffer

memoria *f* **intermedia de entrada/salida** *sustantivo* **1.** input/output buffer **2.** I/O buffer

memoria *f* **intermedia de imágenes** *sustantivo* frame buffer

memoria *f* **intermedia de la impresora** *sustantivo* printer buffer

memoria *f* **intermedia de la unidad** *sustantivo* unit buffer

memoria *f* **intermedia de vídeo** *sustantivo* video buffer

memoria *f* **intermedia dinámica** *sustantivo* dynamic buffer

memoria *f* **intermedia para imágenes** *sustantivo* image buffer

memoria *f* **intermedia z** *sustantivo* z buffer

memoria *f* **interna** *sustantivo* **1.** internal memory **2.** internal store

memoria *f* **local** *sustantivo* local memory

memoria *f* **magnética** *sustantivo* **1.** magnetic memory **2.** magnetic storage

memoria *f* **magnética pelicular** *sustantivo* thin-film memory

memoria *f* **MOS** *sustantivo* MOS memory

memoria *f* **no volátil** *sustantivo* **1.** non volatile memory **2.** non volatile storage *o* nonvolatile store

memoria *f* **óptica** *sustantivo* **1.** optical memory **2.** optical storage

memoria *f* **periférica** *sustantivo* peripheral memory

memoria *f* **permanente** *sustantivo* **1.** nonerasable storage **2.** permanent memory ◇ **la cinta de papel es una memoria permanente** paper tape is a nonerasable storage

memoria *f* **por bloques** *sustantivo* flash memory

memoria *f* **principal** *sustantivo* **1.** central memory **2.** CM **3.** main memory **4.** main storage **5.** primary storage

memoria *f* **(de) programa** *sustantivo* program storage

memoria *f* **programable** *abrev* FROM ■ *sustantivo* **1.** fusible read only memory **2.** programmable memory **3.** PROM

memoria *f* **programable de solo lectura** *sustantivo* PROM

memoria *f* **PROM** *sustantivo* PROM

memoria *f* **protegida** *sustantivo* protected storage

memoria *f* **que contiene un microprograma** *sustantivo* microprogram store

memoria *f* **RAM** *sustantivo* random access memory

memoria *f* **RAM en modo página** *sustantivo* page-mode RAM ◇ **el adaptador de vídeo utiliza memoria RAM en modo página para acelerar la visualización** the video adapter uses page-mode RAM to speed up the display

memoria *f* **real** *sustantivo* real memory

memoria *f* **regenerativa** *sustantivo* regenerative memory ◇ **la pantalla puede compararse con una memoria regenerativa; necesita barridos regulares de actualización para evitar el parpadeo** the CRT display can be thought of as regenerative memory, it requires regular refresh picture scans to prevent flicker ◇ **la RAM dinámica es una memoria regenerativa que necesita ser regenerada cada 250 ns** dynamic RAM is regenerative memory – it needs to be refreshed every 250ns

memoria *f* **reutilizable** *sustantivo* erasable storage

memoria *f* **ROM** *sustantivo* read only memory ■ *abrev* ROM

memoria *f* **ROM auxiliar** *sustantivo* sideways ROM

memoria *f* **ROM enmascarada** *sustantivo* masked ROM

memoria *f* **ROM programable** *sustantivo* programmable read only memory

memoria *f* **ROM programable, modificable eléctricamente** *sustantivo* electrically alterable read-only memory

memoria *f* **secuencial** *sustantivo* serial memory ◇ **la cinta magnética constituye una memoria secuencial de gran capacidad** magnetic tape is a high capacity serial memory

memoria *f* **secuencial indexada** *sustantivo* indexed sequential storage

memoria *f* **secundaria** *sustantivo* **1.** backing store *o* backing storage *o* backing memory **2.** secondary memory **3.** secondary storage

memoria *f* **semiconductora** *sustantivo* semiconductor memory

memoria *f* **sombra** *sustantivo* shadow memory *o* shadow page

memoria *f* **superior** *sustantivo* upper memory

memoria *f* **temporal** *sustantivo* **1.** scratchpad **2.** scratchpad memory **3.** temporary storage **4.** working store

memoria *f* **temporal de instrucción** *sustantivo* instruction cache

memoria *f* **temporal de pantalla** *sustantivo* screen buffer

memoria *f* **transitoria** *sustantivo* **1.** scratchpad **2.** scratchpad memory

memoria *f* **virtual** *sustantivo* **1.** virtual memory **2.** virtual storage ■ *abrev* VS

memoria *f* **viva** *sustantivo* random access memory

memoria *f* **volátil** *sustantivo* volatile memory *o* volatile store *o* volatile dynamic storage

mencionar *verbo vt* to quote ◇ **al responder haga referencia a este número, por favor** in reply please quote this number ◇ **cuando presente una reclamación por favor haga referencia al número del lote situado en la caja del ordenador** when making a complaint please quote the batch number printed on the computer case ◇ **mencionó unas cifras procedentes del artículo del periódico** he quoted figures from the newspaper report

mensaje *sustantivo* message ◇ **conmutación de mensajes** message switching ◇ **el mensaje READY indica que el sistema está disponible para recibir instrucciones** the prompt READY indicates that the system is available to receive instructions ◇ **el sistema MS-DOS normalmente muestra el mensaje C:\> para indicar que está preparado para procesar instrucciones introducidas por el usuario** o **la usuaria** MS-DOS normally displays the command prompt C:\> to indicate that it is ready to process instructions typed in by a user ◇ **mensaje** *m* **(de una instrucción)** prompt ◇ **mensaje del día** message of the day (MOTD) ◇ **mensaje** *m* **incorporado** built-in message ◇ **numeración de mensajes** message numbering ◇ **servicio de transferencia de mensajes** message handling service (MHS)

mensaje *m* **cifrado** *sustantivo* **1.** ciphertext **2.** encryption

mensaje *m* **con acuse de recibo** *sustantivo* acknowledged mail

mensaje *m* **de alerta** *sustantivo* beacon frame

mensaje *m* **de aviso** *sustantivo* notification message ◇ **si se mueve un objeto, la aplicación genera un mensaje de notificación para indicar a otros procesos cuando se ha terminado de mover el objeto** if an object is moved, the application will generate a notification message to tell other processes when it has finished moving the object

mensaje *m* **de consulta** *sustantivo* query message

mensaje *m* **de diagnóstico** *sustantivo* diagnostic message

mensaje *m* **de dirección única** *sustantivo* single address message

mensaje *m* **de entrada** *sustantivo* input statement

mensaje *m* **de error** *sustantivo* error message

mensaje *m* **de instrucción** *sustantivo* command message

mensaje *m* **de intervención** *sustantivo* action message

mensaje *m* **de notificación** *sustantivo* notification message ◇ **si se mueve un objeto, la aplicación genera un mensaje de notificación para indicar a otros procesos cuando se ha terminado de mover el objeto** if an object is moved, the application will generate a notification message to tell other processes when it has finished moving the object

mensaje *m* **de texto** *sustantivo* text message

mensaje *m* **de una sola dirección** *sustantivo* single address message

mensaje *m* **difundido** *sustantivo* broadcast message ◇ **cinco minutos antes de cerrar la red local, emitimos un mensaje a todos los usuarios** five minutes before we shut down the LAN, we send a broadcast message to all users

mensaje *m* **electrónico** *sustantivo* mail

mensaje *m* **emitido** *sustantivo* broadcast message ◇ **cinco minutos antes de cerrar la red local, emitimos un mensaje a todos los usuarios** five minutes before we shut down the LAN, we send a broadcast message to all users

mensaje *m* **recibido** *sustantivo* incoming message

mensajería *f sustantivo* messaging

menú *sustantivo* menu ◇ **menú** *m* **de ayuda con la función de cada tecla** key overlay ◇ **menú** *m* **de ayuda del teclado** keyboard overlay ◇ **menú** *m* **del botón derecho del ratón** right-click menu ◇ **menú** *m* **de programas (en Windows)** Programs menu ◇ **sin un menú de ayuda, nunca recordaría qué es lo que hace cada tecla de función** without the key overlay, I would never remember which function key does what

menú *m* **activo** *sustantivo* active menu

menú *m* **de control** *sustantivo* control menu

menú *m* **desplegable** *sustantivo* **1.** drop-down menu **2.** pop-down menu **3.** pop-up menu **4.** pull-down menu ◇ **el menú desplegable aparece cuando se hace clic sobre la barra del menú en la parte superior de la pantalla** the pull-down menu is viewed by clicking on the menu bar at the top of the screen

menú *m* **principal** *sustantivo* main menu

menú *m* **secundario** *sustantivo* submenu

meollo *m sustantivo* kernel

mesa *f sustantivo* console

mesa *f* **de control** *sustantivo* operator's console

metabit *m sustantivo* metabit

metacompilación *f sustantivo* metacompilation

metacompilador *m sustantivo* metacompiler

metafichero *m sustantivo* metafile ◇ **el sistema operativo usa un metafichero para guardar datos que define dónde se almacena cada fichero en el disco** the operating system uses a metafile to hold data that defines where each file is stored on disk

metafichero *m* **de gráficos** *sustantivo* **1.** CGM **2.** computer graphics metafile

metalenguaje *m sustantivo* **1.** Backus-Naur-Form **2.** BNF **3.** metalanguage

metamorfosis *f sustantivo* morphing

método *sustantivo* technique ◇ **método** *m* **básico de acceso a telecomunicaciones** basic telecommunications access method; BTAM ◇ **método** *m* **de acceso secuencial en cola de espera** QSAM; queued sequential access method ◇ **método** *m* **de acceso secuencial indexado en cola de espera** QISAM; queued indexed sequential access method ◇ **método** *m* **de gestión de la cola de espera** queued access method ◇ **método** *m* **de paginación de la memoria** paged-memory scheme

método *m* **ascendente** *sustantivo* **1.** bottom up method *o* bottom up programming **2.** hill climbing

método *m* **a seguir** *sustantivo* procedure ◇ **debería utilizar este procedimiento para recuperar los ficheros perdidos** you should use this procedure to retrieve lost files ◇ **el procedimiento se explica en el manual de instrucciones** the procedure is given in the manual

método *m* **básico de acceso directo** *sustantivo* basic direct access method ■ *abrev* BDAM

método *m* **BTAM** *sustantivo* **1.** basic telecommunications access method **2.** BTAM

método *m* **de acceso** *sustantivo* access method

método *m* **de acceso secuencial indexado** *sustantivo* indexed sequential access method ■ *abrev* ISAM

método *m* **de asignación de nombres** *sustantivo* naming services

método *m* **de borrado** *sustantivo* eraser

método *m* **de direccionamiento** *sustantivo* addressing method

método *m* **de fuerza bruta** *sustantivo* brute force method

método *m* **del camino crítico** *abrev* CPM

método *m* **de matizado de Gouraud** *sustantivo* Gouraud shading

método *m* **de Monte Carlo** *sustantivo* Monte Carlo method

método *m* **de ruta crítica** *sustantivo* critical path method

método *m* **FTAM** *sustantivo* file transfer access and management

método *m* **no calculado** *sustantivo* brute force method

método *m* **secuencial básico de acceso** *sustantivo* basic sequential access method

métodos formales *plural noun* formal methods

micra *f sustantivo* micron

micro *m sustantivo* microphone

micro- *prefijo* micro-

microcasete *f sustantivo* microcassette

microchip *f sustantivo* microchip

microciclo *m sustantivo* microcycle

microcircuito *m sustantivo* microcircuit

microcódigo *m sustantivo* microcode

microcontrolador *m sustantivo* microcontroller

microcontrolador *m* **de un solo chip** *sustantivo* single-chip microcontroller

microdispositivo *m sustantivo* microdevice

microelectrónica *f sustantivo* microelectronics

micrófono *m sustantivo* microphone ◇ **micrófono de bobina móvil** moving coil microphone ◇ **micrófono dinámico** dynamic microphone

microinformática *f adj* microcomputing ◇ **industria de la microinformática** *o* **de los microordenadores** the microcomputing industry

microinstrucción *f sustantivo* microinstruction

micrómetro *m sustantivo* micrometre

micromódulo *m sustantivo* medallion

micrón *m sustantivo* micron

microordenador *m sustantivo* **1.** micro **2.** microcomputer

microordenador *m* **de escritorio** *sustantivo* desktop computer *o* desktop computer system

microordenador *m* **de mesa** *sustantivo* desktop computer *o* desktop computer system

microordenador *m* **portátil** *sustantivo* microwriter

microplaca *f sustantivo* chip

microplaqueta *f sustantivo* **1.** chip **2.** wafer

microplaqueta *f* **de silicio** *sustantivo* silicon chip

microprocesador *sustantivo* **1.** microdevice **2.** microprocessor

'Los microprocesadores son diminutos cerebros artificiales capaces de realizar millones de combinaciones por segundo.' [*La Red*]

microprograma *m sustantivo* microprogram

microprogramación *f sustantivo* microprogramming

microsecuencia *f sustantivo* microsequence

microsegundo *m sustantivo* microsecond

Microsoft *abrev* MS

Microsoft™ Microsoft

Microsoft Exchange™ (*programa de Windows 95*) Microsoft Exchange

Microsoft Internet Explorer™ Microsoft Internet Explorer

Microsoft Network™ **1.** Microsoft Network **2.** (*marca comercial*) MSN

Microsoft Outlook™ (*marca comercial*) Microsoft Outlook

Microsoft Outlook Express™ (*marca comercial*) Microsoft Outlook Express

Microsoft Windows Microsoft Windows

midi ◇ **interfaz** *f* **digital para instrumentos musicales** musical instrument digital interface

MIDI *sustantivo* MIDI

migración *f* **de datos** *sustantivo* data migration

mili- *prefijo* milli- ◇ **miliculombio (mC)** millicoulomb (mC) ◇ **milisegundo (ms)** millisecond (ms)

miliamperio (mA) *m sustantivo* milliampere

miliamperio *m* **(mA)** *sustantivo* mA

mil instrucciones *fpl* **por segundo** *sustantivo* **1.** kilo instructions per second **2.** KIPS

milisegundo (ms) *m sustantivo* millisecond

millón ◇ **millón** *m* **de instrucciones por segundo** million instructions per second

millón *m* **de instrucciones por segundo** *sustantivo* MIPS

millones ◇ **millones** *mpl* **de operaciones de coma flotante por segundo** megaflop

mil millones *mpl abrev* bn

mi *m* **maletín** *sustantivo* Briefcase utility

MIMD *sustantivo* multiple instruction stream-multiple data stream

mini *m sustantivo* minicomputer

mini- *prefijo* mini-

miniatura *f sustantivo* thumbnail

minicomputador *m sustantivo* minicomputer

minidisco ◇ **minidisco** *m* **duro (de tipo Winchester)** miniwinny

minidisquete *m sustantivo* **1.** minidisk **2.** minifloppy

minimizar *verbo vt* to minimise *o* to minimize

miniordenador *m sustantivo* **1.** mini **2.** minicomputer

minuendo *m sustantivo* minuend

minúscula(s) *f(pl) sustantivo* lower case

Mi PC *sustantivo* My Computer

MIPS *sustantivo* million instructions per second

MISD *sustantivo* multiple instruction stream-single data stream

MKDIR ◇ **MKDIR (de creación de un directorio)** MD

MKDIR (de creación de un directorio) *abrev* MKDIR

MMX (*marca comercial*) Intel MMX

mnemónico *m sustantivo* mnemonic

mnemotécnico *m sustantivo* assembler mnemonic

modal *adj* modal

modalidad *f sustantivo* mode ◇ **cuando quiera mecanografiar un texto, presione esta tecla de función para activar el modo alfanumérico del terminal** when you want to type in text, press this function key which will put the terminal in its alphanumeric mode

modalidad *f* **(de) carácter** *sustantivo* character mode

modalidad *f* **de respuesta** *sustantivo* answer mode

modalidad *f* **en octetos** *sustantivo* byte mode

modalidad *f* **en ráfagas** *sustantivo* burst mode

modalidad *f* **ruidosa** *sustantivo* noisy mode

Mode 1 *sustantivo* Mode 1

Mode 2 *sustantivo* Mode 2

modelación *f* **impresa** *sustantivo* form overlay

modelar *verbo* to model

modelo *sustantivo* **1.** mock-up **2.** model ■ *adj* model ■ *sustantivo* **1.** pattern **2.** stencil **3.** template ◇ **el nuevo modelo B ha sustituido al modelo A** the new model B has taken the place of model A ◇ **éste es el último modelo** this is the latest model ◇ **este modelo contiene todos los componentes electrónicos** the stencil has all the electronic components on it ◇ **modelo** *m* **ar-**

quitectónico de referencia para la interconexión de sistemas abiertos OSI ◇ **modelo** *m* **de (gestión de acceso a la) memoria** memory model ◇ **modelo** *m* **medio de gestión de memoria** medium model

modelo *m* **binario** *sustantivo* bit pattern

modelo *m* **clónico** *sustantivo* clone

modelo *m* **compacto** *sustantivo* compact model

modelo *m* **conceptual** *sustantivo* conceptual model

modelo *m* **de objetos componentes** *sustantivo* Component Object Model

modelo *m* **de trama de rejilla** *sustantivo* **1.** polygon mesh model **2.** stick model **3.** wire frame model **4.** wire mesh model

modelo *m* **de un organigrama** *sustantivo* flowchart template

modelo *m* **de un sistema** *sustantivo* system design

modelo *m* **estocástico** *sustantivo* stochastic model

modelo *m* **grande** *sustantivo* (*de memoria de los procesadores INTEL*) large model

modelo *m* **matemático** *sustantivo* mathematical model

modelo *m* **pequeño** *sustantivo* (*de memoria Intel de 64 Kb*) tiny model

módem *m sustantivo* modem *o* MODEM

módem *sustantivo* dataset ◇ **módem** *m* **de distancia de transmisión limitada** limited distance modem

> 'Son cada día más los que deciden establecer su oficina en el hogar, construyendo en él un lugar dedicado exclusivamente a ello, equipado con al menos una segunda línea telefónica, un fax y un módem para la computadora.' [*La Red*]

módem *m* **compatible con Bell** *sustantivo* Bell-compatible modem

módem *m* **de banda de base** *sustantivo* base band modem ◇ **no debe utilizarse un módem de banda de base con una línea telefónica normal** do not use a base band modem with a normal phone line

módem *m* **de cable** *sustantivo* cable modem

módem *m* **de corto arrastre** *sustantivo* short haul modem

módem *m* **de devolución de llamadas** *sustantivo* call back modem

módem *m* **de fax** *sustantivo* fax modem

módem *m* **de llamada** *sustantivo* originate modem

módem *m* **de llamada automática** *sustantivo* dial-in modem

módem *m* **de respuesta** *sustantivo* answer modem

módem *m* **de retorno** *sustantivo* answer modem

módem *m* **de retrodemanda** *sustantivo* call back modem

módem *m* **de software** *sustantivo* software modem

módem *m* **de una sola dirección** *sustantivo* half-duplex modem

módem *m* **en banda base** *sustantivo* base band modem

módem *m* **externo** *sustantivo* external modem

módem *m* **incorporado** *sustantivo* integrated modem

módem *m* **integrado** *sustantivo* integrated modem

módem *m* **interno** *sustantivo* internal modem

módem *m* **nulo** *sustantivo* null modem ◊ **este cable está configurado como una conexión directa, lo que me permite interconectar fácilmente estos dos ordenadores** this cable is configured as a null modem, which will allow me to connect these 2 computers together easily

módem *m* **para red local** *sustantivo* limited distance modem

módem *m* **semidúplex** *sustantivo* half-duplex modem

moderador *mf sustantivo* moderator

moderar *verbo vt* to moderate

modificable ◊ **modificable por el usuario según sus necesidades** user-selectable

modificación *f sustantivo* **1.** adjustment **2.** change **3.** modification

modificación *f* **de direcciones** *sustantivo* address modification

modificación *f* **de la perspectiva** *sustantivo* perspective correction

modificación *f* **de una instrucción** *sustantivo* instruction modification

modificación *f* **provisional** *sustantivo* patch

modificador *m sustantivo* modifier

modificador *m* **(de instrucción)** *sustantivo* switch ◊ **añada el modificador 'or W' a la instrucción DIR del sistema DOS y el listado del directorio aparecerá a lo ancho de la pantalla** add the switch '/W' to the DOS command DIR and the directory listing will be displayed across the screen

modificadores *mpl* **de impresión** *plural noun* print modifiers

modificar *verbo* **1.** *vt* to modify **2.** *vt* to revise ◊ **estamos ejecutando una versión modificada del programa de edición de cartas modelo** we are running a modified version of the mail-merge system ◊ **se modificó el teclado para los usuarios europeos** the keyboard was modified for European users ◊ **tendremos que modificar el software para poder funcionar en un ordenador personal** the software will have to be modified to run on a small PC

modificar el tamaño *verbo* to size

modo *sustantivo* mode ◊ **cuando quiera mecanografiar un texto, presione esta tecla de función para activar el modo alfanumérico del terminal** when you want to type in text, press this function key which will put the terminal in its alphanumeric mode ◊ **modo** *m* **de carga en función de la tasa de actividad** activity loading ◊ **modo** *m* **de transferencia asíncrona ATM** asynchronous transfer mode; ATM ◊ **modo de transformación por bits** bit-map mode ◊ **modo** *m* **direccionable de una matriz activa** all points addressable mode ◊ **modo** *m* **secundario** background mode

modo *m* **activo** *sustantivo* active state

modo *m* **alterno** *sustantivo* alternate mode

modo *m* **APA** *sustantivo* all points addressable mode

modo *m* **asíncrono** *sustantivo* asynchronous mode

modo *m* **AT** *sustantivo* AT mode

modo *m* **conversacional** *sustantivo* conversational mode

modo *m* **Ctrl** *sustantivo* control mode

modo *m* **de control** *sustantivo* control mode

modo *m* **de desplazamiento** *sustantivo* scroll mode

modo *m* **de direccionamiento** *sustantivo* addressing mode

modo *m* **de ejecución** *sustantivo* execute mode

modo *m* **de ejecución por encauzamiento** *sustantivo* pipelining *o* pipeline memory

modo *m* **de ejecución preferente** *plural noun* foreground mode

modo *m* **de entrada** *sustantivo* input mode

modo *m* **de inserción** *sustantivo* insert mode

modo *m* **de instrucción** *sustantivo* command mode

modo *m* **de intercalación de dígitos** *sustantivo* noisy mode

modo *m* **de presentación** *sustantivo* display mode

modo *m* **de procesos por lotes** *sustantivo* batch mode

modo *m* **de respuesta** *sustantivo* answer mode

modo *m* **de salida** *sustantivo* output mode

modo *m* **de sustitución** *sustantivo* replace mode

modo *m* **de tratamiento por encauzamiento** *sustantivo* pipelining *o* pipeline memory

modo *m* **de trazado** *sustantivo* plotting mode

modo *m* **de visualización** *sustantivo* display mode

modo *m* **diferido** *sustantivo* deferred mode

modo *m* **directo** *sustantivo* **1.** direct mode **2.** raw mode

modo *m* **(de) ejecución** *sustantivo* execute mode

modo *m* **estacionario** *sustantivo* steady state

modo *m* **gráfico** *sustantivo* **1.** graphics mode **2.** plotting mode

modo *m* **hacia atrás** *sustantivo* backward mode

modo *m* **inmediato** *sustantivo* immediate mode

modo *m* **interactivo** *sustantivo* **1.** conversational mode **2.** interactive mode **3.** interactive processing

modo *m* **local** *sustantivo* local mode

modo *m* **multi-usuario** *sustantivo* free running mode

modo *m* **prioritario** *sustantivo* privileged mode

modo *m* **protegido** *sustantivo* **1.** privileged mode **2.** protected mode

modo *m* **reactivo** *sustantivo* reactive mode

modo *m* **ruidoso** *sustantivo* noisy mode

modo *m* **secuencial** *sustantivo* sequential mode

modo *m* **seguro** *sustantivo* safe mode

modo *m* **sincrónico** *sustantivo* synchronous mode

modo *m* **síncrono** *sustantivo* synchronous mode

modo *m* **(de) texto** *sustantivo* text mode ◇ **normalmente el MS-DOS funciona en modo texto** MS-DOS normally operates in a text mode

modulación ◇ **modulación** *f* **de Amplitud en Cuadratura** QAM ◇ **modulación** *f* **de código de impulso diferencial** differential pulse coded modulation; DPCM ◇ **modulación** *f* **diferencial dinámica por impulsos y códigos** adaptive differential pulse code modulation; ADPCM ◇ **modulación** *f* **por codificación de impulsos codificados** PCM; pulse-code modulation

modulación *f* **de amplitud** *abrev* AM ■ *sustantivo* amplitude modulation

modulación *f* **de amplitud en cuadratura** *sustantivo* quadrature amplitude modulation

modulación *f* **de frecuencia modificada** *sustantivo* **1.** MFM **2.** modified frequency modulation

modulación *f* **de frecuencias** *sustantivo* frequency modulation

modulación *f* **por codificación de impulsos** *sustantivo* pulse-code modulation

modulador *m sustantivo* modulator

modular *adj* modular ■ *verbo* *vt* to modulate ◇ **contador modular** modular counter

modularidad *f sustantivo* modularity ◇ **la modularidad del software o del hardware permite modificar el sistema** the modularity of the software or hardware allows the system to be changed

modularidad *f* **de la memoria** *sustantivo* granularity

modularización *f sustantivo* modularisation *o* modularization

modulator-desmodulador *m sustantivo* modulator/demodulator

módulo *sustantivo* **1.** bead **2.** chapter **3.** module ◇ **módulo** *m* **(de un sistema)** building block ◇ **módulo** *m* **de memoria doble en línea** DIMM; dual in-line memory module ◇ **módulo** *m* **simple de memoria en línea** SIMM; single in-line memory module ◇ **un módulo de interfaz analógico multifunción incluye convertidores de analógico a digital y de digital a analógico** a multifunction analog interface module includes analog to digital and digital to analog converters

'La necesidad de respetar el equilibrio entre prestaciones y agilidad es lo que genera el espacio para que existan pequeñas empresas desarrolladoras de módulos (plug-ins) que añaden funcionalidades específicas al programa principal.' [*Ciberp@ís*]

módulo *m* **aritmético** *sustantivo* modulo arithmetic

módulo *m* **N** *sustantivo* modulo-N

monitor *m sustantivo* **1.** monitor **2.** monitor unit **3.** supervisor ◇ **monitor** *m* **(de tipo) TTL** TTL monitor

monitor *m* **(de ordenador)** *sustantivo* cathode ray tube storage

monitor *m* **analógico** *sustantivo* analog monitor

monitor *m* **de color** *sustantivo* colour monitor ◇ **el monitor de color es excelente para los juegos electrónicos** the colour monitor is great for games

Monitor *m* **del Sistema** *sustantivo* System Monitor

monitor *m* **de multifrecuencias** *sustantivo* multifrequency monitor

monitor *m* **de televisión** *sustantivo* television monitor

monitor *m* **de vídeo** *sustantivo* **1.** video display **2.** video monitor

monitor *m* **digital** *sustantivo* digital monitor

monitor *m* **en blanco y negro** *sustantivo* monochrome monitor

monitor *m* **integrado** *sustantivo* firmware monitor

monitor *m* **monocromo** *sustantivo* monochrome monitor

monitor *m* **multisincrónico** *sustantivo* **1.** multi-scan monitor **2.** multisync monitor

monitor/televisor *m sustantivo* television receiver/monitor

mono- *prefijo* mono-

monoaural *adj* monoaural

monocromo *sustantivo* black and white ■ *adj*, *sustantivo* monochrome

montado *m* **en serie** *sustantivo* series circuit

montador *m* **de enlaces** *sustantivo* linkage editing

montaje *m sustantivo* **1.** assembly **2.** linkage editing ◇ **cadena de montaje** assembly line ◇ **montaje** *m* **de un documento a partir de otros textos** boilerplating ◇ **no hay instrucciones de montaje del ordenador** there are no assembly instructions to show you how to put the computer together

montaje *m* **experimental** *sustantivo* breadboard

montaje *m* **provisional** *sustantivo* breadboard

montar *verbo* **1.** *vt* to assemble **2.** *vt* to mount **3.** *vt* to piggyback

Mosaic (*marca comercial*) Mosaic

mosaico *m sustantivo* **1.** mosaic **2.** tile

mostrar *verbo* to window ◇ **mostrar una imagen (por desplazamiento horizontal)** pan

mostrar en pantalla *verbo* to call up ◇ **mostró en pantalla todas las direcciones de los clientes** all the customers addresses were called up ◇ **recuperar en pantalla el fichero anterior** call up the previous file

mostrar información en ventanas *verbo* to window

motor *m* **de base de datos** *sustantivo* database engine

motor *m* **de búsqueda** *sustantivo* search engine

motor *m* **de inferencia** *sustantivo* inference engine *o* inference machine

motor *m* **de pasos** *sustantivo* stepper motor *o* stepping motor

Motorola™ (*empresa productora de procesadores*) Motorola

motor *m* **paso a paso** *sustantivo* stepper motor *o* stepping motor

mover *verbo* **1.** *vt* to bleed **2.** *vt* to drag **3.** *vt* to justify **4.** *vt* to move ◇ **mover (un texto) punto por punto** to smooth scroll ◇ **mover un texto línea a línea por la pantalla** to roll scroll

'Mover' (Apple Macintosh) *sustantivo* Font/DA Mover

moverse *verbo* *vr* to roam

(instrucción de) mover un bloque *sustantivo* move block

movible *adj* movable

móvil *adj* movable

movimiento *m sustantivo* **1.** movement **2.** traffic **3.** transaction ◇ **movimiento** *m* **de rotación (manual)** spindling ◇ **movimiento** *m* **vertical (en la pantalla)** vertical scrolling ◇ **nuestra red Ethernet comienza a reducir la velocidad si el movimiento alcanza el 60 por ciento de la anchura de banda** our Ethernet network begins to slow down if the traffic reaches 60 per cent of the bandwidth

movimiento *m* **de banda de goma** *sustantivo* rubber banding

movimiento *m* **excesivo** *sustantivo* thrashing

MP3 *sustantivo* MP3

MS *abrev* MS

MS-DOS 1. Microsoft DOS **2.** (*marca comercial*) MS-DOS

MSN (*marca comercial*) MSN

MS-Windows MS-Windows

muestra *f sustantivo* sample

muestreo *m* **de aceptación** *sustantivo* acceptance sampling

muestreo *m* **por puntos** *sustantivo* point size

multi- *prefijo* multi- ◇ **tarjeta** *f* **de memoria de muchos megabytes** multimegabyte memory card

multiacceso *m sustantivo* **1.** multi-access system **2.** multiple access system

multicanal *adj* multichannel

multicolor *adj* multicolour

multidimensional *adj* multidimensional

multidireccionado *m sustantivo* multithread

multidisco *adj* multi-disk

MultiFinder™ *sustantivo* MultiFinder

multiflujo ◇ **multiflujo** *m* **de instrucciones – monoflujo de datos** MISD; (*arquitectura*) multiple instruction stream-single data stream ◇ **multiflujo** *m* **de instrucciones – multiflujo de datos** (*arquitectura*) multiple instruction stream-multiple data stream

multifrecuencia *f* **de tono dual** *sustantivo* dual tone multi-frequency

multifunción *adj* multifunction *o* multifunctional ◇ **un módulo de interfaz analógico multifunción incluye convertidores de analógico a digital y de digital a analógico** a multifunction analog interface module includes analog to digital and digital to analog converters

'Los equipos multifunción, llamados así porque reúnen en un mismo aparato compacto las funciones de impresora, escáner, copiadora y fax, tienen la ventaja evidente de que se gana espacio de mesa y cuestan poco más que cualquiera de estos productos por separado.' [*Ciberp@ís*]

multimedia *adj* multimedia

multimedia *m* **interactivo** *sustantivo* interactive multimedia ◇ **este programa multimedia interactivo permite que el usuario componga música con un programa de sintetizador** this interactive multimedia title allows a user to make music with a synthesizer program

multinivel *adj* multilevel

multiplataforma *adj* multi platform

múltiple *adj* multiple

multiplexado *m* **dinámico** *sustantivo* dynamic multiplexing

multiplexado *m* **por división de tiempos** *sustantivo* **1.** TDM **2.** time division multiplexing

multiplexaje *m* **de datos** *sustantivo* dataplex

multiplexar *verbo* *vt* to multiplex

multiplexión ◇ **multiplexión** *f* **de división de longitud de onda** wavelength division multiplexing

multiplexión *f* **de división de frecuencias** *sustantivo* **1.** FDM **2.** frequency division multiplexing

multiplexión *f* **de división de longitud de onda** *abrev* WDM

múltiplexión *f* **dinámica** *sustantivo* dynamic multiplexing

multiplexión *f* **heterogénea** *sustantivo* heterogeneous multiplexing

multiplexión *f* **homogénea** *sustantivo* homogeneous multiplexing

multiplexión *f* **por división de tiempos** *sustantivo* **1.** TDM **2.** time division multiplexing

multiplexor *m sustantivo* **1.** multiplexor **2.** MUX ◇ **un multiplexor de 4 a 1 combina 4 entradas con una sola salida** a 4 to 1 multiplexor combines four inputs into a single output

multiplicación *f sustantivo* multiplication

multiplicador *m sustantivo* multiplier

multiplicando *m sustantivo* **1.** icand **2.** multiplicand

multiplicar *verbo vti* to multiply

multiprocesador *m sustantivo* multiprocessor

multiproceso *m sustantivo* multiprocessor interleaving

multiprogramación *f sustantivo* **1.** multiprocessor interleaving **2.** multi-programming system

multipunto *adj* multipoint

multirepetidor *m* **activo** *sustantivo* active hub

multitarea *f sustantivo* multitasking ■ *adj* multitasking ◇ **el sistema es multiusario y multitarea** the system is multi-user and multi-tasking

multitarea *f* **en tiempo compartido** *sustantivo* preemptive multitasking

multitarea *f* **en tiempo real** *sustantivo* real-time multi-tasking

multitarea *f* **preferente** *sustantivo* preemptive multitasking

mundo *m sustantivo* world

muy *prefijo* ultra-

muy importante *adj* prime

N

n *abrev* (*nano-*) n
nano- *abrev* (*nano-*) n
nano- (n) *prefijo* nano-
nanosegundo (ns) *m sustantivo* nanosecond
Napster (*marca comercial*) Napster
nativo *adj* native
navegable *adj* navigable
navegación *f* **(por Internet)** *sustantivo* navigation
navegador *m sustantivo* browser
navegador *m* **de Internet** *sustantivo* web browser
navegar *verbo vi* to browse
navegar por Internet *verbo* to surf
navegar por la red *verbo* to surf
negación *f sustantivo* 1. denial 2. negation
negación *f* **alternativa** *sustantivo* alternative denial
negación *f* **conexa** *sustantivo* joint denial
negación *f* **conjunta** *sustantivo* joint denial
negativo *adj* negative
negocios *mpl* **electrónicos** *sustantivo* e-business
NetBIOS *m sustantivo* NetBIOS
NetBIOS *m* **en Modo Protegido** *sustantivo* 1. NetBEUI 2. NetBIOS extended user interface
Netscape Navigator™ (*marca comercial*) Netscape Navigator
NetShow™ NetShow
NetWare™ NetWare
neuro-red *f sustantivo* neural network
neutral *adj* neutral
neutro *adj* neutral
Newton™ (*gama de asistentes personales de Apple*) Newton
nexo *m sustantivo* nexus
NI *sustantivo* joint denial
NI *m* **exclusivo** *sustantivo* 1. exclusive NOR 2. EXNOR
nivel *m sustantivo* level ◇ **nivel** *m* **de jerarquización (de bucles)** nesting level ◇ **nivel** *m* **de transmisión de una línea** line level
nivel *m* **A** *sustantivo* Level A
nivel *m* **B** *sustantivo* 1. Level B 2. MID-F1
nivel *m* **C** *sustantivo* Level C
nivel *m* **de acceso** *sustantivo* access level
nivel *m* **de actividad** *sustantivo* activity level
nivel *m* **de autor** *sustantivo* author level

nivel *m* **de complejidad** *sustantivo* complexity measure
nivel *m* **de confianza** *sustantivo* confidence level
nivel *m* **de datos** *sustantivo* data level
nivel *m* **de direccionamiento** *sustantivo* addressing level
nivel *m* **de interrupción** *sustantivo* interrupt level
nivel *m* **de lector** *sustantivo* reader level
nivel *m* **de luminosidad** *sustantivo* brightness range
nivel *m* **de negro** *sustantivo* black level
nivel *m* **de presión acústica** *sustantivo* 1. sound pressure level 2. SPL
nivel *m* **de registro** *sustantivo* recording level
nivel *m* **de usuario** *sustantivo* user level
niveles *mpl* **de gris** *sustantivo* grey scale
nivel *m* **lógico** *sustantivo* logic level
nivel *m* **máximo de producción** *sustantivo* peak output
nivel *m* **objetivo** *sustantivo* target level
no *prefijo* non- ◇ **circuito no lineal** nonlinear circuit ◇ **código no impresor** *o* **que no imprime** non-printing code ◇ **después de terminar de hablar por teléfono ella colgó** after she had finished talking on the telephone, she hung up ◇ **el uso de una cinta magnética proporciona memoria no volátil** using magnetic tape provides non-volatile memory ◇ **instrucciones no desplegables** non-scrollable instructions ◇ **interrupción obligatoria** *o* **que no puede ser invalidada** non-maskable interrupt (NMI) ◇ **la anchura de línea puede establecerse utilizando uno de los códigos no impresores, .LW, seguidos de un número** the line width can be set using one of the non-printing codes, .LW, then a number ◇ **la memoria de burbujas es una memoria no volátil** bubble memory is a non-volatile storage ◇ **la pantalla se hace ilegible rápidamente cuando se usa un cursor no destructivo** the screen quickly becomes unreadable when using a non-destructive cursor ◇ **lectura no destructiva** non-destructive readout (NDR) ◇ **memoria de acceso aleatorio no volátil** non-volatile random access memory (NVRAM) ◇ **no responder después de un fallo** hang ◇ **no retorno** non return to zero (NRZ) ◇ **no tener éxito en una cosa** fail ◇ **realizaré una serie de pruebas no destructivas en su ordenador y, si las pasa, podrá empezar a utilizarlo de**

nuevo I will carry out a number of non-destructive tests on your computer: if it passes, you can start using it again ◊ **sistema no entrelazado** non-interlaced system

no alineado, -a *adj* nonaligned

no clasificado *adj* unsorted ◊ **tardamos cuatro veces más en buscar el fichero no clasificado** it took four times as long to search the unsorted file

no compatibilidad *f sustantivo* noncompatibility

no compatible *adj* 1. alien 2. incompatible

no corregido *adj* unedited

no desplegable *adj* non scrollable

no disponibilidad *f sustantivo* outage

no disponible *adj* configured-off *o* configured-out

nodo *m sustantivo* node ◊ **esta red tiene una conexión de fibra óptica con nodos separados entre sí hasta por un máximo de un kilómetro de distancia** this network has fibre optic connection with nodes up to one kilometre apart ◊ **un árbol está hecho de ramas que se conectan en nodos** a tree is made of branches that connect together at nodes

nodo *m* **activo** *sustantivo* active node

nodos *mpl* **adyacentes** *plural noun* adjacent nodes

no editado *adj* unedited

no ejecutar (una orden) *verbo* to undo ◊ **acaba de borrar el párrafo, pero puede anular esta acción desde el menú Editar** you've just deleted the paragraph, but you can undo it from the option in the Edit menu

no entrelazado, -a *adj* non interlaced

no equipada *adj* unpopulated

no estándar *adj* machine-dependent

no formateado *adj* unformatted ◊ **la unidad cargadora proporciona 12,7 Mbytes de memoria no formateada** the cartridge drive provides 12.7Mbyte of unformatted storage

no hacer (una cosa) *verbo* to fail

no inteligente *adj* dumb

no lineal *adj* nonlinear

nombre *m sustantivo* 1. data name 2. heading 3. name 4. title ◊ **hay problemas cuando se elige un nombre de datos ambiguo** problems occur if an ambiguous data name is chosen ◊ **nombre** *m* **de datos de servidor huésped** host name ◊ **nombre** *m* **(de grupo) de datos de variable** variable name ◊ **nombre** *m* **de dominio totalmente calificado** FQDN ◊ **nombre** *m* **de periférico** (*en forma de abreviatura*) device name ◊ **nombre de un disco** *o* **de un disquete** title of disk

nombre *m* **de acceso** *sustantivo* (*en una base de datos*) access name

nombre *m* **de cadena** *sustantivo* string name

nombre *m* **de dominio** *sustantivo* domain name

nombre *m* **de fichero ambiguo** *sustantivo* ambiguous filename

nombre *m* **de fichero largo** *sustantivo* long filename

nombre *m* **de la cuenta** *sustantivo* account name ◊ **el nombre de la cuenta de John Smith es JSMITH** John Smith's account name is JSMITH

nombre *m* **de la ruta** *sustantivo* pathname ◊ **el nombre de la ruta de acceso del fichero de la carta es \FILES\SIMON\DOCS\LETTER.DOC** the pathname for the letter file is \FILES\SIMON\DOCS\LETTER.DOC

nombre *m* **del volumen** *sustantivo* volume label *o* volume name

nombre *m* **de ordenador huésped** *sustantivo* host name

nombre *m* **de un fichero** *sustantivo* filename ◊ **en MS-DOS, el nombre del fichero puede tener hasta ocho caracteres además de una extensión de tres caracteres** in MS-DOS, a filename can be up to eight characters long together with a three character filename extension ◊ **la extensión SYS que se añade al nombre de un fichero indica que es un fichero del sistema** the filename extension SYS indicates that this is a system file

nombre *m* **de usuario** *sustantivo* user name

nombre *m* **simbólico** *sustantivo* symbolic name

nombre *m* **(de) un programa** *sustantivo* program name

nomenclatura *f sustantivo* nomenclature

no modulado *adj* unmodulated

nomograma *m sustantivo* nomogram *o* nomograph

non-repudiación *f sustantivo* nonrepudiation

no protegido *adj* unprotected

no retorno *m sustantivo* non-return to zero

NOR *m* **exclusivo** *sustantivo* 1. exclusive NOR 2. EXNOR

norma *sustantivo* rule ◊ **la norma dice que se debe esperar la señal de línea antes de transmitir** the rule states that you wait for the clear signal before transmitting ◊ **norma** *f* **de puesta en clave de datos** data encryption standard ◊ **norma** *f* **V21 de transmisión en dúplex de 300 bps en emisión y recepción** V.21 ◊ **norma** *f* **V22 bis (de transmisión en dúplex de 1200 bps en emisión y recepción** V.22bis ◊ **norma** *f* **V22 de transmisión en semi-dúplex de 1200 bps en emisión y recepción** V.22 ◊ **norma** *f* **V29** (*de módem de 9600 bps en la red pública conmutada o en líneas arrendadas*) V.29 ◊ **norma** *f* **V32 bis (con velocidad de transmisión de 14400 bps)** V.32bis ◊ **norma** *f* **V42 bis (de compresión de datos con control de errores V42)** V.42bis ◊ **norma** *f* **V42 de protocolo de control y de corrección de errores** V.42

norma *f* **de conversión ADPCM** *sustantivo* 1. adaptive differential pulse code modulation 2. ADPCM

norma *f* **de línea pequeña** *sustantivo* hairline rule

normal *adj* normal ◇ **el procedimiento normal es que se hagan copias de seguridad al final de cada jornada laboral** the normal procedure is for backup copies to be made at the end of each day's work

normales *plural noun* normals

normalización *f sustantivo* normalisation *o* normalization

normalizar *verbo* **1.** *vt* to normalise *o* to normalize **2.** *vt* to standardise

norma *f* **MSX** *sustantivo* MSX

norma *f* **muy delgada** *sustantivo* hairline rule

norma *f* **RS-422** *sustantivo* RS-422

norma *f* **RS-423** *sustantivo* RS-423

normas *fpl* **de producción** *plural noun* production standards

normas *fpl* **de programación** *plural noun* programming standards

normas *fpl* **de protocolo de transmisión** *plural noun* protocol standards

normas *fpl* **para módems** *plural noun* modem standards

norma *f* **V32** *sustantivo* (*con velocidad de transmisión de 9600 bps*) V.32

NOS *sustantivo* network operating system ■ *abrev* NOS

nota *f sustantivo* **1.** annotation **2.** comment

nota *f* **a pie de página** *sustantivo* footnote

notación *f sustantivo* notation ◇ **cuando en la notación normal se escribe (x-y) + z, en la notación polaca (por prefijo) se escribe – xy + z** normal notation: (x-y) + z, but using prefix notation: – xy + z ◇ **notación decimal** decimal notation ◇ **notación** *f* **polaca (por prefijo)** prefix notation

notación *f* **binaria** *sustantivo* **1.** binary notation **2.** binary representation

notación *f* **de coma fija** *sustantivo* fixed-point notation

notación *f* **de coma flotante** *sustantivo* floating point notation

notación *f* **hexadecimal** *abrev* H ■ *sustantivo* hex *o* hexadecimal notation

notación *f* **infija** *sustantivo* infix notation

notación *f* **octal** *sustantivo* octal *o* octal notation

notación *f* **polaca** *sustantivo* Polish notation

notación *f* **polaca inversa** *sustantivo* **1.** postfix notation **2.** reverse Polish notation **3.** suffix notation ◇ **cuando en la notación normal se escribe (x-y) + z, en la notación polaca inversa se escribe xy – z +** normal notation: (x-y) + z, but using postfix notation: xy – z + ◇ **en notación normal se escribe (x-y) + z, pero en notación por sufijos se escribe xy – z +** normal notation: (x-y) + z, but using postfix notation: xy – z +

notación *f* **polaca prefijada** *sustantivo* prefix notation ◇ **(x-y) + z es la notación normal,** pero la prefijada es – xy + z normal notation: (x-y) + z, but using prefix notation: – xy + z

notación *f* **por infijos** *sustantivo* infix notation

notación *f* **por postfijos** *sustantivo* postfix notation ◇ **cuando en la notación normal se escribe (x-y) + z, en la notación polaca inversa se escribe xy – z +** normal notation: (x-y) + z, but using postfix notation: xy – z +

notación *f* **por prefijo** *sustantivo* prefix notation ◇ **cuando en la notación normal se escribe (x-y) + z, en la notación polaca (por prefijo) se escribe – xy + z** normal notation: (x-y) + z, but using prefix notation: – xy + z

notación *f* **por sufijos** *sustantivo* **1.** postfix notation **2.** suffix notation ◇ **en notación normal se escribe (x-y) + z, pero en notación por sufijos se escribe xy – z +** normal notation: (x-y) + z, but using postfix notation: xy – z +

notación *f* **prefijada** *sustantivo* prefix notation ◇ **(x-y) + z es la notación normal, pero la prefijada es – xy + z** normal notation: (x-y) + z, but using prefix notation: – xy + z

no válido *adj* illegal

novato(-a) *m sustantivo* newbie

Novell™ Novell

no vuelta *f* **a cero** *sustantivo* non-return to zero

ns *abrev* ns

NuBus™ *sustantivo* (*extensión de enlace para ordenadores Macintosh*) NuBus

núcleo *m* **(del sistema)** *sustantivo* kernel ◇ **sistema para entrada** *or* **salida de gráficos** graphics kernel system (GKS)

núcleo *m* **magnético** *sustantivo* magnetic core

nudo ◇ **nudo** *m* **de acceso a la red** concentrator

nueva paginación *f sustantivo* repagination

nueva tecnología *f sustantivo* new technology

nueva *f* **versión** *sustantivo* update

nueva versión *f* **de un fichero** *sustantivo* file update

nuevo, -a *adj* new ◇ **han instalado un nuevo sistema informático** they have installed a new computer system

'Un conocido editor … esperaba encontrarse en la última feria del libro de Chicago con novedades acerca de la nueva economía y el e-business, pero se topó con catálogos enteros dedicados al e-clienting, e-commerce, e-corporations, las marcas digitales, la gestión virtual de los recursos humanos y un largo etcétera.' [*Nueva economía*]

nulo *adj* null ◇ **conjunto vacío** *o* **nulo** null set

numeración *f sustantivo* notation

numeración *f* **de base** *sustantivo* radix notation

numerar *verbo* *vt* to number ◇ **las páginas del manual están numeradas del 1 al 395** the pages of the manual are numbered 1 to 395

numérico *adj* **1.** digital **2.** numeric **3.** numerical
número *sustantivo* **1.** number **2.** numeral ◇ **cada una de las piezas del ordenador tiene un número de fabricación** each piece of hardware has a production number ◇ **número** *m* **de entradas en un circuito lógico** fan-in ◇ **número** *m* **de identificación de un fichero** handle ◇ **número** *m* **de línea (de programa)** line number ◇ **número** *m* **de palabras** (*en un fichero texto*) word count ◇ **número** *m* **de referencia de una línea de un programa** program line number ◇ **número** *m* **de salidas en un circuito lógico** fan-out

número *m* **aleatorio** *sustantivo* random number

número *m* **binario** *sustantivo* **1.** binary number **2.** bit

número *m* **cardinal** *sustantivo* cardinal number

número *m* **de acceso** *sustantivo* **1.** accession number **2.** access number

número *m* **de caracteres por línea** *sustantivo* line length

número *m* **de caracteres por pulgada** *sustantivo* pitch

número *m* **de chips** *sustantivo* chip count ◇ **no sirve; el número de chips es todavía demasiado alto** it's no good, the chip count is still too high

número *m* **de ciclos** *sustantivo* cycle count

número *m* **de código personal** *sustantivo* identity number ◇ **no olvide introducir su número de código personal** don't forget to log in your identity number

número *m* **de coma flotante** *sustantivo* floating point number

número *m* **de entrada** *sustantivo* accession number

número *m* **de equivalencia de llamadas** *sustantivo* **1.** REN **2.** ringer equivalence number

número *m* **de fichero** *sustantivo* file handle ◇ **los nuevos datos son introducidos en el fichero identificado con el número 1** the new data is written to the file identified by file handle 1

número *m* **de identidad** *sustantivo* identity number ◇ **no olvide introducir su número de código personal** don't forget to log in your identity number

número *m* **de identificación personal** *sustantivo* **1.** personal identification number **2.** PIN

número *m* **de instrucción** *sustantivo* statement number

número *m* **de líneas por página** *sustantivo* page length

número *m* **de mensajes recibidos** *sustantivo* incoming traffic

número *m* **de página** *sustantivo* **1.** page makeup **2.** page number

número *m* **de pulsaciones** *sustantivo* keystroke count

número *m* **de referencia** *sustantivo* accession number

número *m* **de tareas en cola** *sustantivo* job number

número *m* **de teléfono** *sustantivo* phone number

número *m* **de trabajos pendientes** *sustantivo* job number

número *m* **de versión** *sustantivo* **1.** release number **2.** version number

número *m* **elegido al azar** *sustantivo* random number

número *m* **entero** *sustantivo* integer

número *m* **entero de doble precisión** *sustantivo* double-precision integer

número *m* **entero largo** *sustantivo* long integer

número hexadecimal 11 *símbolo* B
número hexadecimal 12 *símbolo* C
número hexadecimal 13 *símbolo* D
número hexadecimal 14 *símbolo* E

número *m* **indicativo** *sustantivo* index number

número *m* **máximo de usuarios** *plural noun* maximum users

número *m* **negativo** *sustantivo* negative number

número *m* **octal** *sustantivo* octal digit

número *m* **racional** *sustantivo* rational number ◇ **24** *or* **7 es un número racional** 24 over 7 is a rational number ◇ **se puede escribir 0,333 bajo la forma del número racional 1** *or* **3** 0.333 can be written as the rational number 1/3

número *m* **real** *sustantivo* real number

números *mpl* **arábigos** *plural noun* Arabic figures ■ *sustantivo* Arabic numbers *o* Arabic figures *o* Arabic numerals

números *mpl* **asignados** *plural noun* assigned numbers

números *mpl* **completos** *sustantivo* complementation

números *mpl* **de precisión finita** *sustantivo* finite-precision numbers

O

objetivo *m sustantivo* **1.** goal **2.** objective

objeto *m sustantivo* object ◇ **este programa de gráficos orientados a objetos le permite desplazar figuras muy fácilmente** this object-oriented graphics program lets you move shapes around very easily ◇ **programación orientada a objetos** object-oriented programming (OOP)

objeto *m* **de acción** *sustantivo* action-object

objeto *m* **(de) destino** *sustantivo* destination object

objeto *m* **disponible** *sustantivo* instance

objeto *m* **encerrado** *sustantivo* enclosed object

objeto *m* **enlazado** *sustantivo* linked object

objeto *m* **enmarcado** *sustantivo* enclosed object

objeto *m* **en movimiento** *sustantivo* sprite

objeto *m* **fuente** *sustantivo* source object

objeto *m* **incrustado** *sustantivo* embedded object

objeto *m* **vinculado** *sustantivo* linked object

oblea *f sustantivo* wafer

oblea *f* **de silicio** *sustantivo* silicon wafer

oblicuidad *f sustantivo* skew

observación *f sustantivo* **1.** REM **2.** remark ◇ **enunciado de observación** remark statement

obstrucción *f sustantivo* congestion

obtención *f* **de datos** *sustantivo* data capture

obtener *verbo vt* to obtain ◇ **el filtrado permite obtener una señal clara** a clear signal is obtained after filtering ◇ **obtener datos de un dispositivo de almacenamiento** to obtain data from a storage device

octeto *m abrev* B ■ *sustantivo* **1.** byte **2.** eight-bit byte *o* eight-bit octet **3.** eight-bit octet **4.** octet ◇ **kilo-octeto** KB (kilobyte)

octeto *m* **de control de acceso** *sustantivo* access control byte

ocultar *verbo vt* to conceal ◇ **las líneas escondidas se ocultan a la vista con este algoritmo** the hidden lines are concealed from view with this algorithm

ocupado *adj* busy ■ *adv* off-hook

ocurrir *verbo vi* to occur

O *m* **exclusivo** *sustantivo* **1.** exclusive OR **2.** EXOR ■ *abrev* NEQ ■ *sustantivo* **1.** NEQ function **2.** nonequivalence function **3.** nonequivalence gate

oferta *f* **de promoción** *sustantivo* bundle

oferta *f* **promocional** *sustantivo* bundle

offset *m sustantivo* offset ◇ **impresión (en) offset** offset printing ◇ **litografía offset** offset lithography

oficina *f* **de datos impresos** *sustantivo* output bureau

oficina *f* **electrónica** *sustantivo* paperless office

oficina *f* **integrada** *sustantivo* integrated office

Oficina Postal *sustantivo* post office

oficina *f* **sin papel** *sustantivo* paperless office

ofimática *f* **burótica** *sustantivo* office automation

OIN (Organización Internacional de Normalización) *abrev* ISO

OLE *sustantivo* OLE

omitir *verbo vt* to skip

onda *f sustantivo* wave ◇ **onda sonora** sound wave

onda *f* **cuadrada** *sustantivo* square wave

onda *f* **decimétrica** *sustantivo* **1.** UHF **2.** ultra high frequency

onda *f* **portadora** *sustantivo* **1.** carrier **2.** carrier wave

onda *f* **portadora de datos** *sustantivo* data carrier

ondas *fpl* **sonoras** *plural noun* sound waves

opción *f sustantivo* option

opcional *adj* optional ◇ **el sistema viene con disqueteras opcionales de 3.5 o 5.25 pulgadas** the system comes with optional 3.5 or 5.25 disk drives

opción *f* **de configuración** *sustantivo* setup option

opción *f* **implícita** *sustantivo* default option

opción *f* **multidisco** *sustantivo* multi-disk option

opción *f* **por defecto** *sustantivo* default option

operación *sustantivo* **1.** operation **2.** order **3.** test run ◇ **operación** *f* **booleana monádica de un operando** monadic Boolean operation ◇ **operación** *f* **de entrada en la pila** non-synchronous sound ◇ **operación** *f* **(de longitud) simple** single length working

operacional *adj* operational ◇ **amplificador operacional** operational amplifier (op amp)

operación *f* **ambos o uno** *sustantivo* either-or operation

operación f **aritmética** *sustantivo* arithmetic operation

operación f **asistida** *sustantivo* attended operation

operación f **bidireccional** *sustantivo* either-way operation

operación f **binaria** *sustantivo* binary operation

operación f **booleana** *sustantivo* Boolean operation

operación f **booleana diádica** *sustantivo* dyadic Boolean operation

operación f **complementaria** *sustantivo* complementary operation

operación f **completa** *sustantivo* complete operation

operación f **con dos operandos** *sustantivo* dyadic operation

operación f **de bifurcación** *sustantivo* jump operation

operación f **de ciclo fijo** *sustantivo* fixed cycle operation

operación f **de coincidencia** *sustantivo* 1. AND operation 2. coincidence operation

operación f **de coma flotante** *sustantivo* floating point operation ■ *abrev* FLOP

operación f **de ejecución automática** *sustantivo* unattended operation

operación f **de equivalencia** *sustantivo* 1. equivalence function 2. equivalence operation

operación f **de identidad** *sustantivo* identity operation

operación f **de salto** *sustantivo* jump operation

operación f **de una sola palabra** *sustantivo* single length working

operación f **de una sola pasada** *sustantivo* single pass operation

operación f **de un operando** *sustantivo* unary operation

operación f **diádica** *sustantivo* dyadic operation

operación f **EITHER-OR** *sustantivo* either-or operation

operación f **en dúplex** *sustantivo* duplex operation

operación f **en paralelo** *sustantivo* parallel operation

operación f **en serie** *sustantivo* serial operation

operaciones *fpl* **de mantenimiento** *sustantivo* housekeeping

operaciones *fpl* **numéricas ultra rápidas** *sustantivo* number crunching ◇ **se necesita un procesador muy potente para las aplicaciones gráficas ya que éstas requieren una capacidad de cálculo ultra rápido** a very powerful processor is needed for graphics applications which require extensive number crunching capabilities

operación f **incontrolable** *sustantivo* (*debido a un error*) runaway

operación f **lógica** *sustantivo* 1. conjunction 2. logic operation

operación f **monádica** *sustantivo* 1. monadic operation 2. unary operation

operación f **no direccionable** *sustantivo* no-address operation

operación f **NO-O** *sustantivo* joint denial

operación f **no prioritaria** *sustantivo* background operation

operación f **no válida** *sustantivo* illegal operation

operación f **O** *sustantivo* 1. join 2. union

operación f **O-O** *sustantivo* either-or operation

operación f **programada informáticamente** *sustantivo* program trading

operación f **prohibida** *sustantivo* illegal operation

operación f **secuencial** *sustantivo* sequential operation

operación f **simple** *sustantivo* single operation

operación f **sincronizada** *sustantivo* fixed cycle operation

operación f **sin dirección** *sustantivo* no-address operation

operación f **subordinada** *sustantivo* background operation

operación f **terminada** *sustantivo* complete operation

operación f **unaria** *sustantivo* unary operation

operación f **unidireccional** *sustantivo* single operation

operación f **Y** *sustantivo* 1. AND operation 2. coincidence operation

operador, -a *sustantivo* 1. computer operator 2. operator ◇ **el operador estaba sentado frente a la pantalla del ordenador** the operator was sitting at his console ◇ **operador** m **booleano monádico** monadic Boolean operator ◇ **operador** m **de redirección (del DOS)** redirect operator ◇ **operador** m **de teclado que introduce información en un ordenador** keyboarder ◇ **x es el operador de la multiplicación** x is the multiplication operator

'La separación entre la propiedad de las redes y los operadores y proveedores de contenidos parece deseable si se quiere garantizar la competencia al tiempo que maximizar las posibilidades económicas.' [*La Red*]

operador m **agregado** *sustantivo* aggregate operator

operador m **aritmético** *sustantivo* arithmetic operator

operador m **booleano** *sustantivo* Boolean operator

operador m **booleano monádico** *sustantivo* monadic operator

operador m **central** *sustantivo* centre operator

operador *m* **de derivación** *sustantivo* pipe

operador *m* **de desigualdad** *sustantivo* inequality operator ◇ **el lenguaje de programación C emplea el símbolo '!=' como su operador de desigualdad** the C programming language uses the symbol '!=' as its inequality operator

operador *m* **de globalización** *sustantivo* aggregate operator

operador *m* **del sistema (de una BBS)** *sustantivo* sysop

operador *m* **de sistema** *sustantivo* system operator

operador *m* **informático** *sustantivo* computer operator

operador *m* **lógico** *sustantivo* **1.** logical operator **2.** relational operator

operador *m* **relacional** *sustantivo* relational operator

operando *m* *sustantivo* operand ◇ **en la instrucción ADD 74, el operador ADD añade el operando 74 al acumulador** in the instruction ADD 74, the operator ADD will add the operand 74 to the accumulator

operando *m* **alfanumérico** *sustantivo* alphanumeric operand

operando *m* **de una conjunción** *sustantivo* conjunct

operando *m* **de una instrucción AND** *sustantivo* conjunct

operando *m* **inmediato** *sustantivo* immediate operand

operando *m* **literal** *sustantivo* literal operand

operando *m* **numérico** *sustantivo* numeric operand

opinión *f* *sustantivo* contention

óptico *adj* optical ◇ **lector óptico de caracteres** optical character reader (OCR) ◇ **lector óptico de marcas** optical mark reader (OMR) ◇ **reconocimiento óptico de marcas** *o* **de signos** *o* **de símbolos** optical mark recognition (OMR) ◇ **sistema (electro)óptico de comunicaciones** optical communications system ◇ **un lector óptico emplea un haz de luz para escanear caracteres, símbolos o líneas** an optical reader uses a light beam to scan characters, patterns or lines

optimación *f* *sustantivo* enhancement

optimización *f* *sustantivo* **1.** enhancement **2.** optimisation *o* optimization **3.** upgrade ◇ **los tres modelos tienen una utilidad integrada de optimización** all three models have an on-site upgrade facility

optimizador *m* *sustantivo* **1.** enhancer **2.** optimiser *o* optimizer **3.** optimizer

optimizar *verbo vt* to optimise *o* to optimize

óptimo *adj* optimum ■ *sustantivo* optimum

OR *sustantivo* OR

orden *m* *sustantivo* **1.** array **2.** command **3.** keyword **4.** order **5.** sequence ◇ **en** *o* **por orden alfabético** in alphabetical order ◇ **la palabra 'or-**

denador' **es una palabra clave en la tecnología de la información** computer is a keyword in IT ◇ **la secuencia de nombres está organizada por orden alfabético** the sequence of names is arranged alphabetically ◇ **las instrucciones del programa están organizadas por orden según los números de línea** the program instructions are arranged in sequence according to line numbers ◇ **orden** *m* **de llamadas de los terminales** polling list ◇ **orden lógica** *o* **matriz lógica** logic array

ordenada *f* *sustantivo* y-coordinate

ordenador *sustantivo* **1.** appliance computer **2.** computer **3.** computer system **4.** machine ◇ **estándar** *o* **universal** *o* **que funciona en la mayoría de los ordenadores** machine-independent ◇ **(programa) no estándar** *o* **que sólo funciona con un solo tipo de ordenador** machine-dependent ◇ **ordenador** *m* **con juego de instrucciones modificables** WISC; writable instruction set computer ◇ **ordenador** *m* **de conjunto de arquitectura RISC** reduced instruction set computer; RISC ◇ **ordenador** *m* **de conjunto de instrucciones complejas** complex instruction set computer ◇ **ordenador** *m* **de conjunto de instrucciones reducido** RISC; reduced instruction set computer ◇ **ordenador** *m* **de control de las transmisiones** communications computer ◇ **ordenador** *m* **de palabras de longitud variable** variable word length computer ◇ **ordenador** *m* **de tarjeta única** *or* **de una sola dirección** single-board microcomputer ◇ **ordenador** *m* **intercalado (en otro)** embedded computer ◇ **ordenador** *m* **objeto** (*de ejecución de un programa*) object computer

'El ordenador zombi es una máquina en la que se ha instalado un troyano y se niega a obedecer a su propietario, haciendo caso sólo de las instrucciones dictadas por el hacker.' [*Ciberp@ís*]

'Utilizo, indistintamente, los términos computadora y ordenador. El primero es el más usual en América Latina, y el segundo el más extendido en España.' [*La Red*]

ordenador *m* **a gran escala** *sustantivo* large-scale computer

ordenador *m* **analógico** *sustantivo* analog computer

ordenador *m* **asíncrono** *sustantivo* asynchronous computer

ordenador *m* **auxiliar** *sustantivo* satellite computer

ordenador *m* **central** *sustantivo* **1.** central computer **2.** master computer ◇ **el ordenador central controla todo lo demás** the master computer controls everything else

ordenador *m* **compatible** *sustantivo* compatible

ordenador *m* **conectado a la red** *abrev* NC ■ *sustantivo* network computer

ordenador *m* **de bolsillo** *sustantivo* **1.** handheld computer *o* hand-held programmable **2.** (*que cabe en la mano*) palmtop ◇ **este ordenador de bolsillo dispone de un teclado muy pequeño**

y de una pantalla de 20 líneas this palmtop has a tiny keyboard and twenty-line LCD screen

ordenador *m* **de chip único** *sustantivo* single chip computer

ordenador *m* **de comunicaciones** *sustantivo* communications computer

ordenador *m* **de control** *sustantivo* control computer

ordenador *m* **de control de proceso** *sustantivo* process control computer

ordenador *m* **de cuarta generación** *sustantivo* fourth generation computer

ordenador *m* **de dirección única** *sustantivo* one-address computer

ordenador *m* **de empresa** *sustantivo* business computer

ordenador *m* **de gestión** *sustantivo* business computer

ordenador *m* **de gran capacidad** *sustantivo* supercomputer

ordenador *m* **de lápiz óptico** *sustantivo* pen computer

ordenador *m* **de oficina** *sustantivo* **1.** business computer **2.** office computer

ordenador *m* **de primera generación** *sustantivo* first generation computer

ordenador *m* **de programas fijos** *sustantivo* fixed program computer

ordenador *m* **de quinta generación** *sustantivo* fifth generation computer

ordenador *m* **de red** *abrev* NC ■ *sustantivo* network computer

ordenador *m* **desplazable** *sustantivo* luggable

ordenador *m* **destino** *sustantivo* target computer

ordenador *m* **de tarjeta única** *sustantivo* **1.** SBC **2.** single board computer

ordenador *m* **de tercera generación** *sustantivo* third generation computer

ordenador *m* **de una sola dirección** *sustantivo* **1.** SBC **2.** single board computer

ordenador *m* **de un solo chip** *sustantivo* single chip computer

ordenador *m* **de un solo microchip** *sustantivo* single chip computer

ordenador *m* **de uso profesional** *sustantivo* office computer

ordenador *m* **digital** *sustantivo* digital computer

ordenador *m* **digital electrónico** *sustantivo* electronic digital computer

ordenador *m* **doméstico** *sustantivo* home computer

ordenador *m* **dúplex** *sustantivo* duplex computer

ordenadores *mpl* **de segunda generación** *sustantivo* second generation computers

ordenador *m* **especializado** *sustantivo* dedicated computer

ordenador *m* **familiar** *sustantivo* home computer

ordenador *m* **gigante** *sustantivo* supercomputer

ordenador *m* **grande** *sustantivo* large-scale computer

ordenador *m* **híbrido** *sustantivo* hybrid computer

ordenador *m* **IBM AT** (*marca comercial*) IBM AT

ordenador *m* **incremental** *sustantivo* incremental computer

ordenador *m* **individual** *sustantivo* **1.** PC **2.** single-user system

ordenador *m* **infectado** *sustantivo* infected computer

ordenador Mac/Macintosh™ (*marca comercial*) Apple Mac *o* Apple Macintosh computer

ordenador *m* **maestro** *sustantivo* master computer ◇ **el ordenador central controla todo lo demás** the master computer controls everything else

ordenador *m* **(personal) multimedia** *sustantivo* **1.** MPC **2.** multimedia PC

ordenador *m* **multitarjeta** *sustantivo* multiboard computer

ordenador *m* **neuronal** *sustantivo* **1.** neural computer **2.** neurocomputer

ordenador *m* **numérico** *sustantivo* digital computer

ordenador *m* **objeto** *sustantivo* target computer

ordenador *m* **óptico** *sustantivo* optical computer

ordenador *m* **para la casa** *sustantivo* home computer

ordenador *m* **paralelo** *sustantivo* parallel computer

ordenador *m* **para usos generales** *sustantivo* general purpose computer

ordenador *m* **personal** *sustantivo* **1.** PC **2.** personal computer

ordenador *m* **personal compatible** *adj* PC-compatible

ordenador *m* **personal de bolsillo** *sustantivo* **1.** PDA **2.** personal digital assistant

ordenador *m* **personal IBM** (*marca comercial*) IBM PC

ordenador *m* **portátil** *sustantivo* **1.** laptop *o* laptop computer **2.** notebook computer **3.** notepad **4.** portable ◇ **interfaz portátil de sistema operativo** portable operating system interface (POSIX)

ordenador *m* **principal** *sustantivo* **1.** host computer **2.** mainframe *o* mainframe computer **3.** master computer ◇ **el ordenador central controla todo lo demás** the master computer controls everything else

ordenador *m* **satélite** *sustantivo* satellite computer

ordenador *m* **secuencial** *sustantivo* **1.** sequential computer **2.** serial computer

ordenador *m* **serial** *sustantivo* serial computer

ordenador *m* **sincrónico** *sustantivo* synchronous computer

ordenador *m* **síncrono** *sustantivo* synchronous computer

ordenador *m* **sin teclado** *sustantivo* pen computer

ordenador *m* **universal** *sustantivo* general purpose computer

orden *m* **alfanumérica** *sustantivo* alphanumeric array

ordenar *verbo* **1.** *vt* to order **2.** *vt* to tab

ordenar por orden alfabético *verbo* to alphasort

orden *m* **ascendente** *sustantivo* ascending order

orden *m* **bidimensional** *sustantivo* two-dimensional array

orden *m* **de encadenamiento de operaciones** *sustantivo* operator precedence

orden *m* **de los operadores** *sustantivo* operator precedence

orden *m* **de prioridad** *sustantivo* **1.** operator precedence **2.** priority sequence

orden *m* **de tabulación** *sustantivo* tabbing order

orden *f* **interna** *sustantivo* internal command ◇ **en MS-DOS, la instrucción interna DIR se emplea con frecuencia** in MS-DOS, the internal command DIR is used frequently

orden *m* **lógico programable** *sustantivo* PLA ■ *abrev* PLD ■ *sustantivo* **1.** programmable logic array **2.** programmable logic device

orden *m* **multidimensional** *sustantivo* multidimensional array

orden *m* **tridimensional** *sustantivo* three-dimensional array

ordinograma *m* *sustantivo* **1.** flowchart **2.** flow diagram ◇ **el ordinograma representa el primer paso de un programa bien diseñado** a flowchart is the first step to a well designed program ◇ **modelo de un ordinograma** flowchart template

ordinograma *m* **de flujo** *sustantivo* flowchart

ordinograma *m* **de macro** *sustantivo* macro flowchart

ordinograma *m* **de un sistema** *sustantivo* system flowchart

ordinograma *m* **lógico** *sustantivo* logical flowchart

OR *m* **exclusivo** *sustantivo* exclusive OR

organigrama *m* *sustantivo* **1.** flowchart **2.** system flowchart

organigrama *m* **de flujo** *sustantivo* flowchart

organigrama *m* **del flujo de datos** *sustantivo* data flowchart

organigrama *m* **de programación** *sustantivo* program flowchart

Organismo *m* **internacional de Normalización** *sustantivo* International Standards Organization

Organismo *m* **ISO** *sustantivo* International Standards Organization

organización *sustantivo* scheduling ◇ **organización** *f* **académica** ac

organización *f* **de la página** *sustantivo* page makeup

organización *f* **del campo** *sustantivo* fielding

organización *f* **de trabajos** *sustantivo* job scheduling

organización *f* **de un fichero** *sustantivo* **1.** file layout **2.** file organisation

organizado en serie *adv* serially

organizador *m* *sustantivo* scheduler

organizar *verbo* *vt* to structure

organizar por encauzamiento *verbo* to pipeline

orientable *adj* tilt and swivel

orientación ◇ **orientación** *f* **(horizontal o vertical)** orientation ◇ **orientación** *f* **horizontal (de la página)** landscape

orientación *f* **de la página** *sustantivo* page orientation

orientación *f* **vertical de la página** *adj* portrait

orientada ◇ **orientada en tira de cómic** comic-strip oriented

orientado *adj* orientated ◇ **orientado a la conexión** connection-oriented

orientado, ◇ **este tratamiento de textos facilita el trabajo en grupo al incluir una conexión con el correo electrónico desde los menús estándares** this word-processor is workgroup enabled which adds an email gateway from the standard menus ◇ **orientado, -a al trabajo en grupo** workgroup enabled

orientado a objetos *adj* object-oriented

origen *m* *sustantivo* **1.** origin **2.** source

original *adj* original ■ *sustantivo* original ◇ **el original está demasiado difuminado para hacer fotocopias** the original is too faint to photocopy well

originar *verbo* *vt* to originate

OR *m* **inclusivo** *sustantivo* inclusive OR

ortogonal *adj* orthogonal

OS/2™ OS/2

oscilación *f* **momentánea** *sustantivo* transient

oscilar *verbo* *vi* to range

óxido *m* **férrico** *sustantivo* ferric oxide *o* ferrite

P

página *sustantivo* **1.** form **2.** leaf **3.** page ◇ **cuando en un hipervínculo un usuario se stiúa en un objeto activo, el programa muestra la página destino** when a user clicks on the active object in a hyperlink, the software displays the destination page ◇ **diseñamos todas nuestras páginas con el software de autoedición** we do all our page layouts using desktop publishing software ◇ **esta impresora láser imprime ocho páginas por minuto** this laser printer can output eight pages per minute ◇ **página f (de la red)** site ◇ **página f de servidor activo** Active Server Page; ASP ◇ **página f destino (en un hipervínculo)** destination page ◇ **página f (de memoria) sin modificación** clean page ◇ **(número de) páginas por minuto (ppm)** pages per minute (ppm) ◇ **tecla de avance de página o Av Pág (en un teclado español)** page down key (PgDn) ◇ **tecla de retroceso de página o tecla Re Pág (en un teclado español)** page up key (PgUp)

'Las páginas web, además de ser portadoras de la información empresarial, contienen los elementos de canalización del tráfico de los usuarios y de obtención de datos de interés para los responsables del márketing.' [*PC Plus*]

paginación *f sustantivo* **1.** pagination **2.** paging

paginación *f* **discrecional** *sustantivo* demand paging

paginación *f* **transparente** *sustantivo* transparent paging

página f de código *sustantivo* code page ◇ **para introducir caracteres suecos desde un teclado británico, se tiene que cambiar la página de códigos del sistema** in order to enter Swedish characters from an English keyboard, you have to change the system code page

página f de envío *sustantivo* routing page

página f de inicio *sustantivo* home page

página f de portada *sustantivo* banner page

página f duplicada *sustantivo* shadow memory *o* shadow page

página f índice *sustantivo* index page

página f inicial *sustantivo* home page

página f (de) memoria *sustantivo* memory page

página f principal *sustantivo* home page

paginar *verbo vt* to page

paginar de nuevo *sustantivo* renumber ■ *verbo* to repaginate ◇ **el sistema de publicación asistida por ordenador permite rehacer la**

paginación the dtp package allows simple repagination ◇ **se rehizo la paginación del texto con una nueva longitud de línea** the text was repaginated with a new line width

páginas *fpl* **blancas** *plural noun* white pages

página f siguiente *sustantivo* continuation page

página f sombra *sustantivo* shadow memory *o* shadow page

páginas *fpl* **por minuto (ppm)** *sustantivo* ppm

páginas por minuto (ppm) *sustantivo* pages per minute

página f web *sustantivo* webpage

Paint *m sustantivo* Paintbrush/Paint

paisaje *m sustantivo* landscape

palabra *sustantivo* word ◇ **palabra f indicadora del estado de funcionamiento** device status word; DSW

palabra f (de información) *sustantivo* data word

palabra f clave *sustantivo* **1.** descriptor **2.** key **3.** keyword

palabra f de control *sustantivo* control word

palabra f de cuatro bits *sustantivo* quadbit

palabra f de direcciones *sustantivo* address word ◇ **una palabra de dirección más larga aumenta la cantidad de memoria que un ordenador puede definir** a larger address word increases the amount of memory a computer can address

palabra f de estado de entrada/salida *sustantivo* input/output status word

palabra f de estado del procesador *sustantivo* processor status word ■ *abrev* PSW

palabra f de estado de programa *sustantivo* program status word

palabra f de identificación *sustantivo* identifier word

palabra f de índice *sustantivo* index value word

palabra f de información *sustantivo* computer word

palabra f de instrucción *sustantivo* instruction word ◇ **los fabricantes de esta unidad central de proceso decidieron que JMP será la palabra de instrucción para llamar la función de salto** the manufacturers of this CPU have decided that JMP will be the instruction word to call the jump function

palabra *f* **de longitud determinada** *sustantivo* fixed-length word

palabra *f* **de longitud fija** *sustantivo* fixed-length word

palabra *f* **de longitud finita** *sustantivo* fixed-length word

palabra *f* **de máquina** *sustantivo* machine word

palabra *f* **de parámetro** *sustantivo* parameter word

palabra *f* **de paso** *sustantivo* password ◇ **el usuario debe escribir su contraseña para poder acceder a la base de datos** the user has to key in the password before he can access the database ◇ **protegido, -a por una contraseña** password-protected

palabra *f* **de vínculo activo** *sustantivo* hotword

palabra *f* **doble** *sustantivo* double word

palabra *f* **larga** *sustantivo* double word

palabra *f* **relativa** *sustantivo* offset value *o* offset word

palabra *f* **reservada** *sustantivo* reserved word

palabras ◇ **palabras** *fpl* **que se destacan (visualmente)** display highlights

palabras por minuto *sustantivo* **1.** words per minute **2.** WPM *o* wpm

palanca *f sustantivo* **1.** joystick **2.** paddle

paleta *f* **de colores** *sustantivo* **1.** colour palette **2.** palette

paleta *f* **de diseño** *sustantivo* pattern palette

paleta *f* **de identificación** *sustantivo* identity palette

paleta *f* **lógica** *sustantivo* logical palette

palo *m* **de memoria** *sustantivo* memory stick

pancarta *f sustantivo* banner *o* banner advertisement *o* banner ad

panel *sustantivo* panel ◇ **el enchufe está en el panel trasero** the socket is on the back panel ◇ **panel** *m* **de control de un sistema** system control panel

'En contra de la creencia de que en Linux hay que 'tirar' de línea de comandos cada vez que el usuario quiere modificar algo, muchas distribuciones han desarrollado utilidades que, cualquier 'Panel de Control' de Windows, permiten modificar la configuración del sistema.' [*Computer Hoy*]

panel *m* **acústico** *sustantivo* acoustic panel

panel *m* **básico** *sustantivo* backplane

panel *m* **básico de un microordenador** *sustantivo* microcomputer backplane

panel *m* **de atrás** *sustantivo* back panel ◇ **el enchufe está en el panel trasero** the socket is on the back panel

panel *m* **de conexión** *sustantivo* patch panel

panel *m* **de control** *sustantivo* control panel

panel *m* **delantero** *sustantivo* front panel

panel *m* **frontal** *sustantivo* front panel

panel *m* **posterior** *sustantivo* back panel

panel *m* **trasero** *sustantivo* back panel ◇ **el enchufe está en el panel trasero** the socket is on the back panel

pantalla *sustantivo* **1.** display unit **2.** form mode **3.** screen **4.** shield ◇ **el paquete de publicación asistida por ordenador incluye la visualización de la fuente de caracteres en la pantalla** the dtp package offers on-screen font display ◇ **en pantalla** on-screen ◇ **pantalla** *f* **con fondo blanco y texto en negro** paper-white monitor ◇ **pantalla** *f* **con luz de fondo activada** backlit display ◇ **pantalla** *f* **de cristal líquido de matriz activa** active matrix display ◇ **pantalla** *f* **llena (de información)** screenful

'La pantalla táctil ocupa poco espacio y permite navegar pulsando en pantalla.' [*Ciberp@ís*]

pantalla *f* **(de ordenador)** *sustantivo* cathode ray tube storage

pantalla *f* **(de visualización)** *sustantivo* monitor ■ *abrev* VDU ■ *sustantivo* visual display terminal *o* visual display unit

pantalla *f* **acústica** *sustantivo* loudspeaker

pantalla *f* **alfanumérica** *sustantivo* alphanumeric display

pantalla *f* **analógica** *sustantivo* analog display

pantalla *f* **completa** *adj* full-screen

pantalla *f* **compuesta** *sustantivo* composite display

pantalla *f* **de arranque** *sustantivo* (*de un programa*) splash screen ◇ **la pantalla de arranque normalmente muestra el logotipo del producto y la información básica de los derechos de autor** the splash screen normally displays the product logo and gives basic copyright information

pantalla *f* **de ayuda** *sustantivo* help screen

pantalla *f* **de color** *sustantivo* colour monitor ◇ **el monitor de color es excelente para los juegos electrónicos** the colour monitor is great for games

pantalla *f* **de cristal líquido** *sustantivo* **1.** LCD **2.** LCD screen **3.** liquid crystal display

pantalla *f* **de desviación** *sustantivo* baffle

pantalla *f* **de doble barrido** *sustantivo* dual-scan display

pantalla *f* **de emisión de campo** *abrev* FED ■ *sustantivo* field emission display

pantalla *f* **de inicio** *sustantivo* startup screen

pantalla *f* **de ochenta columnas** *sustantivo* eighty-column screen *o* 80-column screen

pantalla *f* **de página completa** *sustantivo* full-size display

pantalla *f* **de plasma** *sustantivo* gas discharge display *o* gas plasma display

pantalla *f* **de texto** *sustantivo* text screen

pantalla *f* **de toda la página** *sustantivo* full-size display

pantalla *f* **de una línea** *sustantivo* single line display

pantalla *f* **de vídeo** *sustantivo* **1.** video display **2.** video monitor ◊ **entrada a la pantalla de vídeo** video display input (VDI)

pantalla *f* **de vídeo con teclado** *sustantivo* video terminal

pantalla *f* **de visualización** *sustantivo* **1.** display screen **2.** readout device ■ *abrev* VDT

pantalla *f* **de visualización gráfica** *sustantivo* graphics VDU

pantalla *f* **digital** *sustantivo* digital display

pantalla *f* **dividida** *sustantivo* split screen ◊ **utilizamos la pantalla dividida para contrastar el texto sobre el que se está trabajando con otro texto de la memoria que sirve de referencia** we use split screen mode to show the text being worked on and another text from memory for comparison

pantalla *f* **electroluminiscente** *sustantivo* electroluminescent display

pantalla *f* **electrostática** *sustantivo* electrostatic screen

pantalla *f* **esclava** *sustantivo* slave tube

pantalla *f* **magnética** *sustantivo* magnetic screen

pantalla *f* **plana** *sustantivo* **1.** flat panel **2.** flat screen

pantalla *f* **táctil** *sustantivo* touch screen

pantalla *f* **virtual** *sustantivo* **1.** virtual desktop **2.** virtual screen

papel ◊ **papel** *m* **(doblado) de hojas múltiples** accordion fold ◊ **papel** *m* **(doblado) en forma de acordeón** fanfold ◊ **papel** *m* **(continuo) para impresora** computer stationery

'El fax de papel térmico siempre ha sido el tipo más solicitado en nuestro país, por la simple razón de que es el más barato.' [*Ciberp@ís*]

papel *m* **calco** *sustantivo* detail paper

papel *m* **con cabecera** *sustantivo* preprinted stationery

papel *m* **con copia** *adj* two-part

papel *m* **continuo** *sustantivo* **1.** accordion fold *o* accordion fanfold **2.** concertina fold **3.** continuous stationery **4.** fanfold **5.** listing paper

papel *m* **de autocopia** *sustantivo* NCR paper

papel *m* **de listado** *sustantivo* **1.** computer stationery **2.** listing paper

papel *m* **de transferencia térmica** *sustantivo* electrosensitive paper

papel *m* **electrosensible** *sustantivo* electrosensitive paper

papel *m* **en acordeón** *sustantivo* concertina fold

papelera *f* *sustantivo* trashcan

papelera *f* **de bits** *sustantivo* bit bucket

papelera *f* **de reciclaje** *sustantivo* Recycle Bin

papel *m* **fotosensible de doble cara** *sustantivo* duplex

papel *m* **informático** *sustantivo* computer stationery

papel *m* **NCR** *sustantivo* NCR paper

papel *m* **perforado** *sustantivo* punched tape *o* punched paper tape

papel *m* **personalizado** *sustantivo* preprinted stationery

papel *m* **pintado** *sustantivo* (*de la pantalla de Windows*) wallpaper

papel *m* **preimpreso** *sustantivo* preprinted stationery

papel *m* **térmico** *sustantivo* **1.** heat-sensitive paper **2.** thermal paper

papel *m* **termosensible** *sustantivo* heat-sensitive paper

paquete *m* *sustantivo* packaging

paquete *sustantivo* **1.** batch **2.** package **3.** package deal **4.** packet ◊ **el ordenador se vende con un paquete de programas de contabilidad y tratamiento de textos** the computer is sold with accounting and word-processing packages ◊ **llegaron a un acuerdo de conjunto que incluye el desarrollo de software, la personalización del hardware y la formación del personal** they agreed a package deal, which involves the development of software, customizing hardware and training of staff ◊ **paquete** *m* **(de tarjetas perforadas)** pack ◊ **paquete** *m* **(de datos) de multidifusión** multicast packet ◊ **paquete** *m* **de programas (informáticos)** packaged software ◊ **red de conmutación de paquetes** packet switched network (PSN) ◊ **sistema de conmutación de paquetes** packet switching system (PSS)

'La Red es, sobre todo, un medio colosal que permite mandar, recibir y localizar a la velocidad de la luz paquetes de información en una superautopista electrónica, que va de un extremo a otro del planeta.' [*Nueva economía*]

paquete *m* **de aplicación** *sustantivo* applications package

paquete *m* **de aplicaciones** *sustantivo* application package

paquete *m* **de comunicaciones** *sustantivo* communications package

paquete *m* **de discos** *sustantivo* disk pack

paquete *m* **de programas** *sustantivo* application package

paquete *m* **de software** *sustantivo* software package

paquete *m* **de software empresarial** *sustantivo* business package

paquete *m* **IP** *sustantivo* IP Datagram

paquete *m* **lineal** *sustantivo* (*de circuitos integrados*) flat pack

paquete *m* **plano** *sustantivo* flat pack

paquete *m* **rápido** *sustantivo* fast packet

paquete *m* **simple en línea** *sustantivo* single in-line package ■ *abrev* SIP

par *m* *sustantivo* peer

parada *f* *sustantivo* **1.** crash **2.** fault **3.** halt **4.** termination ◊ **parada** *f* **imprevista (en una rutina)** hangup

parada *f* **(anormal)** *sustantivo* abend

parada *f* **anormal** *sustantivo* abnormal termination

parada *f* **automática** *sustantivo* **1.** automatic power off **2.** auto stop

parada *f* **condicional** *sustantivo* conditional breakpoint

parada *f* **de comprobación** *sustantivo* machine check

parada *f* **de formularios** *sustantivo* form stop

parada *f* **del sistema** *sustantivo* system crash

parada *f* **dinámica** *sustantivo* dynamic stop

parada *f* **fatal** *sustantivo* catastrophic failure

parada *f* **por falta de papel** *sustantivo* form stop

parada *f* **programada** *sustantivo* programmed halt

paradas *fpl* **de tabulación** *plural noun* tabulation stops

parada *f* **total** *sustantivo* **1.** dead halt **2.** drop dead halt

paralelo *adj* parallel ◇ **entrada en paralelo** *or* **salida en paralelo** parallel input/parallel output (PIPO) ◇ **entrada** *or* **salida en paralelo** parallel input/output (PIO) ◇ **su velocidad normal de transmisión es de 60.000 bps mediante una conexión en paralelo** their average transmission rate is 60,000 bps through parallel connection

paralizar *verbo vt* to freeze ◇ **congelar** *o* **fijar** *o* **parar (una imagen)** to freeze (frame)

parametrización *f* *sustantivo* parameterisation *o* parameterization

parámetro *m* *sustantivo* parameter ◇ **el parámetro X define el número de caracteres mostrados en pantalla** the X parameter defines the number of characters displayed across a screen ◇ **el tamaño de la matriz se establece con este parámetro** the size of the array is set with this parameter ◇ **parámetro de palabra clave** keyword parameter

parámetro *m* **físico** *sustantivo* physical parameter

parámetros *mpl* **de diseño** *plural noun* design parameters

parámetros *mpl* **de impresión** *plural noun* print modifiers

parar *verbo* **1.** *vi* to block **2.** *vi* to inhibit **3.** *vi* to shut down

pararse *verbo vr* to crash

para tu información *sustantivo* for your information

parche *sustantivo* **1.** bug patch **2.** kludge *o* kluge

paréntesis *m* *sustantivo* bracket

paréntesis *m* **(s&pl)** *plural noun* round brackets

paridad *f* *sustantivo* parity

paridad *f* **de bloque** *sustantivo* block parity

paridad *f* **de columna(s)** *sustantivo* column parity

paridad *f* **impar** *sustantivo* odd parity *o* odd parity check

(hacer) parpadear *verbo* to flash

parpadear *verbo vt* to flicker ■ *sustantivo* jitter

parpadeo *m* *sustantivo* **1.** blinking **2.** flicker **3.** flutter ◇ **el parpadeo de la pantalla me da dolor de cabeza** looking at this screen jitter is giving me a headache ◇ **parpadeo** *m* **(de la imagen)** jitter

parpadeo *m* **de (un) carácter** *sustantivo* character blink

parpadeo *m* **de pantalla** *sustantivo* screen flicker

párrafo *m* *sustantivo* paragraph

párrafo *m* **estándar** *sustantivo* **1.** standard paragraph **2.** template

parte *sustantivo* part ◇ **parte** *f* **principal (de un programa)** main body ◇ **parte** *f* **superior del trazo vertical** ascender

parte *f* **fraccionaria** *sustantivo* **1.** fractional part **2.** mantissa

parte *f* **mantisa** *sustantivo* fractional part

parte *f* **posterior de un microordenador** *sustantivo* microcomputer backplane

partición *f* *sustantivo* partition

partición *f* **binaria** *sustantivo* binary split

partición *f* **de arranque** *sustantivo* boot partition

participación *f* **en las tareas** *sustantivo* load sharing

partícula *f* **alfa** *sustantivo* alpha-particle

partir *verbo vti* to cut

pasaje *m* *sustantivo* pass

pasajero *adj* transient

pasar ◇ **pasar (de un sistema a otro)** change over

pasarela *f* *sustantivo* gateway

pasarela *f* **(de comunicación)** *sustantivo* gateway ◇ **utilizamos una puerta para conectar la red de área local con la red de área extendida** we use a gateway to link the LAN to WAN

pasarela *f* **de pago** *sustantivo* payment gateway

paso *m* *sustantivo* **1.** crossover **2.** pass **3.** step ◇ **de paso único** single step ◇ **de un solo paso** single step

paso a paso *adj* single step

paso *m* **a paso** *sustantivo* step through

paso *m* **de clasificación** *sustantivo* sorting pass

paso *m* **de parámetro** *sustantivo* parameter passing

paso *m* **de programación** *sustantivo* program step

paso *m* **de señales** *sustantivo* token-passing

patilla *f* **de alineamiento** *sustantivo* alignment pin

pausa *f* *sustantivo* holdup

pausa *f* **de la impresión** *sustantivo* print pause

pausa *f* **de un dispositivo** *sustantivo* holdup

PC *m sustantivo* PC ■ *adj* PC-compatible ■ *sustantivo* personal computer ◇ **PC** *o* **ordenador personal compatible** PC compatible

PC/AT *sustantivo* PC/AT

PC-DOS ◇ **PC-DOS (versión IBM de MS-DOS)** PC-DOS

PCMCIA *sustantivo* 1. PCMCIA 2. Personal Computer Memory Card International Association

PC/XT *sustantivo* PC/XT

pedir *verbo* 1. *vt* to bid 2. *vt* to borrow ◇ **el terminal tuvo que pedir línea tres veces antes de que hubiera un hueco en las transmisiones de la red** the terminal had to bid three times before there was a gap in transmissions on the network

pegar *verbo* 1. *vt* to paste 2. *vt* to splice ◇ **puede usar pegamento o cinta adhesiva para unir los extremos (de la película)** you can use glue or splicing tape to splice the ends ◇ **una vez he cortado este párrafo del final del documento, puedo pegarlo aquí** now that I have cut this paragraph from the end of the document, I can paste it in here

película *f* **delgada** *sustantivo* thin film

película *f* **fina** *sustantivo* thin film

película *f* **gruesa** *sustantivo* thick film

Pentium (*marca comercial*) Intel Pentium

Pentium Pro (*marca comercial de un procesador*) Intel Pentium Pro

pequeña aplicación *f sustantivo* applet

pequeña *f* **aplicación** *sustantivo* applet

pequeña escala *adj* small-scale

percentil *m sustantivo* percentile

perceptible al oído *adj* audible

perder intensidad *verbo* to fade

pérdida *f sustantivo* 1. decrement 2. insertion loss ◇ **pérdida** *f* **de alineamiento en el entrehierro** gap loss

pérdida *f* **de la información** *sustantivo* drop out

pérdida *f* **de nivel** *sustantivo* drop out

pérdida *f* **de tensión** *sustantivo* power loss

pérdida *f* **de transmisión inexplicable** *sustantivo* line gremlin

pérdida *f* **de una señal** *sustantivo* breakup

perfil *m sustantivo* outline

perfil *m* **(de usuario)** *sustantivo* profile

perfilar *verbo vt* to tweak

perfil *m* **gubernamental OSI** *sustantivo* 1. GOSIP 2. Government Open Systems Interconnect Profile

perforacion ◇ **perforación** *f* **del margen (del papel)** feed hole

perforación *f sustantivo* key punch ◇ **perforación** *f* **(de la línea) 11** x punch ◇ **perforación** *f* **(de la línea) 12** y punch

perforación *f sustantivo* feed hole

perforación *f* **de acceso** *sustantivo* (*de un disco o de un disquete*) access hole

perforación *f* **de sector** *sustantivo* sectoring hole

perforaciones ◇ **perforaciones** *fpl* **que marcan el borde de un disco** disk index holes

perforaciones *fpl* **de arrastre** *plural noun* sprocket holes

perforación *f* **numérica** *sustantivo* numeric punch

perforación *f* **X** *sustantivo* x punch

perforación *f* **Y** *sustantivo* y punch

perforadora *f sustantivo* 1. key punch 2. perforator 3. punch

perforadora *f* **de cintas de papel** *sustantivo* paper tape punch

perforar *verbo vt* to punch

periférico *m sustantivo* 1. device 2. output device ■ *adj* peripheral ■ *sustantivo* 1. peripheral 2. peripheral unit ◇ **adaptador de interconexiones de periféricos** peripheral interface adapter (PIA) ◇ **los periféricos, como los lectores de disquetes o las impresoras, permiten transferir datos y son controlados por un sistema, pero contienen circuitos independientes para su funcionamiento** peripherals such as disk drives or printers allow data transfer and are controlled by a system, but contain independent circuits for their operation ◇ **procesador periférico** peripheral processing unit (PPU)

periférico *m* **de entrada** *sustantivo* input device

periférico *m* **de entrada/salida** *sustantivo* 1. input/output device 2. input/output unit 3. I/O device

periférico *m* **de salida** *sustantivo* output device

periférico *m* **lento** *sustantivo* slow peripheral

periférico *m* **rápido** *sustantivo* fast peripheral

periféricos *mpl sustantivo* peripheral equipment

periódicamente *adv* periodically

periódico *adj* periodic *o* periodical

periodo *m sustantivo* period ◇ **durante seis años** *o* **en un periodo de seis años** for a six-year period ◇ **durante un espacio** *o* **periodo de tiempo** for a period of time

periodo *m* **de acceso** *sustantivo* access period

periodo *m* **de ensamblaje** *sustantivo* assembly time

periodo *m* **de latencia** *sustantivo* latency

periodo *m* **de máxima demanda** *sustantivo* time of peak demand

periodo *m* **de referencia** *sustantivo* reference time

permiso *m sustantivo* 1. authorisation *o* authorization 2. licence

permiso *m* **(de acceso)** *sustantivo* permission ◇ **este usuario no puede acceder al fichero del servidor porque no tiene autorización** this user cannot access the file on the server because he does not have permission

permiso *m* **de acceso** *sustantivo* access permission

permiso *m* **de utilización** *sustantivo* runtime licence

permiso *m* **para duplicar** *sustantivo* **1.** ATC **2.** authorisation to copy

permutación *f* *sustantivo* **1.** permutation **2.** ring shift

permutación *f* **de bits** *sustantivo* rotate operation

permuta *f* **de tareas** *sustantivo* task swapping

permutar *verbo* **1.** *vi* to exchange **2.** *vi* to swap

persistencia *f* *sustantivo* **1.** afterglow **2.** persistence

persona *sustantivo* caller ◇ **persona** *f* **autorizada (para utilizar un sistema)** authorised user

personal *m* **informático** *sustantivo* liveware

personalización *f* *sustantivo* personalising *o* personalizing

personalizado *adj* custom-built

personalizar *verbo vt* to customise *o* to customize ◇ **utilizamos software hecho a medida** we use customized software

perspectiva *f* *sustantivo* perspective

perspectiva *f* **con punto de fuga** *sustantivo* vanishing point perspective

pestillo *m* *sustantivo* latch

peta *m* *prefijo* peta

petabyte *m* *sustantivo* petabyte

petaocteto *m* *sustantivo* petabyte

petición *f* **de comentario** *sustantivo* **1.** request for comment **2.** RFC

petición *f* **de entrada/salida** *sustantivo* input/output request ■ *abrev* IORQ

petición *f* **de envió** *sustantivo* request to send

petición *f* **de interrupción** *sustantivo* **1.** interrupt request **2.** IRQ

petición *f* **de lectura/grabación** *sustantivo* demand reading/writing

petición *f* **de transmisión** *sustantivo* request to send signal ■ *abrev* RTS

PhotoCD™ Kodak PhotoCD ■ *sustantivo* PhotoCD

pica *f* *sustantivo* pica

PICK™ *sustantivo* PICK

pico- *prefijo* pico- ◇ **picofaradio (pF)** picofarad (pF)

picosegundo (ps) *m* *sustantivo* picosecond ■ *abrev* pS

PICS *sustantivo* **1.** PICS **2.** PING

PICT *sustantivo* PICT

PICture *sustantivo* PICture

pie *m* *sustantivo* foot ◇ **estampó su firma al pie de la carta** he signed his name at the foot of the letter

pie *m* **de página** *sustantivo* footer *o* footing

pieza *f* **de recambio** *sustantivo* spare part ◇ **la impresora no funciona; tenemos que con-** seguir una pieza de repuesto the printer won't work – we need to get a spare part

pieza *f* **de repuesto** *sustantivo* spare part ◇ **la impresora no funciona; tenemos que conseguir una pieza de repuesto** the printer won't work – we need to get a spare part

pila *sustantivo* **1.** heap **2.** nesting store **3.** (*de datos en memoria*) stack ◇ **equipado, -a con una pila (auxiliar)** battery-backed ◇ **pila** *f* **(de datos en memoria)** cellar ◇ **pila** *f* **de instrucciones de un programa** program stack

pila *f* **auxiliar** *sustantivo* battery backup

pila *f* **binaria** *sustantivo* heap

pila *f* **de desplazamiento ascendente** *sustantivo* push-up list *o* push-up stack

pila *f* **de desplazamiento descendente** *sustantivo* push-down list *o* push-down stack

pila *f* **de interrupciones** *sustantivo* interrupt stacking

pila *f* **del protocolo** *sustantivo* protocol stack

pila *f* **de memoria virtual** *sustantivo* virtual memory stack

pila *f* **de reserva** *sustantivo* battery backup

pila *f* **recargable** *sustantivo* re-chargeable battery ◇ **se utiliza una batería recargable como alimentación auxiliar para la memoria RAM cuando se apaga el sistema** a re-chargeable battery is used for RAM back-up when the system is switched off

piloto *m* *sustantivo* control

PIM *sustantivo* **1.** personal information manager **2.** PIM

pincel *m* *sustantivo* brush ◇ **el paquete de dibujo le permite cambiar la anchura (en pixels) del pincel y el color que produce** the paint package lets you vary the width of the brush (in pixels) and the colour it produces

pinchar *verbo vt* to click

pintar *verbo vt* to paint

pintura *f* *sustantivo* paint

pirata *mf* *sustantivo* pirate ■ *adj* pirate ◇ **la empresa está intentando llevar a los piratas de software ante los tribunales** the company is trying to take the software pirates to court

pirateado *m* *adj* pirate

piratear *verbo* **1.** *vt* to hack **2.** *vt* to pirate ◇ **cinta pirateada** a pirated tape ◇ **los diseños del nuevo sistema fueron pirateados en el Extremo Oriente** the designs for the new system were pirated in the Far East ◇ **utilizó un disquete pirateado a buen precio y descubrió que el programa contenía errores** he used a cheap pirated disk and found the program had bugs in it

piratería *f* *sustantivo* piracy

piratería *f* **informática** *sustantivo* software piracy

pista *sustantivo* **1.** track **2.** tracking ◇ **pistas** *fpl* **por pulgada** TPI

pista *f* **de bits** *sustantivo* bit track

pista *f* **de control** *sustantivo* audit trail

pista *f* **de datos binarios** *sustantivo* bit track

pista *f* **de direccion(es)** *sustantivo* address track

pista *f* **de paridad** *sustantivo* parity track

pista *f* **de referencia** *sustantivo* library track

pista *f* **de reloj** *sustantivo* clock track

pista *f* **de un disco** *sustantivo* disk track

pista *f* **de verificación** *sustantivo* audit trail

pista *f* **magnética** *sustantivo* 1. magnetic strip 2. magnetic stripe

pistas por pulgada *sustantivo* tracks per inch

píxel *m sustantivo* 1. pel 2. pixel

píxel *m sustantivo* picture element

pixelado, -a *adj* pixelated

pizarra *f* **electrónica** *sustantivo* electronic blackboard

pizarra *f* **gráfica** *sustantivo* 1. data tablet 2. digitising pad *o* digitising tablet *o* digitizing pad *o* digitizing tablet

placa *f sustantivo* board ◇ **placa** *f* **de circuito impresa a doble cara** double-sided printed circuit board ◇ **placa de circuito impreso** printed circuit board (PCB)

placa *f* **aceleradora** *sustantivo* accelerator board *o* accelerator card

placa *f* **base** *sustantivo* 1. circuit board 2. circuit card

placa *f* **con perforaciones al margen** *sustantivo* edge notched card

placa *f* **de borde** *sustantivo* 1. edge board 2. edge card

placa *f* **de circuito impreso** *abrev* 1. PC 2. PCB ■ *sustantivo* printed circuit *o* printed circuit board

placa *f* **hija** *sustantivo* daughter board

placa *f* **lógica** *sustantivo* 1. logic board 2. logic card ■ *verbo* to logoff ■ *sustantivo* logout

placa *f* **madre** *sustantivo* motherboard

plan *m sustantivo* schedule

plan *sustantivo* plan

'A punto de acabar el primer año del ambicioso plan Info XXI, Ciberp@ís ha revisado los proyectos, plazos y objetivos que se había marcado el Gobierno para 2001. La conclusión no puede resultar más desesperanzadora.' [*Ciberp@ís*]

planar *m adj* planar

plan *m* **de emergencia** *sustantivo* contingency plan

plan *m* **de seguridad** *sustantivo* backup plan ◇ **el suministro ininterrumpido de energía (UPS) normal ha fallado, así que tendremos que utilizar nuestro plan de seguridad para intentar restablecer la electricidad** the normal UPS has gone wrong, so we will have to use our backup plan to try and restore power

plan *m* **de urgencia** *sustantivo* contingency plan

planificación *sustantivo* 1. job scheduling 2. planning 3. scheduling ◇ **planificación a corto plazo** short-term planning ◇ **planificación a largo plazo** long-term planning ◇ **planificación** *f* **de una base de datos** database mapping

planificación *f* **de tareas** *sustantivo* job scheduling

planificador *m* **(de multiprogramación)** *sustantivo* scheduler

planificador *m* **de paquetes** *sustantivo* packet scheduler

planificar *verbo vt* to plan

plano *m sustantivo* 1. plan 2. plane ◇ **conjunto de planos** plans ◇ **plano de la ciudad** street plan *o* town plan ◇ **plano de una planta** floor plan

plano *m* **binario** *sustantivo* bit plane

plano *m* **posterior** *sustantivo* backplane

planta *f* **de montaje** *sustantivo* assembly plant

plantar(se) *sustantivo vr* lock up

plantilla *sustantivo* 1. flowchart template 2. stencil 3. telnet 4. template ◇ **plantilla** *f* **con las funciones del teclado** keyboard overlay ◇ **plantilla** *f* **de un diagrama de flujo** flowchart stencil

plantilla *f* **de organigrama** *sustantivo* flowchart stencil

plataforma *f sustantivo* platform ◇ **este software sólo funcionará sobre una plataforma IBM** this software will only work on the IBM PC platform

plataforma *f* **del equipo** *sustantivo* hardware platform

plataforma *f* **de recogida de datos** *sustantivo* data collection platform

plato ◇ **plato** *m* **(de un disco duro)** platter

Plug and Play™ *sustantivo* plug and play ■ *abrev* PNP

pluma *f sustantivo* pen

pluma *f* **electrónica** *sustantivo* stylus

pluma *f* **trazadora** *sustantivo* plotter pen

plumilla *f* **trazadora** *sustantivo* plotter pen

poblar *verbo vt* to populate

poder *m* **de cálculo** *sustantivo* computing power

poder *m* **de resolución** *sustantivo* resolving power

POKE (de inserción) *sustantivo* poke ◇ **la instrucción POKE 1423.74 insertará el dato 74 en la ubicación 1423** poke 1423.74 will write the data 74 into location 1423

polar *adj* polar ◇ **diagrama de coordenadas polares** polar diagram ◇ **órbita polar** polar orbit

polaridad *f sustantivo* polarity

polaridad *f* **eléctrica** *sustantivo* electrical polarity

polaridad *f* **inversa** *sustantivo* reverse polarity

polaridad *f* **invertida** *sustantivo* reverse polarity

polaridad *f* **magnética** *sustantivo* magnetic polarity

polarizado *adj* polarised

polígono *m sustantivo* polygon

política *f* **de uso aceptable** *sustantivo* acceptable use policy ■ *abrev* AUP ■ *sustantivo* policy

polución *f* **electrónica** *sustantivo* electronic smog

polyphony *m sustantivo* polyphony

ponderación *f sustantivo* weighting

poner ◊ **poner (datos) en la pila** put

poner al día *verbo* to update

poner a prueba *verbo* to pilot ◊ **están poniendo a prueba el nuevo sistema** they are piloting the new system

poner a punto *verbo* 1. to fine-tune 2. to tune 3. to tweak

poner de relieve *verbo* to highlight

poner en clave *verbo* to code

poner en funcionamiento *verbo* 1. to activate 2. to bring up 3. to operate ◊ **¿sabe cómo hacer funcionar la centralita telefónica?** do you know how to operate the telephone switchboard?

poner en marcha *verbo* 1. to activate 2. to bring up 3. to power up

poner en órbita *verbo* to launch

poner en orden alfabético *verbo* to alphabetise *o* to alphabetize ◊ **introduzca la información bibliográfica y póngala en orden alfabético** enter the bibliographical information and alphabetize it

poner en páginas *verbo* to page

por *preposition* 1. per 2. via ◊ **¿cuál es el porcentaje de aumento?** what is the increase per cent? ◊ **diez por ciento** 10 per cent ◊ **el cincuenta por ciento de nada sigue siendo nada** fifty per cent of nothing is still nothing ◊ **la tasa de errores ha descendido al doce por ciento** the error rate has fallen to twelve per hundred ◊ **la tasa se eleva a veinticinco por mil** the rate is twenty-five per thousand ◊ **puede cargar los datos en la unidad central por medio de un módem** you can download the data to the CPU via a modem

por año *adv* per year

por anticipado *prefijo* pre-

porcentaje *m* **de la muestra** *sustantivo* sample rate

porción *f* **de un microprograma** *sustantivo* microsequence

por día *phrase* per day

por etapas *adj* staged

por hora *adv* per hour

por medio de *preposition* via ◊ **puede cargar los datos en la unidad central por medio de un módem** you can download the data to the CPU via a modem

por semana *adv* per week

portabilidad *f sustantivo* portability

portabilidad *f* **de una fórmula** *sustantivo* formula portability

portadiscos *m sustantivo* 1. caddy 2. CD caddy

portadora *f* **T** *sustantivo* T carrier

portador *m* **de compactos** *sustantivo* CD caddy

portal *sustantivo* portal

'Las previsiones apuntan a que la pléyade de portales en general, los que actualmente se anuncian, y los que se anunciarán, se va a reducir drásticamente en un par de años debido a intensos procesos de concentración, principalmente.' [*Nueva economía*]

portal *m* **vertical** *sustantivo* vertical portal

portal *m* **web** *sustantivo* website

portapapeles *m sustantivo* clipboard

portátil *adj* portable

posición *sustantivo* 1. location 2. place ◊ **posición** *f* **de transporte de la cabeza** head park

posicional *adj* positional

posicionamiento *m* **absoluto** *sustantivo* absolute positioning

posicionamiento *m* **de la cabeza** *sustantivo* head positioning

posicionar *verbo vt* to align

posición *f* **binaria** *sustantivo* bit position

posición *f* **de respuesta** *sustantivo* response position

posición *f* **de salida** *sustantivo* home

posición *f* **de signo** *sustantivo* sign position

posición *f* **de una cifra** *sustantivo* digit place *o* digit position

posición *f* **direccionable por el contenido** *sustantivo* content-addressable location

posición *f* **inicial** *sustantivo* home

posición *f* **protegida** *sustantivo* protected location

positivo *adj* 1. affirmative 2. positive

posproducción *f sustantivo* post production

postbyte *m sustantivo* postbyte

postcompilador *m sustantivo* postprocessor

postocteto *m sustantivo* postbyte

postprocesador *m sustantivo* postprocessor

PostScript *m* **encapsulado** *sustantivo* encapsulated PostScript

potencia *sustantivo* power ◊ **potencia** *f* **de cálculo de un ordenador** computer power

potencia *f* **(en voltios)** *sustantivo* voltage ◊ **bajada de tensión** voltage dip *o* dip in voltage ◊ **caída** voltage dip *o* dip in voltage

potencia *f* **de ordenador** *sustantivo* computer power

potencia *f* **fraccionaria** *sustantivo* root

potenciar *verbo vt* to upgrade ◊ **el monoprocesador con 2 Mbytes de memoria puede potenciarse a 4 Mbytes** the single processor with 2Mbytes of memory can be upgraded to 4Mbytes

PowerBook™ PowerBook

PowerPC™ PowerPC

ppp *plural noun* dots per inch ■ *abrev* d.p.i. *o* dpi

practicabilidad *f sustantivo* feasibility

pre- *prefijo* pre-

prealmacenar *verbo vt* to prestore

preamplificador *m sustantivo* pre-amplifier

preasignación *f sustantivo* pre-allocation

precedencia *f sustantivo* precedence

preceder *verbo vt* to precede

precisión *f sustantivo* **1.** accuracy **2.** precision ◇ **precisión** *f* **(de longitud) simple** single length precision

precisión *f* **de una sola palabra** *sustantivo* single length precision

precisión *f* **de un número** *sustantivo* precision of a number

precisión *f* **doble** *sustantivo* double precision

precisión *f* **múltiple** *sustantivo* **1.** multiple precision **2.** multiprecision

precisión *f* **simple** *sustantivo* single precision

preciso *adj* precise

precompilador *m sustantivo* preprocessor

precondicionar *verbo vt* to precondition

predefinido *adj* predefined

predicado *m sustantivo* predicate

preeditar *verbo vt* to pre-edit

preferencia *f sustantivo* priority

prefijo *m sustantivo* prefix

preformateado *adj* preformatted ◇ **un disco preformateado** a preformatted disk

pregunta *f sustantivo* **1.** enquiry **2.** inquiry

pregunta *f* **relacional** *sustantivo* relational query ◇ **la consulta relacional 'encontrar todos los hombres de menos de 35 años' no funciona en este sistema** the relational query 'find all men under 35 years old' will not work on this system

preguntas *fpl* **más frecuentes** *sustantivo* FAQ ■ *plural noun* frequently asked questions

prensador *m sustantivo* clapper

preparación *f* **de datos** *sustantivo* data preparation

preparación *f* **de señal** *sustantivo* signal conditioning

preparado *sustantivo* OK ■ *adj* ready ◇ **la luz verde indica que el sistema está preparado para otro programa** the green light indicates the system is ready for another program

preparado, -a en la impresión *adj* post-formatted

preparado, -a para funcionar *adj* configured-in

preparado para programas multimedia *adj* multimedia-ready

preparado para transmitir *sustantivo* **1.** data terminal ready **2.** DTR

preparar *verbo vt* to arm

preparar un índice *verbo* to index

preprocesador *m sustantivo* preprocessor

preprocesar *verbo vt* to preprocess

preprogramado *adj* preprogrammed

preprogramar *verbo* **1.** *vt* to preprogram **2.** *vt* to preset ◇ **la impresora se preprogramó con**

nuevos parámetros de página the printer was preset with new page parameters

presentación *sustantivo* **1.** form **2.** page layout ◇ **ha sido fácil preparar a los operadores en la utilización del nuevo programa ya que su presentación en pantalla se parece a los impresos existentes** it's been easy to train the operators to use the new software since its display looks like the existing printed forms ◇ **presentación** *f* **(gráfica) en columnas** columnar working

presentaciónes ◇ **presentaciones** *fpl* **(de página) asistidas por ordenador** desktop presentations

presentación *f* **gráfica** *plural noun* presentation graphics ◇ **las ventas del último mes parecieron aún mejores gracias a la presentación gráfica** the sales for last month looked even better thanks to the use of presentation graphics

presentación *f* **por plasma** *sustantivo* plasma display

presentación *f* **positiva** *sustantivo* positive presentation

presentación *f* **visual** *sustantivo* **1.** display **2.** soft copy ◇ **representación visual de siete segmentos** seven-segment display

presentación *f* **visual de pantalla grande** *sustantivo* widescreen display

Presentation Manager™ *sustantivo* Presentation Manager

preservador *m* **de pantalla** *sustantivo* screen saver

prestación *f sustantivo* facility

prevención *f* **de errores** *sustantivo* error trapping

preventivo *adj* preventative *o* preventive

prever *verbo vt* to project ◇ **las ventas previstas del nuevo PC** *o* **ordenador personal** the projected sales of the new PC

previsión *f sustantivo* projection

previsualizar *verbo vt* to preview

primario *adj* primary ◇ **colores primarios** *o* **fundamentales** primary colours ◇ **grupo primario** primary group

primera generación *f sustantivo* first generation

primero ◇ **los dos ordenadores funcionan a velocidades distintas, pero pueden transmitir datos mediante el sistema FIFO** the two computers operate at different rates, but can transmit data using a FIFO memory ◇ **primero en entrar, primero en salir** FIFO

primer *m* **plano** *sustantivo* foreground

primer término *m* **de una suma** *sustantivo* augend

principal *adj* **1.** main **2.** master **3.** prime ◇ **distribuidor general** *o* **principal** main distributing frame ◇ **haz principal** main beam

principio ◇ **principio** *m* **de una página (de una lista)** head of form

principio *m* **de fichero** *sustantivo* beginning of file ■ *abrev* bof *o* BOF

prioridad *f sustantivo* **1.** precedence **2.** priority ◇ **el sistema operativo tiene prioridad sobre la aplicación cuando se asigna el espacio del disco** the operating system has priority over the application when disk space is allocated ◇ **la disquetera es más importante que la impresora, de modo que tiene una mayor prioridad** the disk drive is more important than the printer, so it has a higher priority

prioridad *f* **absoluta** *sustantivo* absolute priority

prioridad *f* **de interrupciones** *plural noun* interrupt priorities

prioridad *f* **de un aparato** *sustantivo* device priority ◇ **la consola de instrucción tiene mayor prioridad que las impresoras y otros terminales** the master console has a higher device priority than the printers and other terminals

prioridad *f* **de una tarea** *sustantivo* job priority

prioridad *f* **de un periférico** *sustantivo* device priority ◇ **la consola de instrucción tiene mayor prioridad que las impresoras y otros terminales** the master console has a higher device priority than the printers and other terminals

privacidad *f sustantivo* privacy

privado *adj* private ◇ **sistema telefónico privado** private telephone system

privativo *adj* private

privilegio *m sustantivo* privilege

privilegio *m* **de acceso** *sustantivo* access privilege

PRN *sustantivo* PRN

probado sobre el terreno *adj* field-tested

probar *verbo vt* to test ◇ **antes de entregarlo probamos el dispositivo durante un largo período** the device was soak-tested prior to delivery ◇ **probar un sistema durante un período largo** soak

problema *m sustantivo* glitch

problema *m* **de contraste** *sustantivo* benchmark problem

problema *m* **de evaluación** *sustantivo* benchmark problem

procedimental *adj* procedural

procedimiento *sustantivo* **1.** procedure **2.** process ◇ **debería utilizar este procedimiento para recuperar los ficheros perdidos** you should use this procedure to retrieve lost files ◇ **el procedimiento se explica en el manual de instrucciones** the procedure is given in the manual ◇ **este procedimiento clasifica todos los ficheros en orden alfabético** this procedure sorts all the files into alphabetic order, you can call it from the main program by the instruction SORT ◇ **procedimiento** *m* **de enlace e incorporación de objetos** object linking and embedding; OLE ◇ **procedimiento** *m* **minimax** *or* **de aproximación al mínimo máximo** minmax

procedimiento *m* **aleatorio** *sustantivo* random process

procedimiento *m* **de acceso a enlace** *sustantivo* link access protocol

procedimiento *m* **de cola de espera** *sustantivo* queue discipline

procedimiento *m* **de control de encaminamiento** *plural noun* routing overheads ◇ **el índice de transferencia de información es mucho menor cuando se tienen en cuenta los protocolos de envío** the information transfer rate is very much less once all routing overheads have been accommodated

procedimiento *m* **de emergencia** *sustantivo* fall back

procedimiento *m* **de operador** *sustantivo* operator procedure

procedimiento *m* **de recuperación** *sustantivo* recovery procedure ◇ **la recuperación de los ficheros perdidos puede realizarse utilizando un procedimiento de recuperación** the recovery of lost files can be carried out using a recovery procedure

procedimiento *m* **de segunda generación** *sustantivo* child process *o* child program

procedimiento *m* **de seguridad** *sustantivo* backup procedure

procedimiento *m* **recursivo** *sustantivo* recursive call

procedimientos *mpl* **de emergencia** *plural noun* (*en case de fallo*) fall back routines

procesador *sustantivo* **1.** machine **2.** processor ◇ **(procesador de) corriente** *f* **de instrucciones múltiples – corriente de un solo dato** multiple instruction stream-single data stream ◇ **palabra de estado del procesador** processor status word (PSW) ◇ **procesador** *m* **de códigos de operación** OCP; order code processor ◇ **procesador** *m* **de conjunto de arquitectura RISC** RISC; reduced instruction set computer ◇ **procesador** *m* **de conjunto de instrucciones reducido** RISC; reduced instruction set computer ◇ **procesador** *m* **de texto de lógica compartida** shared logic text processor ◇ **procesador** *m* **de textos con interfaz de comunicación** communicating word processor ◇ **procesador** *m* **gráfico por barrido de trama** raster image processor

procesador *m* **auxiliar** *sustantivo* **1.** (*conectado al procesador central*) attached processor **2.** attached processor **3.** auxiliary processor **4.** coprocessor **5.** support chip ◇ **el procesador aritmético auxiliar puede conectarse aquí** the maths support chip can be plugged in here

procesador *m* **central** *sustantivo* CPU

procesador *m* **con memoria asociativa** *sustantivo* associative processor

procesador *m* **de consola de instrucciones** *sustantivo* **1.** CCP **2.** command console processor

procesador *m* **de entrada/salida** *sustantivo* input/output processor ■ *abrev* IOP

procesador *m* **de fichero de instrucciones** *sustantivo* command file processor

procesador *m* **de imágenes** *sustantivo* image processor

procesador *m* **de imagen matricial** *sustantivo* raster image processor ■ *abrev* RIP

procesador *m* **de instrucción** *sustantivo* instruction processor

procesador *m* **de interfaz** *sustantivo* interface processor

procesador *m* **de la imagen** *sustantivo* image processor

procesador *m* **de la información** *sustantivo* information processor

procesador *m* **de lenguaje** *sustantivo* language processor

procesador *m* **de matrices** *sustantivo* array processor ◊ **el procesador de matrices permite que la matriz que contiene la imagen de la pantalla pueda girar con una sola instrucción** the array processor allows the array that contains the screen image to be rotated with one simple command

procesador *m* **de mensajes de interfaz** *sustantivo* interface message processor

procesador *m* **de órdenes** *sustantivo* array processor

procesador *m* **de pantalla** *sustantivo* display processor

procesador *m* **de programa fuente** *sustantivo* source machine

procesador *m* **de red** *sustantivo* network processor

procesador *m* **de red de comunicaciones** *sustantivo* communications network processor

procesador *m* **de representación visual** *sustantivo* display processor

procesador *m* **de texto** *sustantivo* word-processor

procesador *m* **de textos con interfaz de comunicación** *abrev* CWP

procesador *m* **de visualización** *sustantivo* display processor

procesador *m* **distribuido** *sustantivo* distributed processor

procesador *m* **doble** *sustantivo* dual processor

procesador *m* **en modalidad carácter** *sustantivo* character machine

procesador *m* **escalar** *sustantivo* scalar processor

procesador *m* **esclavo** *sustantivo* slave processor

procesadores *mpl* **en equipo** *plural noun* tandem processors

procesadores *mpl* **en tándem** *plural noun* tandem processors

procesador *m* **especializado** *sustantivo* back-end processor

procesadores *mpl* **V20, V30** *sustantivo* V20

procesador *m* **frontal** *sustantivo* front-end processor

procesador *m* **gráfico** *sustantivo* graphics processor

procesador *m* **gráfico por barrido de trama** *abrev* RIP

procesador *m* **MMX** *plural noun* multimedia extensions

procesador *m* **nuevo** *sustantivo* clean machine

procesador *m* **periférico** *sustantivo* peripheral processing unit ■ *abrev* PPU

procesador *m* **por lotes** *sustantivo* batch processor

procesador *m* **vectorial** *sustantivo* **1.** array processor **2.** vector processor

procesador *m* **Z80** *sustantivo* Z80

procesamiento *m* **de textos** *sustantivo* word-processing ◊ **cargue el programa de tratamiento de textos antes de empezar a introducir datos** load the word-processing program before you start keyboarding

procesamiento *m* **distribuido** *sustantivo* distributed processing

procesar *verbo vt* to process ◊ **hemos procesado los nuevos datos** we processed the new data ◊ **llevará mucho tiempo procesar toda la información** processing all the information will take a long time

proceso *sustantivo* **1.** process **2.** processing ◊ **cámara de proceso (de imagen en color)** process camera ◊ **el proceso consta de cinco etapas** there are five stages in the process ◊ **el proceso de poner el ordenador en funcionamiento requiere mucho tiempo** the process of setting up the computer takes a long time ◊ **proceso** *m* **(de datos) inmediato** demand processing ◊ **proceso** *m* **no prioritario** background ◊ **proceso** *m* **por lotes de forma secuencial** sequential batch processing

proceso *m* **aleatorio** *sustantivo* random process

proceso *m* **automático de datos** *sustantivo* **1.** ADP **2.** automatic data processing

proceso *m* **centralizado de la información** *sustantivo* centralised data processing *o* centralized data processing

proceso *m* **concurrente** *sustantivo* concurrent processing ◊ **tres transordenadores proporcionan utilidades simultáneas de proceso para todo el departamento** three transputers provide concurrent processing capabilities for the entire department

proceso *m* **cooperativo** *sustantivo* cooperative processing

proceso *m* **de colaboración** *sustantivo* co-operative processing

proceso *m* **de consulta(s)** *sustantivo* query processing

proceso *m* **de datos distribuido** *sustantivo* **1.** DDP **2.** distributed data processing

proceso *m* **de datos integrados** *abrev* IDP
■ *sustantivo* integrated data processing

proceso *m* **de entrada de bloques** *sustantivo* block input processing

proceso *m* **de evaluación del funcionamiento** *sustantivo* benchmark ◇ **la revista dio los resultados de la prueba de evaluación del nuevo programa** the magazine gave the new program's benchmark test results ◇ **prueba comparativa** *o* **de contraste** benchmark test

proceso *m* **de imágenes** *sustantivo* image processing

proceso *m* **de información** *sustantivo* EDP

proceso *m* **de la información** *sustantivo* data processing

proceso *m* **de la información manual** *sustantivo* manual data processing

proceso *m* **de listas** *sustantivo* list processing

proceso *m* **de señales digitales** *sustantivo* 1. digital signal processing 2. DSP

proceso *m* **de tarea** *sustantivo* job processing

proceso *m* **directo** *sustantivo* random process

proceso *m* **distribuido de datos** *sustantivo* distributed data processing

proceso *m* **doble** *sustantivo* parallel running

proceso *m* **electrónico de datos** *sustantivo* 1. EDP 2. electronic data processing

proceso *m* **electrónico de la información** *sustantivo* electronic data processing

proceso *m* **en línea** *sustantivo* online processing

proceso *m* **en paralelo** *sustantivo* 1. parallel processing 2. parallel running

proceso *m* **en red** *sustantivo* online processing

proceso *m* **en serie** *sustantivo* serial processing

proceso *m* **en tiempo real** *sustantivo* real-time processing

proceso *m* **geométrico** *sustantivo* geometry processing

proceso *m* **hijo** *sustantivo* child process *o* child program

proceso *m* **informático** *sustantivo* computer image processing

proceso *m* **iterativo** *sustantivo* iterative process

proceso *m* **no prioritario** *sustantivo* background processing

proceso *m* **por lotes** *sustantivo* batch processing

proceso *m* **preferente** *sustantivo* foregrounding

proceso *m* **secuencial** *sustantivo* sequential processing

proceso *m* **según demanda** *sustantivo* demand processing

proceso *m* **simultáneo** *sustantivo* 1. concurrent processing 2. simultaneous processing ◇ **tres transordenadores proporcionan utilidades simultáneas de proceso para todo el departamento** three transputers provide concurrent processing capabilities for the entire department

proceso *m* **subordinado** *sustantivo* background processing

proceso *m* **tratamiento** *m* **de ficheros** *sustantivo* file processing

producción *f sustantivo* 1. generation 2. origination 3. production ◇ **ciclo de producción** production run ◇ **la producción de códigos es automática** code generation is automatic ◇ **la producción del material gráfico requerirá varias semanas** the origination of the artwork will take several weeks ◇ **la producción se verá probablemente interrumpida por la acción sindical** production will probably be held up by industrial action; we are hoping to speed up production by installing new machinery ◇ **pero esperamos acelerar la producción instalando nueva maquinaria** production will probably be held up by industrial action; we are hoping to speed up production by installing new machinery ◇ **producción en serie de monitores** *o* **de calculadoras** mass production of monitors *o* of calculators

producción *f* **a gran escala** *sustantivo* mass production

producción *f* **en serie** *sustantivo* mass production

producción *f* **específica** *sustantivo* throughput

producido por ordenador *adj* computer-generated

producir *verbo* 1. *vt* to generate 2. *vt* to originate 3. *vt* to output 4. *vt* to produce

producirse *verbo vr* to occur ◇ **se puede producir una pérdida de datos a causa de las bajadas de tensión** data loss can occur because of power supply variations

producir una corriente inducida *verbo* to induce

producir una etiqueta *verbo* to label

producir una inducción *verbo* to induce

productivo *adj* productive

producto *m sustantivo* product

producto *m sustantivo* product

producto *m* **acabado** *sustantivo* 1. end product 2. final product

producto *m* **básico** *sustantivo* basic product

producto *m* **final** *sustantivo* 1. end product 2. final product

productor *m sustantivo* producer

productos *mpl* **ficticios** *sustantivo* vapourware

PROFS™ PROFS

programa *sustantivo* 1. formatter 2. program ◇ **en caso de fallo, el nuevo programa de recuperación de ficheros minimizará la pérdida de datos** if a fault occurs, data loss will be minimized due to the improved abend recovery program ◇ **ensamblador de macros** *o* **de macroinstrucciones** *o* **programa de ensamblaje**

assembly program ◇ **es imposible encontrar un fichero perdido sin un programa de recuperación de ficheros** a lost file cannot be found without a file-recovery utility ◇ **especificaciones de un programa** program specifications ◇ **fichero PIF (de información de un programa en el entorno MS-Windows)** program information file (PIF) ◇ **interfaz f de los programas de Microsoft que sirve para conectar los programas con los datos** data access objects ◇ **lenguaje de diseño de programas** program design language (PDL) ◇ **lo que ve es lo que consigue** WYSIWYG ◇ **olvidé insertar una instrucción importante lo cual ocasionó que el programa se bloqueara, borrando todos los ficheros del disco** I forgot to insert an important instruction which caused a program to crash, erasing all the files on the disk ◇ **para iniciar un programa, haga un doble clic sobre el icono del programa** to run the program, double-click on the program icon ◇ **programa** m **de arranque (de un sistema)** bootstrap ◇ **programa** m **de cargar y ejecutar (automática)** load and go ◇ **programa** m **de diseño de páginas web** webpage design software ◇ **programa de ejecución** o **ejecutivo** executive program ◇ **programa** m **de grupo (de trabajo)** groupware ◇ **programa** m **de recuperación de ficheros** (*después de una interrupción terminación anormal*) abend recovery program ◇ **programa** m **de tratamiento de textos de ventanas múltiples** multi-window editor ◇ **programa** m **(almacenado) en memoria** stored program ◇ **programa** m **gráfico** animation software ◇ **programa** m **para copias de seguridad** backup agent ◇ **programa que muestra por pantalla el documento tal y como será impreso** WYSIWYG ◇ **programa** m **sin errores** blue-ribbon program ◇ **programa** m **utilidad** f **de recuperación de ficheros** (*después de un fallo*) file-recovery utility ◇ **técnica f de evaluación y revisión de programas** PERT; program evaluation and review technique ◇ **técnica de evaluación y revisión de un programa** program evaluation and review technique (PERT)

programa m *sustantivo* schedule

programa(s) m(pl) *sustantivo* software

programa m **a base de menús** *sustantivo* menu-driven software

programa m **absoluto** *sustantivo* absolute program

programa m **activado por instrucciones** *sustantivo* command-driven program

programa m **activo** *sustantivo* active program

programa m **adaptador** *sustantivo* postprocessor

programa m **antivirus** *sustantivo* 1. anti-virus program 2. vaccine 3. virus checker

programable *adj* 1. programmable 2. user-selectable ◇ **memoria programable** o **(memoria) PROM** programmable memory (PROM) ◇ **orden lógico programable** o **dispositivo lógico programable** programmable logic array (PLA) o programmable logic device (PLD)

programable (por el usuario) *adj* user-definable ◇ **la hoja de cálculo contiene 125 símbolos programables** the style sheet contains 125 user-definable symbols

programa m **cableado** *sustantivo* hardwired program

programación f *sustantivo* 1. coding 2. programming

programación f **automática** *sustantivo* automatic programming

programación f **bien concebida** *sustantivo* elegant programming

programación f **concurrente** *sustantivo* concurrent programming

programación f **de abajo a arriba** *sustantivo* bottom up method o bottom up programming

programación f **de campo** *sustantivo* field programming

programación f **defensiva** *sustantivo* defensive computing

programación f **de llamadas** *sustantivo* call scheduling

programación f **de macros** *sustantivo* macro programming

programación f **de una PROM** *sustantivo* programming

programación f **elegante** *sustantivo* elegant programming

programación f **en lenguaje máquina** *sustantivo* machine language programming

programación f **en lenguaje universal** *sustantivo* universal programming

programación f **estructurada** *sustantivo* 1. structured programming 2. top down programming

programación f **lineal** *sustantivo* linear programming

programación f **modular** *sustantivo* modular programming

programación f **orientada a objetos** *sustantivo* object-oriented programming ■ *abrev* OOP

programación f **simbólica** *sustantivo* symbolic programming

programación f **simultánea** *sustantivo* concurrent programming

programación f **visual** *sustantivo* visual programming

programa m **con autodocumentación** *sustantivo* self-documenting program

programa m **concha** *sustantivo* shell

programa m **con documentación en línea** *sustantivo* self-documenting program

programa m **con extremo(s) abierto(s)** *sustantivo* open-ended program

programa m **convertidor** *sustantivo* conversion program

programa m **corregido** *sustantivo* debugged program

programa m **de alta prioridad** *sustantivo* high priority program

programa *m* **de aplicaciones** *sustantivo* application program

programa *m* **de biblioteca** *sustantivo* library program

programa *m* **de calendario** *sustantivo* calendar program

programa *m* **de cargar y ejecutar (automática)** *sustantivo* load and run

programa *m* **de comprobación** *sustantivo* exerciser

programa *m* **de configuración** *sustantivo* setup program

programa *m* **de contabilidad** *sustantivo* **1.** accounting package **2.** accounts package

programa *m* **de control** *sustantivo* **1.** checking program **2.** monitor program

programa *m* **de control de entrada/salida** *sustantivo* input/output control program

programa *m* **de control de red** *sustantivo* network control program

programa *m* **de control de tareas** *sustantivo* job control program

programa *m* **de control maestro** *sustantivo* master control program

programa *m* **de corrección de errores** *sustantivo* debugger ◊ **el depurador de errores no puede gestionar instrucciones compuestas** the debugger cannot handle compound statements

programa *m* **de demostración** *sustantivo* demonstration software ◊ **la compañía proporcionó un programa de demostración que permite hacerlo todo menos guardar los datos** the company gave away demonstration software that lets you do everything except save your data

programa *m* **de depuración** *sustantivo* debugger ◊ **el depurador de errores no puede gestionar instrucciones compuestas** the debugger cannot handle compound statements

programa *m* **de depuración simbólico** *sustantivo* symbolic debugger

programa *m* **de detección de fallos** *sustantivo* malfunction routine

programa *m* **de diagnóstico** *sustantivo* diagnostic program

programa *m* **de dibujo** *sustantivo* drawing program

programa *m* **de diseño** *sustantivo* paint program ◊ **hice un bosquejo de nuestro nuevo logotipo con este programa de diseño** I drew a rough of our new logo with this paint program

programa *m* **de edición de textos** *sustantivo* text editor

programa *m* **de ejecución** *sustantivo* executive program

programa *m* **de especificación** *sustantivo* program specification

programa *m* **de fusión de datos** *sustantivo* collator

programa *m* **de grupo de trabajo** *sustantivo* workgroup software

programa *m* **de herramientas** *sustantivo* toolkit

programa *m* **de instalación** *sustantivo* install program

programa *m* **de instrucciones** *sustantivo* handler

programa *m* **de localización de fallos** *sustantivo* fault location program

programa *m* **del sistema** *sustantivo* systems program

programa *m* **de mantenimiento** *sustantivo* **1.** housekeeping routine **2.** service program

programa *m* **de ordenador** *sustantivo* computer program ◊ **el usuario no puede escribir un programa informático con este sistema** the user cannot write a computer program with this system

programa *m* **de pintura** *sustantivo* paint program ◊ **hice un bosquejo de nuestro nuevo logotipo con este programa de diseño** I drew a rough of our new logo with this paint program

programa *m* **de pretratamiento** *sustantivo* preprocessor

programa *m* **depurado** *sustantivo* debugged program

programa *m* **de rastreo** *sustantivo* trace program

programa *m* **de reasignación automática** *sustantivo* self-relocating program

programa *m* **de recuperación automática** *sustantivo* automatic recovery program

programa *m* **de segunda generación** *sustantivo* child process *o* child program

programa *m* **de seguridad cortafuegos** *sustantivo* firewall

programa *m* **de servicio** *sustantivo* utility program

programa *m* **de traducción** *sustantivo* translator *o* translator program

programa *m* **de transferencia de ficheros** *sustantivo* file transfer utility

programa *m* **de transferencia de mensajes** *sustantivo* **1.** message transfer agent **2.** MTA

programa *m* **de tratamiento de textos** *sustantivo* word-processor

programa *m* **de usuario** *sustantivo* **1.** user program **2.** user's program

programa *m* **de utilidades** *sustantivo* **1.** housekeeping routine **2.** utility program

programado *adj* user-selectable

programado, -a previamente *adj* preprogrammed

programador *m* *sustantivo* **1.** computer programmer **2.** programmer ◊ **analista-programador, -a** analyst/programmer *o* programmer/analyst ◊ **el programador** *o* **la programadora está todavía trabajando en el nuevo software** the programmer is still working on the new software

programador *m* **de aplicaciones** *sustantivo* applications programmer

programador *m* **de PROM** *sustantivo* PROM blaster *o* PROM burner *o* PROM programmer

programador *m* **de ROM** *sustantivo* burner

programador *m* **de sistemas** *sustantivo* systems programmer

programa *m* **ejecutivo** *sustantivo* executive program

programa *m* **en estrella** *sustantivo* star program

programa *m* **en la memoria central** *sustantivo* core program

programa *m* **en lenguaje máquina** *sustantivo* absolute program

programa *m* **en línea** *sustantivo* in-line program

programa *m* **ensamblador** *sustantivo* 1. assembler 2. assembler program 3. language assembler

programa *m* **en serie** *sustantivo* thread

programa *m* **escrito por el usuario** *sustantivo* user's program

programa *m* **fijo** *sustantivo* hardwired program ◇ **ordenador con programa cableado** *o* **fijo** wired *o* hardwired program computer

programa *m* **fuente** *sustantivo* source program

programa *m* **gráfico** *sustantivo* graphics software

programa *m* **ilegal** *sustantivo* pirate software

programa *m* **informático** *sustantivo* computer program ◇ **el usuario no puede escribir un programa informático con este sistema** the user cannot write a computer program with this system

programa *m* **inteligente** *sustantivo* agent

programa *m* **intermedio** *sustantivo* middleware

programa *m* **interpretativo** *sustantivo* interpretative program

programa *m* **intérprete** *sustantivo* 1. interpreter 2. language interpreter

programa *m* **iterativo** *sustantivo* 1. looping program 2. loop program

programa *m* **lineal** *sustantivo* linear program

programa *m* **ludo-educativo** *sustantivo* edutainment

programa *m* **modelo** *sustantivo* blue-ribbon program

programa *m* **monitor** *sustantivo* monitor program

programa *m* **multifase** *sustantivo* multiphase program

programa *m* **multiusuario** *sustantivo* 1. multiuser program 2. network calendar program

programa *m* **no prioritario** *sustantivo* background program

programa *m* **objeto** *sustantivo* 1. object program 2. target program

programa *m* **padre** *sustantivo* parent program

programa *m* **para formato de texto** *sustantivo* text formatter ◇ **se utiliza el programa de formato de texto como programa básico de edición asistida por ordenador** people use the text formatter as a basic desk-top publishing program

programa *m* **para usos generales** *sustantivo* general purpose program

programa *m* **personalizado** *sustantivo* middleware

programa *m* **pirateado** *sustantivo* pirate software

programa *m* **por la usuaria** *sustantivo* user's program

programa *m* **preferente** *sustantivo* foreground program

programa *m* **prioritario** *sustantivo* 1. foreground program 2. high priority program

programar *verbo* 1. *vt* to blast 2. *vt* to burn in ◇ **programar los puntos de parada** to set breakpoints

programar con anterioridad *verbo* to preset ◇ **la impresora se preprogramó con nuevos parámetros de página** the printer was preset with new page parameters

programar de nuevo *verbo* to reprogram

programa *m* **reentrante** *sustantivo* re-entrant program *o* re-entrant code *o* re-entrant routine

programa *m* **repetitivo** *sustantivo* loop program

programa *m* **residente** *sustantivo* 1. internally stored program 2. terminate and stay resident program

programa *m* **residente en memoria** *sustantivo* terminate and stay resident software ■ *abrev* TSR

programa *m* **residente RAM** *sustantivo* RAM resident program

programa *m* **reubicable** *sustantivo* relocatable program ◇ **el sistema operativo puede cargar y ejecutar un programa reubicable desde cualquier área de la memoria** the operating system can load and run a relocatable program from any area of memory

programa *m* **reubicable automáticamente** *sustantivo* self-relocating program

programar un PROM *verbo* to blow

programas *mpl* *sustantivo* system software ◇ **programas** *mpl* **no incluidos en la compra de un ordenador** unbundled software

programa *m* **Schedule+** *sustantivo* Schedule+

programas *mpl* **de la red** *sustantivo* telesoftware ■ *abrev* TSW ◇ **ayer descargamos los programas de la red** the telesoftware was downloaded yesterday

programas *mpl* **en ROM** *sustantivo* romware

programas *mpl* **fijos** *sustantivo* firmware

programas *mpl* **fijos del sistema** *sustantivo* system firmware

programas *mpl* **integrados** *sustantivo* integrated software

programas *mpl* **portátiles** *sustantivo* **1.** portable programs **2.** portable software

programas *mpl* **transferibles** *sustantivo* portable software

programa *m* **subordinado** *sustantivo* background program

programa *m* **supervisor** *sustantivo* **1.** run-time system **2.** supervisor **3.** supervisor program **4.** supervisory program

programático, -a *adj* programmatic

programa *m* **TSR** *sustantivo* terminate and stay resident program

progresivo ◊ **progresivo (a un nuevo sistema)** staged change-over

prohibido *adj* unauthorised *o* unauthorized

PROM *sustantivo* **1.** programmable memory **2.** programmable read only memory ◊ **programar un PROM** burn ◊ **quemar un PROM** burn

pronosticar *verbo vt* to project

propagación *f* **de error** *sustantivo* error propagation

propaganda ◊ **propaganda** *f* **que se recibe por correo** unsolicited mail

propagar *verbo vt* to propagate

propiedad *f* **de archivo** *sustantivo* archival quality

propiedades *fpl* *sustantivo* properties

propiedades *fpl* **de energía** *sustantivo* meter – power supply

propio de la máquina *adj* machine-intimate

proporción *f* *sustantivo* ratio ◊ **la proporción de bits corruptos por mensaje transmitido está disminuyendo con la nueva teconología** the ratio of corrupt bits per transmitted message is falling with new technology

proporcionar *verbo vt* to supply ◊ **el ordenador nos lo proporcionó un distribuidor conocido** the computer was supplied by a recognized dealer ◊ **han firmado un contrato para proporcionar información en línea** they have signed a contract to supply on-line information

proporcionar una conexión *verbo* to interface

proporción *f* **entre señal y ruido** *sustantivo* signal to noise ratio ■ *abrev* S/N

propósito *m* **especial** *sustantivo* special purpose

proseguir *verbo vi* to roll forward

protección *sustantivo* **1.** interlock **2.** shield ◊ **protección** *f* **del acceso a la memoria** fetch-protect ◊ **protección** *f* **de límites de la memoria** boundary protection

'El sistema PGP (Pretty Good Privacy) fue pionero en su género, pero en la actualidad ha sido superado por otros sistemas de protección, por lo que ya no entra en competencia con ellos en el ámbito de los negocios.' [*PC Plus*]

protección *f* **contra la copia** *sustantivo* copy protection ◊ **el nuevo programa no llevará dispositivo de protección de copia** the new program will come without copy protection ◊ **un disco duro puede fallar debido a un sistema defectuoso de protección de copia** a hard disk may crash because of faulty copy protection

protección *f* **de bloques** *sustantivo* block protection

protección *f* **de celda** *sustantivo* cell protection

protección *f* **de datos** *sustantivo* data protection

protección *f* **de ficheros** *sustantivo* file security

protección *f* **del sistema** *sustantivo* system security

protección *f* **de página** *sustantivo* page protection

protección *f* **por contraseña** *sustantivo* password protection

protección *f* **por palabra de paso** *sustantivo* password protection

proteger *verbo vt* to shield ◊ **proteger un disquete contra la escritura no deseada** to write protect

proteger contra copias *verbo* to copy protect

protegido, -a *adj* secured

'En el futuro toda nuestra información privada será protegida por cifrado, sin importar cómo es generada, guardada o transmitida.' [*Ciberp@ís*]

protocolo *sustantivo* protocol ◊ **protocolo** *m* **común de gestión de la información** common management information protocol ◊ **protocolo** *m* **de acceso a la configuración de aplicaciones** ACAP; application configuration access protocol ◊ **protocolo** *m* **de acceso a mensajes de Internet** Internet message access protocol ◊ **protocolo** *m* **de comunicación carácter por carácter** byte-orientated protocol ◊ **protocolo** *m* **de comunicación de red Microcom (MNP)** Microcom Networking Protocol ◊ **protocolo** *m* **de comunicaciones de UNIX a UNIX** UUCP ◊ **protocolo** *m* **de control de enlaces** LCP ◊ **protocolo** *m* **de datagrama de usuario, -a** UDP; user datagram protocol ◊ **protocolo** *m* **de gestión de ficheros Apple** (*marca comercial*) Apple filing protocol ◊ **protocolo** *m* **de intercambio de información en la red** (*marca comercial*) Internetwork Packet Exchange; IPX ◊ **protocolo** *m* **de intercambio de información entre CPU y periférico** CPU handshaking ◊ **protocolo** *m* **de internet de control de mensajes** ICMP; Internet control message protocol ◊ **protocolo** *m* **de internet de línea secuencial** serial line Internet protocol ◊ **protocolo** *m* **de línea serie comprimido** CSLIP ◊ **protocolo** *m* **de pago electrónico seguro** secure encryption payment protocol; SEPP ◊ **protocolo** *m* **de pasarela fronteriza** BGP ◊ **protocolo** *m* **(de comunicaciones) de red** network protocol ◊ **protocolo** *m* **de red (para transmisión de da-**

protocolo

146

tos) fibre over Ethernet ◊ **protocolo** *m* **de red de rank Xerox XNS** ◊ **protocolo** *m* **de redes de Microcom** MNP ◊ **protocolo** *m* **de red no orientado a la conexión** connectionless network protocol ◊ **protocolo** *m* **de resolución de direcciones** address resolution protocol; ARP ◊ **protocolo** *m* **de transferencia para los grupos de noticias de red** NNTP ◊ **protocolo** *m* **de transmisión sincrónica de datos** SDLC; synchronous data link control ◊ **protocolo** *m* **de validación de transferencia de datos** handshake ◊ **protocolo GENDER>m de información común de gestión** CMIP ◊ **protocolo** *m* **ligero de acceso a directorios** lightweight directory access protocol ◊ **protocolo** *m* **seguro de transferencia de hipertexto** secure hypertext transfer protocol ◊ **protocolo** *m* **simple de gestión de red** simple network management protocol ◊ **protocolo** *m* **simple de transferencia de correo (electrónico)** simple mail transfer protocol; SMTP ◊ **protocolo** *m* **XMODEM** (*transmisión de ficheros*) XMODEM ◊ **protocolo** *m* **XMODEM CRC con dispositivo de control de errores** XMODEM CRC

'Durante las primeras etapas del comercio electrónico a través de los protocolos EDI, comerciantes y empresas no sintieron la necesidad de proteger las redes y las comunicaciones, porque éstas se desarrollaban sobre redes privadas no accesibles a personas ajenas a las transacciones.' [*PC Plus*]

protocolo *m* **AFP** *sustantivo* AFP ■ **1.** (*marca comercial*) Apple filing protocol **2.** AppleTalk Filing Protocol

protocolo *m* **APPC** *sustantivo* advanced program to program communications

protocolo *m* **ARP** *sustantivo* **1.** address resolution protocol **2.** ARP

protocolo *m* **CMIP** *sustantivo* **1.** CMIP **2.** common management information protocol

protocolo *m* **de acceso** *sustantivo* **1.** access log **2.** server access log

protocolo *m* **de aplicación inalámbrica** *sustantivo* **1.** WAP **2.** Wireless Application Protocol

protocolo *m* **de arranque-asignación** *sustantivo* **1.** BOOTP **2.** bootstrap protocol

protocolo *m* **de comunicación** *sustantivo* **1.** CPU handshaking **2.** full handshaking

protocolo *m* **de comunicaciones** *sustantivo* **1.** communications protocol **2.** TCP ◊ **el protocolo de comunicaciones para la mayoría de servicios en línea es una palabra de ocho bits, sin bit de parada y paridad par** the communications protocol for most dial-up online services is eight-bit words, no stop bit and even parity

protocolo *m* **de control de enlaces** *sustantivo* link control procedure

protocolo *m* **de control de línea** *sustantivo* line control

protocolo *m* **de Emisión** *abrev* RTP

protocolo *m* **de encaminamiento** *plural noun* (*de un mensaje*) routing overheads

protocolo *m* **de envío** *plural noun* (*de un mensaje*) routing overheads ◊ **el índice de transferencia de información es mucho menor cuando se tienen en cuenta los protocolos de envío** the information transfer rate is very much less once all routing overheads have been accommodated

protocolo *m* **de gestión de ficheros AppleTalk** *sustantivo* AFP ■ AppleTalk Filing Protocol

protocolo *m* **de información de encaminamiento** *abrev* RIP ■ *sustantivo* routing information protocol

protocolo *m* **de intercambio de información** *sustantivo* handshake *o* handshaking

protocolo *m* **de internet** *sustantivo* **1.** Internet protocol **2.** IP

protocolo *m* **de parada y espera** *sustantivo* stop and wait protocol

protocolo *m* **de puerta interior** *sustantivo* **1.** IGP **2.** interior gateway protocol

protocolo *m* **de red no orientado a la conexión** *abrev* CLNP

protocolo *m* **de transferencia de ficheros** *sustantivo* **1.** file transfer protocol **2.** FTP

protocolo *m* **de transmisión CSMA-CD** *sustantivo* **1.** carrier sense multiple access-collision detection **2.** CSMA-CD

protocolo *m* **de trazado** *sustantivo* audit trail

protocolo *m* **entre redes** *sustantivo* **1.** Internet protocol **2.** IP

protocolo *m* **estándar de servidor a sistema intermedio** *sustantivo* end system to intermediate system

protocolo *m* **FTP** *sustantivo* file transfer protocol

protocolo *m* **IP** *sustantivo* **1.** Internet protocol **2.** IP

protocolo *m* **LAP-M** *sustantivo* LAP-M

protocolo *m* **MNP 2–4** *sustantivo* MNP 2–4

protocolo *m* **MNP 10** *sustantivo* MNP 10

protocolo *m* **punto a punto** *sustantivo* **1.** point to point protocol **2.** PPP

protocolos *mpl* **de distancia vectorial** *plural noun* distance vector protocols

protocolo *m* **SDLC** *sustantivo* **1.** SDLC **2.** synchronous data link control

protocolo SET *plural noun* SET

protocolo *m* **simple de gestión de red** *abrev* SNMP

protocolo *m* **SMTP** *sustantivo* **1.** simple mail transfer protocol **2.** SMTP

protocolo *m* **SNMP** *sustantivo* simple network management protocol ■ *abrev* SNMP

protocolo *m* **SSL** *sustantivo* **1.** secure sockets layer **2.** SSL

protocolo *m* **XMODEM 1K** *sustantivo* XMODEM 1K

protocolo *m* **XNS** Xerox Network System

prototipo *m* *sustantivo* prototype

proveedor, -a *sustantivo* **1.** provider **2.** supplier ◇ **nuestros proveedores japoneses han establecido un almacén en Inglaterra** our Japanese suppliers have set up a warehouse in England ◇ **proveedor** *m* **de servicios de internet** Internet service provider ◇ **un proveedor de componentes informáticos** a supplier of computer parts ◇ **un proveedor de unidades lectoras de disquetes** *o* **discos** a supplier of disk drives *o* a disk drive supplier

'Con o sin censura, la revolución Internet también está en marcha. Reporteros sin Fronteras cifra en 200 el número de proveedores de acceso a la red.' [*Ciberp@ís*]

proveedor *m* **de acceso a Internet** *sustantivo* **1.** access provider **2.** ISP

proveedor *m* **de aplicaciones** *sustantivo* application service provider ■ *abrev* ASP

proveedor *m* **de contenido** *sustantivo* content provider

proveedor *m* **del servicio** *sustantivo* service provider

proveer *verbo vt* to supply

provenir (de) *verbo vi* to derive

'proxy' *sustantivo* **1.** proxy agent **2.** proxy server

proyección *f sustantivo* projection

proyección *f* **de fondo** *sustantivo* back projection

proyección *f* **por transparencia** *sustantivo* back projection

proyectar *verbo* **1.** *vt* to cast **2.** *vt* to plan **3.** *vt* to project

proyecto *sustantivo* **1.** plan **2.** project ◇ **su último proyecto consiste en informatizar el departamento de ventas** his latest project is computerizing the sales team ◇ **todo el proyecto se diseñó por ordenador** the design project was entirely worked out on computer ◇ **un programa de diseño CAD resulta esencial para la realización de proyectos con mayor precisión** CAD is essential for accurate project design

'Un caso pionero de ciudad digital fue el proyecto Infoville. En 1997 crearon una comunidad virtual en Villena (Alicante) después ampliada a otros municipios de la comunidad valenciana.' [*Ciberp@ís*]

proyector *m* **de datos** *sustantivo* data projector

prueba *sustantivo* **1.** print **2.** test ◇ **la prueba de funcionamiento pronto descubrirá posibles errores** a test run will soon show up any errors ◇ **prueba** *f* **de bucle de retorno** loopback test ◇ **prueba** *f* **de evaluación del funcionamiento Dhrystone** Dhrystone benchmark

prueba *f* **alfa** *sustantivo* **1.** alpha **2.** alpha test

prueba *f* **asistida por ordenador** *sustantivo* **1.** CAT **2.** computer-aided testing

prueba *f* **beta** *sustantivo* beta test ◇ **la aplicación ha superado las pruebas alfa y acaba de entrar en la fase de pruebas beta** the application has passed the alpha tests and is just entering the beta test phase

prueba *f* **cíclica de redundancia** *sustantivo* cyclic redundancy check

prueba *f* **de aceptación** *sustantivo* acceptance test

prueba *f* **de diagnóstico** *sustantivo* diagnostic test

prueba *f* **de funcionamiento** *sustantivo* test run ◇ **la prueba de funcionamiento pronto descubrirá posibles errores** a test run will soon show up any errors

prueba *f* **de parámetros** *sustantivo* parameter testing

prueba *f* **de polaridad** *sustantivo* polarity test

prueba *f* **de Turing** *sustantivo* Turing test

prueba *f* **de una operación** *sustantivo* operation trial

prueba *f* **de un programa** *sustantivo* program testing

prueba *f* **de verificación** *sustantivo* validity check

prueba *f* **en anillo cerrado** *sustantivo* loopback

prueba *f* **interna total de lectura/escritura** *sustantivo* leap-frog test

prueba *f* **modelo N** *sustantivo* modulo-N check

prueba *f* **no destructiva** *sustantivo* non destructive test

prueba *f* **piloto** *adj* pilot

prueba *f* **positiva** *adj* positive

prueba *f* **restringida** *sustantivo* crippled leapfrog test

prueba *f* **retrospectiva en paralelo** *sustantivo* retrospective parallel running

pruebas *fpl* **de control de enlaces** *plural noun* link trials

pruebas *fpl* **de saturación** *sustantivo* saturation testing

prueba *f* **selectiva limitada** *sustantivo* crippled leapfrog test

pseudo- *prefijo* pseudo-

pseudo-aleatorio *sustantivo* pseudo-random

pseudocódigo *m sustantivo* **1.** P-code **2.** pseudo-code

pseudodigital *adj* pseudo-digital

pseudoinstrucción *f sustantivo* P-code

pseudo-instrucción *f sustantivo* pseudo-instruction

pseudónimo *m sustantivo* alias name

pseudooperación *sustantivo* pseudo-operation

publicación *f* **asistida por ordenador** *sustantivo* **1.** desktop publishing **2.** electronic publishing

publicación *f* **electrónica** *sustantivo* electronic publishing

publicación *f* **multimedia electrónica** *sustantivo* **1.** ebook **2.** electronic book

publicar *verbo vt* to publish ◇ **el instituto ha publicado una lista de cifras de ventas para**

una serie de ordenadores personales the institute has published a list of sales figures for different home computers ◊ **la empresa está especializada en la publicación de libros de referencia** the company specializes in publishing reference books

puente *m sustantivo* bridge

puente *m* **conector (temporal)** *sustantivo* jumper

puente *m* **de ruta** *sustantivo* brouter ◊ **el puente de direccionamiento proporciona una ruta dinámica y puede unir dos redes locales** the brouter provides dynamic routing and can bridge two local area networks

puente *m* **de transición** *sustantivo* bridge

puente *m* **local** *sustantivo* local bridge ◊ **utilizamos un puente local para conectar dos redes locales en la oficina** we use a local bridge to link the two LANs in the office

puerta *f sustantivo* **1.** gate **2.** gateway ◊ **utilizamos una puerta para conectar la red de área local con la red de área extendida** we use a gateway to link the LAN to WAN

puerta *f sustantivo* nonequivalence gate

puerta *f* **(de comunicación)** *sustantivo* gateway

puerta *f* **activa** *sustantivo* active gateway

puerta *f* **analógica** *sustantivo* analog gate

puerta *f* **de coincidencia** *sustantivo* **1.** AND gate **2.** coincidence gate *o* coincidence circuit *o* coincidence element

puerta *f* **de equivalencia** *sustantivo* equivalence gate

puerta *f* **de fax** *sustantivo* fax gateway ◊ **para enviar mensajes por fax en vez de por red, hay que instalar una puerta de fax** to send messages by fax instead of across the network, you'll need to install a fax gateway

puerta *f* **de identidad** *sustantivo* identity gate *o* identity element

puerta *f* **electrónica** *sustantivo* gate circuit

puerta *f* **EXOR** *sustantivo* EXOR gate

puerta *f* **lógica** *sustantivo* logic gate

puerta *f* **NAND** *sustantivo* NAND gate

puerta *f* **NI** *sustantivo* NOR gate

puerta *f* **NI exclusivo** *sustantivo* EXNOR gate

puerta *f* **NOR** *sustantivo* NOR gate

puerta *f* **NOR exclusivo** *sustantivo* EXNOR gate

puerta *f* **NOT** *sustantivo* **1.** negation gate **2.** NOT gate

puerta *f* **NOY** *sustantivo* NAND gate

puerta *f* **O** *sustantivo* OR gate

puerta *f* **O exclusivo** *sustantivo* **1.** except gate **2.** EXOR gate **3.** NEQ gate

puerta *f* **OR** *sustantivo* OR gate

puerta *f* **para el 'joystick'** *sustantivo* joystick port ◊ **el ordenador familiar está provisto de un mando para juegos** a joystick port is provided with the home computer

puerta *f* **para mando de juego** *sustantivo* joystick port

puerta-trampa *f sustantivo* trapdoor

puerta *f* **Y** *sustantivo* AND gate

puerto *sustantivo* port ◊ **puerto** *m* **de comunicaciones** COM port ◊ **puerto** *m* **paralelo LPT1 en un PC** LPT1

'La tecnología puerto a puerto (P2P de 'peer to peer') ... otorga a cada ordenador capacidades y responsabilidades equivalentes.' [*Ciberp@ís*]

puerto *m* **asíncrono** *sustantivo* asynchronous port

puerto *m* **asíncrono de acceso** *sustantivo* asynchronous port

puerto *m* **Centronics** *sustantivo* Centronics port

puerto *m* **compartido** *sustantivo* port sharing

puerto *m* **de comunicación ampliada** *sustantivo* **1.** ECP **2.** enhanced communication port

puerto *m* **de comunicaciones** *sustantivo* communications port

puerto *m* **de datos** *sustantivo* dataport

puerto *m* **de entrada** *sustantivo* input port

puerto *m* **de entrada/salida** *sustantivo* **1.** input/output port **2.** I/O port ◊ **el mando de juego puede conectarse al puerto de entrada** *or* **salida** the joystick can be connected to the input/output port

puerto *m* **de (la) impresora** *sustantivo* printer port

puerto *m* **de juego** *sustantivo* game port

puerto *m* **de periférico(s)** *sustantivo* user port

puerto *m* **de salida** *sustantivo* output port ◊ **conecte la impresora al puerto de salida de la impresora** connect the printer to the printer output port

puerto *m* **en paralelo** *sustantivo* parallel port

puerto *m* **en serie** *sustantivo* serial port

puerto *m* **para el 'joystick'** *sustantivo* joystick port

puerto *m* **paralelo ampliado** *sustantivo* **1.** enhanced parallel port **2.** EPP

puerto *m* **rápido de gráficos** *sustantivo* **1.** accelerated graphics port **2.** AGP

puesta ◊ **comunicado de prensa** press release ◊ **el nuevo software es la versión 5** the latest software is release 5 ◊ **puesta** *f* **en venta de un producto** release

puesta *f* **al día** *sustantivo* **1.** update **2.** upkeep ◊ **agentes de actualización** update agents

puesta *f* **a punto** *sustantivo* file maintenance

puesta *f* **de instrucción** *sustantivo* instruction storage

puesta *f* **en clave de datos** *sustantivo* **1.** data encryption **2.** encryption ◊ **estándar de puesta en clave de datos** data encryption standard (DES)

puesta *f* **en funcionamiento automática** *sustantivo* auto start

puesta *f* **en marcha** *sustantivo* **1.** cold start **2.** restart

puesta *f* **en marcha en frío** *sustantivo* cold boot

puesto *m* *sustantivo* **1.** console **2.** operating console **3.** station ◇ **puesto** *m* **de trabajo de un operador** operator's console

puesto *m* **de trabajo** *sustantivo* **1.** terminal **2.** workstation ◇ **el controlador de red tiene 16 interfaces para terminales** the network controller has 16 terminal interfaces ◇ **el gestor del sistema utiliza el terminal principal para reiniciar el sistema** the system manager uses the master terminal to restart the system ◇ **fanático, -a** *o* **adicto, -a de la informática** terminal junky (TJ) ◇ **mi hijo se ha vuelto un verdadero fanático de la informática** my son has turned into a real terminal junky ◇ **servidor de terminal** terminal server ◇ **todos los mensajes van a todos los terminales ya que ninguno es de direccionamiento protegido** all the messages go to all the terminals since none are addressable terminals

pulsación *f* *sustantivo* **1.** keystroke **2.** stroke ◇ **pulsación** *f* **del teclado controlada por ordenador** processor controlled keying

pulsación *f* **simultánea de dos teclas** *sustantivo* chord keying

pulsar *verbo* **1.** *vt* to click **2.** *vt* to hit ◇ **pulsar dos veces (el ratón)** to double-click ◇ **sitúe el puntero sobre el icono y pulse dos veces el ratón para iniciar el programa** move the pointer to the icon then start the program with a double-click

pulso *m* *sustantivo* pulse ◇ **generador de impulsos** pulse generator ◇ **modulación de amplitud de impulsos** *o* **de impulsos en amplitud** pulse amplitude modulation (PAM) ◇ **modulación de duración de impulsos** pulse width modulation (PWM) ◇ **modulación de impulsos** pulse modulation ◇ **modulación por** *o* **de duración de impulsos** pulse duration modulation (PDM) ◇ **modulación por posición de impulsos** *o* **por impulsos de posición variable** pulse position modulation (PPM)

punta *f* **de tensión** *sustantivo* **1.** spike **2.** voltage transient

punta *f* **máxima** *sustantivo* peak

puntero *m* *sustantivo* **1.** arrow pointer **2.** back pointer **3.** pointer ◇ **el uso del puntero y del ratón facilita la edición electrónica de textos (en un PC)** desktop publishing on a PC is greatly helped by the use of a pointer and mouse ◇ **puntero** *m* **(de posición) de datos** data pointer ◇ **puntero** *m* **en forma de cruz** crosshair

puntero *m* **controlado por el ratón** *sustantivo* mouse pointer

puntero *m* **de datos** *sustantivo* data pointer

puntero *m* **de instrucción** *sustantivo* instruction pointer

puntero *m* **del DOS** *sustantivo* DOS prompt

puntero *m* **del ratón** *sustantivo* mouse pointer

puntero *m* **de pila** *abrev* SP ■ *sustantivo* stack pointer

punto *sustantivo* **1.** available point **2.** period ◇ **punto** *m* **(de acceso** *or* **de entrada** *or* **salida)** port ◇ **punto** *m* **de control** (*en un programa de rastreo*) trace trap ◇ **punto** *m* **de entrada en un sistema** backdoor; trapdoor ◇ **punto** *m* **de inserción (de código)** hook ◇ **punto** *m* **de parada** (*de un programa de rastreo*) trace trap ◇ **todos los puntos direccionables** APA

punto *m* **a punto** *sustantivo* point to point

punto *m* **condicional de interrupción** *sustantivo* conditional breakpoint

punto *m* **de acceso** *sustantivo* access point

punto *m* **de arranque** *sustantivo* starting point

punto *m* **de bifurcación** *sustantivo* branch-point

punto *m* **de conexión** *sustantivo* terminal ◇ **bloque de conexiones** *o* **de empalmes** terminal block

punto *m* **de conexión/de presencia** *sustantivo* **1.** point of presence **2.** POP

punto *m* **de control** *sustantivo* **1.** access point **2.** check point

punto *m* **de empalme** *sustantivo* terminal ◇ **bloque de conexiones** *o* **de empalmes** terminal block

punto *m* **de enganche** *sustantivo* hook

punto *m* **de entrada** *sustantivo* **1.** access point **2.** entry point

punto *m* **de inicio del registro** *sustantivo* **1.** load point **2.** (*de una cinta magnética*) tape load-point

punto *m* **de inserción** *sustantivo* insertion point

punto *m* **de interrupción** *sustantivo* **1.** breakpoint **2.** regional breakpoint

punto *m* **de reanudación** *sustantivo* **1.** check point **2.** re-entry point **3.** rerun point

punto *m* **de reentrada** *sustantivo* re-entry point

punto *m* **de re-entrada** *sustantivo* re-entry point

punto *m* **de referencia** *sustantivo* benchmark

punto *m* **de ruptura** *sustantivo* **1.** breakpoint **2.** regional breakpoint

punto *m* **de salida** *sustantivo* **1.** exit point **2.** starting point

punto *m* **de tensión** *sustantivo* voltage transient

punto *m* **de transición** *sustantivo* transition point

punto *m* **de vaciado** *sustantivo* dump point

punto *m* **de venta** *sustantivo* **1.** outlet **2.** point-of-sale ■ *abrev* POS

punto *m* **de venta electrónico** *sustantivo* **1.** electronic point-of-sale **2.** EPOS

punto *m* **direccionable** *sustantivo* addressable point

punto *m* **grueso** *sustantivo* bullet

punto *m* **indicador de color** *sustantivo* bullet

punto *m* **máximo** *sustantivo* peak

punto *m* **muerto** *sustantivo* deadlock *o* deadly embrace

punto *m* **porcentual** *sustantivo* percentage point

puntos *mpl* **de fósforo** *plural noun* phosphor dots

puntos *mpl* **por pulgada** *plural noun* dots per inch

punto *m* **y coma** *sustantivo* semicolon

punzón *m* **(de perforación) de cintas** *sustantivo* tape punch

punzón *m* **de perforación** *sustantivo* perforator

purgar *verbo vt* to purge

Q

quantum *m sustantivo* quantum

quedarse bloqueado *verbo* to crash ◇ **la cabeza del disco se ha estropeado y puede que los datos se hayan perdido** the disk head has crashed and the data may have been lost

quemado *m* **de pantalla** *sustantivo* screen burn

quemadura *f* **láser** *sustantivo* ablation

quemar *verbo* **1.** *vt* to burn **2.** *vt* to burn in

quemar un PROM *verbo* to blow

que puede ser modificado *adj* user-selectable

que puede ser redefinido *adj* redefinable

que puede ser seleccionado *adj* jumper-selectable

querer decir *verbo* to signify

que se puede gestionar *adj* manageable

que se puede leer *adj* readable

QuickDraw™ QuickDraw

QuickTime™ QuickTime

quinteto *m sustantivo* quintet

quiosco *sustantivo* kiosk ◇ **modo de quiosco** kiosk mode

'Los quioscos interactivos son casetas de información informáticas, situadas en lugares públicos como museos y exposiciones, para obtener información fácilmente mediante una pantalla táctil para el usuario.' [*Computer Hoy*]

R

radiofrecuencia *f sustantivo* RF *o* R/F

ráfaga *f sustantivo* burst ◇ **ráfaga de sincronización cromática** *o* **de señales de color** colour burst

ráfaga *f* **de errores** *sustantivo* error burst

ráfaga *f* **de identificación** *sustantivo* identity burst

raíz *f sustantivo* **1.** radix **2.** root ◇ **la raíz cuadrada de la media de los cuadrados de la señal sinusoidal perfecta equivale a 0,7071 de su amplitud** the root mean square of the pure sinusoidal signal is 0.7071 of its amplitude ◇ **raíz cuadrada de la media de los cuadrados** root mean square (RMS)

raíz *f* **cuadrada** *sustantivo* square root ◇ **la raíz cuadrada de 25 es 5** the square root of 25 is 5

RAM *f sustantivo* RAM

rama *f sustantivo* leg

RAM *f* **auto-actualizada** *sustantivo* self-refreshing RAM

RAM *f* **auto-renovadora** *sustantivo* self-refreshing RAM

RAM *f* **de página rápida** *sustantivo* fast page RAM

RAM *f* **de vídeo** *sustantivo* **1.** video memory **2.** video RAM **3.** video random access memory *o* video RAM

RAM *f* **dinámica** *abrev* DRAM ■ *sustantivo* **1.** dynamic RAM **2.** dynamic random access memory

RAM *f* **estática** *sustantivo* **1.** SRAM **2.** static RAM

ramificación *f* **de recursos** *sustantivo* resource fork

RAM *f* **incompleta** *sustantivo* partial RAM

RAM *f* **parcial** *sustantivo* partial RAM

RAM *f* **sombra** *sustantivo* shadow RAM

rango *m* **de valores** *sustantivo* number range

ranura *f sustantivo* expansion slot ◇ **ranura** *f* **(para una tarjeta) PCMCIA** PCMCIA slot

ranura *f* **de expansión** *sustantivo* expansion slot

ranura *f* **láser** *sustantivo* ablation

ranura *f* **para un mensaje** *sustantivo* message slot

ranura *f* **vacía** *sustantivo* empty slot

rastreador *m sustantivo* crawler

rastreo *sustantivo* **1.** trace **2.** tracing ◇ **rastreo** *m* **automático del rendimiento de una señal** auto-baud scanning

rastreo *m* **automático** *sustantivo* auto trace

rastreo *m* **por rayos** *sustantivo* ray tracing ◇ **se tardarán bastantes horas para generar esta imagen con rastreo por rayos en este potente PC** to generate this picture with ray tracing will take several hours on this powerful PC

rastro *m sustantivo* trace

rastro *m* **de clics** *sustantivo* clickstream

ratio *sustantivo* ratio

'El ratio de compresión es el porcentaje de disminución de tamaño después de comprimir un archivo. Por ejemplo, un ratio de compresión 10:1 indica que el archivo ha disminuido 10 veces de tamaño.' [*Computer hoy*]

ratón *sustantivo* mouse ◇ **(programa) controlado** *o* **dirigido por un ratón** mouse-driven (software) ◇ **velocidad del ratón** mouse accelaration

'El ratón es uno de los regalos más clásicos porque no plantea especiales problemas de elección para el que lo compra ni de instalación para el que lo recibe.' [*Ciberp@ís*]

ratón *m* **conectado al puerto de serie** *sustantivo* serial mouse

ratón *m* **en serie** *sustantivo* serial mouse

ratón *m* **mecánico** *sustantivo* mechanical mouse

ratón *m* **óptico** *sustantivo* optical mouse

ratón *m* **optomecánico** *sustantivo* optomechanical mouse

ratón *m* **zurdo** *sustantivo* left-handed mouse

raya *f sustantivo* scratch ◇ **esta raya impide la lectura del disco** this scratch makes the disk unreadable

rayo *m sustantivo* beam ◇ **desdoblamiento de un rayo** beam diversity ◇ **el láser emite un fino rayo de luz** the laser produces a thin beam of light ◇ **en esta impresora se emplea un rayo de luz láser para producir gráficos de alta resolución** a beam of laser light is used in this printer to produce high-resolution graphics ◇ **se utiliza un campo magnético para la desviación de un haz en un tubo de rayos catódicos (CRT)** a magnetic field is used for beam deflection in a CRT

razón *f* **1 a 0** *sustantivo* one to zero ratio

RDSI de banda ancha *abrev* B-ISDN

reabastecer *verbo vt* to replenish

reaccionar *verbo vi* to react ◇ **entrar en reacción con otra sustancia** to react with something ◇ **reaccionar a algo** *o* **alguna cosa** to react to something

reagrupamiento *m sustantivo* ganged switch ◇ **un reagrupamiento de conmutadores se emplea para seleccionar el bus de datos al que responde una impresora** a ganged switch is used to select which data bus a printer will respond to

reagrupar *verbo vt* to batch

real (*marca comercial*) Real ■ *adj* true ◇ **en un sistema de tiempo real, al mover el mando de juegos hacia la izquierda, la imagen de la pantalla se mueve hacia la izquierda. En cambio, no es un verdadero sistema en tiempo real si hay una pausa para su proceso** in a real-time system, as you move the joystick left, the image on the screen moves left. If there is a pause for processing it is not a true real-time system ◇ **programa visto en tiempo real** *o* **emisión en directo** program shown in real time ◇ **protocolo de transferencia (de datos) en tiempo real** real time transport protocol (RTP) ◇ **un sistema de navegación debe poder procesar la posición de un barco en tiempo real para tomar las decisiones adecuadas antes de dar contra una roca** a navigation system needs to be able to process the position of a ship in real time and take suitable action before she hits a rock

RealAudio™ (de transmisión de sonido por internet) (*marca comercial*) RealAudio

realce *m sustantivo* emphasis

realidad *f* **virtual** *sustantivo* 1. virtual reality 2. VR ◇ **este nuevo programa de realidad virtual puede crear una habitación tridimensional por la que uno se puede desplazar** this new virtual reality software can create a three-dimensional room that you can navigate around

realizador *m sustantivo* producer

realzar *verbo vt* to highlight

reanudación *sustantivo* re-entry ◇ **reanudación** *f* **después de una instrucción de parada** warm start ◇ **reanudación** *f* **después de una interrupción de la alimentación** cold start ◇ **reanudación** *f* **de un programa después de un fallo** roll back ◇ **reanudación** *f* **en el punto de parada** warm start

reanudar *verbo* 1. *vt* to rerun 2. *vt* to resume 3. *vt* to rollback

reasignación *f sustantivo* relocation

reasignación *f* **estática** *sustantivo* static relocation

rebobinar *verbo vt* to rewind ◇ **la cinta se rebobina automáticamente en el carrete** the tape rewinds onto the spool automatically

rebote ◇ **rebote** *m* **(de un correo electrónico)** bounce ◇ **rebote** *m* **de una tecla del teclado** bounce; keyboard contact bounce

rebusca *f* **de datos fraudulenta** *sustantivo* scavenging

recalcar *verbo vt* to underline

recalentarse *verbo vr* to overheat

recargar *verbo* 1. *vt* to reload 2. *vt* to replenish ◇ **después del fallo, recargamos el programa** we reloaded the program after the crash

receptor *m sustantivo* receiver ■ *abrev* RX ◇ **el receptor de radio captó muy claramente su señal** the radio receiver picked up your signal very strongly ◇ **receptor de radio** radio receiver

receptor *m* **de datos** *sustantivo* data sink

receptor/emisor *m sustantivo* answer/originate *o* answer/originate device

recibir *verbo vt* to receive ■ *abrev vt* RX ◇ **el ordenador recibió datos a través de la línea telefónica** the computer received data via the telephone line

reciente *adj* new

recobrar *verbo vt* to recover

recodificar *verbo vt* to recode

recoger *verbo* 1. *vt* to capture 2. *vt* to collect 3. *vt* to fetch ◇ **el programa permite modificar las imágenes recogidas** the software allows captured images to be edited ◇ **este escáner recoge imágenes con una resolución de 300 puntos por pulgada** this scanner captures images at a resolution of 300 dots per inch (dpi)

recogida *f sustantivo* capture ◇ **la recogida de datos se inicia cuando se recibe una señal de interrupción** data capture starts when an interrupt is received

recogida *f* **(de datos)** *sustantivo* entering

recogida *f* **automática de datos** *sustantivo* automatic data capture

recogida *f* **de datos** *sustantivo* 1. data capture 2. data collection 3. logging ◇ **la recogida de datos se inicia cuando se recibe una señal de interrupción** data capture starts when an interrupt is received ◇ **registro de llamadas** call logging

recompilar *verbo vt* to recompile

reconfiguración *f sustantivo* reconfiguration

reconfigurar *verbo vt* to reconfigure ◇ **este programa nos permite reconfigurar el sistema según nuestras necesidades** this program allows us to reconfigure the system to our own requirements ◇ **reconfigurar los píxeles de una imagen** to resample ◇ **reconfiguré la estructura de campos en el fichero** I reconfigured the field structure in the file

reconocer *verbo vt* to recognise *o* to recognize ◇ **el escáner reconoce la mayor parte de los caracteres** the scanner will recognize most character fonts

reconocible *adj* recognisable *o* recognizable

reconocimiento *m sustantivo* recognition

reconocimiento *sustantivo* sense ◇ **el nuevo programa PDA tiene un excelente sistema de reconocimiento caligráfico** the new PDA has excellent handwriting recognition ◇ **reconocimiento** *m* **automático del rendimiento de una señal** auto-baud scanning ◇ **reconocimiento** *m* **(óptico) de caracteres** character recognition ◇ **reconocimiento** *m* **de caracteres de tin-**

ta magnética magnetic ink character recognition; MICR ◇ **reconocimiento** *m* **de escritura (a mano)** handwriting recognition

'El reconocimiento de voz (lenguaje-texto), la conversión texto-voz (generación automática del lenguaje), la identificación del locutor y la codificación de los sonidos humanos precisan de la resolución de algoritmos complejos a gran velocidad, para gozar de las características de tiempo real y respuesta inmediata.' [*La Red*]

reconocimiento *m* **caligráfico** *sustantivo* handwriting recognition ◇ **el nuevo programa PDA tiene un excelente sistema de reconocimiento caligráfico** the new PDA has excellent handwriting recognition

reconocimiento *m* **de la voz** *sustantivo* voice recognition

reconocimiento *m* **del habla** *sustantivo* **1.** speech recognition **2.** voice recognition

reconocimiento *m* **del modelo** *sustantivo* pattern recognition

reconocimiento *m* **de signos** *sustantivo* **1.** OMR **2.** optical mark recognition

reconocimiento *m* **de símbolos** *sustantivo* **1.** OMR **2.** optical mark recognition

reconocimiento *m* **de voz** *sustantivo* speech recognition

reconocimiento *m* **óptico de caracteres** *sustantivo* **1.** OCR **2.** optical character recognition

reconocimiento *m* **óptico de marcas** *sustantivo* **1.** OMR **2.** optical mark recognition

reconocimiento *m* **vocal** *sustantivo* voice recognition

reconstituir *verbo vt* to reconstitute

recopilación *f* **de datos** *sustantivo* data collection

recopilación *f* **de información** *sustantivo* data collection

recorrido *m sustantivo* route

recortar *verbo vt* to crop ◇ **recortar (el reborde de una imagen)** to crop

recuadro *m sustantivo* border

recuadro *m* **delimitador** *sustantivo* bounding box

recuadro *m* **de selección** *sustantivo* marquee

recubrimiento *m sustantivo* **1.** overlap **2.** overlay

recubrir de mosaico *verbo* to tessellate

recuperación *sustantivo* **1.** recall **2.** recovery **3.** retrieval ◇ **recuperación** *f* **del proceso después de la corrección de un fallo** fall back recovery

recuperación *f* **de bloques** *sustantivo* block retrieval

recuperación *f* **de datos** *sustantivo* data retrieval

recuperación *f* **de errores** *sustantivo* error recovery

recuperación *f* **de información en línea** *sustantivo* online information retrieval

recuperación *f* **de la información** *sustantivo* information retrieval ■ *abrev* IR

recuperación *f* **después de un fallo** *sustantivo* failure recovery

recuperación *f* **de texto** *sustantivo* text retrieval

recuperación *f* **de un documento** *sustantivo* document recovery

recuperación *f* **errónea** *sustantivo* **1.** false drop **2.** false retrieval

recuperación *f* **falsa** *sustantivo* **1.** false drop **2.** false retrieval

recuperación *f* **hacia atrás** *sustantivo* (*de un procedimiento fichero*) backward recovery

recuperación *f* **tras un fallo** *sustantivo* failure recovery

recuperar *verbo* **1.** *vt* to call up **2.** *vt* to recall **3.** *vt* to recover **4.** *vt* to restore **5.** *vt* to retrieve **6.** *vt* (*un fichero o un texto suprimido*) to undelete ◇ **afortunadamente pudimos recuperar los ficheros borrados** thankfully we could undelete the files ◇ **después de recibir una entrada, se recupera la primera función** after an input is received, the first function is called up ◇ **es posible recuperar los datos, pero se tarda mucho tiempo** it is possible to recover the data but it can take a long time ◇ **esta instrucción recupera todos los nombres que empiezan por S** this command will retrieve all names beginning with S ◇ **éstos son los registros recuperados en esa búsqueda** these are the records retrieved in that search ◇ **no se preocupe, esta función nos permitirá recuperar las partes que ha eliminado de la carta** don't worry, this function will undelete your cuts to the letter ◇ **recuperar en pantalla el fichero anterior** call up the previous file

recurrir a fuentes externas *verbo* to outsource

recursión *f sustantivo* recursion

recurso *f sustantivo* resource

recurso *m* **crítico** *sustantivo* critical resource

recurso *m* **de emergencia** *sustantivo* fall back

recursos *mpl* **compartidos** *sustantivo* resource sharing

red *sustantivo* network ◇ **arquitecto, -a de la red** network architect ◇ **gestor de red** network manager ◇ **norma de interfaz gestora de red** *o* **norma NDIS** network driver interface specification (NDIS) ◇ **protocolo de transferencia de noticias en red** Network News Transfer Protocol (NNTP) ◇ **red** *f* **avanzada de terminal a terminal** advanced peer-to-peer networking; APPN ◇ **red** *f* **(de tipo) bus** bus network ◇ **red** *o* **cadena** *o* **canal de televisión** television network ◇ **red** *f* **(en forma) de anillo** mesh network ◇ **red** *f* **de enlace común de señales** token bus network ◇ **red** *f* **de la agencia de proyectos de investigación avanzada** ARPANET ◇ **red** *f* **del campus (universitario)** campus network ◇ **red** *f* **di-**

recta de acceso a la información direct information access network for Europe ◇ **red** *f* **internacional de transmisión de datos** web; World Wide Web ◇ **red** *f* **local de banda (de) base** base band local area network ◇ **red** *f* **(en forma de) malla** mesh network ◇ **red** *f* **pública (de transmisión de datos)** public data network ◇ **red radiofónica** *o* **cadena de radio** radio network ◇ **red telefónica básica (RTB)** basic telephone network

'El acceso a la información que facilita la Red está cambiando radicalmente el funcionamiento de importantes instituciones y mercados al aumentar el grado de intervención de los ciudadanos.' [*Ciberp@ís*]

redactor *m sustantivo* editor

red *f* **APPN** *sustantivo* **1.** advanced peer-to-peer networking **2.** APPN

red *f* **ARCNET** *sustantivo* attached resource computer network

red *f* **ARPA** *sustantivo* ARPANET

red *f* **auxiliar** *sustantivo* back-end network

red *f* **avanzada par a par** *sustantivo* **1.** advanced peer-to-peer networking **2.** APPN

red *f* **base** *sustantivo* backbone

red *f* **cableada** *sustantivo* cabling

red *f* **cliente-servidor** *sustantivo* client-server network

red *f* **con conmutación de paquetes** *abrev* PSN

red *f* **de área local** *sustantivo* **1.** LAN *o* lan **2.** local area network ◇ **LAN Manager™** LAN Manager™ ◇ **LAN Server™** LAN Server™

red *f* **de área metropolitana** *sustantivo* MAN

red *f* **de bus** *sustantivo* token bus network

red *f* **de comunicación de datos** *sustantivo* data communications network

red *f* **de comunicaciones** *sustantivo* communications network

red *f* **de datos** *sustantivo* data network

red *f* **de datos sincrónica** *sustantivo* synchronous data network

red *f* **de difusión** *sustantivo* broadcast network

red *f* **de distancia** *sustantivo* wide area network

red *f* **de distribución** *sustantivo* **1.** distributed network **2.** distribution network

red *f* **de electricidad** *sustantivo* mains electricity

red *f* **de empresa** *sustantivo* enterprise network

red *f* **de estrella** *sustantivo* star network

red *f* **de gran alcance** *sustantivo* wide area network

red *f* **de gran distancia** *sustantivo* long haul network

red *f* **de igual a igual** *sustantivo* peer-to-peer network ◇ **hemos conectado los cuatro PC de nuestra pequeña oficina mediante una red de igual a igual** we have linked the four PCs in our small office using a peer-to-peer network

red *f* **de integración de servicios** *sustantivo* value-added network ■ *abrev* VAN

red *f* **de la empresa** *sustantivo* intranet

red *f* **de larga distancia** *sustantivo* long haul network

red *f* **democrática** *sustantivo* democratic network

red *f* **de neuronas artificiales** *sustantivo* artificial neural network

red *f* **de ordenadores** *sustantivo* computer network

red *f* **departamental de área local** *sustantivo* departmental LAN

red *f* **de redes** *sustantivo* Internet

red *f* **despótica** *sustantivo* despotic network

red *f* **de telecomunicaciones** *sustantivo* communications network

red *f* **de topología en anillo** *sustantivo* ring topology network

red *f* **de valor añadido** *sustantivo* value-added network ■ *abrev* VAN

red *f* **digital de servicios integrados** *sustantivo* **1.** integrated services digital network **2.** ISDN

redefinir *verbo vt* to redefine ◇ **redefinimos los parámetros iniciales** we redefined the initial parameters ◇ **redefinir (la función) de una tecla** *o* **reprogramar una tecla** to redefine a key

red *f* **en anillo** *sustantivo* Token Ring network ◇ **las redes en anillo son muy democráticas y conservan su eficacia al aumentar la carga (de trabajo)** Token Ring networks are very democratic and retain performance against increasing load

red *f* **Ethernet de cable fino** *sustantivo* cheapernet ◇ **cable (coaxial) fino de red** cheapernet cable

red *f* **extendida** *sustantivo* **1.** long haul network **2.** wide area network

red *f* **extensa** *sustantivo* WAN

red *f* **inalámbrica de área local** *sustantivo* **1.** wireless LAN **2.** wireless network *o* wireless LAN

red *f* **informática** *sustantivo* **1.** computer network **2.** information network

red *f* **informática centralizada** *sustantivo* centralised computer network *o* centralized computer network

red *f* **informática descentralizada** *sustantivo* decentralised computer network *o* decentralized computer network

red *f* **informática heterogénea** *sustantivo* heterogeneous network

red *f* **informática homogénea** *sustantivo* homogeneous computer network

red *f* **informática internacional** *sustantivo* Internet

red *f* **informática jerárquica** *sustantivo* hierarchical computer network

red *f* **interna** *sustantivo* intranet

redirección *sustantivo* redirection ◇ **el desvío de llamadas consiste en la redirección automática de llamadas** call forwarding is automatic redirection of calls ◇ **redirección** *f* **(automática) de llamadas** redirection

redireccionamiento *sustantivo* relocation ◇ **redireccionamiento** *m* **por desplazamiento que convierte una dirección relativa en absoluta** float relocate

redireccionamiento *m* **dinámico** *sustantivo* dynamic relocation

redireccionamiento *m* **flotante** *sustantivo* float relocate

redireccionar *verbo vt* to forward

redirección *f* **de entrada/salida** *sustantivo* I/O redirection ◇ **utilizando la redirección de entrada** *or* **salida, enviamos desde el teclado todos los datos al puerto de la impresora y no al monitor** using I/O redirection, we send all the data from the keyboard to the printer port instead of the monitor

redirigir *verbo* **1.** *vt* to redirect **2.** *vt* to re-route ◇ **el dispositivo de desvío de llamadas redirige una llamada** the call diverter re-routes a call

redirigir (por ruta distinta) *verbo* to redirect

red *f* **isócrona** *sustantivo* isochronous network

red *f* **local con adaptador externo** *sustantivo* zero slot LAN

red *f* **LocalTalk™** LocalTalk

red *f* **metropolitana** *sustantivo* metropolitan area network

red *f* **neural** *sustantivo* neural network

redondear *verbo vt* to round ◇ **error de redondeo** round off error ◇ **podemos redondear 2,647 a 2,65 por exceso** we can round up 2.647 to 2.65 ◇ **podemos redondear 2,651 a 2,65 por defecto** we can round down 2.651 to 2.65 ◇ **redondear (un número)** to round off ◇ **redondear (un número por defecto)** to round down ◇ **redondear 23,456 a 23,46** round off 23.456 to 23.46 ◇ **redondear por exceso** to round up

redondeo *sustantivo* rounding ◇ **redondeo** *m* **(de los ángulos)** rounding ◇ **redondeo** *m* **a un número determinado de decimales** automatic decimal adjustment

redondeo *m* **de caracteres** *sustantivo* character rounding

red *f* **principal** *sustantivo* backbone

red *f* **principal invertida** *sustantivo* inverted backbone

red *f* **pública (de transmisión de datos)** *abrev* PDN

red *f* **punto a punto** *sustantivo* point to point

red *f* **síncrona** *sustantivo* synchronous network

red *f* **sincrónica** *sustantivo* synchronous network

red *f* **'Token Ring'** *sustantivo* Token Ring network ◇ **las redes en anillo son muy democráticas y conservan su eficacia al aumentar la carga (de trabajo)** Token Ring networks are very democratic and retain performance against increasing load

red *f* **totalmente interconectada** *sustantivo* plex structure

reducción *f* **de datos** *sustantivo* data reduction

reducir *verbo* **1.** *vt* to cut **2.** *vt* to kern **3.** *vt* to minimise *o* to minimize ◇ **hemos reducido el espacio entre la 'T' y la 'o' para que estén más juntas** we have kerned 'T' and 'o' so they are closer together ◇ **se pidió al autor que redujera su manuscrito a 250 páginas** the author was asked to cut his manuscript to 250 pages

reducir la escala *verbo* to scale down

reducir la escala de *verbo* (*una configuración informática*) to downsize ◇ **la reducción de la escala de una configuración informática es más rentable y proporciona más capacidad de proceso al usuario final** downsizing is more cost effective and gives more processing power to the end-user

redundancia *f sustantivo* redundancy

redundante *adj* redundant

red *f* **urbana** *sustantivo* metropolitan area network

(instrucción) reemplazar *verbo* to replace

reemplazar *verbo* **1.** *vt* to overwrite **2.** *vt* to replace **3.** *vt* to supersede ◇ **los nuevos datos introducidos han reemplazado la información anterior** the latest data input has overwritten the old information ◇ **(función de) reemplazar en todo el texto** global exchange

reencaminar *verbo vt* to re-route

reensamblaje *m sustantivo* folding

reentrada *f sustantivo* re-entry

reestablecer *verbo vt* to retrain

referencia *f sustantivo* **1.** benchmark **2.** reference ◇ **modelo de referencia de siete categorías** seven-layer reference model ◇ **nivel de referencia** reference level

referencia *f sustantivo* reference

referencia *f* **circular** *sustantivo* circular reference

referencia *f* **de celda absoluta** *sustantivo* absolute cell reference

referencia *f* **explícita** *sustantivo* explicit reference

referencia *f* **implícita** *sustantivo* implicit reference

referenciar *verbo vt* to reference ◇ **se necesita poco tiempo de acceso para referenciar un ítem de la memoria** the access time taken to reference an item in memory is short

reflectometría *f* **de dominio temporal** *sustantivo* **1.** TDR **2.** time domain reflectometry

reflejar *verbo vt* to mirror ◇ **disco espejo** mirror disk ◇ **imagen inversa** *o* **de espejo** mirror image

reflejo *m sustantivo* glare ◊ **el reflejo de la pantalla me cansa la vista** the glare from the screen makes my eyes hurt

reflejo *m* **de fondo** *sustantivo* background reflectance

reformateado *m sustantivo* reformatting ◊ **el reformateado destruye todos los datos de un disco** reformatting destroys all the data on a disk

reformatear *verbo vt* to reformat ◊ **evite reformatear el disco duro a menos que no haya ninguna otra solución** do not reformat your hard disk unless you can't do anything else

reformateo *m sustantivo* reformatting

refracción *f sustantivo* **1.** beam deflection **2.** refraction

refrescar el contenido de la pantalla *verbo* to screen refresh

regenerador *m sustantivo* regenerator

regenerar *verbo* **1.** *vt* to refresh **2.** *vt* to regenerate

región *f sustantivo* region ◊ **región** *f* **de California donde se concentran gran número de empresas de informática productoras de semiconductores** Silicon Valley

región *f* **activa** *sustantivo* active region

registrador *m sustantivo* logger

registrador *m* **de llamadas** *sustantivo* call logger

registrar *verbo* **1.** *vt* to deposit **2.** *vt* to log **3.** *vt* to post **4.** *vt* to read in **5.** *vt* to register **6.** *vt* to write ◊ **las películas fotosensibles registran la intensidad de la luz** light-sensitive films register light intensity

registro *sustantivo* **1.** entry **2.** log **3.** record **4.** register **5.** Registry ◊ **compatibilidad a nivel de registros** register level compatibility ◊ **entre las características del programa se incluye el registro (automático) de errores** features of the program include error logging ◊ **este registro contiene todos sus detalles personales** this record contains all their personal details ◊ **marcas de registro** register marks ◊ **registro automático y cronológico de datos** data logging ◊ **registro** *m* **(de instrucciones) de control** control register ◊ **registro de control de secuencias** sequence control register (SCR) ◊ **registro** *m* **de datos de la memoria** MDR; memory data register ◊ **registro de dirección de instrucciones** instruction address register (IAR) → **registro** *m* **(automático) de errores** error logging ◊ **registro** *m* **(automático) de incidencias** failure logging ◊ **registro de índice** index register ◊ **registro** *m* **de instrucciones en curso** CIR; current instruction register ◊ **registro** *m* **de la instrucción para ejecutar** next instruction register ◊ **registro de la palabra de estado del programa** *o* **registro PSW** program status word register (PSW register) ◊ **registro** *m* **de la ruta de acceso** access path journalling ◊ **registro** *m* **de memoria intermedia de salida** output buffer register ◊ **registro** *m* **de paginación de acceso directo** direct page register ◊ **registro** *m* **directo sobre disco mediante un teclado** keyboard to

disk entry ◊ **registro externo** external register ◊ **su registro contiene varios campos que han sido agrupados bajo una misma cabecera** your record contains several fields that have been grouped together under the one heading

registro *m* **activo** *sustantivo* active record

registro *m* **acumulador** *sustantivo* accumulator *o* accumulator register

registro *m* **adjunto** *sustantivo* adjunct register

registro *m* **agrupado por pares** *sustantivo* paired register

registro *m* **analógico** *sustantivo* analog recording

registro *m* **aritmético** *sustantivo* arithmetic register

registro *m* **asociado** *sustantivo* paired register

registro *m* **auxiliar de dirección** *sustantivo* B-line counter

registro *m* **B** *sustantivo* B register

registro *m* **base** *sustantivo* base register

registro *m* **binario** *sustantivo* binary cell

registro *m* **circulante** *sustantivo* circulating register

registro *m* **de actividades** *sustantivo* activity trail

registro *m* **de adición** *sustantivo* **1.** addition record **2.** add register

registro *m* **de arranque** *sustantivo* **1.** boot block **2.** boot record

registro *m* **de auditoría** *sustantivo* audit trail

registro *m* **de base** *sustantivo* base register

registro *m* **de cabeza** *sustantivo* leader record

registro *m* **de cambio** *sustantivo* **1.** change record **2.** transaction record

registro *m* **de códigos de condición** *sustantivo* condition code register

registro *m* **de control** *sustantivo* **1.** check register **2.** control register

registro *m* **de control de secuencia** *sustantivo* instruction address register ■ *abrev* SCR ■ *sustantivo* **1.** sequence control register *o* sequence counter **2.** sequence register

registro *m* **de datos** *sustantivo* **1.** data record **2.** data register

registro *m* **de datos en memoria** *sustantivo* **1.** SDR **2.** store data register

registro *m* **de desplazamiento** *sustantivo* shift register

registro *m* **de desplazamiento circular** *sustantivo* circulating register

registro *m* **de dirección de base** *sustantivo* base address register

registro *m* **de dirección de instrucciones** *abrev* PC ■ *sustantivo* **1.** program address counter **2.** program counter

registro *m* **de dirección en memoria** *sustantivo* **1.** MAR **2.** memory address register **3.** SAR **4.** store address register

registro *m* **de direcciones** *sustantivo* 1. address register 2. base register

registro *m* **de direcciones en curso** *abrev* CAR ■ *sustantivo* current address register

registro *m* **de entrada** *sustantivo* input register

registro *m* **de entradas** *sustantivo* receiver register

registro *m* **de entrada/salida** *sustantivo* input/output register

registro *m* **de errores** *sustantivo* error logging ◊ **entre las características del programa se incluye el registro (automático) de errores** features of the program include error logging

registro *m* **de estado** *sustantivo* status register

registro *m* **de etiquetas** *sustantivo* label record

registro *m* **de fallos** *sustantivo* failure logging

registro *m* **de final de fichero** *sustantivo* trailer record

registro *m* **de identificadores** *sustantivo* label record

registro *m* **de indicadores** *sustantivo* flag register

registro *m* **de índice** *sustantivo* index register ■ *abrev* IR

registro *m* **de inicio** *sustantivo* home record

registro *m* **de instrucción** *sustantivo* instruction register ■ *abrev* IR ■ *sustantivo* program register

registro *m* **de instrucciones** *sustantivo* 1. check register 2. command register 3. control register

registro *m* **de la instrucción siguiente** *sustantivo* next instruction register

registro *m* **de la memoria intermedia** *sustantivo* buffer register

registro *m* **de la siguiente instrucción** *sustantivo* next instruction register

registro *m* **de la unidad** *sustantivo* unit record

registro *m* **de límites** *sustantivo* boundary register

registro *m* **de longitud determinada** *sustantivo* fixed-length record

registro *m* **de longitud fija** *sustantivo* fixed-length record

registro *m* **de longitud finita** *sustantivo* fixed-length record

registro *m* **de longitud variable** *sustantivo* variable length record

registro *m* **de máscara** *sustantivo* mask register

registro *m* **de memoria asociativa** *sustantivo* associative storage register

registro *m* **de memoria intermedia** *sustantivo* 1. MBR 2. memory buffer register

registro *m* **de microprograma** *sustantivo* microprogram counter

registro *m* **de modificaciones** *sustantivo* 1. amendment record 2. change record 3. transaction record

registro *m* **de nombre de dominio** *sustantivo* 1. domain name registration 2. name registration

registro *m* **de operación** *sustantivo* 1. operation register 2. op register

registro *m* **de programa** *sustantivo* program register

registro *m* **de salida** *sustantivo* output register

registro *m* **de suma** *sustantivo* add register

registro *m* **de testigos** *sustantivo* flag register

registro *m* **de texto** *sustantivo* text register

registro *m* **de un fallo** *sustantivo* fault trace

registro *m* **de visualización** *sustantivo* display register

registro *m* **directo sobre disco** *sustantivo* key-to-disk

registro *m* **encadenado** *sustantivo* chained record

registro *m* **externo** *sustantivo* external register

registro *m* **físico** *sustantivo* physical record

registro *m* **general** *sustantivo* 1. general register 2. gpr

registro *m* **gráfico** *sustantivo* pen recorder

registro *m* **intermedio de entrada** *sustantivo* input buffer register

registro *m* **lógico** *sustantivo* logical record

registro *m* **para usos generales** *sustantivo* 1. general register 2. gpr

registros *mpl* **de suma** *plural noun* S-registers

registro *m* **secundario** *sustantivo* B box

registro *m* **temporal** *sustantivo* temporary register

registro *m* **último** *sustantivo* trailer record

regla *f* *sustantivo* 1. rule 2. ruler

regla *f* **DE OTRA MANERA** *sustantivo* else rule ◊ **si X=20 PRINT 'X igual a 20' ELSE PRINT 'X distinto de 20'** IF X=20 THEN PRINT 'X is 20' ELSE PRINT 'X not 20'

regla *f* **DE OTRO MODO** *sustantivo* else rule ◊ **si X=20 PRINT 'X igual a 20' ELSE PRINT 'X distinto de 20'** IF X=20 THEN PRINT 'X is 20' ELSE PRINT 'X not 20'

regla *f* **de tabulación** *sustantivo* 1. ruler line 2. tab rack

regla *f* **ELSE** *sustantivo* else rule

reglas *plural noun* rules ◊ **que va contra las reglas** illegal

reglas *fpl* **de codificación básicas** *plural noun* basic encoding rules ■ *sustantivo* BER

reglas *fpl* **de transformación** *sustantivo* transformational rules

reglas *fpl* **de un lenguaje** *plural noun* language rules

regla *f* **SI NO** *sustantivo* else rule

regleta *f* **de conexión** *sustantivo* fanning strip

regleta *f* **de conexiones** *sustantivo* terminal strip

regleta *f* **distribuidora** *sustantivo* fanning strip

regulación *f sustantivo* adjustment

regulador *m* **de tensión** *sustantivo* voltage regulator

regular *verbo vt* to regulate

rehacer desde el inicio *verbo* to redo from start

rehacer la numeración *sustantivo* renumber

rehacer la paginación *verbo* to repaginate ◇ **el sistema de publicación asistida por ordenador permite rehacer la paginación** the dtp package allows simple repagination ◇ **se rehizo la paginación del texto con una nueva longitud de línea** the text was repaginated with a new line width

reincorporar (a la memoria) *verbo* to roll in

reiniciación *f sustantivo* failure recovery

reiniciar *verbo* **1.** *vt* to reboot **2.** *vt* to reset **3.** *vt* to resume ◇ **reiniciamos el sistema y los ficheros reaparecieron en la pantalla** we rebooted and the files reappeared ◇ **reiniciar y arrancar** reset and start

reinicio *m sustantivo* **1.** failure recovery **2.** restart ◇ **reinicio** *m* **(apagando el sistema)** hard reset ◇ **reinicio** *m* **en el punto de recuperación** fall back recovery

reinicio *m* **apagando el sistema** *sustantivo* hard reset

reinicio *m* **automático** *sustantivo* auto restart

reinicio *m* **sin apagar el sistema** *sustantivo* soft reset

reiteración *f sustantivo* iteration

rejilla *f sustantivo* grid

relación *sustantivo* ratio ◇ **la relación 10 a 5 es (igual a) 2:1** the ratio of 10 to 5 is 2:1 ◇ **relación** *f* **de la altura y la anchura de un píxel** aspect ratio

relación *f* **de compresión** *sustantivo* compression ratio

relación *f* **entre señal y ruido** *sustantivo* signal to noise ratio ■ *abrev* S/N

relaciones ◇ **relaciones** *fpl* **comerciales entre empresas** B2B ◇ **relaciones** *fpl* **comerciales entre empresa y consumador** B2C

relanzar *verbo* **1.** *vt* to reboot **2.** *vt* to reload

relé *m sustantivo* relay ◇ **está protegido por un relé de 5 amperios** it is relay-rated at 5 Amps ◇ **hay un relé en el circuito** there is a relay in the circuit ◇ **relé de microondas** microwave relay

rellamada *f* **automática** *sustantivo* callback ■ *abrev* CB

rellenar *verbo vt* to fill

relleno *sustantivo* padding ◇ **relleno** *m* **(con caracteres en blanco)** character stuffing

relleno *m* **de área** *sustantivo* area fill

relleno *m* **de caracteres** *sustantivo* character fill

relleno *m* **de zona** *sustantivo* region fill

relleno *m* **por asteriscos** *sustantivo* asterisk fill

reloj *m sustantivo* **1.** clock **2.** egg timer

reloj *m* **de cuarzo** *sustantivo* quartz clock *o* quartz crystal clock

reloj *m* **de la unidad central** *sustantivo* CPU clock

reloj *m* **del bus** *sustantivo* bus clock

reloj *m* **del sistema** *sustantivo* system clock

reloj *m* **delta** *sustantivo* delta clock

reloj *m* **digital** *sustantivo* digital clock

reloj *m* **en tiempo real** *sustantivo* real-time clock

reloj *m* **exterior** *sustantivo* external clock

reloj *m* **externo** *sustantivo* external clock

reloj *m* **maestro** *sustantivo* **1.** master clock **2.** timing master

reloj *m* **principal** *sustantivo* **1.** main clock **2.** master clock

reloj *m* **programable** *sustantivo* programmable clock

reloj *m* **relativo** *sustantivo* relative-time clock

remoto *adj* remote ◇ **software de acceso remoto** remote access software

rendimiento *m sustantivo* performance ◇ **(de) alto rendimiento** high performance ◇ **como medida del rendimiento del sistema** as a measure of the system's performance

rendimiento *m* **de fosforescencia** *sustantivo* phosphor efficiency

rendimiento *m* **de transmisión** *sustantivo* transmission rate

rendimiento *m* **de una línea** *sustantivo* line speed

rendimiento *m* **efectivo** *sustantivo* **1.** effective throughput **2.** throughput

rendimiento *m* **estimado** *sustantivo* rated throughput

rendimiento *m* **máximo** *sustantivo* peak output

rendimiento *m* **nominal** *sustantivo* rated throughput

rendimiento *m* **teórico** *sustantivo* rated throughput

renglón *m sustantivo* line

renovar *verbo* **1.** *vt* to refresh **2.** *vt* to regenerate

reordenación *f* **de bloques** *sustantivo* frame relay

reorganizar *verbo vt* to reorganise *o* to reorganize ◇ **espere mientras la base de datos de corrección ortográfica se está reorganizando** wait while the spelling checker database is being reorganized

reparación *f sustantivo* corrective maintenance

reparación *f* **en caliente** *sustantivo* hot fix

reparado, -a temporalmente *adj* kluged

reparar *verbo vt* to service ◇ **ayer revisaron o repararon las unidades de lectura de discos y funcionan bien** the disk drives were serviced yesterday and are working well

repartición *f* **de puerto** *sustantivo* port sharing

repartir *verbo vt* to allocate ◇ **el sistema operativo asignó la mayor parte de la memoria principal a la hoja de cálculo** the operating system allocated most of main memory to the spreadsheet program

reparto *m* **de tareas** *sustantivo* job scheduling

reperforadora *f sustantivo* reperforator

repertorio *m sustantivo* repertoire ◇ **el manual describe el repertorio completo** the manual describes the full repertoire

repertorio *m* **de caracteres** *sustantivo* character repertoire

repertorio *m* **de excepciones** *sustantivo* exception dictionary

repertorio *m* **de instrucciones** *sustantivo* instruction repertoire *o* instruction set

repertorio *m* **tipográfico** *sustantivo* character repertoire

repetición *f sustantivo* replay

repetición *f* **automática** *sustantivo* 1. automatic repeat 2. auto repeat

repetidor *m sustantivo* repeater

repetir *verbo* 1. *vt* to replay 2. *vt* to rollback ◇ **este grabador de vídeo tiene la función de repetición** this video recorder has a replay feature ◇ **la repetición a cámara lenta mostró claramente quién era el ganador** the replay clearly showed the winner

repetir la ejecución *verbo* to rerun

reponer *verbo vt* to replenish

reposición *f sustantivo* recovery

reposicionable *adj* relocatable

representación ◇ **representación** *f* **(binaria) de caracteres** character representation ◇ **representación** *f* **gráfica en forma de trama** raster graphics ◇ **representación** *f* **visual en color de un carácter** character representation ◇ **representación** *f* **visual por cristal líquido** LCD; liquid crystal display

representación *f* **analógica** *sustantivo* analog representation

representación *f* **digital** *sustantivo* digital representation

representaciones *fpl* **gráficas** *sustantivo* graphics

representación *f* **gráfica** *sustantivo* graphic display

representación *f* **visual** *sustantivo* display

representación *f* **visual en color** *sustantivo* colour display

representación *f* **visual por plasma** *sustantivo* plasma display

representar *verbo vt* to render ◇ **hemos representado el modelo de trama de rejilla** we rendered the wire-frame model

reproducción *sustantivo* replication ◇ **reproducción** *f* **de datos terminados en un disco maestro** mastering

reproducir *verbo* 1. *vt* to replay 2. *vt* to reproduce ◇ **visionó de nuevo la cinta** he replayed the tape

reproducir (un registro) *verbo* to play back

reproducir un documento *verbo* to copy

reproductor *m* **de CD-ROM** *sustantivo* CD-ROM player

reproductor *m* **de CDs** *sustantivo* jukebox

reproductor *m* **de discos automático** *sustantivo* jukebox

reproductor *m* **de discos compactos** *sustantivo* CD Player

reprogramable *adj* redefinable

reprogramado *adj* redefinable

reprogramar *verbo* 1. *vt* to redefine 2. *vt* to reprogram ◇ **he reprogramado esta tecla para obtener el número cinco** I have redefined this key to display the figure five when pressed ◇ **redefinir (la función) de una tecla** *o* **reprogramar una tecla** to redefine a key

requisitos *mpl plural noun* requirements

reservar *verbo vt* to lock

reservas *fpl* **de energía** *sustantivo* meter – power supply

residente *mf sustantivo* built-in font ■ *adj* resident ◇ **fuente (de caracteres) residente** resident font

residual *adj* residual

residuos *mpl sustantivo* garbage

resistir *vt sustantivo* resist

resolución *f sustantivo* 1. res 2. resolution ◇ **la pantalla de alta definición puede obtener una resolución de 640 por 450 pixels** the high resolution screen can display 640 by 450 pixels ◇ **la resolución de la mayoría de las pantallas de los ordenadores personales es apenas superior a los 70 ppp (puntos por pulgada)** the resolution of most personal computer screens is not much more than 70 dpi (dots per inch)

resolución *f* **de direcciones** *sustantivo* address resolution

resolución *f* **de nombre** *sustantivo* name resolution

resolución *f* **de pantalla** *sustantivo* display resolution

resolución *f* **de visualización gráfica** *sustantivo* graphic display resolution

resolución *f* **digital** *sustantivo* digital resolution

resonancia *f sustantivo* resonance

resonar *verbo vi* to echo

respaldar *verbo vt* to back up ◇ **respaldó su razonamiento para la adquisición de un nuevo sistema con la copia impresa** the printout backed up his argument for a new system

responder *verbo vt* to reply

responder a una llamada *verbo* to answer ◇ **el primer módem genera la llamada y el segundo la contesta** the first modem originates the call and the second answers it ◇ **servicio de contestador** *o* **de contestación automática** answering service

responsable *m&f* **del correo electrónico** *sustantivo* postmaster

responsable *m&f* **del sistema informático** *sustantivo* system manager

responsable *m&f* **de servicio informático** *sustantivo* data processing manager ■ *abrev* DPM

responsable *m&f* **de un portal** *sustantivo* webmaster

responsable *m&f* **de un sitio web** *sustantivo* webmaster

respuesta ◇ **respuesta** *f* **activada por una sola tecla** single key response

respuesta *f* **afirmativa** *sustantivo* positive response

respuesta *f* **automática** *sustantivo* auto-answer

respuesta *f* **en cardioide** *sustantivo* cardioid response

respuesta *f* **intrínseca** *sustantivo* default response

respuesta *f* **por defecto** *sustantivo* default response

respuesta *f* **positiva** *sustantivo* **1.** hit **2.** positive response

restadora *f* **de tres entradas** *sustantivo* full subtractor

restadora *f* **total** *sustantivo* full subtractor

restauración *f* *sustantivo* recovery

restaurar *verbo* **1.** *vt* to reconstitute **2.** *vt* to restore ◇ **restaurar un fichero a su forma original** backout

resto *m* *sustantivo* remainder ◇ **7 dividido por 3 es igual a 2 y 1 de resto** 7 divided by 3 is equal to 2 remainder 1

resto *m* **de supresiones** *sustantivo* deletion tracking

resto *m* **de una imagen** *sustantivo* hangover

restricción *f* *sustantivo* restriction

restringir *verbo vt* to restrict ◇ **el documento es de acceso restringido y, por lo tanto, no debe disponer de acceso público** the document is restricted, and cannot be placed on open access

resultado *sustantivo* result ◇ **resultado** *m* **erróneo (de una búsqueda)** false drop

resultado *m* **de la transcripción** *sustantivo* dump

retardo *m* *sustantivo* lag

retardo *m* **de contención** *sustantivo* contention delay

retardo *m* **de mercurio** *sustantivo* mercury delay line

retardo *m* **medio** *sustantivo* average delay ◇ **después de las nueve y media el tiempo medio de espera aumenta debido a que todo el mundo intenta conectarse (al sistema)** the average delay increases at nine-thirty when everyone tries to log-in

retención *f* **de (la) imagen** *sustantivo* image retention

retirar *verbo* **1.** *vt* to pull **2.** *vt* to unmount

retocar *verbo vt* to tweak

retorno *sustantivo* return ◇ **el programa no funciona porque se ha olvidado de la instrucción de retorno al final de la subrutina** the program is not working because you missed out the return instruction at the end of the subroutine ◇ **retorno** *m* **(de un barrido)** flyback

retorno *m* **automático de carro** *sustantivo* automatic carriage return

retorno *m* **automático de línea** *sustantivo* **1.** automatic carriage return **2.** word wrap **3.** wraparound

retorno *m* **de carro** *sustantivo* carriage return

retorno *m* **del cursor** *sustantivo* horizontal wraparound

retorno *m* **de línea** *sustantivo* line flyback

retorno *m* **horizontal de línea** *sustantivo* horizontal wraparound

retransmitir *verbo vt* to relay ◇ **todos los mensajes se retransmiten a través de este pequeño micrófono** all messages are relayed through this small micro

retraso *m* **de contención** *sustantivo* contention delay

retraso *m* **medio** *sustantivo* average delay ◇ **después de las nueve y media el tiempo medio de espera aumenta debido a que todo el mundo intenta conectarse (al sistema)** the average delay increases at nine-thirty when everyone tries to log-in

retrato *m* *adj* portrait

retro- *prefijo* retro-

retroceder un paso *verbo* to step

reubicable *adj* relocatable

reubicación *f* *sustantivo* relocation

reubicar *verbo vt* to relocate

reunir *verbo* **1.** *vt* to collect **2.** *vt* to gather

revelar *verbo vt* to reveal

revendedor *m* **de valor añadido** *sustantivo* value-added reseller ■ *abrev* VAR

reverberación *f* *sustantivo* reverb *o* reverberation

revestimiento *m* *sustantivo* cladding ◇ **revestimiento** *m* **de un cable de radiofrecuencia** RF shielding ◇ **si el revestimiento está raspado, el cable de fibra óptica no funciona bien** if the cladding is chipped, the fibre-optic cable will not function well ◇ **sin el revestimiento del cable, la señal transmitida sería distorsionada por las interferencias** without RF shielding, the transmitted signal would be distorted by the interference

revisar *verbo* **1.** *vt (texto, programa)* to edit **2.** *vt* to revise

revisar la ortografía *verbo* to spellcheck

revista *f sustantivo* magazine

revista *f* **electrónica** *sustantivo* **1.** e-zine **2.** webzine

riesgo *m sustantivo* hazard

ritmo *m sustantivo* tempo

RJ11 *sustantivo* RJ-11

RJ45 *sustantivo* RJ-45

robot *m sustantivo* **1.** robot **2.** robot

robótica *f sustantivo* robotics

robustez *f sustantivo* robustness

robusto *adj* robust

rojo, verde, azul *sustantivo* **1.** red, green, blue **2.** RGB

rollo *m* **de papel para teleimpresora** *sustantivo* teleprinter roll

ROM *abrev* ROM ◇ **ROM** *m* **modificable mediante una señal eléctrica especial** flash ROM

ROM *f* **BIOS** *sustantivo* ROM BIOS

ROM *f* **fantasma** *sustantivo* phantom ROM

ROM *f* **'flash'** *sustantivo* flash ROM

romperse *verbo vr* to fail

ROM *f* **personalizada** *sustantivo* custom ROM

ROM *f* **(en la) sombra** *sustantivo* shadow ROM

rotación *f sustantivo* rotation

rotación *f* **binaria** *sustantivo* bit rotation

rotación *f* **de matriz** *sustantivo* matrix rotation

rótulo *m sustantivo* **1.** label **2.** tag ◇ **clasificación por rótulo** tag sort

rúbrica *f sustantivo* heading

rueda ◇ **rueda** *f* **de cabezas (magnéticas)** head wheel

rueda *f* **de cadena** *sustantivo* sprocket wheel

rueda *f* **de espigas** *sustantivo* **1.** sprocket **2.** sprocket wheel

rueda *f* **de margarita** *sustantivo* printwheel

rueda *f* **dentada** *sustantivo* pinchwheel

ruido *m sustantivo* noise ◇ **margen de ruido** *o* **límite de tolerancia al ruido** noise margin ◇ **ruido** *m* **de saturación (magnética)** saturation noise ◇ **ruido térmico** thermal noise ◇ **temperatura de ruido** noise temperature

ruido(s) *m(pl) sustantivo* static

ruido *m* **de circuito** *sustantivo* line noise

ruido *m* **de fondo** *sustantivo* **1.** ambient noise **2.** babble **3.** background noise ◇ **el módem es sensible al ruido de fondo** the modem is sensitive to background noise ◇ **los otros aparatos alrededor de este equipo producen mucho ruido de fondo** the other machines around this device will produce a lot of background noise ◇ **nivel de ruido de fondo** *o* **de sonido ambiente** ambient noise level

ruido *m* **de línea** *sustantivo* line noise

ruido *m* **impulsivo** *sustantivo* impulsive noise

ruido *m* **intermitente** *sustantivo* impulsive noise

ruido(s) *m(pl)* **m(pl) de cuantificación** *sustantivo* quantising noise

ruido *m* **parásito** *sustantivo* jabber

ruta *f sustantivo* **1.** access path **2.** facility **3.** path **4.** route ◇ **la ruta elegida no fue la más directa ya que muchos nodos estaban ocupados** the route taken was not the most direct since a lot of nodes were busy

ruta *f* **adaptable** *sustantivo* adaptive routing

ruta *f* **alterna** *sustantivo* alternate route

ruta *f* **completa** *sustantivo* full path

ruta *f* **de acceso** *sustantivo* path

ruta *f* **de seguridad** *sustantivo* backup path

ruta *f* **dinámica** *sustantivo* dynamic routing

ruta *f* **equilibrada** *sustantivo* balanced routing

ruta *f* **fija** *sustantivo* fixed routing

ruta *f* **fuente** *sustantivo* source routing

ruta *f* **preseleccionada** *sustantivo* fixed routing

rutina *sustantivo* **1.** malfunction routine **2.** routine ◇ **la instrucción RETURN al final de la rutina devuelve el control al programa principal** the RETURN instruction at the end of the routine sends control back to the main program ◇ **la rutina permite imprimir el contenido de la pantalla** the routine copies the screen display onto a printer ◇ **rutina** *f* **de carga del sistema operativo (en la memoria principal)** initial program loader; IPL ◇ **rutina** *f* **(de gestión) de errores** error routine

rutina *f* **abierta** *sustantivo* open routine

rutina *f* **auxiliar** *sustantivo* open routine

rutina *f* **cerrada** *sustantivo* closed routine

rutina *f* **de almacenamiento** *sustantivo* packing routine

rutina *f* **de asignación** *sustantivo* allocation routine

rutina *f* **de biblioteca** *sustantivo* library routine

rutina *f* **de coma flotante** *sustantivo* floating point routine

rutina *f* **de compresión** *sustantivo* packing routine

rutina *f* **de diagnóstico** *sustantivo* diagnostic routine

rutina *f* **de ensamblaje** *sustantivo* assembly routine

rutina *f* **de entrada** *sustantivo* input routine

rutina *f* **de gestión de periféricos** *sustantivo* peripheral software driver

rutina *f* **de inserción directa** *sustantivo* direct-insert routine

rutina *f* **de instalación LAP-B** *sustantivo* LAP-B

rutina *f* **de manipulación de ficheros** *sustantivo* file handling routine

rutina *f* **de mantenimiento** *sustantivo* maintenance routine

rutina *f* **de normalización** *sustantivo* normalisation routine

rutina *f* **interactiva** *sustantivo* interactive routine

rutina *f* **iterativa** *sustantivo* **1.** iterate **2.** iterative routine

rutina *f* **primitiva** *sustantivo* primitive

rutina *f* **principal** *sustantivo* main routine

rutina *f* **recursiva** *sustantivo* recursive routine

rutinas *fpl* **de acceso** *plural noun* access method routines

rutinas *fpl* **de ayuda** *plural noun* fall back routines

rutinas *fpl* **de cierre** *plural noun* end of run routines

rutinas *fpl* **de emergencia** *plural noun* fall back routines

rutinas *fpl* **de final** *plural noun* end of run routines

rutinas *fpl* **de interfaz** *plural noun* interface routines

S

SAA (*marca comercial*) SAA

sabotear *verbo vt* to hack

sacar *verbo* **1.** *vt* to output **2.** *vt* to unmount ◇ **los documentos terminados se pueden sacar por la impresora láser** finished documents can be output to the laser printer

saco ◇ **saco** *m* **(de elementos en desorden)** bag

sacudida *f* **eléctrica** *sustantivo* surge

salida *f sustantivo* **1.** fan-out **2.** output

salida *f* **de datos impresos** *sustantivo* information output

salida *f* **de impresora** *sustantivo* hard copy

salida *f* **de (la) impresora** *sustantivo* computer listing

salida *f* **de la impresora** *sustantivo* **1.** computer printout **2.** printout

salida *f* **de (un) ordenador** *sustantivo* computer output

salida *f* **de ordenador en microfilm** *sustantivo* **1.** COM **2.** computer output on microfilm

salida *f* **de sesión** *sustantivo* timeout

salida *f* **digital** *sustantivo* digital output

salida *f* **por impresora** *sustantivo* information output

salida *f* **vocal** *sustantivo* voice output

salir *verbo* **1.** *vi* to abort **2.** *vi* to exit **3.** *vi* to quit ◇ **no olvide guardar el texto antes de salir del sistema** do not forget to save your text before you quit the system ◇ **salir temporalmente (de un programa)** to shell out

salir (sin guardar) *verbo* to abandon ◇ **si se sale de la hoja de cálculo sin guardarla, no podrá recuperarla posteriormente** once you have abandoned your spreadsheet, you cannot retrieve it again

saltador *m sustantivo* jumper

saltar *verbo* **1.** *vi* to branch **2.** *vt* to pop **3.** *vt* to skip

saltar(se) *verbo vr* to jump

salto *m sustantivo* **1.** branch **2.** jump

salto *m* **automático de línea** *sustantivo* horizontal wraparound

salto *m* **de alta velocidad** *sustantivo* high-speed skip

salto *m* **de contacto** *sustantivo* contact bounce

salto *m* **de línea** *abrev* LF ■ *sustantivo* word wrap

salto *m* **de página forzado** *sustantivo* forced page break

salto *m* **de página programado** *sustantivo* forced page break

salto *m* **de papel** *sustantivo* paper throw

salto *m* **incondicional** *sustantivo* unconditional branch *o* unconditional jump *o* unconditional transfer

salto *m* **por defecto** *sustantivo* defect skipping

salto *m* **rápido** *sustantivo* high-speed skip

salvapantallas *m sustantivo* screen saver

salvar *verbo vt* to bridge

sangrado *m sustantivo* **1.** indent **2.** indentation

sangrado *m* **de una línea** *sustantivo* bleed

sangrar *verbo vi* to bleed

saturación *f sustantivo* saturation

saturación *f* **de color** *sustantivo* colour saturation

saturación *f* **de un canal** *sustantivo* channel overload

ScanDisk *sustantivo* ScanDisk

scavenging de datos fraudulenta *sustantivo* scavenging

ScriptX™ *sustantivo* ScriptX

sección *f sustantivo* **1.** body **2.** part **3.** partition **4.** section ◇ **cuerpo (de un carácter)** body size ◇ **longitud** body size ◇ **tamaño de una sección (de texto)** body size

sector *sustantivo* sector

'Las nuevas tecnologías de la información han ocasionado transformaciones notables en la definición de los negocios y de los sectores.' [*Nueva Economía*]

sector *m* **de disco** *sustantivo* disk sector

sector *m* **de discos flexibles** *sustantivo* floppy disk sector

sector *m* **de disquetes** *sustantivo* floppy disk sector

sector *m* **defectuoso** *sustantivo* **1.** bad sector **2.** defective sector **3.** faulty sector

sector *m* **eléctrico** *sustantivo* mains electricity

sectores *mpl* **contiguos** *sustantivo* cluster

sectorizar *verbo vt* to sector ◇ **formateado de sectores (de un disco)** (disk) sector formatting

sector *m* **reservado** *sustantivo* reserved sector

secuencia *sustantivo* 1. sequence 2. string ◇ **la secuencia de nombres está organizada por orden alfabético** the sequence of names is arranged alphabetically ◇ **secuencia de conexión de inicio de sesión** *o* **de identificación** the logon sequence ◇ **secuencia** *f* **(de instrucciones) de control** control sequence

secuencia *f* **binaria** *sustantivo* binary sequence

secuenciación *f* **automática** *sustantivo* automatic sequencing

secuencia *f* **de abandono** *sustantivo* escape sequence

secuencia *f* **de cierre anormal** *sustantivo* abort sequence

secuencia *f* **de control** *sustantivo* 1. control sequence 2. supervisory sequence

secuencia *f* **de final** *sustantivo* abort sequence

secuencia *f* **de indicadores** *sustantivo* flag sequence

secuencia *f* **de intercalación** *sustantivo* collating sequence

secuencia *f* **de interrupción anormal** *sustantivo* abort sequence

secuencia *f* **de llamadas** *sustantivo* calling sequence

secuencia *f* **de marcadores** *sustantivo* flag sequence

secuencia *f* **de microinstrucciones** *sustantivo* microsequence

secuencia *f* **de prioridad** *sustantivo* priority sequence

secuencia *f* **de salida ANSI** *sustantivo* ANSI escape sequence

secuencia *f* **de teclas** *sustantivo* accelerator key ◇ **en vez de seleccionar el menú Archivo y a continuación la opción Guardar, utilice la instrucción de aceleración Alt-G para guardar el fichero** instead of selecting the File menu then the Save option, use the accelerator keys Alt and S to do the same thing and save the file

secuenciador *m* *sustantivo* sequencer

secuenciador *m* **MIDI** *sustantivo* MIDI sequencer

secuencial *adj* 1. linear 2. sequential 3. serial ◇ **intercambio secuencial de paquetes** sequential packet exchange (SPX)™ ◇ **interfaz en serie** *o* **acoplamiento mutuo en serie** *o* **interconexión en serie** serial interface ◇ **las conexiones en paralelo son normalmente menos problemáticas de instalar y utilizar que las interconexiones en serie, pero generalmente se limitan a una longitud de 6 metros** parallel connections are usually less trouble to set up and use than serial interfaces, but are usually limited to 6 metres in length ◇ **método de acceso secuencial en cola de espera** queued sequential access method (QSAM) ◇ **si la secuencia de entrada al circuito de lógica secuencial es 1101 la salida siempre es (0)** if the input sequence to the sequential logic circuit is 1101 the output will always be zero (0)

secuencialmente *adv* sequentially

secuencia *f* **MIDI** *sustantivo* MIDI sequence

secundario *adj* 1. peripheral 2. secondary ■ *prefijo* sub- ◇ **color secundario** secondary colour

segmentación *f* *sustantivo* fragmentation

segmentación *f* *sustantivo* fragmentation

segmento *m* *sustantivo* segment ◇ **segmento** *m* **de tiempo (en modo multitarea)** time slice

segmento *m* **de código** *sustantivo* code segment

segmento *m* **de programa** *sustantivo* program segment

segmento *m* **de tiempo** *sustantivo* time slice

segmento *m* **ejecutable** *sustantivo* section

segmentos *mpl* **superponibles** *plural noun* overlay segments

seguimiento *m* *sustantivo* activity trail ◇ **seguimiento** *m* **(de un programa)** trace

seguimiento *m* **automático** *sustantivo* auto trace

seguimiento *m* **de supresiones** *sustantivo* deletion tracking

seguir *verbo vt* to monitor

segunda pantalla *f* *sustantivo* slave tube

segundo *m* **plano** *sustantivo* background ◇ **el nuevo procesador de gráficos puede gestionar independientemente el movimiento del primer plano, del segundo plano y de otros objetos móviles planos** the new graphics processor chip can handle background, foreground and sprite movement independently

segundo término *m* **de una suma** *sustantivo* augmenter

según necesidades (del usuario) *adj* user-definable ◇ **la hoja de cálculo contiene 125 símbolos programables** the style sheet contains 125 user-definable symbols

seguridad ◇ **de seguridad** backup ◇ **seguridad** *f* **por nivel de operaciones compartidas** share level security

seguridad *f* **de (los) datos** *sustantivo* data protection

seguridad *f* **de la información** *sustantivo* data security

seguridad *f* **del equipo** *sustantivo* hardware security

seguridad *f* **de los datos** *sustantivo* data security

seguridad *f* **del sistema** *sustantivo* system security

seleccionable *adj* 1. selectable 2. user-selectable

seleccionar *verbo* 1. *vt* to enable 2. *vt* to filter 3. *vt* to select 4. *vt* to set ◇ **seleccionar colores de la paleta** to realise

selección *f* **de colores** *sustantivo* colour separation

selección *f* **de un chip** *sustantivo* chip select ■ *abrev* CS

selección *f* **en orden creciente** *sustantivo* forward mode

selección *f* **por intercambio** *sustantivo* exchange selection

selección *f* **por menú** *sustantivo* menu selection

selección *f* **por permutación** *sustantivo* bubble sort

selección *f* **por tonos** *sustantivo* tone dialling

selector *m* *sustantivo* selector ◇ **canal selector** *o* **de selección** selector channel ◇ **el mando del selector de amplitud se encuentra allí** the selector knob for the amplification is located there ◇ **gire el control del selector** turn the selector control

selector *m* **de puerto** *sustantivo* port selector

semáforo *m* *sustantivo* semaphore

semántica *f* *sustantivo* semantics

semi- *prefijo* semi-

semicompilado *adj* semicompiled

semiconductor *m* *sustantivo* semiconductor ◇ **láser semiconductor** semiconductor laser

semiconductor *m* **complementario de óxido metálico** *sustantivo* **1.** CMOS **2.** complementary metal oxide semiconductor

semiconductor *m* **de CMOS** *sustantivo* **1.** CMOS **2.** complementary metal oxide semiconductor

semiconductor *m* **de óxido metálico** *sustantivo* metal oxide semiconductor

semi-conductor *m* **de tipo N** *sustantivo* n-type material *o* n-type semiconductor

semi-conductor *m* **MOS** *sustantivo* MOS

semidúplex *m* *abrev* HDX

semidúplex *m* *sustantivo* **1.** half duplex **2.** HD

semilla *f* *sustantivo* seed

semi-octeto *m* *sustantivo* nibble

semi-octeto *m* *sustantivo* nybble *o* nibble

semiprocesados *sustantivo* semi-processed data

semisumador *sustantivo* half adder ■ *adj* two-input adder

semisumadora *f* **binaria** *sustantivo* binary half adder

semisumador *m* **binario** *sustantivo* binary half adder

señal *sustantivo* **1.** bookmark **2.** mark **3.** signal **4.** token ◇ **el elemento de señal de este sistema es un breve impulso de voltaje, que indica uno binario** the signal element in this system is a short voltage pulse, indicating a binary one ◇ **enviar una señal a la red para indicar que estamos ocupados** signal to the network that we are busy ◇ **generador de señal** signal generator ◇ **la señal recibida del ordenador contenía la respuesta** the signal received from the computer contained the answer ◇ **los elementos de señal del sistema de transmisión por radio son 10**

ms de 40 KHz para el binario 0 y 10 ms de 60 KHz para el binario 1 the signal elements for the radio transmission system are 10ms of 40KHz and 10ms of 60KHz for binary 0 and 1 respectively ◇ **relación entre señal y ruido** signal to noise ratio (S/N) ◇ **señal** *f* **de acuse de recibo positivo** ACK; acknowledge ◇ **señal** *f* **de captura de una instrucción** fetch signal ◇ **señal** *f* **de respuesta de un módem** answertone ◇ **señal** *f* **de validez de la dirección** address strobe ◇ **señales** proof correction marks

señal *f* **alta activa** *sustantivo* active high

señal *f* **analógica** *sustantivo* analog signal

señalar *verbo* **1.** *vt* to flag **2.** *vt* to point **3.** *vt* to signify ◇ **un código de retorno de carro señala el final de la línea** a carriage return code signifies the end of an input line

señal *f* **baja activa** *sustantivo* active low

señal *f* **bipolar** *sustantivo* bipolar signal

señal *f* **CD** *sustantivo* carrier detect

señal *f* **continua** *sustantivo* continuous signal

señal *f* **de aceptación de llamadas** *sustantivo* call accepted signal *o* call accept signal

señal *f* **de activación** *sustantivo* enabling signal

señal *f* **de alerta** *verbo* to beacon

señal *f* **de alineamiento** *sustantivo* alignment pin

señal *f* **de bloqueo** *sustantivo* inhibiting input

señal *f* **de control** *sustantivo* control token

señal *f* **de control de llamadas** *sustantivo* call control signal

señal *f* **de crominancia** *sustantivo* chrominance signal

señal *f* **de detección de portadora** *sustantivo* carrier detect

señal *f* **de ejecución** *sustantivo* execute signal

señal *f* **de entrada** *sustantivo* input

señal *f* **de fallo** *verbo* to beacon

señal *f* **de fin de arrastre** *sustantivo* carry complete signal

señal *f* **de incidente** *verbo* to beacon

señal *f* **de inicio de cinta** *sustantivo* BOT marker

señal *f* **de interrupción** *sustantivo* interrupt signal

señal *f* **de línea ocupada** *sustantivo* line busy tone

señal *f* **de llamada** *sustantivo* calling ◇ **dispositivo de llamadas** calling feature ◇ **sistema de llamadas** calling unit ◇ **unidad** calling unit

señal *f* **de modulación** *sustantivo* modulating signal

señal *f* **de portadora** *sustantivo* carrier signal

señal *f* **de preparado para recibir** *sustantivo* **1.** data set ready **2.** DSR

señal *f* **de profundidad** *sustantivo* depth cueing

señal f **de protección de escritura** *sustantivo* write-protect tab

señal f **de respuesta** *sustantivo* answer back

señal f **de retorno** *sustantivo* return to zero signal

señal f **de selección** *sustantivo* enabling signal

señal f **de sincronismo vertical** *sustantivo* vertical sync signal

señal f **de sincronización** *sustantivo* hold

señal f **de sincronización vertical** *sustantivo* vertical sync signal

señal f **de supervisión** *sustantivo* supervisory signal

señal f **de validación** *sustantivo* enabling signal

señal f **de vídeo** *sustantivo* video signal

señal f **de vídeo compuesta** *sustantivo* composite video

señal f **digital** *sustantivo* digital signal

señal f **digital de nivel cero** *sustantivo* **1.** digital signal level zero **2.** DS-0

señal f **digital de nivel uno** *sustantivo* **1.** digital signal level one **2.** DS-1

señales ◇ **señales** *fpl* **sincronizadas a los impulsos del reloj** clocked signals

señales *fpl* **cronometradas** *plural noun* clocked signals

señales *fpl* **de control** *plural noun* control signals

señales *fpl* **de instrucciones** *plural noun* control signals

señales *fpl* **de transmisión de datos** *plural noun* data signals

señales *fpl* **digitales** *sustantivo* digital signalling

señal f **espúrea** *sustantivo* drop in

señalización f *sustantivo* **1.** flagging **2.** signalling ◇ **señalización** f **de un programa almacenado en la memoria** stored program signalling

señalización f **binaria** *sustantivo* binary signalling

señalización f **de frecuencia única** *sustantivo* **1.** sf signalling **2.** single frequency signalling

señalización f **de límites** *sustantivo* (*de un fichero*) boundary punctuation

señalización f **dentro de banda** *sustantivo* in-band signalling

señalización f **en banda** *sustantivo* in-band signalling

señalización f **por canal común** *sustantivo* common channel signalling

señalización f **por frecuencia vocal** *sustantivo* in-band signalling

señalización f **por vía común** *sustantivo* common channel signalling

señalizador m *sustantivo* flag

señal f **modulada** *sustantivo* modulated signal

señal f **unipolar** *sustantivo* unipolar signal

sensibilidad f **a los rayos alfa** *sustantivo* alpha-particle sensitivity

sensibilidad f **del ratón** *sustantivo* mouse sensitivity

sensible *adj* sensitive ◇ **el ordenador es sensible incluso a los más mínimos cambios de tensión** the computer is sensitive even to very slight changes in current ◇ **las películas fotosensibles cambian cuando se exponen a la luz** light-sensitive films change when exposed to light

sensor m *sustantivo* sensor ◇ **la señal de salida del sensor varía según la temperatura** the sensor's output varies with temperature ◇ **una serie de sensores controlan el proceso** the process is monitored by a bank of sensors

sensor m **de imágenes** *sustantivo* image sensor

sentencia *sustantivo* statement ◇ **enunciado de observación** remark statement ◇ **sentencia** f **REM en un programa en BASIC** remark

sentencia f **de asignación** *sustantivo* assignment statement

sentencia f **de ejecución** *sustantivo* execute statement

sentencia f **de programa** *sustantivo* program statement

separación f **de colores** *sustantivo* colour separation

separación f **entre bloques** *abrev* IBG ■ *sustantivo* **1.** interblock gap **2.** interrecord gap

separación f **entre ficheros** *sustantivo* file gap

separación f **por guiones y justificación** *sustantivo* hyphenation and justification

separación f **silábica** *sustantivo* break

separación f **silábica de palabra** *sustantivo* word break

separación f **silábica inadecuada** *sustantivo* bad break

separador m *sustantivo* decollator

separador m **(de información)** *sustantivo* delimiter

separador, m f **-a de hojas** *sustantivo* burster

separador m **de argumentos** *sustantivo* argument separator ◇ **en la instrucción 'MULTIPLY A, B' se utiliza una coma como separador de argumentos** the command 'MULTIPLY A, B' uses a comma as the argument separator

separador m **de columnas** *sustantivo* column guide

separar *verbo* **1.** *vt* to decollate **2.** *vt* to filter ◇ **separar los elementos de un bloque** deblock

septeto m *sustantivo* septet

ser cabeza de lista *verbo* to head ◇ **mi fichero encabezaba la cola** the queue was headed by my file

serie f *sustantivo* **1.** array **2.** row **3.** series **4.** string ◇ **cada entrada se separa con una serie de puntos** each entry is separated by a row of dots ◇ **(en) serie** serial ◇ **serie** *f* **de programas** **(uno a continuación del otro)** suite of programs

serie *f* **(de productos)** *sustantivo* family

serie *f* **de cadenas de caracteres** *sustantivo* string array

serie *f* **de cifras** *sustantivo* numeric array

serie *f* **de errores consecutivos** *sustantivo* error burst

serie *f* **de instrucciones** *sustantivo* script ◇ **conecto automáticamente con el softwarede comunicación utilizando esta serie de instrucciones** I log in automatically using this script with my communications software

serie *f* **de palabras** *sustantivo* word serial

serie *f* **de tareas** *sustantivo* job stream

serie *f* **multidimensional** *sustantivo* multidimensional array

serie *f* **V** *sustantivo* V series

servicio *m* *sustantivo* **1.** facility **2.** service ◇ **ofrecemos servicios a nuestros clientes para el tratamiento de sus discos** we offer facilities for processing a customer's own disks ◇ **servicio** *m* **de comunicación de datos de conmutación de paquetes** packet switched data service ◇ **servicio** *m* **de conversación (en tiempo real) a través de internet** Internet relay chat; IRC ◇ **servicio** *m* **(proveedor) de información** information provider

servicio *m* **de acogida** *sustantivo* **1.** hosting service provider **2.** host service

servicio *m* **de asistencia técnica** *sustantivo* help desk

servicio *m* **de conmutación de paquetes** *sustantivo* packet switching service

servicio *m* **de contactos** *sustantivo* computer dating

servicio *m* **de información de gestión común** *sustantivo* common management information specification

servicio *m* **de llamadas** *sustantivo* **1.** dialup **2.** dial-up service

servicio *m* **del servidor de nombres** *sustantivo* naming services

servicio *m* **de mantenimiento** *sustantivo* maintenance ◇ **mantenimiento a distancia** remote maintenance ◇ **servicio de asistencia técnica en el propio lugar de trabajo** on-site maintenance

servicio *m* **de mensajes cortes** *sustantivo* short message service ■ *abrev* SMS

servicio *m* **de transferencia de mensajes** *sustantivo* **1.** message handling service **2.** MHS

servicio *m* **informático** *sustantivo* computer department

servicio *m* **informático de gestión** *sustantivo* management information service ■ *abrev* MIS

servicio *m* **postventa** *sustantivo* maintenance

servicio *m* **posventa** *sustantivo* customer service department

servicio *m* **proveedor secundario** *sustantivo* secondary service provider

servicios *plural noun* services ◇ **servicios** *mpl* **de red orientados a la conexión** connection-oriented network services

servicios *mpl* **de comunicaciones personales** *abrev* PCS ■ *plural noun* personal communications services

servicios *mpl* **de teleinformática** *plural noun* teleinformatic services

servicios *mpl* **disponibles en línea** *sustantivo* directory services ◇ **con los servicios en línea disponibles e incorporados al sistema, es mucho más fácil para nuestros usuarios encontrar y conectarse a las impresoras compartidas** with directory services installed, it's much easier for our users to find and connect to the shared printers

servicios *mpl* **fraccionados** *plural noun* fractional services ◇ **el operador (comercial) les venderá servicios fraccionados que proporcionan una transmisión de datos de 64 Kbps** the commercial carrier will sell you fractional services that provide 64Kbps data transmission

servicios *mpl* **fraccionales** *plural noun* fractional services ◇ **el operador (comercial) les venderá servicios fraccionados que proporcionan una transmisión de datos de 64 Kbps** the commercial carrier will sell you fractional services that provide 64Kbps data transmission

servicios *mpl* **informáticos** *plural noun* computer services

servicios *mpl* **partidos** *plural noun* fractional services ◇ **el operador (comercial) les venderá servicios fraccionados que proporcionan una transmisión de datos de 64 Kbps** the commercial carrier will sell you fractional services that provide 64Kbps data transmission

servidor *m* *sustantivo* host computer

servidor *sustantivo* **1.** end system **2.** host computer **3.** server ◇ **(programa) ejecutado por el servidor** server side ◇ **servidor** *m* **de correo (electrónico)** mail server ◇ **servidor** *m* **de información gratuito de área extendida** free WAIS

'La web, como universalmente se la conoce, es algo hecho a base de un cierto voluntarismo de los usuarios, aunque naturalmente ha sido ocupada por las grandes multinacionales y por los dueños de los servidores, los ordenadores que operan como incipientes reguladores del tráfico.' [*La Red*]

servidor *m* **auxiliar** *sustantivo* **1.** back-end server **2.** backup server

servidor *m* **de comunicaciones** *sustantivo* communications server

servidor *m* **de comunicaciones asíncronas** *sustantivo* **1.** ACS **2.** asynchronous communication server

servidor *m* **de control de acceso** *sustantivo* log on server

servidor *m* **de fax** *sustantivo* fax server

servidor *m* **de ficheros** *sustantivo* file server

servidor *m* **de impresión** *sustantivo* print server

servidor *m* **de impresora especializada** *sustantivo* dedicated print server

servidor *m* **de información de área amplia** *sustantivo* wide area information server

servidor *m* **de información de Internet** *sustantivo* Internet Information Server

servidor *m* **de nombres** *sustantivo* name server

servidor *m* **de páginas web** *sustantivo* web server

servidor *m* **de red** *sustantivo* network server

servidor *m* **de red local** *sustantivo* **1.** LAN server **2.** local area network server

servidor *m* **de seguridad** *sustantivo* backup server

servidores *mpl* **de información de área amplia** *sustantivo* WAIS

servidor *m* **intermediario** *sustantivo* proxy server

servidor *m* **seguro** *sustantivo* secure server

servidor *m* **WAIS** *sustantivo* free WAIS

sesgo *m* *sustantivo* skew

sesión ◇ **sesión** *f* **(de trabajo)** session

sesión *f* **de terminal** *sustantivo* terminal session

seudoestática *adj* pseudo-static

sexteto *m* *sustantivo* sextet

Shockwave (*marca comercial*) Shockwave

signatura *f* *sustantivo* signature

signatura *f* **electrónica** *sustantivo* electronic signature

significación *f* *sustantivo* significance

significado *m* *sustantivo* significance

significar *verbo* **1.** *vt* to mean **2.** *vt* to signify

significativo *adj* significant

signo *m* *sustantivo* sign

signo *m* **de interrogación** *sustantivo* question mark

signo *m* **de multiplicación (x)** *sustantivo* multiplication sign

signo *m* **de puntuación** *sustantivo* punctuation mark

signo *m* **de substracción** *sustantivo* minus *o* minus sign

signo *m* **de sumar** *sustantivo* plus *o* plus sign

signo *m* **menos** *sustantivo* minus *o* minus sign

signo *m* **tipográfico** *sustantivo* hashmark *o* hash mark

signo *m* **tipográfico #** *sustantivo* **1.** hash **2.** hash

signo y módulo *sustantivo* sign and modulus

silicio *m* *sustantivo* silicon ◇ **puerta de silicio** silicon gate ◇ **silicio sobre zafiro** silicon on sap-

phire (SOS) ◇ **transistor de silicio** silicon transistor

simbólico *adj* symbolic

símbolo *sustantivo* **1.** paragraph marker **2.** symbol ◇ **este lenguaje utiliza el símbolo ? para representar la instrucción de imprimir** this language uses the symbol ? to represent the print command ◇ **símbolo** *m* **^ (de la tecla Ctrl)** caret ◇ **símbolo gráfico** graphic symbol

símbolo *m* **aritmético** *sustantivo* arithmetic operator

símbolo *m* **de anotación** *sustantivo* annotation symbol

símbolo *m* **de detección** *sustantivo* aiming symbol *o* aiming field

símbolo *m* **de final de línea** *sustantivo* line ending

símbolo *m* **de intercalación** *sustantivo* caret

símbolo *m* **de interrupción** *sustantivo* breakpoint symbol

símbolo *m* **del dólar** *sustantivo* dollar sign

símbolo *m* **de punto y aparte** *sustantivo* paragraph marker

símbolo *m* **lógico** *sustantivo* logic symbol

símbolos ◇ **símbolos** *mpl* **de un diagrama de flujo** flowchart symbol

símbolos *mpl* **de un organigrama** *plural noun* flowchart symbol

símbolo *m* **separador de información** *sustantivo* separator

simetría *f* *sustantivo* balance

Simplex *m* *sustantivo* simplex

simulación *f* *sustantivo* simulation ◇ **las técnicas de simulación han alcanzado un nivel de sofisticación muy elevada** simulation techniques have reached a high degree of sophistication ◇ **programa de simulación** simulation software

simulación *f* **en tiempo real** *sustantivo* real-time simulation

simulador *m* *sustantivo* simulator

simulador *m* **de vuelo** *sustantivo* flight simulator

simular *verbo* *vt* to simulate ◇ **este programa simula el funcionamiento de un avión** this software simulates the action of an aeroplane

simultaneidad *f* *sustantivo* simultaneity

simultáneo *adj* simultaneous

sin acceso al ordenador *adj* hands off

sin componentes *adj* unpopulated

sin conexión *adj* connectionless

sin correcciones *adj* clean ◇ **prueba sin correcciones** clean proof

sincrónico *adj* synchronous

sincronización *f* *sustantivo* **1.** sync **2.** synchronisation

sincronización *f* **automática** *sustantivo* autosync

sincronización *f* **de bloques** *sustantivo* block synchronisation

sincronización *f* **del directorio** *sustantivo* directory synchronisation

sincronización *f* **de microprocesadores** *sustantivo* microprocessor timing

sincronización *f* **de red** *sustantivo* network timing

sincronizado *adj* synchronous

sincronizador *m sustantivo* synchroniser

sincronizador *m* **de canales** *sustantivo* channel synchroniser *o* channel synchronizer

sincronizador *m* **de vías** *sustantivo* channel synchroniser *o* channel synchronizer

sincronizar *verbo* **1.** *vt* to clock **2.** *vt* to synchronise ◇ **memoria dinámica sincrónica de acceso aleatorio** synchronized dynamic RAM (SDRAM)

síncrono *adj* synchronous

sin disco *adj* diskless

sin error *adj* clean

sin (estado de) espera *sustantivo* zero wait state

sin funcionar *adj, adv* down ◇ **el sistema informático quedó sin funcionar en dos ocasiones durante la tarde** the computer system went down twice during the afternoon

sin intervención manual *adj* hands off

sin justificar *adj* unjustified

sin módem *sustantivo* null modem

sin oscilación *adj* flicker-free

sin papel *adj* paperless

sin paridad *sustantivo* no parity

sin (bit de) paridad *sustantivo* no parity

sin parpadeo *adj* flicker-free

sin reflejos *adj* flicker-free

sin reserva *adj* unconditional

sin signo *adj* unsigned

sintaxis *f sustantivo* grammar ■ *plural noun* language rules ■ *sustantivo* syntax

síntesis *f sustantivo* synthesis

síntesis *f* **de voz** *sustantivo* **1.** speech synthesis **2.** speech synthesiser

síntesis *f* **vocal** *sustantivo* voice synthesis

sintetizador *m* **vocal** *sustantivo* voice synthesiser

sintonizar *verbo* *vt* to tune

'Según este modelo, el comerciante inicia el envío de información a unos nodos que actúan como canales de forma semejante a los de la radio y televisión, y que son 'sintonizados' por los usuarios.' [*PC Plus*]

sintonizar con precisión *verbo* to fine-tune

sistema *sustantivo* system ◇ **arquitectura SNA** *o* **arquitectura de red(es) de sistemas** Systems Network Architecture (SNA) ◇ **el nuevo programa no tendrá protección contra la copia** the new program will come without copy protection ◇ **ingeniero, -a de sistemas** systems engineer ◇ **sistema** *m* **automático de compen-**sación bancaria BACS; Bankers Automated Clearing Services ◇ **sistema** *m* **básico de control (vía satélite)** basic control system satellite; BCS ◇ **sistema** *m* **básico de E** *or* **S de red** Network Basic Input Output System ◇ **sistema** *m* **de administración de bases de datos** database management system; DBMS ◇ **sistema** *m* **de alternancia de fase por línea** PAL; phase alternation line ◇ **sistema** *m* **de arrastre (del papel)** feeder ◇ **sistema** *m* **de ayuda a la decisión** decision support system ◇ **sistema** *m* **de base de datos distribuida** distributed database system ◇ **sistema** *m* **de bases de conocimiento inteligentes** intelligent knowledge-based system ◇ **sistema** *m* **de codificación de caracteres de 8 bits** EBCDIC; extended binary coded decimal interchange code ◇ **sistema** *m* **de código de comprobación al azar** hash-code system ◇ **sistema** *m* **(Microsoft) de compartición de ficheros** server message block; SMB ◇ **sistema** *m* **de compensación y liquidación en el que intervien más de 130 bancos, trabajando con divisas y Eurodólares** Clearing House Interbank Payment System ◇ **sistema** *m* **de corrección de errores interactivo** interactive debugging system ◇ **sistema** *m* **de definición de colores: azul verdoso, morado, amarillo, negro** CMYK ◇ **sistema** *m* **de ficheros de alto rendimiento** high performance filing system; HPFS ◇ **sistema** *m* **de gestión de base de datos** database server ◇ **sistema** *m* **de gestión de la información** information management system ◇ **sistema** *m* **de información para la gestión** EIS; executive information system ◇ **sistema** *m* **de nombres y direcciones por dominios (en Internet)** DNS; domain name system ◇ **sistema** *m* **de páginas múltiples (para varios usuarios)** multiple base page ◇ **sistema** *m* **de (corriente) portadora** carrier system ◇ **sistema** *m* **de protección contra la copia** copy protection ◇ **sistema** *m* **de protección en caso de fallos** fail safe system ◇ **sistema** *m* **de reconocimiento de caracteres (por identificación de símbolos combinados)** combined symbol matching; CSM ◇ **sistema** *m* **de reserva de arranque semiautomático** warm standby ◇ **sistema** *m* **de reserva preparado para funcionar** hot standby ◇ **sistema** *m* **de seguridad en caso de fallos** fail safe system ◇ **sistema** *m* **interactivo de vídeo digital (DV-I)** digital video interactive; DV-I ◇ **sistema** *m* **intercalado (en otro)** embedded system ◇ **sistema** *m* **intermedio a sistema intermedio** intermediate system to intermediate system; IS-IS ◇ **sistema operativo** operating system (op sys) ◇ **sistema** *m* **operativo básico de entrada y salida** basic input/output operating system; BIOS ◇ **sistema** *m* **operativo de CD en tiempo real** CDRTOS ◇ **sistema** *m* **operativo de línea de instrucciones** command line operating system ◇ **sistema** *m* **(de tratamiento) por lotes** batch system ◇ **un disco duro puede fallar debido a una protección contra la copia defectuosa** a hard disk may crash because of faulty copy protection

'El reconocimiento de habla trata de identificar qué palabras dice el hablante. Una de las formas típicas en las que aparece pueden ser los sistemas de información telefónica: 'Si quiere hablar con Ventas diga en voz clara y fuerte: uno; si quiere hablar con Atención al cliente, dos ...'.' *[Internet y el español]*

sistema *m* **abierto** *sustantivo* open system

sistema *m* **adaptable** *sustantivo* adaptive system

sistema *m* **arborescente de red** *sustantivo* tree and branch network system

sistema *m* **asesor** *sustantivo* advisory system

sistema *m* **autoadaptable** *sustantivo* adaptive system

sistema *m* **auto-adaptable** *sustantivo* self-adapting system

sistema *m* **autocomprobador** *sustantivo* self-checking system

sistema *m* **automático de llamada** *sustantivo* auto-dial

sistema *m* **automático de llamadas** *sustantivo* 1. ACU 2. automatic calling unit

sistema *m* **automático de nueva llamada** *sustantivo* auto-redial

sistema *m* **autoverificador** *sustantivo* self-checking system

sistema *m* **basado en el conocimiento** *sustantivo* knowledge-based system

sistema *m* **basado en reglas** *sustantivo* rule-based system

sistema *m* **binario** *sustantivo* binary system

sistema *m* **BIOS** *sustantivo* 1. basic input/output operating system 2. BIOS

sistema *m* **cifrado** *sustantivo* cipher system

sistema *m* **cifrado de clave pública** *sustantivo* public key cipher system

sistema *m* **con muchos terminales** *sustantivo* multi terminal system

sistema *m* **de 32 bits** *sustantivo* thirty-two bit system *o* 32-bit system

sistema *m* **de acceso múltiple** *sustantivo* multiple access system

sistema *m* **de alimentación** *sustantivo* feeder

sistema *m* **de almacenaje e indexación** *sustantivo* aspect system

sistema *m* **de almacenamiento masivo** *sustantivo* mass storage system

sistema *m* **de archivo** *sustantivo* filing system

sistema *m* **de archivos de red** *sustantivo* network file system

sistema *m* **de autor** *sustantivo* 1. authoring software *o* authoring system 2. authoring software *o* authoring system

sistema *m* **de base de datos** *sustantivo* database system

sistema *m* **de bus múltiple** *sustantivo* 1. multibus system *o* multibus architecture 2. multiple bus system *o* multiple bus architecture

sistema *m* **de clasificación** *sustantivo* filing system

sistema *m* **de comandos numéricos** *sustantivo* 1. flexible machining system 2. FMS

sistema *m* **de conmutación de paquetes** *abrev* PSS

sistema *m* **de control de proceso** *sustantivo* process control system

sistema *m* **de desarrollo de programas** *sustantivo* program development system

sistema *m* **de desconexión progresiva** *sustantivo* fail soft system

sistema *m* **de doble densidad** *sustantivo* double density

sistema *m* **de emergencia** *sustantivo* (*preparado para funcionar*) hot standby

sistema *m* **de enlace común cerrado** *sustantivo* closed bus system

sistema *m* **de enlace común doble** *sustantivo* dual bus system

sistema *m* **de ensamblaje** *sustantivo* 1. assembly routine 2. assembly system

sistema *m* **de entrega** *sustantivo* delivery system

sistema *m* **de fabricación flexible** *sustantivo* flexible manufacturing system

sistema *m* **de ficheros compartidos** *sustantivo* distributed file system

sistema *m* **de ficheros distribuidos** *sustantivo* distributed file system

sistema *m* **de gestión de la información** *abrev* IMS

sistema *m* **de imagen** *sustantivo* imaging system

sistema *m* **de información** *sustantivo* information system

sistema *m* **de información para administración** *abrev* MIS

sistema *m* **de llamada automática** *sustantivo* ring back system

sistema *m* **de llave en mano** *sustantivo* turnkey system

sistema *m* **de lógica compartida** *sustantivo* shared logic system

sistema *m* **de mensajería electrónica** *sustantivo* computer-based message system

sistema *m* **de microprocesador** *abrev* MPS

sistema *m* **de monoprogramación** *sustantivo* monoprogramming system

sistema *m* **de múltiples conexiones** *sustantivo* multilink system

sistema *m* **de multiproceso** *sustantivo* multiprocessing system

sistema *m* **de operación** *sustantivo* executive control program

sistema *m* **de primero en entrar primero en salir** *sustantivo* first in first out

sistema *m* **de prioridades en paralelo** *sustantivo* parallel priority system

sistema *m* **de recuperación de referencia** *sustantivo* reference retrieval system

sistema *m* **de recursos compartidos** *sustantivo* shared resources system

sistema *m* **de red Xerox** Xerox Network System

sistema *m* **de reserva** *sustantivo* **1.** low-power standby **2.** standby equipment

sistema *m* **de reserva en frío** *sustantivo* cold standby

sistema *m* **de reserva manual** *sustantivo* cold standby

sistema *m* **de seguridad** *sustantivo* secure system

sistema *m* **de software** *sustantivo* software system

sistema *m* **de tablón de anuncios** *sustantivo* **1.** BBS **2.** bulletin board *o* bulletin board system

sistema *m* **de transferencia de memoria** *sustantivo* memory switching system

sistema *m* **de transmisión digital** *sustantivo* digital transmission system

sistema *m* **de tratamiento de imágenes** *sustantivo* image processor

sistema *m* **de un solo usuario** *sustantivo* single-user system

sistema *m* **digital** *sustantivo* digital system

sistema *m* **dinámico** *sustantivo* adaptive system

sistema *m* **distribuido** *sustantivo* distributed system

sistema *m* **DNS** *sustantivo* **1.** DNS **2.** domain name system

sistema *m* **doble** *plural noun* dual systems

sistema *m* **duodecimal** *sustantivo* duodecimal number system

sistema *m* **dúplex** *sustantivo* duplex computer

sistema *m* **EIS** *sustantivo* **1.** EIS **2.** executive information system

sistema *m* **(informático) empresarial** *sustantivo* business system

sistema *m* **en caliente** *sustantivo* hot standby

sistema *m* **en línea** *sustantivo* online system

sistema *m* **en tiempo real** *sustantivo* real-time system ◇ **en un sistema de tiempo real, al mover el mando de juegos hacia la izquierda, la imagen de la pantalla se mueve hacia la izquierda. En cambio, no es un verdadero sistema en tiempo real si hay una pausa para su proceso** in a real-time system, as you move the joystick left, the image on the screen moves left. If there is a pause for processing it is not a true real-time system

sistema *m* **experto** *sustantivo* **1.** expert system **2.** intelligent knowledge-based system **3.** knowledge-based system

sistema *m* **extensible** *sustantivo* expandable system

sistema *m* **global de comunicaciones móviles** *sustantivo* **1.** global system for mobile communications **2.** GSM

sistema *m* **híbrido** *sustantivo* hybrid system

sistema *m* **independiente** *sustantivo* stand-alone system

sistema *m* **indeterminado** *sustantivo* indeterminate system

sistema *m* **informático** *sustantivo* **1.** computer system **2.** information system

sistema *m* **informático de gestión** *sustantivo* management information system

sistema *m* **informático integrado** *sustantivo* computer-integrated system

sistema *m* **informático maestro/maestro** *sustantivo* master/master computer system

sistema *m* **informático maestro/satélite** *sustantivo* master/slave computer system

sistema *m* **informático para oficinas** *sustantivo* computer office system

sistema *m* **integrada por ordenador** *sustantivo* computer-integrated system

sistema *m* **interactivo** *sustantivo* interactive system

sistema *m* **intermedio** *sustantivo* intermediate system ■ *abrev* IS

sistema *m* **jerárquico de comunicación** *sustantivo* hierarchical communications system

sistema *m* **jerárquico de ficheros** *sustantivo* **1.** HFS **2.** hierarchical filing system

sistema *m* **latente** *sustantivo* sleep

sistema *m* **manual** *adj* hands on

sistema *m* **multibús** *sustantivo* **1.** multibus system *o* multibus architecture **2.** multiple bus system *o* multiple bus architecture

sistema *m* **multiplexado** *sustantivo* carrier system

sistema *m* **multiterminal** *sustantivo* multi terminal system

sistema *m* **multiusuario** *sustantivo* **1.** multi-user system **2.** shared resources system **3.** TOPS

sistema *m* **ofimático** *sustantivo* computer office system

sistema *m* **operativo** *sustantivo* **1.** operating system **2.** OS

sistema *m* **operativo de disco** *sustantivo* **1.** disk operating system **2.** DOS ◇ **arranque el sistema operativo DOS después de conectar el ordenador** boot up the DOS after you switch on the PC ◇ **(sistema operativo) DR-DOS™** DR-DOS™

sistema *m* **operativo de red** *sustantivo* network operating system ■ *abrev* NOS

sistema *m* **operativo DOS** *sustantivo* DOS ◇ **arranque el sistema operativo DOS después de conectar el ordenador** boot up the DOS after you switch on the PC

sistema *m* **operativo en tiempo real** *sustantivo* real-time operating system

sistema *m* **operativo simultáneo** *sustantivo* concurrent operating system

sistema *m* **operativo transparente** *sustantivo* TOPS

sistema *m* **(electro)óptico de comunicaciones** *sustantivo* optical communication system

sistema *m* **PAL** *sustantivo* **1.** PAL **2.** phase alternation line

sistema *m* **para entrada/salida gráfica** *sustantivo* **1.** GKS **2.** graphics kernel system

sistema *m* **para máquina flexible** *sustantivo* **1.** flexible machining system **2.** FMS

sistema *m* **piloto** *sustantivo* pilot system

sistemas *mpl* **de control** *plural noun* control systems

sistema *m* **secundario** *sustantivo* subsystem

sistema *m* **seguro** *sustantivo* secure system

sistema *m* **sincrónico** *sustantivo* synchronous system

sistema *m* **síncrono** *sustantivo* synchronous system

sistema *m* **supervisor** *sustantivo* run-time system

sistema *m* **tolerante al fallo** *sustantivo* fail soft system

sistema *m* **TOPS** *sustantivo* TOPS

sistema *m* **transaccional** *sustantivo* **1.** TDS **2.** transaction-driven system

sistema *m* **tutorial inteligente** *sustantivo* intelligent tutoring system

sitio *sustantivo* **1.** place **2.** site

'Los candidatos a las elecciones sentirán vivamente la necesidad de ocupar su 'sitio', crear su 'página' y responder en directo a las preguntas de sus electores.' [*La Red*]

sitio *m* **anquilosado** *sustantivo* cobweb site

sitio *m* **de archivo** *sustantivo* archive site

sitio *m* **de espejo** *sustantivo* mirror site

sitio *m* **seguro** *sustantivo* **1.** secure site **2.** secure website

sitio *m* **web** *sustantivo* website

situación *f* **para recepción de instrucciones** *sustantivo* command state

situar *verbo vt* to locate

situarse en la cola *verbo* to queue ◇ **método de acceso secuencial en cola de espera** queued sequential access method (QSAM)

Smalltalk™ Smalltalk

smiley *m* *sustantivo* smiley

snd *sustantivo* snd

SNOBOL *sustantivo* SNOBOL

sobrebarrido *m* *sustantivo* overscan

sobrebarrido *m* *sustantivo* overscan

sobrecarga *f* *sustantivo* **1.** overflow **2.** overrun

sobrecarga *f* **de canal** *sustantivo* channel overload

sobrecarga *f* **de funciones** *sustantivo* function overloading

sobrecarga *f* **de una vía** *sustantivo* channel overload

sobrecarga *f* **de un operador** *sustantivo* operator overloading

sobrecargar *verbo vt* to overload

sobredesviación *f* *sustantivo* overscan

sobreescribir *verbo vt* to overwrite ◇ **los nuevos datos introducidos han reemplazado la información anterior** the latest data input has overwritten the old information

sobreimpresión *f* *sustantivo* multipass overlap

sobreperforación *f* *sustantivo* overpunching

sobretensión *f* **transitoria** *sustantivo* surge

sobrevoltaje *m* *sustantivo* surge

sociedad ◇ **sociedad** *m* **internet** Internet Society

'Una de las mayores repercusiones de la Sociedad de la Información sobre la empresa está en el ámbito del empleo, en donde se registra una demanda creciente de expertos en las tecnologías de la información y la comunicación (TIC).' [*PC Plus*]

'Una nueva estructura social, la sociedad red, se está estableciendo en todo el planeta, en formas diversas y con consecuencias bastante diferentes para la vida de las personas, según su historia, cultura e instituciones.' [*La galaxia Internet*]

sofisticación *f* *sustantivo* sophistication

sofisticado *adj* sophisticated

software *sustantivo* **1.** communications package **2.** software ◇ **software** *m* **(programado) a medida** bespoke software ◇ **software** *m* **(en versión) beta** beta software; betaware ◇ **software de red** network software ◇ **software** *m* **espía** spyware ◇ **software** *m* **incluido en la compra de un ordenador** bundled software ◇ **software** *m* **para realiza exposiciones orales o escritas** presentation software ◇ **software** *m* **por definir (mediante parámetros)** parameter-driven software ◇ **software** *m* **sólo para reproducción de vídeo** software-only video playback ◇ **software** *m* **variable** (*adaptable al número de usuarios*) scalable software

'¿Sería factible un sistema software libre para la creación de herramientas lingüísticas en una lengua? Digamos, por una parte, que ya ha demostrado que sirve para crear softwares complejos.' [*Internet y el español*]

software *m* **a distancia** *sustantivo* remote control software ◇ **este software de control remoto funciona con Windows y me permite utilizar el ordenador de mi oficina desde mi casa con una conexión por módem** this remote control software will work with Windows and lets me operate my office PC from home over a modem link

software *m* **al servicio del público** *sustantivo* freeware

software *m* **antivirus** *sustantivo* **1.** anti-virus software **2.** virus checker

software *m* **antropomórfico** *sustantivo* anthropomorphic software

software *m* **compartido** *sustantivo* common software

software *m* **común** *sustantivo* common software

software *m* **de adaptación** *sustantivo* bridgeware

software *m* **de agenda** *sustantivo* scheduler

software *m* **de aplicaciones** *sustantivo* application software

software *m* **de aplicación especializada** *sustantivo* single function software

software *m* **de barrido** *sustantivo* scanning software

software *m* **de calendario** *sustantivo* calendar program

software *m* **de compresión de disco** *sustantivo* disk compression software

software *m* **de comunicación** *sustantivo* communications software

software *m* **de control de periféricos** *sustantivo* device driver

software *m* **de control remoto** *sustantivo* remote control software ◇ **este software de control remoto funciona con Windows y me permite utilizar el ordenador de mi oficina desde mi casa con una conexión por módem** this remote control software will work with Windows and lets me operate my office PC from home over a modem link

software *m* **de desarrollo** *sustantivo* development software

software *m* **de diseño gráfico** *sustantivo* graphics software

software *m* **de fácil uso** *sustantivo* user-friendly software

software *m* **definido** *sustantivo* parameter-driven software

software *m* **de función única** *sustantivo* single function software

software *m* **de gestión de periféricos** *sustantivo* device driver

software *m* **del sistema** *sustantivo* system software

software *m* **de memoria intensiva** *sustantivo* memory-intensive software

software *m* **de red** *sustantivo* **1.** common software **2.** networking software **3.** network software

software *m* **didáctico** *sustantivo* courseware

software *m* **gráfico** *sustantivo* graphics software

software *m* **gratuito** *sustantivo* freeware

software *m* **residente** *sustantivo* **1.** memory-resident software **2.** resident software

solapamiento *m* *sustantivo* **1.** lap **2.** overlap

solapamiento *m* **multiciclo** *sustantivo* multipass overlap

solapar(se) *verbo vr* to overlap

solicitar línea *verbo* to bid ◇ **el terminal tuvo que pedir línea tres veces antes de que hubiera un hueco en las transmisiones de la red** the terminal had to bid three times before there was a gap in transmissions on the network

solicitud ◇ **solicitud** *f* **automática de corrección (de errores) ARQ** ARQ; automatic repeat request ◇ **solicitud** *f* **automática de repetición (de errores) ARQ** ARQ; automatic repeat request

sólido *adj* **1.** hard **2.** robust **3.** solid ◇ **este disco duro no es muy sólido** this hard disk is not very robust

soltar *verbo vt* to release

solución *f* **improvisada** *sustantivo* kludge *o* kluge

sondeo *m* *sustantivo* polling

sonido *m* *sustantivo* sound

sonido *m* **ambiente** *sustantivo* ambient noise ◇ **el nivel de sonido ambiente de la oficina es superior al de la biblioteca** the ambient noise level in the office is greater than in the library

sonido *m* **binaural** *sustantivo* binaural sound

Sony (*empresa innovadora*) Sony

soportar *verbo vt* to support

soporte *sustantivo* support ◇ **en soporte magnético** soft ◇ **los componentes lógicos de comunicaciones dependen del equipo y sólo funcionan con un módem compatible de tipo Hayes** the communications software is hardware dependent and will only work with Hayes-compatible modems ◇ **soporte** *m* **de fuerza de introducción nula** zero insertion force socket ◇ **soporte** *m* **de tarjetas (de circuitos impresos)** card chassis ◇ **soporte** *m* **físico (del ordenador)** hardware

soporte *m* **de datos** *sustantivo* **1.** data carrier **2.** data medium

soporte *m* **de fuerza de introducción nula** *sustantivo* ZIF socket

soporte *m* **de información** *sustantivo* data medium

soporte *m* **de tarjeta de extensión** *sustantivo* card extender

soporte *m* **lógico** *sustantivo* software

soporte *m* **lógico del sistema informático** *sustantivo* firmware

soporte *m* **lógico gratuito** *sustantivo* freeware

soporte *m* **lógico inalterable** *sustantivo* firmware

soporte *m* **lógico por cuota** *sustantivo* shareware

soporte *m* **magnético** *sustantivo* **1.** magnetic material **2.** magnetic medium

soporte *m* **magnético original** *sustantivo* magnetic master

soporte *m* **magnético vacío** *sustantivo* empty medium

soporte *m* **puente informático** *sustantivo* bridgeware

soportes *mpl* **magnéticos** *plural noun* magnetic media

soporte *m* **vacío** *sustantivo* empty medium

Sound Blaster (*marca comercial*) Sound Blaster

spam *m sustantivo* spam

'spooler' *m sustantivo* spooler

'spooling' *m sustantivo* spooling

'sprite' *m sustantivo* sprite

suave *adj* soft

suavizar *verbo* 1. *vt* to deaden 2. *vt* to dither

sub- *prefijo* sub-

subclase *f sustantivo* subclass

subconjunto *m sustantivo* subset

subdirección *f sustantivo* subaddress

subdirectorio *m sustantivo* subdirectory

subdividir *verbo vt* to partition

subdominio *m sustantivo* sub-domain

subida *f sustantivo* upgrade

subíndice *m sustantivo* 1. inferior figure 2. subscript

subir *verbo vi* to ascend

submenú *m sustantivo* submenu

subprograma *sustantivo* 1. subprogram 2. subroutine ◇ **subprograma** *m* **de un (solo) nivel** one-level subroutine

sub-programa *m sustantivo* bead

subprograma *m* **paramétrica** *sustantivo* parametric subroutine

subrayado *m sustantivo* 1. underline 2. underlining ◇ **a los títulos de los capítulos se les pone un doble subrayado y a los párrafos un subrayado simple** the chapter headings are given a double underline and the paragraphs a single underline

subrayar *verbo* 1. *vt* to underline 2. *vt* to underscore

subred *f sustantivo* subnet

subrutina *f sustantivo* 1. one-level subroutine 2. subroutine

subrutina *f* **abierta** *sustantivo* open subroutine

sub-rutina *f* **cerrada** *sustantivo* closed subroutine

subrutina *f* **de biblioteca** *sustantivo* library subroutine

subrutina *f* **de dos niveles** *sustantivo* two-level subroutine

subrutina *f* **de inserción directa** *sustantivo* direct-insert routine

subrutina *f* **dinámica** *sustantivo* dynamic subroutine

subrutina *f* **enlazada** *sustantivo* linked subroutine

subrutina *f* **estándar** *sustantivo* standard subroutine

subrutina *f* **estática** *sustantivo* static subroutine

subrutina *f* **insertada** *sustantivo* inserted subroutine

subrutina *f* **paramétrica** *sustantivo* parametric subroutine

subrutinas matemáticas *plural noun* mathematical subroutines

subsegmento *m sustantivo* subsegment

subsistema *m sustantivo* subsystem

sucesión *f* **de impulsos** *sustantivo* 1. pulse stream 2. pulse train

suceso *m sustantivo* event

sufijo *m sustantivo* postfix

suma *f sustantivo* 1. addition 2. sum

suma *f* **de comprobación** *sustantivo* checksum *o* check total

suma *f* **de control** *sustantivo* checksum *o* check total

suma *f* **destructiva** *sustantivo* destructive addition

suma *f* **de verificación** *sustantivo* 1. checksum *o* check total 2. residue check ◇ **los datos deben ser erróneos si el total de verificación es distinto** the data must be corrupted if the checksum is different

sumador *m sustantivo* adder

sumadora *f sustantivo* adder

sumadora *f* **de tres entradas** *sustantivo* 1. full adder 2. three input adder

sumadora *f* **total** *sustantivo* 1. full adder 2. three input adder

sumador *m* **BCD** *sustantivo* BCD adder

sumador *m* **binario** *sustantivo* 1. BCD adder 2. binary adder

sumador *m* **en paralelo** *sustantivo* parallel adder

sumador *m* **en serie** *sustantivo* serial adder

sumador-restador *m sustantivo* adder-subtractor

sumador *m* **serial** *sustantivo* serial adder

sumando *m sustantivo* 1. augend 2. augmenter

sumando *m sustantivo* (*cada una de las cantidades que se suman*) addend

sumar *verbo vt* to add ◇ **en la hoja de cálculo debe sumarse cada columna para obtener un total parcial** in the spreadsheet each column should be added to make a subtotal

suma *f* **sin llevar** *sustantivo* addition without carry

suma *f* **total** *sustantivo* checksum *o* check total ◇ **los datos deben ser erróneos si el total de verificación es distinto** the data must be corrupted if the checksum is different

sumidero *m sustantivo* sink

sumidero *m* **térmico** *sustantivo* heat-sink

suministrador ◇ **suministrador** *m* **de servicios de internet** Internet service provider

suministrar *verbo* 1. *vt* to power 2. *vt* to supply ◇ **el monitor se alimenta del suministro eléctrico de la unidad central** the monitor is powered from a supply in the main PC ◇ **el ordenador nos lo proporcionó un distribuidor conocido** the computer was supplied by a recognized dealer ◇ **(aparato) que funciona** *o* **accionado (con electricidad, etc.)** powered (by)

suministro *m sustantivo* supply ◇ **han firmado un contrato para el suministro de papel**

continuo they signed a contract for the supply of computer stationery

suministro *m* **de alimentación** *sustantivo* PSU

suministro *m* **de corriente controlada** *sustantivo* regulated power supply

suministro *m* **de energía** *sustantivo* PSU

suministro *m* **de energía/de alimentación** *sustantivo* power supply

suministro *m* **eléctrico ininterrumpido** *sustantivo* **1.** uninterruptible power supply **2.** UPS

suministro *m* **ininterrumpible de energía** *sustantivo* **1.** uninterruptible power supply **2.** UPS

super- *prefijo* **1.** super- **2.** ultra- ◇ **super-alta frecuencia (UHF)** *o* **onda decimétrica** ultra high frequency (UHF) ◇ **supergrupo** supergroup ◇ **(estándar de pantalla) super VGA** *o* **SVGA** super VGA (SVGA)

super-alta frecuencia *f* **(UHF)** *sustantivo* UHF

super-alta frecuencia *f* **UHF)** *sustantivo* ultra high frequency

superficie *f sustantivo* deck

superfluo *adj* redundant ◇ **los bits de paridad de los datos recibidos son superfluos y pueden eliminarse** the parity bits on the received data are redundant and can be removed

superíndice *m sustantivo* **1.** superior number **2.** superscript

superordenador *m sustantivo* **1.** number cruncher **2.** supercomputer

superponer *verbo* **1.** *vt* to piggyback **2.** *vt* to superimpose ◇ **los nuevos datos introducidos han reemplazado la información anterior** the latest data input has overwritten the old information ◇ **superponer datos y destruir los datos de la memoria** overwrite ◇ **superponga los dos chips para potenciar la capacidad de memoria** piggyback those two memory chips to boost the memory capacity

superponer(se) *verbo* vr to overlap

superponer información en ventanas *verbo* to window

superposición *f sustantivo* overlap ◇ **tiempo de superposición** overlap time

super VGA/SVGA *sustantivo* super VGA

supervisar *verbo* vt to monitor

supervisión *f* **hacia atrás** *sustantivo* backwards supervision

supervisor *m sustantivo* supervisor

supervisor *m* **de entrada/salida** *sustantivo* input/output executive

supresión *sustantivo* deletion ◇ **supresión** *f* **de señal de llamada parásita** anti-tinkle suppression

supresión *f* **de eco(s)** *sustantivo* echo cancellation

supresión *f* **de ficheros** *sustantivo* file deletion

supresión *f* **de una señal** *sustantivo* blanking

supresor *m sustantivo* suppressor ◇ **supresor de ecos** echo suppressor

supresor *m* **de módem** *sustantivo* modem eliminator

suprimir *verbo* **1.** *vt* to delete **2.** *vt* to kill **3.** *vt* to scrub ◇ **el tratamiento de textos nos permite suprimir un fichero completo al pulsar esta tecla** the word-processor allows us to delete the whole file by pressing this key

suscribir *verbo* vt to subscribe

suspender *verbo* vt to hang ■ *sustantivo* vt suspend

sustancia *f* **protectora fotosensible** *sustantivo* photoresist ◇ **para hacer una placa de circuito impreso, recubra la placa con una sustancia protectora fotosensible, coloque encima el diseño opaco, expóngalo, revélelo y grábelo dejando las guías conductoras** to make the PCB, coat the board with photoresist, place the opaque pattern above, expose, then develop and etch, leaving the conducting tracks

sustancia *f* **protectora fotosensible en positivo** *sustantivo* positive photoresist

sustituir *verbo* **1.** *vt* to substitute **2.** *vt* to supersede ◇ **el nuevo programa sustituye al anterior y, además, es mucho más rápido** the new program supersedes the earlier one, and is much faster

sustracción *f sustantivo* subtraction

sustraendo *m sustantivo* subtrahend

sustrato *m sustantivo* substrate

SVGA (conjunto de gráficos de supervídeo) *sustantivo* SVGA

SX *sustantivo* SX

T

T-1 fraccional *sustantivo* fractional T-1

tabla *sustantivo* **1.** spreadsheet **2.** table ◇ **tabla** *f* **de asignación de ficheros** file allocation table ◇ **tabla** *f* **de clasificación de los ficheros de un disco** disk map ◇ **tabla** *f* **de control de colores de pantalla** video lookup table ◇ **tabla de ficheros del sistema** system file table ◇ **tabla** *f* **de páginas** (*de la memoria paginada*) page table ◇ **tabla** *f* **de referencia de un programa** reference program table ◇ **tabla de referencias cruzadas** cross-reference table ◇ **tabla** *f* **flexible (de dimensiones variables)** flexible array

tabla *f sustantivo* table

tabla *f* **(impresa)** *sustantivo* spreadsheet

tabla *f* **de bifurcación** *sustantivo* branch table

tabla *f* **de Boole** *sustantivo* Boolean operation table

tabla *f* **de comprobación al azar** *sustantivo* hash table

tabla *f* **de consulta de colores** *sustantivo* colour look-up table

tabla *f* **de control** *sustantivo* (*de dispositivos procesos*) image table

tabla *f* **de correspondencia de direcciones** *sustantivo* address mapping

tabla *f* **de decisión** *sustantivo* decision table

tabla *f* **de decisión lógica** *sustantivo* truth table

tabla *f* **de envío** *sustantivo* routing table

tabla *f* **de equivalencia** *sustantivo* substitution table

tabla *f* **de funciones** *sustantivo* function table

tabla *f* **de indicadores** *sustantivo* indicator chart

tabla *f* **de interrupciones prioritarias** *sustantivo* priority interrupt table

tabla *f* **de nombres** *sustantivo* name table

tabla *f* **de onda** *sustantivo* wavetable ◇ **síntesis de tabla de onda** wave table synthesis

tabla *f* **de operaciones booleanas** *sustantivo* Boolean operation table

tabla *f* **de página(s) sombra duplicada(s)** *sustantivo* shadow page table

tabla *f* **de prioridades de interrupción** *sustantivo* priority interrupt table

tabla *f* **de proceso** *sustantivo* process chart

tabla *f* **de referencia** *sustantivo* **1.** look-up table **2.** LUT **3.** reference table ◇ **utilice la tabla de equivalencia para encontrar el valor ASCII** this is the value of the key pressed, use a lookup table to find its ASCII value

tabla *f* **de símbolos** *sustantivo* name table

tabla *f* **de sustitución** *sustantivo* substitution table

tabla *f* **de verdad** *sustantivo* truth table

tabla *f* **FAT** *sustantivo* file allocation table

tabla *f* **gráfica** *sustantivo* graphics pad

tablas *f* **de conversión** *plural noun* translation tables

tablas *fpl* **de conversión** *plural noun* conversion tables

tablas *f* **de equivalencias** *plural noun* translation tables

tablas *fpl* **de equivalencias** *plural noun* conversion tables

tablas *f* **de referencia** *plural noun* translation tables

tablero *m sustantivo* notice board

tablero *m* **de control** *sustantivo* control panel

tableta *f* **(de datos)** *sustantivo* tablet

tableta *f* **gráfica** *sustantivo* graphics tablet

tablilla *f sustantivo* digitising pad *o* digitising tablet *o* digitizing pad *o* digitizing tablet

tablilla *f* **(de datos)** *sustantivo* tablet

tablilla *f* **gráfica** *sustantivo* data tablet

tablón *m* **de anuncios** *sustantivo* notice board

tablón *m* **de mensajes** *sustantivo* message board

tablón *m* **digital** *sustantivo* digital read-out

tabulación *f sustantivo* **1.** tabbing **2.** tabulation ◇ **la tabulación puede hacerse desde el interior del programa** tabbing can be done from inside the program

tabulación *f* **decimal** *sustantivo* decimal tabbing

tabulación *f* **vertical** *sustantivo* vertical tab

tabulado *m sustantivo* tabbing

tabulador *m sustantivo* tabulator

tabular *verbo* vt to tab ■ *abrev* vt TAB ■ *verbo* vt to tabulate ◇ **la lista quedó bien alineada al tabular hasta la columna 10 al inicio de cada nueva línea** the list was neatly lined up by tabbing to column 10 at the start of each new line

tabular hacia atrás *verbo* to backtab

táctil *adj* touch

Taligent *sustantivo* Taligent

taller *m* **de encuadernación** *sustantivo* Bindery

tamaño *m sustantivo* size ◇ **hemos aumentado el tamaño de la letra para que resulte más fácil de leer** the size of the print has been increased to make it easier to read ◇ **tamaño** *o* **formato de la página** page size

tamaño *m* **de (los) caracteres** *sustantivo* (*medidos en puntos*) type size

tamaño *m* **de la memoria** *sustantivo* storage capacity

tamaño *m* **de la memoria intermedia** *sustantivo* buffer size

tamaño *m* **de la muestra** *sustantivo* sample size

tamaño *m* **del entorno** *sustantivo* environment space

tamaño *m* **del equipo** *sustantivo* environment space

tamaño *m* **del fichero** *sustantivo* file extent

tamaño *m* **de (la) pantalla** *sustantivo* screen size

tamaño *m* **de un campo** *sustantivo* field length

tamaño *m* **de un contador** *sustantivo* register length

tamaño *m* **de un fichero** *sustantivo* **1.** file length **2.** file size

tamaño *m* **de un ítem** *sustantivo* item size

tamaño *m* **de un registro** *sustantivo* **1.** record length **2.** register length

tambor *m sustantivo* drum

tambor *m* **magnético** *sustantivo* magnetic drum

tándem *m sustantivo* tandem

tapa *f sustantivo* hood

tarea *f sustantivo* **1.** job **2.** task ◇ **la siguiente tarea consiste en clasificar todos los registros** the next job to be processed is to sort all the records ◇ **tarea** *f* **de ejecución automática** (*de un sistema*) unattended operation

tarea *f* **de baja prioridad** *sustantivo* low-priority work

tarea *f* **de funcionamiento automático** *sustantivo* unattended operation

tarea *f* **de impresión** *sustantivo* print job

tarea *f* **de prioridad alta** *sustantivo* foreground

tarea *f* **no prioritaria** *sustantivo* **1.** background job **2.** background task **3.** low-priority work

tarea *f* **prioritaria** *sustantivo* foreground

tareas ◇ **tareas** *fpl* **(de un ordenador)** activities

tareas *fpl* **en cola de espera** *sustantivo* job queue

tarea *f* **subordinada** *sustantivo* **1.** background job **2.** background task

Targa *sustantivo* **1.** (*formato de archivos de gráficos*) Targa **2.** Targa ◇ **tarjeta Targa** Targa board

tarifa *sustantivo* tariff ◇ **hay una tarifa establecida para conectarse, además de una tasa por cada minuto de tiempo de ordenador utilizado** there is a set tariff for logging on, then a rate for every minute of computer time used

'Hasta ahora, las huelgas más populares en la red han sido las de miles de usuarios que se abstienen de operar en ella, en una fecha concreta, como protesta por la carestía de las tarifas.' [*La Red*]

tarifa *f* **plana** *sustantivo* flat rate

tarjeta *sustantivo* **1.** board **2.** card ◇ **tarjeta** index card ◇ **tarjeta archivadora** filing card ◇ **tarjeta** *f* **controladara de interfaz de red** network interface card ◇ **tarjeta** *f* **para la obtención (de imágenes) de vídeo** video capture board ◇ **tarjeta** *f* **(de memoria) sin componentes** bare board

'El futuro DNI electrónico es una tarjeta inteligente que guarda en su chip el certificado y las claves criptográficas del ciudadano o ciudadana.' [*Ciberp@ís*]

tarjeta *f* **adaptadora** *sustantivo* adapter card

tarjeta *f* **bus** *sustantivo* bus board

tarjeta *f* **con contactos** *sustantivo* contact card

tarjeta *f* **conectora** *sustantivo* bus

tarjeta *f* **controlador** *m* **de vídeo** *sustantivo* **1.** video adapter **2.** video board **3.** video controller

tarjeta *f* **corta** *sustantivo* **1.** half card **2.** short card

tarjeta *f* **de audio** *sustantivo* **1.** audio board **2.** sound card ◇ **este programa le permite crear prácticamente cualquier sonido, pero sólo le es posible escucharlos si dispone de una tarjeta de sonido incorporada al sistema** this software lets you create almost any sound – but you can only hear them if you have a sound card fitted

tarjeta *f* **de chip** *sustantivo* chip card

tarjeta *f* **de circuito impreso** *sustantivo* card

tarjeta *f* **de control de disco** *sustantivo* disk-controller card

tarjeta *f* **de disco duro** *sustantivo* hard card

tarjeta *f* **de encabezamiento** *sustantivo* header card

tarjeta *f* **de enlace** *sustantivo* bus board

tarjeta *f* **de entrada analógica** *sustantivo* analog input card

tarjeta *f* **de extensión** *sustantivo* **1.** add on board **2.** expansion board **3.** expansion card

tarjeta *f* **de extensión de enlaces** *abrev* BEC ■ *sustantivo* bus extender *o* bus extension card

tarjeta *f* **de extensión de memoria** *sustantivo* expanded memory board

tarjeta *f* **de FAX** *sustantivo* fax card *o* fax adapter *o* fax board

tarjeta *f* **de fuentes de caracteres** *sustantivo* font card

tarjeta *f* **de interfaz** *sustantivo* interface card

tarjeta *f* **del sistema** *sustantivo* system board

tarjeta *f* **de marcas detectables** *sustantivo* mark sensing card

tarjeta *f* **de memoria** *sustantivo* **1.** chip card **2.** memory board

tarjeta *f* **de red** *sustantivo* network adapter

tarjeta *f* **de salida analógica** *sustantivo* analog output card

tarjeta *f* **de sonido** *sustantivo* **1.** audio board **2.** sound card ◇ **este programa le permite crear prácticamente cualquier sonido, pero sólo le es posible escucharlos si dispone de una tarjeta de sonido incorporada al sistema** this software lets you create almost any sound – but you can only hear them if you have a sound card fitted

tarjeta *f* **de sonido AdLib™** *sustantivo* AdLib™

tarjeta *f* **gráfica** *sustantivo* graphics adapter ◇ **el nuevo adaptador de gráficos proporciona una mayor resolución** the new graphics adapter is capable of displaying higher resolution graphics

tarjeta *f* **gráfica de expansión** *sustantivo* graphics overlay card

tarjeta *f* **gráfica de vídeo** *sustantivo* **1.** overlay card **2.** video graphics card

tarjeta *f* **inteligente** *sustantivo* smart card ◇ **las tarjetas magnéticas del futuro podrían llevar las huellas digitales del usuario para su identificación** future smart cards could contain an image of the user's fingerprint for identification ◇ **las tarjetas magnéticas reducen el fraude** smart cards reduce fraud

tarjeta *f* **interfaz MIDI** *sustantivo* MIDI interface card

tarjeta *f* **interna** *sustantivo* inlay card

tarjeta *f* **lógica** *sustantivo* **1.** logic board **2.** logic card

tarjeta *f* **maestra** *sustantivo* master card

tarjeta *f* **magnética** *sustantivo* **1.** magnetic card **2.** smart card

tarjeta *f* **magnética de identificación personal** *sustantivo* **1.** personal identification device **2.** PID

tarjeta *f* **MDA** *sustantivo* **1.** MDA **2.** monochrome display adapter

tarjeta *f* **media** *sustantivo* half card

tarjeta *f* **multifunción** *sustantivo* multifunction card

tarjeta *f* **multimedia** *sustantivo* multimedia card

tarjeta *f* **PCMCIA** *sustantivo* PCMCIA card ◇ **la memoria adicional se almacena en esta tarjeta PCMCIA y la puedo usar en mi (ordenador) portátil** the extra memory is stored on this PCMCIA card and I use it on my laptop

tarjeta *f* **RAM** *sustantivo* RAM card

tarjetas *fpl* **de programa** *plural noun* program cards

tasa *sustantivo* rate ◇ **la velocidad de transmisión de la señal binaria fue de 300 bits por segundo** the baud rate of the binary signal was 300 bits per second ◇ **tasa** *f* **de actualización de la memoria RAM** RAM refresh rate ◇ **tasa** *f* **de errores de transmisión (por fibra óptica)** bit error rate ◇ **tasa** *f* **de la altura y la anchura de un píxel** aspect ratio ◇ **tasa** *f* **(de transmisión) en baudios** baud rate ◇ **tasa** *f* **predeterminada (de un módem)** default rate ◇ **tasa** *f* **real de transferencia de datos** actual data transfer rate ◇ **un módem equipado con un escáner de reconocimiento de baudios se ajusta automáticamente a la velocidad a la que debe funcionar** a modem with auto-baud scanner can automatically sense at which baud rate it should operate

tasa *f* **bps** *sustantivo* bps rate

tasa *f* **de acceso al sistema** *sustantivo* access charge

tasa *f* **de actividad** *sustantivo* activity ratio

tasa *f* **de barrido** *sustantivo* scanning rate

tasa *f* **de bits por segundo** *sustantivo* bps rate

tasa *f* **de errores** *sustantivo* error rate ◇ **la tasa de error es inferior a 1%** the error rate is less than 1%

tasa *f* **de errores por bloque** *sustantivo* block error rate

tasa *f* **de fallos** *sustantivo* failure rate

tasa *f* **de muestreo** *sustantivo* sampling rate

tasa *f* **de transferencia** *sustantivo* transfer rate ◇ **con una buena línea telefónica, este par de módems pueden alcanzar una velocidad de transferencia de 14,4 Kbps** with a good telephone line, this pair of modems can achieve a transfer rate of 14.4Kbps

tasa *f* **de transferencia de datos** *sustantivo* data transfer rate

tasa *f* **de transmisión de bits** *sustantivo* debit

tasa *f* **de transmisión de datos** *sustantivo* data signalling rate

tasa *f* **disponible de bits** *sustantivo* available bit rate

tasa *f* **en bits** *sustantivo* bit rate

tasa *f* **máxima absoluta** *sustantivo* absolute maximum rating

tasa *f* **por defecto** *sustantivo* default rate

tecla *sustantivo* **1.** control **2.** key ◇ **hay 84 teclas en el teclado** there are 84 keys on the keyboard ◇ **hay varias teclas especiales de edición; ésta da un nuevo formato al texto** there are several special edit keys – this one will re-format the text ◇ **para parar un programa, pulse Ctrl-C -es decir, la tecla de control y la letra C- simultáneamente** to halt a program, press Ctrl-C – the control key and letter C – at the same time ◇ **presión (necesaria) para accionar una tecla** key force ◇ **recorrido de una tecla (para activar su función)** key travel ◇ **tecla** *f* **de avance de página** *or* **Av Pág (en un teclado**

español) page down key; PgDn ◇ **tecla *f* de bloqueo de las mayúsculas** caps lock ◇ **tecla de carácter** character key ◇ **tecla *f* (de función) de edición** edit key ◇ **tecla de mayúsculas** shift key ◇ **tecla *f* de retroceso de página** PgUp; page up key ◇ **tecla *f* Impr Pant** (*en un teclado español*) Print Screen key; (*de impresión de pantalla en un teclado español*) PrtSc ◇ **tecla *f* (de función) programable** programmable key ◇ **tecla *f* Re Pág (en un teclado español)** PgUp; page up key

tecla *f* aceleradora *sustantivo* shortcut

tecla *f* alfanumérica *sustantivo* alphanumeric key

tecla *f* ALT *sustantivo* Alt key

tecla *f* Apple (*marca comercial*) Apple Key

tecla *f* Bloq Num *sustantivo* Num Lock key

tecla *f* (de) carácter *sustantivo* character key

tecla *f* CTR *sustantivo* CTR *o* CTRL *o* Ctrl

tecla *f* Ctrl *sustantivo* control key ◇ **para parar un programa, pulse Ctrl-C -es decir, la tecla de control y la letra C- simultáneamente** to halt a program, press Ctrl-C – the control key and letter C – at the same time

tecla *f* de aceleración *sustantivo* accelerator key ◇ **en vez de seleccionar el menú Archivo y a continuación la opción Guardar, utilice la instrucción de aceleración Alt-G para guardar el fichero** instead of selecting the File menu then the Save option, use the accelerator keys Alt and S to do the same thing and save the file

tecla *f* de activación *sustantivo* hot key

tecla *f* de acuerdo *sustantivo* OK button

tecla *f* de ayuda *sustantivo* help key ◇ **pulse la tecla de ayuda si necesita información sobre el siguiente paso** hit the HELP key if you want information about what to do next

tecla *f* de bloqueo de desplazamiento *sustantivo* Scroll Lock key

tecla *f* de bloqueo de números *sustantivo* Num Lock key

tecla *f* de borrado *sustantivo* DEL key ◇ **para eliminar una palabra de la pantalla, apriete la tecla DEL de forma repetida** to remove a word from the screen, press the DEL key repeatedly

tecla *f* de búsqueda *sustantivo* search key

tecla *f* de conforme *sustantivo* OK button

tecla *f* de contraste *sustantivo* contrast ◇ **palanca de contraste** contrast lever

tecla *f* de control *sustantivo* 1. control key 2. CTR *o* CTRL *o* Ctrl

tecla *f* de dirección *sustantivo* arrow key

tecla *f* de eliminación DEL *sustantivo* DEL key ◇ **para eliminar una palabra de la pantalla, apriete la tecla DEL de forma repetida** to remove a word from the screen, press the DEL key repeatedly

tecla *f* de escape *sustantivo* escape key

tecla *f* de flechas *sustantivo* arrow key

tecla *f* de función *sustantivo* function key ◇ **las etiquetas pueden asignarse a las teclas de función** tags can be allocated to function keys

tecla *f* de impresión de pantalla *sustantivo* Print Screen key

tecla *f* de instrucciones *sustantivo* command key

tecla *f* de interrupción *sustantivo* Break key

tecla *f* de intervención *sustantivo* attention key

tecla *f* de mayúsculas *sustantivo* 1. case change 2. Shift key

tecla *f* de opciones *sustantivo* Option key

tecla *f* de registro *sustantivo* record button

tecla *f* de reinicio *sustantivo* reset button *o* reset key

tecla *f* de repetición *sustantivo* repeat key

tecla *f* de retorno *sustantivo* return ◇ **escriba su nombre y número de código, y luego pulse la tecla Intro** you type in your name and code number then press return

tecla *f* de retorno de carro *sustantivo* carriage return key ◇ **la tecla de retorno de carro está muy mal colocada para los mecanógrafos al tacto** the carriage return key is badly placed for touch-typists

tecla *f* de retroceso *sustantivo* backspace key ◇ **si comete un error al introducir datos, utilice la tecla de retroceso para corregirlo** if you make a mistake entering data, use the backspace key to correct it

tecla *f* de tabulación *sustantivo* tab key

tecla *f* de tabulación decimal *sustantivo* decimal tab key

tecla *f* de tabulado *sustantivo* tab key

teclado *m* *sustantivo* 1. keyboard 2. pad ◇ **control del teclado** keyboard scan

teclado *m* alfanumérico *sustantivo* alphanumeric keyboard

teclado *m* ANSI *sustantivo* ANSI keyboard

teclado *m* ASCII *sustantivo* ASCII keyboard

teclado *m* ASR *sustantivo* ASR keyboard

teclado *m* AT *sustantivo* AT-keyboard

teclado *m* (IBM) AT IBM AT keyboard

teclado *m* AZERTY *sustantivo* azerty keyboard

teclado *m* ciego *sustantivo* blind keyboard

teclado *m* compacto *sustantivo* keypad

teclado *m* con memoria intermedia *sustantivo* key rollover

teclado *m* de burbujas de plástico *sustantivo* plastic bubble keyboard

teclado *m* de contacto *sustantivo* touch-sensitive keyboard

teclado *m* de membrana *sustantivo* membrane keyboard

teclado *m* de memoria intermedia *sustantivo* rollover

teclado *m* de terminal *sustantivo* terminal keyboard

teclado *m* **DVORAK** *sustantivo* Dvorak keyboard

teclado *m* **emisor/receptor** *sustantivo* ASR keyboard

teclado *m* **extendido** *sustantivo* enhanced keyboard

teclado *m* **francés acentuado** *sustantivo* azerty keyboard

teclado *m* **hexadecimal** *sustantivo* hex keypad

teclado *m* **interactivo** *sustantivo* interactive keyboard

teclado *m* **internacional** *sustantivo* (*utilizado sobre todo en los países anglosajones*) QWERTY keyboard

teclado *m* **numérico** *sustantivo* **1.** keypad **2.** numeric keypad **3.** numeric pad ◇ **usted puede utilizar el teclado numérico para introducir las cifras** you can use the numeric keypad to enter the figures

teclado *m* **para un ordenador IBM** IBM PC keyboard

teclado *m* **PC/AT** *sustantivo* PC/AT keyboard

teclado *m* **PC/XT** *sustantivo* PC/XT keyboard

teclado *m* **programable** *sustantivo* soft keyboard

teclado *m* **QWERTY** *sustantivo* QWERTY keyboard ◇ **el ordenador tiene un teclado QWERTY normal** the computer has a normal QWERTY keyboard

teclado *m* **rápido** *sustantivo* **1.** key rollover **2.** rollover

teclado *m* **sensible** *sustantivo* tactile keyboard

teclado *m* **suave** *sustantivo* soft keyboard

teclado *m* **táctil** *sustantivo* **1.** tactile keyboard **2.** touch-sensitive keyboard

teclado *m* **XT** *sustantivo* XT keyboard

tecla *f* **End** *sustantivo* end key

tecla *f* **'Enter'** *sustantivo* enter key

tecla *f* **ESC** *sustantivo* escape key

tecla *f* **Fin** *sustantivo* (*en un teclado español*) end key

tecla *f* **'Home'** *sustantivo* home key

tecla *f* **Inicio** *sustantivo* (*en un teclado español*) home key

tecla *f* **Ins** *sustantivo* Ins key

tecla *f* **insertar** *sustantivo* insert key

tecla *f* **Intro** *sustantivo* (*en un teclado español*) enter key

tecla *f* **manzana** (*marca comercial*) Apple Key

tecla *f* **Pausa** *sustantivo* pause key

tecla *f* **Print Screen** *sustantivo* PrtSc

tecla *f* **rápida** *sustantivo* hot key

teclas ◇ **tecla** *f* **de función inutilizadas (que no producen caracteres)** dead key

teclas *fpl* **blandas** *plural noun* soft keys

teclas *fpl* **de control del cursor** *plural noun* cursor control keys ■ *sustantivo* cursor pad

tecla *f* **secundaria** *sustantivo* alternate key

teclas *fpl* **programables** *plural noun* soft keys

teclas *fpl* **suaves** *plural noun* soft keys

tecla *f* **Tab** *sustantivo* tab key

teclear *verbo vt* to click ◇ **utilice el ratón para agrandar el recuadro tecleando dentro de su borde y arrastrándolo a la posición deseada** use the mouse to enlarge a frame by clicking inside its border and dragging to the position wanted

técnica *f* *sustantivo* technique ◇ **la compañía ha desarrollado una nueva técnica para tratar los disquetes de los clientes** the company has developed a new technique for processing customers' disks

técnica *f* **alfa beta** *sustantivo* alpha beta technique

técnicas *fpl* *sustantivo* technology

técnicas *fpl* **punta** *sustantivo* new technology

técnico *adj* technical ■ *sustantivo* technician ◇ **el documento ofrece todos los detalles técnicos sobre el nuevo ordenador** the document gives all the technical details on the new computer ◇ **los técnicos informáticos instalaron el nuevo sistema** the computer technicians installed the new system ◇ **técnico, -a de laboratorio** laboratory technician

tecnología *sustantivo* technology ◇ **la introducción de la nueva tecnología** the introduction of new technology ◇ **tecnología** *f* **de la transmisión por fibra óptica** fibre optics

'Si se tiene en cuenta que las TIC han invadido todos los campos de actividad de las empresas sin excepción, y que los puestos de trabajo en informática y comunicaciones son intercambiables de unas empresas a otras, el resultado es que las empresas tienen que competir en un mercado laboral global, lo que va a incidir en un aumento de gastos salariales, de inversión y de pagos por servicios.' [*PC Plus*]

tecnología *f* **avanzada** *adj* high-tech ■ *sustantivo* high technology

tecnología *f* **de ensamblaje SMT** *sustantivo* **1.** SMT **2.** surface-mount technology

tecnología *f* **de la fibra óptica** *plural noun* fibre optics

tecnología *f* **de la información** *sustantivo* **1.** computing **2.** information technology

tecnología *f* **de transacción segura** *sustantivo* STT

tecnología *f* **segura de transacciones** *sustantivo* secure transaction technology

tecnológico *adj* technological

tele- *prefijo* tele-

telecomunicaciones *fpl* *sustantivo* telecommunications

teleconferencia *f* *sustantivo* **1.** conferencing **2.** teleconference **3.** teleconferencing ◇ **el multiusuario del sistema de tablón de anuncios tiene un servicio de comunicación entre ordenadores** *o* **de teleconferencia** the multi-user BBS has a computer conferencing facility

teleconferencia *f sustantivo (a través de la red informática)* computer conferencing

teleconferencia *f* **vídeo** *sustantivo* video teleconferencing

telefonear *verbo vi* to call

telefonía *sustantivo* telephony

'El desarrollo fulgurante de la telefonía móvil, primero, y su convergencia inmediata con el ciberespacio han cambiado la cadena de valor.' [*La Red*]

telefonía *f* **integrada por ordenador** *abrev* CIT

teléfono *sustantivo* **1.** phone **2.** telephone ◊ **abonado, -a de teléfonos** telephone subscriber ◊ **busque su dirección en la guía de teléfonos** look up his address in the phone book ◊ **cableado de teléfono** telephone wiring ◊ **centralita (de teléfonos)** telephone switchboard ◊ **conferencia telefónica** *o* **por teléfono** conference telephone ◊ **contestar al teléfono** to answer the phone *o* to take a phone call ◊ **contestar** *o* **responder al teléfono** *o* **tomar una llamada** to answer the telephone *o* to take a telephone call ◊ **el número de teléfono figura en el papel con el membrete de la empresa** the phone number is on the company notepaper ◊ **está hablando por teléfono con Hong Kong** she is on the telephone to Hong Kong ◊ **guía telefónica** *o* **listín telefónico** *o* **de teléfonos** phone book ◊ **hablar por teléfono** *o* **estar en línea** to be on the telephone ◊ **hablar por teléfono** *o* **estar en línea (con alguien)** to be on the phone ◊ **habló con el director por teléfono** he spoke to the manager on the phone ◊ **hacer un pedido por teléfono** to place an order by telephone ◊ **listín de teléfonos** *o* **guía telefónica** telephone book *o* telephone directory ◊ **número de teléfono** telephone number ◊ **por teléfono** by phone; by telephone ◊ **¿puede darme su número de teléfono?** can you give me your phone number?; can you give me your telephone number? ◊ **repetidor de teléfono** telephone repeater ◊ **se ha pasado toda la mañana en el teléfono** she has been on the phone all morning ◊ **telefonear** *o* **llamar (por teléfono)** *o* **hacer una llamada (telefónica)** to make a phone call ◊ **teléfono celular** cellular telephone ◊ **teléfono de tarjeta** card phone ◊ **teléfono (de impulsión numérica) Digipulse™** Digipulse telephone™ ◊ **teléfono interno** house phone *o* internal phone; house telephone *o* internal telephone ◊ **tiene una lista de números de teléfono en un cuaderno negro** he keeps a list of phone numbers in a black notebook ◊ **transmisor de datos por teléfono** *o* **por la red** telephone data carrier

'Habría que matizar, no obstante, que si bien el correo electrónico ha restringido el uso de teléfono, también es cierto que el creciente uso de los teléfonos móviles está reduciendo el uso de correo electrónico.' [*Ciberpragmática*]

teléfono *m* **celular** *sustantivo* cellular phone

teléfono *m* **móvil** *sustantivo* mobile phone

teleimpresora *f sustantivo* **1.** teleprinter **2.** teletypewriter ◊ **desde este puerto en serie modificado, se puede conectar una teleimpresora** you can drive a teleprinter from this modified serial port ◊ **operador, -a de teleimpresora** teleprinter operator

telemática *f sustantivo* **1.** data communications **2.** telematics

telemática *f* **médica** *sustantivo* medical telematics

Teletexto™ *m sustantivo* teletext

teletexto *m* **interactivo** *sustantivo* interactive videotext

teletipo *m sustantivo* **1.** teleprinter **2.** teletype ■ *abrev* TTY

teletrabajo *sustantivo* telecommuting

'La aplicación del teletrabajo de manera intensiva a la organización de la empresa acabará, en cambio, con la cultura tradicional de la misma.' [*La Red*]

televisión *f sustantivo* television ■ *abrev* TV ◊ **cámara de televisión** television camera ◊ **proyector de televisión** television projector ◊ **receptor de televisión** television receiver

televisión *f* **de alta definición** *abrev* HDTV ■ *sustantivo* high definition television

televisión *f* **de barrido lento** *sustantivo* slow scan TV

televisión *f* **de definición extendida** *sustantivo* **1.** EDTV **2.** enhanced-definition television **3.** extended-definition television

televisión *f* **de exploración lenta** *sustantivo* slow scan TV

televisión *f* **digital** *sustantivo* digital TV

televisor *m sustantivo* television ◊ **televisor** television receiver

telnet *m sustantivo* telnet

temblar *vi sustantivo* jitter

temperatura *f* **ambiente** *sustantivo* ambient temperature

temperatura *f* **cromática** *sustantivo* colour temperature

tempo *m sustantivo* tempo ◊ **el tempo normal del dispositivo musical MIDI es de 120 bpm** a typical MIDI tempo is 120bpm

tempo *m sustantivo* tempo

temporal *adj* **1.** temporary **2.** transient

tenacidad *f sustantivo* persistence

tener acceso a *verbo* to access ◊ **ella accedió al fichero del empleado archivado en el ordenador** she accessed the employee's file stored on the computer

tener lugar *verbo* to occur

tener ocupada (la línea) *verbo* to hold ◊ **corriente de mantenimiento** hold current ◊ **línea de delimitación** *o* **de retención** holding line

tensión *f sustantivo* voltage ◊ **bajada de tensión** voltage dip *o* dip in voltage

tensión *f* **baja** *adj* logical low

teoría *f* **de conjuntos** *sustantivo* set theory

teoría *f* **de la información** *sustantivo* information theory

teoría *f* **de lógica polivalente** *sustantivo* fuzzy logic *o* fuzzy theory

tera *f* T ■ *prefijo* tera-

terabyte *sustantivo* terabyte

'Al incorporar las capacidades que ofrece la arquitectura P2P, las corporaciones pueden aprovechar los teraflops ya existentes en una red y los terabytes de almacenamiento, para hacer las aplicaciones de hoy día más eficientes e incluso crear nuevas aplicaciones en el futuro.' [*Ciberp@ís*]

teraocteto *m sustantivo* terabyte

tercera generación *f sustantivo* **1.** 3G **2.** third generation

tercera parte *f sustantivo* third party

terminación *f sustantivo* **1.** completion **2.** termination ◊ **la fecha de terminación del nuevo paquete de software es el 15 de noviembre** completion date for the new software package is November 15th

terminación *f* **anormal** *sustantivo* abnormal termination

terminador *m* **(de red)** *sustantivo* terminator ◊ **dispositivo de final de línea** line terminator

terminador *m* **SCSI** *sustantivo* terminator

terminal *sustantivo* terminal ■ *adj* terminal ■ *sustantivo* workstation ◊ **el controlador de red tiene 16 interfaces para terminales** the network controller has 16 terminal interfaces ◊ **servidor de terminal** terminal server ◊ **terminal** *m* **de aplicación (sobre control de tareas)** job orientated terminal ◊ **terminal** *m* **de control de enlace de datos de alto nivel** high-level data link control station ◊ **terminal** *m* **de transferencia electrónica de fondos** EFTPOS; electronic funds transfer point-of-sale ◊ **terminal** *m* **especializado (sobre control de tareas)** job orientated terminal ◊ **terminal inteligente** intelligent terminal ◊ **todos los mensajes van a todos los terminales ya que ninguno es de direccionamiento protegido** all the messages go to all the terminals since none are addressable terminals

'El diseño de los terminales, pasada la euforia de los primeros y dubitativos descubrimientos, estará más relacionado con el comportamiento y formas de conducta del usuario que con las necesidades o prestaciones tecnológicas.' [*La Red*]

terminal *m* **(de trabajo)** *sustantivo* station

terminal *m* **(de visualización)** *abrev* VDU ■ *sustantivo* visual display terminal *o* visual display unit

terminal *m* **a distancia** *sustantivo* remote terminal

terminal *m* **auxiliar** *sustantivo* secondary station

terminal *m* **central** *sustantivo* central terminal

terminal *m* **de acceso público** *sustantivo* public access terminal

terminal *m* **de actualización rápido** *sustantivo* bulk update terminal

terminal *m* **de aplicaciones** *sustantivo* **1.** applications terminal **2.** application terminal

terminal *m* **de consulta** *sustantivo* inquiry station

terminal *m* **de datos** *sustantivo* data terminal ◊ **una impresora es un terminal informático para la salida de datos** a printer is a data terminal for computer output

terminal *m* **de direccionamiento protegido** *sustantivo* addressable terminal

terminal *m* **de entrada de datos** *sustantivo* IP terminal

terminal *m* **de llegada** *sustantivo* **1.** receive only **2.** RO

terminal *m* **de trabajo** *sustantivo* console ◊ **la consola consiste en un dispositivo de entrada de datos, como el teclado, y un dispositivo de salida de datos, como una impresora o una pantalla** the console consists of input device such as a keyboard, and an output device such as a printer or CRT

terminal *m* **de transmisión de datos** *sustantivo* **1.** data terminal equipment **2.** DTE

terminal *m* **de vídeo** *abrev* VDT

terminal *m* **de vídeo con teclado** *sustantivo* video terminal

terminal *m* **de visualización** *abrev* VDT

terminal *m* **direccionable** *sustantivo* addressable terminal

terminal *m* **emisor/receptor con teclado** *sustantivo* keyboard send/receive

terminal *m* **esclavo** *sustantivo* slave terminal

terminal *m* **gráfico** *sustantivo* graphics terminal

terminal *m* **independiente** *sustantivo* stand-alone terminal

terminal *m* **informático** *sustantivo* data terminal ◊ **una impresora es un terminal informático para la salida de datos** a printer is a data terminal for computer output

terminal *m* **inteligente** *sustantivo* **1.** intelligent terminal **2.** smart terminal ◊ **el nuevo terminal inteligente tiene un editor de texto incorporado** the new intelligent terminal has a built-in text editor

terminal *m* **interactivo** *sustantivo* interactive terminal

terminal *m* **maestro** *sustantivo* master terminal ◊ **el gestor del sistema utiliza el terminal principal para reiniciar el sistema** the system manager uses the master terminal to restart the system

terminal *m* **no inteligente** *sustantivo* dumb terminal

terminal *m* **periférico** *sustantivo* external device

terminal *m* **positivo** *sustantivo* positive terminal

terminal *m* **principal** *sustantivo* **1.** central terminal **2.** key terminal **3.** master terminal

terminal *m* **remoto** *sustantivo* remote terminal

terminal *m* **satélite** *sustantivo* satellite terminal

terminal *m* **virtual** *sustantivo* virtual terminal

terminar *verbo* **1.** *vt* to close **2.** *vt* to terminate

ternario *adj* ternary

tesauro *m sustantivo* thesaurus

teselar *verbo vt* to tessellate

test *m sustantivo* test

test *m* **de homologación** *sustantivo* acceptance test

testigo *m sustantivo* **1.** flag **2.** indicator flag ◇ **testigo** *m* **de desbordamiento (de la capacidad)** overflow bit; overflow flag ◇ **testigo** *o* **indicador de retención** *o* **de arrastre** carry flag

testigo *m* **de actividad** *sustantivo* activity light

testigo *m* **de funcionamiento** *sustantivo* device flag

testigo *m* **de utilización** *sustantivo* device flag

tetra- *prefijo* quadr-

'texel' *m sustantivo* texel

texto *m sustantivo* text ◇ **campo de texto** text field ◇ **editor de texto** text editor ◇ **el editor de textos sólo lee ficheros de menos de 64 Kb** the text editor will only read files smaller than 64Kbytes long ◇ **el programa lleva una función de tratamiento de textos incorporada** the program includes a built-in text-editing function ◇ **normalmente el MS-DOS funciona en modo texto** MS-DOS normally operates in a text mode ◇ **programa de tratamiento de textos** *o* **procesador de textos** text processor ◇ **se utiliza el programa de formato de texto como programa básico de edición asistida por ordenador** people use the text formatter as a basic desk-top publishing program ◇ **tratamiento de textos** text processing

texto *m* **ASCII** *sustantivo* ASCII text

texto *m* **de un mensaje** *sustantivo* message text

texto *m* **enriquecido** *sustantivo* rich text

texto *m* **estándar** *sustantivo* standard text

texto *m* **mudo** *adj* greeked

texto *m* **no cifrado** *sustantivo* plaintext ◇ **introduzca el mensaje de texto no cifrado en la máquina codificadora** enter the plaintext message into the cipher machine ◇ **los mensajes fueron enviados por teléfono como texto no cifrado** the messages were sent as plaintext by telephone

texto *m* **no justificado** *sustantivo* ragged text

texto *m* **preestablecido** *sustantivo* form overlay

texto *m* **sin errores** *sustantivo* clean copy

texto *m* **sin modificaciones** *sustantivo* clean copy

textura *f sustantivo* texture

3D *adj* three-dimensional

tiempo *sustantivo* run-time *o* run duration ◇ **tiempo** *m* **de acceso a la dirección** address ac-

cess time ◇ **tiempo** *m* **de acceso a la memoria** memory access time ◇ **tiempo** *m* **de conexión de un terminal** terminal session ◇ **tiempo** *m* **de ejecución de una instrucción** instruction execution time; instruction time ◇ **tiempo** *m* **de ejecución de una operación** operation time ◇ **tiempo** *m* **de ejecución de una tarea** elapsed time ◇ **tiempo** *m* **de espera (entre dos operaciones)** dead time ◇ **tiempo** *m* **de llamada y comprobación de terminal de red** polling overhead ◇ **tiempo** *m* **de puesta a punto de un nuevo producto** development time ◇ **tiempo** *m* **de retención de la línea** holding time ◇ **tiempo** *m* **de transferencia de una palabra** word time ◇ **tiempo** *m* **de utilización de la unidad central** CPU time ◇ **tiempo** *m* **medio de funcionamiento correcto entre fallos** MTBF; mean time between failures

tiempo *m* **absoluto** *sustantivo* absolute time

tiempo *m* **compartido** *sustantivo* time-sharing

tiempo *m* **de acceso** *sustantivo* **1.** access time **2.** positioning time **3.** reaction time ◇ **el tiempo de acceso de este chip de RAM dinámico es de aproximadamente 200 ns: disponemos de versiones más rápidas si el reloj de su sistema funciona a más velocidad** the access time of this dynamic RAM chip is around 200ns – we have faster versions if your system clock is running faster

tiempo *m* **de aceleración** *sustantivo* acceleration time

tiempo *m* **de actualización** *sustantivo* refresh cycle

tiempo *m* **de adición** *sustantivo* **1.** addition time **2.** add time

tiempo *m* **de barrido** *sustantivo* scanning rate

tiempo *m* **de buen funcionamiento** *sustantivo* uptime *o* up time

tiempo *m* **de búsqueda** *sustantivo* seek time

tiempo *m* **de ciclo** *sustantivo* cycle time

tiempo *m* **de colocación** *sustantivo* positioning time

tiempo *m* **de compilación** *sustantivo* compilation time

tiempo *m* **de conexión** *sustantivo* connect time

tiempo *m* **de configuración** *sustantivo* set-up time

tiempo *m* **de conversión** *sustantivo* sense recovery time

tiempo *m* **de deceleración** *sustantivo* deceleration time

tiempo *m* **de desarrollo** *sustantivo* development time

tiempo *m* **de detención** *sustantivo* holdup

tiempo *m* **de disponibilidad** *sustantivo* available time

tiempo *m* **de ejecución** *sustantivo* **1.** execute time **2.** execution time **3.** (*de una tarea*) operating time ■ *sustantivo*, *adj* run-duration ■ *sustantivo*

(*de un programa*) run-time *o* run duration ■
abrev TAT ■ *sustantivo* turnaround time

tiempo *m* **de enlace** *sustantivo* (*de una direc-ción*) binding time

tiempo *m* **de ensamblaje** *sustantivo* assembly time

tiempo *m* **de escritura** *sustantivo* write time

tiempo *m* **de espera** *sustantivo* **1.** (*entre dos operaciones*) downtime *o* down time **2.** (*entre dos operaciones*) idle time **3.** wait time

tiempo *m* **de espera (en cola)** *sustantivo* queuing time

tiempo *m* **de inactividad** *sustantivo* idle time

tiempo *m* **de inmovilización** *sustantivo* stop time

tiempo *m* **de la CPU** *sustantivo* CPU time

tiempo *m* **de latencia** *sustantivo* latency

tiempo *m* **del ciclo de instrucciones** *sustantivo* instruction cycle time

tiempo *m* **de llamadas selectivas** *sustantivo* polling overhead

tiempo *m* **de localización** *sustantivo* seek time

tiempo *m* **de ocupación** *sustantivo* holding time

tiempo *m* **de ordenador** *sustantivo* computer time ◇ **la gestión de todos esos informes de ventas cuesta mucho en tiempo de ordenador** running all those sales reports costs a lot in computer time

tiempo *m* **de organización** *sustantivo* setup time

tiempo *m* **de parada** *sustantivo* stop time

tiempo *m* **de preparación** *sustantivo* **1.** set-up time **2.** (*entre dos tareas*) takedown time

tiempo *m* **de proceso** *sustantivo, adj* run-duration ■ *sustantivo* run-time *o* run duration

tiempo *m* **de propagación** *sustantivo* **1.** propagation delay **2.** propagation time

tiempo *m* **de recuperación** *sustantivo* sense recovery time

tiempo *m* **de referencia** *sustantivo* reference time

tiempo *m* **de registro** *sustantivo* write time

tiempo *m* **de respuesta** *sustantivo* **1.** answer time **2.** gate delay **3.** response time ■ *abrev* TAT ■ *sustantivo* turnaround time

tiempo *m* **de retorno** *abrev* TAT ■ *sustantivo* turnaround time

tiempo *m* **de suma** *sustantivo* **1.** addition time **2.** add time

tiempo *m* **de transferencia** *sustantivo* **1.** carry time **2.** transfer time

tiempo *m* **de tratamiento** *sustantivo, adj* run-duration ■ *sustantivo* run-time *o* run duration

tiempo *m* **de un fallo** *sustantivo* fault time

tiempo *m* **de utilización del procesador** *sustantivo* CPU time

tiempo *m* **disponible** *sustantivo* **1.** available time **2.** idle time

tiempo *m* **medio de acceso** *sustantivo* average access time

tiempo *m* **medio de espera** *sustantivo* average delay ◇ **después de las nueve y media el tiempo medio de espera aumenta debido a que todo el mundo intenta conectarse (al sistema)** the average delay increases at nine-thirty when everyone tries to log-in

tiempo *m* **medio sin averías** *sustantivo* **1.** mean time to failure **2.** MTF

tiempo *m* **muerto** *sustantivo* **1.** dead time **2.** downtime *o* down time **3.** idle time

tiempo *m* **productivo** *sustantivo* **1.** productive time **2.** uptime *o* up time

tiempo *m* **real** *sustantivo* real time ◇ **ejecución (de un programa) en tiempo real** real time execution (RTE)

tiempo *m* **transcurrido** *sustantivo* elapsed time

tierra *f* *sustantivo* earth

timbre *m* *sustantivo* timbre

tinta *f* **magnética** *sustantivo* magnetic ink

tintura *f* *sustantivo* toner

tipo *sustantivo* sort ◇ **tipo** *m* **de caracteres de una sección** body type ◇ **tipo** *m* **de letra en la planificación de fibras** raster font

tipo *m* **1 (de IBM)** *sustantivo* Type 1

tipo *m* **2 (de IBM)** *sustantivo* Type 2

tipo *m* **3 (de IBM)** *sustantivo* Type 3

tipo *m* **5 (de IBM)** *sustantivo* Type 5

tipo *m* **6 (de IBM)** *sustantivo* Type 6

tipo *m* **8 (de IBM)** *sustantivo* Type 8

tipo *m* **de acceso** *sustantivo* access category

tipo *m* **de brocha** *sustantivo* brush style ◇ **para rellenar un área grande, selecciono un estilo de pincel ancho y cuadrado** to fill in a big area, I select a wide, square brush style

tipo *m* **de cadena de caracteres** *sustantivo* string type

tipo *m* **de datos** *sustantivo* data type

tipo *m* **de fichero** *sustantivo* file type ◇ **los ficheros con la extensión EXE son tipos de ficheros que contienen un código de programa** files with the extension EXE are file types that contain program code

tipo *m* **de letra** *sustantivo* **1.** case **2.** face **3.** special sort **4.** typeface ◇ **corrigió la palabra 'coMputer' sustituyendo la M mayúscula por una letra minúscula** he corrected the word 'coMputer', replacing the upper case M with a lower case letter

tipo *m* **enumerado** *sustantivo* enumerated type

tipógrafo *mf* *sustantivo* printer

tipo *m* **variable de datos** *sustantivo* variable data type

tirar *verbo* **1.** *vi* to drag **2.** *vt* to junk

título *m* *sustantivo* **1.** heading **2.** running head **3.** title ◇ **página de título** title page

título *m* **actual** *sustantivo* header

toda la panoplia *plural noun* bells and whistles ◇ **este tratamiento de textos lleva todo lo necesario, incluso la instrucción vista preliminar** this word-processor has all the bells and whistles you would expect – including page preview

todo lo necesario *plural noun* bells and whistles ◇ **este tratamiento de textos lleva todo lo necesario, incluso la instrucción vista preliminar** this word-processor has all the bells and whistles you would expect – including page preview

tolerancia *f* (al fallo) *sustantivo* robustness

tolerancia *f* al ruido *sustantivo* noise immunity

tolerante al fallo *adj* fault-tolerant ◇ **comercializan con mucho éxito una gama de miniordenadores tolerantes a los fallos** they market a highly successful range of fault-tolerant minis

tomacorriente *m sustantivo* plug

toma *f* **de corriente** *sustantivo* outlet

toma *f* **de sonido** *sustantivo* sound capture

toma *f* **de tierra** *sustantivo* 1. earth 2. GND 3. ground ◇ **todos los alambres sueltos deberían tener una toma de tierra** all loose wires should be tied to earth

toma *f* **hembra del conector** *sustantivo* connector receptacle

toma *f* **macho del conector** *sustantivo* connector plug

tomar *verbo* 1. *vt* to capture 2. *vt* (*un símbolo de una red Token-Ring*) to capture

tomar muestras *verbo* to sample

tomar prestado *verbo* to borrow ◇ **pidió prestado un libro sobre fabricación de ordenadores** she borrowed a book on computer construction

tonel *m sustantivo* barrel

tóner *m sustantivo* toner ◇ **cuando se acaba el tóner, el cartucho y el tambor se pueden cambiar en una sola operación** the toner cartridge and the imaging drum can be replaced as one unit when the toner runs out ◇ **si se mancha las manos con tóner, sólo se lo puede lavar con agua fría** if you get toner on your hands, you can only wash it off with cold water

tono *m sustantivo* hue

tono *m* **continuo** *sustantivo* continuous tone

Toolbox *m sustantivo* (*de Macintosh*) Toolbox

ToolTips *sustantivo* (*etiquetas explicativas de icono*) ToolTips

topografía *f* **de las direcciones** *sustantivo* address mapping

topología *f sustantivo* 1. database mapping 2. topology ◇ **en una red en estrella, si el cable de una estación de trabajo falla, las otras estaciones siguen funcionando, al contrario de lo que sucede en una topología en bus** if one workstation cable snaps in a star topology, the rest continue, unlike a bus topology ◇ **la red de**

anillo de señales utiliza una topología en anillo token ring uses a ring topology

topología *f* **de enlaces** *sustantivo* bus topology

topología *f* **de red** *sustantivo* network topology

topología *f* **en anillo** *sustantivo* ring topology

topología *f* **en bus** *sustantivo* bus topology ◇ **Ethernet es una red que usa una topología en bus** Ethernet is a network that uses the bus topology

topología *f* **en estrella** *sustantivo* star topology ◇ **en una red en estrella, si el cable de una estación de trabajo falla, las otras estaciones siguen funcionando, al contrario de lo que sucede en una topología en bus** if one workstation cable snaps in a star topology, the rest continue, unlike a bus topology

topología *f* **física** *sustantivo* physical topology

tortuga *f sustantivo* turtle

total *adj* global ■ *sustantivo* total ◇ **sistema de comunicaciones de acceso total o norma TACS (para un sistema de radioteléfono celular)** total access communication system (TACS)

total *m* **de comprobación al azar** *sustantivo* hash total

total *m* **de control** *sustantivo* control total

total *m* **de verificación** *sustantivo* control total

total *m* **por lotes** *sustantivo* batch total

trabajo *m sustantivo* 1. job 2. work ◇ **este tratamiento de textos facilita el trabajo en grupo al incluir una conexión con el correo electrónico desde los menús estándares** this word-processor is workgroup enabled which adds an email gateway from the standard menus ◇ **que facilita el trabajo en grupo** workgroup enabled ◇ **trabajo en equipo** team work

trabajo *m* **atrasado** *sustantivo* backlog

trabajo *m* **pendiente** *sustantivo* backlog

trabar con intercierre *verbo* to interlock

tracción *f* **automática del papel** *sustantivo* auto advance

tradicional *adj* (*comercio*) bricks-and-mortar

traducción ◇ **traducción** *f* **de un lenguaje a otro** language translation

traducción *f* **asistida por ordenador** *sustantivo* machine translation

traducción *f* **automática** *sustantivo* machine translation

traducción *f* **de datos** *sustantivo* data translation

traducción *f* **de direcciones** *sustantivo* address translation

traducir *verbo* 1. *vt* to interpret 2. *vt* to translate

traductor *m* **de fórmulas** *sustantivo* formula translator

tráfico *m sustantivo* 1. peak period 2. traffic

tráfico *m* **de entrada** *sustantivo* incoming traffic

trama *f sustantivo* **1.** matte **2.** raster ◊ **un procesador gráfico por barrido de trama permite transformar una página electrónica en una imagen de vídeo imprimible** an electronic page can be converted to a printer-readable video image by an on-board raster image processor

trama *f* **de imagen** *sustantivo* field ◊ **barrido vertical** *o* **exploración de campo** field sweep ◊ **frecuencia de campo** *o* **de trama** field frequency ◊ **impulso de control** *o* **de sincronización del barrido** field sync pulse ◊ **intervalo de campo** *o* **supresión vertical de campo** field blanking (interval) ◊ **pantalla de emisión de campo** field emision display (FED) ◊ **retorno de campo** field flyback

tramo *sustantivo* **1.** leg **2.** page frame ◊ **tramo** *m* **de inicialización de red bajo el protocolo FDDI** claim frame

trampa *f sustantivo* trap

transacción *f sustantivo* **1.** package deal **2.** transaction ◊ **hemos propuesto una oferta global que comprende un sistema informático completo para la oficina, la formación del personal y el mantenimiento del equipo** we are offering a package deal which includes the whole office computer system, staff training and hardware maintenance

transacción *f* **de datos** *sustantivo* data transaction

transacciones *fpl* **electrónicas seguras** *plural noun* secure electronic transactions

transceptor *m sustantivo* transceiver

transcribir *verbo vt* to transcribe

transferencia *f sustantivo* **1.** bridging **2.** carry **3.** (*a un disco o un soporte magnético*) dump **4.** transfer **5.** transmission ◊ **transferencia condicional** *o* **instrucción condicional de bifurcación** conditional transfer ◊ **transferencia** *f* **de un programa a través de un puente** bridging product ◊ **transferencia** *f* **de un soporte magnético a otro** magnetic transfer ◊ **transferencia** *f* **en serie de palabras binarias** word serial ◊ **transferencia** *f* **entre la unidad central y periférico** peripheral transfer ◊ **transferencia** *f* **incontrolada de páginas (entre la memoria y el disco)** thrashing ◊ **transferencia** *f* **radial de datos de programas** radial transfer

transferencia *f* **asíncrona de datos** *sustantivo* asynchronous data transfer

transferencia *f* **automática** *sustantivo* unconditional branch *o* unconditional jump *o* unconditional transfer

transferencia *f* **condicional** *sustantivo* conditional transfer

transferencia *f* **de bits por bloques** *sustantivo* bit block transfer

transferencia *f* **de control** *sustantivo* control transfer

transferencia *f* **de datos** *sustantivo* (*en línea a dispositivo fuera de línea*) data migration

transferencia *f* **de ficheros** *sustantivo* file transfer

transferencia *f* **de un párrafo** *sustantivo* block transfer

transferencia *f* **de un programa** *sustantivo* program relocation

transferencia *f* **directa** *sustantivo* **1.** direct change-over **2.** direct transfer

transferencia *f* **electrónica de fondos** *sustantivo* **1.** EFT **2.** electronic funds transfer

transferencia *f* **en paralelo** *sustantivo* parallel transfer

transferencia *f* **entre capas** *sustantivo* radial transfer

transferencia *f* **incondicional** *sustantivo* unconditional branch *o* unconditional jump *o* unconditional transfer

transferencia *f* **incontrolada de páginas** *sustantivo* (*entre la memoria y el disco*) thrashing

transferencia *f* **magnética** *sustantivo* magnetic transfer

transferencia *f* **radial** *sustantivo* radial transfer

transferencia *f* **sobre demanda** *sustantivo* (*de una memoria a otra*) demand staging

transferencia *f* **térmica de cera** *sustantivo* thermal transfer *o* thermal wax *o* thermal wax transfer printer

transferir *abrev vt* DL ■ *verbo* **1.** vt to dump **2.** vt to transfer ◊ **el usuario puede transferir datos del PC para actualizar las aplicaciones del ordenador central** the user can upload PC data to update mainframe applications ◊ **todas las operaciones de proceso de datos han sido transferidas al ordenador principal** all processing activities have been transferred to the mainframe ◊ **transferir datos de un ordenador pequeño a otro grande a la red** to upload

transformación *f sustantivo* conversion

transformación *f* **discreta de cosenos** *abrev* DCT ■ *sustantivo* discrete cosine transform

transformación *f* **en serie** *sustantivo* tweening ◊ **con el procedimiento de transformación en serie, se puede mostrar como una rana se convierte en una princesa en cinco pasos** using tweening, we can show how a frog turns into a princess in five steps

transformación *f* **gradual** *sustantivo* shading

transformador *m* **de aislamiento** *sustantivo* isolation transformer

transformador *m* **de separación** *sustantivo* isolation transformer

transformador *m* **MIDI** *sustantivo* MIDI Mapper ◊ **se podría utilizar el acoplador MIDI para desviar al piano electrónico todas las notas destinadas a la batería** you could use the MIDI Mapper to re-direct all the notes meant for the drum machine to the electronic piano

transformar *verbo vt* to transform ◊ **transformar una ventana en un icono** minimise

transformar bits *verbo* to bit-map *o* to bitmap

transformar en mayúsculas *verbo* to shift

transición *f sustantivo* crossover ◇ **la transición a la indexación informatizada de ficheros fue difícil** the crossover to computerized file indexing was difficult

transistor *sustantivo* transistor ◇ **lógica de transistor-transistor** transistor-transistor logic (TTL) ◇ **lógica (de) transistor-resistor** transistor-resistor logic (TRL) ◇ **transistor de conexión bipolar** bipolar junction transistor (BJT) ◇ **transistor** *m* **(de tipo) npn** npn transistor ◇ **transistor** *m* **(de tipo) pnp** pnp transistor

transistor *m* **bipolar** *sustantivo* **1.** bipolar transistor **2.** junction transistor

transistor *m* **de efecto de campo** *sustantivo* **1.** FET **2.** field effect transistor

transistor *m* **(de) MOS** *sustantivo* metal oxide semiconductor

transistor *m* **óptico** *sustantivo* transphasor

transistor *m* **unipolar** *sustantivo* unipolar transistor

transitorio *adj* transient

transmisión *sustantivo* **1.** (*de características de un objeto o una clase*) inheritance **2.** networking **3.** transmission ◇ **protocolo de control de transmisión** *o* **protocolo TCP (de transmisión)** transmission control protocol (TCP) ◇ **su velocidad media de transmisión es de 64.000 bits por segundo (bps), mediante una conexión en paralelo, o de 19.200 bps con una conexión en serie** their average transmission is 64,000 bits per second (bps) through a parallel connection or 19,200 bps through a serial connection ◇ **transmisión** *f* **paralela (bit a bit)** bit parallel ◇ **ventana de transmisión** transmission window

transmisión *f* **analógica** *sustantivo* analog transmission

transmisión *f* **asimétrica** *sustantivo* asymmetric transmission

transmisión *f* **asíncrona** *sustantivo* asynchronous transmission

transmisión *f* **bidireccional** *sustantivo* bidirectional transmission

transmisión *f* **ciega** *sustantivo* blind dialling

transmisión *f* **de banda base** *sustantivo* baseband signalling

transmisión *f* **de bytes en serie** *sustantivo* **1.** byte serial mode **2.** byte serial transmission

transmisión *f* **de datos** *sustantivo* data communications

transmisión *f* **de datos en paralelo** *sustantivo* parallel data transmission

transmisión *f* **de datos en serie** *sustantivo* **1.** serial data communications **2.** serial data transmission

transmisión *f* **de datos/información** *sustantivo* data transmission

transmisión *f* **de la imagen** *sustantivo* picture transmission

transmisión *f* **de señales en binario** *sustantivo* binary signalling

transmisión *f* **directa de señales** *sustantivo* DC signalling

transmisión *f* **electrónica** *sustantivo* electronic traffic

transmisión *f* **en dúplex** *sustantivo* duplex operation

transmisión *f* **en paralelo** *sustantivo* parallel transmission

transmisión *f* **en serie** *sustantivo* serial transmission

transmisión *f* **isócrona** *sustantivo* isochronous transmission

transmisión *f* **neutra** *sustantivo* neutral transmission

transmisión *f* **óptica** *sustantivo* optical transmission

transmisión *f* **paralela** *sustantivo* parallel transmission

transmisión *f* **por fax** *sustantivo* facsimile transmission

transmisión *f* **por onda portadora** *sustantivo* carrier signalling

transmisión *f* **simultánea** *sustantivo* simultaneous transmission

transmisión *f* **sin control de retorno** *sustantivo* free wheeling

transmisión *f* **síncrona** *sustantivo* synchronous transmission

transmisión *f* **sincrónica** *sustantivo* synchronous transmission

transmisor *m sustantivo* transmitter ■ *abrev* TX

transmisor *m* **de cinta con perforadora** *sustantivo* reperforator transmitter

transmisor *m* **perforador** *sustantivo* reperforator transmitter

transmitir *verbo* **1.** *vt* to broadcast **2.** *vt* to conduct **3.** *vt* to forward **4.** *vt* to propagate **5.** *vt* to transmit ◇ **el cobre transmite bien (la señal o la electricidad)** copper conducts well

transmitir una señal *verbo* to signal

transparencia *f sustantivo* transparency

transparente *adj* transparent

transportabilidad *f sustantivo* portability

transportable *adj* transportable ◇ **un ordenador transportable no es tan pequeño como un (ordenador) portátil** a transportable computer is not as small as a portable

transporte *m* **de alta velocidad** *sustantivo* high-speed carry

transporte *m* **de cinta** *sustantivo* tape transport

transporte *m* **rápido** *sustantivo* high-speed carry

trascendencia *f sustantivo* significance

trasladar *verbo vt* to translate

traslado *m* **(en memoria)** *sustantivo* relocation

traslado *m* **de un programa** *sustantivo* program relocation

traslapo *m sustantivo* lap

trastienda *f sustantivo* back office

tratamiento *m sustantivo* **1.** process **2.** processing **3.** word-processing ◇ **cargue el programa de tratamiento de textos antes de empezar a introducir datos** load the word-processing program before you start keyboarding ◇ **equipo de tabulación** tabulating equipment ◇ **tratamiento** *m* **de datos mediante tarjetas perforadas** tabulating

tratamiento *m* **aleatorio** *sustantivo* random processing

tratamiento *m* **automático de datos** *sustantivo* **1.** ADP **2.** automatic data processing

tratamiento *m* **centralizado de la información** *sustantivo* centralised data processing *o* centralized data processing

tratamiento *m* **de bits** *sustantivo* bit handling

tratamiento *m* **de datos** *sustantivo* **1.** data processing **2.** information processing

tratamiento *m* **de documentos** *sustantivo* document processing

tratamiento *m* **de errores** *sustantivo* **1.** error handling **2.** error management **3.** exception handling

tratamiento *m* **de excepciones** *sustantivo* **1.** error handling **2.** error management **3.** exception handling

tratamiento *m* **de imágenes de documentos** *sustantivo* document image processing

tratamiento *m* **de la imagen** *sustantivo* **1.** image processing **2.** picture processing

tratamiento *m* **de la información** *sustantivo* information processing

tratamiento *m* **del lenguaje natural** *sustantivo* natural language processing

tratamiento *m* **de movimientos** *abrev* TP ■ *sustantivo* transaction processing

tratamiento *m* **descentralizado de datos** *sustantivo* decentralised data processing *o* decentralized data processing

tratamiento *m* **de señal** *sustantivo* signal processing ◇ **los estudiantes que investigan sobre técnicas de procesamiento de señales utilizan este sistema** the system is used by students doing research on signal processing techniques

tratamiento *m* **de texto** *abrev* WP

tratamiento *m* **de textos** *sustantivo* **1.** document processing **2.** text processing ◇ **máquina de tratamiento de textos** text processor

tratamiento *m* **de textos especializado** *sustantivo* dedicated word-processor

tratamiento *m* **de transacciones** *abrev* TP ■ *sustantivo* transaction processing

tratamiento *m* **de transacciones en línea** *sustantivo* online transaction processing

tratamiento *m* **de transacciones en red** *sustantivo* online transaction processing

tratamiento *m* **en línea** *sustantivo* **1.** in-line processing **2.** online processing

tratamiento *m* **en red** *sustantivo* online processing

tratamiento *m* **en serie** *sustantivo* serial processing

tratamiento *m* **en tiempo real** *sustantivo* real-time processing

tratamiento *m* **fuera (de) red** *sustantivo* off-line processing

tratamiento *m* **informático de la imagen** *sustantivo* computer image processing

tratamiento *m* **inmediato** *sustantivo* **1.** immediate processing **2.** in-line processing

tratamiento *m* **preferente** *sustantivo* foregrounding

tratamiento *m* **secuencial** *sustantivo* **1.** sequential processing **2.** serial processing

tratamiento *m* **simultáneo** *sustantivo* simultaneous processing

tratamiento *m* **sin ayuda del ordenador** *sustantivo* manual data processing

tratar *verbo* **1.** *vt* to process **2.** *vt* to word-process ◇ **hemos procesado los nuevos datos** we processed the new data ◇ **llevará mucho tiempo procesar toda la información** processing all the information will take a long time ◇ **tratar (las instrucciones) por encauzamiento** pipeline

trayecto *m* **de datos** *sustantivo* data path

trazado *m sustantivo* bar

trazado *m* **de rayos** *sustantivo* ray tracing ◇ **se tardarán bastantes horas para generar esta imagen con rastreo por rayos en este potente PC** to generate this picture with ray tracing will take several hours on this powerful PC

trazado *m* **de un circuito** *sustantivo* circuit design

trazador *m sustantivo* printer-plotter

trazador *m* **(de grafos)** *sustantivo* plotter

trazador *m* **de curvas** *sustantivo* x-y plotter

trazador *m* **de gráficos** *sustantivo* x-y plotter

trazador *m* **de grafos** *sustantivo* graph plotter

trazador *m* **de pluma** *sustantivo* pen plotter

trazador *m* **de plumilla** *sustantivo* pen plotter

trazador *m* **de superficie plana** *sustantivo* flatbed plotter

trazador *m* **de tambor** *sustantivo* drum plotter

trazador *m* **digital** *sustantivo* digital plotter

trazador *m* **gráfico** *sustantivo* **1.** graph plotter **2.** pen recorder

trazador *m* **incremental** *sustantivo* incremental plotter

trazar *verbo vt* (*una curva o un grafo por puntos numerados*) to plot

trazo *m sustantivo* plot

tren *m* **de impulsos** *sustantivo* **1.** pulse stream **2.** pulse train

tríada *f sustantivo* triad

tridimensional *adj* **1.** 3D **2.** three-dimensional

truncamiento *m sustantivo* truncation

truncar *verbo vt* to truncate

Tseng Labs (*empresa productora de conjunto de chips*) Tseng Labs

TSR *sustantivo* RAM resident program

tubo *m sustantivo* conduit ◇ **tubo** *m* **catódico (para el televisor)** television tube

tubo *m* **de almacenamiento** *sustantivo* storage tube

tubo *m* **de rayos catódicos** *sustantivo* **1.** cathode ray tube **2.** CRT

tunelado *m sustantivo* tunnelling

tunelización *f sustantivo* tunnelling

TV *f abrev* TV

TV *f* **interactiva** *sustantivo* interactive TV

TWAIN *sustantivo* (*estándar de interfaz de programación*) TWAIN

12 puntos ingleses *sustantivo* pica

2D (*imagen gráfica*) 2D

U

ubicación ◇ **el programa se rodó en España** the programme was shot on location in Spain ◇ **(rodaje) en los exteriores** on location ◇ **exteriores (de una película)** location shots ◇ **ubicación** *f* **(de la memoria)** location

Ultimedia™ *(marca comercial)* Ultimedia

último ◇ **último en entrar primero en salir** LIFO

último en entrar primero en salir *adj* last in first out

ultra- *prefijo* ultra- ◇ **ultrasonido** ultrasound ◇ **ultrasonoro, -a** *o* **ultrasónico, -a** ultrasonic

ultrasensible *adj* high-speed

umbral *m sustantivo* threshold ◇ **puerta umbral** threshold gate ◇ **valor umbral** threshold value

un billón *m* **de bytes** *sustantivo* terabyte

uni- *prefijo* uni-

unidad *sustantivo* **1.** plug-in unit **2.** unit ◇ **nuestro nuevo producto tiene una unidad de flujo de cinta de 96 Mb** our new product has a 96Mb streaming tape drive ◇ **unidad aritmética y lógica** arithmetic and logic unit (ALU) ◇ **unidad** *f* **con cabeza de lectura fija** fixed head disk ◇ **unidad** *f* **de cinta (magnética)** tape drive ◇ **unidad** *f* **de control de periféricos** PCU; peripheral control unit ◇ **unidad** *f* **de control de periféricos dispuestos en forma de racimo** cluster controller ◇ **unidad** *f* **de disco de doble velocidad** double-speed drive ◇ **unidad** *f* **de gestión de la memoria** memory management unit; MMU ◇ **unidad** *f* **de gestión de la memoria paginada** paged-memory management unit ◇ **unidad** *f* **en buen estado de funcionamiento** functional unit

'En la tecnología P2P, cada unidad funciona a su vez como servidor y como terminal, en contraposición a las de cliente servidor, en las que unos servidores centrales aportan los datos a otros.' [*Ciberp@ís*]

unidad *f* **adaptadora de datos** *sustantivo* data adapter unit

unidad *f* **aritmética y lógica (UAL)** *sustantivo* **1.** arithmetic logic unit **2.** arithmetic unit

unidad *f* **automática de llamadas** *sustantivo* **1.** ACU **2.** automatic calling unit

unidad *f* **cargadora** *sustantivo* cartridge drive

unidad *f* **central (de proceso)** *sustantivo* CPU

unidad *f* **central de cálculo** *sustantivo* central processing element

unidad *f* **central de proceso** *sustantivo* central processing unit *o* central processor

unidad *f* **de acceso** *sustantivo* access unit

unidad *f* **de asignación** *sustantivo* allocation unit

unidad *f* **de asignación perdida** *sustantivo* lost cluster

unidad *f* **de cintas** *sustantivo* tape deck

unidad *f* **de coma flotante** *sustantivo* **1.** floating point processor **2.** floating point unit ■ *abrev* FPU

unidad *f* **de control** *sustantivo* control unit ■ *abrev* CU

unidad *f* **de disco(s)** *sustantivo* disk unit

unidad *f* **de disco duro** *sustantivo* **1.** hard disk drive **2.** hard drive ■ *abrev* HDD

unidad *f* **de disco flexible** *abrev* FDD ■ *sustantivo* floppy disk unit

unidad *f* **de disco magnético** *sustantivo* magnetic disk unit

unidad *f* **de disquete** *sustantivo* floppy disk drive

unidad *f* **de flujo de cinta** *sustantivo* streaming tape drive

unidad *f* **de formateo vertical** *sustantivo* vertical format unit ■ *abrev* VFU

unidad *f* **de información** *sustantivo* computer word

unidad *f* **de lectura por defecto** *sustantivo* default drive ◇ **el sistema operativo permite que el usuario seleccione el lector por defecto** the operating system allows the user to select the default drive

unidad *f* **del sistema** *sustantivo* system unit

unidad *f* **de microprocesador** *sustantivo* microprocessor unit ■ *abrev* MPU

unidad *f* **de respuesta audio** *sustantivo* audio response unit

unidad *f* **de respuesta vocal** *sustantivo* audio response unit

unidad *f* **de sincronización** *sustantivo* synchroniser

unidad *f* **de visualización** *sustantivo* display unit

unidad *f* **lógica** *sustantivo* **1.** logical drive **2.** logical unit **3.** LU ◇ **la unidad lógica F: en realidad almacena datos en una parte del disco del servidor** the logical drive F: actually stores data on part of the server's disk drive

unidad *f* **periférica** *sustantivo* peripheral unit

unidifusión *f sustantivo* unicast
uniformar *verbo vt* to normalise *o* to normalize
unión *sustantivo* **1.** interfacing **2.** junction **3.** union ◇ **unión** *f* **en grupo de varios periféricos** clustering
unión *f* **en cadena** *sustantivo* daisy-chaining ◇ **la conexión en cadena ahorra mucho cable** daisy-chaining saves a lot of cable
unión *f* **en T** *sustantivo* T junction
unión *f* **tierra/satélite** *sustantivo* uplink
unipolar *adj* unipolar
unir *verbo* **1.** *vt* to add **2.** *vt* to merge **3.** *vt* to splice ◇ **puede usar pegamento o cinta adhesiva para unir los extremos (de la película)** you can use glue or splicing tape to splice the ends
unir(se) *verbo vr* to join
universal *adj* **1.** machine-independent **2.** universal ◇ **canal universal de transmisión por bloques** universal block channel (UBC) ◇ **dispositivo universal** universal device (UART, USRT, USART) ◇ **el conjunto universal de números primos inferiores a diez y superiores a dos es 3,5,7** the universal set of prime numbers less than ten and greater than two is 3,5,7
UNIX™ *sustantivo* UNIX
UNIX BSD *sustantivo* Berkeley UNIX
un millón *m* **de millones** *sustantivo* billion
URL *m sustantivo* **1.** uniform resource locator **2.** URL
USB *sustantivo* universal serial bus
Usenet *sustantivo* Usenet
uso *m* **de mayúsculas** *sustantivo* capitalisation *o* capitalization
usuario, -a *sustantivo* **1.** mid-user **2.** user ◇ **usuario** *m* **(con derecho de acceso)** accessor ◇ **usuario** *m* **autorizado (para utilizar un sistema)** authorised user
'Las compañías de software han desarrollado diversos métodos de codificación que, aseguran, garantizan una confidencialidad total sobre los datos transmitidos, pero la desconfianza de los usuarios es todavía grande.' [*La Red*]
usuario *m* **avanzado** *sustantivo* power user
usuario *m* **final** *sustantivo* end user ◇ **la empresa está creando un ordenador pensando en un usuario final específico** the company is creating a computer with a specific end user in mind
utilidad ◇ **utilidad** *f* **de copia UNIX a UNIX** UNIX-to-UNIX copy
utilidad *f sustantivo* applet

utilidad *f* **antivirus** *sustantivo* **1.** anti-virus program **2.** vaccine
utilidad *f* **Chooser™** Chooser™
utilidad *f* **de consulta** *sustantivo* query facility
utilidad *f* **de corrección gramatical** *sustantivo* grammar checker
utilidad *f* **de defragmentación** *sustantivo* defragmentation utility
utilidad *f* **de la aplicación** *sustantivo* application service element
utilidad *f* **de mantenimiento** *sustantivo* service program
utilidad *f* **de pregunta** *sustantivo* query facility
utilidad *f* **de seguridad** *sustantivo* backup utility
utilidad *f* **de transferencia de ficheros** *sustantivo* file transfer utility
utilidad *f* **EDLIN** *sustantivo* EDLIN
utilidad *f* **genia** *sustantivo* wizard
utilidad *f* **que almacena imágenes** *sustantivo* scrapbook ◇ **guardamos nuestro logotipo en el álbum de recortes** we store our logo in the scrapbook
utilidad *f* **UNIX demonio** *sustantivo* daemon
utilidad *f* **UUCP** *sustantivo* UNIX-to-UNIX copy
utilización ◇ **utilización** *f* **de una segunda fuente (de producción de componentes)** second sourcing
utilización *f* **compartida de ficheros** *sustantivo* file sharing
utilización *f* **compartida de los datos** *sustantivo* data sharing
utilización *f* **de doble memoria intermedia** *sustantivo* double buffering
utilización *f* **de la memoria intermedia** *sustantivo* buffering
utilización GENDER>f de datos compartidos *sustantivo* data sharing
utilizar la memoria temporal *verbo* to cache ◇ **este programa puede almacenar en memoria temporal fuentes de caracteres de cualquier tamaño** this program can cache any size font ◇ **las instrucciones de la memoria temporal de este procesador mejoran su rendimiento en un 15 por ciento** this CPU cache instructions improve performance by 15 percent

V

v (voltio) *abrev* V

vaciado *sustantivo* dump ◇ **vaciado** *m* **de la memoria mediante la impresora** memory dump ◇ **vaciado** *m* **de la pantalla mediante la impresora** screen dump ◇ **vaciado** *m* **de pantalla (por impresora)** screen dump ◇ **vaciado** *m* **de punto de control** check point dump ◇ **vaciado** *m* **instantáneo (mediante la impresora)** snapshot dump

vaciado *m* **binario** *sustantivo* binary dump

vaciado *m* **de ficheros** *sustantivo* file clean-up

vaciado *m* **de la memoria** *sustantivo* storage dump

vaciado *m* **del formato** *sustantivo* formatted dump

vaciado *m* **de movimientos** *sustantivo* change dump

vaciado *m* **de seguridad** *sustantivo* rescue dump

vaciado *m* **dinámico** *sustantivo* dynamic dump

vaciado *m* **en binario** *sustantivo* binary dump

vaciado *m* **estático** *sustantivo* static dump

vaciado *m* **hexadecimal** *sustantivo* hex dump

vaciado *m* **irreversible** *sustantivo* disaster dump

vaciado *m* **volcado** *sustantivo* selective dump

vaciado y reinicio *sustantivo* dump and re-start

vaciar *verbo* **1.** *vt* to clear **2.** *vt* to dump **3.** *vt* to purge

vaciar la pantalla *verbo* to zap

vacío *m* *sustantivo* gap

vacío *m* **de aire** *sustantivo* **1.** air gap **2.** head gap

validación *f* *sustantivo* validation

validación *f* **de datos** *sustantivo* **1.** data validation **2.** data vetting

validación *f* **de ficheros** *sustantivo* file validation

validación *f* **de un chip** *sustantivo* chip select ■ *abrev* CS

validado ◇ **el usuario puede seleccionar una resolución de pantalla de 640 por 300, 240 o 200 pixels** the video resolution of 640 by 300, 240 or 200 pixels is user-selectable ◇ **validado según las necesidades del usuario** user-selectable

validar *verbo* **1.** *vt* to arm **2.** *vt* to enable **3.** *vt* to validate

validez *f* *sustantivo* validity

válido *adj* **1.** legal **2.** valid

válido como puente conector *adj* jumper-selectable

valor *m* *sustantivo* value ◇ **red de valor añadido** *o* **red de integración de servicios** value-added network (VAN)

valor *m* **absoluto** *sustantivo* absolute value ◇ **el valor absoluto de –62,34 es 62,34** the absolute value of –62.34 is 62.34

valor añadido *adj* value-added

valor *m* **binario** *sustantivo* truth value

valor *m* **booleano** *sustantivo* Boolean value

valor *m* **complementario** *sustantivo* offset

valor *m* **de comprobación al azar** *sustantivo* hash value

valor *m* **de salida** *sustantivo* seed

valor *m* **de una matriz** *sustantivo* array element

valor *m* **de verdad** *sustantivo* truth value

valor *m* **escalar** *sustantivo* scalar value

valor *m* **inicial** *sustantivo* initial value

valor *m* **por defecto** *sustantivo* default value ◇ **la anchura de la pantalla tiene un valor por defecto de 80** screen width has a default value of 80

valor *m* **por omisión** *sustantivo* default value ◇ **la anchura de la pantalla tiene un valor por defecto de 80** screen width has a default value of 80

valor *m* **relativo** *sustantivo* offset value *o* offset word

vanguardia ◇ **a la vanguardia** bleeding edge

variable *adj* variable ■ *sustantivo* variable ◇ **control de velocidad variable** variable speed control ◇ **variable** *f* **de referencia de una celda** cell reference variable

variable *f* **binaria** *sustantivo* binary variable

variable *f* **booleana** *sustantivo* **1.** Boolean data type **2.** Boolean variable

variable *f* **con subíndice** *sustantivo* subscripted variable

variable *f* **de cadena** *sustantivo* string variable

variable *f* **del entorno** *sustantivo* environment variable

variable *f* **del equipo** *sustantivo* environment variable

variable *f* **del sistema** *sustantivo* system variable

variable *f* **de valor único** *sustantivo* scalar ◇ **una magnitud escalar tiene un valor de magnitud único, un vector tiene dos o más valores posicionales** a scalar has a single magnitude value, a vector has two or more positional values

variable *f* **escalar** *sustantivo* scalar variable

variable *f* **ficticia** *sustantivo* dummy variable

variable *f* **global** *sustantivo* global variable

variable *f* **local** *sustantivo* local variable

variación *f* **de la velocidad** *sustantivo* flutter ◇ **la oscilación y la distorsión del tono son los fallos más comunes en las grabadoras baratas** wow and flutter are common faults on cheap tape recorders

variar *verbo vi* to range

vatio *m sustantivo* watt

VÁYASE A *sustantivo* GOTO

VBScript *abrev* VBScript

véase el manual *abrev* RTFM

vector *m sustantivo* vector ◇ **imagen vectorial** vector image ◇ **vectores por segundo** vectors per second (VPS)

vector *m* **de retardo** *sustantivo* delay vector

vectorial *adj* scalable

vehicular *verbo vt* to channel

vehículo *m* **dirigido por ordenador** *sustantivo* buggy

velocidad *sustantivo* 1. line speed 2. rate ◇ **la velocidad de ejecución de instrucciones del procesador es mejor que la de la versión anterior** the processor's instruction execution rate is better than the older version ◇ **la velocidad de transmisión de la señal binaria fue de 300 bits por segundo** the baud rate of the binary signal was 300 bits per second ◇ **un módem equipado con un escáner de reconocimiento de baudios se ajusta automáticamente a la velocidad a la que debe funcionar** a modem with auto-baud scanner can automatically sense at which baud rate it should operate ◇ **velocidad** *f* **angular constante** CAV ◇ **velocidad** *f* **de acceso a la dirección** address access time ◇ **velocidad** *f* **de cálculo (por ordenador)** computing speed ◇ **velocidad** *f* **del reloj de la unidad central** CPU clock speed ◇ **velocidad** *f* **de salida de la información** information rate ◇ **velocidad** *f* **(de transmisión) en baudios** baud rate ◇ **velocidad** *f* **real de transferencia de datos** actual data transfer rate

velocidad *f* **angular constante** *sustantivo* constant angular velocity

velocidad *f* **constante de bits** *abrev* CBR ■ *sustantivo* constant bit rate

velocidad *f* **de barrido** *sustantivo* scanning speed ◇ **el rendimiento específico es de una velocidad de lectura de 1,3 pulgadas por segundo** throughput is 1.3 inches per second scanning speed ◇ **la velocidad de lectura es de 9,9 segundos para un documento de 8,5 por 11 pulgadas** its scanning speed is 9.9 seconds for an 8.5 inch by 11 inch document

velocidad *f* **de bucle** *sustantivo* speed of loop

velocidad *f* **de búsqueda efectiva** *sustantivo* effective search speed

velocidad *f* **de cronómetro** *sustantivo* 1. clock rate 2. clock speed

velocidad *f* **de lectura** *sustantivo* read rate

velocidad *f* **de línea agregada** *sustantivo* aggregate line speed

velocidad *f* **del ratón** *sustantivo* mouse acceleration

velocidad *f* **del reloj del bus** *sustantivo* bus clock speed

velocidad *f* **de reloj** *sustantivo* 1. clock rate 2. clock speed

velocidad *f* **de reproducción** *sustantivo* playback speed

velocidad *f* **de transferencia** *sustantivo* transfer rate ◇ **con una buena línea telefónica, este par de módems pueden alcanzar una velocidad de transferencia de 14,4 Kbps** with a good telephone line, this pair of modems can achieve a transfer rate of 14.4Kbps

velocidad *f* **de transferencia de datos** *sustantivo* data transfer rate

velocidad *f* **de transmisión** *sustantivo* 1. bit rate 2. transmission rate

velocidad *f* **de transmisión de datos** *sustantivo* 1. data rate 2. data signalling rate

velocidad *f* **de tratamiento** *sustantivo* data rate

velocidad *f* **lineal constante** *sustantivo* 1. CLV 2. constant linear velocity

velocidad *f* **máxima de transmisión** *sustantivo* maximum transmission rate

velocidad *f* **media** *sustantivo* medium speed

velocidad *f* **secuencial** *sustantivo* frame rate

velocidad *f* **única** *sustantivo* single speed

vendedor *m sustantivo* vendor

venir de *verbo* to originate

ventana *f sustantivo* 1. access hole 2. message box 3. window ◇ **el sistema operativo permite visualizar simultáneamente en pantalla otros programas en ventanas diferentes** the operating system will allow other programs to be displayed on-screen at the same time in different windows ◇ **emplee la ventana de control de la interfaz para ver qué señales están activas** the serial interface doesn't seem to be working – use the breakout box to see which signals are present ◇ **entorno gráfico WIMP (con ventana, icono, ratón, puntero)** window, icon, mouse, pointer (WIMP) ◇ **hay varias estaciones de trabajo remotas conectadas a la red y cada una de ellas dispone de su propia ventana de acceso al disco duro** several remote stations are connected to the network and each has its own window onto the hard disk ◇ **la interfaz en serie no parece que esté funcionando** the serial interface doesn't seem to be working – use the breakout box to see which signals are present ◊ **ventana** *f* **de control de la interfaz** breakout box

ventana *f* **activa** *sustantivo* **1.** active window **2.** focus window

ventana *f* **(del) bloc de notas** *sustantivo* screen notepad

ventana *f* **de aplicaciones** *sustantivo* application window

ventana *f* **de compatibilidad** *sustantivo* compatibility box ◊ **el OS** *or* **2 tiene una ventana de compatibilidad que le permite ejecutar aplicaciones de DOS** OS/2 has a compatibility box to allow it to run DOS applications

ventana *f* **de consulta** *sustantivo* query window

ventana *f* **de consulta/de búsqueda** *sustantivo* query window

ventana *f* **de diálogo** *sustantivo* dialog box

ventana *f* **de edición** *sustantivo* edit window

ventana *f* **de instrucción** *sustantivo* command window ◊ **la ventana de instrucción es una sola línea en la parte inferior de la pantalla** the command window is a single line at the bottom of the screen

ventana *f* **de instrucciones** *sustantivo* command window ◊ **el usuario puede definir el tamaño de la ventana de instrucciones** the user can define the size of the command window

ventana *f* **delgada** *sustantivo* thin window

ventana *f* **del menú** *sustantivo* **1.** pop-down menu **2.** pop-up menu

ventana *f* **de mensaje de alerta** *sustantivo* alert box ◊ **el mensaje de alerta me advirtió de que estaba a punto de borrar todos mis ficheros** the alert box warned me that I was about to delete all my files

ventana *f* **de texto** *sustantivo* text window

ventana *f* **de una sola línea** *sustantivo* **1.** strip window **2.** thin window

ventana *f* **estrecha** *sustantivo* thin window

ventana *f* **flottante** *sustantivo* floating window

ventana *f* **inactiva** *sustantivo* inactive window

ventana *f* **objeto** *sustantivo* target window

ventanas *fpl* **en cascada** *plural noun* cascading windows

ventana *f* **superpuesta** *sustantivo* pop-up window

ver *verbo* **1.** *vt* to browse **2.** *vt* to view

verdadero *adj* true ◊ **color verdadero** true colour

verificación *sustantivo* **1.** echo check **2.** verification ◊ **verificación** *f* **(de un programa)** desk check ◊ **verificación** *f* **del buen funcionamiento de un programa** program verification

verificación *f* **aritmética** *sustantivo* arithmetic check

verificación *f* **automática** *sustantivo* **1.** automatic checking **2.** auto verify

verificación *f* **de bucle** *sustantivo* loop check

verificación *f* **de datos** *sustantivo* data vetting

verificación *f* **horizontal** *sustantivo* horizontal check

verificación *f* **por lectura** *sustantivo* read back check

verificación *f* **por residuo** *sustantivo* residue check

verificación *f* **por suma** *sustantivo* summation check

verificación *f* **y validación** *sustantivo* V & V

verificación y validación *sustantivo* verification and validation

verificador *m* *sustantivo* **1.** exerciser **2.** verifier

verificador *m* **de cable** *sustantivo* cable tester

verificar *verbo* **1.** *vt* to monitor **2.** *vt* to verify ◊ **está verificando cómo progresan los aprendices de programación** he is monitoring the progress of the trainee programmers

Verónica Veronica

versión *f* *sustantivo* **1.** build **2.** release **3.** version ◊ **el nuevo software es la versión 5** the latest software is release 5 ◊ **ésta es la última versión del nuevo software** this is the latest build of the new software ◊ **la última versión del software incluye una rutina gráfica actualizada** the latest version of the software includes an improved graphics routine ◊ **versión** *f* **XT basada en el procesador Inter 8088** XT

versión *f* **avanzada** *sustantivo* advanced version

versión *f* **beta** *sustantivo* beta version

versión *f* **de aplicación** *sustantivo* run-time version

versión *f* **de control** *sustantivo* version control

versión *f* **de demostración** *sustantivo* (*de un programa*) demonstration software ◊ **la compañía proporcionó un programa de demostración que permite hacerlo todo menos guardar los datos** the company gave away demonstration software that lets you do everything except save your data

versión *f* **de seguridad** *sustantivo* backup version

versión *f* **ejecutable** *sustantivo* run-time version

versión *f* **elemental** *sustantivo* **1.** lo-res **2.** low resolution

versión *f* **inicial** *sustantivo* **1.** lo-res **2.** low resolution

versión *f* **previa** *sustantivo* (*de un producto que ya no realiza algunas funciones*) back-level

vertical *adj* vertical ■ *sustantivo* y-direction ◊ **barrido vertical** vertical scanning ◊ **impulso de sincronismo vertical** vertical drive pulse ◊ **su nuevo programa para la gestión de una floristería es una buena aplicación vertical** your new software to manage a florist's is a good vertical application ◊ **unidad de formateo vertical** vertical format unit (VFU)

verticalmente *adv* vertically ◇ **señal de polarización vertical** *o* **señal polarizada verticalmente** vertically polarized signal

vértice *m sustantivo* vertex

VGA *sustantivo* VGA

vía *sustantivo* **1.** channel **2.** facility ■ *preposition* via ◇ **cable de envío (de la señal)** *o* **cable de antena-circuito** *o* **alimentador** feeder cable ◇ **grupo de canales** *o* **de vías** channel group ◇ **las señales nos han llegado vía satélite** the signals have reached us via satellite ◇ **vía** *f* **de acceso directo a la memoria** direct memory access channel ◇ **vía** *f* **de retorno de una red local** backward LAN channel ◇ **vía** *f* **de transmisión (de la señal)** feeder ◇ **vía** *f* **de transmisión de la información** information transfer channel

vía *f* **alterna** *sustantivo* alternate route

vía *f* **analógica** *sustantivo* analog channel

vía *f* **asíncrona de acceso** *sustantivo* asynchronous port

vía *f* **de acceso** *sustantivo* pathname

vía *f* **de entrada/salida** *sustantivo* **1.** input/output channel **2.** I/O channel

vía *f* **de envío** *sustantivo* feeder ◇ **cable de envío (de la señal)** *o* **cable de antena-circuito** *o* **alimentador** feeder cable

vía *f* **de lectura/escritura** *sustantivo* read/write channel

vía *f* **de seguridad** *sustantivo* backup path

vía *f* **de transmisión** *sustantivo* transmission channel

vía *f* **de transmisión de información** *sustantivo* information bearer channel

vía *f* **doble** *sustantivo* dual channel

vía *f* **hacia atrás** *sustantivo* backward channel

vía *f* **secundaria** *sustantivo* secondary channel

vida *f* **artificial** *sustantivo* artificial life

VidCap *sustantivo* VidCap

video ◇ **vídeo** *m* **entrelazado** interlaced video

vídeo *m sustantivo* video ◇ **arquitectura** *f* **de control de sistema de vídeo** ViSCA ◇ **asociación normalizadora de la electrónica del vídeo** Video Electronics Standards Association (VESA) ◇ **cinta de vídeo** videotape ◇ **conmutador del nivel de salida de vídeo** video output level selector ◇ **con un procesador de imágenes se puede congelar una imagen de vídeo** with an image processor you can freeze a video frame ◇ **el nuevo escáner de vídeo está diseñado para escanear objetos tridimensionales** the new video scanner is designed to scan three-dimensional objects ◇ **entrada a la pantalla de vídeo** video display input (VDI) ◇ **imagen de vídeo** video frame; video image ◇ **lector de vídeo** video player ◇ **matriz gráfica de vídeo (VGA)** video graphics array (VGA) ◇ **mezclador, -a de vídeo** video mixer ◇ **normas de vídeo** video standards ◇ **operador, -a de vídeo** video engineer *o* video operator ◇ **panel de conexiones de vídeo** video patch panel ◇ **películas de terror** *o* **(pornography) películas porno (en vídeo)** video nasties ◇ **puerto de**

vídeo video port ◇ **RAM de vídeo** *o* **memoria de acceso aleatorio de vídeo** video random access memory (VRAM) ◇ **se puede enviar una imagen de vídeo imprimible a una impresora láser básica a través del puerto de vídeo** a printer-readable video image can be sent to a basic laser printer through a video port ◇ **tarjeta de expansión de vídeo** video expander ◇ **tarjeta de vídeo** video card ◇ **tituladora de vídeo** video character adder ◇ **(reproductor** *or* **grabador de) vídeo** video recorder; videotape recorder ◇ **vídeo para Windows** Video for Windows™ (VFW)

vídeo *m* **activo** *sustantivo* active video *o* active video signal

video-clip *m sustantivo* video clip

vídeo *m* **comprimido** *sustantivo* compressed video

videoconferencia *sustantivo* video conferencing

'Los sistemas de videoconferencias más habituales son los denominados set-top, que lo llevan todo integrado excepto el televisor o el equipo de proyección y representan alrededor del 80% de la venta total.' [*Ciberp@ís*]

vídeo *m* **digital** *sustantivo* digital video

videodisco *m sustantivo* videodisc

vídeo *m* **interactivo** *sustantivo* **1.** interactive video **2.** IV

vídeo *m* **inverso** *sustantivo* inverse video

vídeo *m* **invertido** *sustantivo* reverse video

videojuego *m sustantivo* **1.** computer game **2.** video game

vídeo *m* **lineal** *sustantivo* linear video

vídeo para Windows *abrev* VFW

Video para Windows (*marca comercial*) Video for Windows

videotexto *m sustantivo* videotext *o* videotex

videotexto *m* **interactivo** *sustantivo* interactive videotext

vinculación *f* **activa** *sustantivo* hot link

vínculo *m sustantivo* link

vínculo *m* **activo** *sustantivo* hot link

viral *adj* viral

virgen *adj* **1.** clean **2.** virgin

virtual *adj* virtual ◇ **complejo de procesadores virtuales** virtual processor complex (VPC) ◇ **procesador virtual** virtual processor (VP)

virus *sustantivo* virus ◇ **si su PC se infecta con un virus, los datos están en peligro** if your PC is infected with a virus, your data is at risk

'El aspecto más interesante de un virus informático desde un punto de vista ciberbélico es probablemente su capacidad de difundirse con gran rapidez y expandir cualquier cadena de código infeccioso por cantidad de ordenadores, pasando completamente desapercibido.' [*Ciberp@ís*]

'Periódicamente adquieren notoriedad los virus, programas informáticos cuya presencia en el ordenador propio nadie desea, que son capaces de crear, modificar o destruir información haciéndola inservible y que pueden propagarse a otros pro-

gramas y sistemas de forma espontánea.'
[*PC Plus*]

virus *m* **informático** *sustantivo* computer virus

visionado *m* **de datos** *sustantivo* information output

visionar *verbo vt* to browse

visión *f* **del usuario** *sustantivo* external schema

visitante *m sustantivo* eyeball

visor *m sustantivo* viewer

vista ◇ **(función de) vista** *f* **previa de página (antes de imprimir)** page preview

vista *f* **isométrica** *sustantivo* isometric view ◇ **en una visualización isométrica no se aprecia la perspectiva** an isometric view does not show any perspective

vista *f* **preliminar** *sustantivo* page preview

vista *f* **previa** *sustantivo* **1.** previewer **2.** print preview ◇ **el procedimiento de vista previa permite al usuario localizar errores** the built-in previewer allows the user to check for mistakes

visto *m* **bueno de mantenimiento** *sustantivo* maintenance release ◇ **la puesta a punto correctiva de la base de datos, versión 2.01, corrige el problema de los márgenes** the maintenance release of the database program, version 2.01, corrects the problem with the margins

visual *adj* visual ◇ **(herramienta de programación) Visual Basic™** Visual Basic™ ◇ **(herramienta de programación) Visual Basic para aplicaciones** Visual Basic for Applications™ ◇ **(lenguaje de programación) Visual C™** Visual C™

Visual Basic™ *abrev* VB ■ *(marca comercial)* Visual Basic

Visual Basic para aplicaciones *abrev* VBA ■ *(marca comercial)* Visual Basic for Applications

Visual C™ *(marca comercial)* Visual C

visualización *f sustantivo* **1.** display **2.** readout **3.** visualisation *o* visualization ◇ **dimensión tamaño de visualización** *o* **de pantalla** display size ◇ **visualización** *f* **de negro sobre fondo blanco** positive display ◇ **visualización** *f* **de una parte de la página** part page display ◇ **visualización (previa) PostScript™** Display PostScript™

visualización *f* **alfanumérica** *sustantivo* alphanumeric display

visualización *f* **analógica** *sustantivo* analog display

visualización *f* **compuesta** *sustantivo* composite display

visualización *f* **de caracteres** *sustantivo* character display

visualización *f* **de información en recuadro** *sustantivo* windowing

visualización *f* **de información en ventana** *sustantivo* windowing

visualización *f* **de texto** *sustantivo* character display

visualización *f* **de una línea** *sustantivo* single line display

visualización *f* **de una página** *sustantivo* page display

visualización *f* **electroluminiscente** *sustantivo* electroluminescent display

visualización *f* **en color** *sustantivo* colour display

visualización *f* **gráfica** *sustantivo* graphic display

visualización *f* **isométrica** *sustantivo* isometric view ◇ **en una visualización isométrica no se aprecia la perspectiva** an isometric view does not show any perspective

visualización *f* **PostScript** *(marca comercial)* Display PostScript™

visualización *f* **reducida** *sustantivo* part page display

visualizado *adj* on-screen

visualizador *m abrev* VDU ■ *sustantivo* visual display terminal *o* visual display unit

visualizador *m* **de cristal líquido** *sustantivo* **1.** LCD **2.** liquid crystal display

visualizar *verbo* **1.** *vt* to picture **2.** *vt* to view ◇ **el usuario tiene que pagar para visualizar las páginas en un sistema de tablón de anuncios** the user has to pay a charge for viewing pages on a bulletin board ◇ **intente visualizar el esquema antes de comenzar a dibujar** try to picture the layout before starting to draw it in

vital *adj* mission-critical

Vivo™ *(formato de vídeo por la red)* Vivo

vocabulario *m* **controlado** *sustantivo* controlled vocabulary

volatilidad *f sustantivo* volatility

volcado ◇ **volcado** *m* **automático de fuentes de caracteres** automatic font downloading

volcado *m* **de la memoria** *sustantivo* storage dump

volcado *m* **estático** *sustantivo* static dump

volcado *m* **final** *sustantivo* post mortem

volcado *m* **postmortem** *sustantivo* post mortem

volcado *m* **selectivo** *sustantivo* selective dump

volcar (un texto) *verbo* to flow text

voltaje *m sustantivo* voltage ◇ **caída** voltage dip *o* dip in voltage

voltio *m sustantivo* volt

volumen *m sustantivo* **1.** level **2.** volume ◇ **baje el volumen** turn the sound level down, it's far too loud

volumen *m* **de trabajo** *sustantivo* workload

volver a cero *verbo* to zero ◇ **inserción sin fricción** *o* **fuerza de inserción cero** zero insertion force (ZIF) ◇ **volver un dispositivo a cero** *o* **limpiar un dispositivo programable** to zero a device

volver a dar formato *verbo* to reformat ◇ **evite reformatear el disco duro a menos que**

no haya ninguna otra solución do not reformat your hard disk unless you can't do anything else

volver a enviar *verbo* to redirect

volver a poner en marcha *verbo* to restart

volver hacia atrás *verbo* to rollback

vóxtel *m sustantivo* voxel

voz *f* **de transmisión de datos** *sustantivo* data path

voz *f* **digitalizada** *sustantivo* digital speech

voz *f* **sintetizada** *sustantivo* synthesised voice

vuelco *sustantivo* formatted dump ◇ **vuelco** *m* **de punto de control** check point dump

vuelco *m* **(de memoria)** *sustantivo* dump

vuelco *m* **de la memoria** *sustantivo* memory dump

vuelco *m* **de modificaciones** *sustantivo* change dump

vuelta *f* **a cero** *sustantivo* return to zero signal

vuelta *f* **automática a la línea** *sustantivo* horizontal wraparound

WXYZ

W3 *abrev* W3

webBot WebBot

Windows ◇ **Windows para grupos de trabajo** (*marca comercial*) Windows for Workgroups

Windows 3.1 (*marca comercial*) Windows 3.1

Windows 3.1x (*marca comercial*) Windows 3.1x

Windows 3.11 Windows 3.11

Windows 95 (*marca comercial*) Windows 95

Windows 98 (*marca comercial*) Windows 98

Windows 2000 (*marca comercial*) Windows 2000

Windows CE (*marca comercial*) Windows CE

Windows Explorer (*marca comercial*) Windows Explorer

Windows GDI (*marca comercial*) Windows GDI

Windows ME (*marca comercial*) Windows ME

Windows NT™ (*marca comercial*) Windows NT

Windows SDK™ (*marca comercial*) Windows SDK

Windows XP (*marca comercial*) Windows XP

WINS *sustantivo* WINS

Winsock (para el módem) *sustantivo* socket driver

wireless modem *sustantivo* wireless modem

wireless point *sustantivo* wireless access point

'wizard' *sustantivo* wizard

WordPad WordPad

workaround *m sustantivo* workaround

Xerox PARC (*centro de desarrollo*) Xerox PARC

XGA *sustantivo* XGA

XHMTL *sustantivo* XHTML

XML *sustantivo* XML

X-Windows (*interfaz gráfico*) X-Window System

YMCK *sustantivo* (*definición de colores basados en: amarillo, morado, azul verdoso, negro*) YMCK

YMODEM *sustantivo* YMODEM

yugo *m sustantivo* yoke

yugos *mpl* **de desviación** *plural noun* deflection yokes

zapear *verbo vi* to zap

ZIP *sustantivo* ZIP

ZMODEM *sustantivo* ZMODEM

zona *f sustantivo* **1.** area **2.** region **3.** zone ◇ **zona** *f* **de aparcamiento de la cabeza de lectura** landing zone ◇ **zona** *f* **(de memoria) de programas no residentes** transient area ◇ **zona** *f* **de trabajo en la memoria** memory workspace ◇ **zona** *f* **(de tratamiento) por lotes** batch region

zona *f* **activa** *sustantivo* **1.** active area **2.** hotspot

zona *f* **aislada** *sustantivo* isolated location

zona *f* **común de la memoria** *sustantivo* common storage area ◇ **la memoria central del servidor de ficheros es sobre todo una zona común de almacenamiento, con una sección reservada para el sistema operativo** the file server memory is mainly common storage area, with a section reserved for the operating system

zona *f* **de barrido** *sustantivo* scan area

zona *f* **de cadena** *sustantivo* string area

zona *f* **de código** *sustantivo* code area

zona *f* **de conexiones** *sustantivo* terminal area

zona *f* **de datos** *sustantivo* data area

zona *f* **de detección** *sustantivo* aiming symbol *o* aiming field

zona *f* **de memoria temporal** *sustantivo* save area

zona *f* **de texto** *sustantivo* **1.** hot zone **2.** soft zone

zona *f* **de trabajo** *sustantivo* work area

zona *f* **de visualización** *sustantivo* image area

zona *f* **de visualización del texto** *sustantivo* text screen

zona *f* **protegida** *sustantivo* isolated location

zona *f* **usuario** *sustantivo* user area

zurdo ◇ **ratón** *m* **(configurado) para una persona zurda** left-handed mouse

ENGLISH-SPANISH
INGLÉS-ESPAÑOL

A

A¹ /eɪ/ *symbol* A

A² /eɪ/ *abbr* (*ampere*) A

A: (*first disk drive on an operating system*) A:

Å *abbr* (*angstrom*) angstrom *m*

AAL *abbr* (*ATM adaptation layer*) capa *f* de adaptación en modo de transferencia asíncrona

abandon /ə'bændən/ *verb* salir (sin guardar) ◊ **once you have abandoned your spreadsheet, you cannot retrieve it again** si se sale de la hoja de cálculo sin guardarla, no podrá recuperarla posteriormente

abb. add. *abbr* (*abbreviated addressing*) direccionamiento *m* abreviado; direccionamiento *m* simplificado

abbreviated address /ə,briːvieɪtid ə'dres/ *noun* dirección *f* abreviada; dirección *f* simplificada ◊ **my full network address is over 60 characters long, so you will find it easier to use my abbreviated address** mi dirección electrónica completa tiene más de 60 caracteres, por lo que le será más fácil utilizar mi dirección abreviada

abbreviated addressing /ə,briːvieɪtid ə'dresɪŋ/ *noun* direccionamiento *m* abreviado; direccionamiento *m* simplificado

abbreviated installation /ə,briːvieɪtid ,instə'leɪʃ(ə)n/ *noun* instalación *f* simplificada

abbreviation /ə,briːvi'eɪʃ(ə)n/ *noun* abreviatura *f* ◊ **within the text, the abbreviation 'proc' is used instead of processor** en el texto, se utiliza la abreviatura 'proc' en vez de procesador

ABD *abbr* (*Apple Desktop Bus*) enlace *m* común de Apple Desktop

abend /'æbend/ *noun* (*end of a program*) finalización *f*; interrupción *f*; parada *f* (anormal) ◊ **an interrupt from a faulty printer caused an abend** una señal de interrupción debida a una impresora defectuosa provocó una terminación anormal

abend code /'æbend kəʊd/ *noun* código *m* de terminación; código *m* de interrupción anormal

abend recovery program /,æbend rɪ'kʌv(ə)ri ,prəʊgræm/ *noun* programa *m* de recuperación de ficheros ◊ **if a fault occurs, data loss will be minimized due to the improved abend recovery program** en caso de fallo, el nuevo programa de recuperación de ficheros minimizará la pérdida de datos

aberration /,æbə'reɪʃ(ə)n/ *noun* **1.** (*of light beam or image, etc.*) aberración *f*; anomalía *f* **2.** (*of TV picture*) distorsión *f*

ablation /ə'bleɪʃ(ə)n/ *noun* (*method of writing data to an optical storage device*) ranura *f* láser; quemadura *f* láser

abnormal end /æb,nɔːm(ə)l 'end/ *noun* (*end of a program end of a program end of a program*) finalización *f* anormal

abnormal termination /æb,nɔːm(ə)l ,tɜːmɪ'neɪʃ(ə)n/ *noun* parada *f* anormal; terminación *f* anormal

abort /ə'bɔːt/ *verb* (*to interrupt a process*) abortar *vt*; abandonar *vt*; salir *vi*; cancelar anormalmente ◊ **the program was aborted by pressing the red button** el programa se interrumpió pulsando el botón rojo

aborted connection /ə,bɔːtid kə'nekʃ(ə)n/ *noun* conexión *f* abortada

abort sequence /ə'bɔːt ,siːkwəns/ *noun* (*indication of transmission failure*) secuencia *f* de final; secuencia *f* de cierre anormal; secuencia *f* de interrupción anormal

About... /ə'baʊt/ (*menu selection that displays program information*) Acerca de ...

AB roll /,eɪ 'biː ,rəʊl/ *noun* (*two video or music segments that are synchronised*) encadenado *m* de imágenes

ABS /,eɪ biː 'es/ *noun* función *f* absoluta; función *f* de valor absoluto

absolute address /,æbsəluːt ə'dres/ *noun* dirección *f* absoluta de máquina

absolute addressing /,æbsəluːt ə'dresɪŋ/ *noun* direccionamiento *m* absoluto

absolute assembler /,æbsəluːt ə'semblə/ *noun* ensamblador *m* absoluto

absolute cell reference /,æbsəluːt sel 'ref(ə)rəns/ *noun* referencia *f* de celda absoluta

absolute code /'æbsəluːt kəʊd/ *noun* código *m* absoluto

absolute coordinates /,æbsəluːt kəʊ'ɔːdɪnətz/ *plural noun* coordenadas *fpl* absolutas

absolute device /,æbsəluːt dɪ'vaɪs/ *noun* dispositivo *m* absoluto

absolute error /,æbsəluːt 'erə/ *noun* error *m* absoluto

absolute expression /,æbsəluːt ɪk'spreʃ(ə)n/ *noun* expresión *f* absoluta

absolute instruction /,æbsəluːt ɪn'strʌkʃən/ *noun* instrucción *f* absoluta

absolute loader /'æbsəluːt ,ləʊdə/ *noun* cargador *m* absoluto

absolute maximum rating /ˌæbsəluːt 'mæksɪməm ˌreɪtɪŋ/ *noun* capacidad *f* máxima absoluta; tasa *f* máxima absoluta

absolute positioning /ˌæbsəluːt pə'zɪʃ(ə)nɪŋ/ *noun* posicionamiento *m* absoluto

absolute priority /ˌæbsəluːt praɪ'ɒrɪti/ *noun* prioridad *f* absoluta

absolute program /ˌæbsəluːt 'prəʊgræm/ *noun* programa *m* absoluto; programa *m* en lenguaje máquina

absolute time /'æbsəluːt taɪm/ *noun* tiempo *m* absoluto

absolute value /ˌæbsəluːt 'væljuː/ *noun* valor *m* absoluto ◇ **the absolute value of –62.34 is 62.34** el valor absoluto de –62,34 es 62,34

absorb /əb'zɔːb/ *verb* absorber *vt*

absorption /əb'zɔːpʃən/ *noun* absorción *f*

abstract data type /ˌbstrækt 'deɪtə ˌtaɪp/ *noun* (*general data type that can store any kind of information*) datos *mpl* de tipo general ◇ **the stack is a structure of abstract data types, it can store any type of data from an integer to an address** la pila es una estructura de datos de tipo abstracto que puede almacenar cualquier tipo de datos, desde un número entero hasta una dirección

A-bus /eɪ bʌs/ *noun* (*main internal bus*) enlace *m* común; bus *m* principal; bus *m* A

ac *abbr* (*academic organisation*) organización *f* académica

AC *abbr* (*alternating current*) corriente *f* alterna

ACAP /ˌeɪ siː eɪ 'piː/ *noun* protocolo *m* de acceso a la configuración de aplicaciones

ACC /ˌeɪ siː 'siː/ *noun* acumulador *m*

accelerated graphics port /əkˌseləreɪtɪd 'græfɪks ˌpɔːt/ *noun* puerto *m* rápido de gráficos

acceleration time /əkˌselə'reɪʃ(ə)n taɪm/ *noun* 1. (*to spin a disk at correct speed*) tiempo *m* de aceleración 2. (*time between access instruction and data transfer*) tiempo *m* de aceleración

accelerator board /ək'seləˌreɪtə bɔːd/, **accelerator card** /ək'seləˌreɪtə kɑːd/ *noun* placa *f* aceleradora

accelerator key /ək'seləˌreɪtə kiː/ *noun* (*key on a keyboard*) tecla *f* de aceleración; instrucción *f* de aceleración; (*may also be a combination of keys that carry out a function*) secuencia *f* de teclas ◇ **instead of selecting the File menu then the Save option, use the accelerator keys Alt and S to do the same thing and save the file** en vez de seleccionar el menú Archivo y a continuación la opción Guardar, utilice la instrucción de aceleración Alt-G para guardar el fichero

accept /ək'sept/ *verb* (*to establish a session or connection*) aceptar *vt*

acceptable use policy /əkˌseptəb(ə)l juːz 'pɒlɪsi/ *noun* política *f* de uso aceptable

acceptance sampling /ək'septəns ˌsɑːmplɪŋ/ *noun* muestreo *m* de aceptación

acceptance test /ək'septəns test/ *noun* prueba *f* de aceptación; test *m* de homologación

access /'ækses/ *noun* 1. (*ability to use something*) acceso *m* 2. (*being allowed to use a computer*) acceso *m* ■ *verb* (*call up data stored on a computer*) acceder *vi*; tener acceso a ◇ **access card** (*one of several possible predefined access levels*) tarjeta *f* de acceso ◇ **after he was discovered hacking, he was barred access to the system** después de que se descubriera que estaba accediendo ilegalmente al sistema, se le prohibió el acceso ◇ **direct access storage device (DASD)** dispositivo *m* de almacenamiento de acceso directo ◇ **he has access to numerous sensitive files** él tiene acceso a numerosos ficheros confidenciales ◇ **she accessed the employee's file stored on the computer** ella accedió al fichero del empleado archivado en el ordenador ◇ **the access time of this dynamic RAM chip is around 200ns – we have faster versions if your system clock is running faster** tiempo *m* de acceso (a un fichero, etc.) ◇ **the instantaneous access of the RAM disk was welcome** el acceso instantáneo al disco RAM fue bien acogido ◇ **to bar access to a system** prohibir al acceso a un sistema ◇ **to have access to a file of data** tener acceso *or* acceder a un fichero de datos ◇ **to have access to something** tener acceso a algo

access arm /'ækses ɑːm/ *noun* (*device in a disk drive*) brazo *m* de acceso; brazo *m* de lectura/escritura ◇ **the access arm moves to the parking region during transport** el brazo de acceso se sitúa en la posición de 'parking' durante el transporte

access authority /'ækses ɔːˌθɒrəti/ *noun* autorización *f* de acceso

access-barred /ˌækses 'bɑːd/ *adjective* de acceso prohibido

access category /'ækses ˌkætəg(ə)ri/ *noun* tipo *m* de acceso; categoría *f* de acceso

access channel control /ˌækses ˌtʃæn(ə)l kən'trəʊl/ *noun* control *m* del canal de acceso

access charge /'ækses tʃɑːdʒ/ *noun* gastos *mpl* de acceso al sistema; tasa *f* de acceso al sistema

access code /'ækses kəʊd/ *noun* código *m* de acceso

access control /'ækses kənˌtrəʊl/ *noun* control *m* de acceso (al sistema)

access control byte /ˌækses kən'trəʊl baɪt/ *noun* byte *m* de control de acceso; octeto *m* de control de acceso

access controller /'ækses kənˌtrəʊlə/ *noun* control *m* de acceso (al sistema)

access control list /ˌækses kən'trəʊl lɪst/ *noun* ACL; lista *f* de control de acceso

access hole /'ækses həʊl/ *noun* ventana *f*; perforación *f* de acceso

accession number /ək'seʃ(ə)n ˌnʌmbə/ *noun* (*number in a record*) número *m* de referencia; número *m* de acceso; número *m* de entrada

access level /'ækses ˌlev(ə)l/ *noun* nivel *m* de acceso

access line /'ækses laɪn/ *noun* línea *f* de acceso

access log /'ækses lɒg/ *noun* protocolo *m* de acceso

access mechanism /'ækses ˌmekənɪz(ə)m/ *noun* mecanismo *m* de acceso

access method /'ækses ˌmeθəd/ *noun* método *m* de acceso

access method routines /'ækses ˌmeθəd ruːˌtiːnz/ *plural noun* rutinas *fpl* de acceso; instrucciones *fpl* de acceso

access name /'ækses neɪm/ *noun* nombre *m* de acceso

access number /'ækses ˌnʌmbə/ *noun* número *m* de acceso

accessor /'æksesə/ *noun* (*person who accesses data*) usuario *m* (con derecho de acceso)

accessory /ək'sesəri/ *noun* accesorio *m* ◇ **the printer comes with several accessories, such as a soundproof hood** la impresora viene con diversos accesorios, como por ejemplo una cubierta insonorizada ◇ **this popular home computer has a large range of accessories** este popular ordenador personal dispone de una amplia gama de accesorios

access path /'ækses pɑːθ/ *noun* ruta *f*; camino *m* de acceso

access path journalling /ˌækses ˌpɑːθ 'dʒɜːnəlɪŋ/ *noun* registro *m* de la ruta de acceso

access period /'ækses ˌpɪəriəd/ *noun* periodo *m* de acceso

access permission /'ækses pəˌmɪʃ(ə)n/ *noun* permiso *m* de acceso

access point /'ækses pɔɪnt/ *noun* (*test point to check signals or data*) punto *m* de acceso; punto *m* de entrada; punto *m* de control

access privilege /'ækses ˌprɪvɪlɪdʒ/ *noun* privilegio *m* de acceso

access provider /'ækses prəˌvaɪdə/ *noun* proveedor *m* de acceso a Internet

access rights /'ækses raɪts/ *plural noun* derechos *mpl* de acceso

access time /'ækses ˌtaɪm/ *noun* **1.** (*time needed between request and data being shown*) tiempo *m* de acceso **2.** (*time needed to find a file, etc.*) tiempo *m* de acceso ◇ **the access time of this dynamic RAM chip is around 200ns – we have faster versions if your system clock is running faster** el tiempo de acceso de este chip de RAM dinámico es de aproximadamente 200 ns: disponemos de versiones más rápidas si el reloj de su sistema funciona a más velocidad

access unit /'ækses ˌjuːnɪt/ *noun* unidad *f* de acceso

accidental /ˌæksɪ'dent(ə)l/ *adjective* accidental

accordion fold /ə'kɔːdiən fəʊld/, **accordion fanfold** *noun* (*printing*) papel *m* continuo; papel *m* en forma de acordeón; papel *m* (doblado) de hojas múltiples

account /ə'kaʊnt/ *noun* (*record of a user's name, password and rights*) cuenta *f* ■ *verb* (*to log how much time and resources each user uses*) contabilizar *vt* ◇ **if you are a new user, you will have to ask the supervisor to create an account for you** si es usted un nuevo usuario, deberá solicitar del operador la creación de una nueva cuenta (de acceso) ◇ **John Smith's account name is JSMITH** el nombre de la cuenta de John Smith es JSMITH

accounting package /ə'kaʊntɪŋ ˌpækɪdʒ/ *noun* programa *m* de contabilidad

account name /ə'kaʊnt neɪm/ *noun* nombre *m* de la cuenta ◇ **John Smith's account name is JSMITH** el nombre de la cuenta de John Smith es JSMITH

accounts package /ə'kaʊnts ˌpækɪdʒ/ *noun* programa *m* de contabilidad

accumulate /ə'kjuːmjʊleɪt/ *verb* acumular *vt* ◇ **we have gradually accumulated a large databank of names and addresses** hemos acumulado de forma gradual un gran banco de datos de nombres y direcciones

accumulator /ə'kjuːmjʊleɪtə/, **accumulator register** /ˌeɪ siː 'siː/ *noun* acumulador *m*; registro *m* acumulador

accumulator address /ə'kjuːmjʊleɪtə əˌdres/ *noun* dirección *f* del acumulador

accumulator shift instruction /ə ˌkjuːmjʊleɪtə 'ʃɪft ɪnˌstrʌkʃən/ *noun* instrucción *f* de desplazamiento del acumulador

accuracy /'ækjʊrəsi/ *noun* **1.** (*extent to which something is correct*) exactitud *f*; precisión *f* **2.** (*extent to which someone avoids errors*) exactitud *f*; precisión *f* **3.** (*number of bits used to define number*) exactitud *f*; precisión *f*

accuracy control character /ˌækjʊrəsi kən 'trəʊl ˌkærɪktə/ *noun* carácter *m* de control de precisión

ACD /ˌeɪ siː 'diː/ *noun* distribución *f* automática de llamadas; distribuidor *m* automático de llamadas

ACF *abbr* (*advanced communications function*) función *f* avanzada de comunicaciones

ACH /ˌeɪ siː 'eɪtʃ/ *noun* cámara *f* de compensación electrónica

achromatic colour /ˌeɪkrəʊmætɪk 'kʌlə/ *noun* color *m* acromático

ACIA /ˌeɪ siː aɪ 'eɪ/ *noun* adaptador *m* para interfaz de comunicaciones asíncronas

ACK /ˌeɪ siː 'keɪ/ *noun* señal *f* de acuse de recibo positivo

Ackerman's function /'ækəmənz ˌfʌŋkʃən/ *noun* función *f* de Ackerman

acknowledge /ək'nɒlɪdʒ/ *noun* (*signal that message has been received*) señal *f* de acuse de recibo positivo ■ *verb* **1.** (*to confirm receipt of letter or message*) asentir *vt*; confirmar *vt* **2.** (*to send signal confirming receipt*) acusar recibo (de un mensaje); enviar un acuse de recibo

acknowledge character /ək'nɒlɪdʒ 'kærɪktə/ *noun* carácter *m* de acuse de recibo

acknowledged mail /ək'nɒlɪdʒd 'meɪl/ *noun* (*signals to the sender when an electronic mail* *message has been read*) mensaje *m* con acuse de recibo

ACL /ˌeɪ siː 'el/ *noun* ACL; lista *f* de control de acceso

acoustic /əˈkuːstɪk/ *adjective* acústico *or* -a

acoustic coupler /əˌkuːstɪk 'kʌplə/ *noun* acoplador *m* acústico ◇ **I use an acoustic coupler with my lap-top computer** utilizo un acoplador acústico en mi ordenador portátil

acoustic delay line /əˌkuːstɪk dɪ'leɪ laɪn/ *noun* línea *f* de retraso acústico

acoustic hood /əˈkuːstɪk hʊd/ *noun* (*soundproof cover*) cubierta *f* insonorizada; campana *f* de insonorización

acoustic memory /əˌkuːstɪk 'mem(ə)ri/ *noun* memoria *f* acústica

acoustic panel /əˌkuːstɪk 'pæn(ə)l/ *noun* panel *m* acústico

acoustic store /əˈkuːstɪk stɔː/ *noun* memoria *f* acústica

ACPI /ˌeɪ siː piː 'aɪ/ *noun* ACPI; administrator *mf* ACPI

acquisition /ˌækwɪ'zɪʃ(ə)n/ *noun* adquisición *f*

Acrobat (*file format developed by Adobe Systems*) formato *m* de ficheros gráficos desarrollado por Adobe Acrobat

ACS /ˌeɪ siː 'es/ *noun* servidor *m* de comunicaciones asíncronas

action /ˈækʃən/ *noun* (*in SAA CUA front-end: user event, such as pressing a key*) acción *f* ◇ **action field** (*photography*) campo *m* de acción *or* de movimiento

action bar /ˈækʃən bɑː/ *noun* barra *f* del menú

action bar pull-down /ˈækʃən bɑː pʊl/ *noun* barra *f* desplegable del menú

action code /ˈækʃən kəʊd/ *noun* código *m* de acción

action cycle /ˈækʃən 'saɪk(ə)l/ *noun* ciclo *m* de acción; ciclo *m* funcional

action list /ˈækʃən lɪst/ *noun* lista *f* de acciones

ActionMedia /ˈækʃənˈmiːdiə/ (*trade name for a digital video system developed by Intel*) ActionMedia

action message /ˌækʃən 'mesɪdʒ/ *noun* mensaje *m* de intervención

action-object /ˌækʃən əb'dʒekt/ *noun* objeto *m* de acción

activate /ˈæktɪˌveɪt/ *verb* **1.** (*to start*) activar *vt*; poner en marcha; poner en funcionamiento **2.** (*to make available*) activar *vt*; poner en funcionamiento ◇ **pressing CR activates the printer** al pulsar la tecla CR se activa la impresora

active /ˈæktɪv/ *adjective* activo *or* -a ◇ **active circuit** circuito activo

active application /ˌæktɪv ˌæplɪ'keɪʃ(ə)n/ *noun* aplicación *f* activa

active area /ˌæktɪv 'eəriə/ *noun* zona *f* activa

active cell /ˈæktɪv sel/ *noun* celda *f* activa; celda *f* de trabajo

active code page /ˌæktɪv 'kəʊd ˌpeɪdʒ/ *noun* código *m* de página activo; código *m* de página en vigor

active database /ˌæktɪv 'deɪtəbeɪs/ *noun* base *f* de datos activa

active device /ˌæktɪv dɪ'vaɪs/ *noun* dispositivo *m* activo

Active Document /ˌæktɪv 'dɒkjʊmənt/ *noun* documento *m* activo

active file /ˌæktɪv 'faɪl/ *noun* fichero *m* activo

active gateway /ˌæktɪv 'geɪtweɪ/ *noun* puerta *f* activa

active high /ˈæktɪv haɪ/ *noun* señal *f* alta activa

active hub /ˌæktɪv 'hʌb/ *noun* concentrador *m* activo; multirepetidor *m* activo

active line /ˌæktɪv 'laɪn/ *noun* línea *f* activa

active link /ˌæktɪv 'lɪŋk/ *noun* conexión *f* activa; enlace *m* activo

active low /ˌæktɪv 'ləʊ/ *noun* señal *f* baja activa

active matrix display /ˌæktɪv ˌmeɪtrɪks dɪs'pleɪ/ *noun* pantalla *f* de cristal líquido de matriz activa

active menu /ˌæktɪv 'menjuː/ *noun* menú *m* activo

active node /ˌæktɪv 'nəʊd/ *noun* nodo *m* activo

active pixel region /ˌæktɪv 'pɪks(ə)l ˌriːdʒən/ *noun* área *f* activa de píxeles

active printer /ˌæktɪv 'prɪntə/ *noun* impresora *f* activa

active program /ˌæktɪv 'prəʊɡræm/ *noun* programa *m* activo

active record /ˌæktɪv 'rekɔːd/ *noun* registro *m* activo

active region /ˌæktɪv 'riːdʒ(ə)n/ *noun* región *f* activa

Active Server Page /ˌæktɪv 'sɜːvə peɪdʒ/ *noun* página *f* de servidor activo

active star /ˈæktɪv stɑː/ *noun* estrella *f* activa

active state /ˌæktɪv 'steɪt/ *noun* modo *m* activo

active storage /ˌæktɪv 'stɔːrɪdʒ/ *noun* almacenamiento *m* activo

active streaming format /ˌæktɪv 'striːmɪŋ ˌfɔːmæt/ *noun* formato *m* activo de flujo continuo

active video /ˌæktɪv 'vɪdiəʊ/, **active video signal** /ˌæktɪv 'vɪdiəʊ ˌsɪgn(ə)l/ *noun* vídeo *m* activo

ActiveVRML /ˌæktɪv viː ɑː em 'el/ *noun* ActiveVRML

active window /ˌæktɪv 'wɪndəʊ/ *noun* ventana *f* activa

ActiveX /ˌæktɪv 'eks/ (*trade name for a programming language*) ActiveX

activities /æk'tɪvɪtiz/ *plural noun* tareas *fpl* (de un ordenador)

activity level /æk,tɪvəti 'lev(ə)l/ *noun* nivel *m* de actividad

activity light /æk'tɪvəti laɪt/ *noun (small light or LED)* testigo *m* de actividad; luz *f* testigo; indicador *m* luminoso

activity loading /æk,tɪvəti 'ləʊdɪŋ/ *noun* modo *m* de carga en función de la tasa de actividad

activity ratio /æk,tɪvəti 'reɪʃiəʊ/ *noun* tasa *f* de actividad

activity trail /æk'tɪvəti treɪl/ *noun* seguimiento *m*; registro *m* de actividades

actual address /,æktʃuəl ə'dres/ *noun* dirección *f* real

actual code /'æktʃuəl kəʊd/ *noun* código *m* absoluto; código *m* máquina

actual data transfer rate /,æktʃuəl ,deɪtə 'trænsfɜː ,reɪt/ *noun* tasa *f* real de transferencia de datos; velocidad *f* real de transferencia de datos

actual instruction /,æktʃuəl ɪn'strʌkʃən/ *noun* instrucción *f* absoluta

actuator /'æktʃʊeɪtə/ *noun (mechanical device)* activador *m*; *(mechanical device controlled by an external signal)* accionador *m*; brazo *m* de lectura

ACU /,eɪ siː 'juː/ *noun* sistema *m* automático de llamadas; unidad *f* automática de llamadas

ad *abbr (Andorra)* Andorra

A/D *abbr (analog to digital)* analógico a digital; analógico a numérico

ADA /,eɪ diː 'eɪ/ *noun* lenguaje *m* (de programación) ADA

adapt /ə'dæpt/ *verb* adaptar *vt* ◊ **can this computer be adapted to take 5.25 inch disks?** ¿se puede adaptar este ordenador para que acepte disquetes de 5,25 pulgadas?

adaptation /,ædæp'teɪʃ(ə)n/ *noun* adaptación *f* ◊ **the adaptation of the eye to respond to different levels of brightness** la adaptación del ojo para responder a los distintos niveles de luminosidad

adapter /ə'dæptə/, **adaptor** /ə'dæptə/ *noun (connector)* adaptador *m* ◊ **the cable adapter allows attachment of the scanner to the SCSI interface** el adaptador de cable permite conectar el escáner a la interfaz SCSI ◊ **the cable to connect the scanner to the adapter is included in the package** el paquete informático incluye el cable para conectar el escáner al adaptador

adapter card /ə'dæptə kɑːd/ *noun* tarjeta *f* adaptadora

adapter plug /ə'dæptə plʌg/ *noun* adaptador *m*

adaptive channel allocation /ə,dæptɪv 'tʃæn(ə)l ælə,keɪʃ(ə)n/ *noun* asignación *f* de canal adaptable

adaptive differential pulse code modulation /ə,dæptɪv dɪfə,renʃ(ə)l 'pʌls kəʊd mɒdju,leɪʃ(ə)n/ *noun* modulación *f* diferencial dinámica por impulsos y códigos; norma *f* de conversión ADPCM

adaptive packet assembly /ə,dæptɪv 'pækɪt ə,sembli/ *noun* ensamblaje *m* adaptable de paquetes; agrupación *f* adaptable de datos para corrección de errores MNP

adaptive routing /ə,dæptɪv 'ruːtɪŋ/ *noun* direccionamiento *m* adaptable; ruta *f* adaptable

adaptive system /ə,dæptɪv 'sɪstəm/ *noun (system that can alter its responses and processes)* sistema *m* adaptable; sistema *m* autoadaptable; sistema *m* dinámico

adaptor /ə'dæptə/ *noun* adaptador *m*

ADC /,eɪ diː 'siː/ *noun* convertidor *m* de digital a analógico

add /æd/ *verb* **1.** *(figures)* sumar *vt*; añadir *vt* **2.** *(parts or text)* juntar *vt*; unir *vt*; añadir *vt* ◊ **adding or deleting material from the text is easy using function keys** con las teclas de función es muy fácil añadir o suprimir material de un texto ◊ **in the spreadsheet each column should be added to make a subtotal** en la hoja de cálculo debe sumarse cada columna para obtener un total parcial ◊ **the software house has added a new management package to its range of products** la empresa de software ha añadido un nuevo paquete de gestión a su gama de productos

addend /'ædend/ *noun* sumando *m*

adder /'ædə/ *noun* sumador *m*; sumadora *f*

adder-subtractor /,ædə səb'træktə/ *noun* sumador-restador *m*

add-in /'æd ɪn/ *noun, adjective (supplementary device)* dispositivo *m* adicional; dispositivo *m* complementario ■ *adjective (additional)* de expansión; adicional; complementario *or* -a

addition /ə'dɪʃ(ə)n/ *noun (in arithmetic)* suma *f*; adición *f*; ampliación *f*

additional /ə'dɪʃ(ə)nəl/ *adjective* adicional; complementario *or* -a ◊ **can we add three additional workstations to the network?** ¿podemos añadir tres estaciones de trabajo adicionales a la red?

addition record /ə,dɪʃ(ə)n 'rekɔːd/ *noun* registro *m* de adición; fichero *m* de suma

addition time /ə'dɪʃ(ə)n taɪm/ *noun (time to carry out an addition operation)* tiempo *m* de suma; tiempo *m* de adición

addition without carry /ə,dɪʃ(ə)n wɪð,aʊt 'kæri/ *noun* suma *f* sin llevar

additive colour /,ædətɪv 'kʌlə/ *noun* color *m* aditivo

add-on /'æd ɒn/ *adjective (added to a computer system)* complementario; adicional; añadido *or* -a ■ *noun (additional software or hardware)* dispositivo *m* complementario; dispositivo *m* adicional; dispositivo *m* añadido ◊ **add-on board** tarjeta *f* ◊ **add-on equipment** equipo *m* complementario ◊ **add-on products** productos *mpl* complementarios ◊ **the add-on hard disk will boost the computer's storage capabilities** un disco duro adicional aumentará la capacidad de memoria del ordenador ◊ **the new add-on board allows colour graphics to be displayed** la nueva tarjeta de ampliación permite mostrar gráficos en color

add on board /'æd ɒn bɔːd/ *noun* tarjeta *f* de extensión

add register /æd 'redʒɪstə/ *noun* registro *m* de suma; registro *m* de adición

address /ə'dres/ *noun* (*number allowing a central processing unit to reference a physical location in a storage medium*) dirección *f*; domicilio *m* ■ *verb* (*to enter location data into an address bus*) dirigir *vt*; enviar *vt*; direccionar *vt*; definir una dirección ◇ **to address a letter** *or* **a parcel** dirigir una carta *or* un paquete

addressability /ə,dresə'bɪlɪti/ *noun* (*of pixels*) capacidad *f* de direccionamiento

addressable /ə'dresəb(ə)l/ *adjective* direccionable ◇ **with the new operating system, all of the 5MB of RAM is addressable** con el nuevo sistema operativo, la totalidad de los 5 MB de RAM resulta direccionable

addressable cursor /ə,dresəb(ə)l 'kɜːsə/ *noun* cursor *m* direccionable

addressable point /ə,dresəb(ə)l 'pɔint/ *noun* punto *m* direccionable

addressable terminal /ə,dresəb(ə)l 'tɜːmɪn(ə)l/ *noun* terminal *m* direccionable; terminal *m* de direccionamiento protegido

address access time /ə,dres 'ækses taɪm/ *noun* tiempo *m* de acceso a la dirección; velocidad *f* de acceso a la dirección

address base /ə'dres beɪs/ *noun* base *f* de dirección

address book /ə'dres bʊk/ *noun* libro *m* de direcciones

address bus /ə'dres bʌs/ *noun* (*physical connection that carries address data*) enlace *m* común de direcciones; bus *m* de direcciones

address code /ə'dres kəʊd/ *noun* código *m* de direcciones

address computation /ə,dres ,kɒmpjʊ'teɪʃ(ə)n/ *noun* cálculo *m* de una dirección

address decoder /ə'dres diː,kəʊdə/ *noun* descodificador *m* de direcciones

address field /ə'dres fiːld/ *noun* campo *m* de dirección

address format /ə'dres ,fɔːmæt/ *noun* formato *m* de direccion(es)

address highway /ə'dres ,haɪweɪ/ *noun* enlace *m* común; bus *m* de direcciones

addressing /ə'dresɪŋ/ *noun* (*process of accessing a location in memory*) direccionamiento *m*

addressing capacity /ə'dresɪŋ kə,pæsɪti/ *noun* (*memory*) disponibilidad *f* de memoria; capacidad *f* de direccionamiento

addressing level /ə'dresɪŋ ,lev(ə)l/ *noun* nivel *m* de direccionamiento

addressing method /ə'dresɪŋ ,meθəd/ *noun* método *m* de direccionamiento

addressing mode /ə'dresɪŋ məʊd/ *noun* modo *m* de direccionamiento

address mapping /ə'dres ,mæpɪŋ/ *noun* tabla *f* de correspondencia de direcciones; topografía *f* de las direcciones

address mark /ə'dres mɑːk/ *noun* marca *f* de direcciones

address mask /ə'dres mɑːsk/ *noun* máscara *f* de dirección

address modification /ə,dres ,mɒdɪfɪ'keɪʃ(ə)n/ *noun* modificación *f* de direcciones

address register /ə'dres ,redʒɪstə/ *noun* registro *m* de direcciones

address resolution /ə'dres ,rezəluːʃ(ə)n/ *noun* resolución *f* de direcciones

address resolution protocol /ə,dres ,rezə'luːʃ(ə)n ,prəʊtəkɒl/ *noun* protocolo *m* de resolución de direcciones; protocolo *m* ARP

address space /ə'dres speɪs/ *noun* espacio *m* de direcciones; espacio *m* direccionable

address strobe /ə'dres strəʊb/ *noun* (*signal*) señal *f* de validez de la dirección; impulso *m* de validez de la dirección

address track /ə'dres træk/ *noun* pista *f* de direccion(es)

address translation /ə,dres træns'leɪʃ(ə)n/ *noun* traducción *f* de direcciones

address word /ə'dres wɜːd/ *noun* palabra *f* de direcciones ◇ **a larger address word increases the amount of memory a computer can address** una palabra de dirección más larga aumenta la cantidad de memoria que un ordenador puede definir

add time /'æd taɪm/ *noun* tiempo *m* de suma; tiempo *m* de adición

adjacent domains /ə,dʒeɪs(ə)nt dəʊ'meɪnz/ *plural noun* dominios *mpl* adyacentes

adjacent nodes /ə'dʒeɪs(ə)nt nəʊdz/ *plural noun* nodos *mpl* adyacentes

adjunct register /,ædʒʌŋkt 'redʒɪstə/ *noun* (*where the top 16 bits are used for control information and the bottom 16 bits are available for use by a program*) registro *m* adjunto

adjustment /ə'dʒʌstmənt/ *noun* (*minor change made to improve a system*) ajuste *m*; regulación *f*; modificación *f* ◇ **I think the joystick needs adjustment as it sometimes gets stuck** creo que el mando de juegos necesita un ajuste ya que a veces se atasca ◇ **the brightness needs adjustment** el brillo necesita ajuste

AdLib™ /æd'lɪb/ *noun* (*type of sound card for the PC with basic sound playback and MIDI functions*) tarjeta *f* de sonido AdLib™

administrator /əd'mɪnɪstreɪtə/ *noun* (*person who is responsible for looking after a network*) administrador *m or* -a *f*

Adobe Acrobat /ə,dəʊbi 'ækrəbæt/ (*trade name for a piece of software that converts documents and formatted pages into a file format that can be viewed on almost any computer platform or Internet browser*) Adobe Acrobat

Adobe Systems /ə,dəʊbi 'sɪstəmz/ (*software company*) Adobe™

Adobe Type Manager /ə,dəʊbi taɪp 'mænɪdʒə/ (*trade name for a standard for describing scalable fonts*) gestor *m* de fuentes Adobe

ADP /ˌeɪ diː 'piː/ *noun* proceso *m* automático de datos; tratamiento *m* automático de datos

ADPCM /ˌeɪ diː piː siː 'em/ *noun* norma *f* de conversión ADPCM; modulación *f* diferencial dinámica por impulsos y códigos

ADSL /ˌeɪ diː es 'el/ *noun* línea *f* ADSL

advanced configuration and power interface /ədˌvɑːnst kənˌfɪgjəˌreɪʃ(ə)n ən ˌpaʊə 'ɪntəfeɪs/ *noun* configuración *f* avanzada e interfaz de potencia

advanced peer-to-peer networking /ədˌvɑːnst ˌpɪə tə ˌpɪə 'netwɜːkɪŋ/ *noun* (*extension to the IBM SNA protocol*) red *f* avanzada de terminal a terminal; red *f* avanzada par a par; red *f* APPN

advanced power management /ədˌvɑːnst ˌpaʊə 'mænɪdʒmənt/ *noun* APM; administración *f* avanzada de corriente

advanced program to program communications /ədˌvɑːnst ˌprəʊgræm tə ˌprəʊgræm kəˌmjuːnɪ'keɪʃ(ə)nz/ *noun* (*set of protocols for peer-to-peer communication*) comunicaciones *fpl* avanzadas programa a programa (APPC); comunicaciones *fpl* en condiciones *fpl* de igualdad; protocolo *m* APPC

Advanced Research Projects Agency Network /ədˌvɑːnst ˌriːsɜːtʃ ˌprɒdʒekts ˌeɪdʒ(ə)nsi 'netwɜːk/ *noun* ARPA

advanced run-length limited /ədˌvɑːnst 'rʌn leŋθ ˌlɪmɪtɪd/ *noun* codificación *f* ARLL

advanced technology attachment /əd ˌvɑːnst tek,nɒlədʒi ə'tætʃmənt/ *noun* ATA; adición *f* a tecnología avanzada

advanced technology attachment packet interface /ədˌvɑːnst tek,nɒlədʒi ə ˌtætʃmənt ˌpækɪt 'ɪntəfeɪs/ *noun* accesorio *m* de tecnología avanzada

Advanced Television Systems Committee /ədˌvɑːnst 'telɪvɪʒ(ə)n ˌsɪstəmz kəˌmɪti/ *noun* comité *m* de sistemas avanzados

advanced version /ədˌvɑːnst 'vɜːʃ(ə)n/ *noun* versión *f* avanzada

advisory lock /əd'vaɪz(ə)ri lɒk/ *noun* (*lock placed on a region of a file*) cierre *m* de protección; bloqueo *m* de protección

advisory system /ədˌvaɪz(ə)ri 'sɪstəm/ *noun* (*expert system that provides advice to a user*) sistema *m* asesor

AFAIK *abbr* (*as far as I know*) por lo que sé

affiliate marketing /ə'fɪliət ˌmɑːkɪtɪŋ/ *noun* marketing *m* de empresas afiliadas

affirmative /ə'fɜːmətɪv/ *adjective* afirmativo *or* -a; positivo *or* -a

affirmative acknowledgement /əˌfɜːmətɪv ək'nɒlɪdʒmənt/ *noun* acuse *m* de recibo positivo; confirmación *f* positiva

AFIPS *abbr* (*American Federation of Information Processing Societies*) federación *f* americana de sociedades de tratamiento de información

AFP /ˌeɪ ef 'piː/ *noun* protocolo *m* AFP; protocolo *m* de gestión de ficheros AppleTalk

afterglow /'ɑːftəgləʊ/ *noun* persistencia *f*

after-image /ˌɑːftə 'ɪmɪdʒ/ *noun* (*copy of a block of data that has been modified*) imagen *f* copia; imagen *f* de salida

AGC /ˌeɪ dʒiː 'siː/ *noun* control *m* automático de amplificación

agent /'eɪdʒənt/ *noun* **1.** (*program or software that runs on a workstation in a network*) programa *m* inteligente **2.** (*series of commands or actions carried out automatically*) agente *m*

aggregate /'ægrɪgət/ *noun* agregado *m or* -a

aggregate bandwidth /ˌægrɪgət 'bændwɪdθ/ *noun* anchura *f* de banda agregada

aggregate function /ˌægrɪgət 'fʌŋkʃən/ *noun* función *f* agregada; función *f* de globalización

aggregate line speed /ˌægrɪgət 'laɪn ˌspiːd/ *noun* velocidad *f* de línea agregada

aggregate operator /ˌægrɪgət 'ɒpəreɪtə/ *noun* operador *m* agregado; operador *m* de globalización

AGP /ˌeɪ dʒiː 'piː/ *noun* puerto *m* rápido de gráficos

AI /ˌeɪ 'aɪ/ *noun* inteligencia *f* artificial

aiming symbol /ˌeɪmɪŋ 'sɪmbəl/, **aiming field** /fiːld/ *noun* (*defines the area in which a light-pen can be detected*) símbolo *m* de detección; zona *f* de detección

airbrush /'eə,brʌʃ/ *noun* (*painting tool that creates a diffuse pattern of dots*) aerógrafo *m*

air gap /'eə gæp/ *noun* vacío *m* de aire

alert /ə'lɜːt/ *noun* (*warning message*) alerta *f*

alert box /ə'lɜːt bɒks/ *noun* ventana *f* de mensaje de alerta ◇ **the alert box warned me that I was about to delete all my files** el mensaje de alerta me advirtió de que estaba a punto de borrar todos mis ficheros

alert condition /əˌlɜːt kən'dɪʃ(ə)n/ *noun* condición *f* de alerta

algebra /'ældʒɪbrə/ *noun* álgebra *f*

algebraic language /ˌældʒɪbreɪɪk 'læŋgwɪdʒ/ *noun* (*context-free language*) lenguaje *m* algebraico

ALGOL /'ælgɒl/ *noun* lenguaje *m* algorítmico; ALGOL

algorithm /'ælgərɪð(ə)m/ *noun* algoritmo *m*

'…image processing algorithms are step by step procedures for performing image processing operations' [*Byte*]

'…the steps are: acquiring a digitized image, developing an algorithm to process it, processing the image, modifying the algorithm until you are satisfied with the result' [*Byte*]

algorithmic /ˌælgə'rɪðmɪk/ *adjective* algorítmico *or* -a

algorithmic language /ˌælgərɪðmɪk 'læŋgwɪdʒ/ *noun* lenguaje *m* algorítmico; ALGOL

alias /'eɪliəs/ *noun* (*name given to a file, port, device, etc.*) alias *m* ◇ **the operating system uses the alias COM1 to represent the serial port address 3FCh** el sistema operativo utiliza el alias COM1 para designar la terminal de dirección 3FCh del puerto en serie

aliasing /'eɪliəsɪŋ/ *noun* (*jagged edges along diagonal or curved lines on a computer screen*) efecto *m* escalera

alias name /'eɪliəs neɪm/ *noun* alias *m*; pseudónimo *m*

alien /'eɪliən/ *adjective* extraño *or* -a; no compatible

alien disk /'eɪliən dɪsk/ *noun* disquete *m* no compatible

alien disk reader /ˌeɪliən 'dɪsk ˌriːdə/ *noun* lector *m* de disquetes no compatibles; lector *m* multidisco ◇ **when you have an alien disk select the multi-disk option to allow you to turn the disk drive into an alien disk reader** cuando tenga un disquete no compatible seleccione la opción multidisco para que la disquetera se convierta en un lector de discos no compatibles

align /ə'laɪn/ *verb* **1.** (*to make sure that characters are spaced and levelled correctly*) alinear *vt*; justificar *vt* **2.** (*to arrange numbers into a column with all figured lines up against the left or right hand side*) posicionar *vt*; alinear *vt* **3.** (*to position read/write head*) alinear *vt*; justificar *vt*

aligner /ə'laɪnə/ *noun* (*device for printing*) dispositivo *m* de alineación; dispositivo *m* de justificación; dispositivo *m* de posicionamiento

aligning edge /ə'laɪnɪŋ edʒ/ *noun* (*of optical character recognition system*) borde *m* de alineación; borde *m* de referencia

alignment /ə'laɪnmənt/ *noun* alineamiento *m*

alignment pin /ə'laɪnmənt pɪn/ *noun* (*device to check alignment*) señal *f* de alineamiento; clavija *f* de alineamiento; patilla *f* de alineamiento

allocate /'æləˌkeɪt/ *verb* (*to divide time or work between different people or computers*) asignar *vt*; atribuir *vt*; repartir *vt* ◇ **the operating system allocated most of main memory to the spreadsheet program** el sistema operativo asignó la mayor parte de la memoria principal a la hoja de cálculo

allocation /ˌælə'keɪʃ(ə)n/ *noun* (*dividing something in various ways*) asignación *f*; atribución *f*; distribución *f* ◇ **band allocation** asignación de bandas (de frecuencias *or* de longitud de ondas) ◇ **the new band allocation means we will have more channels** la nueva asignación de bandas de frecuencias significa que tendremos más canales (de transmisión)

allocation routine /ˌælə'keɪʃ(ə)n ruːˌtiːn/ *noun* rutina *f* de asignación; instrucción *f* de asignación

allocation unit /ˌælə'keɪʃ(ə)n ˌjuːnɪt/ *noun* unidad *f* de asignación

all points addressable mode /ˌɔːl ˌpɔɪnts ə 'dresəb(ə)l ˌməʊd/ *noun* (*graphics mode in which each pixel can be individually addressed*) modo *m* direccionable de una matriz activa; modo *m* APA

alpha /'ælfə/ *noun* prueba *f* alfa

ALPHA /'ælfə/ *noun* (*first letter of the Greek alphabet*) ALPHA™

alpha beta technique /ˌælfə 'biːtə tekˌniːk/ *noun* (*technique used in artificial intelligence*) técnica *f* alfa beta

alphabetic character set /ˌælfəbetɪk 'kærɪktə ˌset/ *noun* letras *fpl* del alfabeto

alphabetic string /ˌælfəbetɪk 'strɪŋ/ *noun* cadena *f* de caracteres alfabéticos

alphabetise /'ælfəbetaɪz/, **alphabetize** *verb* alfabetizar *vt*; poner en orden alfabético ◇ **enter the bibliographical information and alphabetize it** introduzca la información bibliográfica y póngala en orden alfabético

alpha channel /'ælfə ˌtʃæn(ə)l/ *noun* (*top eight bits that define the properties of a pixel*) canal *m* alfa

alphageometric /ˌælfədʒiːəʊ'metrɪk/ *adjective* alfageométrico *or* -a

alphameric /ˌælfə'merɪk/ *adjective* US alfanumérico *or* -a

alphamosaic /ˌælfəməʊ'zeɪɪk/ *adjective* alfamosaico *or* -a

alphanumeric /ˌælfənjʊ'merɪk/ *adjective* alfanumérico *or* -a

alphanumeric array /ˌælfənjʊmerɪk ə'reɪ/ *noun* orden *m* alfanumérica

alphanumeric characters /ˌælfənjʊmerɪk 'kærɪktəz/ *plural noun* caracteres *mpl* alfanuméricos

alphanumeric data /ˌælfənjʊmerɪk 'deɪtə/ *noun* datos *mpl* alfanuméricos

alphanumeric display /ˌælfənjʊmerɪk dɪ'spleɪ/ *noun* pantalla *f* alfanumérica; visualización *f* alfanumérica

alphanumeric key /ˌælfənjʊmerɪk 'kiː/ *noun* tecla *f* alfanumérica

alphanumeric keyboard /ˌælfənjʊmerɪk 'kiːbɔːd/ *noun* teclado *m* alfanumérico

alphanumeric operand /ˌælfənjʊmerɪk 'ɒpərænd/ *noun* operando *m* alfanumérico

alphanumerics /ˌælfənjʊ'merɪks/ *plural noun* caracteres *mpl* alfanuméricos

alphanumeric string /ˌælfənjʊmerɪk 'strɪŋ/ *noun* cadena *f* de caracteres alfanuméricos

alpha-particle /'ælfə ˌpɑːtɪk(ə)l/ *noun* partícula *f* alfa

alpha-particle sensitivity /ˌælfə ˌpɑːtɪk(ə)l ˌsensə'tɪvəti/ *noun* sensibilidad *f* a los rayos alfa

alphaphotographic /ˌælfəfəʊtəʊ'græfɪk/ *adjective* alfafotográfico *or* -a

alphasort /ˌælfə'sɔːt/ *verb* ordenar por orden alfabético; clasificar (datos) en orden alfabético

alpha test /'ælfə test/ *noun* (*first test of a computer product*) prueba *f* alfa

alternate /'ɒltəneɪt/ *verb* alternar *vi*

alternate character set /ɔːlˌtɜːnət 'kærɪktə ˌset/ *noun* (*second set of characters*) grupo *m* de caracteres alternativos; conjunto *m* de caracteres alternos ◇ **we can print Greek characters by selecting the alternate character set** podemos imprimir caracteres griegos al seleccionar el conjunto de caracteres alternos

alternate key /ɔːl'tɜːnət kiː/ *noun* tecla *f* secundaria

alternate mode /ɔːl'tɜːnət məʊd/ *noun* modo *m* alterno

alternate route /ɔːl'tɜːnət ruːt/ *noun* (*backup path*) ruta *f* alterna; vía *f* alterna; desviación *f*

alternating current /,ɔːltəneɪtɪŋ 'kʌrənt/ *noun* corriente *f* alterna

alternation /,ɔːltə'neɪʃ(ə)n/ *noun* alternancia *f*

alternative denial /ɔːl,tɜːnətɪv dɪ'naɪəl/ *noun* denegación *f* alternativa; negación *f* alternativa

Alt key /'ɔːlt kiː/ *noun* tecla *f* ALT

ALU /,eɪ el 'juː/ *noun* ALU; dispositivo *m* ALU

always on /'ɔːlweɪz ɒn/ *adjective* 'always-on'

AM *abbr* (*amplitude modulation*) modulación *f* de amplitud

ambience /'æmbiəns/ *noun* acústica *f* ambiental

ambient /'æmbiənt/ *adjective* ambiente; ambiental

ambient noise /,æmbiənt 'nɔɪz/ *noun* ruido *m* de fondo; sonido *m* ambiente ◇ **ambient noise level** nivel *m* de ruido de fondo *or* de sonido ambiente ◇ **the ambient noise level in the office is greater than in the library** el nivel de sonido ambiente de la oficina es superior al de la biblioteca

ambient temperature /,æmbiənt 'temprɪtʃə/ *noun* temperatura *f* ambiente

ambiguity /,æmbɪ'gjuːɪti/ *noun* ambigüedad *f*

ambiguity error /,æmbɪ'gjuːɪti ,erə/ *noun* error *m* de ambigüedad

ambiguous /æm'bɪgjuəs/ *adjective* ambiguo *or* -a; equívoco *or* -a

ambiguous filename /æm,bɪgjuəs 'faɪlneɪm/ *noun* nombre *m* de fichero ambiguo

AMD (*company that develops and produces processor components*) AMD

amendment record /ə,men(d)mənt 'rekɔːd/ *noun* registro *m* de modificaciones

American National Standards Institute /ə,merɪkən ,næʃ(ə)nəl 'stændədz ,ɪnstɪtjuːt/ *noun* (*American equivalent of*) instituto *m* nacional americano de estándares

American Standard Code for Information Interchange /ə,merɪkən ,stændəd kəʊd fər ,ɪnfəmeɪʃ(ə)n 'ɪntətʃeɪndʒ/ *noun* código *m* estándar americano para el intercambio de información

America Online /ə,merɪkə 'ɒnlaɪn/ (*largest Internet service provider in the world*) America Online

amp /æmp/ *noun* amperio *m* (A)

ampere /'æmpeə/ *noun* amperio *m*

amplification /,æmplɪfɪ'keɪʃ(ə)n/ *noun* amplificación *f*; ampliación *f* ◇ **increase the amplification of the input signal** aumente la amplificación de la señal de entrada ◇ **the amplification**

is so high, the signal is distorting la amplificación es tan alta que distorsiona la señal

amplifier /'æmplɪ,faɪə/ *noun* amplificador *m* ◇ **amplifier class** tipo *m* de amplificador ◇ **audio amplifier** amplificador de audio ◇ **low noise amplifier** amplificador de bajo ruido

amplify /'æmplɪ,faɪ/ *verb* amplificar *vt* ◇ **amplified telephone** teléfono *m* amplificado ◇ **the received signal needs to be amplified before it can be processed** la señal recibida necesita ser amplificada antes de que se pueda procesar

amplitude /'æmplɪ,tjuːd/ *noun* amplitud *f* ◇ **amplitude distortion** distorsión *f* de amplitud ◇ **amplitude shift keying (ASK)** codificación *f* por desplazamiento de amplitud

amplitude modulation /'æmplɪtjuːd mɒdju,leɪʃ(ə)n/ *noun* modulación *f* de amplitud

amplitude quantisation /,æmplɪtjuːd ,kwɒntaɪ'zeɪʃ(ə)n/ *noun* cuantificación *f* de la amplitud

analog, analogue ◇ **analog to digital converter (ADC** *or* **A to D converter)** convertidor *m* de analógico a digital *or* de analógico a numérico ◇ **digital to analog converter (DAC** *or* **D to A converter)** convertidor de digital a analógico

analog channel /,ænəlɒg 'tʃæn(ə)l/ *noun* vía *f* analógica; canal *m* analógico

analog computer /,ænəlɒg kəm'pjuːtə/ *noun* ordenador *m* analógico

analog data /,ænəlɒg 'deɪtə/ *noun* datos *mpl* analógicos

analog display /,ænəlɒg dɪ'spleɪ/ *noun* pantalla *f* analógica; visualización *f* analógica

analog gate /'ænəlɒg geɪt/ *noun* puerta *f* analógica; circuito *m* analógico

analog input card /,ænəlɒg 'ɪnpʊt ,kɑːd/ *noun* tarjeta *f* de entrada analógica

analog line /,ænəlɒg 'laɪn/ *noun* línea *f* analógica

analog loopback /,ænəlɒg 'luːpbæk/ *noun* bucle *m* analógico

analog monitor /,ænəlɒg 'mɒnɪtə/ *noun* monitor *m* analógico

analog output card /,ænəlɒg ,aʊt'pʊt ,kɑːd/ *noun* tarjeta *f* de salida analógica

analog recording /,ænəlɒg rɪ'kɔːdɪŋ/ *noun* registro *m* analógico; grabación *f* analógica

analog representation /,ænəlɒg ,reprɪzen'teɪʃ(ə)n/ *noun* representación *f* analógica

analog signal /,ænəlɒg 'sɪgn(ə)l/ *noun* señal *f* analógica

analog to digital /,ænəlɒg tə 'dɪdʒɪt(ə)l/ *adjective* analógico a digital; analógico a numérico

analog to digital converter /,ænəlɒg tə ,dɪdʒɪt(ə)l kən'vɜːtə/ *noun* convertidor *m* de digital a analógico

analog transmission /,ænəlɒg trænz'mɪʃ(ə)n/ *noun* transmisión *f* analógica

analyser /'ænəlaɪzə/ *noun* analizador *m* ◇ **frequency analyzer** analizador de frecuencias

analyst /'ænəlɪst/ *noun* analista *m&f*

analytical engine /ˌænəlɪtɪk(ə)l 'endʒɪn/ *noun* máquina *f* analítica

anamorphic /ˌænə'mɔːfɪk/ *adjective* anamórfico *or* -a

ancestral file /æn͵sestrəl 'faɪl/ *noun* fichero *m* ancestral; fichero *m* precursor

anchor cell /'æŋkə sel/ *noun* (*cell that defines the start of a range of cells*) celda *f* de anclaje

ancillary equipment /æn͵sɪləri ɪ'kwɪpmənt/ *noun* (*useful, but not essential, accessories*) accesorios *mpl*; equipo *m* accesorio; materiales *mpl* auxiliares

AND /ænd/ *noun* función *f* Y; función *f* de coincidencia

AND circuit /ænd 'sɜːkɪt/, **AND element** /ænd 'elɪmənt/ *noun* (*electronic gate*) circuito *m* Y; circuito *m* de coincidencia; elemento *m* Y; elemento *m* de coincidencia

AND function /'ænd ͵fʌŋkʃən/ *noun* función *f* Y; función *f* de coincidencia

AND gate /'ænd geɪt/ *noun* (*electronic gate*) puerta *f* Y; puerta *f* de coincidencia

AND operation /'ænd ͵ɒpəreɪʃ(ə)n/ *noun* operación *f* Y; operación *f* de coincidencia

anechoic chamber /ˌænekəʊɪk 'tʃeɪmbə/ *noun* cámara *f* anecoica

angle /'æŋɡəl/ *noun* (*measure of the change in direction*) ángulo *m*

angstrom /'æŋstrɒm/ *noun* ángstrom *m*; angstromio *m*

ANI /ˌeɪ en 'aɪ/ *noun* identificación *f* automática de los números (de teléfono)

animation /ˌænɪ'meɪʃ(ə)n/ *noun* animación *f*

animation software /ˌænɪ'meɪʃ(ə)n ͵sɒftweə/ *noun* programa *m* gráfico

animatronics /ˌænɪmə'trɒnɪks/ *noun* animatronics

annotation /ˌænə'teɪʃ(ə)n/ *noun* (*comment or note*) anotación *f*; nota *f*; comentario *m*

annotation symbol /ˌænəʊ'teɪʃ(ə)n ͵sɪmb(ə)l/ *noun* símbolo *m* de anotación

announce /ə'naʊns/ *verb* anunciar *vt*

annunciator /ə'nʌnsieɪtə/ *noun* (*signal*) anunciador *m*

anode /'ænəʊd/ *noun* ánodo *m*

anonymous FTP /ə͵nɒnɪməs ef tiː 'piː/ *noun* FTP *m* anónimo

ANSI C /ˌænsi 'siː/ *noun* C ANSI

ANSI driver /'ænsi ͵draɪvə/ *noun* controlador *m* de la instrucción ANSI; activador *m* de la instrucción ANSI

ANSI escape sequence /ˌænsi ɪ'skeɪp ͵siːkwəns/ *noun* secuencia *f* de salida ANSI

ANSI keyboard /ˌænsi 'kiːbɔːd/ *noun* teclado *m* ANSI

ANSI screen control /ˌænsi 'skriːn kən͵trəʊl/ *noun* control *m* de pantalla ANSI

answer /'ɑːnsə/ *verb* (*replying a call*) responder a una llamada ◇ **answering service** servicio *m* de contestador *or* de contestación automática ◇ **the first modem originates the call and the**

second answers it el primer módem genera la llamada y el segundo la contesta

answer back /'ɑːnsə bæk/ *noun* señal *f* de respuesta

answering machine /'ɑːns(ə)rɪŋ mə͵ʃiːn/ *noun* contestador *m* (telefónico) automático

answer mode /'ɑːnsə məʊd/ *noun* modalidad *f* de respuesta; modo *m* de respuesta

answer modem /'ɑːnsə ͵məʊdem/ *noun* módem *m* de retorno; módem *m* de respuesta

answer/originate, answer/originate device *noun* (*device, such as a modem, that can receive or send data*) receptor/emisor *m*

answer time /'ɑːnsə taɪm/ *noun* tiempo *m* de respuesta

answertone /'ɑːnsətəʊn/ *noun* (*signal*) señal *f* de respuesta de un módem

anthropomorphic software /ˌænθrəpəmɔːfɪk 'sɒftweə/ *noun* (*software that appears to react to what a user says*) software *m* antropomórfico

anticoincidence circuit /ˌæntikəʊ'ɪnsɪdəns ͵sɜːkɪt/, **anticoincidence function** *noun* circuito *m* de anti-coincidencia; función *f* de anti-coincidencia

anti-static mat /ˌænti ͵stætɪk 'mæt/ *noun* alfombrilla *f* antiestática

anti-tinkle suppression /ˌænti 'tɪŋk(ə)l sə ͵preʃ(ə)n/ *noun* supresión *f* de señal de llamada parásita

anti-virus program /ˌænti 'vaɪrəs ͵prəʊɡræm/ *noun* programa *m* antivirus; utilidad *f* antivirus

anti-virus software /ˌænti 'vaɪrəs ͵sɒftweə/ *noun* software *m* antivirus

anycast /'enikɑːst/ *noun* anycast *m*

APA *abbr* (*all points addressable*) todos los puntos direccionables

Apache™ HTTPD /ə͵pætʃi ͵eɪtʃ tiː tiː piː 'diː/ *noun* (*web server software product*) Apache™ HTTP

APC *abbr* (*asynchronous procedure call*) llamada *f* de procedimiento asíncrono

aperture /'æpətʃə/ *noun* abertura *f* (de un objetivo)

aperture mask /'æpətʃə mɑːsk/ *noun* máscara *f* de abertura

API /ˌeɪ piː 'aɪ/ *noun* interfaz *f* de programación de aplicaciones

APL /ˌeɪ piː 'el/ *noun* lenguaje *m* (de programación) APL

APM /ˌeɪ piː 'em/ *noun* APM; administración *f* avanzada de corriente

APPC /ˌeɪ piː piː 'siː/ *noun* comunicaciones *fpl* avanzadas programa a programa; comunicaciones *fpl* en condiciones de igualdad

append /ə'pend/ *verb* (*file or data*) agregar *vt*; añadir *vt*; anexar *vt* ◇ **if you enter the DOS command COPY A+B, the file B will be appended to the end of file A** si se utiliza la instrucción de

DOS COPY A+B, el fichero B se añade al final del fichero A

Apple Computer Corporation /ˌæp(ə)l kəmˈpjuːtə ˌkɔːpəreɪʃ(ə)n/ (*company that has developed a range of personal computers, including Apple Mac*) Apple Computer Corporation 'Apple Computer has fleshed out details of a migration path to the PowerPC RISC architecture for its 7 million Apple Macintosh users. Developments in the pipeline include PowerPC versions of the AppleTalk Remote Access networking protocol.' [*Computing*]

Apple Desktop Bus /ˌæp(ə)l ˌdesktɒp ˈbʌs/ (*trade name for a serial bus built into Apple Macs*) enlace *m* común de Apple Desktop; bus *m* de Apple Desktop

Apple file exchange /ˌæp(ə)l ˈfaɪl ɪks ˌtʃeɪndʒ/ (*trade name for a software program that runs on an Apple Mac allowing it to read disks from a PC*) intercambio *m* de ficheros Apple™

Apple filing protocol /ˌæp(ə)l ˈfaɪlɪŋ ˌprəʊtəkɒl/ (*trade name for a method of storing files on a network server*) protocolo *m* de gestión de ficheros Apple; protocolo *m* AFP

Apple Key /ˈæp(ə)l kiː/ (*trade name for a special key on the keyboard of an Apple Mac*) tecla *f* Apple; tecla *f* manzana

Apple Mac /ˈæp(ə)l mæk/, **Apple Macintosh computer** /ˌæp(ə)l ˌmækɪntɒʃ kəmˈpjuːtə/ (*trade name for any of a range of personal computers developed by Apple Computer Corporation*) ordenador Mac/Macintosh™

Appleshare /ˈæp(ə)lʃeə/ (*trade name for software that allows Apple Macs to share files and printers using a file server*) Appleshare™

applet /ˈæplət/ *noun* **1.** (*utility application program*) pequeña aplicación *f* **2.** (*small application on the Internet*) aplique *m*; utilidad *f*; pequeña *f* aplicación

AppleTalk™ /ˈæp(ə)ltɑːk/ (*trade name for a communications protocol developed by the Apple Computer Corporation*) AppleTalk™

AppleTalk Filing Protocol /ˌæp(ə)ltɑːk ˈfaɪlɪŋ ˌprəʊtəkɒl/ protocolo *m* de gestión de ficheros AppleTalk; protocolo *m* AFP

appliance computer /əˌplaɪəns kəmˈpjuːtə/ *noun* ordenador *m*

application /ˌæplɪˈkeɪʃ(ə)n/ *noun* (*task which a computer performs or problem that a computer solves*) aplicación *f* ◊ **application parent** aplicación principal

application configuration access protocol /ˌæplɪkeɪʃ(ə)n kənˌfɪgjʊreɪʃ(ə)n ˈækses ˌprəʊtəkɒl/ *noun* protocolo *m* de acceso a la configuración de aplicaciones

application developer /ˌæplɪkeɪʃ(ə)n dɪˈveləpə/ *noun* diseñador *m* de aplicaciones

application file /ˌæplɪˈkeɪʃ(ə)n faɪl/ *noun* fichero *m* de aplicaciones

application form /ˌæplɪˈkeɪʃ(ə)n ˌfɔːm/ *noun* formulario *m* de solicitud

application generator /ˌæplɪˈkeɪʃ(ə)n ˌdʒenəreɪtə/ *noun* generador *m* de aplicaciones

application icon /ˌæplɪˈkeɪʃ(ə)n ˌaɪkɒn/ *noun* icono *m* de aplicaciones

application layer /ˌæplɪˈkeɪʃ(ə)n ˌleɪə/ *noun* capa *f* de aplicación

application orientated language /ˌæplɪkeɪʃ(ə)n ˌɔːriənteɪtɪd ˈlæŋgwɪdʒ/ *noun* lenguaje *m* de aplicación

application package /ˌæplɪˈkeɪʃ(ə)n ˌpækɪdʒ/ *noun* paquete *m* de aplicaciones; paquete *m* de programas

application program /ˌæplɪˈkeɪʃ(ə)n ˌprəʊgræm/ *noun* programa *m* de aplicaciones

application programming interface /ˌæplɪkeɪʃ(ə)n ˈprəʊgræmɪŋ ˌɪntəfeɪs/ *noun* interfaz *f* de programación de aplicaciones ◊ **if I follow the published API for this system, my program will work properly** si sigo la interfaz de programas de la aplicación (API), publicada para este sistema, el programa funcionará adecuadamente

application service element /ˌæplɪkeɪʃ(ə)n ˈsɜːvɪs ˌelɪmənt/ *noun* utilidad *f* de la aplicación

application service provider /ˌæplɪkeɪʃ(ə)n ˈsɜːvɪs prəˌvaɪdə/ *noun* proveedor *m* de aplicaciones

application software /ˌæplɪkeɪʃ(ə)n ˈsɒftweə/ *noun* software *m* de aplicaciones

applications package /ˌæplɪˈkeɪʃ(ə)nz ˌpækɪdʒ/ *noun* paquete *m* de aplicación

application specific integrated circuits /ˌæplɪkeɪʃ(ə)n spəˌsɪfɪk ˌɪntɪgreɪtɪd ˈsɜːkɪts/ *noun* circuito *m* integrado para aplicaciones específicas

applications programmer /ˌæplɪˈkeɪʃ(ə)nz ˌprəʊgræmə/ *noun* programador *m* de aplicaciones

applications software /ˌæplɪˈkeɪʃ(ə)nz ˌsɒftweə/ *noun* aplicación *f*

applications terminal /ˌæplɪˈkeɪʃ(ə)nz ˌtɜːmɪn(ə)l/ *noun* terminal *m* de aplicaciones

application terminal /ˌæplɪˈkeɪʃ(ə)n ˌtɜːmɪn(ə)l/ *noun* terminal *m* de aplicaciones

application window /ˌæplɪˈkeɪʃ(ə)n ˌwɪndəʊ/ *noun* ventana *f* de aplicaciones

APPN /ˌeɪ piː piː ˈen/ *noun* red *f* APPN; red *f* avanzada par a par; red *f* avanzada de terminal a terminal

approximation error /əˌprɒksɪˈmeɪʃ(ə)n ˌerə/ *noun* error *m* de estimación; error *m* de redondeo

A programming language /ˌeɪ ˈprəʊgræmɪŋ ˌlæŋgwɪdʒ/ *noun* lenguaje *m* de programación APL

APT /ˌeɪ piː ˈtiː/ *noun* herramientas *fpl* de programación automática

Arabic figures /ˌærəbɪk ˈfɪgəz/ *plural noun* números *mpl* arábigos

Arabic numbers /ˌærəbɪk ˈnʌmbəz/, **Arabic figures** /ˌærəbɪk ˈfɪgəz/, **Arabic numerals** /ˌærəbɪk ˈnjuːmərəl/ *noun* números *mpl* arábigos

Archie /'ɑːtʃiː/ *noun (old system of servers on the internet)* Archie

architecture /'ɑːkɪtektʃə/ *noun* arquitectura *f*

'Software giant Microsoft is also interested in using Xerox' Glyph technology as part of its Microsoft At Work architecture that seeks to unite office computers with fax machines and copiers.' [*Computing*]

archival quality /'ɑːkaɪv(ə)l ˌkwɒləti/ *noun* propiedad *f* de archivo

archive /'ɑːkaɪv/ *noun* archivos *mpl* ■ *verb* archivar *vt*

archive attribute /ˌɑːkaɪv ə'trɪbjuːt/**, archive bit** /'ɑːkaɪv bɪt/ *noun (attribute attached to a file)* atributo *m* de archivos; bit *m* de archivos

archived copy /ˌɑːkaɪvd 'kɒpi/ *noun* copia *f* archivada; copia *f* de archivos

archive file /'ɑːkaɪv faɪl/ *noun* fichero *m* de archivos

archive flag /'ɑːkaɪv flæg/ *noun (attribute attached to a file)* indicador *m* de archivos

archive site /'ɑːkaɪv saɪt/ *noun* sitio *m* de archivo

archive storage /ˌɑːkaɪv 'stɔːrɪdʒ/ *noun* memoria *f* de archivo

area /'eəriə/ *noun (section in memory)* zona *f*

area fill /'eəriə fɪl/ *noun* relleno *m* de área

area graph /'eəriə grɑːf/ *noun* grafo *m* de área

area search /'eəriə sɜːtʃ/ *noun* búsqueda *f* de zona; búsqueda *f* selectiva

arg /ɑːg/ *noun* argumento *m* (de una función)

argument /'ɑːgjʊmənt/ *noun* argumento *m* (de una función)

argument separator /'ɑːgjʊmənt ˌsepəreɪtə/ *noun* separador *m* de argumentos ◇ **the command 'MULTIPLY A, B' uses a comma as the argument separator** en la instrucción 'MULTIPLY A, B' se utiliza una coma como separador de argumentos

arithmetic capability /ˌærɪθmetɪk ˌkeɪpə'bɪlɪti/ *noun* capacidad *f* de cálculo aritmético

arithmetic check /ə'rɪθmətɪk tʃek/ *noun* verificación *f* aritmética

arithmetic functions /ə,rɪθmətɪk 'fʌŋkʃənz/ *plural noun* funciones *fpl* aritméticas

arithmetic instruction /ˌærɪθmetɪk ɪn'strʌkʃən/ *noun* instrucción *f* aritmética

arithmetic logic unit /ˌærɪθmetɪk 'lɒdʒɪk ˌjuːnɪt/ *noun* unidad *f* aritmética y lógica (UAL)

arithmetic operation /ˌærɪθmetɪk ˌɒpə'reɪʃ(ə)n/ *noun* operación *f* aritmética

arithmetic operator /ˌærɪθmetɪk 'ɒpəreɪtə/ *noun* operador *m* aritmético; símbolo *m* aritmético

arithmetic register /ˌærɪθmetɪk 'redʒɪstə/ *noun* registro *m* aritmético

arithmetic shift /ˌærɪθmetɪk 'ʃɪft/ *noun* desplazamiento *m* aritmético

arithmetic unit /ˌærɪθmetɪk 'juːnɪt/ *noun* unidad *f* aritmética y lógica (UAL)

ARLL *abbr (advanced run-length limited)* codificación *f* ARLL

arm /ɑːm/ *verb* **1.** *(device or machine or routine)* preparar *vt*; disponer *vt*; armar *vt* **2.** *(to activate)* validar *vt*; activar *vt*

armed interrupt /ɑːmd 'ɪntərʌpt/ *noun* interrupción *f* validada; interrupción *f* activada

ARP /ˌeɪ ɑː 'piː/ *noun* protocolo *m* ARP; protocolo *m* de resolución de direcciones

ARPANET /'ɑːpənet/ *noun* red *f* ARPA; red *f* de la agencia de proyectos de investigación avanzada

ARQ /ˌeɪ ɑː 'kjuː/ *noun* solicitud *f* automática de repetición (de errores) ARQ; solicitud *f* automática de corrección (de errores) ARQ

array /ə'reɪ/ *noun (ordered structure of figures or data)* orden *m*; serie *f*; formación *f*; *(antennae or circuits)* matriz *f* ◇ **logic array** orden lógica *or* matriz lógica ◇ **the array processor allows the array that contains the screen image to be rotated with one simple command** el procesador de matrices permite que la matriz que contiene la imagen de la pantalla pueda girar con una sola instrucción

array bounds /ə'reɪ baʊndz/ *plural noun* límites *mpl* de matriz

array dimension /ə'reɪ daɪˌmenʃ(ə)n/ *noun* dimensión *f* de una matriz; dimensión *f* de una serie

array element /ə'reɪ ˌelɪmənt/ *noun* valor *m* de una matriz; elemento *m* de una matriz

array processor /ə'reɪ ˌprəʊsesə/ *noun (computer for fast applications)* procesador *m* vectorial; procesador *m* de órdenes; procesador *m* de matrices ◇ **the array processor allows the array that contains the screen image to be rotated with one simple command** el procesador de matrices permite que la matriz que contiene la imagen de la pantalla pueda girar con una sola instrucción

arrow key /'ærəʊ kiː/ *noun* tecla *f* de dirección; tecla *f* de flechas

arrow pointer /'ærəʊ 'pɔɪntə/ *noun (on-screen arrow)* flecha *f*; puntero *m*; indicador *m* (en forma de) flecha

artefact /'ɑːtɪfækt/**, artifact** *noun* artefacto *m*

article /'ɑːtɪk(ə)l/ *noun (of newspaper or magazine)* artículo *m* ◇ **he wrote an article about the user group for the local newspaper** escribió un artículo para el periódico local sobre el grupo de usuarios

artifact /'ɑːtɪfækt/ *noun* artefacto *m*

artificial intelligence /ˌɑːtɪfɪʃ(ə)l ɪn'telɪdʒ(ə)ns/ *noun* inteligencia *f* artificial

artificial life /ˌɑːtɪfɪʃ(ə)l 'laɪf/ *noun* vida *f* artificial

artificial neural network /ˌɑːtɪfɪʃ(ə)l 'njʊərəl ˌnetwɜːk/ *noun* red *f* de neuronas artificiales

artwork /'ɑːtˌwɜːk/ *noun (graphical work or images which are to be printed)* material *m* gráfico; ilustraciones *fpl*

ascend /ə'send/ *verb (increase)* subir *vi*; aumentar *vt*; ascender *vi*

ascender /ə'sendə/ *noun* (*of a character*) parte *f* superior del trazo vertical

ascending order /ə,sendɪŋ 'ɔːdə/ *noun* orden *m* ascendente

ASCII /'æskiː/ *noun* código *m* estándar americano para el intercambio de información

ASCII character /'æski ,kærɪktə/ *noun* carácter *m* ASCII

ASCII file /'æski faɪl/ *noun* fichero *m* ASCII

ASCII keyboard /,æski 'kiːbɔːd/ *noun* teclado *m* ASCII

ASCII text /'æski tekst/ *noun* texto *m* ASCII

ASCIIZ string /,æski: 'zed ,strɪŋ/ *noun* cadena *f* de caracteres ASCIIZ

ASF /,eɪ es 'ef/ *noun* formato *m* activo de flujo continuo

ASIC /,eɪ es aɪ 'siː/ *plural noun* circuito *m* integrado para aplicaciones específicas

ASP *abbr* **1.** (*Active Server Page*) ASP; página *f* de servidor activo **2.** (*application service provider*) proveedor *m* de aplicaciones

aspect ratio /,æspekt 'reɪʃiəʊ/ *noun* tasa *f* de la altura y la anchura de un píxel; relación *f* de la altura y la anchura de un píxel

aspect system /,æspekt 'sɪstəm/ *noun* sistema *m* de almacenaje e indexación

ASR /,eɪ es 'ɑː/ *noun* emisor-receptor *m* automático

ASR keyboard /,eɪ es ɑː 'kiːbɔːd/ *noun* teclado *m* ASR; teclado *m* emisor/receptor

assemble /ə'semb(ə)l/ *verb* **1.** (*to put together*) ensamblar *vt*; montar *vt* **2.** (*to translate assembly code into machine code*) ensamblar *vt* **3.** (*to insert something into a program*) ensamblar *vt* ◇ **syntax errors spotted whilst the source program is being assembled** los errores de sintaxis detectados mientras se ensambla el programa fuente ◇ **the parts for the disk drive are made in Japan and assembled in Spain** las piezas de la disquetera se manufacturan en Japón y se ensamblan en España ◇ **there is a short wait during which time the program is assembled into object code** hay una espera breve durante la que el programa se ensambla en código objeto

assembler /ə'semblə/ *noun* programa *m* ensamblador; ensamblador *m*

assembler error messages /ə,semblə 'erə ,mesɪdʒ/ *plural noun* mensaje *m* de error del ensamblador

assembler language /ə'semblə ,læŋgwɪdʒ/ *noun* lenguaje *m* de ensamblaje

assembler mnemonic /ə,semblə nɪ'mɒnɪk/ *noun* mnemotécnico *m or* -a *f*

assembler program /ə'semblə ,prəʊgræm/ *noun* (*assembly program*) ensamblador *m*; programa *m* ensamblador

assembly /ə'semblɪ/ *noun* (*putting together*) ensamblaje *m*; montaje *m* ◇ **assembly line** cadena *f* de montaje ◇ **there are no assembly instructions to show you how to put the com-** puter together no hay instrucciones de montaje del ordenador

assembly code /ə'sembli kəʊd/ *noun* código *m* de ensamblaje

assembly language /ə'sembli ,læŋgwɪdʒ/ *noun* lenguaje *m* de ensamblaje

assembly listing /ə'sembli ,lɪstɪŋ/ *noun* (*display of an assembler*) lista *f* de ensamblaje; listado *m* de ensamblaje; impresión *f* de un programa de montaje

assembly plant /ə'sembli plɑːnt/ *noun* planta *f* de montaje; fábrica *f* de montaje

assembly routine /ə'sembli ruː,tiːn/ *noun* rutina *f* de ensamblaje; sistema *m* de ensamblaje

assembly system /ə'semblɪ ,sɪstəm/ *noun* sistema *m* de ensamblaje

assembly time /ə'sembli taɪm/ *noun* (*for the translation of a program*) duración *f* de ensamblaje; tiempo *m* de ensamblaje; periodo *m* de ensamblaje

assertion /ə'sɜːʃ(ə)n/ *noun* (*program statement of a fact or rule*) aserción *f*; aserto *m*

assets /'æsets/ *plural noun* (*separate data elements, such as video or audio, that are used in a multimedia application*) elementos *mpl* disponibles; bienes *mpl* disponibles

assign /ə'saɪn/ *verb* **1.** (*to allocate task*) asignar *vt* **2.** (*to set a variable*) definir *vt* **3.** (*to allocate part of memory*) asignar *vt*; asignar una zona de la memoria a una tarea determinada ◇ **assigned frequency** frecuencia *f* asignada ◇ **two PCs have been assigned to outputting the labels** se han asignado dos ordenadores PC para producir las etiquetas

assigned numbers /ə,saɪnd 'nʌmbəz/ *plural noun* números *mpl* asignados

assignment /ə'saɪnmənt/ *noun* asignación *f*; distribución *f*

assignment compatible /ə,saɪnmənt kəm 'pætəb(ə)l/ *adjective* compatible con la asignación

assignment conversion /ə,saɪnmənt kən 'vɜːʃ(ə)n/ *noun* conversión *f* de asignación

assignment statement /ə,saɪnmənt 'steɪtmənt/ *noun* instrucción *f*; sentencia *f* de asignación

associated document /ə,səʊsieɪtɪd 'dɒkjʊmənt/, **associated file** /faɪl/ *noun* (*document or file linked to its originating application*) documento *m* asociado; fichero *m* asociado

associative addressing /ə,səʊsiətɪv ə 'dresɪŋ/ *noun* direccionamiento *m* asociativo; direccionamiento *m* de contenido direccionable

associative memory /ə,səʊsiətɪv 'mem(ə)ri/ *noun* memoria *f* asociativa

associative processor /ə,səʊsiətɪv 'prəʊsesə/ *noun* procesador *m* con memoria asociativa

associative storage /ə,səʊsiətɪv 'stɔːrɪdʒ/ *noun* almacenamiento *m* asociativo

associative storage register /əˌsəʊsiətɪv ˈstɔːrɪdʒ ˌredʒɪstə/ noun registro m de memoria asociativa

asterisk /ˈæstərɪsk/ noun **1.** (*multiplication symbol*) asterisco m **2.** (*wildcard symbol*) asterisco m

asterisk fill /ˈæst(ə)rɪsk fɪl/ noun relleno m por asteriscos

asymmetric compression /ˌæsɪˌmetrɪk kəmˈpreʃ(ə)n/ noun compresión f asimétrica

Asymmetric Digital Subscriber Line /ˌæsɪ ˌmetrɪk ˌdɪdʒɪt(ə)l səbˈskraɪbə ˌlaɪn/ noun línea f digital asimétrica de abonado

asymmetric transmission /eɪsɪˌmetrɪk trænzˈmɪʃ(ə)n/ noun (*data transmission used in high-speed modems*) transmisión f asimétrica

asymmetric video compression /eɪsɪ ˌmetrɪk ˈvɪdiəʊ kəmˌpreʃ(ə)n/ noun (*using a powerful computer to compress video*) compresión f asimétrica de vídeo

async /ˈeɪsɪŋk/ adjective informal asincrónico m or -a f; asíncrono m or -a f

asynchronous /əˈsɪŋkrənəs/ adjective asíncrono or -a; asincrónico or -a ◇ **asynchronous balanced mode (ABM)** modo asíncrono equilibrado ◇ **asynchronous balanced mode extended (ABME)** modo asíncrono equilibrado extendido ◇ **asynchronous response mode (ARM)** modo asíncrono de respuesta ◇ **when asynchronous ports are used no special hardware is required** cuando se utilizan puertos asíncronos de acceso no se requiere ningún hardware especial

asynchronous access /eɪˌsɪŋkrənəs ˈækses/ noun acceso m asíncrono

asynchronous cache /eɪˌsɪŋkrənəs ˈkæʃ/ noun memoria f caché asíncrona

asynchronous communication /eɪ ˌsɪŋkrənəs kəˌmjuːnɪˈkeɪʃ(ə)n/ noun comunicación f asíncrona

asynchronous communication server /eɪˌsɪŋkrənəs kəˌmjuːnɪˈkeɪʃ(ə)n ˌsɜːvə/ noun servidor m de comunicaciones asíncronas

asynchronous communications interface adapter /əˌsɪŋkrənəs kə ˌmjuːnɪkeɪʃ(ə)nz ˈɪntəfeɪs əˌdæptə/ noun adaptador m para interfaz de comunicaciones asíncronas

asynchronous computer /eɪˌsɪŋkrənəs kəmˈpjuːtə/ noun ordenador m asíncrono

asynchronous data transfer /eɪˌsɪŋkrənəs ˌdeɪtə ˈtrænsfɜː/ noun transferencia f asíncrona de datos

asynchronous mode /eɪˈsɪŋkrənəs məʊd/ noun modo m asíncrono

asynchronous port /eɪˌsɪŋkrənəs ˈpɔːt/ noun (*connection*) puerto m asíncrono de acceso; puerto m asíncrono; vía f asíncrona de acceso

asynchronous procedure call /eɪ ˌsɪŋkrənəs prəˈsiːdʒə ˌkɔːl/ noun llamada f de procedimiento asíncrono

asynchronous transfer mode /eɪ ˌsɪŋkrənəs ˈtrænsfɜː ˌməʊd/ noun modo m de transferencia asíncrona ATM; conmutación f temporal asíncrona

asynchronous transmission /eɪˌsɪŋkrənəs trænzˈmɪʃ(ə)n/ noun transmisión f asíncrona

AT /ˌeɪ ˈtiː/ noun (*standard of PC that uses a 16-bit 80286 processor*) AT

ATA /ˌeɪ tiː ˈeɪ/ noun ATA; adición f a tecnología avanzada

ATA Fast /ˌeɪ tiː ˌeɪ ˈfɑːst/ noun accesorio m rápido de tecnología avanzada

ATA packet interface /ˌeɪ tiː ˌeɪ ˈpækɪt ˌɪntəfeɪs/ noun interfaz f de tecnología avanzada

ATAPI abbr (*advanced technology attachment packet interface*) accesorio m de tecnología avanzada

AT attachment /ˌeɪ ˈtiː əˌtætʃmənt/ noun adición f a tecnología avanzada

ATA Ultra /ˌeɪ tiː ˌeɪ ˈʌltrə/ noun accesorio m ultra-rápido de tecnología avanzada

AT-bus /ət bʌs/ noun bus m AT

ATC /ˌeɪ tiː ˈsiː/ noun autorización f para copiar; permiso m para duplicar

AT command set /ˌeɪ tiː kəˈmɑːnd set/ noun juego m de instrucciones AT

ATD /ˌeɪ tiː ˈdiː/ noun (*modems*) ATD

ATE /ˌeɪ tiː ˈiː/ noun equipo m automático de verificación

Athlon XP /ˈæθlɒn eks ˌpiː/ (*trade name for a 32-bit processor, developed by AMD*) Athlon XP

AT-keyboard /ət ˈkiːˌbɔːd/ noun teclado m AT

ATM¹ /ˌeɪ tiː ˈem/ abbr (*Adobe Type Manager*) gestor m de fuentes Adobe

ATM² /ˌeɪ tiː ˈem/ noun conmutación f temporal asíncrona; modo m de transferencia asíncrona ATM

ATM³ /ˌeɪ tiː ˈem/ noun cajero m automático

ATM adaptation layer /ˌeɪ tiː ˌem ˌædæp ˈteɪʃ(ə)n ˌleɪə/ noun capa f de adaptación en modo de transferencia asíncrona; capa f de adaptación ATM

ATM cell format /ˌeɪ tiː ˈem sel/ noun formato m de célula ATM; formato m en modo de transferencia asíncrona

ATM layers /ˌeɪ tiː ˌem ˈleɪəs/ noun capas fpl ATM; capas fpl en modo de transferencia asíncrona

AT mode /ˌeɪ ˈtiː ˌməʊd/ noun modo m AT

ATM payload /ˌeɪ tiː ˌem ˌpeɪˈləʊd/ noun carga f útil ATM; carga f en modo de transferencia asíncrona

A to D /eɪ tə diː/ adjective analógico-digital

A to D converter /ˈə tə tʊ diː/ noun convertidor m analógico-digital ◇ **the speech signal was first passed through an A to D converter before being analysed** la señal de voz se pasó primero a través de un convertidor analógico-digital antes de ser analizada

atom /ˈætəm/ noun **1.** (*smallest particle of an element*) átomo m **2.** (*value or string that cannot be reduced to a simpler form*) dato m absoluto; átomo m

atomic /ə'tɒmɪk/ *adjective* (*referring to atoms; operation that returns data to its original state if it is stopped during processing*) atómico *or* -a

ATSC /ˌeɪ tiː es 'siː/ *noun* comité *m* de sistemas avanzados

attach /ə'tætʃ/ *verb* (*to connect a node or login to a server on a network*) conectarse *vt*; enlazar (con un servidor) ◊ **I issued the command to attach to the local server** he dado la instrucción para conectarme al servidor local

attached processor /əˌtætʃt 'prəʊsesə/ *noun* procesador *m* auxiliar

attached resource computer network /ə ˌtætʃt rɪˌzɔːs kəm'pjuːtə ˌnetwɜːk/ *noun* red *f* ARCNET

attachment /ə'tætʃmənt/ *noun* (*named file with an electronic mail message*) documento *m* adjunto

attack /ə'tæk/ *noun* (*start of a sound*) ataque *m*

attended operation /əˌtendɪd ˌɒpə'reɪʃ(ə)n/ *noun* operación *f* asistida

attention code /ə'tenʃən kəʊd/ *noun* (*the characters AT used within the Hayes AT command set to tell a modem that a command follows*) código *m* de intervención; código *m* AT

attention interruption /əˌtenʃ(ə)n ˌɪntə 'rʌpʃən/ *noun* interrupción *f* de la intervención

attention key /ə'tenʃ(ə)n kiː/ *noun* tecla *f* de intervención

attenuation /əˌtenju'eɪʃ(ə)n/ *noun* **1.** (*reduction of a signal*) debilitamiento *m* (de la señal) **2.** (*difference in power*) atenuación *f*; debilitamiento *m* ◊ **if the cable is too long, the signal attenuation will start to cause data errors** si el cable es demasiado largo, el debilitamiento de la señal comenzará a ocasionar errores en los datos

attribute /'ætrɪbjuːt/ *noun* **1.** (*characteristic*) atributo *m*; característica *f* **2.** (*control data*) característica *f*; atributo *m* ◊ **pressing Ctrl and B keys at the same time will set the bold attribute for this paragraph of text** al pulsar al mismo tiempo las teclas Ctrl y B se activa el atributo negrita para este párrafo de texto ◊ **this attribute controls the colour of the screen** este atributo controla el color de la pantalla

auctioneering device /ˌɔːkʃə'nɪərɪŋ dɪ ˌvaɪs/ *noun* dispositivo *m* de selección de señal máxima; dispositivo *m* de selección de señal mínima

audible /'ɔːdɪb(ə)l/ *adjective* (*signal*) audible; perceptible al oído ◊ **the printer makes an audible signal when it runs out of paper** la impresora emite una señal audible cuando se le acaba el papel

audio /'ɔːdiəʊ/ *adjective* audio ◊ **active audio system** sistema *m* de audio interactivo ◊ **audio compressor** reductor *m* (de la señal) de audio ◊ **audio conferencing** audioconferencia *f* ◊ **audio frequency** frecuencia *f* audio *or* audiofrecuencia *f* ◊ **audio *or* video interleaved (AVI)** (*Windows multimedia video format developed by Microsoft*) audio/vídeo intercalados ◊ **audio port** puer-

to *m* (de) audio ◊ **audio slide** diapositiva *f* (de) audio

audio board /'ɔːdiəʊ bɔːd/ *noun* tarjeta *f* de audio; tarjeta *f* de sonido

audio file /'ɔːdiəʊ faɪl/ *noun* fichero *m* de audio

audio range /'ɔːdiəʊ reɪndʒ/ *noun* (*frequency range*) límites *mpl* de audiofrecuencias; campo *m* de audiofrecuencias; gama *f* de audiofrecuencias

audio response unit /ˌɔːdiəʊ rɪ'spɒns ˌjuːnɪt/ *noun* unidad *f* de respuesta audio; unidad *f* de respuesta vocal

audiotex /'ɔːdiəʊteks/ *noun* (*interactive voice response over the telephone*) audiotex *m*

audio/video interleaved /ˌɔːdiəʊ ˌvɪdiəʊ ˌɪntə'liːvd/ *noun* audio/vídeo intercalados

audit /'ɔːdɪt/ *noun* (*noting tasks carried out by a computer*) auditoría *f* ■ *verb* (*checking of a system*) hacer una auditoría

audit trail /'ɔːdɪt treɪl/ *noun* (*record of details of the use of a system*) protocolo *m* de trazado; pista *f* de control; (*record of details of the use made of a system*) pista *f* de verificación; registro *m* de auditoría

augend /'ɔːgend/ *noun* (*number to which another number is added to produce a sum*) sumando *m*; primer término *m* de una suma

augmented addressing /ɔːgˌmentɪd ə 'dresɪŋ/ *noun* direccionamiento *m* ampliado

augmenter /ˌɔːg'mentə/ *noun* (*value added to another*) sumando *m*; segundo término *m* de una suma

AUI connector /ˌeɪ juː 'aɪ kəˌnektə/ *noun* (*connector used to connect Ethernet cable to a network adapter*) conector *m* AUI

AUP *abbr* (*acceptable use policy*) política *f* de uso aceptable

authentication of messages /ɔː ˌθentɪkeɪʃ(ə)n əv 'mesɪdʒɪz/ *noun* autentificación *f* de mensajes

authenticator /ɔː'θentɪkeɪtə/ *noun* autenticador *m*

author /'ɔːθə/ *noun* (*person who wrote a program*) autor *m*

'The authoring system is a software product that integrates text and fractally compressed images, using any wordprocessor line editor, to create an electronic book with hypertext links between different pages.' [*Computing*]

authoring language /ˌɔːθərɪŋ 'læŋgwɪdʒ/ *noun* lenguaje *m* de autor

authoring software /ˌɔːθərɪŋ 'sɒftweə/, **authoring system** /ˌɔːθərɪŋ 'sɪstəm/ *noun* **1.** (*multimedia software*) sistema *m* de autor **2.** (*webpage design software*) sistema *m* de autor

authorisation /ˌɔːθəraɪ'zeɪʃ(ə)n/, **authorization** *noun* **1.** autorización *f*; permiso *m* **2.** (*to access a system*) autorización *f* ◊ **authorization to copy (ATC)** autorización *f*

authorisation code /ˌɔːθəraɪ'zeɪʃ(ə)n kəʊd/ *noun* código *m* de acceso

authorisation to copy /ˌɔːθəraɪzeɪʃ(ə)n tə 'kɒpɪ/ *noun* autorización *f* para copiar; permiso *m* para duplicar

authorised user /ˌɔːθəˌraɪzd 'juːzə/, **authorized user** *noun* usuario *m* autorizado (para utilizar un sistema); persona *f* autorizada (para utilizar un sistema)

authority file /ɔː'θɒrɪti faɪl/, **authority list** /ɔː'θɒrɪti lɪst/ *noun* fichero *m* de referencia; lista *f* de referencia

author level /ˌɔːθə 'lev(ə)l/ *noun* nivel *m* de autor

auto advance /ˌɔːtəʊ əd'vɑːns/ *noun* alimentación *f* automática del papel; tracción *f* automática del papel

auto-answer /ˌɔːtəʊ 'ɑːnsə/ *noun* auto-respuesta *f*; respuesta *f* automática

auto-baud scanning /'ɔːtəʊ bɔːd/, **auto-baud sensing** /'ɔːtəʊ bɔːd/ *noun* (*modem*) reconocimiento *m* automático del rendimiento de una señal; rastreo *m* automático del rendimiento de una señal; autoescaneado *m* de baudios

auto-boot /'ɔːtəʊ buːt/ *noun* arranque *m* automático (de un sistema); iniciación *f* automática (de un sistema)

auto-dial /ˌɔːtəʊ 'daɪəl/ *noun* sistema *m* automático de llamada

AUTOEXEC.BAT /ˌɔːtəʊɪg'zek bæt/ *noun* (*batch file*) autoexec.bat

autoflow /'ɔːtəʊfləʊ/ *noun* autoflujo *m*

auto-login /ˌɔːtəʊ 'lɒgɪn/, **auto-logon** /ˌɔːtəʊ 'lɒgɒn/ *noun* apertura *f* automática de una sesión

automated teller machine /ˌɔːtəmeɪtɪd 'telə məˌʃiːn/ *noun* cajero *m* automático

automatically programmed tools /ˌɔːtəmætɪkli ˌprəʊgræmd 'tuːlz/ *plural noun* herramientas *fpl* de programación automática

automatic backup /ˌɔːtəmætɪk 'bækʌp/ *noun* copia *f* automática de seguridad

automatic call distribution /ˌɔːtəmætɪk 'kɔːl ˌdɪstrɪbjuːʃ(ə)n/ *noun* distribución *f* automática de llamadas; distribuidor *m* automático de llamadas

automatic calling unit /ˌɔːtəmætɪk 'kɔːlɪŋ ˌjuːnɪt/ *noun* sistema *m* automático de llamadas; unidad *f* automática de llamadas

automatic carriage return /ˌɔːtəmætɪk 'kærɪdʒ rɪˌtɜːn/ *noun* retorno *m* automático de línea; retorno *m* automático de carro

automatic checking /ˌɔːtəmætɪk 'tʃekɪŋ/ *noun* verificación *f* automática

automatic data capture /ˌɔːtəmætɪk 'deɪtə ˌkæptʃə/ *noun* recogida *f* automática de datos

automatic data processing /ˌɔːtəmætɪk 'deɪtə ˌprəʊsesɪŋ/ *noun* proceso *m* automático de datos; tratamiento *m* automático de datos

automatic decimal adjustment /ˌɔːtəmætɪk 'desɪm(ə)l əˌdʒʌstmənt/ *noun* (*process of lining up all the decimal points in a column of figures*) ajuste *m* automático de decimales; alineación *f* automática de decimales; redondeo *m* a un número determinado de decimales

automatic error correction /ˌɔːtəmætɪk 'erə kəˌrekʃ(ə)n/ *noun* corrección *f* automática de errores

automatic error detection /ˌɔːtəmætɪk 'erə dɪˌtekʃ(ə)n/ *noun* detección *f* automática de errores

automatic font downloading /ˌɔːtəmætɪk 'fɒnt dəʊnˌləʊdɪŋ/ *noun* carga *f* automática de fuentes de caracteres; volcado *m* automático de fuentes de caracteres

automatic frequency switching /ˌɔːtəmætɪk 'friːkwənsi ˌswɪtʃɪŋ/ *noun* conmutación *f* automática de frecuencias; conmutación *f* automática de modo

automatic gain control /ˌɔːtəmætɪk ˌgeɪn kən'trəʊl/ *noun* control *m* automático de amplificación

automatic hyphenation /ˌɔːtəmætɪk ˌhaɪfə'naɪʃ(ə)n/ *noun* división *f* automática

automatic letter writing /ˌɔːtəmætɪk 'letə ˌraɪtɪŋ/ *noun* composición *f* automática de tipos de cartas

automatic loader /ˌɔːtəmætɪk 'ləʊdə/ *noun* cargador *m* automático

automatic log on /ˌɔːtəmætɪk 'lɒg ˌɒn/ *noun* acceso *m* automático a una sesión

automatic mailing list /ˌɔːtəmætɪk 'meɪlɪŋ ˌlɪst/ *noun* lista *f* de direcciones

automatic mode /ˌɔːtə'mætɪk məʊd/ *noun* conmutación *f* automática de modo; conmutación *f* automática de frecuencias

automatic number identification /ˌɔːtəmætɪk 'nʌmbə aɪˌdentɪfɪkeɪʃ(ə)n/ *noun* identificación *f* automática de los números (de teléfono)

automatic power off /ˌɔːtəmætɪk ˌpaʊə 'ɒf/ *noun* parada *f* automática; apagado *m* automático

automatic programming /ˌɔːtəmætɪk 'prəʊgræmɪŋ/ *noun* programación *f* automática

automatic recalculation /ˌɔːtəmætɪk riːˌkælkjuː'leɪʃ(ə)n/ *noun* cálculo *m* automático nuevo

automatic recovery program /ˌɔːtəmætɪk rɪ'kʌv(ə)ri ˌprəʊgræm/ *noun* programa *m* de recuperación automática

automatic repeat /ˌɔːtəmætɪk rɪ'piːt/ *noun* repetición *f* automática

automatic repeat request /ˌɔːtəmætɪk rɪ'piːt rɪˌkwest/ *noun* solicitud *f* automática de repetición (de errores) ARQ; solicitud *f* automática de corrección (de errores) ARQ

automatic send/receive /ˌɔːtəmætɪk ˌsend rɪ'siːv/ *noun* emisor/receptor *m* automático

automatic sequencing /ˌɔːtəmætɪk 'siːkwənsɪŋ/ *noun* secuenciación *f* automática

automatic speed matching /ˌɔːtəmætɪk 'spiːd ˌmætʃɪŋ/ *noun* emparejamiento *m* automático de las velocidades

automatic test equipment /ˌɔːtəmætɪk 'test ɪˌkwɪpmənt/ *noun* equipo *m* automático de verificación

auto-redial /ˌɔːtəʊ ˈriːdaɪəl/ *noun* sistema *m* automático de nueva llamada

auto repeat /ˌɔːtəʊ rɪˈpiːt/ *noun* repetición *f* automática

autoresponder /ˌɔːtəʊrɪˈspɒndə/ *noun* emisor *m* de respuestas automáticas

auto restart /ˌɔːtəʊ ˈriːstɑːt/ *noun* reinicio *m* automático

auto start /ˈɔːtəʊ stɑːt/ *noun* (*facility to load a program automatically*) inicio *m* automático; arranque *m* automático; puesta *f* en funcionamiento automática

auto stop /ˈɔːtəʊ stɒp/ *noun* parada *f* automática

autosync /ˈɔːtəʊsɪŋk/ *noun* (*of modem*) sincronización *f* automática

auto trace /ˈɔːtəʊ treɪs/ *noun* rastreo *m* automático; seguimiento *m* automático

auto verify /ˌɔːtəʊ ˈverɪfaɪ/ *noun* verificación *f* automática

A/UX (*trade name for a version of the Unix operating system for the Apple Mac range of computers*) A/UX

auxiliary equipment /ɔːgˌzɪliəri ɪˈkwɪpmənt/ *noun* (*backup equipment*) material *m* auxiliar; equipo *m* auxiliar; equipo *m* de repuesto

auxiliary memory /ɔːgˌzɪliəri ˈmem(ə)ri/ *noun* almacenamiento *m* auxiliar

auxiliary processor /ɔːgˌzɪliəri ˈprəʊsesə/ *noun* procesador *m* auxiliar

auxiliary storage /ɔːgˌzɪliəri ˈstɔːrɪdʒ/, **auxiliary store** /ɔːgˈzɪliəri stɔː/ *noun* almacenamiento *m* auxiliar

available bit rate /əˌveɪləb(ə)l ˈbɪt ˌreɪt/ *noun* tasa *f* disponible de bits

available list /əˈveɪləb(ə)l lɪst/ *noun* lista *f* de recursos disponibles

available point /əˈveɪləb(ə)l pɔɪnt/ *noun* punto *m*; elemento *m* de imagen

available power /əˌveɪləb(ə)l ˈpaʊə/ *noun* energía *f* disponible; electricidad *f* disponible

available time /əˈveɪləb(ə)l taɪm/ *noun* tiempo *m* disponible; tiempo *m* de disponibilidad

avalanche /ˈævəlɑːntʃ/ *noun* (*one action starting a number of other actions*) avalancha *f* ◇ **avalanche photodiode (APD)** fotodiodo *m* de avalanchas ◇ **there was an avalanche of errors after I pressed the wrong key** hubo una avalancha de errores después de apretar la tecla equivocada

avatar /ˈævətɑː/ *noun* **1.** (*graphical image*) avatar *m* **2.** (*superuser account in UNIX*) avatar *m*

average access time /ˌæv(ə)rɪdʒ ˈækses ˌtaɪm/ *noun* tiempo *m* medio de acceso

average delay /ˌæv(ə)rɪdʒ dɪˈleɪ/ *noun* (*time taken to access a communication network*) retraso *m* medio; retardo *m* medio; tiempo *m* medio de espera ◇ **the average delay increases at nine-thirty when everyone tries to log-in** después de las nueve y media el tiempo medio de espera aumenta debido a que todo el mundo intenta conectarse (al sistema)

AVI /ˌeɪ viː ˈaɪ/ *noun* audio/vídeo intercalados

axis /ˈæksɪs/ *noun* **1.** (*around which something turns*) eje *m* **2.** (*on a graph*) eje *m* de coordenadas ◇ **the CAD package allows an axis to be placed anywhere** el paquete de diseño asistido por ordenador (CAD) permite colocar el eje en cualquier sitio (de la pantalla)

azerty keyboard /əˌzɜːti ˈkiːbɔːd/ *noun* teclado *m* AZERTY; teclado *m* francés acentuado

azimuth /ˈæzɪməθ/ *noun* acimut *m*; azimut *m* ◇ **azimuth alignment might not be correct for tape recorded on a different machine** la alineación acimutal puede no ser la correcta para cintas grabadas en una máquina distinta

azimuth alignment /ˌæzɪməθ əˈlaɪnmənt/ *noun* (*horizontal angle of a tape head*) alineación *f* acimutal; alineación *f* de cabezas; alineación *f* de los ángulos de acimut ◇ **azimuth alignment is adjusted with this small screw** con este pequeño tornillo se ajusta la alineación acimutal ◇ **azimuth alignment might not be correct for tape recorded on a different machine** la alineación acimutal puede no ser la correcta para cintas grabadas en una máquina distinta

B

b *abbr* (*one bit*) (*bit*) b; bit *m*; dígito *m* binario; bi-tio *m* ◇ **bps (bits per second)** bit(s) por segundo

B¹ *abbr* (*one byte*) (*byte*) byte *m*; octeto *m*; B ◇ **KB (kilobyte)** (*1024 bytes*) KB *or* kilo-byte *m*; kilo-octeto *m*

B² *symbol* (*hexadecimal number equivalent to decimal 11*) número hexadecimal 11; B

B: (*second disk drive*) B:

B2B /ˌbiː tə ˈbiː/ *adjective* relaciones *fpl* comerciales entre empresas

B2C /ˌbiː tə ˈsiː/ *adjective* relaciones *fpl* comerciales entre empresa y consumador

babble /ˈbæb(ə)l/ *noun* diafonía *f*; ruido *m* de fondo

backbone /ˈbækˌbəʊn/ *noun* (*high-speed, high-capacity connection path*) red *f* principal; red *f* base; eje *m* principal (de red) ◇ **we have linked the networks in each office using a high-speed backbone** hemos interconectado las redes en cada oficina mediante una red principal de alta velocidad

backbone ring /ˈbækˌbəʊn rɪŋ/ *noun* anillo *m* de red principal

back buffer /bæk ˈbʌfə/ *noun* bufér *m* secundario

backdoor /ˈbækˌdɔː/ *noun* punto *m* de entrada en un sistema

back-end /bæk end/ (*informatics jargon*) auxiliar; especial

back-end network /ˌbæk end ˈnetwɜːk/ *noun* (*connection between a mainframe computer and a high-speed mass storage device*) red *f* auxiliar

back-end processor /ˌbæk end ˈprəʊsesə/ *noun* (*special purpose auxiliary processor*) procesador *m* especializado

back-end server /ˌbæk end ˈsɜːvə/ *noun* (*computer that carries out tasks requested by client workstations*) servidor *m* auxiliar

background /ˈbækɡraʊnd/ *noun* **1.** (*part of a picture*) segundo *m* plano; fondo *m* **2.** proceso *m* no prioritario ◇ **black text on a white background is less stressful for the eyes** el texto en negro sobre un fondo blanco fatiga menos la vista ◇ **the new graphics processor chip can handle background, foreground and sprite movement independently** el nuevo procesador de gráficos puede gestionar independientemente el movimiento del primer plano, del segundo plano y de otros objetos móviles planos

background colour /ˌbækɡraʊnd ˈkʌlə/ *noun* color *m* de fondo

background communication /ˌbækɡraʊnd kəˌmjuːnɪˈkeɪʃ(ə)n/ *noun* comunicación *f* subordinada; comunicación *f* no prioritaria

background image /ˌbækɡraʊnd ˈɪmɪdʒ/ *noun* imagen *f* de fondo; imagen *f* de segundo plano

background job /'bækgraʊnd dʒɒb/ *noun* tarea *f* subordinada; tarea *f* no prioritaria

background mode /'bækgraʊnd ˌməʊd/ *noun* modo *m* secundario

background noise /ˌbækgraʊnd 'nɔɪz/ *noun* ruido *m* de fondo ◇ **the modem is sensitive to background noise** el módem es sensible al ruido de fondo ◇ **the other machines around this device will produce a lot of background noise** los otros aparatos alrededor de este equipo producen mucho ruido de fondo

background operation /ˌbækgraʊnd ˌɒpə'reɪʃ(ə)n/ *noun* operación *f* subordinada; operación *f* no prioritaria

background printing /ˌbækgraʊnd 'prɪntɪŋ/ *noun* (*printing done while a computer processes another task*) impresión *f* subordinada; impresión *f* de fondo; impresión *f* en cola ◇ **background printing can be carried out whilst you are editing another document** se puede ejecutar una impresión de segundo plano mientras corriges otro documento

background processing /ˌbækgraʊnd 'prəʊsesɪŋ/ *noun* (*low priority job*) proceso *m* subordinado; proceso *m* no prioritario

background program /ˌbækgraʊnd 'prəʊgræm/ *noun* (*low-priority computer program*) programa *m* no prioritario; programa *m* subordinado

background recalculation /ˌbækgraʊnd riː ˌkælkju'leɪʃ(ə)n/ *noun* cálculo *m* subordinado

background reflectance /ˌbækgraʊnd rɪ 'flektəns/ *noun* reflejo *m* de fondo

background task /'bækgraʊnd tɑːsk/ *noun* tarea *f* subordinada; tarea *f* no prioritaria

backing /'bækɪŋ/ *noun* auxiliar *m* ◇ **by adding another disk drive, I will increase the backing store capabilities** al añadir otra disquetera aumentaré la capacidad de la memoria auxiliar

backing memory /ˌbækɪŋ 'mem(ə)ri/ *noun* memoria *f* auxiliar

backing storage /ˌbækɪŋ ˌstɔːrɪdʒ/ *noun* memoria *f* auxiliar

backing store /'bækɪŋ stɔː/, **backing storage** /'bækɪŋ ˌstɔːrɪdʒ/, **backing memory** /ˌbækɪŋ 'mem(ə)ri/ *noun* memoria *f* auxiliar; memoria *f* secundaria ◇ **by adding another disk drive, I will increase the backing store capabilities** al añadir otra disquetera aumentaré la capacidad de la memoria auxiliar ◇ **paper tape is one of the slowest access backing stores** la cinta de papel (perforada) es una de las memorias auxiliares de acceso más lento

back-level /bæk 'lev(ə)l/ *noun* (*earlier release of a product*) versión *f* previa

backlight /'bæklaɪt/ *noun* (*light behind a LCD*) luz *f* de fondo

backlit display /ˌbæklɪt dɪ'spleɪ/ *noun* pantalla *f* con luz de fondo activada

backlog /'bæk,lɒg/ *noun* (*work or tasks to be done*) trabajo *m* atrasado; trabajo *m* pendiente

back office /ˌbæk 'ɒfɪs/ *noun* trastienda *f*

backout /ˌbæk'aʊt/ *verb* (*restore a file to its original condition*) restaurar un fichero a su forma original

back panel /bæk 'pæn(ə)l/ *noun* (*at the rear of a computer*) panel *m* de atrás; panel *m* trasero; panel *m* posterior ◇ **the socket is on the back panel** el enchufe está en el panel trasero

backplane /'bækpleɪn/ *noun* panel *m* básico; plano *m* posterior

back pointer /bæk 'pɔɪntə/ *noun* puntero *m*; indicador *m* de retorno

back projection /bæk prə'dʒekʃ(ə)n/ *noun* (*cinema*) proyección *f* de fondo; proyección *f* por transparencia

backslash /'bækslæʃ/ *noun* (*ASCII character 92: the sign* \) barra *f* oblicua inversa (\)

backspace /'bæk,speɪs/ *noun* (*of cursor*) espacio *m* hacia atrás; espacio *m* de retroceso ◇ **if you make a mistake entering data, use the backspace key to correct it** si comete un error al introducir datos, utilice la tecla de retroceso para corregirlo

backspace character /'bækspeɪs ˌkærɪktə/ *noun* carácter *m* de retroceso

backspace key /'bæk,speɪs kiː/ *noun* tecla *f* de retroceso ◇ **if you make a mistake entering data, use the backspace key to correct it** si comete un error al introducir datos, utilice la tecla de retroceso para corregirlo

backtab /'bæktæb/ *verb* (*action using the cursor*) tabular hacia atrás

backtrack /'bæktræk/ *verb* buscar hacia atrás

back up /bæk ʌp/ *verb* **1.** (*to support or help*) ayudar *vt*; apoyar *vt*; respaldar *vt* **2.** (*to make a copy of a file or data or disk*) hacer una copia de seguridad ◇ **he brought along a file of documents to back up his claim** trajo consigo un fichero con documentos para apoyar su reclamación ◇ **the company accounts were backed up on disk as a protection against fire damage** se hizo una copia de seguridad de la contabilidad de la empresa en un disco para protegerla en caso de incendio ◇ **the printout backed up his argument for a new system** respaldó su razonamiento para la adquisición de un nuevo sistema con la copia impresa ◇ **the program enables users to back up hard disk files with a single command** el programa permite a los usuarios hacer copias de seguridad de ficheros del disco duro con una sola instrucción

backup /'bækʌp/ *noun* **1.** (*support*) appoyo *m*; (*technical support*) apoyo *m* técnico **2.** (*copy for security*) copia *f* de reserva; copia *f* de seguridad; copia *f* de protección **3.** (*process of making a copy*) duplicación *f* ■ *adjective*, *noun* (*of a file*) de seguridad; (*of memory*) de apoyo

'...the previous version is retained, but its extension is changed to .BAK indicating that it's a back-up' [*Personal Computer World*]

BACKUP *noun* (*MS-DOS command*) BACKUP

backup agent /'bækʌp ˌeɪdʒənt/ *noun* programa *m* para copias de seguridad

backup copy /'bækʌp ˌkɒpi/ *noun* copia *f* de seguridad

backup disk /'bækʌp dɪsk/ *noun* disco *m* de seguridad; disquete *m* de seguridad

backup domain controller /ˌbækʌp dəʊ 'meɪn kənˌtrəʊlə/ *noun* controlador *m* de seguridad por dominio(s)

backup file /'bækʌp faɪl/ *noun* fichero *m* de seguridad

backup path /'bækʌp pɑːθ/ *noun* vía *f* de seguridad; ruta *f* de seguridad

backup plan /'bækʌp plæn/ *noun* plan *m* de seguridad ◇ **the normal UPS has gone wrong, so we will have to use our backup plan to try and restore power** el suministro ininterrumpido de energía (UPS) normal ha fallado, así que tendremos que utilizar nuestro plan de seguridad para intentar restablecer la electricidad

backup procedure /ˌbækʌp prə'siːdʒə/ *noun* procedimiento *m* de seguridad

backup server /ˌbækʌp 'sɜːvə/ *noun* servidor *m* de seguridad; servidor *m* auxiliar

backup utility /ˌbækʌp juː'tɪlɪti/ *noun* utilidad *f* de seguridad

backup version /ˌbækʌp 'vɜːʃ(ə)n/ *noun* versión *f* de seguridad; copia *f* de seguridad

Backus-Naur-Form /ˌbækəs 'naʊə ˌfɔːm/ *noun* (*programming language*) convención *f*; metalenguaje *m*; forma *f* BNF

backward chaining /'bækwəd tʃeɪnɪŋ/ *noun* encadenamiento *m* hacia atrás; encadenamiento *m* en retroceso

backward channel /ˌbækwəd 'tʃæn(ə)l/ *noun* vía *f* hacia atrás; canal *m* hacia atrás

backward error correction /ˌbækwəd 'erə kəˌrekʃ(ə)n/ *noun* corrección *f* de errores hacia atrás; corrección *f* en retroceso

backward LAN channel /ˌbækwəd 'læn ˌtʃæn(ə)l/ *noun* vía *f* de retorno de una red local; canal *m* de retorno de una red local

backward mode /'bækwəd məʊd/ *noun* modo *m* hacia atrás; marcha *f* atrás

backward recovery /ˌbækwəd rɪ'kʌv(ə)ri/ *noun* recuperación *f* hacia atrás

backwards compatible /ˌbækwədz kəm 'pætəb(ə)l/ *adjective* **1.** compatible con versiones anteriores; compatible hacia atrás **2.** compatible con ficheros de versiones anteriores; compatible hacia atrás

backwards search /ˌbækwədz 'sɜːtʃ/ *noun* búsqueda *f* hacia atrás; búsqueda *f* en retroceso

backwards supervision /ˌbækwədz ˌsuːpə 'vɪʒ(ə)n/ *noun* control *m* hacia atrás; supervisión *f* hacia atrás

BACS /bæks/ *noun* sistema *m* automático de compensación bancaria

bad break /ˌbæd 'breɪk/ *noun* (*incorrect hyphenation*) interrupción *f* impropia; separación *f* silábica inadecuada; interrupción *f* inadecuada

badge reader /bædʒ 'riːdə/ *noun* lector *m* de tarjetas; lector *m* de placas de identificación ◇ **a badge reader makes sure that only author-** ized personnel can gain access to a computer room un lector de tarjetas de identificación garantiza que sólo el personal autorizado pueda acceder a la sala de ordenadores

bad sector /bæd 'sektə/ *noun* sector *m* defectuoso

baffle /'bæf(ə)l/ *noun* (*sound absorber and deflector*) deflector *m*; pantalla *f* de desviación

bag /bæg/ *noun* (*of elements*) bolsa *f*; saco *m* (de elementos en desorden)

BAK file extension /ˌbæk faɪl ɪg'stenʃ(ə)n/ *noun* (*MS-DOS systems*) extensión *f* BAK

balance /'bæləns/ *noun* (*placing of text and graphics*) equilibrio *m*; (*attractive placing of text and graphics*) simetría *f*; disposición *f* ◇ **the DTP package allows the user to see if the overall page balance is correct** el paquete de software DTP permite al usuario ver si la disposición general de la página es correcta

balanced circuit /ˌbælənst 'sɜːkɪt/ *noun* circuito *m* equilibrado; circuito *m* compensado

balanced error /ˌbælənst 'erə/ *noun* error *m* equilibrado; error *m* compensado

balanced line /'bælənst laɪn/ *noun* línea *f* equilibrada

balanced routing /'bælənst raʊtɪŋ/ *noun* ruta *f* equilibrada

balun /'bælən/ *noun* (*transformer*) balún *m*; estabilizador *m* de impedancia ◇ **we have used a balun to connect the coaxial cable to the twisted-pair circuit** hemos utilizado un estabilizador de impedancia para conectar el cable coaxial al circuito de par retorcido

band /bænd/ *noun* **1.** (*of frequencies*) banda *f* **2.** (*on magnetic disk*) banda *f* multipista ◇ **voice base band ranges from 20Hz to 15KHz** la banda de base de frecuencias vocales oscila entre 20Hz y 15Hz

bandpass filter /'bændpɑːs ˌfɪltə/ *noun* filtro *m* de paso de banda

bandwidth /'bændwɪdθ/ *noun* **1.** (*range of frequencies*) ancho *m* de banda **2.** (*amount of data that can be transmitted*) anchura *f* de banda (de frecuencias); capacidad *f* de transferencia ◇ **telephone bandwidth is 3100Hz** la capacidad de transferencia de un teléfono es de 3100Hz ◇ **this fibre-optic cable has a greater bandwidth than the old copper cable and so it can carry data at higher speeds** este cable de fibra óptica tiene una mayor capacidad de transferencia que el viejo cable de cobre, por lo que puede transportar datos a mayor velocidad

bandwidth on demand /ˌbændˌwɪdθ ɒn dɪ 'mɑːnd/ *noun* ancho *m* de banda a petición

bank /bæŋk/ *noun* (*collection of similar devices*) banco *m*; grupo *m*; bloque *m* ◇ **a bank of minicomputers process all the raw data** un grupo de miniordenadores procesa todos los datos en bruto

Bankers Automated Clearing Services /ˌbæŋkəz ˌɔːtəmeɪtɪd 'klɪərɪŋ ˌsɜːvɪsɪz/ *noun* (*system to transfer money between banks*) sistema *m* automático de compensación bancaria

bank switching /'bæŋk ˌswɪtʃɪŋ/ *noun* conmutación *f* de bancos

banner /'bænə/, **banner advertisement** /ˌbænə əd'vɜːtɪsmənt/, **banner ad** /'bænə æd/ *noun* pancarta *f*; estandarte *m*

banner page /'bænə peɪdʒ/ *noun* página *f* de portada; cubierta *f*

bar /bɑː/ *noun* (*thick line*) barra *f*; línea *f*; trazado *m*

bar chart /'bɑː tʃɑːt/ *noun* gráfico *m* de barras; histograma *m*

bar code /'bɑː kəʊd/ *noun* código *m* de barras

bar code reader /'bɑː kəʊd ˌriːdə/ *noun* lector *m* (óptico) de código de barras; lápiz *m* óptico

bare board /'beə bɔːd/ *noun* (*circuit board with no components*) tarjeta *f* (de memoria) sin componentes

bar graph /'bɑː grɑːf/ *noun* código *m* de barras

bar graphics /bɑː 'græfɪks/ *noun* US código *m* de barras

barrel /'bærəl/ *noun* tonel *m*; barril *m*

base /beɪs/ *noun* **1.** (*lowest position*) base *f* **2.** (*collection of files*) base *f* **3.** (*initial position*) base *f* **4.** (*notation referring to a number system*) lenguaje *m* base **5.** (*class in C++*) base *f* ■ *verb* **1.** (*to calculate from*) basar(se) en **2.** (*to set something up somewhere*) basar *vt*

base 2 /'beɪs tuː/ *noun* base *f* binaria; base *f* 2

base 8 /'beɪs eɪt/ *noun* base *f* octal; base *f* 8

base 10 /ˌbeɪs 'ten/ *noun* base *f* decimal; base *f* 10

base 16 /ˌbeɪs sɪks'tiːn/ *noun* base *f* hexadecimal; base *f* 16

base address /beɪs ə'dres/ *noun* dirección *f* base; dirección *f* de base

base address register /ˌbeɪs ə'dres ˌredʒɪstə/ *noun* registro *m* de dirección de base

baseband /'beɪsbænd/, **base band** *noun* **1.** (*frequency range of a signal*) banda *f* base **2.** (*digital signals without modulation*) banda *f* base **3.** (*information modulated*) banda *f* base

base band local area network /ˌbeɪs bænd ˌləʊk(ə)l ˌeəriə 'netwɜːk/ *noun* red *f* local de banda (de) base

base band modem /ˌbeɪs bænd 'məʊdem/ *noun* módem *m* de banda de base; módem *m* en banda base ◊ **do not use a base band modem with a normal phone line** no debe utilizarse un módem de banda de base con una línea telefónica normal

baseband signalling /ˌbeɪsbænd 'sɪgnəlɪŋ/ *noun* transmisión *f* de banda base

base font /'beɪs fɒnt/ *noun* fuente *f* (de caracteres) base; fuente *f* por defecto

base hardware /beɪs 'hɑːdˌweə/ *noun* equipo *m* base; hardware *m* base

base language /beɪs 'læŋgwɪdʒ/ *noun* lenguaje *m* base; ensamblador *m*

base line /'beɪs laɪn/ *noun* línea *f* base

base memory /beɪs 'mem(ə)ri/, **base RAM** /beɪs ræm/ *noun* memoria *f* base

base register /beɪs 'redʒɪstə/ *noun* (*register that contains the start of a program*) registro *m* base; registro *m* de base; registro *m* de direcciones

base station /beɪs 'steɪʃ(ə)n/ *noun* estación *f* base

BASIC /'beɪsɪk/ *noun* lenguaje *m* (de alto nivel) BASIC

basic code /'beɪsɪk kəʊd/ *noun* código *m* básico; código *m* elemental

basic controller /ˌbeɪsɪk kən'trəʊlə/ *noun* controlador *m* básico

basic control system satellite /ˌbeɪsɪk kən ˌtrəʊl ˌsɪstəm 'sætəlaɪt/ *noun* sistema *m* básico de control (vía satélite)

basic direct access method /ˌbeɪsɪk ˌdaɪrekt 'ækses ˌmeθəd/ *noun* método *m* básico de acceso directo

basic encoding rules /ˌbeɪsɪk ɪn'kəʊdɪŋ ˌruːlz/ *plural noun* reglas *fpl* de codificación básicas

basic exchange format /ˌbeɪsɪk ɪks'tʃeɪndʒ ˌfɔːmæt/ *noun* formato *m* estándar de intercambio

basic input/output operating system /ˌbeɪsɪk ˌɪnpʊt ˌaʊtpʊt 'ɒpəreɪtɪŋ ˌsɪstəm/ *noun* sistema *m* operativo básico de entrada y salida; sistema *m* BIOS

basic instruction /ˌbeɪsɪk ɪn'strʌkʃən/ *noun* instrucción *f* básica

basic mode link control /ˌbeɪsɪk məʊd 'lɪŋk kən,trəʊl/ *noun* control *m* estándar de enlaces

basic product /ˌbeɪsɪk 'prɒdʌkt/ *noun* producto *m* básico

basic rate access /ˌbeɪsɪk reɪt 'ækses/ *noun* acceso *m* básico RDSI

basic rate interface /ˌbeɪsɪk reɪt 'ɪntəfeɪs/ *noun* interfaz *f* de velocidad primaria

basic sequential access method /ˌbeɪsɪk sɪ,kwenʃ(ə)l ˌækses 'meθəd/ *noun* método *m* secuencial básico de acceso

basic telecommunications access method /ˌbeɪsɪk ˌtelikəmjuːnɪkeɪʃ(ə)nz 'ækses ˌmeθəd/ *noun* método *m* básico de acceso a telecomunicaciones; método *m* BTAM

BAT /bæt/ *noun* BAT

batch /bætʃ/ *noun* **1.** (*documents processed at same time*) paquete *m*; lote *m* **2.** (*tasks or data processed as single unit*) paquete *m*; lote *m* ■ *verb* (*to put data or tasks together*) reagrupar *vt*; agrupar *vt* ◊ **batch processor** procesador *m* por lotes

batched communication /ˌbætʃ kə,mjuːnɪ 'keɪʃ(ə)n/ *noun* comunicación *f* agrupada (por lotes)

batch file /'bætʃ faɪl/ *noun* fichero *m* de instrucciones; fichero *m* por lotes ◊ **this batch file is used to save time and effort when carrying out a routine task** este fichero de instrucciones se utiliza para ahorrar tiempo y esfuerzo al realizar una rutina

batch mode *noun* modo *m* de procesos por lotes

batch processing /'bætʃ ˌprəʊsesɪŋ/ *noun* proceso *m* por lotes

batch processor /'bætʃ ˌprəʊsesə/ *noun* procesador *m* por lotes

batch region /bætʃ 'riːdʒ(ə)n/ *noun* zona *f* (de tratamiento) por lotes

batch system /bætʃ 'sɪstəm/ *noun* sistema *m* (de tratamiento) por lotes

batch total /bætʃ 'təʊt(ə)l/ *noun* total *m* por lotes

BAT file extension /ˌbæt faɪl ɪk'stenʃən/ *noun* (*MS-DOS systems*) extensión *f* (de un fichero) BAT

battery-backed /'bæt(ə)ri bækd/ *adjective* (*volatile storage devices*) equipado, -a con una pila (auxiliar); equipado, -a con una batería (auxiliar) ◊ **battery-backed CMOS memory replaces a disk drive in this portable** la memoria CMOS, equipada con una batería auxiliar, sustituye la disquetera en este (modelo de ordenador) portátil ◊ **the RAM disk card has the option to be battery-backed** la tarjeta RAM puede ir opcionalmente equipada con una pila auxiliar

battery backup /ˌbæt(ə)ri 'bækʌp/ *noun* (*battery to provide power to volatile storage devices*) pila *f* de reserva; pila *f* auxiliar; batería *f* de reserva; batería *f* auxiliar

battery charging /'bæt(ə)ri ˌtʃɑːdʒɪŋ/ *noun* (tiempo de) carga *f* de una pila; carga *f* de una batería

battery meter /ˌbæt(ə)ri 'miːtə/ *noun* determinador *m* de pilas

baud /bɔːd/ *noun* baudio *m*

baud rate /'bɔːd reɪt/ *noun* tasa *f* (de transmisión) en baudios; velocidad *f* (de transmisión) en baudios ◊ **a modem with auto-baud scanner can automatically sense at which baud rate it should operate** un módem equipado con un escáner de reconocimiento de baudios se ajusta automáticamente a la velocidad a la que debe funcionar ◊ **the baud rate of the binary signal was 300 bits per second** la velocidad de transmisión de la señal binaria fue de 300 bits por segundo

baud rate generator /ˌbɔːd ˌreɪt 'dʒenəreɪtə/ *noun* generador *m* de la tasa en baudios

bay /beɪ/ *noun* (*space where a disk drive is fitted*) lugar *m* de la disquetera; emplazamiento *m* de la disquetera; lugar *m* del lector de discos; emplazamiento *m* del lector de discos

B box /'biː bɒks/ *noun* registro *m* secundario; caja *f* secundaria

BBS /ˌbiː biː 'es/ *noun* sistema *m* de tablón de anuncios

bcc *noun* copia *f* de cortesía

BCC /ˌbiː siː 'siː/ *noun* control *m* de bloques de caracteres

BCD /ˌbiː siː 'diː/ *noun* decimal *m* codificado en binario; BCD ◊ **the BCD representation of decimal 8 is 1000** la representación decimal codificada en binario del decimal 8 es 1000

BCD adder /ˌbiː siː ˌdiː 'ædə/ *noun* sumador *m* binario; sumador *m* BCD

BCH code /ˌbiː ˌsiː'eɪtʃ kəʊd/ *noun* código *m* BCH

BCPL /ˌbiː siː piː 'el/ *noun* lenguaje *m* (de alto nivel) BCPL

BCS *abbr* (*basic control system satellite*) sistema *m* básico de control (vía satélite)

BDAM *abbr* (*basic direct access method*) método *m* básico de acceso directo

beacon /'biːkən/ *verb* (*signal*) señal *f* de alerta; señal *f* de incidente; señal *f* de fallo

beacon frame /'biːkən freɪm/ *noun* (*frame that is sent after a network break has occurred*) mensaje *m* de alerta

bead /biːd/ *noun* (*small section of a program*) módulo *m*; sub-programa *m*; función *f*

beam /biːm/ *noun* rayo *m*; haz *m* ◊ **a beam of laser light is used in this printer to produce high-resolution graphics** en esta impresora se emplea un rayo de luz láser para producir gráficos de alta resolución ◊ **a magnetic field is used for beam deflection in a CRT** se utiliza un campo magnético para la desviación de un haz en un tubo de rayos catódicos (CRT) ◊ **beam diversity** desdoblamiento *m* de un rayo ◊ **beam width** anchura *f* de un haz ◊ **the laser produces a thin beam of light** el láser emite un fino rayo de luz

beam deflection /biːm dɪ'flekʃ(ə)n/ *noun* refracción *f*; desviación *f* de un rayo ◊ **a magnetic field is used for beam deflection in a CRT** se utiliza un campo magnético para la desviación de un haz en un tubo de rayos catódicos (CRT)

BEC *abbr* (*bus extension card*) tarjeta *f* de extensión de enlaces

beginner's all-purpose symbolic instruction code /bɪˌgɪnəz ɔːl ˌpɜːpəs sɪm ˌbɒlɪk ɪn'strʌkʃən ˌkəʊd/ *noun* lenguaje *m* de alto nivel BASIC

beginning of file /bɪˌgɪnɪŋ əv 'faɪl/ *noun* principio *m* de fichero

beginning of information mark /bɪˌgɪnɪŋ əv ˌɪnfə'meɪʃ(ə)n ˌmɑːk/ *noun* marca *f* del principio de la información; indicador *m* del principio de la información

beginning of tape marker /bɪˌgɪnɪŋ əv 'teɪp ˌmɑːkə/ *noun* marca *f* del principio de la cinta; indicador *m* del principio de la cinta

bell character /bel 'kærɪktə/, **BEL** *noun* carácter *m* de alarma

Bell-compatible modem /ˌbel kəm ˌpætɪb(ə)l 'məʊdem/ *noun* (*modem that operates according to standards set by AT&T*) módem *m* compatible con Bell

bells and whistles /ˌbelz ənd 'wɪs(ə)lz/ *plural noun* (*advanced features*) toda la panoplia; todo lo necesario ◊ **this word-processor has all the bells and whistles you would expect – including page preview** este tratamiento de textos lleva todo lo necesario, incluso la instrucción vista preliminar

benchmark /'bentʃmɑːk/ noun 1. (important point in an index which can be used for comparison) referencia f; punto m de referencia 2. (program used to test performance) proceso m de evaluación del funcionamiento; ensayo m comparativo del rendimiento ◇ **benchmark test** prueba f comparativa or de contraste ◇ **the magazine gave the new program's benchmark test results** la revista dio los resultados de la prueba de evaluación del nuevo programa

benchmarking /'bentʃmɑːkɪŋ/ noun contraste m del rendimiento; evaluación f comparativa del rendimiento

benchmark problem /ˌbentʃmɑːk 'prɒbləm/ noun problema m de evaluación; problema m de contraste

BER /ˌbiː iː 'ɑː/ noun reglas fpl de codificación básicas

Berkeley UNIX /ˌbɜːkli 'juːnɪks/ noun UNIX BSD

bespoke software /bɪˌspəʊk 'sɒftweə/ noun (software that has been written especially for a customer) software m (programado) a medida

best fit /best 'fɪt/ noun la mejor elección; la (elección) más adecuada

beta site /'biːtə saɪt/ noun (company that tests new software before it is released) empresa f de pruebas beta

beta software /'biːtə ˌsɒf(t)weə/ noun (software that has not finished all its testing) software m (en versión) beta

beta test /'biːtə ˌtest/ noun (second stage of tests performed on new software) prueba f beta; comprobación f beta ◇ **the application has passed the alpha tests and is just entering the beta test phase** la aplicación ha superado las pruebas alfa y acaba de entrar en la fase de pruebas beta

‘The client was so eager to get his hands on the product that the managing director bypassed internal testing and decided to let it go straight out to beta test.’ [Computing]

beta version /'biːtə ˌvɜːʒn/ noun (version of software that is almost ready to be released) versión f beta

betaware /'biːtəweə/ noun software m (en versión) beta

bezel /'bez(ə)l/ noun (front cover of a computer's casing) cubierta f; marco m frontal (de un ordenador)

Bézier curve /'bezieɪ kɜːv/ noun (geometric curve) curva f de Bézier

BGP /ˌbiː dʒiː 'piː/ noun protocolo m de pasarela fronteriza

biased exponent /ˌbaɪəst ɪk'spəʊnənt/ noun exponente m sesgado

bid /bɪd/ verb (of a computer) pedir vt; solicitar línea ◇ **the terminal had to bid three times before there was a gap in transmissions on the network** el terminal tuvo que pedir línea tres veces antes de que hubiera un hueco en las transmisiones de la red

bi-directional bus /ˌbaɪ daɪˌrekʃ(ə)n(ə)l 'bʌs/ noun enlace m común bidireccional

bi-directional printer /ˌbaɪ daɪˌrekʃ(ə)n(ə)l 'prɪntə/ noun impresora f bidireccional

bi-directional transmission /ˌbaɪ daɪˌrekʃ(ə)n(ə)l trænz'mɪʃ(ə)n/ noun transmisión f bidireccional

Big Blue /bɪg 'bluː/ noun informal la empresa f IBM

bilinear filtering /baɪˌlɪniə 'fɪltərɪŋ/ noun filtrado m bilineal

billion /'bɪljən/ noun (one thousand million or one million million) billón m; un millón m de millones

BIM /ˌbiː aɪ 'em/ noun indicador m del principio de la información; marca f del principio de la información

bin /bɪn/ noun (tray used to hold a supply of paper ready to be fed into a printer) bandeja f de papel ◇ **lower bin** bandeja inferior ◇ **upper bin** bandeja superior

binary /'baɪnəri/ adjective binario or -a ■ noun dígito m binario ◇ **your letter is a text file, not a binary file** su carta es un fichero de texto, no un fichero binario

binary adder /ˌbaɪnəri 'ædə/ noun sumador m binario

binary arithmetic /ˌbaɪnəri ə'rɪθmətɪk/ noun cálculo m binario

binary bit /'baɪnəri bɪt/ noun bit m binario

binary cell /'baɪnəri sel/ noun registro m binario; célula f binaria

binary chop /'baɪnəri tʃɒp/ noun búsqueda f binaria

binary code /'baɪnəri kəʊd/ noun código m binario

binary coded characters /ˌbaɪnəri ˌkəʊdɪd 'kærɪktəz/ plural noun caracteres mpl codificados en binario

binary coded decimal /ˌbaɪnəri ˌkəʊdɪd 'desɪm(ə)l/ noun decimal m codificado en binario

binary counter /ˌbaɪnəri 'kaʊntə/ noun contador m binario

binary digit /ˌbaɪnəri 'dɪdʒɪt/ noun bit m; dígito m binario

binary dump /'baɪnəri dʌmp/ noun vaciado m en binario; vaciado m binario

binary encoding /ˌbaɪnəri ɪn'kəʊdɪŋ/ noun (representation of characters with bits) codificación f binaria; codificación f en binario

binary exponent /ˌbaɪnəri ɪk'spəʊnənt/ noun exponente m binario

binary field /'baɪnəri fiːld/ noun campo m binario

binary file /'baɪnəri faɪl/ noun fichero m binario ◇ **the program instructions are stored in the binary file** las instrucciones del programa se guardan en un fichero binario ◇ **your letter is a text file, not a binary file** su carta es un fichero de texto, no un fichero binario

binary fraction /ˌbaɪnəri 'frækʃən/ *noun* fracción *f* binaria ◇ **the binary fraction 0.011 is equal to one quarter plus one eighth (i.e. three eighths)** la fracción binaria 0,011 es igual a un cuarto más un octavo (es decir, tres octavos)

binary half adder /ˌbaɪnəri 'hɑːf ˌædə/ *noun* semisumador *m* binario; semisumadora *f* binaria

binary large object /ˌbaɪnəri lɑːdʒ 'ɒbdʒekt/ *noun* campo *m* (de gran capacidad) para datos binarios

binary loader /ˌbaɪnəri 'ləʊdə/ *noun* cargador *m* binario

binary look-up /'baɪnəri lʊk/ *noun* búsqueda *f* binaria

binary mantissa /ˌbaɪnəri mæn'tɪsə/ *noun* mantisa *f* binaria

binary notation /ˌbaɪnəri nəʊ'teɪʃ(ə)n/ *noun* notación *f* binaria

binary number /ˌbaɪnəri 'nʌmbə/ *noun* número *m* binario

binary operation /ˌbaɪnəri ˌɒpə'reɪʃ(ə)n/ *noun* operación *f* binaria

binary point /'baɪnəri pɔɪnt/ *noun* coma *f* binaria

binary representation /ˌbaɪnəri ˌreprɪzen'teɪʃ(ə)n/ *noun* notación *f* binaria

binary scale /'baɪnəri skeɪl/ *noun* escala *f* binaria ◇ **in a four bit word, the binary scale is 1,2,4,8** en una palabra de cuatro bits, la escala binaria es 1,2,4,8

binary search /'baɪnəri sɜːtʃ/ *noun* búsqueda *f* binaria

binary sequence /ˌbaɪnəri 'siːkwəns/ *noun* secuencia *f* binaria

binary signalling /ˌbaɪnəri 'sɪgnəlɪŋ/ *noun* señalización *f* binaria; transmisión *f* de señales en binario

binary split /'baɪnəri splɪt/ *noun* partición *f* binaria

binary synchronous communications /ˌbaɪnəri ˌsɪŋkrənəs kəˌmjuːnɪ'keɪʃ(ə)nz/ *noun* comunicaciones *fpl* sincrónicas en binario

binary system /'baɪnəri ˌsɪstəm/ *noun* sistema *m* binario

binary-to-decimal conversion /ˌbaɪnəri tə, tʊ 'desɪm(ə)l/ *noun* conversión *f* binario a decimal

binary tree /'baɪnəri triː/ *noun* árbol *m* binario

binary variable /ˌbaɪnəri 'veəriəb(ə)l/ *noun* variable *f* binaria

binaural sound /baɪn'ɔːrl saʊnd/ *noun* sonido *m* binaural

bind /baɪnd/ *verb* (*to link*) enlazar *vt*; (*address*) establecer un enlace

BIND /ˌbiː aɪ en 'diː/ *noun* BIND

binder /'baɪndə/ *noun* (*software program*) editor *m* de enlaces

Bindery /'baɪndəri/ *noun* (*special database used in a Novell NetWare network operating system*) taller *m* de encuadernación; fichero *m* de enlaces; biblioteca *f* de enlaces (Netware)

binding offset /ˌbaɪndɪŋ 'ɒfset/ *noun* margen *m* de encuadernación

binding time /'baɪndɪŋ taɪm/ *noun* tiempo *m* de enlace

BinHex /bɪn'heks/ *noun* BinHex

biochip /'baɪəʊtʃɪp/ *noun* biopastilla *f*

BIOS /'baɪɒs/ *noun* sistema *m* BIOS; sistema *m* operativo básico de entrada y salida

bipolar /baɪ'pəʊlə/ *adjective* bipolar ◇ **bipolar junction transistor (BJT)** transistor *m* de conexión bipolar

bipolar coding /ˌbaɪpəʊlə 'kɒdɪŋ/ *noun* codificación *f* bipolar

bipolar signal /ˌbaɪpəʊlə 'sɪgn(ə)l/ *noun* señal *f* bipolar

bipolar transistor /ˌbaɪpəʊlə træn'zɪstə/ *noun* transistor *m* bipolar

biquinary code /baɪˌkwɪnəri 'kəʊd/ *noun* código *m* biquinario

B-ISDN /biː ˌaɪ es diː 'en/ *abbr* (*broadband ISDN*) RDSI de banda ancha

bistable /baɪ'steɪb(ə)l/ *adjective* biestable

bit /bɪt/ *noun* 1. (*binary digit*) bit *m*; bitio *m*; dígito *m*; número *m* binario 2. (*smallest unit of data*) bit *m* ◇ **bits per pixel (BPP)** (*number of bits assigned to store the colour of each pixel*) (número de) bits por píxel ◇ **bits per second (bps)** (número de) bits por segundo *or* bps ◇ **least significant bit (LSB)** bit menos significativo ◇ **most significant bit (MSB)** (el) bit más significativo ◇ **significant bit** (el) bit significativo ◇ **testing bit six of a byte containing an ASCII character is bit significant and determines if the ASCII character is upper or lower case** la prueba del sexto bit de un byte que contiene un carácter ASCII determina si el carácter es bit significativo y si debe ir en mayúscula o en minúscula ◇ **the bit slice design uses four 4-bit word processors to construct a 16-bit processor** el diseño en elementos de bits utiliza cuatro procesadores de texto de 4 bits para crear un procesador de 16 bits

bit addressing /bɪt ə'dresɪŋ/ *noun* direccionamiento *m* binario

bit blit /'bɪt blɪt/ *noun* desplazamiento *m* de bits (en memoria)

bit block /'bɪt blɒk/ *noun* bloque *m* de bits

bit block transfer /ˌbɪt blɒk 'trænsfɜː/ *noun* transferencia *f* de bits por bloques

bit bucket /bɪt 'bʌkɪt/ *noun* papelera *f* de bits

bit density /bɪt 'densəti/ *noun* densidad *f* binaria; densidad *f* de bits

bit error rate /ˌbɪt 'erə ˌreɪt/ *noun* tasa *f* de errores de transmisión (por fibra óptica)

bit flipping /bɪt 'flɪpɪŋ/ *noun* inversión *f* binaria

bit handling /bɪt 'hændlɪŋ/ *noun* manipulación *f* de bits; tratamiento *m* de bits

bit image /bɪt 'ɪmɪdʒ/ *noun* imagen *f* binaria

bit interleaving /'bɪt ɪntəˌliːvɪŋ/ *noun* entrelazado *m* de bits

bit manipulation /bɪt məˌnɪpjʊ'leɪʃ(ə)n/ noun manipulación f de bits

bitmap /'bɪtmæp/ noun **1.** (of an image) mapa m de bits **2.** (of a binary representation) mapa m de bits **3.** (file format) mapa m de bits '...microcomputers invariably use raster-scan cathode ray tube displays, and frequently use a bit-map to store graphic images' [Soft]

bit-map /bɪt mæp/, **bitmap** /'bɪtmæp/ verb transformar bits; definir una tabla (de direccionamiento binario) '...the expansion cards fit into the PC's expansion slot and convert bit-mapped screen images to video signals' [Publish]

bit-mapped font /ˌbɪt mæpt 'fɒnt/ noun fuente f (de caracteres) transformada por bits

bit-mapped graphics /ˌbɪt mæpt 'græfɪks/ plural noun gráficos mpl transformados por bits

bitmp /'bɪtmæp/ abbr (bit-map) mapa m de bits

BitNet /'bɪtnet/ noun BitNet

bit parallel /bɪt 'pærəlel/ noun transmisión f paralela (bit a bit)

bit pattern /bɪt 'pæt(ə)nn/ noun modelo m binario

bit plane /'bɪt pleɪn/ noun plano m binario; capa f binaria

bit position /bɪt pə'zɪʃ(ə)n/ noun posición f binaria

bit rate /'bɪt reɪt/ noun tasa f en bits; velocidad f de transmisión

bit rotation /bɪt rəʊ'teɪʃ(ə)n/ noun rotación f binaria

bit-slice architecture /ˌbɪt slaɪs 'ɑːkɪtektʃə/, **bit-slice design** /ˌbɪt slaɪs dɪ 'zaɪn/ noun arquitectura f en elementos de bits; diseño m en elementos de bits

bits per inch /ˌbɪts pɜː 'ɪntʃ/ noun bits por pulgada

bits per pixel /ˌbɪts pɜː 'pɪks(ə)l/ noun bits por píxel

bits per second /ˌbɪts pɜː 'sekənd/ noun bits por segundo; bps ◇ **their transmission rate is 60,000 bits per second (bps) through a parallel connection** su velocidad de transmisión es de 60.000 bits por segundo (bps) a través de una conexión en paralelo

bit stream /'bɪt striːm/ noun flujo m de bits; corriente f de bits

bit stuffing /bɪt 'stʌfɪŋ/ noun inserción f de bits

bit track /'bɪt træk/ noun pista f de bits; pista f de datos binarios

bitwise /'bɪtwaɪz/ adverb a nivel binario

BIX /ˌbiː aɪ 'eks/ noun (commercial online system) BIX

biz /bɪz/ noun (for business discussions and opportunities) biz

black and white /ˌblæk ən 'waɪt/ noun blanco y negro; monocromo

black box /blæk 'bɒks/ noun caja f negra

black level /blæk 'lev(ə)l/ noun nivel m de negro

black matrix /blæk 'meɪtrɪks/ noun matriz f negra

black writer /blæk 'raɪtə/ noun impresora f con definición de tonos negros

blank cell /blæŋk 'sel/ noun celda f vacía

blank character /blæŋk 'kærɪktə/ noun carácter m en blanco; carácter m de espacio

blank disk /blæŋk 'dɪsk/ noun disco m vacío; disquete m en blanco

blanking /'blæŋkɪŋ/ noun (loss of signal) supresión f de una señal; inhibición f de una señal; eliminación f de una señal

blanking interval /'blæŋkɪŋ ˌɪntəvəl/ noun intervalo m de supresión

blank instruction /blæŋk ɪn'strʌkʃən/ noun instrucción f de relleno; instrucción f de espacios en blanco

blank string /blæŋk 'strɪŋ/ noun cadena f vacía; cadena f en blanco

blank tape /blæŋk 'teɪp/ noun cinta f virgen

blast /blɑːst/ verb **1.** (in relation to PROM) escribir vt; programar vt **2.** (in relation to memory or resources) liberar memoria

blast-through alphanumerics /ˌblɑːst θruː ˌælfənjuː'merɪks/ plural noun (characters which can be displayed on a videotext terminal when it is in graphics mode) caracteres mpl alfanuméricos mostrados

bleed /bliːd/ noun **1.** (printing) sangrado m de una línea **2.** (badly adjusted colour monitor) desajuste m (de pantalla) ■ verb sangrar vi; mover vt

bleeding edge /ˌbliːdɪŋ 'edʒ/ adjective 'bleeding edge'; a la vanguardia

blessed folder /ˌblesɪd 'fəʊldə/ noun (the System Folder that contains files loaded when the Macintosh is switched on) carpeta f preferencial (Macintosh)

blind /blaɪnd/ adjective ciego or -a

blind carbon copy /ˌblaɪnd ˌkɑːbən 'kɒpɪ/ noun copia f oculta

blind certificate /ˌblaɪnd sə'tɪfɪkət/ noun cookie sin el nombre del usuario

blind copy receipt /blaɪnd ˌkɒpɪ rɪ'siːt/ noun (in electronic mail, method of sending a message to several users whose identities are not known) aviso m de recepción de copia discreta

blind dialling /ˌblaɪnd 'daɪəlɪŋ/ noun transmisión f ciega

blind keyboard /ˌblaɪnd 'kiːbɔːd/ noun teclado m ciego

B-line counter /ˌbiː laɪn 'kaʊntə/ noun registro m auxiliar de dirección

blinking /'blɪŋkɪŋ/ noun parpadeo m; intermitencia f

blitter /'blɪtə/ noun (component designed to process or move a bit-mapped image) acelerador m binario

bloatware /'bləʊtweə/ noun bloatware m

blob /blɒb/ *noun* campo *m* (de gran capacidad) para datos binarios

block /blɒk/ *noun* 1. (*records treated as single unit*) bloc *m* 2. (*wide printed bar*) barra *f* ■ *verb* (*to stop*) parar *vi*; bloquear *vt* ◇ **the system manager blocked his request for more CPU time** el director del sistema bloqueó su petición de más tiempo en la unidad central

block capitals /ˌblɒk ˈkæpɪt(ə)lz/ *plural noun* caracteres *mpl* dóricos

block character check /ˌblɒk ˈkærɪktə tʃek/ *noun* control *m* de bloques de caracteres

block code /blɒk ˈkəʊd/ *noun* código *m* de bloques

block-copy /ˌblɒk ˈkɒpi/ *verb* 1. (*to copy data in a block*) copiar bloques 2. (*to copy text in a block*) copiar bloques

block cursor /blɒk ˈkɜːsə/ *noun* cursor *m* (de forma) rectangular

block-delete /ˌblɒk dɪˈliːt/ *verb* borrar bloques

block device /blɒk dɪˈvaɪs/ *noun* dispositivo *m* de bloques ◇ **the disk drive is a block device that can transfer 256 bytes of data at a time** la disquetera es un dispositivo de bloques que puede transferir 256 bytes de datos a la vez

block diagram /blɒk ˈdaɪəˌɡræm/ *noun* (*illustration of how the main components in a system are connected*) diagrama *m* de bloques; esquema *m* de bloques ◇ **the first step to designing a new computer is to draw out a block diagram of its main components** el primer paso para diseñar un nuevo ordenador es dibujar un diagrama (de bloques) de sus componentes principales

block error rate /blɒk ˈerə reɪt/ *noun* tasa *f* de errores por bloque

block header /blɒk ˈhedə/ *noun* encabezamiento *m* de bloque

block ignore character /ˌblɒk ɪɡˈnɔː ˌkærɪktə/ *noun* carácter *m* de rechazo de bloque

blocking factor /blɒkɪŋ ˈfæktə/ *noun* (*records in a block*) factor *m* de bloques

block input processing /ˌblɒk ˈɪnpʊt ˌprəʊsesɪŋ/ *noun* proceso *m* de entrada de bloques

block length /blɒk ˈleŋθ/ *noun* (*data*) longitud *f* de bloque; longitud *f* de palabra de entrada

block letters /ˌblɒk ˈletəz/ *plural noun* caracteres *mpl* dóricos

block list /ˈblɒk lɪst/ *noun* lista *f* de bloques

block mark /ˈblɒk mɑːk/ *noun* marca *f* de bloque

block move /ˈblɒk muːv/ *verb* mover bloques

block operation /blɒk ˌɒpəˈreɪʃ(ə)n/ *noun* manipulación *f* de bloques

block parity /blɒk ˈpærəti/ *noun* paridad *f* de bloque

block protection /blɒk prəˈtekʃən/ *noun* protección *f* de bloques

block retrieval /blɒk rɪˈtriːv(ə)l/ *noun* recuperación *f* de bloques

block synchronisation /ˌblɒk ˌsɪŋkrənaɪˈzeɪʃ(ə)n/ *noun* sincronización *f* de bloques

block transfer /blɒk ˈtrænsfɜː/ *noun* (*data transfer*) transferencia *f* de un párrafo; inserción *f* de un bloque

blog /blɒɡ/ *noun* blog *m*

blogger /ˈblɒɡə/ *noun* blogger *m*

blogging *noun* blogging *m*

'Over the past year, blogging has grown, in both importance and size. The original hardcore blogging community is still there, and still vociferous. But every month, thousands of others are trying their hand at this unique publishing form.' [*The Guardian*]

blogosphere /ˈblɒɡəˌsfɪə/ *noun informal* blogosfera *f*

blogware /ˈblɒɡweə/ *noun* blogware *m*

bloop /bluːp/ *verb* desmagnetizar *vt*

blow /bləʊ/ *verb* (*burn*) quemar un PROM; programar un PROM

Blue Book Ethernet /ˌbluː bʊk ˈiːθənet/ *noun* Ethernet *f* Blue Book

blueprint /ˈbluːˌprɪnt/ *noun* (*set of specifications or design*) especificaciones *fpl*; diseño *m* gráfico; cianotipo *m*

blue-ribbon program /ˌbluː ˈrɪbən ˌprəʊɡræm/ *noun informal* programa *m* modelo; programa *m* sin errores

Bluetooth /ˈbluːtuːθ/ (*trade name for a short-range radio communications system*) Bluetooth

blur /blɜː/ *noun* imagen *f* borrosa ■ *verb* desdibujar(se); hacer(se) borroso *or* -a ◇ **the image becomes blurred when you turn the focus knob** la imagen se hace borrosa al girar el mando de enfocar

BMP /ˌbiː em ˈpiː/ *noun* (*bit-mapped imaging*) extensión *f* BMP ◇ **this paint package lets you import BMP files** este paquete de software de dibujo permite importar ficheros BMP

bn *abbr* (*billion*) mil milliones *mpl*

BNC connector /ˌbiː en ˈsiː kəˌnektə/ *noun* (*cylindrical metal connector with a copper core*) conector *m* (coaxial) BNC

BNC T-piece connector /ˌbiː en ˌsiː ˈtiː piːs kəˌnektə/ *noun* (*T-shaped metal connector*) conector *m* BNC en forma de T

BNF /ˌbiː en ˈef/ *noun* forma *f* BNF; metalenguaje *m*

board /bɔːd/ *noun* (*flat insulation material*) tarjeta *f*; placa *f*; junta *f* ◇ **printed circuit board (PCB)** placa de circuito impreso

body /ˈbɒdi/ *noun* (*main section of text or program*) cuerpo *m*; sección *f* ◇ **body size** (*of text*) cuerpo *m* (de un carácter); longitud *f*; tamaño *m* de una sección (de texto)

body type /ˈbɒdi taɪp/ *noun* tipo *m* de caracteres de una sección

bof, BOF *abbr* (*beginning of file*) (*beginning of file*) BOF; bof; principio *m* de fichero

boilerplate /ˈbɔɪləpleɪt/ *noun* documento *m* definitivo

boilerplating /'bɔɪləpleɪtɪŋ/ *noun* montaje *m* de un documento a partir de otros textos

bold face /'bəʊld feɪs/ *noun* carácter *m* en negrita

bomb /bɒm/ *noun* (*routine designed to crash the system*) bomba *f* ■ *verb informal* (*to fail*) bombardear *vt*; hacer saltar; fallar *vi* ◇ **the program bombed, and we lost all the data** el programa falló y perdimos totos los datos ◇ **the system can bomb if you set up several desk accessories or memory-resident programs at the same time** el sistema puede fallar si se instalan al mismo tiempo varios accesorios de escritorio o programas de memoria residente

book /bʊk/ *noun* libro *m* ◇ **the book is available in paperback and hard cover** el libro está disponible en rústica y en tapas duras ◇ **they can print books of up to 96 pages** pueden imprimir libros de hasta 96 páginas

bookmark /'bʊkmaːk/ *noun* (*coding*) señal *f*; marca *f* para localizar una sección del documento

Boolean algebra /ˌbuːliən 'ældʒɪbrə/ *noun* álgebra *f* booleana

Boolean connective /ˌbuːliən kə'nektɪv/ *noun* conector *m* booleano

Boolean data type /ˌbuːliən 'deɪtə ˌtaɪp/ *noun* variable *f* booleana

Boolean logic /ˌbuːliən 'lɒdʒɪk/ *noun* (*Boolean algebra*) álgebra *f* de Boole; álgebra *f* booleana; lógica *f* booleana

Boolean operation /ˌbuːliən ˌɒpə'reɪʃ(ə)n/ *noun* operación *f* booleana

Boolean operation table /ˌbuːliən ˌɒpə 'reɪʃ(ə)n ˌteɪb(ə)l/ *noun* tabla *f* de Boole; tabla *f* de operaciones booleanas

Boolean operator /ˌbuːliən 'ɒpəreɪtə/ *noun* operador *m* booleano

Boolean search /ˌbuːliən 'sɜːtʃ/ *noun* búsqueda *f* de Boole

Boolean value /ˌbuːliən 'væljuː/ *noun* valor *m* booleano

Boolean variable /ˌbuːliən 'veəriəb(ə)l/ *noun* variable *f* booleana

boot /buːt/ *verb* arrancar *vt*; inicializar *vt*

bootable /'buːtəb(ə)l/ *adjective* que puede iniciarse; que se puede cargar

boot block /'buːt blɒk/ *noun* bloque *m* de arranque; registro *m* de arranque

boot disk /'buːt dɪsk/ *noun* disco *m* de arranque; disquete *m* de arranque ◇ **after you switch on the computer, insert the boot disk** después de encender el ordenador, inserte el disquete de arranque

booting /'buːtɪŋ/ *noun* arranque *m*; iniciación *f*

bootleg /'buːtˌleg/ *noun* copia *f* ilegal; copia *f* pirata

BOOTP /ˌbiː əʊ əʊ tiː 'piː/ *noun* protocolo *m* de arranque-asignación

boot partition /buːt paː'tɪʃ(ə)n/ *noun* partición *f* de arranque

boot record /'buːt ˌrekɔːd/ *noun* bloque *m* de arranque; registro *m* de arranque

bootstrap, bootstrap loader *noun* arranque *m* (de un sistema); programa *m* de arranque (de un sistema)

bootstrap memory /'buːtstræp ˌmem(ə)ri/ *noun* memoria *f* de arranque

bootstrap protocol /ˌbuːtstræp 'prəʊtəkɒl/ *noun* protocolo *m* de arranque-asignación

boot up /buːt 'ʌp/ *noun* (*booting – of system*) arranque *m*; iniciación *f*

border /'bɔːdə/ *noun* 1. (*area around printed or displayed text*) borde *m*; marco *m*; recuadro *m* 2. (*line*) borde *m*; marco *m*; recuadro *m*

borrow /'bɒrəʊ/ *noun* acarreo *m* negativo ■ *verb* pedir *vt*; tomar prestado ◇ **she borrowed a book on computer construction** pidió prestado un libro sobre fabricación de ordenadores

Bose-Chandhuri-Hocquenghem code *noun* código *m* BCH

bot /bɒt/ *noun* bot *m*

BOT marker /'bɒt ˌmaːkə/ *noun* marca *f* de inicio de cinta; señal *f* de inicio de cinta

bottom up method /ˌbɒtəm ʌp 'meθəd/**, bottom up programming** /'prəʊgræmɪŋ/ *noun* método *m* ascendente; programación *f* de abajo a arriba

bounce /baʊns/ *noun* 1. (*of key*) rebote *m* de una tecla del teclado 2. (*of an email*) rebote *m* (de un correo electrónico)

boundary /'baʊnd(ə)ri/ *noun* límite *m*

boundary protection /ˌbaʊnd(ə)ri prə 'tekʃən/ *noun* protección *f* de límites de la memoria

boundary punctuation /ˌbaʊnd(ə)ri ˌpʌŋktʃu'eɪʃ(ə)n/ *noun* marcado *m* de límites (de un fichero); señalización *f* de límites

boundary register /ˌbaʊnd(ə)ri 'redʒɪstə/ *noun* registro *m* de límites

bounding box /'baʊndɪŋ bɒks/ *noun* (*rectangle that determines the shape and position of an image*) caja *f* delimitadora; recuadro *m* delimitador

Boyce-Codd normal form /ˌbɔɪs kɒd 'nɔːməl ˌfɔːm/ *noun* formato *m* normal Boyce-Codd; formato *m* BCNF

bozo bit /'bəʊzəʊ bɪt/ *noun* (*Apple Macintosh system*) bit *m* de protección; bozo *m* (Apple Macintosh)

BPI, bpi *noun* bpp (bitios por pulgada)

BPP /ˌbiː piː 'piː/ *noun* bits *mpl* por píxel

bps /ˌbiː piː 'es/ *noun* bps (bitios por segundo)

Bps /ˌbiː piː 'es/ *noun* bytes *mpl* por segundo

bps rate /ˌbiː piː 'es reɪt/ *noun* tasa *f* bps; tasa *f* de bits por segundo

bps rate adjust /ˌbiː piː 'es reɪt ə'dʒʌst/ *noun* ajuste *m* de la tasa en bps

BRA /ˌbiː aː 'eɪ/ *noun* acceso *m* básico RDSI

braces /'breɪsɪz/ *plural noun* (*curly bracket characters { }*) llaves *fpl*

bracket /'brækɪt/ *noun* paréntesis *m*; corchete *m*

branch /brɑːntʃ/ noun 1. (path or jump from one instruction to another) bifurcación f; salto m 2. (link to network) bifurcación ■ verb (to jump section in program) saltar vi ◇ **the faulty station is on this branch** la estación defectuosa está en esta bifurcación

branch cable /brɑːntʃ 'keɪb(ə)l/ noun cable m de bifurcación

branch instruction /brɑːntʃ ɪn'strʌkʃən/ noun instrucción f de bifurcación; instrucción f de salto

branchpoint /'brɑːntʃpɔɪnt/ noun punto m de bifurcación

branch table /'brɑːntʃ ˌteɪb(ə)l/ noun tabla f de bifurcación

breach /briːtʃ/ noun incumplimiento m

breadboard /'bredbɔːd/ noun (electronic circuits) montaje m experimental; montaje m provisional

break /breɪk/ noun (action performed, or a key pressed, to stop the execution of a program) corte m (de palabra); separación f silábica; interrupción f

Break key /'breɪk kiː/ noun tecla f de interrupción

breakout box /'breɪkaut bɒks/ noun (device that displays the status of lines within an interface) ventana f de control de la interfaz ◇ **the serial interface doesn't seem to be working – use the breakout box to see which signals are present** la interfaz en serie no parece que esté funcionando; emplee la ventana de control de la interfaz para ver qué señales están activas

breakpoint /'breɪkpɔɪnt/ noun (control point) punto m de interrupción; punto m de ruptura

breakpoint halt /'breɪkpɔɪnt ˌhɔːlt/ noun instrucción f de interrupción; instrucción f de parada

breakpoint instruction /'breɪkpɔɪnt ɪnˌstrʌkʃən/ noun instrucción f de parada; instrucción f de interrupción

breakpoint symbol /'breɪkpɔɪnt ˌsɪmb(ə)l/ noun símbolo m de interrupción

breakup /'breɪkʌp/ noun (loss or distortion of a signal) corte m de una señal; pérdida f de una señal; distorsión f de una señal

B register /biː 'redʒɪstə/ noun registro m B

BRI /ˌbiː ɑː 'aɪ/ noun interfaz f de velocidad primaria

bricks-and-mortar /ˌbrɪks ən 'mɔːtə/ adjective tradicional

bridge /brɪdʒ/ verb (transfer programs) llenar vt; salvar vt ■ noun 1. (communications equipment between two networks) puente m; puente m de transición 2. (matching computer equipment to prevent power problems) puente m 3. (hardware or software allowing old system to be used on new system) puente m

'Lotus Development and IMRS are jointly developing a bridge linking their respective spreadsheet and client server reporting tools. It will allow users of IMRS' Hyperion reporting tool to manipulate live data from Lotus Improv.' [Computing]

bridgeware /'brɪdʒweə/ noun (hardware of software used to facilitate the transfer between computers) equipo m de adaptación; (hardware or software used to facilitate the transfer between computers) software m de adaptación; soporte m puente informático

bridging /'brɪdʒɪŋ/ noun (communications equipment) derivación f; transferencia f

bridging product /'brɪdʒɪŋ ˌprɒdʌkt/ noun interfaz f de transición; transferencia f de un programa a través de un puente

Briefcase utility /'briːfkeɪs juːˌtɪlɪti/ noun (Windows utility) mi m maletín

brightness /'braɪtnəs/ noun luminosidad f; brillo m ◇ **a control knob allows you to adjust brightness and contrast** un mando de control le permite ajustar el brillo y el contraste ◇ **the brightness of the monitor can hurt the eyes** el brillo del monitor puede dañar la vista

brightness range /'braɪtnəs reɪndʒ/ noun nivel m de luminosidad

brilliant /'brɪljənt/ adjective brillante ◇ **he used brilliant white for the highlights** empleó blanco brillante para lo más destacado ◇ **the background colour is a brilliant red** el color de fondo es rojo brillante

bring up /ˌbrɪŋ 'ʌp/ verb (start a computer system) poner en marcha; poner en funcionamiento

British Standards Institute /ˌbrɪtɪʃ 'stændədz ˌɪnstɪtjuːt/ noun (British equivalent of) asociación f británica de normativa sobre diseño y seguridad

broadband /'brɔːdbænd/ noun (transmission method) banda f ancha

broadband ISDN /ˌbrɔːdbænd ˌaɪ es diː 'en/ noun banda f ancha ISDN; banda f B-ISDN

broadcast /'brɔːdkɑːst/ noun (data transmission to many receivers) emisión f; comunicación f radiofónica ■ verb transmitir vt; emitir vt ◇ **broadcast satellite technique** técnica f de difusión por satélite or de emisión vía satélite

broadcast message /ˌbrɔːdkɑːst 'mesɪdʒ/ noun mensaje m difundido; mensaje m emitido ◇ **five minutes before we shut down the LAN, we send a broadcast message to all users** cinco minutos antes de cerrar la red local, emitimos un mensaje a todos los usuarios

broadcast network /ˌbrɔːdkɑːst 'netwɜːk/ noun red f de difusión

broadcast quality /ˌbrɔːdkɑːst 'kwɒlɪti/ noun calidad f de transmisión ◇ **we can use your multimedia presentation as the advert on TV if it's of broadcast quality** podemos utilizar su presentación multimedia como anuncio en televisión si tiene calidad para ser emitido

brochure site /'brəʊʃə saɪt/ noun folleto m electrónico

brouter /'bruːtə/ noun (device that combines the functions of a router and bridge) puente m de ruta; direccionamiento m ◇ **the brouter provides dynamic routing and can bridge two lo-**

cal area networks el puente de direccionamiento proporciona una ruta dinámica y puede unir dos redes locales

brown-out /'braʊn aʊt/ *noun* (*electricity*) bajada *f* de la corriente; apagón *m* parcial

browse /braʊz/ *verb* **1.** (*to view data in a database or online system*) examinar *vt*; navegar *vi*; consultar la red; visionar *vt*; ver *vt*; fisgonear *vi*; curiosear *vi* **2.** (*to search database material without permission*) visionar *vt*; ver *vt*

browser /'braʊzə/ *noun* (*software program that is used to navigate through WWW pages*) navegador *m*; (*software program that is used to navigate through WWW pages stored on the internet*) explorador *m*

browsing /'braʊzɪŋ/ *noun* lectura *f*

brush /brʌʃ/ *noun* (*tool in paint package software that draws pixels on screen*) pincel *m*; brocha *f* ◊ **the paint package lets you vary the width of the brush (in pixels) and the colour it produces** el paquete de dibujo le permite cambiar la anchura (en pixels) del pincel y el color que produce

brush style /'brʌʃ staɪl/ *noun* (*width and shape of brush tool*) tipo *m* de brocha; estilo *m* de pincel ◊ **to fill in a big area, I select a wide, square brush style** para rellenar un área grande, selecciono un estilo de pincel ancho y cuadrado

brute force method /ˌbruːt fɔːs 'meθəd/ *noun* método *m* de fuerza bruta; método *m* no calculado

BS *abbr* (*backspace*) (*backspace*) espacio *m* hacia atrás; espacio *m* de retroceso; carácter *m* BS

BSC /ˌbiː es 'siː/ *noun* comunicaciones *fpl* sincrónicas en binario

BSI /ˌbiː es 'aɪ/ *abbr* (*British Standards Institute*) asociación *f* británica de normativa sobre diseño y seguridad

BTAM /ˌbiː tiː eɪ 'em/ *noun* método *m* BTAM; método *m* básico de acceso a telecomunicaciones

btree /'biː triː/ *noun* árbol *m* binario

bubble-help /'bʌb(ə)l help/ *noun* (*single line that appears on screen to describe what you are pointing at*) etiqueta *f* de ayuda (que identifica la función del icono)

bubble jet printer /ˌbʌb(ə)l dʒet 'prɪntə/ *noun* impresora *f* de chorro de tinta

bubble memory /ˌbʌb(ə)l 'mem(ə)ri/ *noun* (*method of storing binary data*) memoria *f* de burbujas (magnéticas)

bubble memory cassette /ˌbʌb(ə)l 'mem(ə)ri kəˌset/ *noun* casete *f* de memoria de burbujas

bubble sort /'bʌb(ə)l sɔːt/ *noun* (*sorting method*) clasificación *f* por burbujas; selección *f* por permutación

bucket /'bʌkɪt/ *noun* cubeta *f* sector; condensador *m* (en memoria RAM)

buffer /'bʌfə/ *noun* **1.** (*circuit*) 'buffer' *m*; búfer *m*; circuito *m* intermedio **2.** (*temporary storage area for data*) memoria *f* intermedia; memoria *f*

amortiguadora; 'buffer' *m* ◼ *verb* (*to use temporary memory*) utilizar una memoria intermedia

buffered input/output /ˌbʌfəd ˌɪnpʊt 'aʊtpʊt/ *noun* entrada/salida *f* de la memoria intermedia

buffered memory /ˌbʌfəd 'mem(ə)ri/ *noun* memoria *f* almacenada temporalmente

buffering /'bʌfərɪŋ/ *noun* utilización *f* de la memoria intermedia; introducción *f* en memoria intermedia

buffer length /'bʌfə leŋθ/ *noun* longitud *f* de la memoria intermedia

buffer register /ˌbʌfə 'redʒɪstə/ *noun* registro *m* de la memoria intermedia

buffer size /'bʌfə saɪz/ *noun* tamaño *m* de la memoria intermedia

bug /bʌg/ *noun* (*error in program*) error *m*; defecto *m*

buggy /'bʌgi/ *noun* (*small computer-controlled vehicle*) vehículo *m* dirigido por ordenador

bug patch /'bʌg pætʃ/ *noun* **1.** (*temporary correction to program*) arreglo *m* provisional; parche **2.** (*correction to software*) arreglo *m* provisional; parche

build /bɪld/ *noun* (*particular version of a program*) versión *f* ◊ **this is the latest build of the new software** ésta es la última versión del nuevo software

building block /'bɪldɪŋ blɒk/ *noun* (*self-contained unit*) elemento *m*; módulo *m* (de un sistema)

built-in /ˌbɪlt 'ɪn/ *adjective* integrado *or* -a; incorporado *or* -a

built-in check /ˌbɪlt ɪn 'tʃek/ *noun* control *m* integrado

built-in font /ˌbɪlt ɪn 'fɒnt/ *noun* fuente *f* (de caracteres) incorporada; residente *mf*

built-in function /ˌbɪlt ɪn 'fʌŋkʃ(ə)n/ *noun* función *f* incorporada

built-in message /ˌbɪlt ɪn 'mesɪdʒ/ *noun* mensaje *m* incorporado

bulk erase /bʌlk ɪ'reɪz/ *verb* borrar *m* completamente

bulk storage medium /ˌbʌlk 'stɔːrɪdʒ ˌmiːdiəm/ *noun* medio *m* de almacenamiento de gran capacidad ◊ **magnetic tape is a reliable bulk storage medium** la cinta magnética es un medio muy fiable de almacenamiento de gran capacidad

bulk update terminal /ˌbʌlk 'ʌpdeɪt ˌtɜːmɪn(ə)l/ *noun* terminal *m* de actualización rápido

bullet /'bʊlɪt/ *noun* (*symbol on printed text*) punto *m* grueso; punto *m* indicador de color; (*filled circle or square in front of a line of text in a list*) marcador *m* de enumeración

'For a bullet chart use four to six bullet points and no more than six to eight words each' [*Computing*]

bulletin board /'bʊlɪtɪn bɔːd/, **bulletin board system** /ˌbʊlɪtɪn bɔːd 'sɪstəm/ *noun* sistema *m* de tablón de anuncios

bundle /ˈbʌnd(ə)l/ *noun* **1.** (*of optic fibres*) haz *m* (de fibras ópticas) **2.** (*package containing a computer with software or accessories*) oferta *f* promocional; oferta *f* de promoción ■ *verb* (*to market a computer together with a range of software at a special price*) hacer una oferta global

bundled software /ˌbʌnd(ə)ld ˈsɒftweə/ *noun* software *m* incluido en la compra de un ordenador

bureau /ˈbjʊərəu/ *noun* agencia *f*; empresa *f* de servicios ◇ **our data manipulation is handled by a bureau** nuestros datos son gestionados por una agencia de servicios ◇ **the company offers a number of bureau services, such as printing and data collection** la empresa ofrece diversos servicios ofimáticos, como los de impresión y recogida de datos ◇ **we farm out the office typing to a local bureau** confiamos nuestros escritos de oficina a una empresa informática local

'IMC has a colour output bureau that puts images onto the uncommon CD-ROM XA format.' [*Computing*]

burn /bɜːn/ *verb* **1.** programar un PROM; quemar un PROM **2.** quemar *vt*; arder *vi*

burner /ˈbɜːnə/ *noun* programador *m* de ROM

burn in /bɜːn ˈɪn/ *verb* **1.** (*to mark a television or monitor screen*) hacer un quemado de pantalla **2.** (*to write data into a PROM chip*) grabar *vt*; programar *vt*; quemar *vt*

burn-in /ˈbɜːn ɪn/ *noun* (*for electronic components*) envejecimiento *m*

burn out /ˌbɜːn ˈaut/ *noun* (*electronic circuit or device*) fallo *m* por calentamiento; fallo *m* por avería

burst /bɜːst/ *noun* (*short sequence of signals*) ráfaga *f* ◇ **colour burst** (*TV*) ráfaga de sincronización cromática *or* de señales de color

burster /ˈbɜːstə/ *noun* (*for paper*) separador, *mf* -a de hojas

burst mode /ˈbɜːst məud/ *noun* modalidad *f* en ráfagas

bus /bʌs/ *noun* **1.** (*communication link*) enlace *m* común; conductor *m* común; bus *m* **2.** (*central source of information*) tarjeta *f* conectora; enlace *m* común central ◇ **input** *or* **output data bus (I** *or* **O bus)** enlace común de entrada/salida *or* enlace común E/S

bus address lines /ˌbʌs əˈdres ˌlaɪnz/ *plural noun* líneas *fpl* de dirección de un enlace común

bus arbitration /bʌs ˌɑːbɪˈtreɪʃ(ə)n/ *noun* arbitraje *m* del bus; gestión *f* de enlace común

'The slot controller detects when a new board is inserted, it activates power up and assigns a bus arbitration and card slot ID to the board.' [*Computing*]

bus bar /ˈbʌs bɑː/ *noun* barra *f* ómnibus

bus board /ˈbʌs bɔːd/ *noun* (*PCB containing conducting paths*) tarjeta *f* de enlace; tarjeta *f* bus

bus clock /ˈbʌs klɒk/ *noun* reloj *m* del bus

bus clock speed /ˌbʌs klɒk ˈspiːd/ *noun* velocidad *f* del reloj del bus

bus control lines /ˌbʌs kənˈtrəul ˌlaɪnz/ *plural noun* líneas *fpl* de control de enlaces

bus data lines /ˌbʌs ˈdeɪtə ˌlaɪnz/ *plural noun* líneas de transmisión de datos de un enlace común

bus driver /bʌs ˈdraɪvə/ *noun* controlador *m* de enlaces

bus extender /ˌbʌs ɪksˈtendə/, **bus extension card** /bʌs ɪkˈstenʃən kɑːd/ *noun* tarjeta *f* de extensión de enlaces

business computer /ˈbɪznɪs kəmˌpjuːtə/ *noun* (*computer for business tasks*) ordenador *m* de gestión; ordenador *m* de empresa; ordenador *m* de oficina

business package /ˈbɪznɪs ˌpækɪdʒ/ *noun* paquete *m* de software empresarial

business system /ˈbɪznɪs ˌsɪstəm/ *noun* sistema *m* (informático) empresarial

bus master /bʌs ˈmɑːstə/ *noun* (*emisor de datos*) maestro *m* de un enlace común

bus master adapter /ˌbʌs ˌmɑːstə əˈdæptə/ *noun* adaptador *m* maestro de enlaces ◇ **the bus master network adapter provides much faster data throughput than the old adapter** el adaptador maestro de enlaces de red proporciona una trasferencia mucho más rápida que el adaptador antiguo

bus network /bʌs ˈnetwɜːk/ *noun* red *f* (de tipo) bus

bus slave /ˈbʌs sleɪv/ *noun* esclavo *m* de un enlace común

bus structure /bʌs ˈstrʌktʃə/ *noun* estructura *f* de un enlace común

bus topology /ˌbʌs təˈpɒlədʒi/ *noun* topología *f* de enlaces; topología *f* en bus ◇ **Ethernet is a network that uses the bus topology** Ethernet es una red que usa una topología en bus

busy /ˈbɪzi/ *adjective* (*background to a film shot*) fondo *m* animado; (*tone or signal*) ocupado *or* en servicio

button /ˈbʌt(ə)n/ *noun* **1.** (*switch that carries out an action*) botón *m* **2.** (*square shape that can be selected by a pointer*) botón *m* ◇ **there are two buttons at the bottom of the status line, select the left button to cancel the operation or the right to continue** seleccione el botón de la izquierda para cancelar la operación o el de la derecha para continuar ◇ **use the mouse to move the cursor to the icon and start the application by pressing the mouse button** utilice el ratón para situar el cursor sobre el icono e inicie la aplicación pulsando el botón del ratón

bypass /ˈbaɪˌpɑːs/ *noun* (*alternative route*) desviación *f*; desvío *m*

byte /baɪt/ *noun* byte *m*; octeto *m*

byte address /ˈbaɪt əˌdres/ *plural noun* direcciones *fpl* de bytes; direcciones *fpl* de octetos

bytecode /ˈbaɪtkəud/ *noun* código *m* byte

byte machine /baɪt məˈʃiːn/ *noun* máquina *f* de bytes; máquina *f* de octetos

byte manipulation /baɪt məˌnɪpjuˈleɪʃ(ə)n/ *noun* manipulación *f* de bytes; manipulación *f* de octetos

byte mode /'baɪt məʊd/ *noun* modalidad *f* en octetos

byte-orientated protocol /ˌbaɪt ˌɔːriənteɪtɪd 'prəʊtəkɒl/ *noun* protocolo *m* de comunicación carácter por carácter

byte serial mode /ˌbaɪt 'sɪəriəl ˌməʊd/ *noun* transmisión *f* de bytes en serie

byte serial transmission /ˌbaɪt ˌsɪəriəl trænz'mɪʃ(ə)n/ *noun* transmisión *f* de bytes en serie

bytes-per-inch /baɪtz pə/ *noun* bytes *mpl* por pulgada

bytes per second /ˌbaɪts pɜː 'sekənd/ *noun* bytes *mpl* por segundo

C

C¹ *symbol* C; número hexadecimal 12

C² *noun* (*high level programming language providing object oriented programming functions*) lenguaje *m* (de alto nivel) C

C++ /ˌsiː plʌs 'plʌs/ *noun* C++

CA *abbr* (*certificate authority*) autoridad *f* certificadora

cable /'keɪb(ə)l/ *noun* cable *m* ◇ **cable television** *or* **cable TV** (*communications system*) televisión por cable *or* TV por cable ◇ **cable TV relay station** repetidor *m* de televisión por cable

cable connector /ˌkeɪb(ə)l kə'nektə/ *noun* conector *m* (de cable)

cable matcher /'keɪb(ə)l ˌmætʃə/ *noun* acoplador *m* de impedancia

cable modem /ˌkeɪb(ə)l 'məʊdem/ *noun* módem *m* de cable

cable plant /'keɪb(ə)l plɑːnt/ *noun* cableado *m*

cable tester /ˌkeɪb(ə)l 'testə/ *noun* verificador *m* de cable

cabling /'keɪblɪŋ/ *noun* (*cable as a material*) cableado *m*; cables *mpl*; red *f* cableada ◇ **cabling costs up to £2 a foot** cada pie (30,5 cms) de cableado cuesta hasta dos libras ◇ **using high-quality cabling will allow the user to achieve very high data transfer rates** el uso de cables de alta calidad permite al usuario alcanzar una velocidad de transferencia de datos muy alta

'It has won a £500,000 contract to supply a structured voice and data cabling system to the bank and its stockbrocking subsidiary.' [*Computing*]

cabling diagram /'keɪb(ə)lɪŋ ˌdaɪəɡræm/ *noun* diagrama *m* cableado; diagrama *m* de circuito cableado

cache /kæʃ/ *noun* (*section of memory*) memoria *f* (de almacenamiento) temporal; antememoria *f*; memoria *f* caché ■ *verb* almacenar en memoria temporal; utilizar la memoria temporal ◇ **this CPU cache instructions improve performance by 15 percent** las instrucciones de la memoria temporal de este procesador mejoran su rendimiento en un 15 por ciento ◇ **this program can cache any size font** este programa puede almacenar en memoria temporal fuentes de caracteres de cualquier tamaño

cache controller /kæʃ kən'trəʊlə/ *noun* controlador *m* de memoria temporal

cache hit /'kæʃ hɪt/ *noun* dato *m* extraído directamente de la memoria temporal

cache memory /'kæʃ ˌmem(ə)ri/ *noun* (*cache*) memoria *f* de almacenamiento temporal; antememoria *f* ◇ **file access time is much quicker if the most frequently used data is stored in cache memory** el tiempo de acceso a los ficheros es mucho menor si los datos usados con mayor frecuencia se almacenan en la memoria temporal

CAD /kæd/ *noun* diseño *m* asistido por ordenador; CAD ◇ **all our engineers design on CAD workstations** todos nuestros ingenieros diseñan en terminales equipados con CAD

'John Smith of CAD supplier CAD/CAM Limited has moved into sales with responsibilities for the North of England. He was previously a technical support specialist.' [*Computing*]

CAD/CAM *noun* CAD/CAM

caddy /'kædi/ *noun* portadiscos *m*

CAE /ˌsiː eɪ 'iː/ *noun* ingeniería *f* asistida por ordenador

CAI /ˌsiː eɪ 'aɪ/ *noun* instrucción *f* asistida por ordenador

CAL /ˌsiː eɪ 'el/ *noun* aprendizaje *m* asistido por ordenador

calculated field /'kælkjʊˌleɪtɪd fiːld/ *noun* (*field that contains the results of calculations*) campo *m* estimado; campo *m* calculado

Calculator /'kælkjʊˌleɪtə/ (*software utility that is part of Microsoft Windows*) Calculadora *f*

calendar program /ˌkælɪndə 'prəʊɡræm/ *noun* (*software diary utility*) programa *m* de calendario; software *m* de calendario

calibrate /'kælɪbreɪt/ *verb* (*to adjust a monitor or joystick*) calibrar *vt*; ajustar *vt*

calibration /ˌkælə'breɪʃ(ə)n/ *noun* calibrado *m*

call /kɔːl/ *verb* **1.** (*to transfer control to a separate program or routine from a main program*) llamar un programa **2.** (*communicate*) telefonear *vi*; llamar *vt* ◇ **I'll call you at your office tomorrow** le llamaré mañana a su oficina

call accepted signal /kɔːl ək'septɪd/, **call accept signal** /kɔːl ək'sept/ *noun* señal *f* de aceptación de llamadas

callback /'kɔːlbæk/ *noun* (*security system*) rellamada *f* automática

call back modem /'kɔːl bæk ˌməʊdem/ *noun* módem *m* de devolución de llamadas; módem *m* de retrodemanda

call control signal /'kɔːl kənˌtrəʊl ˌsɪɡn(ə)l/ *noun* señal *f* de control de llamadas

call discrimination /kɔːl dɪˌskrɪmɪ'neɪʃ(ə)n/ *noun* identificación *f* de llamadas

call duration /kɔːl djʊˈreɪʃ(ə)n/ *noun* duración *f* de una llamada ◇ **call duration depends on the complexity of the transaction** la duración de una llamada depende de la complejidad de la transmisión ◇ **charges are related to call duration** los precios están relacionados con la duración de la llamada

called party /kɔːld ˈpɑːti/ *noun* comunicante *m&f*; interlocutor *or* -a

caller /ˈkɔːlə/ *noun* persona *f*; abonado *m* que llama (por teléfono) ◇ **caller ID** identificación *f* de abonado que llama (por teléfono)

calling /ˈkɔːlɪŋ/ *noun* (*signal*) señal *f* de llamada ◇ **calling feature** (*device or system*) dispositivo *m* de llamadas ◇ **calling unit** unidad *f*; sistema *m* de llamadas

calling sequence /ˌkɔːlɪŋ ˈsiːkwəns/ *noun* secuencia *f* de llamadas

call instruction /kɔːl ɪnˈstrʌkʃən/ *noun* instrucción *f* de llamada ◇ **the subroutine call instruction should be at this point** la subrutina de instrucción de llamada debería encontrarse en este punto

call logger /kɔːl ˈlɒɡə/ *noun* registrador *m* de llamadas

call scheduling /ˈkɔːl ˌʃedjuːlɪŋ/ *noun* programación *f* de llamadas

call up /ˌkɔːl ˈʌp/ *verb* (*to ask for information from a backing store to be displayed*) llamar *vt*; recuperar *vt*; mostrar en pantalla ◇ **after an input is received, the first function is called up** después de recibir una entrada, se recupera la primera función ◇ **all the customers addresses were called up** mostró en pantalla todas las direcciones de los clientes ◇ **call up the previous file** recuperar en pantalla el fichero anterior

CAM /ˌsiː eɪ ˈem/ *noun* fabricación *f* asistida por ordenador ■ *abbr* (*content addressable memory*) memoria *f* asociativa; memoria *f* direccionable por el contenido

Cambridge ring /ˌkeɪmbrɪdʒ ˈrɪŋ/ *noun* (red en) anillo *m* de Cambridge

campus environment /ˌkæmpəs ɪnˈvaɪrənmənt/ *noun* entorno *m* universitario; ambiente *m* universitario

campus network /ˌkæmpəs ˈnetwɜːk/ *noun* red *f* del campus (universitario)

cancel /ˈkænsəl/ *verb* anular *vt*; cancelar *vt*

cancel character /ˌkæns(ə)l ˈkærɪktə/ *noun* carácter *m* de anulación ◇ **the software automatically sends a cancel character after any error** después de cualquier error, el programa envía automáticamente un carácter de cancelación

cancellation /ˌkænsəˈleɪʃ(ə)n/ *noun* cancelación *f*; anulación *f*

canonical schema /kəˌnɒnɪkl ˈskiːmə/ *noun* esquema *m* estándar

capability list /ˌkeɪpəˈbɪləti lɪst/ *noun* lista *f* de capacidades

capacitance /kæˈpæsɪtəns/ *noun* capacitancia *f*

capacitative /kəˈpæsɪtətɪv/, **capacititive** *adjective* capacitivo *or* -a

capacitor /kəˈpæsɪtə/ *noun* condensador *m*; (dispositivo con) capacidad *f* de condensación ◇ **capacitor microphone** micrófono *m* electrostático (de condensador) ◇ **ceramic capacitor** condensador cerámico ◇ **electrolytic capacitor** condensador electrolítico ◇ **non-electrolytic capacitor** condensador no electrolítico ◇ **variable capacitor** condensador variable

capacitor storage /kəˌpæsɪtə ˈstɔːrɪdʒ/ *noun* memoria *f* con condensador

capacity /kəˈpæsɪti/ *noun* (*space*) capacidad *f*

capitalisation /ˌkæpɪt(ə)laɪˈzeɪʃ(ə)n/, **capitalization** *noun* (*converts text into capitals*) uso *m* de mayúsculas; (*word-processor function that converts text into capitals*) función *f* mayúsculas

capitals /ˈkæpɪt(ə)lz/, **caps** *plural noun* mayúsculas *fpl*

caps lock /ˈkæps lɒk/ *noun* tecla *f* de bloqueo de las mayúsculas; Bloq Mayús

capstan /ˈkæpstən/ *noun* (*of tape player*) cabrestante *m* de arrastre

caption /ˈkæpʃən/ *noun* leyenda *f*; encabezamiento *m* ◇ **the captions are printed in italics** las leyendas se imprimen en cursiva

capture /ˈkæptʃə/ *noun* captura *f*; recogida *f* ■ *verb* **1.** (*of data*) recoger *vt*; capturar *vt*; tomar *vt* **2.** (*remove a token from the network*) tomar *vt* ◇ **data capture starts when an interrupt is received** la recogida de datos se inicia cuando se recibe una señal de interrupción ◇ **the software allows captured images to be edited** el programa permite modificar las imágenes recogidas ◇ **this scanner captures images at a resolution of 300 dots per inch (dpi)** este escáner recoge imágenes con una resolución de 300 puntos por pulgada

CAR *abbr* (*current address register*) registro *m* de direcciones en curso

carbon copy /ˌkɑːbən ˈkɒpi/ *noun* copia *f* de papel carbón; calco *m*

carbon ribbon /ˌkɑːbən ˈrɪbən/ *noun* cinta *f* de carbón

card /kɑːd/ *noun* (*sheet of insulating material*) tarjeta *f*; ficha *f*; tarjeta *f* de circuito impreso ◇ **filing card** tarjeta archivadora ◇ **index card** tarjeta *f*; ficha *f*

'A smart card carries an encryption chip, which codifies your ID and password prior to their being transmitted across a network.' [*Computing*]

card cage /ˈkɑːd keɪdʒ/ *noun* caja *f* de placa de circuito; estuche *m* de circuito

card chassis /kɑːd ˈʃæsi/ *noun* marco *m* de tarjetas (de circuitos impresos); soporte *m* de tarjetas (de circuitos impresos)

card edge connector /ˌkɑːd edʒ kəˈnektə/ *noun* conector *m* de borde de tarjetas

card extender /ˈkɑːd ɪkˌstendə/ *noun* soporte *m* de tarjeta de extensión

card frame /'kɑːd freɪm/ *noun* marco *m* de tarjetas (de circuitos impresos); soporte *m* de tarjetas (de circuitos impresos)

cardinal number /ˌkɑːdɪn(ə)l 'nʌmbə/ *noun* (*positive integer*) número *m* cardinal

cardioid response /ˌkɑːdɪɔɪd rɪ'spɒns/ *noun* respuesta *f* en cardioide

card reader /kɑːd 'riːdə/ *noun* lector *m* de tarjetas

caret /'kærət/ *noun* (*symbol of the Control key*) símbolo *m* de intercalación; símbolo *m* ^ (de la tecla Ctrl); (*used in proofreading*) marca *f* de intercalación

carpal tunnel syndrome /ˌkɑːp(ə)l 'tʌn(ə)l ˌsɪndrəʊm/ *noun* lesión *f* por fatiga crónica

carriage /'kærɪdʒ/ *noun* (*of typewriter or printer*) carro *m* ◇ **carriage return** *or* **line feed (CR** *or* **LF)** retorno de carro/avance *m* de línea

carriage control /'kærɪdʒ kənˌtrəʊl/ *noun* control *m* de carro ◇ **carriage control codes can be used to move the paper forward two lines between each line of text** los códigos de control de carro pueden emplearse para hacer avanzar el papel dos líneas entre cada línea de texto

carriage return /ˌkærɪdʒ rɪ't3ːn/ *noun* retorno *m* de carro

carriage return key /ˌkærɪdʒ rɪ't3ːn ˌkiː/ *noun* tecla *f* de retorno de carro ◇ **the carriage return key is badly placed for touch-typists** la tecla de retorno de carro está muy mal colocada para los mecanógrafos al tacto

carrier /'kærɪə/ *noun* (*high frequency waveform*) onda *f* portadora

carrier detect /ˌkærɪə dɪ'tekt/ *noun* señal *f* CD; señal *f* de detección de portadora

carrier frequency /ˌkærɪə 'friːkwənsi/ *noun* frecuencia *f* de portadora

carrier sense multiple access-collision avoidance /ˌkærɪə sens ˌmʌltɪp(ə)l ˌækses kə 'lɪʒ(ə)n əˌvɔɪdəns/ *noun* acceso *m* múltiple con detección de portadora evitando colisiones

carrier sense multiple access-collision detection /ˌkærɪə sens ˌmʌltɪp(ə)l ˌækses kə 'lɪʒ(ə)n dɪˌtekʃ(ə)n/ *noun* acceso *m* múltiple de detección de portadora con detección de colisión; protocolo *m* de transmisión CSMA-CD

carrier signal /ˌkærɪə 'sɪgn(ə)l/ *noun* señal *f* de portadora

carrier signalling /'kærɪə ˌsɪgnəlɪŋ/ *noun* transmisión *f* por onda portadora

carrier system /ˌkærɪə 'sɪstəm/ *noun* (*analog or digital*) sistema *m* de (corriente) portadora; (*analog*) sistema *m* multiplexado

carrier wave /ˌkærɪə weɪv/ *noun* onda *f* portadora

carry /'kæri/ *noun* (*maths*) arrastre *m*; transferencia *f*; dígito *m* que se lleva en una suma ◇ **when 5 and 7 are added, there is an answer of 2 and a carry which is put in the next column, giving 12** cuando se suman 5 más 7, hay una respuesta de dos y un dígito, que se suma a la columna siguiente, lo cual da 12

carry bit /'kæri bɪt/ *noun* bit *m* de arrastre; bit *m* de transferencia

carry complete signal /ˌkæri kəm'pliːt ˌsɪgn(ə)l/ *noun* señal *f* de fin de arrastre

carry flag /'kæri flæg/ *noun* indicador *m* de retención; indicador *m* de arrastre

carry look ahead /ˌkæri lʊk ə'hed/ *noun* arrastre *m* hacia adelante

carry time /'kæri taɪm/ *noun* tiempo *m* de transferencia

cartesian coordinates /kɑːˌtiːziən kəʊ 'ɔːdɪnəts/ *plural noun* coordenadas *fpl* cartesianas

cartesian structure /kɑːˌtiːziən 'strʌktʃə/ *noun* estructura *f* cartesiana

cartridge /'kɑːtrɪdʒ/ *noun* cartucho *m*; cargador *m* ◇ **the portable computer has no disk drives, but has a slot for ROM cartridges** este ordenador portátil no tiene disqueteras, pero dispone de una ranura para cargadores ROM

cartridge drive /'kɑːtrɪdʒ draɪv/ *noun* unidad *f* cargadora

cartridge fonts /'kɑːtrɪdʒ fɒntz/ *plural noun* fuentes *fpl* de caracteres de cargador

cartridge ribbon /ˌkɑːtrɪdʒ 'rɪbən/ *noun* cinta *f* de cartucho

cascade carry /kæˌskeɪd 'kæri/ *noun* arrastre *m* en cascada

cascade connection /kæˌskeɪd kə 'nekʃ(ə)n/ *noun* conexión *f* en cascada

cascade control /kæˌskeɪd kən'trəʊl/ *noun* control *m* en cascada

cascading style sheet /kæˌskeɪdɪŋ 'staɪl ˌʃiːt/ *noun* hoja *f* de estilo en cascada

cascading windows /kæˌskeɪdɪŋ 'wɪndəʊz/ *plural noun* ventanas *fpl* en cascada

case /keɪs/ *noun* **1.** (*typography*) tipo *m* de letra **2.** (*programming command*) CASE; instrucción *f* de bifurcación condicional ◇ **he corrected the word 'coMputer', replacing the upper case M with a lower case letter** corrigió la palabra 'coMputer' sustituyendo la M mayúscula por una letra minúscula

case branch /'keɪs brɑːntʃ/ *noun* bifurcación *f* condicional

case change /'keɪs tʃeɪndʒ/ *noun* tecla *f* de mayúsculas

case sensitive /keɪs 'sensətɪv/ *adjective* que distingue las mayúsculas de las minúsculas ◇ **the password is case sensitive** la contraseña tiene en cuenta las mayúsculas y las minúsculas

case sensitive search /ˌkeɪs ˌsensətɪv 's3ːtʃ/ *noun* búsqueda *f* que distingue las mayúsculas de las minúsculas

cassette /kə'set/ *noun* casete *mf* ◇ **video cassette** videocasete *or* casete de vídeo ◇ **you must back up the information from the computer onto a cassette** debe hacer una copia de seguridad de la información del ordenador en una casete

cassette recorder /kə'set rɪˌkɔːdə/ *noun* casete *m*; grabadora *f*

cassette tape /kə'set teɪp/ *noun* (*reel of magnetic tape*) cinta *f* casete; cinta *f* magnética; casete *m*

cast /kɑːst/ *noun* (*instruction*) CAST ■ *verb* lanzar *vt*; proyectar *vt*

CAT /kæt/ *noun* 1. (*computer-aided training or computer-assisted training*) prueba *f* asistida por ordenador 2. (*computer-aided testing or computer-assisted testing*) comprobación *f* asistida por ordenador

catalogue /'kæt(ə)lɒg/ *noun* catálogo *m* ■ *verb* catalogar *vt*; hacer un listado ◇ **all the terminals are catalogued, with their location, call sign and attribute table** todos los terminales son catalogados con su ubicación, signo de llamada y tabla de atributos ◇ **disk catalogue** (*directory*) catálogo *m* ◇ **the entry in the disk catalogue is removed when the file is deleted** la entrada en el catálogo de ficheros de disco queda eliminada cuando se borra el fichero

catastrophe /kə'tæstrəfi/ *noun* catástrofe *f*

catastrophic error /ˌkætəstrɒfɪk 'erə/ *noun* error *m* catastrófico; error *m* fatal

catastrophic failure /ˌkætəstrɒfɪk 'feɪljə/ *noun* parada *f* fatal; fallo *m* catastrófico

Category 1 /ˌkætəg(ə)ri 'wʌn/ *noun* categoría 1

Category 2 /ˌkætəg(ə)ri 'tuː/ *noun* categoría 2

Category 3 /ˌkætəg(ə)ri 'θriː/ *noun* categoría 3

Category 4 /ˌkætəg(ə)ri 'fɔː/ *noun* categoría 4

Category 5 /ˌkætəg(ə)ri 'faɪv/ *noun* categoría 5

category wiring /ˌkætəg(ə)ri 'waɪərɪŋ/ *noun* cableado *m* según categoría (de cable)

catena /kə'tiːnə/ *noun* 1. (*items in a chained list*) (número de) caracteres *mpl* en una lista 2. (*character chain*) cadena *f* de caracteres

catenate /'kætəneɪt/ *verb* concatenar *vt*; encadenar *vt*

cathode ray tube /ˌkæθəʊd 'reɪ tjuːb/ *noun* tubo *m* de rayos catódicos

cathode ray tube storage /ˌkæθəʊd reɪ ˌtjuːb 'stɔːrɪdʒ/ *noun* monitor *m* (de ordenador); pantalla *f* (de ordenador)

CAV /ˌsiː eɪ 'viː/ *noun* velocidad *f* angular constante

CB *abbr* (*call back*) rellamada *f* automática

CBI /n/ *abbr* (*computer-based instruction*) formación *f* por ordenador

CBL /ˌsiː biː 'el/ *noun* aprendizaje *m* asistido por ordenador

CBR *abbr* (*constant bit rate*) velocidad *f* constante de bits

CBT /ˌsiː biː 'tiː/ *noun* formación *f* por ordenador

cc /ˌsiː 'siː/ *noun* copia *f* de cortesía

CCD *abbr* (*charge-coupled device*) CCD; dispositivo *m* de cargamentos adyacentes

CCD memory /ˌsiː siː diː 'mem(ə)ri/ *noun* memoria *f* CCD

CCITT /ˌsiː siː aɪ tiː 'tiː/ *noun* comité *m* consultivo internacional en teléfonos y telégrafos

CCP /ˌsiː siː 'piː/ *noun* procesador *m* de consola de instrucciones

CD /siː'diː/ *abbr* (*compact disc*) CD *m*

CD32 /ˌsiː diː ˌθɜːti 'tuː/ *noun* (*processor and CD-ROM developed by Commodore for Amiga computer*) CF32

CD caddy /ˌsiː 'diː ˌkædi/ *noun* portadiscos *m*; portador *m* de compactos

CD-I /ˌsiː 'diː aɪ/ *noun* (*standards that combine sound, data, video and text onto a CD*) CD-I

CD Player /ˌsiː 'diː ˌpleɪə/ *noun* reproductor *m* de discos compactos

CD quality /ˌsiː 'diː ˌkwɒlɪti/ *adjective* (*recording*) de calidad CD

CD-R /ˌsiː diː 'ɑː/ *noun* (*technology that allows a user to write data to and read from a CD-R disc*) CD-R

C: drive /'siː draɪv/ *noun* disco *m* duro C:

CD-ROM /ˌsiː diː 'rɒm/ *noun* (*disc drive*) disco *m* compacto de sólo lectura

''Customers' images will be captured, digitised, and stored on optical disk or CD-ROM, and produced if queries arise about responsibility for ATM transactions.'' [*Computing*]

CD-ROM Extended Architecture /ˌsiː ˌdiː rɒm ɪkˌstendɪd 'ɑːkɪtektʃə/ *noun* arquitectura *f* ampliada de CD-ROM

CD-ROM Extensions /ˌsiː 'diː rɒm/ *plural noun* extensiones *fpl* de CD-ROM

CD-ROM player /ˌsiː 'diː rɒm/ *noun* lector *m* de CD-ROM; reproductor *m* de CD-ROM

CD-ROM Re-Writable /ˌsiː 'diː rɒm reɪ/ *noun* CD *m* regrabable

CDRTOS /ˌsiː diː ɑː tiː əʊ 'es/ *noun* (*operating system*) sistema *m* operativo de CD en tiempo real

CD-RW /ˌsiː diː ɑː 'dʌb(ə)ljuː/ *noun* CD-RW *m*

cel /sel/ *noun* (*single frame in an animation sequence*) fotograma *m* de animación digital

cell /sel/ *noun* 1. (*single function in a spreadsheet*) celda *f* 2. (*single memory location*) celda *f* 3. (*in transmission system*) celda *f*

cell address /sel ə'dres/ *noun* dirección *f* de celda

cellar /'selə/ *noun* pila *f* (de datos en memoria)

cell definition /sel ˌdefə'nɪʃ(ə)n/ *noun* definición *f* de celda

cell format /sel 'fɔːmæt/ *noun* formato *m* de celda ◇ **the cell format is right-aligned and emboldened** las celdas tienen un formato de justificación a la derecha y negrita

cell protection /sel prə'tekʃən/ *noun* protección *f* de celda

cell reference variable /ˌsel ˌref(ə)rəns 'veəriəb(ə)l/ *noun* variable *f* de referencia de una celda

cellular phone /ˌseljʊlə 'fəʊn/ *noun* teléfono *m* celular

central computer /ˌsentrəl kəmˈpjuːtə/ *noun* ordenador *m* central

centralised computer network /ˌsentrə ˌlaɪzd kəmˈpjuːtə/, **centralized computer network** *noun* red *f* informática centralizada

centralised data processing /ˌsentrəˌlaɪzd ˈdeɪtə/, **centralized data processing** *noun* proceso *m* centralizado de la información; tratamiento *m* centralizado de la información

central memory /ˌsentrəl ˈmem(ə)ri/ *noun* memoria *f* central; memoria *f* principal

central processing element /ˌsentrəl ˈprəʊsesɪŋ ˌelɪmənt/ *noun* unidad *f* central de cálculo

central processing unit /ˌsentrəl ˌprəʊsesɪŋ ˈjuːnɪt/, **central processor** /ˌsentrəl ˌprəʊˈsesə/ *noun* unidad *f* central de proceso

central terminal /ˌsentrəl ˈtɜːmɪn(ə)l/ *noun* terminal *m* principal; terminal *m* central

centre /ˈsentə/ *verb* **1.** (*to align read/write head*) centrar las cabezas; alinear (las cabezas); (*to format*) ajustar (las cabezas) **2.** (*in text or on screen*) centrar *vt*

centre channel /ˌsentə ˈtʃæn(ə)l/ *noun* canal *m* central

centre operator /ˌsentə ˈɒpəreɪtə/ *noun* operador *m* central

Centronics interface /senˈtrɒnɪks ˌɪntəfeɪs/ *noun* interfaz *f* Centronics

Centronics port /senˈtrɒnɪks ˌpɔːt/ *noun* puerto *m* Centronics

CERN /sɜːn/ *noun* (*research laboratory in Switzerland where the world wide web was originally invented*) Consejo *m* Europeo para la Investigación Nuclear

certificate /səˈtɪfɪkət/ *noun* certificado *m*

certificate authority /səˈtɪfɪkət ɔːˌθɒrɪti/ *noun* autoridad *f* certificadora

certificate of approval /səˌtɪfɪkət əv ə ˈpruːv(ə)l/ *noun* certificado *m* de homologación

CF *abbr* (*compact Flash*) compact Flash

CGI /ˌsiː dʒiː ˈaɪ/ *noun* interfaz *f* de acceso común

CGM /ˌsiː dʒiː ˈem/ *noun* fichero *m* de gráficos CGM; metafichero *m* de gráficos

chain /tʃeɪn/ *noun* **1.** (*linked data or files*) cadena *f* **2.** (*sequential instructions*) cadena *f* ■ *verb* (*to link files or data*) encadenar(se) *vr* ◇ **chain delivery mechanism** (*for paper*) mecanismo *m* alimentador (de hojas) en cadena ◇ **more than 1,000 articles or chapters can be chained together when printing** cuando se imprime, se pueden encadenar más de 1.000 artículos o capítulos

chain code /ˈtʃeɪn kəʊd/ *noun* (*series of words*) código *m* encadenado; código *m* en cadena

chained file /ˌtʃeɪnd ˈfaɪl/ *noun* fichero *m* encadenado

chained list /ˈtʃeɪnd lɪst/ *noun* (*list containing data and an address*) lista *f* en cadena; lista *f* encadenada; lista *f* enlazada

chained record /tʃeɪnd ˈrekɔːd/ *noun* registro *m* encadenado

chaining /ˈtʃeɪnɪŋ/ *noun* encadenamiento *m*; encadenado *m*

chaining search /ˈtʃeɪnɪŋ sɜːtʃ/ *noun* búsqueda *f* en cadena; búsqueda *f* asociativa

chain list /ˈtʃeɪn lɪst/ *noun* lista *f* en cadena; lista *f* encadenada

chain printer /tʃeɪn ˈprɪntə/ *noun* impresora *f* de cadena; impresora *f* en cadena

change /tʃeɪndʒ/ *noun* cambio *m*; modificación *f*

change directory /ˈtʃeɪndʒ daɪˌrekt(ə)ri/ *noun* (*instrucción*) CD

change dump /ˈtʃeɪndʒ dʌmp/ *noun* vaciado *m* de movimientos; vuelco *m* de modificaciones

change file /ˈtʃeɪndʒ faɪl/ *noun* fichero *m* de modificaciones

change over /ˌtʃeɪndʒ ˈəʊvə/ *noun* cambiar *vt*; pasar (de un sistema a otro)

changer /ˈtʃeɪndʒə/ *noun* conversor *m* ◇ **record changer** cambiadiscos *m* ◇ **you can interconnect all these peripherals with just two cables and a gender changer** se pueden interconectar todos estos periféricos con sólo dos cables y un conversor de género

change record /tʃeɪndʒ ˈrekɔːd/ *noun* registro *m* de modificaciones; registro *m* de cambio

change tape /ˌtʃeɪndʒ ˈteɪp/ *noun* cinta *f* de modificaciones

channel /ˈtʃæn(ə)l/ *noun* (*physical connection*) canal *m*; vía *f*; enlace *m* ■ *verb* (*signals or data*) canalizar *vt*; vehicular *vt* ◇ **channel address word** palabra *f* de dirección de canal ◇ **channel connector** conector *m* de canales ◇ **channel controler** controlador *m* de canal ◇ **channel control field** campo *m* de control de canales ◇ **channel error** error *m* de canal ◇ **channel group** grupo *m* de canales *or* de vías ◇ **channel status condition** condición *f* de estado del canal ◇ **channel switching** conmutación *f* de canal ◇ **channel time response** respuesta *f* de tiempo de canal ◇ **channel work area expansion** extensión *f* de área de memoria para la gestión de canales

channel adapter /ˈtʃæn(ə)l əˌdæptə/ *noun* interfaz *f* de canal de transmisión; adaptador *m* de canal de transmisión

channel bank /ˈtʃæn(ə)l bæŋk/ *noun* banco *m* de canales

channel capacity /ˈtʃæn(ə)l kəˌpæsɪti/ *noun* capacidad *f* de canal

channel command /ˈtʃæn(ə)l kəˌmɑːnd/ *noun* instrucción *f* de canal

channel isolation /ˌtʃæn(ə)l ˌaɪsəˈleɪʃ(ə)n/ *noun* aislamiento *m* de canales

channelling /ˈtʃænəlɪŋ/ *noun* (*protective pipes*) conducto *m*; canalización *f*

channel overload /ˈtʃæn(ə)l ˌəʊvələʊd/ *noun* (*transmission of data*) sobrecarga *f* de una vía; sobrecarga *f* de canal; saturación *f* de un canal

channel queue /'tʃæn(ə)l kjuː/ *noun* **1.** cola *f* de espera **2.** cola *f* de transmisión de datos

channel synchroniser /'tʃæn(ə)l ˌsɪŋkrənaɪzə/, **channel synchronizer** *noun* sincronizador *m* de canales; sincronizador *m* de vías

channel-to-channel connection /ˌtʃæn(ə)l tə ˌtʃæn(ə)l kə'nekʃ(ə)n/ *noun* conexión *f* directa entre canales

chapter /'tʃæptə/ *noun* (*of program*) módulo *m*

char /tʃɑː/ *noun* (*in programming*) (variable de tipo carácter) char

character /'kærɪktə/ *noun* carácter *m* ◇ **character key** (*word processor control*) tecla *f* (de) carácter ◇ **character oriented protocols (COP)** protocolos *mpl* orientados al carácter ◇ **character skew** inclinación de un carácter

character assembly /'kærɪktə əˌsembli/ *noun* (*designing characters with pixels*) agrupación *f*; grupo *m* de caracteres

character-based /'kærɪktə ˌbeɪst/ *adjective* basada en caracteres

character blink /'kærɪktə blɪŋk/ *noun* parpadeo *m* de (un) carácter

character block /'kærɪktə blɒk/ *noun* bloque *m* de caracteres

character byte /'kærɪktə baɪt/ *noun* byte *m* de caracteres

character check /'kærɪktə tʃek/ *noun* control *m* de caracteres

character code /'kærɪktə kəʊd/ *noun* código *m* de caracteres

character density /'kærɪktə ˌdensɪti/ *noun* densidad *f* de caracteres

character display /'kærɪktə dɪˌspleɪ/ *noun* visualización *f* de caracteres; visualización *f* de texto

character fill /'kærɪktə fɪl/ *noun* relleno *m* de caracteres; inserción *f* de caracteres (en memoria)

character generator /'kærɪktə ˌdʒenəreɪtə/ *noun* generador *m* de caracteres ◇ **the ROM used as a character generator can be changed to provide different fonts** la ROM utilizada como generadora de caracteres se puede cambiar para proporcionar fuentes distintas

character interleaving /ˌkærɪktə ˌɪntə'liːvɪŋ/ *noun* entrelazado *m* de caracteres

characteristic /ˌkærɪktə'rɪstɪk/ *noun* **1.** (*typical or special*) característico *m* **2.** (*measurement or property of a component*) exponente *m*; característico *m* ◇ **this fault is characteristic of this make and model of personal computer** este defecto es característico de esta marca y modelo de ordenador personal

characteristic overflow /ˌkærɪktərɪstɪk 'əʊvəfləʊ/ *noun* desbordamiento *m* de la característica

character key /'kærɪktə kiː/ *noun* tecla *f* (de) carácter

character machine /'kærɪktə məˌʃiːn/ *noun* máquina *f* en modalidad carácter; procesador *m* en modalidad carácter

Character Map /'kærɪktə mæp/ *noun* mapa *m* de caracteres

character matrix /'kærɪktə ˌmeɪtrɪks/ *noun* matriz *f* de caracteres

character mode /'kærɪktə məʊd/ *noun* modalidad *f* (de) carácter

character-orientated /'kærɪktə ˌɔːriənteɪtɪd/ *adjective* (ordenador) en modalidad carácter

character printer /'kærɪktə ˌprɪntə/ *noun* impresora *f* carácter por carácter ◇ **a daisy-wheel printer is a character printer** la impresora de margarita imprime carácter por carácter

character recognition /ˌkærɪktə ˌrekəg'nɪʃ(ə)n/ *noun* reconocimiento *m* (óptico) de caracteres

character repertoire /ˌkærɪktə ˌrepə'twɑː/ *noun* (*list of characters*) repertorio *m* de caracteres; repertorio *m* tipográfico; fuentes *fpl* de caracteres

character representation /ˌkærɪktə ˌreprɪzen'teɪʃ(ə)n/ *noun* representación *f* visual en color de un carácter; representación *f* (binaria) de caracteres

character rounding /'kærɪktə ˌraʊndɪŋ/ *noun* redondeo *m* de caracteres

character set /'kærɪktə set/ *noun* (*list of characters*) conjunto *m*; conjunto *m* de caracteres; juego *m* de caracteres; fuente *f* de caracteres

characters per inch /ˌkærɪktəz pɜːr 'ɪntʃ/ *plural noun* caracteres *mpl* por pulgada

characters per second /ˌkærɪktəz pə 'sekənd/ *noun* caracteres *mpl* por segundo (cps)

character string /'kærɪktə strɪŋ/ *noun* cadena *f* de caracteres

'This explains a multitude of the database's problems – three-letter months are treated like character strings instead of as dates.' [*Computing*]

character stuffing /'kærɪktə ˌstʌfɪŋ/ *noun* (*addition of blank characters to a file*) relleno *m* (con caracteres en blanco); inserción *f* de caracteres en blanco; inserción *f* de caracteres de relleno

charge /tʃɑːdʒ/ *noun* **1.** (*of electricity*) carga *f* **2.** (*of electrons*) carga *f* ■ *verb* (*to supply device with electric charge*) cargar *vt*

charge-coupled device /ˌtʃɑːdʒ ˌkʌp(ə)ld dɪ'vaɪs/ *noun* dispositivo *m* CCD; dispositivo *m* acoplado de carga

charge-coupled device memory /tʃɑːdʒ ˌkʌp(ə)ld dɪ'vaɪs/ *noun* memoria *f* CCD; memoria *f* de dispositivo acoplado de carga

chart /tʃɑːt/ *noun* diagrama *m*; gráfico *m* ◇ **chart recorder** registrador *m* gráfico *or* de gráficos ◇ **the memory allocation is shown on this pie chart** este diagrama de sectores muestra la asignación de memoria

chassis /'ʃæsi/ *noun* chasis *m*

chat /tʃæt/ *verb* (*on the Internet*) charlar *vi*

chat group /'tʃæt gruːp/ *noun* grupo *m* de discusión

chat room /'tʃæt ruːm/ *noun* (*on the Internet*) cuarto *m* de charlas en el Internet

CHCP /ˌsiː aɪtʃ siː 'piː/ *noun* (*system command in MS-DOS OS/2*) CHCP

CHDIR /ˌsiː aɪtʃ diː aɪ 'ɑː/ *abbr* (*change directory*) (instrucción) CHDIR (de cambio de directorio)

cheapernet /'tʃiːpənet/ *noun informal* (*informal term for thin-Ethernet*) red *f* Ethernet de cable fino ◇ **cheapernet cable** cable *m* (coaxial) fino de red

check bit /'tʃek bɪt/ *noun* (*one bit of a binary word*) bit *m* de control; bit *m* de comprobación

check box /'tʃek bɒks/ *noun* caja *f* de selección; caja *f* de control ◇ **select the option by moving the cursor to the check box and pressing the mouse button** seleccione la opción desplazando el cursor a la caja de selección y pulsando el botón del ratón

check character /tʃek 'kærɪktə/ *noun* carácter *m* de control

check digit /'tʃek ˌdɪdʒɪt/ *noun* cifra *f* (numérica) de control; clave *f* (numérica) de control

checkerboarding /'tʃekəˌbɔːdɪŋ/ *noun* supresión *f* parcial (de la memoria) *f*; borrado *m* parcial (de la memoria)

check indicator /tʃek 'ɪndɪˌkeɪtə/ *noun* indicador *m* de control

checking program /tʃekɪŋ 'prəʊɡræm/ *noun* programa *m* de control

check key /'tʃek kiː/ *noun* clave *f* de control

check mark /'tʃek mɑːk/ *noun* marca *f* de verificación

check number /tʃek 'nʌmbə/ *noun* cifra *f*; clave *f* (numérica) de control

check point /'tʃek pɔɪnt/ *noun* punto *m* de control; punto *m* de reanudación

check point dump /ˌtʃek pɔɪnt 'dʌmp/ *noun* vaciado *m* de punto de control; vuelco *m* de punto de control

check register /tʃek 'redʒɪstə/ *noun* registro *m* de control; registro *m* de instrucciones

checksum /tʃek 'təʊt(ə)l/, **check total** *noun* (*program that checks data*) suma *f* total; suma *f* de verificación; suma *f* de control; suma *f* de comprobación ◇ **the data must be corrupted if the checksum is different** los datos deben ser erróneos si el total de verificación es distinto

child process /tʃaɪld prəʊ'ses/, **child program** /tʃaɪld 'prəʊɡræm/ *noun* (*routine or program*) procedimiento *m* de segunda generación; programa *m* de segunda generación; proceso *m* hijo

chip /tʃɪp/ *noun* (*device used in transistors, resistors and capacitors*) chip *m*; componente *m*; microplaca *f*; microplaqueta *f*; circuito *m* integrado ◇ **the data strobe line is connected to the latch chip select line** la línea de validación de datos está conectada a la línea de selección del chip de pestillo

chip architecture /tʃɪp 'ɑːkɪˌtektʃə/ *noun* arquitectura *f* de un chip; arquitectura *f* de un circuito integrado

chip card /ˌtʃɪp 'kɑːd/ *noun* tarjeta *f* de chip; tarjeta *f* de memoria

chip count /ˌtʃɪp 'kaʊnt/ *noun* número *m* de chips ◇ **it's no good, the chip count is still too high** no sirve; el número de chips es todavía demasiado alto

'Where the display is provided by an LCD system, high levels of performance must be achieved with the lowest cost, smallest chip count and lowest power consumption.' [*Computing*]

chip select /ˌtʃɪp sɪ'lekt/ *noun* validación *f* de un chip; selección *f* de un chip

chip select line /ˌtʃɪp sɪ'lekt ˌlaɪn/ *noun* línea *f* de selección; línea *f* de validación de un chip ◇ **the data strobe line is connected to the latch chip select line** la línea de validación de datos está conectada a la línea de selección del chip de pestillo

chip set /ˌtʃɪp 'set/ *noun* conjunto *m* de chips; conjunto *m* de circuitos integrados

CHKDSK /'tʃekdɪsk/ *noun* (*system command in MS-DOS*) (instrucción) CHKDSK (de control de disquetera)

Chooser™ /'tʃuːzə/ (*Apple Macintosh operating system*) utilidad *f* Chooser™

chord keying /'kɔːd kiːɪŋ/ *noun* pulsación *f* simultánea de dos teclas

chroma /'krəʊmə/ *noun* crominancia *f*; croma *f* ◇ **chroma control** (*TV*) control *m* de croma ◇ **chroma detector** detector *m* de croma

chrominance /'krəʊmɪnəns/ *noun* croma *f*; crominancia *f*

chrominance signal /'krəʊmɪnəns ˌsɪɡn(ə)l/ *noun* señal *f* de crominancia

CIF /ˌsiː aɪ 'ef/ *abbr* (*common intermediate format*) formato *m* intermedio común (para vídeo)

CIM /ˌsiː aɪ 'em/ *noun* **1.** (*computer input microfilm*) fabricación *f* integrada por ordenador **2.** (*computer-integrated manufacturing*) fabricación *f* asistida por ordenador

cipher /'saɪfə/ *noun* (*system, method*) código *m* cifrado; escritura *f* cifrada

cipher key /'saɪfə kiː/ *noun* clave *f* cifrada

cipher system /'saɪfə ˌsɪstəm/ *noun* sistema *m* cifrado

ciphertext /'saɪfətekst/ *noun* mensaje *m* cifrado

CIR /ˌsiː aɪ 'ɑː/ *noun* registro *m* de instrucciones en curso

circuit /'sɜːkɪt/ *noun* (*electric*) circuito *m* ◇ **circuit grade** características *fpl* de un circuito ◇ **circuit noise level** nivel *m* de ruido de un circuito ◇ **circuit switched digital circuitry (CSDC)** conjunto digital conmutado de circuitos ◇ **circuit switched network** red *f* conmutada de circuitos ◇ **printed circuit board (PCB)** (*with circuit printed*) (tarjeta de) circuito impreso

circuit analyser /'sɜːkɪt ˌænəlaɪzə/ *noun* analizador *m* de circuitos

circuit board /'sɜːkɪt bɔːd/ *noun* placa *f* base

'The biggest shock was to open up the PC and find the motherboard smothered in patch wires (usually a sign that a design fault in the printed circuit board was rectified at the last minute).' [*Computing*]

circuit breaker /'sɜːkɪt ˌbreɪkə/ *noun* (*device which protects equipment by cutting off electrical supply if appropriate*) interruptor *m* de corriente; cortacircuitos *m*; interruptor *m*

circuit capacity /'sɜːkɪt kəˌpæsɪti/ *noun* capacidad *f* de un circuito

circuit card /'sɜːkɪt kɑːd/ *noun* placa *f* base

circuit design /'sɜːkɪt dɪˌzaɪn/ *noun* trazado *m* de un circuito; diseño *m* de un circuito

circuit diagram /'sɜːkɪt ˌdaɪəgræm/ *noun* diagrama *m* de un circuito ◇ **the CAD program will plot the circuit diagram rapidly** el programa CAD traza el diagrama del circuito con rapidez

circuit switching /'sɜːkɪt ˌswɪtʃɪŋ/ *noun* conmutación *f* de circuitos

circular buffer /ˌsɜːkjʊlə 'bʌfə/ *noun* memoria *f* intermedia circular

circular file /'sɜːkjʊlə faɪl/ *noun* fichero *m* en bucle; fichero *m* circular

circularity /ˌsɜːkjʊ'lærɪti/ *noun* falta *f* de lógica

circular list /'sɜːkjʊlə lɪst/ *noun* lista *f* en bucle

circular reference /ˌsɜːkjʊlə 'ref(ə)rəns/ *noun* referencia *f* circular

circular shift /'sɜːkjʊlə ʃɪft/ *noun* desplazamiento *m* circular

circulate /'sɜːkjʊˌleɪt/ *verb* (*to go in circle*) describir un círculo; (*to send information to*) (hacer) circular

circulating register /ˌsɜːkjuleɪtɪŋ 'redʒɪstə/ *noun* registro *m* circulante; registro *m* de desplazamiento circular

circulating storage /ˌsɜːkjuleɪtɪŋ 'stɔːrɪdʒ/ *noun* memoria *f* circulante; memoria *f* dinámica

CIS /ˌsiː aɪ 'es/ *noun* detector *m* de imágenes por contacto

CIT *abbr* (*computer-integrated telephony*) telefonía *f* integrada por ordenador

CIX *abbr* (*commercial Internet exchange*) intercambio *m* comercial internet

cladding /'klædɪŋ/ *noun* (*surrounding a conducting core*) revestimiento *m*; cubierta *f* ◇ **if the cladding is chipped, the fibre-optic cable will not function well** si el revestimiento está raspado, el cable de fibra óptica no funciona bien

claim frame /'kleɪm freɪm/ *noun* (*FDDI protocol network: frame used to determine which station will initialise the network*) tramo *m* de inicialización de red bajo el protocolo FDDI

clamper /'klæmpə/ *noun* estabilizador *m* de la señal

clapper /'klæpə/ *noun* (*on printer*) prensador *m*

class /klɑːs/ *noun* (*definition of what a software routine will do*) clase *f*

class interval /klɑːs 'ɪntəv(ə)l/ *noun* intervalo *m* de clase

clean /kliːn/ *adjective* (*error-free*) limpio *or* -a; sin error; sin correcciones; virgen ■ *verb* (*to make clean*) limpiar *vt*; eliminar *vt* ◇ **clean proof** prueba *f* sin correcciones ◇ **write errors occur if you do not use a head cleaning kit regularly** ocurren errores de escritura si no utiliza con regularidad un juego de limpieza de cabezas

clean copy /kliːn 'kɒpi/ *noun* (*text that does not need changing*) copia *f* final; texto *m* sin errores; texto *m* sin modificaciones

clean machine /kliːn mə'ʃiːn/ *noun* (*computer that contains only the minimum of ROM-based code*) procesador *m* nuevo; máquina *f* desnuda

clean page /'kliːn peɪdʒ/ *noun* página *f* (de memoria) sin modificación

clean room /'kliːn ruːm/ *noun* cámara *f* estéril

clear /klɪə/ *verb* **1.** (*free*) borrar *vt*; (*to wipe out*) vaciar *vt* **2.** (*to release a communications link*) liberar la línea

clearance /'klɪərəns/ *noun* autorización *f* ◇ **you do not have the required clearance for this processor** usted no tiene la autorización necesaria para este procesador

Clearing House Interbank Payment System /ˌklɪərɪŋ haʊs ˌɪntəbæŋk 'peɪmənts ˌsɪstəm/ *noun* sistema *m* de compensación y liquidación en el que intervien más de 130 bancos, trabajando con divisas y Eurodólares

clear to send /ˌklɪə tə 'send/ *noun* CTS; (señal de) preparado para transmitir

click /klɪk/ *noun* (*pressing a key or button*) clic *m* ■ *verb* (*to press a key or button or mouse*) teclear *vt*; pulsar *vt*; pinchar *vt* ◇ **use the mouse to enlarge a frame by clicking inside its border and dragging to the position wanted** utilice el ratón para agrandar el recuadro tecleando dentro de su borde y arrastrándolo a la posición deseada ◇ **you move through text and graphics with a click of the button** al pinchar el ratón uno se puede desplazar por el texto y los gráficos

click rate /'klɪk reɪt/ *noun* coeficiente *m* de clics en anuncios

clickstream /'klɪkstriːm/ *noun* rastro *m* de clics

'…the only way of achieving it would be to monitor the clickstreams of every single UK user of the net.' [*The Guardian*]

client /'klaɪənt/ *noun* (*in a network, a workstation connected to a network*) cliente *m* ◇ **client-to-client protocol (CTCP)** protocolo *m* cliente a cliente

client-server architecture /ˌklaɪənt ˌsɜːvə 'ɑːkɪtektʃə/ *noun* (*in a network*) arquitectura *f* cliente-servidor

client-server network /ˌklaɪənt 'sɜːvə ˌnetwɜːk/ *noun* red *f* cliente-servidor

client-side /'klaɪənt saɪd/ *adjective* ejecutado por el cliente

clip /klɪp/ *verb* (*short piece of live film*) fragmento *m* de película

clip-art /klɪp ɑːt/ *noun* imágenes *fpl* de biblioteca; galería *f* de imágenes

clipboard /'klɪp,bɔːd/ *noun* (*temporary storage area for data*) portapapeles *m*; almacén *m* temporal; (*utility that temporarily stores any type of data*) Bloc *m* de Notas™; bloc *m* de notas ◇ **copy the text to the clipboard, then paste it back into a new document** copie el texto en el bloc de ntoas, luego péguelo en un nuevo documento

CLNP *abbr* (*connectionless network protocol*) protocolo *m* de red no orientado a la conexión

clock /klɒk/ *noun* (*used to synchronize equipment*) reloj *m*; cronómetro *m* ■ *verb* sincronizar *vt*

clock cycle /klɒk 'saɪk(ə)l/ *noun* ciclo *m* del reloj

clock doubler /'klɒk ,dʌb(ə)lə/ *noun* doblador *m* de reloj ◇ **the new CPU from Intel has an optional clock doubler that will double performance** el nuevo procesador de Intel tiene un doblador opcional de reloj que dobla el redimiento

clocked signals /klɒkd 'sɪgn(ə)lz/ *plural noun* señales *fpl* cronometradas; señales *fpl* sincronizadas a los impulsos del reloj

clock frequency /klɒk 'friːkwənsi/ *noun* frecuencia *f* de reloj ◇ **the main clock frequency is 10MHz** la principal frecuencia de reloj es de 10 MHz

clock pulse /'klɒk pʌls/ *noun* impulso *m* de reloj

clock rate /klɒk reɪt/ *noun* velocidad *f* de reloj; velocidad *f* de cronómetro

clock speed /'klɒk spiːd/ *noun* velocidad *f* de cronómetro; velocidad *f* de reloj

clock track /'klɒk træk/ *noun* pista *f* de reloj

clone /kləʊn/ *noun* modelo *m* clónico; clon *m*

'On the desktop, the IBM/Motorola/Apple triumvirate is planning to energise a worldwide clone industry based on the PowerPC chip.' [*Computing*]

close /kləʊz/ *verb* (*to shut down*) cerrar *vt*; terminar *vt*; acabar *vi* ◇ **closed circuit television (CCTV)** televisión *f* en circuito cerrado

CLOSE /kləʊz/ *noun* (*in a programming language*) (instrucción) CLOSE (de fin de acceso de un equipo o de un fichero)

closed bus system /,kləʊzd 'bʌs ,sɪstəm/ *noun* sistema *m* de enlace común cerrado

closed loop /,kləʊzd 'luːp/ *noun* bucle *m* cerrado

closed routine /kləʊzd ruː'tiːn/ *noun* rutina *f* cerrada

closed subroutine /kləʊzd 'sʌbruː,tiːn/ *noun* sub-rutina *f* cerrada

closed user group /,kləʊzd ,juːzə 'gruːp/ *noun* grupo *m* de usuario cerrado

cloud /klaʊd/ *noun* codificación *f* directa

CLS /,si: el 'es/ *noun* (*in MS-DOS*) (instrucción MS-DOS) CLS (de borrado de pantalla)

cluster /'klʌstə/ *noun* **1.** (*sectors on a hard disk*) grupo *m* racimo; agrupamiento *m*; sectores *mpl* contiguos **2.** (*of terminals*) grupo *m* de terminales; grupo *m* de periféricos

cluster controller /'klʌstə kən,trəʊlə/ *noun* unidad *f* de control de periféricos dispuestos en forma de racimo

clustering /'klʌstərɪŋ/ *noun* unión *f* en grupo de varios periféricos

'...these include IBM networking and clustering hardware   and   software' [*Personal Computer World*]

CLV /,si: el 'viː/ *noun* velocidad *f* lineal constante

CM /,si: 'em/ *noun* memoria *f* central; memoria *f* principal

CMIP /,si: em aɪ 'piː/ *noun* protocolo *m* CMIP; protocolo GENDER>m de información común de gestión

CMOS /,si: em əʊ 'piː/ *noun* semiconductor *m* complementario de óxido metálico; semiconductor *m* de CMOS

'Similarly, customers who do not rush to acquire CMOS companion processors for their mainframes will be rewarded with lower prices when they finally do migrate.' [*Computergram*]

CMOT /,si: em əʊ 'tiː/ *noun* (*using of CMIP and CMIS network management protocols to manage gateways*) CMOT

CMYK /,si: em waɪ 'keɪ/ *noun* (*method of describing a colour*) sistema *m* de definición de colores: azul verdoso, morado, amarillo, negro

coalesce /,kəʊə'les/ *verb* (*to merge files*) combinar *vt*; fusionar *vt*; fundir *vt*

co-axial cable /kəʊks/, **coax** *noun* cable *m* co-axial

COBOL /'kəʊbɒl/ *noun* lenguage *m* COBOL

cobweb site /'kɒbweb saɪt/ *noun* sitio *m* anquilosado

code /kəʊd/ *noun* (*sequence of computer instructions*) código *m* ■ *verb* (*to write a program in a programming language*) codificar *vt*; cifrar *vt*; poner en clave ◇ **code translator feature** dispositivo *m* de conversión de códigos ◇ **escape code** código de escape

{Unrecovered Error: TEMP7D52C53A-
2926-4E08-8415-6100D08EEA58 post
code = US zip code TEMP2A8E4BB8-
064F-4BA0-AB6D-8327B07057B6
TEMPE3023A4C-8E3E-4B5D-9A01-
1B4AFE9D8552   código   postal
TEMP31D3EB63-6F54-4B88-B11A-
9D7AD05259F7   stock   code
TEMP74A91F32-3994-487E-8850-
36400DD8F87A   TEMP768D55F6-1E6E-
4F99-96D2-C0038B7A9FCC código de
existencias & exor; de stock}

code area /kəʊd 'eəriə/ *noun* zona *f* de código

code bit /'kəʊd bɪt/ *noun* bit *m* de código

CODEC /'kəʊdek/ *noun* codificador *m* / descodificador

code conversion /kəʊd kən'vɜːʃ(ə)n/ *noun* conversión f de código(s)

code element /kəʊd 'elɪmənt/ *noun* elemento *m* de un código

code group /'kəʊd gruːp/ *noun* grupo *m* de código

code line /'kəʊd laɪn/ *noun* línea f de código

code page /'kəʊd peɪdʒ/ *noun* página f de código ◊ **in order to enter Swedish characters from an English keyboard, you have to change the system code page** para introducir caracteres suecos desde un teclado británico, se tiene que cambiar la página de códigos del sistema

coder /'kəʊdə/ *noun* codificador *m*

coder/decoder /ˌkəʊdə diː'kəʊdə/ *noun* codificador/descodificador *m*

code segment /kəʊd 'segmənt/ *noun* segmento *m* de código

coding /'kəʊdɪŋ/ *noun* codificación f; programación f ◊ **coding line** línea f de codificación

coding form /'kɒdɪŋ fɔːm/ *noun* formulario *m* de programación; formulario *m* de codificación

coding sheet /'kɒdɪŋ ʃiːt/ *noun* hoja f de programación; hoja f de codificación

coincidence circuit /kəʊˌɪnsɪd(ə)ns 'sɜːkɪt/, **coincidence element** /'elɪmənt/ *noun* circuito *m* de coincidencia; elemento *m* de coincidencia

coincidence function /kəʊ'ɪnsɪd(ə)ns ˌfʌŋkʃən/ *noun* función f de coincidencia; función f Y

coincidence gate /kəʊ'ɪnsɪd(ə)ns geɪt/, **coincidence circuit** /kəʊˌɪnsɪd(ə)ns 'sɜːkɪt/, **coincidence element** /kəʊˌɪnsɪd(ə)ns 'elɪmənt/ *noun* (*electronic circuit*) puerta f de coincidencia; circuito *m* de coincidencia; elemento *m* de coincidencia

coincidence operation /kəʊ'ɪnsɪd(ə)ns ˌɒpəreɪʃ(ə)n/ *noun* operación f Y; operación f de coincidencia

cold boot /ˌkəʊld 'buːt/ *noun* arranque *m* en frío; puesta f en marcha en frío

coldboot /'kəʊldbuːt/ *verb* arrancar en frio

cold fault /'kəʊld fɔːlt/ *noun* error *m* de arranque

cold standby /kəʊld 'stændbaɪ/ *noun* (*backup system*) sistema *m* de reserva manual; sistema *m* de reserva en frío

cold start /ˌkəʊld 'stɑːt/ *noun* (*computer or program*) arranque *m* en frío; puesta f en marcha; reanudación f después de una interrupción de la alimentación

collating sequence /kə'leɪtɪŋ ˌsiːkwəns/ *noun* secuencia f de intercalación

collator /kə'leɪtə/ *noun* **1.** (*of data*) programa *m* de fusión de datos; clasificador *m or* -a f; ensambladora f **2.** (*of punched cards*) clasificador *m or* -a f

collect /kə'lekt/ *verb* (*data*) reunir *vt*; (*to receive or capture data*) recoger *vt*; reunir *vt*

collision /kə'lɪʒ(ə)n/ *noun* (*of two signals*) colisión f; choque *m*

collision detection /kə'lɪʒ(ə)n dɪˌtekʃ(ə)n/ *noun* detección f de colisión

co-location /kəʊ ləʊ'keɪʃ(ə)n/ *noun* coemplazamiento *m*

colour balance /'kʌlə ˌbæləns/ *noun* equilibrio *m* de colores

colour bits /'kʌlə bɪts/ *plural noun* bits *mpl* de descripción de color

colour cell /'kʌlə sel/ *noun* celda f de control de colores

colour depth /'kʌlə depθ/ *noun* intensidad f de color

colour display /ˌkʌlə dɪ'spleɪ/ *noun* visualización f en color; representación f visual en color

colour look-up table /ˌkʌlə 'lʊk ʌp ˌteɪb(ə)l/ *noun* tabla f de consulta de colores

colour monitor /ˌkʌlə 'mɒnɪtə/ *noun* monitor *m* de color; pantalla f de color ◊ **the colour monitor is great for games** el monitor de color es excelente para los juegos electrónicos

colour palette /ˌkʌlə 'pælət/ *noun* paleta f de colores

colour printer /ˌkʌlə 'prɪntə/ *noun* impresora f de color

colour saturation /ˌkʌlə ˌsætʃə'reɪʃ(ə)n/ *noun* saturación f de color

colour separation /ˌkʌlə ˌsepə'reɪʃ(ə)n/ *noun* (*colour printing*) separación f de colores; selección f de colores

colour standard /'kʌlə ˌstændəd/ *noun* color *m* estándar

colour temperature /'kʌlə ˌtemprɪtʃə/ *noun* temperatura f cromática

column /'kɒləm/ *noun* columna f ◊ **an 80-column printer is included in the price** el precio incluye una impresora de 80 columnas ◊ **put the total at the bottom of the column** escriba el total al final de la columna ◊ **to add up a column of figures** sumar una columna de cifras

columnar graph /kə,lʌmnə 'grɑːf/ *noun* (*graph on which values are shown as vertical or horizontal bars*) diagrama *m* en columnas; gráfico *m* en columnas; histograma *m*

columnar working /kə,lʌmnə 'wɜːkɪŋ/ *noun* presentación f (gráfica) en columnas

column balance /'kɒləm ˌbæləns/ *noun* equilibrio *m* de las columnas

column guide /'kɒləm gaɪd/ *noun* guía *m*; separador *m* de columnas

column indicator /'kɒləm ˌɪndɪkeɪtə/ *noun* indicador *m* de columna

column parity /ˌkɒləm 'pærɪti/ *noun* paridad f de columna(s)

column report /'kɒləm rɪˌpɔːt/ *noun* informe *m* en columnas

com /kɒm/ *suffix* com

COM /ˌsiː əʊ 'em/ *noun* (*computer output on microfilm*) salida f de ordenador en microfilm

COM1 /ˌkɒm 'wʌn/ *noun* (*first serial port in a PC*) COM1

comb filter /kəʊm 'fɪltə/ *noun* filtro *m* de peine

combinational circuit /ˌkɒmbɪneɪʃən(ə)l 'sɜːkɪt/ *noun* circuito *m* combinatorio

combinational logic /ˌkɒmbɪneɪʃən(ə)l 'lɒdʒɪk/ *noun* lógica *f* combinatoria

combined head /kəm'baɪnd hed/ *noun* cabeza *f* de lectura/escritura

combined station /kəmˌbaɪnd 'steɪʃ(ə)n/ *noun* estación *f* combinada

combined symbol matching /kəmˌbaɪnd 'sɪmbəl ˌmætʃɪŋ/ *noun* sistema *m* de reconocimiento de caracteres (por identificación de símbolos combinados)

combi player /'kɒmbi ˌpleɪə/ *noun* reproductor *m* de CD-ROM de varios formatos

combo box /'kɒmbəu bɒks/ *noun* (*box that displays a number of different input and output objects*) caja *f* de útiles; caja *f* de objetos de E/S

COM file /'kɒm faɪl/ *noun* (*three-letter extension to a file name*) fichero *m* COM; fichero *m* binario ejecutable ◇ **to start the program, type the name of the COM file at the MS-DOS prompt** para iniciar un programa, escriba el nombre del fichero COM en el (indicador del) MS-DOS

comic-strip oriented /ˌkɒmɪk strɪp 'ɔːrientɪd/ *adjective* orientada en tira de cómic

Comité Consultatif Internationale de Télégraphie et Téléphonie *noun* comité *m* Consultivo Internacional en Teléfonos y Telégrafos

comma /'kɒmə/ *noun* (*typography*) coma *f*

comma-delimited file /ˌkɒmə diːˌlɪmɪtd 'faɪl/ *noun* fichero *m* delimitado por una coma ◇ **all databases can import and export to a comma-delimited file format** todas las bases de datos pueden importar y exportar datos a un formato de archivo delimitado por una coma

command /kə'mɑːnd/ *noun* **1.** (*electrical pulse or signal*) instrucción *f*; orden *m*; comando *m* **2.** (*word recognized by a computer*) instrucción *f* ◇ **interrupt command** instrucción de interrupción (de un programa) ◇ **the command to execute the program is RUN** RUN es la instrucción de ejecución de un programa ◇ **type the command 'DIR' to get the list of files** escriba la instrucción DIR para obtener la lista de ficheros ◇ **use the command 'DIR' to view the files on disk, add the command line argument 'A:' to view the files on drive A:** utilice la instrucción DIR para ver los ficheros en el disco

command chain /kə'mɑːnd tʃeɪn/ *noun* cadena *f* de instrucciones

command code /kə'mɑːnd kəud/ *noun* código *m* de operación; código *m* de instrucciones

COMMAND.COM /kə'mɑːnd kɒm/ *noun* (*program file that contains the command interpreter*) fichero *m* COMMAND.COM

command console processor /kə'mɑːnd ˌkɒnsəul ˌprəusesə/ *noun* procesador *m* de consola de instrucciones

command control language /kəˌmɑːnd kən'trəul ˌlæŋgwɪdʒ/ *noun* lenguaje *m* de control de instrucciones

command-driven program /kəˌmɑːnd ˌdrɪv(ə)n 'prəugræm/ *noun* programa *m* activado por instrucciones

command file /kə'mɑːnd faɪl/ *noun* fichero *m* de instrucciones

command file processor /kə'mɑːnd faɪl ˌprəusesə/ *noun* procesador *m* de fichero de instrucciones

command interface /kə'mɑːnd ˌɪntəfeɪs/ *noun* interfaz *f* de instrucciones; interfaz *f* de control

command interpreter /kə'mɑːnd ɪnˌtɜːprɪtə/ *noun* intérprete *m* de instrucciones

command key /kə'mɑːnd kiː/ *noun* tecla *f* de instrucciones

command language /kə'mɑːnd ˌlæŋgwɪdʒ/ *noun* lenguaje *m* de instrucción; lenguaje *m* de instrucciones

command line /kə'mɑːnd laɪn/ *noun* **1.** (*of a program line*) línea *f* de instrucciones **2.** (*of a prompt*) línea *f* de instrucciones

'This gives Unix a friendly face instead of the terrifyingly complex command-line prompts that make most users reach for their manuals.' [*Computing*]

command line argument /kəˌmɑːnd laɪn 'ɑːgjumənt/ *noun* argumento *m* de línea de instrucciones ◇ **use the command 'DIR' to view the files on disk, add the command line argument 'A:' to view the files on drive A:** utilice la instrucción DIR para ver los ficheros en el disco; añada el argumento de línea de instrucciones A: para ver los ficheros en la disquetera A:

command line interface /kəˌmɑːnd laɪn 'ɪntəfeɪs/ *noun* interfaz *f* de línea de instrucciones

command line operating system /kə ˌmɑːnd laɪn 'ɒpəreɪtɪŋ ˌsɪstəm/ *noun* sistema *m* operativo de línea de instrucciones

command message /kə'mɑːnd ˌmesɪdʒ/ *noun* mensaje *m* de instrucción

command mode /kə'mɑːnd məud/ *noun* modo *m* de instrucción

command prompt /kə'mɑːnd prɒmpt/ *noun* indicación *f* de instrucción

command register /kə'mɑːnd ˌredʒɪstə/ *noun* registro *m* de instrucciones

command state /kə'mɑːnd steɪt/ *noun* estado *m* para recepción de instrucciones; situación *f* para recepción de instrucciones

command string /kə'mɑːnd strɪŋ/ *noun* cadena *f* de comando

command window /kə'mɑːnd ˌwɪndəu/ *noun* ventana *f* de instrucciones; ventana *f* de instrucción ◇ **the command window is a single line at the bottom of the screen** la ventana de instrucción es una sola línea en la parte inferior de la pantalla ◇ **the user can define the size of the command window** el usuario puede definir el tamaño de la ventana de instrucciones

comment /'kɒment/ *noun* (*note in a program*) nota *f*; explicación *f*; comentario *m* ◇ **BASIC allows comments to be written after a REM instruction** en BASIC se pueden introducir comentarios después de la instrucción REM

comment field /'kɒment fiːld/ *noun* campo *m* de notas

comment out /'kɒment aʊt/ *noun* comentario *m* que inhabilita una instrucción

commerce /'kɒmɜːs/ comercio *m*

commercial Internet exchange /kə,mɜːʃ(ə)l 'ɪntənet ɪks,tʃeɪndʒ/ *noun* intercambio *m* comercial internet

common algorithmic language /,kɒmən ,ælgərɪðmɪk 'læŋgwɪdʒ/ *noun* COMAL

common business orientated language /,kɒmən ,bɪznɪs ,ɔːriənteɪtɪd 'læŋgwɪdʒ/ *noun* COBOL

common carrier /,kɒmən 'kæriə/ *noun* (*private company that supplies data*) empresa *f* pública de servicios informativos; línea *f* común; canal *m* común

common channel signalling /,kɒmən 'tʃæn(ə)l ,sɪgn(ə)lɪŋ/ *noun* señalización *f* por canal común; señalización *f* por vía común

common gateway interface /,kɒmən 'geɪtweɪ ,ɪntəfeɪs/ *noun* interfaz *f* común de pasarela

common hardware /,kɒmən 'hɑːdweə/ *noun* hardware *m* corriente; hardware *m* común

common intermediate format /,kɒmən ,ɪntəmiːdiət 'fɔːmæt/ *noun* formato *m* intermedio común (para vídeo)

common language /,kɒmən 'læŋgwɪdʒ/ *noun* lenguaje *m* común; lenguaje *m* compartido

common management information protocol /,kɒmən ,mænɪdʒmənt ,ɪnfə'meɪʃ(ə)n ,prəʊtəkɒl/ *noun* protocolo *m* común de gestión de la información; protocolo *m* CMIP

common management information specification /,kɒmən ,mænɪdʒmənt ,ɪnfə'meɪʃ(ə)n ,spesɪfɪkeɪʃ(ə)n/ *noun* servicio *m* de información de gestión común

common object request broker architecture /,kɒmən əb,dʒekt rɪ,kwest ,brəʊkə 'ɑːkɪtektʃə/ *noun* arquitectura *f* común de agente de solicitud de objetos

common ordinary business-oriented language /,kɒmən ,ɔːd(ə)n(ə)ri ,bɪznɪs ,ɔːriəntɪd 'læŋgwɪdʒ/ *noun* COBOL

common software /,kɒmən 'sɒftweə/ *noun* (*routine used by any program*) software *m* común; software *m* compartido; software *m* de red

common storage area /,kɒmən 'stɔːrɪdʒ ,eəriə/ *noun* zona *f* común de la memoria ◇ **the file server memory is mainly common storage area, with a section reserved for the operating system** la memoria central del servidor de ficheros es sobre todo una zona común de almacenamiento, con una sección reservada para el sistema operativo

communicating word processor /kə,mjuːnɪkeɪtɪŋ 'wɜːd ,prəʊsesə/ *noun* procesador *m* de textos con interfaz de comunicación

communications buffer /kə,mjuːnɪ'keɪʃ(ə)nz ,bʌfə/ *noun* memoria *f* intermedia de comunicaciones; memoria *f* de transmisión de datos

communications channel /kə,mjuːnɪ'keɪʃ(ə)nz ,tʃæn(ə)l/ *noun* canal *m* de transmisión; canal *m* de comunicaciones

communications computer /kə,mjuːnɪ'keɪʃ(ə)nz kəm,pjuːtə/ *noun* ordenador *m* de comunicaciones; ordenador *m* de control de las transmisiones

communications control unit /kə,mjuːnɪkeɪʃ(ə)nz kən'trəʊl ,juːnɪt/ *noun* controlador *m* de comunicaciones; controlador *m* de transmisiones

communications executive /kə,mjuːnɪ'keɪʃ(ə)nz ɪg,zekjʊtɪv/ *noun* gestor *m* de telecomunicaciones

communications interface adapter /kə,mjuːnɪkeɪʃ(ə)nz 'ɪntəfeɪs ə,dæptə/ *noun* adaptator *m* de interfaz de comunicaciones

communications link /kə,mjuːnɪ'keɪʃ(ə)nz lɪŋk/ *noun* enlace *m* de comunicaciones; enlace *m* de transmisiones

communications link control /kə,mjuːnɪkeɪʃ(ə)nz lɪŋk kən'trəʊl/ *noun* control *m* de enlace de comunicaciones; control *m* de transmisiones

communications network /kə,mjuːnɪ'keɪʃ(ə)nz ,netwɜːk/ *noun* (*transfer of data*) red *f* de comunicaciones; red *f* de telecomunicaciones

communications network processor /kə,mjuːnɪkeɪʃ(ə)nz ,netwɜːk 'prəʊsesə/ *noun* procesador *m* de red de comunicaciones

communications package /kə,mjuːnɪ'keɪʃ(ə)nz ,pækɪdʒ/ *noun* software *m*; paquete *m* de comunicaciones

communications port /kə,mjuːnɪ'keɪʃ(ə)nz pɔːt/ *noun* puerto *m* de comunicaciones

communications protocol /kə,mjuːnɪ'keɪʃ(ə)nz ,prəʊtəkɒl/ *noun* protocolo *m* de comunicaciones ◇ **the communications protocol for most dial-up online services is eight-bit words, no stop bit and even parity** el protocolo de comunicaciones para la mayoría de servicios en línea es una palabra de ocho bits, sin bit de parada y paridad par

communications scanner /kə,mjuːnɪ'keɪʃ(ə)nz ,skænə/ *noun* (*monitoring equipment*) escáner *m* de comunicaciones; explorador *m* de comunicaciones; analizador *m* de comunicaciones; analizador *m* de control de llamadas

communications server /kə,mjuːnɪ'keɪʃ(ə)nz ,sɜːvə/ *noun* servidor *m* de comunicaciones

communications software /kə,mjuːnɪ'keɪʃ(ə)nz ,sɒftweə/ *noun* software *m* de comunicación

community /kə'mjuːnɪti/ *noun* comunidad *f* virtual

comp /kɒmp/ *noun* (grupo de noticias) comp (sobre ordenadores y programación)

compact code /'kɒmpækt kəʊd/ *noun* código *m* compacto

compact disc /ˌkɒmpækt 'dɪsk/ *noun* disco *m* compacto; CD *m*

compact disc-digital audio /ˌkɒmpækt ˌdɪsk ˌdɪdʒɪt(ə)l 'ɔːdiəʊ/ *noun* disco *m* compacto de audio

compact disc erasable /ˌkɒmpækt ˌdɪsk ɪ 'reɪzəb(ə)l/ *noun* disco *m* compacto borrable

compact disc-interactive /ˌkɒmpækt dɪsk ˌɪntər'æktɪv/ *noun* disco *m* compacto interactivo; CD *m* interactivo

compact disc player /ˌkɒmpækt 'dɪsk ˌpleɪə/ *noun* lector *m* de discos compactos; lector *m* de CD

compact disc ROM /ˌkɒmpækt ˌdɪsk 'rɒm/ *noun* disco *m* compacto CD-ROM

compact disc write once /ˌkɒmpækt dɪsk ˌraɪt 'wʌns/ *noun* disco *m* compacto de una sola grabación

compact Flash /kəmˌpækt 'flæʃ/ *noun* compact Flash

compacting algorithm /ˌkɒmpæktɪŋ 'ælgə ˌrɪð(ə)m/ *noun* algoritmo *m* de compactación

compact model /'kɒmpækt ˌmɒd(ə)l/ *noun* modelo *m* compacto

companding /kɒm'pændɪŋ/ *noun* compresión *f*; expansión *f*

COMPAQ /'kɒmpæk/ (*US personal computer company*) Compaq™

comparator /kəm'pærətə/ *noun* comparador *m*

compatibility /kəmˌpætɪ'bɪlɪti/ *noun* (*ability of two devices to function together*) compatibilidad *f*

'The manufacturer claims that this card does not require special drivers on the host machine… and therefore has fewer compatibility problems.' [*Computing*]

compatibility box /kəmˌpætə'bɪlɪti bɒks/ *noun* ventana *f* de compatibilidad ◇ **OS *or* 2 has a compatibility box to allow it to run DOS applications** el OS/2 tiene una ventana de compatibilidad que le permite ejecutar aplicaciones de DOS

compatible /kəm'pætɪb(ə)l/ *adjective* compatible ■ *noun* ordenador *m* compatible

'…this was the only piece of software I found that wouldn't work, but it does show that there is no such thing as a totally compatible PC clone' [*Personal Computer World*]

compilation /ˌkɒmpɪ'leɪʃ(ə)n/ *noun* compilación *f*

'This utility divides the compilation of software into pieces and performs the compile in parallel across available machines on the network.' [*Computergram*]

compilation error /ˌkɒmpɪ'leɪʃ(ə)n ˌerə/ *noun* error *m* de compilación ◇ **compilation errors result in the job being aborted** los errores de compilación hacen que se aborte la tarea

compilation time /ˌkɒmpɪ'leɪʃ(ə)n taɪm/ *noun* tiempo *m* de compilación; duración *f* de la compilación

compile /kəm'paɪl/ *verb* compilar *vt* ◇ **compiled BASIC programs run much faster than the interpretor version** los programas de BASIC compilados son mucho más rápidos que la versión intérprete ◇ **compiling takes a long time with this old version** con esta versión antigua del programa se tarda mucho en compilar ◇ **debug your program, then compile it** corrija los errores de su programa antes de compilarlo

compile phase /kəm'paɪl feɪz/ *noun* fase *f* de compilación

compiler /kəmˌpaɪlə 'prəʊgræm/, **compiler program** *noun* compilador *m*

compiler diagnostics /kəmˌpaɪlə ˌdaɪəg 'nɒstɪks/ *plural noun* herramientas *fpl* de diagnóstico del compilador; diagnóstico *m* mediante el compilador ◇ **thorough compiler diagnostics make debugging easy** un detallado diagnóstico mediante el compilador facilita el proceso de corrección de errores

compiler language /kəm'paɪlə ˌlæŋgwɪdʒ/ *noun* lenguaje *m* de compilación

complement /'kɒmplɪmənt/ *noun* **1.** (*inversion of binary digit*) complemento *m* **2.** (*result of subtraction*) complemento *m* ■ *verb* (*to invert a binary digit*) determinar el complemento (de una cantidad) ◇ **the complement is found by changing the 1s to 0s and 0s to 1s** se encuentra el complemento cambiando los unos a ceros y los ceros a unos

complementary metal oxide semiconductor /ˌkɒmplɪmənt(ə)ri ˌmet(ə)l ˌɒksaɪd 'semɪkənˌdʌktə/ *noun* semiconductor *m* de CMOS; semiconductor *m* complementario de óxido metálico

complementary operation /ˌkɒmplɪmənt(ə)ri ˌɒpə'reɪʃ(ə)n/ *noun* operación *f* complementaria

complementation /ˌkɒmplɪmən'teɪʃ(ə)n/ *noun* números *mpl* completos

complemented /'kɒmplɪməntɪd/ *adjective* complementado *or* -a

complete operation /kəmˌpliːt ˌɒpə 'reɪʃ(ə)n/ *noun* operación *f* completa; operación *f* terminada

completion /kəm'pliːʃ(ə)n/ *noun* terminación *f*; finalización *f* ◇ **completion date for the new software package is November 15th** la fecha de terminación del nuevo paquete de software es el 15 de noviembre

complex instruction set computer /ˌkɒmpleks ɪnˌstrʌkʃən ˌset kəm'pjuːtə/ *noun* ordenador *m* de conjunto de instrucciones complejas

complexity measure /kəm'pleksɪti ˌmeʒə/ *noun* nivel *m* de complejidad; medida *f* de complejidad

compliant /kəm'plaɪənt/ *adjective* acomodaticio *or* -a; compatible ◇ **if you want to read PhotoCD compact discs in your computer you must be sure that the CD-ROM drive is PhotoCD or CD-ROM XA compliant** si desea leer discos compactos de tipo PhotoCD en su ordenador, asegúrese de que su disquetera de CD-ROM es compatible con PhotoCD o con CD-ROM XA

component density /kəmˌpəʊnənt 'densɪti/ *noun* densidad *f* de los componentes

component error /kəm'pəʊnənt ˌerə/ *noun* error *m* de un componente (defectuoso)

Component Object Model /kəmˌpəʊnənt 'ɒbdʒekt ˌmɒd(ə)l/ *noun* modelo *m* de objetos componentes

COM port /'kɒm pɔːt/ *noun* puerto *m* de comunicaciones

composite circuit /ˌkɒmpəzɪt 'sɜːkɪt/ *noun* circuito *m* compuesto

composite display /ˌkɒmpəzɪt dɪ'spleɪ/ *noun* pantalla *f* compuesta; visualización *f* compuesta

composite video /ˌkɒmpəzɪt 'vɪdiəʊ/ *noun* señal *f* de vídeo compuesta

compound /'kɒmpaʊnd/ *adjective* compuesto *or* -a

compound device /ˌkɒmpaʊnd dɪ'vaɪs/ *noun* dispositivo *m* compuesto

compound document /'kɒmpaʊnd ˌdɒkjʊmənt/ *noun* documento *m* compuesto

compound file /'kɒmpaʊnd faɪl/ *noun* fichero *m* compuesto

compound logical element /ˌkɒmpaʊnd ˌlɒdʒɪk(ə)l 'elɪmənt/ *noun* elemento *m* lógico compuesto; elemento *m* lógico múltiple

compound statement /ˌkɒmpaʊnd 'steɪtmənt/ *noun* instrucción *f* compuesta ◇ **the debugger cannot handle compound statements** el depurador de errores no puede gestionar instrucciones compuestas

compressed video /ˌkɒmprest 'vɪdiəʊ/ *noun* vídeo *m* comprimido

compression /kəm'preʃ(ə)n/ *noun* compresión *f*

compression ratio /kəm'preʃ(ə)n ˌreɪʃiəʊ/ *noun* relación *f* de compresión

CompuServe /'kɒmpjuːsɜːv/ (*online information service*) CompuServe™

computer /kəm'pjuːtə/ *noun* (*calculating machine*) ordenador *m*

computer-aided /kəmˌpjuːtə 'eɪdɪd/ *adjective* asistido, -a por ordenador

computer-aided design /kəmˌpjuːtər ˌeɪdɪd dɪ'zaɪn/ *noun* diseño *m* asistido por ordenador (CAD)

computer-aided engineering /kəmˌpjuːtər ˌeɪdɪd ˌendʒɪ'nɪərɪŋ/ *noun* ingeniería *f* asistida por ordenador

computer-aided instruction /kəmˌpjuːtər ˌeɪdɪd ɪn'strʌkʃən/ *noun* instrucción *f* asistida por ordenador

computer-aided learning /kəmˌpjuːtər ˌeɪdɪd 'lɜːnɪŋ/ *noun* aprendizaje *m* asistido por ordenador

computer-aided manufacture /kəmˌpjuːtər ˌeɪdɪd ˌmænjʊ'fæktʃə/ *noun* fabricación *f* asistida por ordenador

computer-aided testing /kəmˌpjuːtər ˌeɪdɪd 'testɪŋ/ *noun* evaluación *f* asistida por ordenador; prueba *f* asistida por ordenador

computer-aided training /kəmˌpjuːtər ˌeɪdɪd 'treɪnɪŋ/ *noun* instrucción *f* asistida por ordenador

computer animation /kəmˌpjuːtə ˌænɪ 'meɪʃ(ə)n/ *noun* animación *f* (de imágenes) por ordenador; animación *f* por ordenador

computer applications /kəmˌpjuːtə ˌæplɪ 'keɪʃ(ə)nz/ *plural noun* aplicaciones *fpl* informáticas

computer architecture /kəmˌpjuːtə 'ɑːkɪtektʃə/ *noun* arquitectura *f* de ordenador

computer-assisted /kəmˌpjuːtər ə'sɪstɪd/ *adjective* asistido, -a por ordenador

computer-assisted design /kəmˌpjuːtər ə ˌsɪstɪd dɪ'zaɪn/ *noun* diseño *m* asistido por ordenador (CAD)

computer-assisted engineering /kəm ˌpjuːtər əˌsɪstɪd ˌendʒɪ'nɪərɪŋ/ *noun* ingeniería *f* asistida por ordenador

computer-assisted instruction /kəm ˌpjuːtər əˌsɪstɪd ɪn'strʌkʃən/ *noun* instrucción *f* asistida por ordenador

computer-assisted learning /kəmˌpjuːtər əˌsɪstɪd 'lɜːnɪŋ/ *noun* aprendizaje *m* asistido por ordenador

computer-assisted manufacture /kəm ˌpjuːtər əˌsɪstɪd ˌmænjʊ'fæktʃə/ *noun* fabricación *f* asistida por ordenador

computer-assisted testing /kəmˌpjuːtər ə ˌsɪstɪd 'testɪŋ/ *noun* comprobación *f* asistida por ordenador

computer-assisted training /kəmˌpjuːtər əˌsɪstɪd 'treɪnɪŋ/ *noun* formación *f* por ordenador

computer-based learning /kəmˌpjuːtə beɪst 'lɜːnɪŋ/ *noun* aprendizaje *m* asistido por ordenador

computer-based message system /kəm ˌpjuːtə beɪst 'mesɪdʒ ˌsɪstəm/ *noun* sistema *m* de mensajería electrónica

computer-based training /kəmˌpjuːtə beɪst 'treɪnɪŋ/ *noun* instrucción *f* asistida por ordenador

computer bureau /kəm'pjuːtə ˌbjʊərəʊ/ *noun* empresa *f* de servicios informáticos

computer code /kəm'pjuːtə kəʊd/ *noun* código *m* de instrucción; código *m* máquina

computer conferencing /kəmˌpjuːtə 'kɒnf(ə)rənsɪŋ/ *noun* (*use of computers and terminals to communicate*) teleconferencia *f*; conexión *f* de ordenadores en modo conversacional; comunicación *f* entre ordenadores ◇ **the multiuser BBS has a computer conferencing facility** el multiusuario del sistema de tablón de anuncios tiene un servicio de comunicación entre ordenadores *or* de teleconferencia

computer crime /kəm'pju:tə kraɪm/ *noun* fraude *m* informático; delito *m* informático

computer dating /kəm,pju:tə 'deɪtɪŋ/ *noun* servicio *m* de contactos; citas *fpl* por ordenador

computer department /kəm'pju:tə dɪ,pɑːtmənt/ *noun* servicio *m* informático; departamento *m* informático

computer engineer /kəm,pju:tə ,endʒɪ'nɪə/ *noun* ingeniero *m* informático

computer error /kəm,pju:tər 'erə/ *noun* error *m* del ordenador

computer file /kəm'pju:tə faɪl/ *noun* fichero *m* informático; fichero *m* de ordenador

computer fraud /kəm'pju:tə frɔːd/ *noun* fraude *m* informático

computer game /kəm'pju:tə geɪm/ *noun* (*game played on a computer*) juego *m* electrónico; videojuego *m*; juego *m* de ordenador

computer-generated /kəm,pju:tə 'dʒenəreɪtɪd/ *adjective* creado por ordenador *or* -a; generado por ordenador *or* -a; producido por ordenador *or* -a; diseñado, -a por ordenador ◇ **computer-generated graphics** gráficos *mpl* diseñados por ordenador *or* infografía *f* ◇ **they analyzed the computer-generated image** analizaron la imagen diseñada por ordenador

computer generation /kəm,pju:tə ,dʒenə'reɪʃ(ə)n/ *noun* generación *f* de ordenadores

computer graphics /kəm,pju:tə 'græfɪks/ *plural noun* (*information displayed graphically*) gráficos *mpl* de ordenador; gráficos *mpl* por ordenador; infografía *f*

computer graphics metafile /kəm,pju:tə ,græfɪks 'metəfaɪl/ *noun* metafichero *m* de gráficos; fichero *m* de gráficos CGM

computer illiterate /kəm,pju:tə ɪ'lɪtərət/ *adjective* (persona) que carece de cualquier conocimiento sobre informática; analfabeto, -a en informática

computer image processing /kəm,pju:tə 'ɪmɪdʒ ,prəʊsesɪŋ/ *noun* proceso *m* informático; tratamiento *m* informático de la imagen

computer-independent language /kəm,pju:tə ,ɪndɪpendənt 'læŋgwɪdʒ/ *noun* lenguaje *m* informático estándar; lenguaje *m* informático independiente

computer indexing /kəm,pju:tə 'ɪndeksɪŋ/ *noun* indexación *f* informática; indexación *f* asistida por ordenador

computer-integrated manufacturing /kəm,pju:tə ,ɪntɪgreɪtɪd ,mænjʊ'fæktʃərɪŋ/ *noun* fabricación *f* integrada por ordenador

computer-integrated system /kəm,pju:tə ,ɪntɪgreɪtɪd 'sɪstəm/ *noun* sistema *m* informático integrado; sistema *m* integrada por ordenador

computerisation /kəm,pjʊtəraɪ'zeɪʃ(ə)n/, **computerization** *noun* informatización *f* ◇ **computerization of the financial sector is proceeding very fast** la informatización del sector financiero se está produciendo muy rápidamente

computerise /kəm'pju:təraɪz/, **computerize** *verb* informatizar *vt*; computarizar *vt* ◇ **our stock control has been completely computerized** nuestra gestión de existencias ha sido totalmente informatizada ◇ **they operate a computerized invoicing system** funcionan con un sistema informatizado de facturación

computer language /kəm'pju:tə ,læŋgwɪdʒ/ *noun* lenguaje *m* informático

computer listing /kəm,pju:tə 'lɪstɪŋ/ *noun* (*printout of a list of items*) listado *m* informático; salida *f* de (la) impresora

computer literacy /kəm,pju:tə 'lɪt(ə)rəsi/ *noun* conocimientos *mpl* informáticos; (nivel de) conocimientos *mpl* de informática

computer-literate /kəm,pju:tə 'lɪt(ə)rət/ *adjective* que tiene conocimientos de informática; (persona) con conocimientos de informática ◇ **the managing director is simply not computer-literate** el director general no posee conocimientos de informática

computer logic /kəm,pju:tə 'lɒdʒɪk/ *noun* lógica *f* de ordenador; lógica *f* informática

computer manager /kəm'pju:tə ,mænɪdʒə/ *noun* director *m* informático

computer network /kəm,pju:tə 'netwɜːk/ *noun* (*shared use of computers, terminals and peripherals*) red *f* de ordenadores; red *f* informática

computer numerical control /kəm,pju:tə nju:,merɪk(ə)l kən'trəʊl/ *noun* control *m* numérico

computer office system /kəm,pju:tər 'ɒfɪs ,sɪstəm/ *noun* sistema *m* informático para oficinas; sistema *m* ofimático

computer operator /kəm'pju:tər ,ɒpəreɪtə/ *noun* operador *m* informático; operador *m or* -a *f*

computer organisation /kəm'pju:tər ,ɔːgənaɪzeɪʃ(ə)n/, **computer organization** *noun* arquitectura *f* de ordenador

computer output /kəm,pju:tər 'aʊtpʊt/ *noun* (*data processed by a computer*) datos *mpl* de salida; salida *f* de (un) ordenador

computer output on microfilm /kəm,pju:tər ,aʊtpʊt ɒn 'maɪkrəʊfɪlm/ *noun* salida *f* de ordenador en microfilm

computer power /kəm'pju:tə ,paʊə/ *noun* potencia *f* de ordenador; potencia *f* de cálculo de un ordenador

computer printer /kəm,pju:tə 'prɪntə/ *noun* impresora *f* de ordenador; impresora *f* (para ordenador)

computer printout /kəm,pju:tə 'prɪntaʊt/ *noun* (*printed information*) salida *f* de la impresora; copia *f* impresa; impresión *f* de ordenador

computer program /kəm'pjuːtə ˌprəʊgræm/ *noun* programa *m* informático; programa *m* de ordenador ◇ **the user cannot write a computer program with this system** el usuario no puede escribir un programa informático con este sistema

computer programmer /kəmˌpjuːtə 'prəʊgræmə/ *noun* programador *m or* -a *f*

computer run /kəm'pjuːtə rʌn/ *noun* ejecución *f* de un programa

computer science /kəmˌpjuːtə 'saɪəns/ *noun* informática *f*

computer services /kəmˌpjuːtə 'sɜːvɪsɪz/ *plural noun* servicios *mpl* informáticos

computer stationery /kəmˌpjuːtə 'steɪʃ(ə)n(ə)ri/ *noun* (*computer printer*) papel *m* informático; papel *m* (continuo) para impresora; papel *m* de listado

computer system /kəm'pjuːtə ˌsɪstəm/ *noun* sistema *m* informático; ordenador *m*

computer-telephony integration /kəm ˌpjuːtə təˌlefəni ˌɪntɪ'greɪʃ(ə)n/ *noun* integración *f* de telefonía e informática

computer time /kəm'pjuːtə taɪm/ *noun* tiempo *m* de ordenador ◇ **running all those sales reports costs a lot in computer time** la gestión de todos esos informes de ventas cuesta mucho en tiempo de ordenador

computer virus /kəm'pjuːtə ˌvaɪrəs/ *noun* virus *m* informático

computer-word /kəm'pjuːtə wɜːd/ *noun* palabra *f* de información; unidad *f* de información

computing /kəm'pjuːtɪŋ/ *adjective, noun* (*science*) informático *or* -a; informática *f*; (*calculation*) cálculo *m* ■ *noun* informática *f*; tecnología *f* de la información

computing power /kəm'pjuːtɪŋ ˌpaʊə/ *noun* poder *m* de cálculo; capacidad *f* de cálculo

computing speed /kəm'pjuːtɪŋ spiːd/ *noun* velocidad *f* de cálculo (por ordenador)

CON /kɒn/ *noun* (*in IBM-PC compatible systems*) consola *f* (IBM o compatible)

concatenate /kən'kætəneɪt/ *verb* encadenar *vt*; concatenar *vt*

concatenated data set /kənˌkætəneɪtɪd 'deɪtə ˌset/ *noun* concatenación *f* de datos; conjunto *m* de datos encadenados

conceal /kən'siːl/ *verb* (*information or graphics*) ocultar *vt*; (*to hide information or graphics*) disimular *vt*; enmascarar *vt* ◇ **the hidden lines are concealed from view with this algorithm** las líneas escondidas se ocultan a la vista con este algoritmo

concentrate /'kɒnsəntreɪt/ *verb* (*to combine line or circuit or data*) concentrar *vt*; condensar *vt*; comprimir *vt*; compactar *vt* ◇ **the concentrated data was transmitted cheaply** los datos comprimidos fueron transmitidos con poco gasto ◇ **to concentrate a beam of light on a lens** concentrar un rayo de luz con una lente

concentrator /'kɒnsəntreɪtə/ *noun* **1.** (*in a Token-Ring network*) concentrador *m* **2.** (*in an*

FDDI network) nudo *m* de acceso a la red **3.** (*in a 10Base-T Ethernet network*) concentrador *m* 10base-T **4.** (*in general networking*) concentrador *m* de red

conceptual model /kənˌseptʃuəl 'mɒd(ə)l/ *noun* (*description of a database*) modelo *m* conceptual

concertina fold /ˌkɒnsə'tiːnə fəʊld/ *noun* papel *m* en acordeón; papel *m* continuo

concurrency /kən'kʌrənsi/ *noun* acceso *m* concurrente

concurrent operating system /kənˌkʌrənt 'ɒpəreɪtɪŋ ˌsɪstəm/ *noun* sistema *m* operativo simultáneo

concurrent processing /kənˌkʌrənt 'prəʊsesɪŋ/ *noun* proceso *m* concurrente; proceso *m* simultáneo ◇ **three transputers provide concurrent processing capabilities for the entire department** tres transordenadores proporcionan utilidades simultáneas de proceso para todo el departamento

concurrent programming /kənˌkʌrənt 'prəʊgræmɪŋ/ *noun* programación *f* concurrente; programación *f* simultánea

condition /kən'dɪʃ(ə)n/ *noun* **1.** (*state of device etc*) condición *f* **2.** (*requirement for action*) condición *f* ■ *verb* (*to modify data*) condicionar *vt*; adaptar *vt* ◇ **condition the raw data to a standard format** adapte los datos en bruto a un formato estándar

conditional /kən'dɪʃ(ə)n(ə)l/ *adjective* **1.** condicional **2.** (*of a process*) condicional ◇ **the conditional branch will select routine one if the response is yes and routine two if no** la bifurcación condicional seleccionará la rutina 1 ó la 2 según sea la respuesta sí o no

conditional branch /kənˌdɪʃ(ə)n(ə)l 'brɑːntʃ/ *noun* bifurcación *f* condicional

conditional breakpoint /kənˌdɪʃ(ə)nəl 'breɪkpɔɪnt/ *noun* parada *f* condicional; punto *m* condicional de interrupción

conditional jump /kən'dɪʃ(ə)nəl dʒʌmp/ *noun* bifurcación *f* condicional

conditional statement /kənˌdɪʃ(ə)nəl 'steɪtmənt/ *noun* instrucción *f* condicional

conditional transfer /kənˌdɪʃ(ə)nəl 'trænsfɜː/ *noun* transferencia *f* condicional; instrucción *f* condicional de bifurcación

condition code /kən'dɪʃ(ə)n kəʊd/ *noun* código *m* de condición

condition code register /kənˌdɪʃ(ə)n 'kəʊd ˌredʒɪstə/ *noun* registro *m* de códigos de condición

conduct /kən'dʌkt/ *verb* conducir *vt*; transmitir *vt* ◇ **copper conducts well** el cobre transmite bien (la señal *or* la electricidad) ◇ **to conduct electricity** conducir la electricidad

conduction /kən'dʌkʃən/ *noun* conductibilidad *f*; conducción *f* ◇ **the conduction of electricity by gold contacts** la conducción de electricidad mediante contactos de oro

conductive /kən'dʌktɪv/ *adjective* conductor *or* -a

conductor /kən'dʌktə/ *noun* conductor *m* ◇ **copper is a good conductor of electricity** el cobre es un buen conductor de la electricidad

conduit /'kɒndjuɪt/ *noun* (*for wires or or cables*) conducto *m*; tubo *m*; manguera *f*; canalización *f* ◇ **the cables from each terminal are channelled to the computer centre by metal conduit** los cables de cada terminal se canalizan al servicio de informática mediante un conducto metálico

conferencing /'kɒnf(ə)rənsɪŋ/ *noun* (*connection by modem*) teleconferencia *f* ◇ **the multiuser BBS has a computer conferencing facility** el multiusuario del sistema de tablón de anuncios tiene un servicio de comunicación entre ordenadores *or* de teleconferencia

'Small organisations and individuals find it convenient to use online services, offering email, conferencing and information services.' [*Computing*]

confidence level /'kɒnfɪd(ə)ns ,lev(ə)l/ *noun* (*statistics*) nivel *m* de confianza

CONFIG.SYS /kən'fɪg sɪs/ *noun* (*configuration text file*) CONFIG.SYS ◇ **if you add a new adapter card to your PC you will have to add a new command to the CONFIG.SYS file** si añade una nueva tarjeta adaptadora a su ordenador personal, tendrá que añadir una instrucción nueva al fichero CONFIG.SYS

configuration /kən,fɪgjə'reɪʃ(ə)n/ *noun* configuración *f*

'He said only Banyan Vines had the network configuration and administration capabilities required for implementing an international business plan based on client-server computing.' [*Computing*]

configuration file /kən,fɪgjə'reɪʃ(ə)n faɪl/ *noun* fichero *m* de configuración

configuration state /kən,fɪgjə'reɪʃ(ə)n steɪt/ *noun* estado *m* de configuración

configure /kən'fɪgə/ *verb* configurar *vt* ◇ **this terminal has been configured to display graphics** este terminal ha sido configurado para visualizar gráficos ◇ **you only have to configure the PC once – when you first buy it** sólo tiene que configurar su ordenador personal una vez, cuando lo compra

configured-in /kən'fɪgəd ɪn/ *adjective* (*device: ready*) configurado *or* -a; (con) configuración válida; preparado, -a para funcionar; disponible

configured-off /kən'fɪgəd ɒf/, **configured-out** /kən'fɪgəd aʊt/ *adjective* (sin) configuración válida; no disponible

congestion /kən'dʒestʃən/ *noun* (*of system*) obstrucción *f*; aglomeración *f*

conjunct /'kɒndʒʌŋkt/ *noun* (*in an logical function*) operando *m* de una instrucción AND; operando *m* de una conjunción

conjunction /kən'dʒʌŋkʃən/ *noun* (*logical function*) conjunción *f*; operación *f* lógica

connect /kə'nekt/ *verb* (*to link circuits or communication networks*) conectar *vt*; establecer una comunicación; asociar *vt*

connect charge /kə'nekt tʃɑːdʒ/ *noun* coste *m* de conexión

connectionless /kə'nekʃənləs/ *adjective* sin conexión

connectionless network protocol /kə,nekʃənləs 'netwɜːk ,prəʊtəkɒl/ *noun* protocolo *m* de red no orientado a la conexión

connection-oriented /kə'nekʃ(ə)n ,ɔːrientɪd/ *adjective* orientado a la conexión

connection-oriented network services /kə,nekʃən ,ɔːrientɪd 'netwɜːk ,sɜːvɪsɪz/ *plural noun* servicios *mpl* de red orientados a la conexión

connective /kə'nektɪv/ *noun* (*symbol between two operands*) conector *m*

connectivity /,kɒnek'tɪvɪti/ *noun* (*ability of a device to connect with other devices*) conectividad *f*

connector /kə'nektə/ *noun* conector *m*; conectador *m* ◇ **the connector at the end of the cable will fit any standard serial port** el conector al final del cable se adapta a cualquier puerta estándar en serie

connector plug /kə'nektə plʌg/ *noun* toma *f* macho del conector

connector receptacle /kə'nektə rɪ,septək(ə)l/ *noun* toma *f* hembra del conector

connect state /kə'nekt steɪt/ *noun* estado *m* de conexión

connect time /kə'nekt taɪm/ *noun* tiempo *m* de conexión

CONS *abbr* (*connection-oriented network services*) servicio *m* de red orientado a la conexión

conscious error /,kɒnʃəs 'erə/ *noun* error *m* consciente

consistency check /kən'sɪstənsi tʃek/ *noun* (*to make sure that data or items conform*) control *m* de coherencia; control *m* de regularidad

console /'kɒnsəʊl/ *noun* (*unit connected to a computer system*) consola *f*; puesto *m*; terminal *m* de trabajo; mesa *f*; consola *f* (de instrucciones) ◇ **the console consists of input device such as a keyboard, and an output device such as a printer or CRT** la consola consiste en un dispositivo de entrada de datos, como el teclado, y un dispositivo de salida de datos, como una impresora o una pantalla

constant /'kɒnstənt/ *noun* (*which does not change*) constante *f*; fijo *m or* -a *f* ■ *adjective* (*as opposed to a variable*) constante *f* ◇ **constant angular velocity (CAV)** velocidad *f* angular constante ◇ **the disk drive motor spins at a constant velocity** el motor de la disquetera gira a una velocidad constante

constant angular velocity /,kɒnstənt ,æŋgjʊlə və'lɒsɪti/ *noun* velocidad *f* angular constante

constant bit rate /,kɒnstənt 'bɪt ,reɪt/ *noun* velocidad *f* constante de bits

constant length field /ˌkɒnstənt leŋθ 'fiːld/ *noun* campo *m* de tamaño fijo

constant linear velocity /ˌkɒnstənt ˌlɪniə vəˈlɒsɪti/ *noun* velocidad *f* lineal constante

constant ratio code /ˌkɒnstənt 'reɪʃiəʊ ˌkəʊd/ *noun* código *m* de proporción constante

constrain /kənˈstreɪn/ *verb* constreñir *vt*

consumables /kənˈsjuːməb(ə)lz/ *plural noun* material *m* fungible

contact /ˈkɒntækt/ *noun* (*section of a switch or connector*) contacto *m*; conexión *f* ■ *verb* contactar *vt* ◇ **contact negative** (*photography*) (film) negativo *m* de contacto ◇ **contact print** prueba *f* (impresa) de contacto ◇ **the circuit is not working because the contact is dirty** el circuito no funciona porque la conexión está sucia

contact bounce /ˈkɒntækt baʊns/ *noun* salto *m* de contacto

contact card /ˈkɒntækt kɑːd/ *noun* tarjeta *f* con contactos

contact image sensor /ˌkɒntækt 'ɪmɪdʒ ˌsensə/ *noun* detector *m* de imágenes por contacto

content /ˈkɒntent/ *noun* (*ideas*) contenido *m*

content-addressable addressing /ˌkɒntent əˌdresəb(ə)l əˈdresɪŋ/ *noun* direccionamiento *m* asociativo; direccionamiento *m* de contenido direccionable

content-addressable file /ˌkɒntent əˌdresəb(ə)l 'faɪl/ *noun* fichero *m* direccionable por el contenido

content-addressable location /ˌkɒntent əˌdresəb(ə)l ləʊˈkeɪʃ(ə)n/ *noun* posición *f* direccionable por el contenido

content-addressable memory /ˌkɒntent əˌdresəb(ə)l 'mem(ə)ri/, **content-addressable storage** /ə,səʊsiətɪv 'stɔːrɪdʒ/ *noun* memoria *f* direccionable por el contenido; memoria *f* asociativa

contention /kənˈtenʃən/ *noun* contención *f*; opinión *f*

contention bus /kənˈtenʃ(ə)n bʌs/ *noun* bus *m* de arbitraje; bus *m* de regulación

contention delay /kənˈtenʃ(ə)n dɪˌleɪ/ *noun* retraso *m* de contención; retardo *m* de contención

content provider /ˈkɒntent prəˌvaɪdə/ *noun* proveedor *m* de contenido

contents /ˈkɒntents/ *plural noun* contenido *m*

context /ˈkɒntekst/ *noun* contexto *m*

context-sensitive /ˌkɒntekst 'sensɪtɪv/ *adjective* (*relating to the particular context*) en función del contexto

context-sensitive help /ˌkɒntekst ˌsensɪtɪv 'help/ *noun* ayuda *f* en función del contexto

context-switching /ˈkɒntekst ˌswɪtʃɪŋ/ *noun* cambio *m* de aplicación

contiguous file /kənˌtɪgjuəs 'faɪl/ *noun* fichero *m* contiguo

contiguous graphics /kənˌtɪgjuəs 'græfɪks/ *plural noun* gráficos *mpl* contiguos ◇ **most display units do not provide contiguous graphics: their characters have a small** space on each side to improve legibility la mayoría de pantallas no disponen de visualización de gráficos contiguos; cada carácter (gráfico) tiene un pequeño espacio a cada lado para mejorar la legibilidad

contingency plan /kənˈtɪndʒənsi plæn/ *noun* plan *m* de urgencia; plan *m* de emergencia

continuation page /kənˌtɪnjʊˈeɪʃ(ə)n peɪdʒ/ *noun* página *f* siguiente; continuación *f*

continuity /ˌkɒntɪˈnjuːɪti/ *noun* (*conduction path*) continuidad *f*

continuous data stream /kənˌtɪnjuəs 'deɪtə ˌstriːm/ *noun* flujo *m* continuo; flujo *m* ininterrumpido de datos

continuous feed /kənˌtɪnjuəs 'fiːd/ *noun* alimentación *f* continua; alimentación *f* ininterrumpida

continuous labels /kənˌtɪnjuəs 'leɪb(ə)lz/ *plural noun* etiquetas *fpl* continuas

continuous loop /kənˌtɪnjuəs 'luːp/ *noun* bucle *m* continuo; ciclo *m* sin fin

continuous signal /kənˌtɪnjuəs 'sɪgn(ə)l/ *noun* señal *f* continua

continuous stationery /kənˌtɪnjuəs 'steɪʃ(ə)n(ə)ri/ *noun* papel *m* continuo

continuous tone /kənˈtɪnjuəs təʊn/ *noun* tono *m* continuo

contouring /ˈkɒntʊərɪŋ/ *noun* hormado *m*

contrast /ˈkɒntrɑːst/ *noun* **1.** (*differences in colours*) contraste *m* **2.** (*knob or key*) botón *m* de contraste; tecla *f* de contraste ◇ **contrast lever** palanca *f* de contraste ◇ **the control allows you to adjust brightness and contrast** la tecla le permite ajustar el brillo y el contraste

contrast enhancement filter /ˌkɒntrɑːst ɪn 'hɑːnsmənt ˌfɪltə/ *noun* filtro *m* de mejora del contraste

control /kənˈtrəʊl/ *noun* **1.** (*section of computer or device that carries out instructions*) control *m*; piloto *m* **2.** (*conditional statement in a program*) instrucción *f* de bifurcación **3.** (*key sending control character*) tecla *f*; datos *mpl* de control **4.** (*data or key that controls*) tecla *f*; datos *mpl* de control ◇ **control card** tarjeta *f* de control ◇ **control program for microcomputers (CP or M)** programa *m* de control para microordenadores ◇ **control signal** señal *f* de control *or* de instrucciones ◇ **control unit (CU)** unidad de control ◇ **to halt a program, press Ctrl-C – the control key and letter C – at the same time** para parar un programa, pulse Ctrl-C -es decir, la tecla de control y la letra C- simultáneamente ◇ **to reset your PC, press Ctrl-Alt-Del** para reiniciar su ordenador personal, pulse Ctrl-Alt-Del

control block /kənˈtrəʊl blɒk/ *noun* bloque *m* (de datos) de control

control bus /kənˈtrəʊl bʌs/ *noun* bus *m* de control; enlace *m* común de control

control change /kənˈtrəʊl tʃeɪndʒ/ *noun* cambio *m* de control

control character /kənˈtrəʊl ˌkærɪktə/ *noun* carácter *m* de control

'...there are seven print control characters which can be placed in a document' [*Personal Computer World*]

control computer /kən'trəʊl kəm,pjuːtə/ *noun* ordenador *m* de control

control cycle /kən'trəʊl ,saɪk(ə)l/ *noun* ciclo *m* de control

control data /kən'trəʊl ,deɪtə/ *noun* datos *mpl* de control; datos *mpl* de instrucción

control-driven /kən'trəʊl ,drɪv(ə)n/ *adjective* accionado, -a por la tecla de control; accionado, -a por la tecla Ctrl

control field /kən'trəʊl fiːld/ *noun* campo *m* de control

control group /kən'trəʊl gruːp/ *noun* grupo *m* testigo; grupo *m* de control

control instruction /kən'trəʊl ɪn,strʌkʃən/ *noun* instrucción *f* de control ◊ **the next control instruction will switch to italics** la próxima intrucción de control cambiará a letra cursiva

control key /kən'trəʊl kiː/ *noun* tecla *f* de control; tecla *f* Ctrl ◊ **to halt a program, press Ctrl-C – the control key and letter C – at the same time** para parar un programa, pulse Ctrl-C -es decir, la tecla de control y la letra C- simultáneamente

control language /kən'trəʊl ,læŋgwɪdʒ/ *noun* lenguaje *m* de control

controlled vocabulary /kən,trəʊld vəʊ'kæbjʊləri/ *noun* vocabulario *m* controlado

controller /kən'trəʊlə/ *noun* controlador *m* de periférico(s)

'...a printer's controller is the brains of the machine. It translates the signals coming from your computer into printing instructions that result in a hard copy of your electronic document' [*Publish*]

control memory /kən'trəʊl ,mem(ə)ri/ *noun* memoria *f* de control

control menu /kən'trəʊl ,menjuː/ *noun* menú *m* de control

control mode /kən'trəʊl məʊd/ *noun* (*state of a device*) modo *m* de control; modo *m* Ctrl

control panel /kən'trəʊl ,pæn(ə)l/ *noun* **1.** tablero *m* de control; cuadro *m* de control **2.** panel *m* de control

control register /kən'trəʊl ,redʒɪstə/ *noun* (*storage location*) registro *m* de control; registro *m* (de instrucciones) de control; registro *m* de instrucciones

control ROM /kən,trəʊl 'rɒm/ *noun* control *m* ROM

control sequence /kən'trəʊl ,siːkwəns/ *noun* secuencia *f* de control; secuencia *f* (de instrucciones) de control

control signals /kən'trəʊl ,sɪgn(ə)lz/ *plural noun* señales *fpl* de control; señales *fpl* de instrucciones

control statement /kən'trəʊl ,steɪtmənt/ *noun* **1.** instrucción *f* de control **2.** instrucción *f* de bifurcación

control structure /kən'trəʊl ,strʌktʃə/ *noun* estructura *f* de control

control systems /kən'trəʊl ,sɪstəmz/ *plural noun* sistemas *mpl* de control

control token /kən'trəʊl ,təʊkən/ *noun* señal *f* de control; ficha *f* de control

control total /kən'trəʊl ,təʊt(ə)l/ *noun* total *m* de verificación; total *m* de control

control transfer /kən'trəʊl ,trænsfɜː/ *noun* transferencia *f* de control

control unit /kən'trəʊl ,juːnɪt/ *noun* unidad *f* de control

control word /kən'trəʊl wɜːd/ *noun* palabra *f* de control

convention /kən'venʃən/ *noun* convención *f*

conventional memory /kən,venʃ(ə)n(ə)l 'mem(ə)ri/ *noun* memoria *f* convencional; memoria *f* base

convergence /kən'vɜːdʒəns/ *noun* convergencia *f*

conversation /,kɒnvə'seɪʃ(ə)n/ *noun* conversación *f*

conversational mode /,kɒnvə'seɪʃ(ə)n(ə)l məʊd/ *noun* modo *m* conversacional; modo *m* interactivo

converse /kən'vɜːs/ *verb* conversar *vt*

conversion /kən'vɜːʃ(ə)n/ *noun* conversión *f*; transformación *f* ◊ **conversion factor** factor *m* de conversión

conversion equipment /kən'vɜːʃ(ə)n ɪ,kwɪpmənt/ *noun* convertidor *m*; equipo *m* convertidor

conversion program /kən'vɜːʃ(ə)n ,prəʊgræm/ *noun* **1.** (*of programs*) programa *m* convertidor; instrucción *f* de conversión **2.** (*of formatting, etc.*) instrucción *f* de conversión

conversion tables /kən'vɜːʃ(ə)n ,teɪb(ə)lz/ *plural noun* **1.** (*of source codes*) tablas *fpl* de equivalencias **2.** (*of stored results*) tablas *fpl* de conversión

converter /kən'vɜːtə/ *noun* convertidor *m* ◊ **analog to digital converter (ADC)** convertidor de analógico a digital ◊ **digital to analog converter (DAC)** convertidor de digital a analógico ◊ **the convertor allowed the old data to be used on the new system** el convertidor permitió que se usaran los datos antiguos en el nuevo sistema

convertibility /kən,vɜːtə'bɪləti/ *noun* convertibilidad *f*

convertible /kən'vɜːtəb(ə)l/ *adjective* convertible

convertor /kən'vɜːtə/ *noun* convertidor *m*

cookie /'kʊki/ *noun* (*data supplied by a remote internet site and stored on the user's hard disk*) cookie *m*

cookie file /'kʊki faɪl/ *noun* fichero *m* favorito

cooperative processing /kəʊ,ɒp(ə)rətɪv 'prəʊsesɪŋ/ *noun* (*system in which computers in a distributed network can execute a part of a program*) proceso *m* cooperativo; proceso *m* de colaboración

coordinate graph /kəʊ'ɔːdɪnət grɑːf/ *noun* gráfico *m* (expresado) en coordenadas

coordinates /kəʊ'ɔːdɪnəts/ *plural noun* co-ordenadas *fpl*

coordination /kəʊˌɔːdɪ'neɪʃ(ə)n/ *noun* coordinación *f*

coprocessor /kəʊ'prəʊsesə/ *noun* coprocesador *m*; procesador *m* auxiliar

'Inmos is hiring designers to create highly integrated transputers and co-processors for diverse computer and telecoms systems.' [*Computing*]

copy /'kɒpɪ/ *verb* (*to duplicate something*) copiar *vt*; hacer una copia; reproducir un documento ◇ **I kept yesterday's copy of 'The Times'** me llevé el ejemplar de 'The Times' de ayer ◇ **make a copy of your data using the COPY command before you edit it** haga una copia de sus datos con la instrucción COPY antes de modificarlos ◇ **there is a memory resident utility which copies the latest files onto backing store every 40 minutes** hay una utilidad residente que copia los últimos ficheros en memoria auxiliar cada 40 minutos

copy protect /ˌkɒpi prə'tekt/ *noun* dispositivo *m* anticopia ■ *verb* proteger contra copias ◇ **all the disks are copy protected** todos los disquetes tienen un dispositivo anticopia ◇ **the program is not copy protected** el programa no está protegido (contra la copia)

copy protection /'kɒpi prəˌtekʃən/ *noun* (*preventing copies from being made*) protección *f* contra la copia; codificación *f* anticopia; sistema *m* de protección contra la copia ◇ **a hard disk may crash because of faulty copy protection** un disco duro puede fallar debido a un sistema defectuoso de protección de copia; un disco duro puede fallar debido a una protección contra la copia defectuosa ◇ **the new program will come without copy protection** el nuevo programa no llevará dispositivo de protección de copia; el nuevo programa no tendrá protección contra la copia

CORAL /'kɒpi/ *noun* CORAL

core /kɔː/ *noun* (*of cable*) alma *f*

core memory /kɔː 'mem(ə)ri/ *noun* memoria *f* central

core program /kɔː 'prəʊgræm/ *noun* programa *m* en la memoria central

coresident /kəʊ'rezɪd(ə)nt/ *adjective* (*program*) corresidente

core store /'kɔː stɔː/ *noun* memoria *f* de núcleos

corona /kə'rəʊnə/ *noun* (*electric discharge that charges toner*) efecto *m* corona; carga *f* estática

corona wire /kə'rəʊnə ˌwaɪə/ *noun* hilo *m* de carga estática ◇ **if your printouts are smudged, you may have to clean the corona wire** si la impresión sale borrosa, quizá deba limpiar el hilo de carga estática

coroutine /'kəʊruːˌtiːn/ *noun* corrutina *f*

corrective maintenance /kəˌrektɪv 'meɪntənəns/ *noun* mantenimiento *m* correctivo; reparación *f*

corrupt /kə'rʌpt/ *adjective* corrompido *or* -a; corrupto *or* -a ■ *verb* (*to introduce errors into something*) corromper *vt*; deteriorar *vt* ◇ **power loss during disk access can corrupt the data** la pérdida de energía durante el acceso al disco puede deteriorar los datos

corruption /kə'rʌpʃən/ *noun* (*faulty data*) corrupción *f*; deterioro *m*; deformación *f* ◇ **acoustic couplers suffer from data corruption more than the direct connect form of modem** los acopladores acústicos son más susceptibles al deterioro de los datos que el módem de conexión directa a la línea

cost analysis /'kɒst əˌnæləsɪs/ *noun* análisis *m* de los costes

counter /'kaʊntə/ *noun* contador *m*

counter-rotating ring /ˌkaʊntə rəʊˌeɪtɪŋ 'rɪŋ/ *noun* anillo *m* de contrarrotación

country file /'kʌntri faɪl/ *noun* (*file in an operating system that defines parameters*) fichero *m* de localización; fichero *m* de país

coupler /'kʌplə/ *noun* acoplador *m*

courseware /'kɔːsweə/ *noun* software *m* didáctico

cpi /ˌsiː piː 'aɪ/ *noun* caracteres *mpl* por pulgada

CPM *abbr* (*critical path method*) método *m* del camino crítico

cps /ˌsiː piː 'es/ *noun* caracteres *mpl* por segundo (cps)

CPU /ˌsiː piː 'juː/ *noun* unidad *f* central (de proceso); procesador *m* central

CPU bound /ˌsiː piː 'juː baʊnd/ *adjective* limitado a la unidad central

CPU clock /ˌsiː piː 'juː klɒk/ *noun* reloj *m* de la unidad central

CPU clock speed /ˌsiː piː 'juː klɒk/ *noun* velocidad *f* del reloj de la unidad central

CPU cycle /ˌsiː piː ˌjuː 'saɪk(ə)l/ *noun* ciclo *m* de la unidad central; ciclo *m* de la CPU

CPU elements /ˌsiː piː ˌjuː 'elɪmənts/ *plural noun* elementos *mpl* de la unidad central; elementos *mpl* de la CPU

CPU handshaking /ˌsiː piː juː 'hændʃeɪkɪŋ/ *noun* protocolo *m* de comunicación; protocolo *m* de intercambio de información entre CPU y periférico

CPU time /ˌsiː piː 'juː taɪm/ *noun* (*time to process instructions*) tiempo *m* de utilización de la unidad central; tiempo *m* de utilización del procesador; tiempo *m* de la CPU

crash /kræʃ/ *noun* (*failure*) fallo *m*; parada *f*; bloqueo *m* ■ *verb* (*to fail suddenly and completely*) fallar *vi*; pararse *vr*; bloquearse *vr*; quedarse bloqueado; deteriorar(se) *vr*; estropear(se) *vr* ◇ **the disk head has crashed and the data may have been lost** la cabeza del disco se ha estropeado y puede que los datos se hayan perdido

crash-protected /kræʃ prə'tektɪd/ *adjective* protegido contra el fallo la destrucción accidental ◇ **if the disk is crash-protected, you will never lose your data** si se dispone de un disco protegido contra el fallo, nunca perderá sus datos

crawler /'krɔːlə/ *noun* araña *f*; rastreador *m*

CRC *abbr* (*cyclic redundancy check*) código *m* de redundancia cíclica

crippled leapfrog test /ˌkrɪp(ə)ld 'liːpfrɒg ˌtest/ *noun* (*standard leapfrog test*) prueba *f* selectiva limitada; comprobación *f* interna parcial de lectura escritura; prueba *f* restringida

critical error /ˌkrɪtɪk(ə)l 'erə/ *noun* error *m* crítico

critical fusion frequency /ˌkrɪtɪk(ə)l 'fjuːʒ(ə)n ˌfriːkwənsi/ *noun* frecuencia *f* crítica de fusión

critical path analysis /ˌkrɪtɪk(ə)l 'pɑːθ ə ˌnæləsɪs/ *noun* análisis *m* de ruta crítica

'Surprisingly, critical path analysis and project management, frequently the next career step for engineers, did not seem to warrant a mention.' [*Computing*]

critical path method /ˌkrɪtɪk(ə)l 'pɑːθ ˌmeθəd/ *noun* método *m* de ruta crítica

critical resource /ˌkrɪtɪk(ə)l rɪ'zɔːs/ *noun* recurso *m* crítico

crop /krɒp/ *verb* **1.** (*reduce the size of an image*) recortar *vt*; cuadrar *vi* **2.** (*cut a rectangular section of image*) recortar (el reborde de una imagen)

crop mark /'krɒp mɑːk/ *noun* (*printed marks that show the edge of a page*) marco *m* de encuadre

cross-assembler /krɒs ə'semblə/ *noun* ensamblador *m* cruzado

cross-compiler /krɒs kəm'paɪlə/ *noun* (*assembler that compiles programs*) compilador *m* cruzado; compilador *m* en cruce ◇ **we can use the cross-compiler to develop the software before the new system arrives** podemos utilizar el compilador cruzado para desarrollar el software antes de que llegue el nuevo sistema

crosshair /'krɒsheə/ *noun* puntero *m* en forma de cruz

cross-linked files /ˌkrɒs lɪŋkt 'faɪlz/ *plural noun* (*error in which two files claim to be using the same cluster on disk*) ficheros *mpl* mezclados; interferencia *f* de ficheros

crossover /'krɒs,əʊvə/ *noun* (*change from one system to another*) transición *f*; cruce *m*; paso *m* ◇ **the crossover to computerized file indexing was difficult** la transición a la indexación informatizada de ficheros fue difícil

cross-reference generator /ˌkrɒs 'ref(ə)rəns ˌdʒenəreɪtə/ *noun* generador *m* de referencias cruzadas

crosstalk /'krɒstɑːk/ *noun* diafonía *f*; interferencia *f* (entre canales de comunicación) ◇ **the crosstalk was so bad, the signal was unreadable** la interferencia era tan fuerte que la señal era ilegible

CRT /ˌsiː ɑː 'tiː/ *noun* tubo *m* de rayos catódicos

crunch /krʌntʃ/ *verb* calcular *vt*

cryogenic memory /ˌkraɪəʊdʒenɪk 'mem(ə)ri/ *noun* memoria *f* criogénica

cryptanalysis /ˌkrɪptə'næləsɪs/ *noun* análisis *m* criptográfico

cryptographic /ˌkrɪptə'græfɪk/ *adjective* criptográfico *or* -a

cryptographic algorithm /ˌkrɪptəgræfɪk 'ælgərɪð(ə)m/ *noun* algoritmo *m* criptográfico

cryptographic key /ˌkrɪptəgræfɪk 'kiː/ *noun* clave *f* criptográfica; clave *f* cifrada

cryptography /ˌkrɪp'tɒgrəfi/ *noun* criptografía *f*

crystal /'krɪstəl/ *noun* cristal *m* ◇ **crystal microphone** micrófono *m* de cristal *or* piezoeléctrico ◇ **crystal oscillator** oscilador *m* de cristal

crystal shutter printer /ˌkrɪst(ə)l ˌʃʌtə 'prɪntə/ *noun* impresora *f* de transferencia LCD

CS *abbr* (*chip select*) selección *f* de un chip; validación *f* de un chip

CSLIP *noun* (*version of the SLIP protocol that compresses data before it is transmitted*) protocolo *m* de línea serie comprimido

CSM /ˌsiː es 'em/ *noun* sistema *m* de reconocimiento de caracteres (por identificación de símbolos combinados)

CSMA-CA /ˌsiː es em siː 'eɪ/ *noun* acceso *m* múltiple con detección de portadora evitando colisiones

CSMA-CD /ˌsiː es em siː 'diː/ *noun* protocolo *m* de transmisión CSMA-CD; acceso *m* múltiple de detección de portadora con detección de colisión

CTI /ˌsiː tiː 'aɪ/ *noun* integración *f* de telefonía e informática

CTR /kən'trəʊl/, **CTRL, Ctrl** *noun* (*control key*) tecla *f* de control; tecla *f* CTR; CTRL; Ctrl

CTS /ˌsiː tiː 'es/ *noun* CTS; (señal de) preparado para transmitir

CU *abbr* (*control unit*) unidad *f* de control

cue /kjuː/ *noun* (mensaje de) invitación *f* a iniciar una instrucción

CUG /ˌsiː juː 'dʒiː/ *noun* grupo *m* de usuario cerrado

cumulative trauma disorder /ˌkjuːmjʊlətɪv 'trɔːmə dɪsˌɔːdə/ *noun* lesión *f* por fatiga crónica

curly brackets /'kɜːli 'brækɪts/, **curly braces** /ˌkɜːli 'breɪsɪz/ *plural noun* llaves *fpl*

current address /ˌkʌrənt ə'dres/ *noun* dirección *f* actual

current address register /ˌkʌrənt ə'dres ˌredʒɪstə/ *noun* registro *m* de direcciones en curso

current directory /ˌkʌrənt daɪ'rekt(ə)ri/ *noun* directorio *m* actual

current drive /ˌkʌrənt 'draɪv/ *noun* disquetera *f* actual

current instruction register /ˌkʌrənt ɪn 'strʌkʃən ˌredʒɪstə/ *noun* registro *m* de instrucciones en curso

cursor /'kɜːsə/ *noun* cursor *m*

'Probably the most exciting technology demonstrated was ScreenCam, which allows users to combine voice, cursor movement and on-screen

activities into a movie which can be replayed.'
[*Computing*]
'...further quick cursor movements are available for editing by combining one of the arrow keys with the control function' [*Personal Computer World*]

cursor control keys /'kɜːsə kən‚trəʊl kiːz/ *plural noun* teclas *fpl* de control del cursor

cursor home /'kɜːsə həʊm/ *noun* esquina *f* izquierda superior; inicio *m* de la pantalla

cursor pad /'kɜːsə pæd/ *noun* teclas *fpl* de control del cursor

custom-built /'kʌstəm bɪlt/ *adjective* personalizado *or* -a; hecho a medida

custom colours /‚kʌstəm 'kʌləs/ *plural noun* colores *m* personalizados

customer engineering /‚kʌstəmə ‚endʒɪ'nɪərɪŋ/ *noun* mantenimiento *m* del equipo de clientes

customer service department /‚kʌstəmə 'sɜːvɪs dɪ‚pɑːtmənt/ *noun* departamento *m* posventa; servicio *m* posventa; departamento *m* de servicio al cliente

customise /'kʌstəmaɪz/, **customize** *verb* (*to modify something so that it meets customers' requirements*) fabricar por encargo; personalizar *vt*; hacer según los requisitos del cliente ◇ **we use customized software** utilizamos software hecho a medida

custom ROM /‚kʌstəm 'rɒm/ *noun* ROM *f* personalizada

cut /kʌt/ *noun* **1.** (*process of deletion*) corte *m* **2.** (*piece removed*) corte *m* ■ *verb* **1.** (*to remove sections of text*) cortar *vt*; reducir *vt* **2.** (*to divide into parts*) partir *vti*; dividir *vt* ◇ **the author was asked to cut his manuscript to 250 pages** se pidió al autor que redujera su manuscrito a 250 páginas ◇ **the editors have asked for cuts in the first chapter** los editores han pedido que se hagan algunos recortes en el primer capítulo

cut and paste /‚kʌt ən 'peɪst/ *noun* cortar y insertar

cut sheet feeder /‚kʌt 'ʃiːt ‚fiːdə/ *noun* (*printing*) alimentador *m* de folios; alimentador *m* de papel cortado; alimentador *m* hoja a hoja

CWP *abbr* (*communicating word processor*) procesador *m* de textos con interfaz de comunicación

cyber- /saɪbə/ *prefix* ciber-

cybercafé /'saɪbə‚kæfeɪ/ *noun* (*internet*) ciber-café *m*

cyberlaw /'saɪbəlɔː/ *noun* ciberley *f*

cybernetics /‚saɪbə'netɪks/ *noun* cibernética *f*

cyberspace /'saɪbəspeɪs/ *noun* ciberespacio *m*

cybersquatting /'saɪbə‚skwɒtɪŋ/ *noun* ciberocupación *f*

cycle /'saɪk(ə)l/ *noun* ciclo *m*

cycle availability /‚saɪk(ə)l ə‚veɪlə'bɪlɪti/ *noun* disponibilidad *f* de ciclo

cycle count /'saɪk(ə)l kaʊnt/ *noun* número *m* de ciclos

cycle index /'saɪk(ə)l ‚ɪndeks/ *noun* índice *m* de ciclo

cycle shift /'saɪk(ə)l ʃɪft/ *verb* desplazamiento *m* de ciclo

cycle stealing /'saɪk(ə)l ‚stiːlɪŋ/ *noun* (utilización en) robo *m* de ciclo

cycle time /'saɪk(ə)l taɪm/ *noun* tiempo *m* de ciclo

cyclic /'sɪklɪk, 'saɪklɪk/ *adjective* cíclico *or* -a; circular

cyclic access /‚saɪklɪk 'ækses/ *noun* acceso *m* cíclico

cyclic check /‚saɪklɪk 'tʃek/ *noun* control *m* cíclico

cyclic code /‚saɪklɪk 'kəʊd/ *noun* código *m* cíclico

cyclic decimal code /‚saɪklɪk 'desɪm(ə)l kəʊd/ *noun* código *m* decimal cíclico

cyclic redundancy check /‚sɪklɪk rɪ'dʌndənsi ‚tʃek/ *noun* prueba *f* cíclica de redundancia

cyclic shift /‚saɪklɪk 'ʃɪft/ *noun* desplazamiento *m* cíclico

cylinder /'sɪlɪndə/ *noun* **1.** (*group of tracks on a disk*) cilindro *m* **2.** (*tracks on a multidisk device*) cilindro *m*

cypher /'saɪfə/ *noun* cifra *f*

D

D *symbol* (*hexadecimal number equivalent to decimal 13*) número hexadecimal 13; D

DA *abbr* (*desk accessory*) accesorio *m* de escritorio

DAC /ˌdiː eɪ 'siː/ *noun* convertidor *m* digital-analógico

d/a converter /ˌdiː tʊ eɪ kən'vɜːtə/ *noun* convertidor *m* digital/analógico

daemon /'diːmən/ *noun* (*utility program in a UNIX system*) utilidad *f* UNIX demonio; demonio *m*

daisy chain /'deɪzi tʃeɪn/ *noun* cadena *f* margarita; cadena *f* mariposa

daisy chain bus /ˌdeɪzi tʃeɪn 'bʌs/ *noun* (*communication bus*) encadenamiento *m* mariposa; enlace *m* común de cadena mariposa; enlace *m* de cadena (margarita); encadenamiento *m* margarita

daisy-chaining /'deɪzi tʃeɪnɪŋ/ *noun* (*connecting equipment*) conexión *f* en cadena; unión *f* en cadena; conexión *f* en cascada ◇ **daisy-chaining saves a lot of cable** la conexión en cadena ahorra mucho cable

daisy chain interrupt /ˌdeɪzi tʃeɪn 'ɪntərʌpt/ *noun* interrupción *f* en serie; interrupción *f* en cadena

daisy chain recursion /ˌdeɪzi tʃeɪn rɪ'kɜːʒ(ə)n/ *noun* bucle *m* de recurrencia; bucle *m* de cadena margarita

DAL *abbr* (*data access language*) lenguaje *m* de acceso a los datos

DAMA *abbr* (*demand assigned multiple access*) acceso *m* múltiple según demanda

DAO /ˌdiː eɪ 'əʊ/ *noun* interfase de los programas de Microsoft que sirve para conectar los programas con los datos

dark fibre /ˌdɑːk 'faɪbə/ *noun* fibra *f* vacía; fibra *f* sin señal

DAS *abbr* (*dual attached station*) estación *f* de doble conexión

DASD /ˌdiː eɪ es 'diː/ *noun* dispositivo *m* de almacenamiento de acceso directo

DAT /ˌdiː eɪ 'tiː/ *noun* (*system of recording sound as digital information on DAT tape*) cinta *f* audiodigital; grabación *f*

data /'deɪtə/ *noun* datos *mpl*; información *f* ◇ **all the files were stored on one disk with this new data compacting routine** se grabaron todos los ficheros en un solo disco mediante esta nueva rutina de compresión de datos ◇ **a user needs a password to access data** un usuario necesita una contraseña para acceder a los datos ◇ **data above voice (DAV)** (transmisión de) datos supravocales ◇ **data area** área *f* de datos ◇ **data below voice (DBV)** (transmisión de) datos infravocales ◇ **data communications equipment (DCE)** equipo *m* de comunicación de datos *or* de información ◇ **data corruption occurs each time the motor is switched on** cada vez que se enciende el motor hay un deterioro de los datos ◇ **data description language (DDL)** lenguaje *m* de descripción de datos *or* de información ◇ **data dictionary** *or* **directory (DD** *or* **D)** diccionario/directorio *m* de datos ◇ **data encryption standard (DES)** estándar *m* de puesta en clave de datos ◇ **data flow diagram (DFD)** diagrama *m* de flujo datos ◇ **data input bus (DIB)** bus *m* de entrada de datos ◇ **data interchange format (DIF)** (*standard method of storing spreadsheet data*) formato *m* de intercambio de datos *or* formato DIF ◇ **data is input at one of several workstations** los datos se introducen en una de las diversas estaciones de trabajo ◇ **scanners use a technique called data compression which manages to reduce, even by a third, the storage required** los escáners utilizan una técnica denominada compresión de datos que consigue reducir, hasta un tercio, la memoria necesaria ◇ **the company stores data on customers in its main computer file** la empresa almacena la información sobre los clientes en su ordenador central ◇ **the data file has to be analysed** se tiene que analizar el fichero de datos ◇ **the data flowchart allowed us to improve throughput, by using a better structure** el diagrama de flujo de datos nos permitió mejorar los resultados al utilizar una estructura mejor

data access language /ˌdeɪtə 'ækses ˌlæŋgwɪdʒ/ *noun* lenguaje *m* de acceso a los datos

data access management /ˌdeɪtə 'ækses ˌmænɪdʒmənt/ *noun* gestión *f* de acceso a los datos

data access objects /ˌdeɪtə 'ækses ˌɒbjekts/ *plural noun* interfaz *f* de los programas de Microsoft que sirve para conectar los programas con los datos

data acquisition /'deɪtə ækwɪˌzɪʃ(ə)n/ *noun* adquisición *f* de datos

data adapter unit /ˌdeɪtə ə'dæptə ˌjuːnɪt/ *noun* (*device that interfaces a CPU*) unidad *f* adaptadora de datos; adaptador *m* de canal de transmisión de datos

data administrator /ˌdeɪtə əd'mɪnɪstreɪtə/ *noun* (*database management system*) gestor *m* de datos; administrador *m* de (base de) datos

data aggregate /'deɪtə ˌægrɪgət/ *noun* (*collection of related data items*) agregado *m* de datos

data analysis /ˌdeɪtə ə'næləsɪs/ *noun* análisis *m* de datos

data area /'deɪtə ˌeəriə/ *noun* zona *f* de datos; área *f* de datos

databank /'deɪtəbæŋk/ *noun* banco *m* de datos

database /'deɪtəbeɪs/ *noun* base *f* de datos
'This information could include hypertext references to information held within a computer database, or spreadsheet formulae.' [*Computing*]

database administrator /ˌdeɪtəbeɪs əd'mɪnɪstreɪtə/ *noun* administrador *m* de base de datos

database engine /'deɪtəbeɪs ˌendʒɪn/ *noun* motor *m* de base de datos

database language /'deɪtəbeɪs ˌlæŋgwɪdʒ/ *noun* lenguaje *m* de base de datos

database machine /ˌdeɪtəbeɪs mə'ʃiːn/ *noun* máquina *f* de base de datos

database management system /ˌdeɪtəbeɪs 'mænɪdʒmənt ˌsɪstəm/, **database manager** /ˌdeɪtəbeɪs 'mænɪdʒə/ *noun* sistema *m* de administración de bases de datos

database mapping /'deɪtəbeɪs ˌmæpɪŋ/ *noun* (*database management system*) topología *f*; configuración *f*; planificación *f* de una base de datos; (*device which receives data*) configuración *f* de una base de datos

database schema /ˌdeɪtəbeɪs 'skiːmə/ *noun* esquema *m* de base de datos

database server /ˌdeɪtəbeɪs 'sɜːvə/ *noun* sistema *m* de gestión de base de datos

database system /'deɪtəbeɪs ˌsɪstəm/ *noun* sistema *m* de base de datos

data block /'deɪtə blɒk/ *noun* bloque *m* de datos

data break /'deɪtə breɪk/ *noun* interrupción *f* (de transmisión) de datos; interrupción *f* de información

data buffer /'deɪtə ˌbʌfə/ *noun* memoria *f* intermedia de datos

data bus /'deɪtə bʌs/ *noun* (*bus carrying data*) enlace *m* común *m*; enlace *m*; bus *m* de datos

data bus connector /ˌdeɪtə 'bʌs kəˌnektə/ *noun* conector *m* DB

data capture /'deɪtə ˌkæptʃə/ *noun* (*obtaining data into a computer system*) captura *f* de datos; obtención *f* de datos; recogida *f* de datos; captación *f* de datos ◇ **data capture starts when an interrupt is received** la recogida de datos se inicia cuando se recibe una señal de interrupción

data carrier /'deɪtə ˌkæriə/ *noun* **1.** soporte *m* de datos **2.** onda *f* portadora de datos

data cartridge /'deɪtə ˌkɑːtrɪdʒ/ *noun* (*cartridge that contains data*) cargador *m* de datos; cargador *m* de información; cartucho *m* de datos

data cassette /'deɪtə kəˌset/ *noun* casete *f* de datos

data chaining /'deɪtə ˌtʃeɪnɪŋ/ *noun* (*data storage*) encadenamiento *m* de datos; encadenamiento *m* de información; enlace *m* de datos en cadena

data channel /'deɪtə ˌtʃæn(ə)l/ *noun* canal *m* de datos; canal *m* (de transmisión) de datos

data check /'deɪtə tʃek/ *noun* breve interrupción *f* en la transmisión de datos; comprobación *f* de datos

data circuit /'deɪtə ˌsɜːkɪt/ *noun* circuito *m* de datos

data cleaning /'deɪtə ˌkliːnɪŋ/ *noun* (*data storage*) limpieza *f* de datos; depuración *f* de datos; limpieza *f* de información; corrección *f* de errores; eliminación *f* de errores

data collection /'deɪtə kəˌlekʃən/ *noun* (*data storage*) recogida *f* de datos; recopilación *f* de datos; recopilación *f* de información

data collection platform /ˌdeɪtə kə'lekʃən ˌplætfɔːm/ *noun* (*station that transmits collected data*) plataforma *f* de recogida de datos

data communications /ˌdeɪtə kəˌmjuːnɪ'keɪʃ(ə)nz/ *noun* (*transmission and reception of data*) comunicación *f*; telemática *f*; transmisión *f* de datos; comunicaciones *fpl* de datos; comunicaciones *fpl* de información

data communications buffer /ˌdeɪtə kəˌmjuːnɪ'keɪʃ(ə)nz ˌbʌfə/ *noun* memoria *f* intermedia de transmisión de datos

data communications equipment /ˌdeɪtə kəˌmjuːnɪ'keɪʃ(ə)nz ɪˌkwɪpmənt/ *noun* equipo *m* de comunicación de datos; equipo *m* de información

data communications network /ˌdeɪtə kəˌmjuːnɪ'keɪʃ(ə)nz ˌnetwɜːk/ *noun* red *f* de comunicación de datos

data compacting /'deɪtə ˌkɒmpæktɪŋ/ *noun* (*reducing data storage*) concentración *f* de datos; compactación *f* de datos; condensación *f* de datos; compresión *f* de datos; compresión *f* de información ◇ **all the files were stored on one disk with this new data compacting routine** se grabaron todos los ficheros en un solo disco mediante esta nueva rutina de compresión de datos

data compression /ˌdeɪtə kəm'preʃ(ə)n/ *noun* (*reducing size of data*) compresión *f* de datos; concentración *f* de datos; condensación *f* de datos; condensación *f* de información ◇ **scanners use a technique called data compression which manages to reduce, even by a third, the storage required** los escáners utilizan una técnica denominada compresión de datos que consigue reducir, hasta un tercio, la memoria necesaria

data concentrator /'deɪtə ˌkɒns(ə)ntreɪtə/ *noun* concentrador *m* de datos; concentrador *m* de información

data connection /ˌdeɪtə kə'nekʃ(ə)n/ *noun* conexión *f* (por transmisión) de datos

data control /'deɪtə kənˌtrəʊl/ *noun* control *m* de datos

data corruption /'deɪtə kə,rʌpʃ(ə)n/ *noun* (*introduction of errors into data*) deterioro *m* de datos; corrupción *f* de datos; deterioro *m* de los datos ◇ **acoustic couplers suffer from data corruption more than the direct connect form of modem** los acopladores acústicos son más susceptibles al deterioro de los datos que el módem de conexión directa a la línea ◇ **data corruption occurs each time the motor is switched on** cada vez que se enciende el motor hay un deterioro de los datos ◇ **data corruption on the disk has made one file unreadable** el deterioro de datos en el disco ha resultado en un fichero ilegible

data delimiter /'deɪtə diː,lɪmɪtə/ *noun* delimitador *m* de datos

data description language /,deɪtə dɪ 'skrɪpʃən ,læŋgwɪdʒ/ *noun* lenguaje *m* de descripción de datos; lenguaje *m* de información ◇ **many of DDL's advantages come from the fact that it is a second generation language** muchas de las ventajas de un lenguaje de descripción de datos provienen del hecho de que se trata de un lenguaje de segunda generación

data dictionary/directory /,deɪtə ,dɪkʃən(ə)ri daɪ'rekt(ə)ri/ *noun* diccionario/directorio *m* de datos

data division /'deɪtə dɪ,vɪʒ(ə)n/ *noun* (sección de programa para la) descripción *f* de datos

data-driven /'deɪtə ,drɪv(ə)n/ *adjective* activado, -a por reconocimiento de datos

data element /'deɪtə ,elɪmənt/ *noun* elemento *m* de datos

data element chain /,deɪtə 'elɪmənt ,tʃeɪn/ *noun* cadena *f* de elementos de datos

data encryption /'deɪtə ɪn,krɪpʃ(ə)n/ *noun* (*process of encrypting data using a cipher system*) puesta *f* en clave de datos; encriptado *m* de datos; encriptado *m* de información

data encryption standard /,deɪtə ɪn 'krɪpʃən ,stændəd/ *noun* norma *f* de puesta en clave de datos; estándar *m* de puesta en clave de datos

data entry /,deɪtə 'entri/ *noun* (*entering data into a system*) entrada *f* de datos; introducción *f* de datos; introducción *f* de información

data error /'deɪtə ,erə/ *noun* error *m* de datos

data field /'deɪtə fiːld/ *noun* campo *m* de datos

data file /'deɪtə faɪl/ *noun* fichero *m* de datos ◇ **the data file has to be analysed** se tiene que analizar el fichero de datos

data flow /'deɪtə fləʊ/ *noun* flujo *m* de datos

data flowchart /,deɪtə 'fləʊtʃɑːt/ *noun* organigrama *m* del flujo de datos; diagrama *m* del flujo de datos ◇ **the data flowchart allowed us to improve throughput, by using a better structure** el diagrama de flujo de datos nos permitió mejorar los resultados al utilizar una estructura mejor

data flow diagram /'deɪtə fləʊ ,daɪəgræm/ *noun* diagrama *m* de flujo de datos

data format /'deɪtə ,fɔːmæt/ *noun* formato *m* de datos

data glove /'deɪtə glʌv/ *noun* guante *m* de datos; guante *m* electrónico

datagram /'deɪtəgræm/ *noun* diagrama *m* de datos; datagrama *m*

data hierarchy /,deɪtə 'haɪərɑːki/ *noun* estructura *f* jerárquica de datos; jerarquía *f* de datos

data highway /,deɪtə 'haɪweɪ/ *noun* (*transfer of data*) enlace *m* común; enlace *m* de transferencia de datos; bus *m* de transferencia de datos

data independence /,deɪtə ,ɪndɪ'pendəns/ *noun* independencia *f* de datos

data input /,deɪtə 'ɪnpʊt/ *noun* entrada *f* de datos; introducción *f* de datos

data input bus /,deɪtə 'ɪnpʊt ,bʌs/ *noun* bus *m* de entrada de datos

data integrity /,deɪtə ɪn'tegrɪti/ *noun* integridad *f* de datos; integridad *f* de información

data interchange format /,deɪtə 'ɪntətʃeɪndʒ ,fɔːmæt/ *noun* formato *m* de intercambio de datos; formato *m* DIF

data item /'deɪtə ,aɪtəm/ *noun* elemento *m* de datos

data jack /'deɪtə dʒæk/ *noun* clavija *f* para teléfono; clavija *f* para módem

data level /'deɪtə ,lev(ə)l/ *noun* nivel *m* de datos

data link /'deɪtə lɪŋk/ *noun* enlace *m* de datos

data link control /,deɪtə lɪŋk kən'trəʊl/ *noun* control *m* de enlace de datos

data link layer /'deɪtə lɪŋk ,leɪə/ *noun* (*data transmission*) capa *f* de enlace de datos

data logging /'deɪtə ,lɒgɪŋ/ *noun* (*automatic data collection*) registro *m* automático y cronológico de datos; inscripción *f* de datos; inscripción *f* de información

data management /'deɪtə ,mænɪdʒmənt/ *noun* gestión *f* de datos

data manipulation language /,deɪtə mə ,nɪpjʊ'leɪʃ(ə)n ,læŋgwɪdʒ/ *noun* lenguaje *m* de manipulación de datos

data medium /'deɪtə ,miːdiəm/ *noun* soporte *m* de datos; soporte *m* de información

data migration /,deɪtə maɪ'greɪʃ(ə)n/ *noun* (*data transfer*) transferencia *f* de datos; migración *f* de datos

data mining /'deɪtə ,maɪnɪŋ/ *noun* extracción *f* de datos

'Both companies specialise in decision support, statistical analysis and data mining.' [*The Guardian*]

data name /'deɪtə neɪm/ *noun* nombre *m* ◇ **problems occur if an ambiguous data name is chosen** hay problemas cuando se elige un nombre de datos ambiguo

data network /'deɪtə ,netwɜːk/ *noun* red *f* de datos

data origination /'deɪtə ə,rɪdʒɪneɪʃ(ə)n/ *noun* generación *f* de datos; creación *f* de datos

data path /'deɪtə pɑːθ/ *noun* (*data transfer*) camino *m* de datos; trayecto *m* de datos; voz *f* de transmisión de datos

dataplex /'deɪtəpleks/ *noun* multiplexaje *m* de datos

data pointer /'deɪtə ˌpɔɪntə/ *noun* (*data storage*) puntero *m* de datos; puntero *m* (de posición) de datos; indicador *m* de datos

dataport /'deɪtəpɔːt/ *noun* puerto *m* de datos

data preparation /ˌdeɪtə ˌprepə'reɪʃ(ə)n/ *noun* preparación *f* de datos

data processing /ˌdeɪtə 'prəʊsesɪŋ/ *noun* tratamiento *m* de datos; proceso *m* de la información

data processing manager /ˌdeɪtə 'prəʊsesɪŋ ˌmænɪdʒə/ *noun* responsable *m&f* de servicio informático

data projector /'deɪtə prəˌdʒektə/ *noun* proyector *m* de datos; cañón *m*

data protection /'deɪtə prəˌtekʃən/ *noun* (*data storage*) protección *f* de datos; seguridad *f* de (los) datos

Data Protection Act /ˌdeɪtə prə'tekʃən ˌækt/ *noun* ley *f* de seguridad informática; Ley *f* de Protección de Datos

data rate /'deɪtə reɪt/ *noun* velocidad *f* de tratamiento; velocidad *f* de transmisión de datos

data record /'deɪtə ˌrekɔːd/ *noun* registro *m* de datos

data reduction /ˌdeɪtə rɪ'dʌkʃən/ *noun* reducción *f* de datos

data register /'deɪtə ˌredʒɪstə/ *noun* registro *m* de datos

data reliability /'deɪtə rɪˌlaɪəbɪlɪti/ *noun* calidad *f* de datos; fiabilidad *f* de datos

data retrieval /ˌdeɪtə rɪ'triːv(ə)l/ *noun* recuperación *f* de datos; búsqueda *f* documental

data routing /'deɪtə ˌruːtɪŋ/ *noun* encaminamiento *m*; (asignación de) ruta *f* de datos

data security /'deɪtə sɪˌkjʊərɪti/ *noun* seguridad *f* de los datos; seguridad *f* de la información

dataset /'deɪtəset/ *noun US* módem *m*; convertidor *m* de señal

data set ready /ˌdeɪtə set 'redi/ *noun* señal *f* de preparado para recibir

data sharing /'deɪtə ˌʃeərɪŋ/ *noun* utilización *f* compartida de los datos; utilización GENDER>f de datos compartidos

data signalling rate /ˌdeɪtə 'sɪɡn(ə)lɪŋ ˌreɪt/ *noun* tasa *f* de transmisión de datos; velocidad *f* de transmisión de datos

data signals /'deɪtə ˌsɪɡn(ə)lz/ *plural noun* señales *fpl* de transmisión de datos

data sink /'deɪtə sɪŋk/ *noun* (*device which receives data*) receptor *m* de datos; depósito *m* de datos; destino *m* de datos

data source /'deɪtə sɔːs/ *noun* fuente *f* de datos

data station /'deɪtə ˌsteɪʃ(ə)n/ *noun* estación *f* de datos

data storage /'deɪtə ˌstɔːrɪdʒ/ *noun* (*medium for holding information*) memoria *f* de datos; almacenamiento *m* de datos

data stream /'deɪtə striːm/ *noun* flujo *m* de datos; flujo *m* de información

data strobe /'deɪtə strəʊb/ *noun* (señal de) validación *f* de datos (transmitidos)

data structure /'deɪtə ˌstrʌktʃə/ *noun* estructura *f* de datos

data switching exchange /ˌdeɪtə 'swɪtʃɪŋ ɪks,tʃeɪndʒ/ *noun* dispositivo *m* de intercambio de datos

data tablet /'deɪtə ˌtæblət/ *noun* tablilla *f* gráfica; pizarra *f* gráfica

data terminal /'deɪtə ˌtɜːmɪn(ə)l/ *noun* terminal *m* de datos; terminal *m* informático ◇ **a printer is a data terminal for computer output** una impresora es un terminal informático para la salida de datos

data terminal equipment /'deɪtə ˌtɜːmɪn(ə)l ɪˌkwɪpmənt/ *noun* terminal *m* de transmisión de datos

data terminal ready /ˌdeɪtə ˌtɜːmɪn(ə)l 'redi/ *noun* preparado para transmitir

data transaction /'deɪtə træn,zækʃən/ *noun* transacción *f* de datos

data transfer rate /ˌdeɪtə 'trænsfɜː ˌreɪt/ *noun* tasa *f* de transferencia de datos; velocidad *f* de transferencia de datos

data translation /'deɪtə træns,leɪʃ(ə)n/ *noun* conversión *f* de datos; traducción *f* de datos

data transmission /'deɪtə trænz,mɪʃ(ə)n/ *noun* transmisión *f* de datos/información

data type /'deɪtə taɪp/ *noun* tipo *m* de datos

data validation /'deɪtə ˌvælɪdeɪʃ(ə)n/ *noun* validación *f* de datos; comprobación *f* de datos

data vetting /'deɪtə ˌvetɪŋ/ *noun* validación *f* de datos; verificación *f* de datos

data warehouse /'deɪtə ˌweəhaʊs/ *noun* almacén *m* de datos

data word /'deɪtə wɜːd/ *noun* palabra *f* (de información)

data word length /ˌdeɪtə 'wɜːd ˌleŋθ/ *noun* longitud *f* de una palabra de información

DAT drive /'dæt draɪv/ *noun* (*to record and retrieve data*) lector *m* de cinta audionumérica; lector *m* de cinta audio digital; lector *m* audio digital; lector *m* DAT ◇ **we use a DAT drive as the backup device for our network** utilizamos un lector DAT como dispositivo de seguridad de la red

date /deɪt/ *noun* fecha *f*

date-time /ˌdeɪt 'taɪm/ *noun* fecha/hora *f*

daughter board /'dɔːtə bɔːd/ *noun* placa *f* hija

daylight saving time /ˌdeɪlaɪt 'seɪvɪŋ ˌtaɪm/ *noun* horario *m* de verano

dB *abbr* (*decibel*) decibelio (dB) *m*

DBA /ˌdiː biː 'eɪ/ *noun* administrador *m* de base de datos

DB connector /ˌdiː biː kə'nektə/ *noun* (*D-shape connector*) conector *m* DB

DBMS /ˌdiː biː em ˈes/ *noun* sistema *m* de administración de bases de datos

DC *abbr* (*direct current*) corriente *m* continua

DCC /ˌdiː siː ˈsiː/ *noun* casete *f* digital compacto

DCD /ˌdiː siː ˈdiː/ *noun* detección *f* de portadora de datos

DCE *abbr* (*data communications equipment*) equipo *m* de comunicación de datos

DC signalling /ˌdiː siː ˈsɪgn(ə)lɪŋ/ *noun* transmisión *f* directa de señales

DCT *abbr* (*discrete cosine transform*) transformación *f* discreta de cosenos

DD *abbr* (*double density*) doble densidad *f*

DDC /ˌdiː diː ˈsiː/ *noun* control *m* digital directo

DD/D /ˌdiː diː ˈdiː/ *noun* diccionario/directorio *m* de datos

DDE /ˌdiː diː ˈiː/ *noun* **1.** (*direct data entry*) entrada *f* directa de datos (mediante el teclado) **2.** (*dynamic data exchange*) intercambio *m* dinámico de datos

DDL /ˌdiː diː ˈel/ *noun* lenguaje *m* de información; lenguaje *m* de descripción de datos

DDP /ˌdiː diː ˈpiː/ *noun* proceso *m* de datos distribuido

dead /ded/ *adjective* (*not working*) fuera de servicio; inutilizado *or* -a

deaden /ˈded(ə)n/ *verb* (*sound or colour*) amortiguar *vt*; atenuar *vt*; suavizar *vt* ◇ **acoustic hoods are used to deaden the noise of printers** se utilizan unas cubiertas insonorizadas para amortiguar el ruido de las impresoras

dead halt /ˈded hɔːlt/ *noun* parada *f* total

dead key /ˈded kiː/ *noun* tecla *f* de función inutilizadas (que no producen caracteres)

deadlock /ˈded.lɒk/, **deadly embrace** /ˈdedli ɪmˈbreɪs/ *noun* interbloqueo *m*; punto *m* muerto

dead time /ˈded taɪm/ *noun* tiempo *m* muerto; tiempo *m* de espera (entre dos operaciones)

deallocate /diːˈæləkeɪt/ *verb* liberar *vt* ◇ **when a reset button is pressed all resources are deallocated** cuando se presiona la tecla de reinicio se liberan todos los recursos

debit /ˈdebɪt/ *noun* (*in informatics*) débito *m* debe; tasa *f* de transmisión de bits

deblock /diːˈblɒk/ *verb* separar los elementos de un bloque

de-bounce /diː ˈbaʊns/ *noun* antirrebote *m*

de-bounce circuit /diː ˈbaʊns ˌsɜːkɪt/ *noun* circuito *m* antirrebote

debug /diːˈbʌg/ *verb* depurar *vt*; eliminar errores

'Further questions, such as how you debug an application built from multi-sourced software to run on multisourced hardware, must be resolved at this stage.' [*Computing*]

DEBUG /diːˈbʌg/ *noun* (*software utility in MS-DOS*) DEBUG

debugged program /ˌdiːbʌgd ˈprəʊgræm/ *noun* programa *m* corregido; programa *m* depurado

debugger /diːˈbʌgə/ *noun* (*identification of errors in a program*) depurador *m*; programa *m* de depuración; programa *m* de corrección de errores ◇ **the debugger cannot handle compound statements** el depurador de errores no puede gestionar instrucciones compuestas

decade /ˈdekeɪd/ *noun* decena *f*; década *f* ◇ **decade counter** contador *m* de decenas

decay /dɪˈkeɪ/ *noun* (*process of a sound signal fading away*) debilitamiento *m*; extinción *f*; decaimiento *m* (de un sonido) ◇ **decay time** (*of signal*) tiempo *m*; intervalo *m* de amortiguamiento *or* descenso *or* decaimiento de una señal ◇ **with a short decay, it sounds very sharp** con una pequeña debilitación, suena de forma muy aguda

deceleration time /diːˌseləˈreɪʃ(ə)n ˌtaɪm/ *noun* (*time taken for an access arm to come to a stop*) tiempo *m* de deceleración

decentralised computer network /diːˌsentrəˌlaɪzd kəmˈpjuːtə/, **decentralized computer network** *noun* red *f* informática descentralizada

decentralised data processing /diːˌsentrəˌlaɪzd ˈdeɪtə/, **decentralized data processing** *noun* tratamiento *m* descentralizado de datos

decibel /ˈdesɪbel/ *noun* decibelio *m* (dB)

deciding factor /dɪˌsaɪdɪŋ ˈfæktə/ *noun* factor *m* de decisión; argumento *m* decisivo ◇ **the deciding factor was the superb graphics** el factor decisivo fue la excelente calidad de los gráficos

decimal tabbing /ˌdesɪm(ə)l ˈtæbɪŋ/ *noun* tabulación *f* decimal

decimal tab key /ˌdesɪm(ə)l ˈtæb ˌkiː/ *noun* tecla *f* de tabulación decimal

decimal-to-binary conversion /ˌdesɪm(ə)l tə ˌbaɪnəri kənˈvɜːʃ(ə)n/ *noun* conversión *f* decimal-binaria

decipher /dɪˈsaɪfə/ *verb* descifrar *vt*

decision box /dɪˈsɪʒ(ə)n bɒks/ *noun* caja *f* de decisión

decision circuit /dɪˈsɪʒ(ə)n ˌsɜːkɪt/ *noun* circuito *m* de decisión

decision instruction /dɪˈsɪʒ(ə)n ɪnˌstrʌkʃən/ *noun* instrucción *f* de decisión; instrucción *f* condicional

decision support system /dɪˌsɪʒ(ə)n sə ˈpɔːt ˌsɪstəm/ *noun* sistema *m* de ayuda a la decisión

decision table /dɪˈsɪʒ(ə)n ˌteɪb(ə)l/ *noun* tabla *f* de decisión

decision tree /dɪˈsɪʒ(ə)n triː/ *noun* árbol *m* de decisiones

deck /dek/ *noun* cubierta *f*; superficie *f*

declaration /ˌdeklə'reɪʃ(ə)n/ *noun* declaración *f*

declarative language /dɪˌklærətɪv ˈlæŋgwɪdʒ/ *noun* lenguaje *m* declarativo

declarative statement /dɪˌklærətɪv ˈsteɪtmənt/ *noun* declaración *f*

decode /diːˈkəʊd/ *verb* descodificar *vt*; descifrar *vt*

decoder /diːˈkəʊdə/ *noun* descodificador *m*

decode unit /diːˈkəʊd ˌjuːnɪt/ *noun* decodificador *m*

decollate /ˌdiːkəˈleɪt/ *verb* (*continuous stationery*) separar *vt*

decollator /ˌdiːkəˈleɪtə/ *noun* separador *m or -* a *f*

decompilation /diːˌkɒmpɪˈleɪʃ(ə)n/ *noun* descompilación *f*

decompress /ˌdiːkəmˈpres/ *verb* **1.** descomprimir *vt* **2.** descomprimir *vi*

decompression /ˌdiːkəmˈpreʃ(ə)n/ *noun* (*expanding a compressed image or data file*) descompresión *f*

decrement /ˈdekrɪmənt/ *verb* decrecer *vi* ■ *noun* coeficiente *m* de amortiguación; pérdida *f*

decrypt /diːˈkrɪpt/ *verb* descifrar *vt*

decryption /diːˈkrɪpʃ(ə)n/ *noun* descifrado *m*; descriptografía *f* ◇ **decryption is done using hardware to increase speed** el descifrado se realiza utilizando el hardware para aumentar la velocidad

dedicated /ˈdedɪkeɪtɪd/ *adjective* (*reserved for a particular use*) dedicado *or* -a; especializado *or* -a

'The PBX is changing from a dedicated proprietary hardware product into an open application software development platform.' [*Computing*]

dedicated channel /ˌdedɪkeɪtɪd ˈtʃæn(ə)l/ *noun* canal *m* especializado; canal *m* dedicado

dedicated computer /ˌdedɪkeɪtɪd kəmˈpjuːtə/ *noun* ordenador *m* especializado

dedicated line /ˌdedɪkeɪtɪd ˈlaɪn/ *noun* línea *f* telefónica especializada; línea *f* dedicada

dedicated logic /ˌdedɪkeɪtɪd ˈlɒdʒɪk/ *noun* lógica *f* especializada ◇ **the person appointed should have a knowledge of micro-based hardware and dedicated logic** la persona seleccionada debería tener conocimientos de hardware para microordenadores y de lógica especializada

dedicated print server /ˌdedɪkeɪtɪd ˈprɪnt ˌsɜːvə/ *noun* servidor *m* de impresora especializada

dedicated word-processor /ˌdedɪkeɪtɪd ˈwɜːd ˌprəʊsesə/ *noun* tratamiento *m* de textos especializado

de facto standard /deɪ ˌfæktəʊ ˈstændəd/ *noun* (*system which has become a standard*) estándar *m* común

default /dɪˈfɔːlt/ *adjective* defecto *m* ◇ **by default** por defecto *or* implícito ◇ **screen width has a default value of 80** la anchura de la pantalla tiene un valor por defecto de 80

default drive /dɪˈfɔːlt draɪv/ *noun* unidad *f* de lectura por defecto ◇ **the operating system allows the user to select the default drive** el sistema operativo permite al usuario seleccione el lector por defecto

default option /dɪˈfɔːlt ˈɒpʃən/ *noun* opción *f* implícita; opción *f* por defecto

default printer /dɪˌfɔːlt ˈprɪntə/ *noun* impresora *f* por defecto

default rate /dɪˌfɔːlt ˈreɪt/ *noun* tasa *f* por defecto; tasa *f* predeterminada (de un módem)

default response /dɪˌfɔːlt rɪˈspɒns/ *noun* respuesta *f* intrínseca; respuesta *f* por defecto

default value /dɪˌfɔːlt ˈvæljuː/ *noun* valor *m* por defecto; valor *m* por omisión ◇ **screen width has a default value of 80** la anchura de la pantalla tiene un valor por defecto de 80

'The default values of columns cannot be set in the database schema, so different applications can trash the database.' [*Computing*]

defective sector /dɪˌfektɪv ˈsektə/ *noun* sector *m* defectuoso

defect skipping /ˈdiːfekt ˌskɪpɪŋ/ *noun* salto *m* por defecto

defensive computing /dɪˌfensɪv kəmˈpjuːtɪŋ/ *noun* informática *f* defensiva; programación *f* defensiva

deferred addressing /dɪˌfɜːd əˈdresɪŋ/ *noun* direccionamiento *m* diferido; direccionamiento *m* directo

deferred mode /dɪˈfɜːd məʊd/ *noun* modo *m* diferido

deferred printing /dɪˌfɜːd ˈprɪntɪŋ/ *noun* impresión *f* diferida

define /dɪˈfaɪn/ *verb* definir *vt* ◇ **all the variables were defined at initialization** todas las variables fueron definidas en la inicialización

definition /ˌdefɪˈnɪʃ(ə)n/ *noun* **1.** (*of a screen*) definición *f* **2.** (*of a value*) definición *f*

deflect /dɪˈflekt/ *verb* (*object or beam*) hacer desviar

deflection /dɪˈflekʃ(ə)n/ *noun* desviación *f*

deflection yokes /dɪˈflekʃ(ə)n jəʊkz/ *plural noun* yugos *mpl* de desviación

DEFRAG /ˈdiːfræɡ/ *noun* (*defragmentation utility in MS-DOS*) DEFRAG

defragmentation /ˌdiːfræɡmenˈteɪʃ(ə)n/ *noun* (*reorganisation of files*) defragmentación *f*

defragmentation utility /ˌdiːfræɡmenˈteɪʃ(ə)n juːˌtɪlɪti/ *noun* utilidad *f* de defragmentación

degauss /diːˈɡaʊs/ *verb* desmagnetizar *vt* ◇ **the R or W heads have to be degaussed each week to ensure optimum performance** hay que desmagnetizar los cabezales de lectura/escritura para asegurar un funcionamiento óptimo

degausser /diːˈɡaʊsə/ *noun* desmagnetizador *m*

degradation /ˌdeɡrəˈdeɪʃ(ə)n/ *noun* **1.** (*loss of picture quality*) degradación *f* **2.** (*loss of processing capacity*) degradación *f* del funcionamiento

dejagging /diːˈdʒæɡɪŋ/ *noun* antimelladura *f*

DEL /del/ *noun* (*MS-DOS command*) instrucción *f* de borrar; instrucción *f* eliminar ◇ **to delete all files with the extension BAK, use the command DEL** *or* **.BAK** para borrar todos los ficheros con la extensión BAK, utilice la instrucción DEL *or* .BAK ◇ **to remove a word from the screen, press the DEL key repeatedly** para eliminar una palabra de la pantalla, apriete la tecla DEL de forma repetida

delay line /dɪ'leɪ laɪn/ *noun* línea *f* de retardo

delay line store /dɪ'leɪ laɪn ˌstɔ:/ *noun* memoria *f* de línea de retardo

delay vector /dɪ'leɪ ˌvektə/ *noun* vector *m* de retardo

delete /dɪ'li:t/ *verb* **1.** (*word in text*) borrar *vt*; eliminar *vt*; suprimir *vt* **2.** (*text or data or file*) borrar *vt*; destruir *vt*; suprimir *vt* ◇ **the word-processor allows us to delete the whole file by pressing this key** el tratamiento de textos nos permite suprimir un fichero completo al pulsar esta tecla

delete character /dɪˌli:t 'kærɪktə/ *noun* carácter *m* de supresión; carácter *m* de eliminación

deletion /dɪ'li:ʃ(ə)n/ *noun* **1.** (*cutting text*) eliminación *f*; (*cutting or erasing text*) supresión *f*; (*erasing text*) borrado *m* **2.** (*removal from storage device*) eliminación *f*; supresión *f* **3.** (*text cut*) eliminación *f*; supresión *f*

deletion record /dɪ'li:ʃ(ə)n ˌrekɔ:d/ *noun* fichero *m* de supresiones; fichero *m* de correcciones

deletion tracking /dɪ'li:ʃ(ə)n ˌtrækɪŋ/ *noun* seguimiento *m* de supresiones; resto *m* de supresiones

delimit /di:'lɪmɪt/ *verb* delimitar *vt*

delimited-field file /di:ˌlɪmɪtd fi:ld 'faɪl/ *noun* fichero *m* de campos delimitados

delimiter /di:'lɪmɪtə/ *noun* **1.** (*symbol for start or end of data, etc.*) delimitador *m*; separador *m* (de información) **2.** (*boundary between instruction and argument*) delimitador *m* (de información); separador *m* (de información)

delivery system /dɪˌlɪv(ə)ri 'sɪstəm/ *noun* sistema *m* de entrega

DEL key /'del ki:/ *noun* tecla *f* de borrado; tecla *f* de eliminación DEL ◇ **to remove a word from the screen, press the DEL key repeatedly** para eliminar una palabra de la pantalla, apriete la tecla DEL de forma repetida

Delphi /'delfi:/ (*commercial online information provider*) Delphi

delta clock /'deltə klɒk/ *noun* reloj *m* delta

demagnetise, demagnetize *verb* desmagnetizar *vt*

demagnetiser, demagnetizer *noun* desmagnetizador *m* ◇ **he used the demagnetizer to degauss the tape heads** utilizó un desmagnetizador para desmagnetizar los cabezales de lectura

demand assigned multiple access /dɪˌmɑ:nd əˌsaɪnd ˌmʌltɪp(ə)l 'ækses/ *noun* acceso *m* múltiple según demanda

demand fetching /dɪ'mɑ:nd ˌfetʃɪŋ/ *noun* acceso *m* por demanda de la memoria paginada; captura *f* por demanda de la memoria paginada

demand paging /dɪ'mɑ:nd ˌpeɪdʒɪŋ/ *noun* demanda *f* de página; paginación *f* discrecional

demand processing /dɪ'mɑ:nd ˌprəʊsesɪŋ/ *noun* proceso *m* (de datos) inmediato; proceso *m* según demanda

demand protocol architecture /dɪˌmɑ:nd ˌprəʊtəkɒl 'a:kɪtektʃə/ *noun* arquitectura *f* de protocolo de demanda; arquitectura *f* DPA

demand reading/writing /dɪˌmɑ:nd ˌri:dɪŋ 'raɪtɪŋ/ *noun* (*direct data transfer*) demanda *f* de lectura/escritura; demanda *f* de transferencia de datos; petición *f* de lectura/grabación

demand staging /dɪ'mɑ:nd ˌsteɪdʒɪŋ/ *noun* transferencia *f* sobre demanda

demarcation /ˌdi:mɑ:'keɪʃ(ə)n/ *noun* demarcación *f*

democratic network /ˌdeməkrætɪk 'netwɜ:k/ *noun* red *f* democrática

demodulation /di:ˌmɒdju'leɪʃ(ə)n/ *noun* demodulación *f*

demonstration software /ˌdemənstreɪʃ(ə)n 'sɒftweə/ *noun* (*software that only shows the functions of a computer*) programa *m* de demostración; versión *f* de demostración; demo *f* ◇ **the company gave away demonstration software that lets you do everything except save your data** la compañía proporcionó un programa de demostración que permite hacerlo todo menos guardar los datos

denial /dɪ'naɪəl/ *noun* denegación *f*; negación *f*

dense index /dens 'ɪndeks/ *noun* índice *m* completo

dense list /'dens lɪst/ *noun* lista *f* completa

density /'densɪti/ *noun* (*amount of light that a negative blocks*) densidad *f*

'…diode lasers with shorter wavelengths will make doubling of the bit and track densities possible' [*Byte*]

departmental LAN /ˌdi:pɑ:t'ment(ə)l læn/ *noun* red *f* departamental de área local

dependent /dɪ'pendənt/ *adjective* dependiente

deposit /dɪ'pɒzɪt/ *noun* (*to print out the content of memory*) impresión *f* del contenido de una memoria) ■ *verb* (*to write data into a register or storage location*) registrar *vt*; introducir en un registro; introducir en la memoria auxiliar

deposition /ˌdepə'zɪʃ(ə)n/ *noun* (*on semiconductor*) deposición *f*; depósito *m*

depth cueing /'depθ ˌkju:ɪŋ/ *noun* señal *f* de profundidad

deque /ˌdi: 'i: ˌkju:/ *noun* fichero *m* de espera de dos entradas

derivation graph /ˌderɪ'veɪʃ(ə)n grɑ:f/ *noun* gráfico *m* de derivación

derive /dɪ'raɪv/ *verb* provenir (de) *vi*; derivar (de) *vi* ◇ **derived indexing** indexación derivada ◇ **derived sound** sonido derivado

DES /ˌdi: i: 'es/ *noun* algoritmo *m* de encriptación estándar

descender /dɪ'sendə/ *noun* (*of the letters 'q' or 'p'*) cola *f* (descendente de una letra)

de-scramble /di: 'skræmb(ə)l/ *verb* (*coded message*) descifrar *vt*; descodificar *vt*

de-scrambler /di: 'skræmblə/ *noun* descodificador *m*

description list /dɪ'skrɪpʃən lɪst/ *noun* lista *f* descriptiva

descriptor /dɪ'skrɪptə/ *noun* descriptor *m*; palabra *f* clave

deselect /ˌdiːsɪ'lekt/ *verb* deseleccionar *vt*

design parameters /dɪ'zaɪn pəˌræmɪtəz/ *plural noun* especificaciones *fpl*; parámetros *mpl* de diseño

desk accessory /'desk əkˌsesəri/ *noun* (*Apple Macintosh utility that enhances the system*) accesorio *m* de escritorio

desk check /'desk tʃek/ *noun* (*dry run of a program*) control *m*; control *m* de un programa; verificación *f* (de un programa)

desktop /'desktɒp/ *adjective* escritorio *m* ■ *noun* (*workspace that is a graphical representation of a real-life desktop*) escritorio *m*

desktop background /ˌdesktɒp 'bækɡraʊnd/ *noun* fondo *m* del escritorio (de la pantalla de Windows)

desktop computer /ˌdesktɒp kəm'pjuːtə/, **desktop computer system** /ˌdesktɒp kəm 'pjuːtə ˌsɪstəm/ *noun* microordenador *m* de escritorio; microordenador *m* de mesa

desktop file /ˌdesktɒp 'faɪl/ *noun* fichero *m* de escritorio (Apple Macintosh)

desktop icons /ˌdesktɒp 'aɪkɒnz/ *plural noun* iconos *mpl* del escritorio (de Windows)

desktop media /ˌdesktɒp 'miːdiə/ *plural noun* escritorio multimedia

desktop presentations /ˌdesktɒp ˌprez(ə)n 'teɪʃ(ə)nz/ *plural noun* presentaciones *fpl* (de página) asistidas por ordenador

desktop publishing /ˌdesktɒp 'pʌblɪʃɪŋ/ *noun* publicación *f* asistida por ordenador; edición *f* electrónica

'...desktop publishing or the ability to produce high-quality publications using a minicomputer, essentially boils down to combining words and images on pages' [*Byte*]

desktop video /ˌdesktɒp 'vɪdiəʊ/ *noun* edición *f* de vídeo asistida por ordenador

despatch /dɪ'spætʃ/ *noun* envío *m*

despool /diː'spuːl/ *verb* imprimir la cola de impresión

despotic network /dɪˌspɒtɪk 'netwɜːk/ *noun* red *f* despótica

destination address /ˌdestɪneɪʃ(ə)n ə'dres/ *noun* dirección *f* de destino

destination object /ˌdestɪneɪʃ(ə)n 'ɒbdʒekt/ *noun* objeto *m* (de) destino

destination page /ˌdestɪ'neɪʃ(ə)n peɪdʒ/ *noun* página *f* destino (en un hipervínculo) ◇ **when a user clicks on the active object in a hyperlink, the software displays the destination page** cuando en un hipervínculo un usuario se stiúa en un objeto activo, el programa muestra la página destino

destructive addition /dɪˌstrʌktɪv ə'dɪʃ(ə)n/ *noun* suma *f* destructiva; adición *f* destructiva

destructive cursor /dɪˌstrʌktɪv 'kɜːsə/ *noun* cursor *m* destructivo; cursor *m* supresor ◇ **read-**

ing the screen becomes difficult without a destructive cursor resulta difícil leer la pantalla sin un cursor destructivo

destructive read /dɪ'strʌktɪv riːd/ *noun* lectura *f* destructiva

destructive readout /dɪˌstrʌktɪv 'riːdaʊt/ *noun* lectura *f* destructiva

detail file /'diːteɪl faɪl/ *noun* fichero *m* de movimientos

detail paper /'diːteɪl ˌpeɪpə/ *noun* papel *m* calco

detected error /dɪˌtektɪd 'erə/ *noun* error *m* detectado; error *m* notificado

deterministic /dɪˌtɜːmɪ'nɪstɪk/ *adjective* determinista

Deutsche Industrienorm /ˌdɔɪtʃə 'ɪndustriː ˌnɔːm/ *noun* DIN

developer /dɪ'veləpə/ *noun* (*person*) diseñador *m or* -a *f*

development software /dɪ'veləpmənt ˌsɒftweə/ *noun* software *m* de desarrollo

development time /dɪ'veləpmənt taɪm/ *noun* tiempo *m* de desarrollo; tiempo *m* de puesta a punto de un nuevo producto

device /dɪ'vaɪs/ *noun* (*machine linked to a computer*) dispositivo *m*; aparato *m*; periférico *m*

'Users in remote locations can share ideas on the Liveboard through the use of a wireless pen-input device and network connections.' [*Computing*]

device address /dɪ'vaɪs əˌdres/ *noun* dirección *f* de control de periféricos

device character control /dɪˌvaɪs ˌkærɪktə kən'trəʊl/ *noun* (sistema de) control *m* de periféricos por caracteres

device code /dɪ'vaɪs kəʊd/ *noun* código *m* de identificación de periféricos; código *m* de dispositivo

device control character /dɪˌvaɪs kən'trəʊl ˌkærɪktə/ *noun* (*code transmitted to a device*) carácter *m* de control de dispositivo; carácter *m* de control; carácter *m* de periféricos; carácter *m* de instrucción de periféricos

device-dependent /dɪˌvaɪs dɪ'pendənt/ *adjective* dependiente del dispositivo

device driver /dɪ'vaɪs ˌdraɪvə/ *noun* (*driver*) software *m* de gestión de periféricos; software *m* de control de periféricos; gestor *m* de periféricos

device flag /dɪ'vaɪs flæg/ *noun* (*indication of a device's state*) indicador *m* de funcionamiento; testigo *m* de utilización; testigo *m* de funcionamiento; lector *m* de cinta audio digital

device handler /dɪˌvaɪs 'hændlə/ *noun* gestor *m* de periféricos

device-independent /dɪˌvaɪs ˌɪndɪ'pendənt/ *adjective* independiente

device name /dɪ'vaɪs neɪm/ *noun* nombre *m* de periférico

device priority /dɪ'vaɪs praɪˌɒrɪti/ *noun* prioridad *f* de un periférico; prioridad *f* de un aparato ◇ **the master console has a higher device priority than the printers and other terminals** la consola de instrucción tiene mayor prioridad que las impresoras y otros terminales

device queue /dɪ'vaɪs kjuː/ *noun* cola *f* de espera (de periféricos)

device status word /dɪˌvaɪs 'steɪtəs ˌwɜːd/ *noun* palabra *f* indicadora del estado de funcionamiento

devise /dɪ'vaɪz/ *verb* idear *vt*; inventar *vt*

DFD /ˌdiː ef 'diː/ *noun* diagrama *m* de flujo de datos

Dhrystone benchmark /ˌdraɪstəun 'bentʃmɑːk/ *noun* (*benchmarking system*) prueba *f* de evaluación del funcionamiento Dhrystone

DIA/DCA /ˌdiː aɪ eɪ ˌdiː siː 'eɪ/ *noun* arquitectura *f* de contenido de documentos; arquitectura *f* de transmisión de documentos

diagnose /'daɪəgnəuz/ *verb* diagnosticar *vt*; encontrar *vt*

diagnosis /ˌdaɪəg'nəusɪs/ *noun* diagnosis *f*

diagnostic /ˌdaɪəg'nɒstɪk/ *noun* diagnóstico *m*

'...the implementation of on-line diagnostic devices that measure key observable parameters' [*Byte*]

'...to check for any hardware problems, a diagnostic disk is provided' [*Personal Computer World*]

diagnostic aid /ˌdaɪəgnɒstɪk 'eɪd/ *noun* ayuda *f* para el diagnóstico

diagnostic chip /ˌdaɪəgnɒstɪk 'tʃɪp/ *noun* chip *m* de diagnóstico ◇ **they are carrying out research on diagnostic chips to test computers that contain processors** están haciendo una investigación sobre chips de diagnóstico para probar ordenadores equipados con procesadores

diagnostic message /ˌdaɪəgnɒstɪk 'mesɪdʒ/ *noun* mensaje *m* de diagnóstico

diagnostic program /ˌdaɪəgnɒstɪk 'prəugræm/ *noun* programa *m* de diagnóstico

diagnostic routine /ˌdaɪəgnɒstɪk ruː'tiːn/ *noun* rutina *f* de diagnóstico

diagnostics /ˌdaɪəg'nɒstɪks/ *plural noun* diagnóstico *m*

diagnostic test /ˌdaɪəgnɒstɪk 'test/ *noun* prueba *f* de diagnóstico

dial /'daɪəl/ *noun* (*used to select or validate*) mando *m*; dial *m*; esfera *f*; (*on telephone or clock*) cuadrante *m* ◇ **density dial** mando de densidad ◇ **if the text fades, turn the density dial on the printer to full black** si el texto sale muy claro, gire el mando de densidad de la impresora a negro ◇ **to tune into the radio station, turn the dial** para sintonizar emisora de radio, gire el dial

'Customers will be able to choose a wide variety of telephony products, from basic auto-dial programs to call-centre applications.' [*Computing*]

dialect /'daɪəlekt/ *noun* dialecto *m* ◇ **this manufacturer's dialect of BASIC is a little different to the one I'm used to** el dialecto de BASIC de este fabricante es un poco diferente al que yo estoy acostumbrado

Dialer /'daɪələ/ (*Windows 95 utility*) marcador *m* telefónico

dial-in modem /ˌdaɪəl ɪn 'məudem/ *noun* (*auto-answer modem*) módem *m* de llamada automática

dialog /'daɪəlɒg/ *noun US* diálogo *m*

dialog box /'daɪəlɒg bɒks/ *noun* caja *f* de diálogo; ventana *f* de diálogo

dialogue /'daɪəlɒg/, **dialog** *noun* diálogo *m*

dialup *noun* servicio *m* de llamadas

dial-up access /ˌdaɪəl ʌp 'ækses/ *noun* acceso *m* de mercado

dial-up connection /ˌdaɪəl ʌp kə'nekʃ(ə)n/ *noun* conexión *f* de mercado

dial-up service /ˌdaɪəl ʌp 'sɜːvɪs/ *noun* servicio *m* de llamadas

diaphragm /'daɪəfræm/ *noun* (*photography*) diafragma *m*

DIB /ˌdiː aɪ 'biː/ *noun* **1.** bus *m* de entrada de datos **2.** bus *m* dual independiente

dibit /'dɪbɪt/ *noun* (*two binary bits*) dibit *m*; dos bits *mpl*; grupo *m* de dos cifras binarias

dichotomising search /daɪ'kɒtəmaɪzɪŋ ˌsɜːtʃ/, **dichotomizing search** *noun* búsqueda *f* dicotómica; búsqueda *f* por dicotomía

dichroic /daɪ'krəuɪk/ *adjective* dicroico

dichroic filter /daɪˌkrəuɪk 'fɪltə/ *noun* filtro *m* decroico

dictionary /'dɪkʃən(ə)ri/ *noun* **1.** (*data management structure*) diccionario *m* **2.** (*spell checker*) diccionario *m*

dielectric /ˌdaɪɪ'lektrɪk/ *adjective* dieléctrico *m*

differential pulse coded modulation /ˌdɪfərenʃəl ˌpʌls ˌkəudɪd ˌmɒdjʊ'leɪʃ(ə)n/ *noun* modulación *f* de código de impulso diferencial

DIF file /'dɪf faɪl/ *noun* fichero *m* DIF

diffusion /dɪ'fjuːʒ(ə)n/ *noun* difusión *f*

digit /'dɪdʒɪt/ *noun* cifra *f*; dígito *m* ◇ **a phone number with eight digits or an eight-digit phone number** un número de teléfono de ocho cifras ◇ **the decimal number system uses the digits 0123456789** el sistema de números de base decimal utiliza los dígitos 0123456789

digital /'dɪdʒɪt(ə)l/ *adjective* numérico *or* -a; digital

'Xerox Parc's LCD breakthrough promises the digital equivalent of paper, by producing thin, low-cost flat displays with a 600dpi resolution.' [*Computing*]

digital audio tape /ˌdɪdʒɪt(ə)l 'ɔːdiəu ˌteɪp/ *noun* grabación *f*; cinta *f* audiodigital

digital camera /ˌdɪdʒɪt(ə)l 'kæm(ə)rə/ *noun* cámara *f* digital

digital cash /ˌdɪdʒɪt(ə)l 'kæʃ/ *noun* dinero *m* electrónico

digital cassette /ˌdɪdʒɪt(ə)l kə'set/ *noun* casete *f* digital; casete *f* audionumérica

digital channel /ˌdɪdʒɪt(ə)l 'tʃæn(ə)l/ *noun* canal *m* digital

digital circuit /ˌdɪdʒɪt(ə)l 'sɜːkɪt/ *noun* circuito *m* digital

digital clock /ˌdɪdʒɪt(ə)l ˈklɒk/ *noun* reloj *m* digital

digital compact cassette /ˌdɪdʒɪt(ə)l ˌkɒmpækt kəˈset/ *noun* casete *f* digital compacto

digital computer /ˌdɪdʒɪt(ə)l kəmˈpjuːtə/ *noun* ordenador *m* digital; ordenador *m* numérico

digital data /ˌdɪdʒɪt(ə)l ˈdeɪtə/ *noun* datos *mpl* digitales

digital display /ˌdɪdʒɪt(ə)l dɪˈspleɪ/ *noun* (*video display unit*) pantalla *f* digital; tablón *m* (de anuncios) digital

digital logic /ˌdɪdʒɪt(ə)l ˈlɒdʒɪk/ *noun* lógica *f* digital

digital monitor /ˌdɪdʒɪt(ə)l ˈmɒnɪtə/ *noun* monitor *m* digital

digital optical recording /ˌdɪdʒɪt(ə)l ˌɒptɪk(ə)l rɪˈkɔːdɪŋ/ *noun* lectura *f* óptica digital (de datos)

digital output /ˌdɪdʒɪt(ə)l ˈaʊtpʊt/ *noun* salida *f* digital

digital plotter /ˌdɪdʒɪt(ə)l ˈplɒtə/ *noun* trazador *m* digital

digital read-out /ˌdɪdʒɪt(ə)l ˈriːdaʊt/ *noun* tablón *m* digital

digital representation /ˌdɪdʒɪt(ə)l ˌreprɪzenˈteɪʃ(ə)n/ *noun* representación *f* digital

digital resolution /ˌdɪdʒɪt(ə)l ˌrezəˈluːʃ(ə)n/ *noun* resolución *f* digital

digital signal /ˌdɪdʒɪt(ə)l ˈsɪgn(ə)l/ *noun* señal *f* digital

digital signal level one /ˌdɪdʒɪt(ə)l ˌsɪgn(ə)l ˌlev(ə)l ˈwʌn/ *noun* señal *f* digital de nivel uno

digital signal level zero /ˌdɪdʒɪt(ə)l ˌsɪgn(ə)l ˌlev(ə)l ˈzɪərəʊ/ *noun* señal *f* digital de nivel cero

digital signalling /ˌdɪdʒɪt(ə)l ˈsɪgnəlɪŋ/ *noun* señales *fpl* digitales

digital signal processing /ˌdɪdʒɪt(ə)l ˈsɪgn(ə)l ˌprəʊsesɪŋ/ *noun* proceso *m* de señales digitales

digital signature /ˌdɪdʒɪt(ə)l ˈsɪgnətʃə/ *noun* firma *f* digital

digital speech /ˌdɪdʒɪt(ə)l ˈspiːtʃ/ *noun* voz *f* digitalizada

digital subscriber line /ˌdɪdʒɪt(ə)l səbˈskraɪbə ˌlaɪn/ *noun* línea *f* de abonado digital

digital switching /ˌdɪdʒɪt(ə)l ˈswɪtʃɪŋ/ *noun* conmutación *f* digital

digital system /ˌdɪdʒɪt(ə)l ˈsɪstəm/ *noun* sistema *m* digital

digital to analog converter /ˌdɪdʒɪt(ə)l tə ˌænəlɒg kənˈvɜːtə/ *noun* convertidor *m* digital/analógico

digital transmission system /ˌdɪdʒɪt(ə)l trænzˈmɪʃ(ə)n ˌsɪstəm/ *noun* sistema *m* de transmisión digital

digital TV /ˌdɪdʒɪt(ə)l tiːˈviː/ *noun* televisión *f* digital

digital versatile disc /ˌdɪdʒɪt(ə)l ˌvɜːsətaɪl ˈdɪsk/ *noun* disco *m* vídeo digital

digital video /ˌdɪdʒɪt(ə)l ˈvɪdiəʊ/ *noun* vídeo *m* digital

digital videodisc /ˌdɪdʒɪt(ə)l ˈvɪdiəʊdɪsk/ *noun* disco *m* de vídeo digital

digital video interactive /ˌdɪdʒɪt(ə)l ˌvɪdiəʊ ˌɪntərˈæktɪv/ *noun* sistema *m* interactivo de vídeo digital (DV-I)

digitise /ˈdɪdʒɪˌtaɪz/, **digitize** *verb* digitalizar *vt*

'The contract covers fibre optic cable and Synchronous Digital Hierarchy transmission equipment to be used to digitize the telecommunications network.' [*Computergram*]

digitised photograph /ˌdɪdʒɪˌtaɪzd ˌfəʊtəˈgrɑːf/, **digitized photograph** *noun* fotografía *f* digitalizada

digitiser, digitizer *noun* digitalizador *m*

digitising pad /ˈdɪdʒɪtaɪzɪŋ ˌpæd/, **digitising tablet, digitizing pad, digitizing tablet** *noun* tablilla *f*; pizarra *f* gráfica

digit place /ˈdɪdʒɪt pleɪs/, **digit position** /ˌdɪdʒɪt pəˈzɪʃ(ə)n/ *noun* lugar *m* de una cifra; posición *f* de una cifra

DIM /ˌdiː aɪ ˈem/ *noun* gestión *f* de documentos de imágenes

dimension /daɪˈmenʃən/ *noun* dimensión *f*

dimensioning /daɪˈmenʃənɪŋ/ *noun* cálculo *m* de dimensiones ◇ **array dimensioning occurs at this line** el cálculo de las dimensiones de la red tiene lugar en esta línea

diminished radix complement /dɪˌmɪnɪʃt ˈreɪdɪks ˌkɒmpleks/ *noun* complemento *m* de raíz reducida

DIMM /ˌdiː aɪ em ˈem/ *noun* módulo *m* de memoria doble en línea

DIN /ˌdiː aɪ ˈen/ *noun* (*German industry standards organisation*) DIN *m*

Dingbat™ /ˈdɪŋbæt/ *noun* (*font*) Dingbat™; fuente *f* de caracteres especiales ◇ **to insert a copyright symbol, use the Dingbat font** para insertar el símbolo de 'copyright', emplee la fuente Dingbat

diode /ˈdaɪəʊd/ *noun* diodo *m*

DIP /ˌdiː aɪ ˈpiː/ *noun* empaquetamiento *m* doble en línea; encapsulado *m* dual en línea

DIP switch /ˈdɪp swɪtʃ/ *noun* conmutador *m* DIP

DIR /ˌdiː aɪ ˈɑː/ *noun* (*MS-DOS system command*) (instrucción) DIR (de búsqueda de ficheros)

direct /daɪˈrekt/ *adjective, adverb* **1.** (*straight*) directo **2.** (*without interruption*) directo; directamente **3.** (*with no processing*) directo *or* -a ◇ **to dial direct** marcar (el número) directamente ◇ **you can dial New York direct from London if you want** si quiere puede llamar a Nueva York desde Londres marcando el número directamente

direct access /ˌdaɪrekt ˈækses/ *noun* acceso *m* directo

direct access storage device /daɪˌrekt ˌækses ˈstɔːrɪdʒ dɪˌvaɪs/ *noun* dispositivo *m* de almacenamiento de acceso directo

direct addressing /ˌdaɪrekt əˈdresɪŋ/ *noun* direccionamiento *m* directo

direct cable connection /ˌdaɪrekt ˈkeɪb(ə)l kəˌneks(ə)n/ *noun* conexión *f* directa por cable

direct change-over /daɪˈrekt tʃeɪndʒ/ *noun* transferencia *f* directa

direct code /daɪˈrekt kəʊd/ *noun* código *m* directo

direct coding /daɪˈrekt kɒdɪŋ/ *noun* codificación *f* directa

direct connect /ˌdaɪrekt kəˈnekt/ *adjective* de conexión directa

direct connection /daɪˌrekt kəˈnekʃən/ *noun* conexión *f* directa

direct current /dɪˌrekt ˈkʌrənt/ *noun* corriente *f* continua

direct data entry /daɪˌrekt ˌdeɪtə ˈentri/ *noun* entrada *f* directa de datos (mediante el teclado)

direct digital control /daɪˌrekt ˌdɪdʒɪt(ə)l kənˈtrəʊl/ *noun* control *m* digital directo

directed scan /daɪˈrektd skæn/ *noun* escaneado *m* dirigido; exploración *f* dirigida

direct information access network for Europe /daɪˌrekt ˌɪnfəmeɪʃ(ə)n ˌækses ˌnetwɜːk fə ˈjʊərəp/ *noun* red *f* directa de acceso a la información

direct-insert routine /ˌdaɪrekt ɪnˈsɜːt ruːˌtiːn/ *noun* rutina *f* de inserción directa; subrutina *f* de inserción directa

direct instruction /ˌdaɪrekt ɪnˈstrʌkʃən/ *noun* instrucción *f* directa

directive /daɪˈrektɪv/ *noun* directiva *f*

'...directives are very useful for selecting parts of the code for particular purposes' [*Personal Computer World*]

directive statement /daɪˌrektɪv ˈsteɪtmənt/ *noun* instrucción *f* directiva

direct memory access /daɪˌrekt ˈmem(ə)ri ˌækses/ *noun* acceso *m* directo a la memoria

direct memory access channel /daɪˌrekt ˌmem(ə)ri ˈækses ˌtʃæn(ə)l/ *noun* vía *f* de acceso directo a la memoria

direct mode /daɪˈrekt məʊd/ *noun* modo *m* directo

directory /daɪˈrekt(ə)ri/ *noun* directorio *m*

directory services /daɪˈrekt(ə)ri ˌsɜːvɪsɪz/ *noun* servicios *mpl* disponibles en línea ◇ **with directory services installed, it's much easier for our users to find and connect to the shared printers** con los servicios en línea disponibles e incorporados al sistema, es mucho más fácil para nuestros usuarios encontrar y conectarse a las impresoras compartidas

directory synchronisation /daɪˌrekt(ə)ri ˌsɪŋkrənaɪˈzeɪʃ(ə)n/ *noun* sincronización *f* del directorio

direct page register /daɪˌrekt ˈpeɪdʒ ˌredʒɪstə/ *noun* registro *m* de paginación de acceso directo

direct reference address /ˌdaɪrekt ˌref(ə)rəns əˈdres/ *noun* dirección *f* de referencia directa

direct transfer /ˌdaɪrekt ˈtrænsfɜː/ *noun* transferencia *f* directa

dirty bit /ˈdɜːti bɪt/ *noun* (*flag bit indicating the loading of programs*) bit *m* marcado; bitio *m* marcado; bitio *m* sucio

disable interrupt /dɪsˌeɪb(ə)l ˈɪntərʌpt/ *noun* instrucción *f* de supresión de una interrupción

disarm /dɪsˈɑːm/ *verb* desconectar *vt*; desactivar *vt*

disarmed state /dɪsˈɑːmd steɪt/ *noun* estado *m* desactivado

disassemble /ˌdɪsəˈsemb(ə)l/ *verb* (*translation of machine instructions*) desensamblar *vt*; desarmar *vt*; (*translation of instructions*) desmontar *vt*

disassembler /ˌdɪsəˈsemblə/ *noun* desensamblador *m or* -a *f*

disaster dump /dɪˈzɑːstə dʌmp/ *noun* vaciado *m* irreversible

disc /dɪsk/ *noun* disco *m* compacto

disconnect /ˌdɪskəˈnekt/ *verb* desconectar *vt* ◇ **do not forget to disconnect the cable before moving the printer** no olvide desconectar el cable antes de trasladar la impresora

discrete /dɪˈskriːt/ *adjective* (*in small individual units*) discreto *or* -a ◇ **a data word is made up of discrete bits** una palabra de datos se compone de (una serie de) bits discretos

discrete cosine transform /dɪˌskriːt ˈkəʊsaɪn trænsˌfɔːm/ *noun* transformación *f* discreta de cosenos

discretionary hyphen *noun* guión *m* discrecional

discrimination instruction /dɪˌskrɪmɪˌneɪʃ(ə)n ɪnˈstrʌkʃən/ *noun* instrucción *f* de salto condicional

discussion group /dɪˈskʌʃ(ə)n gruːp/ *noun* grupo *m* de discusión

disjunction /dɪsˈdʒʌŋkʃ(ə)n/ *noun* (*logical function*) disyunción *f*; función *f* OR

disjunctive search /dɪsˌdʒʌnktɪv ˈsɜːtʃ/ *noun* búsqueda *f* disyuntiva; búsqueda *f* mediante palabras clave

disk /dɪsk/ *noun* (*record or computer hard disk*) disco *m*; (*floppy*) disquete *m* ◇ **optical disk** disco óptico

disk access /dɪsk ˈækses/ *noun* acceso *m* al disco

disk access management /ˌdɪsk ˌækses ˈmænɪdʒmənt/ *noun* gestión *f* de acceso a los discos

disk-based /ˈdɪsk beɪsd/ *adjective* (sistema operativo) basado en un disco (duro); basado en disquetes

disk cartridge /dɪsk ˈkɑːtrɪdʒ/ *noun* cargador *m* de disco(s)

disk compression software /ˌdɪsk kəm
'preʃ(ə)n ˌsɒftweə/ *noun* software *m* de compresión de disco

disk controller /dɪsk kən'trəʊlə/ *noun* controlador *m* de disco; controlador *m* de disquete

disk-controller card /'dɪsk kənˌtrəʊlə ˌkɑːd/ *noun* tarjeta *f* de control de disco

disk crash /'dɪsk kræʃ/ *noun* (*faulty disk*) fallo *m* de un disquete; avería *f* total de un disco; destrucción *f* (accidental) del disco

disk directory /dɪsk də'rekt(ə)ri/ *noun* directorio *m* (de ficheros) ◊ **the disk directory shows file name, date and time of creation** el drectorio del disco muestra el nombre, la fecha y la hora de creación de un fichero

disk doctor /dɪsk 'dɒktə/ *noun* corrector *m* de disco

disk drive /'dɪsk draɪv/ *noun* controlador *m* de discos

disk duplexing /'dɪsk ˌdjuːpleksɪŋ/ *noun* copia *f* espejo de datos (sobre un disco espejo); duplicación *f* de datos sobre un disco espejo

diskette /dɪ'sket/ *noun* disquete *m*

disk file /'dɪsk faɪl/ *noun* (*data stored on disk*) fichero *m* de disco; fichero *m* de disquete; archivo *m* de disco

disk formatting /'dɪsk ˌfɔːmætɪŋ/ *noun* (*setting up of a blank disk*) formateado *m* de disco; formateo *m* de un disco; formateado *m* de disquete; formateo *m* de un disquete ◊ **disk formatting has to be done before you can use a new floppy disk** antes de utilizar un disco flexible hay que formatearlo

disk head /'dɪsk hed/ *noun* cabeza *f* de lectura; cabeza *f* de lectura/escritura de disquetes

disk index holes /ˌdɪsk 'ɪndeks ˌhəʊlz/ *plural noun* perforaciones *fpl* que marcan el borde de un disco

diskless /'dɪskləs/ *adjective* sin disco

disk map /'dɪsk mæp/ *noun* tabla *f* de clasificación de los ficheros de un disco

disk memory /dɪsk 'mem(ə)ri/ *noun* (*memory on disk*) memoria *f* de disco; disquete *m*

disk mirroring /'dɪsk ˌmɪrərɪŋ/ *noun* copia *f* espejo de datos (sobre un disco espejo); duplicación *f* de datos sobre un disco espejo

disk operating system /ˌdɪsk 'ɒpəreɪtɪŋ ˌsɪstəm/ *noun* sistema *m* operativo de disco; (sistema operativo) DOS

disk pack /'dɪsk pæk/ *noun* (*disks on a single hub*) lote *m* cargador; cargador *m* de discos; paquete *m* de discos

disk sector /dɪsk 'sektə/ *noun* sector *m* de disco

disk sector formatting /ˌdɪsk ˌsektə 'fɔːmætɪŋ/ *noun* formateado *m* de sectores (de un disco)

disk storage /dɪsk 'stɔːrɪdʒ/ *noun* (*using disks for storage*) memoria *f* de disco

disk track /'dɪsk træk/ *noun* pista *f* de un disco

disk unit /dɪsk 'juːnɪt/ *noun* unidad *f* de disco(s); lector *m* de disco(s)

dispatch /dɪ'spætʃ/**, despatch** /dɪ'spætʃ/ *noun* envío *m*

dispersion /dɪ'spɜːʃ(ə)n/ *noun* (*of beam*) dispersión *f*

displacement /dɪs'pleɪsmənt/ *noun* desplazamiento *m*

display /dɪ'spleɪ/ *noun* (*of information or images*) representación *f* visual; visualización *f*; indicador *m* visual; presentación *f* visual ◊ **Display PostScript™** visualización (previa) PostScript™ ◊ **display size** dimensión *f* tamaño *m* de visualización *or* de pantalla ◊ **seven-segment display** representación visual de siete segmentos

display adapter /dɪ'spleɪ əˌdæptə/ *noun* adaptador *m* de pantalla

display attribute /dɪ'spleɪ ˌætrɪbjuːt/ *noun* atributo *m* de pantalla

display character /dɪ'spleɪ ˌkærɪktə/ *noun* carácter *m* de pantalla

display character generator /dɪ'spleɪ ˌkærɪktə ˌdʒenəreɪtə/ *noun* generador *m* de caracteres de pantalla

display colour /dɪ'spleɪ ˌkʌlə/ *noun* color *m* de visualización; color *m* de pantalla

display controller /dɪ'spleɪ kənˌtrəʊlə/ *noun* (*device used for displaying dot-matrix patterns*) controlador *m* de pantalla; controlador *m* de la representación visual

display element /dɪ'spleɪ ˌelɪmənt/ *noun* elemento *m* visualizado

display format /dɪ'spleɪ ˌfɔːmæt/ *noun* formato *m* de pantalla

display highlights /dɪ'spleɪ ˌhaɪlaɪts/ *plural noun* palabras *fpl* que se destacan (visualmente); caracteres *mpl* que se destacan visualmente

display line /dɪ'spleɪ laɪn/ *noun* línea *f* de pantalla

display mode /dɪ'spleɪ məʊd/ *noun* modo *m* de presentación; modo *m* de visualización

Display PostScript™ /dɪˌspleɪ 'pəʊstskrɪpt/ (*trade name for an extension of PostScript*) visualización *f* PostScript

display processor /dɪ'spleɪ ˌprəʊsesə/ *noun* (*to make data suitable for a display controller*) procesador *m* de representación visual; procesador *m* de visualización; procesador *m* de pantalla

display register /dɪ'spleɪ ˌredʒɪstə/ *noun* registro *m* de visualización

display resolution /dɪˌspleɪ ˌrezə'luːʃ(ə)n/ *noun* definición *f*; resolución *f* de pantalla

display screen /dɪ'spleɪ skriːn/ *noun* pantalla *f* de visualización

display scrolling /dɪ'spleɪ ˌskrəʊlɪŋ/ *noun* desplazamiento *m* del texto sobre la pantalla

display space /dɪ'spleɪ speɪs/ *noun* espacio *m* de visualización

display unit /dɪ'spleɪ ˌjuːnɪt/ *noun* unidad *f* de visualización; pantalla *f*

dissolve /dɪ'zɒlv/ noun (special effect in presentation graphics software) disolver(se) vr; desaparecer progresivamente (la imagen)

distance vector protocols /ˌdɪstəns 'vektə ˌprəʊtəkɒlz/ plural noun protocolos mpl de distancia vectorial

distort /dɪ'stɔːt/ verb distorsionar vt; deformar vt

distortion /dɪ'stɔːʃ(ə)n/ noun (unwanted differences in a signal) distorsión f; aberración f; alteración f ◇ **distortion optics** óptica f de distorsión ◇ **image distortion** deformación or distorsión de una imagen

distribute /dɪ'strɪbjuːt/ verb distribuir vt; hacer circular ◇ **distributed data processing (DDP)** proceso m de datos distribuido

distributed adaptive routing /dɪˌstrɪbjʊtɪd əˌdæptɪv 'ruːtɪŋ/ noun direccionamiento m adaptable distribuido

distributed database system /dɪˌstrɪbjʊtɪd 'deɪtəbeɪs ˌsɪstəm/ noun sistema m de base de datos distribuida

distributed data processing /dɪˌstrɪbjʊtɪd 'deɪtə ˌprəʊsesɪŋ/ noun proceso m distribuido de datos; proceso m de datos distribuido

distributed file system /dɪˌstrɪbjʊtɪd 'faɪl ˌsɪstəm/ noun sistema m de ficheros distribuidos; sistema m de ficheros compartidos

distributed intelligence /dɪˌstrɪbjʊtɪd ɪn'telɪdʒ(ə)ns/ noun inteligencia f distribuida

distributed network /dɪˌstrɪbjʊtɪd 'netwɜːk/ noun red f de distribución

distributed processing /dɪˌstrɪbjʊtɪd 'prəʊsesɪŋ/ noun procesamiento m distribuido

distributed processor /dɪˌstrɪbjʊtɪd 'prəʊsesə/ noun procesador m distribuido

distributed system /dɪˌstrɪbjʊtɪd 'sɪstəm/ noun sistema m distribuido

distribution /ˌdɪstrɪ'bjuːʃ(ə)n/ noun distribución f ◇ **distribution point** centro m de distribución

distribution network /ˌdɪstrɪ'bjuːʃ(ə)n ˌnetwɜːk/ noun red f de distribución

dither /'dɪðə/ verb (pixels) suavizar vt

dithered colour /ˌdɪðəd 'kʌlə/ noun color m suavizado

dividend /'dɪvɪdend/ noun dividendo m

divisor /dɪ'vaɪzə/ noun divisor m

DL abbr (download) transferir vt

DLL /ˌdiː el 'el/ noun biblioteca f dinámica de enlaces; DLL

DLL file /ˌdiː el 'el ˌfaɪl/ noun fichero m DLL

DMA /ˌdiː em 'eɪ/ noun (interface IC that controls high-speed data transfer) acceso m directo a la memoria; DMA

'A 32-bit DMA controller, 16-bit video I/O ports and I/O filters complete the chip.' [Computing]

DMA controller /ˌdiː em 'eɪ kənˌtrəʊlə/ noun controlador m DMA; controlador m de acceso directo a la memoria

DMA cycle stealing /ˌdiː em eɪ 'saɪk(ə)l ˌstiːlɪŋ/ noun acceso m directo a la memoria mediante utilización en robo de ciclo

DML abbr (data manipulation language) lenguaje m de manipulación de datos

DNS /ˌdiː en 'es/ noun sistema m DNS; sistema m de nombres y direcciones por dominios (en Internet)

dock /dɒk/ verb acoplar vt

docking station /'dɒkɪŋ ˌsteɪʃ(ə)n/ noun estación f de atrancamiento

document noun /'dɒkjʊmənt/ documento m ■ verb /'dɒkjʊˌment/ documentar vt

document assembly /'dɒkjʊmənt əˌsembli/ noun fusión f de documentos; ensamblaje m de documentos

documentation /ˌdɒkjʊmen'teɪʃ(ə)n/ noun (information, notes, etc.) documentos mpl

document image management /ˌdɒkjʊmənt ˌɪmɪdʒ 'mænɪdʒmənt/ noun gestión f de documentos de imágenes

document image processing /ˌdɒkjʊmənt 'ɪmɪdʒ ˌprəʊsesɪŋ/ noun tratamiento m de imágenes de documentos

document interchange architecture/document content architecture /ˌdɒkjʊmənt ˌɪntətʃeɪndʒ ˌɑːkɪtektʃə ˌdɒkjʊmənt 'kɒntent ˌɑːkɪtektʃə/ noun arquitectura f de transmisión de documentos; arquitectura f de contenido de documentos

document merge /'dɒkjʊmənt mɜːdʒ/ noun ensamblaje m de documentos; fusión f de documentos

document processing /ˌdɒkjʊmənt 'prəʊsesɪŋ/ noun tratamiento m de textos; tratamiento m de documentos

document reader /'dɒkjʊmənt ˌriːdə/ noun lector m de documentos

document recovery /ˌdɒkjʊmənt rɪ'kʌv(ə)ri/ noun recuperación f de un documento

Dolby Digital™ /ˌdɒlbi 'dɪdʒɪt(ə)l/ (trade name for a multichannel audio compression and transmission system) Dolby Digital™

Dolby system™ /'dɒlbi ˌsɪstəm/ (trade name for a system for reducing background noise for recordings) Dolby system™

dollar sign /'dɒlə saɪn/ noun símbolo m del dólar

domain /dəʊ'meɪn/ noun (scope) dominio m

domain name /dəʊ'meɪn neɪm/ noun nombre m de dominio

domain name registration /dəʊˌmeɪn neɪm ˌredʒɪ'streɪʃ(ə)n/ noun registro m de nombre de dominio

domain name system /dəʊ'meɪn neɪm ˌsɪstəm/ noun sistema m de nombres y direcciones por dominios (en Internet); sistema m DNS

dongle /'dɒŋgl/ noun circuito m encriptado de protección de software; clave f electrónica

do-nothing instruction /ˌdəʊ 'nʌθɪŋ ɪn ˌstrʌkʃən/ *noun* instrucción *f* de no hacer nada; instrucción *f* sin efecto

dopant /'dəʊpənt/ *noun* adulterante *m*; agente *m* impurificador

doped /'dəʊpt/ *adjective* adulterado *or* -a; con impurezas

DOR /ˌdiː əʊ 'ɑː/ *noun* lectura *f* óptica digital (de datos)

DOS /dɒs/ *noun* sistema *m* operativo de disco; sistema *m* operativo DOS ◇ **boot up the DOS after you switch on the PC** arranque el sistema operativo DOS después de conectar el ordenador ◇ **DR-DOS™** (*operating system developed by Digital Research*) DR-DOS™

DOS prompt /'dɒs prɒmpt/ *noun* indicador *m* del DOS; puntero *m* del DOS

dot addressable /'dɒt əˌdresəb(ə)l/ *adjective* direccionable de píxeles

dot command /dɒt kə'mɑːnd/ *noun* instrucción *f* (precedida de un) punto

dot matrix /ˌdɒt 'meɪtrɪks/ *noun* matriz *f* de puntos

dot-matrix printer /ˌdɒt 'meɪtrɪks ˌprɪntə/ *noun* (*a printer whose output is made up of characters formed by a series of closely spaced dots*) impresora *f* matricial; impresora *f* por puntos; impresora *f* de matriz por puntos

dot pitch /'dɒt pɪtʃ/ *noun* espacio *m* entre puntos

dot prompt /'dɒt prɒmpt/ *noun* indicador *m* de punto

dots per inch /ˌdɒtz pɜːr 'ɪntʃ/ *plural noun* puntos *mpl* por pulgada; ppp

double buffering /ˌdʌb(ə)l 'bʌfərɪŋ/ *noun* (*use of two buffers*) introducción *f* doble en memoria intermedia; utilización *f* de doble memoria intermedia

double-click /ˌdʌb(ə)l 'klɪk/ *noun* (*to click twice on the mouse*) doble-clic *m* ■ *verb* (*two clicks on the mouse*) pulsar dos veces (el ratón); hacer clic dos veces (con el ratón) ◇ **move the pointer to the icon then start the program with a double-click** sitúe el puntero sobre el icono y pulse dos veces el ratón para iniciar el programa

double density /ˌdʌb(ə)l 'densəti/ *noun* sistema *m* de doble densidad

double density disk /ˌdʌb(ə)l ˌdensɪti 'dɪsk/ *noun* disquete *m* de doble densidad

double ended queue /ˌdʌb(ə)l ˌendɪd 'kjuː/ *noun* fichero *m* de espera de dos entradas

double-length arithmetic /ˌdʌb(ə)l ˌleŋθ ə'rɪθmətɪk/ *noun* aritmética *f* de doble precisión

double precision /ˌdʌb(ə)l prɪ'sɪʒ(ə)n/ *noun* precisión *f* doble

double-precision integer /ˌdʌb(ə)l prɪ ˌsɪʒ(ə)n 'ɪntɪdʒə/ *noun* número *m* entero de doble precisión

double-sided disk /ˌdʌb(ə)l ˌsaɪdɪd 'dɪsk/ *noun* disquete *m* de doble cara

double-sided disk drive /ˌdʌb(ə)l ˌsaɪdɪd 'dɪsk ˌdraɪv/ *noun* lector *m* de disquetes de doble cara

double-sided printed circuit board /ˌdʌb(ə)l ˌsaɪdɪd ˌprɪntɪd 'sɜːkɪt ˌbɔːd/ *noun* placa *f* de circuito impresa a doble cara

DoubleSpace /ˌdʌb(ə)l'speɪs/ (*software program that is part of MS-DOS 6*) compresión *f* de los datos del disco

double-speed drive /ˌdʌb(ə)l spiːd 'draɪv/ *noun* unidad *f* de disco de doble velocidad

double strike /'dʌb(ə)l straɪk/ *noun* doble subrayado *m*

doublet /'dʌblət/ *noun* doblete *m*; dipolo *m*

double word /'dʌb(ə)l wɜːd/ *noun* palabra *f* doble; palabra *f* larga

down /daʊn/ *adjective, adverb* (*not working*) sin funcionar ◇ **the computer system went down twice during the afternoon** el sistema informático quedó sin funcionar en dos ocasiones durante la tarde

download /ˌdaʊn'ləʊd/ *verb* **1.** (*to load a program or retrieve a section of data*) bajar *vt*; copiar *vt* **2.** (*to load data from a CPU to a small computer*) bajar *vt*; copiar *vt* **3.** (*to send print font data stored on disk to a printer, etc.*) bajar *vt*; copiar *vt* ◇ **there is no charge for downloading public domain software from the BBS** no es necesario pagar para copiar software de dominio público procedente de un tablón de anuncios (de la red)

'The cards will also download the latest version of the network drivers from the server.' [*Computing*]

downloadable font /ˌdaʊnləʊdəb(ə)l 'fɒnt/ *noun* fuente *f* de caracteres que se puede copiar

downsize /'daʊnsaɪz/ *verb* (*change from a central mainframe to a network*) reducir la escala de ◇ **downsizing is more cost effective and gives more processing power to the end-user** la reducción de la escala de una configuración informática es más rentable y proporciona más capacidad de proceso al usuario final

downtime /'daʊn taɪm/, **down time** *noun* tiempo *m* muerto; tiempo *m* de espera

downward compatibility /ˌdaʊnwəd kəm ˌpætə'bɪlɪti/ *noun* compatibilidad *f* con un sistema de nivel inferior

downward compatible /ˌdaʊnwəd kəm 'pætɪb(ə)l/ *adjective* compatible con un sistema de nivel inferior

DPCM /ˌdiː piː siː 'em/ *noun* modulación *f* de código de impulso diferencial

d.p.i. /ˌdiː piː 'aɪ/, **dpi** *abbr* (*dots per inch*) (número de) puntos *mpl* por pulgada; ppp ◇ **a 300 d.p.i. black and white A4 monitor** un monitor de tamaño A4, en blanco y negro y de 300 puntos por pulgada ◇ **a 300 dpi image scanner** un escáner de imágenes de 300 puntos por pulgada

DPM /ˌdiː piː 'em/ *abbr* (*data processing manager*) responsable *m&f* de servicio informático

draft printing /drɑːft 'prɪntɪŋ/ *noun* impresión *f* de baja calidad; impresión *f* de calidad de borrador

draft quality /drɑːft 'kwɒlɪti/ *noun* calidad *f* borrador

drag /dræg/ *verb* (*a mouse*) desplazar *vt*; deslizar *vt*; mover *vt*; tirar *vi*

'...press the mouse button and drag the mouse: this produces a dotted rectangle on the screen; you can easily enlarge the frame by dragging from any of the eight black rectangles round the border, showing that it is selected' [*Desktop Publishing*]

drag and click /ˌdræg ən 'klɪk/ *verb* arrastrar y hacer clic

drag and drop /ˌdræg ən 'drɒp/ *verb* arrastrar y soltar ◇ **drag and drop the document icon onto the word-processor icon and the system will start the program and load the document** arrastre y suelte el icono del documento sobre el icono del tratamiento de textos y el sistema arrancará el programa y cargará el documento

drag image /dræg 'ɪmɪdʒ/ *noun* imagen *f* de arrastre

DRAM /'diː ræm/ *abbr* (*dynamic random access memory*) memoria *f* de acceso aleatorio dinámica; RAM *f* dinámica

draw direct /ˌdrɔː daɪ'rekt/ *noun* (proceso de) dibujo *m* directo (sobre la pantalla)

drawing program /'drɔːɪŋ ˌprəʊgræm/ *noun* programa *m* de dibujo

drawing tool /'drɔːɪŋ tuːl/ *noun* herramienta *f* de dibujo; función *f* de dibujo

drive /draɪv/ *noun* lector *m*

drive bay /'draɪv beɪ/ *noun* emplazamiento *m* de la disquetera; emplazamiento *m* del lector de discos

drive designator /'draɪv ˌdezɪgneɪtə/ *noun* letra *f* de identificación de un lector; letra *f* de identificación de la unidad de disco

drive letter /draɪv 'letə/, **drive designator** /'draɪv ˌdezɪgneɪtə/ *noun* letra *f* de identificación de un lector; letra *f* de identificación de la unidad de disco

driver /'draɪvə/ *noun* (*device driver or device handler*) controlador *m*; excitador *m*

DRO /ˌdiː ɑːr 'əʊ/ *noun* lectura *f* destructiva

drop /drɒp/ *verb* caer *vi*

drop cable /drɒp 'keɪb(ə)l/ *noun* (*cable that links an adapter to the main network cable*) cable *m* de derivación; cable *m* de bajada

drop dead halt /ˌdrɒp ded 'hɔːlt/ *noun* parada *f* total

drop-down list box /ˌdrɒp daʊn 'lɪst/ *noun* (*list of options for an entry*) lista *f* desplegable

drop-down menu /ˌdrɒp daʊn 'menjuː/ *noun* (*menu that appears below a menu title*) menú *m* desplegable

drop in /ˌdrɒp 'ɪn/ *noun* (*piece of dirt on a disk or tape surface*) información *f* parásita; aberración *f* por exceso; señal *f* espúrea

drop out /ˌdrɒp 'aʊt/ *noun* (*data storage*) pérdida *f* de la información; aberración *f* por defecto; (*of signal*) pérdida *f* de nivel

drum /drʌm/ *noun* cilindro *m*; tambor *m*

drum plotter /'drʌm ˌplɒtə/ *noun* trazador *m* de tambor

dry contact /draɪ 'kɒntækt/ *noun* contacto *m* seco; contacto *m* en circuito sin corriente

dry run /ˌdraɪ 'rʌn/ *noun* ejecución *f* seca; ejecución *f* en seco

DS-0 /ˌdiː es 'zɪərəʊ/ *noun* señal *f* digital de nivel cero

DS-1 /ˌdiː es 'wʌn/ *noun* señal *f* digital de nivel uno

DSL /ˌdiː es 'el/ *noun* línea *f* de abonado digital

DSP /ˌdiː es 'piː/ *noun* proceso *m* de señales digitales

DSR /ˌdiː es 'ɑː/ *noun* señal *f* de preparado para recibir

D-SUB connector /ˌdiː sʌb kə'nektə/ *noun* (*connector commonly used on PC monitors*) conector *m* D-SUB

DSW /ˌdiː es 'dʌb(ə)l juː/ *noun* palabra *f* indicadora del estado de funcionamiento

DTE /ˌdiː tiː 'iː/ *noun* terminal *m* de transmisión de datos

D to A converter /ˌdiː tʊ ˌeɪ kən'vɜːtə/ *noun* convertidor *m* digital/analógico

DTP /ˌdiː tiː 'piː/ *noun* autoedición *f*

DTR /ˌdiː tiː 'ɑː/ *noun* preparado para transmitir

DTV /ˌdiː tiː 'viː/ *noun* edición *f* de vídeo asistida por ordenador

D-type connector /ˌdiː taɪp kə'nektə/ *noun* (*connector shaped like the letter D*) conector *m* en D; conector *m* de tipo D ◇ **the serial port on a PC uses a 9-pin D-type connector** el puerto en serie de un PC usa un conector de tipo D con nueve contactos

dual /'djuːəl/ *adjective* dual ◇ **dual tone multi-frequency (DTMF)** multifrecuencia *f* de tono dual

dual attachment /'djuːəl ə'tætʃmənt/, **dual attached station** /ˌdjuːəl əˌtætʃt 'steɪʃ(ə)n/ *noun* estación *f* de doble conexión

dual bus system /ˌdjuːəl 'bʌs ˌsɪstəm/ *noun* sistema *m* de enlace común doble

dual channel /ˌdjuːəl 'tʃæn(ə)l/ *noun* vía *f* doble; canal *m* doble

dual clocking /'djuːəl klɒkɪŋ/ *noun* cronometraje *m* doble

dual column /ˌdjuːəl 'kɒləm/ *noun* columna *f* doble

dual homing /ˌdjuːəl 'həʊmɪŋ/ *noun* base *f* doble

dual in-line memory module /ˌdjuːəl ˌɪn laɪn 'mem(ə)ri ˌmɒdjuːl/ *noun* módulo *m* de memoria doble en línea

dual-in-line package /ˌdjuːəl ɪn laɪn 'pækɪdʒ/ *noun* encapsulado *m* dual en línea; empaquetamiento *m* doble en línea

dual port memory /ˌdjuːəl pɔːt 'mem(ə)ri/ *noun* memoria *f* con doble acceso

dual processor /ˌdjuːəl 'prəʊsesə/ *noun* procesador *m* doble

dual-scan display /ˌdjuːəl skæn dɪ'spleɪ/ *noun* pantalla *f* de doble barrido

dual systems /ˌdjuːəl 'sɪstəmz/ *plural noun* sistema *m* doble

dual tone multi-frequency /ˌdjuːəl təʊn ˌmʌlti 'friːkwənsi/ *noun* multifrecuencia *f* de tono dual

dub /dʌb/ *verb* doblar *vt* ◇ **dubbed sound** sonido *m* doblado

duct /dʌkt/ *noun* conducto *m*

dumb /dʌm/ *adjective* no inteligente

dumb terminal /dʌm 'tɜːmɪn(ə)l/ *noun* terminal *m* no inteligente

dummy /'dʌmi/ *noun* maqueta *f*

dummy instruction /'dʌmi ɪnˌstrʌkʃən/ *noun* (*blank instruction*) instrucción *f* nula; instrucción *f* falsa; instrucción *f* ficticia; instrucción *f* simulada

dummy variable /ˌdʌmi 'veəriəb(ə)l/ *noun* variable *f* ficticia

dump /dʌmp/ *noun* **1.** (*data copied*) resultado *m* de la transcripción **2.** (*transferring of data*) vaciado *m*; vuelco *m* (de memoria); transferencia *f* ■ *verb* (*to transfer data*) copiar *vti*; transferir *vt*; vaciar *vt*

dump and restart /ˌdʌmp ən 'riːstɑːt/ *noun* vaciado y reinicio

dump point /'dʌmp pɔɪnt/ *noun* punto *m* de vaciado

duodecimal number system /djuːəʊ ˌdesɪm(ə)l 'nʌmbə ˌsɪstəm/ *noun* sistema *m* duodecimal

duplex /'djuːpleks/ *noun* (*photographic paper*) papel *m* fotosensible de doble cara; (*transmission of two signals*) dúplex *m*

duplex circuit /'djuːpleks ˌsɜːkɪt/ *noun* circuito *m* dúplex

duplex computer /'djuːpleks kəmˌpjuːtə/ *noun* ordenador *m* dúplex; sistema *m* dúplex

duplexing /'djuːpleksɪŋ/ *noun* duplexado *m*

duplex operation /ˌdjuːpleks ˌɒpə'reɪʃ(ə)n/ *noun* operación *f* en dúplex; transmisión *f* en dúplex

duty-rated /'djuːti rætd/ *adjective* medido por el coeficiente de trabajo

DVD /ˌdiː viː 'diː/ *noun* disco DVD *m*

DVD-R /ˌdiː viː 'diː ɑː/ *abbr* (*DVD-Recordable*) DVD-R

DVD-RAM /ˌdiː viː 'diː ræm/ *noun* DVD-RAM

DVD-Recordable /ˌdiː viː diː rɪ'kɔːdəb(ə)l/ *noun* disco *m* de vídeo digital recordable

DVD-ROM /ˌdiː viː 'diː rɒm/ *noun* DVD-ROM

DVD+RW /ˌdiː viː diː plʌs ɑː 'dʌb(ə)l juː/ *noun* DVD+RW

DVD-video /ˌdiː viː 'diː 'vɪdiəʊ/ *noun* DVD-vídeo *m*

DV-I /ˌdiː viː 'aɪ/ *noun* sistema *m* interactivo de vídeo digital (DV-I)

Dvorak keyboard /ˌdvɔːræk 'kiːbɔːd/ *noun* (*special keyboard layout*) teclado *m* DVORAK

DX /diː eks/ *suffix* DX (del procesador Intel)

dyadic Boolean operation /daɪˌædɪk ˌbuːliən ˌɒpə'reɪʃ(ə)n/ *noun* operación *f* booleana diádica

dyadic operation /daɪˌædɪk ˌɒpə'reɪʃ(ə)n/ *noun* operación *f* diádica; operación *f* con dos operandos

dye-polymer recording /ˌdaɪ 'pɒlɪmə rɪ ˌkɔːdɪŋ/ *noun* (*optical disk recording method*) grabación *f* por capa polimerizada

dye-sublimation printer /daɪ sʌblɪ ˌmeɪʃ(ə)n 'prɪntə/ *noun* (*high-quality colour printer*) impresora *f* con sublimación térmica ◇ **the new dye-sublimation printer can produce colour images at a resolution of 300dpi** la nueva impresora con sublimación térmica puede producir imágenes con una resolución de 300 puntos por pulgada

dynamic /daɪ'næmɪk/ *adjective* dinámico *or* -a ◇ **dynamic hypertext markup language (DHTML)** lenguaje *m* de escritura hipertextual dinámico ◇ **dynamic microphone** micrófono dinámico ◇ **dynamic RAM** *or* **dynamic random access memory (DRAM)** RAM dinámico *or* memoria de acceso aleatorio dinámica

dynamic allocation /daɪˌnæmɪk ˌælə 'keɪʃ(ə)n/ *noun* asignación *f* dinámica

dynamically redefinable character set /daɪˌnæmɪkli riːdɪˌfaɪnəb(ə)l 'kærɪktə ˌset/ *noun* conjunto *m* de caracteres redefinibles dinámicamente

dynamic buffer /daɪˌnæmɪk 'bʌfə/ *noun* memoria *f* intermedia dinámica

dynamic data exchange /daɪˌnæmɪk 'deɪtə ɪksˌtʃeɪndʒ/ *noun* intercambio *m* dinámico de datos

dynamic data structure /daɪˌnæmɪk 'deɪtə ˌstrʌktʃə/ *noun* (*transferring of data*) estructura *f* de datos dinámica

dynamic dump /daɪˌnæmɪk 'dʌmp/ *noun* vaciado *m* dinámico

dynamic link library /daɪˌnæmɪk 'lɪŋk ˌlaɪbrəri/ *noun* (*Microsoft Windows and OS/2 library of utility programs*) biblioteca *f* dinámica de enlaces; DLL

dynamic memory /daɪˌnæmɪk 'mem(ə)ri/ *noun* (*dynamic storage*) memoria *f* dinámica

dynamic multiplexing /daɪˌnæmɪk 'mʌltɪpleksɪŋ/ *noun* múltiplexión *f* dinámica; multiplexado *m* dinámico

dynamic RAM /daɪˌnæmɪk 'ræm/ *noun* RAM *f* dinámica

dynamic random access memory /daɪ ˌnæmɪk ˌrændəm ˌækses 'mem(ə)ri/ *noun* RAM *f* dinámica; memoria *f* de acceso aleatorio dinámica

dynamic relocation /daɪ,næmɪk ,riːləʊ 'keɪʃ(ə)n/ *noun* redireccionamiento *m* dinámico

dynamic relocation program /daɪ,næmɪk ,riːləʊ'keɪʃ(ə)n ,prəʊgræm/ *noun* desplazamiento *m* dinámico

dynamic routing /daɪ,næmɪk 'ruːtɪŋ/ *noun* ruta *f* dinámica

dynamic stop /daɪ,næmɪk 'stɒp/ *noun* parada *f* dinámica

dynamic storage /daɪ,næmɪk 'stɔːrɪdʒ/ *noun* memoria *f* dinámica

dynamic storage allocation /daɪ,næmɪk 'stɔːrɪdʒ ,æləkeɪʃ(ə)n/ *noun* asignación *f* dinámica de la memoria

dynamic subroutine /daɪ,næmɪk 'sʌbruːtiːn/ *noun* subrutina *f* dinámica

dynamic update /daɪ'næmɪk ,ʌpdeɪt/ *noun* actualización *f* dinámica

E

E *symbol* (*hexadecimal number equivalent to decimal 14*) número hexadecimal 14; electrónico; (*hexadecimal number equivalent to decimal 14*) E *or* -a ◇ **e-commerce consultant** consultor, -a *or* asesor, -a de comercio electrónico

E-1 /iː wʌn/ *noun* línea *f* E-1 (de telecomunicaciones)

EAPROM /ˌiː eɪ ˈpiː ˌrɒm/ *noun* memoria *f* EAPROM

early token release /ˌɜːli ˈtəʊkən rɪˌliːs/ *noun* (*Token-Ring or FDDI network system*) liberación *f* anticipada de ficha

EAROM /ˌiː eɪ ˌrɒm/ *noun* memoria *f* EAROM

earth /ɜːθ/ *noun* (*in circuit connection*) tierra *f*; (*to connect an electrical device to earth*) toma *f* de tierra ■ *verb* (*to connect an electrical device to earth*) conectar a tierra; instalar una toma de tierra ◇ **all appliances must be earthed** todos los aparatos eléctricos deben tener toma de tierra ◇ **all loose wires should be tied to earth** todos los alambres sueltos deberían tener una toma de tierra

earth wire /ɜːθ ˈwaɪə/ *noun* cable *m* de tierra; cable *m* de toma de tierra

EBCDIC /ˌiː biː biː siː diː aɪ ˈsiː/ *noun* código *m* EBCDIC; código *m* de intercambio decimal de codificación binaria extendida; sistema *m* de codificación de caracteres de 8 bits

ebook /ˈiːbʊk/ *noun* (*electronic book*) libro *m* electrónico; publicación *f* multimedia electrónica

e-business /ˈiː ˌbɪznəs/ *noun* **1.** empresa *f* electrónica **2.** negocios *mpl* electrónicos

echo /ˈekəʊ/ *noun* eco *m* ■ *verb* hacer eco; resonar *vi* ◇ **echo chamber** cámara *f* de ecos ◇ **echo suppressor** supresor *m* de eco

echo cancellation /ˈekəʊ ˌkænsəleɪʃ(ə)n/ *noun* supresión *f* de eco(s)

echo check /ˈekəʊ tʃek/ *noun* verificación *f*; control *m* por eco

ECMA *abbr* (*European Computer Manufacturers Association*) asociación *f* europea de fabricantes de ordenadores

ECML /ˌiː siː em ˈel/ *abbr* (*electronic commerce modelling language*) lenguaje *m* de modelado de comercio electrónico

e-commerce /ˈiː ˌkɒmɜːs/ *noun* comercio *m* electrónico

ECP /ˌiː siː ˈpiː/ *noun* puerto *m* de comunicación ampliada

EDAC /ˌiː diː eɪ ˈsiː/ *noun* detección y corrección de errores

edge /edʒ/ *noun* **1.** (*of flat object or signal or clock pulse*) borde *m*; límite *m* **2.** borde *m*; límite *m*

edge board /ˈedʒ bɔːd/ *noun* placa *f* de borde

edge card /ˈedʒ kɑːd/ *noun* placa *f* de borde

edge connector /edʒ kəˈnektə/ *noun* conector *m* de borde

'Connections to the target board are made via IC test clips or the edge connector.' [*Electronics Today*]

edge detection /edʒ dɪˈtekʃ(ə)n/ *noun* detección *f* de límites; detección *f* de bordes

edge notched card /ˌedʒ nɒtʃt ˈkɑːd/ *noun* placa *f* con perforaciones al margen

edge-triggered /edʒ ˈtrɪɡəd/ *adjective* de borde activado

EDI /ˌiː diː ˈaɪ/ *noun* intercambio *m* electrónico de datos

edit /ˈedɪt/ *verb* (*to format*) editar *vt*; dar formato; (*to correct text*) corregir *vt*; revisar *vt* ◇ **there are several special edit keys – this one will re-format the text** ésta da un nuevo formato al texto

edit command /ˈedɪt kəˌmɑːnd/ *plural noun* instrucción *f* de edición

editing run /ˈedɪtɪŋ rʌn/ *noun* ejecución *f* de un programa de edición

editing term /ˈedɪtɪŋ tɜːm/ *noun* instrucción *f* de edición

edit key /ˈedɪt kiː/ *noun* tecla *f* (de función) de edición ◇ **there are several special edit keys – this one will re-format the text** hay varias teclas especiales de edición; ésta da un nuevo formato al texto

editor /ˈedɪtə/ *noun* (*person who edits films or books*) editor *m or* -a *f*; redactor *m or* -a; corrector, -a de estilo ◇ **linkage editor** editor *or* montador *m* de enlaces

'The Smartbook authoring system is a software product that integrates text and fractally compressed images, using any wordprocessor line editor.' [*Computing*]

'…while it has many formatting facilities, it does not include an editor with which to create the template for the report' [*Personal Computer World*]

editor program /ˈedɪtə ˌprəʊɡræm/ *noun* editor *m* de programa

edit window /ˈedɪt ˌwɪndəʊ/ *noun* ventana *f* de edición

EDLIN /ˌiː diː el aɪ ˈen/ *noun* (*MS-DOS system utility*) utilidad *f* EDLIN; editor *m* de línea

EDO memory /,i: di: əʊ 'mem(ə)ri/ *noun* memoria *f* EDO

EDP /,i: di: 'pi:/ *noun* proceso *m* electrónico de datos; proceso *m* de información

EDP capability /,i: di: pi: ,keɪpə'bɪlɪti/ *noun* capacidad *f* de proceso (electrónico) de datos

EDS /,i: di: 'es/ *noun* almacenamiento *m* de discos intercambiables

EDTV /,i: di: ti: 'vi:/ *noun* televisión *f* de definición extendida

edu *suffix* (*at the end of an internet domain*) - edu; (sufijo que identifica la dirección digital de un centro) educativo

edutainment /,edjʊ'teɪnmənt/ *noun* programa *m* ludo-educativo

EEPROM *abbr* (*electrically erasable programmable read-only memory*) memoria *f* EEPROM

EEROM *abbr* (*electrically erasable read-only memory*) memoria *f* EEROM

effective address /ɪ,fektɪv ə'dres/ *noun* dirección *f* efectiva; dirección *f* real

effective instruction /ɪ,fektɪv ɪn'strʌkʃən/ *noun* instrucción *f* efectiva

effective search speed /ɪ,fektɪv 'sɜ:tʃ ,spi:d/ *noun* velocidad *f* de búsqueda efectiva

effective throughput /ɪ,fektɪv 'θru:pʊt/ *noun* rendimiento *m* efectivo

EFT /,i: ef 'ti:/ *noun* transferencia *f* electrónica de fondos

EFTPOS /,i: ef ,ti: pi: əʊ 'es/ *noun* terminal *m* de transferencia electrónica de fondos

'Alphameric has extended its range specifically for the hospitality market and has developed an eftpos package which allows most credit and debit cards to be processed.' [*Computing*]

egg timer /'eg ,taɪmə/ *noun* reloj *m*

EIA *abbr* (*Electronics Industry Association*) asociación *f* de industrias electrónicas

EIA interface /,i: ,aɪ ,eɪ ,ɪntə'feɪs/ *noun* interfaz *f* de normas EIA; interfaz *f* EIA

eight-bit /eɪt bɪt/, **8-bit** /eɪt bɪt/ *adjective* de ocho bits

eight-bit byte /eɪt bɪt/, **eight-bit octet** /,eɪt bɪt ɒk'tet/ *noun* octeto *m*

eight-bit octet /,eɪt bɪt ɒk'tet/ *noun* octeto *m*

eight-inch disk /eɪt ɪntʃ dɪsk/, **8-inch disk** *noun* disquete *m* de ocho pulgadas

eight-inch drive /eɪt ɪntʃ draɪv/, **8-inch drive** *noun* lector *m* de disquetes de ocho pulgadas

eighty-column screen /,eɪti 'kɒləm skri:n/, **80-column screen** *noun* (*screen that displays 80 characters horizontally*) pantalla *f* de ochenta columnas

eighty-track disk /'eɪti træk dɪsk/, **80-track disk** *noun* disco *m* de ochenta pistas

EIS /,i: aɪ 'es/ *noun* sistema *m* EIS; sistema *m* de información para la gestión

EISA /,i: aɪ es 'eɪ/ *noun* EISA

either-or operation /,aɪðə 'ɔ: ,ɒpəreɪʃ(ə)n/ *noun* (*logical function*) operación *f* O-O; operación *f* ambos o uno; operación *f* EITHER-OR

either-way operation /,aɪðə 'weɪ ,ɒpəreɪʃ(ə)n/ *noun* operación *f* bidireccional

elapsed time /ɪ,læpst 'taɪm/ *noun* tiempo *m* transcurrido; tiempo *m* de ejecución de una tarea

elastic banding /ɪ'læstɪk bændɪŋ/ *noun* (*defining the limits of an image on a screen*) encuadre *m* (de una imagen en la pantalla) ◊ **elastic banding is much easier to control with a mouse** con el ratón se controla mucho mejor el encuadre de una imagen

elastic buffer /ɪ,læstɪk 'bʌfə/ *noun* memoria *f* intermedia de capacidad variable

electrically alterable programmable read-only memory /ɪ,lektrɪkli ,ɔ:ltərəb(ə)l ,prəʊgræməb(ə)l ,ri:d ,əʊnli 'mem(ə)ri/ *noun* memoria *f* EAPROM

electrically alterable read-only memory /ɪ,lektrɪkli ,ɔ:ltərəb(ə)l ,ri:d ,əʊnli 'mem(ə)ri/ *noun* memoria *f* EAPROM, modificable eléctricamente; memoria *f* ROM programable, modificable eléctricamente

electrically erasable programmable read-only memory /ɪ,lektrɪkli ɪ,reɪzəb(ə)l ,prəʊgræməb(ə)l ,ri:d ,əʊnli 'mem(ə)ri/ *noun* memoria *f* EEPROM; memoria *f* de lectura programable y borrable eléctricamente

electrically erasable read-only memory /ɪ,lektrɪkli ɪ,reɪzəb(ə)l ,ri:d ,əʊnli 'mem(ə)ri/ *noun* memoria *f* EEROM; memoria *f* de lectura borrable eléctricamente

electrical polarity /ɪ,lektrɪk(ə)l pəʊ'lærɪti/ *noun* polaridad *f* eléctrica

electric charge /ɪ'lektrɪk tʃɑ:dʒ/ *noun* carga *f* eléctrica

electric current /ɪ,lektrɪk 'kʌrənt/ *noun* corriente *f* eléctrica

electricity /ɪ,lek'trɪsɪti/ *noun* electricidad *f*; corriente *f* ◊ **electricity prices are an important factor in the production costs** los precios de la electricidad son un factor importante en los costos de producción ◊ **the electricity was cut off, and the computer crashed** hubo un corte de la corriente eléctrica y el ordenador falló

electrographic printer /ɪ,lektrəʊgræfɪk 'prɪntə/ *noun* impresora *f* electrostática

electroluminescence /ɪ,elektrəʊ,lu:mɪ'nes(ə)ns/ *noun* electroluminiscencia *f*

electroluminescent /ɪ,elektrəʊ,lu:mɪ'nes(ə)nt/ *adjective* electroluminiscente ◊ **the screen coating is electroluminescent** la pantalla está recubierta de una capa electroluminiscente

electroluminescent display /ɪ,lektrəʊlu:mɪnesənt dɪ'spleɪ/ *noun* visualización *f* electroluminiscente; pantalla *f* electroluminiscente

electroluminescing /ɪ,elektrəʊ,lu:mɪ'nesɪŋ/ *adjective* electroluminiscente

electromagnetic /ɪ,lektrəʊmæg'netɪk/ *adjective* electromagnético *or* -a ◊ **electromagnetic spectrum** espectro electromagnético

electromagnetic interference /ˌlektrəʊmægnetɪk ˌɪntəˈfɪərəns/ *noun* interferencia *f* electromagnética

electron beam /ɪˈlekˌtrɒn biːm/ *noun* haz *m* electrónico; haz *m* de electrones ◇ **the electron beam draws the image on the inside of a CRT screen** el haz de electrones dibuja la imagen en el interior de una pantalla de rayos catódicos

electron beam recording /ɪˌlektrɒn ˌbiːm rɪˈkɔːdɪŋ/ *noun* grabación *f* por medio de un haz electrónico

electron gun /ɪˈlekˌtrɒn gʌn/ *noun* cañón *m* de electrones

electronic agenda /ˌelektrɒnɪk əˈdʒendə/ *noun* agenda *f* electrónica

electronic blackboard /ˌelektrɒnɪk ˈblækbɔːd/ *noun* pizarra *f* electrónica

electronic book /ˌelektrɒnɪk ˈbʊk/ *noun* libro *m* electrónico; publicación *f* multimedia electrónica

electronic commerce /ˌelektrɒnɪk ˈkɒmɜːs/ *noun* comercio *m* electrónico

electronic data interchange /ˌelektrɒnɪk ˈdeɪtə ˌɪntətʃeɪndʒ/ *noun* intercambio *m* electrónico de datos

electronic data processing /ˌelektrɒnɪk ˈdeɪtə ˌprəʊsesɪŋ/ *noun* proceso *m* electrónico de datos; proceso *m* electrónico de la información

electronic data processing capability /ˌelektrɒnɪk ˌdeɪtə ˌprəʊsesɪŋ ˌkeɪpəˈbɪlɪti/ *noun* capacidad *f* de proceso electrónico de datos

electronic digital computer /ˌelektrɒnɪk ˌdɪdʒɪt(ə)l kəmˈpjuːtə/ *noun* ordenador *m* digital electrónico; calculadora *f* digital electrónica

electronic filing /ˌelektrɒnɪk ˈfaɪlɪŋ/ *noun* (*storage of documents*) clasificación *f* electrónica; catalogación *f* electrónica; catalogación *f* por ordenador

electronic funds transfer /ˌelektrɒnɪk ˈfʌndz ˌtrænsfɜː/ *noun* transferencia *f* electrónica de fondos

electronic funds transfer point-of-sale /ˌelektrɒnɪk ˌfʌndz ˌtrænsfɜː ˌpɔɪnt əv ˈseɪl/ *noun* terminal *m* de transferencia electrónica de fondos

electronic mail /ˌelɪktrɒnɪk ˈmeɪl/ *noun* correo *m* electrónico

electronic mailbox /ˌelektrɒnɪk ˈmeɪlbɒks/ *noun* buzón *m* electrónico ◇ **when I log onto the network, I always check my electronic mailbox for new messages** cuando contacto con la red, siempre examino mi buzón electrónico por si hay algún mensaje nuevo

electronic pen /ˌelektrɒnɪk ˈpen/ *noun* lápiz *m* óptico

electronic point-of-sale /ˌelektrɒnɪk ˌpɔɪnt əv ˈseɪl/ *noun* punto *m* de venta electrónico

electronic publishing /ˌelektrɒnɪk ˈpʌblɪʃɪŋ/ *noun* publicación *f* electrónica; publicación *f* asistida por ordenador

electronic pulse /ˌelektrɒnɪk ˈpʌls/ *noun* impulso *m* electrónico

electronics /ˌelekˈtrɒnɪks/ *noun* (*science*) electrónica *f* ◇ **electronics specialist** experto, -a en electrónica; especialista *m&f* en electrónica ◇ **the electronics industry** la industria electrónica

electronic shopping /ˌelektrɒnɪk ˈʃɒpɪŋ/ *noun* compra *f* por ordenador

electronic signature /ˌelektrɒnɪk ˈsɪgnɪtʃə/ *noun* firma *f* electrónica; signatura *f* electrónica

electronics industry association interface /ˌelektrɒnɪks ˌɪndəstri əˌsəʊsieɪʃ(ə)n ˈɪntəfeɪs/ *noun* interfaz *f* de normas EIA

Electronics Industry Standards Association /elekˌtrɒnɪks ˌɪndəstri ˈstændədz əˌsəʊsieɪʃ(ə)n/ *noun* EISA

electronic smog /ˌelektrɒnɪk ˈsmɒg/ *noun* contaminación *f* electrónica; polución *f* electrónica

electronic stylus /ˌelektrɒnɪk ˈstaɪləs/ *noun* lápiz *m* óptico

electronic traffic /ˌelektrɒnɪk ˈtræfɪk/ *noun* transmisión *f* electrónica

electronic wand /ˌelektrɒnɪk ˈwɒnd/ *noun* lápiz *m* óptico

electrophotographic /ˌelektrəʊˌfəʊtəˈgræfɪk/ *adjective* electrofotográfico

electrosensitive /ˌelektrəʊˈsensɪtɪv/ *adjective* electrosensible

electrosensitive paper /ɪˌlektrəʊsensɪtɪv ˈpeɪpə/ *noun* papel *m* electrosensible; papel *m* de transferencia térmica

electrosensitive printing /ɪˌlektrəʊsensɪtɪv ˈprɪntɪŋ/ *noun* impresión *f* electrosensible; impresión *f* térmica

electrostatic /ɪlektrəʊˈstætɪk/ *adjective* electrostático *or* -a ◇ **electrostatic speaker** altavoz electrostático

electrostatic printer /ɪˌlektrəʊstætɪk ˈprɪntə/ *noun* impresora *f* electrostática

electrostatic screen /ɪˌlektrəʊstætɪk ˈskriːn/ *noun* pantalla *f* electrostática

electrostatic storage /ɪˌlektrəʊstætɪk ˈstɔːrɪdʒ/ *noun* memoria *f* electrostática

electrothermal printer /ɪˌlektrəʊθɜːməl ˈprɪntə/ *noun* impresora *f* electrotérmica

elegant programming /ˌelɪgənt ˌprəʊˈgræmɪŋ/ *noun* programación *f* elegante; programación *f* bien concebida

element /ˈelɪmənt/ *noun* **1.** (*small part of an object*) elemento *m*; componente *m* **2.** (*cell of a matrix*) elemento *m*; célula *f*

elementary /ˌelɪˈment(ə)ri/ *adjective* (*made of many similar small sections or objects*) elemental ◇ **elementary cable section** sección *f* elemental de cable

elevator /ˈelɪveɪtə/ *noun* (*small, square indicator displayed within a scroll*) ascensor *m*; (*small, square indicator displayed within a scroll bar*) cursor *m* de la barra lateral ◇ **the user can scroll through the image or text by dragging the elevator up or down the scroll bar** un usuario se puede mover por la imagen o por el texto arrastrando el cursor de la barra lateral de desplazamiento hacia arriba o hacia abajo

elimination factor /ɪ,lɪmɪ'neɪʃ(ə)n ,fæktə/ *noun* factor *m* de eliminación

else rule /'els ruːl/ *noun* (*program logical rule*) regla *f* DE OTRO MODO; regla *f* SI NO; regla *f* DE OTRA MANERA; regla *f* ELSE ◇ **IF X=20 THEN PRINT 'X is 20' ELSE PRINT 'X not 20'** si X=20 PRINT 'X igual a 20' ELSE PRINT 'X distinto de 20'

email /'iː meɪl/, **e-mail** *noun* (*message*) correo *m* electrónico

embedded code /ɪm,bedɪd 'kəʊd/ *noun* código *m* incorporado

embedded command /ɪm,bedɪd kə'mɑːnd/ *noun* instrucción *f* intercalada

embedded computer /ɪm,bedɪd kəm'pjuːtə/ *noun* ordenador *m* intercalado (en otro)

embedded object /ɪm,bedɪd əb'dʒekt/ *noun* (*feature of Windows OLE*) objeto *m* incrustado; archivo *m* incrustado

embedded system /ɪm,bedɪd 'sɪstəm/ *noun* sistema *m* intercalado (en otro)

EMI /,iː em 'aɪ/ *noun* interferencia *f* electromagnética

emitter-coupled logic /ɪ,mɪtə ,kʌp(ə)ld 'lɒdʒɪk/ *noun* lógica *f* de emisor acoplado (ECL)

EMM /,iː em 'em/ *noun* gestor *m* de memoria extendida

emoticon /ɪ'məʊtɪkɒn/ *noun* (*combination of colons, hyphens and parentheses, etc., which becomes a 'smiley' to show feelings*) emoticón *m*; expreicono *m*

'Smileys, or emoticons, have been around for a long time: the simplest ones, such as :-), can indicate in a tense-sounding email or text message that you are not feeling as angry as you may appear.' [*The Guardian*]

emphasis /'emfəsɪs/ *noun* **1.** acentuación *f* **2.** realce *m*

empty medium /,empti 'miːdiəm/ *noun* (*blank storage medium*) soporte *m* vacío; medio *m* vacío; soporte *m* magnético vacío

empty slot /'empti slɒt/ *noun* **1.** (*for card*) ranura *f* vacía **2.** conector *m* (de tarjeta adicional) vacío

EMS /,iː em 'es/ *noun* especificación *f* de memoria expandida

emulate /'emjʊ,leɪt/ *verb* emular *vt* ◇ **a laser printer which emulates a wide range of office printers** una impresora láser que puede emular una amplia gama de impresoras de oficina

'...some application programs do not have the right drivers for a laser printer, so look out for laser printers which are able to emulate the more popular office printers' [*Publish*]

emulation /,emjʊ'leɪʃ(ə)n/ *noun* emulación *f*

emulation facility /,emjʊ'leɪʃ(ə)n fə,sɪlɪti/ *noun* capacidad *f* de emulación

'...full communications error checking built into the software ensures reliable file transfers and a

terminal emulation facility enables a user's terminal to be used as if it were a terminal to the remote computer' [*Byte*]

emulator /'emjʊleɪtə/ *noun* emulador *m*

'...for an authentic retro coding experience, download an emulator and turn your computer into a virtual BBC Micro.' [*The Guardian*]

emulsion laser storage /ɪ,mʌlʃ(ə)n 'leɪzə ,stɔːrɪdʒ/ *noun* (técnica de) almacenamiento *m* láser por emulsión

en /en/ *noun* en; medio *m* em

enable /ɪn'eɪb(ə)l/ *verb* (*to use an electronic signal to start a process*) seleccionar *vt*; activar *vt*; validar *vt*

enabled /ɪn'eɪb(ə)ld/ *adjective* activo

enabling signal /ɪn'eɪblɪŋ ,sɪgn(ə)l/ *noun* (*signal that starts a process*) señal *f* de selección; señal *f* de validación; señal *f* de activación

encapsulated /ɪn'kæpsjʊleɪtɪd/ *adjective* (*contained in something else*) encapsulado *or* -a

encapsulated PostScript /ɪn,kæpsjʊleɪtɪd 'pəʊstskrɪpt/ *noun* PostScript *m* encapsulado; EPS

encapsulated PostScript file /ɪn ,kæpsjʊleɪtɪd 'pəʊstskrɪpt ,faɪl/ *noun* fichero *m* PostScript encapsulado; EPSF

encapsulation /ɪn'kæpsjʊleɪʃ(ə)n/ *noun* (*system of sending a frame of data in another frame*) encapsulación *f*

encipher /ɪn'saɪfə/ *verb* cifrar *vt*; codificar *vt* ◇ **our competitors cannot understand our files – they have all been enciphered** están en lenguaje cifrado

enclosed object /ɪn,kləʊzd əb'dʒekt/ *noun* objeto *m* encerrado; objeto *m* enmarcado

encode /ɪn'kəʊd/ *verb* cifrar *vt*; codificar *vt*

encoder /ɪn'kəʊdə/ *noun* codificador *m* ◇ **colour encoder** codificador de colores

encoding /ɪn'kəʊdɪŋ/ *noun* codificación *f*

encoding format /ɪn'kəʊdɪŋ ,fɔːmæt/ *noun* formato *m* de codificación

encrypt /ɪn'krɪpt/ *verb* (*to encode plaintext*) cifrar *vt*; codificar *vt*; encriptar *vt* ◇ **the encrypted text can be sent along ordinary telephone lines, and no one will be able to understand it** se puede transmitir un texto codificado por una línea de teléfono normal de forma que nadie pueda entenderlo

encryption /ɪn'krɪpʃən/ *noun* (*encoding of plaintext*) codificación *f*; mensaje *m* cifrado; puesta *f* en clave de datos ◇ **data encryption standard (DES)** estándar *m* de puesta en clave de datos

end /end/ *noun* final *m*

end about carry /,end ə'baʊt ,kæri/ *noun* arrastre *m* en esquema circular; arrastre *m* en bucle

end about shift /,end ə'baʊt ,ʃɪft/ *noun* desplazamiento *m* circular

end around carry /,end ə'raʊnd ,kæri/ *noun* arrastre *m* en esquema circular/en bucle

end key /'end kiː/ *noun* tecla *f* End; tecla *f* Fin

endless loop /'endləs luːp/ *noun* (*repetition of information or instructions*) bucle *m* sin fin; bucle *m* continuo; bucle *m* infinito

end of address /ˌend əv ə'dres/ *noun* código *m* de final de dirección

end of block /ˌend əv 'blɒk/ *noun* código *m* de final de bloque

end of data /ˌend əv 'deɪtə/ *noun* código *m* de final de datos

end of document /ˌend əv 'dɒkjʊmənt/ *noun* código *m* de final de documento

end of file /ˌend əv 'faɪl/ *noun* fin *m* de archivo

end of job /ˌend əv 'dʒɒb/ *noun* código *m* de final de tarea

end of line /ˌend əv 'laɪn/ *noun* código *m* de final de línea

end of medium /ˌend əv 'miːdiəm/ *noun* código *m* de final de medio; código *m* de soporte de datos

end of message /ˌend əv 'mesɪdʒ/ *noun* código *m* de final de mensaje

end of record /ˌend əv 'rekɔːd/ *noun* código *m* de final de registro

end of run routines /ˌend əv 'rʌn ruːˌtiːnz/ *plural noun* rutinas *fpl* de final; rutinas *fpl* de cierre

end of tape /ˌend əv 'teɪp/ *noun* código *m* de final de cinta (magnética)

end of text /ˌend əv 'tekst/ *noun* código *m* de final de texto

end of transmission /ˌend əv trænz 'mɪʃ(ə)n/ *noun* final *m* de transmisión

end product /ˌend 'prɒdʌkt/ *noun* producto *m* final; producto *m* acabado

end system /end 'sɪstəm/ *noun* servidor *m*

end system to intermediate system /ˌend ˌsɪstəm tə ˌɪntə'miːdiət ˌsɪstəm/ *noun* protocolo *m* estándar de servidor a sistema intermedio

end user /ˌend 'juːzə/ *noun* usuario *m* final ◇ **the company is creating a computer with a specific end user in mind** la empresa está creando un ordenador pensando en un usuario final específico

Energy Star /'enədʒi stɑː/ *noun* (logotipo de) Estrella *f* de (ahorro de) Energía

engine /'endʒɪn/ *noun* (*part of a software package that carries out a particular function*) máquina *f*

enhanced communication port /ɪnˌhɑːnst kəˌmjuːnɪ'keɪʃ(ə)n pɔːt/ *noun* puerto *m* de comunicación ampliada

enhanced-definition television /ɪnˌhɑːnst ˌdefɪnɪʃ(ə)n ˌtelɪ'vɪʒ(ə)n/ *noun* televisión *f* de definición extendida

enhanced dot matrix /ɪnˌhɑːnst ˌdɒt 'meɪtrɪks/ *noun* matriz *f* de impresión de alta definición

enhanced expanded memory specification /ɪnˌhɑːnst ɪkˌspændɪd 'mem(ə)ri ˌspesɪfɪkeɪʃ(ə)n/ *noun* gestión *f* avanzada de la memoria extendida; memoria *f* EEMS

enhanced keyboard /ɪnˌhɑːnst 'kiːbɔːd/ *noun* teclado *m* extendido

enhanced parallel port /ɪnˌhɑːnst 'pærəlel ˌpɔːt/ *noun* puerto *m* paralelo ampliado

enhanced small device interface /ɪn ˌhɑːnst smɔːl dɪ'vaɪs ˌɪntəfeɪs/ *noun* interfaz *f* ESDI; interfaz *f* de pequeño dispositivo avanzado

enhancement /ɪn'hɑːnsmənt/ *noun* (*add-on facility*) optimización *f*; mejora *f*; ampliación *f*; optimación *f*

enhancer /ɪn'hɑːnsə/ *noun* optimizador *m*

ENQ *abbr* (*enquiry*) consulta *f*

enquiry /ɪn'kwaɪri/ *noun* **1.** pregunta *f*; investigación *f* **2.** pregunta *f*; investigación *f*

enquiry character /ɪn'kwaɪri ˌkærɪktə/ *noun* carácter *m* de petición

enter /'entə/ *verb* (*data or code*) entrar *vt*; introducir *vt* ◇ **the data has been entered** se han introducido los datos ◇ **to enter a name on a list** introducir un nombre en una lista

entering /'entərɪŋ/ *noun* (*typing in data*) entrada *f*; introducción *f*; recogida *f* (de datos)

enter key /'entə kiː/ *noun* tecla *f* 'Enter'; tecla *f* Intro

enterprise network /'entəpraɪz ˌnetwɜːk/ *noun* (*network connecting all the workstations in a company*) red *f* de empresa

entity /'entɪti/ *noun* entidad *f*

entry /'entri/ *noun* (*single record*) entrada *f*; registro *m*

entry condition /'entri kənˌdɪʃ(ə)n/ *noun* condición *f* de entrada

entry instruction /ˌentri ɪn'strʌkʃən/ *noun* instrucción *f* de entrada

entry point /'entri pɔɪnt/ *noun* punto *m* de entrada; dirección *f* de entrada

entry time /'entri taɪm/ *noun* hora *f* de entrada

enumerated type /ɪ'njuːməreɪtd taɪp/ *noun* tipo *m* enumerado; datos *mpl* numerados

enumeration /ɪˌnjuːmə'reɪʃ(ə)n/ *noun* enumeración *f*

envelope /'envələʊp/ *noun* **1.** (*variation of amplitude of signal or sound*) envolvente *m*; curva *f* envolvente **2.** (*transmitted packet of data containing error-detection and control information*) byte *m* de datos con bits de error y control ◇ **attack envelope** (forma de la) parte *f* inicial de un envolvente ◇ **envelope delay** retardo *f* de envolvente ◇ **envelope detection** detección *f* de (curva) envolvente

envelope feeder /'envələʊp ˌfiːdə/ *noun* alimentador *m* de sobres

envelope printer /'envələʊp ˌprɪntə/ *noun* impresora *f* de sobres

environment /ɪn'vaɪrənmənt/ *noun* **1.** (*condition in a computer system of all registers and memory locations*) entorno *m* **2.** entorno *m*

environment space /ɪn'vaɪrənmənt speɪs/ *noun* tamaño *m* del entorno; tamaño *m* del equipo

environment variable /ɪn'vaɪrənmənt ˌveəriəb(ə)l/ *noun* variable *f* del entorno; variable *f* del equipo

EOA *abbr* (*end of address*) fin *m* de dirección

EOB *abbr* (*end of block*) fin *m* de bloque

EOD /ˌiː əʊ 'diː/ *abbr* (*end of data*) fin *m* de datos

EOF *abbr* (*end of file*) fin *m* de archivo

EOJ *abbr* (*end of job*) fin *m* de tarea

EOL *abbr* (*end of line*) fin *m* de línea

EOM *abbr* (*end of message*) fin *m* de mensaje

EOR *abbr* (*end of record*) fin *m* de registro

EOT *abbr* **1.** (*end of text*) fin *m* de texto **2.** (*end of transmission*) fin *m* de transmisión

EPOS /'iːpɒs/ *noun* punto *m* de venta electrónico

EPP /ˌiː piː 'piː/ *noun* puerto *m* paralelo ampliado

EPROM /ˌiː 'piː ˌrɒm/ *abbr* (*erasable programmable read-only memory*) memoria *f* de sólo lectura programable electrónicamente

EPS *abbr* (*encapsulated PostScript*) extensión *f* EPS

equality /ɪ'kwɒlɪti/ *noun* igualdad *f*

equipment failure /ɪ'kwɪpmənt ˌfeɪljə/ *noun* fallo *m* del material; fallo *m* del ordenador

equivalence /ɪ'kwɪvələns/ *noun* (*logical operation*) equivalencia *f*

equivalence function /ɪ'kwɪvələns 'fʌŋkʃən/ *noun* función *f* de equivalencia; operación *f* de equivalencia

equivalence gate /ɪ'kwɪvələns geɪt/ *noun* puerta *f* de equivalencia; circuito *m* de equivalencia

equivalence operation /ɪ'kwɪvələns ˌɒpəreɪʃ(ə)n/ *noun* función *f* de equivalencia; operación *f* de equivalencia

erasable memory /ɪˌreɪzəb(ə)l 'mem(ə)ri/ *noun* almacenamiento *m* borrable; memoria *f* borrable

erasable programmable read-only memory /ɪˌreɪzəb(ə)l ˌprəʊgræməb(ə)l ˌriːd ˌəʊnli 'mem(ə)ri/ *noun* (*memory chip which can be programmed and erased*) memoria *f* EPROM; memoria *f* ROM programable y borrable; memoria *f* de solo lectura programable y borrable

erasable read-only memory /ɪˌreɪzəb(ə)l ˌriːd ˌəʊnli 'mem(ə)ri/ *noun* memoria *f* de sólo lectura que puede borrarse

erasable storage /ɪˌreɪzəb(ə)l 'stɔːrɪdʒ/ *noun* **1.** almacenamiento *m* borrable; memoria *f* borrable **2.** almacenamiento *m* reutilizable; memoria *f* reutilizable

erase /ɪ'reɪz/ *verb* **1.** (*to set all the digits in a storage area to zero*) borrar *vt*; dejar a cero **2.** (*to remove any signal from a magnetic medium*) borrar *vt*; destruir *vt*; eliminar *vt*

erase character /ɪ'reɪz ˌkærɪktə/ *noun* carácter *m* de borrado

erase head /ɪ'reɪz hed/ *noun* cabeza *f* de borrado

eraser /ɪ'reɪzə/ *noun* (*device that removes the contents of something*) borrador *m*; dispositivo *m*; método *m* de borrado

eraser tool /ɪ'reɪzə tuːl/ *noun* herramienta *f* de borrar; goma *f*

EROM /'iː rɒm/ *noun* memoria *f* de sólo lectura que puede borrarse

error /'erə/ *noun* **1.** (*due to a human operator*) error *m*; falta *f*; anomalía *f* **2.** (*caused by hardware or software fault*) error *m*; falta *f*; anomalía *f* **3.** (*in a program*) error *m*; falta *f*; anomalía *f* ◇ **a wrinkled or torn page may be the cause of scanning errors** una página arrugada o rota puede ser la causa de un error de exploración ◇ **diagnostic (error) message** mensaje *m* de diagnóstico de error ◇ **error correcting codes** códigos *mpl* de corrección de errores ◇ **error detecting codes** códigos de detección de errores ◇ **error detection and correction (EDAC)** detección y corrección de errores ◇ **error interrupt** (señal de) interrupción *f* por un error *or* por un incidente ◇ **features of the program include error logging** entre las características del programa se incluye el registro (automático) de errores ◇ **he made an error in calculating the total** cometió un error al calcular el total ◇ **in error** *or* **by error** por error ◇ **printer's error** error de imprenta ◇ **the secretary must have made a typing error** la secretaria *or* el secretario debe haber cometido un error mecanográfico

'…syntax errors, like omitting a bracket, will produce an error message from the compiler' [*Personal Computer World*]

error ambiguity /ˌerə ˌæmbɪ'gjuːɪti/ *noun* error *m* de ambigüedad; ambigüedad *f* (causada) por un error

error burst /'erə bɜːst/ *noun* (*group of errors*) ráfaga *f* de errores; serie *f* de errores consecutivos; error *m* en ráfagas

error checking code /'erə ˌtʃekɪŋ ˌkəʊd/ *noun* código *m* de verificación y corrección de errores

error code /'erə kəʊd/ *noun* código *m* de errores; código *m* indicador de error

error condition /'erə kən,dɪʃ(ə)n/ *noun* condición *f* de error

error control /'erə kən,trəʊl/ *noun* control *m* de errores

error correcting code /'erə kə,rektɪŋ ˌkəʊd/ *noun* código *m* corrector de error(es)

error correction /'erə kə,rekʃ(ə)n/ *noun* corrección *f* de errores

error detecting code /'erə dɪ,tektɪŋ ˌkəʊd/ *noun* código *m* detector de error

error detection /'erə dɪ,tekʃ(ə)n/ *noun* detección *f* de errores

error detection and correction /ˌerə dɪ,tekʃən ən kə'rekʃən/ *noun* detección y corrección de errores

error diagnosis /'erə ˌdaɪəgnəʊsɪs/ *noun* diagnóstico *m* de errores

error diagnostics /'erə ˌdaɪəgnɒstɪks/ *noun* diagnóstico *m* de errores; herramientas *fpl* de diagnóstico de errores

error handler /'erə ˌhændlə/ *noun* controlador *m* de errores

error handling /'erə ˌhændlɪŋ/ *noun* tratamiento *m* de errores; tratamiento *m* de excepciones

error interrupt /'erə ˌɪntərʌpt/ *plural noun* (señal de) interrupción *f* por un error; (señal de) interrupción *f* por un incidente

error logging /'erə ˌlɒgɪŋ/ *noun* registro *m* de errores; registro *m* (automático) de errores ◇ **features of the program include error logging** entre las características del programa se incluye el registro (automático) de errores

error management /'erə ˌmænɪdʒmənt/ *noun* tratamiento *m* de errores; tratamiento *m* de excepciones

error message /'erə ˌmesɪdʒ/ *noun* mensaje *m* de error

error propagation /'erə ˌprɒpəgeɪʃ(ə)n/ *noun* propagación *f* de error

error rate /'erə reɪt/ *noun* tasa *f* de errores ◇ **the error rate is less than 1%** la tasa de error es inferior a 1%

error recovery /'erə rɪˌkʌv(ə)ri/ *noun* recuperación *f* de errores; depuración *f* de errores

error routine /'erə ruːˌtiːn/ *noun* rutina *f* (de gestión) de errores

error trapping /'erə ˌtræpɪŋ/ *noun* (*process of detecting and correcting errors*) detección *f* de errores; prevención *f* de errores

ESC /ɪˈskeɪp/ *noun* **1.** (*key on a computer keyboard*) escape *m*; código *m* ESC **2.** escape *m* **3.** escape *m*

escape character /ɪˈskeɪp ˌkærɪktə/ *noun* carácter *m* de escape

escape code /ɪˈskeɪp kəʊd/ *noun* código *m* de escape

escape key /ɪˈskeɪp kiː/ *noun* tecla *f* ESC; tecla *f* de escape

escape sequence /ɪˈskeɪp ˌsiːkwəns/ *noun* secuencia *f* de abandono

Esc key /ɪˈskeɪp kiː/ *noun* escape *m*

Ethernet /'iːθənet/ *noun* (*network*) Ethernet *f*

EtherTalk /'iːθətɑːk/ (*Apple Macintosh variation of Ethernet*) EtherTalk

ETX *abbr* (*end of text*) fin *m* de texto

Eudora /juːˈdɔːrə/ (*email software*) Eudora

even parity /ˌiːv(ə)n ˈpærɪti/, **even parity check** /ˌiːv(ə)n ˈpærɪti tʃek/ *noun* control *m* de paridad par

event /ɪˈvent/ *noun* suceso *m*; evento *m*; acontecimiento *m*

event-driven /ɪˈvent ˌdrɪv(ə)n/ *adjective* activado por un suceso *or* -a; accionado, -a por un suceso

'Forthcoming language extensions will include object-oriented features, including classes with full inheritance, as well as event-driven programming.' [*Computing*]

event focus /ɪˈvent ˌfəʊkəs/ *noun* foco *m* de evento

event handler /ɪˈvent ˌhændlə/ *noun* gestor *m* de eventos; gestor *m* de sucesos

except gate /ɪkˈsept geɪt/ *noun* puerta *f* O exclusivo

exception /ɪkˈsepʃən/ *noun* excepción *f*

exception dictionary /ɪkˈsepʃ(ə)n ˌdɪkʃ(ə)n(ə)ri/ *noun* (*for word-processing and photocomposition*) lista *f*; listado *m* de excepciones; repertorio *m* de excepciones

exception handling /ɪkˈsepʃ(ə)n ˌhændlɪŋ/ *noun* tratamiento *m* de excepciones; tratamiento *m* de errores

excess-3 code /ˌekses ˈθriː kəʊd/ *noun* código *m* de exceso de 3 ◇ **the excess-3 code representation of 6 is 1001** la representación del código de exceso de 3 del número 6 es 1001

exchange /ɪksˈtʃeɪndʒ/ *noun* (*telephone equipment*) central *f* telefónica ■ *verb* (*to swap data between two locations*) hacer un intercambio; intercambiar *vt*; permutar *vi*

exchangeable /ɪksˈtʃeɪndʒəb(ə)l/ *adjective* (*returnable*) intercambiable; canjeable; (*moveable*) amovible

exchangeable disk storage /ɪks ˌtʃeɪndʒəb(ə)l dɪsk ˈstɔːrɪdʒ/ *noun* almacenamiento *m* de discos intercambiables

exchange selection /ɪksˈtʃeɪndʒ sɪˌlekʃən/ *noun* selección *f* por intercambio

exclusion /ɪkˈskluːʒ(ə)n/ *noun* (*restriction of access to a telephone line*) exclusión *f*

exclusive NOR /ɪkˌskluːsɪv ˈnɔː/ *noun* NI *m* exclusivo; NOR *m* exclusivo

exclusive OR /ɪkˌskluːsɪv ˈɔː/ *noun* (*logical function*) O *m* exclusivo; OR *m* exclusivo; EXOR *m*

executable file /'eksɪˌkjuːtəb(ə)l faɪl/ *noun* (*file containing a program*) fichero *m* ejecutable

executable form /'eksɪˌkjuːtəb(ə)l fɔːm/ *noun* (programa con) formato *m* para funcionar; formato *m* para ejecutar

execute /'eksɪˌkjuːt/ *verb* (*computer program*) ejecutar *vt*

execute cycle /'eksɪkjuːt ˌsaɪk(ə)l/ *noun* ciclo *m* de ejecución

execute mode /'eksɪkjuːt məʊd/ *noun* modo *m* (de) ejecución; modo *m* de ejecución

execute phase /'eksɪkjuːt feɪz/ *noun* fase *f* de ejecución

execute signal /'eksɪkjuːt ˌsɪgn(ə)l/ *noun* señal *f* de ejecución

execute statement /'eksɪkjuːt ˌsteɪtmənt/ *noun* sentencia *f* de ejecución; instrucción *f* de ejecución

execute time /'eksɪkjuːt taɪm/ *noun* duración *f* de ejecución; tiempo *m* de ejecución

execution /ˌeksɪˈkjuːʃ(ə)n/ *noun* (*carrying out of a computer program*) ejecución *f*

execution address /ˌeksɪˈkjuːʃ(ə)n əˌdres/ *noun* dirección *f* de ejecución

execution cycle /ˌeksɪ'kjuːʃ(ə)n ˌsaɪk(ə)l/ *noun* ciclo *m* de ejecución

execution error /ˌeksɪ'kjuːʃ(ə)n ˌerə/ *noun* error *m* de ejecución

execution phase /ˌeksɪ'kjuːʃ(ə)n ˌfeɪz/ *noun* fase *f* de ejecución

execution time /ˌeksɪ'kjuːʃ(ə)n ˌtaɪm/ *noun* tiempo *m* de ejecución

executive /ɪg'zekjʊtɪv/ *adjective* (*operating system*) ejecutivo *or* -a

executive control program /ɪg,zekjʊtɪv kən'trəʊl ˌprəʊgræm/ *noun* sistema *m* de operación

executive information system /ɪg ˌzekjʊtɪv ɪnfə'meɪʃ(ə)n ˌsɪstəm/ *noun* sistema *m* de información para la gestión; sistema *m* EIS

executive instruction /ɪg,zekjʊtɪv ɪn 'strʌkʃən/ *noun* instrucción *f* ejecutiva; instrucción *f* de supervisión

executive program /ɪg,zekjʊtɪv 'prəʊgræm/ *noun* programa *m* de ejecución; programa *m* ejecutivo ◇ **in DOS, to start a program type in its EXE file name** para iniciar un programa en DOS, escriba el nombre de su fichero EXE

exerciser /'eksəsaɪzə/ *noun* (*tester for a device*) verificador *m*; programa *m* de comprobación

exhaustive search /ɪg'zɔːstɪv sɜːtʃ/ *noun* búsqueda *f* exhaustiva

exit /'egzɪt/ *verb* (*to stop program execution*) salir *vi*

EXIT /'eksɪt/ *noun* (*MS-DOS system command*) EXIT

exit point /'eksɪt pɔɪnt/ *noun* punto *m* de salida

exjunction /'eks,dʒʌŋkʃən/ *noun* (*logical function*) disyunción *f*

EXNOR /ˌeks 'nɔː/ *noun* (*logical function*) NI *m* exclusivo; NOR *m* exclusivo

EXNOR gate /ˌeks 'nɔː ˌgeɪt/ *noun* puerta *f* NI exclusivo; puerta *f* NOR exclusivo

EXOR /ˌeks 'ɔː/ *noun* (*logical function*) O *m* exclusivo

EXOR gate /ˌeks 'ɔː ˌgeɪt/ *noun* puerta *f* O exclusivo; puerta *f* EXOR

expandable system /ɪk,spændəb(ə)l 'sɪstəm/ *noun* sistema *m* extensible

expanded memory /ɪk,spændɪd 'mem(ə)ri/ *noun* (*IBM PC standard*) memoria *f* extendida

expanded memory board /ɪk,spændɪd 'mem(ə)ri ˌbɔːd/ *noun* tarjeta *f* de extensión de memoria

expanded memory manager /ɪk,spændɪd 'mem(ə)ri ˌmænɪdʒə/ *noun* gestor *m* de memoria extendida

expansion /ɪk'spænʃən/ *noun* expansión *f*; extensión *f* ◇ **insert the board in the free expansion slot** inserte la tarjeta en la ranura de extensión disponible

expansion board /ɪk'spænʃən bɔːd/ *noun* tarjeta *f* de extensión

expansion box /ɪk'spænʃ(ə)n bɒks/ *noun* caja *f* de expansión

'...it can be attached to most kinds of printer, and, if that is not enough, an expansion box can be fitted to the bus connector' [*Personal Computer World*]

expansion bus /ɪk'spænʃ(ə)n bʌs/ *noun* (*data and address lines leading to a connector*) enlace *m* común de expansión; bus *m* de extensión

expansion card /ɪk'spænʃ(ə)n kɑːd/ *noun* tarjeta *f* de extensión

expansion slot /ɪk'spænʃ(ə)n slɒt/ *noun* (*connector*) ranura *f*; ranura *f* de expansión; conector *m*; emplazamiento *m* para la tarjeta de extensión

expert system /'ekspɜːt ˌsɪstəm/ *noun* sistema *m* experto

explicit address /ɪk,splɪsɪt ə'dres/ *noun* dirección *f* explícita

explicit reference /ɪk,splɪsɪt 'ref(ə)rəns/ *noun* referencia *f* explícita

Explorer™ /ɪk'splɔːrə/ (*Windows 95 program that lets you manage all the files stored on a disk*) Explorer™

exponentiation /ˌekspə,nenʃi'eɪʃ(ə)n/ *noun* elevación *f* de un número a la potencia x

export /ɪk'spɔːt/ *verb* (*save data*) exportar *vt* ◇ **to use this data with dBASE, you will have to export it as a DBF file** para utilizar estos datos con dBase, se tienen que exportar como fichero DBF

expression /ɪk'spreʃ(ə)n/ *noun* **1.** (*mathematical formula*) expresión *f*; fórmula *f* **2.** (*definition of a variable in a program*) expresión *f*

extended arithmetic element /ɪk,stendɪd ˌærɪθmetɪk 'elɪmənt/ *noun* elemento *m* aritmético extendido

extended binary coded decimal interchange code /ɪk,stendɪd ˌbaɪnəri ˌkəʊdɪd ˌdesɪm(ə)l 'ɪntətʃeɪndʒ ˌkəʊd/ *noun* (*numerical system*) código *m* de intercambio decimal de codificación binaria extendida; código *m* EBCDIC; sistema *m* de codificación de caracteres de 8 bits

extended character set /ɪk,stendɪd 'kærɪktə ˌset/ *noun* juego *m* de caracteres ampliado

extended data output memory /ɪk,stendɪd ˌdeɪtə 'aʊtpʊt ˌmem(ə)ri/ *noun* memoria *f* ampliada de salida de datos

extended-definition television /ɪk,stendɪd ˌdefɪnɪʃ(ə)n ˌtelɪ'vɪʒ(ə)n/ *noun* televisión *f* de definición extendida

extended graphics array /ɪk,stendɪd 'græfɪks ə,reɪ/ *noun* estándar *m* XGA; matriz *f* de gráficos ampliada

extended integrated drive electronics /ɪk ,stendɪd ˌɪntɪ,greɪtɪd 'draɪv ˌelektrɒnɪks/ *noun* electrónica *f* de unidad (de lectura) integrada ampliada

extended memory /ɪk,stendɪd 'mem(ə)ri/ *noun* memoria *f* ampliada; memoria *f* extendida

extended memory manager /ɪk,stendɪd 'mem(ə)ri ˌmænɪdʒə/ *noun* administrador *m* de memoria extendida

extended memory specification /ɪk
ˌstendɪd 'mem(ə)ri ˌspesɪfɪkeɪʃ(ə)n/ *noun* estándar *m* XMS (de memoria extendida)

extending serial file /ɪkˌstendɪŋ 'sɪərɪəl
ˌfaɪl/ *noun* fichero *m* de serie extensible

extensible hypertext markup language
/ɪkˌstensɪb(ə)l ˌhaɪpətekst 'mɑːkʌp
ˌlæŋgwɪdʒ/ *noun* language *m* XHTML

extensible language /ɪkˌstensɪb(ə)l
'læŋgwɪdʒ/ *noun* lenguaje *m* extensible; lenguaje
m adaptable

extensible markup language /ɪk
ˌstensɪb(ə)l 'mɑːkʌp ˌlæŋgwɪdʒ/ *noun* lenguage *m* XML

extension memory /ɪk'stenʃən ˌmem(ə)ri/
noun memoria *f* de extensión

external arithmetic /ɪkˌstɜːn(ə)l ə'rɪθmətɪk/
noun aritmética *f* externa

external clock /ɪk'stɜːn(ə)l klɒk/ *noun* reloj *m*
externo; reloj *m* exterior

external data file /ɪkˌstɜːn(ə)l 'deɪtə ˌfaɪl/
noun fichero *m* de datos externo

external device /ɪkˌstɜːn(ə)l dɪ'vaɪs/ *noun* **1.**
terminal *m* periférico; dispositivo *m* externo **2.**
dispositivo *m* externo

external disk drive /ɪkˌstɜːn(ə)l 'dɪsk
draɪv/ *noun* lector *m* externo; disquetera *f* externa

external interrupt /ɪkˌstɜːn(ə)l 'ɪntərʌpt/
noun interrupción *f* externa

external label /ɪkˌstɜːn(ə)l 'leɪb(ə)l/ *noun* (*of
a device or disk*) etiqueta *f* externa; etiqueta *f* fijada en el exterior

external memory /ɪkˌstɜːn(ə)l 'mem(ə)ri/
noun memoria *f* externa; memoria *f* auxiliar

external modem /ɪkˌstɜːn(ə)l 'məʊdem/
noun módem *m* externo

external register /ɪkˌstɜːn(ə)l 'redʒɪstə/
noun registro *m* externo

external schema /ɪkˌstɜːn(ə)l 'skiːmə/ *noun*
(*user's view of data or program*) esquema *m* del
usuario; visión *f* del usuario; esquema *m* externo

external sort /ɪkˌstɜːn(ə)l 'sɔːt/ *noun* clasificación *f* externa; clasificación *f* con soporte externo

external storage /ɪkˌstɜːn(ə)l 'stɔːrɪdʒ/, **external store** /ɪkˌstɜːn(ə)l 'stɔː/ *noun* memoria *f*
externa

extracode /'ekstrəkəʊd/ *noun* (*routines within
the operating system that emulate a hardware
system*) extracódigo *m*

extract /ɪk'strækt/ *verb* extraer *vt* ◇ **we can extract the files required for typesetting** podemos extraer los ficheros necesarios para la composición (de tipos)

extract instruction /ek'strækt ɪnˌstrʌkʃən/
noun instrucción *f* de extracción

extractor /ɪk'stræktə/ *noun* extractor *m*

extranet /'ekstrənet/ *noun* extranet *m*

eyeball /'aɪbɔːl/ *noun slang* visitante *m*

e-zine /'iː ziːn/ *noun* folletín *m* electrónico; revista *f* electrónica

F

f /ef/ *symbol* (*equal to one thousandth of a million millionth or 10–15*) f; femto-

face /feɪs/ *noun* estilo *m* de letra; fuente *f* de caracteres; tipo *m* de letra

faceted code /ˈfæsɪtd kəʊd/ *noun* código *m* por facetas

facility /fəˈsɪlɪti/ *noun* **1.** (*being able to do something easily*) facilidad *f*; (*service*) servicio *m*; prestación *f* **2.** (*communication path*) ruta *f*; vía *f*; dispositivo *m* de acceso ◇ **storage facilities** almacén *m*; medios *mpl* de almacenamiento ◇ **we offer facilities for processing a customer's own disks** ofrecemos servicios a nuestros clientes para el tratamiento de sus discos

facsimile character generator /fækˌsɪmɪli ˈkærɪktə ˌdʒenəreɪtə/ *noun* generador *m* de caracteres facsímiles

facsimile copy /fækˌsɪmɪli ˈkɒpi/ *noun* **1.** facsímil *m*; fax *m* **2.** copia *f* facsímil

facsimile transmission /fækˈsɪmɪli trænz ˌmɪʃ(ə)n/ *noun* transmisión *f* por fax

factor /ˈfæktə/ *noun* (*number*) factor *m*; coeficiente *m* ◇ **by a factor of ten** por un factor de diez *or* diez veces *or* multiplicado por diez

factorial /fækˈtɔːriəl/ *noun* factorial *m*

factorise /ˈfæktəraɪz/, **factorize** *verb* (*numbers*) sacar el factorial de; descomponer en factores

fade /feɪd/ *verb* (*radio or electrical signal*) debilitarse *vr*; bajar *vi*; perder intensidad; atenuarse *vr*

fade out /ˌfeɪd ˈaʊt/ *noun* (*of an image*) fundido *m* en negro

fail /feɪl/ *verb* **1.** (*not to do something*) no hacer (una cosa); fallar *vi*; no tener éxito en una cosa; (*machine*) averiarse *vr*; romperse *vr*; estropearse *vr* **2.** (*machine*) averiarse *vr*; romperse *vr*; estropearse *vr* ◇ **a computer has failed if you turn on the power supply and nothing happens** si al encender el ordenador no pasa nada, es que está estropeado ◇ **the prototype disk drive failed its first test** el prototipo de la unidad de disco falló en su primera prueba

fail safe system /feɪl seɪf ˌsɪstəm/ *noun* sistema *m* de seguridad en caso de fallos; mecanismo *m* de seguridad en caso de fallos; sistema *m* de protección en caso de fallos; mecanismo *m* de protección en caso de fallos

'The DTI is publishing a new code of best practice which covers hardware reliability and fail-safe software systems.' [*Computing*]

fail soft system /feɪl sɒft ˌsɪstəm/ *noun* sistema *m* de desconexión progresiva; sistema *m* tolerante al fallo

failure logging /ˈfeɪljə ˌlɒɡɪŋ/ *noun* registro *m* (automático) de incidencias; registro *m* de fallos

failure rate /ˈfeɪljə reɪt/ *noun* tasa *f* de fallos; índice *m* de fallos

failure recovery /ˈfeɪljə rɪˈkʌv(ə)ri/ *noun* (*resuming a process*) recuperación *f* después de un fallo; reinicio *m*; reiniciación *f*; recuperación *f* tras un fallo

fall back /ˌfɔːl ˈbæk/ *noun* procedimiento *m* de emergencia; recurso *m* de emergencia

fall back recovery /ˌfɔːl bæk rɪˈkʌv(ə)ri/ *noun* (*resuming a program*) recuperación *f* del proceso después de la corrección de un fallo; reinicio *m* en el punto de recuperación

fall back routines /ˈfɔːl bæk ruːˌtiːnz/ *plural noun* (*when a system or machine has failed*) rutinas *fpl* de emergencia; rutinas *fpl* de ayuda; procedimientos *mpl* de emergencia

false /fɔːls/ *adjective* **1.** (*not true or wrong*) falso *or* -a; incorrecto *or* -a; erróneo *or* -a **2.** (*logic*) falso *or* -a

false code /ˌfɔːls ˈkəʊd/ *noun* código *m* erróneo; error *m* de código

false drop /ˌfɔːls ˈdrɒp/ *noun* resultado *m* erróneo (de una búsqueda); recuperación *f* falsa; recuperación *f* errónea

false error /fɔːls ˈerə/ *noun* error *m* falso

false retrieval /ˌfɔːls rɪˈtriːv(ə)l/ *noun* recuperación *f* errónea; recuperación *f* falsa

FAM *abbr* (*fast access memory*) memoria *f* de acceso rápido

family /ˈfæm(ə)li/ *noun* **1.** (*range of typefaces*) familia *f* **2.** (*range of machines*) familia *f*; gama *f*; serie *f* (de productos)

fanfold /ˈfænfəʊld/ *noun* papel *m* (doblado) en forma de acordeón; papel *m* continuo

fan-in /fæn ɪn/ *noun* entrada *f*; número *m* de entradas en un circuito lógico

fanning strip /ˈfænɪŋ strɪp/ *noun* regleta *f* distribuidora; regleta *f* de conexión

fan-out /fæn aʊt/ *noun* (*maximum number of outputs*) salida *f*; factor *m* piramidal; número *m* de salidas en un circuito lógico

FAQ /fæk, ˌef eɪ ˈkjuː/ *noun* preguntas *fpl* más frecuentes

Faraday cage /ˈfærədeɪ keɪdʒ/ *noun* caja *f* de Faraday; jaula *f* de Faraday

fast access memory /ˌfɑːst ˌækses ˈmem(ə)ri/ *noun* memoria *f* de acceso rápido

fast core /ˈfɑːst kɔː/ *noun* memoria *f* central rápida ◊ **the fast core is used as a scratchpad for all calculations in this system** en este sistema, se emplea la memoria central rápida como bloc de notas para todas las operaciones de cálculo

fast line /ˈfɑːst laɪn/ *noun* línea *f* rápida; línea *f* de transmisión rápida

fast packet /fɑːst ˈpækɪt/ *noun* paquete *m* rápido

fast page RAM /ˌfɑːst peɪdʒ ˈræm/ *noun* RAM *f* de página rápida

fast peripheral /fɑːst pəˈrɪf(ə)rəl/ *noun* periférico *m* rápido

Fast-SCSI /fɑːst ˈskʌzi/ *noun* interfaz *f* SCSI-rápido

fast time-scale /ˈfɑːst taɪm/ *noun* (*operation*) base *f* de tiempo rápida; escala *f* de tiempo rápida; base *f* de tiempo reducida

FAT /ˌef eɪ ˈtiː/ *noun* listado *m* de archivos

fatal error /ˌfeɪt(ə)l ˈerə/ *noun* error *m* fatal

FatBits /ˈfætbɪts/ (*MacPaint option*) FatBits

father file /ˈfɑːðə faɪl/ *noun* fichero *m* padre; archivo *m* padre

fault /fɔːlt/ *noun* (*defect*) defecto *m*; (*mistake*) fallo *m*; error *m*; (*stoppage*) parada *f*; incidente *m* ◊ **fault tracer** localizador *m* de fallos ◊ **the technical staff are trying to correct a programming fault** el personal técnico intenta corregir un fallo de programación ◊ **we think there is a basic fault in the product design** pensamos que existe un error de base en el diseño del producto

fault detection /fɔːlt dɪˈtekʃ(ə)n/ *noun* localización *f*; detección *f* (automática) de fallos

fault diagnosis /fɔːlt ˌdaɪəgˈnəʊsɪs/ *noun* diagnóstico *m* de fallos

fault location program /ˌfɔːlt ləʊˈkeɪʃ(ə)n ˌprəʊɡræm/ *noun* programa *m* de localización de fallos

fault management /fɔːlt ˈmænɪdʒmənt/ *noun* gestión *f* de fallos

fault time /ˌfɔːlt ˈtaɪm/ *noun* duración *f*; tiempo *m* de un fallo

fault tolerance /fɔːlt ˈtɒlərəns/ *noun* (nivel de) tolerancia *f* a los fallos

fault-tolerant /fɔːlt ˈtɒlərənt/ *adjective* tolerante al fallo ◊ **they market a highly successful range of fault-tolerant minis** comercializan con mucho éxito una gama de mini-ordenadores tolerantes a los fallos

fault trace /ˌfɔːlt ˈtreɪs/ *noun* registro *m* de un fallo; indicio *m* de un fallo

faulty sector /ˌfɔːlti ˈsektə/ *noun* sector *m* defectuoso

fax /fæks/, **FAX** *noun* **1.** *informal* (*method of sending images digitally*) fax *m* **2.** (*copy of document sent digitally*) fax *m* ■ *verb* (*to send message by fax*) enviar por fax ◊ **fax machine** fax *m* ◊ **fax paper** papel para fax ◊ **the fax machine is next to the telephone switchboard** el fax está junto a la centralita (de teléfonos) ◊ **we will send a fax of the design plan** enviaremos los planos por fax

fax card /fæks kɑːd/, **fax adapter** /fæks ə ˈdæptə/, **fax board** /fæks bɔːd/ *noun* tarjeta *f* de FAX; adaptador *m* de FAX

fax gateway /fæks ˈɡeɪtweɪ/ *noun* puerta *f* de fax; fax *m* de telecopia ◊ **to send messages by fax instead of across the network, you'll need to install a fax gateway** para enviar mensajes por fax en vez de por red, hay que instalar una puerta de fax

fax modem /fæks ˈməʊˌdem/ *noun* módem *m* de fax

fax server /fæks ˈsɜːvə/ *noun* servidor *m* de fax

fd, FD *abbr* (*floppy disk*) disco *m* flexible; disquete *m* flexible

FDC /ˌef diː ˈsiː/ *noun* controlador *m* de discos flexibles; controlador *m* de disquetes

FDD *abbr* (*floppy disk drive*) unidad *f* de disco flexible

FDDI /ˌef diː diː ˈaɪ/ *noun* interconexión *f* de datos distribuidos por fibra óptica; interfaz *f* de datos distribuidos por fibra óptica

FDDI II /ˌef diː diː aɪ ˈtuː/ *noun* estándar *m* FDDI II

FDISK /ˈef dɪsk/ *noun* (*MS-DOS system utility*) FDISK

FDM /ˌef diː ˈem/ *noun* multiplexión *f* de división de frecuencias

fdx, FDX *abbr* (*full duplex*) dúplex *m* completo; dúplex *m* integral

feasibility /ˌfiːzəˈbɪlɪti/ *noun* practicabilidad *f*

feasibility study /ˌfiːzəˈbɪlɪti ˌstʌdi/ *noun* estudio *m* de viabilidad

FED *abbr* (*field emission display*) pantalla *f* de emisión de campo

FEDS /ˌef iː diː ˈes/ *noun* FEDS; almacenamiento *m* con discos fijos e intercambiables

feed /fiːd/ *noun* (*printer or photocopier*) arrastre *m*; alimentación *f* ◊ **feed form** (*command*) (instrucción de) alimentación *f* de página

feedback /ˈfiːdbæk/ *noun* (*information which can be used to modify something*) intercambio *m* de información

feedback control /ˈfiːdbæk kənˌtrəʊl/ *noun* control *m* de retorno

feeder /ˈfiːdə/ *noun* **1.** (*channel*) vía *f* de envío; vía *f* de transmisión (de la señal) **2.** (*for paper*) sistema *m* de alimentación; sistema *m* de arrastre (del papel) ◊ **feeder cable** cable *m* de envío (de la señal) *or* cable de antena-circuito *or* alimentador

feed hole /ˈfiːd həʊl/ *noun* (*printing*) perforación *f*; guía *f* de arrastre (del papel); perforación *f* del margen (del papel)

female /ˈfiːmeɪl/ *adjective* hembra

female connector /ˌfiːmeɪl kəˈnektə/ *noun* conector *m* hembra

female socket /ˌfiːmeɪl ˈsɒkɪt/ *noun* enchufe *m* hembra

femto- /femtəʊ/ *prefix* femto-

femtosecond /'femtəʊˌsekənd/ *noun* femtosegundo *m*

ferric oxide /ˌferɪk 'ɒksaɪd/, **ferrite** /'feraɪt/ *noun* óxido *m* férrico

ferrite /'feraɪt/ *noun* ferrita *f*

ferromagnetic material /ˌferəʊmægnetɪk məˈtɪəriəl/ *noun* material *m* ferromagnético

FET /ˌef iː 'tiː/ *noun* transistor *m* de efecto de campo

fetch /fetʃ/ *verb* (*command that retrieves the next instruction*) recoger *vt*; (*command*) capturar *vt*; localizar y leer; (*command that retrieves the next instruction*) llamar *vt* ■ *noun* búsqueda y carga de instrucciones

fetch cycle /fetʃ 'saɪk(ə)l/ *noun* (*series of events that retrieve the next instruction*) ciclo *m* de lectura; captura *f*; extracción *f* (de una instrucción)

fetch-execute cycle /ˌfetʃ 'eksɪkjuːt ˌsaɪk(ə)l/ *noun* ciclo *m* de captura (de una instrucción); ciclo *m* de ejecución (de una instrucción)

fetch instruction /fetʃ ɪnˈstrʌkʃən/ *noun* instrucción *f* de captura; búsqueda *f* de una instrucción

fetch phase /'fetʃ feɪz/ *noun* (*section of the fetch-execute cycle*) fase *f*; intervalo *m* de captura; búsqueda *f* (de una instrucción)

fetch-protect /ˌfetʃ prəˈtekt/ *verb* protección *f* del acceso a la memoria

fetch signal /fetʃ 'sɪgn(ə)l/ *noun* señal *f* de captura de una instrucción

fibre /'faɪbə/ *noun* (*very thin glass or plastic strand that can carry data in the form of light signals*) fibra *f*

fibre channel /'faɪbə ˌtʃæn(ə)l/ *noun* canal *m* de fibra

fibre connector /'faɪbə kəˌnektə/ *noun* conector *m* de fibra óptica

fibre distributed data interface /ˌfaɪbə dɪ ˌstrɪbjutɪd 'deɪtə ˌɪntəfeɪs/ *noun* interconexión *f* de datos distribuidos por fibra óptica; interfaz *f* de datos distribuidos por fibra óptica

fibre distributed data interface II /ˌfaɪbə dɪ ˌstrɪbjutɪd ˌdeɪtə ˌɪntəfeɪs 'tuː/ *noun* interconexión *f* de datos distribuidos por fibra óptica II; interfaz *f* de datos distribuidos por fibra óptica II

fibre optic cable /'faɪbə 'ɒptɪk/, **fibre optic connection** /ˌfaɪbə ˌɒptɪk kəˈnekʃən/ *noun* (*material for data transfer*) cable *m* de fibra óptica; conexión *f* de fibra óptica; cable *m* óptico

fibre optics /ˌfaɪbə 'ɒptɪks/ *plural noun* (*used for transmission of light signals*) fibroóptica *f*; tecnología *f* de la fibra óptica; tecnología *f* de la transmisión por fibra óptica

fibre over Ethernet /ˌfaɪbə 'əʊvə ˌiːθənet/ *noun* protocolo *m* de red (para transmisión de datos)

field /fiːld/ *noun* 1. (*area of force*) campo *m* 2. (*in a record*) campo *m* 3. (*of picture on a television screen*) trama *f* de imagen ◇ **field blanking (interval)** intervalo *m* de campo *or* supresión *f* vertical de campo ◇ **field emision display**

(FED) pantalla *f* de emisión de campo ◇ **field flyback** retorno *m* de campo ◇ **field frequency** frecuencia *f* de campo *or* de trama ◇ **field strength** intensidad *f* de campo *or* **field sweep** barrido *m* vertical *or* exploración *m* de campo ◇ **field sync pulse** impulso *m* de control *or* de sincronización del barrido ◇ **the employee record has a field for age** el registro 'empleado' tiene un campo para la (variable) 'edad'

field effect transistor /ˌfiːld ɪˌfekt trænˈzɪstə/ *noun* transistor *m* de efecto de campo

field emission display /ˌfiːld ɪˈmɪʃ(ə)n dɪ ˌspleɪ/ *noun* pantalla *f* de emisión de campo

field engineer /fiːld ˌendʒɪˈnɪə/ *noun* (*person who carries maintenance work off-site*) ingeniero *m* de campo post venta; ingeniero *m* de mantenimiento (en el lugar)

fielding /'fiːldɪŋ/ *noun* organización *f* del campo

field label /fiːld 'leɪb(ə)l/ *noun* etiqueta *f* de campo

field length /'fiːld leŋθ/ *noun* (*number of characters*) longitud *f*; longitud *f* de campo; tamaño *m* de un campo

field marker /fiːld 'mɑːkə/ *noun* marcador *m* de campo

field name /'fiːld neɪm/ *noun* etiqueta *f* de campo

field programmable device /ˌfiːld ˌprəʊgræməb(ə)l dɪˈvaɪs/ *noun* dispositivo *m* programable de campo

field programming /fiːld 'prəʊˌgræmɪŋ/ *noun* programación *f* de campo

field separator /'fiːld ˌsepəreɪtə/ *noun* marcador *m* de campo

field-tested /'fiːld ˌtestɪd/ *adjective* probado sobre el terreno

FIF /ˌef aɪ 'ef/ *noun* formato *m* FIF; formato *m* de imagen fractal

FIFO /'faɪfəʊ/ *noun* primero en entrar, primero en salir; FIFO ◇ **the two computers operate at different rates, but can transmit data using a FIFO memory** los dos ordenadores funcionan a velocidades distintas, pero pueden transmitir datos mediante el sistema FIFO

FIFO memory /ˌfaɪfəʊ 'mem(ə)ri/ *noun* memoria *f* FIFO; memoria *f* que funciona bajo el principio de primero en entrar primero en salir ◇ **the two computers operate at different rates, but can transmit data using a FIFO memory** los dos ordenadores funcionan a velocidades distintas, pero pueden transmitir datos mediante el sistema FIFO

FIFO queue /'faɪfəʊ kjuː/ *noun* cola *f*; almacenamiento *m* temporal que funciona bajo el principio de 'primero en entrar primero en salir'

fifth generation computer /ˌfɪfθ ˌdʒenəreɪʃ(ə)n kəmˈpjuːtə/ *noun* ordenador *m* de quinta generación

file /faɪl/ *noun* (*documents*) expediente *m*; (*section of data on a computer*) fichero *m*; archivo *m* ■ *verb* archivar *vt* ◇ **a lost file cannot be found without a file-recovery utility** es imposible encontrar un fichero perdido sin un programa de recuperación de ficheros ◇ **file control block (FCB)** bloque *m* de control de ficheros ◇ **files with the extension EXE are file types that contain program code** los ficheros con la extensión EXE son tipos de ficheros que contienen un código de programa ◇ **file transfer access and management (FTAM)** (*method of transferring files*) gestión, acceso y transferencia de ficheros *or* método FTAM ◇ **hidden file** fichero escondido ◇ **the file header in the database file shows the total number of records and lists the index fields** la cabecera del fichero de la base de datos muestra el número total de registros y hace un listado de los campos indexados ◇ **the new data is written to the file identified by file handle 1** los nuevos datos son introducidos en el fichero identificado con el número 1 ◇ **to place (something) on file** colocar (un documento) en un expediente *or* introducir (información) en un fichero

'The first problem was solved by configuring a Windows swap file, which I hadn't done before because my 4Mb 486 had never been overloaded.' [*Computing*]

'...the lost file, while inaccessible without a file-recovery utility, remains on disk until new information writes over it' [*Publish*]

file activity ratio /ˌfaɪl ækˈtɪvɪti ˌreɪʃiəʊ/ *noun* índice *m* de actividad; índice *m* de movimiento de un fichero

file allocation table /ˌfaɪl ˌæləˈkeɪʃ(ə)n ˌteɪb(ə)l/ *noun* tabla *f* de asignación de ficheros; tabla *f* FAT

file attribute /ˈfaɪl ˌætrɪbjuːt/ *plural noun* atributo *m* de un fichero

file cleanup /ˈfaɪl ˌkliːnʌp/ *noun* limpieza *f* de ficheros; vaciado *m* de ficheros

file collating /ˈfaɪl kəˌleɪtɪŋ/ *noun* fusión *f*; intercalación *f* de ficheros

file conversion /ˈfaɪl kənˌvɜːʃ(ə)n/ *noun* conversión *f* de ficheros

file copy /ˈfaɪl ˌkɒpi/ *noun* copia *f* para archivar

file creation /ˈfaɪl kriˌeɪʃ(ə)n/ *noun* creación *f* de ficheros

file defragmentation /ˈfaɪl ˌdiːfrægmenteɪʃ(ə)n/ *noun* defragmentación *f* de ficheros

file deletion /ˈfaɪl dɪˌliːʃ(ə)n/ *noun* eliminación *f* de ficheros; supresión *f* de ficheros

file descriptor /ˈfaɪl dɪˌskrɪptə/ *noun* descriptor *m* de ficheros

file directory /ˈfaɪl daɪˌrekt(ə)ri/ *noun* directorio *m* de ficheros

file extent /ˈfaɪl ɪkˌstent/ *noun* extensión *f* del fichero; tamaño *m* del fichero

file format /ˈfaɪl ˌfɔːmæt/ *noun* formato *m* de fichero

file fragmentation /ˈfaɪl ˌfrægmənteɪʃ(ə)n/ *noun* fragmentación *f* de ficheros

file gap /ˈfaɪl gæp/ *noun* espacio *m* neutro; separación *f* entre ficheros

file handle /ˈfaɪl ˌhænd(ə)l/ *noun* número *m* de fichero ◇ **the new data is written to the file identified by file handle 1** los nuevos datos son introducidos en el fichero identificado con el número 1

file handling routine /ˈfaɪl ˌhændlɪŋ ruːˌtiːn/ *noun* rutina *f* de manipulación de ficheros

file header /ˈfaɪl ˌhedə/ *noun* cabecera *f* de fichero ◇ **the file header in the database file shows the total number of records and lists the index fields** la cabecera del fichero de la base de datos muestra el número total de registros y hace un listado de los campos indexados

file identification /ˈfaɪl aɪˌdentɪfɪkeɪʃ(ə)n/ *noun* identificación *f* de ficheros

file index /ˈfaɪl ˌɪndeks/ *noun* índice *m* de ficheros

file interrogation /ˈfaɪl ɪnˌterəgeɪʃ(ə)n/ *noun* interrogación *f* de fichero

file label /ˈfaɪl ˌleɪb(ə)l/ *noun* etiqueta *f*; descriptor *m* de ficheros

file layout /ˈfaɪl ˌleɪaʊt/ *noun* diseño *m* de un fichero; organización *f* de un fichero

file length /ˈfaɪl leŋθ/ *noun* longitud *f*; tamaño *m* de un fichero

file locking /ˈfaɪl ˌlɒkɪŋ/ *noun* bloqueo *m*; cierre *m* de ficheros

file maintenance /ˈfaɪl ˌmeɪntənəns/ *noun* (*updating files*) mantenimiento *m*; puesta *f* a punto; mantenimiento *m* de un fichero; actualización *f* de ficheros

file management /ˈfaɪl ˌmænɪdʒmənt/, **file management system** /ˈfaɪl ˌmænɪdʒmənt ˌsɪstəm/ *noun* gestión *f* de ficheros

file manager /ˈfaɪl ˌmænɪdʒə/ *noun* (*section of a disk operating system*) gestor *m* de ficheros

file merger /ˈfaɪl ˌmɜːdʒə/ *noun* fusión *f* de ficheros

filename /ˈfaɪlneɪm/ *noun* nombre *m* de un fichero ◇ **in MS-DOS, a filename can be up to eight characters long together with a three character filename extension** en MS-DOS, el nombre del fichero puede tener hasta ocho caracteres además de una extensión de tres caracteres ◇ **the filename extension SYS indicates that this is a system file** la extensión SYS que se añade al nombre de un fichero indica que es un fichero del sistema

'...when the filename is entered at the prompt, the operating system looks in the file and executes any instructions stored there' [*PC User*]

filename extension /ˈfaɪlneɪm ɪkˌstenʃ(ə)n/ *noun* extensión *f* del nombre del fichero; extensión *f* del nombre ◇ **in MS-DOS, a filename can be up to eight characters long together with a three character filename extension** en MS-DOS, el nombre del fichero puede tener hasta ocho caracteres además de una extensión de tres caracteres ◇ **the filename extension SYS indicates that this is a system file** la extensión SYS que se añade al nombre de un fichero indica que es un fichero del sistema

file organisation /'faɪl ˌɔːgənaɪzeɪʃ(ə)n/ noun diseño m de un fichero; organización f de un fichero

file processing /'faɪl ˌprəʊsesɪŋ/ noun proceso m tratamiento m de ficheros

file protection /ˌfaɪl prə'tekʃən/ noun (dispositivo de) protección f de ficheros

file protect tab /ˌfaɪl prə'tekt ˌtæb/ noun dispositivo m de protección de la escritura de un fichero

file purge /'faɪl pɜːdʒ/ noun depuración f de ficheros

file queue /'faɪl kjuː/ noun cola f de ficheros; ficheros mpl en cola de espera ◇ **output devices such as laser printers are connected on-line with an automatic file queue** los periféricos como las impresoras láser entán conectados en línea con una cola automática de ficheros en espera

file-recovery utility /ˌfaɪl rɪ'kʌv(ə)ri juː ˌtɪlɪti/ noun programa m utilidad f de recuperación de ficheros ◇ **a lost file cannot be found without a file-recovery utility** es imposible encontrar un fichero perdido sin un programa de recuperación de ficheros

file security /'faɪl sɪˌkjʊərɪti/ noun protección f de ficheros

file server /'faɪl ˌsɜːvə/ noun servidor m de ficheros

file set /'faɪl set/ noun grupo m de ficheros (conectados)

file sharing /'faɪl ˌʃeərɪŋ/ noun utilización f compartida de ficheros

file size /'faɪl saɪz/ noun tamaño m de un fichero

file sort /'faɪl sɔːt/ verb clasificación f de ficheros

file storage /'faɪl ˌstɔːrɪdʒ/ noun (data storage) depósito m de memoria; almacenamiento m de ficheros; medio m de almacenamiento (de datos); memoria f (que contiene los ficheros)

file store /'faɪl stɔː/ noun ficheros mpl en memoria

file structure /'faɪl ˌstrʌktʃə/ noun estructura f de un fichero

file transfer /'faɪl ˌtrænsfɜː/ noun transferencia f de ficheros

file transfer access and management /ˌfaɪl ˌtrænsfɜː ˌækses ən 'mænɪdʒmənt/ noun gestión, acceso y transferencia de ficheros; método m FTAM

file transfer protocol /ˌfaɪl 'trænsfɜː ˌprəʊtəkɒl/ noun protocolo m de transferencia de ficheros; protocolo m FTP

file transfer utility /ˌfaɪl 'trænsfɜː juːˌtɪlɪti/ noun programa m de transferencia de ficheros; utilidad f de transferencia de ficheros

file type /'faɪl taɪp/ noun tipo m de fichero ◇ **files with the extension EXE are file types that contain program code** los ficheros con la extensión EXE son tipos de ficheros que contienen un código de programa

file update /'faɪl ˌʌpdeɪt/ noun 1. (corrected version) nueva versión f de un fichero 2. nueva versión f de un fichero

file validation /'faɪl ˌvælɪdeɪʃ(ə)n/ noun validación f de ficheros

filing system /'faɪlɪŋ ˌsɪstəm/ noun 1. (way of putting documents in order) sistema m de clasificación; sistema m de archivo 2. (software) sistema m de archivo

fill /fɪl/ verb 1. (to put characters into gaps) rellenar vt; completar vt 2. (to draw) llenar vt ◇ **the disk was quickly filled up** el disquete se llenó en seguida

fill character /fɪl 'kærɪktə/ noun carácter m de relleno

filter /'fɪltə/ noun 1. (electronic circuit) filtro m; (pattern of binary digits) máscara f 2. (coloured glass) filtro m ■ verb 1. (to select various bits) filtrar vt 2. (to remove unwanted elements) filtrar vt 3. (to select various bits) separar vt; eliminar mediante un filtrado; seleccionar vt ◇ **high pass filter** filtro de paso alto ◇ **low pass filter** filtro de paso bajo

final product /ˌfaɪn(ə)l 'prɒdʌkt/ noun producto m acabado; producto m final

find /faɪnd/ verb (command) encontrar vt; localizar vt; detectar vt ◇ **it took a lot of time to find the faulty chip** llevó mucho tiempo localizar el chip defectuoso ◇ **the debugger found the error very quickly** el detector (de fallos) localizó el error rápidamente

find and replace /ˌfaɪnd ən rɪ'pleɪs/ noun (dispositivo de) buscar y sustituir

Finder /'faɪndə/ (Apple Macintosh graphical user interface) Finder™ m

fine-tune /ˌfaɪn 'tjuːn/ verb (to carry out small adjustments) poner a punto; ajustar con precisión; sintonizar con precisión

finger /'fɪŋgə/ noun (on the internet – software program that will retrieve information about a user) dedo m; (software on the internet) (programa) dedo

finite-precision numbers /ˌfaɪnaɪt prɪ ˌsɪʒ(ə)n 'nʌmbəz/ noun números mpl de precisión finita

firewall /'faɪəwɔːl/ noun (security system hardware or software) programa m de seguridad cortafuegos

Firewire /'faɪəwaɪə/ (trade name for a high-speed serial interface developed by the Apple Computer Corporation) Firewire

firmware /'fɜːmweə/ noun (program or data stored in a hardware memory chip) soporte m lógico inalterable; soporte m lógico del sistema informático; programas mpl fijos; 'firmware' m

firmware monitor /'fɜːmweə ˌmɒnɪtə/ noun monitor m integrado

first fit /'fɜːst fɪt/ noun algoritmo m del primer emplazamiento posible

first generation /ˌfɜːst dʒenə'reɪʃ(ə)n/ noun primera generación f

first generation computer /ˌfɜːst ˌdʒenəreɪʃ(ə)n kəʉˈpjuːtə/ *noun* ordenador *m* de primera generación

first generation image /ˌfɜːst ˌdʒenəreɪʃ(ə)n ˈɪmɪdʒ/ *noun* imagen *f* original; imagen *f* de primera generación

first in first out /ˌfɜːst ɪn ˌfɜːst ˈaʊt/ *noun* (*storage read/write method*) sistema *m* de primero en entrar primero en salir; almacenamiento *m* FIFO; cola *f* de espera

first-level address /ˌfɜːst ˌlev(ə)l əˈdres/ *noun* dirección *f* de primer nivel; dirección *f* real

fit /fɪt/ *verb* (*calculate a curve*) ajustar *vt*

fixed and exchangeable disk storage /ˌfɪkst ən ɪksˌtʃeɪndʒəb(ə)l ˈdɪsk ˌstɔːrɪdʒ/ *noun* almacenamiento *m* con discos fijos e intercambiables; FEDS

fixed cycle operation /ˌfɪkst ˌsaɪk(ə)l ˌɒprəˈreɪʃ(ə)n/ *noun* **1.** operación *f* de ciclo fijo **2.** operación *f* sincronizada

fixed data /ˌfɪkst ˈdeɪtə/ *noun* datos *mpl* fijos; datos *mpl* permanentes

fixed disk /ˌfɪkst ˈdɪsk/ *noun* (*disk which cannot be removed*) disco *m* fijo; disco *m* duro fijo; disco *m* no intercambiable

fixed disk storage /ˌfɪkst dɪsk ˈstɔːrɪdʒ/ *noun* memoria *f* del disco duro

fixed field /ˌfɪkst ˈfiːld/ *noun* campo *m* fijo

fixed head disk /ˌfɪkst hed ˈdɪsk/**, fixed head disk drive** /ˌfɪkst hed ˈdɪsk ˌdraɪv/ *noun* (*separate immovable read/write head*) lector *m* (de discos); disquetera *f*; unidad *f* con cabeza de lectura fija

fixed-length field /ˌfɪkst leŋθ ˈfiːld/ *noun* campo *m* de longitud fija

fixed-length record /ˌfɪkst leŋθ ˈrekɔːd/ *noun* registro *m* de longitud fija; registro *m* de longitud finita; registro *m* de longitud determinada

fixed-length word /ˌfɪkst leŋθ ˈwɜːd/ *noun* (*preset number of bits*) palabra *f* de longitud fija; palabra *f* de longitud finita; palabra *f* de longitud determinada

fixed-point arithmetic /ˌfɪkst pɔɪnt əˈrɪθmətɪk/ *noun* aritmética *f* de coma fija; cálculo *m* de coma fija

fixed-point notation /ˌfɪkst pɔɪnt nəʊˈteɪʃ(ə)n/ *noun* notación *f* de coma fija

fixed program computer /ˌfɪkst ˌprəʊɡræm kəʉˈpjuːtə/ *noun* ordenador *m* de programas fijos

fixed routing /ˌfɪkst ˈraʊtɪŋ/ *noun* ruta *f* fija; ruta *f* preseleccionada

fixed word length /ˌfɪkst ˈwɜːd ˌleŋθ/ *noun* (ordenador de) longitud *f* fija de palabra

flag /flæɡ/ *noun* (*for block or field*) señalizador *m*; indicador *m*; marcador *m*; (*to indicate status*) indicador *m*; testigo *m* ■ *verb* (*to indicate status*) marcar *vt*; señalar *vt*; indicar *vt* ◇ **carry flag** testigo *or* indicador de retención *or* de arrastre ◇ **if the result is zero, the zero flag is set** si el resultado es cero se activa el indicador cero

flag bit /ˈflæɡ bɪt/ *noun* indicador *m* de bit; indicador *m* binario

flag code /ˈflæɡ kəʊd/ *noun* código *m* indicador

flag event /flæɡ ɪˈvent/ *noun* (*a process or condition that sets a flag*) función *f* de un evento; condición *f* de un evento; condición *f* que provoca un indicador; función *f* que genera una señalización

flagging /ˈflæɡɪŋ/ *noun* (*putting an indicator next to something*) señalización *f*; demarcación *f*; colocación *f* de un indicador

flag register /flæɡ ˈredʒɪstə/ *noun* registro *m* de testigos; registro *m* de indicadores

flag sequence /flæɡ ˈsiːkwəns/ *noun* secuencia *f* de marcadores; secuencia *f* de indicadores

flame /fleɪm/ *verb* (*on the internet – to send a rude or angry message to a user*) insultar (por la red)

flash /flæʃ/ *verb* **1.** hacer parpadear **2.** (hacer) parpadear

flash A/D /ˌflæʃ eɪ ˈdiː/ *noun* convertidor *m* A/D; convertidor *m* en paralelo de señales analógico-digitales

flashing character /flæʃɪŋ ˈkærɪktə/ *noun* carácter *m* intermitente

flash memory /flæʃ ˈmem(ə)ri/ *noun* memoria *f* por bloques; memoria *f* 'flash'

flash ROM /ˈflæʃ rɒm/ *noun* ROM *m* modificable mediante una señal eléctrica especial; ROM *f* 'flash'

flat address space /ˌflæt əˈdres ˌspeɪs/ *noun* espacio *m* de dirección plana

flatbed /ˈflætˌbed/ *adjective* (*printer or scanner*) de superficie plana; de plataforma; de tipo 'flatbed' ◇ **flatbed transmitter** transmisor *m* de superficie plana *or* de tipo 'flatbed' ◇ **scanners are either flatbed models or platen type, paper-fed models** los escáners son o bien de superficie plana o de rodillo con autoalimentación de papel

flatbed plotter /ˌflætbed ˈplɒtə/ *noun* trazador *m* de superficie plana

flatbed scanner /ˌflætbed ˈskænə/ *noun* escáner *m* de superficie plana ◇ **paper cannot be rolled through flatbed scanners** no se puede hacer rodar el papel a través de escáners de superficie plana

flat file /ˈflæt faɪl/ *noun* fichero *m* plano; fichero *m* bidimensional

flat file database /ˌflæt faɪl ˈdeɪtəbeɪs/ *noun* base *f* de datos lineal

flat pack /ˈflæt pæk/ *noun* paquete *m* plano; paquete *m* lineal

flat panel /ˌflæt ˈpæn(ə)l/ *noun* pantalla *f* plana

flat rate /ˌflæt ˈreɪt/ *noun* tarifa *f* plana; cuota *f* fija

flat screen /ˈflæt skriːn/ *noun* pantalla *f* plana

flexible array /ˌfleksəb(ə)l əˈreɪ/ *noun* matriz *f* flexible; tabla *f* flexible (de dimensiones variables)

flexible machining system /ˌfleksɪb(ə)l mə'ʃiːnɪŋ ˌsɪstəm/ *noun* sistema *m* para máquina flexible; sistema *m* de comandos numéricos

flexible manufacturing system /ˌfleksɪb(ə)l ˌmænjʊ'fæktʃərɪŋ ˌsɪstəm/ *noun* sistema *m* de fabricación flexible

flicker /'flɪkə/ *noun* (*variation of brightness*) parpadeo *m*; centelleo *m* ■ *verb* parpadear *vt*; centellear *vi*

flicker-free /'flɪkə friː/ *adjective* (*display*) sin parpadeo; sin reflejos; sin oscilación

'A CRT (cathode ray tube) monitor paints the screen from top to bottom, and is usually considered 'flicker free' if it refreshes the image 75 times a second, or more' [*The Guardian*]

flight simulator /'flaɪt ˌsɪmjʊleɪtə/ *noun* simulador *m* de vuelo

flip-flop /flɪp flɒp/ *noun* (*electronic circuit or chip*) circuito *m* biestable; circuito *m* basculante

flippy /'flɪpi/ *noun* disquete *m* reversible

float /fləʊt/ *noun* diferencia *f*; desplazamiento *m*

float factor /fləʊt 'fæktə/ *noun* factor *m* flotante

floating /'fləʊtɪŋ/ *adjective* flotante ◇ **floating accent** acento flotante ◇ **floating point** coma *f* flotante ◇ **floating point notation** notación *f* de coma flotante ◇ **floating voltage** voltaje *m* flotante ◇ **the fixed number 56.47 in floating-point arithmetic would be 0.5647 and a power of 2** en un cálculo de coma flotante, el número 56,47 sería 0,5647 elevado a la potencia de 2 ◇ **the floating point processor speeds up the processing of the graphics software** el procesador de coma flotante acelera el tratamiento del programa de gráficos ◇ **this model includes a built-in floating point processor** este modelo tiene incorporado un procesador de coma flotante

floating address /ˌfləʊtɪŋ ə'dres/ *noun* dirección *f* flotante; dirección *f* relativa

floating point arithmetic /ˌfləʊtɪŋ pɔɪnt ə'rɪθmətɪk/ *noun* cálculo *m* de coma flotante; aritmética *f* de coma flotante

floating point notation /ˌfləʊtɪŋ pɔɪnt nəʊ'teɪʃ(ə)n/ *noun* notación *f* de coma flotante

floating point number /ˌfləʊtɪŋ pɔɪnt 'nʌmbə/ *noun* número *m* de coma flotante

floating point operation /ˌfləʊtɪŋ pɔɪnt ˌɒpə'reɪʃ(ə)n/ *noun* operación *f* de coma flotante

floating point processor /ˌfləʊtɪŋ pɔɪnt 'prəʊsesə/ *noun* unidad *f* de coma flotante

floating point routine /ˌfləʊtɪŋ pɔɪnt ruː'tiːn/ *noun* rutina *f* de coma flotante

floating point unit /ˌfləʊtɪŋ pɔɪnt 'juːnɪt/ *noun* unidad *f* de coma flotante

floating symbolic address /ˌfləʊtɪŋ sɪm ˌbɒlɪk ə'dres/ *noun* dirección *f* simbólica flotante; dirección *f* simbólica relativa

floating window /ˌfləʊtɪŋ 'wɪndəʊ/ *noun* ventana *f* flottante

float relocate /fləʊt ˌriːləʊ'keɪt/ *noun* redireccionamiento *m* flotante; redireccionamiento *m* por desplazamiento que convierte una dirección relativa en absoluta

FLOP /flɒp/ *abbr* (*floating point operation*) operación *f* de coma flotante

floppy disk /ˌflɒpi 'dɪsk/, **floppy** /'flɒpi/ *noun* disco *m* flexible; disquete *m*

floppy disk controller /ˌflɒpi 'dɪsk kən ˌtrəʊlə/ *noun* controlador *m* de disquetes; controlador *m* de discos flexibles

floppy disk drive /ˌflɒpi 'dɪsk ˌdraɪv/ *noun* (*of a computer*) disquetera *f*; unidad *f* de disquete

floppy disk sector /ˌflɒpi 'dɪsk ˌsektə/ *noun* sector *m* de discos flexibles; sector *m* de disquetes

floppy disk unit /ˌflɒpi 'dɪsk ˌjuːnɪt/ *noun* unidad *f* de disco flexible

FLOPs per second /ˌflɒps pɜː 'sekənd/ *noun* (número de) operaciones *fpl* de coma flotante por segundo

flowchart /'fləʊtʃɑːt/ *noun* (*graphic description of a process*) ordinograma *m*; organigrama *m*; diagrama *m* de flujo; ordinograma *m* de flujo; organigrama *m* de flujo ◇ **a flowchart is the first step to a well designed program** el ordinograma representa el primer paso de un programa bien diseñado ◇ **flowchart template** modelo *m* de un ordinograma; plantilla *f*

flowchart stencil /'fləʊtʃɑːt ˌstens(ə)l/ *noun* plantilla *f* de organigrama; plantilla *f* de un diagrama de flujo

flowchart symbol /'fləʊtʃɑːt ˌsɪmb(ə)l/ *plural noun* símbolos *mpl* de un organigrama; símbolos *mpl* de un diagrama de flujo

flowchart template /'fləʊtʃɑːt ˌtempleɪt/ *noun* plantilla *f*; modelo *m* de un organigrama

flow control /fləʊ kən'trəʊl/ *noun* control *m* del flujo (de datos)

flow diagram /'fləʊ ˌdaɪəgræm/ *noun* ordinograma *m*; diagrama *m* de flujo

flow direction /fləʊ daɪ'rekʃən/ *noun* dirección *f* del flujo

flowline /'fləʊlaɪn/ *noun* línea *f* de flujo; línea *f* de unión

flow text /ˌfləʊ 'tekst/ *verb* volcar (un texto); introducir (un texto)

flush /flʌʃ/ *verb* (*levelled*) en línea con ■ *adjective* al mismo nivel; en línea con ◇ **the cover is trimmed flush with the pages** la cubierta se recorta en línea con las páginas

flutter /'flʌtə/ *noun* variación *f* de la velocidad; parpadeo *m* ◇ **wow and flutter are common faults on cheap tape recorders** la oscilación y la distorsión del tono son los fallos más comunes en las grabadoras baratas

flyback /'flaɪbæk/ *noun* retorno *m* (de un barrido)

flying head /'flaɪɪŋ hed/ *noun* (*floating head*) cabeza *f* flotante

FMS /ˌef em 'es/ *noun* sistema *m* de comandos numéricos; sistema *m* para máquina flexible

focus /'fəʊkəs/ *noun* foco *m*; enfoque *m* ■ *verb* enfocar *vt* ◇ **the camera is focused on the foreground** la cámara está enfocando un primer plano ◇ **they adjusted the lens position so that the beam focused correctly** han ajustado la posición de la lente de modo que el rayo de luz esté correctamente enfocado

focus window /ˈfəʊkəs ˌwɪndəʊ/ *noun* ventana *f* activa

fogging /ˈfɒgɪŋ/ *noun* efecto *m* niebla

folder /ˈfəʊldə/ *noun* (*Apple Macintosh, e-mail, Windows group of files*) carpeta *f*; clasificador *m* or -a *f*

folding /ˈfəʊldɪŋ/ *noun* (*hashing method*) codificación *f*; desdoblamiento *m*; reensamblaje *m*; dualidad *f* funcional

font /fɒnt/ *noun* fuente *f* (de caracteres tipográficos)

'Word Assistant is designed to help wordprocessing users produce better- looking documents. It has style templates and forms providing 25 TrueType fonts, 100 clip-art images and two font utility programs.' [*Computing*]

'...laser printers store fonts in several ways: as resident, cartridge and downloadable fonts' [*Desktop Publishing Today*]

font card /ˈfɒnt kɑːd/ *noun* tarjeta *f* de fuentes de caracteres

font change /ˈfɒnt tʃeɪndʒ/ *noun* cambio *m* de fuente de caracteres

Font/DA Mover /ˌfɒnt ˌdiː eɪ ˈmuːvə/ *noun* gestor *m* de fuentes y accesorios del escritorio; 'Mover' (Apple Macintosh)

font disk /ˈfɒnt dɪsk/ *noun* disquete *m* de fuentes

Fonts Folder /ˈfɒnts ˌfəʊldə/ *noun* carpeta *f* de fuentes (de caracteres)

foot /fʊt/ *noun* (*bottom part*) pie *m*; base *f* ◇ **he signed his name at the foot of the letter** estampó su firma al pie de la carta

footer /ˈfʊtə/, **footing** /ˈfʊtɪŋ/ *noun* (*message at the bottom of pages*) pie *m* de página

footnote /ˈfʊtˌnəʊt/ *noun* nota *f* a pie de página; anotación *f* a pie de página

footprint /ˈfʊtˌprɪnt/ *noun* 1. (*area covered by a beam*) huella *f* (de un haz luminoso, etc.) 2. (*desk space*) espacio *m* (que ocupa un ordenador)

'...signals from satellites in orbit 36,000km above the earth don't care very much whether you are close to an exchange or not....as long as you have a dish within their footprint.' [*The Guardian*]

forbidden character /fəˈbɪd(ə)n ˈkærɪktə/, **forbidden combination** /fəˌbɪd(ə)n ˌkɒmbɪˈneɪʃ(ə)n/ *noun* carácter *m* prohibido; cadena *f* (de caracteres) prohibida

forced page break /ˌfɔːst ˈpeɪdʒ ˌbreɪk/ *noun* salto *m* de página forzado; salto *m* de página programado

foreground /ˈfɔːgraʊnd/ *noun* 1. (*front part*) primer *m* plano 2. (*high priority task*) tarea *f* prioritaria; tarea *f* de prioridad alta

'This brighter – but still anti-glare – type of screen is especially useful for people using colourful graphic applications, where both the background and foreground are visually important.' [*Computing*]

foreground colour /ˌfɔːgraʊnd ˈkʌlə/ *noun* color *m* de primer plano

foregrounding /ˈfɔːgraʊndɪŋ/ *noun* tratamiento *m* preferente; proceso *m* preferente

foreground mode /ˈfɔːgraʊnd məʊd/ *plural noun* modo *m* de ejecución preferente

foreground processing memory /ˌfɔːgraʊnd ˈprəʊsesɪŋ ˌmem(ə)ri/ *noun* memoria *f* de proceso preferente

foreground program /ˌfɔːgraʊnd ˈprəʊgræm/ *noun* programa *m* prioritario; programa *m* preferente

forest /ˈfɒrɪst/ *noun* arborescencia *f*; bosque *m*

form /fɔːm/ *noun* 1. (*preprinted document*) formulario *m*; impreso *m*; (*preset computer layout for addresses, etc.*) presentación *f*; modelo *m* para introducir (datos); formato *m* de pantalla (para introducir datos) 2. (*page of computer stationery*) hoja *f*; página *f* 3. (*size and shape of a device*) constituir *vt*; formar *vt* ◇ **it's been easy to train the operators to use the new software since its display looks like the existing printed forms** ha sido fácil preparar a los operadores en la utilización del nuevo programa ya que su presentación en pantalla se parece a los impresos existentes ◇ **the system is formed of five separate modules** el sistema está constituido por cinco módulos independientes

formal methods /ˈfɔːm(ə)l ˌmeθədz/ *plural noun* métodos formales

format /ˈfɔːmæt/ *noun* 1. (*of book*) formato *m* 2. (*of text*) formato *m* ■ *verb* (*syntax of instructions*) formatear; (*to arrange text*) dar formato ◇ **style sheets are used to format documents** se utilizan hojas de estilo para dar formato a los documentos ◇ **the printer can deal with all formats up to quarto** la impresora puede gestionar todo tipo de formatos hasta tamaño en cuarto

'As an increasing amount of information within businesses is generated in wordprocessed format, text retrieval tools are becoming a highly attractive pragmatic solution.' [*Computing*]

format mode /ˈfɔːmæt məʊd/ *noun* formato *m* de pantalla

formatted dump /ˌfɔːmætɪd ˈdʌmp/ *noun* vuelco *m*; vaciado *m* del formato

formatter /ˈfɔːmætə/ *noun* (*piece of hardware or software*) programa *m*; instrucción *f* para formatear; instrucción *f* para ejecutar una función de formateado

form factor /ˈfɔːm ˈfæktə/ *noun* factor *m* de forma

form feed /ˈfɔːm fiːd/ *verb* cambio *m* de página

form flash /ˌfɔːm ˈflæʃ/ *noun* cabecera *f* preestablecida (guardada en memoria); encabezamiento *m* preestablecido (guardado en memoria)

form handling equipment /ˌfɔːm ˈhændlɪŋ ɪˌkwɪpmənt/ *noun* equipo *m* para la gestión de formularios; equipo *m* de impresos

form letter /ˈfɔːm ˌletə/ *noun* (*standard letter*) carta *f* tipo; carta *f* estándar; carta *f* modelo

form mode /'fɔːm məʊd/ *noun* (*display method-od on a data entry terminal*) pantalla *f*; máscara *f* (para introducir) de datos; máscara *f* (para introducción) de datos

form overlay /fɔːm ˌəʊvə'leɪ/ *noun* (*printing*) texto *m* preestablecido; gráfico *m* preestablecido (guardado en memoria); modelación *f* impresa

form stop /ˌfɔːm 'stɒp/ *noun* (*sensor on a printer*) parada *f* por falta de papel; parada *f* de formularios; indicador *m* de final de papel

form type /'fɔːm taɪp/ *noun* código *m* identificador

formula /'fɔːmjʊlə/ *noun* fórmula *f*

formula portability /ˌfɔːmjʊlə ˌpɔːtə'bɪlɪti/ *noun* portabilidad *f* de una fórmula

formula translator /'fɔːmjələ trænsˌleɪtə/ *noun* traductor *m* de fórmulas; lenguaje *m* de programación (de alto nivel)

for-next loop /ˌfɔː 'nekst ˌluːp/ *noun* bucle *m* FOR-NEXT

FORTH /fɔːθ/ *noun* lenguaje *m* (de programación) FORTH

FORTRAN /'fɔːtræn/ *noun* lenguaje de programación de alto nivel *m* FORTRAN

forum /'fɔːrəm/ *noun* foro *m*

forward /'fɔːwəd/ *verb* **1.** (*to send an email message that you have received on to another user*) transmitir *vt*; hacer llegar; redireccionar *vt*; enviar *vt* **2.** transmitir *vt*

forward error correction /ˌfɔːwəd 'erə kəˌrekʃ(ə)n/ *noun* corrección *f* de errores hacia adelante

forward mode /'fɔːwəd məʊd/ *noun* (*positive displacement to an origin*) selección *f* en orden creciente; clasificación *f* en orden creciente; hacia *f* adelante

forward pointer /ˌfɔːwəd 'pɔɪntə/ *noun* indicador *m* hacia adelante

for your information /fə ˌjɔːʀ ˌɪnfə 'meɪʃ(ə)n/ *noun* FYI; para tu información

four-address instruction /ˌfɔː əˌdres ɪn 'strʌkʃən/ *noun* instrucción *f* de cuatro direcciones

4GL *abbr* (*fourth-generation language*) lenguaje *m* de cuarta generación

fourth generation computer /ˌfɔːθ ˌdʒenəreɪʃ(ə)n kəm'pjuːtə/ *noun* ordenador *m* de cuarta generación

fourth generation language /ˌfɔːθ ˌdʒenəreɪʃ(ə)n 'læŋgwɪdʒ/ *noun* lenguaje *m* de cuarta generación

FPU *abbr* (*floating point unit*) unidad *f* de coma flotante

FQDN /ˌef kjuː diː 'en/ *noun* nombre *m* de dominio totalmente calificado

fractal /'frækt(ə)l/ *noun* (*shape that repeats itself*) fractal *m*

fractal compression /ˌfrækt(ə)l kəm 'preʃ(ə)n/ *noun* compresión *f* fractal

fractal image format /ˌfrækt(ə)l 'ɪmɪdʒ ˌfɔːmæt/ *noun* formato *m* de imagen fractal

fraction /'frækʃən/ *noun* **1.** fracción *f* **2.** fracción *f*

fractional part /'frækʃənəl pɑːt/ *noun* parte *f* fraccionaria; parte *f* mantisa

fractional services /ˌfrækʃənəl 'sɜːvɪsɪz/ *plural noun* (*parts of a bandwidth*) servicios *mpl* partidos; servicios *mpl* fraccionados; servicios *mpl* fraccionales ◇ **the commercial carrier will sell you fractional services that provide 64Kbps data transmission** el operador (comercial) les venderá servicios fraccionados que proporcionan una transmisión de datos de 64 Kbps

fractional T-1 /'frækʃənəl tiː/ *noun* T-1 fraccional

fragment /'frægmənt/ *noun* fragmento *m*

fragmentation /ˌfrægmən'teɪʃ(ə)n/ *noun* **1.** (*memory allocation to a number of files*) fragmentación *f*; segmentación *f*; fraccionamiento *m* **2.** (*of files on a disk*) fragmentación *f*; segmentación *f*; fraccionamiento *m*

frame /freɪm/ *noun* (*one image*) fotograma *m*; imagen *f* completa ◇ **video frame** imagen de vídeo *or* fotograma ◇ **with the image processor you can freeze a video frame** con el procesador de imágenes se puede congelar un fotograma del vídeo

frame buffer /freɪm 'bʌfə/ *noun* memoria *f* intermedia de imágenes

frame error /freɪm 'erə/ *noun* error *m* de tramo; error *m* de sección

frame grabber /'freɪm ˌgræbə/ *noun* (*high speed digital sampling circuit*) captador *m* de imágenes; captador *m* de imágenes (de vídeo); dispositivo *m* de grabación de imágenes

'…the frame grabber is distinguished by its ability to acquire a TV image in a single frame interval' [*Electronics & Wireless World*]

frame rate /'freɪm reɪt/ *noun* velocidad *f* secuencial

frame relay /freɪm rɪ'leɪ/ *noun* (*communications protocol*) cambio *m* de tramos; reordenación *f* de bloques

frame window /freɪm 'wɪndəʊ/ *noun* marco *m* de ventana (en pantalla)

framework /'freɪmwɜːk/ *noun* esquema *m*; estructura *f* ◇ **the program framework was designed first** primero se diseñó la estructura del programa

free /friː/ *adjective* (*not currently being used*) libre ■ *noun* (*of bytes*) libre ■ *verb* (*to clear space in memory*) liberar (espacio en la memoria) ◇ **free indexing** indexado *m* libre ◇ **free line** línea *f* libre ◇ **free space loss** pérdida *f* de espacios libres ◇ **free space media** soportes *mpl* de espacios libres

freedom of information /ˌfriːdəm əv ɪnfə 'meɪʃ(ə)n/ *noun* libertad *f* de información

free form database /ˌfriː fɔːm 'deɪtəbeɪs/ *noun* base *f* de datos con estructura libre

free running mode /ˌfriː 'rʌnɪŋ ˌməʊd/ *noun* modo *m* multi-usuario

free WAIS /ˌfriː ˌdʌb(ə)l juː eɪ aɪ 'es/ *noun* servidor *m* de información gratuito de área extendida; servidor *m* WAIS

freeware /'friːweə/ *noun* (*software in the public domain*) soporte *m* lógico gratuito; software *m* gratuito; software *m* al servicio del público

free wheeling /'friː wiːlɪŋ/ *noun* transmisión *f* sin control de retorno

freeze /friːz/ *verb* paralizar *vt*; congelar *vt* ◇ **the image processor will freeze a single TV frame** el procesador de imágenes puede congelar una imagen de televisión aislada ◇ **to freeze (frame)** congelar *or* fijar *or* parar (una imagen)

frequency /'friːkwənsi/ *noun* frecuencia *f* ◇ **extremely high frequency (EHF)** (*from 30 – 300 GHz*) frecuencia *f* de ondas extremadamente altas *or* de ondas milimétricas ◇ **extremely low frequency (ELF)** (*of less than 100 Hz*) frecuencia de ondas extremadamente bajas *or* de ondas miriamétricas ◇ **frequency changer** convertidor *m* de frecuencia ◇ **frequency deviation** desviación *f* de frecuencia ◇ **frequency distribution** distribución *f* de frecuencia ◇ **frequency divider** divisor *m* de frecuencia ◇ **frequency domain** dominio *m* de frecuencias ◇ **frequency range** ámbito *m* de frecuencias ◇ **frequency response** respuesta *f* de frecuencias ◇ **frequency shift keying (FSK)** (sistema de) modulación *or* manipulación *f* por desplazamiento de frecuencias ◇ **frequency swing** excursión *f* de frecuencia ◇ **frequency variation** variación *f* de frecuencias ◇ **the main clock frequency is 10MHz** la principal frecuencia de reloj es de 10 MHz ◇ **using FDM we can transmit 100 telephone calls along one main cable** la multiplexión de división de frecuencias permite transferir 100 llamadas telefónicas con un único cable principal

frequency division multiplexing /ˌfriːkwənsi dɪˌvɪʒ(ə)n 'mʌltɪˌpleksɪŋ/ *noun* multiplexión *f* de división de frecuencias

frequency modulation /ˌfriːkwənsi mɒdjuˈleɪʃ(ə)n/ *noun* modulación *f* de frecuencias

frequently asked questions /ˌfriːkwənt(ə)li ɑːskd 'kwestʃənz/ *plural noun* preguntas *fpl* más frecuentes

friendly front end /ˌfrendli ˌfrʌnt 'end/ *noun* (*display that is easy to use and understand*) interfaz *f* de fácil utilización

FROM /'ef rɒm/ *abbr* (*fusible read only memory*) dispositivo *m* PROM; memoria *f* programable

front end /ˌfrʌnt 'end/ *adjective* (*program that is seen by an end user*) interfaz *f* (de usuario); interconexión *f* ◇ **the program is very easy to use thanks to the uncomplicated front-end** el programa es de fácil utilización gracias a la interfaz poco complicada

front-end processor /ˌfrʌnt end 'prəʊsesə/ *noun* procesador *m* frontal

front panel /frʌnt 'pæn(ə)l/ *noun* panel *m* delantero; panel *m* frontal

FTAM /ˌef tiː eɪ 'em/ *noun* transferencia, acceso y gestión de ficheros

FTP /ˌef tiː 'piː/ *noun* FTP; protocolo *m* de transferencia de ficheros

full adder /ˌfʊl 'ædə/ *noun* sumadora *f* total; sumadora *f* de tres entradas

full duplex /ˌfʊl 'djuːpleks/ *noun* dúplex *m* bidireccional

full handshaking /ˌfʊl 'hændʃeɪkɪŋ/ *noun* protocolo *m* de comunicación

full-motion video adapter /ˌfʊl ˌməʊʃ(ə)n 'vɪdiəʊ əˌdæptə/ *noun* adaptador *m* de vídeo de animación completa

full path /ˌfʊl 'pɑːθ/ *noun* camino *m* completo; ruta *f* completa

full-screen /fʊl skriːn/ *adjective* pantalla *f* completa

full-size display /ˌfʊl saɪz dɪs'pleɪ/ *noun* pantalla *f* de página completa; pantalla *f* de toda la página

full subtractor /ˌfʊl səb'træktə/ *noun* restadora *f* total; restadora *f* de tres entradas

full-text search /ˌfʊl tekst 'sɜːtʃ/ *noun* búsqueda *f* global; búsqueda *f* en todo el texto

fully formed character /ˌfʊli fɔːmd 'kærɪktə/ *plural noun* carácter *m* completo ◇ **a daisy wheel printer produces fully formed characters** una impresora de margarita produce caracteres completos

fully-populated /ˌfʊli 'pɒpjuˌleɪtɪd/ *adjective* (*PCB with components in all free sockets*) con todos sus componentes

function /'fʌŋkʃən/ *noun* **1.** (*mathematical formula*) función *f* **2.** (*sequence of computer program instructions*) función *f* **3.** (*special feature on a computer*) función *f* ◇ **hitting F5 will put you into insert mode** la función de insertar se activa pulsando la tecla F5 ◇ **the word-processor had a spelling-checker function but no built-in text-editing function** el procesador de textos disponía de una función de corrección ortográfica, pero no de una función de edición de textos

functional diagram /ˌfʌŋkʃ(ə)nəl 'daɪəgræm/ *noun* esquema *m* funcional; diagrama *m* funcional

functional specification /ˌfʌŋkʃ(ə)nəl ˌspesɪfɪ'keɪʃ(ə)n/ *noun* especificación *f* funcional; análisis *m* funcional

functional unit /ˌfʌŋkʃən(ə)l 'juːnɪt/ *noun* aparato *m* en buen estado; unidad *f* en buen estado de funcionamiento

function call /'fʌŋkʃən kɔːl/ *noun* llamada *f* de función

function code /'fʌŋkʃən kəʊd/ *noun* código *m* de función

function digit /'fʌŋkʃən ˌdɪdʒɪt/ *noun* (*code used to instruct a computer*) dígito *m*; carácter *m*; código *m* de función

function key /'fʌŋkʃən kiː/ *noun* tecla *f* de función ◇ **tags can be allocated to function keys**

las etiquetas pueden asignarse a las teclas de función

function library /'fʌŋkʃən ˌlaɪbrəri/ *noun* biblioteca *f* de funciones

function overloading /'fʌŋkʃ(ə)n ˌəʊvələʊdɪŋ/ *noun* sobrecarga *f* de funciones

function table /'fʌŋkʃən ˌteɪb(ə)l/ *noun* tabla *f* de funciones

fusible link /ˌfjuːzɪb(ə)l 'lɪŋk/ *noun* elemento *m* fusible; enlace *m* fusible

fusible read only memory /ˌfjuːzɪb(ə)l riːd ˌəʊnli 'mem(ə)ri/ *noun* dispositivo *m* PROM; memoria *f* programable

fuzzy logic /ˌfʌzi 'lɒdʒɪk/, **fuzzy theory** /ˌfʌzi 'θɪəri/ *noun* lógica *f* confusa; teoría *f* de lógica polivalente

G

gain /geɪn/ *noun* **1.** (*increase*) ganancia *f*; (*becoming larger*) amplificación *f* **2.** (*in signal amplitude*) amplificación *f* ◇ **gain control** control *m* de amplificación *or* de ganancia

gallium arsenide /ˌgæliəm ˈɑːs(ə)naɪd/ *noun* arseniuro *m* de galio

game cartridge /ˈgeɪm ˌkɑːtrɪdʒ/ *noun* cartucho *m* de juego

game console /ˈgeɪm ˌkɒnsəʊl/ *noun* consola *f* de juego

game port /ˈgeɪm pɔːt/ *noun* puerto *m* de juego

games console /ˈgeɪmz ˌkɒnsəʊl/ *noun* consola *f* de juego

ganged /gæŋd/ *adjective* (*mechanically linked*) acoplados mecánicamente

ganged switch /ˌgæŋd ˈswɪtʃ/ *noun* (*series of switches*) reagrupamiento *m*; conjunto *m* de conmutadores; conmutadores *mpl* montados en serie ◇ **a ganged switch is used to select which data bus a printer will respond to** un reagrupamiento de conmutadores se emplea para seleccionar el bus de datos al que responde una impresora

gap /gæp/ *noun* **1.** (*between recorded data*) espacio *m* intermedio; intervalo *m* vacío **2.** (*space*) espacio *m* intermedio; intervalo *m*; vacío *m*

gap character /gæp ˈkærɪktə/ *noun* carácter *m* de relleno

gap digit /gæp ˈdɪdʒɪt/ *noun* dígito *m* de relleno

gap loss /ˌgæp ˈlɒs/ *noun* pérdida *f* de alineamiento en el entrehierro

garbage /ˈgɑːbɪdʒ/ *noun* **1.** (*radio interference*) residuos *mpl*; desechos *mpl*; basura *f*; interferencias *fpl* **2.** (*information no longer required*) información *f* no válida

garbage collection /ˈgɑːbɪdʒ kəˌlekʃən/ *noun* limpieza *f* de memoria

garbage in garbage out /ˌgɑːbɪdʒ ɪn ˌgɑːbɪdʒ ˈaʊt/ *noun* datos *mpl* erróneos, resultados erróneos; basura *f* en la entrada, basura *f* en la salida

gas discharge display /gæs dɪsˌtʃɑːdʒ dɪ ˈspleɪ/, **gas plasma display** /gæs ˌplæzmə dɪ ˈspleɪ/ *noun* pantalla *f* de plasma

gate /geɪt/ *noun* **1.** (*logical electronic switch*) puerta *f* **2.** (*connection pin of a FET device*) conector *m* (de un transistor)

gate array /geɪt əˈreɪ/ *noun* circuito *m* lógico complejo; circuito *m* en red

gate circuit /geɪt ˈsɜːkɪt/ *noun* circuito *m* lógico; puerta *f* electrónica

gate delay /geɪt dɪˈleɪ/ *noun* tiempo *m* de respuesta

gateway /ˈgeɪtweɪ/ *noun* **1.** (*networks*) puerta *f*; pasarela *f* (de comunicación) **2.** (*electronic mail software*) pasarela *f* **3.** (*allowing access to network*) puerta *f* (de comunicación); pasarela *f* (de comunicación) ◇ **we use a gateway to link the LAN to WAN** utilizamos una puerta para conectar la red de área local con la red de área extendida

gather /ˈgæðə/ *verb* agrupar *vt*; reunir *vt*

gather write /ˈgæðə raɪt/ *verb* escritura *f* agrupada; grabación *f* agrupada

Gb *abbr* (*gigabyte*) gigabyte (Gb) *m*; gigaocteto *m*

gender changer /ˈdʒendə ˌtʃeɪndʒə/ *noun* informal (*connection*) conversor *m* de género; cambiador *m* de género; conmutador *m* de género ◇ **you can interconnect all these peripherals with just two cables and a gender changer** se pueden interconectar todos estos periféricos con sólo dos cables y un conversor de género

general purpose computer /ˌdʒen(ə)rəl ˌpɜːpəs kəmˈpjuːtə/ *noun* ordenador *m* universal; ordenador *m* para usos generales

general purpose interface adapter /ˌdʒen(ə)rəl ˌpɜːpəs ˈɪntəfeɪs əˌdæptə/ *noun* adaptador *m* de interfaces de interconexión general

general purpose interface bus /ˌdʒen(ə)rəl ˌpɜːpəs ˈɪntəfeɪs ˌbʌs/ *noun* enlace *m* común de interconexión general

general purpose program /ˌdʒen(ə)rəl ˌpɜːpəs ˈprəʊgræm/ *noun* programa *m* para usos generales

general register /ˌdʒen(ə)rəl ˈredʒɪstə/ *noun* registro *m* general; registro *m* para usos generales

generate /ˈdʒenəˌreɪt/ *verb* (*codes or programs*) producir *vt*; generar *vt*; crear *vt* ◇ **the graphics tablet generates a pair of co-ordinates each time the pen is moved** cada vez que se mueve el lápiz óptico la pizarra gráfica genera un par de coordenadas ◇ **to generate an image from digitally recorded data** crear una imagen a partir de datos grabados digitalmente

generated address /ˌdʒenəreɪtɪd əˈdres/ *noun* dirección *f* generada

generated error /ˌdʒenəreɪtɪd ˈerə/ *noun* error *m* generado (por redondeo)

generation /ˌdʒenəˈreɪʃ(ə)n/ *noun* **1.** (*producing data*) producción *f*; creación *f* **2.** (*age of the technology*) generación *f* **3.** (*of file*) creación *f*;

generación *f* ◇ **code generation is automatic** la producción de códigos es automática ◇ **the father file is a first generation backup** el fichero padre es una copia de seguridad de primera generación

generator /'dʒenə,reɪtə/ *noun* (*program*) generador *m*

generator lock /'dʒenə,reɪtə lɒk/ *noun* generador *m* de sincronismos

generic /dʒə'nerɪk/ *adjective* genérico *or* -a

genlock /'dʒenlɒk/ *noun* generador *m* de sincronismos

geometry /dʒi'ɒmətri/ *noun* geometría *f*

geometry processing /dʒi:'ɒmətri ,prəʊsesɪŋ/ *noun* proceso *m* geométrico

get /get/ *noun* instrucción *f* 'GET'; instrucción *f* 'buscar'

ghost /gəʊst/ *noun* imagen *f* fantasma

ghost cursor /gəʊst 'kɜːsə/ *noun* cursor *m* secundario

GHz *abbr* (*gigahertz*) GHz; gigahercio (GHz) *m*

GIF /gɪf/ (*trade name for a graphics file format*) formato *m* gráfico de intercambio

GIF file /,dʒi: aɪ 'ef faɪl/ *noun* (*graphics file format*) fichero *m* gráfico

giga- /gɪgə/ *prefix* **1.** (*meaning one thousand million*) giga-; G **2.** giga-

gigabit /'gɪgəbɪt/ *noun* gigabit *m*

gigabyte /'gɪgəbaɪt/ *noun* gigabyte *m* (Gb); gigaocteto *m*

gigaflop /'gɪgəflɒp/ *noun* (*one thousand million floating-point operations per second*) gigaflop *m*; mil millones de operaciones de coma flotante por segundo

gigahertz /'gɪgəhɜːts/ *noun* gigahercio (GHz) *m*; GHz

GIGO /'gaɪgəʊ/ *noun* datos *mpl* erróneos, resultados erróneos; basura *f* en la entrada, basura en la salida

GKS /,dʒi: keɪ 'es/ *noun* sistema *m* para entrada/salida gráfica

glare /gleə/ *noun* reflejo *m* ◇ **the glare from the screen makes my eyes hurt** el reflejo de la pantalla me cansa la vista

glare filter /gleə 'fɪltə/ *noun* filtro *m* de pantalla; antirreflejo *m*

glitch /glɪtʃ/ *noun informal* (*something that causes a sudden or unexpected failure*) problema *m*; fallo *m*

'The programmer was upgrading a verification system at Visa's UK data centre when his work triggered a software glitch causing hundreds of valid cards to be rejected for several hours.' [*Computing*]

global /'gləʊb(ə)l/ *adjective* global; total

'In an attempt to bring order to an electronic Tower of Babel, pharmaceutical giant Rhone-Poulenc has assembled an X.400-based global messaging network and a patchwork directory system that will be used until a single email system is deployed worldwide.' [*Computing*]

global exchange /,gləʊb(ə)l ɪks'tʃeɪndʒ/ *noun* (función de) reemplazar en todo el texto

global knowledge /,gləʊb(ə)l 'nɒlɪdʒ/ *noun* conocimiento *m* global

global memory /,gləʊb(ə)l 'mem(ə)ri/ *noun* memoria *f* global

global search and replace /,gləʊb(ə)l ,sɜːtʃ ən rɪ'pleɪs/ *noun* (función de) buscar y reemplazar en todo el texto

global system for mobile communications /,gləʊb(ə)l ,sɪstəm fə ,məʊbaɪl kə ,mjuːnɪ'keɪʃ(ə)nz/ *noun* sistema *m* global de comunicaciones móviles

global variable /,gləʊb(ə)l 'veəriəb(ə)l/ *noun* variable *f* global

glyph /glɪf/ *noun* glifo *m*

GND /,dʒi: en 'di:/ *abbr* (*ground*) toma *f* de tierra

goal /gəʊl/ *noun* objetivo *m*

go down /,gəʊ 'daʊn/ *verb* bloquearse *vr*; dejar de funcionar *vi*

Google /'guːg(ə)l/ (*trade name for a popular Internet search engine*) Google

Gopher /'gəʊfə/ *noun* (*internet system*) Gopher

GOSIP /'gɒsɪp/ *noun* perfil *m* gubernamental OSI

GOSUB /'gəʊsʌb/ *noun* (*programming command to execute a routine*) GOSUB

GOTO /'gəʊtuː/ *noun* (*command which instructs a jump*) VÁYASE A; GOTO

Gouraud shading /'guːrəʊ ,ʃeɪdɪŋ/ *noun* método *m* de matizado de Gouraud

Government Open Systems Interconnect Profile /,gʌv(ə)nmənt ,əʊpən ,sɪstəm 'ɪntəkənekt ,prəʊfaɪl/ *noun* perfil *m* gubernamental OSI

GPIB /,dʒi: pi: aɪ 'bi:/ *noun* enlace *m* común de interconexión general

gpr /,dʒi: pi: 'ɑː/ *noun* registro *m* general; registro *m* para usos generales

grabber /'græbə/ *noun* captador *m*

graceful degradation /,greɪsf(ə)l ,degrə 'deɪʃ(ə)n/ *noun* (*process of allowing some parts of a system to continue to function after a part has broken down*) degradación *f* limitada; degradación *f* progresiva; degradación *f* leve

gradient /'greɪdiənt/ *noun* gradiente

grammar /'græmə/ *noun* (*rules for language use*) sintaxis *f*; gramática *f*

grammar checker /'græmə ,tʃekə/ *noun* corrector *m* gramatical; utilidad *f* de corrección gramatical

grammatical error /grə,mætɪk(ə)l 'erə/ *noun* error *m* de sintaxis; fallo *m* de sintaxis

grandfather cycle /'grænfɑːðə ,saɪk(ə)l/ *noun* ciclo *m* abuelo; ciclo *m* de rotación de los ficheros de seguridad

grandfather file /'grænfɑːðə faɪl/ *noun* (*when followed by two other files: father and son*) fichero *m* abuelo

granularity /ˌgrænjʊ'lærɪti/ *noun* (*size of memory segments*) granulosidad *f*; modularidad *f* de la memoria; grado *m* de segmentación de la memoria

graphic /'græfɪk/ *adjective* gráfico *or* -a

graphical user interface /ˌgræfɪkl 'juːzə ˌɪntəfeɪs/ *noun* (*interface between an operating system and the user*) interfaz *f* gráfica (del usuario); GUI

graphic data /'græfɪk ˌdeɪtə/ *noun* datos *mpl* gráficos

graphic display /'græfɪk dɪˌpleɪ/ *noun* representación *f* gráfica; visualización *f* gráfica

graphic display resolution /'græfɪk dɪ ˌspleɪ ˌrezəluːʃ(ə)n/ *noun* resolución *f* de visualización gráfica; definición *f* de visualización gráfica

graphic language /'græfɪk ˌlæŋgwɪdʒ/ *noun* lenguaje *m* gráfico ◇ **this graphic language can plot lines, circles and graphs with a single command** este lenguaje gráfico puede trazar líneas, círculos y gráficos con una sola instrucción

graphics /'græfɪks/ *noun* gráficos *mpl*; representaciones *fpl* gráficas ◇ **graphics output such as bar charts, pie charts, etc.** las representaciones gráficas como los histogramas, los gráficos sectoriales, etc. ◇ **there are many standards for graphics files including TIFF, IMG and EPS** hay muchos estándares para ficheros gráficos como TIFF, IMG y EPS

graphics adapter /'græfɪks əˌdæptə/ *noun* (*electronic device to display graphics*) adaptador *m* gráfico; tarjeta *f* gráfica ◇ **the new graphics adapter is capable of displaying higher resolution graphics** el nuevo adaptador gráfico es capaz de producir gráficos de mayor definición; el nuevo adaptador de gráficos proporciona una mayor resolución

graphics character /'græfɪks ˌkærɪktə/ *noun* carácter *m* gráfico

graphics coprocessor /'græfɪks kəʊ ˌprəʊsesə/ *noun* coprocesador *m* gráfico

graphics file /'græfɪks faɪl/ *noun* fichero *m* gráfico ◇ **there are many standards for graphics files including TIFF, IMG and EPS** hay muchos estándares para ficheros gráficos como TIFF, IMG y EPS

graphics file format /'græfɪks faɪl ˌfɔːmæt/ *noun* formato *m* de fichero gráfico

graphics interface format /ˌgræfɪks 'ɪntəfeɪs ˌfɔːmæt/ *noun* formato *m* de intercambio gráfico

graphics kernel system /ˌgræfɪks 'kɜːn(ə)l ˌsɪstəm/ *noun* sistema *m* para entrada/salida gráfica

graphics library /'græfɪks ˌlaɪbr(ə)ri/ *noun* biblioteca *f* gráfica; biblioteca *f* de gráficos

graphics light pen /ˌgræfɪks 'laɪt ˌpen/ *noun* lápiz *m* óptico gráfico

graphics mode /'græfɪks məʊd/ *noun* modo *m* gráfico

graphics overlay card /ˌgræfɪks 'əʊvəleɪ ˌkɑːd/ *noun* tarjeta *f* gráfica de expansión

graphics pad /'græfɪks pæd/ *noun* tabla *f* gráfica

graphics primitive /ˌgræfɪks 'prɪmɪtɪv/ *noun* forma *f* primitiva; forma *f* de base

graphics printer /'græfɪks ˌprɪntə/ *noun* impresora *f* gráfica

graphics processor /'græfɪks ˌprəʊsesə/ *noun* procesador *m* gráfico

graphics software /'græfɪks ˌsɒftweə/ *noun* (*routines which perform standard graphics commands*) programa *m* gráfico; software *m* gráfico; software *m* de diseño gráfico

graphics tablet /'græfɪks ˌtæblət/ *noun* tableta *f* gráfica

graphics terminal /'græfɪks ˌtɜːmɪn(ə)l/ *noun* terminal *m* gráfico

graphics VDU /ˌgræfɪks ˌviː diː 'juː/ *noun* pantalla *f* de visualización gráfica

graph plotter /'grɑːf ˌplɒtə/ *noun* trazador *m* gráfico; trazador *m* de grafos

Gray code /'greɪ kəʊd/ *noun* código *m* de Gray

gray scale /'greɪ skeɪl/ *noun US* escala *f* de grises

greeked /griːkd/ *adjective* (*font with a point size too small to display*) texto *m* mudo

Green Book /griːn 'bʊk/ *noun* Green Book

gremlin /'gremlɪn/ *noun informal* (*unexplained fault in a system*) duende *m*; error *m* inexplicable

grey scale /'greɪ skeɪl/ *noun* (*shades of grey on a monochrome monitor*) niveles *mpl* de gris; (*used to measure the correct exposure when filming*) escala *f* de grises

grid /grɪd/ *noun* **1.** (*when drawing*) rejilla *f* **2.** (*matrix*) rejilla *f*

grid snap /'grɪd snæp/ *noun* dispositivo *m* de rejilla (en pantalla) ◇ **if you want to draw accurate lines, you'll find it easier with grid snap turned on** si quiere dibujar con líneas precisas, le resultará más fácil con el dispositivo de rejilla activado

ground /graʊnd/ *noun* (*electrical connection to earth or GND*) toma *f* de tierra

group /gruːp/ *noun* **1.** (*set of computer records*) grupo *m* **2.** (*in telegraphic communications*) grupo *m* (de caracteres/de palabras) **3.** (*collection of icons in a GUI*) grupo *m* de programas; iconos *mpl* **4.** (*collection of users*) grupo *m* de usuarios ■ *verb* (*bring together*) agrupar *vt* ◇ **all the icons in this group are to do with painting** todos los iconos de este grupo están relacionados con la pintura

group icon /gruːp 'aɪkɒn/ *noun* icono *m* de grupo

group mark /gruːp mɑːk/, **group marker** /gruːp 'mɑːkə/ *noun* marca *f* de grupo; marcador *m* de grupo

group poll /'gruːp pəʊl/ *noun* llamada *f* (selectiva) de grupo

groupware /'gruːpweə/ *noun* (*software written to be used by a group*) programa *m* de grupo (de trabajo)

GSM /ˌdʒiː es 'em/ *noun* sistema *m* global de comunicaciones móviles

guard band /'gaːd bænd/ *noun* (*section of magnetic tape*) banda *f* de guarda; banda *f* de frecuencia no utilizada; banda *f* de protección; banda *f* intermedia

guard bit /'gaːd bɪt/ *noun* bit *m* de guarda

GUI /'guːi/ *noun* GUI; interfaz *f* gráfico (del usuario)

guide bar /'gaɪd baː/ *noun* línea *f* guía; línea *f* de referencia

gulp /gʌlp/ *noun* grupo *m* de bytes; grupo *m* de dos bytes

gun /gʌn/ *noun* cañón *m*

gutter /'gʌtə/ *noun* (*margin*) margen *m* interior

H

H *abbr* (*hex*) notación *f* hexadecimal

hack /hæk/ *verb* **1.** (*for criminal purposes*) introducirse en un sistema informático sin autorización; piratear *vt*; sabotear *vt* **2.** (*to gain access to a computer system for criminal purposes*) introducirse en un sistema informático sin autorización; (*for criminal purposes*) piratear *vt*; sabotear *vt*

hacker /'hækə/ *noun* (*person who explores computer software and hardware*) aficionado, -a a la informática *mf*; fanático, -a informático, -a; (*person who breaks into a computer system for criminal purposes*) intruso *m* informático

'The two were also charged with offences under the Computer Misuse Act and found guilty of the very actions upon which every hacker is intent.' [*Computing*]

hairline rule /'heə,laɪn ruːl/ *noun* (*in DTP system: very thin line*) norma *f* de línea pequeña; norma *f* muy delgada

half adder /hɑːf 'ædə/ *noun* semisumador *or* -a

half card /,hɑːf 'kɑːd/ *noun* tarjeta *f* media; tarjeta *f* corta

half duplex /hɑːf 'djuːpleks/ *noun* semidúplex *m*; dúplex *m* en alternativa

half-duplex modem /,hɑːf ,djuːpleks 'məʊdem/ *noun* módem *m* semidúplex; módem *m* de una sola dirección

half-height drive /,hɑːf haɪt 'draɪv/ *noun* disquetera *f* de altura media

half-intensity /hɑːf ɪn'tensɪti/ *adjective* de intensidad media

halftone /,hɑːf'təʊn/ *noun* mediotono *m*; media tinta *f*

half word /,hɑːf 'wɜːd/ *noun* media *f* palabra

Hall effect /hɔːl ɪ'fekt/ *noun* efecto *m* Hall

halt /hɔːlt/ *noun* parada *f*

halt condition /hɔːlt kən'dɪʃ(ə)n/ *noun* condición *f* de parada

halt instruction /hɔːlt ɪn'strʌkʃən/ *noun* instrucción *f* de parada

Hamming code /'hæmɪŋ kəʊd/ *noun* código *m* de Hamming

Hamming distance /'hæmɪŋ ,dɪstəns/ *noun* distancia *f* de Hamming

hand /hænd/ *noun* mano *f* ◇ **hand viewer** visor *m* de mano

hand-held computer /,hænd held kəm'pjuːtə/, **hand-held programmable** /,hænd held 'prəʊɡræməb(ə)l/ *noun* ordenador *m* de bolsillo

hand-held scanner /,hænd held 'skænə/ *noun* escáner *m* de mano; escáner *m* de bolsillo

H & J /,eɪtʃ ənd 'dʒeɪ/ *noun* código *m* de Hamming; codificación *f* de Hamming

handle /'hænd(ə)l/ *noun* **1.** (*number to identify an active file*) número *m* de identificación de un fichero **2.** (*small square to change a shape*) cuadro *m* pequeño de manipulación de una figura ◇ **to stretch the box in the DTP program, select it once to display the handles then drag one handle to change its shape** para agrandar un recuadro en el programa DTP, selecciónelo primero (con el ratón) y a continuación arrastre uno de los cuadros pequeños de manipulación hasta lograr la figura deseada

handler /'hændlə/ *noun* (*control of a function or device*) controlador *m*; programa *m* de instrucciones; gestor *m* de periféricos

handshake /'hæn(d),ʃeɪk/, **handshaking** *noun* (*between transmitter and receptor*) protocolo *m* de validación de transferencia de datos; protocolo *m* de intercambio de información

handshake I/O control /,hæn(d)ʃeɪk aɪ 'əʊ kən,trəʊl/ *noun* control *m* de intercambio de comunicaciones entrada/salida; control *m* de intercambio E/S

hands off /,hændz 'ɒf/ *adjective* (*automatic working system*) con sistema automático; sin intervención manual; sin acceso al ordenador

hands on /,hændz 'ɒn/ *adjective* (*manual*) sistema *m* manual; (*training*) formación *f* práctica

handwriting recognition /'hændraɪtɪŋ ,rekəɡnɪʃ(ə)n/ *noun* (*of software – that recognises handwritten text*) reconocimiento *m* caligráfico; reconocimiento *m* de escritura (a mano) ◇ **the new PDA has excellent handwriting recognition** el nuevo programa PDA tiene un excelente sistema de reconocimiento caligráfico

hang /hæŋ/ *verb* (*to stop responding*) suspender *vt*; no responder después de un fallo; engancharse en un bucle ◇ **after she had finished talking on the telephone, she hung up** después de terminar de hablar por teléfono ella colgó

hangover /'hæŋəʊvə/ *noun* (*of fax machine*) cola *f*; resto *m* de una imagen; arrastre *m* de la tonalidad

hangup /'hæŋʌp/ *noun* parada *f* imprevista (en una rutina)

hard /hɑːd/ *adjective* (*solid*) duro *or* -a; sólido *or* -a; (*not programmable*) cerrado *or* -a

hardboot /'hɑːdbuːt/ *verb* arrancar en frío

hard card /ˌhɑːd ˈkɑːd/ noun tarjeta f de disco duro

hard copy /ˌhɑːd ˈkɒpi/ noun (printed document or copy of information) copia f impresa; salida f de impresora; impresión f de pantalla; documento m impreso

hard copy interface /ˌhɑːd ˈkɒpi ˌɪntəfeɪs/ noun interfaz f de copia impresa

hard disk /ˌhɑːd ˈdɪsk/ noun disco m duro

hard disk drive /ˌhɑːd ˈdɪsk ˌdraɪv/ noun (to store and retrieve data) controlador m de disco duro; unidad f de disco duro

hard drive /ˈhɑːd draɪv/ noun controlador m de disco duro; unidad f de disco duro

hard error /hɑːd ˈerə/ noun error m permanente; anomalía f permanente

hard failure /hɑːd ˈfeɪljə/ noun fallo m serio ◇ **the hard failure was due to a burnt-out chip** el fallo del equipo se debió a un chip quemado

hard reset /hɑːd ˌriːˈset/ noun reinicio m apagando el sistema; reinicio m (apagando el sistema)

hard return /hɑːd rɪˈtɜːn/ noun código m de final de párrafo

hardware /ˈhɑːdˌweə/ noun (physical components of a computer) hardware m; equipo m; soporte m físico (del ordenador) ◇ **the communications software is hardware dependent and will only work with Hayes-compatible modems** los componentes lógicos de comunicaciones dependen del equipo y sólo funcionan con un módem compatible de tipo Hayes

'Seuqent's Platform division will focus on hardware and software manufacture, procurement and marketing, with the Enterprise division concentrating on services and client-server implementation.' [Computing]

hardware compatibility /ˌhɑːdweə kəmˌpætəˈbɪlɪti/ noun compatibilidad f del equipo

hardware configuration /ˌhɑːdweə kənˌfɪɡjəˈreɪʃ(ə)n/ noun configuración f del equipo

hardware dependent /ˌhɑːdweə dɪˈpendənt/ adjective dependiente del equipo ◇ **the communications software is hardware dependent and will only work with Hayes-compatible modems** los componentes lógicos de comunicaciones dependen del equipo y sólo funcionan con un módem compatible de tipo Hayes

hardware failure /ˈhɑːdweə ˌfeɪljə/ noun fallo m del equipo; avería f provocada por el equipo

hardware interrupt /ˈhɑːdweə ˌɪntərʌpt/ noun señal f de interrupción provocada por el equipo

hardware platform /ˈhɑːdweə ˌplætfɔːm/ noun plataforma f del equipo

hardware reliability /ˌhɑːdweə rɪˌlaɪəˈbɪlɪti/ noun fiabilidad f del equipo

hardware reset /ˌhɑːdweə ˈriːset/ noun interruptor m para reiniciar el equipo

hardware security /ˌhɑːdweə sɪˈkjʊərɪti/ noun seguridad f del equipo

hardwired connection /ˌhɑːdwaɪəd kəˈnekʃ(ə)n/ noun conexión f cableada; conexión f fija

hardwired logic /ˌhɑːdwaɪəd ˈlɒdʒɪk/ noun lógica f cableada

hardwired program /ˌhɑːdwaɪəd ˈprəʊɡræm/ noun programa m cableado; programa m fijo ◇ **wired** or **hardwired program computer** ordenador m con programa cableado or fijo

harmonics /hɑːˈmɒnɪks/ noun armónicos mpl

hartley /ˈhɑːtli/ noun (unit of information equal to 3.32 bits) hartley m

hash /hæʃ/ noun **1.** (printed sign #) signo m tipográfico # **2.** (printed sign #) signo m tipográfico # ■ verb generar un código de comprobación al azar

hash code /ˌhæʃ ˈkəʊd/ noun código m de comprobación al azar

hash-code system /ˈhæʃ kəʊd ˌsɪstəm/ noun sistema m de código de comprobación al azar

hash index /hæʃ ˈɪndeks/ noun índice m de comprobación al azar

hashing function /hæʃɪŋ ˈfʌŋkʃən/ noun función f de comprobación al azar; función f de comprobación aleatoria

hashmark /ˈhæʃmɑːk/, **hash mark** /ˈhæʃ mɑːk/ noun (printed sign &#;) signo m tipográfico

hash table /hæʃ ˈteɪb(ə)l/ noun tabla f de comprobación al azar

hash total /hæʃ ˈtəʊt(ə)l/ noun (total of a number of hashed entries) total m de comprobación al azar; aleatoria

hash value /hæʃ ˈvæljuː/ noun valor m de comprobación al azar

Hayes AT command set /ˌheɪz eɪ tiː kə ˈmɑːnd set/ noun conjunto m de instrucciones Hayes AT

Hayes-compatible /ˌheɪz kəmˈpætɪb(ə)l/ adjective compatible Hayes

Hayes Corporation /ˈheɪz ˌkɔːpəreɪʃ(ə)n/ (modem manufacturer) Hayes Corporation™

hazard /ˈhæzəd/ noun riesgo m; fallo m (por defecto del reloj)

hazard-free implementation /ˌhæzəd friː ˌɪmplɪmenˈteɪʃ(ə)n/ noun aplicación f que tolera y resuelve posibles fallos

haze /heɪz/ noun efecto m niebla

HD /ˌeɪtʃ ˈdiː/ noun dúplex m en alternativa; semidúplex m

HDD abbr (hard disk drive) unidad f de disco duro

HDLC abbr (high-level data link control) control m de enlace de datos de alto nivel

HDTV abbr (high definition television) televisión f de alta definición

HDX abbr (half duplex) dúplex m en alternativa; semidúplex m

head /hed/ noun **1.** cabeza f **2.** (device) cabeza f de bobina **3.** (data) inicio m de fichero **4.** (of book

or page) cabecera f **5.** (of film or tape) cabeza f ■
verb (to be the first item in a list) encabezar vt; ser
cabeza de lista; estar al frente de ◇ **the queue
was headed by my file** mi fichero encabezaba la
cola

head cleaning disk /'hed ˌkliːnɪŋ dɪsk/ noun
disquete m de limpieza de cabezales; disquete m
de limpieza de cabezas ◇ **use a head cleaning
disk every week** utilice un disquete de limpieza
de cabezas una vez por semana

head crash /'hed kræʃ/ noun fallo m de la cabeza de lectura

head demagnetiser /'hed diːˌmægnətaɪzə/
noun desimantador m de cabezas; desmagnetizador m de cabezas

head end /'hed end/ noun cabeza f de red

header /'hedə/ noun **1.** (in a local area network) bloque m de identificación **2.** (at top of a list
of data) cabecera f de fichero **3.** (at top of page)
cabecera f; título m actual

header block /'hedə blɒk/ noun bloque m de
identificación

header card /'hedə kɑːd/ noun tarjeta f de encabezamiento

header label /'hedə ˌleɪb(ə)l/ noun etiqueta f
de identificación; etiqueta f de reconocimiento de
banda

head gap /'hed gæp/ noun vacío m de aire

heading /'hedɪŋ/ noun **1.** (name or title of document or file) encabezamiento m; membrete m;
rúbrica f; nombre m **2.** (at the top of each page)
cabecera f; encabezado m; título m

headlife /'hedlaɪf/ noun duración f de vida de la
cabeza lectora o grabadora

head of form /ˌhed əv 'fɔːm/ noun cabecera f
de una página (de una lista); principio m de una
página (de una lista)

head park /'hed pɑːk/ noun posición f de transporte de la cabeza; estacionamiento m de la cabeza

head positioning /hed pəˈzɪʃ(ə)nɪŋ/ noun
posicionamiento m de la cabeza

head wheel /'hed wiːl/ noun rueda f de cabezas
(magnéticas); cabeza f múltiple rotativa

heap /hiːp/ noun **1.** (temporary storage area)
pila f **2.** (binary tree) pila f binaria

heat-sensitive paper /ˌhiːt ˌsensɪtɪv 'peɪpə/
noun papel m térmico; papel m termosensible

heat-sink /hiːt sɪŋk/ noun sumidero m térmico;
disipador m térmico

helical scan /ˌhelɪk(ə)l 'skæn/ noun lectura f
helicoidal; exploración f helicoidal

help /help/ noun (function) ayuda f

help desk /'help desk/ noun servicio m de
asistencia técnica

help key /'help kiː/ noun tecla f de ayuda ◇ **hit
the HELP key if you want information about
what to do next** pulse la tecla de ayuda si necesita información sobre el siguiente paso

help screen /'help skriːn/ noun pantalla f de
ayuda

hertz /hɜːts/ noun (unit of frequency) hertz m;
hercio m

heterogeneous   multiplexing
/ˌhetərəʊdʒiːniəs 'mʌltɪˌpleksɪŋ/ noun multiplexión f heterogénea

heterogeneous network /ˌhetərəʊdʒiːniəs
'netwɜːk/ noun red f informática heterogénea

heuristic /hjʊəˈrɪstɪk/ adjective heurístico or -
a ◇ **a heuristic program learns from its previous actions and decisions** un programa heurístico aprende de sus acciones y decisiones previas

Hewlett Packard /ˌhewlət 'pækɑːd/ (manufacturer of computers, etc.) Hewlett Packard™ ◇
Hewlett Packard Interface Bus (HPIB) (standard method of interfacing peripheral devices)
bus m; enlace m de interfaz HP ◇ **Hewlett Packard Printer Control Language (HP-PCL)**
(standard set of commands) lenguaje m de control de la impresora HP or lenguaje HP-PCL

Hewlett Packard Graphics Language
/ˌhewlət ˌpækɑːd 'græfɪks ˌlæŋgwɪdʒ/ (standard set of commands used to describe graphics)
lenguaje m gráfico HP; lenguaje m HPGL

Hewlett Packard Interface Bus /ˌhewlət
ˌpækɑːd 'ɪntəfeɪs bʌs/ (standard method of interfacing peripheral devices) bus m de interfaz
HP; enlace m de interfaz HP

Hewlett   Packard   LaserJet /ˌhewlət
ˌpækɑːd 'leɪzədʒet/ (trade name for a laser
printer that uses its PCL language to describe a
page) impresora f gráfica HP Laserjet

**Hewlett Packard Printer Control Lan-
guage** /ˌhewlət ˌpækɑːd ˌprɪntə kənˈtrəʊl
ˌlæŋgwɪdʒ/ (standard set of commands that allows a software application to control a laser
printer's functions) lenguaje m de control de la
impresora HP; lenguaje m HP-PCL

hex /heksə,desɪm(ə)l nəʊˈteɪʃ(ə)n/, **hexadecimal notation** noun notación f hexadecimal

hex dump /'heks dʌmp/ noun vaciado m hexadecimal

hex keypad /heks 'kiːˌpæd/ noun teclado m
hexadecimal

HFS /ˌeɪtʃ ef 'es/ noun sistema m jerárquico de
ficheros

hidden files /'hɪd(ə)n faɪlz/ plural noun ficheros mpl ocultos

hidden   line   algorithm /ˌhɪd(ə)n laɪn
'ælgərɪð(ə)m/ noun algoritmo m de líneas ocultas

hidden line removal /ˌhɪd(ə)n 'laɪn rɪ
ˌmuːvəl/ noun borrado m de líneas ocultas

hidden lines /'hɪd(ə)n laɪnz/ plural noun
líneas ocultas

hierarchical /haɪəˈrɑːkɪk(ə)l/ adjective jerárquico or -a

hierarchical communications system
/ˌhaɪərɑːkɪk(ə)l kəˌmjuːnɪˈkeɪʃ(ə)nz ˌsɪstəm/
noun sistema m jerárquico de comunicación

hierarchical   computer   network
/ˌhaɪərɑːkɪk(ə)l kəmˈpjuːtə ˌnetwɜːk/ noun red
f informática jerárquica

hierarchical database /ˌhaɪərɑːkɪk(ə)l ˈdeɪtəbeɪs/ *noun* base *f* de datos jerárquica

hierarchical directory /ˌhaɪərɑːkɪk(ə)l daɪ ˈrekt(ə)ri/ *noun* directorio *m* jerárquico

hierarchical filing system /ˌhaɪərɑːkɪk(ə)l ˈfaɪlɪŋ ˌsɪstəm/ *noun* sistema *m* jerárquico de ficheros

hierarchy /ˈhaɪərɑːki/ *noun* jerarquía *f*

high definition television /ˌhaɪ ˌdefɪnɪʃ(ə)n ˈtelɪˌvɪʒ(ə)n/ *noun* televisión *f* de alta definición

high density storage /ˌhaɪ ˌdensɪ ˈstɔːrɪdʒti/ *noun* memoria *f* de alta densidad ◊ **a hard disk is a high density storage medium compared to paper tape** un disco duro, comparado con una cinta perforada, es un medio de almacenamiento de alta densidad

high-end /ˈhaɪ end/ *adjective* alto *m* rendimiento

high fidelity /ˌhaɪ fɪˈdeləti/ *noun* alta fidelidad *f*; hi-fi

high-level data link control /ˌhaɪ ˌlev(ə)l ˌdeɪtə lɪŋk kənˈtrəʊl/ *noun* control *m* de enlace de datos de alto nivel

high-level data link control station /ˌhaɪ ˌlev(ə)l ˌdeɪtə lɪŋk kənˈtrəʊl ˌsteɪʃ(ə)n/ *noun* estación *f* de control de enlace de datos de alto nivel *f*; terminal *m* de control de enlace de datos de alto nivel

high-level language /ˌhaɪ ˌlev(ə)l ˈlæŋgwɪdʒ/, **high-level programming language** /ˌhaɪ ˌlev(ə)l ˌprəʊgræmɪŋ ˈlæŋgwɪdʒ/ *noun* lenguaje *m* de programación de alto nivel

highlight /ˈhaɪlaɪt/ *noun* lo más destacado ■ *verb* (*underscore*) destacar *vt*; poner de relieve; (*on screen*) realzar *vt*; dar realce

highlight bar /ˈhaɪˌlaɪt bɑː/ *noun* barra *f* de selección

high memory /ˌhaɪ ˈmem(ə)ri/ *noun* memoria *f* alta

high memory area /ˌhaɪ ˈmem(ə)ri ˌeəriə/ *noun* área *f* de memoria alta

high order /ˌhaɪ ˈɔːdə/ *noun* cifra *f* de alto nivel; dígito *m* de alto nivel

high performance filing system /ˌhaɪ pə ˌfɔːməns ˈfaɪlɪŋ ˌsɪstəm/ *noun* sistema *m* de ficheros de alto rendimiento

high priority program /ˌhaɪ praɪˌɒrɪti ˈprəʊgræm/ *noun* programa *m* de alta prioridad; programa *m* prioritario

high-resolution /ˌhaɪ ˌrezəˈluːʃ(ə)n/, **high-res** /ˌhaɪ rez/ *noun* alta resolución *f*; alta definición *f* ◊ **the high resolution screen can display 640 by 450 pixels** la pantalla de alta definición puede obtener una resolución de 640 por 450 pixels

high resolution graphics /ˌhaɪ ˌrezəluːʃ(ə)n ˈgræfɪks/ *noun* gráficos *mpl* de alta definición

high-spec /ˌhaɪ spek/ *plural noun* de alta precisión; de tecnología avanzada

high specification /ˌhaɪ ˌspesɪfɪˈkeɪʃ(ə)n/ *noun* alta precisión *f*; alta tecnología *f*

high-speed /ˈhaɪ spiːd/ *adjective* (*film*) de alta velocidad; ultrasensible

high-speed carry /ˌhaɪ spiːd ˈkæri/ *noun* transporte *m* rápido; transporte *m* de alta velocidad

high-speed serial interface /ˌhaɪ spiːd ˌsɪəriəl ˈɪntəfeɪs/ *noun* interfaz *f* en serie de alta velocidad

high-speed skip /ˌhaɪ spiːd ˈskɪp/ *noun* (*printing*) salto *m* rápido; salto *m* de alta velocidad

high-tech /ˌhaɪ ˈtek/ *adjective* (*advanced*) alta tecnología *f*; tecnología *f* avanzada

high technology /ˌhaɪ tekˈnɒlədʒi/ *noun* alta tecnología *f*; tecnología *f* avanzada

highway /ˈhaɪweɪ/ *noun* (*bus*) enlace *m* común; conductor *m* común

hill climbing /hɪl ˈklaɪmɪŋ/ *noun* (*in an expert system*) escalada *f* ascendente; método *m* ascendente

hi-res /ˌhaɪ reɪz/ *noun* alta definición *f*; alta resolución *f*

histogram /ˈhɪstəgræm/ *noun* histograma *m*

history /ˈhɪst(ə)ri/ *noun* historial *m*

hit /hɪt/ *noun* (*successful search*) éxito *m*; acierto *m*; respuesta *f* positiva ■ *verb* (*to press a key*) pulsar *vt*

HLDLC *abbr* (*high-level data link control*) control *m* de enlace de datos de alto nivel

HLL *abbr* (*high-level language*) lenguaje *m* de programación de alto nivel

HMA *abbr* (*high memory area*) área *f* de memoria alta

HMI *abbr* (*human-machine interface*) interfaz *f* hombre/máquina; interfaz *f* usuario/máquina

hold /həʊld/ *noun* (*TV*) señal *f* de sincronización; (*oscilloscope*) instrucción *f* de estabilización de la señal ■ *verb* (*in memory*) guardar *vt*; (*value*) mantener *vt*; (*telephone*) tener ocupada (la línea) ◊ **hold current** corriente *f* de mantenimiento ◊ **holding line** (*artwork*) línea *f* de delimitación *or* de retención

holding loop /ˈhəʊldɪŋ luːp/ *noun* bucle *m* de mantenimiento; bucle *m* de soporte

holding time /ˈhəʊldɪŋ taɪm/ *noun* tiempo *m* de ocupación; tiempo *m* de retención de la línea

holdup /ˈhɒldʌp/ *noun* **1.** (*pause in a program*) tiempo *m* de detención; pausa *f* de un dispositivo; corte *m* accidental **2.** (*pause in a program*) pausa *f*; corte *m* accidental

hologram /ˈhɒləˌgræm/ *noun* holograma *m*

holographic image /ˌhɒləgræfɪk ˈɪmɪdʒ/ *noun* holograma *m*

holographic storage /ˌhɒləgræfɪk ˈstɔːrɪdʒ/ *noun* almacenamiento *m* de holograma; memoria *f* holográfica

home /həʊm/ *noun* (*starting point for printing on a screen*) posición *f* inicial; posición *f* de salida

home banking /ˌhəʊm ˈbæŋkɪŋ/ *noun* (sistema de) transacciones *fpl* (bancarias) a domicilio

home computer /həʊm kəmˈpjuːtə/ *noun* (*computer designed for home use*) ordenador *m* familiar; ordenador *m* para la casa; ordenador *m* doméstico

home key /'həʊm kiː/ *noun* tecla *f* 'Home'; tecla *f* Inicio

home page /'həʊm peɪdʒ/ *noun* (*opening page of a website*) página *f* de inicio; página *f* inicial; página *f* principal

home record /həʊm 'rekɔːd/ *noun* registro *m* de inicio

homogeneous computer network /ˌhəʊməʊdʒiːniəs kəm'pjuːtə ˌnetwɜːk/ *noun* red *f* informática homogénea

homogeneous multiplexing /ˌhəʊməʊdʒiːniəs 'mʌltɪˌpleksɪŋ/ *noun* (*switching multiplexer system*) multiplexión *f* homogénea

hood /hʊd/ *noun* cubierta *f*; tapa *f*

hook /hʊk/ *noun* (*code*) punto *m* de enganche; punto *m* de inserción (de código)

hop /hɒp/ *noun* (*transmission*) ruta *f* (de transmisión directa) *f*

hopper /'hɒpə/ *noun* cargador *m* de tarjetas perforadas

horizontal axis /ˌhɒrɪzɒnt(ə)l 'æksɪs/ *noun* eje *m* horizontal; eje *m* de abscisas

horizontal check /ˌhɒrɪzɒnt(ə)l 'tʃek/ *noun* verificación *f* horizontal; control *m* horizontal

horizontal scrollbar /ˌhɒrɪzɒnt(ə)l 'skrəʊlbɑː/ *noun* barra *f* de desplazamiento horizontal

horizontal scrolling /ˌhɒrɪzɒnt(ə)l 'skrəʊlɪŋ/ *noun* desplazamiento *m* horizontal

horizontal wraparound /ˌhɒrɪzɒnt(ə)l 'ræpəˌraʊnd/ *noun* (*movement of cursor*) retorno *m* horizontal de línea; vuelta *f* automática a la línea; salto *m* automático de línea; retorno *m* del cursor

host /həʊst/ *noun, adjective* huésped *m&f*; huésped *m*

'...you select fonts manually or through commands sent from the host computer along with the text' [*Byte*]

host adapter /həʊst ə'dæptə/ *noun* adaptador *m* del ordenador principal ◇ **the cable to connect the scanner to the host adapter is included** se incluye el cable para conectar el escáner con el adaptador huésped

host address /'həʊst əˌdres/ *noun* dirección *f* Internet

host computer /həʊst kəm'pjuːtə/ *noun* **1.** (*main controlling computer*) ordenador *m* principal **2.** (*used to write and debug software*) ordenador *m* principal; servidor *m* **3.** (*in a network*) servidor *m*

'...you select fonts manually or through commands sent from the host computer along with the text' [*Byte*]

hosting service provider /'həʊstɪŋ ˌsɜːvɪs prəˌvaɪdə/ *noun* servicio *m* de acogida

host name /'həʊst ˌneɪm/ *noun* nombre *m* de ordenador huésped; nombre *m* de datos de servidor huésped

host number /'həʊst ˌnʌmbə/ *noun* dirección *f* Internet

host service /'həʊst ˌsɜːvɪs/ *noun* servicio *m* de acogida

hot /hɒt/ *adjective* caliente ◇ **hot metal composition** composición *f* al plomo *or* composición caliente ◇ **hot type** carácter *m* fundido *or* composición *f* caliente *or* al plomo

hot chassis /hɒt 'ʃæsi/ *noun* chasis *m* bajo tensión

hot fix /ˌhɒt 'fɪks/ *noun* (*repairing*) corrección *f* inmediata; acción *f* inmediata; reparación *f* en caliente

hot key /'hɒt kiː/ *noun* (*key which starts a process*) tecla *f* de activación; tecla *f* rápida

hot link /ˌhɒt 'lɪŋk/ *noun* (*command within a hypertext program*) vinculación *f* activa; vínculo *m* activo

hotspot /'hɒtspɒt/ *noun* (*area or image*) zona *f* activa

hot standby /hɒt 'stændbaɪ/ *noun* (*piece of hardware used as backup*) sistema *m* de emergencia; sistema *m* de reserva preparado para funcionar; sistema *m* en caliente

hotword /'hɒtwɜːd/ *noun* palabra *f* de vínculo activo

hot zone /'hɒt zəʊn/ *noun* zona *f* de texto

housekeeping /'haʊsˌkiːpɪŋ/ *noun* operaciones *fpl* de mantenimiento

housekeeping routine /'haʊskiːpɪŋ ruːˌtiːn/ *noun* programa *m* de mantenimiento; programa *m* de utilidades

housing /'haʊzɪŋ/ *noun* estuche *m*; caja *f* ◇ **the computer housing was damaged when it fell on the floor** cuando el ordenador se cayó al suelo, su caja se estropeó

howler /'haʊlə/ *noun* (*sound device*) indicador *m* sonoro

HP *abbr* (*Hewlett Packard*) HP

HPFS /ˌeɪtʃ piː ef 'es/ *noun* sistema *m* de ficheros de alto rendimiento

HPGL *abbr* (*Hewlett Packard Graphics Language*) lenguaje *m* gráfico HP; lenguaje sistema *m* HPGL

HPIB *abbr* (*Hewlett Packard Interface Bus*) bus *m* de interfaz HP; enlace *m* de interfaz HP

HP-PCL /ˌeɪtʃ ˌpiː ˌpiː siː 'el/ *abbr* (*Hewlett Packard Printer Control Language*) lenguaje HP-PCL *m*; lenguaje *m* de control de la impresora HP

HRG /ˌeɪtʃ ɑː 'dʒiː/ *noun* gráficos *mpl* de alta definición

HTML /ˌeɪtʃ tiː em 'el/ *noun* HTML; lenguaje *m* de marcado de hipertexto

HTTP /ˌeɪtʃ tiː tiː 'piː/ *noun* HTTP

HTTPd /ˌeɪtʃ tiː tiː piː 'diː/ *noun* demonio *m* de protocolo de transferencia de hipertexto

hub /hʌb/ *noun* **1.** (*of disk*) centro *m* **2.** (*central ring in a star-topology network*) concentrador *m* multirepetidor; boca *f* de conexiones

hue /hjuː/ *noun* **1.** tono *m* **2.** color *m*

Huffman code /'hʌfmən kəʊd/ *noun* (*data compression code*) código *m* de Huffman

human-computer interface /ˌhjuːmən kəm ˌpjuːtə 'ɪntəfeɪs/ *noun* interfaz *f* usuario/máquina; interfaz *f* hombre/máquina

human-machine interface /ˌhjuːmən mə ˌʃiːn 'ɪntəfeɪs/ *noun* interfaz *f* usuario/máquina; interfaz *f* hombre/máquina

hunting /'hʌntɪŋ/ *noun* (proceso de) búsqueda *f* (de datos en un fichero)

hybrid circuit /ˌhaɪbrɪd 'sɜːkɪt/ *noun* (*connection of electronic components*) circuito *m* híbrido; circuito *m* mixto; circuito *m* compuesto

hybrid computer /ˌhaɪbrɪd kəm'pjuːtə/ *noun* ordenador *m* híbrido

hybrid interface /ˌhaɪbrɪd 'ɪntəfeɪs/ *noun* interfaz *f* híbrida

hybrid system /ˌhaɪbrɪd 'sɪstəm/ *noun* sistema *m* híbrido

HyperCard /'haɪpəkɑːd/ (*database system*) HyperCard™

hyperlink /'haɪpəlɪŋk/ *noun* (*word or image or button in a Web page or multimedia title that moves the user to another page when clicked*) hipervínculo *m*; hiperenlace *m*

hypermedia /'haɪpəmiːdiə/ *noun* (*hypertext document*) hiperdocumento *m* (con imágenes y sonido)

HyperTalk /'haɪpətɔːk/ (*programming language*) HyperTalk™

HyperTerminal /'haɪpəˌtɜːmɪn(ə)l/ *noun* hiperterminal *m*

hypertext /'haɪpətekst/ *noun* **1.** (*system of organising information*) hipertexto *m* **2.** (*linking one word or image to another page*) hipertexto *m* ◇ **hypertext transfer protocol (HTTP)** protocolo *m* de transferencia de hipertexto ◇ **in this hypertext page, click once on the word 'computer' and it will tell you what a computer is** en esta página de hipertexto, pulse una vez sobre la palabra 'ordenador' y le explicará qué es un ordenador

hypertext markup language /ˌhaɪpətekst 'mɑːkʌp ˌlæŋgwɪdʒ/ *noun* HTML; lenguaje *m* de marcado de hipertexto

hypertext transfer protocol /ˌhaɪpətekst 'trænsfɜː ˌprəʊtəkɒl/ *noun* HTTP

hypertext transfer protocol daemon /ˌhaɪpətekst 'trænsfɜː ˌprəʊtəkɒl ˌdiːmən/ *noun* demonio *m* de protocolo de transferencia de hipertexto

hyphenated /'haɪfəneɪtɪd/ *adjective* (palabra) con guión

hyphenation /ˌhaɪfə'neɪʃ(ə)n/ *noun* división *f* silábica (por guiones)

hyphenation and justification /haɪfə ˌnaɪʃ(ə)n ən ˌdʒʌstɪfɪ'keɪʃ(ə)n/ *noun* separación *f* por guiones y justificación

I

IAB /ˌaɪ eɪ 'biː/ *noun* comité *m* de actividades de internet

IAM /ˌaɪ eɪ 'em/ *noun* memoria *f* de acceso intermedio

IAS /ˌaɪ eɪ 'es/ *noun* memoria *f* de acceso inmediato

I-beam /aɪ biːm/ *noun* (*cursor shaped like 'I'*) cursor *m* en I

IBG *abbr* (*interblock gap*) espacio *m* entre bloques; separación *f* entre bloques; intervalo *m* entre bloques

IBM /ˌaɪ biː 'em/ (*largest computer company in the world*) IBM

IBM AT /ˌaɪ biː em eɪ 'tiː/ (*trade name for a personal computer based on the Intel 80286 16-bit processor*) ordenador *m* IBM AT

IBM AT keyboard /ˌaɪ biː em eɪ ˌtiː 'kiːbɔːd/ (*keyboard layout that features 12 function keys in a row along the top of the keyboard, with a separate numeric keypad*) teclado *m* (IBM) AT

IBM-compatible /ˌaɪ biː em kəm'pætɪb(ə)l/ *adjective* IBM compatible

IBM PC /ˌaɪ biː em piː 'siː/ (*trade name for a personal computer based on the Intel 8088 8-bit processor*) ordenador *m* personal IBM

IBM PC keyboard /ˌaɪ biː em piː ˌsiː 'kiːbɔːd/ (*keyboard layout that features 10 function keys arranged to the left of the main keys, with no separate numeric keypad*) teclado *m* para un ordenador IBM

IBM PS/2 /ˌaɪ biː em ˌem 'pɜːs(ə)nəl/, **IBM Personal System/2** (*trade name for a range of personal computers*) IBM PS/2

IBM XT /ˌaɪ biː em eks 'tiː/ (*trade name for a personal computer based on the IBM PC*) IBM-XT

IC *abbr* (*integrated circuit*) circuito *m* integrado

icand /'ɪkænd/ *noun* multiplicando *m*

ICMP /ˌaɪ ciː em 'piː/ *noun* protocolo *m* de internet de control de mensajes

icon /'aɪkɒn/, **ikon** *noun* icono *m* ◇ **click twice over the wordprocessor icon – the picture of the typewriter** haga clic dos veces sobre el icono del tratamiento de textos-el dibujo de una máquina de escribir ◇ **the icon for the graphics program is a small picture of a palette** el icono del programa de gráficos tiene la forma de paleta de pintor

'Despite (or because of?) the swap file, loading was slow and the hourglass icon of the mouse pointer frequently returned to the arrow symbol well before loading was complete.' [*Computing*]

ID *abbr* **1.** (*identification*) identificación *f* **2.** (*identifier*) cadena *f* de caracteres de identificación; carácter *m* de identificación; identificador *m*

ID code /,aɪ'diː kəʊd/ *noun* código *m* personal; código *m* de identificación ◇ **after you wake up the system, you have to input your ID code then your password** después de activar el sistema, tiene que introducir su código de identificación y a continuación su contraseña

IDE /ˌaɪ diː 'iː/ *noun* entorno *m* de desarrollos integrados

identification /aɪˌdentɪfɪ'keɪʃ(ə)n/ *noun* identificación *f*

identification character /aɪˌdentɪfɪ'keɪʃ(ə)n ˌkærɪktə/ *noun* carácter *m* de identificación

identification division /aɪˌdentɪfɪ'keɪʃ(ə)n dɪˌvɪʒ(ə)n/ *noun* división *f* con parámetros de identificación

identifier /aɪ'dentɪfaɪə/ *noun* (*set of characters used to distinguish between different blocks of data or files*) identificador *m*; (*set of characters*) carácter *m* de identificación; (*set of characters used to distinguish between different blocks of data or files*) cadena *f* de caracteres de identificación

identifier word /aɪ'dentɪfaɪə wɜːd/ *noun* identificador *m*; palabra *f* de identificación

identity burst /aɪ'dentɪti bɜːst/ *noun* ráfaga *f* de identificación

identity gate /aɪ'dentɪti geɪt/, **identity element** /aɪ'dentɪti ˌelɪmənt/ *noun* puerta *f* de identidad; elemento *m* de identidad

identity number /aɪ'dentɪti ˌnʌmbə/ *noun* número *m* de código personal; número *m* de identidad ◇ **don't forget to log in your identity number** no olvide introducir su número de código personal

identity operation /aɪˌdentɪti ˌɒpə'reɪʃ(ə)n/ *noun* operación *f* de identidad

identity palette /aɪ'dentɪti ˌpælət/ *noun* paleta *f* de identificación

idle /'aɪd(ə)l/ *adjective* (*unused machine, telephone line or device*) libre; disponible; en reposo

idle character /ˌaɪd(ə)l 'kærɪktə/ *noun* carácter *m* nulo

idle time /'aɪd(ə)l taɪm/ *noun* (*of a device*) tiempo *m* disponible; tiempo *m* muerto; tiempo *m* de espera; tiempo *m* de inactividad

IDP *abbr* (*integrated data processing*) proceso *m* de datos integrados

IE *abbr* (*Internet Explorer*) explorador *m* de internet (de Microsoft)

IEC connector /ˌaɪ iː 'siː kəˌnektə/ *noun* (*standard for a three-pin connector*) conector *m* IEC

IEE *abbr* (*Institution of Electrical Engineers*) instituto *m* de ingenieros eléctricos

IEEE *abbr* (*Institute of Electrical and Electronic Engineers*) instituto *m* de ingenieros eléctricos y electrónicos

IEEE-488 *noun* (norma de interfaz paralela estándar) IEEE-488

IEEE-802.2 *noun* estándar *m* IEEE 802.2 que define los enlaces entre los datos

IEEE-802.3 *noun* estándar *m* IEEE 802.3 que define el sistema de red Ethernet

IEEE-802.4 *noun* estándar *m* IEEE 802.4 que define el bus en anillo

IEEE-802.5 *noun* estándar *m* IEEE-802.5 que define la red en anillo de IBM

IEEE bus *noun* bus *m* IEEE; enlace *m* común IEEE

IETF /ˌaɪ iː tiː 'ef/ *noun* grupo *m* de tareas de ingeniería de Internet

IFF /ˌaɪ ef 'ef/ *noun* **1.** formato *m* de fichero internacional **2.** formato *m* de fichero intercambiable

IF statement /ɪf 'steɪtmənt/ *noun* instrucción *f* IF (si)

IF-THEN-ELSE /ɪf ðen/ *noun* instrucción *f* IF-THEN-ELSE (si, en otro caso si, si no)

ignore character /ɪg'nɔː ˌkærɪktə/ *noun* carácter *m* de relleno

IGP /ˌaɪ dʒiː 'piː/ *noun* protocolo *m* de puerta interior

IH *abbr* (*interrupt handler*) controlador *m* de interrupciones

ikon /'aɪkɒn/ *noun* icono *m*

illegal /ɪ'liːg(ə)l/ *adjective* **1.** (*against the rules*) ilegal; (*against the law*) no válido *or* -a; (*against the rules*) que va contra las reglas **2.** no válido *or* -a

illegal character /ɪˌliːg(ə)l 'kærɪktə/ *noun* carácter *m* no válido; carácter *m* prohibido

illegal instruction /ɪˌliːg(ə)l ɪn'strʌkʃən/ *noun* instrucción *f* no válida; instrucción *f* prohibida

illegal operation /ɪˌliːg(ə)l ˌɒpə'reɪʃ(ə)n/ *noun* operación *f* no válida; operación *f* prohibida

IMA /ˌaɪ em 'eɪ/ *noun* asociación *f* de sistemas multimedia interactivos

image /'ɪmɪdʒ/ *noun* **1.** (*duplicate of an area of memory*) imagen *f* **2.** (*copy of a picture or design*) imagen *f* ◇ **image carrier** (*in phototypesetting*) portadora *f* de imagen *or* de señal de vídeo ◇ **image distortion** distorsión *f* de la imagen ◇ **im-**

age enhancer intensificador *m* de (la) imagen ◇ **image plane** (*in a camera*) plano *m* focal *or* de imagen

image area /'ɪmɪdʒ ˌeərɪə/ *noun* (*region of microfilm or display screen*) área *f* de visualización; zona *f* de visualización; área *f* de imagen

image buffer /'ɪmɪdʒ ˌbʌfə/ *noun* memoria *f* intermedia para imágenes

image compression /'ɪmɪdʒ kəmˌpreʃ(ə)n/ *noun* compresión *f* de (la) imagen

image degradation /'ɪmɪdʒ ˌdegrədeɪʃ(ə)n/ *noun* degradación *f* de la imagen

image editing /'ɪmɪdʒ ˌedɪtɪŋ/ *noun* edición *f* de imágenes

image editor /'ɪmɪdʒ ˌedɪtə/ *noun* editor *m* de imagen

image enhancement /'ɪmɪdʒ ɪnˌhɑːnsmənt/ *noun* amplificación *f* de imágenes; intensificación *f* de imágenes

image processing /'ɪmɪdʒ ˌprəʊsesɪŋ/ *noun* proceso *m* de imágenes; tratamiento *m* de la imagen

image processor /'ɪmɪdʒ ˌprəʊsesə/ *noun* (*electronic or computer system used for image processing*) procesador *m* de la imagen; procesador *m* de imágenes; sistema *m* de tratamiento de imágenes; analizador *m* de la imagen

'The Max FX also acts as a server to a growing number of printers, including a Varityper 5300 with emerald raster image processor and a Canon CLC 500 colour photocopier.' [*Computing*]

image retention /'ɪmɪdʒ rɪˌtenʃən/ *noun* retención *f* de (la) imagen

image scanner /'ɪmɪdʒ ˌskænə/ *noun* escáner *m* de imágenes

image sensor /'ɪmɪdʒ ˌsensə/ *noun* sensor *m* de imágenes

image stability /'ɪmɪdʒ stəˌbɪlɪti/ *noun* estabilidad *f* de (la) imagen

image storage space /ˌɪmɪdʒ 'stɔːrɪdʒ ˌspeɪs/ *noun* espacio *m* de memoria de imágenes

image table /'ɪmɪdʒ ˌteɪb(ə)l/ *noun* tabla *f* de control

imaging /'ɪmɪdʒɪŋ/ *noun* (sistema de) formación *f* de imágenes ◇ **magnetic resonance imaging (MRI)** (sistema de) formación *f* de imágenes por resonancia magnética ◇ **X-ray imaging** radioscopia *f*; (sistema de) formación de imágenes por rayos X

imaging system /ˌɪmɪdʒɪŋ 'sɪstəm/ *noun* sistema *m* de imagen

immediate access store /ɪˌmiːdɪət ˌækses 'stɔː/ *noun* memoria *f* de acceso inmediato

immediate address /ɪˌmiːdɪət ə'dres/ *noun* dirección *f* inmediata; dirección *f* directa

immediate addressing /ɪˌmiːdɪət ə'dresɪŋ/ *noun* direccionamiento *m* inmediato

immediate instruction /ɪˌmiːdɪət ɪn'strʌkʃən/ *noun* instrucción *f* inmediata

immediate mode /ɪ'miːdɪət məʊd/ *noun* modo *m* inmediato

immediate operand /ɪ'miːdiət ˌɒpərænd/ *noun* operando *m* inmediato

immediate processing /ɪˌmiːdiət 'prəʊsesɪŋ/ *noun* tratamiento *m* inmediato

impedance /ɪm'piːd(ə)ns/ *noun* impedancia *f* ◇ **impedance matching** adaptación *f* de impedancia; igualación de impedancia ◇ **impedance matching between a transmitter and a receiver minimizes power losses to transmitted signals** la adaptación de impedancia entre un transmisor y un receptor minimiza las pérdidas de potencia de las señales transmitidas ◇ **impedance mismatch** desacoplo *m* de impedancia

implication /ˌɪmplɪ'keɪʃ(ə)n/ *noun* (*logical operation*) implicación *f*

implicit reference /ɪmˌplɪsɪt 'ref(ə)rəns/ *noun* referencia *f* implícita

implied addressing /ɪmˌplaɪd ə'dresɪŋ/ *noun* direccionamiento *m* implicado; direccionamiento *m* inherente ◇ **implied addressing for the accumulator is used in the instruction LDA,16** el direccionamiento inherente del acumulador se utiliza en la instrucción LDA, 16

import /ɪm'pɔːt/ *verb* 1. (*to bring something in from outside a system*) importar *vt* 2. (*to convert a file to default format*) importar *vt* ◇ **imported signal** señal *f* importada ◇ **you can import images from the CAD package into the DTP program** puede importar imágenes procedentes de un paquete de CAD en el programa de edición DTP

'At the moment, Acrobat supports only the sending and viewing of documents. There are legal implications associated with allowing users to edit documents in the style of the original application, without having the tool itself on their desks, and there is no import facility back into applications.' [*Computing*]

impulse /'ɪmpʌls/ *noun* impulso *m*; excitación *f*

impulsive noise /ɪm'pʌlsɪv nɔɪz/ *noun* (*interference on a signal*) ruido *m* intermitente; ruido *m* impulsivo; interferencia *f* impulsiva

IMS *abbr* (*information management system*) sistema *m* de gestión de la información

inactive window /ɪnˌæktɪv 'wɪndəʊ/ *noun* ventana *f* inactiva

in-band signalling /ˌɪn bænd 'sɪɡn(ə)lɪŋ/ *noun* (*data transmission*) señalización *f* en banda; señalización *f* dentro de banda; señalización *f* por frecuencia vocal

InBox /'ɪnbɒks/ *noun* (*Windows messaging system*) bandeja *f* de entrada del correo electrónico

inbuilt /'ɪnbɪlt/ *adjective* integrado *or* -a; incorporado *or* -a ◇ **this software has inbuilt error correction** este software tiene incorporado un sistema de corrección de errores

in-circuit emulator /ˌɪn ˌsɜːkɪt 'emjʊleɪtə/ *noun* emulador *m* integrado en el circuito; incorporado *m* al circuito ◇ **this in-circuit emulator is used to test the floppy disk controller by emulating a disk drive** este emulador incorporado al circuito actúa como emulador de una dis-

quetera para comprobar el funcionamiento del controlador de disquetes

inclusion /ɪn'kluːʒ(ə)n/ *noun* inclusión *f*

inclusive OR /ɪn'kluːsɪv ɔː/ *noun* OR *m* inclusivo

incoming message /ˌɪnkʌmɪŋ 'mesɪdʒ/ *noun* mensaje *m* recibido

incoming traffic /ˌɪnkʌmɪŋ 'træfɪk/ *noun* (*data received*) número *m* de mensajes recibidos; tráfico *m* de entrada; datos *mpl* de llegada; datos *mpl* recibidos

incompatible /ˌɪnkəm'pætɪb(ə)l/ *adjective* incompatible; no compatible ◇ **they tried to link the two systems, but found they were incompatible** intentaron conectar los dos sistemas, pero se encontraron con que eran incompatibles

increment /'ɪŋkrɪmənt/ *noun* 1. (*addition of a number*) incremento *m*; aumento *m* 2. (*number added*) incremento *m* ■ *verb* 1. (*to increase a number*) aumentar *vt*; incrementar *vt* 2. (*to move forward*) avanzar *vi* ◇ **an increment is added to the counter each time a pulse is detected** cada vez que se detecta un impulso se añade un incremento al contador ◇ **increase the increment to three** aumente el incremento a tres ◇ **the counter is incremented each time an instruction is executed** el contador se incrementa cada vez que se ejecuta una instrucción

incremental backup /ˌɪŋkrɪment(ə)l 'bækʌp/ *noun* copia *f* de seguridad incremental

incremental computer /ˌɪŋkrɪment(ə)l kəm'pjuːtə/ *noun* ordenador *m* incremental

incremental data /ˌɪŋkrɪment(ə)l 'deɪtə/ *noun* datos *mpl* incrementales; datos *mpl* adicionales

incremental plotter /ɪŋkrɪment(ə)l 'plɒtə/ *noun* trazador *m* incremental

indent *noun* /'ɪndent/ sangrado *m* ■ *verb* /ɪn'dent/ hacer un sangrado ◇ **the first line of the paragraph is indented two spaces** la primera línea de cada párrafo tiene un sangrado de dos espacios

indentation /ˌɪnden'teɪʃ(ə)n/ *noun* sangrado *m*

Indeo /'ɪndiəʊ/ (*Intel software technology for video sequences*) Indeo

indeterminate system /ˌɪndɪtɜːmɪnət 'sɪstəm/ *noun* sistema *m* indeterminado

index /'ɪndeks/ *noun* 1. (*list of items in a computer memory*) índice *m* 2. (*computer address*) índice *m* ■ *verb* (*a book*) preparar un índice; indexar *vt*

index build /'ɪndeks bɪld/ *noun* indexación *f*

indexed address /ˌɪndeksd ə'dres/ *noun* dirección *f* indexada

indexed addressing /ˌɪndeksd ə'dresɪŋ/ *noun* (*addressing mode*) direccionamiento *m* indexado; direccionamiento *m* indizado

indexed file /'ɪndeksd faɪl/ *noun* fichero *m* indexado

indexed instruction /ˌɪndeksd ɪn'strʌkʃən/ *noun* instrucción *f* indexada

indexed sequential access method /ˌɪndeks sɪˌkwensəl ˈækses ˌmeθəd/ *noun* método *m* de acceso secuencial indexado

indexed sequential storage /ˌɪndeksd sɪˌkwenʃ(ə)l ˈstɔːrɪdʒ/ *noun* memoria *f* secuencial indexada

index.html /ˌɪndeks dɒt ˌeɪtʃ tiː em ˈel/ *noun* index.html

indexing /ˈɪndeksɪŋ/ *noun* **1.** (*in a computer*) indexación *f* **2.** (*process of building and sorting a list of records*) indexación *f*

index key /ˈɪndeks kiː/ *noun* clave *f* de índice

index letter /ˈɪndeks ˌletə/ *noun* letra *f* indicativa

index number /ˈɪndeks ˌnʌmbə/ *noun* número *m* indicativo

index page /ˈɪndeks peɪdʒ/ *noun* página *f* índice

index register /ˈɪndeks ˌredʒɪstə/ *noun* registro *m* de índice

index value word /ˌɪndeks ˌvæljuː ˈwɜːd/ *noun* palabra *f* de índice

indicator /ˈɪndɪˌkeɪtə/ *noun* indicador *m*

indicator chart /ˈɪndɪˌkeɪtə tʃɑːt/ *noun* tabla *f* de indicadores

indicator flag /ˈɪndɪˌkeɪtə flæg/ *noun* (*register or single bit*) indicador *m*; testigo *m*; marcador *m*

indicator light /ˈɪndɪˌkeɪtə laɪt/ *noun* luz *f* indicadora

indirect address /ˌɪndaɪrekt əˈdres/ *noun* dirección *f* relativa

indirect addressing /ˌɪndaɪrekt əˈdresɪŋ/ *noun* direccionamiento *m* indirecto

induce /ɪnˈdjuːs/ *verb* **1.** (*electricity*) producir una corriente inducida; producir una inducción **2.** inducir *vt*

induced failure /ɪnˌdjuːsd ˈfeɪljə/ *noun* (*failure due to external effects*) fallo *m* inducido; fallo *m* provocado (por una causa externa); debido *m* a una causa externa

induced interference /ɪnˌdjuːsd ˌɪntə ˈfɪərəns/ *noun* (*electrical noise on a signal*) interferencia *f* inducida; interferencia *f* causada por las máquinas; interferencia *f* causada por otra máquina

inductance /ɪnˈdʌktəns/ *noun* inductancia *f*

induction /ɪnˈdʌkʃən/ *noun* **1.** (*in electricity*) inducción *f* **2.** (*in mathematics*) inducción *f* ◇ **induction coil** bobina *f* de inducción

inductive coordination /ɪnˌdʌktɪv kəʊˌɔːdɪ ˈneɪʃ(ə)n/ *noun* coordinación *f* inductiva

inductor /ɪnˈdʌktə/ *noun* inductor *m*; bobina *f* de inducción

Industry Standard Architecture /ˌɪndəstri ˌstændəd ˈɑːkɪˌtektʃə/ *noun* (*standard for 16-bit expansion bus*) arquitectura *f* ISA

inequality operator /ˌɪnɪˈkwɒlɪti ˌɒpəreɪtə/ *noun* (*symbol indicating that two variables are not equal*) operador *m* de desigualdad ◇ **the C programming language uses the symbol '!='**

as its inequality operator el lenguaje de programación C emplea el símbolo '!=' como su operador de desigualdad

inequivalence /ˌɪnɪˈkwɪvələns/ *noun* (*logical function*) exclusión *f* recíproca

infect /ɪnˈfekt/ *verb* infectar *vt*

infected computer /ɪnˌfektɪd kəmˈpjuːtə/ *noun* (*computer with a virus program*) ordenador *m* infectado

inference /ˈɪnf(ə)rəns/ *noun* **1.** (*operation*) inferencia *f*; deducción *f* **2.** (*result*) inferencia *f*; deducción *f*

inference control /ˈɪnf(ə)rəns kənˌtrəʊl/ *noun* control *m* de inferencia

inference engine /ˈɪnf(ə)rəns ˈendʒɪn/, **inference machine** /ˌɪnf(ə)rəns məˈʃiːn/ *noun* motor *m* de inferencia; máquina *f* de inferencia

inferior figure /ɪnˌfɪəriə ˈfɪgə/ *noun* (*smaller number printed slightly below normal characters*) subíndice *m*

infinite loop /ˈɪnfɪnət luːp/ *noun* bucle *m* sin fin; bucle *m* infinito

infinity /ɪnˈfɪnɪti/ *noun* **1.** (*quantity*) infinito *m* **2.** (*distance*) infinito *m*

infix notation /ɪnˌfɪks nəʊˈteɪʃ(ə)n/ *noun* notación *f* infija; notación *f* por infijos

informatics /ˌɪnfɔːˈmætɪks/ *noun* informática *f*

information /ˌɪnfəˈmeɪʃ(ə)n/ *noun* (*data*) información *f*; datos *mpl* ◇ **information architect** arquitecto, -a de la información

information bearer channel /ˌɪnfəmeɪʃ(ə)n ˈbeərə ˌtʃæn(ə)l/ *noun* vía *f* de transmisión de información

information content /ˌɪnfəˈmeɪʃ(ə)n ˌkɒntent/ *noun* contenido *m* de la información

information flow control /ˌɪnfəˈmeɪʃ(ə)n fləʊ kənˌtrəʊl/ *noun* control *m* del flujo de la información

information input /ˌɪnfəˈmeɪʃ(ə)n ˌɪnpʊt/ *noun* entrada *f* de información; introducción *f* de datos

information line /ˌɪnfəˈmeɪʃ(ə)n laɪn/ *noun* línea *f* de información

information management system /ˌɪnfəmeɪʃ(ə)n ˈmænɪdʒmənt ˌsɪstəm/ *noun* sistema *m* de gestión de la información

information network /ˌɪnfəˈmeɪʃ(ə)n ˌnetwɜːk/ *noun* red *f* informática

information output /ˌɪnfəmeɪʃ(ə)n ˈaʊtpʊt/ *noun* (*display of information*) visionado *m* de datos; salida *f* de datos impresos; salida *f* por impresora

information processing /ˌɪnfəmeɪʃ(ə)n ˈprəʊsesɪŋ/ *noun* tratamiento *m* de datos; tratamiento *m* de la información

information processor /ˌɪnfəmeɪʃ(ə)n ˈprəʊsesə/ *noun* procesador *m* de la información

information provider /ˌɪnfəˈmeɪʃ(ə)n prəˌvaɪdə/ *noun* (*company or user who provides information*) fuente *f* de información; servicio *m* (proveedor) de información; agencia *f* de información

information rate /ˌɪnfəˈmeɪʃ(ə)n reɪt/ *noun* capacidad *f* de transmisión de información; velocidad *f* de salida de la información

information retrieval /ˌɪnfəmeɪʃ(ə)n rɪˈtriːv(ə)l/ *noun* recuperación *f* de la información

information retrieval centre /ˌɪnfəmeɪʃ(ə)n rɪˈtriːv(ə)l ˌsentə/ *noun* centro *m* de recuperación de (la) información

information storage /ˌɪnfəmeɪʃ(ə)n ˈstɔːrɪdʒ/ *noun* (*data storage*) almacenamiento *m* de datos; almacenamiento *m* de la información

information storage and retrieval /ˌɪnfəmeɪʃ(ə)n ˌstɔːrɪdʒ ən rɪˈtriːv(ə)l/ *noun* almacenamiento *m* de la información; almacenamiento *m* de datos

information structure /ˌɪnfəˈmeɪʃ(ə)n ˌstrʌktʃə/ *noun* estructura *f* de la información

information system /ˌɪnfəˈmeɪʃ(ə)n ˌsɪstəm/ *noun* sistema *m* de información; sistema *m* informático

information technology /ˌɪnfəmeɪʃ(ə)n tek ˈnɒlədʒi/ *noun* informática *f*; tecnología *f* de la información

information theory /ˌɪnfəˈmeɪʃ(ə)n ˌθɪəri/ *noun* teoría *f* de la información

information transfer channel /ˌɪnfəmeɪʃ(ə)n ˈtrænsfɜː ˌtʃæn(ə)l/ *noun* canal *m* de transmisión de la información; vía *f* de transmisión de la información

infrared /ˌɪnfrəˈred/ *noun* infrarrojo *or* -a

infrared controller /ˌɪnfrəred kənˈtrəʊlə/ *noun* control *m* a distancia por rayos infrarrojos

Infrared Data Association /ˌɪnfrəred ˈdeɪtə əˌsəʊsieɪʃ(ə)n/ *noun* Asociación *f* de transferencia de datos por infrarrojo

infra-red link /ˌɪnfrə red ˈlɪŋk/ *noun* enlace *m* por infrarrojo

infrastructure /ˈɪnfrəˌstrʌktʃə/ *noun* infraestructura *f*

inherent addressing /ɪnˌhɪərənt əˈdresɪŋ/ *noun* direccionamiento *m* inherente; direccionamiento *m* implícito

inherit /ɪnˈherɪt/ *verb* (*data*) heredar (características de otro objeto)

inheritance /ɪnˈherɪt(ə)ns/ *noun* (*data*) herencia *f*; transmisión *f*

inherited error /ɪnˌherɪtɪd ˈerə/ *noun* error *m* heredado; error *m* transmitido

inhibit /ɪnˈhɪbɪt/ *verb* (*process or circuit or gate*) inhibir *vt*; impedir *vt*; bloquear *vt*; parar *vi*

inhibiting input /ɪnˌhɪbɪtɪŋ ˈɪnpʊt/ *noun* señal *f* de bloqueo; inhibición *f* de la transmisión

initial address /ɪˌnɪʃ(ə)l əˈdres/ *noun* dirección *f* inicial; dirección *f* de origen

initial condition /ɪˌnɪʃ(ə)l kənˈdɪʃ(ə)n/ *noun* condición *f* inicial

initial error /ɪˌnɪʃ(ə)l ˈerə/ *noun* error *m* inicial

initial instructions /ɪˌnɪʃ(ə)l ɪnˈstrʌkʃənz/ *plural noun* instrucciones *fpl* iniciales

initialisation, initialization *noun* inicialización *f*

initialisation string /ɪˌnɪʃ(ə)laɪˈzeɪʃ(ə)n ˌstrɪŋ/, **initialization string** *noun* cadena *f* de inicialización

initialise /ɪˈnɪʃəˌlaɪz/, **initialize** *verb* inicializar *vt*

initial program header /ɪˌnɪʃ(ə)l ˈprəʊgræm ˌhedə/ *noun* bloque *m* de identificación de un programa de carga

initial program loader /ɪˌnɪʃ(ə)l ˈprəʊgræm ˌləʊdə/ *noun* rutina *f* de carga del sistema operativo (en la memoria principal)

initial value /ɪˌnɪʃ(ə)l ˈvæljuː/ *noun* valor *m* inicial

ink /ɪŋk/ *verb* impregnar con tinta; entintar *vt*

ink cartridge /ɪŋk ˈkɑːtrɪdʒ/ *noun* cartucho *m* de tinta

ink-jet printer /ˈɪŋk dʒet ˌprɪntə/ *noun* impresora *f* de chorro de tinta

'…ink-jet printers work by squirting a fine stream of ink onto the paper' [*Personal Computer World*]

inlay card /ˈɪnleɪ kɑːd/ *noun* (*inside tape or disk box*) tarjeta *f* interna

in-line /ɪn laɪn/ *adjective* en línea ■ *noun* (*connection pins arranged in one or two rows*) en línea

in-line processing /ˌɪn laɪn ˈprəʊsesɪŋ/ *noun* tratamiento *m* en línea; tratamiento *m* inmediato

in-line program /ˌɪn laɪn ˈpeʊgræm/ *noun* programa *m* en línea

inner loop /ˈɪnə luːp/ *noun* bucle *m* interior

input /ˈɪnpʊt/ *verb* (*to transfer data*) introducir *vt* ■ *noun* 1. (*to transfer data*) introducción *f* (de datos) 2. (*action*) entrada *f*; (*data*) datos *mpl* de entrada 3. (*electrical signals*) señal *f* de entrada ◇ **input speed** velocidad *m* de entrada (de datos) ◇ **the data is input via a modem** los datos se introducen mediante un módem ◇ **the input unit accepts coded information from human operators, from electromechanical devices, or from other computers** la unidad de entrada acepta información codificada que proviene de operadores humanos, de dispositivos electromagnéticos o de otras computadoras

'In fact, the non-Qwerty format of the Maltron keyboard did cause a few gasps when it was first shown to the staff, but within a month all the Maltron users had regained normal input speeds.' [*Computing*]

input area /ˈɪnpʊt ˌeəriə/ *noun* área *f* de entrada

input block /ˈɪnpʊt blɒk/ *noun* bloque *m* de entrada

input-bound /ˈɪnpʊt ˌbaʊnd/ *adjective* lento en la introducción de datos

input buffer register /ˌɪnpʊt ˈbʌfə ˌredʒɪstə/ *noun* registro *m* intermedio de entrada

input device /ˈɪnpʊt dɪˌvaɪs/ *noun* periférico *m* de entrada

input lead /'ɪnpʊt liːd/ *noun* cable *m* de entrada; conexión *f* de un periférico de entrada

input-limited /,ɪnpʊt 'lɪmɪtɪd/ *adjective* limitado en la entrada de datos

input mode /'ɪnpʊt məʊd/ *noun* (*of data*) modo *m* de entrada

input/output /,ɪnpʊt 'aʊtpʊt/ *noun* **1.** entrada/salida *f* (E/S) **2.** datos *mpl* de entrada/salida (E/S)

input/output buffer /,ɪnpʊt 'aʊtpʊt ,bʌfə/ *noun* memoria *f* intermedia de entrada/salida

input/output bus /,ɪnpʊt 'aʊtpʊt bʌs/ *noun* enlace *m* común de entrada/salida

input/output channel /,ɪnpʊt 'aʊtpʊt ,tʃæn(ə)l/ *noun* canal *m* de entrada/salida; vía *f* de entrada/salida

input/output controller /,ɪnpʊt 'aʊtpʊt kən,trəʊlə/ *noun* controlador *m* de entrada/salida

input/output control program /,ɪnpʊt 'aʊtpʊt kən,trəʊl/ *noun* programa *m* de control de entrada/salida

input/output device /,ɪnpʊt 'aʊtpʊt dɪ,vaɪs/ *noun* dispositivo *m* de entrada/salida; periférico *m* de entrada/salida

input/output executive /,ɪnpʊt 'aʊtpʊt ɪg,zekjʊtɪv/ *noun* supervisor *m* de entrada/salida

input/output instruction /,ɪnpʊt 'aʊtpʊt ɪn,strʌkʃən/ *noun* instrucción *f* de entrada/salida

input/output interface /,ɪnpʊt 'aʊtpʊt ɪntə,feɪs/ *noun* interfaz *f* de entrada/salida

input/output interrupt /,ɪnpʊt 'aʊtpʊt ɪntə,rʌpt/ *noun* (señal de) interrupción *f* de entrada/salida

input/output library /,ɪnpʊt 'aʊtpʊt ,laɪbrəri/ *noun* biblioteca *f* (de programas) de entrada/salida

input/output port /,ɪnpʊt 'aʊtpʊt ,pɔːt/ *noun* puerto *m* de entrada/salida ◊ **the joystick can be connected to the input *or* output port** el mando de juego puede conectarse al puerto de entrada/salida

input/output processor /,ɪnpʊt 'aʊtpʊt ,prəʊsesə/ *noun* procesador *m* de entrada/salida

input/output referencing /,ɪnpʊt 'aʊtpʊt ,ref(ə)rənsɪŋ/ *noun* (sistema de) referencia *m* de entrada/salida

input/output register /,ɪnpʊt 'aʊtpʊt ,redʒɪstə/ *noun* registro *m* de entrada/salida

input/output request /,ɪnpʊt 'aʊtpʊt rɪ,kwest/ *noun* petición *f* de entrada/salida

input/output status word /,ɪnpʊt ,aʊtpʊt 'steɪtəs wɜːd/ *noun* palabra *f* de estado de entrada/salida

input/output unit /,ɪnpʊt 'aʊtpʊt ,juːnɪt/ *noun* dispositivo *m* de entrada/salida; periférico *m* de entrada/salida

input port /'ɪnpʊt pɔːt/ *noun* puerto *m* de entrada

input register /'ɪnpʊt ,redʒɪstə/ *noun* registro *m* de entrada

input routine /'ɪnpʊt ruː,tiːn/ *noun* rutina *f* de entrada

input statement /'ɪnpʊt ,steɪtmənt/ *noun* instrucción *f* de entrada; mensaje *m* de entrada

input storage /'ɪnpʊt ,stɔːrɪdʒ/ *noun* memoria *f* de entrada

input work queue /,ɪnpʊt 'wɜːk ,kjuː/ *noun* cola *f* de espera de entrada de datos

inquiry /ɪn'kwaɪəri/ *noun* consulta *f*; pregunta *f*

inquiry character /ɪn'kwaɪəri ,kærɪktə/ *noun* carácter *m* de consulta

inquiry/response /ɪn,kwaɪəri rɪ'spɒns/ *noun* consulta/respuesta *f*

inquiry station /ɪn'kwaɪri ,steɪʃ(ə)n/ *noun* estación *f*; terminal *m* de consulta

insert /ɪn'sɜːt/ *verb* (*to add new text*) añadir *vt*

inserted subroutine /,ɪnsɜːtɪd 'sʌbruːtiːn/ *noun* subrutina *f* insertada

insertion loss /ɪn'sɜːʃ(ə)n lɒs/ *noun* (*attenuation to a signal*) pérdida *f*; debilitamiento *m* por inserción

insertion point /ɪn'sɜːʃ(ə)n pɔɪnt/ *noun* (*cursor*) punto *m* de inserción

insert key /ɪn'sɜːt kiː/ *noun* tecla *f* insertar

insert mode /'ɪnsɜːt məʊd/ *noun* (*mode for correcting and editing documents*) modo *m* de inserción

Ins key /'ɪns kiː/ *noun* (*insert key – key that switches into insert mode*) tecla *f* Ins

install /ɪn'stɔːl/ *verb* instalar *vt* ◊ **the system is easy to install and simple to use** el sistema es fácil de instalar y sencillo de utilizar

installable device driver /ɪn,stɔːləb(ə)l dɪ 'vaɪs ,draɪvə/ *noun* (*device driver loaded into memory*) gestor *m* de periféricos instalable

installation /,ɪnstə'leɪʃ(ə)n/ *noun* **1.** (*equipment*) instalación *f* informática; material *m*; equipamiento *m* informático **2.** (*setting up*) instalación *f* ◊ **the installation of the equipment took only a few hours** la instalación del equipo sólo llevó unas pocas horas

installation manual /,ɪnstə'leɪʃ(ə)n ,mænjʊəl/ *noun* manual *m* de instalación

install program /'ɪnstɔːl ,prəʊgræm/ *noun* programa *m* de instalación

instance /'ɪnstəns/ *noun* (*duplicate object*) objeto *m* disponible; instancia *f* en programación orientada a objetos

instantaneous access /,ɪnstənteɪniəs 'ækses/ *noun* acceso *m* instantáneo ◊ **the instantaneous access of the RAM disk was welcome** el acceso instantáneo al disco RAM fue bien acogido

instruction /ɪn'strʌkʃən/ *noun* instrucción *f* ◊ **do-nothing instruction** instrucción *f* e no hacer nada *or* instrucción *f* in efecto ◊ **dummy instruction** instrucción *f* nula *or* ficticia *or* simulada ◊ **jump instruction** instrucción de salto ◊ **macro instruction** macro-instrucción *f* ◊ **the instruction PRINT is used in this BASIC dialect as an operand to display the following data** la instrucción PRINT se utiliza en este dialecto de BA-

SIC como un operando para mostrar los siguientes datos ◊ **the manufacturers of this CPU have decided that JMP will be the instruction word to call the jump function** los fabricantes de esta unidad central de proceso decidieron que JMP será la palabra de instrucción para llamar la función de salto

'A Taos kernel, typically 15Kb in size, resides at each processing node to 'translate', non-native instructions – on the fly when needed. This kernel contains the only code which has to be written in the processor's native instruction set.' [*Computing*]

instruction address /ɪn'strʌkʃən ə,dres/ *noun* dirección *f* de instrucción

instruction address register /ɪn,strʌkʃən ə'dres ,redʒɪstə/ *noun* registro *m* de control de secuencia

instruction area /ɪn'strʌkʃən ,eəriə/ *noun* área *f* de instrucción en la memoria

instruction cache /ɪn'strʌkʃən kæʃ/ *noun* memoria *f* temporal de instrucción

instruction character /ɪn'strʌkʃən ,kærɪktə/ *noun* carácter *m* de instrucción

instruction codes /ɪn'strʌkʃən kəʊdz/ *plural noun* códigos *mpl* de instrucción

instruction counter /ɪn'strʌkʃən ,kaʊntə/ *noun* contador *m* de instrucciones

instruction cycle /ɪn'strʌkʃən ,saɪk(ə)l/ *noun* ciclo *m* de instrucciones

instruction cycle time /ɪn,strʌkʃən 'saɪk(ə)l ,taɪm/ *noun* tiempo *m* del ciclo de instrucciones

instruction decoder /ɪn'strʌkʃən diː,kəʊdə/ *noun* descodificador *m* de instrucciones

instruction execution time /ɪn,strʌkʃən ,eksɪ'kjuːʃ(ə)n ,taɪm/ *noun* tiempo *m* de ejecución de una instrucción

instruction format /ɪn'strʌkʃən ,fɔːmæt/ *noun* formato *m* de instrucciones; formato *m* de instrucción

instruction manual /ɪn'strʌkʃən ,mænjuəl/ *noun* manual *m* de instrucciones; manual *m* de uso

instruction modification /ɪn,strʌkʃən ,mɒdɪfɪ'keɪʃ(ə)n/ *noun* modificación *f* de una instrucción

instruction pipelining /ɪn'strʌkʃən ,paɪplaɪnɪŋ/ *noun* (proceso de) encauzamiento *m* de una instrucción

instruction pointer /ɪn'strʌkʃən ,pɔɪntə/ *noun* puntero *m* de instrucción

instruction processor /ɪn'strʌkʃən ,prəʊsesə/ *noun* procesador *m* de instrucción

instruction register /ɪn'strʌkʃən ,redʒɪstə/ *noun* registro *m* de instrucción

instruction repertoire /ɪn'strʌkʃən ,repətwɑː/, **instruction set** /set/ *noun* repertorio *m* de instrucciones; conjunto *m* de instrucciones

instruction storage /ɪn'strʌkʃən ,stɔːrɪdʒ/ *noun* (*memory*) memoria *f* de instrucción; puesta *f* de instrucción; introducción *f* en memoria

instruction time /ɪn'strʌkʃən taɪm/ *noun* tiempo *m* de ejecución de una instrucción

instruction word /ɪn'strʌkʃən wɜːd/ *noun* palabra *f* de instrucción ◊ **the manufacturers of this CPU have decided that JMP will be the instruction word to call the jump function** los fabricantes de esta unidad central de proceso decidieron que JMP será la palabra de instrucción para llamar la función de salto

instrument /'ɪnstrʊmənt/ *noun* instrumento *m*

integer /'ɪntɪdʒə/ *noun* número *m* entero

integral /ɪntɪgrəl, ɪn'tegəl/ *adjective* (*device*) integral

integrated /'ɪntɪ,greɪtɪd/ *adjective* integrado *or* -a ◊ **integrated device** dispositivo integrado ◊ **integrated digital access (IDA)** acceso *m* digital integrado ◊ **integrated digital network** red *f* digital integrada ◊ **integrated optical circuit** circuito *m* óptico integrado ◊ **integrated program** programa *m* integrado ◊ **integrated project support environment (IPSE)** entorno *m* de apoyo a proyectos integrados ◊ **our competitor's computer doesn't have an integrated disk drive like this model** el ordenador de nuestro competidor no dispone de una disquetera integrada como este modelo

integrated circuit /,ɪntɪgreɪtɪd 'sɜːkɪt/ *noun* circuito *m* integrado

integrated database /,ɪntɪgreɪtɪd 'deɪtəbeɪs/ *noun* base *f* de datos integrada

integrated data processing /,ɪntɪgreɪtɪd 'deɪtə ,prəʊsesɪŋ/ *noun* proceso *m* de datos integrados

integrated device electronics /,ɪntɪ,greɪtɪd dɪ,vaɪs ,elek'trɒnɪks/, **integrated drive electronics** /,ɪntɪ,greɪtɪd draɪv ,elek'trɒnɪks/ *noun* electrónica *f* de dispositivo integrado ◊ **IDE drives are the standard fitted to most PCs** las disqueteras electrónicas de dispositivo integrado son el estándar incorporado en la mayoría de los ordenadores personales

integrated emulator /,ɪntɪgreɪtɪd 'emjʊleɪtə/ *noun* emulador *m* integrado

integrated injection logic /,ɪntɪgreɪtɪd ɪn 'dʒekʃən ,lɒdʒɪk/ *noun* lógica *f* de inyección integrada

integrated modem /,ɪntɪgreɪtɪd 'məʊdem/ *noun* módem *m* integrado; módem *m* incorporado

integrated office /,ɪntɪgreɪtɪd 'ɒfɪs/ *noun* oficina *f* integrada

integrated services digital network /,ɪntɪgreɪtɪd ,sɜːvɪsɪz ,dɪdʒɪt(ə)l 'netwɜːk/ *noun* red *f* digital de servicios integrados

integrated software /,ɪntɪgreɪtɪd 'sɒftweə/ *noun* programas *mpl* integrados

integration /,ɪntɪ'greɪʃ(ə)n/ *noun* integración *f* ◊ **large scale integration (LSI)** integración a gran escala ◊ **medium scale integration (MSI)** (*10 – 500 components*) integración a media escala ◊ **super large scale integration (SLSI)** integración a super gran escala ◊ **very large scale integration (VLSI)** integración a muy gran escala

integrity /ɪn'tegrɪti/ *noun* integridad *f* ◇ **integrity of a file** integridad de un fichero ◇ **the data in this file has integrity** los datos de este fichero tienen integridad

Intel /'ɪntel/ (*company which developed the first microprocessor*) Intel™

Intel 8086 (*trade name for a microprocessor that uses a 16-bit data bus and can address up to 1Mb of RAM*) Intel 8086

Intel 8088 (*trade name for a microprocessor that uses a 16-bit data bus internally, but uses an 8-bit data bus externally*) Intel 8088

Intel 80286 (*trade name for a microprocessor that uses a 16-bit data bus and can address up to 16Mb of RAM*) Intel 80286

Intel 80386 (*trade name for a microprocessor that uses a 32-bit data bus and can address up to 4Gb of RAM*) Intel 80386

Intel 80486 (*trade name for a microprocessor that uses a 32-bit data bus and can address up to 64Gb of RAM*) Intel 80486

Intel Indeo /ˌɪntel 'ɪndiəʊ/ (*trade name for software technology that allows a computer to store and play back compressed video sequences*) Indeo

intelligence /ɪn'telɪdʒəns/ *noun* (*of person or machine*) inteligencia *f*

intelligent /ɪn'telɪdʒənt/ *adjective* (*person or program or machine*) inteligente

intelligent device /ɪn,telɪdʒ(ə)nt dɪ'vaɪs/ *noun* máquina *f* inteligente; dispositivo *m* inteligente

intelligent knowledge-based system /ɪn ,telɪdʒ(ə)nt ,nɒlɪdʒ beɪsd 'sɪstəm/ *noun* sistema *m* de bases de conocimiento inteligentes; sistema *m* experto

intelligent spacer /ɪn,telɪdʒ(ə)nt 'speɪsə/ *noun* espaciador *m* inteligente; gestor *m* de espacios inteligente

intelligent terminal /ɪn,telɪdʒ(ə)nt 't3:mɪn(ə)l/ *noun* terminal *m* inteligente ◇ **the new intelligent terminal has a built-in text editor** el nuevo terminal inteligente tiene un editor de texto incorporado

intelligent tutoring system /ɪn,telɪdʒ(ə)nt 'tju:tərɪŋ ,sɪstəm/ *noun* sistema *m* tutorial inteligente

intelligent wiring hub /ɪn,telɪdʒ(ə)nt 'waɪərɪŋ hʌb/ *noun* boca *f* de conexión inteligente

Intel MMX /ˌɪntel em em 'eks/ (*trade name for a range of processors*) MMX

Intel Pentium /ˌɪntel 'pentiəm/ (*trade name for a range of advanced microprocessors*) Pentium

Intel Pentium Pro /ˌɪntel ,pentiəm 'prəʊ/ (*trade name for a 32-bit processor*) Pentium Pro

intensity /ɪn'tensɪti/ *noun* (*of signal or light or sound*) intensidad *f*

interactive /ˌɪntər'æktɪv/ *adjective* (*that allows communication between the computer and the user*) interactivo *or* -a; dialogado *or* -a; conversacional ◇ **the space invaders machine has great interactive graphics, the player controls the position of his spaceship with the joystick** el juego de los invasores del espacio tiene unos gráficos interactivos excelentes ◇ **this interactive multimedia title allows a user to make music with a synthesizer program** este programa multimedia interactivo permite que el usuario componga música con un programa de sintetizador

'Oracle today details its interactive information superhighway aims, endorsed by 17 industry partners. The lynchpin to the announcement will be software based on the Oracle Media Server, a multimedia database designed to run on massively parallel computers.' [*Computing*]

interactive debugging system /ˌɪntəræktɪv di:'bʌgɪŋ ,sɪstəm/ *noun* sistema *m* de corrección de errores interactivo

interactive graphics /ˌɪntəræktɪv 'græfɪks/ *plural noun* (*display system*) gráficos *mpl* interactivos; infografía *f* interactiva

interactive keyboard /ˌɪntəræktɪv 'ki:bɔ:d/ *noun* teclado *m* interactivo

interactive media /ˌɪntəræktɪv 'mi:diə/ *plural noun* medios *mpl* de comunicación interactivos

interactive mode /ˌɪntər'æktɪv ,məʊd/ *noun* modo *m* interactivo

interactive multimedia /ˌɪntəræktɪv ,mʌlti 'mi:diə/ *noun* multimedia *m* interactivo ◇ **this interactive multimedia title allows a user to make music with a synthesizer program** este programa multimedia interactivo permite que el usuario componga música con un programa de sintetizador

Interactive Multimedia Association /ˌɪntəræktɪv ,mʌlti'mi:diə ə,səʊsieɪʃ(ə)n/ *noun* asociación *f* de sistemas multimedia interactivos

interactive processing /ˌɪntəræktɪv 'prəʊsesɪŋ/ *noun* modo *m* interactivo

interactive routine /ˌɪntəræktɪv ru:'ti:n/ *noun* rutina *f* interactiva

interactive system /ˌɪntəræktɪv 'sɪstəm/ *noun* sistema *m* interactivo

interactive terminal /ˌɪntəræktɪv 't3:mɪn(ə)l/ *noun* terminal *m* interactivo

interactive TV /ˌɪntəræktɪv ti: 'vi:/ *noun* TV *f* interactiva

interactive video /ˌɪntəræktɪv 'vɪdiəʊ/ *noun* vídeo *m* interactivo

interactive videotext /ˌɪntəræktɪv 'vɪdiəʊtekst/ *noun* teletexto *m* interactivo; videotexto *m* interactivo

interactivity /ˌɪntəræk'tɪvɪti/ *noun* interactividad *f*

'…interactivity is a buzzword you've been hearing a lot lately. Resign yourself to it because you're going to be hearing a lot more of it' [*Music Technology*]

interblock /'ɪntəblɒk/ *adjective* entre bloques

interblock gap /'ɪntəblɒk gæp/ *noun* (*blank magnetic tape*) espacio *m* entre bloques; separación *f* entre bloques; intervalo *m* entre bloques

interchange file format /,ɪntətʃeɪndʒ 'faɪl ,fɔːmæt/ *noun* formato *m* de fichero intercambiable

intercharacter spacing /ɪntə,kærəktə 'speɪsɪŋ/ *noun* (*DTP*) espaciado *m* (proporcional) de caracteres

interconnection /,ɪntəkə'nekʃən/ *noun* (*connecting material*) interconexión *f*

interface /'ɪntəfeɪs/ *noun* **1.** (*point at which one computer system ends and another begins*) interfaz *f*; interconexión *f* **2.** (*linking device in communications system*) intermediario *m*; acoplamiento *m* mutuo **3.** (*section of a program which allows transmission of data to another program*) interfaz *f*; interconexión *f* ■ *verb* **1.** (*to modify device in communications system*) proporcionar una conexión **2.** (*to connect incompatible devices*) interactuar *vi* ◇ **serial interface** interfaz en serie

'The original release of ODBC only included a driver for Microsoft's own SQL Server database. Microsoft has subsequently published the ODBC application program interface enabling third-party vendors to create drivers for other databases and tools.' [*Computing*]

interface card /'ɪntəfeɪs kɑːd/ *noun* tarjeta *f* de interfaz

interface message processor /,ɪntəfeɪs 'mesɪdʒ ,prəʊsesə/ *noun* procesador *m* de mensajes de interfaz

interface processor /'ɪntəfeɪs ,prəʊsesə/ *noun* procesador *m* de interfaz

interface routines /'ɪntəfeɪs ruː,tiːnz/ *plural noun* rutinas *fpl* de interfaz

interfacing /'ɪntəfeɪsɪŋ/ *noun* (*hardware or software*) conexión *f*; intercomunicación *f*; unión *f*

interfere /,ɪntə'fɪə/ ◇ **to interfere with something** interferir *vt*

interference /,ɪntə'fɪərəns/ *noun* (*unwanted addition of signal*) interferencia *f*

interior gateway protocol /ɪn,tɪəriə ,geɪtweɪ ,prəʊtəʊ'kɒl/ *noun* protocolo *m* de puerta interior

interior label /ɪn,tɪəriə 'leɪb(ə)l/ *noun* etiqueta *f* interior (de identificación)

interlace /,ɪntə'leɪs/ *verb* entrelazar *vt*

interlaced scanning /,ɪntəleɪsd 'skænɪŋ/ *noun* exploración *f* entrelazada

interlaced video /,ɪntəleɪsd 'vɪdiəʊ/ *noun* vídeo *m* entrelazado

interleave /,ɪntər'liːv/ *noun* intercalar hojas; interpaginar

interleaved memory /,ɪntərliːvd 'mem(ə)ri/ *noun* memoria *f* intercalada

interleave factor /,ɪntər,liːv 'fæktə/ *noun* (*ratio of sectors skipped between access operations*) factor *m* de intercalación

interlock /,ɪntə'lɒk/ *noun* (*security device*) interbloqueo *m*; protección *f* ■ *verb* interbloquear *vt*; trabar con intercierre

interlude /'ɪntə,luːd/ *noun* (*routine*) intervalo *m*; intermedio *m*

intermediate access memory /,ɪntəmiːdiət ,ækses 'mem(ə)ri/ *noun* memoria *f* de acceso intermedio

intermediate code /,ɪntəmiːdiət 'kəʊd/ *noun* código *m* intermedio

intermediate file /,ɪntəmiːdiət 'faɪl/ *noun* fichero *m* intermedio

intermediate storage /,ɪntəmiːdiət 'stɔːrɪdʒ/ *noun* (*temporary area of memory*) memoria *f* intermedia; almacenamiento *m* intermedio

intermediate system /,ɪntəmiːdiət 'sɪstəm/ *noun* sistema *m* intermedio

intermediate system to intermediate system /,ɪntəmiːdiət ,sɪstəm tə ,ɪntəmiːdiət 'sɪstəm/ *noun* sistema *m* intermedio a sistema intermedio

intermittent error /,ɪntəmɪt(ə)nt 'erə/ *noun* error *m* intermitente

internal arithmetic /ɪn,tɜːn(ə)l ə'rɪθmətɪk/ *noun* aritmética *f* interna

internal character code /ɪn,tɜːn(ə)l 'kærɪktə ,kəʊd/ *noun* código *m* de caracteres interno

internal command /ɪn,tɜːn(ə)l kə'mɑːnd/ *noun* orden *f* interna; instrucción *f* interna ◇ **in MS-DOS, the internal command DIR is used frequently** en MS-DOS, la instrucción interna DIR se emplea con frecuencia

internal format /ɪn,tɜːn(ə)l 'fɔːmæt/ *noun* formato *m* interno

internal hard disk /ɪn,tɜːn(ə)l 'hɑːd ,dɪsk/ *noun* disco *m* duro interno

internal language /ɪn,tɜːn(ə)l 'læŋgwɪdʒ/ *noun* lenguaje *m* interno; lenguaje *m* máquina

internally stored program /ɪn,tɜːn(ə)li stɔːd 'prəʊgræm/ *noun* programa *m* residente

internal memory /ɪn,tɜːn(ə)l 'mem(ə)ri/ *noun* memoria *f* interna

internal modem /ɪn,tɜːn(ə)l ,məʊ'dem/ *noun* (*modem that transfers information to the processor through the bus*) módem *m* interno

internal sort /ɪn'tɜːn(ə)l sɔːt/ *noun* clasificación *f* interna

internal store /ɪn,tɜːn(ə)l 'stɔː/ *noun* memoria *f* interna

international file format /,ɪntənæʃ(ə)nəl 'faɪl ,fɔːmæt/ *noun* formato *m* de fichero internacional

International Standards Organization /,ɪntənæʃ(ə)nəl 'stændədz ,ɔːgənaɪzeɪʃ(ə)n/ *noun* Organismo *m* internacional de Normalización; Organismo *m* ISO

International Standards Organization Open System Interconnection /,ɪntənæʃ(ə)nəl ,stændədz ,ɔːgənaɪzeɪʃ(ə)n ,əʊpən ,sɪstəm ,ɪntəkə'nekʃ(ə)n/ *noun* arquitectura *f* ISO/OSI

Internet /'ɪntənet/ *noun (wide area network formed of local area networks)* internet *f*; red *f* de redes; red *f* informática internacional ◇ **Internet coorporation for assigned names and numbers (ICANN)** corporación de asignación de números y nombres Internet

Internet Activities Board /ˌɪntənet æk'tɪvɪtiz ˌbɔːd/ *noun* comité *m* de actividades de internet

Internet address /'ɪntənet əˌdres/ *noun* dirección *f* Internet

Internet architecture board /ˌɪntənet 'ɑːkɪtektʃə ˌbɔːd/ *noun* comité *m* de actividades de internet

Internet café /'ɪntənet ˌkæfeɪ/ *noun* cibercafé *m*

Internet control message protocol /ˌɪntənet kənˌtrəʊl 'mesɪdʒ ˌprəʊtəkɒl/ *noun* protocolo *m* de internet de control de mensajes

Internet engineering task force /ˌɪntənet ˌendʒɪnɪərɪŋ 'tɑːsk ˌfɔːs/ *noun* comité *m* de normalización de internet; comité *m* de ingeniería de internet

Internet Information Server /ˌɪntənet ˌɪnfə'meɪʃ(ə)n ˌsɜːvə/ *noun* servidor *m* de información de Internet

Internet message access protocol /ˌɪntənet 'mesɪdʒ ˌækses ˌprəʊtəkɒl/ *noun* protocolo *m* de acceso a mensajes de Internet

Internet number /'ɪntənet ˌnʌmbə/ *noun* dirección *f* Internet

Internet protocol /ˌɪntənet 'prəʊtəkɒl/ *noun (transmission of data over a network)* protocolo *m* de internet; protocolo *m* IP; protocolo *m* entre redes

Internet protocol address /ˌɪntənet ˌprəʊtəkɒl ə'dres/ *noun* dirección *f* en internet; dirección *f* de internet

Internet relay chat /ˌɪntənet ˌriːleɪ 'tʃæt/ *noun* servicio *m* de conversación (en tiempo real) a través de internet

Internet research task force /ˌɪntənet rɪˌsɜːtʃ 'tɑːsk fɔːs/ *noun* comité *m* de investigación de internet

Internet service provider /ˌɪntənet 'sɜːvɪs prəˌvaɪdə/ *noun* proveedor *m* de servicios de internet; suministrador *m* de servicios de internet

Internet Society /'ɪntənet səˌsaɪəti/ *noun* sociedad *m* internet

Internetwork /ˌɪntə'netwɜːk/ *noun (interconnected networks allowing users to access resources on other networks)* interconexión *f* de redes

Internetwork Packet Exchange /ˌɪntənetwɜːk 'pækɪt ɪksˌtʃeɪndʒ/ *(trade name for a network protocol developed by Novell)* protocolo *m* de intercambio de información en la red

interoperability /ˌɪntəˌɒpərə'bɪlɪti/ *noun (the ability of two devices or computers to exchange information)* interoperabilidad *f*

interpolation /ɪnˌtɜːpə'leɪʃ(ə)n/ *noun* interpolación *f*

interpret /ɪn'tɜːprɪt/ *verb* interpretar *vt*; traducir *vt*

interpretative /ɪn'tɜːrprɪtətɪv/ *adjective* interpretativo *or* -a

interpretative code /ɪnˌtɜːrprɪtətɪv 'kəʊd/ *noun* código *m* interpretativo

interpretative program /ɪnˌtɜːrprɪtətɪv 'prəʊɡræm/ *noun* programa *m* interpretativo

interpreted language /ɪnˌtɜːprɪtd 'læŋɡwɪdʒ/ *noun* lenguaje *m* interpretado

interpreter /ɪn'tɜːprɪtə/ *noun (software)* interpretador *m or* -a *f*; programa *m* intérprete

interrecord gap /ˌɪntərekɔːd 'ɡæp/ *noun* espacio *m* entre bloques; intervalo *m* entre bloques; separación *f* entre bloques

interrogate /ɪn'terəɡeɪt/ *verb* interrogar *vt*

interrupt /ˌɪntə'rʌpt/ *noun* **1.** *(stopping of a transmission)* interrupción *f* **2.** *(signal)* interrupción *f*

interrupt handler /'ɪntərʌpt ˌhændlə/ *noun* controlador *m* de interrupciones

interrupt level /'ɪntərʌpt ˌlev(ə)l/ *noun* nivel *m* de interrupción

interrupt line /'ɪntərʌpt laɪn/ *noun* línea *f* de interrupción

interrupt mask /'ɪntərʌpt mɑːsk/ *noun (computer programming)* máscara *f* de interrupción

interrupt priorities /'ɪntərʌpt praɪˌɒrɪtiz/ *plural noun* prioridad *f* de interrupciones

interrupt request /'ɪntərʌpt rɪˌkwest/ *noun* petición *f* de interrupción

interrupt servicing /'ɪntərʌpt ˌsɜːvɪsɪŋ/ *noun* (operaciones de) control y ejecución de la interrupción

interrupt signal /'ɪntərʌpt ˌsɪɡn(ə)l/ *noun* señal *f* de interrupción

interrupt stacking /'ɪntərʌpt ˌstækɪŋ/ *noun* pila *f* de interrupciones; lote *m* de interrupciones

intersection /'ɪntəˌsekʃən/ *noun* intersección *f*

interval /'ɪntəv(ə)l/ *noun* intervalo *m* ◇ **there was an interval between pressing the key and the starting of the printout** había un intervalo entre el instante en el que se apretaba la tecla y el comienzo de la impresión

interword spacing /ɪntəˌwɜːd 'speɪsɪŋ/ *noun* espacio *m* entre palabra y palabra

intimate /'ɪntɪmət/ *adjective (software)* (programa) que opera con el sistema

intranet /'ɪntrənet/ *noun (private network of computers within a company)* red *f* interna; red *f* de la empresa

intruder /ɪn'truːdə/ *noun (person who is not authorized to use a computer)* intruso *m or* -a *f*

inverse /ˌɪn'vɜːs/ *noun* inverso *or* -a

inverse video /ˌɪnvɜːs 'vɪdiəʊ/ *noun* vídeo *m* inverso

inversion /ɪn'vɜːʃ(ə)n/ *noun* **1.** *(of numbers)* inversión *f* **2.** *(of signal or device)* inversión *f* ◇ **the inversion of a binary digit takes place in one's complement** la inversión de un dígito binario tiene lugar en el complemento de uno

invert /ˌɪn'vɜːt/ *verb* invertir *vt*

inverted backbone /ɪn,vɜːtɪd 'bækbəʊn/ *noun* red *f* principal invertida

inverted commas /ɪn,vɜːtɪd 'kɒməz/ *plural noun* comillas *fpl*

inverted file /ɪn,vɜːtɪd 'faɪl/ *noun* fichero *m* invertido; archivo *m* invertido

inverter /ɪn'vɜːtə/ *noun* **1.** (*logical gate*) inversor *m* **2.** (*circuit*) inversor *m* ◇ **inverter (AC or DC)** (*circuit*) inversor *m* de corriente

invisible /ɪn'vɪzɪb(ə)l/ *adjective* invisible

invitation /ˌɪnvɪ'teɪʃ(ə)n/ *noun* invitación *f*

invitation to send /ˌɪnvɪteɪʃ(ə)n tə 'send/ *noun* invitación *f* a transmitir

invoke /ɪn'vəʊk/ *verb* (*a program*) llamar *vt*

'...when an error is detected, the editor may be invoked and positioned at the statement in error' [*Personal Computer World*]

I/O /ˌaɪ 'əʊ/ *noun* entrada/salida *f* ◇ **I or O processor** procesador *m* de entrada/salida ◇ **I or O request** petición *f* de entrada/salida

I/O address /ˌaɪ 'əʊ ə,dres/ *noun* dirección *f* de los puertos de entrada/salida

I/O bound /ˌaɪ əʊ 'baʊnd/ *adjective* limitado a entrada/salida

I/O buffer /ˌaɪ 'əʊ ˌbʌfə/ *noun* (*temporary storage area*) almacenamiento *m* temporal de entrada/salida; memoria *f* intermedia de entrada/salida; almacenamiento *m* en memoria intermedia de entrada/salida; 'buffer' *m* de E/S

I/O bus /ˌaɪ 'əʊ ˌbʌs/ *noun* (*for transmission of data and control signals*) enlace *m*; conductor *m* común; bus *m* de entrada/salida

I/O channel /ˌaɪ 'əʊ ˌtʃæn(ə)l/ *noun* (*data transfer*) vía *f* de entrada/salida; canal *m* de entrada/salida; canal *m* E/S

I/O device /ˌaɪ 'əʊ dɪ,vaɪs/ *noun* (*peripheral for inputting and outputting data*) dispositivo *m* de entrada/salida; aparato *m* de entrada/salida; periférico *m* de entrada/salida

I/O file /ˌaɪ 'əʊ ˌfaɪl/ *noun* fichero *m* de entrada/salida; archivo *m* de entrada/salida

I/O instruction /ˌaɪ 'əʊ ˌɪnstrʌkʃ(ə)n/ *noun* instrucción *f* de entrada/salida

I/O mapping /ˌaɪ əʊ 'mæpɪŋ/ *noun* (*assigning a special address to I/O port*) configuración *f* de entrada/salida; acoplamiento *m* de entrada/salida

ion deposition /'aɪən ˌdepəzɪʃ(ə)n/ *noun* (*impresión por*) depósito *m* de iones

IOP *abbr* (*input/output processor*) procesador *m* de entrada/salida

I/O port /ˌaɪ 'əʊ ˌpɔːt/ *noun* puerto *m* de entrada/salida

I/O redirection /ˌaɪ əʊ ˌriːdaɪ'rekʃ(ə)n/ *noun* redirección *f* de entrada/salida ◇ **using I or O redirection, we send all the data from the keyboard to the printer port instead of the monitor** utilizando la redirección de entrada/salida, enviamos desde el teclado todos los datos al puerto de la impresora y no al monitor

IORQ *abbr* (*input/output request*) petición *f* de entrada/salida

IP /ˌaɪ 'piː/ *noun* protocolo *m* de internet; protocolo *m* entre redes; protocolo *m* IP

i/p, I/P *abbr* (*input*) entrada *f*

IP address /aɪ 'piː ə,dres/ *noun* dirección *f* en internet

IP Datagram /ˌaɪ piː 'deɪtəɡræm/ *noun* paquete *m* IP; datagrama *m* IP

IPL *abbr* (*initial program loader*) rutina *f* de carga del sistema operativo (en la memoria principal)

IPSE *abbr* (*integrated project support environment*) entornos *mpl* integrados de proyectos

IP terminal /ˌaɪ ˌpiː 'tɜːmɪn(ə)l/ *noun* terminal *m* de entrada de datos

IPX *abbr* (*Internetwork Packet Exchange*) protocolo *m* de intercambio de información en la red

IR *abbr* **1.** (*information retrieval*) recuperación *f* de la información **2.** (*index register*) registro *m* de índice **3.** (*instruction register*) registro *m* de instrucción

IRC *abbr* (*Internet relay chat*) servicio *m* de conversación (en tiempo real) a través de internet

IRQ /ˌaɪ ɑː 'kjuː/ *noun* petición *f* de interrupción

IRTF /ˌaɪ ɑː tiː 'ef/ *noun* comité *m* de investigación de internet

IS *abbr* (*intermediate system*) sistema *m* intermedio

ISA /'aɪsə/ *noun* arquitectura *f* estándar industrial, Arquitectura *f* ISA; arquitectura *f* ISA

ISAM *abbr* (*indexed sequential access method*) método *m* de acceso secuencial indexado

ISDN /ˌaɪ es diː 'en/ *noun* red *f* digital de servicios integrados

IS-IS /ɪz ɪz/ *noun* sistema *m* intermedio a sistema intermedio

ISO *abbr* (*International Standards Organization*) OIN (Organización Internacional de Normalización)

isochronous network /aɪ,sɒkrən(ə)s 'netwɜːk/ *noun* red *f* isócrona

isochronous transmission /aɪ,sɒkrən(ə)s trænz'mɪʃ(ə)n/ *noun* transmisión *f* isócrona

isolate /'aɪsə,leɪt/ *verb* (*to separate or to insulate*) aislar *vt* ◇ **isolated adaptive routing** direccionamiento *m* adaptable aislado *or* ruta *f* adaptable aislada

isolated location /ˌaɪsəleɪtɪd ləʊ'keɪʃ(ə)n/ *noun* zona *f* protegida; zona *f* aislada

isolation transformer /ˌaɪsə,leɪʃ(ə)n træns 'fɔːmə/ *noun* transformador *m* de aislamiento; transformador *m* de separación

isolator /'aɪsəleɪtə/ *noun* (*device or material*) desconectador *m* disyuntor; aislante *m*

isometric view /ˌaɪsəʊ'metrɪk vjuː/ *noun* (*in graphics – a drawing that shows all three dimensions of an object in equal proportion*) visualización *f* isométrica; vista *f* isométrica ◇ **an isometric view does not show any perspective** en una visualización isométrica no se aprecia la perspectiva

ISP /ˌaɪ es 'piː/ *noun* proveedor *m* de acceso a Internet

ISR *abbr* (*information storage and retrieval*) almacenamiento *m* de datos; almacenamiento *m* de la información

IT *abbr* (*information technology*) informática *f*

italic /ɪ'tælɪk/ *noun* cursiva *f* ◇ **all the footnotes are printed in italics** todas las notas a pie de página están impresas en cursiva ◇ **hit CTRL I to print the text in italics** apriete CTRL I para imprimir el texto en cursiva ◇ **the headline is printed in italic and underlined** el título viene impreso en cursiva y subrayado

item size /'aɪtəm saɪz/ *noun* tamaño *m* de un ítem; dimensión *f* de una unidad de información

iterate /'ɪtəreɪt/ *noun* rutina *f* iterativa

iteration /ˌɪtə'reɪʃ(ə)n/ *noun* iteración *f*; reiteración *f*

iterative process /ˌɪtərətɪv 'prəʊses/ *noun* proceso *m* iterativo

iterative routine /ˌɪtərətɪv ruː'tiːn/ *noun* rutina *f* iterativa

ITS *abbr* (*invitation to send*) invitación *f* a transmitir

IV /ˌaɪ 'viː/ *noun* vídeo *m* interactivo

J

jabber /'dʒæbə/ *noun* (*continuous random signal*) ruido *m* parásito

jack /dʒæk/, **jack plug** /dʒæk plʌg/ *noun* clavija *f*; conjuntor *m*

jaggies /'dʒægiːz/ *plural noun* (*jagged edges*) dentado *m*; efecto *m* escalera

Java /'dʒɑːvə/ (*trade name for a programming language and program definition developed by Sun Microsystems*) Java *m*

Java Beans /'dʒɑːvə biːnz/ (*trade name for a software system developed by Sun Microsystems*) Java Beans

Java Database Connectivity /ˌdʒɑːvə ˌdeɪtəbeɪs ˌkɒnekˈtɪvɪti/ (*trade name for a set of standard functions*) conectividad *f* de una base de datos Java

JavaScript /'dʒɑːvəskrɪpt/ (*trade name for set of programming commands that can be included within a normal webpage written using HTML commands*) JavaScript

JCL /ˌdʒeɪ siː ˈel/ *noun* lenguaje *m* de control de tareas

jitter /'dʒɪtə/ *noun* 1. (*in a facsimile transmission*) inestabilidad *f*; fluctuación *f*; parpadeo *m* (de la imagen) 2. (*image or screen*) temblar *vi*; parpadear *vi* ◇ **looking at this screen jitter is giving me a headache** el parpadeo de la pantalla me da dolor de cabeza

JK-flip-flop /ˌdʒeɪ keɪ 'flɪp flɒp/ *noun* circuito *m* biestable de tipo JK

job /dʒɒb/ *noun* tarea *f*; trabajo *m* ◇ **the next job to be processed is to sort all the records** la siguiente tarea consiste en clasificar todos los registros

job control file /'dʒɒb kənˌtrəʊl faɪl/ *noun* fichero *m* de control de tareas

job control language /ˌdʒɒb kənˈtrəʊl ˌlæŋgwɪdʒ/ *noun* lenguaje *m* de control de tareas

job control program /'dʒɒb kənˌtrəʊl ˌprəʊgræm/ *noun* programa *m* de control de tareas

job file /'dʒɒb ˌfaɪl/ *noun* fichero *m* de trabajos; fichero *m* de tareas

job mix /'dʒɒb ˌmɪks/ *noun* conjunto *m* de trabajos; conjunto *m* de tareas en curso

job number /dʒɒb 'nʌmbə/ *noun* número *m* de tareas en cola; número *m* de trabajos pendientes

job orientated language /ˌdʒɒb ˌɔːriənteɪtɪd 'læŋgwɪdʒ/ *noun* lenguaje *m* de control de tareas; lenguaje *m* de control de trabajos

job orientated terminal /ˌdʒɒb ˌɔːriənteɪtɪd 'tɜːmɪn(ə)l/ *noun* terminal *m* de aplicación (sobre control de tareas); terminal *m* especializado (sobre control de tareas)

job priority /dʒɒb praɪˈɒrɪti/ *noun* prioridad *f* de una tarea

job processing /dʒɒb ˌprəˈsesɪŋ/ *noun* proceso *m* de tarea

job queue /'dʒɒb ˌkjuː/ *noun* cola *f* de tareas (en espera); tareas *fpl* en cola de espera

job scheduling /'dʒɒb ˌʃedjuːlɪŋ/ *noun* (*arranging the order of jobs to be processed*) planificación *f* de tareas; planificación *f*; gestión *f* de trabajos; reparto *m* de tareas; (*production*) organización *f* de trabajos

job statement control /'dʒɒb ˌsteɪtmənt kənˌtrəʊl/ *noun* control *m* de ejecución de tareas

job step /'dʒɒb ˌstep/ *noun* etapa *f* de un trabajo

job stream /'dʒɒb ˌstriːm/ *noun* (*job queue*) serie *f* de tareas; flujo *m* de trabajos; flujo *m* de tareas

join /dʒɔɪn/ *verb* (*combine pieces of information*) juntar *vt*; empalmar *vt*; unir(se) *vr* ■ *noun* (*logical function*) operación *f* O

joint denial /dʒɔɪnt dɪ'naɪəl/ *noun* (*logical function*) negación *f* conjunta; negación *f* conexa; operación *f* NO-O; NI

Joint Photographic Experts Group /ˌdʒɔɪnt fəʊtəˌgræfɪks 'ekspɜːts gruːp/ *noun* JPEG

journal /'dʒɜːn(ə)l/ *noun* 1. (*record of communications*) diario *m* 2. (*list of changes to a file*) diario *m*; lista *f* de modificaciones ◇ **the modified records were added to the master file and noted in the journal** los registros modificados fueron añadidos al fichero maestro y anotados en el diario de modificaciones

journal file /'dʒɜːn(ə)l faɪl/ *noun* fichero *m* de comunicaciones diarias entre el usuario y el ordenador central

joystick /'dʒɔɪˌstɪk/ *noun* (*device that allows a user to move a cursor*) palanca *f*; mando *m*; 'joystick' *m*

joystick port /'dʒɔɪˌstɪk pɔːt/ *noun* (*socket and interfacing circuit*) conector *m*; puerto *m* para el 'joystick'; puerta *f* para el 'joystick'; puerta *f* para mando de juego ◇ **a joystick port is provided with the home computer** el ordenador familiar está provisto de un mando para juegos

JPEG /'dʒeɪ peg/ *noun* JPEG

JPEG++ /ˌdʒeɪ peg plʌs 'plʌs/ *noun* JPEG++

JScript /'dʒaɪskrɪpt/ (*trade name for a version of JavaScript developed by Microsoft*) Jscript

jukebox /'dʒuːkˌbɒks/ *noun* (*CD-ROM drive*) reproductor *m* de CDs; reproductor *m* de discos automático; gramola *f*

Julian date /'dʒuːliən deɪt/ *noun* fecha *f* juliana

jump /dʒʌmp/ *noun* salto *m*; bifurcación *f* ■ *verb* saltar(se) *vr*

jumper /'dʒʌmpə/ *noun* (*on circuit board*) saltador *m*; puente *m* conector (temporal)

jumper-selectable /ˌdʒʌmpə sɪ'lektəb(ə)l/ *adjective* que puede ser seleccionado; válido como puente conector

jump instruction /'dʒʌmp ɪnˌstrʌkʃən/ *noun* instrucción *f* de salto

jump on zero /ˌdʒʌmp ɒn 'zɪərəʊ/ *verb* efectuar una bifurcación; efectuar una bifurcación (condicional) de cero; bifurcar cuando un registro es cero

jump operation /dʒʌmp ˌɒpə'reɪʃ(ə)n/ *noun* operación *f* de salto; operación *f* de bifurcación

junction /'dʒʌŋkʃən/ *noun* (*connection*) empalme *m*; unión *f*; conexión *f*

junction box /'dʒʌŋkʃən bɒks/ *noun* (*connection of wires*) caja *f* de empalme(s); caja *f* de conexiones; caja *f* de derivación

junction transistor /ˌdʒʌŋkʃən træn'zɪstə/ *noun* transistor *m* bipolar

junk /dʒʌŋk/ *noun* baratija *f*; basura *f* ■ *verb* tirar *vt* ◇ **junk mail** correo *m* basura *or* propaganda *f* sin interés

justification /ˌdʒʌstɪfɪ'keɪʃ(ə)n/ *noun* justificación *f*

justify /'dʒʌstɪˌfaɪ/ *verb* **1.** (*changes of characters in a document*) alinear *vt*; justificar *vt* **2.** (*change or shift in the contents of a computer register*) mover *vt*; justificar *vt*

K

K *symbol* (*represents 1,024 or 210*) K; kilo; (*thousand*) k

K6 (*64-bit processor developed by AMD Corporation*) K6™

Karnaugh map /ˈkɑːnəʊ mæp/ *noun* mapa *m* de Karnaugh ◇ **the prototype was checked for hazards with a Karnaugh map** se comprobó si el prototipo tenía riesgos mediante un mapa de Karnaugh

Kbps /ˌkeɪ biː piː ˈes/ *noun* kilobits *mpl* por segundo

Kermit /ˈkɜːmɪt/ *noun* (*file transfer protocol*) Kermit

kern /kɜːn/ *verb* (*adjust space between letters*) reducir *vt*; ajustar el espacio entre dos caracteres ◇ **we have kerned 'T' and 'o' so they are closer together** hemos reducido el espacio entre la 'T' y la 'o' para que estén más juntas

kernel /ˈkɜːn(ə)l/ *noun* (*essential instruction routines*) núcleo *m* (del sistema); corazón *m*; meollo *m* ◇ **graphics kernel system (GKS)** sistema *m* para entrada/salida de gráficos

key /kiː/ *noun* **1.** (*on a keyboard*) tecla *f* **2.** (*important object*) clave *f* **3.** (*numbers to encrypt or decrypt a message*) clave *f* de un código **4.** (*identification code*) clave *f* de identificación; palabra *f* clave ■ *verb* (*to activate a key*) accionar una tecla ◇ **character key** tecla *f* de carácter; tecla de carácter ◇ **key force** presión *f* (necesaria) para accionar una tecla ◇ **key management** gestión *f* de la clave ◇ **key travel** recorrido *f* de una tecla (para activar su función) ◇ **shift key** tecla de mayúsculas ◇ **there are 84 keys on the keyboard** hay 84 teclas en el teclado ◇ **to key in** introducir (un texto *or* datos) con *or* mediante el teclado *or* teclear *or* mecanografiar ◇ **type this key into the machine, that will decode the last message** teclee esta clave en la máquina; eso descodificará el último mensaje

keyboard /ˈkiːbɔːd/ *noun* teclado *m* ■ *verb* introducir datos en un ordenador ◇ **it was cheaper to have the manuscript keyboarded by another company** resultaba más barato dejar que otra compañía pasara el manuscrito al ordenador ◇ **keyboard scan** (*method of control*) control *m* del teclado

'…the main QWERTY typing area is in the centre of the keyboard with the 10 function keys on the left' [*Personal Computer World*]

keyboard contact bounce /ˌkiːbɔːd ˌkɒntækt ˈbaʊns/ *noun* rebote *m* de una tecla del teclado

keyboard encoder /ˈkiːbɔːd ɪnˌkəʊdə/ *noun* codificador *m* de teclas; codificador *m* de teclado

keyboarder /ˈkiːbɔːdə/ *noun* operador *m* de teclado que introduce información en un ordenador

keyboarding /ˈkiːbɔːdɪŋ/ *noun* introducción *f* de datos (mediante un teclado) ◇ **the cost of keyboarding is calculated in keystrokes per hour** el coste de la introducción de datos se calcula por el número de pulsaciones por hora

keyboard layout /ˈkiːbɔːd ˌleɪaʊt/ *noun* disposición *f* de las teclas de un teclado

keyboard overlay /ˈkiːbɔːd ˌəʊvəleɪ/ *noun* plantilla *f* con las funciones del teclado; menú *m* de ayuda del teclado

keyboard send/receive /ˌkiːbɔːd send rɪ ˈsiːv/ *noun* terminal *m* emisor/receptor con teclado

keyboard to disk entry /ˌkiːbɔːd tə ˈdɪsk ˌentri/ *noun* introducción *f* directa en un disco mediante el teclado; registro *m* directo sobre disco mediante un teclado

key click /ˈkiː klɪk/ *noun* clic *m* de tecla

key combination /ˈkiː ˌkɒmbɪneɪʃ(ə)n/ *noun* combinación *f* de teclas; acceso *m* directo

key escrow /ˌkiː ˈeskrəʊ/ *noun* depósito *m* de la clave

key feature /ˌkiː ˈfiːtʃə/ *noun* característica *f* principal; característica *f* más importante ◇ **the key features of this system are: 20Mb of formatted storage with an access time of 60ms** las principales características de este sistema son: 20 Mb de memoria formateada con un tiempo de acceso de 60 ms

key field /ˌkiː ˈfiːld/ *noun* campo *m* clave

key matrix /ˌkiː ˈmeɪtrɪks/ *noun* (*keyboard*) matriz *f* del teclado

key number /ˈkiː ˌnʌmbə/ *noun* código *m* numérico de una tecla

key overlay /ˌkiː ˈəʊvəleɪ/ *noun* menú *m* de ayuda con la función de cada tecla ◇ **without the key overlay, I would never remember which function key does what** sin un menú de ayuda, nunca recordaría qué es lo que hace cada tecla de función

keypad /ˈkiːˌpæd/ *noun* teclado *m* compacto; teclado *m* numérico ◇ **you can use the numeric keypad to enter the figures** usted puede utilizar el teclado numérico para introducir las cifras

'…it uses a six button keypad to select the devices and functions' [*Byte*]

key punch /'kiː pʌntʃ/ *noun* perforadora *f*; perforación *f*

key rollover /ˌkiː 'rəʊləʊvə/ *noun* teclado *m* con memoria intermedia; teclado *m* rápido

key shortcut /ˌkiː 'ʃɔːtkʌt/ *noun* acceso *m* directo; combinación *f* de teclas

keystone distortion /ˌkiːstəʊn dɪ'stɔːʃ(ə)n/ *noun* distorsión *f* trapezoidal

key strip /'kiː strɪp/ *noun* adhesivo *m* identificador de la función de una tecla

keystroke /'kiːstrəʊk/ *noun* pulsación *f*

keystroke count /'kiːstrəʊk ˌkaʊnt/ *noun* número *m* de pulsaciones

keystroke verification /ˌkiːstrəʊk ˌverɪfɪ 'keɪʃ(ə)n/ *noun* control *m* de teclas; control *m* de pulsaciones

key terminal /ˌkiː 'tɜːmɪn(ə)l/ *noun* terminal *m* principal

key-to-disk /ˌkiː tə 'dɪsk/ *noun* registro *m* directo sobre disco

keyword /'kiːwɜːd/ *noun* (*command word*) orden *f*; instrucción *f*; (*important word in title or text*) palabra *f* clave ◇ **computer is a keyword in IT** la palabra 'ordenador' es una palabra clave en la tecnología de la información

KHz *abbr* (*kilohertz*) kilohercio *m* (kHz)

kill /kɪl/ *verb* (*file or program*) destruir *vt*; eliminar *vt*; suprimir *vt*

kilo /'kɪləʊ/ *prefix* **1.** (*1,024 units, equal to 2¹⁰*) kilo *m* **2.** kilo *m* ◇ **kiloword (KW)** kilo-palabra *m*

kilobaud /'kɪləbɔːd/ *noun* kilobaudio *m*

kilobit /'kɪləbɪt/ *noun* kilobit *m*

kilo bits per second /ˌkiːləʊ bɪts pɜː 'sekənd/ *noun* kilobits por segundo

kilobyte /'kɪləʊˌbaɪt/ *noun* kilo-byte *m* (KB); kilo-octeto *m* (Ko)

kilohertz /'kɪləhɜːts/ *noun* kilohercio *m* (kHz)

kilo instructions per second /ˌkɪləʊ ɪn ˌstrʌkʃənz pɜː 'sekənd/ *noun* mil instrucciones *fpl* por segundo

Kilostream /'kɪləstriːm/ (*trade name for a leased line connection supplied by British Telecom*) Kilostream

kiloword /'kɪləwɜːd/ *noun* K palabras; kilopalabra *f*

kiosk /'kiːɒsk/ *noun* (*information*) quiosco *m* ◇ **kiosk mode** (*in a web navigator*) modo *m* de quiosco

KIPS /ˌkeɪ aɪ piː 'es/ *noun* mil instrucciones *fpl* por segundo

Klamath /'klæmæθ/ (*Intel Pentium Pro processor*) Klamath™

kludge, kluge *noun informal* **1.** (*software or hardware*) parche *m*; solución *f* improvisada **2.** (*software or hardware*) equipo *m* sólo para demostraciones

kluged /kluːdʒd/ *adjective* reparado, -a temporalmente

knob /nɒb/ *noun* botón *m*; mando *m* (de regulación) ◇ **the brightness can be regulated by turning a knob at the back of the monitor** el brillo puede regularse al girar un mando que está en la parte posterior del monitor ◇ **turn the on or off knob** girar el mando de encedido/apagado *or* conectado/desconectado

knowledge base /'nɒlɪdʒ beɪs/ *noun* banco *m* de conocimientos

knowledge-based system /ˌnɒlɪdʒ beɪst 'sɪstəm/ *noun* sistema *m* basado en el conocimiento; sistema *m* experto

knowledge engineering /'nɒlɪdʒ ˌendʒɪnɪərɪŋ/ *noun* ingeniería *f* del conocimiento

Kodak PhotoCD /ˌkəʊdæk 'fəʊtəʊ siː ˌdiː/ PhotoCD™

L

L1 cache /ˌel ˈwʌn ˌkæʃ/ *noun* caché *m* de nivel 1

L2 cache /ˌel ˈtuː ˌkæʃ/ *noun* caché *m* de nivel 2

label /ˈleɪb(ə)l/ *noun* **1.** (*in a computer program*) etiqueta *f*; rótulo *m*; identificador *m* **2.** (*piece of paper*) etiqueta *f*; (*for quality*) etiqueta *f* de calidad ■ *verb* (*to put a label on a product*) producir una etiqueta ◇ **BASIC uses many program labels such as line numbers** los programas en lenguaje BASIC utilizan numerosas etiquetas de programa tales como la numeración de las líneas ◇ **internal label** etiqueta interna (de identificación en soporte magnético)

label field /ˈleɪb(ə)l fiːld/ *noun* campo *m* de etiqueta; campo *m* de identificación

labelling /ˈleɪb(ə)lɪŋ/ *noun* **1.** (*on a product*) etiquetado *m*; (*printing labels*) impresión *f* de etiquetas **2.** impresión *f* de etiquetas ◇ **the word-processor has a special utility allowing simple and rapid labelling** el tratamiento de textos tiene una utilidad especial que permite una simple y rápida impresión de etiquetas

label printer /ˈleɪb(ə)l ˌprɪntə/ *noun* impresora *f* de etiquetas

label record /ˈleɪb(ə)l ˌrekɔːd/ *noun* registro *m* de etiquetas; registro *m* de identificadores

lag /læg/ *noun* (*of signal*) retardo *m*; desfase *m* ◇ **time lag is noticeable on international phone calls** se percibe un desfase horario en las llamadas telefónicas internacionales

LAN, lan *noun* red *f* de área local ◇ **LAN Manager™** (*MicroSoft network operating system*) LAN Manager™ ◇ **LAN Server™** (*IBM network operating system*) LAN Server™

'The opportunities to delete and destroy data are far greater on our LAN than in the days when we had a mainframe. PC people are culturally different from mainframe people. You really don't think about security problems when you can physically lock your system up in a closet.' [*Computing*]

landing zone /ˈlændɪŋ zəʊn/ *noun* (*area of a hard disk which does not carry data*) zona *f* de aparcamiento de la cabeza de lectura

landline /ˈlæn(d)ˌlaɪn/ *noun* (*cable*) cable *m* terrestre; línea *f* terrestre

landscape /ˈlændskeɪp/ *noun* (*page where the longest edge is horizontal*) paisaje *m*; (*horizontal page setup*) apaisado *or* -a; orientación *f* horizontal (de la página)

language /ˈlæŋgwɪdʒ/ *noun* (*spoken or written*) lenguaje *m*; lengua *f*; idioma *m* ◇ **foreign language** lengua extranjera *or* idioma extranjero ◇ **he speaks several European languages** habla varios idiomas europeos

language assembler /ˈlæŋgwɪdʒ əˌsemblə/ *noun* programa *m* ensamblador; lenguaje *m* ensamblador

language compiler /ˈlæŋgwɪdʒ kəmˌpaɪlə/ *noun* (*encoding of a source program*) compilador *m* (de un lenguaje); compilador *m*; lenguaje *m* compilador

language interpreter /ˈlæŋgwɪdʒ ɪnˌtɜːprɪtə/ *noun* programa *m* intérprete; lenguaje *m* interpretador

language processor /ˌlæŋgwɪdʒ ˌprəʊsesə/ *noun* procesador *m* de lenguaje

language rules /ˈlæŋgwɪdʒ ruːlz/ *plural noun* sintaxis *f*; reglas *fpl* de un lenguaje

language support environment /ˌlæŋgwɪdʒ səˈpɔːt ɪnˌvaɪərənmənt/ *noun* entorno *m* de soporte de un lenguaje

language translation /ˈlæŋgwɪdʒ trænsˌleɪʃ(ə)n/ *noun* traducción *f* de un lenguaje a otro

language translator /ˈlæŋgwɪdʒ trænsˌleɪtə/ *noun* (*programa*) traductor *m* (de un lenguaje)

LAN Manager /ˈlæn ˌmænɪdʒə/ (*trade name for a network operating system developed for the PC by Microsoft*) LAN Manager™

LAN server /læn ˈsɜːvə/ *noun* (*IBM network operating system*) servidor *m* de red local

LAN Server /ˈlæn ˌsɜːvə/ (*trade name for a network operating system developed for the PC by Microsoft*) LAN Server™

lap /læp/ *noun* (*overlap*) solapamiento *m*; traslapo *m*

LAP /ˌel eɪ ˈpiː/ *noun* (*CCITT standard protocol*) estándar *m* LAP

LAP-B /læp biː/ *noun* rutina *f* de instalación LAP-B

LAP-M /læp em/ *noun* protocolo *m* LAP-M

laptop /ˈlæptɒp/, **laptop computer** /ˌlæptɒp kəmˈpjuːtə/ *noun* ordenador *m* portátil; laptop *m*

'Michael Business Systems has provided research company BMRB with 240 Toshiba laptop computers in a deal valued at £300,000. The deal includes a three-year maintenance contract.' [*Computing*]

large model /lɑːdʒ ˈmɒd(ə)l/ *noun* (*memory model in an Intel processor*) modelo *m* grande

large-scale /ˈlɑːdʒ skeɪl/ *adjective* a gran escala

large-scale computer /ˌlɑːdʒ skeɪl kəm
'pjuːtə/ *noun* ordenador *m* grande; ordenador *m* a
gran escala

large-scale integration /ˌlɑːdʒ skeɪl ˌɪntɪ
'greɪʃ(ə)n/ *noun* integración *f* a gran escala

laser /'leɪzə/ *noun* (*Light Amplification by Stim-
ulated Emission of Radiation*) láser *m* ◇ **laser
beam communications** comunicaciones *fpl* por
rayos láser ◇ **laser beam recording (LBR)** grabación *f* por rayos láser

laser disc /'leɪzə dɪsk/ *noun* disco *m* láser

laser emulsion storage /ˌleɪzə ɪˌmʌlʃ(ə)n
'stɔːrɪdʒ/ *noun* memoria *f* de escritura láser

LaserJet /'leɪzədʒet/ (*Hewlett Packard laser
printer*) impresora *f* LaserJet de Hewlett Pack-
ard™

laser printer /'leɪzə ˌprɪntə/ *noun* impresora *f*
láser

LaserWriter /'leɪzəraɪtə/ (*Apple laser printer*)
impresora *f* LaserWriter de Apple™

last in first out /ˌlɑːst ɪn ˌfɜːst 'aʊt/ *adjective*
último en entrar primero en salir; (método) LIFO

last in last out /ˌlɑːst ɪn lɑːst 'aʊt/ *adjective*
(método) LILO

latch /lætʃ/ *noun* (*electronic component that
maintains an output value*) pestillo *m*; dispositivo
m de bloqueo

latency /'leɪt(ə)nsi/ *noun* periodo *m* de latencia;
tiempo *m* de latencia

launch /lɔːntʃ/ *noun* (*of new product*) lanzamiento *m* ■ *verb* **1.** (*to introduce a new product to
market*) lanzar *vt*; (*to send a satellite into orbit*)
poner en órbita **2.** (*to start a program*) iniciar *vt*;
ejecutar *vt* ◇ **the launch date for the network
will be September** la fecha de lanzamiento de la
red es el mes de septiembre ◇ **the launch of the
new PC has been put back six months** el lanzamiento del nuevo ordenador personal ha sido retrasado seis meses ◇ **you launch the word-processor by double-clicking on this icon** se inicia
el tratamiento de textos al pulsar dos veces sobre
este icono

layer /'leɪə/ *noun* (*division of space*) capa *f*;
(*ISO/OSI standards*) capa *f* de protocolo

layered /'leɪəd/ *adjective* estratificador *or* -a;
dispuesto, -a en capas

layout /'leɪaʊt/ *noun* **1.** (*outline or design*) esquema *m*; esbozo *m*; diseño *m* **2.** (*distribution*) especificaciones *fpl* de la presentación de datos ◇
**the design team is working on the layouts for
the new magazine** el equipo de diseño está realizando la maquetación de la nueva revista =

LCD /ˌel siː 'diː/ *noun* (*display that uses liquid
crystals*) pantalla *f* de cristal líquido; representación *f* visual por cristal líquido; visualizador *m* de
cristal líquido

LCD screen /ˌel siː 'diː skriːn/ *noun* pantalla *f*
de cristal líquido

LCD shutter printer /ˌel siː ˌdiː 'ʃʌtə/ *noun*
impresora *f* por transmisión LCD

LCP /ˌel siː 'piː/ *noun* protocolo *m* de control de
enlaces

lead /liːd/ *noun* (*wire*) conductor *m*; cable *m*;
alambre *m* de conducción; hilo *m* conductor

leader /'liːdə/ *noun* (*beginning of the reel*) cabecera *f* de cinta magnética

leader record /'liːdə ˌrekɔːd/ *noun* registro *m*
de cabeza

leading /'liːdɪŋ/ *noun* (*space between lines*)
interlínea *f*; interlineado *m*

leading edge /'liːdɪŋ edʒ/ *noun* (*first edge of
a punched card*) borde *m* de guía; borde *m* de entrada; borde *m* anterior

leading zero /ˌliːdɪŋ 'zɪərəʊ/ *noun* cero *m* de
cabeza

leaf /liːf/ *noun* (*of paper*) hoja *f*; (*of book*) página
f; (*in a tree structure*) elemento *m* final de una arborescencia

leap-frog test /'liːp frɒg ˌtest/ *noun* prueba *f*
interna total de lectura/escritura; comprobación *f*
interna total de lectura/escritura

learning curve /'lɜːnɪŋ kɜːv/ *noun* (*graph of
how someone can acquire knowledge*) curva *f* de
aprendizaje

lease /liːs/ *noun* contrato *m* de arrendamiento ■
verb arrendar *vt*; alquilar *vt* ◇ **leased circuit** circuito *m* arrendado ◇ **the company has a policy
of only using leased equipment** la política de
la empresa es utilizar sólo material alquilado ◇
the company leases all its computers la empresa alquila todos sus ordenadores

leased line /'liːsd ˌlaɪn/ *noun* (*communication
channel*) línea *f* arrendada; línea *f* especializada;
circuito *m* alquilado

least cost design /ˌliːst kɒst dɪ'zaɪn/ *noun*
diseño *m* más económico; diseño *m* de menor
coste ◇ **the budget is only £1,000, we need the
least cost design for the new circuit** el presupuesto es de sólo 1.000 libras esterlinas; necesitamos el diseño más económico para el nuevo circuito

least recently used algorithm /ˌliːst
ˌriːs(ə)ntli juːzd 'ælgəˌrɪð(ə)m/ *noun* algoritmo
m usado menos recientemente; algoritmo *m* de la
página menos utilizada recientemente

least significant bit /ˌliːst sɪgˌnɪfɪkənt 'bɪt/
noun bit *m* menos significativo

least significant digit /ˌliːst sɪgˌnɪfɪkənt
'dɪdʒɪt/ *noun* dígito *m* menos significativo

LED /ˌel iː 'diː/ *noun* diodo *m* electroluminesc-
cente; diodo *m* emisor de luz

LED printer /ˌel iː ˌdiː 'prɪntə/ *noun* impresora
f por diodos; impresora *f* LED

left-handed mouse /ˌeft ˌhændɪd 'maʊs/
noun (*configuration of a mouse so that the function of the two buttons are reversed*) ratón *m* zurdo; ratón *m* (configurado) para una persona zurda

left justification /left ˌdʒʌstɪfɪ'keɪʃ(ə)n/
noun justificación *f* a la izquierda

left justify /left 'dʒʌstɪˌfaɪ/ *verb* (*printing or binary number*) (instrucción de) justificación a la
izquierda; (instrucción de) justificar a la izquierda

left shift /ˌleft 'ʃɪft/ *noun* (efectuar un) desplazamiento *m* hacia la izquierda

leg /leg/ *noun* tramo *m*; rama *f*

legal /'liːg(ə)l/ *adjective* (*acceptable within language syntax rules*) legal; válido *or* -a; autorizado *or* -a

length /leŋθ/ *noun* longitud *f*

length of filename /ˌleŋθ əv 'faɪlneɪm/ *noun* longitud *f* del nombre de un fichero

level /'lev(ə)l/ *noun* (*of electrical signal*) nivel *m*; (*of sound*) volumen *m* ◇ **turn the sound level down, it's far too loud** baje el volumen

Level A /'lev(ə)l eɪ/ *noun* nivel *m* A

Level B /'lev(ə)l biː/ *noun* nivel *m* B

Level C /'lev(ə)l siː/ *noun* nivel *m* C

lexical analysis /ˌleksɪk(ə)l ə'næləsɪs/ *noun* análisis *m* léxico

LF *abbr* (*line feed*) avance *m* de línea; salto *m* de línea

library /'laɪbrəri/ *noun* **1.** (*of files, books, etc.*) biblioteca *f* **2.** (*of programs*) biblioteca *f* **3.** (*of computer routines*) biblioteca *f* ◇ **he has a large library of computer games** tiene una enorme biblioteca de juegos de ordenador ◇ **look up the bibliographical details in the library catalogue** busque las referencias bibliográficas en el catálogo de la biblioteca ◇ **the editors have checked all the references in the local library** los editores han verificado todas las referencias en la biblioteca local ◇ **the square root function is already in the library program** la función de la raíz cuadrada ya está en el programa de biblioteca

library function /'laɪbrəri ˌfʌŋkʃən/ *noun* función *f* (de) biblioteca

library program /'laɪbrəri ˌprəʊgræm/ *noun* programa *m* de biblioteca

library routine /'laɪbrəri ruːˌtiːn/ *noun* rutina *f* de biblioteca

library subroutine /ˌlaɪbrəri 'sʌbruːtiːn/ *noun* subrutina *f* de biblioteca

library track /'laɪbrəri træk/ *noun* pista *f* de referencia

licence /'laɪs(ə)ns/ *noun* permiso *m*; licencia *f* ◇ **this software is manufactured under licence** este software está fabricado bajo licencia

licence agreement /'laɪs(ə)ns əˌgriːmənt/ *noun* acuerdo *m* de licencia

lifetime /'laɪftaɪm/ *noun* (*time during which a device is useful*) duración *f* de vida ◇ **this new computer has a four-year lifetime** este nuevo ordenador tiene una duración de vida de cuatro años

LIFO /'laɪfəʊ/ *adjective* último en entrar primero en salir; LIFO

lifter /'lɪftə/ *noun* levantador *m* de cinta; levantador *m* de banda

light /laɪt/ *noun* luz *f* ◇ **coherent light** luz coherente ◇ **light conduit** conductor *m* de luz ◇ **light guide** guía *m&f* de luz *or* guía óptico, -a ◇ **the VDU should not be placed under a bright light** la pantalla no debería colocarse bajo una luz demasiado intensa ◇ **ultra-violet light (UV light)** luz ultravioleta *or* radiación *f* ultravioleta ◇ **visible light** luz visible

light-emitting diode /ˌlaɪt ɪˌmɪtɪŋ 'daɪəʊd/ *noun* diodo *m* electroluminescente; diodo *m* emisor de luz

light pen /'laɪt pen/ *noun* lápiz *m* fotosensible; lápiz *m* óptico

lightweight /'laɪtweɪt/ *adjective* ligero *or* -a ◇ **a lightweight computer which can easily fit into a suitcase** un ordenador ligero que pueda fácilmente caber en una maleta

lightweight directory access protocol /ˌlaɪtweɪt daɪ'rekt(ə)ri ˌækses ˌprəʊtəkɒl/ *noun* protocolo *m* ligero de acceso a directorios

LILO /'laɪləʊ/ *adjective* LILO

limited distance modem /ˌlɪmɪtɪd ˌdɪstəns 'məʊdem/ *noun* módem *m* para red local; módem *m* de distancia de transmisión limitada

limiter /'lɪmɪtə/ *noun* (*electricity*) limitador *m*; fusible *m*

limiting resolution /ˌlɪmɪtɪŋ ˌrezə'luːʃ(ə)n/ *noun* definición *f* límite

limits /'lɪmɪts/ *noun* (*for numbers in a computer*) límites *mpl*

line /laɪn/ *noun* **1.** (*cable*) cable *m*; renglón *m* **2.** (*of text*) línea *f*; (*printing*) renglón *m* **3.** (*one trace by the electron picture beam on a television screen*) renglón *m* **4.** (*row of characters on screen or page*) línea *f* **5.** (*row of commands*) línea *f* de programa ◇ **line extender** (*in cable TV*) unidad *f* de extensión de una línea ◇ **line impedance** impedancia *f* de línea ◇ **line load** tráfico *m*; carga *f* de una línea ◇ **line terminator** (*connection*) dispositivo *m* de final de línea ◇ **line transient** sobretensiones *fpl* transitorias de línea

'…straight lines are drawn by clicking the points on the screen where you would like the line to start and finish' [*Personal Computer World*]

line adapter /laɪn ə'dæptə/ *noun* adaptador *m* de línea

line analyser /'laɪn ˌænəlaɪzə/ *noun* analizador *m* de línea

linear /'lɪniə/ *adjective* lineal; secuencial ◇ **linear array** (*antenna*) ordenamiento *m* lineal ◇ **linear function** función *f* lineal ◇ **linear integrated circuit** circuito *m* integrado lineal ◇ **the expression Y = 10 + 5X − 3W is a linear function** la expresión Y = 10 + 5X − 3W es una función lineal ◇ **the expression Y = (10 + 5X2) is not a linear function** la expresión Y = (10 + 5X2) no es una función lineal

linearity /ˌlɪni'ærɪti/ *noun* linealidad *f*

linear list /'lɪniə lɪst/ *noun* lista *f* secuencial; lista *f* lineal

linear program /ˌlɪniə 'prəʊgræm/ *noun* programa *m* lineal

linear programming /ˌlɪniə 'prəʊgræmɪŋ/ *noun* programación *f* lineal

linear search /ˌlɪniə 'sɜːtʃ/ *noun* búsqueda *f* secuencial; búsqueda *f* lineal

linear video /ˌlɪniə 'vɪdiəʊ/ *noun* vídeo *m* lineal

line break *noun* corte *m* de líneas

line busy tone /ˌlaɪn 'bɪzi ˌtəʊn/ *noun* señal *f* de línea ocupada

line communications /laɪn kəˌmjuːnɪ'keɪʃ(ə)ns/ *plural noun* comunicaciones *fpl* por cable; comunicaciones *fpl* por línea

line conditioning /laɪn kən'dɪʃ(ə)nɪŋ/ *noun* mantenimiento *m* de la línea

line control /laɪn kən'trəʊl/ *noun* (*communication channel*) instrucciones *fpl* de línea; control *m* de canal; instrucción *f* de línea; protocolo *m* de control de línea

line doubling /'laɪn ˌdʌb(ə)lɪŋ/ *noun* conversión *f* de barrido

line drawing /'laɪn ˌdrɔːɪŋ/ *noun* dibujo *m* lineal

line driver /laɪn 'draɪvə/ *noun* amplificador *m* de señal

line editor /laɪn 'edɪtə/ *noun* (*of source program*) editor *m* de línea; (*or source program*) editor *m* de línea; (*of source program*) editor *m* línea a línea

line ending /laɪn 'endɪŋ/ *noun* carácter *m* de final de línea; símbolo *m* de final de línea

line feed /'laɪn fiːd/ *noun* avance *m* de línea

line flyback /'laɪn ˌflaɪbæk/ *noun* retorno *m* de línea

line frequency /laɪn 'friːkwənsi/ *noun* frecuencia *f* (de barrido) de líneas; frecuencia *f* de líneas

line gremlin /laɪn 'gremlɪn/ *noun* error *m* en la línea; pérdida *f* de transmisión inexplicable

line input /ˌlaɪn 'ɪnpʊt/ *noun* (instrucción de) validación *f* de línea

line length /'laɪn leŋθ/ *noun* (*horizontal display of characters*) longitud *f* de una línea; longitud *f* de línea; número *m* de caracteres por línea

line level /laɪn 'lev(ə)l/ *noun* nivel *m* de transmisión de una línea

line noise /'laɪn nɔɪz/ *noun* ruido *m* de circuito; ruido *m* de línea

line number /laɪn 'nʌmbə/ *noun* número *m* de línea (de programa)

line printer /'laɪn ˌprɪntə/ *noun* impresora *f* por líneas

line spacing /laɪn 'speɪsɪŋ/ *noun* interlínea *m*; interlineado *m*

line speed /'laɪn spiːd/ *noun* velocidad *f*; rendimiento *m* de una línea

lines per minute /ˌlaɪnz pɜː 'mɪnət/ *noun* líneas por minuto

line width /'laɪn ˌwɪdθ/ *noun* longitud *f* de línea

link /lɪŋk/ *noun* **1.** (*communication path*) enlace *m*; vínculo *m*; (*in Latin America*) liga *f* **2.** (*software routine*) vínculo *m*; enlace *m* ■ *verb* (*with interface*) enlazar *vt*; conectar *vt* ◇ **link loss** pérdida *f* de enlace *or* de transmisión ◇ **satellite link** enlace *or* transmisión *f* por satélite ◇ **the two computers are linked** los dos ordenadores están conectados ◇ **to transmit faster, you can use the direct link with the mainframe** para una

transmisión más rápida, se puede utilizar un enlace directo con el ordenador principal

link access protocol /ˌlɪŋk 'ækses ˌprəʊtəkɒl/ *noun* procedimiento *m* de acceso a enlace

linkage /'lɪŋkɪdʒ/ *noun* (*of devices*) acoplamiento *m*; (*for program*) creación *f* de enlaces

linkage editing /'lɪŋkɪdʒ ˌedɪtɪŋ/ *noun* (*combining separate programs together*) editor *m*; montaje *m*; montador *m* de enlaces; edición *f* de enlaces

linkage software /'lɪŋkɪdʒ ˌsɒftweə/ *noun* generador *m* de enlaces ◇ **graphics and text are joined without linkage software** los gráficos y el texto se unen sin el programa generador de enlaces

link control procedure /ˌlɪŋk kən'trəʊl prəˌsiːdʒə/ *noun* protocolo *m* de control de enlaces

link control protocol /ˌlɪŋk kən'trəʊl ˌprəʊtəkɒl/ *noun* estándar *m* LAP

linked list /ˌlɪŋkd 'lɪst/ *noun* lista *f* encadenada; lista *f* enlazada

linked object /lɪŋkd 'ɒbdʒekt/ *noun* objeto *m* vinculado; objeto *m* enlazado

linked subroutine /ˌlɪŋkɪd ˌsʌbruː'tiːn/ *noun* subrutina *f* enlazada

linking /'lɪŋkɪŋ/ *noun* (*merging of small programs*) enlace *m*; encadenamiento *m*; conexión *f*; ensamblaje *m* ◇ **intersegment linking** enlace *or* conexión entre segmentos

linking information /'lɪŋkɪŋ ˌɪnfəmeɪʃ(ə)n/ *noun* (instrucción de) insertar información (de una aplicación a otra)

linking loader /'lɪŋkɪŋ ˌləʊdə/ *noun* cargador *m* de enlaces

link trials /lɪŋk 'traɪəlz/ *plural noun* pruebas *fpl* de control de enlaces

Linux /'lɪnəks/ (*trade name for a version of the UNIX operating system originally developed by Linus Torvalds*) Linux

liquid crystal display /ˌlɪkwɪd ˌkrɪst(ə)l dɪs 'pleɪ/ *noun* (*for watches, calculators and digital displays*) pantalla *f* de cristal líquido; representación *f* visual por cristal líquido; visualizador *m* de cristal líquido

liquid crystal display shutter printer /ˌlɪkwɪd ˌkrɪstəl dɪˌspleɪ 'ʃʌtə ˌprɪntə/ *noun* impresora *f* por transmisión LCD

LISP /lɪsp/ *noun* lenguaje *m* LISP

list /lɪst/ *noun* lista *f* ■ *verb* (*to print or display information*) hacer una lista; enumerar *vt*; editar en forma de lista ◇ **to list a program** hacer una lista de (las líneas de instrucción de) un programa

listing /'lɪstɪŋ/ *noun* listado *m*; lista *f*

listing paper /'lɪstɪŋ ˌpeɪpə/ *noun* papel *m* de listado; papel *m* continuo

list processing /'lɪst ˌprəʊsesɪŋ/ *noun* **1.** proceso *m* de listas **2.** lenguaje *m* LISP

literal /'lɪt(ə)rəl/ *noun* **1.** (*operand*) literal *m* **2.** (*printing error*) errata *f*

literal operand /'lɪt(ə)rəl ˌɒpərænd/ *noun* operando *m* literal

lithium-Ion battery /ˌlɪθiəm ˈaɪən ˌbæt(ə)ri/ *noun* batería *f* de ion-litio

liveware /ˈlaɪvweə/ *noun* personal *m* informático

LLC /ˌel el ˈsiː/ *noun* control *m* lógico de enlaces

load /ləʊd/ *verb* (*impedance*) cargar ◇ **load impedance** impedancia *f* de carga ◇ **load life** tiempo *m* de descarga ◇ **matched load** carga equilibrada

'…this windowing system is particularly handy when you want to load or save a file or change directories' [*Byte*]

load and go /ˌləʊd ən ˈgəʊ/ *noun* programa *m* de cargar y ejecutar (automática)

load and run /ˌləʊd ən ˈrʌn/ *noun* programa *m* de cargar y ejecutar (automática)

loader /ˈləʊdə/ *noun* (*program*) cargador *m*

load high /ˈləʊd ˌhaɪ/ *verb* instrucción LOAD HIGH; LH *vt*

loading /ˈləʊdɪŋ/ *noun* (*of file*) carga *f* ◇ **loading can be a long process** cargar (un programa) puede ser un proceso largo

load point /ˈləʊd pɔɪnt/ *noun* (*start of a recording section*) punto *m* de inicio del registro

load sharing /ˈləʊd ˌʃeərɪŋ/ *noun* participación *f* en las tareas

local /ˈləʊk(ə)l/ *adjective* **1.** (*used in a certain section of a computer program*) local **2.** (*system with limited access*) local; localizado *or* -a **3.** (*physically attached and close to the controlling computer*) local ◇ **local area wireless network (LAWN)** red inalámbrica de área local ◇ **local exchange** (*telephony*) central *f* urbana *or* estación *f* local ◇ **the fastest expansion cards fit into this local bus connector** las tarjetas de extensión más rápidas encajan en este conector de enlace local

local area network /ˌləʊk(ə)l ˌeəriə ˈnetwɜːk/ *noun* red *f* de área local

local area network server /ˌləʊk(ə)l ˌeəriə ˈnetwɜːk ˌsɜːvə/ *noun* servidor *m* de red local

local bridge /ˈləʊk(ə)l brɪdʒ/ *noun* puente *m* local ◇ **we use a local bridge to link the two LANs in the office** utilizamos un puente local para conectar dos redes locales en la oficina

local bus /ˌləʊk(ə)l ˈbʌs/ *noun* enlace *m* local; bus *m* local ◇ **the fastest expansion cards fit into this local bus connector** las tarjetas de extensión más rápidas encajan en este conector de enlace local

local declaration /ˌləʊk(ə)l ˌdeklə'reɪʃ(ə)n/ *noun* declaración *f* de una variable local

local drive /ˈləʊk(ə)l draɪv/ *noun* lector *m* (de disquetes) local

local format storage /ˌləʊk(ə)l ˌfɔːmæt ˈstɔːrɪdʒ/ *noun* memoria *f* de formato local; memoria *f* en curso

local memory /ˌləʊk(ə)l ˈmem(ə)ri/ *noun* memoria *f* local

local mode /ˈləʊk(ə)l məʊd/ *noun* modo *m* local

local printer /ˌləʊk(ə)l ˈprɪntə/ *noun* impresora *f* local; impresora *f* no compartida

LocalTalk /ˈləʊkəltɔːk/ (*cabling system in AppleTalk network*) red *f* LocalTalk™

local variable /ˌləʊk(ə)l ˈveəriəb(ə)l/ *noun* variable *f* local

locate /ləʊˈkeɪt/ *verb* **1.** (*place*) encontrar(se) *vr*; localizar *vt*; identificar *vt*; situar *vt* **2.** (*find*) encontrar(se) *vr*; (*fault*) localizar *vt*; (*find*) identificar *vt*; situar *vt* ◇ **have you managed to locate the programming fault?** ¿ha conseguido localizar el error de programación? ◇ **the computer is located in the main office building** el ordenador se encuentra en el edificio de la oficina principal

location /ləʊˈkeɪʃ(ə)n/ *noun* (*number or absolute address*) emplazamiento *m*; posición *f*; ubicación *f* (de la memoria) ◇ **location shots** exteriores *mpl* (de una película) *or* ◇ **on location** (*filming*) (rodaje) en los exteriores ◇ **the programme was shot on location in Spain** el programa se rodó en España

lock /lɒk/ *verb* (*system or file*) bloquear *vt*; reservar *vt*; cerrar *vt* ◇ **locking a file** bloquear (el acceso a) un fichero

lockdown /ˈlɒkdəʊn/ *noun* bloqueo *m*

lockout /ˈlɒkaʊt/ *noun* (*over a network*) bloqueo *m*; cierre *m* de línea ◇ **receiver lockout system** (*radiocommunications*) sistema *m* de bloqueo de receptores

lock up /ˌlɒk ˈʌp/ *noun* (*of computer*) bloquear(se); plantar(se)

log /lɒg/ *noun* (*computer science*) registro *m*; entrada *f* (en un registro de funcionamiento) ■ *verb* **1.** (*telecommunications*) registrar *vt* **2.** (*connection*) registrar *vt*; anotar *vt*; llevar un diario

log file /ˈlɒg faɪl/ *noun* archivo *m* de registro

logger /ˈlɒgə/ *noun* registrador *m*

logging /ˈlɒgɪŋ/ *noun* (*input of data*) adquisición *f*; recogida *f* de datos ◇ **call logging** registro *m* de llamadas

logging in /ˈlɒgɪŋ ɪn/ *noun* inicio *m* de sesión

logging off /ˈlɒgɪŋ ɒf/ *noun* cierre *m* de sesión

logging on /ˈlɒgɪŋ ɒn/ *noun* inicio *m* de sesión

logging out /ˈlɒgɪŋ aʊt/ *noun* cierre *m* de sesión

logic /ˈlɒdʒɪk/ *noun* **1.** (*mathematical treatment*) lógica *f* **2.** (*for deducing results from binary data*) lógica *f* **3.** (*components of a computer system*) lógica *f* (de un sistema) ◇ **logic array** orden lógica *or* circuito lógico ◇ **uncommitted logic array (ULA)** circuito lógico no conectado

logical /ˈlɒdʒɪk(ə)l/ *adjective* lógico *or* -a ◇ **logical reasoning can be simulated by an artificial intelligence machine** el razonamiento lógico puede simularse mediante una máquina de inteligencia artificial

logical channel /ˌlɒdʒɪk(ə)l ˈtʃæn(ə)l/ *noun* canal *m* lógico

logical chart /ˈlɒdʒɪk(ə)l tʃɑːt/ *noun* diagrama *m* lógico

logical comparison /ˌlɒdʒɪk(ə)l kəmˈpærɪs(ə)n/ *noun* comparación *f* lógica

logical decision /ˌlɒdʒɪk(ə)l dɪˈsɪʒ(ə)n/ *noun* decisión *f* lógica

logical drive /ˈlɒdʒɪk(ə)l draɪv/ *noun* unidad *f* lógica; letra *f* que designa una unidad de disco ◇ **the logical drive F: actually stores data on part of the server's disk drive** la unidad lógica F: en realidad almacena datos en una parte del disco del servidor

logical error /ˌlɒdʒɪk(ə)l ˈerə/ *noun* error *m* lógico

logical expression /ˌlɒdʒɪk(ə)l ɪkˈspreʃ(ə)n/ *noun* expresión *f* lógica

logical flowchart /ˈlɒdʒɪk(ə)l ˌfləʊtʃɑːt/ *noun* ordinograma *m* lógico

logical link control /ˌlɒdʒɪk(ə)l ˈlɪŋk kən ˌtrəʊl/ *noun* control *m* lógico de enlaces

logical low /ˈlɒdʒɪk(ə)l ləʊ/ *adjective* estado *m* lógico bajo; tensión *f* baja

logical operator /ˌlɒdʒɪk(ə)l ˌɒpəˈreɪtə/ *noun* operador *m* lógico

logical palette /ˌlɒdʒɪk(ə)l ˈpælət/ *noun* paleta *f* lógica

logical record /ˌlɒdʒɪk(ə)l ˈrekɔːd/ *noun* registro *m* lógico; artículo *m* lógico

logical ring /ˈlɒdʒɪk(ə)l rɪŋ/ *noun* anillo *m* lógico

logical shift /ˈlɒdʒɪk(ə)l ʃɪft/ *noun* (*data movement*) desplazamiento *m* lógico; desplazamiento *m* no aritmético

logical unit /ˌlɒdʒɪk(ə)l ˈjuːnɪt/ *noun* unidad *f* lógica

logic board /ˈlɒdʒɪk bɔːd/ *noun* placa *f* lógica; tarjeta *f* lógica

logic bomb /ˈlɒdʒɪk bɒm/ *noun* bomba *f* lógica ◇ **the system programmer installed a logic bomb when they made him redundant** el programador de sistemas instaló una bomba lógica cuando le despidieron

logic card /ˈlɒdʒɪk kɑːd/ *noun* tarjeta *f* lógica; placa *f* lógica

logic circuit /ˈlɒdʒɪk ˌsɜːkɪt/ *noun* circuito *m* lógico

logic element /ˈlɒdʒɪk ˌelɪmənt/ *noun* elemento *m* lógico

logic flowchart /ˈlɒdʒɪk ˌfləʊtʃɑːt/ *noun* diagrama *m* lógico

logic gate /ˈlɒdʒɪk geɪt/ *noun* puerta *f* lógica; circuito *m* lógico

logic level /ˈlɒdʒɪk ˌlev(ə)l/ *noun* nivel *m* lógico

logic map /ˈlɒdʒɪk mæp/ *noun* (*in a logic circuit*) configuración *f* lógica; mapa *m* lógico

logic operation /ˈlɒdʒɪk ˌɒpəreɪʃ(ə)n/ *noun* operación *f* lógica

logic-seeking /ˈlɒdʒɪk ˌsiːkɪŋ/ *adjective* búsqueda *f* lógica

logic state /ˈlɒdʒɪk steɪt/ *noun* estado *m* lógico

logic state analyser /ˈlɒdʒɪk steɪt ˌænəlaɪzə/ *noun* analizador *m* de estado lógico

logic symbol /ˈlɒdʒɪk ˌsɪmbəl/ *noun* símbolo *m* lógico

logo /ˈləʊgəʊ/ *noun* (*high level programming language*) logotipo *m*; distintivo *m*

LOGO /ˈləʊgəʊ/ *noun* (*high level programming language*) lenguaje *m* LOGO

logoff /lɒgˈɒf/ *verb* placa *f* lógica

logon /lɒgˈɒn/ *verb* inicio *m* de sesión

log on server /ˈl ˈɒg ɒn ˌsɜːvə/ *noun* servidor *m* de control de acceso

logout /ˈlɒgaʊt/ *noun* placa *f* lógica

long filename /lɒŋ ˈfaɪlˌneɪm/ *noun* (*feature of Windows 95 that lets a user give files a long name – up to 254 characters long*) nombre *m* de fichero largo

long haul network /ˌlɒŋ hɔːl ˈnetwɜːk/ *noun* (*communications network*) red *f* de larga distancia; red *f* de gran distancia; red *f* extendida

long integer /lɒŋ ˈɪntɪdʒə/ *noun* (*integer represented by several bytes of data*) número *m* entero largo

longitudinal redundancy check /ˌlɒŋgɪtjuːdɪn(ə)l rɪˈdʌndənsi ˌtʃek/ *noun* control *m* por redundancia longitudinal

long persistence phosphor /lɒŋ pə ˌsɪstəns ˈfɒsfə/ *noun* (*television screen coating*) fósforo *m* de gran persistencia; fósforo *m* de larga persistencia

look-ahead /ˈlʊk əˌhed/ *noun* lectura *f* anticipada

look-up /ˈlʊk ʌp/ *noun* búsqueda *f*

look-up table /ˈlʊk ʌp ˌteɪb(ə)l/ *noun* tabla *f* de referencia ◇ **this is the value of the key pressed, use a lookup table to find its ASCII value** utilice la tabla de equivalencias para encontrar el valor ASCII

'…a lookup table changes a pixel's value based on the values in a table' [*Byte*]

loop /luːp/ *noun* (*instruction in computer program*) bucle *m*; circuito *m*; ciclo *m* ◇ **loop film** película *f* en bucle ◇ **loop network** red *f* en anillo *or* en bucle

loopback /ˈluːpbæk/ *noun* (*diagnostic test*) bucle *m* de corrección; prueba *f* en anillo cerrado

loopback test /ˈluːpbæk test/ *noun* prueba *f* de bucle de retorno; diagnóstico *m* de prueba

loop body /luːp ˈbɒdi/ *noun* cuerpo *m* del bucle

loop check /ˈluːp ˌtʃek/ *noun* verificación *f* de bucle; control *m* de bucle

loop counter /luːp ˈkaʊntə/ *noun* contador *m* de bucles

looping program /luːpɪŋ ˈprəʊgræm/ *noun* programa *m* iterativo

loop program /luːp ˈprəʊgræm/ *noun* programa *m* iterativo; programa *m* repetitivo

lo-res /ləʊ riːs/ *noun* versión *f* elemental; versión *f* inicial

lossless compression /ˌlɒsləs kəm ˈpreʃ(ə)nn/ *noun* (*image compression techniques that can reduce the number of bits used for each pixel in an image, without losing any information or quality*) compresión *f* de imágenes sin pérdida de información

lossy compression /ˈlɒsi kəmˌpreʃ(ə)n/ *noun* (*image compression techniques that can reduce the number of bits used for each pixel in an image, but in doing so lose information*) compresión *f* de imágenes con pérdida de información

lost cluster /lɒst ˈklʌstə/ *noun* grupo *m* (de datos) perdido; unidad *f* de asignación perdida

Lotus /ˈləʊtəs/ (*software company*) Lotus™

Lotus-Intel-Microsoft Expanded Memory System /ˌləʊtəs ˌɪntel ˌmaɪkrəsɒft ɪks ˌpændɪd ˈmem(ə)ri ˌsɪstəm/ *noun* memoria *f* extendida LIM EMS

loudspeaker /ˌlaʊdˈspiːkə/ *noun* (*system*) altavoz *m*; pantalla *f* acústica; bafle *m*

low-end /ˌləʊ ˈend/ *adjective* (*hardware that is not very powerful or sophisticated*) elemental; inicial

lower case /ˌləʊə ˈkeɪs/ *noun* minúscula(s) *f(pl)*

low-level format /ˌləʊ ˈlev(ə)l ˌfɔːmæt/ *noun* (*defines the pattern of tracks on a disk*) formato *m* de bajo nivel

low-level language /ˌləʊ ˌlev(ə)l ˈlæŋgwɪdʒ/ *noun* (*programming language similar to assembler*) lenguaje *m* de bajo nivel; lenguaje *m* LLL

low memory /ˌləʊ ˈmem(ə)ri/ *noun* (*memory locations in a PC*) memoria *f* baja

low-order digit /ˌləʊ ˌɔːdə ˈdɪdʒɪt/ *noun* cifra *f* de orden inferior; cifra *f* menos significativa ◇ **the number 234156 has a low-order digit of 6**

el 6 es la cifra menos significativa del número 234156

low-power standby /ˌləʊ ˈpaʊə ˌstændbaɪ/ *noun* sistema *m* de reserva; auxiliar *m* de bajo consumo de energía

low-priority work /ˌləʊ praɪˌɒrɪti ˈwɜːk/ *noun* tarea *f* no prioritaria; tarea *f* de baja prioridad

low resolution /ˌləʊ ˌrezəˈluːʃ(ə)n/ *noun* versión *f* elemental; versión *f* inicial

low-resolution graphics /ləʊ ˌrezəˌluːʃ(ə)n ˈgræfɪks/, **low-res graphics** /ləʊ rez ˈgræfɪks/ *plural noun* gráficos *mpl* de baja definición; gráficos *mpl* de baja resolución

low-speed communications /ˌləʊ spiːd kə ˌmjuːnɪˈkeɪʃ(ə)nz/ *plural noun* comunicaciones *fpl* de baja velocidad

LPM *abbr* (*lines per minute*) líneas por minuto

LPT1 /ˌel piː tiː ˈwʌn/ *noun* (*first parallel printer port*) puerto *m* paralelo LPT1 en un PC

LSB /ˌel es ˈbiː/ *noun* bit *m* menos significativo

LSD /ˌel es ˈdiː/ *noun* dígito *m* menos significativo

LU /ˌel ˈjuː/ *noun* unidad *f* lógica

luggable /ˈlʌgəb(ə)l/ *noun* ordenador *m* desplazable

luminance /ˈluːmɪn(ə)ns/ *noun* luminancia *f*; brillo *m* fotométrico ◇ **luminance signal** señal *f* de luminancia

LUT /ˌel juː ˈtiː/ *noun* tabla *f* de referencia

'…an image processing system can have three LUTs that map the image memory to the display device' [*Byte*]

M

mA /ˌem ˈeɪ/ *noun* miliamperio *m* (mA)

Mac /mæk/ *noun* Mac

MAC /ˌem eɪ ˈsiː/ *noun* control *m* de acceso al medio ■ *abbr* (*media access control*) control *m* de acceso a medios (de transmisión)

MacBinary /mækˈbaɪnəri/ (*file storage and transfer system*) MacBinario™ *m*; (*trade name for a file storage and transfer system for Macintosh files*) MacBinario™ *m*

machine /məˈʃiːn/ *noun* **1.** máquina *f* **2.** (*processors and computers*) ordenador *m*; procesador *m*; máquina *f* ◇ **machine-dependent** (*software*) (programa) no estándar *or* que sólo funciona con un solo tipo de ordenador ◇ **machine-independent** (*software*) estándar *or* universal *or* que funciona en la mayoría de los ordenadores ◇ **machine-intimate** (programa) propio de la máquina *or* hecho a medida *or* adaptado al ordenador ◇ **machine-readable** (*command or data*) (instrucción *or* datos) en lenguaje máquina

machine address /məˈʃiːn əˌdres/ *noun* dirección *f* (de) máquina

machine check /məˈʃiːn tʃek/ *noun* parada *f* de comprobación

machine code /məˈʃiːn kəʊd/ *noun* código *m* de máquina

machine code format /məˈʃiːn kəʊd ˌfɔːmæt/ *noun* (*format for machine code instructions*) instrucción *f* en código; instrucción *f* en lenguaje máquina

machine code instruction /məˈʃiːn kəʊd ɪnˌstrʌkʃən/ *noun* instrucción *f* en código máquina

machine cycle /məˈʃiːn ˌsaɪk(ə)l/ *noun* ciclo *m* de máquina

machine-dependent /məˌʃiːn dɪˈpendənt/ *adjective* (*unable to be used on hardware or software*) no estándar; que sólo funciona con un solo tipo de ordenador

machine equation /məˈʃiːn ɪˌkweɪʒ(ə)n/ *noun* (*formula*) ecuación *f* máquina; lógica *f* de máquina

machine error /məˈʃiːn ˌerə/ *noun* error *m* causado por la máquina

machine-independent /məˌʃiːn ˌɪndɪˈpendənt/ *adjective* (*that can be run on any computer system*) estándar; universal; que funciona en la mayoría de los ordenadores

machine-independent language /məˌʃiːn ˌɪndɪpendənt ˈlæŋgwɪdʒ/ *noun* (*programming language*) lenguaje *m* estándar; lenguaje *m* independiente de la máquina; lenguaje *m* universal

machine instruction /məˈʃiːn ɪnˌstrʌkʃən/ *noun* instrucción *f* en lenguaje máquina

machine intelligence /məˈʃiːn ɪnˌtelɪdʒ(ə)ns/ *noun* inteligencia *f* artificial

machine-intimate /məˌʃiːn ˈɪntɪmət/ *adjective* (*that operates closely with the hardware*) propio de la máquina; hecho a medida; adaptado al ordenador

machine language /məˈʃiːn ˌlæŋgwɪdʒ/ *noun* **1.** código *m* de maquina **2.** lenguaje *m* máquina

machine language compile /məˌʃiːn ˌlæŋgwɪdʒ kəmˈpaɪl/ *noun* compilador *m* en lenguaje máquina

machine language programming /məˌʃiːn ˌlæŋgwɪdʒ ˈprəʊgræmɪŋ/ *noun* programación *f* en lenguaje máquina

machine readable /məˌʃiːn ˈriːdəb(ə)l/ *adjective* en lenguaje máquina ◇ **the disk stores data in machine-readable form** el disco almacena los datos en lenguaje máquina

machine-readable code /məˌʃiːn ˌriːdəb(ə)l ˈkəʊd/ *noun* código *m* legible por máquina

machine run /məˈʃiːn rʌn/ *noun* ejecución *f* de un programa

machine translation /məˌʃiːn trænsˈleɪʃ(ə)n/ *noun* (*texts and commands*) traducción *f* asistida por ordenador; traducción *f* automática

machine word /məˈʃiːn wɜːd/ *noun* palabra *f* de máquina

Macintosh /ˈmækɪntɒʃ/ (*trade name for a range of personal computers designed by Apple Corporation*) Macintosh™ ◇ **Macintosh computers are not compatible with an IBM PC unless you use special emulation software** los ordenadores Macintosh no son compatibles con un ordenador IBM a no ser que utilice un programa de emulación

macro /mækrəʊ/ *noun* macroinstrucción *f*; macro *f*

macro- /mækrəʊ/ *prefix* macro-

macro assembler /ˈmækrəʊ əˌsemblə/, **macro assembly program** /ˌmækrəʊ əˈsemblə ˌprəʊgræm/ *noun* (*program able to decode macro instructions*) macro ensamblador *m*; ensamblador *m* de macros; macroinstrucciones *fpl*

macro block /ˈmækrəʊ blɒk/ *noun* macrobloque *m*

macro call /ˈmækrəʊ kɔːl/ *noun* macroinstrucción *f*

macro code /'mækrəʊ kəʊd/ *noun* (*program writing*) código *m* macro; macrocódigo *m*; código *m* de macros

macro command /'mækrəʊ kə,mɑːnd/ *noun* (*macro code*) macroinstrucción *f*; instrucción *f* de macro

macro definition /'mækrəʊ ,defənɪʃ(ə)n/ *noun* macrodefinición *f*; definición *f* de macro

macroelement /'mækrəʊ,elɪmənt/ *noun* (*data items treated as one element*) macroelemento *m*; elemento *m* de macro

macro expansion /'mækrəʊ ɪk,spænʃ(ə)n/ *noun* (*process*) macroexpansión *f*

macro flowchart /'mækrəʊ ,fləʊtʃɑːt/ *noun* macroordinograma *m*; ordinograma *m* de macro

macroinstruction /'mækrəʊ,ɪnstrʌkʃən/ *noun* macroinstrucción *f*; macro *f*

macro language /'mækrəʊ ,læŋgwɪdʒ/ *noun* macrolenguaje *m*; lenguaje *m* de macros

'Microsoft has released a developer's kit for its Word 6.0 for Windows wordprocessing package. The 900-page kit explains how to use the Word-Basic macro language supplied with the software.' [*Computing*]

macro library /'mækrəʊ ,laɪbrəri/ *noun* (*routines to ease program writing*) biblioteca *f* de macros

macro programming /,mækrəʊ ,prəʊgræmɪŋ/ *noun* (*writing a program using macro instructions*) macroprogramación *f*; programación *f* de macros

macro virus /'mækrəʊ ,vaɪrəs/ *noun* macrovirus *m*

magazine /,mægə'ziːn/ *noun* (*videotext system*) revista *f*; magacín *m*; (número de) páginas *fpl* de un sistema de teletexto

magnet /'mægnɪt/ *noun* imán *m*

magnetic /mæg'netɪk/ *adjective* magnético *or* -a; imantado *or* -a ◇ **magnetic focusing** (*of beam of electrons*) enfoque magnético *or* concentración magnética

magnetic bubble memory /mæg,netɪk 'bʌb(ə)l ,mem(ə)ri/ *noun* memoria *f* de burbujas magnéticas

magnetic card /mæg,netɪk 'kɑːd/ *noun* tarjeta *f* magnética

magnetic card reader /mæg,netɪk 'kɑːd ,riːdə/ *noun* lector *m* de tarjetas magnéticas

magnetic cartridge /mæg,netɪk 'kɑːtrɪdʒ/ *noun* cartucho *m* (de banda magnética)

magnetic cassette /mæg,netɪk kə'set/ *noun* casete *f* (de banda magnética)

magnetic cell /mæg'netɪk sel/ *noun* celda *f* magnética

magnetic core /mæg'netɪk kɔː/ *noun* núcleo *m* magnético

magnetic disk /mæg'netɪk dɪsk/ *noun* disco *m* magnético

magnetic disk unit /mæg,netɪk 'dɪsk ,juːnɪt/ *noun* unidad *f* de disco magnético

magnetic drum /mæg'netɪk drʌm/ *noun* (*cylindrical magnetic storage device*) tambor *m* magnético

magnetic encoding /mæg,netɪk ɪn'kəʊdɪŋ/ *noun* codificación *f* magnética

magnetic field /mæg,netɪk 'fiːld/ *noun* campo *m* magnético

magnetic flux /mæg'netɪk flʌks/ *noun* (*measure of magnetic field strength*) flujo *m* magnético

magnetic head /mæg'netɪk hed/ *noun* cabeza *f* magnética

magnetic ink /mæg,netɪk 'ɪŋk/ *noun* (*printing ink that contains a magnetic material*) tinta *f* magnética

magnetic ink character recognition /mæg,netɪk ɪŋk ,kærɪktə ,rekəg'nɪʃ(ə)n/ *noun* reconocimiento *m* de caracteres de tinta magnética

magnetic master /mæg,netɪk 'mɑːstə/ *noun* (*original version of a recorded tape or disk*) soporte *m* magnético original; banda *f* original; disco *m* original

magnetic material /mæg,netɪk mə'tɪəriəl/ *noun* soporte *m* magnético

magnetic media /mæg,netɪk 'miːdiə/ *plural noun* soportes *mpl* magnéticos

magnetic medium /mæg,netɪk 'miːdiəm/ *noun* soporte *m* magnético

magnetic memory /mæg,netɪk 'mem(ə)ri/ *noun* memoria *f* magnética

magnetic polarity /mæg,netɪk pəʊ'lærɪti/ *noun* polaridad *f* magnética

magnetic recording /mæg,netɪk rɪ'kɔːdɪŋ/ *noun* grabación *f* con soporte magnético

magnetic screen /mæg'netɪk skriːn/ *noun* pantalla *f* magnética

magnetic storage /mæg,netɪk 'stɔːrɪdʒ/ *noun* memoria *f* magnética

magnetic strip /mæg,netɪk 'strɪp/ *noun* (*data recording*) pista *f* magnética

magnetic stripe /mæg,netɪk 'straɪp/ *noun* pista *f* magnética

magnetic strip reader /mæg,netɪk 'strɪp ,riːdə/ *noun* lector *m* de tarjetas magnéticas

magnetic tape /mæg'netɪk teɪp/ *noun* cinta *f* magnética

magnetic tape cartridge /mæg,netɪk teɪp 'kɑːtrɪdʒ/ *noun* cartucho *m* de cinta magnética; cargador *m* de cinta magnética

magnetic tape cassette /mæg,netɪk teɪp kə'set/ *noun* cargador *m* de cinta magnética; cartucho *m* de cinta magnética

magnetic tape encoder /mæg,netɪk teɪp en'kəʊdə/ *noun* (*data writing*) codificador *m* para bandas magnéticas; codificador *m* de bandas magnéticas

magnetic tape reader /mæg,netɪk teɪp 'riːdə/ *noun* lector *m* de bandas; lector *m* de cintas magnéticas

magnetic tape recorder /mæg,netɪk 'teɪp rɪ,kɔːdə/ *noun* (*data writing*) grabadora *f* de banda;

grabadora *f* de cintas magnéticas; magnetófono *m* de cinta magnética

magnetic tape transport /mæg,netɪk teɪp 'trænspɔːt/ *noun* (mecanismo de) transporte *m* de cintas magnéticas

magnetic transfer /mæg,netɪk 'trænsfɜː/ *noun* (*copying of signals*) transferencia *f* magnética; transferencia *f* de un soporte magnético a otro

magnetise /'mægnə,taɪz/, **magnetize** *verb* magnetizar *vt*

magneto-optical disc /mæg,niːtəʊ ,ɒptɪk(ə)l 'dɪsk/ *noun* (*optical disc*) disco *m* magnetoóptico

magneto-optical recording /mæg,niːtəʊ ,ɒptɪk(ə)l rɪ'kɔːdɪŋ/ *noun* grabación *f* en discos magnetoópticos

magnitude /'mægnɪtjuːd/ *noun* (*of a signal or variable*) amplitud *f*; magnitud *f* ◇ **signal magnitude** amplitud de una señal

mag tape /'mæg teɪp/ *noun informal* cinta *f* magnética

mail /meɪl/ *noun* mensaje *m* electrónico

mail application programming interface /,meɪl ,æplɪkeɪʃ(ə)n 'prəʊgræmɪŋ ,ɪntəfeɪs/ *noun* interfaz *f* de programación de aplicaciones para el correo electrónico

mailbox /'meɪlbɒks/, **mail box** /'meɪl bɒks/ *noun* (*electronic*) buzón *m* (de mensajes electrónicos)

mail-enabled /meɪl ɪn'eɪb(ə)ld/ *adjective* (*application that has access to an electronic mail system*) compatible con el correo electrónico ◇ **this word-processor is mail-enabled – you can send messages to other users from within it** este tratamiento de textos es compatible con el correo electrónico y puede enviar mensajes a otros usuarios sin salir del programa

mailing /'meɪlɪŋ/ *noun* (*post or e-mail*) envío *m* por correo; (*e-mail*) envío *m* por correo electrónico; (*post or e-mail*) 'mailing' *m* ◇ **direct mailing** envío *m* por correo directo *or* publicidad *f* directa *or* 'mailing' *m* directo ◇ **mailing piece** prospecto *m*; folleto enviado por correo ◇ **mailing shot** envío *m* de folletos publicitarios ◇ **the mailing of publicity material** el envío por correo (electrónico) de material publicitario ◇ **to build up a mailing list** elaborar una lista de direcciones ◇ **to buy a mailing list** comprar una lista de direcciones

mailing list /'meɪlɪŋ lɪst/ *noun* (*list of e-mail addresses*) fichero *m* de direcciones; lista *f* de direcciones ◇ **his name is on our mailing list** su nombre está en nuestra lista de direcciones

mailmerge /'meɪlmɜːdʒ/ *noun* intercalación *f* de correo

'Spreadsheet views for data and graphical forms for data entry have been added to the Q&A database, with the traditional reporting, mailmerge, and labels improved through Windows facilities.' [*Computing*]

mail server /meɪl 'sɜːvə/ *noun* servidor *m* de correo (electrónico)

main /meɪn/ *adjective* principal ◇ **main beam** (*of antenna transmission*) haz *m* principal ◇

main distributing frame distribuidor *m* general *or* principal

main body /,meɪn 'bɒdi/ *noun* parte *f* principal (de un programa)

main clock /'meɪn klɒk/ *noun* (*clock signal*) reloj *m* principal

main entry /meɪn 'entri/ *noun* entrada *f* principal

mainframe /'meɪnfreɪm kəm,pjuːtə/, **mainframe computer** /,meɪnfreɪm kəm'pjuːtə/ *noun* ordenador *m* principal

mainframe access /'meɪnfreɪm ,ækses/ *noun* acceso *m* al ordenador principal

main index /meɪn 'ɪndeks/ *noun* índice *m* general; índice *m* principal

main loop /,meɪn 'luːp/ *noun* bucle *m* principal (de un programa)

main memory /meɪn 'mem(ə)ri/ *noun* memoria *f* principal; memoria *f* central

main menu /meɪn 'menjuː/ *noun* menú *m* principal

main routine /meɪn ruː'tiːn/ *noun* rutina *f* principal

mains electricity /meɪns ɪ,lek'trɪsəti/ *noun* (*domestic electricity supply*) red *f* de electricidad; sector *m* eléctrico

main storage /meɪn 'stɔːrɪdʒ/ *noun* memoria *f* central; memoria *f* principal

maintain /meɪn'teɪn/ *verb* (*system*) mantener *vt*; conservar *vt*

maintainability /,meɪnteɪnə'bɪlɪti/ *noun* (*repairs*) facilidad *f* de conservación técnica; conservabilidad *f*

maintenance /'meɪntənəns/ *noun* **1.** (*service*) mantenimiento *m*; (*repairs*) conservación *f*; (*service*) servicio *m* de mantenimiento; servicio *m* postventa **2.** (*of database, website*) mantenimiento *m*; conservación *f* ◇ **on-site maintenance** servicio *m* de asistencia técnica en el propio lugar de trabajo ◇ **remote maintenance** mantenimiento a distancia

maintenance contract /'meɪntənəns ,kɒntrækt/ *noun* contrato *m* de mantenimiento

maintenance release /'meɪntənəns rɪ,liːs/ *noun* (*program revision*) conformidad *f*; visto *m* bueno de mantenimiento ◇ **the maintenance release of the database program, version 2.01, corrects the problem with the margins** la puesta a punto correctiva de la base de datos, versión 2.01, corrige el problema de los márgenes

maintenance routine /'meɪntənəns ruː,tiːn/ *noun* rutina *f* de mantenimiento

major cycle /,meɪdʒə 'saɪk(ə)l/ *noun* ciclo *m* principal

make directory /,meɪk daɪ'rekt(ə)ri/ *noun* instrucción *f* MD; MKDIR (de creación de un directorio)

male connector /meɪl kə'nektə/ *noun* conector *m* macho

malfunction /mæl'fʌŋkʃən/ *noun* (*of hardware or software*) mal *m* funcionamiento; fallo *m*; funcionamiento *m* defectuoso ∎ *verb* funcionar mal ◇ **some of the keys on the keyboard have started to malfunction** algunas de las teclas del teclado han empezado a funcionar mal ◇ **the data was lost due to a software malfunction** los datos se perdieron a causa de un fallo de funcionamiento en el programa

malfunctioning /mæl'fʌŋkʃənɪŋ/ *adjective* mal *m* funcionamiento

malfunction routine /mæl'fʌŋkʃən ruː,tiːn/ *noun* (*software routine that detects faults*) rutina *f*; programa *m* de detección de fallos

MAN /mæn/ *noun* red *f* de área metropolitana

manageable /'mænɪdʒəb(ə)l/ *adjective* manejable; que se puede gestionar ◇ **data should be split into manageable files** los datos se deberían dividir en ficheros manejables

management information service /,mænɪdʒmənt ,ɪnfə'meɪʃ(ə)n ,sɜːvɪs/ *noun* servicio *m* informático de gestión

management information system /,mænɪdʒmənt ,ɪnfə'meɪʃ(ə)n ,sɪstəm/ *noun* (*software for managers*) sistema *m* informático de gestión

manager /'mænɪdʒə/ *noun* (*software*) gestor *m*

Manchester coding /'mæntʃestə ,kɒdɪŋ/ *noun* (*method of encoding data*) codificación *f* Manchester

Mandlebrot set /'mænd(ə)lbrɒt set/ *noun* (*mathematical equation*) ecuación *f* de Mandlebrot

manipulate /mə'nɪpjʊ,leɪt/ *verb* manipular *vt* ◇ **an image processor that captures, displays and manipulates video images** un procesador de imágenes que recoge, muestra y manipula imágenes de vídeo

manipulation /mə,nɪpjʊ'leɪʃ(ə)n/ *noun* manipulación *f*

man machine interface /,mæn mə,ʃiːn 'ɪntəfeɪs/ *noun* interfaz *f* hombre/máquina; interfaz *f* usuario/máquina

mantissa /mæn'tɪsə/ *noun* (*numbers*) mantisa *f*; parte *f* fraccionaria; fraccional *m* ◇ **the mantissa of the number 45.897 is 0.897** la mantisa del número 45,897 es 0,897

manual /'mænjuəl/ *noun* (*book or booklet*) manual *m*

manual data processing /,mænjuəl 'deɪtə ,prəʊsesɪŋ/ *noun* tratamiento *m* sin ayuda del ordenador; proceso *m* de la información manual

manual entry /,mænjuəl 'entri/ *noun* entrada *f* de datos manual

manual input /,mænjuəl 'ɪnpʊt/ *noun* entrada *f* de datos mediante el teclado

manually /'mænjuəli/ *adverb* manualmente; de forma manual ◇ **the paper has to be fed into the printer manually** hay que introducir el papel en la impresora de forma manual

map /mæp/ *noun* (*internal layout of computer's memory*) configuración *f*; mapa *m*; diagrama *m* ■ *verb* asignar *vt*

MAPI /,em eɪ piː 'aɪ/ *noun* interfaz *f* de programación de aplicaciones para el correo electrónico

MAR /,em eɪ 'ɑː/ *noun* registro *m* de dirección en memoria

marching display /mɑːtʃɪŋ dɪ'spleɪ/ *noun* (dispositivo de) visualización *f* de los últimos caracteres (introducidos)

margin /'mɑːdʒɪn/ *noun* **1.** (*blank space*) margen *m* **2.** (*extra time or space*) margen *m* ◇ **foot margin** margen *m* inferior ◇ **the left margin and right margin are the two sections of blank paper on either side of the page** el margen izquierdo y el margen derecho son las dos secciones de papel en blanco a cada lado de la página ◇ **top margin** margen superior ◇ **to set a margin** fijar un margen

margin of error /,mɑːdʒɪn əv 'erə/ *noun* margen *m* de error

mark /mɑːk/ *noun* **1.** (*sign*) marca *f*; señal *f* **2.** (*signal*) marca *f* lógica ■ *verb* marcar *vt*; indicar *vt* ◇ **marking interval** intervalo *m* de marca ◇ **proof correction marks** marcas *fpl* de corrección de las galeradas; señales *fpl*

mark block /,mɑːk 'blɒk/ *verb* marcar un bloque

marker /'mɑːkə/ *noun* (*writing or signalling tool*) marcador *m*; indicador *m* ◇ **marker pen** marcador *m*

mark sense /,mɑːk 'sens/ *verb* (*to write detectable characters*) hacer marcas detectables

mark sense device /,mɑːk 'sens dɪ,vaɪs/ *noun* dispositivo *m* de marcas detectables

mark sense reader /,mɑːk 'sens ,riːdə/ *noun* lector *m* de marcas detectables

mark sensing card /'mɑːk ,sensɪŋ kɑːd/ *noun* tarjeta *f* de marcas detectables

mark space /,mɑːk 'speɪs/ *noun* espacio *m* de marca

markup /'mɑːkʌp/ *noun* maquetación *f*

markup language /'mɑːkʌp ,læŋgwɪdʒ/ *noun* lenguaje *m* de marcas

marquee /mɑː'kiː/ *noun* **1.** (*in a graphics application*) recuadro *m* de selección **2.** (*in a website*) recuadro *m* de selección

mask /mɑːsk/ *noun* **1.** (*circuit layout stencil*) máscara *f* **2.** (*photographic*) máscara *f* ■ *verb* (*pattern of binary digits*) cubrir ◇ **a mask or stencil is used to transfer the transistor design onto silicon** se emplea una máscara o clisé para transferir el diseño del transistor al silicio ◇ **the first instruction, UMASK, sets an internal bit mask within the system, which is used to mask off mode bits when a file is created** la primera instrucción, UMASK, asigna un valor a una máscara de bits interna al sistema, utilizada para enmascarar automáticamente los bits de protección cuando se crea un fichero

maskable /'mɑːskəb(ə)l/ *adjective* enmascarable

maskable interrupt /,mɑːskəb(ə)l 'ɪntərʌpt/ *noun* (*interrupt which can be activated by using* *an interrupt mask*) interrupción *f* enmascarable; interrupción *f* que puede ser invalidada; interrupción *f* invalidable

mask bit /'mɑːsk bɪt/ *noun* (*one bit in a mask*) bit *m* de máscara

masked ROM /'mɑːskt rɒm/ *noun* memoria *f* ROM enmascarada

masking /'mɑːskɪŋ/ *noun* enmascaramiento *m*

mask register /mɑːsk 'redʒɪstə/ *noun* registro *m* de máscara

mass production /mæs prə'dʌkʃən/ *noun* producción *f* en serie; producción *f* a gran escala

mass storage /mæs 'stɔːrɪdʒ/ *noun* almacenamiento *m* masivo; almacenamiento *m* de gran capacidad

mass storage device /ˌmæs 'stɔːrɪdʒ dɪ ˌvaɪs/ *noun* dispositivo *m* de almacenamiento masivo

mass storage system /ˌmæs 'stɔːrɪdʒ ˌsɪstəm/ *noun* (*data storage system*) sistema *m* de almacenamiento masivo

master /'mɑːstə/ *adjective* **1.** (*person or device*) maestro *or* -a; principal **2.** (*copy*) maestro *or* -a; principal ■ *verb* (*learn*) dominar *vt* ◇ **master control program (MCP)** programa *m* de control maestro

master card /'mɑːstə kɑːd/ *noun* tarjeta *f* maestra

master clock /'mɑːstə klɒk/ *noun* reloj *m* maestro; reloj *m* principal

master computer /'mɑːstə kəmˌpjuːtə/ *noun* (*computer that controls the other processors*) ordenador *m* maestro; ordenador *m* principal; ordenador *m* central ◇ **the master computer controls everything else** el ordenador central controla todo lo demás

master control program /ˌmɑːstə kən'trəul ˌprəugræm/ *noun* programa *m* de control maestro

master data /ˌmɑːstə 'deɪtə/ *noun* (*reference data*) datos *mpl* maestros; datos *mpl* de referencia; datos *mpl* de base

master disc /'mɑːstə dɪsk/ *noun* disco *m* original; disco *m* maestro

master disk /'mɑːstə dɪsk/ *noun* **1.** disco *m* maestro **2.** disco *m* original

master file /'mɑːstə faɪl/ *noun* fichero *m* maestro; fichero *m* principal

mastering /'mɑːstərɪŋ/ *noun* (*data*) copia *f*; reproducción *f* de datos terminados en un disco maestro

master/master computer system /ˌmɑːstə 'mɑːstə kəmˌpjuːtə ˌsɪstəm/ *noun* sistema *m* informático maestro/maestro

master program file /ˌmɑːstə 'prəugræm ˌfaɪl/ *noun* fichero *m* de programa maestro

master/slave computer system /ˌmɑːstə 'sleɪv kəmˌpjuːtə ˌsɪstəm/ *noun* sistema *m* informático maestro/satélite

master tape /'mɑːstə teɪp/ *noun* cinta *f* original; cinta *f* maestra

master terminal /ˌmɑːstə 'tɜːmɪn(ə)l/ *noun* terminal *m* maestro; terminal *m* principal ◇ **the**

system manager uses the master terminal to restart the system el gestor del sistema utiliza el terminal principal para reiniciar el sistema

mat /mæt/ *noun* (*border displayed around an image*) borde *m*

match /mætʃ/ *verb* **1.** (*in pairs*) clasificar *vt*; emparejar *vt* **2.** (*to set a register*) igualar *vt*; equilibrar *vt* ◇ **matched load** carga *f* equilibrada

material /mə'tɪəriəl/ *noun* (*substance to make a finished product*) material *m* ◇ **gold is the ideal material for electrical connections** el oro es el material ideal para las conexiones eléctricas

math /mæθ/ *noun* US *informal* matemáticas *fpl*

mathematical /ˌmæθə'mætɪk(ə)l/ *adjective* matemático *or* -a

mathematical model /ˌmæθəmætɪk(ə)l 'mɒd(ə)l/ *noun* modelo *m* matemático

mathematical subroutines /ˌmæθəmætɪk(ə)l 'sʌbruːtiːnz/ *plural noun* subrutinas matemáticas

mathematics /ˌmæθə'mætɪks/ *noun* matemáticas *fpl*

maths /mæθs/ *noun informal* (*mathematics*) matemáticas *fpl*

maths chip /'mæθs ˌtʃɪp/ *noun* chip *m* matemático

maths coprocessor /'mæθs kəuˌprəusesə/ *noun* coprocesador *m* matemático

matrix /'meɪtrɪks/ *noun* **1.** (*array of numbers*) matriz *f* **2.** (*array of connections*) matriz *f* de relación **3.** (*printing*) matriz *f* gráfica

matrix printer /'meɪtrɪks ˌprɪntə/ *noun* impresora *f* matricial

matrix rotation /'meɪtrɪks rəuˌteɪʃ(ə)n/ *noun* (*process of swapping the rows with the columns in an array*) rotación *f* de matriz

matte /mæt/ *noun* trama *f*

matter /'mætə/ *noun* (*main section of text*) cuerpo *m* de un texto ◇ **printed matter** impresos *mpl* ◇ **publicity matter** material *m* publicitario

maximise /'mæksɪmaɪz/, **maximize** *verb* (*expand an application icon*) ampliar la pantalla; maximizar *vt*

maximum /'mæksɪməm/ *noun* máximo *m or* -a ■ *adjective* máximo *or* -a

maximum capacity /ˌmæksɪməm kə'pæsɪti/ *noun* capacidad *f* máxima

maximum transmission rate /ˌmæksɪməm trænz'mɪʃ(ə)n ˌreɪt/ *noun* velocidad *f* máxima de transmisión

maximum users /ˌmæksɪməm 'juːzəz/ *plural noun* número *m* máximo de usuarios

Mbps *abbr* (*megabits per second*) (número de) megabits *mpl* por segundo; Mbps; (número de) megabits *mpl* por segundo

MBR /ˌem biː 'ɑː/ *noun* registro *m* de memoria intermedia

MCA /ˌem siː 'eɪ/ (*trade name for the expansion bus within IBM's PS/2 range of personal computers*) arquitectura *f* MCA ■ *abbr* (*media control architecture*) arquitectura *f* micro channel

MCA chipset /ˌem si: eɪ 'tʃɪpset/ *noun* juego *m* de componentes MCA

MCI /ˌem si: 'aɪ/ *noun* interfaz *f* de control de medios (multimedia)

MCI device /ˌem si: 'aɪ dɪˌvaɪs/ *noun* dispositivo *m* de control multimedia

MD /ˌem 'di:/ *noun* instrucción *f* MD; MKDIR (de creación de un directorio)

MDA /ˌem di: 'eɪ/ *noun* tarjeta *f* MDA; adaptador *m* de pantalla monocromo

MDK /ˌem di: 'keɪ/ *noun* conjunto *m* de aplicaciones multimedia

MDR /ˌem di: 'ɑː/ *noun* registro *m* de datos de la memoria

MDRAM /ˌem 'di: ræm/ *noun* memoria *f* de acceso aleatorio dinámica multiuso

mean /miːn/ *noun, adjective* medio *or* -a ■ *verb* significar *vt*

mean time between failures /ˌmiːn taɪm bɪ ˌtwiːn 'feɪljəz/ *noun* tiempo *m* medio de funcionamiento correcto entre fallos; duración *f* media de funcionamiento correcto entre fallos

mean time to failure /ˌmiːn taɪm tə 'feɪljə/ *noun* tiempo *m* medio sin averías

mean time to repair /ˌmiːn 'taɪm tə, tʊ/ *noun* duración *f* media necesaria para una reparación

measure /'meʒə/ *noun* **1.** (*way of calculating size*) medida *f* **2.** (*width of a printed line*) anchura *f* de una línea **3.** (*action*) medida *f* ■ *verb* **1.** (*to find out size, etc.*) medir *vt* **2.** (*to have certain size, etc.*) medir *vt* ◇ **tape measure** metro *m* ◇ **to take measures to prevent something happening** tomar medidas para evitar que algo ocurra

measurement /'meʒəmənt/ *noun* **1.** medición *f*; medida *f* **2.** evaluación *f* ◇ **to write down the measurements of a package** anotar las medidas de un paquete

measurements /'meʒəmənts/ *plural noun* dimensiones *fpl*; medidas *fpl* ◇ **to write down the measurements of a package** anotar las medidas de un paquete

mechanical /mɪ'kænɪk(ə)l/ *adjective* mecánico *or* -a

mechanical mouse /mɪ'kænɪk(ə)l maʊs/ *noun* ratón *m* mecánico

mechanism /'mekəˌnɪz(ə)m/ *noun* mecanismo *m* ◇ **the drive mechanism appears to be faulty** el mecanismo de la disquetera parece que no funciona bien ◇ **the printer mechanism is very simple** el mecanismo de la impresora es muy simple

medallion /mə'dæliən/ *noun* micromódulo *m*

media /'miːdiə/ *plural noun* **1.** (*means of communicating information to the public*) medios *mpl* de comunicación **2.** (*physical material that can be used to store data*) medios *mpl* de comunicación (de masas) ◇ **media access control (MAC)** control *m* de acceso a medios (de transmisión) ◇ **media analysis** *or* **media research** análisis *m*; investigación *f* de los medios (de comunicación) ◇ **media coverage** cobertura *f* periodís-

tica *or* mediática ◇ **the media** los medios informativos *or* de comunicación *mpl* ◇ **the product attracted a lot of interest in the media** el producto despertó mucho interés en los medios de comunicación ◇ **to transfer from magnetic tape to floppy disk, you need a media conversion device** para transferir de una cinta magnética a un disquete, se necesita un dispositivo de conversión de soporte ◇ **we got good media coverage for the launch of the new model** conseguimos una buena cobertura periodística para el lanzamiento del nuevo modelo

media access control /ˌmiːdiə 'ækses kən ˌtrəʊl/ *noun* control *m* de acceso a medios (de transmisión)

media control architecture /ˌmiːdiə kən ˌtrəʊl 'ɑːkɪˌtektʃə/ *noun* arquitectura *f* micro channel

media control interface /ˌmiːdiə kənˌtrəʊl 'ɪntəfeɪs/ *noun* interfaz *f* de control de medios (multimedia)

media conversion /ˌmiːdjə kən'vɜːʃ(ə)n/ *noun* conversión *f* de soporte (de datos) ◇ **to transfer from magnetic tape to floppy disk, you need a media conversion device** para transferir de una cinta magnética a un disquete, se necesita un dispositivo de conversión de soporte (de datos)

media error /ˌmiːdjə 'erə/ *noun* error *m* causado por el soporte

Media Player /'miːdiə ˌpleɪə/ (*trade name for a Windows utility program*) Media Player™

MediaServer /'miːdiəˌsɜːvə/ (*trade name for a system developed by Netscape to provide audio and video delivery over the Internet*) MediaServer™

medical telematics /ˌmedɪk(ə)l ˌtelɪ 'mætɪks/ *noun* telemática *f* médica

medium /'miːdiəm/ *adjective* (*middle or average*) medio *or* -a ■ *noun* **1.** (*for data storage*) medio *m* **2.** (*for transmitting information*) medio *m* ◇ **a medium-sized computer system** un sistema informático de tamaño medio

medium model /ˌmiːdiəm 'mɒd(ə)l/ *noun* modelo *m* medio de gestión de memoria

medium scale integration /ˌmiːdiəm skeɪl ˌɪntɪ'greɪʃ(ə)n/ *noun* integración *f* media

medium speed /'miːdiəm spiːd/ *noun* velocidad *f* media

meet /miːt/ *noun* (*logical function*) conjunción *f*

meg /meg/ *noun informal* (*megabyte*) megabyte *f*; megaocteto *m*

mega- /megə/ *prefix* (*used only in computing and electronic related applications*) mega- ◇ **megabyte (MB** *or* **Mb)** megabyte *m*; megaocteto *m*

megabit /'megəbɪt/ *noun* megabit *m*

megabits per second /ˌmegəbɪts pɜː 'sekənd/ *noun* megabits *mpl* por segundo

megabyte /'megəbaɪt/ *noun* (*storage capacity of hard disk drives or RAM*) megabyte *m*; megaocteto *m*; Mb

'Doing this reduced a bitmap of my desktop from 2.25 megabytes to a 58K GIF' [*The Guardian*]

megaflop /'megəflɒp/ *noun* millones *mpl* de operaciones de coma flotante por segundo; megaflops *mpl* (Mflops)

megahertz /'megə,hɜːts/ *noun* megahercio *m* (MHz)

megapixel display /megə,pɪks(ə)l dɪ'spleɪ/ *noun* (adaptador de) pantalla *f* de resolución superior (a 1024x1024 píxeles)

Megastream /'megəstriːm/ (*trade name for a data link provided by British Telecom*) conexión *f* Megastream™

member /'membə/ *noun* elemento *m* (de un campo)

membrane keyboard /,membreɪn 'kiːbɔːd/ *noun* (*keyboard using a thin plastic sheet*) teclado *m* de membrana

memo field /'meməʊ fiːld/ *noun* (*field in a database*) campo *m* de memorándum

memorise /'memə,raɪz/, **memorize** *verb* introducir en la memoria

memory /'mem(ə)ri/ *noun* memoria *f*

'The lower-power design, together with an additional 8Kb of on-board cache memory, will increase the chip's performance to 75 million instructions per second.' [*Computing*]

'…when a program is loaded into memory, some is used for the code, some for the permanent data, and some is reserved for the stack which grows and shrinks for function calls and local data' [*Personal Computer World*]

memory access time /,mem(ə)ri 'ækses ,taɪm/ *noun* tiempo *m* de acceso a la memoria

memory address register /,mem(ə)ri ə'dres ,redʒɪstə/ *noun* registro *m* de dirección en memoria

memory allocation /'mem(ə)ri ,æləkeɪʃ(ə)n/ *noun* asignación *f* de memoria; distribución *f* de memoria

memory backup capacitor /,mem(ə)ri 'bækʌp kə,pæsɪtə/ *noun* condensador *m* de seguridad de la memoria; condensador *m* para la memoria RAM

memory bank /'mem(ə)ri bæŋk/ *noun* (*small storage devices connected together*) banco *m* de memoria ◇ **an add-on card has a 128KB memory bank made up of 16 chips** una tarjeta de extensión tiene un banco de memoria de 128KB formado por 16 chips

memory board /'mem(ə)ri bɔːd/ *noun* tarjeta *f* de memoria

memory buffer register /'mem(ə)ri ,bʌfə ,redʒɪstə/ *noun* registro *m* de memoria intermedia

memory bus /'mem(ə)ri bʌs/ *noun* enlace *m* común de memoria

memory capacity /'mem(ə)ri kə,pæsɪti/ *noun* capacidad *f* de memoria

memory cell /'mem(ə)ri sel/ *noun* celda *f* de memoria

memory chip /'mem(ə)ri tʃɪp/ *noun* chip *m* de memoria

memory cycle /'mem(ə)ri ,saɪk(ə)l/ *noun* ciclo *m* de memoria

memory data register /,mem(ə)ri 'deɪtə ,redʒɪstə/ *noun* registro *m* de datos de la memoria

memory diagnostic /'mem(ə)ri ,daɪəgnɒstɪk/ *noun* diagnóstico *m* de la memoria

memory dump /'mem(ə)ri dʌmp/ *noun* (*printout of the contents of a memory*) vaciado *m* de la memoria mediante la impresora; vuelco *m* de la memoria; análisis *m* del contenido de la memoria

memory effect /'mem(ə)ri ɪ,fekt/ *noun* efecto *m* memoria

memory expansion /'mem(ə)ri ɪk,spænʃ(ə)n/ *noun* expansión *f* de la memoria

memory hierarchy /,mem(ə)ri ,haɪərɑːki/ *noun* jerarquía *f* de la memoria

memory-intensive software /,mem(ə)ri ɪn,tensɪv 'sɒftweə/ *noun* (*software that uses large amounts of RAM or disk storage*) software *m* de memoria intensiva

memory management /'mem(ə)ri ,mænɪdʒmənt/ *noun* gestión *f* de la memoria

memory management unit /'mem(ə)ri ,mænɪdʒmənt ,juːnɪt/ *noun* unidad *f* de gestión de la memoria

memory map /'mem(ə)ri mæp/ *noun* configuración *f* de la memoria; mapa *m* de la memoria

memory-mapped /'mem(ə)ri ,mæpt/ *adjective* configurado, -a en (la) memoria ◇ **a memory-mapped screen has an address allocated to each pixel, allowing direct access to the screen by the CPU** una pantalla configurada en la memoria dispone de una dirección asignada para cada píxel, lo que permite el acceso directo de la unidad central de proceso a la pantalla

memory-mapped input/output /,mem(ə)ri ,mæpt ,ɪnpʊt 'aʊtpʊt/ *noun* entrada/salida *f* configurada en la memoria

memory-mapped I/O /,mem(ə)ri ,mæpt aɪ 'əʊ/ *noun* entrada/salida *f* configurada en la memoria; E/S configurada en la memoria

memory model /'mem(ə)ri ,mɒd(ə)l/ *noun* modelo *m* de (gestión de acceso a la) memoria

memory page /'mem(ə)ri peɪdʒ/ *noun* página *f* (de) memoria

memory protect /'mem(ə)ri prə,tekt/ *noun* (dispositivo de) protección *f* de la memoria

memory-resident software /,mem(ə)ri ,rezɪd(ə)nt 'sɒftweə/ *noun* software *m* residente

memory stick /'mem(ə)ri stɪk/ *noun* palo *m* de memoria

memory switching system /'mem(ə)ri ,swɪtʃɪŋ ,sɪstəm/ *noun* sistema *m* de transferencia de memoria

memory workspace /'mem(ə)ri ,wɜːkspeɪs/ *noun* zona *f* de trabajo en la memoria

menu /'menjuː/ *noun* menú *m*

menu-bar /'menjuː bɑː/ *noun* barra *f* del menú

menu-driven software /ˌmenjuː ˌdrɪv(ə)n
ˈsɒftweə/ *noun* programa *m* a base de menús

menu item /ˈmenjuː ˌaɪtəm/ *noun* (*choice in a
menu*) elemento *m*; ítem *m* del menú

menu selection /ˈmenjuː sɪˌlekʃən/ *noun* selección *f* por menú

menu shortcut /ˈmenjuː ˈʃɔːtkʌt/ *noun* acceso *m* directo al menú

mercury delay line /ˌmɜːkjʊri dɪˈleɪ ˌlaɪn/
noun (*obsolete method of storing serial data*)
línea *f* de retraso; retardo *m* de mercurio

merge /mɜːdʒ/ *verb* (*to combine two data files*)
fusionar *vt*; integrar *vt*; combinar *vt*; unir *vt* ◇ **the
system automatically merges text and illustrations into the document** el sistema fusiona
or combina automáticamente texto e ilustraciones
dentro del documento

merge sort /ˌmɜːdʒ ˈsɔːt/ *noun* (función de)
clasificar y fusionar

mesh /meʃ/ *noun* malla *f*

mesh network /meʃ ˈnetwɜːk/ *noun* (*network
connection*) red *f* (en forma de) malla; red *f* (en
forma) de anillo

message /ˈmesɪdʒ/ *noun* **1.** (*piece of information sent*) mensaje *m* **2.** (*detailed amount of information*) mensaje *m* ◇ **message handling service (MHS)** servicio *m* de transferencia de mensajes ◇ **message numbering** numeración *f* de
mensajes ◇ **message of the day (MOTD)** (*in
chats*) mensaje del día ◇ **message switching**
conmutación *f* de mensajes

message board /ˈmesɪdʒ bɔːd/ *noun* tablón *m*
de mensajes

message box /ˈmesɪdʒ bɒks/ *noun* (*small
window on screen*) ventana *f*; cuadro *m* de mensaje

message code authentication /ˌmesɪdʒ
kəʊd ɔːˌθentɪˈkeɪʃ(ə)n/ *noun* código *m* de autent-
ticación de mensajes

message format /ˈmesɪdʒ ˌfɔːmæt/ *noun* formato *m* de mensaje

message handling service /ˌmesɪdʒ
ˈhændlɪŋ ˌsɜːvɪs/ *noun* servicio *m* de transferencia de mensajes

message header /ˈmesɪdʒ ˌhedə/ *noun* (*sequence of data*) encabezamiento *m*; cabecera *f* de
mensaje

message routing /ˈmesɪdʒ raʊtɪŋ/ *noun* encaminamiento *m* de mensajes

message slot /ˈmesɪdʒ slɒt/ *noun* (*number of
bits that can hold a message*) ranura *f* para un
mensaje

message text /ˈmesɪdʒ tekst/ *noun* texto *m* de
un mensaje

message transfer agent /ˌmesɪdʒ ˈtrænsfɜː
ˌeɪdʒənt/ *noun* programa *m* de transferencia de
mensajes

messaging /ˈmesɪdʒɪŋ/ *noun* (*sending messages by phone*) mensajería *f*

metabit /ˈmetəbɪt/ *noun* metabit *m*

metacompilation /ˌmetəkɒmpɪˈleɪʃ(ə)n/
noun metacompilación *f*

metacompiler /ˈmetəkɒmˌpaɪlə/ *noun* (*compiler used to create another compiler*) metacompilador *m*

metafile /ˈmetəfaɪl/ *noun* **1.** (*file that contains
other files*) metafichero *m* **2.** (*file with data about
other files*) metafichero *m* ◇ **the operating system uses a metafile to hold the data that defines
where each file is stored on disk** el sistema operativo usa un metafichero para guardar datos que
define dónde se almacena cada fichero en el disco

metalanguage /ˈmetəˌlæŋgwɪdʒ/ *noun* metalenguaje *m*

metal oxide semiconductor /ˌmet(ə)l
ˌɒksaɪd ˈsemikənˌdʌktə/ *noun* semiconductor *m*
de óxido metálico; transistor *m* (de) MOS

meter – power supply /ˌmiːtə ˈpaʊə səˌplaɪ/
noun propiedades *fpl* de energía; reservas *fpl* de
energía

metropolitan area network
/ˌmetrəpɒlɪt(ə)n ˌeəriə ˈnetwɜːk/ *noun* (*network extending over a limited area*) red *f* metropolitana; red *f* urbana

MFLOPS /ˈem flɒps/ *noun* (*measure of computing speed*) megaflops *mpl*; (número de) millones *mpl* de operaciones de coma flotante por segundo

MFM /ˌem ef ˈem/ *noun* modulación *f* de frecuencia modificada

MHS /ˌem eɪtʃ ˈes/ *noun* servicio *m* de transferencia de mensajes

MHz *abbr* (*megahertz*) megahercio (MHz) *m*

MICR /ˌem aɪ siː ˈɑː/ *noun* reconocimiento *m* de
caracteres de tinta magnética

micro /ˈmaɪkrəʊ/ *noun* (*one millionth*) microordenador *m*

micro- /ˈmaɪkrəʊ/ *prefix* **1.** (*one millionth*) mi-
cro- **2.** (*very small*) micro-

microcassette /ˈmaɪkrəʊkəˌset/ *noun* (*very
small cassette used in pocket dictating equipment*) microcasete *f*

Micro Channel Architecture /ˌmaɪkrəʊ
ˌtʃæn(ə)l ˈɑːkɪtektʃə/ arquitectura *f* MCA

Micro Channel Architecture chipset
/ˌmaɪkrəʊ ˌtʃæn(ə)l ˌɑːkɪtektʃə ˈtʃɪpset/ juego
m de componentes MCA

Micro Channel Bus /ˌmaɪkrəʊ ˌtʃæn(ə)l
ˈbʌs/ (*IBM 32-bit expansion bus*) bus *m* Micro-
Channel; (*proprietary 32-bit expansion bus defined by IBM*) bus *m* MCA

microchip /ˈmaɪkrəʊˌtʃɪp/ *noun* microchip *f*

microcircuit /ˈmaɪkrəʊˌkɜːkɪt/ *noun* (*complex integrated circuit*) microcircuito *m*

microcode /ˈmaɪkrəʊkəʊd/ *noun* microcódigo
m

Microcom Networking Protocol
/ˌmaɪkrəkɒm ˈnetwɜːkɪŋ ˌprəʊtəkɒl/ (*error detection and correction system*) protocolo *m* de
comunicación de red Microcom (MNP)

microcomputer /ˈmaɪkrəʊkəmˌpjuːtə/ *noun*
microordenador *m*

microcomputer architecture
/ˌmaɪkrəʊkəmˈpjuːtə ˈɑːkɪtektʃə/ noun arquitectura f de microordenador

microcomputer backplane
/ˌmaɪkrəʊkəmˈpjuːtə ˈbækpleɪn/ noun (main printed circuit board of a system) parte f posterior de un microordenador; panel m básico de un microordenador

microcomputer bus /ˈmaɪkrəʊkəmˌpjuːtə ˌbʌs/ noun (set of the main data, address and control buses) bus m; enlace m común de un microordenador

microcomputer development kit
/ˌmaɪkrəʊkəmˈpjuːtə dɪˈveləpmənt ˌkɪt/ noun equipo m de desarrollo de un microordenador

microcomputing /ˈmaɪkrəʊkəmˌpjuːtɪŋ/ adjective microinformática f ◇ **the microcomputing industry** industria f de la microinformática or de los microordenadores

microcontroller /ˈmaɪkrəʊkənˌtrəʊlə/ noun microcontrolador m

microcycle /ˈmaɪkrəʊˌsaɪk(ə)l/ noun microciclo m

microdevice /ˈmaɪkrəʊdɪˌvaɪs/ noun (very small device) dispositivo m; componente m de dimensiones muy pequeñas; microdispositivo m; (microprocessor) microprocesador m

microelectronics /ˌmaɪkrəʊɪlekˈtrɒnɪks/ noun microelectrónica f

microfloppy /ˈmaɪkrəʊˌflɒpi/ noun (usually refers to 3.5 inch disks) disquete m de 3,5 pulgadas

microinstruction /ˈmaɪkrəʊɪnˌstrʌkʃən/ noun microinstrucción f

micrometre /ˈmaɪkrəʊˌmiːtə/ noun (one millionth of a metre – formerly called 'micron') micrómetro m; formerly micrómetro m

micron /ˈmaɪkrɒn/ noun (one millionth of a metre) micra f; micrón m

microphone /ˈmaɪkrəfəʊn/ noun micrófono m; micro m ◇ **dynamic microphone** micrófono dinámico ◇ **moving coil microphone** micrófono de bobina móvil

microprocessor /ˈmaɪkrəʊˌprəʊsesə/ noun microprocesador m

microprocessor addressing capabilities
/ˌmaɪkrəʊprəʊsesə əˈdresɪŋ ˌkeɪpəbɪlɪtiz/ noun (highest address) capacidad f; facilidad f de direccionamiento de un microprocesador

microprocessor architecture
/ˈmaɪkrəʊprəʊsesə ˌɑːkɪtektʃə/ noun arquitectura f de un microprocesador

microprocessor chip /ˈmaɪkrəʊˌprəʊsesə tʃɪp/ noun chip m de microprocesador

microprocessor timing /ˈmaɪkrəʊˌprəʊsesə ˌtaɪmɪŋ/ noun sincronización f de microprocesadores

microprocessor unit /ˈmaɪkrəʊˌprəʊsesə ˌjuːnɪt/ noun unidad f de microprocesador

microprogram /ˈmaɪkrəʊˌprəʊɡræm/ noun microprograma m

microprogram assembly language
/ˌmaɪkrəʊprəʊɡræm əˈsembli ˌlæŋɡwɪdʒ/ noun lenguaje m ensamblador de un microprograma

microprogram counter /ˈmaɪkrəʊˌprəʊɡræm ˌkaʊntə/ noun (register) registro m de microprograma; contador m de microprograma

microprogram instruction set
/ˌmaɪkrəʊprəʊɡræm ɪnˈstrʌkʃən ˌset/ noun (register) juego m; (set of basic microinstructions) juego m; (register) grupo m de instrucciones de un microprograma; (set of basic microinstructions) grupo m de instrucciones de un microprograma

microprogramming /ˈmaɪkrəʊˌprəʊɡræmɪŋ/ noun microprogramación f

microprogram store /ˈmaɪkrəʊˌprəʊɡræm ˌstɔː/ noun memoria f que contiene un microprograma

microsecond /ˈmaɪkrəʊˌsekənd/ noun microsegundo m

microsequence /ˈmaɪkrəʊˌsiːkwəns/ noun microsecuencia f; porción f de un microprograma; secuencia f de microinstrucciones

Microsoft /ˈmaɪkrəsɒft/ (developer and publisher of software) Microsoft™

Microsoft DOS /ˌmaɪkrəsɒft ˈdɒs/ MS-DOS

Microsoft Exchange /ˌmaɪkrəsɒft ɪks ˈtʃeɪndʒ/ (program included with Windows 95) Microsoft Exchange™

Microsoft Internet Explorer /ˌmaɪkrəsɒft ˌɪntənet ɪksˈplɔːrə/ Microsoft Internet Explorer™

Microsoft Network /ˌmaɪkrəsɒft ˈnetwɜːk/ Microsoft Network™

Microsoft Outlook /ˌmaɪkrəsɒft ˈaʊtlʊk/ (trade name for an application that provides a range of features including managing email, contacts and diary appointments) Microsoft Outlook™

Microsoft Outlook Express /ˌmaɪkrəsɒft ˌaʊtlʊk ɪkˈspres/ (trade name for a free version of Outlook) Microsoft Outlook Express™

Microsoft Windows /ˌmaɪkrəsɒft ˈwɪndəʊz/ Microsoft Windows; (sistema) Windows de Microsoft

microwriter /ˈmaɪkrəʊˌraɪtə/ noun (portable keyboard and display) microordenador m portátil

middleware /ˈmɪd(ə)lweə/ noun (system software that has been customised) programa m personalizado; programa m intermedio

MID-F1 /ˌmɪd ef ˈwʌn/ noun nivel m B

MIDI /ˈmɪdi/ noun MIDI

MIDI channel /ˈmɪdi ˌtʃæn(ə)l/ noun canal m MIDI

MIDI connector /ˈmɪdi kəˌnektə/ noun conector m MIDI

MIDI device /ˈmɪdi ðiˌvaɪs/ noun dispositivo m MIDI

MIDI file /ˈmɪdi faɪl/ noun fichero m MIDI

MIDI interface card /ˌmɪdi 'ɪntəfeɪs kɑːd/ *noun* tarjeta *f* interfaz MIDI

MIDI Mapper /'mɪdi ˌmæpə/ *noun* acoplador *m*; transformador *m* MIDI ◇ **you could use the MIDI Mapper to re-direct all the notes meant for the drum machine to the electronic piano** se podría utilizar el acoplador MIDI para desviar al piano electrónico todas las notas destinadas a la batería

MIDI mapping /'mɪdi ˌmæpɪŋ/ *noun* configuración *f* MIDI

MIDI sequence /'mɪdi ˌsiːkwəns/ *noun* secuencia *f* MIDI

MIDI sequencer /ˌmɪdi 'siːkwənsə/ *noun* secuenciador *m* MIDI

MIDI setup map /ˌmɪdi 'setʌp mæp/ *noun* controlador *m* de instalación del acoplador MIDI

MIDI time code /ˌmɪdi 'taɪm kəʊd/ *noun* código *m* temporal MIDI

mid-user /mɪd 'juːzə/ *noun* usuario *m or* -a *f*; intermediario *m or* -a *f*

migration /maɪ'greɪʃ(ə)n/ *noun* (*moving users from one hardware platform to another*) emigración *f*

milk disk /'mɪlk dɪsk/ *noun* (*disk used to transfer data from a small machine onto a larger computer*) disco *m*; disquete *m* de enlace

milking machine /'mɪlkɪŋ məˌʃiːn/ *noun* concentradora *f* de datos

milli- /mɪlɪ/ *prefix* (*one thousandth*) mili- ◇ **millicoulomb (mC)** miliculombio (mC) *m* ◇ **millisecond (ms)** milisegundo (ms) *m*

milliampere /ˌmɪli'æmpeə/ *noun* miliamperio (mA) *m*

million instructions per second /ˌmɪljən ɪnˌstrʌkʃənz pɜː sɪ'kɒnd/ *noun* millón *m* de instrucciones por segundo; MIPS

millisecond /'mɪlɪˌsekənd/ *noun* milisegundo (ms) *m*

MIME /ˌem aɪ em 'iː/ *noun* extensiones *fpl* multipropósito de correo Internet

mini /'mɪni/ *noun* miniordenador *m*

mini- /mɪni/ *prefix* (*small*) mini-

minicomputer /'mɪnikəmˌpjuːtə/ *noun* (*small computer*) mini *m*; miniordenador *m*; minicomputador *m*

minidisk /'mɪnidɪsk/ *noun* minidisquete *m*

minifloppy /'mɪniˌflɒpi/ *noun* (*disk*) minidisquete *m*

minimal tree /'mɪnɪm(ə)l triː/ *noun* árbol *m* de ejecución mínima

minimise /'mɪnɪmaɪz/, **minimize** *verb* **1.** minimizar *vt* **2.** (*to shrink an application window*) minimizar *vt*; reducir *vt*; transformar una ventana en un icono

miniwinny /'mɪniˌwɪni/ *noun informal* minidisco *m* duro (de tipo Winchester)

minmax /'mɪnimæks/ *noun* procedimiento *m* minimax/de aproximación al mínimo máximo

minuend /'mɪnjuːend/ *noun* minuendo *m*

minus /'maɪnəs/, **minus sign** /'maɪnəs saɪn/ *noun* signo *m* menos; signo *m* de substracción

MIPS /mɪps/ *noun* millón *m* de instrucciones por segundo

'ICL has staked its claim to the massively parallel market with the launch of the Goldrush MegaServer, providing up to 16,000 Unix MIPS of processing power.' [*Computing*]

mirror /'mɪrə/ *verb* **1.** reflejar *vt* **2.** (*to make an identical copy*) hacer una copia idéntica ◇ **mirror disk** disco *m* espejo ◇ **mirror image** imagen *f* inversa *or* de espejo

'Network-attached storage systems which aim to make it easy to mirror data between units' [*The Guardian*]

mirror site /'mɪrə saɪt/ *noun* sitio *m* de espejo

MIS *abbr* **1.** (*management information service*) servicio *m* informático de gestión **2.** (*management information system*) sistema *m* de información para administración

MISD /ˌem aɪ es 'diː/ *noun* (procesador de) corriente *f* de instrucciones múltiples – corriente de un solo dato; multiflujo *m* de instrucciones – monoflujo de datos

mission-critical /ˌmɪʃ(ə)n 'krɪtɪk(ə)l/ *adjective* (*on which a company depends*) crítico *or* -a; vital

MKDIR *abbr* (*make directory*) instrucción *f* MD; MKDIR (de creación de un directorio)

MMU /ˌem em 'juː/ *noun* unidad *f* de gestión de la memoria

MMX (*trade name for an enhanced Intel processor chip*) extensiones *fpl* multimedia

mnemonic /nɪ'mɒnɪk/ *noun* (*shortened form of a word or function*) mnemónico *m*

MNP /ˌem en 'piː/ *noun* protocolo *m* de redes de Microcom

MNP 2–4 /ˌem en 'piː tuː fɔː/ *noun* protocolo *m* MNP 2–4

MNP 5 *noun* estándar *m* MNP 5

MNP 10 *noun* protocolo *m* MNP 10

mobile phone /ˌməʊbaɪl 'fəʊn/ *noun* teléfono *m* móvil

mock-up /'mɒk ʌp/ *noun* modelo *m*; maqueta *f*

modal /'məʊd(ə)l/ *adjective* modal

mode /məʊd/ *noun* **1.** (*way of doing something*) modo *m*; modalidad *f* **2.** (*method of operating computer*) modo *m*; modalidad *f* ◇ **bit-map mode** modo *m* de transformación por bits ◇ **when you want to type in text, press this function key which will put the terminal in its alphanumeric mode** cuando quiera mecanografiar un texto, presione esta tecla de función para activar el modo alfanumérico del terminal

'The approach being established by the Jedec committee provides for burst mode data transfer clocked at up to 100MHz.' [*Computing*]

Mode 1 /'məʊd wʌn/ *noun* Mode 1

Mode 2 /'məʊd tuː/ *noun* Mode 2

model /'mɒd(ə)l/ *noun* **1.** (*small-size copy*) maqueta *f*; modelo *m* **2.** (*version*) modelo *m* ■ *adjective* (*perfect*) modelo ■ *verb* (*to make a mod-*

el) modelar ◇ **he showed us a model of the new computer centre building** nos mostró una maqueta del nuevo edificio del centro informático ◇ **the new model B has taken the place of model A** el nuevo modelo B ha sustituido al modelo A ◇ **this is the latest model** éste es el último modelo

modelling /'mɒd(ə)lɪŋ/ *noun* creación *f* de modelos de programas

modem /'məʊˌdem/, **MODEM** *noun* (*modulator/demodulator*) módem *m*

'AST Research has bundled together a notebook PC with a third-party PCMCIA fax modem technology for a limited-period special offer.' [*Computing*]

modem eliminator /ˌməʊdem ɪ'lɪmɪneɪtə/ *noun* supresor *m* de módem

modem standards /'məʊdem ˌstændədz/ *plural noun* normas *fpl* para módems

moderate /'mɒd(ə)rət/ *verb* moderar *vt*

moderated list /ˌmɒd(ə)rətɪd 'lɪst/, **moderated mailing list** /ˌmɒd(ə)rətd 'meɪlɪŋ lɪst/ *noun* (*mailing list checked and approved*) lista *f* moderada; lista *f* verificada

moderator /'mɒdəˌreɪtə/ *noun* moderador *mf*

modification /ˌmɒdɪfɪ'keɪʃ(ə)n/ *noun* modificación *f*; cambio *m*

modification loop /ˌmɒdɪfɪ'keɪʃ(ə)n luːp/ *noun* (*set of instructions within a loop*) bucle *m* de modificación

modified frequency modulation /ˌmɒdɪfaɪd 'friːkwənsi ˌmɒdjʊleɪʃ(ə)n/ *noun* (*method of storing data on magnetic media*) modulación *f* de frecuencia modificada

modifier /'mɒdɪˌfaɪə/ *noun* modificador *m*

modify /'mɒdɪˌfaɪ/ *verb* modificar *vt*; adaptar *vt* ◇ **the keyboard was modified for European users** se modificó el teclado para los usuarios europeos ◇ **the software will have to be modified to run on a small PC** tendremos que modificar el software para poder funcionar en un ordenador personal ◇ **we are running a modified version of the mail-merge system** estamos ejecutando una versión modificada del programa de edición de cartas modelo

Modula-2 /ˌmɒdjʊlə 'tuː/ *noun* (*programming language*) lenguaje *m* (de alto nivel) Modula-2

modular /'mɒdjʊlə/ *adjective* modular ◇ **modular counter** contador *m* modular

modularisation, modularization *noun* modularización *f*

modularity /ˌmɒdjʊ'lærɪti/ *noun* modularidad *f* ◇ **the modularity of the software or hardware allows the system to be changed** la modularidad del software o del hardware permite modificar el sistema

modular programming /ˌmɒdjʊlə 'prəʊgræmɪŋ/ *noun* programación *f* modular

modulate /'mɒdjʊˌleɪt/ *verb* modular *vt*

modulated signal /ˌmɒdjʊleɪtɪd 'sɪgn(ə)l/ *noun* señal *f* modulada

modulating signal /'mɒdjʊleɪtɪŋ ˌsɪgn(ə)l/ *noun* señal *f* de modulación

modulator /'mɒdjʊleɪtə/ *noun* modulador *m*

modulator/demodulator /ˌmɒdjʊleɪtə diː 'mɒdjʊleɪtə/ *noun* modulator-desmodulador *m*

module /'mɒdjuːl/ *noun* **1.** (*section of program*) módulo *m* **2.** (*piece of hardware*) módulo *m* ◇ **a multifunction analog interface module includes analog to digital and digital to analog converters** un módulo de interfaz analógico multifunción incluye convertidores de analógico a digital y de digital a analógico

modulo arithmetic /'mɒdjʊləʊ əˌrɪθmətɪk/ *noun* módulo *m* aritmético

modulo-N /ˌmɒdjʊləʊ 'en/ *noun* módulo *m* N

modulo-N check /ˌmɒdjʊləʊ 'en tʃek/ *noun* prueba *f* modelo N

moiré effect /'mwɑːreɪ ɪˌfekt/ *noun* efecto *m* muaré

momentary switch /'məʊmənt(ə)ri swɪtʃ/ *noun* (*switch*) interruptor *m* temporal; conmutador *m* de acción momentánea

monadic Boolean operation /mɒˌnædɪk ˌbuːliən ˌɒpə'reɪʃ(ə)n/ *noun* operación *f* booleana monádica de un operando

monadic Boolean operator /mɒˌnædɪk ˌbuːliən 'ɒpəreɪtə/ *noun* operador *m* booleano monádico

monadic operation /mɒˌnædɪk ˌɒpə 'reɪʃ(ə)n/ *noun* operación *f* monádica

monadic operator /mɒˌnædɪk 'ɒpəreɪtə/ *noun* operador *m* booleano monádico

monitor /'mɒnɪtə/ *noun* **1.** (*VDU*) monitor *m*; pantalla *f* (de visualización) **2.** (*system that watches for faults*) monitor *m* ■ *verb* (*to supervise*) verificar *vt*; controlar *vt*; seguir *vt*; supervisar *vt* ◇ **he is monitoring the progress of the trainee programmers** está verificando cómo progresan los aprendices de programación ◇ **the machine monitors each signal as it is sent out** la máquina controla cada señal al mismo tiempo que la envía

monitor program /'mɒnɪtə ˌprəʊgræm/ *noun* (*computer program*) programa *m* de control; programa *m* monitor

monitor unit /'mɒnɪtə ˌjuːnɪt/ *noun* monitor *m*

mono- /mɒnəʊ/ *prefix* mono-

monoaural /ˌmɒnəʊ'ɔːrəl/ *adjective* monoaural

monochrome /'mɒnəkrəʊm/ *adjective, noun* monocromo; (en) blanco y negro

monochrome display adapter /ˌmɒnəkrəʊm dɪ'spleɪ əˌdæptə/ *noun* adaptador *m* de pantalla monocromo; tarjeta *f* MDA

monochrome monitor /ˌmɒnəkrəʊm 'mɒnɪtə/ *noun* (*computer monitor that displays in black or white*) monitor *m* monocromo; monitor *m* en blanco y negro

monolithic driver /mɒnəˌlɪθɪk 'draɪvə/ *noun* controlador *m* monolítico

monomode fibre /'mɒnəʊməʊd ˌfaɪbə/ *noun* fibra *f* (óptica) monomodo

monoprogramming system /'mɒnəʊ ˌprəʊɡræmɪŋ ˌsɪstəm/ *noun* sistema *m* de mono-programación

monospaced font /ˌmɒnəʊspeɪst 'fɒnt/ *noun* (*font in which each character has the same width*) fuente *f* (de caracteres) uniforme; fuente *f* monoespaciada

Monte Carlo method /ˌmɒnti 'kɑːləʊ ˌmeθəd/ *noun* método *m* de Monte Carlo

morphing /'mɔːfɪŋ/ *noun* (*in multimedia and games*) metamorfosis *f*

MOS /ˌem əʊ 'es/ *noun* semi-conductor *m* MOS

mosaic /məʊ'zeɪɪk/ *noun* mosaico *m*

Mosaic /məʊ'zeɪɪk/ (*trade name for a popular browser software used to view webpages on the Internet*) Mosaic

MOS memory /ˌem əʊ es 'mem(ə)ri/ *noun* memoria *f* MOS

most significant bit /ˌməʊst sɪɡˌnɪfɪkənt 'bɪt/ *noun* bit *m* más significativo; BMS

most significant digit /məʊst sɪɡˌnɪfɪkənt 'dɪdʒɪt/, **most significant character** /məʊst sɪɡˌnɪfɪkənt 'kærɪktə/ *noun* carácter *m* más significativo; dígito *m* más significativo (MSD)

motherboard /'mʌðəbɔːd/ *noun* placa *f* madre

Motorola /ˌməʊtə'rəʊlə/ (*company that designs and makes the 68000 range of processors that were used in the original Apple Mac computers*) Motorola™

mount /maʊnt/ *verb* **1.** (*a device or circuit*) montar *vt*; instalar *vt*; armar *vt* **2.** (*insert a disk in a disk drive*) insertar *vt*; introducir *vt* ◇ **the chips are mounted in sockets on the PCB** los chips se instalan en enchufes sobre la placa del circuito impreso

mouse /maʊs/ *noun* ratón *m* ◇ **mouse acceleration** velocidad *f* del ratón ◇ **mouse-driven (software)** (programa) controlado *or* dirigido por un ratón

> 'This project has now borne fruit, with the announcement last week of Windots, a project which allows users to 'see' Windows screens in a Braille form of Ascii. Other areas of research include a sound system which allows a sound to 'move', mirroring the movement of a mouse.'
> [*Computing*]

mouse acceleration /maʊs əkˌselə'reɪʃ(ə)n/ *noun* velocidad *f* del ratón

mouse-driven /maʊs 'drɪv(ə)n/ *adjective* controlado por un ratón; dirigido por un ratón

mouse pointer /maʊs 'pɔɪntə/ *noun* (*small arrow displayed on screen*) puntero *m* del ratón; puntero *m* controlado por el ratón

mouse sensitivity /maʊs ˌsensə'tɪvəti/ *noun* sensibilidad *f* del ratón

mouse tracking /maʊs 'trækɪŋ/ *noun* insensibilidad *f* del ratón

M out of N code /ˌem aʊt əv 'en ˌkəʊd/ *noun* código *m* M de N

movable /'muːvəb(ə)l/ *adjective* (*which can be removed*) movible; (*which can be moved*) móvil; extraíble

movable head disk /ˌmuːvəb(ə)l hed 'dɪsk/ *noun* cabeza *f* de disco (magnético) móvil

move /muːv/ *verb* (*to change the position*) desplazar *vt*; mover *vt*; cambiar de lugar

move block /'muːv ˌblɒk/ *noun* (instrucción de) mover un bloque

movement /'muːvmənt/ *noun* movimiento *m*

movement file /'muːvmənt faɪl/ *noun* fichero *m* de movimientos

Moving Pictures Expert Group /ˌmuːvɪŋ ˌpɪktʃəs 'ekspɜːt ˌɡruːp/ *noun* grupo *m* de expertos en imagen en movimiento

MP3 /ˌem pi: 'θriː/ *noun* MP3

MPC /ˌem pi: 'siː/ *noun* ordenador *m* (personal) multimedia

MPEG /'em peɡ/ *noun* grupo *m* de expertos en imagen en movimiento

MPS *abbr* (*microprocessor system*) sistema *m* de microprocesador

MPU *abbr* (*microprocessor unit*) unidad *f* de microprocesador

MS *abbr* (*Microsoft*) Microsoft; MS

msb /ˌem es 'biː/, **MSB** *noun* BMS; bit *m* más significativo

MSD /ˌem es 'diː/ *noun* carácter *m* más significativo; dígito *m* más significativo (MSD)

MS-DOS /ˌem es 'dɒs/ (*trade name for an operating system for the IBM PC range of personal computers*) MS-DOS

MSI *abbr* (*medium scale integration*) integración *f* media

MSN (*trade name for an Internet portal*) MSN; Microsoft Network™

MS-Windows /ˌem es 'wɪndəʊz/ MS-Windows

MSX /ˌem es 'eks/ *noun* norma *f* MSX; estándar *m* MSX

MTA /ˌem ti: 'eɪ/ *noun* programa *m* de transferencia de mensajes

MTBF /ˌem ti: bi: 'ef/ *noun* duración *f* media de funcionamiento correcto entre fallos; tiempo *m* medio de funcionamiento correcto entre fallos

MTC /ˌem ti: 'siː/ *noun* código *m* temporal MIDI

MTF /ˌem ti: 'ef/ *noun* tiempo *m* medio sin averías

MTTR /ˌem ti: ti: 'ɑː/ *noun* duración *f* media necesaria para una reparación

MUD /ˌem ti: 'eɪ/ *noun* **1.** dimensión *f* multiusuario **2.** dimensión *f* multiusuario

multi- /mʌlti/ *prefix* (*many or more than one*) multi- ◇ **multimegabyte memory card** tarjeta *f* de memoria de muchos megabytes

multi-access system /ˌmʌlti ˌækses 'sɪstəm/ *noun* (*system that allows access to multi-users*) multiacceso *m*

multi-address /ˌmʌlti ə'dres/, **multi-address instruction** /ˌmʌlti əˌdres ɪn'strʌkʃən/ *noun* (*system that allows access to multi-users*) instrucción *f* de multidirección; (*instruction with more than one address*) dirección *f* múltiple

multibank dynamic random access memory /ˌmʌltɪbæŋk daɪˌnæmɪk ˌrændəm ˌækses 'mem(ə)ri/ *noun* memoria *f* de acceso aleatorio dinámica multiuso

multi-board computer /ˌmʌltɪ bɔːd kəm 'pjuːtə/ *noun* ordenador *m* multitarjeta

multibus system /ˌmʌltɪbʌs 'sɪstəm/, **multibus architecture** /ˌmʌltɪbʌs 'aːkɪtektʃə/ *noun* sistema *m* multibús; sistema *m* de bus múltiple

multicast packet /ˌʌltɪkaːst 'pækɪt/ *noun* paquete *m* (de datos) de multidifusión

multichannel /ˌmʌltɪ'tʃæn(ə)l/ *adjective* multicanal

multicolour /ˌmʌlti'kʌlə/ *adjective* multicolor

multidimensional /ˌmʌltidaɪ'menʃən(ə)l/ *adjective* multidimensional

multidimensional array /ˌmʌltɪdaɪmenʃ(ə)n(ə)l ə'reɪ/ *noun* (*arrays arranged in parallel*) orden *m* multidimensional; matriz *f* multidimensional; serie *f* multidimensional

multidimensional language /ˌmʌltɪdaɪmenʃ(ə)n(ə)l 'læŋgwɪdʒ/ *noun* lenguaje *m* multidimensional; lenguaje *m* multinivel

multi-disk /ˌmʌltɪ 'dɪsk/ *adjective* multidisco

multi-disk option /'mʌltɪ dɪsk ˌɒpʃ(ə)n/ *noun* opción *f* multidisco

multi-disk reader /ˌmʌltɪ dɪsk 'riːdə/ *noun* lector *m* multidisco

multidrop circuit /'mʌltɪdrɒp ˌsɜːkɪt/ *noun* circuito *m* multipunto

MultiFinder /'mʌltɪfaɪndə/ *noun* (*Apple Macintosh Finder that supports multitasking*) MultiFinder™

multifrequency monitor /ˌmʌltɪfriːkwənsi 'mɒnɪtə/ *noun* monitor *m* de multifrecuencias

multifunction, multifunctional *adjective* multifunción *f* ◇ **a multifunction analog interface module includes analog to digital and digital to analog converters** un módulo de interfaz analógico multifunción incluye convertidores de analógico a digital y de digital a analógico

multifunction card /ˌmʌltɪfʌnkʃ(ə)n 'kaːd/ *noun* tarjeta *f* multifunción

multifunction workstation /ˌmʌltɪfʌnkʃ(ə)n 'wɜːkˌsteɪʃ(ə)n/ *noun* estación *f* de trabajo multifunción

multilayer /ˌmʌlti'leɪə/ *adjective* de capas múltiples ◇ **multilayer device** dispositivo *m* de capas múltiples

multilevel /ˌmʌlti'lev(ə)l/ *adjective* de niveles múltiples; multinivel

multilink system /'mʌltɪlɪŋk ˌsɪstəm/ *noun* sistema *m* de múltiples conexiones

multimedia /ˌmʌlti'miːdiə/ *adjective* (*combination of sound, graphics, text, etc.*) multimedia

'The Oracle Media Server is a multimedia database designed to run on massively parallel computers, running hundreds of transactions per second and managing multiple data types, such as video, audio and text.' [*Computing*]

multimedia card /ˌmʌltimiːdiə 'kaːd/ *noun* tarjeta *f* multimedia

multimedia developer's kit /ˌmʌltimiːdiə dɪ'veləpəz kɪt/ *noun* conjunto *m* de aplicaciones multimedia

multimedia extensions /ˌmʌltimiːdiə ɪk 'stenʃ(ə)nz/ *plural noun* extensiones *fpl* multimedia; procesador *m* MMX

multimedia PC /ˌmʌltimiːdiə ˌpiː 'siː/ *noun* ordenador *m* (personal) multimedia

multimedia-ready /ˌmʌltimiːdiə 'redi/ *adjective* preparado para programas multimedia

multimode fibre /ˌmʌltiməud 'faɪbə/ *noun* fibra *f* multimoda; fibra *f* (óptica) multimodal

multipass overlap /ˌmʌltipaːs 'əuvəlæp/ *noun* sobreimpresión *f*; solapamiento *m* multiciclo

multiphase program /ˌmʌltifeɪz 'prəugræm/ *noun* programa *m* multifase

multi platform /ˌmʌlti 'plætˌfɔːm/ *adjective* multiplataforma

multiple /'mʌltɪp(ə)l/ *adjective* múltiple

multiple access system /ˌmʌltɪp(ə)l 'ækses ˌsɪstəm/ *noun* multiacceso *m*; sistema *m* de acceso múltiple

multiple address code /ˌmʌltɪp(ə)l ə'dres ˌkəud/ *noun* código *m* de dirección múltiple

multiple base page /ˌmʌltɪp(ə)l beɪs 'peɪdʒ/ *noun* sistema *m* de páginas múltiples

multiple bus architecture /ˌmʌltɪp(ə)l bʌs 'aːkɪtektʃə/ *noun* arquitectura *f* de bus múltiple

multiple bus system /ˌmʌltɪp(ə)l bʌs 'sɪstəm/, **multiple bus architecture** /ˌmʌltɪp(ə)l bʌs 'aːkɪtektʃə/ *noun* sistema *m* de bus múltiple; sistema *m* multibús

multiple instruction stream-multiple data stream /ˌmʌltɪp(ə)l ɪnˌstrʌkʃən ˌstriːm ˌmʌltɪp(ə)l 'deɪtə ˌstriːm/ *noun* multiflujo *m* de instrucciones – multiflujo de datos; MIMD

multiple instruction stream-single data stream /ˌmʌltɪp(ə)l ɪnˌstrʌkʃən ˌstriːm ˌsɪŋg(ə)l 'deɪtə ˌstriːm/ *noun* (*architecture of a parallel computer*) multiflujo *m* de instrucciones – monoflujo de datos; (procesador de) corriente *f* de instrucciones múltiples – corriente de un solo dato; MISD

multiple precision /ˌmʌltɪp(ə)l prɪ'sɪʒ(ə)n/ *noun* (*use of more than one bit of data*) precisión *f* múltiple

multiplex /'mʌltɪpleks/ *verb* multiplexar *vt*

multiplexed bus /ˌmʌltɪpleksd 'bʌs/ *noun* bus *m* multiplexado

multiplexor /'mʌltɪpleksə/ *noun* multiplexor *m*; combinador *m* ◇ **a 4 to 1 multiplexor combines four inputs into a single output** un multiplexor de 4 a 1 combina 4 entradas con una sola salida

multiplicand /ˌmʌltɪplɪ'kænd/ *noun* multiplicando *m*

multiplication /ˌmʌltɪplɪ'keɪʃ(ə)n/ *noun* multiplicación *f*

multiplication sign /ˌmʌltɪplɪ'keɪʃ(ə)n saɪn/ *noun* signo *m* de multiplicación (x)

multiplier /'mʌltɪplaɪə/ *noun* multiplicador *m*

multiply /'mʌltɪˌplaɪ/ *verb* (*perform the multiplication of a number by another number*) multiplicar *vti*

multipoint /'mʌltipɔɪnt/ *adjective* multipunto

multiprecision /ˌmʌltiprɪ'sɪʒ(ə)n/ *noun* precisión *f* múltiple

multiprocessing system /ˌmʌltɪ'prəʊsesɪŋ ˌsɪstəm/ *noun* sistema *m* de multiproceso

multiprocessor /'mʌlti,prəʊsesə/ *noun* multiprocesador *m*

multiprocessor interleaving /ˌmʌltɪprəʊsesə ˌɪntə'liːvɪŋ/ *noun* (*use of more than one bit of data*) multiproceso *m*; multiprogramación *f*

multi-programming system /ˌmʌltɪ 'prəʊgræmɪŋ ˌsɪstəm/ *noun* multiprogramación *f*

multi-scan monitor /ˌmʌltɪ skæn 'mɒnɪtə/ *noun* (*can lock onto the scanning frequency of any type of graphics card*) monitor *m* multisincrónico

multisync monitor /mʌltɪˌsɪŋk 'mɒnɪtə/ *noun* monitor *m* multisincrónico

multitasking /'mʌlti,tɑːskɪŋ/ *noun* multitarea *f* ■ *adjective* multitarea ◇ **the system is multi-user and multi-tasking** el sistema es multiusario y multitarea

'X is the underlying technology which allows Unix applications to run under a multi-user, multitasking GUI. It has been adopted as the standard for the Common Open Software Environment, proposed recently by top Unix vendors including Digital, IBM and Sun.' [*Computing*]

multi terminal system /ˌmʌltɪ ˌtɜːmɪn(ə)l 'sɪstəm/ *noun* sistema *m* con muchos terminales; sistema *m* multiterminal

multithread /'mʌltiθred/ *noun* multidireccionado *m*

multiuser program /ˌmʌltijuːzə 'prəgræm/ *noun* programa *m* multiusuario

multiuser system /ˌmʌltijuːzə 'sɪstəm/ *noun* sistema *m* multiusuario

multi-window editor /ˌmʌlti ˌwɪndəʊ 'edɪtə/ *noun* programa *m* de tratamiento de textos de ventanas múltiples

Murray code /'mʌri: kəʊd/ *noun* código *m* de Murray

musical instrument digital interface /ˌmjuːzɪk(ə)l ˌɪnstrʊmənt ˌdɪdʒɪt(ə)l 'ɪntəfeɪs/ *noun* (*interface that connects electronic instruments*) interfaz *f* digital para instrumentos musicales

music chip /'mjuːzɪk tʃɪp/ *noun* circuito *m* (integrado generador) de sonido

MUX /ˌem juː 'eks/ *noun* multiplexor *m*

My Computer /ˌmaɪ kəm'pjuːtə/ *noun* (*icon that is normally in the upper left-hand corner of the screen on a computer running Windows 95*) Mi PC; (*Windows icon*) Mi PC

N

n *abbr* (*nano-*) n; nano-

NAK *abbr* (*negative acknowledgement*) acuse *m* de recibo negativo

name /neɪm/ *noun* (*address identification*) nombre *m*

name registration /neɪm ˌredʒɪ'streɪʃ(ə)n/ *noun* registro *m* de nombre de dominio

name resolution /neɪm ˌrezə'luːʃ(ə)n/ *noun* resolución *f* de nombre

name server /neɪm 'sɜːvə/ *noun* servidor *m* de nombres

namespace /'neɪmspeɪs/ *noun* espacio *m* nominal

name table /neɪm 'teɪb(ə)l/ *noun* tabla *f* de nombres; tabla *f* de símbolos

naming services /'neɪmɪŋ ˌsɜːvɪsɪz/ *noun* servicio *m* del servidor de nombres; método *m* de asignación de nombres

NAND function /'nænd ˌfʌŋkʃ(ə)n/ *noun* función *f* NOY; función *f* NAND

NAND gate /'nænd geɪt/ *noun* (*electronic circuit*) puerta *f* NOY; puerta *f* NAND; circuito *m* NO-Y

nano- /'nænəʊ/ *prefix* (*one thousand millionth or one billionth*) nano- (n)

nanocircuit /'nænəʊˌsɜːkɪt/ *noun* circuito *m* de respuesta en nanosegundos

nanosecond /'nænəʊˌsekənd/ *noun* nanosegundo (ns) *m*

nanosecond circuit /'nænəʊˌsekənd ˌsɜːkɪt/ *noun* circuito *m* de respuesta en nanosegundos

Napster /'næpstə/ (*trade name for software that allows users to share files*) Napster

narrative /'nærətɪv/ *noun* (*explanatory notes*) comentario *m*

narrative statement /'nærətɪv ˌsteɪtmənt/ *noun* (*program*) declaración *f* de procedimiento; instrucción *f* declarativa; instrucción *f* narrativa

narrow band ISDN /ˌnærəʊ bænd ˌaɪ es diː 'en/ *noun* ISDN *m* de banda estrecha

native /'neɪtɪv/ *adjective* nativo *or* -a

native compiler /ˌneɪtɪv kəm'paɪlə/ *noun* compilador *m* original; compilador *m* nativo

native file format /ˌneɪtɪv 'faɪl ˌfɔːmæt/ *noun* formato *m* de fichero original

native format /ˌneɪtɪv 'fɔːmæt/ *noun* formato *m* original

native language /ˌneɪtɪv 'læŋgwɪdʒ/ *noun* lenguaje *m* nativo; lenguaje *m* de máquina

natural binary coded decimal /ˌnætʃ(ə)rəl ˌbaɪnəri ˌkəʊdɪd 'desɪm(ə)l/ *noun* decimal *m* codificado binario natural

natural language /ˌnætʃ(ə)rəl 'læŋgwɪdʒ/ *noun* lenguaje *m* natural ◇ **the expert system can be programmed in a natural language** el sistema experto puede programarse en lenguaje natural

natural language processing /ˌnætʃ(ə)rəl 'læŋgwɪdʒ ˌprəʊsesɪŋ/ *noun* tratamiento *m* del lenguaje natural

navigable /'nævɪgəb(ə)l/ *adjective* navegable

navigation /ˌnævɪ'geɪʃ(ə)n/ *noun* (*moving around a multimedia title using hotspots, buttons and a user interface*) navegación *f* (por Internet)

NBCD *abbr* (*natural binary coded decimal*) decimal *m* codificado binario natural

NC *abbr* **1.** (*network computer*) ordenador *m* conectado a la red; ordenador *m* de red **2.** (*numerical control*) control *m* numérico

NCR paper /ˌen siː 'ɑː ˌpeɪpə/ *noun* (*special type of carbonless paper*) papel *m* NCR; papel *m* de autocopia

NCSA /ˌen siː es 'eɪ/ *noun* centro *m* nacional de aplicaciones de supercomputación

NDR /ˌen diː 'ɑː/ *noun* lectura *f* no destructiva

needle /'niːd(ə)l/ *noun* (*on dot matrix printer*) aguja *f*

negate /nɪ'geɪt/ *verb* (*to reverse the sign of a number*) invertir *vt*; cambiar *vt*; invalidar *vt*

negation /nɪ'geɪʃ(ə)n/ *noun* (*reversing the sign of a number*) negación *f*; inversión *f*

negation gate /nɪ'geɪʃ(ə)n geɪt/ *noun* circuito *m* NO; puerta *f* NOT

negative /'negətɪv/ *adjective* (*meaning 'no'*) negativo *or* -a

negative acknowledgement /ˌnegətɪv ək'nɒlɪdʒmənt/ *noun* acuse *m* de recibo negativo

negative number /ˌnegətɪv 'nʌmbə/ *noun* número *m* negativo

negative-true logic /ˌnegətɪv 'truː ˌlɒdʒɪk/ *noun* lógica *f* negativa

neither-nor function /ˌnaɪðə 'nɔː ˌfʌŋkʃ(ə)n/ *noun* (*logical function*) función *f* NO-O; función *f* NI

NEQ *abbr* (*nonequivalence function*) función *f* de disyunción; O *m* exclusivo

NEQ function /'nek ˌfʌŋkʃ(ə)n/ *noun* función *f* de disyunción; O *m* exclusivo

NEQ gate /'nek geɪt/ *noun* puerta *f* O exclusivo; circuito *m* O exclusivo

nerd /nɜːd/ *noun slang* (*slang for a person obsessed with computers*) fanático, -a de la información *mf*

nest /nest/ *verb* **1.** (*to insert subroutine*) anidar *vi*; jerarquizar *vt* **2.** (*to use routine*) anidar *vi*; jerarquizar *vt*

nested loop /ˌnestd 'luːp/ *noun* (*program*) bucle *m* anidado; bucle *m* jerarquizado

nested macro call /ˌnestɪd 'mækrəʊ ˌkɔːl/ *noun* llamada *f* de macro anidada

nested structure /nestd 'strʌktʃə/ *noun* estructura *f* anidada; estructura *f* jerarquizada

nesting level /nestɪŋ 'lev(ə)l/ *noun* nivel *m* de jerarquización (de bucles)

nesting store /ˌnestɪŋ 'stɔː/ *noun* memoria *f* de anidamiento; pila *f*

NetBEUI /'net bjuːi/ *noun* NetBIOS *m* en Modo Protegido

NetBIOS /'net ˌbaɪɒs/ *noun* NetBIOS *m*

NetBIOS extended user interface /ˌnet baɪɒs ɪkˌstendɪd 'juːzə ˌɪntəfeɪs/ *noun* NetBIOS *m* en Modo Protegido

netiquette /'netɪket/ *noun* etiqueta *f* de Internet

Netscape Navigator /ˌnetskeɪp 'nævɪgeɪtə/ (*trade name for one of the most popular web browsers*) Netscape Navigator™

NetShow /'netʃəʊ/ (*Microsoft system*) NetShow™

NetView /'netvjuː/ (*network management architecture*) (arquitectura de gestión de redes) NetView™

NetWare /'netweə/ (*Novell operating system*) NetWare™

NetWare Loadable Module /ˌnetweə ˌləʊdəb(ə)l 'mɒdjuːl/ (*trade name for an application that can run under the NetWare operating system*) aplicación *f* para Netware™

network /'netwɜːk/ *noun* red *f*; cadena *f* ■ *verb* (*to link points together in a network*) interconectar *vt*; disponer *vt*; configurar en red ◇ **basic telephone network** red telefónica básica (RTB) ◇ **network architect** arquitecto, -a de la red ◇ **network driver interface specification (NDIS)** (*standard command interface between network driver software and network adapter card – defined by Microsoft*) norma *f* de interfaz gestora de red *or* norma NDIS ◇ **network manager** gestor *m* de red ◇ **Network News Transfer Protocol (NNTP)** protocolo *m* de transferencia de noticias en red ◇ **radio network** red radiofónica *or* cadena de radio ◇ **television network** red *or* cadena *or* canal *m* de televisión ◇ **the workstations have been networked together rather than used as standalone systems** se han interconectado los terminales en lugar de usarlos como sistemas independientes ◇ **they run a system of networked micros** gestionan un sistema de microordenadores interconectados

'Asante Technologies has expanded its range of Ethernet-to-LocalTalk converters with the release of AsantePrint 8, which connects up to eight LocalTalk printers, or other LocalTalk devices, to a high-speed Ethernet network.' [*Computing*]

network adapter /'netwɜːk əˌdæptə/ *noun* tarjeta *f* de red; adaptador *m* de red

network address /'netwɜːk əˌdres/ *noun* dirección *f* de red

network administrator /ˌnetwɜːk ədˈmɪnɪstreɪtə/ *noun* administrador *m* de red

network alert /ˌnetwɜːk əˈlɜːt/ *noun* (mensaje de) alerta *f* en la red

network analysis /'netwɜːk əˌnæləsɪs/ *noun* análisis *m* de red

network architecture /ˌnetwɜːk 'ɑːkɪtektʃə/ *noun* arquitectura *f* de red

Network Basic Input Output System /ˌnetwɜːk ˌbeɪsɪk ˌɪnpʊt 'aʊtpʊt ˌsɪstəm/ *noun* sistema *m* básico de E/S de red

network calendar program /ˌnetwɜːk 'kælɪndə ˌprəʊgræm/ *noun* programa *m* multiusuario

network computer /ˌnetwɜːk kəm'pjuːtə/ *noun* ordenador *m* de red; ordenador *m* conectado a la red

network controller /ˌnetwɜːk kən'trəʊlə/ *noun* controlador *m* de red

network control program /ˌnetwɜːk kən'trəʊl ˌprəʊgræm/ *noun* programa *m* de control de red

network database /ˌnetwɜːk 'deɪtəbeɪs/ *noun* base *f* de datos en red

network device driver /ˌnetˌwɜːk dɪ'vaɪs ˌdraɪvə/ *noun* gestor *m* de periféricos en red

network diagram /ˌnetwɜːk 'daɪəgræm/ *noun* diagrama *m* de red

network directory /ˌnetwɜːk daɪ'rekt(ə)ri/ *noun* directorio *m* de red

network drive /'netwɜːk draɪv/ *noun* lector *m* de red

network file system /ˌnetwɜːk 'faɪl ˌsɪstəm/ *noun* sistema *m* de archivos de red

network hardware /ˌnetwɜːk 'hɑːdweə/ *noun* material *m*; equipo *m* de red (informática)

networking /'netwɜːkɪŋ/ *noun* **1.** (*TV or radio*) transmisión *f*; difusión *f* por la red **2.** (*organization of a computer network*) configuración *f* de red; (*interconnecting computers*) conexión *f* (de ordenadores) en red

networking hardware /ˌnetwɜːkɪŋ 'hɑːdweə/ *noun* material *m* de red; equipo *m* en red

networking software /ˌnetwɜːkɪŋ 'sɒftweə/ *noun* software *m* de red

networking specialist /'netwɜːkɪŋ ˌspeʃəlɪst/ *noun* experto *m or* -a *f*; especialista *m&f* en redes informáticas ◇ **this computer firm is a UK networking specialist** esta empresa informática es una sociedad británica especializada en redes

network interface card /ˌnetwɜːk 'ɪntəfeɪs ˌkɑːd/ *noun* tarjeta *f* controladara de interfaz de red

network-intrinsic application /ˌnetwɜːk ɪn 'trɪnsɪk ˌæplɪkeɪʃ(ə)n/ *noun* aplicación *f* de red; aplicación *f* que usa una red

network layer /'netwɜːk ˌleɪə/ *noun* capa *f* de red

network management /ˌnetwɜːk 'mænɪdʒmənt/ *noun* (*organisation of a network*) gestión *f* de red

Network Neighborhood /ˌnetwɜːk 'neɪbəhʊd/ *noun* Entorno *m* de Red

network operating system /ˌnetwɜːk 'ɒpəreɪtɪŋ ˌsɪstəm/ *noun* sistema *m* operativo de red; NOS

network printer /ˌnetwɜːk 'prɪntə/ *noun* impresora *f* de red; impresora *f* compartida

network processor /ˌnetwɜːk 'prəʊsesə/ *noun* procesador *m* de red

network protocol /ˌnetwɜːk 'prəʊtəkɒl/ *noun* protocolo *m* (de comunicaciones) de red

network redundancy /ˌnetwɜːk rɪ 'dʌndənsi/ *noun* (*organisation of a network*) enlaces *mpl* redundantes; auxiliares de una red

network server /ˌnetwɜːk 'sɜːvə/ *noun* servidor *m* de red

network software /ˌnetwɜːk 'sɒftweə/ *noun* software *m* de red

network structure /ˌnetwɜːk 'strʌktʃə/ *noun* estructura *f* de red; estructura *f* en red

network timing /ˌnetwɜːk 'taɪmɪŋ/ *noun* sincronización *f* de red

network topology /ˌnetwɜːk tə'pɒlədʒi/ *noun* topología *f* de red; configuración *f*

neural computer /ˌnjʊərəl kəm'pjuːtə/ *noun* ordenador *m* neuronal

neural network /ˌnjʊərəl 'netwɜːk/ *noun* (*system running an artificial intelligence*) red *f* neural; neuro-red *f*

neurocomputer /'njʊərəʊkəmˌpjuːtə/ *noun* ordenador *m* neuronal

neutral /'njuːtrəl/ *adjective* neutro *or* -a; neutral

neutral transmission /ˌnjuːtrəl trænz 'mɪʃ(ə)n/ *noun* transmisión *f* neutra

new /njuː/ *adjective* (*recent*) nuevo *or* -a; reciente ◇ **they have installed a new computer system** han instalado un nuevo sistema informático

newbie /'njuːbi/ *noun slang* (*user*) novato(-a) *m*

new line character /ˌnjuː 'laɪn ˌkærɪktə/ *noun* carácter *m* de línea nueva; carácter *m* de retorno de línea

newsgroup /'njuːzˌgruːp/ *noun* (*Internet*) foro *m*; grupo *m* de noticias; foro *m* de discusión (en Internet) ◇ **newsgroup reader** lector *m* de grupos de noticias

news reader /'njuːz ˌriːdə/ *noun* lector *m* de noticias

new technology /ˌnjuː tek'nɒlədʒi/ *noun* (*electronic instruments*) nueva tecnología *f*; técnicas *fpl* punta

Newton /'njuːtən/ (*range of PDAs developed by Apple*) Newton™

next instruction register /ˌnekst ɪn 'strʌkʃən ˌredʒɪstə/ *noun* (*register in a CPU*) registro *m* de la siguiente instrucción; registro *m* de la instrucción siguiente; registro *m* de la instrucción para ejecutar

nexus /'neksəs/ *noun* conexión *f*; nexo *m*

nibble /'nɪb(ə)l/ *noun* (*half the length of a standard byte*) semi-octeto *m*

NiCad /'naɪkæd/ *noun* batería *f* de níquel y cadmio

nickel cadmium /ˌnɪk(ə)l 'kædmiəm/ *noun* cadmio-níquel *m*

nickel metal hydride /ˌnɪk(ə)l ˌmet(ə)l 'haɪdraɪd/ *noun* hidruro *m* metálico de níquel

nil pointer /nɪl 'pɔɪntə/ *noun* marcador *m* nulo; marcador *m* de final de lista

NiMH /ˌen aɪ em 'eɪtʃ/ *noun* hidruro *m* metálico de níquel

nine's complement /'naɪnz ˌkɒmplɪmənt/ *noun* complemento *m* de 9

n-key rollover /ˌen kiː 'rəʊləʊvə/ *noun* (*using a buffer to provide key stroke storage*) memoria *f* intermedia de teclado de n pulsaciones

n-level logic /ˌen ˌlev(ə)l 'lɒdʒɪk/ *noun* lógica *f* de nivel n

NLQ *abbr* (*near-letter-quality*) calidad *m* casi de impresión alta

NMI *abbr* (*non maskable interrupt*) interrupción *f* obligatoria; interrupción *f* que no puede ser invalidada

NNTP /ˌen en tiː 'piː/ *noun* protocolo *m* de transferencia para los grupos de noticias de red

no-address operation /ˌnəʊ ə'dres ˌɒpəreɪʃ(ə)n/ *noun* (*instruction with no address*) operación *f* sin dirección; operación *f* no direccionable

node /nəʊd/ *noun* nodo *m* ◇ **a tree is made of branches that connect together at nodes** un árbol está hecho de ramas que se conectan en nodos ◇ **this network has fibre optic connection with nodes up to one kilometre apart** esta red tiene una conexión de fibra óptica con nodos separados entre sí hasta por un máximo de un kilómetro de distancia

no-drop image /ˌnəʊ 'drɒp ˌɪmɪdʒ/ *noun* (*in a GUI – icon image displayed during a drag and drop operation when the pointer is over an object that cannot be the destination object*) imagen *f* de arrastre

noise /nɔɪz/ *noun* ruido *m*; interferencia *f* ◇ **noise margin** margen *m* de ruido *or* límite *m* de tolerancia al ruido ◇ **noise temperature** temperatura *f* de ruido ◇ **thermal noise** ruido térmico

noise immunity /nɔɪz ɪ'mjuːnəti/ *noun* inmunidad *f*; tolerancia *f* al ruido

noisy digit /ˌnɔɪzi 'dɪdʒɪt/ *noun* dígito *m* ruidoso

noisy mode /'nɔɪzi məʊd/ *noun* (*floating point arithmetic system*) modo *m* ruidoso; modo *m* de intercalación de dígitos; modalidad *f* ruidosa

nomenclature /nəʊ'meŋklətʃə/ *noun* nomenclatura *f*

nomogram /'nɒməgræm/, **nomograph** /'nɒməgrɑːf/ *noun* nomograma *m*; ábaco *m*

non- /nɒn/ *prefix* no; des- ◇ **bubble memory is a non-volatile storage** la memoria de burbujas es una memoria no volátil ◇ **I will carry out a number of non-destructive tests on your computer: if it passes, you can start using it again** realizaré una serie de pruebas no destructivas en su ordenador y, si las pasa, podrá empezar a utilizarlo de nuevo ◇ **non-destructive readout (NDR)** lectura *f* no destructiva ◇ **non-interlaced system** (*system in which the picture electron beam scans each line of the display once*) sistema *m* no entrelazado ◇ **nonlinear circuit** circuito *m* no lineal ◇ **non-maskable interrupt (NMI)** interrupción *f* obligatoria *or* que no puede ser invalidada ◇ **non-printing code** código *m* no impresor *or* que no imprime ◇ **non return to zero (NRZ)** no retorno *m* ◇ **non-scrollable instructions** instrucciones *fpl* no desplegables ◇ **non-volatile random access memory (NVRAM)** memoria de acceso aleatorio no volátil ◇ **the line width can be set using one of the non-printing codes, .LW, then a number** la anchura de línea puede establecerse utilizando uno de los códigos no impresores, .LW, seguidos de un número ◇ **the screen quickly becomes unreadable when using a non-destructive cursor** la pantalla se hace ilegible rápidamente cuando se usa un cursor no destructivo ◇ **using magnetic tape provides non-volatile memory** el uso de una cinta magnética proporciona memoria no volátil

nonaligned /ˌnɒnə'laɪnd/ *adjective* no alineado, -a

nonaligned read head /nɒnəˌlaɪnd 'riːd hed/ *noun* cabeza *f* de lectura desalineada

non arithmetic shift /ˌnɒn ˌærɪθmetɪk 'ʃɪft/ *noun* desplazamiento *m* lógico; desplazamiento *m* no aritmético

non breaking space /ˌnɒn ˌbreɪkɪŋ 'speɪs/ *noun* (*space character that prevents two words being separated*) espacio *m* sin ruptura; espacio *m* sin interrupción

noncompatibility /ˌnɒnkəmˌpætɪ'bɪlɪti/ *noun* incompatibilidad *f*; no compatibilidad *f*

non destructive cursor /ˌnɒn dɪˌstrʌktɪv 'kɜːsə/ *noun* cursor *m* no destructivo

non destructive readout /ˌnɒn dɪˌstrʌktɪv 'riːdaʊt/ *noun* lectura *f* no destructiva

non destructive test /ˌnɒn dɪˌstrʌktɪv 'test/ *noun* prueba *f* no destructiva

nonequivalence function /ˌnɒnɪ'kwɪvələns ˌfʌŋkʃən/ *noun* función *f* de disyunción; O *m* exclusivo

nonequivalence gate /ˌnɒnɪ'kwɪvələns geɪt/ *noun* (*electronic circuit*) puerta *f*; circuito *m*; O *m* exclusivo

nonerasable storage /nɒnɪˌreɪzəb(ə)l 'stɔːrɪdʒ/ *noun* (*storage medium*) memoria *f* permanente; que no puede ser borrada ◇ **paper tape is a nonerasable storage** la cinta de papel es una memoria permanente

non impact printer /ˌnɒn ɪmˌpækt 'prɪntə/ *noun* impresora *f* sin impacto

non interlaced /ˌnɒn 'ɪntəleɪsd/ *adjective* (*system in which the picture electron beam scans each line of the display once*) no entrelazado, -a

nonlinear /nɒn'lɪniə/ *adjective* no lineal

non maskable interrupt /ˌnɒn ˌmɑːskəb(ə)l 'ɪntərʌpt/ *noun* interrupción *f* obligatoria; interrupción *f* que no puede ser invalidada

non operable instruction /ˌnɒn ˌɒp(ə)rəb(ə)l ɪn'strʌkʃən/ *noun* instrucción *f* simulada; instrucción *f* nula; instrucción *f* de relleno

nonprinting code /ˌnɒnprɪntɪŋ 'kəʊd/ *plural noun* código *m* no impresor; código *m* que no imprime

non-procedural language /nɒn prə ˌsiːdʒ(ə)rəl 'læŋgwɪdʒ/ *noun* lenguaje *m* no procedimental

nonrepudiation /ˌnɒnrɪˌpjuːdi'eɪʃ(ə)n/ *noun* non-repudiación *f*

non-return to zero /ˌnɒn rɪˌtɜːn tə'zɪərəʊ/ *noun* no retorno *m*; no vuelta *f* a cero

non scrollable /ˌnɒn 'skrəʊləb(ə)l/ *adjective* no desplegable

non volatile memory /ˌnɒn ˌvɒlətaɪl 'mem(ə)ri/ *noun* memoria *f* no volátil; almacenamiento *m* no volátil

non-volatile random access memory /ˌnɒn ˌvɒlətaɪl ˌrændəm ˌækses 'mem(ə)ri/ *noun* memoria *f* de acceso aleatorio no volátil

non volatile storage /ˌnɒn ˌvɒlətaɪl 'stɔːrɪdʒ/, **nonvolatile store** *noun* memoria *f* no volátil; almacenamiento *m* no volátil

no-op instruction /nəʊ ɒp/, **no op** *noun* instrucción *f* simulada; instrucción *f* nula; instrucción *f* de relleno

no parity /nəʊ 'pærəti/ *noun* (*data transmission which does not use a parity bit*) sin paridad; sin (bit de) paridad

NOR function /nɔːr 'fʌŋkʃən/ *noun* (*logical function*) función *f* NI

NOR gate /'nɔːr geɪt/ *noun* (*electric circuit*) puerta *f* NI; puerta *f* NOR; circuito *m* NO-O

normal /'nɔːm(ə)l/ *adjective* normal ◇ **the normal procedure is for backup copies to be made at the end of each day's work** el procedimiento normal es que se hagan copias de seguridad al final de cada jornada laboral

normal form /'nɔːm(ə)l fɔːm/ *noun* forma *f* normal; configuración *f* normal

normal format /'nɔːm(ə)l ˌfɔːmæt/ *noun* formato *m* normal; formato *m* estándar

normalisation /ˌnɔːməlaɪ'zeɪʃ(ə)n/, **normalization** *noun* normalización *f*

normalisation routine /ˌnɔːməlaɪˈzeɪʃ(ə)n ruːˌtiːn/ *noun* rutina *f* de normalización

normalise /ˈnɔːməˌlaɪz/, **normalize** *verb* **1.** (*to convert data*) normalizar *vt* **2.** (*to convert characters*) uniformar *vt*; ajustar *vt* **3.** (*to store and represent numbers*) normalizar *vt*; ajustar *vt* ◊ **all the new data has been normalized to 10 decimal places** todos los datos nuevos han sido ajustados a diez puntos decimales

normalised form /ˈnɔːməlaɪzd fɔːm/ *noun* forma *f* normalizada

normal range /ˈnɔːm(ə)l reɪndʒ/ *noun* gama *f* normal; ámbito *m* normal

normals /ˈnɔːm(ə)lz/ *plural noun* normales

NOS *abbr* (*network operating system*) NOS; sistema *m* operativo de red

NOT-AND /nɒt ən/ *noun* función *f* NOY; función *f* NAND

notation /nəʊˈteɪʃ(ə)n/ *noun* (*numbers*) numeración *f*; notación *f* ◊ **decimal notation** notación decimal

notebook computer /ˌnəʊtbʊk kəmˈpjuːtə/ *noun* (*very small portable computer – normally smaller than a laptop computer*) ordenador *m* portátil

notepad /ˈnəʊtˌpæd/ *noun* **1.** bloc *m* de notas **2.** ordenador *m* portátil

NOT function /nɒt ˈfʌŋkʃən/ *noun* (*logical inverse function*) función *f* NO; función *f* complementaria

NOT gate /ˈnɒt geɪt/ *noun* puerta *f* NOT; circuito *m* NO

notice board /ˈnəʊtɪs bɔːd/ *noun* **1.** tablero *m* **2.** tablón *m* de anuncios

notification message /ˌnəʊtɪfɪˈkeɪʃ(ə)n ˌmesɪdʒ/ *noun* mensaje *m* de notificación; mensaje *m* de aviso ◊ **if an object is moved, the application will generate a notification message to tell other processes when it has finished moving the object** si se mueve un objeto, la aplicación genera un mensaje de notificación para indicar a otros procesos cuando se ha terminado de mover el objeto

notify handler /ˈnəʊtɪfaɪ ˌhændlə/ *noun* gestor *m* de notificaciones

Novell /nəʊˈvel/ (*company that produces network software*) Novell™

n-plus-one address instruction /en plʌs wʌn əˈdres/ *noun* instrucción *f* de n (direcciones) más una

n-plus-one instruction /ˈen plʌs wʌn/ *noun* instrucción *f* de n (direcciones) más una

npn transistor /ˌen piː ˈen trænˌzɪstə/ *noun* transistor *m* (de tipo) npn

ns *abbr* (*nanosecond*) ns

n-type material /en taɪp məˈtɪəriəl/, **n-type semiconductor** /en taɪp/ *noun* material *m* de tipo N; semi-conductor *m* de tipo N

NuBus /ˈnjuːbʌs/ *noun* (*Macintosh computers*) NuBus™

NUL character /ˈnʌl ˌkærɪktə/ *noun* carácter *m* de relleno; carácter *m* nulo

null /nʌl/ *adjective* (*nothing*) nulo *or* -a ◊ **null set** (*that only contains zeros*) conjunto *m* vacío *or* nulo

null character /ˈnʌl ˌkærɪktə/ *noun* carácter *m* nulo; carácter *m* de relleno

null instruction /ˈnʌl ɪnˈstrʌkʃən/ *noun* instrucción *f* nula; instrucción *f* de relleno

null list /ˌnʌl ˈlɪst/ *noun* lista *f* vacía

null modem /nʌl ˈməʊˌdem/ *noun* (*connection*) sin módem; conexión *f* directa; módem *m* nulo ◊ **this cable is configured as a null modem, which will allow me to connect these 2 computers together easily** este cable está configurado como una conexión directa, lo que me permite interconectar fácilmente estos dos ordenadores

null set /ˌnʌl ˈset/ *noun* conjunto *m* vacío; conjunto *m* nulo

null string /ˌnʌl ˈstrɪŋ/ *noun* cadena *f* vacía; cadena *f* nula

null terminated string /ˌnʌl ˌtɜːmɪneɪtɪd ˈstrɪŋ/ *noun* cadena *f* de caracteres terminada en un carácter nulo

number /ˈnʌmbə/ *noun* **1.** (*representation of quantities*) número *m* **2.** (*written figure*) cifra *f*; número *m*; dígito *m* ■ *verb* (*to assign digits to a list of items in an ordered manner*) numerar *vt* ◊ **each piece of hardware has a production number** cada una de las piezas del ordenador tiene un número de fabricación ◊ **the pages of the manual are numbered 1 to 395** las páginas del manual están numeradas del 1 al 395

number cruncher /ˈnʌmbə ˌkrʌntʃə/ *noun* (*calculations*) superordenador *m*; mascador *m*; triturador *m* de números

number crunching /ˈnʌmbə krʌntʃɪŋ/ *noun* cálculo *m* ultra rápido; operaciones *fpl* numéricas ultra rápidas ◊ **a very powerful processor is needed for graphics applications which require extensive number crunching capabilities** se necesita un procesador muy potente para las aplicaciones gráficas ya que éstas requieren una capacidad de cálculo ultra rápido

number range /ˈnʌmbə reɪndʒ/ *noun* gama *f* de valores; rango *m* de valores

numeral /ˈnjuːm(ə)rəl/ *noun* número *m*; cifra *f*

numeric /njuːˈmerɪk/ *adjective* numérico *or* -a

numerical /njuːˈmerɪk(ə)l/ *adjective* (*referring to numbers*) numérico *or* -a

numerical analysis /njuːˌmerɪk(ə)l əˈnæləsɪs/ *noun* análisis *m* numérico

numerical control /njuːˌmerɪk(ə)l kənˈtrəʊl/ *noun* control *m* numérico

numeric array /njuːˌmerɪk əˈreɪ/ *noun* (*array containing numbers*) cuadro *m* numérico; serie *f* de cifras; matriz *f* numérica

numeric character /njuːˌmerɪk ˈkærɪktə/ *noun* carácter *m* numérico

numeric keypad /njuː,merɪk 'kiːpæd/ *noun* teclado *m* numérico ◇ **you can use the numeric keypad to enter the figures** usted puede utilizar el teclado numérico para introducir las cifras

numeric operand /njuː,merɪk 'ɒpərænd/ *noun* operando *m* numérico

numeric pad /njuː,merɪk 'pæd/ *noun* teclado *m* numérico

numeric punch /njuː,merɪk 'pʌntʃ/ *noun* perforación *f* numérica

numeric string /njuː,merɪk 'strɪŋ/ *noun* cadena *f* numérica

Num Lock key /'nʌm lɒk kiː/ *noun* (*key on a keyboard*) tecla *f* de bloqueo de números; tecla *f* Bloq Num

NVRAM /,en viː 'ræm/ *noun* memoria *f* de acceso aleatorio no volátil

nybble /'nɪb(ə)l/, **nibble** *noun informal* (*half the length of a standard byte*) semi-octeto *m*

O

OA *abbr* (*office automation*) automatización *f* de oficinas

object /ˈɒbdʒekt/ *noun* **1.** (*data that makes a particular image*) objeto *m* **2.** (*variable in expert system*) objeto *m* **3.** (*data in a statement*) objeto *m* ◊ **object-oriented programming (OOP)** (*method of programming, in which each element of the program is treated as an object*) programación orientada a objetos ◊ **this object-oriented graphics program lets you move shapes around very easily** este programa de gráficos orientados a objetos le permite desplazar figuras muy fácilmente

object architecture /ˈɒbdʒekt ˈɑːkɪtektʃə/ *noun* arquitectura *f* de objetos; arquitectura *f* orientada a objetos

object code /əbˈdʒekt kəʊd/ *noun* código *m* objeto

object computer /ˈɒbdʒekt kəmˈpjuːtə/ *noun* ordenador *m* objeto

object deck /əbˈdʒekt dek/ *noun* juego *m* (de tarjetas) objeto

object file /əbˈdʒekt faɪl/ *noun* fichero *m* objeto

objective /əbˈdʒektɪv/ *noun* (*aim*) objetivo *m*; fin *m*; finalidad *f*

object language /ˈɒbdʒekt ˈlæŋɡwɪdʒ/ *noun* lenguaje *m* objeto

object linking and embedding /ˈɒbdʒekt ˈlɪŋkɪŋ ənd ɪmˈbedɪŋ/ *noun* procedimiento *m* de enlace e incorporación de objetos; (procedimiento) OLE

object-orientated architecture /ˈɒbdʒekt ˈɔːriənteɪtɪd ˈɑːkɪtektʃə/ *noun* arquitectura *f* de objetos; arquitectura *f* orientada a objetos

object-oriented /ˈɒbdʒekt ˈɔːrientɪd/ *adjective* (*that uses objects*) orientado a objetos *or*, -a

object-oriented graphics /ˈɒbdʒekt ˈɔːrientɪd ˈɡræfɪks/ *plural noun* gráficos *mpl* orientados a objetos

object-oriented language /ˈɒbdʒekt ˈɔːrientɪd ˈlæŋɡwɪdʒ/ *noun* lenguaje *m* orientado a objetos

object-oriented programming /ˈɒbdʒekt ˈɔːrientɪd ˈprəʊɡræmɪŋ/ *noun* programación *f* orientada a objetos

object program /ˈɒbdʒekt ˈprəʊɡræm/ *noun* programa *m* objeto

obtain /əbˈteɪn/ *verb* obtener *vt* ◊ **a clear signal is obtained after filtering** el filtrado permite obtener una señal clara ◊ **to obtain data from a storage device** obtener datos de un dispositivo de almacenamiento

OCCAM /ˈɒkəm/ *noun* lenguaje *m* (de programación) OCCAM

occur /əˈkɜː/ *verb* ocurrir *vi*; producirse *vr*; tener lugar ◊ **data loss can occur because of power supply variations** se puede producir una pérdida de datos a causa de las bajadas de tensión

OCP /ˌəʊ siː ˈpiː/ *noun* procesador *m* de códigos de operación

OCR /ˌəʊ siː ˈɑː/ *noun* **1.** lector *m* óptico de caracteres **2.** reconocimiento *m* óptico de caracteres

'In 1986, Calera Recognition Systems introduced the first neural-network-based OCR system that could read complex pages containing any mixture of non-decorative fonts without manual training.' [*Computing*]

OCR font /ˌəʊ siː ˈɑː fɒnt/ *noun* fuente *f* OCR; fuente *f* de caracteres reconocible por un lector óptico

octal /ˈɒkt(ə)l/, **octal notation** /ˈɒkt(ə)l nəʊˈteɪʃ(ə)n/ *noun* notación *f* octal

octal digit /ˌɒkt(ə)l ˈdɪdʒɪt/ *noun* número *m* octal; dígito *m* octal

octal scale /ˈɒkt(ə)l skeɪl/ *noun* escala *f*; base *f* octal

octet /ɒkˈtet/ *noun* (*group of eight bits*) octeto *m*

odd-even check /ˌɒd ˈiːv(ə)n ˌtʃek/ *noun* control *m* de paridad par-impar

odd parity /ˌɒd ˈpærɪti/, **odd parity check** /ˌɒd ˈpærɪti tʃek/ *noun* paridad *f* impar

OEM /ˌəʊ iː ˈem/ *noun* empresa *f* de montaje; fabricante *mf* de equipos (informáticos) originales

off-hook /ˌɒf ˈhʊk/ *adverb* (*modem*) ocupado; descolgado

office automation /ˌɒfɪs ˈɔːtəˈmeɪʃ(ə)n/ *noun* ofimática *f* burótica; automatización *f* de la oficina

office computer /ˌɒfɪs kəmˈpjuːtə/ *noun* ordenador *m* de oficina; ordenador *m* de uso profesional

off-line /ˌɒf ˈlaɪn/ *adverb, adjective* **1.** (*peripheral, processing, etc.*) desconectado *or* -a; (*connection*) independiente; fuera de red **2.** (*connection*) desconectado *or* -a; independiente; fuera de red ◊ **before changing the paper in the printer, switch it off-line** antes de cambiar el papel de la impresora, sitúe el interruptor en fuera de red

off-line editing /ˌɒf laɪn ˈedɪtɪŋ/ *noun* edición *f* fuera de línea

off-line printing /ˌɒf laɪn 'prɪntɪŋ/ *noun* impresión *f* fuera de red

off-line processing /ˌɒf laɪn 'prəʊsesɪŋ/ *noun* tratamiento *m* fuera (de) red

off-line storage /ˌɒf laɪn 'stɔːrɪdʒ/ *noun* almacenamiento *m* fuera de red

offload /ɒf'ləʊd/ *verb* descargar *vt*

off-screen image /ˌɒf skriːn 'ɪmɪdʒ/ *noun* imagen *f* fuera de campo; imagen *f* fuera de pantalla

offset /'ɒfset/ *noun* (*printing*) offset *m*; (*quantity added to a number*) valor *m* complementario ◇ **offset lithography** litografía *f* offset ◇ **offset printing** impresión *f* (en) offset

offset value /ˌɒfˌset 'væljuː/, **offset word** /ˌɒf 'set wɜːd/ *noun* (*indexed address*) valor *m* relativo; dirección *f* relativa; palabra *f* relativa

OK /ˌəʊ 'keɪ/ *noun* (*prompt meaning 'ready'*) preparado *or* -a; listo *m or* -a

OK button /əʊ'keɪ ˌbʌt(ə)n/ *noun* tecla *f* de conforme; tecla *f* de acuerdo

OLE /ˌəʊ el 'iː/ *noun* OLE; procedimiento *m* de enlace e incorporación de objetos

omission factor /əʊ'mɪʃ(ə)n ˌfæktə/ *noun* factor *m* de omisión; factor *m* de silencio

OMR /ˌəʊ em 'ɑː/ *noun* **1.** lector *m* óptico de marcas **2.** reconocimiento *m* de signos; reconocimiento *m* de símbolos; reconocimiento *m* óptico de marcas

on-board /ɒn bɔːd/ *adjective* (*on main PCB*) integrado, -a en el circuito

'…the electronic page is converted to a printer-readable video image by the on-board raster image processor the key intelligence features of these laser printers are emulation modes and on-board memory' [*Byte*]

on chip /ˌɒn 'tʃɪp/ *noun* circuito *m* integrado

on-chip /ɒn tʃɪp/ *adjective* integrado *or* -a

on-chip cache /ˌɒn tʃɪp 'kæʃ/ *noun* memoria *f* caché integrada

one-address computer /ˌwʌn əˌdres kəm 'pjuːtə/ *noun* ordenador *m* de dirección única

one-address instruction /ˌwʌn əˌdres ɪn 'strʌkʃən/ *noun* instrucción *f* de dirección única

one element /wʌn 'elɪmənt/ *noun* (*logical function*) elemento *m* único

one for one /ˌwʌn fə 'wʌn/ *noun* (*programming language*) (lenguaje de programación) uno por uno

one-level address /ˌwʌn ˌlev(ə)l ə'dres/ *noun* dirección *f* de un (solo) nivel

one-level code /ˌwʌn ˌlev(ə)l 'kəʊd/ *noun* código *m* de un (solo) nivel

one-level store /ˌwʌn ˌlev(ə)l 'stɔː/ *noun* memoria *f* de un (solo) nivel

one-level subroutine /ˌwʌn ˌlev(ə)l 'sʌbruːtiːn/ *noun* subrutina *f*; subprograma *m* de un (solo) nivel

one-pass assembler /ˌwʌn pɑːs ə'semblə/ *noun* ensamblador *m* de una sola pasada ◇ **this new one-pass assembler is very quick in op-**

eration este nuevo ensamblador de una sola pasada es muy rápido

one-plus-one address /'wʌn plʌs wʌn/ *noun* dirección *f* uno más uno

one's complement /'wʌnz ˌkɒmplɪment/ *noun* complemento *m* de 1 ◇ **the one's complement of 10011 is 01100** el complemento de 1 de 10011 es 01100

one-time pad /ˌwʌn 'taɪm pæd/ *noun* (*for coding system*) clave *f* única

one to zero ratio /wʌn tə, tʊ 'zɪərəʊ/ *noun* razón *f* de salida 1 a salida 0; razón *f* 1 a 0

on-hook /ɒn hʊk/ *adverb* (*modem*) colgado; desocupado

onion skin architecture /'ʌnjən skɪn ˌɑːkɪtektʃə/ *noun* (*computer design*) arquitectura *f* de piel de cebolla ◇ **the onion skin architecture of this computer is made up of a kernel at the centre, an operating system, a low-level language and then the user's program** la arquitectura de piel de cebolla de este ordenador consiste en un núcleo central, un sistema operativo, un lenguaje de bajo nivel y a continuación el programa del usuario ◇ **the onion skin architecture of this computer is made up of a kernel at the centre, an operating system, a low-level language and then the user's programs** la arquitectura de piel de cebolla de este ordenador consiste en un núcleo central, un sistema operativo, un lenguaje de bajo nivel y a continuación los programas de usuario

onion skin language /'ʌnjən skɪn ˌlæŋgwɪdʒ/ *noun* lenguaje *m* de piel de cebolla

online /ɒn'laɪn/ *adverb, adjective* (*connection*) en línea; conectado *or* -a; en red ■ *adverb* (*connection*) en línea; conectado *or* -a ◇ **the terminal is on-line to the mainframe** el terminal está conectado al ordenador principal

online database /ˌɒnlaɪn 'deɪtəbeɪs/ *noun* base *f* de datos en línea

online editing /ɒnˌlaɪn 'edɪtɪŋ/ *noun* edición *f* en línea

online help /ˌɒnlaɪn 'help/ *noun* asistencia *f* en línea

online information retrieval /ˌɒnlaɪn ˌɪnfə 'meɪʃ(ə)n rɪˌtriːvəl/ *noun* recuperación *f* de información en línea

online processing /ˌɒnlaɪn 'prəʊsesɪŋ/ *noun* tratamiento *m* en línea; proceso *m* en línea; tratamiento *m* en red; proceso *m* en red

online storage /ˌɒnlaɪn 'stɔːrɪdʒ/ *noun* almacenamiento *m* (de datos) en línea

online system /ˌɒnlaɪn 'sɪtsəm/ *noun* sistema *m* en línea

online transaction processing /ˌɒnlaɪn træn'zækʃən ˌprəʊsesɪŋ/ *noun* tratamiento *m* de transacciones en línea; tratamiento *m* de transacciones en red

on-screen /ɒn skriːn/ *adjective* (*displayed on screen*) en pantalla; (mostrado, -a) en la pantalla; visualizado *or* -a ◇ **on-screen display** visualización *f* en la pantalla

on-site /ɒn saɪt/ *adjective* en el lugar (de trabajo)

on the fly /ˌɒn ðə ˈflaɪ/ *adverb* (*without stopping the run*) al vuelo

OOP *abbr* (*object-oriented programming*) programación *f* orientada a objetos

op code /ˈɒp kəʊd/ *noun* código *m* de operación

open /ˈəʊpən/ *adjective* **1.** (*file*) abierto *or* -a **2.** (*not closed*) abierto *or* -a ∎ *verb* (*file*) abrir *vt* ◇ **open loop** bucle abierto ◇ **Open Systems Interconnection (OSI)** interconexión *f* de sistemas abiertos (de acuerdo con las normas ISO) ◇ **you cannot access the data unless the file has been opened** no puede acceder a los datos sin abrir el fichero antes ◇ **you cannot access the data while the file is open** no se puede acceder a los datos a no ser que el archivo esté abierto

open access /ˌəʊpən ˈækses/ *noun* (*workstation*) (puesto de trabajo) abierto; libre acceso *m*; acceso *m* sin limitaciones

open architecture /ˌəʊpən ˈɑːkɪtektʃə/ *noun* arquitectura *f* abierta

open code /ˈəʊpən kəʊd/ *noun* código *m* abierto

open-ended program /ˌəʊpən ˌendɪd ˈprəʊɡræm/ *noun* programa *m* con extremo(s) abierto(s)

open file /ˈəʊpən faɪl/ *noun* fichero *m* abierto

open routine /ˌəʊpən ruːˈtiːn/ *noun* rutina *f* abierta; rutina *f* auxiliar

open subroutine /ˌəʊpən ˈsʌbruːtiːn/ *noun* subrutina *f* abierta

open system /ˈəʊpən ˌsɪstəm/ *noun* sistema *m* abierto

open system interconnection /ˌəʊpən ˌsɪstəm ˌɪntəkəˈnekʃ(ə)n/ *noun* interconexión *f* de sistemas abiertos (de acuerdo con las normas ISO)

operand /ˈɒpərænd/ *noun* operando *m* ◇ **in the instruction ADD 74, the operator ADD will add the operand 74 to the accumulator** en la instrucción ADD 74, el operador ADD añade el operando 74 al acumulador

operand field /ˈɒpərænd fiːld/ *noun* campo *m* de datos del operador; campo *m* de operando

operate /ˈɒpəreɪt/ *verb* (*machine*) funcionar *vi*; hacer funcionar; poner en funcionamiento ◇ **do you know how to operate the telephone switchboard?** ¿sabe cómo hacer funcionar la centralita telefónica?

operating code /ˈɒpəreɪtɪŋ kəʊd/ *noun* código *m* operativo

operating console /ˈɒpəreɪtɪŋ ˌkɒnsəʊl/ *noun* puesto *m*; estación *f* de trabajo

operating instructions /ˈɒpəreɪtɪŋ ɪn ˌstrʌkʃənz/ *plural noun* instrucciones *fpl* de trabajo

operating system /ˈɒpəreɪtɪŋ ˌsɪstəm/ *noun* sistema *m* operativo

operating time /ˈɒpəreɪtɪŋ taɪm/ *noun* tiempo *m* de ejecución

operation /ˌɒpəˈreɪʃ(ə)n/ *noun* **1.** (*working of machine*) operación *f* **2.** (*series of actions*) operación *f* **3.** (*mathematical process*) operación *f*

operational /ˌɒpəˈreɪʃ(ə)nəl/ *adjective* operacional ◇ **operational amplifier (op amp)** amplificador *m* operacional

operational information /ˌɒpəˌreɪʃ(ə)nəl ˌɪnfəˈmeɪʃ(ə)n/ *noun* información *f* de uso; información *f* operacional

operation code /ˌɒpəˈreɪʃ(ə)n kəʊd/ *noun* código *m* de operación

operation cycle /ˌɒpəˈreɪʃ(ə)n ˌsaɪk(ə)l/ *noun* ciclo *m* de operación

operation decoder /ˌɒpəˈreɪʃ(ə)n diːˌkəʊdə/ *noun* descodificador *m* de operación; instrucción *f*

operation field /ˌɒpəˈreɪʃ(ə)n ˌfiːld/ *noun* campo *m* de operación

operation priority /ˌɒpəreɪʃ(ə)n praɪˈɒrɪti/ *noun* (orden de) prioridad *f* de las operaciones

operation register /ˌɒpəˈreɪʃ(ə)n ˌredʒɪstə/ *noun* registro *m* de operación

operations manual /ˌɒpəˌreɪʃ(ə)nz ˈmænjʊəl/ *noun* manual *m* de uso

operation time /ˌɒpəˈreɪʃ(ə)n taɪm/ *noun* tiempo *m* de ejecución de una operación

operation trial /ˌɒpəˈreɪʃ(ə)n ˌtraɪəl/ *noun* ensayo *m*; prueba *f* de una operación

operator /ˈɒpəˌreɪtə/ *noun* **1.** (*person*) operador *m or* -a *f* **2.** (*of a function or operation*) operador *m* ◇ **the operator was sitting at his console** el operador estaba sentado frente a la pantalla del ordenador ◇ **x is the multiplication operator** x es el operador de la multiplicación

operator overloading /ˌɒpəreɪtə ˈəʊvələʊdɪŋ/ *noun* sobrecarga *f* de un operador

operator precedence /ˌɒpəreɪtə ˈpresɪdəns/ *noun* (*mathematical operations*) orden *m* de encadenamiento de operaciones; orden *m* de los operadores; orden *m* de prioridad

operator procedure /ˈɒpəreɪtə prəˌsiːdʒə/ *noun* procedimiento *m* de operador

operator's console /ˈɒpəreɪtəz ˌkɒnsəʊl/ *noun* mesa *f* de control; puesto *m* de trabajo de un operador

op register /ɒp ˈredʒɪstə/ *noun* registro *m* de operación

optical /ˈɒptɪk(ə)l/ *adjective* (*referring to or making use of light*) óptico *or* -a ◇ **an optical reader uses a light beam to scan characters, patterns or lines** un lector óptico emplea un haz de luz para escanear caracteres, símbolos o líneas ◇ **optical character reader (OCR)** lector óptico de caracteres ◇ **optical communications system** sistema (electro)óptico de comunicaciones ◇ **optical mark reader (OMR)** lector óptico de marcas ◇ **optical mark recognition (OMR)** reconocimiento óptico de marcas *or* de signos *or* de símbolos

optical bar reader /ˌɒptɪk(ə)l ˈbɑː ˌriːdə/ *noun* lector *m* óptico de códigos de barras

optical character reader /ˌɒptɪk(ə)l ˈkærɪktə ˌriːdə/ *noun* lector *m* óptico de caracteres

optical character recognition /ˌɒptɪk(ə)l ˌkærɪktə ˌrekəgˈnɪʃ(ə)n/ *noun* reconocimiento *m* óptico de caracteres

optical communication system /ˌɒptɪk(ə)l kəˌmjuːnɪˈkeɪʃ(ə)n ˌsɪstəm/ *noun* sistema *m* (electro)óptico de comunicaciones

optical computer /ˌɒptɪk(ə)l kəmˈpjuːtə/ *noun* ordenador *m* óptico

optical data link /ˌɒptɪk(ə)l ˈdeɪtə ˌlɪŋk/ *noun* enlace *m* de datos; enlace *m* óptico de datos

optical disk /ˈɒptɪk(ə)l dɪsk/ *noun* disco *m* óptico

optical fibre /ˌɒptɪk(ə)l ˈfaɪbə/ *noun* fibra *f* óptica

optical font /ˈɒptɪk(ə)l fɒnt/ *noun* fuente *f* óptica de caracteres; fuente *f* de caracteres para lectura óptica

optical mark reader /ˌɒptɪk(ə)l ˈmɑːk ˌriːdə/ *noun* lector *m* óptico de marcas

optical mark recognition /ˌɒptɪk(ə)l mɑːk ˌrekəgˈnɪʃ(ə)n/ *noun* (*optical reading*) reconocimiento *m* óptico de marcas; reconocimiento *m* de signos; reconocimiento *m* de símbolos

optical memory /ˌɒptɪk(ə)l ˈmem(ə)ri/ *noun* memoria *f* óptica

optical mouse /ˈɒptɪk(ə)l maʊs/ *noun* (*optical device*) ratón *m* óptico

optical scanner /ˌɒptɪk(ə)l ˈskænə/ *noun* (*piece of equipment that converts an image into electrical signals*) lector *m* óptico; escáner *m* (de reconocimiento) óptico; escáner *m* de reconocimiento óptico

optical storage /ˌɒptɪk(ə)l ˈstɔːrɪdʒ/ *noun* (*action*) almacenamiento *m* óptico; memoria *f* óptica

optical transmission /ˌɒptɪk(ə)l trænzˈmɪʃ(ə)n/ *noun* transmisión *f* óptica

optic fibre /ˌɒptɪk ˈfaɪbə/ *noun* fibra *f* óptica

optimisation, optimization *noun* optimización *f*

optimise /ˈɒptɪmaɪz/, **optimize** *verb* optimizar *vt*

optimised code /ˈɒptɪˌmaɪzd kəʊd/, **optimized code** *noun* código *m* optimizado

optimiser /ˈɒptɪmaɪzə/, **optimizer** *noun* optimizador *m*

optimising compiler /ˌɒptɪmaɪzɪŋ kəmˈpaɪlə/ *noun* compilador *m* de optimización

optimizer /ˈɒptɪmaɪzə/ *noun* (*program*) optimizador *m*

optimum /ˈɒptɪməm/ *adjective* (*best possible*) óptimo *or* -a ■ *noun* óptimo *or* -a

optimum code /ˈɒptɪməm kəʊd/ *noun* (*coding system*) código *m* óptimo; código *m* con tiempo de acceso mínimo

opt-in mailing list /ˌɒpt ɪn ˈmeɪlɪŋ lɪst/ *noun* lista *f* de direciones suscripción activa

option /ˈɒpʃən/ *noun* opción *f*

optional /ˈɒpʃ(ə)n(ə)l/ *adjective* opcional ◊ **the system comes with optional 3.5 or 5.25 disk drives** el sistema viene con disqueteras opcionales de 3.5 o 5.25 pulgadas

Option key /ˈɒpʃ(ə)n kiː/ *noun* tecla *f* de opciones

optomechanical mouse /ˌɒptəʊmɪˌkænɪk(ə)l ˈmaʊs/ *noun* ratón *m* optomecánico

OR /ˌəʊ ˈɑː/ *noun* OR

order /ˈɔːdə/ *noun* **1.** (*instruction*) orden *f*; instrucción *f*; operación *f* **2.** (*disposition*) orden *m* ■ *verb* **1.** (*to instruct*) dar una instrucción; ordenar *vt* **2.** (*to put in order*) ordenar *vt*; clasificar *vt* ◊ **in alphabetical order** en *or* por orden alfabético

order code /ˈɔːdə kəʊd/ *noun* código *m* de operación

order code processor /ˈɔːdə kəʊd ˌprəʊsesə/ *noun* procesador *m* de códigos de operación

ordered list /ˈɔːdəd lɪst/ *noun* lista *f* ordenada

OR function /ɔː ˈfʌŋkʃən/ *noun* (*logical function*) función *f* O; función *f* OR

OR gate /ˈɔː geɪt/ *noun* (*electronic circuit*) puerta *f* O; circuito *m* O; puerta *f* OR

orientated /ˈɔːriənteɪtɪd/ *adjective* orientado *or* -a

orientation /ˌɔːriənˈteɪʃ(ə)n/ *noun* (*direction of a page*) orientación *f* (horizontal o vertical)

origin /ˈɒrɪdʒɪn/ *noun* **1.** (*position on a screen*) origen *m* **2.** (*location in memory*) dirección *f* origen

original /əˈrɪdʒən(ə)l/ *adjective* original ■ *noun* (*document*) original *m* ◊ **the original is too faint to photocopy well** el original está demasiado difuminado para hacer fotocopias

original equipment manufacturer /əˌrɪdʒən(ə)l ɪˌkwɪpmənt ˌmænjʊˈfæktʃərə/ *noun* fabricante *mf* de equipos (informáticos) originales; empresa *f* de montaje ◊ **he started in business as a manufacturer of PCs for the OEM market** empezó su carrera como montador de ordenadores personales para el mercado de fabricantes de equipos informáticos originales

originate /əˈrɪdʒɪneɪt/ *verb* (*to start*) originar *vt*; producir *vt*; crear *vt*; (*to come from*) venir de

originate modem /əˈrɪdʒəneɪt ˌməʊdem/ *noun* módem *m* de llamada

origination /əˌrɪdʒɪˈneɪʃ(ə)n/ *noun* creación *f*; producción *f* ◊ **the origination of the artwork will take several weeks** la producción del material gráfico requerirá varias semanas

orphan /ˈɔːf(ə)n/ *noun* (*single line at the bottom of a page*) primera línea *f* de párrafo al final de una página o columna que queda aislada del resto del texto

orthogonal /ɔːˈθɒɡənəl/ *adjective* ortogonal

OS /ˌəʊ ˈes/ *noun* sistema *m* operativo

OS/2 (*multitasking operating system for PCs*) OS/2™

OSI /ˌəʊ es ˈaɪ/ *noun* MARISA *f*; modelo *m* arquitectónico de referencia para la interconexión de sistemas abiertos

outage /'aʊtɪdʒ/ *noun* (*of machine*) no disponibilidad *f*; interrupción *f* del servicio (de un aparato)

outlet /'aʊtlet/ *noun* (*electrical*) punto *m* de venta; toma *f* de corriente

outline /'aʊtlaɪn/ *noun* (*main features*) perfil *m*; diseño *m*; esquema *m*

outline flowchart /'aʊt(ə)laɪn ˌfləʊtʃɑːt/ *noun* esquema *m* principal; diagrama *m* principal

outline font /'aʊt(ə)laɪn fɒnt/ *noun* fuente *f* (de caracteres) modelo

outliner /'aʊtlaɪnə/ *noun* (*program used to help a user order sections of a list*) esquematizador *m* de texto

out of alignment /ˌaʊt əv ə'laɪnmənt/ *adjective* desajustado *or* -a

out of control /ˌaʊt əv kən'trəʊl/ *adjective* fuera de control

out of date /ˌaʊt əv 'deɪt/ *adjective* anticuado *or* -a ◇ **their computer system is years out of date** su sistema informático está muy anticuado ◇ **they are still using out-of-date equipment** todavía están utilizando un equipo anticuado

out of range /ˌaʊt əv 'reɪndʒ/ *adjective* fuera de alcance

output /'aʊtpʊt/ *noun* **1.** (*data*) salida *f* **2.** (*action*) salida *f* ■ *verb* (*data*) producir *vt*; sacar *vt* ◇ **finished documents can be output to the laser printer** los documentos terminados se pueden sacar por la impresora láser

output area /'aʊtpʊt ˌeəriə/, **output block** /'aʊtpʊt blɒk/ *noun* área *f* de salida (de la memoria)

output-bound /'aʊtpʊt ˌbaʊnd/ *adjective* limitado por la (velocidad de) salida (de datos)

output buffer register /ˌaʊtpʊt ˌbʌfə 'redʒɪstə/ *noun* registro *m* de memoria intermedia de salida

output bureau /'aʊtpʊt ˌbjʊərəʊ/ *noun* oficina *f* de datos impresos

output device /'aʊtpʊt dɪˌvaɪs/ *noun* (*device which allows information to be displayed*) periférico *m* de salida; aparato *m*; periférico *m*; dispositivo *m* de salida

output file /'aʊtpʊt faɪl/ *noun* fichero *m* de salida

output formatter /'aʊtpʊt ˌfɔːmætə/ *noun* formateador *m* de salida; instrucción *f* para dar formato a los datos de salida

output-limited /ˌaʊtpʊt 'lɪmɪtɪd/ *adjective* limitado por la (velocidad de) salida (de datos)

output mode /'aʊtpʊt məʊd/ *noun* modo *m* de salida

output port /'aʊtpʊt pɔːt/ *noun* puerto *m* de salida ◇ **connect the printer to the printer output port** conecte la impresora al puerto de salida de la impresora

output register /'aʊtpʊt ˌredʒɪstə/ *noun* registro *m* de salida

output stream /'aʊtpʊt striːm/ *noun* flujo *m* (de datos) de salida

outsource /'aʊtˌsɔːs/ *verb* (*to employ another company to manage and support a network for your company*) recurrir a fuentes externas

OV *abbr* (*overflow*) desbordamiento *m* (de capacidad)

overflow /'əʊvəfləʊ/ *noun* **1.** desbordamiento *m* (de capacidad); sobrecarga *f* **2.** desbordamiento *m* de capacidad (de una línea)

overflow bit /ˌəʊvə'fləʊ bɪt/ *noun* bit *m* de desbordamiento (de la capacidad); indicador *m* de desbordamiento (de la capacidad); testigo *m* de desbordamiento (de la capacidad)

overflow check /ˌəʊvə'fləʊ tʃek/ *noun* control *m* de desbordamiento de la capacidad

overflow flag /'əʊvəfləʊ flæg/ *noun* (*single bit in a word set to 1*) indicador *m* de desbordamiento (de la capacidad); testigo *m* de desbordamiento (de la capacidad); bit *m* de desbordamiento (de la capacidad)

overhead /'əʊvəhed/ *noun* (*extra code*) código *m* suplementario

overhead bit /ˌəʊvər'hed bɪt/ *noun* bit *m* suplementario para detección de errores

overheat /ˌəʊvə'hiːt/ *verb* recalentarse *vr*

overlap /ˌəʊvə'læp/ *noun* (*data*) solapamiento *m*; recubrimiento *m*; superposición *f* ■ *verb* solapar(se) *vr*; superponer(se) *vr* ◇ **overlap time** tiempo de superposición *f*

overlay /'əʊvəleɪ/ *noun* **1.** recubrimiento *m* **2.** (*small section of a program*) recubrimiento *m*

'Many packages also boast useful drawing and overlay facilities which enable the user to annotate specific maps.' [*Computing*]

overlay card /'əʊvəleɪ kɑːd/ *noun* tarjeta *f* gráfica de vídeo

overlay manager /'əʊvəleɪ ˌmænɪdʒə/ *noun* gestor *m* de segmento superpuesto

overlay region /'əʊvəleɪ ˌriːdʒ(ə)n/ *noun* área *f* de segmento de recubrimiento

overlay segments /'əʊvəleɪ ˌsegmənts/ *plural noun* segmentos *mpl* superponibles

overload /ˌəʊvə'ləʊd/ *verb* sobrecargar *vt*

overpunching /ˌəʊvə'pʌntʃɪŋ/ *noun* sobreperforación *f*

overrun /ˌəʊvə'rʌn/ *noun* exceso *m* de velocidad; sobrecarga *f*

overscan /'əʊvəskæn/ *noun* **1.** sobrebarrido *m*; sobredesviación *f* **2.** sobrebarrido *m*; sobredesviación *f*

over-voltage protection /ˌəʊvə 'vəʊltɪdʒ prəˌtekʃ(ə)n/ *noun* (*dispositivo de*) protección *f* contra el sobrevoltaje; protección *f* contra la subida de tensión

overwrite /ˌəʊvə'raɪt/ *verb* (*data*) superponer datos y destruir los datos de la memoria; reemplazar *vt*; borrar datos por superposición; sobreescribir *vt* ◇ **the latest data input has overwritten the old information** los nuevos datos introducidos han reemplazado la información anterior

P

pack /pæk/ *noun (punched cards)* paquete *m* (de tarjetas perforadas) ■ *verb (goods)* embalar *vt*; envasar *vt*; empaquetar *vt* ◇ **the diskettes are packed in plastic wrappers** los disquetes están empaquetados en un envoltorio de plástico

package /'pækɪdʒ/ *noun (items joined together in one deal)* paquete *m* ◇ **the computer is sold with accounting and word-processing packages** el ordenador se vende con un paquete de programas de contabilidad y tratamiento de textos

package deal /ˌpækɪdʒ 'diːl/ *noun (agreement)* transacción *f*; acuerdo *m* de conjunto; acuerdo *m* global; contrato *m* global; paquete *m* ◇ **they agreed a package deal, which involves the development of software, customizing hardware and training of staff** llegaron a un acuerdo de conjunto que incluye el desarrollo de software, la personalización del hardware y la formación del personal ◇ **we are offering a package deal which includes the whole office computer system, staff training and hardware maintenance** hemos propuesto una oferta global que comprende un sistema informático completo para la oficina, la formación del personal y el mantenimiento del equipo

packaged software /ˌpækɪdʒd 'sɒftweə/ *noun* paquete *m* de programas (informáticos)

packaging /'pækɪdʒɪŋ/ *noun (creating books for publishers)* paquete *m*; embalaje *m*

packed decimal /pækt 'desɪm(ə)l/ *noun* decimal *m* condensado

packed format /pækt 'fɔːmæt/ *noun* formato *m* condensado

packet /'pækɪt/ *noun (group of bits)* paquete *m* ◇ **packet switched network (PSN)** red *f* de conmutación de paquetes ◇ **packet switching system (PSS)** sistema *m* de conmutación de paquetes

packet assembler/disassembler /ˌpækɪt əˌsemblə ˌdɪsəˈsemblə/ *noun* ensamblador/desensamblador *m* de paquetes

packet scheduler /'pækɪt ˌʃedjuːlə/ *noun* planificador *m* de paquetes;;;;

packet-switched /'pækɪt ˌswɪtʃd/ *adjective* con conmutación de paquetes

packet switched data service /'pækɪt swɪtʃd 'deɪtə/, **packet switched network** /ˌpækɪt ˌswɪtʃɪd 'netwɜːk/ *noun* servicio *m* de comunicación de datos de conmutación de paquetes

packet switching /'pækɪt swɪtʃɪŋ/ *noun* conmutación *f* de paquetes

'The network is based on Northern Telecom DPN data switches over which it will offer X.25 packet switching, IBM SNA, and frame-relay transmission.' [*Computing*]

packet switching service /'pækɪt ˌswɪtʃɪŋ ˌsɜːvɪs/ *noun* servicio *m* de conmutación de paquetes

packing /'pækɪŋ/ *noun (data)* compresión *f*; condensación *f*

packing density /'pækɪŋ ˌdensɪti/ *noun* densidad *f* de almacenamiento; densidad *f* de registro

packing routine /'pækɪŋ ruːˌtiːn/ *noun* rutina *f* de compresión; rutina *f* de almacenamiento

pad /pæd/ *noun (of keys)* teclado *m*

PAD *abbr (packet assembler/disassembler)* ensamblador/desensamblador *m* de paquetes

pad character /pæd 'kærɪktə/ *noun* carácter *m* de relleno

padding /'pædɪŋ/ *noun (characters added to fill out)* relleno *m*

paddle /'pæd(ə)l/ *noun* palanca *f*; mando *m* ◇ **games paddle** mando de juego

page /peɪdʒ/ *noun* **1.** *(sheet of paper)* página *f* **2.** *(side of a printed sheet or text held on a computer screen)* página *f* **3.** *(section of main store)* página *f* **4.** *(section of a main program)* página *f* ■ *verb (to make a text into page)* paginar *vt*; poner en páginas; *(to put numbers onto pages)* paginar *vt* ◇ **page down key (PgDn)** *(key that moves the cursor down in an English keyboard)* tecla *f* de avance de página *or* Av Pág (en un teclado español) ◇ **pages per minute (ppm)** *(speed of printer)* (número de) páginas por minuto (ppm) ◇ **page up key (PgUp)** *(key that moves the cursor up in an English keyboard)* tecla de retroceso de página *or* tecla Re Pág (en un teclado español) ◇ **this laser printer can output eight pages per minute** esta impresora láser imprime ocho páginas por minuto ◇ **we do all our page layouts using desktop publishing software** diseñamos todas nuestras páginas con el software de autoedición

page addressing /peɪdʒ əˈdresɪŋ/ *noun* direccionamiento *m* de página

page boundary /peɪdʒ 'baʊnd(ə)ri/ *noun* límite *m* de página

page break /ˌpeɪdʒ 'breɪk/ *noun* **1.** *(point at which a page ends)* cambio *m* de página **2.** cambio *m* de página

paged address /ˌpeɪdʒd əˈdres/ *noun* dirección *f* paginada

page description language /ˌpeɪdʒ dɪ 'skrɪpʃən ˌlæŋgwɪdʒ/ *noun* lenguaje *m* de descripción de página

page description programming language /peɪdʒ dɪˌskrɪpʃ(ə)n 'prəʊgræmɪŋ ˌlæŋgwɪdʒ/ *noun* lenguaje *m* de descripción de página

page display /peɪdʒ dɪ'spleɪ/ *noun* visualización *f* de una página

paged-memory management unit /ˌpeɪdʒd ˌmem(ə)ri 'mænɪdʒmənt ˌjuːnɪt/ *noun* unidad *f* de gestión de la memoria paginada

paged-memory scheme /ˌpeɪdʒd 'mem(ə)ri ˌskiːm/ *noun* método *m* de paginación de la memoria

page down key /ˌpeɪdʒ 'daʊn ˌkiː/ *noun* tecla *f* de avance de página/ Av Pág (en un teclado español)

page frame /ˌpeɪdʒ 'freɪm/ *noun* tramo *m*; bloque *m* de página

page image buffer /ˌpeɪdʒ 'ɪmɪdʒ ˌbʌfə/ *noun* memoria *f* de imagen de página

page impression /peɪdʒ ɪm'preʃ(ə)n/ *noun* impresiones *fpl* de páginas

page layout /peɪdʒ 'leɪaʊt/ *noun* (*formatting*) presentación *f*; diseño *m*; composición *f* de página

page length /ˌpeɪdʒ 'leŋθ/ *noun* longitud *f* de página; número *m* de líneas por página

page makeup /ˌpeɪdʒ 'meɪkʌp/ *noun* organización *f* de la página; número *m* de página

page-mode RAM /ˌpeɪdʒ məʊd 'ræm/ *noun* memoria *f* RAM en modo página ◇ **the video adapter uses page-mode RAM to speed up the display** el adaptador de vídeo utiliza memoria RAM en modo página para acelerar la visualización

page number /peɪdʒ 'nʌmbə/ *noun* número *m* de página

page orientation /peɪdʒ ˌɔːriən'teɪʃ(ə)n/ *noun* orientación *f* de la página

page preview /peɪdʒ 'priːˌvjuː/ *noun* vista *f* preliminar; (función de) vista *f* previa de página (antes de imprimir)

page printer /peɪdʒ 'prɪntə/ *noun* impresora *f* por páginas ◇ **this dot-matrix printer is not a page printer, it only prints one line at a time** esta impresora matricial no es una impresora de página por página

page protection /peɪdʒ prə'tekʃən/ *noun* protección *f* de página

page reader /peɪdʒ 'riːdə/ *noun* lector *m* de páginas; escáner *m*

page setup /'peɪdʒ ˌsetʌp/ *noun* configuración *f*; distribución *f* de página

pages per minute /ˌpeɪdʒɪz pɜː 'mɪnət/ *noun* páginas por minuto (ppm)

page table /peɪdʒ 'teɪb(ə)l/ *noun* tabla *f* de páginas

page up key /ˌpeɪdʒ 'ʌp ˌkiː/ *noun* tecla *f* de retroceso de página; tecla *f* Re Pág (en un teclado español)

page width /ˌpeɪdʒ ', wɪdθ/ *noun* anchura *f* de página

pagination /ˌpædʒɪ'neɪʃ(ə)n/ *noun* **1.** (*dividing text into pages*) paginación *f* **2.** (*dividing into pages*) paginación *f*

paging /'peɪdʒɪŋ/ *noun* (*technique that splits main memory*) paginación *f*

paging algorithm /'peɪdʒɪŋ ˌælgərɪð(ə)m/ *noun* algoritmo *m* de paginación

paint /peɪnt/ *noun* (*Windows application for creating or editing bitmap images*) pintura *f* ■ *verb* (*in a graphics program*) pintar *vt*; colorear *vt*

Paintbrush/Paint /ˌpaɪntbrʌʃ 'peɪnt/ *noun* (*application supplied with Microsoft Windows 3.1x and Windows 95*) Paint *m*

paint program /'peɪnt ˌprəʊgræm/ *noun* programa *m* de diseño; programa *m* de pintura ◇ **I drew a rough of our new logo with this paint program** hice un bosquejo de nuestro nuevo logotipo con este programa de diseño

paired register /ˌpeəd 'redʒɪstə/ *noun* registro *m* asociado; registro *m* agrupado por pares

PAL /ˌpiː eɪ 'el/ *noun* sistema *m* PAL; sistema *m* de alternancia de fase por línea

palette /'pælət/ *noun* paleta *f* de colores

palette shift /'pælət ʃɪft/ *noun* desplazamiento *m* de la paleta de colores

palmtop /'pɑːmtɒp/ *noun* (*very small PC*) ordenador *m* de bolsillo ◇ **this palmtop has a tiny keyboard and twenty-line LCD screen** este ordenador de bolsillo dispone de un teclado muy pequeño y de una pantalla de 20 líneas

pan /pæn/ *verb* (*move a viewing window horizontally*) mostrar una imagen (por desplazamiento horizontal)

panel /'pæn(ə)l/ *noun* (*flat section of a casing*) panel *m*; cuadro *m* ◇ **the socket is on the back panel** el enchufe está en el panel trasero

paper-fed /'peɪpə fed/ *adjective* con alimentación automática de papel

paper feed /'peɪpə fiːd/ *noun* (*printer*) alimentación *f* de papel; arrastre *m* del papel

paperless /'peɪpələs/ *adjective* sin papel

paperless office /ˌpeɪpələs 'ɒfɪs/ *noun* oficina *f* electrónica; oficina *f* sin papel

'Indeed, the concept of the paperless office may have been a direct attack on Xerox and its close ties to the paper document. Yet, as we all know, the paperless office has so far been an empty promise.' [*Computing*]

paper tape /'peɪpə teɪp/ *noun* cinta *f* de papel; banda *f* de papel

paper tape feed /ˌpeɪpə 'teɪp ˌfiːd/ *noun* (dispositivo de) arrastre *m* de cinta de papel

paper tape punch /ˌpeɪpə 'teɪp ˌpʌntʃ/ *noun* perforadora *f* de cintas de papel

paper tape reader /ˌpeɪpə 'teɪp ˌriːdə/ *noun* lector *m* de cintas de papel perforadas

paper throw /'peɪpə θrəʊ/ *noun* salto *m* de papel

paper tray /'peɪpə treɪ/ *noun* bandeja *f* de papel (para alimentación hoja a hoja)

paper-white monitor /ˌpeɪpə 'waɪt ˌmɒnɪtə/ *noun* (*displays black text on a white background*) pantalla *f* con fondo blanco y texto en negro

paragraph /'pærəgrɑːf/ *noun* **1.** (*in a document*) párrafo *m* **2.** (*in a memory map*) bloque *m* de párrafo (de memoria)

paragraph marker /'pærəgrɑːf ˌmɑːkə/ *noun* (*nonprinting character*) símbolo *m*; marcador *m* de párrafo; símbolo *m* de punto y aparte

parallel /'pærəlel/ *adjective* **1.** (*processors*) paralelo *or* -a; en paralelo **2.** (*bits of words*) paralelo *or* -a; en paralelo ◇ **parallel input** *or* **output (PIO)** entrada/salida *f* en paralelo ◇ **parallel input** *or* **parallel output (PIPO)** entrada en paralelo/salida en paralelo ◇ **their average transmission rate is 60,000 bps through parallel connection** su velocidad normal de transmisión es de 60.000 bps mediante una conexión en paralelo

parallel access /ˌpærəlel 'ækses/ *noun* (*data transfer*) acceso *m* (en) paralelo

parallel adder /ˌpærəlel 'ædə/ *noun* sumador *m* en paralelo

parallel computer /ˌpærəlel kəm'pjuːtə/ *noun* ordenador *m* paralelo

parallel connection /ˌpærəlel kə'nekʃ(ə)n/ *noun* conexión *f* en paralelo ◇ **their transmission rate is 60,000 bps through parallel connection** la velocidad de transmisión es de 60.000 bps mediante una conexión en paralelo

parallel data transmission /ˌpærəlel 'deɪtə trænz͜mɪʃ(ə)n/ *noun* transmisión *f* de datos en paralelo

parallel input/output /ˌpærəlel ˌɪnpʊt 'aʊtpʊt/ *noun* entrada/salida *f* en paralelo

parallel input/output chip /ˌpærəlel ˌɪnpʊt 'aʊtpʊt ˌtʃɪp/ *noun* circuito *m* integrado de entrada/salida en paralelo

parallel input/parallel output /ˌpærəlel ˌɪnpʊt ˌpærəlel 'aʊtpʊt/ *noun* entrada *f* en paralelo/salida en paralelo

parallel input/serial output /ˌpærəlel ˌɪnpʊt ˌsɪəriəl 'aʊtpʊt/ *noun* entrada *f* en paralelo/salida en serie

parallel interface /ˌpærəlel 'ɪntəfeɪs/ *noun* interfaz *f* en paralelo

parallel operation /ˌpærəlel ˌɒpə'reɪʃ(ə)n/ *noun* operación *f* en paralelo

parallel port /'pærəlel pɔːt/ *noun* puerto *m* en paralelo; interfaz *f* en paralelo

parallel printer /ˌpærəlel 'prɪntə/ *noun* impresora *f* en paralelo

'The Wheelwriter 7000 offers 172Kb of document storage and mail-merge capabilities: it can be connected to a PC using the parallel printer port.' [*Computing*]

parallel priority system /ˌpærəlel praɪ'ɒrɪti ˌsɪstəm/ *noun* sistema *m* de prioridades en paralelo

parallel processing /ˌpærəlel 'prəʊsesɪŋ/ *noun* proceso *m* en paralelo

parallel running /ˌpærəlel 'rʌnɪŋ/ *noun* (*running of a new and old system*) funcionamiento *m*; explotación *f*; proceso *m* en paralelo; ejecución *f* en paralelo; proceso *m* doble

parallel search storage /ˌpærəlel 'sɜːtʃ ˌstɔːrɪdʒ/ *noun* memoria *f* de búsquedas paralelas; memoria *f* asociativa

parallel transfer /ˌpærəlel 'trænsfɜː/ *noun* transferencia *f* en paralelo

parallel transmission /ˌpærəlel trænz 'mɪʃ(ə)n/ *noun* (*data transfer*) transmisión *f* paralela; transmisión *f* en paralelo

parameter /pə'ræmɪtə/ *noun* parámetro *m* ◇ **keyword parameter** parámetro de palabra clave ◇ **the size of the array is set with this parameter** el tamaño de la matriz se establece con este parámetro ◇ **the X parameter defines the number of characters displayed across a screen** el parámetro X define el número de caracteres mostrados en pantalla

parameter-driven software /pəˌræmɪtə ˌdrɪv(ə)n 'sɒftweə/ *noun* (*with values fixed*) software *m* por definir (mediante parámetros); software *m* definido

parameterisation /pəˌræmɪtəraɪ'zeɪʃ(ə)n/, **parameterization** *noun* parametrización *f*

parameter passing /pə'ræmɪtə ˌpɑːsɪŋ/ *noun* paso *m* de parámetro

parameter testing /pə'ræmɪtə ˌtestɪŋ/ *noun* prueba *f* de parámetros

parameter word /pə'ræmɪtə wɜːd/ *noun* palabra *f* de parámetro

parametric subroutine /ˌpærəmetrɪk 'sʌbruːtiːn/ *noun* subrutina *f* paramétrica; subprograma *m* paramétrica

parent directory /'peərənt daɪˌrekt(ə)ri/ *noun* (*directory above a sub-directory*) directorio *m* padre

parent folder /'peərənt ˌfəʊldə/ *noun* (*Macintosh system: folder that contains other folders*) carpeta *f* padre

parent program /'peərənt ˌprəʊgræm/ *noun* (*program that starts another program*) programa *m* padre

parity /'pærɪti/ *noun* paridad *f*; igualdad *f*

'The difference between them is that RAID level one offers mirroring, whereas level five stripes records in parity across the disks in the system.' [*Computing*]

parity bit /'pærɪti bɪt/ *noun* bit *m* de paridad

parity check /'pærɪti tʃek/ *noun* control *m* de paridad

parity flag /'pærɪti flæg/ *noun* indicador *m* (de control) de paridad

parity interrupt /'pærɪti ˌɪntərʌpt/ *noun* interrupción *f* (de control) de paridad

parity track /'pærɪti træk/ *noun* pista *f* de paridad

park /pɑːk/ *verb* (*move the read/write head over a point on the disk where no data is stored*) aparcar *vt* ◇ **when parked, the disk head will not damage any data if it touches the disk**

surface cuando está aparcada, la cabeza del disco no daña los datos si toca la superficie del disco

parse /pɑːz/ *verb* (*language*) analizar sintácticamente; analizar gramaticalmente

parser /'pɑːzə/ *noun* analizador *m* sintáctico

part /pɑːt/ *noun* (*section of something*) parte *f*; sección *f*

part exchange /ˌpɑːt ɪks'tʃeɪndʒ/ *noun* intercambio *m* de una pieza

partial carry /ˌpɑːʃ(ə)l 'kæri/ *noun* arrastre *m* parcial

partial RAM /'pɑːʃ(ə)l ræm/ *noun* RAM *f* parcial; RAM *f* incompleta

partition /pɑː'tɪʃ(ə)n/ *noun* 1. (*divider*) división *f* 2. (*area of hard disk treated as a logical drive*) partición *f*; sección *f* ■ *verb* 1. (*to divide a hard disk into logical drives*) subdividir *vt*; dividir *vt*; desglosar *vt*; efectuar una partición 2. (*divide a file or block*) subdividir *vt*; dividir *vt*; desglosar *vt*

partitioned file /pɑː'tɪʃ(ə)nd faɪl/ *noun* fichero *m* subdividido; fichero *m* dividido en varias partes

part page display /ˌpɑːt peɪdʒ dɪ'spleɪ/ *noun* visualización *f* reducida; visualización *f* de una parte de la página

PASCAL /'pæskæl/ *noun* (*programming language*) lenguaje *m* PASCAL

pass /pɑːs/ *noun* paso *m*; pasaje *m* ■ *verb* (*of magnetic tape*) hacer pasar; desfilar *vi*

password /'pɑːs,wɜːd/ *noun* (*access to a system*) contraseña *f*; palabra *f* de paso; clave *f* de acceso ◊ **password-protected** protegido, -a por una contraseña ◊ **the user has to key in the password before he can access the database** el usuario debe escribir su contraseña para poder acceder a la base de datos

'...the system's security features let you divide the disk into up to 256 password-protected sections' [*Byte*]

password protection /ˌpɑːswɜːd prə 'tekʃ(ə)n/ *noun* protección *f* por palabra de paso; protección *f* por contraseña

paste /peɪst/ *verb* (*insert text that has been cut*) pegar *vt*; insertar *vt* ◊ **now that I have cut this paragraph from the end of the document, I can paste it in here** una vez he cortado este párrafo del final del documento, puedo pegarlo aquí

patch /pætʃ/ *noun* (*temporary or small correction to a program or software*) modificación *f* provisional; corrección *f* provisional

patch cord /'pætʃ kɔːd/ *noun* cable *m* de conexión

patch panel /pætʃ 'pæn(ə)l/ *noun* panel *m* de conexión

path /pɑːθ/ *noun* 1. (*program*) camino *m*; ruta *f* de acceso 2. (*network connection*) camino *m*; ruta *f* 3. (*in the DOS system: list of subdirectories*) camino *m* de acceso (DOS)

pathname /ˌpɑːθ'neɪm/ *noun* (*location of a file with a listing of the subdirectories*) nombre *m* de la ruta; vía *f* de acceso ◊ **the pathname for the letter file is \FILES\SIMON\DOCS\LET-**

TER.DOC el nombre de la ruta de acceso del fichero de la carta es \FILES\SIMON\DOCS\LETTER.DOC

pattern /'pæt(ə)n/ *noun* (*shapes or lines*) modelo *m*; diagrama *m*; diseño *m*

patterned /'pæt(ə)nd/ *adjective* con diseño

pattern palette /'pæt(ə)n ˌpælət/ *noun* paleta *f* de diseño

pattern recognition /ˌpæt(ə)n ˌrekəg 'nɪʃ(ə)n/ *noun* reconocimiento *m* del modelo

pause key /'pɔːz kiː/ *noun* (*key that stops a process*) tecla *f* Pausa

payment gateway /'peɪmənt ˌgeɪtweɪ/ *noun* pasarela *f* de pago

PBX *abbr* (*private branch exchange*) conmutador *m* privado (conectado con la red pública)

PC¹ /ˌpiː 'siː/ *noun* (*personal computer*) ordenador *m* personal; ordenador *m* individual; PC *m* ◊ **PC compatible** (*computer compatible with the IBM PC*) PC *or* ordenador personal compatible

PC² /ˌpiː 'siː/ *abbr* 1. (*printed circuit*) placa *f* de circuito impreso 2. (*program counter*) contador *m* de programas; registro *m* de dirección de instrucciones

PC/AT /ˌpiː siː eɪ 'tiː/ *noun* (*IBM PC compatible computer*) PC/AT

PC/AT keyboard /ˌpiː siː eɪ tiː 'kiːbɔːd/ *noun* teclado *m* PC/AT

PCB *abbr* (*printed circuit board*) placa *f* de circuito impreso

PC-compatible /ˌpiː ˌsiː kəm'pætəb(ə)l/ *adjective* PC *m*; ordenador *m* personal compatible

PC-DOS /ˌpiː siː 'dɒs/ *noun* (*version of MS-DOS sold by IBM*) PC-DOS (versión IBM de MS-DOS)

PCI /ˌpiː siː 'eɪ/ *noun* bus *m* local

PCL /ˌpiː siː 'el/ *noun* lenguaje *m* PCL; instrucciones *fpl* de control de la impresora

PCM /ˌpiː siː 'em/ *noun* 1. fabricante *mf* de enchufes conectores 2. modulación *f* por codificación de impulsos codificados

PCMCIA /ˌpiː siː em siː aɪ 'eɪ/ *noun* (*specification for add-in expansion cards*) PCMCIA

PCMCIA card /ˌpiː siː ˌem ˌsiː aɪ 'eɪ kɑːd/ *noun* tarjeta *f* PCMCIA ◊ **the extra memory is stored on this PCMCIA card and I use it on my laptop** la memoria adicional se almacena en esta tarjeta PCMCIA y la puedo usar en mi (ordenador) portátil

PCMCIA connector /ˌpiː siː ˌem ˌsiː aɪ ˌeɪ kə 'nektə/ *noun* conector *m* PCMCIA

PCMCIA slot /ˌpiː siː ˌem ˌsiː aɪ 'eɪ slɒt/ *noun* ranura *f* (para una tarjeta) PCMCIA

P-code /ˌpiː kəʊd/ *noun* pseudocódigo *m*; pseudoinstrucción *f*

PCS *abbr* (*personal communications services*) servicios *mpl* de comunicaciones personales

PCU /ˌpiː siː 'juː/ *noun* controlador *m* de periféricos; unidad *f* de control de periféricos

PCX file /ˌpiː siː eks 'faɪl/ *noun* (*storing of images*) fichero *m* PCX

PC/XT /ˌpiː siː eks 'tiː/ *noun* (*IBM PC compatible computer*) PC/XT

PC/XT keyboard /ˌpiː siː eks tiː 'kiːbɔːd/ *noun* teclado *m* PC/XT

PD *abbr* (*public domain*) dominio *m* público

PDA /ˌpiː diː 'eɪ/ *noun* ordenador *m* personal de bolsillo

PDF /ˌpiː diː 'ef/ *noun* formato *m* de documento transferible

PDL *abbr* **1.** (*page description language*) lenguaje *m* de descripción de página **2.** (*program design language*) lenguaje *m* de diseño de programas

PDN *abbr* (*public data network*) red *f* pública (de transmisión de datos)

peak /piːk/ *noun* **1.** (*highest point*) punta *f* máxima; punto *m* máximo **2.** (*maximum value*) punto *m* máximo ■ *verb* (*to reach highest point*) alcanzar su nivel más alto; alcanzar su punto máximo ◇ **the power peaked at 1,200 volts** la energía alcanzó su máximo nivel de 1.200 voltios

peak output /ˌpiːk 'aʊtpʊt/ *noun* rendimiento *m* máximo; nivel *m* máximo de producción

peak period /'piːk ˌpɪəriəd/ *noun* hora(s) *f(pl)* de máximo consumo; tráfico *m*

peek /piːk/ *noun* instrucción *f* PEEK (de lectura directa de la memoria) ◇ **you need the instruction PEEK 1452 here to examine the contents of memory location 1452** se necesita la instrucción PEEK 1452 para examinar los contenidos en el lugar 1452 de la memoria

peer /pɪə/ *noun* (*any two similar devices*) igual *m*; par *m*

peer-to-peer network /ˌpɪə tə 'pɪə/ *noun* (*local area network*) red *f* de igual a igual ◇ **we have linked the four PCs in our small office using a peer-to-peer network** hemos conectado los cuatro PC de nuestra pequeña oficina mediante una red de igual a igual

pel /pel/ *noun* píxel *m*

pen /pen/ *noun* **1.** (*computer writing device*) lápiz *m*; pluma *f* **2.** lápiz *m* fotosensible; lápiz *m* óptico

pen computer /pen kəm'pjuːtə/ *noun* ordenador *m* de lápiz óptico; ordenador *m* sin teclado

pen plotter /'pen ˌplɒtə/ *noun* trazador *m* de pluma; trazador *m* de plumilla

pen recorder /pen rɪ'kɔːdə/ *noun* trazador *m* gráfico; registro *m* gráfico

Pentium /'pentiəm/ (*processor developed by Intel*) (procesador Intel de 32 bits) Pentium™ ◇ **Pentium Pro™** (*currently the most powerful processor developed by Intel*) (procesador) Pentium Pro™

per /pɜː, pə/ *preposition* **1.** (*at a rate of*) por **2.** (*out of*) por ◇ **10 per cent** diez por ciento ◇ **fifty per cent of nothing is still nothing** el cincuenta por ciento de nada sigue siendo nada ◇ **the error rate has fallen to twelve per hundred** la tasa de errores ha descendido al doce por ciento ◇ **the rate is twenty-five per thousand** la tasa se eleva a veinticinco por mil ◇ **what is the increase per cent?** ¿cuál es el porcentaje de aumento?

percentage point /pə'sentɪdʒ pɔɪnt/ *noun* punto *m* porcentual

percentile /pə'sen,taɪl/ *noun* percentil *m*

per day /pə 'deɪ/ *phrase* por día; al día

perforated tape /'pɜːfə,reɪtɪd teɪp/ *noun* banda *f* perforada; cinta *f* perforada

perforation /ˌpɜːfə'reɪʃ(ə)n/ *noun* (*stationery*) línea *f*; columna *f* de perforaciones; línea *f* perforada

perforator /'pɜːfəreɪtə/ *noun* (*machine*) punzón *m* de perforación; perforadora *f*

perform /pə'fɔːm/ *verb* (*machine*) funcionar *vi*

performance /pə'fɔːməns/ *noun* rendimiento *m*; funcionamiento *m* ◇ **as a measure of the system's performance** como medida del rendimiento del sistema ◇ **high performance** (de) alto rendimiento ◇ **in benchmarking, the performances of several systems or devices are tested against a standard benchmark** para su evaluación, se pone a prueba el funcionamiento de varios sistemas o dispositivos mediante una prueba estándar

per hour /ˌpər 'aʊə/ *adverb* por hora

period /'pɪəriəd/ *noun* **1.** (*length of time*) periodo *m*; espacio *m* (de tiempo) **2.** (*typography*) punto *m* ◇ **for a period of months** durante algunos meses ◇ **for a period of time** durante un espacio *or* periodo de tiempo ◇ **for a six-year period** durante seis años *or* en un periodo de seis años

periodic /ˌpɪəri'ɒdɪk/, **periodical** /ˌpɪəri'ɒdɪk(ə)l/ *adjective* (*from time to time*) periódico *or* -a

periodically /ˌpɪəri'ɒdɪkli/ *adverb* periódicamente; de vez en cuando

peripheral /pə'rɪf(ə)rəl/ *adjective* **1.** (*not essential*) periférico *or* -a; secundario *or* -a **2.** (*attached to something else*) periférico *m* ■ *noun* **1.** (*hardware*) periférico *m* **2.** (*communication device*) periférico *m* ◇ **peripheral interface adapter (PIA)** adaptador *m* de interconexiones de periféricos ◇ **peripheral processing unit (PPU)** procesador periférico ◇ **peripherals such as disk drives or printers allow data transfer and are controlled by a system, but contain independent circuits for their operation** los periféricos, como los lectores de disquetes o las impresoras, permiten transferir datos y son controlados por un sistema, pero contienen circuitos independientes para su funcionamiento

peripheral component interconnect /pə,rɪf(ə)rəl kəm,pəʊnənt 'ɪntəkənekt/ *noun* bus *m* local; enlace *m* común PCI

peripheral control unit /pə,rɪf(ə)rəl kən'trəʊl ˌjuːnɪt/ *noun* unidad *f* de control de periféricos; controlador *m* de periféricos

peripheral driver /pə,rɪf(ə)rəl 'draɪvə/ *noun* controlador *m* de periféricos

peripheral equipment /pə,rɪf(ə)rəl ɪ'kwɪpmənt/ *noun* **1.** (*all equipment*) equipo *m* periférico; (*piece of equipment*) periféricos *mpl* **2.** equipo *m* periférico; periféricos *mpl*

peripheral interface adapter /pə,rɪf(ə)rəl 'ɪntəfeɪs ə,dæptə/ *noun* adaptador *m* de interconexiones de periféricos

peripheral memory /pə,rɪf(ə)rəl 'mem(ə)ri/ *noun* memoria *f* periférica

peripheral processing unit /pə,rɪf(ə)rəl 'prəʊsesɪŋ ,juːnɪt/ *noun* procesador *m* periférico

peripheral software driver /pə,rɪf(ə)rəl 'sɒftweə ,draɪvə/ *noun* rutina *f* de gestión de periféricos

peripheral transfer /pə,rɪf(ə)rəl 'trænsfɜː/ *noun* transferencia *f* entre la unidad central y periférico

peripheral unit /pə,rɪf(ə)rəl 'juːnɪt/ *noun* **1.** periférico *m*; unidad *f* periférica **2.** periférico *m*

Perl /pɜːl/ *noun* lenguaje *m* Perl; lenguaje *m* práctico de extracción y formateado

permanent dynamic memory /,pɜːmənənt daɪ,næmɪk 'mem(ə)ri/ *noun* memoria *f* dinámica permanente

permanent error /,pɜːmənənt 'erə/ *noun* error *m* permanente

permanent file /'pɜːmənənt faɪl/ *noun* fichero *m* permanente

permanent memory /,pɜːmənənt 'mem(ə)ri/ *noun* memoria *f* permanente

permanent swap file /,pɜːmənənt 'swɒp ,faɪl/ *noun* fichero *m* de intercambio permanente

permission /pə'mɪʃ(ə)n/ *noun* (*authorization to access*) autorización *f*; permiso *m* (de acceso) ◇ **this user cannot access the file on the server because he does not have permission** este usuario no puede acceder al fichero del servidor porque no tiene autorización

permutation /,pɜːmjʊ'teɪʃ(ə)n/ *noun* permutación *f*; combinación *f*

persistence /pə'sɪstəns/ *noun* persistencia *f*; tenacidad *f*

personal communications services /,pɜːs(ə)n(ə)l kə,mjuːnɪ'keɪʃ(ə)nz ,sɜːvɪsɪz/ *plural noun* servicios *mpl* de comunicaciones personales

personal computer /,pɜːs(ə)n(ə)l kəm 'pjuːtə/ *noun* ordenador *m* personal; PC *m*

Personal Computer Memory Card International Association /,pɜːs(ə)nəl kəm ,pjuːtə ,mem(ə)ri kɑːd ,ɪntənæʃ(ə)nəl ə,səʊsi 'eɪʃ(ə)n/ *noun* PCMCIA

personal digital assistant /,pɜːs(ə)n(ə)l ,dɪdʒɪt(ə)l ə'sɪstənt/ *noun* ordenador *m* personal de bolsillo

personal identification device /,pɜːs(ə)n(ə)l aɪ,dentɪfɪ'keɪʃ(ə)n dɪ,vaɪs/ *noun* dispositivo *m* de identificación personal; tarjeta *f* magnética de identificación personal

personal identification number /,pɜːs(ə)n(ə)l aɪ,dentɪfɪ'keɪʃ(ə)n ,nʌmbə/ *noun* número *m* de identificación personal

personal information manager /,pɜːs(ə)n(ə)l ,ɪnfə'meɪʃ(ə)n ,mænɪdʒə/ *noun* administrador *m* de información personal; PIM

personalising, personalizing *noun* personalización *f*

perspective /pə'spektɪv/ *noun* perspectiva *f*

perspective correction /pə'spektɪv kə ,rekʃ(ə)n/ *noun* corrección *f*; modificación *f* de la perspectiva

PERT /pɜːt/ *noun* técnica *f* de evaluación y revisión de programas

per week /pə 'wiːk/ *adverb* por semana

per year /pə 'jɪə/ *adverb* por año

peta /petə/ *prefix* (*one quadrillion (250)*) peta *m*

petabyte /'petəbaɪt/ *noun* (*one quadrillion bytes*) petaocteto *m*; petabyte *m*

PgDn /,peɪdʒ 'daʊn/ *abbr* (*page down key*) tecla *f* de avance de página/ Av Pág (en un teclado español)

PGP /,piː dʒiː 'piː/ *noun* confidencialidad *f* segura

PgUp /,peɪdʒ 'ʌp/ *abbr* (*page up key*) tecla *f* de retroceso de página; tecla *f* Re Pág (en un teclado español)

phantom ROM /'fæntəm rɒm/ *noun* (*duplicate area of read-only memory*) ROM *f* fantasma

phase /feɪz/ *noun* (*part of a larger process*) fase *f* ∎ *verb* (*delay*) demorar *vt* ◇ **phase angle** ángulo *m* de fase *or* de desfasamiento ◇ **phase clipping** recorte *m* de fase ◇ **phase equalizer** compensador *m* de fase ◇ **phase modulation** modulación *f* de fase

phase alternation line /,feɪz ,ɔːltə'neɪʃ(ə)n ,laɪn/ *noun* sistema *m* de alternancia de fase por línea; sistema *m* PAL

phased change-over /,feɪzd 'tʃeɪndʒ/ *noun* cambio *m* gradual; cambio *m* progresivo

phone /fəʊn/ *noun* teléfono *m* ◇ **by phone** por teléfono ◇ **can you give me your phone number?** ¿puede darme su número de teléfono? ◇ **card phone** teléfono de tarjeta ◇ **he keeps a list of phone numbers in a black notebook** tiene una lista de números de teléfono en un cuaderno negro ◇ **he spoke to the manager on the phone** habló con el director por teléfono ◇ **house phone** *or* **internal phone** teléfono interno ◇ **look up his address in the phone book** busque su dirección en la guía de teléfonos ◇ **phone book** guía *f* telefónica *or* listín *m* telefónico *or* de teléfonos ◇ **she has been on the phone all morning** se ha pasado toda la mañana en el teléfono ◇ **the phone number is on the company notepaper** el número de teléfono figura en el papel con el membrete de la empresa ◇ **to answer the phone** *or* **to take a phone call** contestar al teléfono ◇ **to be on the phone** hablar por teléfono *or* estar en línea (con alguien) ◇ **to make a phone call** telefonear *or* llamar (por teléfono) *or* hacer una llamada (telefónica)

Phone Dialer /'fəʊn ,daɪələ/ *noun* (*utility supplied with Windows 95*) marcador *m* telefónico

phoneme /'fəʊniːm/ *noun* fonema *m* ◇ **the phoneme 'oo' is present in the words too and zoo** las palabras 'too' y 'zoo' contienen el fonema 'oo'

phone number /'fəʊn ˌnʌmbə/ *noun* número *m* de teléfono

phosphor /'fɒsfə/ *noun* fósforo *m*

phosphor coating /'fɒsfə ˌkəʊtɪŋ/ *noun* capa *f* de fósforo; capa *f* fosforescente

phosphor dots /'fɒsfə dɒtz/ *plural noun* puntos *mpl* de fósforo

phosphor efficiency /'fɒsfə ɪˌfɪʃ(ə)nsi/ *noun* rendimiento *m* de fosforescencia

photo- /fəʊtəʊ/ *prefix* foto-

PhotoCD /'fəʊtəʊ siː ˌdiː/ *noun* (*device to store 35mm slides or negatives in digital format on a CD-ROM*) PhotoCD™

photodigital memory /fəʊtəʊˌdɪdʒɪt(ə)l 'mem(ə)ri/ *noun* memoria *f* fotodigital

photorealistic /ˌfəʊtəʊriə'lɪstɪk/ *adjective* (*high quality computer image*) de calidad fotográfica

photoresist /ˌfəʊtəʊrɪ'zɪst/ *noun* sustancia *f* protectora fotosensible ◇ **to make the PCB, coat the board with photoresist, place the opaque pattern above, expose, then develop and etch, leaving the conducting tracks** para hacer una placa de circuito impreso, recubra la placa con una sustancia protectora fotosensible, coloque encima el diseño opaco, expóngalo, revélelo y grábelo dejando las guías conductoras

phototypesetter /ˌfəʊtəʊ'taɪpsetə/ *noun* (*machine*) fotocompositora *f*; máquina *f* de fotocomposición

physical address /ˌfɪzɪk(ə)l ə'dres/ *noun* dirección *f* física

physical database /ˌfɪzɪk(ə)l 'deɪtəbeɪs/ *noun* base *f* de datos física

physical layer /ˌfɪzɪk(ə)l 'leɪə/ *noun* capa *f* física

physical memory /ˌfɪzɪk(ə)l 'mem(ə)ri/ *noun* memoria *f* física

physical parameter /ˌfɪzɪk(ə)l pə'ræmɪtə/ *noun* parámetro *m* físico

physical record /ˌfɪzɪk(ə)l 'rekɔːd/ *noun* **1.** (*unit of data that can be transmitted*) registro *m* físico **2.** (*all the information for one record*) registro *m* físico

physical topology /ˌfɪzɪk(ə)l tə'pɒlədʒi/ *noun* topología *f* física

PIC /ˌpiː aɪ 'siː/ *noun* controlador *m* de interrupciones programable

pica /'paɪkə/ *noun* (*printing measurement*) pica *f*; 12 puntos ingleses; (*on a printer or typewriter*) fuente *f* de caracteres pica

PICK /pɪk/ *noun* (*operating system*) PICK™

pickup reel /'pɪkʌp riːl/ *noun* bobina *f* receptora

pico- /piːkəʊ/ *prefix* (*one million millionth*) pico- ◇ **picofarad (pF)** picofaradio (pF) *m*

picosecond /'piːkəʊˌsekənd/ *noun* picosegundo (ps) *m*

PICS /pɪks/ *noun* (*file format to import PICT files on a Macintosh*) PICS

PICT /pɪkt/ *noun* (*Apple Macintosh graphics file format*) PICT

picture /'pɪktʃə/ *noun* (*drawing*) dibujo *m*; (*book*) ilustración *f*; (*photograph*) foto *f*; fotografía *f* ■ *verb* imaginar *vt*; visualizar *vt* ◇ **this picture shows the new design** esta foto muestra el nuevo diseño ◇ **try to picture the layout before starting to draw it in** intente visualizar el esquema antes de comenzar a dibujar

PICture /'pɪktʃə/ *noun* PICture

picture beam /'pɪktʃə biːm/ *noun* haz *m* de imagen

picture element /'pɪktʃə ˌelɪmənt/ *noun* elemento *m* de imagen; píxel *m*

picture image compression /ˌpɪktʃə 'ɪmɪdʒ kəmˌpreʃ(ə)n/ *noun* compresión *f* de la imagen

picture processing /ˌpɪktʃə ˌprə'sesɪŋ/ *noun* tratamiento *m* de la imagen

picture transmission /'pɪktʃə trænz ˌmɪʃ(ə)n/ *noun* transmisión *f* de la imagen

PID /ˌpiː aɪ 'diː/ *noun* tarjeta *f* magnética de identificación personal; dispositivo *m* de identificación personal

pie chart /'paɪ tʃɑːt/ *noun* (*diagram*) diagrama *m* de sectores; gráfico *m* circular; diagrama *m* circular ◇ **the memory allocation is shown on this pie chart** este diagrama de sectores muestra la asignación de memoria

PIF /ˌpiː aɪ 'ef/ *noun* fichero *m* PIF (de información de un programa en el entorno MS-Windows)

piggyback /'pɪgibæk/ *verb* (*to connect two integrated circuits in parallel*) montar *vt*; superponer *vt*; incorporar *vt* ◇ **piggyback those two memory chips to boost the memory capacity** superponga los dos chips para potenciar la capacidad de memoria

piggyback entry /'pɪgibæk ˌentri/ *noun* entrada *f* con una clave de acceso pirateada

piggybacking /'pɪgibækɪŋ/ *noun* (*messages*) (mensaje electrónico de) respuesta *f* que incorpora el mensaje recibido

pilot /'paɪlət/ *adjective* (*programming language*) prueba *f* piloto ■ *verb* poner a prueba; ensayar *vt* ◇ **they are piloting the new system** están poniendo a prueba el nuevo sistema

pilot system /'paɪlət ˌsɪstəm/ *noun* sistema *m* piloto

PIM /ˌpiː aɪ 'em/ *noun* administrador *m* de información personal; PIM

pin /pɪn/ *noun* **1.** (*short piece of wire attached to an IC*) contacto *m* **2.** (*part of a plug*) clavija *f*; conector *m* ◇ **pin board** tablero *m* de clavijas *or* de terminales de conexión ◇ **use a three-pin plug to connect the printer to the mains** utilice un enchufe de tres clavijas para conectar la impresora a la red

PIN /pɪn/ *noun* (*short piece of wire attached to an IC*) número *m* de identificación personal

pinchwheel /'pɪntʃwiːl/ *noun* rueda *f* dentada

pin-compatible /ˌpɪn kəm'pætɪb(ə)l/ *adjective* de contactos/conectores compatibles

pincushion distortion /ˌpɪnkʊʃ(ə)n dɪ 'stɔːʃ(ə)n/ noun distorsión f en cojín

pinfeed /'pɪnfiːd/ noun arrastre m; tracción f del papel por rodillo dentado

PING /pɪŋ/ noun (software utility to test all the nodes on a network) PICS

pinout /'pɪnaʊt/ noun (position of pins on an IC) disposición f de los contactos; configuración f de un conector

PIO /ˌpiː aɪ 'əʊ/ noun entrada/salida f en paralelo

pipe /paɪp/ noun (operating system) operador m de derivación

pipeline /'paɪplaɪn/ noun conducto m ■ verb 1. (to schedule inputs) organizar por encauzamiento; encauzar vt 2. tratar (las instrucciones) por encauzamiento; ejecutar (las instrucciones) por encauzamiento

pipeline burst cache /ˌpaɪplaɪn bɜːst 'kæʃ/ noun memoria f caché de ráfagas de canal

pipelining /ˌpaɪpˌlaɪn 'mem(ə)ri/, **pipeline memory** noun (scheduling inputs) modo m de tratamiento por encauzamiento; modo m de ejecución por encauzamiento

PIPO /ˌpiː aɪ piː 'əʊ/ noun entrada f en paralelo/salida en paralelo

piracy /'paɪrəsi/ noun piratería f

pirate /'paɪrət/ noun (person who copies and sells patented invention or a copyright work) pirata mf ■ adjective pirata m&f; (system) pirateado m or -a f ■ verb piratear vt ◇ **a pirated tape** cinta f pirateada ◇ **he used a cheap pirated disk and found the program had bugs in it** utilizó un disquete pirateado a buen precio y descubrió que el programa contenía errores ◇ **the company is trying to take the software pirates to court** la empresa está intentando llevar a los piratas de software ante los tribunales ◇ **the designs for the new system were pirated in the Far East** los diseños del nuevo sistema fueron pirateados en el Extremo Oriente

pirate copy /ˌpaɪrət 'kɒpi/ noun (illegal copy) copia f pirata; copia f pirateada; copia f ilegal ◇ **a pirate copy of a computer program** una copia pirateada de un programa de ordenador

pirate software /ˌpaɪrət 'sɒftweə/ noun programa m pirateado; programa m ilegal

PISO /ˌpiː aɪ es 'əʊ/ noun entrada f en paralelo/salida en serie

pitch /pɪtʃ/ noun (horizontal spacing) espaciado m; (number of characters) densidad f de caracteres; número m de caracteres por pulgada

pix /pɪks/ plural noun (images) imágenes fpl; (illustrations) ilustraciones fpl; (photos) fotos fpl

pixel /'pɪksəl/ noun píxel m; elemento m de una imagen

'…adding 40 to each pixel brightens the image and can improve the display's appearance' [Byte]

pixelated /'pɪksəleɪtɪd/ adjective pixelado, -a

PLA /ˌpiː el 'eɪ/ noun orden m lógico programable; dispositivo m lógico programable

place /pleɪs/ noun (numbers) lugar m; sitio m; posición f

plaintext /ˌpleɪn'tekst/ noun texto m no cifrado ◇ **enter the plaintext message into the cipher machine** introduzca el mensaje de texto no cifrado en la máquina codificadora ◇ **the messages were sent as plaintext by telephone** los mensajes fueron enviados por teléfono como texto no cifrado

plan /plæn/ noun 1. (objective) plan m; proyecto m 2. (drawing) plano m ■ verb (to organise) planificar vt; proyectar vt ◇ **floor plan** plano de una planta ◇ **plans** conjunto m de planos ◇ **street plan** or **town plan** plano de la ciudad

PLAN /plæn/ noun (programming language) lenguaje m PLAN

planar /'pleɪnə/ adjective (method of producing ICs) planar m ■ noun (graphical images arranged on the same plane) gráfico m plano

plane /pleɪn/ noun (in a graphics image) plano m

planner /'plænə/ noun (software) agenda f

planning /'plænɪŋ/ noun planificación f ◇ **long-term planning** planificación a largo plazo ◇ **short-term planning** planificación a corto plazo

plant /plɑːnt/ verb (in memory) colocar vt; almacenar vt

plasma display /'plæzmə dɪˌspleɪ/ noun presentación f por plasma; representación f visual por plasma

plastic bubble keyboard /ˌplæstɪk ˌbʌb(ə)l 'kiːbɔːd/ noun teclado m de burbujas de plástico

platform /'plætfɔːm/ noun (standard type of hardware) plataforma f; conjunto m de estructuras ◇ **this software will only work on the IBM PC platform** este software sólo funcionará sobre una plataforma IBM

platform independence /ˌplætfɔːm ˌɪndɪ 'pendəns/ noun independencia f de plataforma; independencia f del entorno (de trabajo)

platter /'plætə/ noun (disk) plato m (de un disco duro); disco m simple

play back /ˌpleɪ 'bæk/ verb (film, etc.) reproducir (un registro)

playback head /'pleɪˌbæk hed/ noun cabeza f de lectura ◇ **disk playback head** cabeza de lectura de discos ◇ **tape playback head** cabeza de lectura de cintas

playback speed /'pleɪˌbæk spiːd/ noun velocidad f de reproducción

PLD abbr (programmable logic device) orden m lógico programable; dispositivo m lógico programable

plex database /'pleks ˌdeɪtəbeɪs/ noun base f de datos entrelazada

plex structure /'pleks ˌstrʌktʃə/ noun estructura f entrelazada; red f totalmente interconectada

plot /plɒt/ noun (graph or map) grafo m; curva f; trazo m ■ verb trazar vt

plotter /'plɒtə/ noun trazador m (de grafos)

plotter driver /'plɒtə ˌdraɪvə/ noun controlador m or -a; indicador m del trazador

plotter pen /'plɒtə pen/ *noun* pluma *f* trazadora; plumilla *f* trazadora

plotting mode /'plɒtɪŋ məʊd/ *noun* modo *m* gráfico; modo *m* de trazado

plug /plʌg/ *noun* (*connector*) enchufe *m*; clavija *f*; tomacorriente *m* ■ *verb* (*to connect*) enchufar *vt* ◇ **the printer is supplied with a plug** la impresora va provista de un enchufe ◇ **to plug and play** enchufar y usar ◇ **to plug in** (*a machine*) enchufar

plug and play /ˌplʌg ən 'pleɪ/ *noun* (*part of the Windows 95 system – where the user plugs a new adapter card into their PC they do not have to configure it or set any switches*) (dispositivo) conectar y listo; Plug and Play™

plug-compatible /plʌg kəm'pætəb(ə)l/ *adjective* conectable directamente; con conector compatible ◇ **plug-compatible manufacturer (PCM)** fabricante *m&f* de enchufes conectores ◇ **this new plug-compatible board works much faster than any of its rivals, we can install it by simply plugging it into the expansion port** esta nueva placa de conexión es mucho más rápida que cualquier otra; se instala simplemente enchufándola en el puerto de extensión

plug-compatible manufacturer /ˌplʌg kəm ˌpætɪb(ə)l ˌmænjuː'fæktʃərə/ *noun* fabricante *mf* de enchufes conectores

plug-in /'plʌg ɪn/ *noun* (*software to enhance a Web browser*) enchufable *m*

plug-in unit /'plʌg ɪn ˌjuːnɪt/ *noun* unidad *f*; circuito *m* de extensión

plus /plʌs/, **plus sign** /'plʌs saɪn/ *noun* más *m*; signo *m* de sumar

PNP /ˌpiː en 'piː/ *abbr* (*plug and play*) Plug and Play™; (dispositivo) conectar y listo

pnp transistor /ˌpiː en 'piː træn,zɪstə/ *noun* transistor *m* (de tipo) pnp

point /pɔɪnt/ *verb* señalar *vt*

'...the arrow keys, the spacebar or the mouse are used for pointing, and the enter key or the left mouse button are to pick' [*PC User*]

pointer /'pɔɪntə/ *noun* **1.** (*in a computer program*) puntero *m*; indicador *m* **2.** (*graphical symbol*) puntero *m* ◇ **desktop publishing on a PC is greatly helped by the use of a pointer and mouse** el uso del puntero y del ratón facilita la edición electrónica de textos (en un PC) ◇ **increment the contents of the pointer to the address of the next instruction** aumente los contenidos del indicador hasta la dirección de la siguiente instrucción

pointer file /'pɔɪntə faɪl/ *noun* fichero *m* de punteros

pointing device /'pɔɪntɪŋ dɪ,vaɪs/ *noun* (*device that controls the position of a cursor*) dispositivo *m* indicador

point of presence /ˌpɔɪnt əv 'prezəns/ *noun* punto *m* de conexión/de presencia

point-of-sale /ˌpɔɪnt əv 'seɪl/ *noun* punto *m* de venta

point size /ˌpɔɪnt 'saɪz/ *noun* muestreo *m* por puntos

point to point /'pɔɪnt tə, tʊ/ *noun* **1.** punto *m* a punto **2.** red *f* punto a punto

point to point protocol /ˌpɔɪnt tə ˌpɔɪnt 'prəʊtəkɒl/ *noun* protocolo *m* punto a punto

poke /pəʊk/ *noun* POKE (de inserción) ◇ **poke 1423.74 will write the data 74 into location 1423** la instrucción POKE 1423.74 insertará el dato 74 en la ubicación 1423

POL *abbr* (*problem-orientated language*) lenguaje *m* orientado a problemas

polar /'pəʊlə/ *adjective* polar ◇ **polar diagram** diagrama *m* de coordenadas polares ◇ **polar orbit** órbita *f* polar

polar coordinates /ˌpəʊlə kəʊ'ɔːdɪnəts/ *noun* coordenadas *fpl* polares

polarised /'pəʊləraɪzd/ *adjective* polarizado *or* -a

polarised edge connector /ˌpəʊləraɪzd 'edʒ kə,nektə/ *noun* conector *m* de borde polarizado; conector *m* de un solo borde de enchufe

polarised plug /ˌpəʊləraɪzd 'plʌg/ *noun* enchufe *m* polarizado; clavija *f* tomacorriente polarizada

polarity /pəʊ'lærəti/ *noun* polaridad *f*

polarity test /pəʊ'lærəti test/ *noun* prueba *f* de polaridad

policy /'pɒlɪsi/ *noun* política *f* de uso aceptable

Polish notation /ˌpəʊlɪʃ nəʊ'teɪʃ(ə)n/ *noun* notación *f* polaca

poll /pəʊl/ *verb* (*in a network*) llamar *vt*; interrogar *vt*; (*of computer*) emitir *vt*

polled interrupt /ˌpəʊld 'ɪntərʌpt/ *noun* interrupción *f* de llamada

polling /'pəʊlɪŋ/ *noun* (*from controlling computer to terminal*) sondeo *m*; llamada *f* selectiva

polling characters /ˌpəʊlɪŋ 'kærɪktəz/ *plural noun* caracteres *mpl* de llamada selectiva

polling interval /'pəʊlɪŋ ˌɪntəv(ə)l/ *noun* intervalo *m* de llamadas

polling list /'pəʊlɪŋ lɪst/ *noun* lista *f*; orden *m* de llamadas de los terminales

polling overhead /'pəʊlɪŋ ˌəʊvəhed/ *noun* tiempo *m* de llamadas selectivas; tiempo *m* de llamada y comprobación de terminal de red

polygon /'pɒlɪgən/ *noun* (*graphics shape with three or more sides*) polígono *m*

polygon mesh model /ˌpɒlɪgən 'meʃ ˌmɒd(ə)l/ *noun* modelo *m* de trama de rejilla

polynomial code /ˌpɒli'nəʊmiəl kəʊd/ *noun* código *m* polinómico

polyphony /pə'lɪfəni/ *noun* polyphony *m*

pop /pɒp/ *verb* saltar *vt*; hacer saltar

POP /pɒp/ *noun* punto *m* de conexión/de presencia

POP 2 /'pɒp tuː/ *noun* lenguaje *m* POP 2

POP 3 /ˌpɒp 'θriː/ *noun* (*system used to transfer electronic mail messages between a user's computer and a server located at an ISP*) (protocolo de) transferencia *f* de mensajes electrónicos POP 3 (entre usuario y servidor)

pop-down menu /ˌpɒp daʊn 'menjuː/ *noun* ventana *f* del menú; menú *m* desplegable

populate /'pɒpjʊleɪt/ *verb* (*fill the sockets on a printed circuit board with components*) poblar *vt*

pop-up menu /ˌpɒp ʌp 'menjuː/ *noun* ventana *f* del menú; menú *m* desplegable

pop-up window /ˌpɒp ʌp 'wɪndəʊ/ *noun* ventana *f* superpuesta

'...you can use a mouse to access pop-up menus and a keyboard for word processing' [*Byte*]

port /pɔːt/ *noun* (*data transfer*) puerto *m*; conexión *f*; punto *m* (de acceso/de entrada/salida)

portability /ˌpɔːtə'bɪlɪti/ *noun* (*of program*) portabilidad *f*; transportabilidad *f*

'...although portability between machines is there in theory, in practice it just isn't that simple' [*Personal Computer World*]

portable /'pɔːtəb(ə)l/ *noun* (*machine*) ordenador *m* portátil ■ *adjective* (*computer*) portátil ◇ **portable operating system interface (POSIX)** (*IEEE standard*) interfaz *f* portátil de sistema operativo

portable document format /ˌpɔːtəb(ə)l 'dɒkjʊmənt ˌfɔːmæt/ *noun* formato *m* de documento transferible

portable programs /ˌpɔːtəb(ə)l 'prəʊgræmz/ *noun* programas *mpl* portátiles

portable software /ˌpɔːtəb(ə)l 'sɒftweə/ *noun* programas *mpl* portátiles; programas *mpl* transferibles

portal /'pɔːt(ə)l/ *noun* portal *m*

portrait /'pɔːtrɪt/ *adjective* (*page or piece of paper where the longest edge is vertical*) retrato *m*; (*page orientation*) orientación *f* vertical de la página

port selector /pɔːt sɪ'lektə/ *noun* selector *m* de puerto

port sharing /pɔːt 'ʃeərɪŋ/ *noun* puerto *m* compartido; repartición *f* de puerto

POS /pɒz/ *abbr* (*point-of-sale*) punto *m* de venta

positional /pə'zɪʃ(ə)nəl/ *adjective* posicional

positioning time /pə'zɪʃ(ə)nɪŋ taɪm/ *noun* tiempo *m* de colocación; tiempo *m* de acceso

positive /'pɒzɪtɪv/ *adjective* **1.** (*meaning 'yes'*) afirmativo *or* -a **2.** (*image*) prueba *f* positiva **3.** (*electrical*) positivo *or* -a

positive display /ˌpɒzɪtɪv dɪ'spleɪ/ *noun* fijación *f* positiva; visualización *f* de negro sobre fondo blanco

positive logic /ˌpɒzɪtɪv 'lɒdʒɪk/ *noun* lógica *f* positiva

positive photoresist /ˌpɒzɪtɪv ˌfəʊtəʊrɪ'zɪst/ *noun* sustancia *f* protectora fotosensible en positivo

positive presentation /ˌpɒzɪtɪv ˌprez(ə)n'teɪʃ(ə)n/ *noun* presentación *f* positiva

positive response /ˌpɒzɪtɪv rɪ'spɒns/ *noun* respuesta *f* afirmativa; respuesta *f* positiva

positive terminal /ˌpɒzɪtɪv 'tɜːmɪn(ə)l/ *noun* terminal *m* positivo; borne *m* positivo

post /pəʊst/ *verb* (*to enter data*) registrar *vt*; actualizar *vt*

postbyte /'pəʊstbaɪt/ *noun* postbyte *m*; postocteto *m*

post-editing /pəʊst ˌ'edɪtɪŋ/ *noun* (*editing and modifying text*) actualización *f* después de una compilación; actualización *f* después de cálculos

postfix /'pəʊstfɪks/ *noun* sufijo *m*

postfix notation /ˌpəʊstfɪks nəʊ'teɪʃ(ə)n/ *noun* (*mathematical operations*) notación *f* por sufijos; notación *f* por postfijos; notación *f* polaca inversa ◇ **normal notation: (x-y) + z, but using postfix notation: xy – z +** en notación normal se escribe (x-y) + z, pero en la notación por sufijos se escribe xy – z +; cuando en la notación normal se escribe (x-y) + z, en la notación polaca inversa se escribe xy – z +

post-formatted /ˌpəʊst 'fɔːmætɪd/ *adjective* preparado, -a en la impresión

postmaster /'pəʊstmɑːstə/ *noun* responsable *m&f* del correo electrónico

post mortem /pəʊst 'mɔːtəm/ *noun* volcado *m* postmortem; volcado *m* final

post office /'pəʊst ˌɒfɪs/ *noun* Oficina Postal

postprocessor /ˌpəʊst'prəʊsesə/ *noun* **1.** (*microprocessor*) postprocesador *m*; postcompilador *m* **2.** (*program*) programa *m* adaptador

post production /ˌpəʊst prə'dʌkʃən/ *noun* posproducción *f*

PostScript /'pəʊstskrɪpt/ (*description language*) (lenguaje de descripción de página) PostScript™ ◇ **if you do a lot of DTP work, you will benefit from a PostScript printer** si realiza muchas ediciones de textos trabajará mejor con una impresora PostScript

potential difference /pəˌtenʃəl 'dɪf(ə)rəns/ *noun* diferencia *f* de potencial

power /'paʊə/ *noun* **1.** (*unit of energy*) potencia *f*; energía *f*; corriente *f* **2.** (*mathematical term*) potencia *f* ■ *verb* (*to provide electrical energy to a device*) alimentar *vt*; suministrar *vt* ◇ **powered (by)** (aparato) que funciona *or* accionado (con electricidad, etc.) ◇ '**power off**' 'apagado' *or* 'energía desconectada' ◇ '**power on**' 'encendido' *or* 'energía conectada' ◇ **the monitor is powered from a supply in the main PC** el monitor se alimenta del suministro eléctrico de la unidad central

PowerBook /'paʊəbʊk/ (*laptop version of a Macintosh*) PowerBook™

power down /'paʊə daʊn/ *verb* apagar *vt*; desconectar *vt*

power dump /'paʊə dʌmp/ *verb* interrupción *f* total de la alimentación eléctrica

power failure /'paʊə ˌfeɪljə/ *noun* (*loss of electric power supply*) corte *m* del fluido eléctrico; corte *m* de la corriente; interrupción *f* de la corriente; apagón *m*

power loss /'paʊə lɒs/ *noun* caída *f* de potencia; pérdida *f* de tensión

power management /'pauə ˌmænɪdʒmənt/ *noun* gestor *m* de la energía; medidor *m* de batería

power monitor /'pauə ˌmɒnɪtə/ *noun* (dispositivo de) control *m* de (alimentación de) electricidad

power-on reset /ˌpauə 'ɒn ˌriːset/ *noun* reinicialización *f* automática

power on self test /ˌpauə ɒn ˌself 'test/ *noun* auto-test *m* de encendido

power pack /'pauə pæk/ *noun* (*for a circuit*) bloque *m* de energía; bloque *m* de alimentación

PowerPC /'pauə piː ˌsiː/ (*processor*) PowerPC™

power supply /ˌpauə sə'plaɪ/ *noun* fuente *f* de alimentación/de energía; suministro *m* de energía/de alimentación

power transient /ˌpauə 'trænziənt/ *noun* corriente *f* transitoria

power up /'pauə ʌp/ *verb* encender *vt*; poner en marcha

power user /'pauə ˌjuːzə/ *noun* usuario *m* avanzado

ppm /ˌpiː piː 'em/ *noun* páginas *fpl* por minuto (ppm)

PPP /ˌpiː piː 'piː/ *noun* protocolo *m* punto a punto

PPU *abbr* (*peripheral processing unit*) procesador *m* periférico

practical extraction and report language /ˌpræktɪk(ə)l ɪkˌstrækʃ(ə)n ən rɪ'pɔːt ˌlæŋgwɪdʒ/ *noun* lenguaje *m* práctico de extracción y formateado; lenguaje *m* Perl

pre- /priː/ *prefix* (*before*) pre-; con anticipación; por anticipado

pre-agreed /pri ə'griːd/ *adjective* aceptado, -a por anticipado

pre-allocation /pri ˌælə'keɪʃ(ə)n/ *noun* asignación *f* previa; preasignación *f*

pre-amplifier /pri 'æmplɪˌfaɪə/ *noun* preamplificador *m*

precede /prɪ'siːd/ *verb* preceder *vt*; anteceder *vt* ◇ **instruction which cancels the instruction which precedes it** instrucción que anula la instrucción anterior

precedence /'presɪd(ə)ns/ *noun* precedencia *f*; prioridad *f*

precise /prɪ'saɪs/ *adjective* preciso *or* -a; exacto *or* -a

precision /prɪ'sɪʒ(ə)n/ *noun* precisión *f*; exactitud *f*

precision of a number /prɪˌsɪʒ(ə)n əv ə 'nʌmbə/ *noun* precisión *f* de un número

precompiled code /prikəmˌpaɪld 'kəud/ *noun* código *m* precompilado

precondition /ˌpriːkən'dɪʃ(ə)n/ *verb* precondicionar *vt*; condicionar previamente

predefined /ˌpriːdɪ'faɪnd/ *adjective* predefinido *or* -a; definido, -a previamente

predicate /'predɪkət/ *noun* predicado *m*

pre-edit /pri 'edɪt/ *verb* preeditar *vt*; corregir previamente

preemptive multitasking /priˌemptɪv 'mʌltitɑːskɪŋ/ *noun* multitarea *f* preferente; multitarea *f* en tiempo compartido

pre-fetch /priː 'fetʃ/ *verb* llamar anticipadamente (una instrucción)

prefix /'priːˌfɪks/ *noun* (*code*) prefijo *m*

prefix notation /'priːfɪks nəuˌteɪʃ(ə)n/ *noun* (*mathematical operations*) notación *f* por prefijo; notación *f* prefijada; notación *f* polaca (por prefijo); notación *f* polaca prefijada ◇ **normal notation: (x-y) + z, but using prefix notation: – xy + z** cuando en la notación normal se escribe (x-y) + z, en la notación polaca (por prefijo) se escribe – xy + z; (x-y) + z es la notación normal, pero la prefijada es – xy + z

preformatted /priː'fɔːmætɪd/ *adjective* preformateado *or* -a; formateado, -a previamente ◇ **a preformatted disk** un disco preformateado

pre-imaging /pri 'ɪmɪdʒɪŋ/ *noun* diseño *m* previo; anticipado *m* (de una imagen)

preprinted stationery /priˌprɪntɪd 'steɪʃ(ə)n(ə)ri/ *noun* (*computer stationery*) papel *m* preimpreso; formularios *mpl* impresos; papel *m* personalizado; papel *m* con cabecera

preprocess /priː'prəuses/ *verb* preprocesar *vt*

preprocessor /priː'prəusesə/ *noun* **1.** (*software*) programa *m* de pretratamiento **2.** (*small computer*) preprocesador *m*; precompilador *m*

'...the C preprocessor is in the first stage of converting a written program into machine instructions the preprocessor can be directed to read in another file before completion, perhaps because the same information is needed in each module of the program' [*Personal Computer World*]

preprogram /priː'prəugræm/ *verb* preprogramar *vt*

preprogrammed /priː'prəugræmd/ *adjective* preprogramado *or* -a; programado, -a previamente

presentation graphics /ˌprez(ə)nteɪʃ(ə)n 'græfɪks/ *plural noun* (*to represent business information or data*) gráficos *mpl*; diagramas *mpl*; presentación *f* gráfica ◇ **the sales for last month looked even better thanks to the use of presentation graphics** las ventas del último mes parecieron aún mejores gracias a la presentación gráfica

presentation layer /ˌprez(ə)n'teɪʃ(ə)n ˌleɪə/ *noun* (*for the start and end of a connection*) capa *f*; capa *f* de presentación; categoría *f* de presentación

Presentation Manager /ˌprez(ə)n'teɪʃ(ə)n ˌmænɪdʒə/ *noun* (*graphical user interface*) Presentation Manager™

presentation software /ˌprez(ə)nteɪʃ(ə)n 'sɒftweə/ *noun* software *m* para realiza exposiciones orales o escritas

preset /ˌpriː'set/ *verb* (*to set something in advance*) preprogramar *vt*; establecer *vt*; fijar *vt*; programar con anterioridad ◇ **the printer was preset with new page parameters** la impresora se preprogramó con nuevos parámetros de página

prestore /priː'stɔː/ *verb* prealmacenar *vt*

presumptive address /prɪˌzʌmptɪv ə'dres/ *noun* dirección *f* de base; dirección *f* supuesta

presumptive instruction /prɪˌzʌmptɪv ɪn 'strʌkʃən/ *noun* instrucción *f* de base; instrucción *f* supuesta

pretty good privacy /ˌprɪti gʊd 'prɪvəsi/ *noun* confidencialidad *f* segura

preventative /prɪ'ventətɪv/, **preventive** /prɪ 'ventɪv/ *adjective* preventivo *or* -a

preventive maintenance /prɪˌventɪv 'meɪntənəns/ *noun* (*of a system*) mantenimiento *m* preventivo

preview /'priːˌvjuː/ *verb* previsualizar *vt*

previewer /'priːvjuːə/ *noun* (*before printing*) vista *f* previa ◇ **the built-in previewer allows the user to check for mistakes** el procedimiento de vista previa permite al usuario localizar errores

PRI /ˌpiː ɑː 'aɪ/ *noun* interfaz *f* de rendimiento primario (de la transmisión)

primary /'praɪməri/ *adjective* primario *or* -a; elemental; fundamental ◇ **primary colours** colores *fpl* primarios *or* fundamentales ◇ **primary group** (*12 voice channels*) grupo *m* primario

primary channel /ˌpraɪməri 'tʃæn(ə)l/ *noun* canal *m* principal

primary key /'praɪməri kiː/ *noun* clave *f* primaria; clave *f* principal

primary memory /ˌpraɪməri 'mem(ə)ri/ *noun* memoria *f* central

primary rate interface /ˌpraɪməri reɪt 'ɪntəfeɪs/ *noun* interfaz *f* de rendimiento primario (de la transmisión)

primary station /ˌpraɪməri 'steɪʃ(ə)n/ *noun* estación *f* primaria

primary storage /ˌpraɪməri 'stɔːrɪdʒ/ *noun* memoria *f* principal

prime /praɪm/ *adjective* (*very important*) principal; muy importante; esencial

prime attribute /ˌpraɪm ə'trɪbjuːt/ *noun* característica *f* esencial

primer /'praɪmə/ *noun* manual *m* elemental

primitive /'prɪmɪtɪv/ *noun* **1.** (*in programming*) rutina *f* primitiva; instrucciones *fpl* de base; (*in graphics*) forma *f* primitiva **2.** forma *f* primitiva ■ *adjective* de base; de biblioteca

print /prɪnt/ *noun* (*etching*) grabado *m*; (*characters on paper*) prueba *f*; copia *f* ■ *verb* (*to put characters in ink*) imprimir *vt* ◇ **print contrast ratio** relación *f* de contraste de una copia ◇ **printed document** documento *m* impreso *or* escrito ◇ **the printer prints at 60 characters per second** esta impresora imprime 60 caracteres por segundo

print control character /prɪnt kən'trəʊl/, **print control code** *noun* carácter *m* de control de la impresión

printed circuit /ˌprɪntɪd 'sɜːkɪt/, **printed circuit board** *noun* placa *f* de circuito impreso

printer /'prɪntə/ *noun* **1.** (*device*) impresora *f* **2.** (*person*) tipógrafo *mf or* -a; (*company*) impresor *m or* -a

printer buffer /'prɪntə ˌbʌfə/ *noun* memoria *f* intermedia de la impresora

printer control characters /ˌprɪntə kən 'trəʊl ˌkærɪktəz/ *noun* caracteres *mpl* de control de impresión

printer control language /ˌprɪntə kən'trəʊl ˌlæŋgwɪdʒ/ *noun* lenguaje *m* PCL; instrucciones *fpl* de control de la impresora

printer driver /'prɪntə ˌdraɪvə/ *noun* gestor *m* de impresión

printer emulation /'prɪntə emjuˌleɪʃ(ə)n/ *noun* emulación *f* de impresora ◇ **this printer emulation allows my NEC printer to emulate an Epsom** esta emulación de impresora permite que mi impresora NEC emule una Epsom

printer-plotter /'prɪntə ˌplɒtə/ *noun* trazador *m*; impresora *f* gráfica

printer port /'prɪntə pɔːt/ *noun* puerto *m* de (la) impresora

printer quality /'prɪntə ˌkwɒlɪti/ *noun* (*printing*) calidad *f* de impresión; calidad *f* de impresora

printer ribbon /'prɪntə ˌrɪbən/ *noun* cinta *f* de impresora

printer's controller /ˌprɪntəz kən'trəʊlə/ *noun* controlador *m* de impresora

print format /prɪnt 'fɔːmæt/ *noun* formato *m* de impresión

print formatter /'prɪnt ˌfɔːmætə/ *noun* instrucción *f* para formato de impresión

print hammer /prɪnt 'hæmə/ *noun* martillo *m* impresor

printhead /'prɪnthed/ *noun* cabeza *f* de impresora

printing /'prɪntɪŋ/ *noun* (*action*) impresión *f*

print job /'prɪnt dʒɒb/ *noun* tarea *f* de impresión

print life /ˌprɪnt 'laɪf/ *noun* (duración de) vida *f* de una impresora ◇ **the printhead has a print life of over 400 million characters** la cabeza impresora tiene una vida de más de 400 millones de caracteres

Print Manager /'prɪnt ˌmænɪdʒə/ (*software utility that is part of Microsoft Windows*) gestor *m* de impresión

print modifiers /prɪnt 'mɒdɪˌfaɪəs/ *plural noun* modificadores *mpl* de impresión; parámetros *mpl* de impresión

printout /'prɪntˌaʊt/ *noun* (*final printed page*) salida *f* de la impresora; listado *m*; copia *f* impresa

print pause /ˌprɪnt 'pɔːz/ *noun* pausa *f* de la impresión

print preview /prɪnt 'priːˌvjuː/ *noun* vista *f* previa

print quality /prɪnt 'kwɒlɪti/ *noun* calidad *f* de impresión ◇ **a desktop printer with a resolution of 600dpi provides good print quality** una impresora gráfica con una resolución de 600 puntos por pulgada proporciona una buena calidad de impresión

print queue /ˌprɪnt 'kjuː/ *noun* cola *f* de impresión

Print Screen key /ˌprɪnt ˈskriːn ˌkiː/ noun (special key in the top right-hand side of the keyboard – under DOS) tecla f de impresión de pantalla; (under DOS) tecla f Impr Pant

print server /prɪnt ˈsɜːvə/ noun servidor m de impresión

print spooling /ˌprɪnt ˈspuːlɪŋ/ noun gestión f de impresión (por periféricos)

print style /ˌprɪnt ˈstaɪl/ noun estilo m de impresión

printwheel /ˈprɪntwiːl/ noun rueda f de margarita

priority /praɪˈɒrɪti/ noun prioridad f; preferencia f ◇ **the disk drive is more important than the printer, so it has a higher priority** la disquetera es más importante que la impresora, de modo que tiene una mayor prioridad ◇ **the operating system has priority over the application when disk space is allocated** el sistema operativo tiene prioridad sobre la aplicación cuando se asigna el espacio del disco

priority interrupt /praɪˌɒrɪti ˈɪntərʌpt/ noun interrupción f prioritaria

priority interrupt table /praɪˌɒrɪti ˈɪntərʌpt ˌteɪb(ə)l/ noun tabla f de prioridades de interrupción; tabla f de interrupciones prioritarias

priority scheduler /praɪˈɒrɪti ˌʃedjuːlə/ noun gestor m de prioridades

priority sequence /praɪˈɒrɪti ˌsiːkwəns/ noun secuencia f de prioridad; orden m de prioridad

privacy /ˈprɪvəsi/ noun confidencialidad f; privacidad f ◇ **privacy transformation** codificación m (de la información) para asegurar la confidencialidad

privacy of data /ˌprɪvəsi əv ˈdeɪtə/ noun confidencialidad f de datos

privacy of information /ˌprɪvəsi əv ˌɪnfə ˈmeɪʃ(ə)n/ noun confidencialidad f de información

private /ˈpraɪvət/ adjective privado or -a; privativo or -a ◇ **private telephone system** sistema m telefónico privado

private address space /ˌpraɪvət əˈdres ˌspeɪs/ noun espacio m de memoria reservada para utilización de un usuario

private branch exchange /ˌpraɪvət ˈbrɑːntʃ ɪksˌtʃeɪndʒ/ noun conmutador m privado (conectado con la red pública)

privilege /ˈprɪvɪlɪdʒ/ noun privilegio m

privileged account /ˌprɪvəlɪdʒd əˈkaʊnt/ noun cuenta f de acceso privilegiada/prioritaria ◇ **the system manager can access anyone else's account from his privileged account** el director del sistema puede acceder a cualquier otra cuenta desde su cuenta privilegiada

privileged instructions /ˌprɪvəlɪdʒd ɪnˈstrʌkʃənz/ plural noun instrucciones fpl prioritarias

privileged mode /ˈprɪvəlɪdʒd məʊd/ noun modo m protegido; modo m prioritario

PRN /ˌpiː ɑː ˈen/ noun (printing) PRN; impresora f (en el MS-DOS)

problem /ˈprɒbləm/ noun (fault) fallo m; mal m funcionamiento

problem definition /ˈprɒbləm ˌdefənɪʃ(ə)n/ noun exposición f de un problema; definición f de un problema

problem diagnosis /ˈprɒbləm ˌdaɪəgnəʊsɪs/ noun diagnóstico m de problemas

problem-orientated language /ˌprɒbləm ˌɔːriənteɪtɪd ˈlæŋgwɪdʒ/ noun lenguaje m orientado a problemas

procedural /prəˈsiːdʒərəl/ adjective de procedimiento; procedimental

procedural language /prəˌsiːdʒ(ə)rəl ˈlæŋgwɪdʒ/ noun lenguaje m de procedimiento; lenguaje m procedimental

procedure /prəˈsiːdʒə/ noun 1. (instruction code) procedimiento m 2. (method used to solve a problem) procedimiento m; método m a seguir ◇ **the procedure is given in the manual** el procedimiento se explica en el manual de instrucciones ◇ **this procedure sorts all the files into alphabetic order, you can call it from the main program by the instruction SORT** este procedimiento clasifica todos los ficheros en orden alfabético ◇ **you should use this procedure to retrieve lost files** debería utilizar este procedimiento para recuperar los ficheros perdidos

procedure declaration /prəˈsiːdʒə ˌdekləreɪʃ(ə)n/ noun declaración f de procedimiento

procedure-orientated language /prə ˌsiːdʒə ˌɔːriənteɪtɪd ˈlæŋgwɪdʒ/ noun lenguaje m orientado al procedimiento; lenguaje m a procedimientos

process /ˈprəʊses/ noun (number of tasks) procedimiento m; (number of tasks that must be performed to achieve a goal) proceso m; tratamiento m ■ verb procesar vt; tratar vt ◇ **process camera** cámara f de proceso (de imagen en color) ◇ **processing all the information will take a long time** llevará mucho tiempo procesar toda la información ◇ **the process of setting up the computer takes a long time** el proceso de poner el ordenador en funcionamiento requiere mucho tiempo ◇ **there are five stages in the process** el proceso consta de cinco etapas ◇ **we processed the new data** hemos procesado los nuevos datos

process bound /ˈprəʊses baʊnd/ noun limitado por el proceso

process chart /ˈprəʊses tʃɑːt/ noun (diagram) tabla f de proceso; diagrama m de procedimiento; diagrama m de proceso

process control /ˈprəʊses kənˌtrəʊl/ noun control m de proceso

process control computer /ˌprəʊses kən ˌtrəʊl kəmˈpjuːtə/ noun ordenador m de control de proceso

process control system /ˌprəʊses kən'trəʊl ˌsɪstəm/ *noun* sistema *m* de control de proceso

processing /'prəʊsesɪŋ/ *noun* tratamiento *m*; proceso *m*

processor /'prəʊˌsesə/ *noun* procesador *m* ◇ **processor status word (PSW)** palabra *f* de estado del procesador

processor controlled keying /ˌprəʊsesə kənˌtrəʊld 'kiːɪŋ/ *noun* pulsación *f* del teclado controlada por ordenador

processor interrupt /ˌprəʊsesə 'ɪntərʌpt/ *noun* (instrucción de) interrupción *f* del procesador

processor-limited /ˌprəʊsesə 'lɪmɪtɪd/ *adjective* dependiente del procesador; limitado por el procesador

processor status word /ˌprəʊsesə 'steɪtəs ˌwɜːd/ *noun* palabra *f* de estado del procesador

produce /prə'djuːs/ *verb* producir *vt*; crear *vt*

producer /prə'djuːsə/ *noun* (*TV or film*) productor *m or* -a *f*; realizador *m or* -a *f*

producing capacity /prə'djuːsɪŋ kəˌpæsəti/ *noun* capacidad *f* de producción

product /'prɒdʌkt/ *noun* **1.** (*item*) producto *m* **2.** (*result of multiplication*) producto *m* **3.** (*result of multiplication*) producto *m*

product design /'prɒdʌkt dɪˌzaɪn/ *noun* diseño *m* de productos

product engineer /ˌprɒdʌkt ˌendʒɪ'nɪə/ *noun* ingeniero *m* de productos

production /prə'dʌkʃən/ *noun* (*making or manufacturing*) producción *f*; fabricación *f* ◇ **mass production of monitors or of calculators** producción en serie de monitores *or* de calculadoras ◇ **production run** (*of product*) ciclo *m* de producción ◇ **production will probably be held up by industrial action; we are hoping to speed up production by installing new machinery** la producción se verá probablemente interrumpida por la acción sindical; pero esperamos acelerar la producción instalando nueva maquinaria

production control /prə'dʌkʃən kənˌtrəʊl/ *noun* control *m* de producción

production rate /prə'dʌkʃ(ə)n reɪt/ *noun* gasto *m* horario

production standards /prə'dʌkʃən ˌstændədz/ *plural noun* normas *fpl* de producción; estándares *mpl* de producción

productive /prə'dʌktɪv/ *adjective* productivo *or* -a

productive time /prəˌdʌktɪv 'taɪm/ *noun* tiempo *m* productivo

product line /'prɒdʌkt laɪn/, **product range** /'prɒdʌkt reɪndʒ/ *noun* gama *f* de productos; línea *f* de productos

product range /'prɒdʌkt reɪndʒ/ *noun* gama *f* de productos; línea *f* de productos

profile /'prəʊfaɪl/ *noun* (*Windows feature that stores users' settings*) perfil *m* (de usuario)

PROFS /prɒfs/ (*electronic mail system*) PROFS™

program /'prəʊɡræm/ *noun* (*software*) programa *m* ■ *verb* escribir un programa ◇ **assembly program** ensamblador *m* de macros *or* de macroinstrucciones *or* programa de ensamblaje ◇ **executive program** programa de ejecución *or* ejecutivo ◇ **I forgot to insert an important instruction which caused a program to crash, erasing all the files on the disk** olvidé insertar una instrucción importante lo cual ocasionó que el programa se bloqueara, borrando todos los ficheros del disco ◇ **program design language (PDL)** lenguaje *m* de diseño de programas ◇ **program evaluation and review technique (PERT)** técnica *f* de evaluación y revisión de un programa ◇ **program information file (PIF)** (*Microsoft Windows: file that contains environment settings*) fichero PIF (de información de un programa en el entorno MS-Windows) ◇ **program specifications** especificaciones *fpl* de un programa ◇ **to run the program, double-click on the program icon** para iniciar un programa, haga un doble clic sobre el icono del programa

program address counter /ˌprəʊɡræm ə'dres ˌkaʊntə/ *noun* contador *m* de programas; registro *m* de dirección de instrucciones

program branch /'prəʊɡræm brɑːntʃ/ *noun* bifurcación *f* de un programa

program cards /'prəʊɡræm kɑːdz/ *plural noun* tarjetas *fpl* de programa

program coding sheet /ˌprəʊɡræm 'kəʊdɪŋ ˌʃiːt/ *noun* formulario *m* de programación; hoja *f* de codificación de un programa

program compatibility /ˌprəʊɡræm kəmˌpætə'bɪlɪti/ *noun* compatibilidad *f* de un programa

program compilation /ˌprəʊɡræm ˌkɒmpə'leɪʃ(ə)n/ *noun* compilación *f* de programa

program counter /'prəʊɡræm ˌkaʊntə/ *noun* contador *m* de programas; registro *m* de dirección de instrucciones

program crash /'prəʊɡræm kræʃ/ *noun* fallo *m* de un programa; bloqueo *m* de un programa

program design language /ˌprəʊɡræm dɪ'zaɪn ˌlæŋɡwɪdʒ/ *noun* lenguaje *m* de diseño de programas

program development /'prəʊɡræm dɪ'veləpmənt/ *noun* desarrollo *m* de un programa

program development system /ˌprəʊɡræm dɪ'veləpmənt ˌsɪstəm/ *noun* sistema *m* de desarrollo de programas

program documentation /ˌprəʊɡræm ˌdɒkjʊmen'teɪʃ(ə)n/ *noun* documentación *f* sobre el uso de un programa

program editor /'prəʊɡræm ˌedɪtə/ *noun* editor *m* de programa

program evaluation and review technique /ˌprəʊɡræm ɪˌvæljueɪʃ(ə)n ən rɪ'vjuː tekˌniːk/ *noun* técnica *f* de evaluación y revisión de programas

program execution /ˌprəʊɡræm ˌeksɪ'kjuːʃ(ə)n/ *noun* ejecución *f* de un programa

program file /'prəʊgræm faɪl/ *noun* fichero *m* de programa

program flowchart /,prəʊgræm 'fləʊtʃɑːt/ *noun* organigrama *m* de programación

program generation /,prəʊgræm ,dʒenə'reɪʃ(ə)n/ *noun* creación *f* de un programa

program generator /'prəʊgræm ,dʒenəreɪtə/ *noun* generador *m* de programa

program group /'prəʊgræm gruːp/ *noun* grupo *m* de programas

program icon /'prəʊgræm ,aɪkɒn/ *noun* icono *m* de programa

program information file /,prəʊgræm ,ɪnfə'meɪʃ(ə)n ,faɪl/ *noun* fichero *m* PIF (de información de un programa en el entorno MS-Windows)

program instruction /'prəʊgræm ɪn,strʌkʃən/ *noun* instrucción *f* (de un programa)

program item /'prəʊgræm ,aɪtəm/ *noun* icono *m* de programa

program library /'prəʊgræm ,laɪbrəri/ *noun* biblioteca *f* de programas

program line /'prəʊgræm laɪn/ *noun* línea *f* de instrucción de un programa

program line number /,prəʊgræm 'laɪn ,nʌmbə/ *noun* número *m* de referencia de una línea de un programa

program listing /'prəʊgræm ,lɪstɪŋ/ *noun* listado *m* de un programa

programmable /'prəʊgræməb(ə)l/ *adjective* (*device*) programable ◇ **programmable logic array (PLA)** *or* **programmable logic device (PLD)** orden *f* lógico programable *or* dispositivo *m* lógico programable ◇ **programmable memory (PROM)** memoria *f* programable *or* (memoria) PROM

programmable calculator /,prəʊgræməb(ə)l 'kælkjʊleɪtə/ *noun* calculadora *f* programable

programmable clock /,prəʊgræməb(ə)l 'klɒk/ *noun* reloj *m* programable

programmable interrupt controller /,prəʊgræməb(ə)l 'ɪntərʌpt kən,trəʊlə/ *noun* controlador *m* de interrupción programable

programmable key /,prəʊgræməb(ə)l 'kiː/ *noun* tecla *f* (de función) programable

programmable logic array /,prəʊgræməb(ə)l ,lɒdʒɪk ə'reɪ/ *noun* orden *m* lógico programable; dispositivo *m* lógico programable

programmable logic device /,prəʊgræməb(ə)l ,lɒdʒɪk dɪ,vaɪs/ *noun* orden *m* lógico programable; dispositivo *m* lógico programable

programmable memory /,prəʊgræməb(ə)l 'mem(ə)ri/ *noun* memoria *f* programable; PROM

programmable read only memory /,prəʊgræməb(ə)l riːd ,əʊnli 'mem(ə)ri/ *noun* memoria *f* ROM programable; PROM

program maintenance /'prəʊgræm ,meɪntənəns/ *noun* mantenimiento *m* de un programa

Program Manager /,prəʊgræm 'mænɪdʒə/ *noun* gestor *m* de programas

programmatic /,prəʊgrə'mætɪk/ *adjective* programático, -a

programmed halt /'prəʊgræmd hɔːlt/ *noun* parada *f* programada

programmed learning /,prəʊgræmd 'lɜːnɪŋ/ *noun* aprendizaje *m* asistido por ordenador; formación *f* asistida por ordenador

programmer /'prəʊ,græmə/ *noun* 1. (*person*) programador *m or* -a 2. (*device*) programador *m* ◇ **analyst** *or* **programmer** *or* **programmer** *or* **analyst** analista-programador, -a ◇ **the programmer is still working on the new software** el programador *or* la programadora está todavía trabajando en el nuevo software

programming /'prəʊgræmɪŋ/ *noun* 1. (*writing programs*) programación *f* 2. (*writing data*) programación *f* de una PROM

programming language /'prəʊgræmɪŋ ,læŋgwɪdʒ/ *noun* lenguaje *m* de programación

programming standards /'prəʊgræmɪŋ ,stændədz/ *plural noun* normas *fpl* de programación; estándares *mpl* de programación

program name /'prəʊgræm neɪm/ *noun* nombre *m* (de) un programa

program origin /,prəʊgræm 'ɒrɪdʒɪn/ *noun* dirección *f* origen de la primera instrucción de un programa

program register /'prəʊgræm ,redʒɪstə/ *noun* registro *m* de programa; registro *m* de instrucción

program relocation /,prəʊgræm ,riːləʊ'keɪʃ(ə)n/ *noun* (*moving a program*) traslado *m* de un programa; (*moving*) desplazamiento *m* (en memoria); (*moving a program*) transferencia *f* de un programa

program report generator /,prəʊgræm rɪ'pɔːt ,dʒenəreɪtə/ *noun* generador *m* de informes de programas

program run /'prəʊgræm rʌn/ *noun* ejecución *f* de un programa

program segment /'prəʊgræm ,segmənt/ *noun* segmento *m* de programa

Programs menu /'prəʊgræmz ,menjuː/ *noun* menú *m* de programas (en Windows)

program specification /,prəʊgræm ,spesɪfɪ'keɪʃ(ə)n/ *noun* programa *m* de especificación

program stack /'prəʊgræm stæk/ *noun* pila *f* de instrucciones de un programa

program statement /'prəʊgræm ,steɪtmənt/ *noun* instrucción *f* de programa; sentencia *f* de programa

program status word /,prəʊgræm 'steɪtəs ,wɜːd/ *noun* palabra *f* de estado de programa

program step /'prəʊgræm step/ *noun* paso *m* de programación; etapa *f* de programación

program storage /,prəʊgræm 'stɔːrɪdʒ/ *noun* memoria *f* (de) programa

program structure /,prəʊgræm 'strʌktʃə/ *noun* estructura *f* de un programa

program testing /'prəʊgræm ˌtestɪŋ/ noun prueba f de un programa; comprobación f de un programa

program trading /'prəʊgræm ˌtreɪdɪŋ/ noun contratación f contenido electrónica; operación f programada informáticamente

program verification /ˌprəʊgræm ˌverɪfɪ'keɪʃ(ə)n/ noun verificación f del buen funcionamiento de un programa

progressive scanning /prəʊˌgresɪv 'skænɪŋ/ noun barrido m progresivo

project noun /'prɒdʒekt/ proyecto m ■ verb /prə'dʒekt/ (to forecast) proyectar vt; pronosticar vt; prever vt ◇ **CAD is essential for accurate project design** un programa de diseño CAD resulta esencial para la realización de proyectos con mayor precisión ◇ **his latest project is computerizing the sales team** su último proyecto consiste en informatizar el departamento de ventas ◇ **the design project was entirely worked out on computer** todo el proyecto se diseñó por ordenador ◇ **the projected sales of the new PC** las ventas previstas del nuevo PC or ordenador personal

projection /prə'dʒekʃən/ noun (of sales, etc.) previsión f; proyección f

PROM /prɒm/ noun **1.** memoria f programable de solo lectura; memoria f PROM **2.** memoria f programable

PROM blaster /'bɜːnə/, **PROM burner, PROM programmer** /'prəʊˌgræmə/ noun programador m de PROM

prompt /prɒmpt/ noun indicación f; mensaje m (de una instrucción) ◇ **MS-DOS normally displays the command prompt C:\> to indicate that it is ready to process instructions typed in by a user** el sistema MS-DOS normalmente muestra el mensaje C:\> para indicar que está preparado para procesar instrucciones introducidas por el usuario or la usuaria ◇ **the prompt READY indicates that the system is available to receive instructions** el mensaje READY indica que el sistema está disponible para recibir instrucciones

propagate /'prɒpəˌgeɪt/ verb (to spread) propagar vt; difundir vi; transmitir vt

propagated error /ˌprɒpəgeɪtɪd 'erə/ noun error m propagado

propagating error /'prɒpəgeɪtɪŋ ˌerə/ noun error m que se propaga

propagation delay /ˌprɒpə'geɪʃ(ə)n dɪˌleɪ/ noun tiempo m de propagación; demora f de propagación

propagation time /ˌprɒpə'geɪʃ(ə)n ˌtaɪm/ noun tiempo m de propagación

properties /'prɒpətiz/ noun (in Windows 95 – attributes of a file or object) propiedades fpl

proportionally spaced /prəˌpɔːʃ(ə)nəli 'speɪst/ adjective espaciado m proporcional

proprietary file format /prəˌpraɪət(ə)ri 'faɪl ˌfɔːmæt/ noun (data storing method devised by a company) formato m de fichero de propietario; formato m de marca registrada ◇ **you cannot read this spreadsheet file because my software saves it in a proprietary file format** no se puede leer este fichero de hoja de cálculo porque mi programa lo guarda en un formato de marca registrada

protected field /prə'tektɪd fiːld/ noun campo m protegido

protected location /prəˌtektɪd ləʊ'keɪʃ(ə)n/ noun posición f protegida

protected mode /prə'tektɪd məʊd/ noun modo m protegido

protected storage /prəˌtektɪd 'stɔːrɪdʒ/ noun memoria f protegida

protection key /prə'tekʃən kiː/ noun llave f de protección; clave f de protección

protection master /prə'tekʃən ˌmɑːstə/ noun copia f original de seguridad; copia f del original

protocol /'prəʊtəkɒl/ noun protocolo m

protocol stack /'prəʊtəʊkɒl stæk/ noun pila f del protocolo

protocol standards /'prəʊtəʊkɒl ˌstændədz/ plural noun normas fpl de protocolo de transmisión

prototype /'prəʊtəˌtaɪp/ noun prototipo m

prototyping /'prəʊtətaɪpɪŋ/ noun fabricación f de prototipos

provider /prə'vaɪdə/ noun proveedor m; abastecedor m or -a f

proxy agent /'prɒksi ˌeɪdʒənt/ noun agente m intermediario; 'proxy'

proxy server /ˌprɒksi 'sɜːvə/ noun servidor m intermediario; 'proxy'

PrtSc /ˌprɪnt 'skriːn/ noun (printing) tecla f Print Screen; tecla f Impr Pant

pS /ˌpiː 'es/ abbr (picosecond) picosegundo (ps) m

PS/2 (IBM PC computers) PS/2™ (modelo de PC IBM) PS/2

pseudo- /sjuːdəʊ/ prefix pseudo-

pseudo-code /'sjuːdəʊ kəʊd/ noun pseudocódigo m

pseudo-digital /ˌsjuːdəʊ 'dɪdʒɪt(ə)l/ adjective pseudodigital

pseudo-instruction /ˌsjuːdəʊ ɪn'strʌkʃən/ noun instrucción f de relleno; pseudo-instrucción f

pseudo-operation /ˌsjuːdəʊ ˌɒpə'reɪʃ(ə)n/ noun pseudooperación; instrucción f de ensamblaje

pseudo-random /ˌsjuːdəʊ 'rændəm/ noun pseudo-aleatorio or -a

pseudo-random number generator /ˌsjuːdəʊ ˌrændəm 'nʌmbə ˌdʒenəreɪtə/ noun generador m de números pseudo-aleatorios

pseudo-static /ˌsjuːdəʊ 'stætɪk/ adjective seudoestática

PSN abbr (packet switched network) red f con conmutación de paquetes

PSS abbr (packet switching system) sistema m de conmutación de paquetes

PSU /ˌpiː es ˈjuː/ *noun* fuente *f* de alimentación; fuente *f* de energía; suministro *m* de energía; suministro *m* de alimentación

PSW *abbr* (*processor status word*) palabra *f* de estado del procesador

PTR *abbr* (*paper tape reader*) lector *m* de cintas de papel perforadas

public access terminal /ˌpʌblɪk ˌækses ˈtɜːmɪn(ə)l/ *noun* terminal *m* de acceso público

public data network /ˌpʌblɪk ˌdeɪtə ˈnetwɜːk/ *noun* red *f* pública (de transmisión de datos)

public domain /ˌpʌblɪk dəʊˈmeɪn/ *noun* dominio *m* público

public key cipher system /ˌpʌblɪk kiː ˈsaɪfə ˌsɪstəm/ *noun* sistema *m* cifrado de clave pública

public key encryption /ˌpʌblɪk kiː ɪn ˈkrɪpʃ(ə)n/ *noun* encriptado *m* de clave pública

publish /ˈpʌblɪʃ/ *verb* publicar *vt* ◇ **the company specializes in publishing reference books** la empresa está especializada en la publicación de libros de referencia ◇ **the institute has published a list of sales figures for different home computers** el instituto ha publicado una lista de cifras de ventas para una serie de ordenadores personales

pull /pʊl/ *verb* (*data*) extraer *vt*; retirar *vt*

pull-down menu /ˈpʊl daʊn ˌmenjuː/ *noun* menú *m* desplegable ◇ **the pull-down menu is viewed by clicking on the menu bar at the top of the screen** el menú desplegable aparece cuando se hace clic sobre la barra del menú en la parte superior de la pantalla

pulse /pʌls/ *noun* impulso *m*; pulso *m* ■ *verb* emitir impulsos ◇ **pulse amplitude modulation (PAM)** modulación *f* de amplitud de impulsos *or* de impulsos en amplitud ◇ **pulse duration modulation (PDM)** modulación por *or* de duración de impulsos ◇ **pulse generator** generador *m* de impulsos ◇ **pulse modulation** modulación de impulsos ◇ **pulse position modulation (PPM)** modulación por posición de impulsos *or* por impulsos de posición variable ◇ **pulse width modulation (PWM)** modulación de duración de impulsos ◇ **we pulsed the input but it still would not work** emitimos la señal de entrada pero tampoco funcionó

pulse-code modulation /ˌpʌls kəʊd ˌmɒdjʊ ˈleɪʃ(ə)n/ *noun* modulación *f* por codificación de impulsos; modulación *f* por codificación de impulsos codificados

pulse-dialling /ˈpʌls ˌdaɪəlɪŋ/ *noun* (*telephone dialling that sends a series of pulses*) llamada *f* por pulsaciones

pulse stream /ˌpʌls ˈstriːm/ *noun* sucesión *f* de impulsos; tren *m* de impulsos

pulse train /ˈpʌls treɪn/ *noun* sucesión *f* de impulsos; tren *m* de impulsos

punch /pʌntʃ/ *noun* perforadora *f* ■ *verb* perforar *vt*

punch card /ˈpʌntʃ kɑːd/ *noun* (*punched card*) ficha *f* perforada

punch-down block /ˌpʌntʃ daʊn ˈblɒk/ *noun* (*device used to connect UTP cable*) bloque *m* de enchufe

punched card /ˌpʌntʃt ˈkɑːd/ *noun* (*punched card*) ficha *f* perforada

punched card reader /ˌpʌntʃd ˈkɑːd ˌriːdə/ *noun* lector *m* de tarjetas perforadas

punched code /ˌpʌntʃd ˈkəʊd/ *noun* código *m* de perforación

punched tag /ˌpʌntʃd ˈtæg/ *noun* etiqueta *f* perforada

punched tape[1] /ˌpʌntʃd ˈteɪp/, **punched paper tape** /ˌpʌntʃd ˈpeɪpə teɪp/ *noun* cinta *f* perforada; papel *m* perforado

punched tape[2] /ˌpʌntʃd ˈteɪp/ *noun* cinta *f* perforada

punctuation mark /ˌpʌŋktʃuˈeɪʃ(ə)n mɑːk/ *noun* signo *m* de puntuación

pure code /ˌpjʊə ˈkəʊd/ *noun* código *m* puro

purge /pɜːdʒ/ *verb* (*remove unnecessary data from a file*) vaciar *vt*; purgar *vt*

pushbutton /ˈpʊʃbʌt(ə)n/ *adjective* (*on telephone*) de botones; de teclas ◇ **pushbutton telephone** teléfono *m* de teclado *or* de botones

push-down list /ˌpʊʃdaʊn ˈlɪst/, **push-down stack** /pʊʃ daʊn/ *noun* pila *f* de desplazamiento descendente; lista *f* de desplazamiento descendente

push instruction /pʊʃ ɪnˈstrʌkʃən/, **push operation** /pʊʃ ˌɒpəˈreɪʃ(ə)n/ *noun* **non-synchronous sound, non-sync sound** instrucción *f* de entrada en la pila; operación *f* de entrada en la pila

push-up list /pʊʃ ʌp lɪst/, **push-up stack** /stæk/ *noun* pila *f* de desplazamiento ascendente; lista *f* de desplazamiento ascendente

put /pʊt/ *verb* (*to place data onto a stack*) introducir *vt*; poner (datos) en la pila

Q

QAM *abbr* (*quadrature amplitude modulation*) modulación *f* de Amplitud en Cuadratura

QBE /,kjuː biː 'iː/ *noun* lenguaje *m* de consulta

Q Channel /kjuː 'tʃæn(ə)l/ *noun* (*in CDs*) canal *m* Q que identifica un corte del CD y su duración

QISAM *noun* método *m* de acceso secuencial indexado en cola de espera

QL *abbr* (*query language*) lenguaje *m* de consulta

QOS *abbr* (*quality of service*) calidad *f* del servicio (de transmisión de información)

QSAM /,kjuː es eɪ 'em/ *noun* método *m* de acceso secuencial en cola de espera

quad /kwɒd/ *adjective* (*four times*) cuádruple *m*; (*sheet of paper*) cuadrángulo *m*

quadbit /'kwɒdbɪt/ *noun* (*modems*) palabra *f* de cuatro bits

quad density /kwɒd 'densəti/ *noun* densidad *f* cuádruple

quadding /'kwɒdɪŋ/ *noun* (*insertion of spaces*) inserción *f* de espacios

quadr- /kwɒdr/ *prefix* (*meaning four*) cuadr-; tetra-

quadrature amplitude modulation /,kwɒdrətʃə 'æmplɪtjuːd mɒdjuˌleɪʃ(ə)n/ *noun* (*data encoding method*) modulación *f* de amplitud en cuadratura

quadrature encoding /'kwɒdrətʃə ɪn ˌkəʊdɪŋ/ *noun* (*determines the direction of a mouse*) codificado *m* en cuadratura

quadruplex /'kwɒdrʊpleks/ *noun* (*four signals*) cuádruple *m*

quad-speed drive /,kwɒd spiːd 'draɪv/ *noun* lector *m* (CD-ROM) de cuatro velocidades

quality control /'kwɒlɪti kənˌtrəʊl/ *noun* control *m* de calidad

quality of service /,kwɒlɪti əv 'sɜːvɪs/ *noun* calidad *f* del servicio (de transmisión de información)

quantifiable /'kwɒntɪfaɪəb(ə)l/ *adjective* cuantificable

quantifier /'kwɒntɪˌfaɪə/ *noun* cuantificador *m*

quantify /'kwɒntɪˌfaɪ/ *verb* cuantificar *vt* ◇ **it is impossible to quantify the effect of the new computer system on our production** es imposible cuantificar el efecto del nuevo sistema informático en la producción ◇ **to quantify the effect of something** cuantificar *or* calcular el efecto de algo

quantisation error /,kwɒn'teɪʃ(ə)n ˌerə/ *noun* error *m* de cuantificación

quantising noise /,kwɒntaɪzɪŋ 'nɔɪz/ *noun* ruido(s) *m(pl)* m(pl) de cuantificación

quantity /'kwɒntɪti/ *noun* (*amount*) cantidad *f* ■ *adjective* (*large amount*) (gran) cantidad ◇ **a small quantity of illegal copies of the program have been imported** se ha importado una pequeña cantidad de copias ilegales del programa ◇ **he bought a large quantity of spare parts** compró una gran cantidad de piezas de repuesto

quantum /'kwɒntəm/ *noun* (*in communications: packet of data*) cuanto *m*; quantum *m*

quartz clock /,kwɔːts 'klɒk/, **quartz crystal clock** /,kwɔːts ˌkrɪstəl 'klɒk/ *noun* reloj *m* de cuarzo

quasi- /kweɪzaɪ/ *prefix* casi-

quasi-instruction /,kweɪzaɪ ɪn'strʌkʃən/ *noun* etiqueta *f* (de instrucciones); casi instrucción *f*

quaternary /'kwɔːtɜːnəri/ *adjective* cuaternario *or* -a

quaternary level quantization /kwə ˌtɜːnəri ˌlev(ə)l ˌkwɒntaɪ'zeɪʃ(ə)n/ *noun* cuantificación *f* de nivel cuatro; cuantificación *f* de nivel cuaternario

query by example /,kwɪəri baɪ ɪg'zɑːmpəl/ *noun* lenguaje *m* de consulta

query facility /'kwɪəri fəˌsɪlɪti/ *noun* utilidad *f* de consulta; utilidad *f* de pregunta

query language /'kwɪəri ˌlæŋgwɪdʒ/ *noun* lenguaje *m* de consulta

query message /'kwɪəri ˌmesɪdʒ/ *noun* mensaje *m* de consulta

query processing /'kwɪəri ˌprəʊsesɪŋ/ *noun* proceso *m* de consulta(s)

query window /'kwɪəri ˌwɪndəʊ/ *noun* **1.** ventana *f* de consulta **2.** ventana *f* de consulta/de búsqueda

question mark /'kwestʃən mɑːk/ *noun* (*often used as a wildcard*) signo *m* de interrogación; carácter *m* comodín

queue /kjuː/ *noun* (*of data*) cola *f* de espera ■ *verb* situarse en la cola ◇ **queued sequential access method (QSAM)** método de acceso secuencial en cola de espera ◇ **queue manager** gestor *m* de lista *or* de cola de espera

queued access method /,kjuːd 'ækses ˌmeθəd/ *noun* método *m* de gestión de la cola de espera

queued indexed sequential access method /ˌkjuːd ˌɪndeksd sɪˌkwenʃəl ˈækses ˌmeθəd/ *noun* método *m* de acceso secuencial indexado en cola de espera

queue discipline /kjuː ˈdɪsəˌplɪn/ *noun* procedimiento *m* de cola de espera

queued sequential access method /ˌkjuːd sɪˌkwenʃəl ˈækses ˌmeθəd/ *noun* método *m* de acceso secuencial en cola de espera

queue management /kjuː ˈmænɪdʒmənt/, **queue manager** /kjuː ˈmænɪdʒə/ *noun* gestión *f* de lista de espera; gestión *f* de cola de espera

queuing time /ˈkjuːɪŋ taɪm/ *noun* tiempo *m* de espera (en cola)

QuickDraw /ˈkwɪkdrɔː/ (*Apple Macintosh graphics routines*) QuickDraw™

quicksort /ˈkwɪksɔːt/ *noun* clasificación *f* rápida

QuickTime /ˈkwɪktaɪm/ (*Apple Macintosh graphics routines*) QuickTime™

quiescent /kwiˈes(ə)nt/ *adjective* (*process or circuit or device*) desactivado *or* -a; en reposo; inmovilizado *or* -a

quintet /kwɪnˈtet/ *noun* (*five bits*) quinteto *m*

quit /kwɪt/ *verb* (*system or program*) salir *vi*; cerrar *vt* ◇ **do not forget to save your text be-**fore you quit the system no olvide guardar el texto antes de salir del sistema

quotation /kwəʊˈteɪʃ(ə)n/ *noun* (*text borrowed from another text*) cita *f*

quotation marks /kwəʊˈteɪʃ(ə)n mɑːks/ *noun* (*inverted commas*) comillas *fpl*

quote /kwəʊt/ *verb* **1.** citar *vt* **2.** citar **3.** (*to repeat*) citar *vt*; hacer referencia a; mencionar *vt* ◇ **he quoted figures from the newspaper report** mencionó unas cifras procedentes del artículo del periódico ◇ **in reply please quote this number** al responder haga referencia a este número, por favor ◇ **when making a complaint please quote the batch number printed on the computer case** cuando presente una reclamación por favor haga referencia al número del lote situado en la caja del ordenador

quotes /kwəʊts/ *plural noun informal* comillas *fpl*

quotient /ˈkwəʊʃ(ə)nt/ *noun* cociente *m*

quoting /ˈkwəʊtɪŋ/ *noun* respuesta *f* que incluye el mensaje al que se responde

QWERTY keyboard /ˌkwɜːti ˈkiːbɔːd/ *noun* (*standard English language key layout*) teclado *m* QWERTY; teclado *m* internacional

R

race /reɪs/ *noun* (*error condition in digital circuit*) carrera *f* ◇ **race condition** condición *f* de carrera

rack /ræk/ *noun* (*for electronic circuit boards and peripheral devices*) chasis *m* fijo; armazón *f* fija; casillero *m*

rack mounted /ræk ˈmaʊntɪd/ *adjective* chasis *m* preparado; con guías

radial transfer /ˌreɪdiəl ˈtrænsfɜː/ *noun* (*data transfer*) transferencia *f* radial; transferencia *f* entre capas; transferencia *f* radial de datos de programas

radio button /ˈreɪdiəʊ ˌbʌt(ə)n/ *noun* (*in a GUI: circle displayed beside an option*) icono *m* de radio

radio frequency /ˈreɪdiəʊ ˌfriːkwənsi/ *noun* frecuencia *f* de radio

radix /ˈreɪdɪks/ *noun* (*of a number system*) base *f*; raíz *f* ◇ **the hexadecimal number has a radix of 16** el número hexadecimal tiene una base de 16

radix complement /ˈreɪdɪks ˌkɒmplɪmənt/ *noun* complemento *m* de base

radix notation /ˈreɪdɪks nəʊˌteɪʃ(ə)n/ *noun* numeración *f* de base

radix point /ˈreɪdɪks pɔɪnt/ *noun* coma *f* separadora de fracción de decimal

ragged left /ˈrægɪd left/ *noun* (texto) no justificado a la izquierda

ragged right /ˈrægɪd raɪt/ *noun* (texto) no justificado a la derecha

ragged text /ˈrægɪd tekst/ *noun* texto *m* no justificado

RAID /reɪd/ *noun* almacenamiento *m* secundario rápido de discos múltiples

'A Japanese investor group led by system distributor Technography has pumped $4.2 million (#2.8 million) into US disk manufacturer Storage Computer to help with the development costs of RAID 7 hard disk technology.' [*Computing*]

RAM /ræm/ *noun* (*memory*) memoria *f* de acceso aleatorio; memoria *f* de acceso al azar; RAM *f* ◇ **dynamic RAM** (memoria) RAM dinámica ◇ **RAM disk** disco *m* RAM *or* disco de memoria ◇ **when you hit Ctrl-F5, you will activate the RAM resident program and it will display your day's diary** al pulsar Ctrl-F5 se activa el programa residente RAM y muestra la agenda del día ◇ **you can increase the printer's memory by plugging in another RAM cartridge** se puede aumentar la memoria de la impresora conectándole otro cartucho RAM

'The HP Enterprise Desktops have hard-disk capacities of between 260Mb and 1Gb, with RAM ranging from 16Mb up to 128Mb.' [*Computing*]
'...fast memory is RAM that does not have to share bus access with the chip that manages the video display' [*Byte*]

RAM cache /ˈræm kæʃ/ *noun* memoria *f* caché; antememoria *f*

RAM card /ˈræm kɑːd/ *noun* tarjeta *f* RAM

RAM cartridge /ræm ˈkɑːtrɪdʒ/ *noun* cartucho *m* RAM

RAM chip /ˈræm tʃɪp/ *noun* chip *m* RAM

RAM disk /ˈræm dɪsk/ *noun* disco *m* RAM; disco *m* de memoria

RAM loader /ˈræm ˌləʊdə/ *noun* (programa) cargador *m* de memoria RAM

RAM refresh /ræm rɪˈfreʃ/ *noun* (señal de) actualización *f* de la memoria RAM

RAM refresh rate /ˌræm rɪˈfreʃ ˌreɪt/ *noun* frecuencia *f* de actualización de la memoria RAM; tasa *f* de actualización de la memoria RAM

RAM resident program /ˌræm ˌrezɪd(ə)nt ˈprəʊɡræm/ *noun* programa *m* residente RAM; TSR

R & D /ˌɑːr ən ˈdiː/ *noun* investigación y desarrollo

random access /ˌrændəm ˈækses/ *noun* (*memory locations*) acceso *m* aleatorio; (*memory location*) acceso *m* al azar; (*memory locations*) acceso *m* directo ◇ **disk drives are random access, magnetic tape is sequential access memory** los lectores de disquetes son de acceso aleatorio, mientras que las cintas magnéticas son de memoria de acceso secuencial

random access device /ˌrændəm ˈækses dɪˌvaɪs/ *noun* dispositivo *m* de acceso aleatorio

random access digital to analog converter /ˌrændəm ˌækses ˌdɪdʒɪt(ə)l tə ˌænəlɒg kənˈvɜːtə/ *noun* convertidor *m* de digital a analógico de acceso aleatorio

random access files /ˌrændəm ˈækses ˌfaɪlz/ *noun* ficheros *mpl* de acceso aleatorio/directo

random access memory /ˌrændəm ˈækses ˌmem(ə)ri/ *noun* (*memory*) memoria *f* de acceso aleatorio; memoria *f* viva; memoria *f* RAM

random access storage /ˌrændəm ˈækses ˌstɔːrɪdʒ/ *noun* memoria *f* de acceso aleatorio

random number /ˌrændəm ˈnʌmbə/ *noun* número *m* aleatorio; número *m* elegido al azar

random number generation /ˌrændəm ˈnʌmbə ˌdʒenəreɪʃ(ə)n/ *noun* generación *f* aleatoria de números

random number generator /ˌrændəm ˈnʌmbə ˌdʒenəreɪtə/ *noun* generador *m* de números aleatorios

random process /ˌrændəm ˈprəʊses/ *noun* (*system*) proceso *m* directo; proceso *m* aleatorio; procedimiento *m* aleatorio

random processing /ˌrændəm ˈprəʊsesɪŋ/ *noun* tratamiento *m* aleatorio

range /reɪndʒ/ *noun* **1.** (*reach*) ámbito *m*; campo *m* **2.** (*set of values*) gama *f* ■ *verb* **1.** (*to vary*) variar *vi*; oscilar *vi* **2.** (*to put text in order*) alinear *vt*; justificar *vt* ◇ **frequency range** gama de frecuencias ◇ **the telephone channel can accept signals in the frequency range 300 – 3400Hz** la transmisión por teléfono acepta señales dentro de una gama de frecuencias que va de los 300 a los 3400 Hz

rank /ræŋk/ *verb* clasificar por rango

rapid access /ˌræpɪd ˈækses/ *noun* acceso *m* rápido

rapid access memory /ˌræpɪd ˌækses ˈmem(ə)ri/ *noun* memoria *f* de acceso rápido

raster /ˈræstə/ *noun* trama *f* ◇ **an electronic page can be converted to a printer-readable video image by an on-board raster image processor** un procesador gráfico por barrido de trama permite transformar una página electrónica en una imagen de vídeo imprimible

raster font /ˈræstə fɒnt/ *noun* tipo *m* de letra en la planificación de fibras *m*

raster graphics /ˈræstə ˌɡræfɪks/ *plural noun* representación *f* gráfica en forma de trama

raster image processor /ˌræstə ˈɪmɪdʒ ˌprəʊsesə/ *noun* procesador *m* de imagen matricial; procesador *m* gráfico por barrido de trama

raster scan /ˈræstə skæn/ *noun* barrido *m* por trama; exploración *f* de trama

rate /reɪt/ *noun* (*ratio*) tasa *f*; índice *m*; (*speed*) velocidad *f* ◇ **the processor's instruction execution rate is better than the older version** la velocidad de ejecución de instrucciones del procesador es mejor que la de la versión anterior

rated throughput /ˌreɪtɪd ˈθruːpʊt/ *noun* (*maximum throughput of a device*) rendimiento *m* teórico; rendimiento *m* estimado; rendimiento *m* nominal

rate of production /ˌreɪt əv prəˈdʌkʃən/ *noun* gasto *m* horario

ratio /ˈreɪʃiəʊ/ *noun* (*proportion*) ratio *m*; relación *f*; (*coefficient*) coeficiente *m*; (*proportion*) proporción *f* ◇ **the ratio of 10 to 5 is 2:1** la relación 10 a 5 es (igual a) 2:1 ◇ **the ratio of corrupt bits per transmitted message is falling with new technology** la proporción de bits corruptos por mensaje transmitido está disminuyendo con la nueva teconología

rational number /ˌræʃ(ə)nəl ˈnʌmbə/ *noun* número *m* racional ◇ **0.333 can be written as the rational number 1** *or* **3** se puede escribir 0,333 bajo la forma del número racional 1/3 ◇ **24 over 7 is a rational number** 24/7 es un número racional

raw data /ˌrɔː ˈdeɪtə/ *noun* **1.** (*not in computer system*) datos *mpl* en bruto **2.** (*needing to be processed*) datos *mpl* en bruto **3.** (*unprocessed*) datos *mpl* en bruto

raw mode /ˌrɔː ˈməʊd/ *noun* modo *m* directo

ray tracing /reɪ ˈtreɪsɪŋ/ *noun* trazado *m* de rayos; rastreo *m* por rayos ◇ **to generate this picture with ray tracing will take several hours on this powerful PC** se tardarán bastantes horas para generar esta imagen con rastreo por rayos en este potente PC

RDBMS *abbr* (*relational database management system*) base *f* de datos relacional

react /riˈækt/ *verb* reaccionar *vi* ◇ **to react to something** reaccionar a algo *or* alguna cosa ◇ **to react with something** (*of substance*) entrar en reacción con otra sustancia

reaction time /riˈækʃən taɪm/ *noun* tiempo *m* de acceso

reactive mode /riˈæktɪv məʊd/ *noun* modo *m* reactivo

read /riːd/ *verb* **1.** (*to retrieve data*) leer *vt*; extraer *vt* **2.** (*scan printed data*) leer *vt*; extraer *vt* ◇ **access time can be the time taken to read from a record** el tiempo de acceso es el que se requiere para leer un registro

readable /ˈriːdəb(ə)l/ *adjective* legible; que se puede leer

read back check /ˈriːd bæk ˌtʃek/ *noun* control *m* por lectura; verificación *f* por lectura

read cycle /riːd ˈsaɪk(ə)l/ *noun* ciclo *m* de lectura

reader /ˈriːdə/ *noun* (*device*) lector *m*

reader level /ˈriːdə ˌlev(ə)l/ *noun* nivel *m* de lector

read error /riːd ˈerə/ *noun* error *m* de lectura

read head /ˌriːd ˈhed/ *noun* cabeza *f* de lectura

read in /ˌriːd ˈɪn/ *verb* (*data transfer*) introducir *vt*; entrar *vt*; registrar *vt*

reading /ˈriːdɪŋ/ *noun* lectura *f* ◇ **optical reading** lectura óptica

readme file /ˈriːdmi faɪl/ *noun* fichero *m* 'léame'

read only /ˈriːd ˌəʊnli/ *noun* (memoria) de sólo lectura

read only attribute /ˌriːd ˈəʊnli ˌætrɪbjuːt/ *noun* atributo *m* de sólo lectura

read only memory /ˌriːd ˈəʊnli ˈmem(ə)ri/ *noun* memoria *f* de sólo lectura; memoria *f* ROM

readout /ˈriːdaʊt/ *noun* lectura *f*; visualización *f* ◇ **the clock had a digital readout** el reloj tiene una lectura digital ◇ **the readout displayed the time** la lectura mostraba la hora

readout device /ˈriːdaʊt dɪˌvaɪs/ *noun* dispositivo *m* de visualización; pantalla *f* de visualización

read rate /ˌriːd ˈreɪt/ *noun* velocidad *f* de lectura

read/write channel /ˌriːd ˈraɪt ˌtʃæn(ə)l/ noun vía f de lectura/escritura

read/write cycle /ˌriːd ˈraɪt ˌsaɪk(ə)l/ noun ciclo m de lectura/escritura

read/write head /ˌriːd ˈraɪt hed/ noun cabeza f de lectura/escritura

read/write memory /ˌriːd ˌraɪt ˈmem(ə)ri/ noun memoria f de lectura/escritura

ready /ˈredi/ adjective preparado or -a; dispuesto or -a ◇ **the green light indicates the system is ready for another program** la luz verde indica que el sistema está preparado para otro programa

ready state /ˈredi steɪt/ noun estado m preparado; estado m listo

Real /rɪəl/ (trade name for a system used to transmit sound and video over the Internet) real ◇ **a navigation system needs to be able to process the position of a ship in real time and take suitable action before she hits a rock** un sistema de navegación debe poder procesar la posición de un barco en tiempo real para tomar las decisiones adecuadas antes de dar contra una roca ◇ **in a real-time system, as you move the joystick left, the image on the screen moves left. If there is a pause for processing it is not a true real-time system** en un sistema de tiempo real, al mover el mando de juegos hacia la izquierda, la imagen de la pantalla se mueve hacia la izquierda. En cambio, no es un verdadero sistema en tiempo real si hay una pausa para su proceso ◇ **program shown in real time** programa m visto en tiempo real or emisión f en directo ◇ **real time transport protocol (RTP)** protocolo m de transferencia (de datos) en tiempo real

real address /rɪəl əˈdres/ noun dirección f absoluta

RealAudio /ˌrɪəlˈɔːdiəʊ/ (trade name for a system used to transmit sound over the Internet) RealAudio™ (de transmisión de sonido por internet)

realise /ˈrɪəlaɪz/, **realise the palette** /ˌrɪəlaɪz ðə ˈpælət/ verb seleccionar colores de la paleta

real memory /rɪəl ˈmem(ə)ri/ noun memoria f real

real number /rɪəl ˈnʌmbə/ noun número m real

real time /ˈrɪəl taɪm/ noun tiempo m real ◇ **real time execution (RTE)** ejecución f (de un programa) en tiempo real

'Quotron provides real-time quotes, news and analysis on equity securities through a network of 40,000 terminals to US brokers and investors.' [Computing]

'…define a real-time system as any system which is expected to interact with its environment within certain timing constraints' [British Telecom Technology Journal]

real-time animation /ˌrɪəl taɪm ˌænɪˈmeɪʃ(ə)n/ noun animación f en tiempo real

real-time authorisation /ˌrɪəl taɪm ˌɔːθəraɪˈzeɪʃ(ə)n/, **real-time authentication** /ˌrɪəl taɪm ˌɔːθentɪˈkeɪʃ(ə)n/ noun autorización f en tiempo real

real-time clock /ˌrɪəl taɪm ˈklɒk/ noun reloj m en tiempo real

real-time input /ˌrɪəl taɪm ˈɪnpʊt/ noun entrada f en tiempo real

real-time multi-tasking /ˌrɪəl taɪm ˈmʌlti ˌtɑːskɪŋ/ noun multitarea f en tiempo real

real-time operating system /ˌrɪəl taɪm ˈɒpəreɪtɪŋ ˌsɪstəm/ noun sistema m operativo en tiempo real

real-time processing /ˌrɪəl taɪm ˈprəʊsesɪŋ/ noun proceso m en tiempo real; tratamiento m en tiempo real

real-time simulation /ˌrɪəl taɪm ˌsɪmjʊˈleɪʃ(ə)n/ noun simulación f en tiempo real

real-time system /ˈrɪəl taɪm ˌsɪstəm/ noun sistema m en tiempo real ◇ **in a real-time system, as you move the joystick left, the image on the screen moves left. If there is a pause for processing it is not a true real-time system** en un sistema de tiempo real, al mover el mando de juegos hacia la izquierda, la imagen de la pantalla se mueve hacia la izquierda. En cambio, no es un verdadero sistema en tiempo real si hay una pausa para su proceso

reboot /riːˈbuːt/ verb relanzar vt; reiniciar vt ◇ **we rebooted and the files reappeared** reiniciamos el sistema y los ficheros reaparecieron en la pantalla

recall /rɪˈkɔːl/ noun recuperación f ■ verb recuperar vt

receipt notification /rɪˈsiːt ˌnəʊtɪfɪkeɪʃ(ə)n/ noun (of electronic mail applications – to confirm that the recipient has received the message) acuse m de recibo (electrónico)

receive /rɪˈsiːv/ verb recibir vt ◇ **the computer received data via the telephone line** el ordenador recibió datos a través de la línea telefónica

receive only /rɪˌsiːv ˈəʊnli/ noun terminal m de llegada

receiver /rɪˈsiːvə/ noun receptor m ◇ **radio receiver** receptor de radio ◇ **the radio receiver picked up your signal very strongly** el receptor de radio captó muy claramente su señal

receiver register /rɪˈsiːvə ˌredʒɪstə/ noun registro m de entradas

re-chargeable battery /riː ˌtʃɑːdʒəb(ə)l ˈbæt(ə)ri/ noun pila f recargable; batería f recargable ◇ **a re-chargeable battery is used for RAM back-up when the system is switched off** se utiliza una batería recargable como alimentación auxiliar para la memoria RAM cuando se apaga el sistema

recode /riːˈkəʊd/ verb recodificar vt

recognisable /ˈrekəɡnaɪzəb(ə)l/, **recognizable** adjective reconocible

recognise /ˈrekəɡnaɪz/, **recognize** verb reconocer vt; admitir vt ◇ **the scanner will recognize most character fonts** el escáner reconoce la mayor parte de los caracteres

recognition /ˌrekəɡˈnɪʃ(ə)n/ noun reconocimiento m

recognition logic /ˌrekəg'nɪʃ(ə)n ˌlɒdʒɪk/ *noun* lógica *f* de reconocimiento

recompile /ˌriːkəm'paɪl/ *verb* recompilar *vt*; efectuar una nueva compilación

reconfiguration /ˌriːkənfɪgə'reɪʃ(ə)n/ *noun* reconfiguración *f*

reconfigure /ˌriːkən'fɪgə/ *verb* reconfigurar *vt* ◇ **I reconfigured the field structure in the file** reconfiguré la estructura de campos en el fichero ◇ **this program allows us to reconfigure the system to our own requirements** este programa nos permite reconfigurar el sistema según nuestras necesidades

reconstitute /riː'kɒnstɪtjuːt/ *verb* (*after crash or corruption*) reconstituir *vt*; restaurar *vt*

record *noun* /'rekɔːd/ (*items of data*) registro *m*; documento *m* ■ *verb* /rɪ'kɔːd/ (*disk*) inscribir *vt*; anotar registros ◇ **digitally recorded data are used to generate images** los datos registrados digitalmente se utilizan para generar imágenes ◇ **record the results in this column** registre los resultados en este columna ◇ **this device records signals onto magnetic tape** este dispositivo registra las señales sobre cinta magnética ◇ **this record contains all their personal details** este registro contiene todos sus detalles personales ◇ **your record contains several fields that have been grouped together under the one heading** su registro contiene varios campos que han sido agrupados bajo una misma cabecera

recordable CD /rɪˌkɔːdəb(ə)l siː 'diː/ *noun* CD *m* grabable; disco *m* compacto grabable

record button /rɪ'kɔːd ˌbʌt(ə)n/ *noun* tecla *f* de registro; botón *m* de registro

record count /'rekɔːd kaʊnt/ *noun* (número de) registros *mpl* de un fichero

recorder /rɪ'kɔːdə/ *noun* (*equipment*) grabadora *f*

record format /'rekɔːd ˌfɔːmæt/ *noun* formato *m* de un registro; diseño *m* de un registro

record gap /'rekɔːd gæp/ *noun* intervalo *m* en blanco; espacio *m* entre dos registros

record head /re'kɔːd ˌhed/ *noun* cabeza *f* de escritura; cabeza *f* de registro

recording /rɪ'kɔːdɪŋ/ *noun* (*process of storing signals, etc.*) grabación *f*

recording density /rɪ'kɔːdɪŋ ˌdensɪti/ *noun* densidad *f* de registro

recording indicator /rɪ'kɔːdɪŋ ˌɪndɪkeɪtə/ *noun* indicador *m* de registro

recording level /rɪ'kɔːdɪŋ ˌlev(ə)l/ *noun* nivel *m* de registro

record layout /ˌrekɔːd 'leɪaʊt/ *noun* diseño *m* de un registro; formato *m* de un registro

record length /'rekɔːd leŋθ/ *noun* (*total number of characters*) longitud *f* de un registro; tamaño *m* de un registro

record locking /'rekɔːd lɒkɪŋ/ *noun* bloqueo *m* de registros

records manager /'rekɔːdz ˌmænɪdʒə/ *noun* (*program which maintains records*) gestor *m* de

registros ◇ **records management** (programa de) gestión *f* de registros *or* de ficheros

record structure /'rekɔːd ˌstrʌktʃə/ *noun* estructura *f* de un registro

recover /rɪ'kʌvə/ *verb* recobrar *vt*; recuperar *vt* ◇ **it is possible to recover the data but it can take a long time** es posible recuperar los datos, pero se tarda mucho tiempo

recoverable error /rɪˌkʌv(ə)rəb(ə)l 'erə/ *noun* error *m* recuperable; error *m* reparable

recovery /rɪ'kʌv(ə)ri/ *noun* **1.** (*return to normal*) recuperación *f*; reposición *f* **2.** (*getting back something*) recuperación *f*; restauración *f*

recovery procedure /rɪ'kʌv(ə)ri prəˌsiːdʒə/ *noun* procedimiento *m* de recuperación ◇ **the recovery of lost files can be carried out using a recovery procedure** la recuperación de los ficheros perdidos puede realizarse utilizando un procedimiento de recuperación

recursion /rɪ'kɜːʒ(ə)n/ *noun* recursión *f*

recursive call /rɪˌkɜːsɪv 'kɔːl/ *noun* llamada *f* recursiva; procedimiento *m* recursivo

recursive routine /rɪˌkɜːsɪv 'ruːtiːn/ *noun* rutina *f* recursiva

Recycle Bin /riː'saɪk(ə)l bɪn/ *noun* (*icon displayed on the Windows 95 Desktop – like a wastepaper bin*) papelera *f* de reciclaje

red, green, blue /ˌred griːn 'bluː/ *noun* rojo, verde, azul

redefinable /ˌriːdɪ'faɪnəb(ə)l/ *adjective* reprogramable; que puede ser redefinido *or* -a; reprogramado *or* -a

redefine /ˌriːdɪ'faɪn/ *verb* (*to change the function or value*) definir de nuevo; redefinir *vt*; reprogramar *vt* ◇ **I have redefined this key to display the figure five when pressed** he reprogramado esta tecla para obtener el número cinco ◇ **to redefine a key** redefinir (la función) de una tecla *or* reprogramar una tecla ◇ **we redefined the initial parameters** redefinimos los parámetros iniciales

'…one especially useful command lets you redefine the printer's character-translation table' [*Byte*]

redirect /ˌriːdaɪ'rekt/ *verb* **1.** (*a message*) redirigir *vt*; desviar *vt*; volver a enviar **2.** (*to treat the output of one program as input for another program*) redirigir (por ruta distinta); enviar (por ruta distinta); desviar (por ruta distinta) ◇ **you can sort the results from a DIR command by redirecting to the SORT command** puede clasificar los resultados de la instrucción DIR desviándola a la instrucción SORT

redirection /ˌriːdaɪ'rekʃən/ *noun* (*telephone*) redirección *f* (automática) de llamadas; (*message*) redirección *f* ◇ **call forwarding is automatic redirection of calls** el desvío de llamadas consiste en la redirección automática de llamadas

redirect operator /ˌriːdaɪˌrekt ˌɒpə'reɪtə/, **redirection operator** /ˌriːdaɪˌrekʃən 'ɒpəreɪtə/ *noun* operador *m* de redirección (del DOS); carácter *m* de redirección (del DOS)

redliner /'redlaɪnə/ *noun (highlights text in a different colour)* marcador *m* en rojo

redo from start /ˌriːduː frəm 'stɑːt/ *verb* rehacer desde el inicio

reduce /rɪ'djuːs/ *verb (to convert data into a more compact form)* comprimir *vt*

reduced instruction set computer /rɪ ˌdjuːst ɪnˌstrʌkʃən set kəm'pjuːtə/ *noun* ordenador *m* de conjunto de instrucciones reducido; procesador *m* de conjunto de instrucciones reducido; ordenador *m* de conjunto de arquitectura RISC; procesador *m* de conjunto de arquitectura RISC

redundancy /rɪ'dʌndənsi/ *noun* redundancia *f*

redundancy checking /rɪ'dʌndənsi tʃekɪŋ/ *noun* control *m* de redundancia

redundant /rɪ'dʌndənt/ *adjective* **1.** (*data*) redundante; superfluo *or* -a **2.** (*equipment kept ready*) de seguridad; de emergencia; redundante ◇ **the parity bits on the received data are redundant and can be removed** los bits de paridad de los datos recibidos son superfluos y pueden eliminarse

redundant array of inexpensive disks /rɪ ˌdʌndənt əˌreɪ əv ˌɪnɪkspensɪv 'dɪsks/ *noun* almacenamiento *m* secundario rápido de discos múltiples

redundant character /rɪˌdʌndənt 'kærɪktə/ *noun* carácter *m* redundante; carácter *m* de redundancia

redundant code /rɪ'dʌndənt kəʊd/ *noun* código *m* redundante; código *m* de redundancia

reel to reel /ˌriːl tə 'riːl/ *noun* de bobina a bobina

reel to reel recorder /ˌriːl tə riːl rɪ'kɔːdə/ *noun* grabadora *f* de bobina a bobina

re-entrant program /riː ˌentrənt 'prəʊgræm/, **re-entrant code** /kəʊd/, **re-entrant routine** /ruː'tiːn/ *noun* programa *m* reentrante

re-entry /reɪ 'entri/ *noun* reentrada *f*; reanudación *f*

re-entry point /ˌriː 'entri ˌpɔɪnt/ *noun* (*point in a program or routine*) punto *m* de reentrada; punto *m* de re-entrada; punto *m* de reanudación

reference /'ref(ə)rəns/ *noun* **1.** (*value used as a starting point*) referencia *f* **2.** (*mentioning something*) referencia *f* ■ *verb (to access location)* referenciar *vt*; aludir *vi* ◇ **reference level** (*of signal*) nivel *m* de referencia ◇ **seven-layer reference model** modelo *m* de referencia de siete categorías ◇ **the access time taken to reference an item in memory is short** se necesita poco tiempo de acceso para referenciar un ítem de la memoria

reference address /'ref(ə)rəns əˌdres/ *noun* dirección *f* de referencia

reference file /'ref(ə)rəns faɪl/ *noun* fichero *m* de referencia

reference instruction /'ref(ə)rəns ɪnˌstrʌkʃən/ *noun* instrucción *f* de referencia; instrucción *f* de base

reference list /'ref(ə)rəns lɪst/ *noun* lista *f* de referencia

reference mark /'ref(ə)rəns mɑːk/ *noun* marca *f* de referencia; llamada *f* para nota al pie de página

reference program table /ˌref(ə)rəns 'prəʊgræm ˌteɪb(ə)l/ *noun* tabla *f* de referencia de un programa

reference retrieval system /ˌref(ə)rəns rɪ'triːv(ə)l ˌsɪstəm/ *noun* sistema *m* de recuperación de referencia

reference table /'ref(ə)rəns ˌteɪb(ə)l/ *noun* tabla *f* de referencia

reference time /'ref(ə)rəns taɪm/ *noun* periodo *m* de referencia; tiempo *m* de referencia

reflected code /rɪ'flektd kəʊd/ *noun* código *m* reflejado

reformat /ˌriː'fɔːmæt/ *verb* reformatear *vt*; volver a dar formato ◇ **do not reformat your hard disk unless you can't do anything else** evite reformatear el disco duro a menos que no haya ninguna otra solución

reformatting /riː'fɔːmætɪŋ/ *noun* reformateo *m*; reformateado *m* ◇ **reformatting destroys all the data on a disk** el reformateado destruye todos los datos de un disco

refraction /rɪ'frækʃən/ *noun* refracción *f*

refresh /rɪ'freʃ/ *verb (to update a memory)* renovar *vt*; actualizar *vt*; regenerar *vt* ◇ **memory refresh signal** señal *f* de actualización de la memoria

refresh cycle /rɪ'freʃ ˌsaɪk(ə)l/ *noun* ciclo *m* de actualización; tiempo *m* de actualización

refresh rate /rɪ'freʃ reɪt/ *noun* índice *m* de renovación

'Philips autoscan colour monitor, the 4CM6099, has SVGA refresh rates of 72Hz (800 x 600) and EVGA refresh rates of 70Hz (1,024 x 768).' [*Computing*]

regenerate /rɪ'dʒenəˌreɪt/ *verb* **1.** regenerar *vt*; renovar *vt*; actualizar *vt* **2.** (*to process distorted signals*) regenerar *vt*; renovar *vt*; actualizar *vt*

regenerative memory /rɪˌdʒenərətɪv 'mem(ə)ri/ *noun* memoria *f* regenerativa ◇ **dynamic RAM is regenerative memory – it needs to be refreshed every 250ns** la RAM dinámica es una memoria regenerativa que necesita ser regenerada cada 250 ns ◇ **the CRT display can be thought of as regenerative memory, it requires regular refresh picture scans to prevent flicker** la pantalla puede compararse con una memoria regenerativa; necesita barridos regulares de actualización para evitar el parpadeo

regenerative reading /rɪˌdʒenərətɪv 'riːdɪŋ/ *noun* lectura *f* regenerativa

regenerator /riː'dʒenəreɪtə/ *noun* (*device that regenerates a received signal*) regenerador *m*; amplificador *m* de señal

region /'riːdʒən/ *noun* (*area of memory or program*) zona *f*; región *f*

regional breakpoint /ˌriːdʒ(ə)nəl ˈbreɪkpɔɪnt/ *noun* punto *m* de interrupción; punto *m* de ruptura

region fill /ˈriːdʒ(ə)n fɪl/ *noun* relleno *m* de zona

register /ˈredʒɪstə/ *noun* **1.** (*for data*) registro *m* **2.** (*reserved memory location*) registro *m* ■ *verb* (*to react*) registrar *vt* ◊ **external register** registro externo ◊ **index register** registro de índice ◊ **instruction address register (IAR)** registro de dirección de instrucciones ◊ **light-sensitive films register light intensity** las películas fotosensibles registran la intensidad de la luz ◊ **program status word register (PSW register)** registro de la palabra de estado del programa *or* registro PSW ◊ **register level compatibility** compatibilidad *f* a nivel de registros ◊ **register marks** (*printing*) marcas *fpl* de registro ◊ **sequence control register (SCR)** registro de control de secuencias

register addressing /ˌredʒɪstə əˈdresɪŋ/ *noun* direccionamiento *m* de registro(s)

register file /ˈredʒɪstə faɪl/ *noun* fichero *m* de registros

register length /ˈredʒɪstə leŋθ/ *noun* (*number of bits*) tamaño *m* de un registro; tamaño *m* de un contador

register map /ˈredʒɪstə mæp/ *noun* (visualización del) contenido *m* de los registros; (visualización de la) configuración *f* de los registros

Registry /ˈredʒɪstri/ *noun* (*database that forms the basis of Windows*) registro *m*

regulate /ˈregjʊleɪt/ *verb* (*process*) controlar *vt*; ajustar *vt*; regular *vt*

regulated power supply /ˌregjʊleɪt ɪd ˈpaʊə sə,plaɪ/ *noun* suministro *m* de corriente controlada

rehyphenation /riː,haɪfəˈneɪʃ(ə)n/ *noun* actualización *f* de la división silábica

rejection error /rɪˈdʒekʃən ,erə/ *noun* error *m* de rechazo

relational database /rɪ,leɪʃ(ə)n(ə)l ˈdeɪtəbeɪs/, **relational database management system** /rɪ,leɪʃn(ə)l ,deɪtəbeɪs ,mænɪdʒmənt ˈsɪstəm/ *noun* base *f* de datos relacional

relational operator /rɪ,leɪʃ(ə)n(ə)l ˈɒpəreɪtə/ *noun* operador *m* relacional; operador *m* lógico

relational query /rɪ,leɪʃ(ə)n(ə)l ˈkwɪəri/ *noun* consulta *f* relacional; pregunta *f* relacional ◊ **the relational query 'find all men under 35 years old' will not work on this system** la consulta relacional 'encontrar todos los hombres de menos de 35 años' no funciona en este sistema

relative address /ˌrelətɪv əˈdres/ *noun* dirección *f* relativa

relative coding /ˈrelətɪv kɒdɪŋ/ *noun* codificación *f* relativa

relative coordinates /ˌrelətɪv kəʊˈɔːdɪnəts/ *plural noun* coordenadas *fpl* relativas

relative data /ˌrelətɪv ˈdeɪtə/ *noun* datos *mpl* relativos

relative error /ˌrelətɪv ˈerə/ *noun* error *m* relativo

relative pointing device /ˌrelətɪv ˈpɔɪntɪŋ dɪ,vaɪs/ *noun* dispositivo *m* de señalización relativa; indicador *m* relativo

relative-time clock /ˌrelətɪv taɪm ˈklɒk/ *noun* reloj *m* relativo

relay /ˈriːleɪ/ *noun* (*switch*) relé *m* ■ *verb* retransmitir *vt* ◊ **all messages are relayed through this small micro** todos los mensajes se retransmiten a través de este pequeño micrófono ◊ **it is relay-rated at 5 Amps** está protegido por un relé de 5 amperios ◊ **microwave relay** relé de microondas ◊ **there is a relay in the circuit** hay un relé en el circuito

release /rɪˈliːs/ *noun* **1.** (*version of a product*) versión *f*; puesta *f* en venta de un producto **2.** (*putting a new product on the market*) comercialización *f* ■ *verb* **1.** (*of software: relinquish control*) soltar *vt*; (*new product*) lanzar *vt*; comercializar *vt* **2.** (*of software: relinquish control*) liberar *vt* ◊ **press release** (*announcing a product*) comunicado *m* de prensa ◊ **the latest software is release 5** el nuevo software es la versión 5

release number /rɪˈliːs ,nʌmbə/ *noun* número *m* de versión

reliability /rɪ,laɪəˈbɪliti/ *noun* fiabilidad *f* ◊ **it has an excellent reliability record** tiene una excelente fiabilidad ◊ **the product has passed its reliability tests** el producto ha superado las pruebas de fiabilidad

reliable /rɪˈlaɪəb(ə)l/ *adjective* fiable ◊ **the early versions of the software were not completely reliable** las primeras versiones del software no resultaron completamente fiables

reliable connection /rɪ,laɪəb(ə)l kəˈnekʃən/ *noun* conexión segura

reload /riːˈləʊd/ *verb* recargar *vt*; relanzar *vt* ◊ **we reloaded the program after the crash** después del fallo, recargamos el programa

relocatable /ˌriːləʊˈkeɪtəb(ə)l/ *adjective* (*to another area of memory*) reubicable; reposicionable

relocatable program /ˌriːləʊˈkeɪtəb(ə)l ˈprəʊgræm/ *noun* programa *m* reubicable; código *m* de posición independiente ◊ **the operating system can load and run a relocatable program from any area of memory** el sistema operativo puede cargar y ejecutar un programa reubicable desde cualquier área de la memoria

relocate /ˌriːləʊˈkeɪt/ *verb* (*to move data*) reubicar *vt*; cambiar de dirección ◊ **the data is relocated during execution** se cambia la dirección de los datos durante la ejecución

relocation /ˌriːləʊˈkeɪʃ(ə)n/ *noun* (*memory*) reasignación *f*; reubicación *f*; redireccionamiento *m*; desplazamiento *m*; traslado *m* (en memoria)

relocation constant /ˌriːləʊˈkeɪʃ(ə)n ˌkɒnstənt/ *noun* constante *f* de reubicación; constante *f* de reasignación

REM /rem/ *noun* observación *f*; comentario *m*

remainder /rɪ'meɪndə/ *noun* (*in division*) resto *m* ◇ **7 divided by 3 is equal to 2 remainder 1** 7 dividido por 3 es igual a 2 y 1 de resto

remark /rɪ'mɑːk/ *noun* (*statement ignored by the interpreter*) observación *f*; comentario *m*; sentencia *f* REM en un programa en BASIC ◇ **remark statement** enunciado *m* de observación

remedial maintenance /rɪ,miːdiəl 'meɪntənəns/ *noun* (*in a system*) mantenimiento *m* correctivo; mantenimiento *m* de reparación

remote /rɪ'məʊt/ *adjective* remoto *or* -a; a distancia ◇ **remote access software** (*allows a user to control the remote computer*) software *m* de acceso remoto ◇ **remote procedure call (RPC)** (*communication between two programs running on two connected computers*) llamada *f* de procedimiento a distancia ◇ **users can print reports on remote printers** los usuarios pueden imprimir informes en impresoras a distancia

remote access /rɪ,məʊt 'ækses/ *noun* acceso *m* a distancia ◇ **remote access software** (*allows a user to control the remote computer*) software *m* de acceso remoto

remote client /rɪ,məʊt 'klaɪənt/ *noun* cliente *m* remoto

remote console /rɪ,məʊt 'kɒnsəʊl/ *noun* consola *f* de instrucciones a distancia; dispositivo *m* de instrucciones a distancia

remote control /rɪ,məʊt kən'trəʊl/ *noun* (*control of a system from a distance*) mando *m* a distancia; control *m* remoto; control *m* a distancia ◇ **the video recorder has a remote control facility** el vídeo tiene un dispositivo de control remoto

remote control software /rɪ,məʊt kən'trəʊl ,sɒftweə/ *noun* software *m* de control remoto; software *m* a distancia ◇ **this remote control software will work with Windows and lets me operate my office PC from home over a modem link** este software de control remoto funciona con Windows y me permite utilizar el ordenador de mi oficina desde mi casa con una conexión por módem

remote device /rɪ,məʊt dɪ'vaɪs/ *noun* consola *f* de instrucciones a distancia; dispositivo *m* de instrucciones a distancia

remote job entry /rɪ,məʊt dʒɒb 'entri/ *noun* entrada *f* de trabajos a distancia; entrada *f* de tareas remotas

remote procedure call /rɪ,məʊt prə'siːdʒə ,kɔːl/ *noun* llamada *f* de procedimiento a distancia

remote station /rɪ,məʊt 'steɪʃ(ə)n/ *noun* estación *f* remota; estación *f* a distancia

remote terminal /rɪ,məʊt 'tɜːmɪn(ə)l/ *noun* terminal *m* a distancia; terminal *m* remoto

removable /rɪ'muːvəb(ə)l/ *adjective* intercambiable; desmontable ◇ **a removable hard disk** un disco duro intercambiable

removable Winchester disk /rɪ,muːvəb(ə)l 'lɪntʃestə/ *noun* disco *m* intercambiable Winchester

REN /ren/ *noun* número *m* de equivalencia de llamadas

rename /riː'neɪm/ *verb* cambiar el nombre de ◇ **save the file and rename it CLIENT** guarde el fichero y cambie el nombre a 'CLIENT'

render /'rendə/ *verb* (*graphic object*) representar *vt* ◇ **we rendered the wire-frame model** hemos representado el modelo de trama de rejilla

renumber /'riːnʌmbə/ *noun* (*line, etc.*) rehacer la numeración; (*page*) paginar de nuevo

reorganise /riː'ɔːɡənaɪz/, **reorganize** *verb* reorganizar *vt* ◇ **wait while the spelling checker database is being reorganized** espere mientras la base de datos de corrección ortográfica se está reorganizando

repaginate /riː'pædʒɪneɪt/ *verb* (*to change the lengths of pages*) paginar de nuevo; rehacer la paginación ◇ **the dtp package allows simple repagination** el sistema de publicación asistida por ordenador permite rehacer la paginación ◇ **the text was repaginated with a new line width** se rehizo la paginación del texto con una nueva longitud de línea

repagination /riː,pædʒɪ'neɪʃ(ə)n/ *noun* (*changing pages lengths*) nueva paginación *f*

repeat counter /rɪ,piːt 'kaʊntə/ *noun* contador *m* de repeticiones

repeater /rɪ'piːtə/ *noun* (*device that repeats a signal*) repetidor *m*

repeating group /rɪ'piːtɪŋ ɡruːp/ *noun* grupo *m* (de datos) de repetición; grupo *m* de datos que se repiten periódicamente

repeat key /rɪ'piːt kiː/ *noun* tecla *f* de repetición

repeat rate /rɪ'piːt reɪt/ *noun* índice *m* de repetición

reperforator /riː'pɜːfəreɪtə/ *noun* reperforadora *f*

reperforator transmitter /riː'pɜːfəreɪtə trænz,mɪtə/ *noun* transmisor *m* perforador; transmisor *m* de cinta con perforadora

repertoire /'repə,twɑː/ *noun* repertorio *m* ◇ **the manual describes the full repertoire** el manual describe el repertorio completo

repetitive letter /rɪ,petətɪv 'letə/ *noun* carta *f* estándar; carta *f* tipo

repetitive strain injury /rɪ,petɪtɪv 'streɪn ,ɪndʒəri/, **repetitive stress injury** /rɪ,petɪtɪv stres 'ɪndʒəri/ *noun* lesión *f* por esfuerzo repetitivo; lesión *f* por tensión repetitiva

replace /rɪ'pleɪs/ *verb* **1.** (*instruction*) (instrucción) reemplazar **2.** reemplazar *vt*

replace mode /rɪ'pleɪs məʊd/ *noun* modo *m* de sustitución

replay *noun* /'riːpleɪ/ (*data or music*) repetición *f* ■ *verb* /riː'pleɪ/ (*something which has been recorded*) repetir *vt*; reproducir *vt* ◇ **he replayed the tape** visionó de nuevo la cinta ◇ **the replay clearly showed the winner** la repetición a cámara lenta mostró claramente quién era el ganador ◇ **this video recorder has a replay feature** este grabador de vídeo tiene la función de repetición

replenish /rɪ'plenɪʃ/ *verb* (*a battery*) reponer *vt*; (*to recharge a battery*) reabastecer *vt*; recargar *vt*

replication /ˌreplɪ'keɪʃ(ə)n/ *noun* **1.** (*copying a record*) copia *f*; reproducción *f*; (*copy*) duplicado *m* **2.** copia *f*; reproducción *f*

reply /rɪ'plaɪ/ *verb* (*to a letter or e-mail*) responder *vt*; contestar *vi*

report generator /rɪˌpɔːt 'dʒenəreɪtə/ *noun* (*software*) generador *m* de informes

reproduce /ˌriːprə'djuːs/ *verb* reproducir *vt*

reprogram /riː'prəʊɡræm/ *verb* reprogramar *vt*; programar de nuevo

request for comment /rɪˌkwest fə 'kɒment/ *noun* petición *f* de comentario

request to send /rɪˌkwest tə 'send/ *noun* petición *f* de envió

request to send signal /rɪˌkwest tə 'send ˌsɪɡn(ə)l/ *noun* petición *f* de transmisión

requirements /rɪ'kwaɪəmənts/ *plural noun* requisitos *mpl*; exigencias *fpl*

re-route /riː ruːt/ *verb* (*message, data, etc*) reencaminar *vt*; (*to send something by a different route*) redirigir *vt*; cambiar la ruta ◇ **the call diverter re-routes a call** el dispositivo de desvío de llamadas redirige una llamada

rerun /ˌriː'rʌn/ *verb* (*to redo a program or printing job*) reanudar *vt*; repetir la ejecución; ejecutar de nuevo (un programa)

rerun point /'riːˌrʌn pɔɪnt/ *noun* punto *m* de reanudación

res /rez/ *noun* resolución *f*

resample /riː'sɑːmp(ə)l/ *verb* (*to change the number of pixels used to make up an image*) reconfigurar los píxeles de una imagen

resave /riː'seɪv/ *verb* guardar de nuevo ◇ **it automatically resaves the text** automáticamente guarda de nuevo el texto

rescue dump /'reskjuː dʌmp/ *noun* vaciado *m* de seguridad

research /rɪ'sɜːtʃ/ *noun* investigación *f* ◇ **research and development (R & D)** investigación y desarrollo ◇ **the company has spent millions of dollars on R & D** la empresa ha gastado millones de dólares en investigación y desarrollo

research and development /rɪˌsɜːtʃ ən dɪ'veləpmənt/ *noun* investigación y desarrollo

reserved character /rɪˌzɜːvd 'kærɪktə/ *noun* (*special character used by the operating system*) carácter *m* reservado ◇ **in DOS, the reserved character \ is used to represent a directory path** en el DOS, el carácter reservado \ se utiliza para representar el camino de un directorio

reserved sector /rɪˌzɜːvd 'sektə/ *noun* sector *m* reservado

reserved word /rɪˌzɜːvd wɜːd/ *noun* palabra *f* reservada

reset /ˌriː'set/ *verb* **1.** reiniciar *vt* **2.** (*to start again*) reiniciar *vt* ◇ **reset and start** reiniciar y arrancar

reset button /ˌriːˌset 'bʌt(ə)n/, **reset key** /ˌriː 'set kiː/ *noun* botón *m* de reinicio; tecla *f* de reinicio

reshape handle /'riːʃeɪp ˌhænd(ə)l/ *noun* (*icono*) controlador *m* de modificación de tamaño

resident /'rezɪd(ə)nt/ *adjective* (*data or program*) residente ◇ **resident font** (*font data always present in a printer*) fuente *f* (de caracteres) residente

resident engineer /ˌrezɪd(ə)nt ˌendʒɪ'nɪə/ *noun* ingeniero *m* de empresa

resident fonts /ˌrezɪd(ə)nt 'fɒntz/ *plural noun* fuente *f* (de caracteres) residente

resident software /ˌrezɪd(ə)nt 'sɒftweə/ *noun* software *m* residente

residual /rɪ'zɪdjuəl/ *adjective* residual

residual error rate /rɪˌzɪdjuəl 'erə ˌreɪt/ *noun* índice *m* de error residual

residue check /'rezɪˌdjuː tʃek/ *noun* verificación *f* por residuo; suma *f* de verificación

resist /rɪ'zɪst/ *noun* (*substance not affected by etching chemicals*) resistir *vt*

resolution /ˌrezə'luːʃ(ə)n/ *noun* (*number of pixels*) resolución *f*; definición *f* ◇ **the high resolution screen can display 640 by 450 pixels** la pantalla de alta definición puede obtener una resolución de 640 por 450 pixels ◇ **the resolution of most personal computer screens is not much more than 70 dpi (dots per inch)** la resolución de la mayoría de las pantallas de los ordenadores personales es apenas superior a los 70 ppp (puntos por pulgada)

'Group IV fax devices can send a grey or colour A4 page in about four seconds, at a maximum resolution of 15.7 lines per millimetre over an Integrated Services Digital Network circuit.' [*Computing*]

resolving power /rɪ'zɒlvɪŋ ˌpaʊə/ *noun* (*of an optical system*) poder *m* de resolución

resonance /'rez(ə)nəns/ *noun* resonancia *f*

resource /rɪ'zɔːs/ *noun* recurso *f*

resource allocation /rɪ'zɔːs ˌæləkeɪʃ(ə)n/ *noun* asignación *f* de recursos

resource fork /rɪ'zɔːs fɔːk/ *noun* bifurcación *f*; ramificación *f* de recursos

resource interchange file format /rɪˌzɔːs ˌɪntətʃeɪndʒ 'faɪl ˌfɔːmæt/ *noun* formato *m* de intercambio de ficheros

resource sharing /rɪ'zɔːs ˌʃeərɪŋ/ *noun* (*in a network*) compartición *f* de recursos; recursos *mpl* compartidos

response frame /rɪ'spɒns freɪm/ *noun* cuadro *m* de respuesta

response position /rɪ'spɒns pəˌzɪʃ(ə)n/ *noun* posición *f* de respuesta; celda *f* de respuesta

response time /rɪ'spɒns taɪm/ *noun* tiempo *m* de respuesta

restart /rɪ'stɑːt/ *verb* volver a poner en marcha ■ *noun* reinicio *m*; puesta *f* en marcha

restore /rɪ'stɔː/ *verb* recuperar *vt*; restaurar *vt*

'...first you have to restore the directory that contains the list of deleted files' [*Personal Computer World*]

restrict /rɪ'strɪkt/ *verb* restringir *vt*; limitar *vt* ◇ **the document is restricted, and cannot be placed on open access** el documento es de acceso restringido y, por lo tanto, no debe disponer de acceso público

restriction /rɪ'strɪkʃ(ə)n/ *noun* (*data flow or access*) restricción *f*; límite *m*; coacción *f*

result /rɪ'zʌlt/ *noun* resultado *m*

result code /rɪ'zʌlt kəʊd/ *noun* (*indicates the state of a modem*) código *m* de resultado

resume /rɪ'zjuːm/ *verb* (*to restart*) reanudar *vt*; continuar *vi*; reiniciar *vt*

retrain /ˌriː'treɪn/ *verb* (*re-establish a better quality connection*) reestablecer *vt*

retrieval /rɪ'triːv(ə)l/ *noun* recuperación *f*

retrieve /rɪ'triːv/ *verb* recuperar *vt*; extraer *vt* ◇ **these are the records retrieved in that search** éstos son los registros recuperados en esa búsqueda ◇ **this command will retrieve all names beginning with S** esta instrucción recupera todos los nombres que empiezan por S

retro- /retrəʊ/ *prefix* retro-

retrofit /'retrəʊˌfɪt/ *noun* (dispositivo de) actualización *f* (de un sistema)

retrospective parallel running /ˌretrəʊspektɪv 'pærəlel ˌrʌnɪŋ/ *noun* prueba *f* retrospectiva en paralelo

retrospective search /ˌretrəʊspektɪv 'sɜːtʃ/ *noun* búsqueda *f* retrospectiva

return /rɪ't3ːn/ *noun* **1.** (*to the main program*) retorno *m* **2.** (*key on a keyboard*) tecla *f* de retorno; Intro; Enter **3.** (*at end of line*) (símbolo de) final *m* de línea ◇ **carriage return (CR)** (*code or key*) (código *or* tecla de) retorno de carro ◇ **the program is not working because you missed out the return instruction at the end of the subroutine** el programa no funciona porque se ha olvidado de la instrucción de retorno al final de la subrutina ◇ **you type in your name and code number then press return** escriba su nombre y número de código, y luego pulse la tecla Intro

return address /rɪ't3ːn əˌdres/ *noun* dirección *f* de retorno

return to zero signal /rɪˌt3ːn tə 'zɪərəʊ ˌsɪgn(ə)l/ *noun* señal *f* de retorno; vuelta *f* a cero

reveal /rɪ'viːl/ *verb* revelar *vt*; hacer aparecer

reverb, reverberation *noun* reverberación *f*

reverse /rɪ'v3ːs/ *adjective* (*opposite to usual*) inverso *or* -a; contrario *or* -a ■ *verb* **1.** (*with movement*) hacer marcha atrás **2.** (*of data*) invertir *vt*

'...the options are listed on the left side of the screen, with active options shown at the top left in reverse video' [*PC User*]

reverse channel /rɪˌv3ːs 'tʃæn(ə)l/ *noun* canal *m* de retorno

reverse engineering /rɪˌv3ːs ˌendʒɪ'nɪərɪŋ/ *noun* ingeniería *f* inversa

reverse index /rɪˌv3ːs 'ɪndeks/ *noun* índice *m* inverso

reverse interrupt /rɪˌv3ːs 'ɪntərʌpt/ *noun* interrupción *f* inversa

reverse polarity /rɪˌv3ːs pəʊ'lærɪti/ *noun* (*in an electric or electronic circuit*) polaridad *f* inversa; polaridad *f* invertida; inversión *f* de polaridad

reverse Polish notation /rɪˌv3ːs ˌpəʊlɪʃ nəʊ'teɪʃ(ə)n/ *noun* notación *f* polaca inversa

reverse video /rɪˌv3ːs 'vɪdiəʊ/ *noun* vídeo *m* invertido

revert command /rɪ'v3ːt kəˌmɑːnd/ *noun* instrucción *f* de vuelta a la situación inicial

revise /rɪ'vaɪz/ *verb* (*document or file*) revisar *vt*; modificar *vt*; corregir *vt* ◇ **the revised version has no mistakes** la versión corregida no contiene errores

rewind /ˌriː'waɪnd/ *verb* rebobinar *vt* ◇ **the tape rewinds onto the spool automatically** la cinta se rebobina automáticamente en el carrete

RF, R/F *noun* (*electromagnetic spectrum*) radiofrecuencia *f*; frecuencia *f* de radio ◇ **RF modulator** *or* **radio frequency modulator** modulador *m* de frecuencia de radio

RFC /ˌɑː ef 'siː/ *noun* petición *f* de comentario

RF shielding /ˌɑː ef 'ʃiːldɪŋ/ *noun* revestimiento *m* de un cable de radiofrecuencia ◇ **without RF shielding, the transmitted signal would be distorted by the interference** sin el revestimiento del cable, la señal transmitida sería distorsionada por las interferencias

RGB /ˌɑː dʒiː 'biː/ *noun* (*producing colours by mixing three primary colours red, green and blue*) rojo, verde, azul

ribbon cable /'rɪbən ˌkeɪb(ə)l/ *noun* cable *m* de cinta

rich e-mail /ˌrɪtʃ 'iː meɪl/ *noun* e-mail *m* enriquecido

rich text /ˌrɪtʃ 'tekst/ *noun* texto *m* enriquecido

rich text format /ˌrɪtʃ 'tekst ˌfɔːmæt/ *noun* (*way of storing a document with all the commands for page, type, font and formatting*) formato *m* de texto enriquecido

RIFF /rɪf/ *noun* formato *m* de intercambio de ficheros

RIFF file /'rɪf faɪl/ *noun* fichero *m* (con formato) RIFF

right-click menu /ˌraɪt 'klɪk ˌmenjuː/ *noun* (*small pop-up menu that appears when you click on the right button of a two-button mouse*) menú *m* del botón derecho del ratón

right-hand button /ˌraɪt hænd 'bʌt(ə)n/ *noun* botón *m* derecho (del ratón)

right justification /raɪt ˌdʒʌstɪfɪ'keɪʃ(ə)n/ *noun* justificación *f* a la derecha

right justify /raɪt 'dʒʌstɪˌfaɪ/ *verb* (*printing*) (instrucción de) justificar a la derecha

right shift /ˌraɪt 'ʃɪft/ *noun* (*maths*) desplazamiento *m* a la derecha; deslizamiento *m* a la derecha

rightsizing /'raɪt ˌsaɪzɪŋ/ *noun* (*changing a company's IT structure to a new hardware platform*) instalación *f* de un nuevo hardware

rigid disk /'rɪdʒɪd dɪsk/ noun disco m duro

ring /rɪŋ/ noun **1.** (data) lista f circular; lista f en anillo **2.** (network topology) anillo m; en anillo ◇ **ring network** red f en anillo ◇ **Token Ring network** (IEEE 802.5 standard) red en anillo or red 'Token Ring'

ring back system /'rɪŋ bæk ˌsɪstəm/ noun sistema m de llamada automática

ringer equivalence number /ˌrɪŋər ɪ 'kwɪvələns ˌnʌmbə/ noun número m de equivalencia de llamadas

ring shift /ˌrɪŋ 'ʃɪft/ noun (data movement) permutación f; desplazamiento m circular

ring topology /'rɪŋ tə,pɒlədʒi/ noun topología f en anillo

ring topology network /rɪŋ tə,pɒlədʒi 'netwɜːk/ noun red f de topología en anillo

RIP abbr **1.** (raster image processor) procesador m de imagen matricial; procesador m gráfico por barrido de trama **2.** (routing information protocol) protocolo m de información de encaminamiento

ripple-through carry /'rɪp(ə)l θruː ˌkæri/ noun (mathematical operations) arrastre m rápido; arrastre m simultáneo de transmisión

ripple-through effect /'rɪp(ə)l θruː ɪˌfekt/ noun (changes in a spreadsheet when the value in one cell is changed) efecto m en cascada

RISC /ˌɑː aɪ es 'siː/ noun ordenador m de conjunto de arquitectura RISC; ordenador m de conjunto de instrucciones reducido; procesador m de conjunto de arquitectura RISC; procesador m de conjunto de instrucciones reducido

RJ-11 /ˌɑː dʒeɪ ɪ'lev(ə)n/ noun (standard four-wire modular connector) RJ11

RJ-45 /ˌɑː dʒeɪ ˌfɔːti 'faɪv/ noun (modular connector) RJ45

RJE /ˌɑː dʒeɪ 'iː/ noun entrada f de trabajos a distancia; entrada f de tareas remotas

rm /ˌɑː 'em/ noun (UNIX command) (instrucción) rm (de supresión de un subdirectorio UNIX)

RO /ˌɑː 'əʊ/ noun terminal m de llegada

roam /rəʊm/ verb (to move around freely but remain contactable via wireless communications) moverse vr; (in wireless communications) desplazarse (con un transmisor inalámbrico) vr

robot /'rəʊ,bɒt/ noun **1.** robot m **2.** robot m

robotics /rəʊ'bɒtɪks/ noun robótica f

robust /rəʊ'bʌst/ adjective (system) robusto or -a; sólido or -a; fuerte ◇ **this hard disk is not very robust** este disco duro no es muy sólido

robustness /rəʊ'bʌstnəs/ noun (ability to continue functioning even with faults) robustez f; tolerancia f (al fallo)

rogue indicator /rəʊg 'ɪndɪ,keɪtə/ noun indicador m de control

rogue value /ˌrəʊg 'væljuː/ noun (in a list of data) marca f; (in list of data) marcador m de lista; marcador m de final de fichero

role indicator /rəʊl 'ɪndɪ,keɪtə/ noun indicador m de función

roll back /'rəʊl bæk/ noun reanudación f de un programa después de un fallo

rollback verb reanudar vt; volver hacia atrás; repetir vt

roll forward /rəʊl 'fɔːwəd/ verb proseguir vi

roll in /ˌrəʊl 'ɪn/ verb reincorporar (a la memoria)

roll out /ˌrəʊl 'aʊt/ verb descargar al disco; descargar a la memoria externa

rollover /'rəʊləʊvə/ noun teclado m rápido; teclado m de memoria intermedia

roll scroll /'rəʊl skrəʊl/ verb desplazar la imagen en la pantalla línea a línea; mover un texto línea a línea por la pantalla

ROM /rɒm/ abbr (read only memory) memoria f de sólo lectura; ROM f; memoria f ROM

ROM BIOS /rɒm 'baɪɒs/ noun (rutinas de) BIOS en la ROM; ROM f BIOS

ROM cartridge /rɒm 'kɑːtrɪdʒ/ noun cartucho m ROM; cargador m ROM ◇ **the portable computer has no disk drives, but has a slot for ROM cartridges** este ordenador portátil no tiene disqueteras, pero dispone de una ranura para cargadores ROM

romware /'rɒmweə/ noun programas mpl en ROM

root /ruːt/ noun **1.** (in a data tree structure) raíz f **2.** (fractional power of a number) potencia f fraccionaria; raíz f ◇ **root mean square (RMS)** raíz f cuadrada de la media de los cuadrados ◇ **the root mean square of the pure sinusoidal signal is 0.7071 of its amplitude** la raíz cuadrada de la media de los cuadrados de la señal sinusoidal perfecta equivale a 0,7071 de su amplitud

root directory /ruːt də'rekt(ə)ri/ noun directorio m raíz ◇ **in DOS, the root directory on drive C: is called C:** en el sistema DOS, el directorio raíz de la unidad de disco C: se llama C:\

rotate /rəʊ'teɪt/ verb girar vt

rotate operation /rəʊ'teɪt ˌɒpəreɪʃ(ə)n/ noun permutación f de bits

rotation /rəʊ'teɪʃ(ə)n/ noun rotación f

rough copy /ˌrʌf 'kɒpi/ noun borrador m; esbozo m

round /raʊnd/ verb dar la vuelta; redondear vt ◇ **round off 23.456 to 23.46** redondear 23,456 a 23,46 ◇ **round off error** error m de redondeo ◇ **to round down** redondear (un número por defecto) ◇ **to round off** redondear (un número) ◇ **to round up** redondear por exceso ◇ **we can round down 2.651 to 2.65** podemos redondear 2,651 a 2,65 por defecto ◇ **we can round up 2.647 to 2.65** podemos redondear 2,647 a 2,65 por exceso

round brackets /raʊnd 'brækɪts/ plural noun paréntesis m (s&pl)

rounding /'raʊndɪŋ/ noun **1.** (of a number) redondeo m **2.** (giving a smoother look) redondeo m (de los ángulos)

rounding error /'raʊndɪŋ ˌerə/, **round-off error** /'raʊnd ɒf ˌerə/ noun error m por redondeo

round robin /raʊnd 'rɒbɪn/ noun circuito m cíclico; asignación f de ida y vuelta

route /ruːt/ *noun* (*of message*) camino *m*; recorrido *m*; ruta *f* ◇ **the route taken was not the most direct since a lot of nodes were busy** la ruta elegida no fue la más directa ya que muchos nodos estaban ocupados

router /'ruːtɪd/ *noun* **1.** (*communications device*) direccionador *m*; encaminador *m*; director *m* de ruta; dispositivo *m* de ruta **2.** enrutador *m*

routine /ruː'tiːn/ *noun* (*set of instructions to carry out a task*) rutina *f* ◇ **the RETURN instruction at the end of the routine sends control back to the main program** la instrucción RETURN al final de la rutina devuelve el control al programa principal ◇ **the routine copies the screen display onto a printer** la rutina permite imprimir el contenido de la pantalla

'Hewlett-Packard has announced software which aims to reduce PC-network downtime and cut support costs by automating housekeeping routines such as issuing alerts about potential problems.' [*Computing*]

routing /'ruːtɪŋ/ *noun* (*network*) direccionamiento *m*; encaminamiento *m*; envío *m*

routing information protocol /'ruːtɪŋ ˌɪnfəmeɪʃ(ə)n ˌprəʊtəkɒl/ *noun* protocolo *m* de información de encaminamiento

routing overheads /ˌraʊtɪŋ 'əʊvəhedz/ *plural noun* (*protocol used when routing messages*) procedimiento *m* de control de encaminamiento; protocolo *m* de encaminamiento; protocolo *m* de envío ◇ **the information transfer rate is very much less once all routing overheads have been accommodated** el índice de transferencia de información es mucho menor cuando se tienen en cuenta los protocolos de envío

routing page /ˌraʊtɪŋ 'peɪdʒ/ *noun* página *f* de envío

routing table /raʊtɪŋ 'teɪb(ə)l/ *noun* tabla *f* de envío

row /raʊ/ *noun* **1.** (*of characters*) línea *f*; fila *f*; (*of perforations*) serie *f* **2.** (*in an array or matrix*) línea *f* ◇ **each entry is separated by a row of dots** cada entrada se separa con una serie de puntos ◇ **the figures are presented in rows, not in columns** las cifras se presentan en filas, no en columnas

RPC /ˌɑː piː 'siː/ *noun* llamada *f* de procedimiento a distancia

RS-232C *noun* (*EIA approved standard*) interfaz *f* eléctrica RS-232C entre ordenador y dispositivo periférico; interfaz *f* normalizada RS-232C

RS-422 *noun* (*EIA approved standard*) norma *f* RS-422

RS-423 *noun* (*EIA approved standards*) norma *f* RS-423

RSI *abbr* (*repetitive strain injury*) lesión *f* por fatiga crónica

RTF *abbr* (*rich text format*) formato *m* de texto enriquecido

RTFM *abbr* (*abbreviation*) véase el manual

RTP *abbr* (*real time transport protocol*) protocolo *m* de Emisión

RTS *abbr* (*request to send signal*) petición *f* de transmisión

rubber banding /ˌrʌbə 'bændɪŋ/ *noun* movimiento *m* de banda de goma

rub out /ˌrʌb 'aʊt/ *verb* borrar *vt*

rule /ruːl/ *noun* **1.** (*set of conditions*) regla *f*; norma *f* **2.** (*thin line*) regla *f* ◇ **the rule states that you wait for the clear signal before transmitting** la norma dice que se debe esperar la señal de línea antes de transmitir

rule-based system /ˌruːl beɪst 'sɪstəm/ *noun* sistema *m* basado en reglas

ruler /'ruːlə/ *noun* (*bar on screen that is a unit of measurement*) regla *f*; barra *f* graduada

ruler line /'ruːlə laɪn/ *noun* regla *f* de tabulación

rules /ruːlz/ *plural noun* reglas *fpl*

run /rʌn/ *noun* ejecución *f*; impresión *f* ■ *verb* (*a device*) funcionar *vi*; estar en marcha; (*a program*) ejecutar *vt* ◇ **do not interrupt the spelling checker while it is running** no interrumpa el verificador ortográfico mientras está en marcha ◇ **run-length encoding (RLE)** codificación *f* de ejecución longitud ◇ **run-on price** precio *m* de una tirada adicional ◇ **the computer has been running ten hours a day** el ordenador ha estado funcionando diez horas al día ◇ **the new package runs on our PC** el nuevo software funciona en nuestro ordenador personal ◇ **the next invoice run will be on Friday** la próxima impresión de facturas será el viernes

run around /rʌn ə'raʊnd/ *verb* (*to fit text around an image*) colocar texto alrededor

runaway /'rʌnəˌweɪ/ *noun* operación *f* incontrolable

Run command /'rʌn kəˌmɑːnd/ *noun* instrucción *f* de ejecución (de un programa)

run-duration /'rʌn djʊˌreɪʃ(ə)n/ *noun, adjective* tiempo *m* de ejecución; tiempo *m* de proceso; tiempo *m* de tratamiento

run in /'rʌn ɪn/ *verb* funcionar a menor capacidad

run indicator /rʌn 'ɪndɪˌkeɪtə/ *noun* indicador *m* (luminoso) de marcha; indicador *m* de funcionamiento

running head /'rʌnɪŋ hed/ *noun* (*title line*) cabecera *f*; título *m*; encabezamiento *m* actual

run on /ˌrʌn 'ɒn/ *verb* (*text*) componer texto sin interrupción; imprimir más copias ◇ **the line can run on to the next without any space** el texto puede continuar en la línea siguiente sin dejar espacios

run phase /'rʌn feɪz/ *noun* fase *f* objetivo

run-time /rʌn taɪm/, **run duration** /rʌn djʊ 'reɪʃ(ə)n/ *noun* **1.** (*length of time a program takes to run*) tiempo *m*; duración *f* de ejecución **2.** (*time when a computer is executing a program*) tiempo *m* de ejecución; tiempo *m* de tratamiento; tiempo *m* de proceso

run-time error /'rʌn taɪm ˌerə/ *noun* error *m* de ejecución

run-time library /'rʌn taɪm ˌlaɪbrəri/ *noun* biblioteca *f* de rutinas de aplicaciones ◇ **the soft-**